THE UNITED STATES AND GERMANY IN THE ERA OF THE COLD WAR, 1945–1990

The close association between the United States and the Federal Republic of Germany was a key element in the international order of the Cold War era. No country had as wide-reaching or as profound an impact on the western portion of divided Germany as the United States. No country better exemplified the East–West conflict in American thinking than Germany. *The United States and Germany in the Era of the Cold War* examines all facets of German-American relations and interaction in the decades from the defeat of the Third Reich to Germany's re-unification in 1990. In addition to its comprehensive treatment of U.S.–West German political, economic, social, and cultural ties, *The United States and Germany in the Era of the Cold War* provides an overview of the more limited dealings between the United States and the communist German Democratic Republic.

Detlef Junker, Curt-Engelhorn Chair in American History at the University of Heidelberg, received his PhD from the University of Kiel. He has also been affiliated with Yale University, the University of Nebraska, Lincoln, and University of Stuttgart. From 1994 to 1999, he was director of the German Historical Institute in Washington, D.C. In 2003, he became the founding director of the interdisciplinary Heidelberg Center for American Studies.

Junker's research has focused on German politics in the interwar period, American foreign policy in the twentieth century, German-American relations, and the history of the Cold War. He is author and editor of numerous books and articles, among them *Die Deutsche Zentrumspartei und Hitler 1932–33. Ein Beitrag zur Problematik des politischen Katholizismus in Deutschland* (1969), *Der unteilbare Weltmarkt. Das ökonomische Interesse in der Außenpolitik der USA, 1933–1941* (1975), *Von der Weltmacht zur Supermacht. Amerikanische Aussenpolitik im 20. Jahrhundert* (1995), and *Power and Mission. Was Amerika antreibt* (2003).

The United States and Germany in the Era of the Cold War, 1945–1990

A HANDBOOK

Volume 1: 1945–1968

Edited by

DETLEF JUNKER

University of Heidelberg

Associate Editors

Philipp Gassert, Wilfried Mausbach, and
David B. Morris

GERMAN HISTORICAL INSTITUTE
Washington, D.C.
and
 CAMBRIDGE
UNIVERSITY PRESS

PUBLISHED BY THE PRESS SYNDICATE OF THE UNIVERSITY OF CAMBRIDGE
The Pitt Building, Trumpington Street, Cambridge, United Kingdom

CAMBRIDGE UNIVERSITY PRESS
The Edinburgh Building, Cambridge CB2 RU, UK
40 West 20th Street, New York, NY 10011-4211, USA
477 Williamstown Road, Port Melbourne, VIC 3207, Australia
Ruiz de Alarcón 13, 28014 Madrid, Spain
Dock House, The Waterfront, Cape Town 8001, South Africa

http://www.cambridge.org

First published 2004

Printed in the United States of America

Typeface Bembo 10/12 pt.   *System* LaTeX 2$_\varepsilon$ [TB]

A catalog record for this book is available from the British Library.

Library of Congress Cataloging in Publication Data

USA und Deutschland im Zeitalter des Kalten Krieges, 1945–1990. English

The United States and Germany in the era of the Cold War, 1945–1990 : a handbook/
edited by Detlef Junker; associate editors, Philipp Gassert, Wilfried Mausbach, and David B. Morris.

p.   cm. – (Publications of the German Historical Institute)

Includes bibliographical references and index.

Contents: v. 1. 1945–1968 – v. 2. 1968–1990.

ISBN 0-521-79112-X (v.1) – ISBN 0-521-83420-1 (v.2)

1. United States–Relations–Germany.   2. Germany–Relations–United States.   3. United
States–Foreign relations–1945–1989.   I. Junker, Detlef.   II. Gassert, Philipp.   III. Mausbach, Wilfried,
1964–   IV. Morris, David B. (David Brian), 1963–   V. Title.   VI. Series.

E183.8.G3U7213   2004
327.43073′09′045 – dc22   2003060607

ISBN 0 521 79112 X (volume 1)
ISBN 0 521 83420 1 (volume 2)
ISBN 0 521 83731 6 (set)

Contents

Volume 1

The United States and Germany, 1945–1968

POLITICS

SECURITY

ECONOMICS

CULTURE

SOCIETY

List of Contributors for Volumes 1 and 2

WILLI PAUL ADAMS (†), Abteilung für Geschichte Nordamerikas, John F. Kennedy-Institut für Nordamerikastudien, Freie Universität, Berlin

MITCHELL G. ASH, Institut für Geschichte der Universität Wien

DAVID BATHRICK, Department of Theater, Film, and Dance, Cornell University

SIGRID BAUSCHINGER, Department of Germanic Languages and Literatures, University of Massachusetts, Amherst

VOLKER R. BERGHAHN, Department of History, Columbia University, New York

JULIA BERNARD, Kunstgeschichtliches Institut, Johann Wolfgang Goethe-Universität, Frankfurt am Main

RAINER A. BLASIUS, *Frankfurter Allgemeine Zeitung*

REBECCA BOEHLING, Department of History, University of Maryland Baltimore County

CHRISTINE BORRMANN, Hamburgisches Welt-Wirtschafts-Archiv

HEINRICH BORTFELDT, Berlin

STEVEN J. BRADY, Department of History, University of Notre Dame

H. W. BRANDS, Department of History, Texas A&M University

MICHAEL BROER, Institut für Internationale Politik, Universität der Bundeswehr, Hamburg

SUZANNE BROWN-FLEMING, U.S. Holocaust Memorial Museum, Center for Advanced Holocaust Studies

CHRISTOPH BUCHHEIM, Seminar für Wirtschafts- und Sozialgeschichte, Phillipps-Universität Mannheim

WERNER BÜHRER, Institut für Sozialwissenschaften, Technische Universität, München

ECKART CONZE, Seminar für Zeitgeschichte, Eberhard-Karls-Universität, Tübingen

MATTHIAS DEMBINSKI, Hessische Stiftung Friedens- und Konfliktforschung, Frankfurt am Main

MONIKA DICKHAUS, Historisches Institut der Deutschen Bank AG, Frankfurt

JEFFRY M. DIEFENDORF, Department of History, University of New Hampshire, Durham

WERNER DURTH, Fachbereich Architektur, Technische Universität, Darmstadt

MICHAEL ERMARTH, Department of History, Dartmouth College, New Hampshire

BARBARA FAIT, Historisches Seminar der Universität zu Köln

ANDREAS FALKE, Economics Section, U.S. Embassy, Berlin

MICHAEL FICHTER, Arbeitsstelle Nationale und Internationale Gewerkschaftspolitik, Otto-Suhr-Institut für Politikwissenschaft, Freie Universität, Berlin

JÖRG FISCH, Historisches Seminar der Universität, Zürich

ULRIKE FISCHER-INVERARDI, Brussels, Belgium

ERHARD FORNDRAN, Institut für Politikwissenschaft, Otto-von-Guericke-Universität, Magdeburg

ANNETTE FREYBERG, Faculty of Political Sciences, University of Bucharest

LUTZ FRÜHBRODT, Wirtschaftsredaktion, *Die Welt*, Berlin

KARL-HEINZ FÜSSL, Abteilung Historische Erziehungswissenschaft, Philosophische Fakultät IV, Humboldt-Universität zu Berlin

LILY GARDNER FELDMAN, American Institute for Contemporary German Studies, Washington, D.C.

PHILIPP GASSERT, Historisches Seminar, Ruprecht-Karls-Universität, Heidelberg

MICHAEL E. GEISLER, German Department, Middlebury College, Middlebury, Vermont

STEFAN GERMER(†), Kunstgeschichtliches Institut, Johann Wolfgang Goethe-Universität, Frankfurt am Main

JESSICA C. E. GIENOW-HECHT, Johann Wolfgang Goethe-Universität, Frankfurt am Main

PETRA GOEDDE, Department of History, Princeton University, New Jersey

ROBERT F. GOECKEL, Department of Political Science, State University of New York at Geneseo

MANFRED GÖRTEMAKER, Historisches Institut, Universität Potsdam

REGINA URSULA GRAMER, Department of History, Temple University, Philadelphia, Pennsylvania

RONALD J. GRANIERI, Department of History, Furman University, Greenville, South Carolina

THOMAS GRUMKE, Bereich Politik der Bertelsmann Stiftung, Gütersloh

CHRISTIAN HACKE, Seminar für Politische Wissenschaft der Rheinischen Friedrich-Wilhelms-Universität Bonn

HARALD HAGEMANN, Institut für Volkswirtschaftslehre, Universität Hohenheim-Stuttgart

GERD HARDACH, Fachbereich Geschichte und Kulturwissenschaften, Universität Marburg

KLAUS-DIETMAR HENKE, Hannah-Arendt-Institut für Totalitarismusforschung an der Technischen Universität, Dresden

DIETRICH HERRMANN, Sonderforschungsbereich 537: "Institutionalität und Geschichtlichkeit," Technische Universität, Dresden

ANDREAS HÖFELE, Institut für Englische Philologie, Ludwig-Maximilians-Universität, München

HELMUT HUBEL, Institut für Politikwissenschaft, Friedrich-Schiller-Universität, Jena

HAROLD JAMES, Department of History, Princeton University, New Jersey

LOCH K. JOHNSON, Department of Political Science, University of Georgia at Athens

DETLEF JUNKER, Historisches Seminar, Ruprecht-Karls-Universität, Heidelberg

ANTON KAES, German Department and Program in Film Studies, University of California at Berkeley

KARL KAISER, Prof. Emeritus, Rheinische Friedrich-Wilhelms-Universität, Bonn, and Otto-Wolff-Direktor, Forschungsinstitut der Deutschen Gesellschaft für Auswärtige Politik, Berlin

HEIDRUN KÄMPER, Abteilung Historische Lexikographie und Lexikologie, Institut für deutsche Sprache, Mannheim

MANFRED KNAPP, Institut für Internationale Politik, Universität der Bundeswehr, Hamburg

THOMAS KOEBNER, Fachbereich Filmwissenschaft, Universität Mainz

WULF KÖPKE, Prof. Emeritus, Texas A&M University

KNUD KRAKAU, Abteilung für Geschichte, John F. Kennedy-Institut für Nordamerikastudien, Freie Universität, Berlin

WOLFGANG KRIEGER, Historisches Seminar der Philipps-Universität, Marburg

CLAUS-DIETER KROHN, Fachbereich Kulturwissenschaften, Universität Lüneburg

BRIAN LADD, Department of History and Department of Geography and Planning, State University of New York at Albany

RAIMUND LAMMERSDORF, German Historical Institute, Washington, D.C.

CARL LANKOWSKI, U.S. Department of State, Foreign Service Institute, Arlington, Virginia

DAVID CLAY LARGE, Department of History and Philosophy, Montana State University, Bozeman

EDWARD LARKEY, Department of Modern Languages and Linguistics, University of Maryland Baltimore County

KLAUS LARRES, School of Politics, Department of Social and Political Science, Royal Holloway, University of London

DANIEL J. LEAB, Department of History, Seton Hall University, New Jersey

CLAUS LEGGEWIE, Institut für Politikwissenschaft, Justus-Liebig-Universität, Giessen

WERNER LINK, Prof. Emeritus, Forschungsinstitut für Politische Wissenschaft und Europäische Fragen, Universität zu Köln

MICHAEL R. LUCAS, World Policy Institute, New School University, New York

FELIX PHILIPP LUTZ, Prognos AG, Basel

GUNTHER MAI, Historisches Institut, Pädagogische Hochschule, Erfurt

WILFRIED MAUSBACH, Historisches Seminar, Ruprecht-Karls-Universität, Heidelberg

BERNHARD MAY, Forschungsinstitut der Deutschen Gesellschaft für Auswärtige Politik, Berlin

JOHN A. MCCARTHY, Department of Germanic and Slavic Languages, Vanderbilt University, Nashville, Tennessee

MONIKA MEDICK-KRAKAU, Institut für Politikwissenschaft, Technische Universität, Dresden

MARTIN MEYER, Giessen

KLAUS J. MILICH, Institut für Anglistik und Amerikanistik, Philosophische Fakultät II, Humboldt-Universität zu Berlin

DAVID B. MORRIS, European Division, Library of Congress, Washington, D.C.

KERSTIN MÜLLER-NEUHOF, Hamburgisches Welt-Wirtschafts-Archiv

MICHAEL J. NEUFELD, Department of Space History, National Air and Space Museum, Smithsonian Institution, Washington, D.C.

GOTTFRIED NIEDHART, Historisches Institut der Universität, Mannheim

FRANK A. NINKOVICH, Department of History, St. John's University, New York

CHRISTIAN F. OSTERMANN, Director, Cold War International History Project, Woodrow Wilson Center, Washington, D.C.

JEFFREY PECK, Canadian Centre for German and European Studies, York University, Toronto, and Department of German, University of Montreal

MAARTEN L. PEREBOOM, Department of History, Salisbury State University, Maryland

ANN L. PHILLIPS, Department of Political Science, American University, Washington, D.C.

WERNER PLUMPE, Historisches Seminar der Johann Wolfgang Goethe-Universität, Frankfurt am Main

UTA G. POIGER, Department of History, University of Washington, Seattle

DAVID BRADEN POSNER, History Department, Choate Rosemary Hall School, Connecticut

PAMELA M. POTTER, School of Music and Department of German, University of Wisconsin at Madison

DIETHELM PROWE, Department of History, Carleton College, Northfield, Minnesota

CORNELIA RAUH-KÜHNE, Historisches Seminar, Eberhard-Karls-Universität, Tübingen

STEVEN L. REARDEN, Joint History Office, U.S. Department of Defense

THOMAS REUTHER, Rektorat, Universität Dortmund

JOACHIM ROHDE, Stiftung Wissenschaft und Politik, Forschungsinstitut für Internationale Politik und Sicherheit, Ebenhausen

SIGRID RUBY, Institut für Kunstgeschichte, Justus-Liebig-Universität, Giessen

T. MICHAEL RUDDY, Department of History, St. Louis University, Missouri

MARK E. RUFF, Department of Humanities, Concordia University, Portland, Oregon

HERMANN-JOSEF RUPIEPER, Institut für Geschichte, Martin-Luther-Universität, Halle-Wittenberg

KORI N. SCHAKE, Institute for National Strategic Studies, National Defense University, Washington, D.C.

HANS-ECKART SCHARRER, Hamburgisches Welt-Wirtschafts-Archiv

INGRID SCHENK, Atlanta, Georgia

AXEL SCHILDT, Forschungsstelle für Zeitgeschichte in Hamburg und Historisches Seminar der Universität, Hamburg

HANNA SCHISSLER, Georg Eckert Institut Braunschweig und Historisches Seminar der Universität, Hannover

RAINER SCHNOOR, Institut für Anglistik und Amerikanistik, Universität Potsdam

FRANK SCHUMACHER, Lehrstuhl für Nordamerikanische Geschichte, Universität Erfurt

KLAUS SCHWABE, Prof. Emeritus, Historisches Institut, Rheinisch-Westfälische Technische Hochschule, Aachen

THOMAS A. SCHWARTZ, Department of History, Vanderbilt University, Nashville, Tennessee

HANS-PETER SCHWARZ, Prof. Emeritus, Seminar für Politikwissenschaft, Rheinische Friedrich-Wilhelms-Universität, Bonn

SHLOMO SHAFIR, Ramat Hasharon, Israel

EDMUND SPEVACK(†), German Historical Institute, Washington, D.C.

ALAN E. STEINWEIS, History and Judaic Studies, University of Nebraska, Lincoln

RAYMOND G. STOKES, Department of Economic and Social History, University of Glasgow

BERND STÖVER, Historisches Institut, Universität Potsdam

STEPHEN F. SZABO, Paul H. Nitze School of Advanced International Studies, The Johns Hopkins University, Washington, D.C.

JAMES F. TENT, Department of History, University of Alabama at Birmingham

FRANK TROMMLER, Department of German, University of Pennsylvania, Philadelphia

HANS N. TUCH, U.S. Foreign Service (retired)

RUUD VAN DIJK, University of Wisconsin at Milwaukee

BRYAN T. VAN SVERINGEN, United States European Command, Stuttgart

MICHAEL WALA, Amerika Institut, Ludwig-Maximillians-Universität, Munich

WESLEY K. WARK, Department of History, University of Toronto

WELF WERNER, Abteilung für Wirtschaft, John F. Kennedy-Institut für Nordamerikastudien, Freie Universität, Berlin

GODEHARD WEYERER, Bremen Journalisten-Etage, Bremen

S. JONATHAN WIESEN, Department of History, Southern Illinois University at Carbondale

RICHARD WIGGERS, University of New Brunswick, Canada

FREDERICK ZILIAN JR., Department of History, Portsmouth Abbey School, Rhode Island

MATTHIAS ZIMMER, University of Alberta, Edmonton, Canada

HUBERT ZIMMERMANN, Department of Government, Cornell University, New York

Preface

The idea for this history, *The United States and Germany in the Era of the Cold War, 1945–1990*, was conceived in the revolutionary period between 1989 and 1991. With the end of the Cold War, the collapse of the Soviet empire, the reorganization of Central and Eastern Europe, the fall of the Berlin Wall, the unification of Germany, and the end of the Soviet Union in those years, it quickly became obvious that an epoch in U.S.-German relations had drawn to a close. Inspired by the Hegelian dictum that the owl of Minerva, a symbol of wisdom, first takes to flight when night is falling, the editor of this collection decided to document American-German relations between 1945 and 1990 in all their complexity.

The success of this undertaking was made possible through the resources of the German Historical Institute (GHI) in Washington, D.C., whose primary mission is to promote scholarly collaboration between German and American historians, and thus contribute to a better understanding between their respective countries.[1] Since its founding in 1987, the Institute has devoted its scholarly energy to three areas in particular: research into the political, economic, social, and cultural interactions between the United States and Germany since the eighteenth century; comparative studies of the political, economic, social, and cultural developments in these countries in the modern era; and studies focusing on individual themes important to German and American history. Each of these three areas has claimed a place in the present volumes. It seemed fitting that the GHI invite a total of 132 scholars from both sides of the Atlantic to contribute their work – 146 essays in all – to this project.

In many ways these two volumes have no precedent. Never has a work attempted to describe and explain the relations between two states, two societies, and two cultures in such detail for one historical epoch. No comparable analytical study exists for U.S.-Soviet relations, nor for U.S.-British, U.S.-Japanese,

---

[1] See Detlef Junker, ed., with the assistance of Thomas Goebel and Edmund Spevack, *The German Historical Institute, 1987–1997: A Ten-Year Report*, Reference Guide series, no. 10 (Washington, D.C., 1998) (www.ghi-dc.org/10year/index.html); Wissenschaftsrat, *Stellungnahme zu den Geisteswissenschaftlichen Auslandsinstituten* (Cologne, 1999).

or German-French relations. Similarly, no previous study has fully met the oft-invoked challenge of examining the reciprocal ties that run between two nations; no study has done this for the realm of politics, security, and economic policy, while also scrutinizing society, culture, and the role of nonstate actors. Finally, using the concrete example of U.S.-German relations, this history can demonstrate how the character of the international system and thus also bilateral relations were transformed after 1945. The second volume in particular makes clear the extent to which a growing multilateralization of international relations and economic globalization, as well as the globalization of popular culture, which was greatly influenced by the United States, affected the bilateral American-German relationship.

The editor and his associate editors chose the title *The United States and Germany in the Era of the Cold War, 1945–1990*, deliberately. On the one hand, by focusing on the distinctive characteristics of the Cold War, the title distinguishes this particular time period from both an earlier epoch and a later epoch whose contours remain as yet undefined. On the other hand, the title indicates that these relationships as a whole were more than just dependent variables of the Cold War. For nearly half a century, that war shaped the U.S.-German relationship in a decisive way. The global tension between the two superpowers was the starting point and basis for close political and military cooperation between the United States and the Federal Republic; this in turn contributed to increased economic, cultural, and societal interactions between the two countries. Yet, as the essays in these two volumes make clear, developments and factors that originally had nothing to do with the Cold War also influenced German-American relations in this period. This was particularly true for the presence of the past, the lessons that were drawn from the memory of National Socialist Germany on both sides of the Atlantic. It was also true of global economic developments and tendencies toward modernization that arose in both places.

The end of the division of Germany and Europe in 1990 clearly signaled a new era in German-American relations. Taking 1945 as our starting date may seem more problematic, however. Anyone familiar with the extensive literature on the emergence of the Cold War can cite the arguments for instead choosing 1943 or 1947, or even 1917. Depictions of the interwoven actions, events, and intentions contributing to the origins of the Cold War typically begin prior to 1945. Still, it makes sense to begin with this particular date because the new global political conflict gradually became visible for contemporaries between 1945 and 1947. In this short time span, the world was forced to recognize that the Allies' hopes for continued cooperation – beyond the moment when the German Reich capitulated – had come apart with astonishing speed. The future of Germany doubtlessly belonged very centrally to the many arenas of conflict. Even the outcome and contradictions of the Potsdam Conference cannot be explained without reference to the emerging conflict of two world powers that embodied antagonistic values, as well as antagonistic societal and state systems.

Objections to use of the term *Germany* may also arise. It will become apparent that our focus is to a great extent the relations between the superpower of the

West and the Federal Republic, which was gradually integrated into the West. By contrast, relations between the United States and the other German state, the communist German Democratic Republic, are a secondary concern here. Yet, because this volume also scrutinizes those relations to the extent that they did exist, it seemed legitimate to speak of "Germany" here. Finally, by referring to "The United States and Germany" in that order, we wish to indicate that the dominant influence – mutual interactions and connections notwithstanding – flowed from West to East, from superpower to dependent ally.

Dividing the articles into two volumes stems from more than practical considerations. The division also reflects the recognition that 1968 represents a significant turning point for historians, and not only in domestic policy; across the globe, that date also marked a major break with the past in Cold War–era international relations. At the same time, the second volume is considerably shorter because the historical exploration of German-American relations in the 1970s and 1980s remains in its early stages, and can as yet not draw on a substantial body of primary sources. One exception to this is the analysis of German reunification and the decisive role that the United States played in that event.

The authors of these essays live on both sides of the Atlantic and grew up in different cultures. Their contributions are thus often marked by a distinctly American or German perspective. This transatlantic variety does more than substantiate a kind of epistemological relativism along the lines of "where you stand depends on where you sit." It makes a rich and fruitful exchange of perspectives possible, one that is essential for moving forward intellectually.

The general editor and the GHI in Washington have greatly benefited from the help and generous cooperation of many institutions and individuals. My first expression of gratitude must go to the German taxpayer, for the vast majority of the resources that made this project possible came from public funds provided by the Federal Republic of Germany. This is true for the monies that supported the scholarly and administrative staff members of the GHI who were involved with the project but also for the crucial sponsorship provided through the German Economics Ministry; the latter offered financial support through special funds – its *ERP-Sondervermögen*, the Transatlantic Program – on the recommendation of an interministerial committee. Financing of a study of German-American relations through these special funds seems particularly appropriate to us because they give evidence of the ongoing legacy of the Marshall Plan. In connection with these funds, special thanks are due to Wolfgang Rieck, former section head at the Economics Ministry; Michael Mertes, former director in the Chancellor's Office; and Werner Weidenfeld, former coordinator for German-American cooperation at the Foreign Office. His successor in that position, Karsten Voigt, also lent his support during the completion of the project. We are likewise indebted to the Federal Ministry for Education and Research, as well as to members of the GHI's Board of Trustees and Academic Advisory Council under the chairmanship of Klaus Hildebrand (Bonn), whose astute advice was always helpful.

The editors are also deeply indebted to Volker Berghahn (New York), Christoph Buchheim (Mannheim), Lily Gardner Feldman (Washington, D.C.), Harold

James (Princeton, N.J.), Wolfgang Krieger (Marburg), Klaus Schwabe (Aachen), Thomas A. Schwartz (Nashville, Tenn.), and Frank Trommler (Philadelphia), who wrote the introductory essays for each of the main sections in these volumes: politics, security, economics, culture, and society. They also contributed annotated bibliographies for each. In addition, each gave valuable advice on the contributions appearing in his or her section. Carl-Ludwig Holtfrerich (Berlin), Diane B. Kunz (New York), and Hans-Peter Schwarz (Bonn) supported this project with their generous and valuable advice when it was in its early stages. Professor Schwarz also provided a perspective on German-American relations in the post–Cold War world.

It is, unfortunately, not possible to thank all the contributors individually. The editors are deeply in their debt. Not only did we rely on established scholars who had long devoted themselves to the study of German-American relations but also on a number of younger scholars who, in many instances, are presenting the results of their first major research in condensed form.

Because approximately half of the original manuscripts were in German and half were in English, translation proved to be a formidable task. Sally E. Robertson, who coordinated a team of translators for the project, provided crucial support. We extend our warmest gratitude to her and her team.

The efficient administrative support offered by the GHI in Washington aided this project in numerous ways. I extend a special thanks to my successor as director, Professor Christof Mauch, Administrative Director Dieter H. Schneider, and the GHI's foreign-language assistants, Christa Brown and Bärbel Thomas. A range of colleagues in Washington helped to keep the heavy volume of communications with the authors and translators flowing and lent support in the final editorial stages; these included Pamela Abraham, Simone Herrmann, Kathrin Klein, Lusi McKinley, Annette M. Marciel, Afaf E. Morgan, and Richard F. Wetzell, who each contributed to the completion of the manuscript. In Heidelberg, Daniela Eisenstein, Barbara Duttenhöfer, Matthias Kirchner, Thomas Maulucci, Christian Müller, and Christiane Rösch provided support in the final phase of the project. Responsibility for the final editorial work on the present volumes lay primarily in the hands of Jan Ruth Lambertz and Daniel S. Mattern. David Lazar provided the final elegant touch. Frank Smith, publishing director for Social Sciences at Cambridge University Press, took great interest in this project from the beginning, patiently waited to get hold of the completed manuscript, then guided it to publication with his usual professionalism.

My greatest debt as general editor is to my collaborators, Philipp Gassert, Wilfried Mausbach, and David B. Morris. Dr. Gassert and Dr. Mausbach were research Fellows at the Institute in Washington, D.C., while these volumes were assembled, and they devoted a considerable portion of their time to this project. Dr. Morris's main responsibility at the Institute was to oversee the editorial work for the book's publication in English and German. The Deutsche Verlags-Anstalt published a German-language edition in 2001. I am grateful for their expertise, engagement, and skillful command of two languages. Without the team spirit of our Washington

four-leaf clover, it would not have been possible to maintain such a fruitful collaboration with more than 130 authors of varied temperament.

Last, but not least, I thank my Dutch wife, Anja van der Schrieck-Junker, for the
rich conversation that we carried on during our five years in Washington, D.C.,
from 1994 to 1999.

Detlef Junker
Heidelberg/Washington, D.C.
January 2003

Politics, Security, Economics, Culture, and Society
Dimensions of Transatlantic Relations

Detlef Junker

Translated by Sally E. Robertson

THE UNITED STATES AND GERMANY IN THE TWENTIETH CENTURY

When historians attempt to describe and explain the significance of German-American relations in the second half of the twentieth century, they are forced to look at the entire century. This is because the relationship between the two states, societies, and cultures in the era of the Cold War was shaped by history in a twofold manner: by the objective consequences of American intervention in both world wars and, second, by the lessons learned from these historical experiences on both sides of the Atlantic.

When we look at the entire century from an American perspective, we might venture to say that no country in the world has contributed as much to the ascent of the United States to superpower status and to the globalization of its interests as Germany, Europe's central power.[1] The United States had kept its distance from the Eurasian continent in the nineteenth century, particularly in terms of military engagement or alliance politics. It was the triple challenge posed by the German problem in World War I, World War II, and the Cold "World" War that finally established the United States as a military, economic, and cultural power on that continent.[2]

Germany was America's chief adversary in World War I, and the United States waged two wars against it: a military one in Europe and a cultural one against German-Americans at home. The American political and military elite viewed Germany as its most pressing enemy in World War II, even after the Japanese attack on Pearl Harbor. After 1945, the American-Soviet conflict became the major structural principle of international relations, and the German question was to a large extent a dependent variable in the relationship between those two superpowers. Nonetheless, Germany remained America's

[1] On German-American relations in the twentieth century, see Hans W. Gatzke, *Germany and the United States: A "Special Relationship"?* (Cambridge, Mass., 1980); Manfred Jonas, *The United States and Germany: A Diplomatic History* (Ithaca, N.Y., 1984); Frank Trommler and Joseph McVeigh, eds., *America and Germany: An Assessment of a Three-Hundred-Year History*, 2 vols. (Philadelphia, 1985), vol. 2; Carl C. Hodge and Cathal J. Nolan, eds., *Shepherd of Democracy: America and Germany in the Twentieth Century* (Westport, Conn., 1992); Klaus Larres and Torsten Oppelland, eds., *Deutschland und die USA im 20. Jahrhundert: Geschichte der politischen Beziehungen* (Darmstadt, 1997).

[2] Samuel F. Wells, Jr., Robert H. Ferrell, and David Trask, *American Diplomacy Since 1900* (Boston, 1975); Akira Iriye, *The Globalizing of America, 1913–1945* (Cambridge, Mass., 1993); Warren I. Cohen, *America in the Age of Soviet Power, 1945–1991* (Cambridge, Mass., 1993); Robert D. Schulzinger, *American Diplomacy in the Twentieth Century*, 3d ed. (Oxford, 1994); Lloyd C. Gardner, *A Covenant with Power: America and World Order from Wilson to Reagan* (New York, 1984); Detlef Junker, *Von der Weltmacht zur Supermacht: Amerikanische Aussenpolitik im 20. Jahrhundert* (Mannheim, 1995); Frank Ninkovich, *The Wilsonian Century: U.S. Foreign Policy Since 1900* (Chicago, 1999); Michael J. Hogan, ed., *America in the World: The Historiography of American Foreign Relations Since 1941* (Cambridge, Mass., 1995).

central problem in Europe. The power vacuum created in Europe by the unconditional surrender of the German Reich can be viewed as the most important cause of the emergence of Soviet-American antagonism after 1945. The establishment of NATO and the permanent stationing of American troops on German soil – both revolutions in American foreign policy – were direct results of the fact that the major victors of World War II could not agree on a system of domestic order for Germany or on its proper place in Europe. The Berlin crises of 1948–49 and 1958–62 were among the gravest Cold War threats to world peace. The second crisis, closely related to the Cuban Missile Crisis,[3] and the erection of the Berlin Wall sharply exposed the dilemma of the Americans, who wanted neither to die for Berlin and the Germans in an atomic war nor to endanger their prestige and position as a European hegemonic power in Europe by withdrawing from West Berlin.

National Socialism shadowed American foreign policy after 1945. The overriding goal of containing the Soviet Union was linked with the major lesson that a whole generation of American politicians had learned from the failure of democracy in the 1930s. Never again should a policy of appeasement be pursued toward dictators; there must be no second Munich, neither in Europe nor in Asia. This experience also gave rise to the domino theory, which was used in the United States during the Cold War as an all-purpose political weapon for justifying alliances, military interventions, and economic aid to Europe, Asia, Africa, and Latin America, and that ultimately drew the Americans into the Vietnam War.

From a geostrategic perspective, containing the power of the German nation-state in the center of Europe had been a leitmotif of American policy in Europe since the age of imperialism, when Kaiser Wilhelm II's Germany and an imperial America outgrew their status as regional powers and became competing world powers. Yet, Germany did not become a problem for the United States until it threatened to rise to the level of hegemonic power or an oppressor of Europe. Unlike Germany's European neighbors,[4] the distant United States feared not the German nation-state created in 1871 but rather its potential as a rival world power. That is why the United States not only fought the German Empire and the Third Reich in world wars but also sought to contain and stabilize the Weimar Republic through economic integration, just as it attempted to contain and stabilize the Federal Republic through economic, military, and diplomatic integration beginning in 1949. European stability and German containment were among the chief strategic objectives of American foreign policy in the twentieth century, from Woodrow Wilson to George Bush.

In the first half of the century, the Germans not only served twice as the enemy but also twice provided America with the paramount image of an enemy. The American civil religion – that unmistakable mixture of Christian republicanism and democratic faith[5] – certainly facilitated the propagandistic transformation of the German Empire of Kaiser Wilhelm II into the evil empire. It was this Manichaean pattern of distinguishing between good and evil with religious fervor that permitted the Wilson administration to win the battle for the soul of the

---

[3] John C. Ausland, *Kennedy, Khrushchev, and the Berlin-Cuba Crisis, 1961–1964* (Oslo, 1996); Aleksandr Fursenko and Timothy Naftali, *One Hell of a Gamble: Khrushchev, Castro, and Kennedy, 1958–1964* (New York, 1997); Ernest R. May and Philip D. Zelikow, eds., *The Kennedy Tapes: Inside the White House During the Cuban Missile Crisis* (Cambridge, Mass., 1997); Lawrence Freedman, *Kennedy's Wars: Berlin, Cuba, Laos, and Vietnam* (New York, 2000).

[4] Gottfried Niedhart, Detlef Junker, and Michael Richter, eds., *Deutschland in Europa: Nationale Interessen und internationale Ordnung im 20. Jahrhundert* (Mannheim, 1997).

[5] Walter A. McDougall, *Promised Land, Crusader State: The American Encounter with the World Since 1776* (Boston, 1997); Michael H. Hunt, *Ideology and U.S. Foreign Policy* (New Haven, Conn., 1987); Knud Krakau, *Missionsbewusstsein und Völkerrechtsdoktrin in den Vereinigten Staaten von Amerika* (Frankfurt am Main, 1967); Kurt R. Spillmann, *Amerikas Ideologie des Friedens: Ursprünge, Formwandlungen und geschichtliche Auswirkungen des amerikanischen Glaubens an den Mythos einer friedlichen Weltordnung* (Bern, 1984).

American people, who were not eager to go to war in 1917.[6] From 1937 to 1941, the general outline of this process was repeated: The major difference was that Nazi Germany, unlike Wilhelm's empire, really was an evil empire.

The Germans also played a central role in bringing about the positive aspect of this Manichaean pattern in American politics: the mission of bringing freedom and democracy to the world. In this respect, too, the "American century" is difficult to imagine without the Germans.[7] It was the German challenge that forced President Wilson to broaden and globalize America's mission beyond the passive idea of turning America into a new Jerusalem that would serve as a beacon for the world by virtue of its example to the active responsibility of raising to the American level those peoples who were less free, less civilized, and who had been left behind.[8] Wilson's call to make the *world* safe for democracy was the ideological climax of the declaration that he used to justify his country's entry into the war against Germany in April 1917. Segments of the American political elite interpreted the failure of this mission in Germany during the period between the wars partly as a failure of their own country, which withdrew from Europe in its military and alliance policy after the Treaty of Versailles and remained in Europe only in an economic and cultural role.

After 1945, therefore, the pacification and democratization of Germany (and Japan) were among the central goals of American foreign policy. Never before or since have the Americans expended so many resources to remake two foreign and occupied nations in their own political, social, and cultural image. Under the influence of the Cold War, the United States incorporated the western part of Germany into

an Atlantic community – of security, values, production, consumption, information, leisure, travel, and entertainment – under American hegemony. Berlin, which had been the headquarters of evil from 1933 to 1945, became not only a symbol of the Cold War and a divided world but also an outpost of freedom, the "city on the hill" on which the eyes of the world were focused.[9] Nothing was a more obvious symbol of the victory of freedom over communism and dictatorship for the Americans than the fall of the Berlin Wall, and they reacted almost more enthusiastically than many surprised and disconcerted West Germans.

At the outset of the new millennium, ten years after German reunification and the fall of the Soviet empire, these two fundamental experiences of Germany – as evil empire and as democratic ally in a transatlantic community – are united and yet separate in a curious mélange in the American collective consciousness and memory industry. It is not the Cold War but World War II that appears to be the axis of twentieth-century American identity. The morally ambiguous Cold War could easily have ended in nuclear catastrophe[10] and was accompanied by a series of disturbingly opaque and inhuman wars on the periphery, most conspicuously the American debacle in Vietnam. By contrast, the war against the Axis powers is considered the most important event of the century and, at the same time, America's great, noble, and just war.[11] In this war, however, it

---

[6] Detlef Junker, *The Manichaean Trap: American Perceptions of the German Empire, 1871–1945*, German Historical Institute, Occasional Paper 12 (Washington, D.C., 1995).

[7] Tony Smith, *America's Mission: The United States and the Worldwide Struggle for Democracy in the Twentieth Century* (Princeton, N.J., 1994); Emily S. Rosenberg, *Spreading the American Dream: American Economic and Cultural Expansion, 1890–1945* (New York, 1982).

[8] H. W. Brands, *What America Owes the World: The Struggle for the Soul of Foreign Policy* (New York, 1998).

[9] See the chapter by Diethelm Prowe, vol. 1, Politics.

[10] Some scholars of the Cold War think this was only a remote possibility, given the transformed international system after 1945. See John Lewis Gaddis, *The Long Peace: Inquiries into the History of the Cold War* (Oxford, 1987); John Mueller, *Retreat from Doomsday: The Obsolescence of Major War* (New York, 1989).

[11] A 1999 survey asked Americans to name the most important event of the twentieth century and an important, but not most important event. The results were: World War II (71 percent responded most important; 21 percent important but not most important); the granting of the vote to American women in 1920 (66 percent; 22 percent); the dropping of the atomic bomb on Hiroshima (66 percent; 20 percent); the Holocaust (65 percent; 20 percent); the Civil Rights Act of 1964 (58 percent; 26 percent). In sixth to eighth place were: World

was Nazism and not communism that was the paramount foe.

World War II has special significance for America's identity and its culture of remembrance, not only because it objectively marks a qualitative transition from major power to superpower or because, along with the American Civil War, it is particularly well suited for a patriotic and heroic view of history in the American mass media. More importantly, the Holocaust, embodying pure evil, overshadows all other crimes of the century in the American consciousness. Since the 1960s, historians, politicians, artists, and theologians in the United States and elsewhere have devoted increasing attention to the genocide committed against the Jews in Europe. The universalization, commercialization, trivialization, and functionalization of this discussion by the media and politicians have led to a debate on the "Americanization of the Holocaust."[12] This process is related to the growing importance of Holocaust remembrance for Jewish communities in the United States, Israel, and other parts of the world;[13] to the relationship of American Jews to Israel; to their fear of losing their identity without the

Holocaust; and to the successful institutionalization and broadening of research on and remembrance of the Holocaust.[14]

At the beginning of the new millennium it is difficult to predict what significance the Americanization of the Holocaust will have for the American image of Germany, the German image of the United States, and German-American relations in the coming decades. However, for historians, the shadow of the Holocaust cannot obscure the fundamental fact that, from not only a German but also an American perspective, German-American relations after 1945 have been a success story unprecedented in the history of international relations.[15]

The solution of the German problem is among the greatest American foreign policy successes of the twentieth century. No one could have foreseen this success in 1945, when World War II ended and images of the liberation of the concentration camps at Buchenwald and Dachau evoked an elemental revulsion in the United States. For almost forty years, Germany was an integral component of the dual containment policy of the United States in continental Europe: namely, containment of the Soviet and German threats. This policy went hand in hand with the desire to satisfy the French need for protection against Germany and the Soviet Union, while preventing France from ascending to the level of a hegemonic power capable of competing with the United States. The unification of Germany under Western conditions produced nearly the best possible Germany from the American perspective: a medium-sized democratic country in Europe with political influence and international economic significance. Germany lacks any vital conflicts of interest with the United States, is integrated into and contained by European and Atlantic

War I, the 1969 moon landing, and the assassination of President Kennedy. It is striking that the fall of the Berlin Wall in 1989 ranked ninth, ahead of the Great Depression of the 1930s (10), the end of the Soviet Union (11), and the Vietnam War (12). According to this survey, Americans considered World War II to be not only the most important event of the century but also the most just war that the United States has ever waged: *Gallup Poll Releases*, Dec. 6, 1999. Among American Jews, 24 percent consider remembrance of the Holocaust to be "extremely important," 54 percent "very important," 20 percent "somewhat important," and only 2 percent "not important." See also Studs Terkel, *The Good War: An Oral History of World War II* (New York, 1984).

[12] Hilene Flanzbaum, ed., *The Americanization of the Holocaust* (Baltimore, 1999); Peter Novick, *The Holocaust in American Life* (Boston, 1999); Jeffrey Shandler, *While America Watches: Televising the Holocaust* (New York, 1999); Tim Cole, *Selling the Holocaust: From Auschwitz to Schindler. How History Is Bought, Packaged, and Sold* (New York, 1999); Norman G. Finkelstein, *Holocaust Industry: Reflection on the Exploitation of Jewish Suffering* (London, 2000).

[13] David S. Wyman, ed., *The World Reacts to the Holocaust* (Baltimore, 1996).

[14] Shlomo Shafir, *Ambiguous Relations: The American Jewish Community and Germany Since 1945* (Detroit, 1999). See the chapters by Shlomo Shafir, vols. 1 and 2, Society, Alan E. Steinweis, vol. 1, Culture, and Jeffrey Peck, vol. 2, Culture.

[15] See Fritz Stern, "Die zweite Chance? Deutschland am Anfang und am Ende des Jahrhunderts," in Fritz Stern, *Verspielte Grösse: Essays zur deutschen Geschichte* (Munich, 1996), 11–36.

institutions, and – given the Two-Plus-Four Treaty on reunification and its political culture – remains incapable of and uninterested in threatening its European neighbors militarily. Finally, despite the increasing Europeanization of German foreign policy, it remains the most important ally of the United States on the European continent.

From the German perspective, no country in the world had as great an influence on the fate of the Germans in the twentieth century as the United States. Its military and political resistance twice foiled attempts by the German Reich to move beyond a semihegemonic position in Central Europe and become a world power among world powers. At the same time, these two "battles for world power" also represented the conflict between two opposing worldviews. America, as embodied by American President Woodrow Wilson, emerged in World War I as the primary ideological opponent of the antiliberal, authoritarian camp in Germany. Behind the German debate over *Siegfrieden* and unlimited submarine warfare were differing views concerning not only strategy and war objectives but also the internal structure of the German Reich.[16] Images of the enemy established during World War I dominated the German image of America until well into World War II. Even in the years after 1939, two antagonistic ideologies confronted one another. The Americans saw National Socialism as the mortal enemy of democracy; Hitler and many Germans saw democracy as the mortal enemy of National Socialism. Held together by anti-Semitism as its overall ideological framework, Nazi propaganda characterized "Americanism" as a scourge of humanity equal to or even greater than Bolshevism, not least because the United States was becoming the most serious threat to the German domination of Europe as the war went on. Images of America generated by the Nazis built on traditional stereotypes,

but beginning in 1938–9 they were increasingly dominated by the racist, anti-Semitic anti-Americanism of extreme right-wing Germans. Again, it was an American president who personified this ideological enmity toward America. According to Nazi propaganda, Franklin D. Roosevelt, the "main warmonger" and an agent of the world's Jews and the international Jewish-Bolshevist conspiracy, had driven the American people into war with the Third Reich.[17] Occasionally, echoes of this radical, National Socialist criticism of America are still heard from right-wing anti-American elements in the Federal Republic today.[18]

A democratic Germany twice turned to the dominant Western power, the United States, following the end of hostilities. American democratization policies after 1945 thus had their roots in the period between the wars, when the growing economic influence of the United States in Germany was accompanied by the first timorous attempts to create a transatlantic "alliance of ideas."[19]

It is largely because of the United States that the citizens of the "old" Federal Republic enjoyed freedom, democracy, prosperity, consumption, modernity, and mobility like no other generation of Germans before them. On an even more existential level, security or destruction – the physical survival of the Germans or their potential extermination in a nuclear holocaust – depended on the decisions of American presidents. Ultimately, *all* Germans owe their unity, on the one hand, to Soviet General Secretary Mikhail Gorbachev and, on the other, to the determined and consistent support of the United States. It was the superpowers who divided and united Germany. Its European neighbors played

---

[16] Ernst Fraenkel, "Das deutsche Wilson-Bild," *Jahrbuch für Amerikastudien* 5 (1960): 66–120; Torsten Oppelland, *Reichstag und Aussenpolitik im Ersten Weltkrieg: Die deutschen Parteien und die Politik der USA 1914–18* (Düsseldorf, 1995).

[17] Philipp Gassert, *Amerika im Dritten Reich: Ideologie, Propaganda und Volksmeinung 1933–1945* (Stuttgart, 1997); Detlef Junker, "The Continuity of Ambivalence: German Views of America, 1933–1945," in David E. Barclay and Elisabeth Glaser-Schmidt, eds., *Transatlantic Images and Perceptions: Germany and America Since 1776* (New York, 1997), 243–63.

[18] See the chapters by Philipp Gassert, vol. 1, Society, and Thomas Grumke, vol. 2, Society.

[19] Ernst Jäckh, *Amerika und wir: Deutsch-amerikanisches Ideenbündnis, 1929–1959* (Stuttgart, 1959).

a considerable role in both processes, but not a decisive one.

The enormous influence of the United States on the security, politics, economics, culture, and society of the Federal Republic during the Cold War can essentially be attributed to seven factors. The first was the overwhelming political, military, economic, cultural, and technological status of the American superpower after 1945. Second, the foreign policy decision-making elite in the era of President Harry S. Truman from 1945 to 1952 possessed a determination and vision the likes of which the United States had not seen since the time of the Founding Fathers. This elite drew its lessons from history and was determined to do everything in its power to prevent the Germans from ever again posing a threat to the peace of Europe or the world. The third factor was the dramatic transition from the wartime coalition to the Cold War and anticommunism. Fourth, Americans' images of the enemy in Europe gradually shifted from a focus on the Germans to a focus on the Russians.[20] Closely related to this was the fifth factor, the fear Germans and Americans shared of Soviet aggression and expansion. Sixth, out of necessity, insight, enlightened self-interest, and a turning away from the past, the West Germans became willing to open themselves up to the West and to see the United States for the most part as the guarantor of their own security and prosperity. The seventh and final factor was the increasing willingness of the West Germans after the construction of the Berlin Wall on August 13, 1961, to submit to the inevitability of détente by paying the price for the Western alliance: the de facto division of Germany. From that point in time, the postponement of Germany's reunification steadily became less of a burden on German-American relations.

The influence of the American superpower on the western part of Germany was certainly greatest during the era of the Allied Control Council (1945–49) and under the reign of the Allied High Commission (1949–55). Nonetheless, after West Germany joined NATO (without ever becoming completely sovereign either politically or under international law) and after the Conference of Foreign Ministers of the four victorious powers collapsed in Geneva in 1955, Germany still depended on America's hegemonic power, its nuclear umbrella, and the presence of American troops west of the Iron Curtain to guarantee its existence. The Federal Republic's economic recovery and its integration into the world market were possible only in the context of a liberal, capitalist international economic system guaranteed by the economic weight of the United States and by American dominance of crucial institutions such as the World Bank, the International Monetary Fund, the General Agreement on Tariffs and Trade (GATT), and the tariff reduction rounds. American influence in other regions of the world guaranteed a supply of raw materials, particularly oil, to Europe and Germany. The West Germans' internal turn toward the West, their eventual arrival in the West, and the incremental transformation of the values, mentality, society, and culture of the Federal Republic also cannot be explained without the considerable role of American influence.

THE PRESENCE OF THE PAST

In the beginning were Hitler and National Socialism, not Stalin and communism. German-American relations from 1947 on came under the spell of the ultimately global confrontation that formed political blocs in East and West. However, the overriding point of departure for American policy on Germany was the attempt of the German Reich to force the racist domination of National Socialism upon Europe. Never again, according to the great lesson of history, would the Germans be allowed to pose a threat

---

[20] The American image of Germany was not, however, as bad after 1941 or as good before 1955 as has long been assumed. See Thomas Reuther, *Die ambivalente Normalisierung: Deutschlanddiskurs und Deutschlandbilder in den USA 1941–1955* (Stuttgart, 2000). See also Astrid M. Eckert, *Feindbilder im Wandel: Ein Vergleich des Deutschland- und des Japanbildes in den USA 1945 und 1946* (Münster, 1999), and, from the older literature, Christine M. Totten, *Deutschland – Soll und Haben: Amerikas Deutschlandbild* (Munich, 1964).

to the security and welfare of Europe and the world. This starting point dominated America's plans for Germany during World War II. And it influenced American occupation policy through 1949, the formation of the West German state that year, the actions of the High Commission, the release of Germany into a state of limited sovereignty, and its entrance into NATO in 1955. It continued to have an effect during the period of détente and arms control, was partially responsible for the American refusal to grant Germany access to nuclear weapons, and was a leitmotif in the integration of the German economy into a liberal international economic system. Even the American attempt to transform and democratize German society and culture was born of this principle. The legacy of the Third Reich was the raison d'être for inclusion of Germany within European and transatlantic organizations – indeed, even for American policy during German reunification and for the conditions of the Two-Plus-Four Treaty. One glimpse into the abyss of a Europe ruled by the National Socialists was enough to nourish the dominant motive for containing Germany through integration until 1990.

Despite a shared anticommunism, despite the Atlantic community's avowals of shared values that have become almost a ritual, and despite the unrelenting declarations of German gratitude for American aid, the fact that the German past refuses to die in America has irritated generations of German politicians, citizens, and visitors to America. Over the course of contemporary decision making, it has fostered mistrust and even downright crises in German-American relations.

The legacy of the Third Reich can probably be seen most plainly in the forty-five years of American security policy toward Germany. "Program to Prevent Germany from Starting World War III"[21] was the title of one ver-

sion of the notorious plan by Treasury Secretary Henry Morgenthau, Jr., calling for the dismemberment, demilitarization, deindustrialization, and long-term occupation of Germany's fragmented territory by its European neighbors to ensure that the country in the heart of Europe would be forever incapable of waging war. Although Morgenthau's recommendations had been weakened and diluted by the time they found their way into the principles of American occupation policy issued on May 10, 1945 (JCS 1067/8),[22] even Morgenthau's most vehement domestic critics agreed with his ultimate goal. The German people had to be disarmed, denazified, and reeducated. National Socialist organizations had to be dissolved and the war criminals brought to justice. And the possibility of renewed German aggression had to be prevented for all time.

The resolve to use all available means to prevent a repetition of the past remained a constant in American security policy during the decisive decade from 1945 to 1955. Beginning in 1946, however, it became increasingly clear that it was not possible to reach agreement with the Soviet Union over the principles of external disarmament (e.g., long-term military disarmament and future foreign trade policy) and internal disarmament (e.g., denazification, reeducation, reparations, dismantling of industry, and decartelization of the German economy). Like Great Britain and France, the United States was not willing – even after the founding of the Federal Republic – to give up control over German security policy. Despite the developing Western integration of West Germany, a deepseated skepticism about the German capacity for democracy and peace remained.[23]

1996); Bernd Greiner, *Die Morgenthau-Legende: Zur Geschichte eines umstrittenen Plans* (Hamburg, 1995); Warren F. Kimball, *Swords or Ploughshares? The Morgenthau Plan for Defeated Nazi Germany, 1943–1946* (Philadelphia, 1976).

[22] See the chapter by Steven L. Rearden, vol. 1, Security; see also the chapter by Wilfried Mausbach, vol. 1, Economics.

[23] See the chapters by Thomas A. Schwartz, vol. 1, Politics, and Thomas Reuther, vol. 1, Society.

[21] U.S. Department of State, *A Decade of American Foreign Policy: Basic Documents, 1941–1949*, rev. ed. (Washington, D.C., 1985), 269–72. See Wilfried Mausbach, *Zwischen Morgenthau und Marshall: Das wirtschaftspolitische Deutschlandkonzept der USA 1944–1947* (Düsseldorf,

The Germans had an overwhelming need for and interest in shaking off the burden of the past on their long road back to sovereignty and "normality," on the path to becoming a full member of the world community politically, economically, and morally. They would deal with their past in a very selective manner, particularly during the 1940s and 1950s.[24] Nevertheless, the Allies in general and the United States in particular continued to draw their motivation for new actions from the lessons and experiences of the Third Reich.

With the onset of the Cold War, securing the Western occupation zones and Western Europe against possible Soviet aggression increasingly became a major problem for American, British, and French military planners. Nevertheless, until the outbreak of the Korean War, the Truman administration found it impossible to get the American public used to the idea of West Germany contributing militarily to the defense of the West. In light of this deep-seated skepticism, the Americans considered it necessary to cast a safety net of controls and provisos over the West German state founded just four years after the demise of the Third Reich.[25] Security policy, foreign policy, and foreign trade policy were taken out of German hands, and deep incursions into the domestic policies of the Federal Republic were considered necessary until such time as the Federal Republic

proved itself to be a democratic and peaceful state.

This test might have lasted some time had not the outbreak of the Korean War in 1950 sent shock waves around the world and revolutionized American foreign and security policy. The effect of the Korean War on American policy and on the overall course of the Cold War can hardly be exaggerated. The only other events of comparable significance were the Chinese revolution, the explosion of the first Soviet atomic bomb, and the American assumption that the Soviets had developed long-range bombers and missiles capable of crossing the ocean and threatening the security of the continental United States. After the Korean War, the American superpower decided for the first time in its history that it needed more than just potential resources to wage war and promote its own interests. For the first time, the United States began to build a massive fighting force on land, at sea, and in the air. A military-industrial complex developed that put food on the table for millions of people and offered a simple, dualistic worldview on which to fall back. This complex was composed of military forces, government departments and bureaucracies, congressional representatives, senators and lobbyists, think tanks, universities, research and production facilities, intelligence services, nuclear strategists, and Kremlinologists, all producing constantly new images of an enemy, scenarios, missile gaps, and "windows of vulnerability," both real and imagined.[26]

This revolution in American foreign policy necessitated what had previously been unthinkable: the rearming of the (West) Germans. The West's collective experience with the Third Reich and German militarism, the deep-seated fear of an armed Germany, collided with the fear of Soviet aggression. This collision produced

---

[24] They saw themselves primarily as victims of war, imprisonment, displacement, and the terror of Allied bombing. Omer Bartov, "Defining Enemies, Making Victims: Germans, Jews, and the Holocaust," *American Historical Review* 103 (1998): 771–816; Elizabeth D. Heinemann, "The Hour of the Women: Memories of Germany's 'Crisis Years' and West German National Identity," *American Historical Review* 101 (1996): 354–95; Robert G. Moeller, "War Stories: The Search for a Usable Past in the Federal Republic of Germany," *American Historical Review* 101 (1996): 1008–48; Eike Wolgast, "Vergangenheitsbewältigung in der unmittelbaren Nachkriegszeit," *Ruperto Carola: Forschungsmagazin der Universität Heidelberg* 3 (1997): 30–9.

[25] See the chapters by Frank Schumacher and Richard Wiggers, vol. 1, Politics, Steven L. Rearden, vol. 1, Security, and Regina Ursula Gramer, vol. 1, Economics. See also Hermann-Josef Rupieper, *Der besetzte Verbündete: Die amerikanische Deutschlandpolitik 1949–1955* (Opladen, 1991), 34–40.

[26] For the Truman administration's interpretation of the Korean War, which was deeply influenced by the domino theory and the "lessons of Munich," see Melvyn P. Leffler, *A Preponderance of Power: National Security, the Truman Administration, and the Cold War* (Stanford, Calif., 1992), 369–74; Michael J. Hogan, *A Cross of Iron: Harry S. Truman and the Origins of the National Security State* (New York, 1998).

incongruities that can only be explained by the German past: the desire for German weapons that could only be fired toward the East; the desire for German soldiers who would not have their own general staff or high command, but who would unleash into combat a power at least as great as that of the Nazi Wehrmacht in a war against the Soviet Union, the East bloc, and the Germans in the GDR;[27] the desire to use German manpower without setting up a German army;[28] and the desire to defend Europe against Germany while defending Germany and Europe against the Soviet Union.

It speaks for the realism of the Federal Republic's first chancellor, Konrad Adenauer, that he immediately recognized the historic opportunity that this crisis presented to the occupied Federal Republic: The offer of German rearmament could be used to secure an end to the controls, a new sovereignty, and an equal status in the Western alliance. Adenauer and the German government only partially achieved their objective in the complicated negotiations with the Western Allies over Adenauer's bargain (a German defense contribution and sovereignty in exchange for the annulment of the Occupation Statute and the dissolution of the Allied High Commission). The West Germans' failure to gain full sovereignty in either a legal or political sense was due less to the new international constellation of the Cold War (defense of Western Europe and West Germany) than to the legacy of the past (defense against Germany). In the October 23, 1954, Paris Agreements, Adenauer pushed through the following laconic wording: "The Federal Republic shall accordingly [after termination of the occupation regime] have the full authority of a sovereign state over its internal and external affairs."[29] If this was intended

as a statement of fact, it must be conceded that it was partly fiction and, if interpreted as wishful thinking, it was a promise that went unfulfilled until 1990. The Allies maintained their rights and responsibilities regarding Berlin and Germany as a whole, particularly the responsibility for future reunification and a future peace treaty. These provisos were safeguards and veto clauses of great political significance. Their application by the Western powers played a significant role, for example, in the second major Berlin crisis of 1958–62, during the political battle over the Moscow and Warsaw treaties and the entry of the two German states into the United Nations between 1970 and 1973, and during the reunification process in 1989–90. Although these developments transformed Western troops on German soil into allied protective forces, negotiations over their continued stationing in Germany made it clear that the Western powers were not giving up their original rights as occupying powers (*occupatio bellica*). Rather, they reserved their indirect right to station troops in Germany. Even after 1955, the ally could legally become a vanquished enemy again.[30]

Just as significant in the long view was the system of arms control, arms limitation, and arms renunciation that permitted the controlled participation of the Federal Republic in the Western military alliance from the time it joined NATO and the Western European Union (WEU) in 1955 until reunification.[31] Under no circumstances would an independent German army be permitted. The Americans were in agreement on that point with the British,

---

[27] See the chapter by David Clay Large, vol. 1, Security.

[28] See the chapter by Erhard Forndran, vol. 1, Security.

[29] Convention on Relations Between the Three Powers and the Federal Republic of Germany, May 26, 1952, as Amended by Schedule I of the Protocol on Termination of the Occupation Regime in Germany, signed at Paris, Oct. 23, 1954, in U.S. Department of State, *Documents on Germany, 1944–1985* (Washington, D.C., 1985), 425; see Helga Haftendorn and Henry Riecke,

eds., "... *Die volle Macht eines souveränen Staates* ...": *Die Alliierten Vorbehaltsrechte als Rahmenbedingung westdeutscher Aussenpolitik 1949/1950* (Baden-Baden, 1996); Hans-Peter Schwarz, *Adenauer: Der Staatsmann 1952–1967* (Stuttgart, 1991), 153–4; See also the chapters by Richard Wiggers, vols. 1 and 2, Politics.

[30] Daniel Hofmann, *Truppenstationierung in der Bundesrepublik Deutschland: Die Vertragsverhandlungen mit den Westmächten 1951–1959* (Munich, 1997); Sebastian Fries, "Zwischen Sicherheit und Souveränität: Amerikanische Truppenstationierung und aussenpolitischer Handlungsspielraum der Bundesrepublik Deutschland," in Haftendorn and Riecke, eds., *Die volle Macht*, 125–57.

[31] See the chapters by Wolfgang Krieger and Erhard Forndran, vol. 1, Security, and Wolfgang Krieger and Matthias Dembinski, vol. 2, Security.

French, and all of Germany's other European neighbors. In addition, Adenauer was forced to "voluntarily" renounce on behalf of the Federal Republic the right to manufacture nuclear, biological, or chemical weapons, and to agree to additional arms limitations. Adenauer did not, however, completely renounce all German participation in the control of nuclear weapons, because the nuclear arms race between the superpowers and the shifting nuclear strategies of the United States – from "massive retaliation" to "flexible response" – had existential consequences for the Federal Republic. Its geography as a front-line state in the Cold War posed an insoluble dilemma. The strategy of deterrence was based on nuclear weapons, so the failure of deterrence would mean the nuclear annihilation of German territory. For this reason, the Federal Republic attempted to participate in some way in the nuclear arena, either within a multilateral NATO nuclear force or through European options. This attempt failed due to French and British resistance, and the Federal Republic's hope for nuclear participation collapsed when the common American and Soviet interest in a nuclear duopoly (with Great Britain as a junior partner) finally forced the Federal Republic to renounce the manufacture, possession, and use of nuclear weapons by putting its signature on the Non-Proliferation Treaty in 1969. This treaty primarily represented an attempt by the two superpowers to protect their dominance, prevent an uncontrolled proliferation of nuclear powers, and thereby keep the system of deterrence manageable. But it was also the experience with the German past that made the German signature so important for America and, especially, the Soviet Union.

It was these fears fed by the past that in the end made continued military control of Germany a central component of international diplomacy concerning the external conditions of German reunification. Containing Germany through integration was again the overriding objective of American foreign policy. Indeed, it was the prerequisite for America's approval of German unification. The country had to remain part of NATO and an overall Atlantic-European structure. On their own, the land-, air-, and

sea-based armed forces of the Federal Republic are capable of neither offensive nor defensive action. Unified Germany is still bound by the rights and obligations arising from the Non-Proliferation Treaty of 1968. Germany's self-containment through renunciation of nuclear weapons was the factor that made German unity tolerable to its neighbors.[32]

The Americans dictated the framework not only for the security of the West Germans (and West Europeans) but also for their prosperity. In this area, too, lessons from the past were the overriding motivation at first. As the Federal Republic attained the status of a major Western economic power in the early 1960s, however, this motivation disappeared. The social market economy (established with considerable assistance from the United States), its successful integration into the world economy, and the associated dependence of German foreign trade on open markets and raw materials convinced the world that there would be no revival of National Socialist economic policies.

The primary objective of both American wartime planning and American economic policy after 1945 had been to use economic and security policy to prevent any possible recurrence of the Nazi regime's protectionist, highly centralized, armament-oriented economy that had freed itself, through autarkic policies and bilateral barter trade, from dependency on the world economy and had ruthlessly exploited subjugated peoples. As early as the late 1930s, American politicians – especially Secretary of State Cordell Hull – considered the economic policy of the Third Reich to be one of the major causes of German aggression.[33] In the 1940s, this perception of National Socialism would combine with a generally negative view of the world economy in the period between the wars. According to this widely held view, the system of international trade that had been arduously and incompletely rebuilt after World War I was

---

[32] See the chapters by Stephen F. Szabo, vol. 2, Politics, and by Karl Kaiser, vol. 2, Security.

[33] Detlef Junker, *Der unteilbare Weltmarkt: Das ökonomische Interesse in der Aussenpolitik der USA 1933–1941* (Stuttgart, 1975).

devastated by the Great Depression. The international economic crisis undermined the world monetary system. Taking the position of "every man for himself," virtually all countries resorted to protectionist and interventionist measures. The result was an atrophied and fragmented system of international trade that exacerbated worldwide misery and fostered the development of dictatorships and fascist political systems.

This dominant view of the past necessarily led to several conclusions. Only a new international economy based on liberal principles and anchored in international institutions could prevent a repetition of the past. Only the complete elimination of all forms and causes of National Socialist economic policy could make Europe as a whole a productive partner in a new international economic order. Only the United States, the only major power that grew richer in the course of World War II, had the resources to establish this new international economic system. In 1945, the United States held two-thirds of the world's gold reserves. Its share of more than 50 percent of the world's production of industrial goods even exceeded its share in the period from 1925 to 1929. An undamaged economy of extraordinary productivity and great competitive advantage stood in stark contrast to an impoverished and divided Eurasian continent.[34] The Americans dominated the conference at Bretton Woods in July 1944, where 1,500 delegates from forty-four countries established the International Monetary Fund and the World Bank as the central pillars of a liberal international economic order.[35]

According to the Bretton Woods principles and liberal theory, it would have been logical to cleanse the German economy of National Socialist structures and integrate it as quickly as possible into an international system of free trade, but that did not happen right away. The onset of the Cold War very soon divided the German economy, and East Germany disappeared behind the Iron Curtain. The economic

policies of the Western occupying powers – the United States, the United Kingdom, and France – differed considerably. The United States faced several constraints. In the short term, it had to bring down the high mortality rates in its occupation zone. In the medium and long terms, industrial disarmament measures motivated by security considerations and fueled by the spirit of the Morgenthau Plan ran the risk of destroying the basis for German and European economic recovery. These measures included reparations, the dismantling of production units, restrictions on German industrial production, the expropriation of German foreign holdings, and a ban on foreign trade. The ghosts of the past thus paved the winding road by which the West German economy was reintegrated into the international marketplace. A clear direction was found only through the Marshall Plan, the currency reform, the introduction of the social market economy, the U.S.-backed establishment of the European Coal and Steel Community, and Germany's ultimate reintegration into a multilateral system of international trade.[36]

Once the German *Wirtschaftswunder* (economic miracle) began in the 1950s and Germany again rose to the position of Europe's most significant economic and trading power, the legacy of the past no longer played a role in economic policy relations between the two countries.[37] The United States and the Federal Republic became the two largest trading nations in the world. In a mixture of cooperation, competition, and conflict, the two nations sought to adapt to the crises in the economic system of the Western capitalist world that were triggered by the slow-down in the growth of the world economy after 1965, by the oil shocks, and by the Nixon shock when the United States abandoned the Bretton Woods system in 1971

---

[34] Detlef Junker, *Von der Weltmacht zur Supermacht*, 71.
[35] Harold James, *International Monetary Cooperation Since Bretton Woods* (New York, 1996).

[36] See the chapters by Christoph Buchheim, Wilfried Mausbach, Jörg Fisch, Regina Ursula Gramer, Werner Plumpe, Gerd Hardach, and Werner Bührer, vol. 1, Economics.
[37] See the chapter by Welf Werner, vol. 2, Economics. This is why the chapters in the Economics section of volume 2 no longer address the presence of the past.

and thereby forced the industrial nations to convert to a system of floating exchange rates. Although the United States still periodically exerted pressure on the European Economic Community (EEC) and the Federal Republic in transatlantic economic conflicts, the weight of West Germany in German-American economic relations continued to grow. There were essentially four reasons. The primary reason was the Federal Republic's growing economic power and its significant contribution to the growth of the world economy. Second, beginning in 1957, the EEC developed into a zone in which the Federal Republic could exert economic influence and find economic protection. The EEC brought about a broadening and deepening of trade within Europe, reduced dependency on the United States, and faced the Americans as a bloc in trade conflicts. Third, beginning in the early 1980s, the Federal Republic was less and less willing to do what it had been required to do for two decades due to its dependency on the United States in matters of security: to pay not only the costs for its own armed forces but also a share of the cost of stationing American forces in Germany by such means as offset payments and purchases of American armaments.[38] Fourth, despite conflicts with its transatlantic ally, the Federal Republic turned out to be, by and large, an economic power that adhered to the fundamental principles of liberalism and an open world market. It always took a very cooperative stance toward the United States in the various tariff-reduction rounds of the postwar period and at the international economic summits beginning in the 1970s. Above all, it always attempted to mediate the more serious conflicts between the Americans and the French. Bridging economic and other differences between the United States and France was a standard exercise in West German foreign policy.

It is very probable that nothing contributed more to the democratic stabilization of the Federal Republic than the German *Wirtschaftswun-*

der of the 1950s, which enabled the Federal Republic to bear the heavy burden of occupation, reconstruction, integration, and reparations costs. The unprecedented growth of the world economy between 1945 and 1965, as well as the liberalization of international trade and the explosive growth in trade between industrialized nations, proved to be a windfall for the Federal Republic. Therefore, to the extent that it determined the framework for the social market economy and the growth of the world economy, the United States was responsible for laying an economic foundation for democratic development in the Federal Republic of Germany.

It is much more difficult to determine the impact of American denazification and democratization policies on the democratic development of the second German republic.[39] The only certainty is that the attempt to change German society and political culture in a fundamental way was again motivated decisively by the lessons of the past. The "crusade in Europe" (so Eisenhower) must not end with the unconditional surrender of the Third Reich. Rather, all Americans who had been involved in planning for postwar Germany during the war were convinced that the crusade must lead to a radical transformation of German society and, indeed, the German national character.[40] Thus, the packs of the GIs who were

---

[38] See the chapter by Hubert Zimmermann, vol. 1, Economics.

[39] See the chapters by Barbara Fait, Cornelia Rauh-Kühne, and Hermann-Josef Rupieper, vol. 1, Politics; by Rebecca Boehling, James F. Tent, Jessica C. E. Gienow-Hecht, and Karl-Heinz Füssl, vol. 1, Culture; and by Klaus-Dietmar Henke, Petra Gödde, Claus-Dieter Krohn, and Raimund Lammersdorf, vol. 1, Society.

[40] Günter Moltmann, *Amerikas Deutschlandpolitik im Zweiten Weltkrieg: Kriegs- und Friedensziele 1941–1945* (Heidelberg, 1958); Paul Y. Hammond, "Directives for the Occupation of Germany: The Washington Controversy," in Harold Stein, ed., *American Civil-Military Decisions* (Birmingham, AL, 1963), 311–464; Anthony J. Nicholls, "American Views of Germany's Future During World War II," in Lothar Kettenacker, ed., *Das "andere Deutschland" im Zweiten Weltkrieg: Emigration und Widerstand in internationaler Perspektive* (Stuttgart, 1977), 77–87; Uta Gerhardt, "Reeducation als Demokratisierung der Gesellschaft Deutschlands durch das amerikanische Besatzungsregime: Ein historischer Bericht," *Leviathan: Zeitschrift für Sozialwissenschaft* 27 (1999): 355–85; Klaus-Dietmar Henke, *Die amerikanische Besetzung*

shipped across the Atlantic to Europe contained not only weapons and ammunition, but also fifteen million books.[41] The books symbolized the superpower's belief in its 1945 mission of not only defeating Germany, but also transforming the politics, constitution, culture, and mentality of the Germans – of taking up the "fight for the soul of Faust."[42] The lessons of the past could be summed up as follows: never again National Socialism, never again dictatorship, never again racism, never again German subservience to authoritarianism. On account of the Nazi past and their interpretation of German history, leery Americans in 1945 considered the Germans incapable of returning to democracy on their own. They first had to be denazified, reeducated, and led to democracy in measured steps, a process that the Americans controlled very tightly in their zone. This was necessary because the American government, Congress, and public opinion regarded developments in Germany with skepticism. As late as 1949, 55 percent of Americans still did not believe that the Germans were capable of governing themselves in a democratic manner.[43]

Leaving aside the trials against the major war criminals in Nuremberg, which were conducted jointly by the Allied powers, it is difficult to determine the immediate and long-term effects of denazification, reeducation, democratization, and other punitive measures that the United States carried out in the regional states of its occupation zone – Bavaria, Württemberg-Baden, Greater Hesse, and Bremen – either alone or, beginning in 1949, together with Great Britain and France within the framework of the High Commission. There are several reasons for this. These measures were aimed at a "society in ruins"[44] that lacked the characteristics of a normal, structured society. The means and the ends of a prescribed, licensed "democracy from above" were locked into an irreconcilable conflict. Rule by command or decree demands that people obey orders; the essence of democracy is self-determination. The mass denazification and related punitive measures in the American zone confronted a population that used nearly all its energy in the battle for survival, food, heat, shelter, and caring for family members. It was a population that suppressed as much as possible any mention of the Third Reich, the war, and the genocide of the Jews, and that saw itself predominantly as victims rather than perpetrators. Moreover, the advent of the Cold War added a new dimension to democratization and "reorientation" policies. Anti-Nazism turned into an antitotalitarianism that tended to equate Nazism and communism, thus retroactively legitimated the anticommunist propaganda of the Nazis. And it diverted the spiritual and emotional energies of the West Germans away from dealing with the past, turning them instead toward the new front: the free West against the totalitarian communists.

It is difficult in the end to distinguish what part of the incremental development of democratic structures was due to coercion and understanding by decree, what part to the prior existence of German democratic traditions, and what part to insights freely acquired by the Germans living under occupation. Three hypotheses, however, have a high degree of plausibility. Without the trials against war criminals and without forced denazification, the "cleansing" of German society might have been even less extensive than it actually was. Without the American decision to begin a process of controlled democratization in its zone in early 1946, it would have been much more difficult to establish a representative democracy in West

Deutschlands (Munich, 1995), 67–78; Richard L. Merritt, *Democracy Imposed: U.S. Occupation Policy and the German Public, 1945–1949* (New Haven, Conn., 1995), 1–69; Petra Marquardt-Bigman, *Amerikanische Geheimdienstanalysen über Deutschland 1942–1949* (Munich, 1995), 119–68; Michaela Hönicke, "Das nationalsozialistische Deutschland und die Vereinigten Staaten von Amerika (1933–1945)," in Larres and Oppelland, eds., *Deutschland und die USA,* esp. 79–82.

[41] See the chapter by Martin Meyer, vol. 1, Culture.
[42] See the chapter by Thomas A. Schwartz, vol. 1, Politics.
[43] See the chapter by Thomas Reuther, vol. 1, Society.

[44] Christoph Klessmann, *Die doppelte Staatsgründung: Deutsche Geschichte 1945–1955,* 5th ed. (Göttingen, 1991), chap. 3; Theodor Eschenburg, *Jahre der Besatzung 1945–1949* (Stuttgart, 1983).

Germany. Without a democratic, constitutional tradition in Germany, the "prescribed democracy"[45] would not have become a natural, freely accepted part of West German political culture. The most important domestic policy foundations of the Federal Republic – the introduction of the social market economy, the currency reform and abolition of price-fixing, and the promulgation of the Basic Law – are excellent illustrations of the complex relationship between American and Allied influence, on the one hand, and, on the other, Germany's traditions and desire for self-assertion.[46]

Between 1949 and 1955, after the establishment of the Federal Republic of Germany and the intensification of the East-West conflict following the outbreak of the Korean War, the Allied High Commission and its American representative, John J. McCloy, gradually lost control over Germany's policy on its past because they wished to retain control over the present – namely, over West Germany's rearmament and integration into the West. Sometimes reluctantly and sometimes with resignation, the Allies had to recognize that – if they expected to keep their new ally in the Western camp – they had to tolerate the overwhelming longing of most West Germans to put their past behind them. Time and again, the U.S. High Commissioner pointed out to the State Department and the administration in Washington that the fundamental conflict between the United States' role as victor, occupier, and enforcer of Allied justice and its role as ally and friend of Germany was becoming sharper and that this conflict was causing ever clearer damage to American policy toward Germany.[47]

The end of the occupation regime and the establishment of a partially autonomous Federal Republic in 1955 were important turning points for the presence of the past in postwar German-American relations. The American government lost its legal right to intervene in Germany's policies touching upon the past. This did not eradicate the legacy of National Socialism from German-American relations. But from that point until the fall of the Berlin Wall, it seldom provoked confrontation in the official foreign policy of the allied states. The most famous exception was the thoroughly unsuccessful attempt of Chancellor Helmut Kohl in 1985 to force a reconciliation over the past with President Ronald Reagan over the graves at Bitburg. Commenting on the incident, Secretary of State George P. Shultz told Arthur Burns, U.S. ambassador to the Federal Republic, "Hitler is laughing in hell right now."[48]

[45] Theo Pirker, *Die verordnete Demokratie: Grundlagen und Erscheinungen der "Restauration"* (Berlin, 1977).

[46] See the chapters by Christoph Buchheim and Werner Plumpe, vol. 1, Economics, and by Hermann-Josef Rupieper, vol. 1, Politics. For a discussion of American influence on the Basic Law, see the report on the literature in Adolf M. Birke, *Die Bundesrepublik Deutschland: Verfassung, Parlament und Parteien* (Munich, 1997), 64–70; Eberhard Pickart, "Auf dem Weg zum Grundgesetz," in Richard Löwenthal and Hans-Peter Schwarz, eds., *Die zweite Republik: 25 Jahre Bundesrepublik Deutschland – eine Bilanz* (Stuttgart, 1974), 149–76; Erich J. C. Hahn, "The Occupying Powers and the Constitutional Reconstruction of West Germany, 1945–1949," *Cornerstone of Democracy: The West German Grundgesetz 1949–1989*, German Historical Institute, Occasional Paper 13 (Washington, D.C., 1995), 7–36; Karlheinz Niclauss, *Der Weg zum Grundgesetz: Demokratiegründung in Westdeutschland 1945–1949* (Paderborn, 1998); Edmund Spevack, "Amerikanische Einflüsse auf das Grundgesetz: Die Mitglieder des Parlamentarischen Rates und ihre Beziehungen zu den USA," in Heinz Bude and Bernd Greiner, eds., *Westbindungen: Amerika in der Bundesrepublik* (Hamburg, 1999), 55–71.

[47] Thomas A. Schwartz, "John McCloy and the Landsberg Cases," in Jeffry M. Diefendorf, Axel Frohn, and Hermann-Josef Rupieper, eds., *American Policy and the Reconstruction of West Germany, 1945–1955* (New York, 1993), 433–54; Ulrich Brochhagen, *Nach Nürnberg: Vergangenheitsbewältigung und Westintegration in der Ära Adenauer* (Hamburg, 1994); Norbert Frei, *Vergangenheitspolitik: Die Anfänge der Bundesrepublik und die NS-Vergangenheit:* (Munich, 1996); Jeffrey Herf, *Divided Memory: The Nazi Past in the Two Germanies* (Cambridge, Mass., 1997); Aleida Assmann and Ute Frevert, *Geschichtsvergessenheit, Geschichtsversessenheit: Vom Umgang mit deutschen Vergangenheiten nach 1945* (Stuttgart, 1999).

[48] George P. Shultz, *Turmoil and Triumph: My Years as Secretary of State* (New York, 1993), 550. Shultz's sharp criticism of Kohl stands in contrast to the position taken by Reagan, who continued to defend his decision to visit the German military cemetery. See Ronald Reagan, *An American Life* (New York, 1990), 376–84. See also David B. Morris, "Bitburg Revisited: Germany's Search for

Relations between the two nations up to the point of reunification and beyond were generally characterized by careful efforts on both sides to ensure that German-American relations were not adversely affected by the increasing attention accorded the Holocaust inside and outside academia beginning in the 1960s, or by its growing importance in both German and American consciousness. German politicians and diplomats, the party-linked foundations, and German-American organizations such as the Atlantik-Brücke attempted to expand their dialogue with Jewish organizations and leading Jewish personalities in the United States. On the German side, this meant not denying the past but promoting the new, democratic Germany. Although the majority of American Jews were and are still distrustful of the democratic Germany, many Jewish organizations have attempted, even after Bitburg, to keep this dialogue going.[49]

DUAL CONTAINMENT

The prevailing interpretive model of American policy toward Europe beginning in 1947–8 – namely, the concept of double or dual containment – is also impossible to understand without considering the presence of the past. The Soviet Union was to be contained by building up an opposing force in Western Europe while the Federal Republic would *simultaneously* be contained by integration in the Western alliance and the liberal international economy. Political scientist Wolfram F. Hanrieder has written about the significance of this concept. Although he did not coin the term, he has contributed more astutely than anyone else to its diffusion:

Every major event in the postwar history of Europe follows from this: the rearmament and reconstruction of the Federal Republic within the restraints of international organizations, the development of NATO from a loosely organized mutual assistance pact into an integrated military alliance, American

support for West European integration, and the solidification of the division of Germany and Europe. So long as the two components of America's double containment were mutually reinforcing, America's European diplomacy was on a sure footing. In later years, when tensions and contradictions developed between the two components, German-American relations became increasingly strained.[50]

The concept of "dual containment" has been criticized because the nature and scope, the origin and immediacy of the German and Soviet threats to the United States were fundamentally different. An analysis of the situation in Europe after 1945 purely in terms of power politics would need to reject the idea that American policy toward Germany and the Soviet Union could be construed as comparable even on only a conceptual level and would, therefore, also reject the concept of "dual containment."[51] But such a view of the Cold War geopolitical constellation ignores the cultural and mental dispositions that arise during the collective interpretation of historical experiences. For example, the notion of a catastrophic German tradition from Luther to Hitler, popularized by William Shirer's bestseller in the 1960s,[52] demonstrates

---

[50] Wolfram F. Hanrieder, *Germany, America, Europe: Forty Years of German Foreign Policy* (New Haven, Conn., 1989), 6. See also Wilfried Loth, "Die doppelte Eindämmung: Überlegungen zur Genesis des Kalten Krieges 1945–1947," *Historische Zeitschrift* 238 (1984): 611–31; Thomas A. Schwartz, "Dual Containment: John J. McCloy, The American High Commission, and European Integration," in Francis Heller and John R. Gillingham, eds., *NATO: The Founding of the Atlantic Alliance and the Integration of Europe* (New York, 1992): 131–212; Rolf Steininger et al., eds., *Die doppelte Eindämmung: Europäische Sicherheit und deutsche Frage in den Fünfzigern* (Munich, 1993); as well as the chapters by Thomas A. Schwartz, Michael Wala, Ruud van Dijk, Frank Schumacher, and Frank Ninkovich, vol. 1, Politics; Steven L. Rearden, vol. 1, Security; and Klaus Schwabe, Gottfried Niedhart, and H. W. Brands, vol. 2, Politics.
[51] See the chapter by Wolfgang Krieger, vol. 1, Security, and the concluding essay by Hans-Peter Schwarz, vol. 2.
[52] Rohan O'Butler, *The Roots of National Socialism* (London, 1941); William Montgomery McGovern, *From Luther to Hitler: The History of Nazi-Fascist Philosophy* (London, 1946); William L. Shirer, *The Rise and Fall of the Third Reich: A History of Nazi Germany* (New York, 1960).

Normalcy," *German Politics and Society* 13 (1995): 92–109, and the chapter by Jeffrey Peck, vol. 2, Culture.
[49] See Shafir, *Ambiguous Relations*.

that the Americans did not see their military victory over National Socialism as a definitive answer to the German problem. German authoritarianism, Prussian militarism, and National Socialist fantasies of destruction could become virulent again – if not today, then tomorrow; if not in the same form, then in a new form. Skepticism about the German national character linked the past and the future of American policy, which actually sought to "contain" the latent danger of such excesses.

Herein lies the qualitative difference from the kind of hegemonic control that the United States sought to exert over Britain or France. The Western superpower never acknowledged France's *vocation mondiale et européenne*, its claim to the role of a major international power and a hegemonic position within Europe. For decades, American politicians were bent on preventing France from using European integration to push the United States out of Europe and free the Federal Republic from its dependence on the transatlantic colossus by making it France's junior partner in Europe. The United States wanted – and wants – to remain the decisive balancer and pacifier in Europe.[53] Unlike the Federal Republic, France never accepted this claim.

French President Charles de Gaulle, the self-appointed embodiment of "eternal" France, always envisioned a French-led Europe that would achieve parity with the two superpowers.[54] Anglo-Saxon resistance foiled de Gaulle's plans to be accepted into a nuclear directorate consisting of the United States, France,

and the United Kingdom. In response, France took the liberty of denying Great Britain access to the EEC (1963). It also shocked the United States and NATO allies with its decision to withdraw French forces from NATO's integrated military command (1966), called for the withdrawal of all American troops from French soil, undermined the American-dominated monetary system of Bretton Woods, and made a vain but daring attempt to forge a unilateral alliance with the Federal Republic in the Franco-German Treaty of 1963.[55]

Politicians in the Federal Republic dared not even dream of such latitude in dealing with the Western hegemonic power. That was due in part to the greater, indeed, existential dependence of the Federal Republic on the United States in the area of security policy. It was also because the legacy of National Socialism made an independent German claim to power untenable. The United States would not have tolerated it. The American policy of containing Germany through integration was geared precisely toward withholding from the Federal Republic the military, political, or social basis for such a power play. German politicians understood this well and chose multilateral routes for pursuing their interests.

Unlike Germany, France had not forfeited its right to conduct unilateral power politics. De Gaulle's hegemonic plans for Europe may have been inconvenient and annoying, but they could not shake a French-American trust rooted in a two-hundred-year-old shared tradition. The two nations perceived and continue to perceive themselves as standard-bearers of the universal mission of freedom, which began its victory march through the world with the American and French Revolutions. A veiled battle over the birthright of this mission is part of the tradition of French-American rivalry. Despite or perhaps because of this shared tradition, French national pride, born of the consciousness of French greatness and sovereignty, has chafed for several decades against American hegemonic policies in

---

[53] Frank Costigliola, *France and the United States: The Cold Alliance Since World War II* (New York, 1992); Klaus Schwabe, "Atlantic Partnership and European Integration: American-European Policies and the German Problem, 1947–1966," in Geir Lundestad, ed., *No End to Alliance. The United States and Western Europe: Past, Present and Future* (New York, 1998), 37–80; Pierre Melandri, "The Troubled Partnership: France and the United States, 1945–1989," ibid., 112–33.

[54] Georges-Henri Soutou, *L'alliance incertaine: Les rapports politico-stratégiques franco-allemands, 1954–1996* (Paris, 1996), 131; Robert Paxton and Nicholas Wahl, eds., *De Gaulle and the United States. A Centennial Reappraisal* (Oxford, 1994).

[55] Klaus Hildebrand, *Von Erhard zur Grossen Koalition 1963–1969* (Stuttgart, 1984), 99–111.

Europe, while the Federal Republic has viewed these policies primarily as protection and assistance toward the goal of integration. This wounded pride was the underlying reason for the series of French-American conflicts, all of which had repercussions for German-American and Franco-German relations and that forced the Germans into continual diplomatic gymnastics between the United States and France.[56]

INTERNATIONAL ECONOMIC CRISES, MULTIPOLARITY, AND THE SECOND COLD WAR

The Federal Republic did play a more significant role in bilateral relations with the United States beginning in the second half of the 1960s. But military protection by the United States and NATO remained vital to German survival until reunification and the collapse of the Soviet Union, and the price for this protection was the military containment of the Federal Republic and the division of Germany. In the economic sphere as well, neither the Federal Republic nor the European Community (EC) became a truly equal partner in terms of power or rights. This state of affairs is well concealed by the fact that the EC and the Federal Republic were engaged in nearly continuous negotiations with the United States within numerous multilateral organizations for the purpose of resolving economic crises.

The *relative* increase in significance of the Federal Republic in the economic realm was also related to diminishing American hegemony over the world economy. The entanglement of the United States in the Vietnam War and, in particular, the year 1968, in many ways a decisive turning point in the Cold War,[57] played a significant role in this process. The United States appeared to be falling prey to the fate of all great world empires. Its resources were no longer ad-

equate to meet global requirements. America was at risk of losing its dominant position because of imperial overstretch. President Lyndon B. Johnson (1963–69) had hoped to be able to wage two wars at once: the war on poverty at home and the war on communism in Southeast Asia. Congress, however, refused to fill the growing hole in the budget with a tax increase. Loans from the international capital markets – that is, from the European and Asian allies (primarily Germany and Japan) – therefore, had to cover mounting deficits. The consequences – a weak dollar, chronic American balance-of-trade and balance-of-payments deficits, and rising prices at home – began to undermine the stability of the international monetary system of Bretton Woods that had served to institutionalize American domination of the world economy since World War II.[58] Although the currency-exchange mechanism was temporarily restored during the gold crisis of March 1968,[59] that year was the beginning of the end of an era of unparalleled economic growth. During the half-decade from 1968 to 1973–4, political decisions and developments contributed to a slowing of international economic growth. The political reaction of the oil-producing countries to the Arab-Israeli Six Day War in 1967 led to the first oil-price shocks of 1973 and 1974.[60]

In the face of international economic crises and its own weakened position, the United States attempted to do the same thing that the British had done after 1763 and drove the American colonists into the Revolutionary War: to externalize the costs of its own empire in part and recover them from a dependent clientele. The United States was still strong enough to force primarily the Europeans and Japanese – although not itself – to adapt actively to the new

---

[56] See the chapter by Eckhart Conze, vol. 2, Politics.

[57] See the first attempt to interpret 1968 as a global turning point for domestic and foreign policy: Carole Fink, Philipp Gassert, and Detlef Junker, eds., *1968: The World Transformed* (New York, 1998).

[58] Diane B. Kunz, *Butter and Guns: America's Cold War Economic Diplomacy* (New York, 1997).

[59] Robert M. Collins, "The Economic Crisis of 1968 and the Waning of the 'American Century,'" *American Historical Review* 101 (1996): 396–422.

[60] See Daniel Yergin, *The Prize: The Epic Quest for Oil, Money, and Power* (New York, 1991); Jens Hohensee, *Der erste Ölpreisschock 1973/74: Die politischen und gesellschaftlichen Auswirkungen der arabischen Erdölpolitik auf die Bundesrepublik und Westeuropa* (Stuttgart, 1996).

international economic problems, to thwart the largely multilateral economic crisis management with unilateral measures if necessary (much to the aggravation of the Europeans), and to threaten the Federal Republic in particular with the withdrawal of American troops in order to obtain economic concessions. The American colonists had been free to rebel in part because their external enemies, the French and the American Indians, had been conquered with the very effective help of the British in the global war of 1756–63. The West Germans, however, lived in fear of the Warsaw Pact's military potential. President Johnson instructed his staff to demand from the Germans what Congress would not give him: "What you have to do is put great pressure to get the Germans; I want to use all the influence I can to hold the Alliance together and get the Germans to pay the bill; but they don't want to do it, and if they can't do it, I can't do it by myself."[61]

The 1970s and 1980s, which were marked by monetary and trade conflicts between the United States and Europe, began with a unilateral termination of the principles of the Bretton Woods system by the Nixon administration in 1971, the Nixon shock. The United States freed itself of the obligation to exchange dollars for gold at any time. When the major trading nations switched to floating exchange rates in 1973, the United States was able to use the dollar as a political weapon even against its own allies. To respond to what it deemed "unfair" trade practices of other countries, the United States acquired further foreign trade policy tools in 1974 and 1988; these enabled it to respond with retaliatory measures to actual or perceived protectionist practices of other nations.[62]

Foreign trade policy had been a collective task of the EC since 1974. National economic policies had been multilateralized through international institutions such as the Organization for Economic Cooperation and Development (OECD), the GATT, the World Bank, and the International Monetary Fund. Finally, the World Economic Summit of heads of state had been created in 1974 at the initiative of French President Valéry Giscard d'Estaing and German Chancellor Helmut Schmidt, and communications were increasing between finance ministers and central-bank presidents of the major industrial nations. These developments notwithstanding, however, multilateralism remained only a means – albeit one that kept conflicts within limits – by which the nations involved could pursue their own national interests as defined by their political leaders.

The United States remained the most significant power in terms of pursuing its national interests. It secured its access to oil and other raw materials. Despite the various crises, the dollar remained the most important currency. And the enormous American domestic market remained relatively invulnerable to retaliatory measures; the United States remained much less dependent on exports than the Federal Republic and Japan, for example. Neither the Federal Republic nor the EC could change these facts despite improved Franco-German and intra-European cooperation. The unilateral latitude enjoyed by the United States in economic matters became even more visible in the 1980s when President Ronald Reagan terminated the policy of détente in his first term (1981–85), initiated a massive (reactive) arms buildup, and let Japan and the Europeans foot a significant part of the bill.

The American arms buildup had, of course, severe economic consequences. From 1980 to 1984, military expenditures in the United States climbed 40 percent at the same time that Congress was passing tax cuts. The two measures together led to a spiraling budget deficit and an immense foreign debt for the United States. In 1985, the country became a debtor nation for the first time since World War I. Whereas the United States still had a positive net external

---

[61] Memorandum for the Record, Subject: President's Conversation with John McCloy Concerning U.S. Position in Trilateral Negotiations, 10:45–11:40 A.M., Wed., Mar. 1, 1967, Francis Bator papers, box 17, folder: Trilateral-McCloy Meeting, Lyndon B. Johnson Library, Austin, Tex. I am grateful to Philipp Gassert for pointing out this document.

[62] See the lead essay and chapter by Harold James and the chapters by Monika Medick-Krakau, Andreas Falke, and Bernhard May, vol. 2, Economics.

asset position of $106.2 billion in 1980, by the end of the Reagan administration in 1988 it had a negative net external asset position of $532.5 billion.[63] The national debt grew from $914 billion in 1980 to $1.823 trillion in 1985; by 1991, it was approaching the $4 trillion mark.[64] The Americans have been living on credit since the Reagan administration, particularly capital transfers from Europe and Japan. The Bush administration could not provide Mikhail Gorbachev – the great mover and shaker, failed reformer, and sorcerer's apprentice – with the massive economic aid he desired. Given the attitude of Congress, the administration would have had to borrow the money on capital markets. In the 1990-91 Gulf War against Saddam Hussein, the Americans may have been militarily dominant, but they let Saudi Arabia, Japan, and Germany bear most of the costs.

Although the international economic crises and the loss of American economic hegemony presented a challenge mainly to those nations, international organizations, and "summit meetings" that sought to influence the rules of the international "free" market, the loss of American nuclear superiority improved the position of its paramount Cold War enemy, the communist, totalitarian Soviet Union. The atomic stalemate between the superpowers and its political and military consequences were the overriding structural problem of security policy in the 1960s, 1970s, and 1980s. The problems resulting from this strategic situation for Europe and its "frontline" state, the Federal Republic, could in principle only be handled within the triangle consisting of the Soviet Union, the United States, and Western Europe. In security policy, these decades can be seen as a continual attempt by the Europeans to influence the nuclear policies of the Western superpower as the United States simultaneously attempted to reach bilateral agreements with the Soviet Union while

making only as many concessions to its NATO allies as was necessary to preserve the alliance.[65] Much was at stake for the Federal Republic: namely, its security and its hope for reunification.[66]

The nuclear stalemate, reflected in the principle of Mutually Assured Destruction (MAD), offered compelling motivation for arms control, cooperation, and limited détente between the United States and the USSR in order to prevent the worst possible disaster, a nuclear holocaust. The arms race, driven by competing risk scenarios and the interests of the military-industrial complex on both sides, had long since entered the realm of the absurd. By 1972, for example, the United States and the Soviet Union possessed enough nuclear weapons to explode fifteen tons of radioactive TNT over every man, woman, and child on earth.[67] After the shocks of the Berlin Crisis and the Cuban Missile Crisis, the two superpowers had signed several treaties aimed at slowing the arms race and reducing the risk of a nuclear surprise attack. In 1962, the two powers agreed to the joint, peaceful use of outer space in several areas. In 1963, a direct teletype connection, the "hot line," was installed between the Kremlin and the White House. In 1967, the United States, the Soviet Union, and Great Britain signed a treaty on the peaceful exploration and use of outer space. On July 1, 1968, these nations attempted, with the

---

[65] On the problem of cooperation in the hegemonic alliance structure beginning in 1945, see Thomas Risse-Kappen, *Cooperation Among Democracies* (Princeton, N.J., 1995); Geir Lundestad, *"Empire" by Integration: The United States and European Integration 1945–1997* (Oxford, 1998); Josef Joffe, *The Limited Partnership: Europe, the United States, and the Burdens of Alliance* (Cambridge, 1987). An excellent illustration from the German perspective are the memoirs of Helmut Schmidt, *Men and Powers: A Political Retrospective* (New York, 1989), 119–284.

[66] See the chapters by Klaus Schwabe, Gottfried Niedhart, Klaus Larres, Werner Link, H. W. Brands, Steven Brady, and Christian Hacke, vol. 2, Politics; and by Wolfgang Krieger, Kori Schake, Michael Broer, and Matthias Dembinski, vol. 2, Security.

[67] Walter LaFeber, *The American Age: United States Foreign Policy at Home and Abroad Since 1750* (London, 1985), 615.

---

[63] Carl-Ludwig Holtfrerich, *Wirtschaft USA: Strukturen, Institutionen und Prozesse* (Munich, 1991), 369.

[64] Paul M. Kennedy, *The Rise and Fall of the Great Powers: Economic Change and Military Conflict from 1500 to 2000* (New York, 1987), 527; Paul M. Kennedy, *Preparing for the Twenty-First Century* (New York, 1993).

Non-Proliferation Treaty, both to preserve the nuclear powers' monopoly and to prevent an uncontrolled increase in the number of nuclear powers. All three nations had an overriding interest in keeping the Federal Republic of Germany from gaining access to nuclear weapons. The first round of negotiations on strategic arms limitations (SALT I), which had begun in 1970, was brought to a close with President Richard M. Nixon's visit to Moscow in May 1972. The goal was to limit offensive delivery systems by establishing limits on the number of intercontinental ballistic missiles and submarine-launched ballistic missiles that each side could have. At the same time, the two sides agreed to allow each country to build no more than two antiballistic missile (ABM) systems, which were theoretically capable of removing the other side's second-strike capacity and would, therefore, have destroyed the balance of terror.

The policies of arms control and détente on both sides rested on political assumptions and expectations. Soviet objectives included nuclear parity with the United States, recognition as an equal superpower and competitor in all regions of the world, the preservation of the political status quo in Europe (i.e., the division of Europe and Germany), and finally, actual acceptance of a communist bloc under Soviet leadership. For its part, the United States was prepared to enter into arms-control negotiations and – as established by the Final Act of the Helsinki Conference in 1975 – to cement into place the foreign policy status quo in Europe (i.e., renunciation of the use of force, the inviolability of borders). This made a principle – not necessarily binding under international law – out of the pattern of response that the United States had demonstrated at the time of the uprisings of the East Germans in 1953 and the Hungarians in 1956, the erection of the Berlin Wall in 1961, and the invasion of Czechoslovakia by Warsaw Pact troops in 1968: the pattern of not intervening militarily in the communist sphere of influence. However, the United States never recognized the Soviet Union as a politically or morally equal superpower. For the Americans, communism remained an inhumane system with no regard for the right to freedom. In Helsinki, therefore, the Soviet Union reluctantly had to declare its acceptance of the right of peoples to self-determination and its respect for human rights and the fundamental freedoms of the citizen (Basket III). It did so knowing full well that the actual implementation of these freedoms would be the downfall of the communist regimes in the Eastern bloc. The Helsinki Final Act, like the Federal Republic's Moscow and Warsaw treaties, was thus an instrument for both maintaining and overcoming the status quo.[68]

Even after the end of the Vietnam War, the basic antagonistic structure of the Cold War remained in place until the collapse of the Soviet Union. The global competition between the superpowers continued even at the height of the period of limited détente from 1970 to 1975. Midway through Jimmy Carter's presidency, the policy of limited détente began to lose its domestic political support. Americans reached the conclusion that the Soviet Union was attempting to establish itself as the dominant superpower worldwide through its military interventions in the Third World and a dangerous arms buildup that included new intercontinental missiles, new nuclear-powered submarines, the buildup of six deep-sea fleets, and the deployment of new medium-range missiles that were particularly threatening to Europe. President Reagan ended the policy of détente in his first term and led the United States into an ice-cold war with the Soviet Union. Anticommunism and an arms buildup were the pillars of his program. Reagan surprised and shocked the world the most with his announcement in March 1983 that he intended to develop an impenetrable barrier in space – the Strategic Defense Initiative (SDI) – that would protect the United States from nuclear surprise attack by the Soviet Union. Such a barrier promised to return to Americans the unassailable security of the nineteenth century. At the same time, it threatened to decouple Europe from the United

[68] See the chapter by Michael Lucas, vol. 2, Politics.

States and to destroy not only the logic of mutual deterrence but NATO as well.[69] The message of Reagan's first term was clear: The United States would find its security not through détente and arms control but through more armaments and technological advances.

Both the policies of arms control and détente and the second Cold War had severe consequences for German-American relations. As in the early phase of the Cold War, this bilateral relationship was a dependent variable of American policy toward the Soviet Union and Western Europe.[70] The policy of détente deferred the prospect of German reunification to the indefinite future. Adenauer's promise that a policy of strength would lead to reunification was exposed as an illusion by the Berlin Wall. The politics of arms control made the Germans fully aware for the first time of the dilemmas of their security situation in the nuclear age. It was, therefore, no accident that Kennedy's new security policy led to serious conflict with the Adenauer government; that the joint Franco-German reaction to that policy, the 1963 Élysée Treaty, contributed to Adenauer's departure from office; that Johnson's security policy brought about the downfall of Chancellor Ludwig Erhard; that Carter's and Reagan's policies played their part in undermining Helmut Schmidt's position within his own party; and that Chancellor Helmut Kohl had to play the political strongman to push through the NATO double-track decision against the wishes of a formidable German peace movement.

From its founding, the Federal Republic had no alternative to its total dependence on the United States for a credible nuclear deterrent against the Soviet Union. This deterrent could not be permitted to fail; the worst-case scenario – an attack by the Warsaw Pact – could not be permitted to occur. If it did, the Federal Republic, nearly incapable of resisting, would either have been immediately overrun, which would at least have ensured the physical survival of the West Germans ("better red than dead"), or it would have become a battlefield where conventional, nuclear, and possibly chemical and biological weapons would be used. For the Germans, the nightmarish aspect of the decades of bilateral and NATO planning for this worst-case scenario was that the Federal Republic had a say only about the form of its annihilation.[71] Even the "flexible-response" strategy, which was pushed through NATO with difficulty in the 1960s, did not alter the dilemma in which the Federal Republic found itself. Although it provided for a "pause" between the use of conventional and nuclear weapons in the event of an attack from the East, this strategy gave the American president alone the time to negotiate before triggering an intercontinental nuclear holocaust. "A 'limited conflict' from the U.S. standpoint would be a total war for the Federal Republic and would extinguish its national existence."[72] It was, therefore, logical under the circumstances that dissonance and conflict characterized the German-American security relationship. This was so from the time the Bundeswehr was established until shortly before reunification, even if the United States did occasionally accommodate German and European concerns, as with the NATO double-track decision in December 1979, in order to keep the NATO alliance together. Other notable examples of this accommodation included the flexible-response strategy; the poorly developed plan for a sea-based, multilateral nuclear force

[69] The resuscitation of such plans by the U.S. Congress and the Clinton administration at the end of the millennium has aroused similar European fears. See William Drozdiak, "Possible U.S. Missile Shield Alarms Europe," *Washington Post*, Nov. 6, 1999, A1; "Ausbau der amerikanischen Raketenabwehr: Fischer kritisiert US-Pläne," *Süddeutsche Zeitung*, Nov. 5, 1999, 8.

[70] See the chapters by Manfred Görtemaker, Frank Ninkovich, Diethelm Prowe, and Manfred Knapp, vol. 1, Politics; by Wolfgang Krieger, Kori Schake, and Erhard Forndran, vol. 1, Security; and the chapters in vol. 2, Politics and Security.

[71] This was apparent from the time of the first nuclear planning games in the mid-1950s. See the chapters by Kori Schake and Frederick Zilian Jr., vol. 1, Security.

[72] Helga Haftendorn, *Security and Detente: Conflicting Priorities in German Foreign Policy* (New York, 1985), 105.

in Europe that the United States conceived as a placebo for the Germans; the exclusion of the constrained ally from possession of nuclear weapons; the NATO double-track decision; the stationing of short- and medium-range nuclear weapons in Europe; the neutron bomb; and the American SDI program.[73]

The nuclear stalemate and the military, economic, political, spiritual, and emotional strain of the Vietnam War forced the United States into political détente in Europe and the West Germans into the largest change of course in their foreign policy since 1955: namely, the de facto but not de jure recognition of the division of Germany in the Moscow and Warsaw treaties of 1970 and 1973. With this "active adjustment to American détente policy,"[74] many Germans had to give up the illusion of the 1950s that European détente could be made dependent on progress toward German reunification. The great disillusionment occurred when construction of the Berlin Wall began on August 13, 1961, and the West accepted the barricading of the Eastern sector. The highest circulation German newspaper, *Bild*, was enraged on August 16: "The West is doing NOTHING! U.S. President Kennedy is silent.... MacMillan has gone hunting ... and Adenauer is cursing Brandt!"[75] While the arms-control policies of the superpowers were a brutally clear reminder to the Germans of their (in)security dilemma, the Wall symbolized a dead end in Western reunification policy.

The Federal Republic clearly had to adapt twice to new American policies between the time the Wall was built and the revolution in international relations initiated by Mikhail Gorbachev in the late 1980s. Until the middle of Carter's presidency, Germans had to adapt to the American policy of détente and thereafter to Reagan's second Cold War. Again, the dog was wagging the tail and not vice versa. The

reason that the second adaptation became so difficult was that the majority of West Germans had made their peace with détente after the Moscow and Warsaw treaties were signed and had put off any hope of reunification. The Germans had serious problems with the Woodrow Wilson of the nuclear age, Ronald Reagan. They considered his arms buildup and Manichaean worldview dangerous. The "fear of our friends" (Oskar Lafontaine) grew and added fuel to the protest movement against the stationing of American Pershing and cruise missiles in Europe. Adapting left a deep, painful imprint on German-American relations, German society, and the German political parties.[76] Not until the process of German reunification began did we again see, as in the 1950s, a fundamental parallelism in values *and* interests between the Americans and Germans.[77]

ARRIVAL IN THE WEST: AMERICAN
INFLUENCE ON SOCIETY AND CULTURE
IN THE FEDERAL REPUBLIC

When we as historians look back from the perspective of German reunification at the history of German-American relations in the era of the Cold War, we may venture to say that the United States had a greater influence on society and culture in the Federal Republic than any other state or society in the world. As with foreign, security, and economic policy, virtually no area of German society and culture lacked an American dimension.

The Germans experienced the new Western superpower as an "exogenous revolutionary" after 1945, "as prosecutor, judge, and reeducator attempting to radically change the German government, society, and economy,"[78] and attempting to Westernize, democratize, and transform the political culture of the Germans with a targeted "Americanization from above."

---

[73] See the chapters in vols. 1 and 2, Security.

[74] See the chapter by Werner Link, as well as the chapters by Klaus Schwabe, Gottfried Niedhart, Richard Wiggers, and Christian Hacke, vol. 2, Politics.

[75] Quoted in Hans-Peter Schwarz, *Die Ära Adenauer: Epochenwechsel 1957–1963* (Stuttgart, 1983), 146.

[76] See the chapter by Matthias Zimmer, vol. 2, Politics.

[77] See the chapters by Stephen F. Szabo, vol. 2, Politics and Karl Kaiser, vol. 2, Security.

[78] See the chapter by Knud Krakau, vol. 1, Society.

The decade from 1955 to 1965 may be viewed as an incubation period for "Americanization from below," which subsequently encompassed West German society as a whole.[79] This Americanization from below was not the result primarily of U.S. governmental policies, as had been the case from 1945 into the early 1950s, but rather of the influence of nongovernmental American players.

As plausible as these generalizations may sound, it must be conceded that historical research on the Americanization of Germany and the development of a civil society – particularly in the 1960s, 1970s, and 1980s – is in its infancy. In addition, researchers have a great deal of difficulty objectively recording and conceptually defining this influence. The academic discussion of this influence on the mentality, society, and culture of West Germans – and to some extent even on East Germans behind the Iron Curtain – is centered around a few terms ("Americanization," "democratization," "Westernization," "modernization," and "technologization") that are often used synonymously, but entail competing or overlapping meanings.[80] It is all the more

difficult to clarify their meaning because they were not invented by historians but appeared in sources of the time as normative and often pejorative terms as, for instance, in the vocabulary of rigid anti-Americanism.[81]

Moreover, it is extraordinarily difficult, if not impossible, to determine the exact breadth and depth of American influence and the chronological and substantive fluctuations in the relation of American influence versus German tradition, of imitation versus rejection, of active assimilation versus cultural self-assertion, of American mission versus German democratic disposition, of pro-Americanism versus anti-Americanism. A growing number of historians are wondering whether a one-way street can even exist in "intercultural transfer processes."[82] Even a superpower like the United States is not capable of exerting direct and unmediated influence and power in the cultural arena, if we understand cultural power to mean the capacity to force one's own spirit (*Geist*), language, and lifestyle onto another. Intersocietal and intercultural transfer cannot be forced into such binary subject-object categories. Cultural appropriation always means a transformation and a merging into one's own tradition. In the relationship between Germany and the United States, the "westernization," "democratization," and "modernization" of the Federal Republic should thus be interpreted not as "Americanization" but rather as a cultural and

[79] See the chapter by Axel Schildt, vol. 1, Society. See also Axel Schildt, *Ankunft im Westen: Ein Essay zur Erfolgsgeschichte der Bundesrepublik* (Frankfurt am Main, 1999).

[80] See the chapters by Frank Trommler, vol. 1, Culture; Volker Berghahn, Axel Schildt, and Raimund Lammersdorf, vol. 1, Society; Frank Trommler and Klaus Milich, vol. 2, Culture; and Lily Gardner-Feldman and Stephen Kalberg, vol. 2, Society. See also Michael Ermarth, ed., *America and the Shaping of German Society, 1945–1955* (Providence, R.I., 1993); Konrad H. Jarausch and Hannes Siegrist, eds., *Amerikanisierung und Sowjetisierung in Deutschland 1955–1970* (Frankfurt am Main, 1997); Alf Lüdtke, Inge Marssolek, and Adelheid von Saldern, eds., *Amerikanisierung: Traum und Alptraum im Deutschland des 20. Jahrhunderts* (Stuttgart, 1996); Anselm Doering-Manteuffel, *Wie westlich sind die Deutschen? Amerikanisierung und Westernisierung im 20. Jahrhundert* (Göttingen, 1999); Reiner Pommerin, ed., *The American Impact on Postwar Germany* (Providence, R.I., 1995); Axel Schildt and Arnold Sywottek, eds., *Modernisierung im Wiederaufbau: Die westdeutsche Gesellschaft der 50er Jahre* (Bonn, 1998); Manfred Görtemaker, *Geschichte der Bundesrepublik Deutschland: Von der Gründung bis zur Gegenwart* (Munich, 1999), 199–270; "The American Occupation of Germany in Cultural Perspective: A Roundtable," *Diplomatic History* 23 (1999): 1–77; as well

as the instructive bibliographies of Anselm Doering-Manteuffel, "Dimensionen von Amerikanisierung in der deutschen Gesellschaft," *Archiv für Sozialgeschichte* 35 (1995): 1–34; Bernd Greiner, "'Test the West': Über die 'Amerikanisierung' der Bundesrepublik Deutschland," *Mittelweg* 36 (1997): 4–40; Philipp Gassert, "Amerikanismus, Antiamerikanismus, Amerikanisierung: Neue Literatur zur Sozial-, Wirtschafts- und Kulturgeschichte des amerikanischen Einflusses in Deutschland und Europa," *Archiv für Sozialgeschichte* 39 (1999): 531–61.

[81] See the chapters by Knud Krakau and Philipp Gassert, vol. 1, Society; and by Claus Leggewie, David B. Morris, Rainer Schnoor, and Philipp Gassert, vol. 2, Society.

[82] Johannes Paulmann, "Internationaler Vergleich und interkultureller Transfer: Zwei Forschungsansätze zur europäischen Geschichte des 18. bis 20. Jahrhundert," *Historische Zeitschrift* 267 (1998): 649–85.

social synthesis that has both accepted and resisted American influence.[83]

Finally, we must remember that the discussion of American influence on the society and
culture of the Federal Republic is part of a
larger debate in Europe and other regions of
the planet over the "Americanization" of the
world. The ascent of the United States to the
position of global superpower in the twentieth
century was accompanied by an equally global
history of perceptions on the part of those nations and regions, societies and political systems
affected by the American model and influence,
by American hegemony and control in Europe,
Asia, Latin America, and – to a lesser extent –
Africa.[84]

In Germany, too, the discussion about Americanization and modernization began before
1945. American influence on German society
and culture had existed in the first half of the
century.[85] Not until after 1945, however, did

West Germany become part of a "Euroameri-
can" Western civilization in a social and cultural
sense, a civilization under the umbrella of American hegemony and under the influence of the
Cold War and unprecedented economic growth
among the industrial nations on both sides of the
Atlantic.

With some justification, the two decades
from the early 1950s to the early 1970s have
been called the "golden age" of the twentieth century.[86] In contrast to the period before
1945, a tight web of highly diverse German-
American interactions developed during the
half century after the war. There was an expansion of American influence on mass consumption and mass culture – on popular culture, if
popular culture is understood, as in the United
States, as the forms and products of the entertainment and leisure industries. This influence
rested on the triumphant ideology of the social
market-capitalist system, which sought to solve
the problem of poverty and the unequal distribution of wealth through economic growth,
and on the mass prosperity the *Wirtschaftswunder* brought West Germany in the 1950s.[87] The
web of interactions was created by intensified
transatlantic trade, increased reciprocal investment activity,[88] improved communications networks and communications technologies (film,
radio, press, television), and the revolution in
transatlantic travel and tourism brought about
by the airplane. Increased professional collaboration of Americans and Germans in many areas
reinforced these trends, as did the international

[83] For similar conclusions, see Richard Pells, *Not Like
Us: How Europeans Have Loved, Hated, and Transformed
American Culture Since World War II* (New York, 1997).
See also Berndt Ostendorf, "The Final Banal Idiocy
of the Reversed Baseball Cap: Transatlantische Wider-
sprüche in der Amerikanisierungsdebatte," *Amerikastu-
dien/American Studies* 44 (1999): 25–47.

[84] Michael J. Hogan, ed., *The Ambiguous Legacy: U.S.
Foreign Policy in the American Century* (New York, 1999),
provides an excellent introduction to this problem. See
also Peter Duignan and Lewis H. Gann, *The Rebirth of the
West: The Americanization of the Democratic World, 1945–
1958*, 2d ed. (Lanham, Md., 1996); Rob Kroes, *If You've
Seen One, You've Seen the Mall: Europeans and American
Mass Culture* (Urbana, Ill., 1996); Richard F. Kuisel, *Se-
ducing the French: The Dilemma of Americanization*, 2d ed.
(Berkeley, Calif., 1996).

[85] See Alexander Schmidt, *Reisen in die Moderne: Der
Amerika-Diskurs des deutschen Bürgertums vor dem Ersten
Weltkrieg im europäischen Vergleich* (Berlin, 1997); Egbert Klautke, "Amerika im Widerstreit: Vergleichende
Untersuchungen zur Auseinandersetzung mit den Vereinigten Staaten in Deutschland und Frankreich
während der 'Klassischen Moderne,' 1900–1933," Ph.D.
diss., University of Heidelberg, 1999; Detlev J. K. Peukert, *The Weimar Republic: The Crisis of Classical Modernity*
(New York, 1992); Mary Nolan, *Visions of Modernity:
American Business and the Modernization of Germany* (Oxford, 1994); Frank Costigliola, *Awkward Dominion: American Political, Economic, and Cultural Relations with Europe,*

1919–1933 (Ithaca, N.Y., 1984); Gassert, *Amerika im Dritten Reich*; Junker, "Continuity of Ambivalence"; Frank
Trommler, "The Rise and Fall of Americanism in Germany," in Trommler and McVeigh, eds., *America and the
Germans*, 333–42.

[86] Eric J. Hobsbawm, *The Age of Extremes: A History
of the World, 1914–1991* (New York, 1994), 225–402.

[87] Charles S. Maier, "The Politics of Productivity:
Foundations of American Economic Policy After World
War II," *International Organization* 31 (1977): 607–33.

[88] See the chapters by Hans-Eckart Scharrer and
Kerstin Müller-Neuhof, vol. 1, Economics, and by
Hans-Eckart Scharrer and Christine Borrmann, vol. 2,
Economics.

communications of nongovernmental organizations such as churches,[89] business organizations,[90] unions,[91] sports clubs, universities, scientific organizations, and professional societies;[92] of social movements such as the 1968 activists[93] and the women's,[94] peace, and environmental movements;[95] of intelligence services;[96] of political foundations,[97] transatlantic elites, and institutions in general;[98] and even of right-wing extremists.[99]

The history of the assimilation and rejection of America by the West German political, military, social, and cultural elite during the Cold War has yet to be written. Nevertheless, several building blocks are available for such a history. They touch upon the transfer, assimilation, or rejection of American ideas, mentality, institutions, and behavior patterns – the "American way of life" – by these elites, many of whom had made extended stays in the United States. Although attempts by the Americans to influence the German educational system in their occupation zone were largely unsuccessful,[100] the Amerika-Häuser (American cultural and information centers) and the American exchange programs of the early 1950s contributed significantly to the Westernization of a segment of West Germany's budding elite. In 1954, approximately half of all Germans had heard of

the Amerika-Häuser, and of those familiar with them, 84 percent knew their programs well. Media sources such as publishers, newspapers, magazines, and radio stations, which the United States licensed and controlled, were to play a significant role in convincing Germans to open their minds toward the West.[101]

While downplaying the negative sides of the United States – crime, poverty, racism, and the apartheid system in the American South – the Americans promoted the liberal and capitalist values of their polity, such as freedom, tolerance, independent initiative, individualism, the free market, and consumption. From 1950 to 1956, the United States developed an exchange program with West Germany more extensive than any other similar program with another country. By 1956, 14,000 West Germans had visited the United States. The target group consisted of members of the younger generation who were expected to belong to the future elite of the Federal Republic. The fact that the U.S. State Department conducted fourteen studies between 1950 and 1960 to determine the effects of these programs on German participants illustrates how seriously the United States took this exchange program. In 1952, one extrapolation concluded that between 900,000 and 1.6 million Germans "had been exposed to the multiplier effect of the exchange program."[102]

When the U.S. government programs ended in the mid-1950s, the reestablished German exchange organizations and private organizations on both sides of the Atlantic stepped into the breach and managed to provide a firm foundation for the exchange of German and American elites up to the end of the Cold War – and beyond.

Alongside these governmental measures, other U.S.-inspired – and, in some cases, CIA-funded – networks developed. They influenced the noncommunist Left in Western Europe in

[89] See the chapters by Mark E. Ruff, vol. 1, Society, and Robert Goeckel, vol. 2, Society.

[90] See the chapter by Jonathan Wiesen, vol. 1, Society.

[91] See the chapters by Michael Fichter, vol. 1 and vol. 2, Society.

[92] See the chapters by Mitchell G. Ash, vol. 1, Culture, and by Willi Paul Adams and John McCarthy, vol. 2, Culture.

[93] See the chapter by Claus Leggewie, vol. 2, Society.

[94] See the chapters by Hanna Schissler, vol. 1 and vol. 2, Society.

[95] See the chapter by Carl Lankowski, vol. 2, Society.

[96] See the chapters by Wesley Wark, vol. 1, Security, and by Loch Johnson and Annette Freyberg, vol. 2, Security.

[97] See the chapter by Ann Phillips, vol. 2, Society.

[98] See the chapters by Lily Gardner Feldman and Felix Philipp Lutz, vol. 2, Society.

[99] See the chapter by Thomas Grumke, vol. 2, Society.

[100] See the chapter by James F. Tent, vol. 1, Culture.

[101] See the chapter by Jessica C. E. Gienow-Hecht, vol. 1, Culture.

[102] See the chapter by Karl-Heinz Füssl, vol. 1, Culture.

the 1950s and 1960s, particularly in the Federal Republic. The objective of these networks was to offer an anticommunist and antitotalitarian ideology on a high intellectual level. This ideology has often been described as "consensus liberalism." It combined such classical American values as freedom, justice, property, and the "pursuit of happiness" with the American lesson of the 1930s (the New Deal) that the active state as an agent of reform is a necessary part of the free enterprise system. Business and labor unions, as entirely legitimate elements of this system, would negotiate collective bargaining agreements with each other without state intervention. The economic goal of consensus liberalism was neither class warfare nor unrestrained capitalist competition, but rather an increase in mass buying power through productivity and growth. Recent research has shown how strongly German elites were influenced by *Der Monat*, a periodical for intellectuals, and the Congress for Cultural Freedom (*Kongress für kulturelle Freiheit*), a network of intellectuals. The list of persons influenced by this network reads like a "Who's Who" of the early Federal Republic: Willy Brandt, Max Brauer, Adolf Grimme, Eugen Kogon, Siegfried Lenz, Golo Mann, Alexander Mitscherlich, Richard Loewenthal, Marcel Reich-Ranicki, Ernst Reuter, Karl Schiller, Carlo Schmid, Theo Sommer, Dolf Sternberger, Otto Suhr, and many others. Westernization also influenced the West German Protestants associated with the Kronberg circle as well as the most influential publishing house in the early Federal Republic, the Axel Springer Verlag.[103]

These consensus-liberal elites were among the first to be attacked by the New Left and

the 1968 movement as representatives of a bourgeois class society. One of the ironic twists in the Westernization of the Federal Republic is the fact that even the New Left critical of America drew some of its intellectual ammunition, primarily protest slogans and lifestyle models, from the United States.[104] No detailed studies have been done yet on American influence on German elites during the 1970s and 1980s. Given the intensified transatlantic communication in all spheres of life, however, American influence on governmental and nongovernmental figures in the Federal Republic probably increased during that period.

Another possible approach to the question of influence on German elites and German society in general consists of sectoral analyses that attempt to assess American influence on, for example, the German media,[105] sciences,[106] American studies,[107] German literature and German readers,[108] West German theater,[109] the German art scene,[110] architecture,[111] urban and transportation planning,[112] and economic thought.[113] Here, too, influence was a matter of reciprocal interactions and processes of assimilation, but the dominant direction of influence ran from West to East.

American influence on West German mass culture and consumer society is another

---

[103] Michael Hochgeschwender, *Freiheit in der Offensive? Der Kongress für kulturelle Freiheit und die Deutschen* (Munich, 1998); Thomas Sauer, *Westorientierung im deutschen Protestantismus? Vorstellungen und Tätigkeit des Kronberger Kreises* (Munich, 1998); Gudrun Kruip, *Das "Welt"-"Bild" des Axel Springer Verlags: Journalismus zwischen westlichen Werten und deutschen Denktraditionen* (Munich, 1998); Axel Schildt, *Zwischen Abendland und Amerika: Studien zur westdeutschen Ideenlandschaft der 50er Jahre* (Munich, 1999).

[104] See the chapters by Claus Leggewie and Philipp Gassert, vol. 2, Society.

[105] See the chapter by David Posner, vol. 1, Society.

[106] See the chapter by Mitchell G. Ash, vol. 1, Culture.

[107] See the chapter by Willi Paul Adams, vol. 2, Culture.

[108] See the chapters by Martin Meyer, vol. 1 and vol. 2, Culture.

[109] See the chapter by Andreas Höfele, vol. 1, Culture.

[110] See the chapters by Sigrid Ruby, vol. 1, Culture; David Bathrick, vol. 2, Culture; and Stefan Germer and Julia Bernard, vol. 2, Culture.

[111] See the chapters by Werner Durth, vol. 1 and vol. 2, Culture.

[112] See the chapter by Jeffry M. Diefendorf, vol. 1, Society; see also the chapter by Brian Ladd, vol. 2, Society.

[113] See the chapter by Harald Hagemann, vol. 2, Economics.

growing and still developing field of research. The monographic studies published so far have been limited in focus to the 1940s and 1950s or the protest movement of 1968.[114] One thing that appears to be certain is that the initial resistance of traditional German elites to this influence and fears of a possible cultural collapse caused by rock 'n' roll, boogie-woogie, rowdies, hippies, jazz, and jeans had dwindled by the late 1950s. The products of the American leisure, entertainment, and consumer industries had largely become accepted parts of German society. Neither the 1968 movement – with its critical stance against the United States – nor the peace and protest movement against the NATO double-track decision in the early 1980s, nor the periodic jeremiads of German cultural critics have changed this long-term trend, a trend that continues unabated even after the end of the Cold War and that has become a fixture in the cultural "globalization" of the present.

Perhaps nothing illustrates the extent to which the Federal Republic had become part of the American-dominated West by the end of the Cold War as impressively as the Americanization of the German language, which has rightly been described as a "postwar variant of a growing Anglicization of the German language beginning in the eighteenth century."[115] Beginning with a conscious political and thus also linguistic orientation toward the United States in the early postwar period, the Americanization of the German language expanded to nearly all areas of life and nearly all segments of West German society. By the end of the Cold War, it had become a commonplace that American English was the lingua franca of the Western world and that the West Germans were taking part in this globalization by virtue of both their English-language skills and the Americanization of their language.

Ironically, it appears in retrospect that the influence of American popular culture on the second German state, the German Democratic Republic, during the Cold War was in many ways the most threatening and least controllable aspect of the otherwise marginal East German-American relationship.[116] From the time the GDR was founded in 1949 until the belated establishment of diplomatic relations a quarter century later, the United States pursued a strict policy of nonrecognition of the Soviet satellite. Even once recognition was granted, it largely remained a formality, with no political or economic and almost no cultural substance. The American embassy in East Berlin was merely an embassy "to the German Democratic Republic." Neither trade nor cultural agreements were signed. The dependence of the GDR on the Soviet Union – its raison d'être – placed severe restrictions on foreign policy action undertaken by the East German state. Until the end of the Cold War and reunification, the focus of the United States was on the Federal Republic and the Soviet Union. Before the erection of the Berlin Wall, the United States undertook a few half-hearted attempts to destabilize the GDR as part of a poorly conceived "rollback" policy.[117] Although possible recognition of the GDR became a central problem during the Berlin crisis of 1958–62, the United States held firm to its existing policy. When the Wall was built, the GDR became a symbol of a system with no respect for human rights. At the same time, however, the second German state, which had no domestic lobby in the United States, essentially disappeared behind the Wall as far as the American public was concerned.

The cultural contacts between the two states were sporadic before diplomatic recognition, and this did not change fundamentally after 1974 despite a few initiatives by individuals and organizations. The only exception, as indicated previously, was the boundary-breaking attraction of American popular culture and the

---

[114] See note 80 and the chapters by Uta G. Poiger, vol. 1, Culture, and Michael Ermarth, vol. 2, Culture.

[115] See the chapter by Heidrun Kämper, vol. 2, Culture.

[116] See the chapters by Christian Ostermann, vol. 1 and vol. 2, Politics; Uta G. Poiger, vol. 1, Culture; Rainer Schnoor, vol. 1 and vol. 2, Society; and Heinrich Bortfeldt, vol. 2, Culture.

[117] See the chapter by Bernd Stöver, vol. 1, Politics.

products of American mass consumption, which the citizens of the GDR could examine themselves in West Berlin before the Wall went up and which the media, especially television, drummed into their consciousness after the erection of the Wall. For several decades, the governing Socialist Unity Party of Germany (*Sozialistische Einheitspartei Deutschlands*, or SED) and East German authorities fought against these products and expressions of the "American way of life." They attempted to disparage consumption of American pop culture – boogie-woogie, jazz, rock and pop, jeans and cowboy hats, Elvis, and *Dallas* – as cultural barbarism, as targeted infiltration and a threat to the stability of the farmers' and workers' state. Beginning in the 1970s, the SED took a new line. Instead of doing direct battle with the influence of American mass culture, the party attempted to neutralize it, harness it, and use it to stabilize the communist system. Nothing helped; the seductive power of American popular culture could not be stopped at the border with the Federal Republic. There was no remedy on either side of the Wall for the "global, American-style mass cultural ecumenical movements."[118] In this respect, even the East arrived in the West long before reunification.

[118] See the chapter by Rainer Schnoor, vol. 2, Society.

POLITICS

"No Harder Enterprise"

Politics and Policies in the German–American Relationship, 1945–1968

Thomas A. Schwartz

A German colleague once told me that Americans always begin their scholarly presentations with a humorous story or anecdote. Whether or not that national stereotype holds true, I could not resist beginning this chapter with such a story. When my first book was published, it had the title *America's Germany*, an expression that captured the almost proprietary relationship that the American foreign policy establishment – notably John J. McCloy – had with "their" Germany. However, in the post-Cold War atmosphere of the early 1990s, the German publisher did not particularly care for my choice of title, with its connotations of a Germany within the American orbit and under American tutelage. They changed the title to *Die Atlantik-Brücke*, a translation that may have soothed national pride but missed the point of the original moniker entirely.

The relationship between the United States and the Federal Republic of Germany from 1945 to 1968 was unique in the history of relations between highly developed states. The rapid reversal of alliances that began the German-American relationship and the intensity with which it flourished during the Cold War resist comparison. Embedded within the multilateral framework of NATO, the German-American alliance spawned a network of exceptionally close institutional and personal relationships. For all intents and purposes, the Federal Republic of Germany functioned as an integral part of a larger American commonwealth or confederation, a nonvoting but influ-

ential player in the game of American politics, with its concerns and interests woven into the fabric of American decision making.[1] Germany received far more of Washington's attention than that accorded to some parts of the American republic itself, becoming at times a laboratory of political experiments, a vindication of the American political economy, and a "border of freedom" defended by 300,000 American soldiers. (By the early 1960s, about as many Americans lived in Germany as in eleven of the fifty states.[2]) Although this relationship affected Germany most of all, the challenge Secretary of State Dean Acheson once called "no harder enterprise," the integration of Germany into the Western community of nations, changed America as well.[3]

America's role as the guarantor of Germany's security against the Soviet Union had a wide range of profound effects. The most obvious and direct of these was the sharply diminished role of the German military in the German political system, but the effects were no less profound in other areas. The dynamism of the *Wirtschaftswunder* (economic miracle) secured

---

[1] I have elaborated in more detail on this point in Thomas A. Schwartz, "The United States and Germany After 1945: Alliances, Transnational Relations, and the Legacy of the Cold War," *Diplomatic History* 19 (1995): 549–68.

[2] U.S. Department of Commerce, *Statistical Abstract of the United States* (Washington, D.C., 1989), 18.

[3] Dean Acheson, speech before the Pilgrims Club of London, *New York Times*, May 11, 1950.

the process of democratization while boosting America's own confidence in the future of liberal capitalism during a crucial phase of the Cold War. The powerful societal and cultural impact of the United States, especially apparent in such areas of popular culture as movies, music, and fashion, led observers to consider the Federal Republic the most "Americanized" part of Western Europe. Although all these areas must be considered – as this project has done – the articles in this section demonstrate the centrality of politics in the German-American relationship. The American impact on German political culture, the interactions of American and German democratically elected leaders and opposition groups, and the importance of each to the political life and debates of the other – all stem from the politics and policy of the German-American alliance.

The nineteen articles in this section reflect the unsurprising fact that the historical scholarship in this period tends to be richer and more complete for the occupation and the first decade of the relationship, and less definitive – if still suggestive and provocative – for the 1960s. The articles also reflect the areas of consensus and conflict that grew out of the different American and German perspectives on the relationship from 1945 and 1968.

AMERICAN PERSPECTIVES, 1945–1968

On August 26, 1944, President Franklin D. Roosevelt told his secretary of war, Henry Stimson, that "It is of the utmost importance that every person in Germany should realize that this time Germany is a defeated nation." Although Roosevelt did not "want to starve them to death," the Germans should be fed "three times a day with soup from Army soup kitchens."[4] In September 1946, Secretary of State James Byrnes told an audience in Stuttgart that the "American people want to help return the government of Germany to the German people,"

and "help the German people to win their way back to an honorable place among the free and peace-loving nations of the world."[5] Only two years separated Roosevelt's emphasis on severe punishment from Byrnes's commitment to German rehabilitation and self-determination, but the two statements serve to define the spectrum of American policy. Punishment was a significant aspect of the early occupation period, with war-crimes trials, the dismantling of German industries, and wide-scale denazification.[6] However, for many Americans, including General Lucius D. Clay, the military governor, the war itself had severely punished Germany, and their first instinct was to establish a functioning society in a bombed-out landscape.

Clay and other American officials also saw in their defeated enemy a historic opportunity to "democratize" German political culture and fundamentally transform German political life. In their view, they were not only fulfilling America's historic mission in bringing democracy to a hated foe but also ensuring America's own security, since only a democratic Germany could be trusted to break with the hostile traditions of the past. From the earliest days of the occupation, General Clay actively promoted the process of political party formation and elections at the local level, preparing the way for German leaders to take on greater responsibility.[7] Clay insisted, correctly, that Congress would not tolerate a lengthy and expensive occupation of Germany.[8] But Clay also believed that free elections and a democratic political system were essential to Germany's revival. Although the Americans imposed "democracy," Americans and Germans often disagreed over aspects of the new political structure, such as federalism, and the result was either compromise or an acceptance of German ideas.[9] Along with his emphasis on elections,

---

[4] Memorandum for the Secretary of War from the President, Aug. 26, 1944, PSF, War Department, 1944–1945, box 104, FDR papers, Roosevelt Library.

[5] U.S. Department of State, *Documents on Germany, 1944–1985* (Washington, D.C., 1985), 99.
[6] See the chapter by Cornelia Rauh-Kühne in this section.
[7] See the chapter by Barbara Fait in this section.
[8] See the chapter by Steven Brady in this section.
[9] See the chapters by Barbara Fait and Hermann-Josef Rupieper in this section.

Clay himself promoted greater transparency in the political process through his frequent press conferences. As the Cold War began to intensify and the United States scaled back its direct military occupation, Americans placed greater emphasis on a "massive propaganda program" to convince Germans of the merits of European integration, rearmament, and support for the United States in the Cold War.[10] In appearances before Congress, High Commissioner John J. McCloy argued that "At this stage of history there is a better chance to influence the German mind than there has been for a century," and that the United States was engaged with the Soviet Union in a "struggle for the soul of Faust."[11] Such dramatic metaphors may seem overblown, but they captured the sense of many Americans that Germany was the central battlefield of the Cold War, and that whoever prevailed there was most likely to triumph.

And it was in Germany that America seemed to experience real success in the Cold War. The dramatic economic and psychological impact of the Marshall Plan was most apparent in Germany.[12] The success of the Berlin airlift and the outpouring of enthusiastic support by Berliners helped shift public perceptions of Germans within the United States. To Americans, the divided city of Berlin became the foremost symbol of the Cold War; the former capital of Nazi Germany was embraced as a courageous outpost of the Free World surrounded by a communist menace.[13] Along with their special attachment to Berlin, American leaders came to see the Federal Republic of Germany as a ward of the United States, a growing "child" of democracy under the supervision of its powerful patron. During the 1950s, the "golden age" of German-American relations, the American political effort in Germany was intense and extensive, involving both public and private

agencies.[14] The Ford Foundation, with the advice of Shepard Stone, who had been McCloy's public affairs director, sponsored a wide variety of programs aimed at political democratization. Government agencies, universities, businesses, and trade unions promoted exchanges designed to expose Germans to the American model of political democracy and liberal capitalism. Private groups such as the American Council on Germany fostered ties between political and business elites.

The public harmony in German-American relations was reflected in the close relationship between Chancellor Konrad Adenauer and United States secretaries of state Dean Acheson and John Foster Dulles. Congress also echoed this support for the chancellor. Both President Eisenhower and Dulles saw the chancellor's commanding success in the 1953 and 1957 elections as a vindication of their policies, despite setbacks such as the August 1954 defeat of the European Defense Community (EDC) proposal. The gradual change in the political orientation of Germany's Social Democratic Party (*Sozialdemokratische Partei Deutschlands*, or SPD) from Marxist-oriented neutralism toward a pro-NATO support for the social market economy further underscored America's positive assessment of "its" Germany. At a time of increasing concern in the United States about comparative economic growth rates and a missile gap with the Soviet Union, political success in West Germany and Berlin vindicated the American position in the Cold War. As President Kennedy put it to his cheering German audience in his "Ich bin ein Berliner" speech, critics of the United States should "come to Berlin" to see the true difference between the two superpowers.[15]

However, Kennedy himself was an ambivalent figure in the German-American relationship. As a senator, he had criticized the Eisenhower administration for being "lashed too tightly to a single German government and

---

[10] See the chapter by Frank Schumacher in this section.

[11] Testimony by John J. McCloy in U.S. Senate Committee on Appropriations, *Foreign Aid Appropriations for 1951: Hearings Before the Committee on Appropriations*, 81st Cong., 2d sess., Mar. 10, 1950, 68.

[12] See the chapter by Michael Wala in this section.

[13] See the chapter by Diethelm Prowe in this section.

[14] See the chapter by Ronald Granieri in this section.

[15] After his tumultuous reception, Kennedy told Theodore Sorenson, "We'll never have another day like this one, as long as we live" (Richard Reeves, *President Kennedy: Profile in Power* [New York, 1993], 537).

political party."[16] Kennedy was part of a small but growing group in the late 1950s, which included other Democrats such as Mike Mansfield and Hubert Humphrey, that saw the tight American identification with the "unyielding" Adenauer as a barrier to progress with the Soviet Union on disarmament and nuclear test ban issues.[17] George Kennan's call for "disengagement" from Central Europe and the consideration of some type of nuclear-free zone were also evidence of these views. Prodded by Soviet premier Nikita Khrushchev's tough "ultimatum" on Berlin in November 1958, even Dulles hoped to encourage greater flexibility in Adenauer's policy toward East Germany and German reunification. But the failure of the Paris summit in May 1960 left the situation deadlocked. Publicly, German-American relations remained harmonious; privately, President Eisenhower expressed his concern that Adenauer was "too rigid" and should be willing to encourage exchanges and contact with East Germany.[18] Eisenhower's reasoning differed little from that behind Egon Bahr's formula of *Wandel durch Annäherung* (change through rapprochement) three years later.

Although it did not end the Berlin Crisis, the building of the Berlin Wall led to a "maturation in the German-American relationship."[19] Kennedy insisted far more strongly than Eisenhower that the Federal Republic assume a greater military and financial burden in support of America's position in the Cold War. He also demonstrated a much greater interest in the SPD, hoping to encourage its evolution into an acceptable governing partner. Kennedy even received its leader, Willy Brandt, in the White House before his first meeting with Adenauer,

a decision that aroused all of the chancellor's distrust and suspicion. Relations were antagonistic throughout the first two years of the administration, with Kennedy determined, as he put it, to move away from the "emptiness" of demands for German reunification and to "bend" German policy toward a de facto recognition of German division.[20] After the Cuban Missile Crisis – which was much more intimately connected with Berlin than many have realized[21] – the Kennedy administration pushed even more energetically for agreements with the Soviet Union, succeeding with the Limited Nuclear Test Ban Treaty in the summer of 1963. Adenauer's harsh criticism of the treaty, along with his flirtation with President Charles de Gaulle of France, further complicated relations; in 1962 and 1963, official ties between the United States and the Federal Republic were at their nadir.[22] By contrast, Kennedy himself enjoyed an exceptionally high standing among ordinary Germans. This popular sympathy became a permanent symbol of the German-American alliance following Kennedy's assassination in November 1963.

President Lyndon Johnson and Chancellor Ludwig Erhard, who had succeeded Adenauer in October 1963, enjoyed an initially good rapport. An ebullient Erhard declared after his first summit with Johnson, "I love President Johnson and he loves me."[23] But Johnson, like his predecessor, was determined to move forward in relations with the Soviet Union and to bring the Germans with him. In a telephone conversation early in 1964 with his national security adviser, McGeorge Bundy, Johnson discussed the lack of imaginative peace proposals coming from his advisers and complained that "we act like

---

[16] John F. Kennedy, "A Democrat Looks at Foreign Policy," *Foreign Affairs* 36 (1957): 44–59. See also Frank Mayer, *Adenauer and Kennedy* (New York, 1996).

[17] See the chapter by Steven Brady in this section.

[18] Memorandum of a Conference with President Eisenhower, Oct. 16, 1959, in U.S. Department of State, *Foreign Relations of the United States* (hereafter *FRUS*), *1958–1960*, 9:69–72.

[19] See the chapter by Diethelm Prowe in this section.

[20] Memorandum from President Kennedy to Secretary of State Rusk, Sept. 12, 1961, *FRUS, 1961–1963*, 14:402–3.

[21] Ernest R. May and Philip D. Zelikow, eds., *The Kennedy Tapes: Inside the White House During the Cuban Missile Crisis* (Cambridge, Mass., 1997).

[22] See the chapter by Rainer Blasius in this section.

[23] Frank A. Ninkovich, *Germany and the United States: The Transformation of the German Question Since 1945* (New York, 1995), 132.

Adenauer."[24] Johnson hoped to defuse the Cold War in Europe, as he put it, "to build bridges" to Eastern Europe and the Soviet Union, based at least implicitly on an acceptance of the status quo of Germany's and Europe's division.[25] This meant a lessening of the central importance Germany had enjoyed in American thinking during the 1950s. The president's scuttling of the multilateral nuclear force (MLF) in December 1964, a complex proposal for a mixed-manned nuclear fleet originally designed to appease German nuclear ambitions, also indicted the relative priority he gave to reaching a nonproliferation treaty with the Russians.[26] The escalation of the war in Vietnam after July 1965 further reduced the centrality of Germany and Europe to American concerns. The Federal Republic was now repeatedly urged, both privately and publicly, to "grow up" and assume greater responsibilities. In a dramatic Washington meeting in December 1965, Johnson exerted considerable pressure on his "friend" Erhard to provide some symbolic assistance to the American effort in Vietnam.[27] At the same time, the support in the Senate for the Mansfield Resolution indicated that many Americans believed Germany was now strong enough to defend itself. American leaders also urged greater German openness and conciliation toward Eastern Europe. Francis Bator, one of Johnson's key European advisers, argued that "the only tolerably safe path to unification is one which involves lessening the fear of Germany in Eastern Europe and the USSR."[28]

The changing perception of Germany in American eyes is captured in a "hot" argument between two of the "Wise Men," John J. McCloy and W. Averell Harriman, in January 1966. McCloy, adhering to the belief in the crucial importance of Germany for American concerns, expressed reservations about the proposed nuclear Non-Proliferation Treaty (NPT) and its impact on Germany. Recognizing that one of the goals of the NPT was preventing German acquisition of nuclear weapons, McCloy told Harriman that Johnson seemed willing to sacrifice NATO for the benefit of the Russians and that the president was "letting NATO go to hell in a hack." Harriman dismissed these concerns and criticized McCloy for allowing Germany to "dictate" U.S. policy. Harriman emphasized that Asia was the future for American foreign policy; McCloy needed to "get up to date and not be in the past when Germany was his ward."[29]

The signing of the Trilateral Agreements, which readjusted the relative financial burdens of the presence of American troops in Germany, produced what Ambassador George McGhee called a "pervading calm in German-American relations"[30] by the end of 1967. The Grand Coalition government's greater willingness to ease relations with Eastern Europe also removed a significant source of friction between Bonn and Washington. Fortunately, this calm in bilateral relations was not disturbed by the domestic storms that would afflict the Federal Republic and the United States in 1968. Both countries turned inward, and for the first time since the early Adenauer era, there was no meeting between the German chancellor and the American president. Most important, however, was that America increasingly saw the Federal Republic as having "come of age." With this maturity would come greater responsibility. Most American leaders expected greater support from Germany for U.S. policies, but this was no longer a given: Maturity also meant the confidence to say no.

[24] Michael R. Beschloss, *Taking Charge: The Johnson White House Tapes, 1963–1964* (New York, 1997), 145.

[25] The best expression of this came in Johnson's European speech of Oct. 7, 1966: *Public Papers of the President: Lyndon B. Johnson, 1966* (Washington, D.C., 1967), 1125–30.

[26] See the chapter by Erhard Forndran, vol. 1, Security.

[27] See the chapter by T. Michael Ruddy, vol. 2, Security.

[28] Bator to Johnson, "A Nuclear Role for Germany: What Do the Germans Want?" Apr. 4, 1966, Francis M. Bator papers, chronological file, box 3, Lyndon B. Johnson Library.

[29] Harriman memo of Jan. 22, 1966, quoted in Kai Bird, *The Chairman: John J. McCloy and the Making of the American Establishment* (New York, 1992), 586.

[30] George McGhee, *At the Creation of a New Germany* (New Haven, 1989), 228.

GERMAN PERSPECTIVES, 1945–1968

Toward the end of World War II, despite the extraordinary destructiveness of the bombing campaign and the propaganda of the Nazi regime about the Morgenthau Plan, Germans voted with their feet and fled west toward the approaching American army.[31] From the very beginning of the occupation, many Germans believed the Americans, having come from so far away, would treat them fairly, even generously, especially in comparison with the other members of the Allied coalition. The rapid breakdown of the nonfraternization policy, the immediate American attempts to restore order and feed the populace, and General Clay's efforts to jump-start German political life tended to confirm this view. Although uncertainty remained about Germany's future, Byrnes's Stuttgart speech of September 1946 characterized a generous policy that had already begun to take shape.[32] The intensification of the Cold War in 1947–8 and America's determination to defend its position in West Germany and Berlin brought more Germans away from any inclination toward neutrality or *ohne mich* (count-me-out)[33] views of the developing struggle. The application of enormous American economic power in the Marshall Plan and American military power in the Berlin airlift helped to solidify the German view, best expressed in Adenauer's policies, that the United States was the decisive power for Germany's political future.

Although this American connection created important public controversies – most notably over rearmament and the question of Germany's nuclear future – Adenauer was eager to play the role of America's most loyal European ally. Since the earliest days of his chancellorship, Adenauer

had told his cabinet that his policies, even his pursuit of reconciliation with France, were at least partly driven by his determination to keep the United States in Europe.[34] Adenauer's goal of integrating Germany into the West stemmed as well from his belief that "the outcome of foreign policy issues would determine what kind of society would ultimately prevail in Germany."[35] Adenauer's view did not arise from any affection for American culture, which he disdained, but from a recognition of American power and its critical importance to the Federal Republic's survival.[36] The chancellor also wagered correctly that the American connection was good domestic politics, and his trips to Washington produced numerous "photo-ops" for the West German public well before this phrase was coined. During the 1950s, it seemed that very few months would pass without a picture of Adenauer and Dulles emerging arm-in-arm from a meeting, the frostiest of Cold Warriors announcing their continuing determination to resist the godless communism of the Soviet Union. The ritual trip to Washington for consultation became so important to German politics that by the 1957 election, the SPD leader, Erich Ollenhauer, embraced it as well.

During this period, and despite his constant protestations about European integration, Adenauer sought above all a direct bilateral link to the United States. Bonn's efforts in this direction were so intense that Washington often thought it necessary to encourage Germany to be more "European" and enmesh itself further in European institutions. The closeness of the German-American alliance was a secret concern of British and French leaders, who feared it might challenge the territorial settlement of World War II. This set of relationships began to

---

[31] Klaus-Dietmar Henke, *Die amerikanische Besetzung Deutschlands* (Munich, 1995).

[32] See the chapters by Edmund Spevak and Gunther Mai in this section.

[33] The *ohne-mich* movement against German rearmament is discussed fully in David Clay Large, *Germans to the Front: West German Rearmament in the Adenauer Era* (Chapel Hill, N.C., 1996).

[34] Ulrich Enders and Konrad Reisen, eds., *Die Kabinettsprotokolle der Bundesregierung*, vol. 1, *1949* (Boppard am Rhein, 1982), 138.

[35] Wolfram Hanrieder, *Germany, America, Europe: Forty Years of German Foreign Policy* (New Haven, Conn., 1989), xiv.

[36] See the chapter by Ronald Granieri in this section.

change toward the end of the 1950s, with the onset of the Berlin Crisis, the coming to power of Charles de Gaulle in France, and the transition of power in Washington. If Germany had been playing the role of most loyal ally of the United States, its new experience was that of a disappointed – and frequently angry – lover, continually encountering a lack of appreciation from Washington for her unstinting loyalty. The calm acceptance of the Berlin Wall shattered the illusions of many German leaders, including the SPD's Willy Brandt, about the United States' willingness to defend German interests. American plans to compromise the status of Berlin in early 1962 led to a crisis and the recall of Ambassador Wilhelm Grewe. Adenauer complained bitterly of American "appeasement" of the Soviet Union, a word whose powerful political connotations gives a clear indication of how bad relations between the two countries had become.[37]

Although Americans favored Franco-German rapprochement in theory, the signing of the Élysée Treaty in January 1963 elicited a storm of outrage from the Kennedy administration, which feared that Adenauer and de Gaulle intended to build a European bloc independent of American influence. Ludwig Erhard, the preeminent Atlanticist, sought to restore the close connection with Washington, opposing those Gaullists in the Christian Democratic Union (Christlich-Demokratische Union, or CDU) like Adenauer who argued for a closer connection with France. Erhard fashioned himself a mediator between Washington and Paris, as well as the German leader most capable of restoring close bilateral cooperation on security matters. In October 1964, he even sent former ambassador Grewe to Washington to try to convince President Johnson to go ahead with the proposed multilateral nuclear force as a bilateral American and German undertaking. The Bonn government was reluctant to hear that the American attitude toward the MLF was changing and that such a German approach was

unwelcome.[38] Erhard's failure in this approach, and in his subsequent attempt in September 1966 to win relief from the financial burdens of the offset payments,[39] undermined his government. He became the target of charges by the CDU's Gaullists and the SPD that unquestioning loyalty to the United States was now a losing proposition.

When the Grand Coalition came to power in late 1966 and the United States grew increasingly preoccupied with Vietnam, Bonn began to distance itself from Washington; Chancellor Kurt Georg Kiesinger's first official visit was not to the American capital, but to Paris. Kiesinger also ruffled feathers in Washington when he criticized the nuclear NPT, which the Johnson administration hoped to negotiate with the Soviet Union. However, at the same time as it displayed a more public attitude of independence from the United States, Kiesinger's government continued to work quietly with Washington, agreeing to the trilateral accords, helping secure the approval of the Kennedy Round tariff negotiations, and supporting the stability of the dollar and the American position in international monetary negotiations.[40] As foreign minister, Willy Brandt was already proceeding with Ostpolitik, and Germany was moving toward a more European definition of its interests, but its ties to the United States remained a crucial part of its postwar identity. As one prominent German leader wrote, "The German-American alliance . . . is not merely one aspect of modern German history but a decisive element as a result of its preeminent place in our politics. . . . In effect, it provides a second constitution for our country."[41]

[38] See the chapter by Rainer A. Blasius in this section.
[39] See the chapter by Hubert Zimmermann, vol. 1, Economics.
[40] Thomas A. Schwartz, "Lyndon Johnson and Europe: Alliance Politics, Political Economy, and 'Growing Out of the Cold War,'" in H. W. Brands, ed., The Foreign Policies of Lyndon Johnson: Beyond Vietnam (College Station, Tex., 1999), 37–60.
[41] Walther Leisler Kiep, A New Challenge for Western Europe: A View from Bonn (New York, 1974), 111.

[37] Hans-Peter Schwarz, Adenauer, vol. 2: Der Staatsmann 1952–1967 (Stuttgart, 1986), 743.

NO *STUNDE NULL*

This discussion of the different American and German perspectives on the relationship highlights a number of important points. The first is that there was no *Stunde Null* (zero hour) in the German-American relationship. Both Germans and Americans came to their postwar relations with pre-1945 ideas and conceptions, and both came with a certain narrative of the recent past. For the United States, there would be the recurring concern that Germany not become a threat, not in the sense of a new Reich or new Führer, but as a possible unstable force in Europe, spurred on by its chronic nationalism and lured by Soviet offers of reunification. American leaders of the World War II generation, despite their public protestations of alliance and partnership, always perceived the need to keep a wary eye on Germany and its political development, and this became one of the central reasons for their "double containment" policy.[42] Even during the "golden age" of German-American relations, substantial pessimism remained about the degree to which Germany had really changed.[43] Ironically, the substantial American presence in Germany and Europe was no longer seen as a symbol of the Federal Republic's unquestioned allegiance to the West, but as a way to ensure that it resist Soviet pressure and stay on the straight and narrow path of democracy.

For the Germans, there was a similar historical narrative, although this one stressed the fear of a new American betrayal of German democracy and of a return to isolationism that would parallel the retreat after the Senate's defeat of the Treaty of Versailles. Many Germans argued that the Weimar Republic could have survived had it been treated more generously by the Allies, and that this would have happened had the Americans remained engaged in

Europe. Adenauer employed the "Weimar analogy" frequently, and it dominated much of the political discourse of the Bonn Republic in its early years. Whereas the Americans feared a new "Rapallo" between the Soviet Union and Germany, Adenauer feared a new "Potsdam" between the Soviet Union and the United States that would create détente between the superpowers at Germany's expense. All these words – Versailles, Rapallo, Weimar, Potsdam – captured the lingering uneasiness within the alliance and the powerful memories of the recent past. For the most part, American and German leaders came to share a narrative of the recent past that stressed the necessity of the alliance for both countries, emphasizing the importance of the American role in Europe in supporting German democracy and deterring Soviet aggression. Both came to use the Weimar analogy to justify the more conciliatory approach to postwar Germany compared to the interwar period. But even among the most fervent supporters of the German-American alliance, the memory of the Nazi era and America's wars with Germany was just below the surface. In March 1960, when Eisenhower was considering a proposal to place West Berlin under UN control, the ambassador in Bonn told him that the Germans would view "the abandonment of 2 1/4 million people in West Berlin [as raising] a question as to whether we would abandon the population of Norway which is of a similar size." Eisenhower coldly replied that "the Norwegians had not brought this on themselves by initiating an aggressive war."[44]

A "GOLDEN AGE"?

Historians are, for good reason, skeptical of notions like a "golden age," which usually are the product of heavy doses of nostalgia mixed with selective memory. Even with that skepticism in mind, the political relationship between the United States and Germany from 1945 to 1968 was unusually harmonious and showed a

---

[42] See the chapters by Frank Schumacher and Ruud van Dijk in this section.

[43] John Montgomery painted a grim picture of the limited degree to which German political culture had become democratized. See John Montgomery, *Forced to Be Free: The Artificial Revolution in Germany and Japan* (Chicago, 1957).

[44] Memorandum of a Conference with President Eisenhower, Mar. 14, 1960, *FRUS, 1958–1960*, 9:220–1.

rare degree of convergence in the attitudes and ideas of the major policymakers. Despite the various "crises" that invariably sprung up, the two countries deliberately accentuated the areas of agreement between them while minimizing the differences. Obviously, the international environment at the time, dominated as it was by the Cold War, helped the two nations maintain and develop their relationship. The Soviet Union's own behavior – its violent suppression of uprisings in East Germany, Hungary, and Czechoslovakia, the building of the Wall in East Berlin – always seemed to impress upon German and American leaders the importance of their solidarity. Even détente, which might have led to an unraveling of German-American ties, was eventually adopted by both sides as a way to gradually ease tensions in the Cold War.

This German-American solidarity had its ironic moments. The decision to rearm Germany,[45] which many Americans believed would meet with great enthusiasm among the incorrigibly militaristic Germans, actually produced enormous resistance and demonstrated how democratic the political culture of Germany had already become. Popular resistance to the stationing of nuclear weapons in the late 1950s also indicated that the Germans were unwilling to allow such critical decisions to be made without extensive debate and discussion. American and German leaders prevailed in their decisions in both cases, but the attendant friction compelled them to move cautiously and pursue negotiations with the Soviet Union. Even if these talks were ultimately unsuccessful, they helped to legitimate the final decisions and produce a broader consensus in support of them – something postwar German leaders greatly valued.

Germans and Americans were in full agreement in their support of European integration.[46] Although Germany's economic and political recovery by the end of the era brought

with it a greater assertiveness, it is remarkable how well the two countries harmonized their policies in this area.[47] Ever since the Marshall Plan and continuing through to the Schuman Plan and the EDC, the United States insisted that Europe open the door for Germany and that the Germans enter it. Despite setbacks like the EDC, this external support for integration was vital in overcoming the powerful political, institutional, and bureaucratic resistance that might have strangled European unity in its infancy. Further, the enthusiasm with which the Federal Republic embraced the concept of European integration was an important element in reducing the mistrust of Germany in Europe and the United States. By the time Bonn did begin to pursue an active Ostpolitik, the Federal Republic was anchored securely within Western Europe and the Atlantic alliance, which allayed, but never completely eliminated, the suspicions of its neighbors.

Although German-American relations were unusually harmonious during the "golden age," Americans and Germans often differed in their approach toward the central question of German unity.[48] In the aftermath of the failed Moscow conferences of 1947, most American leaders assigned less and less priority to German unity compared to other American foreign policy objectives. (Germany's right to any readjustment of its boundaries in Eastern Europe never seems to have figured in the American calculations about a reunified Germany.) Whether the United States can be held responsible for Germany's division – as Carolyn Eisenberg has argued[49] – remains debatable, but there is little question that with the Marshall Plan and the formation of NATO, the United States pressed ahead with its plans to organize Western Europe against the Soviet Union, and that these plans did not anticipate any immediate end to

---

[45] See the chapter by David Clay Large, vol. 1, Security.

[46] The fullest treatment of the American support for this subject is Geir Lundestad, *"Empire" By Integration:*

The United States and European Integration, 1945–1997 (Oxford, 1998).

[47] See the chapter by Manfred Knapp in this section.

[48] See the chapter by Frank Ninkovich in this section.

[49] Carolyn W. Eisenberg, *Drawing the Line: The American Decision to Divide Germany, 1944–1949* (New York, 1996).

the division of Germany. After the failure of the Four Power talks in Paris in May 1949, Dean Acheson made it clear that his priority was the integration of West Germany into Europe. The militarization of the Cold War after the outbreak of the Korean War only confirmed this view and intensified efforts to link Germany to the West.

Few Americans of Acheson's and Dulles's generation would ever again underestimate the strength and power of German nationalism, and most of them probably expected Germans to demand reunification at some point in the future. A reunified Germany must not again become a "loose cannon," but must remain anchored within NATO and Europe. Acheson and Dulles believed firmly – if rather naively – that the Soviet Union might find such a solution in its own interests as well.[50] The United States continually stressed its commitment to German reunification and encouraged efforts to weaken, even "roll back" the Soviet hold over East Germany.[51] However, after the June 1953 uprising and the powerful response to the American-sponsored food program for East Germany, American policy grew markedly ambivalent. Pushing too hard to undermine Soviet rule in East Germany, it was feared, might endanger the policy of integrating Germany into Western Europe.[52] As John Ausland of the State Department's Office of German Affairs put it in November 1953, "I think it pretty clear that if there is any conflict between our policy of reducing Soviet power in Soviet Occupied Germany (as well as the other satellites) and our policy of integrating the Federal Republic with the West, our policy of integration should be given priority." According to Ausland, the United States' response to Germany's division should be long term: "Our primary problem then will be to keep hope alive, without arousing unwarranted expectations of

early unification."[53] In the interest of this long-term strategy, the United States began to emphasize such ideas as exchange programs and other contacts between West and East Germans that could maintain hope for reunification without spurring a dangerous confrontation.

Not surprisingly, the leaders of the Federal Republic had a far different perspective on the German question. The Federal Republic's participation in America's containment policy against the Soviet Union was always an ambivalent undertaking, in large measure because containment implied the permanent division of Germany.[54] German policymakers hoped to hold open the disposition of the "lost territories" – the millions of refugee voters made this a necessity – but they were even more concerned that American leaders continually show their devotion to the cause of German self-determination and reunification. Reunification was a basic goal of the Federal Republic, whose "Basic Law" was only temporary until reunification allowed for a permanent constitution. No German politician could afford even the appearance of weakness on this subject, and Adenauer had to frame his own interest in Western integration as a "policy of strength" that in some way might lead the Soviet Union to abandon its hold over East Germany. Kurt Schumacher's decision to make reunification the central demand of the SPD further amplified the issue, giving it "doctrinal political status."[55] The commitment to reunification as a concrete policy goal was enshrined in the so-called Hallstein Doctrine, which cut off diplomatic relations with any country that recognized East Germany – with the exception of the Soviet Union. Throughout the 1950s, Adenauer continually asserted that all Western negotiations with the Soviet Union must focus on the issue of German reunification, a demand that was ultimately self-defeating and made the German government appear to be the main obstacle to détente. Bonn's demand was

---

[50] Dulles made this point a number of times to Soviet negotiators. See *FRUS, 1952–1954*, 7:899–900, 933–4.

[51] See the chapter by Bernd Stöver in this section.

[52] See the chapter by Christian Ostermann in this section.

[53] Memorandum by John C. Ausland of Office of German Political Affairs to Director of the Office Brewster H. Morris, Oct. 27, 1953, *FRUS, 1952–1954*, 7:1666.

[54] See the chapter by Ruud van Dijk in this section.

[55] See the chapter by Frank Ninkovich in this section.

fundamentally just: East Germans clearly did not approve of their regime and wanted the right to join West Germany. But as the arms race and the need to prevent nuclear war gradually overshadowed the issue of reunification, the Federal Republic's insistence appeared to "dictate" American foreign policy and prevent agreements with the Soviet Union. The building of the Berlin Wall in August 1961 ended German hopes for imminent reunification and began a slow adjustment to the reality of two Germanys.[56]

Although German reunification lost its centrality in Western diplomacy, the Federal Republic was able to use other means to keep the issue open. The legal foundations of Germany's provisional territorial status assumed greater importance in Bonn's approach. This led to the irony that the Federal Republic preferred the United States remain an occupying power in Berlin rather than settle the status of the city, for this kept the German question open.[57] After toying with alternatives like UN control or an international commission, the United States ultimately preferred this course as well. By remaining in Berlin, the United States could counter challenges to its rights by the Soviet Union and maintain a key role in a future settlement. But although American leaders encouraged their German counterparts to accept the reality of German division, the United States never abandoned its basic support of German self-determination and allowed the Federal Republic – with a great deal of behind-the-scenes encouragement – to determine the pace of its opening toward the East German regime. Even on this contentious issue, the United States and the Federal Republic reached an acceptable compromise.

COSTS

Along with their skepticism about any "golden age," historians are inclined to believe that no

achievement comes without costs. This inclination is more than just the proverbial pessimism of the academic, who must find something negative to balance any positive assessment. Rather, it is the recognition that compromise and trade-offs are an inevitable part of politics. In the case of the German-American relationship, revisionist historians have blamed the alliance between the two countries for the intensification of the Cold War and the arms race, and have interpreted America's policies as a betrayal of Roosevelt's hopes for the Grand Alliance and a peaceful relationship with the Soviet Union. In a detailed study of the first days of the occupation, Rebecca Boehling has blamed the United States for preventing more radical social and economic reforms in the Federal Republic that would have dealt more effectively with the vestiges of Nazism.[58] Carolyn Eisenberg has held the United States responsible for dividing Germany and condemning thirteen million East Germans to life under a dictatorship.[59] Rolf Steininger and others have argued that there were numerous "lost opportunities" to create a unified, neutralist Germany and that these were lost because of Cold War concerns and/or the influence of Adenauer on American leaders.[60]

These views are considered in this section but find no great support. Whatever uncertainty may have existed before its founding, the inclusion of the GDR in the Soviet empire after 1949 was no surprise.[61] Although recent scholarship based on Soviet and East German archives demonstrates considerable confusion in Soviet policy,[62] there is no hard evidence that the Soviet Union was ever willing to abandon

---

[56] See the chapter by Manfred Görtemacher in this section.

[57] See the chapter by Richard Wiggers in this section.

[58] Rebecca Boehling, *A Question of Priorities: Democratic Reforms and Economic Recovery in Postwar Germany* (Providence, R.I., 1996).

[59] Eisenberg, *Drawing the Line.*

[60] Rolf Steininger, *Eine Chance zur Wiedervereinigung? Die Stalin-Note vom 10. März 1952: Darstellung und Dokumentation auf Grundlage unveröffentlichter britischer und amerikanischer Akten,* 2d ed. (Bonn, 1986).

[61] See the chapter by Manfred Görtemaker in this section.

[62] Norman M. Naimark, *The Russians in Germany: A History of the Soviet Zone of Occupation, 1945–1949* (Cambridge, Mass., 1995).

its position in East Germany, its greatest prize in the Great Patriotic War.[63] The East German–Soviet and West German–American relationships did share some characteristics. Both Germanys could use their supposed weakness as an argument for additional support from their benefactors, and both the United States and the Soviet Union felt constrained by the political interests of their German allies. Nevertheless, the West German–American connection existed within a democratic and open political system, whereas the East German–Soviet relationship involved the intrigue of party officials within a closed dictatorship, ruling over a sullen and largely hostile East German population. This ideological and political contrast far outweighs any superficial similarities.

A genuine cost of the Cold War and the rapid construction of the German-American alliance was the refusal to confront the crimes of the Nazi era, which allowed thousands of war criminals to escape justice. Although the Germans were those most responsible for this repression, American policies encouraged it. The United States showed little compunction in exploiting Nazi intelligence services and scientists for its Cold War competition with the Soviets.[64] McCloy's pardon of a number of convicted war criminals, including the prominent industrialist Alfried Krupp, contributed to the impression that the United States was saying, in one of General Eisenhower's more unfortunate expressions, "Let bygones be bygones."[65] This repression of the Nazi past was connected not only with the Cold War but also with the democratization of West Germany. The United States was a driving force for democratization, but with democracy came the demand for the reintegration not only of the Nazi *Mitläufer* (fellow travelers) but also for some who had served in the Nazi elite.[66] Was this a necessary condition for the stability of a nascent democracy? Norbert Frei, in an intensive examination of this issue, argues that the German public's support during the Adenauer years for rapid amnesty for those accused and convicted war criminals was so broad as to imply an "indirect admission of the entire society's involvement in National Socialism."[67] Jeffrey Herf, in a complete and judicious examination of this question, argues simply, "there was no electoral majority in the 1950s for political leaders who spoke bluntly about and sought timely justice for crimes of the Nazi era." Even if the United States had possessed the will to continue its Nuremberg policies into the 1950s – which it clearly did not – "it would have had to pursue justice in opposition to the wishes of the democratically elected government in Bonn. In the postwar decade, daring more democracy meant attaining less memory and justice."[68]

The perception outside Germany that the country was burying its past had an impact on Germany's postwar reputation. The fact that many ex-Nazis – of varying levels of culpability – were walking free in the Federal Republic provoked concern, especially in America. Similarly, the international media closely scrutinized the Federal Republic for any sign of Nazi revival or anti-Semitism. Controversies erupted with extraordinary frequency, most notably the Eichmann trial in 1961 and over extending the statute of limitations in 1965. Reminders of the Nazi past also came in the form of best-selling books such as *The Rise and Fall of the Third Reich* and movies like *Judgment at Nuremberg*.[69] A

[63] Constantine Pleshakov and Vladislav Zubok, *Inside the Kremlin's Cold War: From Stalin to Khrushchev* (Cambridge, Mass., 1996). Pleshakov and Zubok are more certain about Stalin's determination to stay in Germany than they are about his successors, but their book shows the difficulties Soviet leaders had in changing from the great dictator's policies.

[64] Christopher Simpson, *Blowback* (New York, 1988). See also the chapters by Michael Neufeld, vol. 1, Security, and by Mitchell Ash, vol. 2, Culture.

[65] Thomas A. Schwartz, *America's Germany: John J. McCloy and the Federal Republic of Germany* (Cambridge, Mass., 1991), 156–75.

[66] See the chapters by Barbara Fait and Cornelia Rauh-Kühne in this section.

[67] Norbert Frei, *Vergangenheitspolitik: Die Anfänge der Bundesrepublik und die NS-Vergangenheit* (Munich, 1996), 399.

[68] Jeffrey Herf, *Divided Memory: The Nazi Past in the Two Germanies* (Cambridge, Mass., 1997), 387–90.

[69] William Shirer, *The Rise and Fall of the Third Reich* (New York, 1960).

popular American folk-music group, The Mitchell Trio, which specialized in civil rights and antiwar protest songs, had hits in the early 1960s with the "I Was Not a Nazi Polka" and a parody of the "Twelve Days of Christmas," in which young Germans at a holiday party progressively turn into raving Nazis. As the group's founder, Chad Mitchell, said, "the song was about Western permissiveness, about the re-establishment and rebuilding of West Germany. In the face of Communism we forget that a few years ago Fascism was as dangerous as certain aspects of Communism.... Our old enemies are neither watched nor punished."[70]

Recalling the failure of both the Federal Republic and the United States to pursue justice and punish Nazi crimes is a sobering corrective to a blindly positive reading of their relationship during this era. But Herf also notes that there were German politicians, especially Kurt Schumacher and Theodor Heuss, who did confront the issues of the Nazi past, and "inaugurated a tradition of public recollection in which the Holocaust eventually found an enduring place in the dominant West German public narratives of the Nazi era." That tradition was also a consequence of the establishment of a functioning and viable democracy in West Germany, where, as Herf rightly notes, the "decisions of the early years were not final." Although some commentators during the Cold War believed that the East German regime, because of its communist and "antifascist" character, had dealt with the Nazi past more thoroughly, Herf completely rejects this view. Citing the actions of the East German parliament of 1990, which expressed remorse for the crimes of the Nazi past, he argues that "an honest effort to face the Nazi past was inseparable from the development of democracy in Germany."[71] This balanced conclusion about the costs of both the democratization of Germany and its Cold War alliance with the United States is likely to stand the test of time.

CONCLUSION

When the United States was preparing to withdraw its remaining forces from Berlin in 1994, an American colonel commented that "What we did here in Berlin, in Germany, and in the post-war period, was the best thing the United States has ever done."[72] Despite the lofty rhetoric of the ceremonial moment, the colonel was not far off the mark. The United States had promoted the democratization of Germany's political culture by policy and example. Although by 1968 it had become tarnished by racial strife and the Vietnam War, the American model of state and society remained valid for most Germans. Even the protests in the Federal Republic against the Vietnam War, which developed nearly parallel to the antiwar movement in the United States, signified that both countries were now part of the same Western community, where citizens could differ sharply on the types of policies needed to defend it.

For the United States, its experience in Germany helped to accustom its leaders and public to the exercise of international leadership. With memories of isolationism still fresh, American leaders needed the type of cooperation – and success – they experienced in Germany in order to acclimate their people to an enduring internationalist role. The strong consensus in favor of the American presence in Europe – which Eisenhower and others thought would and should be only temporary – testifies to the lasting impact of the German-American alliance.

Long a steadfast member of the West by 1968, the Federal Republic now undertook a more self-assured policy toward the East, including the GDR. Brandt's Ostpolitik offered a new alternative to de Gaulle's discredited vision of détente by seeking to ameliorate the effects of German and European division. Aware of the limits of their power and their need to be far more circumspect than other European states, German leaders had internalized the concerns of

---

[70] Chad Mitchell, *The Mitchell Trio Songbook* (Chicago, 1964), 138. (I owe my knowledge of this to my older brother Bob, who played the Mitchell Trio's music so often that I knew the words by heart.)

[71] Herf, *Divided Memory*, 390.

[72] Col. Alfred Baker quoted in *Berlin: Journey of a City*, written Robert E. Frye, prod. German Information Center New York, 1994, videocassette.

"double containment." They also had become determined multilateralists, working through "Europe" to pursue their objectives. Germany was also grappling with its past, in fits and starts, but still far more conscientiously than many in the 1950s would have thought possible. Acheson's "no harder enterprise" was well on its way toward completion.

SUGGESTIONS FOR FURTHER READING

Among the best overviews of German-American relations during this period are Frank A. Ninkovich, *Germany and the United States: The Transformation of the German Question Since 1945*, 2d ed. (New York, 1995) and Wolfram Hanrieder, *Germany, America, Europe: Forty Years of German Foreign Policy* (New Haven, 1989). See also the pertinent essays in Klaus Larres and Torsten Oppelland, eds., *Deutschland und die USA im 20. Jahrhundert. Geschichte der politischen Beziehungen* (Darmstadt, 1997). On the German question, see Wolfgang-Uwe Friedrich, ed., *Die USA und die deutsche Frage, 1945–1990* (Frankfurt am Main and New York, 1991); Hans-Jürgen Schröder, ed., *Die Deutsche Frage als internationales Problem* (Stuttgart, 1990); W. R. Smyser, *From Yalta to Berlin: The Cold War Struggle over Germany* (New York, 1999).

The literature dealing with German-American relations immediately after the war is particularly rich because many of the authors served in the occupation. For a first orientation, see Wolfgang Benz, ed., *Deutschland unter alliierter Besatzung 1945–1949/55. Ein Handbuch* (Berlin 1999). Among the most important studies are John Gimbel, *The American Occupation of Germany: Politics and the Military, 1945–1949* (Stanford, Calif., 1968); Edward N. Peterson, *The American Occupation of Germany: Retreat to Victory* (Detroit, 1977); John H. Backer, *Winds of History: The German Years of Lucius DuBignon Clay* (New York, 1983); Wolfgang Benz, *Die Gründung der Bundesrepublik Deutschland: Von der Bizone zum souveränen Staat*, 5th. ed. (Munich, 1999). Fresh perspectives on this period can be found in Carolyn Eisenberg, *Drawing the Line: The American Decision to Divide Ger-*

many, 1944–1949 (New York, 1996); Wilfried Mausbach, *Zwischen Morgenthau und Marshall: Das wirtschaftspolitische Deutschlandkonzept der USA 1944–1947* (Düsseldorf, 1996); Hermann-Josef Rupieper, *Der besetzte Verbündete: Die amerikanische Deutschlandpolitik 1949–1955* (Opladen, 1991); Jeffry M. Diefendorf, Axel Frohn, and Hermann-Josef Rupieper, eds., *American Policy and the Reconstruction of West Germany, 1945–1955* (New York, 1993).

Biographies and focused biographical studies are crucial for examining the political relationship between the two countries. The most important are Hans-Peter Schwarz, *Konrad Adenauer: A German Politician and Statesman in a Period of War, Revolution, and Reconstruction*, 2 vols. (Providence, R.I., 1995–7); Jean Edward Smith, *Lucius D. Clay* (New York, 1990); Wolfgang Krieger, *General Lucius D. Clay und die amerikanische Deutschlandpolitik 1945–1949* (Stuttgart, 1987); Volker Hentschel, *Ludwig Erhard. Ein Politikerleben* (Munich, 1996); Thomas A. Schwartz, *America's Germany: John J. McCloy and the Federal Republic of Germany* (Cambridge, Mass., 1991); Kai Bird, *The Chairman: John J. McCloy and the Making of the American Establishment* (New York, 1991); James Hershberg, *James B. Conant: Harvard to Hiroshima and the Making of the Nuclear Age* (New York, 1993); James Chace, *Acheson: The Secretary of State Who Created the American World* (New York, 1998); Detlef Felken, *Dulles und Deutschland* (Berlin and Bonn, 1993); Richard H. Immerman, *John Foster Dulles: Piety, Pragmatism, and Power in U. S. Foreign Policy* (Wilmington, 1999); Gregor Schöllgen, *Willy Brandt: Die Biographie* (Berlin, 2001).

Memoirs are helpful but must be used with great caution. Among the most important are Konrad Adenauer, *Erinnerungen*, 4 vols. (Stuttgart, 1965–1969); Willy Brandt, *People and Politics: The Years 1960–1975* (Boston, 1978); Herbert Blankenhorn, *Verständnis und Verständigung: Blätter eines politischen Tagebuchs 1949–1979* (Frankfurt am Main, 1980); Wilhelm Grewe, *Rückblenden 1976–1951* (Frankfurt am Main, 1979); Kurt Birrenbach, *Meine Sondermissionen* (Düsseldorf, 1984); Lucius D. Clay, *Decision in Germany* (Garden City, N.Y., 1950); Dean

Acheson, *Present at the Creation* (New York, 1969); George Ball, *The Past Has Another Pattern* (New York, 1982); George McGhee, *At the Creation of a New Germany* (New Haven, 1989); Martin J. Hillenbrand, *Fragments of Our Time: Memoirs of a Diplomat* (Athens, GA., 1998).

The importance of economic reconstruction for the political stability of the German-American relationship is underlined in Charles S. Maier and Günter Bischof, eds., *The Marshall Plan and Germany: West German Development Within the Framework of the European Recovery Program* (London, 1991) and Michael Hogan, *The Marshall Plan: America, Britain, and the Reconstruction of Western Europe, 1947–1952* (New York, 1987).

On the central event of this era in German-American relations, the Berlin Crisis, there is still no fully satisfactory study. William Burr, ed., *The Berlin Crisis, 1958–62* (Alexandria, Va., 1991) is a thorough documentary collection with an excellent introduction. Burr has also contributed a number of articles on this subject for the journal *Diplomatic History*. A provocative interpretation of the crisis is Marc Trachtenberg, *History and Strategy* (Princeton, 1991); see also his most recent book, *A Constructed Peace: The Making of the European Settlement 1945–1963* (Princeton, 1999). Works focused on the German-American aspects of the crisis are Christian Bremen, *Die Eisenhower Administration und die zweite Berlin-Krise 1958–1961* (Berlin, 1998) and Frank A. Mayer, *Adenauer and Kennedy* (New York, 1991).

For the Johnson, Erhard, and Grand Coalition eras, there are still relatively few studies.

Erhard's political failure is captured in Heinz Osterheld, *Aussenpolitik unter Bundeskanzler Ludwig Erhard 1963–1966: Ein dokumentarischer Bericht aus dem Kanzleramt* (Düsseldorf, 1992) and Klaus Hildebrand, *Von Erhard zur Grossen Koalition 1963–1969* (Stuttgart, 1984). On the foreign policy of Germany's "forgotten chancellor," see Dirk Kroegel, *Einen Anfang finden! Kurt-Georg Kiesinger in der Aussen- und Deutschlandpolitik der Grossen Koalition* (Munich, 1997). A first try at a book-length study of U.S. policy toward Germany during the 1960s is Adrian W. Schertz, *Die Deutschlandpolitik Kennedys und Johnsons. Unterschiedliche Ansätze in der amerikanischen Regierung* (Cologne, 1992). Greater analytical depth is found in Frank Costigliola, "Lyndon B. Johnson, Germany, and the 'End of the Cold War,'" in Warren I. Cohen and Nancy Bernkopf Tucker, eds., *Lyndon Johnson Confronts the World: American Foreign Policy, 1963–1968* (New York, 1994), 173–210; Thomas A. Schwartz, "Victories and Defeats in the Long Twilight Struggle: The United States and Western Europe in the 1960s," in Diane B. Kunz, ed., *The Diplomacy of the Crucial Decade: American Foreign Relations During the 1960s* (New York, 1994), 115–48; Thomas A. Schwartz, *Lyndon Johnson and Europe: In the Shadow of Vietnam* (Cambridge, 2003). On the financial aspects of security relations, see Hubert Zimmermann, *Money and Security: Troops, Monetary Policy, and West Germany's Relations with the United States and Britain, 1950–1971* (Cambridge and Washington, DC, 2002) and Gregory F. Treverton, *The Dollar Drain and American Forces in Germany* (Athens, OH, 1978).

The Allied Council of Foreign Ministers Conferences and the German Question, 1945–1947

Edmund Spevack

The Potsdam Conference of July–August 1945 established a new international mechanism for the peaceful postwar order of both Germany and the world. Following the suggestion of President Harry S. Truman, it was agreed that a new "Council of Foreign Ministers" (CFM), composed of the foreign ministers of the United States, Britain, France, the USSR, and China, should meet regularly. A group of American foreign policy decision makers had realized that their nation could no longer afford to be isolationist; with the help of other major powers, the Americans now set out to promote the construction of an effective worldwide system of peace and security. Although it was agreed that the smaller countries should be dealt with first, a major problem on the CFM's agenda was a solution to the German question. The victorious powers hoped to find a more effective procedure this time without calling a large peace conference like the one at Versailles at the end of World War I. The Potsdam Protocol of August 2, 1945, consisted largely of rhetoric designed to temporarily secure the status quo; genuine solutions to pressing problems, however, were to be sought at the CFM conferences.[1]

The first CFM conference took place in London from September 12 to October 21, 1945. Although this meeting did not deal directly with the German question, it did provide clear evidence of a growing worldwide struggle between the United States and the USSR for spheres of influence. Particularly in the drafting of peace treaties for Finland, Italy, Romania, Hungary, and Bulgaria, the conference revealed the extent of the Soviet Union's de facto domination of Eastern Europe and how difficult it would be for the West to reverse it. Another sensitive topic was the role of France. Because it had been excluded from the Potsdam Conference, France now renewed its efforts to secure those interests the other powers had previously ignored. These included the revision of France's border with Germany and, in a direct challenge to Russian demands for reparations, the insistence that France receive reparations as well.

The United States, for its part, prevented Moscow from participating in the occupation of Japan by refusing to put this topic on the agenda. Although signs of friction between British foreign secretary Ernest Bevin, French foreign minister Georges Bidault, and Russian foreign minister Molotov increased (at one point

---

[1] Werner Link, "Zielperspektiven der amerikanischen Deutschlandpolitik in der frühen Nachkriegszeit," *Zeitgeschichte* 5 (1977–8): 2–12; Patricia Dawson Ward, *The Threat of Peace: James F. Byrnes and the Council*

of Foreign Ministers, 1945–1946 (Kent, Ohio, 1979), 6–17. Published documents on the CFM are available in U.S. Department of State, *Foreign Relations of the United States* (hereafter *FRUS*), *1946*, vol. 2, and *FRUS*, *1947*, vol. 2, as well as in *Documents on British Policy Overseas*, ser. 1, vol. 2.

during the discussion, Bevin compared Molotov to Hitler), U.S. Secretary of State James Byrnes remained calm and attempted to steer the conference in a more productive direction. But the meeting ended in failure, due mainly to provocative Russian attempts to avoid concessions by excluding France and China from future meetings of the foreign ministers.[2]

Much to the chagrin of the French and the Chinese, the foreign ministers of the United States, Britain, and the USSR next met alone in Moscow from December 16 to 26, 1945. Still hoping to appease the Russians and bind them to a cooperative position, Byrnes had made an appointment with Stalin directly. This improvised move forced the reluctant Bevin to come along to the hastily organized conference. While the United States refused to let the USSR participate in the military administration of Japan, the Russians blocked the West from intervening in the affairs of Hungary. Furthermore, the USSR was requested, without tangible result, to withdraw its troops from Iran. When the foreign ministers returned to the German question, the seeds of mistrust and rivalry had long been sowed. Germany gradually became the focus of a struggle for influence that was also being fought in other regions, such as Eastern Europe and Asia.

FROM ALLIANCE TO CONTAINMENT

Despite the increasingly apparent East-West tension, Byrnes refused to abandon his belief that a comprehensive Four Power agreement could solve the German problem and overcome the deadlock in Allied occupation policies. The Byrnes Demilitarization Plan, placed before Molotov on September 20, 1945, and discussed with Stalin personally on December 24 of the same year, proposed a mandatory twenty-five-year disarmament of Germany under international control. This proposal illustrated Byrnes's belief that the USSR's main diplomatic concern was security; if this concern could be taken seriously, the division of Germany might be successfully avoided.[3] However, Byrnes's view of Soviet-American cooperation would soon give way to a less optimistic assessment. The famous "Long Telegram" written by the American chargé in Moscow, George F. Kennan, and sent to Washington on February 22, 1946, warned of Russia's expansionism, insecurity, and distrust of the West. Kennan argued that American policy must be readjusted in favor of containing the USSR. He followed the telegram with a statement about German policy that sounded similar warning notes and urged the American leadership to secure western Germany from a growing Soviet threat.[4]

American policy began to shift in this direction in 1946-7, when the United States departed from its conciliatory approach toward the Soviet Union and aimed to stabilize Western Europe by securing the Ruhr and the West German industrial base. On February 9, 1946, Stalin had argued in a speech in Moscow that the fundamental incompatibility of communism and capitalism made a stable international peace impossible. Truman sensed this change in tone and felt it necessary to show strength, not offer negotiation. His overriding concern was to bolster Western Europe against the communist threat. The fate of Poland, Hungary, and other countries proved that entire regions could swiftly fall to communism and that the USSR would never back down from a position of strength once attained. Truman, therefore, opted to build up western Germany economically and to integrate it into a consolidated Western Europe.[5]

---

[3] John F. Karl, "Compromise or Confrontation: James F. Byrnes and the United States Policy toward the Soviet Union, 1945–1946," Ph.D. diss., University of Toronto, 1976.

[4] The Chargé in the Soviet Union (Kennan) to the Secretary of State, Feb. 22, 1946, *FRUS, 1946*, 6:696–709; The Chargé in the Soviet Union (Kennan) to the Secretary of State, Mar. 6, 1946, *FRUS, 1946*, 5:516–20.

[5] Melvyn P. Leffler, *A Preponderance of Power: National Security, the Truman Administration, and the Cold War* (Stanford, Calif., 1992), 100–21; and Melvyn P. Leffler,

[2] Hermann Graml, *Die Alliierten und die Teilung Deutschlands: Konflikte und Entscheidungen, 1941–1948* (Frankfurt am Main, 1985), 133–8.

At the Paris Conference (two sessions in April–May and June–July 1946), the critical decisions that led to German national division were formulated. The first phase of the conference was marked by Byrnes's attempt to present his Demilitarization Plan again for the twofold purpose of overcoming French intransigence and testing Russian intentions. Molotov resisted Byrnes's plan, and British support was not forthcoming. It was obvious that the USSR would not abandon its demand for reparations from current production, a concession that the West did not want to make under any circumstances. When the second session began in June 1946, Byrnes had begun to question his central assumption, that the Soviets were motivated above all by security needs; instead, he began to accept the idea that Russian imperialism was dangerous and had to be contained. A memorandum by Byrnes's aides Dean Acheson and John H. Hilldring in May 1946 examined the remaining chances of saving German unity and urged Byrnes to put Soviet policy to a "final test."[6] The failure of this second test, this time aimed exclusively at the USSR, soon demonstrated the futility of Byrnes's previous efforts.

Although the public learned nothing about the new policies and both states pretended to keep the channels of negotiation with the USSR open, Britain and the United States were beginning to discuss the economic unification of their zones into "Bizonia." American negotiators worried that the British would lose patience and pursue their own interests independently, leaving the United States without vital British support. The Soviets now took over from France the role of blocking negotiations and retarding any constructive solution to the German question.

The future form of Germany, therefore, remained undecided. A new Russian plan, related by Molotov during the second Paris session,

sharply criticized the possible dismemberment of Germany. Instead of advocating national division, Molotov called for the establishment of a single German government, the economic and military disarmament of Germany, the establishment of a definite reparations program, and the placing of the Ruhr under Four Power control. Molotov's plan aimed to retain significant Russian influence in Germany and was carefully calculated to appeal to the German public. American negotiators realized they too had to compete for its support.

However, Molotov's suggestions were no longer relevant for the policies of the Western powers.[7] Bidault wanted to create a loose confederation of states, whereas the Americans and the British wished for a single federal state eventually to be composed of all three Western zones of occupation. After the Paris Conference ended in July 1946, the division of Germany was nearly inevitable; all public statements to the contrary were merely a political show.[8] In the months that followed, Britain and the United States began to lay the groundwork for the European order that would prevail until 1989.

The British decided to divide Germany long before the United States did and then bargained hard for American support. In Bevin's opinion, the Soviets had to be kept out of the Ruhr because reparations could not be granted indefinitely and western Germany had to be secured from communist influence. Long before the division of Germany was sealed at the end of 1947, British planners had anticipated the failure of a Four Power compromise on Germany and had advocated national division. They shifted to obstructionism at the CFM conferences and waited for the Americans to come around to their own point of view.[9] The British did not have to wait for long: Byrnes's speech at Stuttgart in September 1946, understood by many contemporaries as a direct answer to Molotov's proposals for a centralized German government,

---

The Struggle for Germany and the Origins of the Cold War, German Historical Institute, Occasional Paper 16 (Washington, D.C., 1996), 29–30, 61–2.

[6] The Acting Secretary of State (Acheson) to the Secretary of State, at Paris, May 9, 1946, *FRUS, 1946*, 5:549–55.

[7] Ward, *Threat of Peace*, 121.

[8] Graml, *Die Alliierten und die Teilung*, 189.

[9] Anne Deighton, *The Impossible Peace: Britain, the Division of Germany, and the Origins of the Cold War* (Oxford, 1990), 70–1.

signified a definite change in U.S. policy toward Germany. Although Byrnes still hesitated to close the door publicly on any cooperation with the Soviets – several passages of his speech were intentionally vague – the American leadership had realized that they needed an economically strong West Germany in order to keep communism out of Western Europe. In return, Byrnes hinted that the West Germans might soon receive an increased amount of control over their own economic fate. By the fall of 1946, it was clear that Kennan's concept of containment had triumphed over Byrnes's original hopes for pragmatic cooperation with the USSR.[10]

The official discussions at the New York CFM conference of November–December 1946 produced only minor progress on the German question. On December 2, 1946, however, senior British and American delegates finalized an agreement on the sidelines of this meeting, calling for zonal fusion in western Germany. Although Four Power negotiations continued and the Russians attempted to keep the German question open, British and American delegates had already abandoned thoughts of the political and economic unity of Germany.[11] The agreement on unifying the economies of the British and American zones went into effect on January 1, 1947. Byrnes resigned after the New York conference. He had failed to secure productive cooperation with the USSR; instead, the confrontation between Americans and Russians had intensified. Byrnes also realized in December 1946 that determining the future form of a divided Germany would involve even longer and more difficult meetings, and he was unwilling to take on this additional burden.[12]

The Moscow conference (March 10–April 24, 1947) exposed the rift among the four Allies to full view. The participants initially failed to agree on an agenda, and none of the central problems concerning Germany could be solved or even discussed productively. Once again, Molotov argued for the creation of a centralized German state. He suggested that the Allied Control Council frame a German constitution, hold elections, form a provisional government, and conduct a plebiscite on the new state.[13] However, instead of pursuing this Soviet plan, the CFM soon demonstrated the breakdown of Four Power negotiations on Germany. Bevin persuaded the new American secretary of state, George Marshall, to accept the Bevin Plan of February 1947, which called for the unification of the Western zones of occupation, as the basis for all Western planning on Germany.

By the time of the Moscow conference, the Bevin Plan had thus become the secret Western blueprint for dividing Germany. The British publicly professed their willingness to continue negotiations with the Russians while privately doing everything in their power to ensure the decisive failure of the Moscow conference and place the blame for the division of Germany on the Soviet Union.[14] Under Marshall, the United States soon followed suit by increasing its toughness on the Soviets while offering generous aid to those countries willing to remain part of the West.

After the president had announced the "Truman Doctrine" before Congress in March 1947, stating that "containment" of the Soviet Union was to be the principal goal of American foreign policy, anticommunism became the most important theme of U.S. policy, at home as well as abroad. The European Recovery Program, popularly known as the Marshall Plan, was announced on June 5, 1947. With this plan, the United States not only stabilized its influence in Western Europe, it also thwarted extremist political movements and

---

[10] Wilfried Mausbach, *Zwischen Morgenthau und Marshall: Das wirtschaftspolitische Deutschlandkonzept der USA, 1944–1947* (Düsseldorf, 1996), 274–6; John Gimbel, "Byrnes' Stuttgarter Rede und die amerikanische Nachkriegspolitik in Deutschland," *Vierteljahrshefte für Zeitgeschichte* 20 (1972): 39–62.

[11] Deighton, *Impossible Peace*, 116–20; Martina Kessel, *Westeuropa und die deutsche Teilung: Englische und französische Deutschlandpolitik auf den Aussenministerkonferenzen von 1945 bis 1947* (Munich, 1989), 154–9.

[12] Ward, *Threat of Peace*, 169–72.

[13] Deighton, *Impossible Peace*, 135–67; Kessel, *Westeuropa und die deutsche Teilung*, 211–56.

[14] Deighton, *Impossible Peace*, 115–34.

parties in the region. Indeed, after 1947, the electoral strength of West European communists declined rapidly.[15]

In May 1947, as Cold War tensions rose, the French communists left the government, and French policies were thereafter dominated by the Socialists under Prime Minister Paul Ramadier. At the Moscow CFM conference, Bidault came to the personal realization that he had to abandon cooperation with the Soviet Union and side with the West. The French generally did not think the Soviet Union seriously threatened their national interests, but Bidault would have the difficult task of convincing his compatriots that it did. He began to play a difficult double role, siding with the West at the CFM conferences while pretending not to do so at home.[16]

FINALIZING GERMAN NATIONAL DIVISION

The London CFM conference of November 25–December 15, 1947, signified the definitive failure of Allied cooperation in the matter of Germany. Molotov reacted to the announcement of the Marshall Plan by alleging that Britain and the United States were waging a "new imperialist war" against the Soviet Union. He demanded the installation of Four Power control over the Ruhr, the abolition of Bizonia, and reparations totaling $10 billion; in return, he offered a long list of concessions. At this point, the Western foreign ministers were convinced that negotiating with the Soviets was no longer necessary and that securing their zones of Germany was more important than preserving an unproductive alliance with the Soviet Union. After mutual accusations, Marshall finally suggested the postponement of the conference; it ended on December 15 without setting a date for a future meeting. The Americans and their

Western allies now took the initiative and independently began to found a West German state.[17]

Only very late in 1947 were Britain and the United States able to secure French cooperation in the amalgamation of the three West German zones into an actual state. The French finally joined Bizonia when they realized that the course of events was leaving them no alternative but to follow the West. The economic and financial boost promised by the Marshall Plan provided an added incentive. When the Western Powers and the Soviet Union broke off communication, France decided to participate as much as possible in the shaping of the new West European order. If France could not decisively weaken Germany, at least it could attempt to integrate it firmly into Western Europe. The next French foreign minister, Robert Schuman, would concentrate on this new policy.[18]

Even in late 1947, the USSR still strove to preserve the unity of Germany in order to expand its influence beyond the Eastern zone. Stalin and Molotov were alarmed when the West decided to divide Germany and unilaterally deprive the Russians of the Ruhr's resources. The Soviets were angered that Britain and the United States managed to place the blame for the division of Germany, in the eyes of the world community, squarely on them. Although the overall Russian policy in eastern Germany was ultimately self-contradictory and self-defeating, forced reforms in the Russian zone of Germany had been progressing rapidly since the beginning of 1946. After the Socialist Unity Party was founded in April 1946, the Russians began to actively shape their zone through the German communists they had installed in power.[19]

Through the East German communist leadership and directly, the Russians had made

[15] Carolyn Eisenberg, *Drawing the Line: The American Decision to Divide Germany, 1944–1949* (New York, 1996), 318–62; Leffler, *Preponderance of Power*, 182–219.

[16] Jacques Bariety, "Die deutsche Frage aus französischer Sicht, 1945–1955," in Wilfried Loth, ed., *Die deutsche Frage in der Nachkriegszeit* (Berlin, 1994), 177; Leffler, *Preponderance of Power*, 186–8.

[17] Deighton, *Impossible Peace*, 207–22; Kessel, *Westeuropa und die deutsche Teilung*, 288–94.

[18] Raymond Poidevin, "Die Neuorientierung der französischen Deutschlandpolitik 1948/49," in Josef Foschepoth, ed., *Kalter Krieg und deutsche Frage* (Göttingen, 1985), 129–31.

[19] See Norman M. Naimark, *The Russians in Germany: A History of the Soviet Zone of Occupation, 1945–1949* (Cambridge, Mass., 1995).

proposals for the neutralization of Germany after 1945. Although these plans had also existed among the Western Allies, after 1947 they originated exclusively from the Soviet Union. Even as the division of Germany and the sealing off of western German industrial potential from Soviet influence became increasingly evident in 1947, Moscow initially refrained from establishing an independent East German state. After the German Democratic Republic was founded in 1949, the Soviet Union continued to view this state as a temporary solution and did not abandon its push for the neutralization of Germany.[20]

After the Russians departed from the process of planning the future of western Germany, the London Six Power Conference, which met in two sessions between February and June 1948, agreed upon definitive guidelines for trizonal fusion and the establishment of an independent West German state.[21] The main American and British objective was now to win over the support of the West Germans for the founding of such a state. The newly formed Western bloc, fiercely attacked in Russian propaganda, had to be consolidated; the unification of Germany's Western zones depended on its integrity. A part of the West German political elite and the majority of the population tolerated this development because they could expect prosperity and the guarantee of military protection against the Soviet Union only from the West.

[20] Leffler, *Struggle for Germany*, 39–42, 48–9.

[21] Gerd Wehner, *Die Westalliierten und das Grundgesetz: Die Londoner Sechsmächtekonferenz* (Freiburg im Breisgau, 1994); see also the chapter by Hermann-Josef Rupieper in this section.

CHAPTER TWO

The United States in the Allied Control Council

From Dualism to Temporary Division

Gunther Mai

Translated by Edward Fichtner

The Potsdam Protocol established the Allied Control Council in Germany[1] by confirming the terms of the agreement that the United States, the Soviet Union, and Great Britain had concluded in the European Advisory Commission on November 14, 1944. The Control Council was assigned duties in the areas of the economy and reparations, and central German administrative departments answered to it as well. Its work was supposed to be governed by certain political principles,[2] but these principles were little more than compromise formulas that were disputed by the powers and, in some cases, contradictory. It remained for the Control Council, therefore, to solve those problems on which the governments had not been able to reach agreement.

When the Control Council held its first organizational meeting on July 30, 1945, a number of preliminary decisions had already been made that proved to be irreversible. First of all, the Soviet Union had obstructed all joint substantive decisions in the European Advisory Commission, with the result that different directives would inevitably be in effect in the respective zones of occupation. Second, at the first meeting

of the four commanders in chief on June 5, 1945, the Soviet Union delayed the establishment of the Control Council; by permitting political parties and unions on its own authority on June 10 and by forming central administrative authorities on July 27, it confronted the other Allies with faits accomplis. Third, France almost immediately announced its veto of the centralized German institutional structures already planned. Fourth, the agreement establishing the Control Council (Control Agreement) was marked by a dualism between the zonal commanders and the Control Council. Because of the veto power of the commanders, it was not possible to prevent unilateral action within the zones.

This dualism arose from the fact that the highest governmental authority in Germany was supposed to be exercised by the commanders in chief of the Four Powers "on instructions from their respective governments," specifically, "each in his own zone of occupation, and also jointly, in matters affecting Germany as a whole."[3] This dualism had been established by the United States as a compromise between, on the one hand, the more centralist proposals of the British, which were linked to a wide-ranging pressure for the Control Council to set unified policies, and, on the other hand, the radically anticentralist notions of the Soviets, who

---

[1] Gunther Mai, *Der Alliierte Kontrollrat in Deutschland 1945–1948: Alliierte Einheit – deutsche Teilung?* (Munich, 1995).

[2] Protocol of the Proceedings of the Berlin Conference, Aug. 1, 1945, in U.S. Department of State, *Foreign Relations of the United States* (hereafter *FRUS*), *The Conference of Berlin (Potsdam) 1945*, 2:1478–85.

[3] Agreement on Control Machinery in Germany, Nov. 14, 1944, *FRUS, The Conferences of Malta and Yalta, 1945*, 124–7, 124.

wanted to concede to the council only the right of coordination among the "sovereign" zones. This dual system of "unified" central political decision making and "uniform" zonal administration, however, also reflected the ambivalence of American plans for Germany.

Although this dualistic construction was already consistent with the demand of the Joint Chiefs of Staff (JCS) for a free hand in their zone, they insisted on an interpretation of the Control Agreement that resembled the Soviet view: The Control Council was intended to be only an advisory body; in the event that its intervention in the American zone conflicted with American policy, it would have to be blocked by a veto of the United States. The JCs found support for this view from Treasury Secretary Henry Morgenthau, who believed that a strong Control Council would endanger the decentralization of Germany, and President Franklin D. Roosevelt, who wanted to defer decisions of principle until the war was over. The State Department, which wanted to prevent the zonal military administrations (including that of the United States) from taking unilateral action, had to yield. The United States, therefore, presented on May 3, 1945, its new interpretation of the Control Agreement to the European Advisory Commission: The Control Council wields the highest authority in all questions affecting Germany as a whole, "and its agreed policies shall be carried out in each zone by the zone commander." But "in the absence of such agreed policies," the commander in chief of each zone has the right to exercise his authority autonomously and independently, pursuant to the directives of his own government.[4] Here, the unwillingness at the Potsdam Conference to formulate binding principles for the treatment of Germany became apparent. This policy of the free hand was rejected by the British and the French. In their view, the proposal was "an invitation to a split and unilateral action"; it would give the zonal commanders "complete liberty of action" because by their own veto they could prevent una-

nimity. The Soviet representative, however, indicated sympathy for the American proposal by "rather marked non-participation" in the debate.[5]

Despite the official rejection of the American position, the British expected a "*de facto* dismemberment*" behind a "façade of central control,"[6] while the French adhered to a combination of zonal autonomy and central coordination. Disappointed by the results of the Berlin meeting of June 5, the Western commanders in chief recommended their governments move toward a joint administration of only the three Western zones. In this they were in accord with Stalin's assessment that, in the long run, there will be "two Germanies."[7] In any case, the Soviet Union had made no secret of its determination to retain maximum autonomy in its zone.

With the arrest of the Dönitz government on May 23, 1945, the last all-German counterpoise to the centrifugal tendencies of zonal autonomy had disappeared. Churchill's attempt to delay the retreat of troops from Thuringia and Saxony until the Soviets had committed themselves to maintain both Allied *and* German unity collapsed in the face of opposition from the United States. In Potsdam, members of the American delegation still could not agree on whether the zones had primary authority (which would have implied a trizonal Western solution) or the Control Council. Central administrations,[8] which the Soviets now pressed for in opposition to the zonal regulation of reparations established by Secretary of State James F. Byrnes, were

[4] *FRUS, 1945*, 3:471 (Memorandum Regarding American Policy for the Treatment of Germany, Mar. 23, 1945) and 3:504n.28.

[5] Sir William Strang, E.A.C. Summary No. 72, May 4, 1945, Public Record Office, London (hereafter PRO), Foreign Office (hereafter FO) 371/46824; The Ambassador in the United Kingdom (Winant) to the Secretary of State, May 7, 1945, *FRUS, 1945*, 3:504–5. For Soviet plans for Germany, see Georgij F. Kynin and Jochen Laufer, eds., *Die UdSSR und die deutsche Frage 1941–1949*, vol. 1. (Moscow, 1996).

[6] Secretary of State for War Sir John Grigg, War Cabinet, APW Committee, Apr. 13, 1945, PRO, FO 942/66.

[7] Rolf Badstübner and Wilfried Loth, eds., *Wilhelm Pieck: Aufzeichnungen zur Deutschlandpolitik 1945–1953* (Berlin, 1994), 50.

[8] Elisabeth Kraus, *Ministerien für das ganze Deutschland? Der Alliierte Kontrollrat und die Frage gesamtdeutscher Zentralverwaltungen* (Munich, 1990).

supposed to lend support to the Control Council without restricting the free hand of the zonal commanders.

This fundamental ambivalence also characterized the work within the Control Council. This work was at first unaffected by the fact that, despite Directive JCS 1067, various "factions" in Office of Military Government United States (OMGUS)[9] were attacking one another well into the higher organs of the Control Council. If the military, primarily General Lucius D. Clay,[10] now advocated Four Power arrangements within the Control Council, it was because of economic pressures and pragmatic considerations, for France's veto of all-German parties, unions, and central administrations on October 1, 1945, was impeding economic unification and with it the effective administration of the American zone. The United States had to watch helplessly as the Soviet and French zones were sealed off and plundered. Only later did the Soviet policies of transformation in the Soviet occupation zone come into focus, first as an economic problem, then as a political one.

Clay's first efforts in the Control Council reflected his desire to maximize the chances for pragmatic action from the center if for no other reason than to be able to administer his own zone efficiently. But even Clay was not able to compel quick Four Power decisions by threatening to block the coordinating committee. For this reason, he immediately made use of the American interpretation of the Control Agreement, according to which, in the absence of joint decisions, he was authorized to act on his own judgment and conclude agreements with other zones. After August 1945 – and, until October 20, without authorization from Washington – he put forward specific solutions on a trizonal level: at times without the Soviet Union, at others without England, and at still others without France. On November 13, 1945, he finally proposed to the British "that you join with us in the establishment of central administrative machinery covering our two zones."[11] Although Clay added that he would also present his offer to the Soviets, the British interpreted it as a proposal to establish a British-American zone. They nevertheless declined.

Clay's attempts to find temporary and interim solutions to deal with acute day-to-day problems – solutions that, as he always emphasized, compromised nothing – were understandable, but they further undermined the pressure for unity. As he well knew, his proposals lay "outside of the formal structure of the Control machinery."[12] His British colleague, Sir Brian Robertson, recognized the disruptive effect of these efforts: To accept Clay's suggestion would "drive a wedge of dissent into the whole conception of quadripartite control."[13] Whereas the British were privately discussing a revision of the Potsdam Agreement and the Soviets were actually practicing one,[14] Clay wanted to force the implementation of the agreement but with means that ultimately promoted the autonomy of the zones. For this reason, Clay initially rejected a compromise that his economic adviser, William H. Draper, had been working on with his French colleague, René Sergent, since October 1945. It foresaw the establishment of "Allied Bureaus," which would be authorities of the Control Council, instead of central German administrations subordinate to it. The United States did not officially present this plan until May 1, 1946, but then only for tactical reasons: A unified position on the part of the three

[9] Christoph Weisz, ed., *OMGUS-Handbuch: Die amerikanische Militärregierung in Deutschland 1945–1949* (Munich, 1994).

[10] Wolfgang Krieger, *General Lucius D. Clay und die amerikanische Deutschlandpolitik 1945–1949* (Stuttgart, 1987); John H. Backer, *Winds of History: The German Years of Lucius DuBignon Clay* (New York, 1983).

[11] Montgomery to Street, Nov. 18, 1945, in *Documents on British Policy Overseas* (hereafter DBPO), ser. 1, vol. 5:382.

[12] French Policy, Nov. 1, 1945, 2, Bundesarchiv, Koblenz, Z 45 F/OMGUS, 2/100–1/11.

[13] Sir William Strang to Oliver Harvey, Sept. 29, 1945, PRO, FO 371/46988/C6744.

[14] Rolf Steininger, ed., *Die Ruhrfrage 1945/46 und die Entstehung des Landes Nordrhein-Westfalen: Britische, französische und amerikanische Akten* (Düsseldorf, 1988); Norman M. Naimark, *The Russians in Germany: A History of the Soviet Zone of Occupation, 1945–1949* (Cambridge, Mass., 1995).

Western powers would force the Soviets either to fulfill their commitment to economic unification or to openly reject normalization on an all-German basis.

The timing of this proposal was deliberate and could not fail to be noticed. It coincided with the forced fusion of the German Social Democratic Party and the German Communist Party in the Soviet zone to form the Socialist Unity Party (*Sozialistische Einheitspartei Deutschlands*, or SED) at the end of April, and with Clay's suspension of reparations deliveries at the beginning of May 1946. Whereas political adviser Robert Murphy was trying to get the Soviet Union to commit itself to democratic principles for parties and labor unions by means of a decision of the Control Council, Clay wanted to force the Soviets to open the economy of their zone by means of a halt to reparations. His demand that the central administrations and/or the Allied Bureaus be granted executive powers throughout the zones without interference from the individual zone commanders was unacceptable to the Soviet Union (and not just to it). Moscow was not ready to give up political control of the Soviet zone for the sake of economic advantages.

At the Conference of Foreign Ministers in Paris in 1946, Byrnes's deputy, Dean Acheson, and Clay urged the hesitant secretary of state to subject the Soviet Union to a "final test": Reparations deliveries would resume for sixty to ninety days, during which time negotiations would be held on the establishment of economic unity and the organization of Allied Bureaus as a transitional measure until central German administrative offices could be set up. If the negotiations should prove unsuccessful, the hold on reparations would be reinstated and the failure of the Potsdam accords confirmed.[15] Byrnes still refused to bring about the definitive break in Germany; in the meantime, British foreign minister Ernest Bevin had reconciled himself to such a step.[16] The Soviet Union did not pass the

"test." It failed it definitively on August 2, 1946, when it withdrew its own draft for a central administration for industry (that is, for reparations) because even this draft seemed likely to undermine the autonomy of the Soviet zone. To be sure, the Soviet Union showed a keen interest in raising the production of reparations commodities by expanding trade among the zones, but it wanted to do so without surrendering exclusive control over its own zone. The Soviet Union was therefore not prepared to accept more than *interzonal cooperation* through informal and closely limited arrangements that it could monitor *within the framework of the Control Council*. At the moment the Control Council, upon Soviet initiative, formally accepted the American view that its inability to act justified bilateral or trilateral cooperation among the zones, the mutually agreed erosion of the Control Council had begun.

After much hesitation, the change in U.S. policy toward Germany was announced by Byrnes in his Stuttgart speech of September 6, 1946. It found expression in plans for a British-American zone. Nevertheless, at this time neither the Americans nor the British intended to divide Germany. Although the Cold War was beginning to unfold, the domestic political conditions for such a move were still absent in the United States and Britain. Furthermore, purely pragmatic considerations effectively prevented both countries, as well as the other two occupying powers, from completely abandoning the economic unity of Germany. On the basis of the contradictory arrangements of the Potsdam Agreement, however, both sides could claim for themselves a "first-charge principle": the British and Americans with regard to the priority of exports and imports over other payments, the Soviets (and the French) with regard to the priority of reparations.

The Control Council was nonetheless able to achieve some initial successes in the economic area. However, these were due to the

[15] The Acting Secretary of State to the Secretary of State, May 9, 1946, *FRUS, 1946,* 5:549–55.

[16] Anne Deighton, *The Impossible Peace: Britain, the Division of Germany and the Origins of the Cold War* (Oxford, 1990); Martina Kessel, *Westeuropa und die deutsche Teilung: Englische und französische Deutschlandpolitik auf den Aussenministerkonferenzen von 1945 bis 1947* (Munich, 1989).

fact that the very disagreement on fundamental questions (exports and imports, reparations, currency reform) required pragmatic interim solutions. As provided in the Potsdam Agreement, nineteen groups of commodities (above all, iron and steel) were assigned to the zones by the Control Council. Modest interzonal trade reduced the need for imports; the comprehensive regulation of wages, prices, and taxes made it possible to postpone the currency reform. Finally, by the end of March 1946, a reparations and level-of-industry plan was worked out that seemed to reduce the conflicting principles to a common denominator. But the plan was only a political compromise that Clay had managed to push through. When the Control Council attempted to put it into effect, the old conflicts about central administration and exports-imports were reopened, and they again proved insuperable.

The United States was determined not to finance German reparations indirectly, as it had after World War I. The USSR, however, in view of the destruction caused by the war and its own need for modernization, did not want to allow Germany to rebuild while its own demands were postponed. Invoking the Potsdam Agreement, the Soviet Union implemented an autonomous reparations policy in its own zone, whereas the distribution of reparations from the Western zones was subject to the Control Council. The Soviet Union's obvious need for reparations lent itself to use as a political weapon. On May 3, 1946, after a brief preliminary notice, Clay suspended the dismantling of factories in the American zone earmarked for reparations; the British sided with the American policy indirectly by means of tactical delay.

The stop in dismantling and the retreat from Control Council distribution of the most important raw materials, the increasing accommodation to the British strategy of open curtness, the decision to establish the British-American zone – all these demonstrated in summer 1946 the growing readiness in both Washington and OMGUS to surrender the economic unity of Germany. As the Americans viewed it, it was impossible to cooperate with the Soviet Union under the prevailing circumstances.

Moreover, they increasingly realized that the reconstruction of Europe was also impossible without a German contribution. Byrnes (like Bevin) was pushed by his advisers to accept a Western solution, but he still refused to abrogate the Potsdam Agreement only one year after the war and to complete the breach in the Control Council.

Clay also hesitated. On the one hand, political considerations persuaded him and economic ones forced him to take pragmatic measures within the framework of the Control Council detrimental to economic unity. On the other hand, he took up the offer of his Soviet colleague, Marshal Vasiliy Sokolovsky, of July–August 1946, which sought to overcome the deadlock in the Control Council and to prevent the splitting of Germany by agreeing on reparations from current production.[17] The positive development of the bilateral negotiations in Berlin made an agreement appear likely at the Moscow Conference of Foreign Ministers in March 1947. But Clay failed because of resistance in his own delegation. The new secretary of state, George C. Marshall, although quite willing to make concessions, acted on President Truman's instructions and rejected the Soviets' offer to agree to raise the level of industrial production in return for reparations from current production. A solution of this kind would only have led to a renewed dependence on the willingness of the Soviet Union to cooperate. Breaking off from the wrong path seemed to offer better prospects than beginning new experiments – the results of which, to judge by all experience, promised very little.

Within the Soviet government, too, there had been considerable resistance to such an arrangement.[18] Ultimately, mutual mistrust prevailed. This was highlighted emphatically in the report

[17] Memorandum from Clay for Byrnes, Nov. 1946, in Jean E. Smith, ed., *The Papers of General Lucius D. Clay: Germany 1945–1949*, 2 vols. (Bloomington, Ind., and London, 1974), 1:279–84.

[18] Jochen Laufer, "Konfrontation oder Kooperation? Zur sowjetischen Politik in Deutschland und im Allierten Kontrollrat 1945–1948," in Alexander Fischer, ed., *Studien zur Geschichte der SBZ/DDR* (Berlin, 1993), 57–80.

of the Control Council that the foreign ministers had ordered for the Moscow conference.[19] After intense negotiations that often teetered on the brink of collapse, the report expressed only the agreement to disagree; the Control Council had certified its own inability to act and to decide. The Moscow conference in spring 1947 made it clear that even the foreign ministers were unable to break the deadlock.

The idea now finally began to take root among all the powers that the division of Germany was all but unavoidable. The Control Council became little more than a stage for propaganda battles mostly for the benefit of the Germans. Even the formal dissolution of Prussia by the Control Council in February 1947, which the British had been promoting through unilateral measures since summer 1946, was another step toward the division rather than the unity of Germany. France's exclusion of the Saar region from the competence of the Control Council in December 1946; the founding of Bizonia on January 1, 1947; the establishment, in the Soviet zone, of state and provincial governments in December 1946, and of the German Economic Commission on February 10, 1947 – all pointed in the same direction. Central administration and Allied Bureaus were once again discussed as intermediate steps toward the formation of a government, but old and new reservations prevented a resolution of this issue. All-German institutions would have been prejudicial to solutions based on division. Only a "temporary" division could satisfy the interests of the occupation powers in their policies toward Germany.

The founding of a divided state implied that the last remnants of economic unity had to be given up as well. Because they were subject to Soviet veto, the decisions of the Control Council on taxes, wages, prices, dismantling, and level of industry obstructed the transition to a liberal, expansionist economic policy. More for the Western powers than for the Soviet Union, the Control Council became a constraint. It was in this body, therefore, that the decision for a

division would have to be reached and implemented. Halfhearted attempts to circumvent the deadlock in the Control Council with German help (e.g., Munich conference of minister presidents, the People's Congress movement) failed while also showing that the Germans would offer no decisive resistance to the division of their country.

Currency reform, which had been postponed again and again since 1946, ultimately proved to be the crucial issue leading to the open breach in the Control Council. Even though all the powers agreed that a change of currency was necessary, they could not reach a unanimous decision because this question was inextricably connected with the political, economic, and social structure of the future Germany. Moreover, the debates in the Control Council about currency reform were by no means always a result of the conflict between East and West. Even between the British and the Americans there were sometimes substantial differences, as in the occupation administrations, which reflected similar conflicts in the capitals. At the end of December 1946, when the British officially proposed negotiations on a joint currency reform for the British-American zone, the American experts were by no means disinclined in principle; yet, such a step was not possible without first arriving at the basic decision to break up the Control Council. With the Marshall Plan, the United States' resolve for an independent course of action grew stronger in 1947, but no one wanted yet to rule out the possibility that the Soviet Union, because of its interest in reparations, would offer better conditions for the economic unification of Germany.[20] Only after October 1947 was the United States (like Great Britain) prepared for a breach in the Control Council.

Even as early as the London CFM in December 1947, the American and British financial advisers decided to seek a decision in the Control Council; the Soviet Union, too, was preparing for a decision. In January 1948, the

[19] Mai, *Der Alliierte Kontrollrat*, 400–15.

[20] S. P. Chambers to G. P. Hampshire, Mar. 28, 1947, PRO, FO 371/65005/CE1323/22/74.

two Western military governors obtained the go-ahead from their governments. On January 21, 1948, Clay (after consulting with the British) issued an ultimatum: If unanimity could not be reached within ninety days, he would, pursuant to the American interpretation of the Control Agreement, act on his own or bi- or trilaterally in agreement with other occupation powers. The Soviet Union made concessions they had obdurately refused to make up to now, but then withdrew them partly or entirely in the follow-up negotiations. It was clear that each side was trying to portray the other in the eyes of the Germans and the world as politically responsible for the end of the Control Council. On March 10–11, 1948,[21] the United States decided to hold to its ultimatum: Clay was instructed to withdraw from the consultations after the deadline of April 12. The Americans dropped any further attempts to reach agreement, which would only have given the Soviet Union another chance to gain influence in the Western zones. However, Clay was relieved of the burden of breaking up the Control

[21] Memorandum by Frank G. Wisner, Mar. 10, 1948, *FRUS, 1948*, 2:879–80.

Council because the Soviet representative left the body on March 20. That also removed the responsibility for the now inevitable division, and thereafter the United States did all it could to prevent a revival of the Control Council. The Soviets themselves did everything possible to eliminate this danger with the Berlin Blockade, which began as a technical measure to protect currency conversion in the Soviet zone (from the influx of devalued reichsmarks) and evolved into Stalin's offensive policy toward Germany.

The history of the Control Council reflects the conflict of the United States between the destruction of Germany and the reconstruction of Europe. The Control Council administered Germany on the basis of the lowest common denominator of the national interests of the victorious great powers. Its significance for American policy toward Germany and Europe lay in the fact that proposals to overcome the deadlock in it (i.e., the Byrnes Plan, the Marshall Plan) became important stepping stones toward the United States' long-term economic and military engagement in Europe. For Germany, the collapse of the Control Council meant the division of the country; for Western Europe and America, it was the beginning of a new era.

CHAPTER THREE

Supervised Democratization

American Occupation and German Politics

Barbara Fait

Translated by Richard Sharp

ALLIED TENSIONS AS THE MOTOR OF DEMOCRATIZATION

In mid-May 1945, General Lucius D. Clay stated that the first and overriding goals of American occupation policy were to render Germany totally powerless and to punish those guilty of war crimes. Not until those goals had been achieved would it be possible to plan any farther ahead. In any event, he added, the vanquished could expect to be kept on a tight rein. Although the United States military government (OMGUS) would be unable to avoid setting up a German administrative machine to assist it, this would for many months to come be no more than an instrument of the real sovereign power in Germany – a low-level administrative apparatus run and supervised by the Allies.[1]

Clay was responsible for the civil aspects of the occupation and exerted a strong influence on American occupation policy. The attitude toward the "defeated enemy nation" he voiced in May 1945 (JCS 1067) hardly suggested that he would soon be urging swifter progress toward giving Germans more responsibilities and toward democratization. The urgent tempo set

by Clay sometimes alarmed not only his political advisers but even the Germans. Clay's decision to hold elections as early as January 1946, for example, was greeted as skeptically by the Germans themselves as it was by most of his own officers. Not without good cause, both occupiers and occupied had their doubts whether Germany's "post-Hitler" society had yet progressed that far.

But Clay had sound reasons for hastening the pace of democratization. First, he was convinced that the democratic way could not be taught as theory; it had to be learned by practice, the sooner the better. Second, Clay had a duty to the American taxpayer to reduce America's manpower commitment. This could be achieved only by allowing the Germans greater responsibility. As Clay saw it, however, the transfer of authority to German institutions was out of the question unless those institutions had first been democratically legitimized. And third, Clay felt that the policy being pursued by France made haste necessary.

In the Potsdam Agreement, Britain, the Soviet Union, and the United States had settled on common principles of occupation policy. One point of agreement was that no central government should be established in Germany for the time being, but that Germany should be treated as a single economic entity and that some German central administrative bodies should be established for that purpose. France had not been invited to the Potsdam Conference. It, therefore, did not consider itself bound by the agreements concluded there and blocked the

---

[1] SHAEF, Public Relations Division, Guest Speaker Lt. Gen. Lucius D. Clay, May 16, 1945, Archiv des Instituts für Zeitgeschichte [hereafter IfZ-Archiv], OMGUS 3/157–1/21. For an important pioneering study on American policy, see John Gimbel, *The American Occupation of Germany: Politics and the Military, 1945–49* (Stanford, Calif., 1968).

implementation of any resolutions that ran counter to its plans for an extreme form of federalism in Germany.

This gave rise to major economic problems, as the particularism of the various zones proved a serious obstacle to urgently needed economic reconstruction. The American zone, especially, was viable only in the context of an economically integrated Germany.[2] When it became apparent after mid-September 1945 that the central administrative units could not be set up quickly, Clay turned his attention increasingly to the political structure of the American zone. Starting with the creation of the *Länder* (states) on September 19, 1945, he accelerated this process as the economic situation became more critical and doubts grew as to whether the Potsdam Agreement could ever be implemented.

On December 10, 1945, Clay argued in favor of a bold alternative: that the United States government should commit itself to the rapid formation of a German government.[3] Although Clay wanted to grant it only limited powers at first, there was little prospect that such an initiative would find favor with the other Allies. Clay's idea met with a cool reception in Washington as well. The War Department replied to his proposals to the effect that any such review of the foundations of American policy toward Germany was impracticable for the present, not least in light of public opinion in the United States. At the same time, however, Clay was unofficially given a free hand to shape practical policy in the American zone as he saw fit.[4]

Clay took advantage of this freedom. He stepped up efforts to democratize the American zone and arranged early in February 1946 for the drafting of *Land* (state) constitutions. In undertaking this "democratic experiment" he had two ends in view. First, the constitutions, which were to be ratified in November 1946, would tip the scale in favor of federalism

and counterbalance the centralist tendencies that were becoming apparent in the Soviet and British zones. Second, the subsequent election of the first democratically legitimized state governments would, at least in the American zone, create all the necessary conditions for the formation of a central government in Germany based on federalist principles. Clay hoped that his policy would send out a signal: If the states in the American zone were willing and able to adopt democratic constitutions, it would prove that the same thing could be done throughout Germany as a whole. That would refute the arguments of those who rejected the idea of a German government on the grounds that the Germans were not yet ready for democracy. For this strategy to work, the framers would, of course, have to be able to complete their work on the constitutions free of American tutelage.[5]

It was because of the economically fatal consequences of France's obstructionist policies and the resulting need to find an alternative to the Potsdam Agreement that the states in the American zone were able to choose their own political leadership and determine their own constitutional form earlier than the rest of Germany. Their political acumen proved equal to the "democratic experiment." They projected an image of themselves as potential junior partners and thereby contributed to the U.S. government's adoption of Clay's position: On September 6, 1946, Secretary of State James F. Byrnes gave official backing to the formation of a provisional German government. Because the democratic advances in the American zone could be matched in other zones, Byrnes said in a widely noted speech in Stuttgart, the Germans should be permitted to make the necessary preparations.[6] As we now know, that would not come

---

[2] See the chapter by Wilfried Mausbach, vol. 1, Economics.

[3] Clay to Hilldring, Dec. 10, 1945, National Archives (hereafter NA), RG 200, box 10, folder 2.

[4] Hilldring to Clay, Dec. 31, 1945, NA, RG 218, box 125, sec. 10.

[5] Barbara Fait, "'In einer Atmosphäre von Freiheit:' Die Rolle der Amerikaner bei der Verfassunggebung in den Ländern der US-Zone," *Vierteljahrshefte für Zeitgeschichte* 33 (1985): 420–55.

[6] This speech given by Byrnes in Stuttgart has often been hailed as a turning point in American occupation policy. In fact, as Clay stated on October 12, 1946, it merely confirmed a policy that had long been practiced. See Division Staff Meeting, Minutes, Oct. 12, 1946, IfZ-Archiv, Fg 12/6. See also John

about until 1948–9, and the Cold War, which by that time dominated every decision affecting occupation policy, resulted in the formation of two German governments and two German states. Unlike the East-West conflict, the initial disagreements, in particular those with France, did have some beneficial effects: They acted as a motor of democratization.

TERRITORIAL AND ADMINISTRATIVE REORGANIZATION

With Proclamation No. 2 of September 19, 1945, the Americans created three administrative units in their zone that they referred to as "states," each of which would have its own government.[7] After the Soviet Union divided its own zone into five states or provinces on July 9, 1945,[8] OMGUS came to a very swift decision on the territorial organization of the American zone.

Territorially, Bavaria had emerged from the war almost unscathed. From the American perspective, the size of Bavaria's territory and population were ideal. All that needed to be done there was to resurrect the administrative machinery that had been undermined during the Nazi period. On May 28, 1945, a "temporary minister president" had been appointed in Bavaria: Fritz Schäffer, former chairman of the Bavarian Peoples Party.

Finding a solution in the southwest proved more difficult. The original plan was that Württemberg and Baden should also remain states. Although relatively small, they seemed

likely to be able to hold their own in the future federation after the planned breakup of Prussia.

These plans became redundant once France had been recognized as the fourth controlling power in Germany. The French zone of occupation was carved out of the British and American zones in the southwest of the country. The border between the French and American zones ran straight through the middle of Württemberg and Baden: In the years that followed, the south of each was under French control, the north under American. American plans for federation would hardly benefit from dividing Württemberg and Baden, with their long traditions and strong sense of regional identity. The loss of their southern parts had made them too small to remain viable on their own. A new territorial arrangement was needed. Eventually, three "states" were called into existence: Bavaria; "Greater Hesse," formed from the former Prussian province of Hesse-Nassau and the "People's State" of Hesse; and "Württemberg-Baden," consisting of the northern parts of the two states. Bremen, as an enclave within the British zone, did not achieve the status of a state of the American zone until January 1947.[9]

The unification of the territory of Hesse corresponded to the wishes of the population.[10] The merging of Württemberg and Baden was less popular. Enormous pressure had to be brought to bear before the people of (north) Baden could bring themselves to recognize the government of Württemberg-Baden, which had existed since September 24, 1945, and, on October 29, to send representatives to it. The minister president selected by the Americans was Reinhold Maier, a left-liberal who had been economics minister of Württemberg from 1930 to 1933. An important part was played in the new "hyphenated state" by Maier's

---

Gimbel, "Byrnes Stuttgarter Rede und die amerikanische Nachkriegspolitik in Deutschland," *Vierteljahrshefte für Zeitgeschichte* 20 (1972): 39–62; Wilfried Mausbach, *Zwischen Morgenthau und Marshall: Das wirtschaftspolitische Deutschlandkonzept der USA 1944–1947* (Düsseldorf, 1996), 274–6.

[7] The proclamation is reprinted in Bayerische Staatskanzlei, *Dokumente zum Aufbau des Bayerischen Staates* (Munich, 1948), 30–3.

[8] Martin Broszat and Hermann Weber, ed., *SBZ-Handbuch: Staatliche Verwaltungen, Parteien, gesellschaftliche Organisationen und ihre Führungskräfte in der Sowjetischen Besatzungszone Deutschlands*, 2d ed. (Munich, 1993).

[9] For the special position of Bremen, see Dirk Bavendamm, "Hamburg und Bremen," in Walter Först, ed., *Die Länder und der Bund: Beiträge zur Entstehung der Bundesrepublik Deutschland* (Essen, 1989), 63–9.

[10] Walter Mühlhausen, "Hessen," in Först, *Die Länder und der Bund*, 77; Helmut Berding, ed., *Die Entstehung der Hessischen Verfassung von 1946: Eine Dokumentation* (Wiesbaden, 1996), xi.

deputy, Heinrich Köhler of Baden, who had also come to the forefront of state politics during the Weimar Republic. Formerly of the Center Party, Köhler was able to negotiate special measures for north Baden that gave the region a degree of independence within the state.[11]

On October 16, 1945, Karl Geiler became the first minister president of "Greater Hesse" (which after December 1946 was called simply "Hesse"). A lawyer by profession, Geiler could be described as a liberal conservative but belonged to no party. In Bavaria, the business of government lay in the hands of Social Democrat Wilhelm Hoegner, who took office on September 28. The reason given by the military government for the removal of his predecessor was Schäffer's lack of zeal in enforcing denazification within the public sector. Schäffer did indeed adopt a critical stance toward overly rigid purging of the public administration, fearing it might collapse altogether. He told the Americans as much, which put him on dangerous ground, given the high priority they attached to denazification.[12]

That, however, was not the main reason for Schäffer's dismissal. Clay had sent his political adviser, Robert D. Murphy, to Munich to investigate the matter, and Murphy formed the impression that Schäffer could not be seriously faulted on the denazification issue. Even so, he recommended that Schäffer be removed from office while urging immediate action to strengthen the Bavarian government.[13] What may seem paradoxical at first glance becomes clear on closer examination: Clay was at that time beginning to press on with the democratic consolidation of the American zone, and Murphy's recommendation reflects the new, constructive tone of Clay's policy. Schäffer was firmly opposed to an early move toward party politics and democracy, and he did not conceal

his views from the Americans.[14] It was this attitude, more than anything else, that cost him his office. What was wanted was a minister president who could support the steps being taken toward accelerated democratization and credibly represent them.

According to Proclamation No. 2, the state premiers wielded full legislative, judicial, and executive powers, subject to the overriding authority of the military government. Intended for public consumption, the proclamation appeared to give the heads of the state governments virtually dictatorial powers but, in fact, their authority was extremely limited. The state governments initially acted as strictly executive organs of the occupying power and agents of its objectives. Externally, however, they had to be seen as independent: No legislation could contain the slightest hint that it had been enacted in the name of the military government or with its approval.[15]

This control, initially very strict, was increasingly relaxed in the course of 1946. Responsibility for the everyday business of administration passed more and more into the hands of the state minister presidents, though their policies still had to be "cleared" daily with the military government.[16] Although the ratification of the state constitutions and the election of democratic state parliaments and governments in November and December 1946 had marked the start of something of a "new era,"[17] unrestricted German self-determination was still out of the question at this point. The occupation

---

[11] Klaus-Jürgen Matz, "Baden und Württemberg," in Först, *Die Länder und der Bund*, 33–6.

[12] See the chapter by Cornelia Rauh-Kühne in this section.

[13] Murphy to the Secretary of State, Oct. 5, 1945, NA, RG 165, box 175, sec. 2.

[14] Barbara Fait, *Die Anfänge der CSU 1945–1948: Der holprige Weg zur Erfolgspartei* (Munich, 1995), 21–6; Christoph Henzler, *Fritz Schäffer (1945–1967): Eine biographische Studie zum ersten bayerischen Nachkriegsministerpräsidenten und ersten Finanzminister der Bundesrepublik Deutschland* (Munich, 1994), 160–1.

[15] Office of Military Government in Bavaria to Wilhelm Hoegner, Dec. 26, 1945, Bayerisches Hauptstaatsarchiv (hereafter BayHStA), Nachlass Pfeiffer 55.

[16] Zusammenarbeit zwischen Bayerischen Behörden und Militärregierung, BayHStA, Nachlass Pfeiffer 32.

[17] Address to the Länderrat by Major General Frank A. Keating (Jan. 1947), IfZ-Archiv, OMGUS 3/157–1/21.

power continued to supervise legislation and, indeed, public life as a whole. Wilhelm Hoegner has aptly summarized the balance of power: "Occupation law takes precedence not just over ordinary laws but even over the constitutional law of the states."[18]

Just one month after the creation of the states, Clay called upon the minister presidents to form a zonal coordination office that would perform the functions of the central administrative units originally envisaged at Potsdam. The Länderrat (Council of States), which began work in Stuttgart on November 6, 1945, had a loose federal structure. The minister presidents met monthly to arrange the requisite cooperation between their states within the framework of the political guidelines laid down by the occupying power. Their decisions had to be adopted unanimously. An office was set up to assist the Council, and its staff grew quickly. Organizationally, too, the Länderrat was expanded, as set out in a statute the minister presidents agreed upon in June 1946.[19]

The substance of that statute was soon rendered obsolete by events. On July 11, 1946, at the Council of Foreign Ministers conference in Paris, Byrnes invited the other Allies to merge their zonal economies, separately or jointly, with the American zone. On July 29, the British accepted the invitation, and negotiations were underway by August on "Bizonia." The "United Economic Area," as it was also known, officially came into being on January 1, 1947. The organization of Bizonia, too, was somewhat loose at first to avoid giving the impression that it might be the precursor of a government. Bizonia's reorganization, following the breakdown of the Moscow Conference of Foreign Ministers (CFM) (March 10–April 24, 1947) did, however, suggest a move in that direction. When the attempt to reach a Four Power agreement

on Germany at the London CFM (November 25–December 15, 1947)[20] also failed, the bizonal apparatus was again reorganized. By February 1948, it was already showing clear structural characteristics of a central government.

POLITICAL PARTIES, ELECTIONS, STATE CONSTITUTIONS

In the Soviet zone, the formation of "antifascist" political parties had been permitted since June 10, 1945, but political groups in the American zone had to wait until August 27 before they were allowed to organize – initially at the local level only. The developing local parties were minutely scrutinized by OMGUS before they were granted (or refused) licenses to begin political activity. That took some time, but was not the only reason why in Bavaria, for example, local political parties – 264 in all – had been formed in only 120 of 164 administrative districts by January 15, 1946. Postwar society was engaged in a struggle for survival. Few people were interested in political matters. For most Germans, the experience of National Socialism and the impression made by the start of denazification made politics suspect.

Those who did commit themselves politically were generally reluctant just to continue in the tradition of the Weimar parties. The memories of Nazi dictatorship and military defeat were still fresh, and there was a very strong desire to turn away from outdated political positions. That created the need, however, to develop new positions and, on account of the strong trend toward political concentration, to integrate divergent currents of political opinion. Conflicts were inevitable and resolving them took time. For example, it was not until November 25, 1945, that the founders of the Munich Christian Social Union (*Christlich-Soziale Union*, or CSU) were able to apply for a license. By that time, however, the parties in the American zone

[18] Wilhelm Hoegner, *Lehrbuch des Bayerischen Verfassungsrechts* (Munich, 1949), 23.

[19] Marie-Elise Foelz-Schröter, *Föderalistische Politik und nationale Repräsentation 1945–1947: Westdeutsche Länderregierungen, zonale Bürokratien und politische Parteien im Widerstreit* (Stuttgart, 1974), 25–9.

[20] On the CFMs, see the chapter by Edmund Spevack in this section.

were being allowed to merge to form state organizations, a directive to that effect having been issued on November 23, 1945.

The decision to permit state parties again took into account the American principle of grassroots democracy, albeit more in theory than in practice. The example of the Munich CSU was not an isolated one, and a consolidation of the local party system was still out of the question. The military government was also aware of this, but there were arguments in favor of pushing ahead, after a hesitant start, with the formation of parties. By this time, Clay was contemplating the formation of a provisional German government in the near future. Whereas in late September 1945 he had still considered it impossible to hold state elections before October 1946, by mid-November 1945 he was considering allowing them as early as June. He wanted to use the elections to usher in the final phase of the institutional democratization of the American zone: the drafting of state constitutions. The Germans learned of this plan at around the turn of the year; they urgently advised against it, as did a team of American experts Clay had consulted, but in vain. Work on the constitutions was officially launched on February 4, 1946.[21] There was another argument in favor of licensing state parties: The first elections, in municipalities of up to 20,000 inhabitants, were scheduled for January 1946. In view of the continuing low level of organization, only the licensing of statewide parties could guarantee a competitive party landscape.

In the elections held on January 20 and 27, 1946, it was still not possible for voters everywhere to choose between all the parties that had been granted statewide licenses in 1945–6. The Union parties (the CSU and the Christian Democratic Union, *Christlich Demokratische Union*) and the Social Democratic and Communist organizations were already licensed in every state, but the Bavarian Communists did not receive their statewide license until January 19 – too late to be able to field candidates throughout the state. The same applied to the liberal groups that had formed under various names. Only in Württemberg-Baden, with its strongly rooted liberal tradition, had the Democratic People's Party (*Demokratische Volkspartei*) obtained a statewide license. The organizational preparations were not sufficiently advanced until May 1946 in Bavaria and June in Hesse.

The party system that evolved in the American zone (as in the other zones) was largely the same in each state. Only in Bavaria were the aforementioned groups joined by a fifth party with a statewide license, the Union for Economic Reconstruction (*Wirtschaftliche Aufbau-Vereinigung*, or WAV), which achieved notable successes in the 1946 elections. Under its enigmatic chairman, Alfred Loritz, the WAV developed into a protest party that attracted the disaffected:[22] nationalists, supporters of the Bavarian monarchy or Bavarian separatism, expellees and refugees – groups the military government tolerated only locally or refused party licenses altogether.

Although the licensing practice helped to ensure that there was no return in 1945 to the party fragmentation of the Weimar era, it would be wrong to deny the German political forces a share in that achievement. Many people at the time had come to realize that the ideological narrowness and obduracy of the Weimar parties had encouraged the process of political disintegration and abetted the progressive discrediting of parliamentary democracy. The *Zeitgeist* also favored unity and solidarity because social barriers and conflicting interests had been swept away by the war, and German society had, for a

---

[21] Pollock to Clay, Jan. 3, 1946, Constitutional Conventions, IfZ-Archiv, Selected Records, MA 1420/9. See also James K. Pollock, *Besatzung und Staatsaufbau nach 1945: Occupation Diary and Private Correspondence 1945–1948*, ed. Ingrid Krüger-Bulcke (Munich, 1994), 123, 126. For the official start of the work on the constitutions, see "Direktive an die Militärregierungen in Bayern, Gross-Hessen und Württemberg-Baden: Elections in the U.S. Zone, February 4, 1946," in James K. Pollock, James H. Meisel, and Henry L. Bretton, eds., *Germany Under Occupation: Illustrative Materials and Documents* (Ann Arbor, Mich., 1949), 120.

[22] Hans Woller, *Die Loritz-Partei: Geschichte, Struktur und Politik der Wirtschaftlichen Aufbau-Vereiningung (WAV) 1945–1955* (Stuttgart, 1982).

brief transitional period, become fused into an emergency alliance of the dispossessed. In general, there was evidence of a strong trend toward more open party platforms. The newly created or re-created parties wanted to work toward social justice and to become broad-based "people's parties" (*Volksparteien*).[23]

The results of the January elections allowed no reliable forecast of the future balance of political power. But the municipal elections could serve as a touchstone for the status of democratization. OMGUS, therefore, awaited the outcome of the elections with great anticipation. The results exceeded its "fondest hopes." The high turnout – more than 85 percent in all three states – was noted with particular favor by the military government. It was also relieved that very few unrepentant Nazi sympathizers had used their ballots to express their views. The predominance of the Union parties and Social Democrats in all three states was regarded by OMGUS as a welcome indication that the Germans were showing no tendency to radicalism "at present."[24] Most important of all in Clay's view, however, was that the results of the elections had defused the main arguments. A few days after the elections, the order was given to begin preparations for the election of constituent assemblies in early summer. These elections were held in all three states on June 30, 1946. Although the turnout on this occasion was significantly lower – 67.5 percent in Württemberg-Baden, 70.9 percent in Hesse, and 72.1 percent in Bavaria – the results confirmed a trend that had been apparent since

January: The Union parties and Social Democrats remained the strongest political forces.

Because a major aim of Clay's "democratic experiment" had been to demonstrate that the Germans had acquired sufficient understanding of democracy since the end of the war to justify risking the creation of a democratic government, more radical interference by America in the constitutional work was both inadvisable and unnecessary. OMGUS had already taken preliminary steps to ensure that the framers of the constitutions were democratically inclined: by a selective licensing policy in party and press affairs, by denazification, and by carefully vetting the candidates put forward. A fundamental democratic consensus thus existed between the Americans and the German framers.

The Germans and Americans did not always see eye to eye on the best way of structuring the new democracy, however. But it suited American policy that there were also differences of opinion among the Germans as well. Proponents of an authoritarian, patriarchal democracy clashed with fervent democrats, socialists were at odds with those who favored a liberal economic order, and representatives of the center moved in between. Because the political parties were concerned to strike a balance between their interests, the military government could count on a functioning, democratic form of self-regulation and in moderate results. On Clay's orders, it limited itself to influencing the constitutional deliberations by "friendly persuasion" when necessary.

The suggestions the Americans offered were sometimes accepted and sometimes rejected by the constitution drafters. Even where massive conflicts of interest existed, the military government consistently refrained from forcing revisions. Its respect for German rights of self-determination extended only to the texts of the constitutions as such, however; the letters of approval that were to be regarded as part of the constitutions for the duration of the occupation reflected certain American interests. This was particularly true in connection with the Americans' desire to establish a functioning German government as quickly as possible. Clay denied

[23] Ossip K. Flechtheim, ed., *Dokumente zur parteipolitischen Entwicklung in Deutschland seit 1945*, 9 vols. (Berlin, 1962–71); Oskar Niedermayer and Richard Stöss, eds., *Stand und Perspektiven der Parteienforschung in Deutschland* (Opladen, 1993); Adolf M. Birke, *Die Bundesrepublik Deutschland: Verfassung, Parlament, Parteien* (Munich, 1997), 92–105; see also the bibliography of contemporary history published annually with the *Vierteljahrshefte für Zeitgeschichte* on the present status of party research, which is currently experiencing a new boom.

[24] Memorandum from Brewster H. Morris (RGCO) to Murphy, Feb. 1, 1946, NA, RG 84, POLAD, CGC, box 2.

the states any right to oppose measures that OMGUS considered necessary for this objective.[25]

Overall, however, it cannot be said that the Americans imposed their own notion of democracy upon Germany.[26] This argument has been advanced, for example, in connection with the socialization article of the constitution of Hesse (Article 41), the enactment of which was suspended by OMGUS on the ground that such a decision could be taken only in the context of Germany as a whole. Historians have long held that the sympathies of the occupying power very often actually lay with the left-liberals and the socialists.[27] And if Clay and, after September 1946, the American government had had their way, the consultations on a federal constitution would have taken place at a time when socialist ideas were still very much in favor even in the Union parties.

The referenda on the state constitutions took place in conjunction with the elections to the first postwar state parliaments – on November 24, 1946, in Württemberg-Baden and December 1 in Bavaria and Hesse. Those qualified to vote gave clear approval to the fact that the framers had tried to reconcile social and political interests. All constitutions were adopted by large majorities (70.6 percent in Bavaria, 76.8 percent in Hesse, and 86.8 percent in Württemberg-Baden). The state parliament elections confirmed the Union parties and the Social Democrats as the leading political forces.

The formation of the first democratic governments also reflected the political parties' desire for cooperation and a greater share of responsibility. In Bavaria, a coalition government was formed by the CSU, SPD, and WAV under Minister President Hans Ehard (CSU), though the coalition survived only until September 1947. In Hesse, the CDU and SPD under Minister President Christian Stock (SPD) shared the responsibilities of government until the end of the legislative period. In Württemberg-Baden, an all-party coalition was formed under the incumbent minister president, Reinhold Maier, and it, too, proved durable, lasting until July 1949. Maier alone among the minister presidents named by OMGUS successfully bridged the democratic transition.[28]

The elections for the first state parliaments in November and December 1946 marked the close of the new political beginning in the American zone. In the Americans' view, the groundwork had now been laid for the rapid formation of a German government. After the elections, American interest centered on establishing multizonal institutions. The attention of German politicians, too, was increasingly shifting to the multizonal stage – reluctantly so in the case of Bavaria, with its deep attachment to independence. Bavaria had many struggles with the Americans and the multizonal organizations in defense of its "national" rights, but it struggled in vain while Clay continued down the path toward the formation of a German government he had embarked upon in late 1945.

[25] A survey of the literature on the origins of the constitutions in the Länder can be found in Barbara Fait, *Demokratische Erneuerung unter dem Sternenbanner: Amerikanische Kontrolle und Verfassunggebung in Bayern* (Düsseldorf, 1998), 24–31.

[26] Theo Pirker, *Die verordnete Demokratie: Grundlagen und Erscheinungen der Restauration* (Berlin, 1977); Eberhard Schmidt, *Die verhinderte Neuordnung 1945–1952: Zur Auseinandersetzung um die Demokratisierung der Wirtschaft in den westlichen Besatzungszonen und in der Bundesrepublik Deutschland* (Frankfurt am Main, 1970).

[27] Dörte Winkler, "Die amerikanische Sozialisierungspolitik in Deutschland 1945–1948," in Heinrich August Winkler, ed., *Politische Weichenstellungen im Nachkriegsdeutschland 1945–1953* (Göttingen, 1979), 88–110. Against this background, clearer distinctions also need to be drawn when considering the prospects of the antifascist committees: Rebecca L. Boehling, *A Question of Priorities: Democratic Reforms and Economic Recovery in Postwar Germany: Frankfurt, Munich, and Stuttgart under U.S. Occupation 1945–51* (Providence, R.I., 1996); Wilfried Mausbach, "Rückkehr nach Weimar? Der politische Neubeginn in Köln in den Augen der amerikanischen Besatzungsmacht," in Georg Mölich and Stefan Wunsch, eds., *Köln nach dem Krieg: Facetten der Stadtgeschichte* (Cologne, 1995), 27–62. For a discussion of research in general, see Rudolf Morsey, *Die Bundesrepublik Deutschland: Entstehung und Entwicklung bis 1969*, 3d rev. and enl. ed. (Munich, 1995), 145–9.

[28] For more detailed surveys of franchise regulations, election results, and governments, see Heinrich Potthoff and Rüdiger Wenzel, eds., *Handbuch politischer Institutionen und Organisationen 1945–1949* (Düsseldorf, 1983), 47–59.

CHAPTER FOUR

Life Rewarded the Latecomers

Denazification During the Cold War

Cornelia Rauh-Kühne

Translated by Edward G. Fichtner and Sally Robertson

According to rough estimates, the denazification policy of the three Western Allies during the postwar period cost nearly 870,000 people their jobs at least temporarily.[1] In addition, about 230,000 persons were detained, some for several years.[2] In the early 1950s, the all too recent memories of these purges were still causing feelings to run high.[3]

Soon afterward, however, the humiliating process of denazification gradually faded from memory. Since the end of the 1960s, denazification has stood as "unfinished business," a project sacrificed to the Cold War.[4] Even the controversies about how to deal with personnel in the

German Democratic Republic in the wake of German reunification were still influenced by the image of denazification in the West as having been nothing but a series of sins of omission.

Clichés of this sort do justice neither to the aims nor the implementation of denazification policy. There was no lack of serious intent about denazification in 1945, nor did it fail solely because of the Cold War. Naturally, the tendency to suppress those memories and the increasing tension between East and West in all the occupation zones helped to hasten the end of denazification and discredit it in the eyes of the German public. However, the failure of the American denazification plan had deeper roots than that. It resulted from the fact that the American guidelines for the purges were irreconcilable with the social reality of the Third Reich.

AMERICAN PLANS FOR DENAZIFICATION

At the end of the war, the United States was the only Western power that had made concrete preparations for denazifying German society. These were set forth in Joint Chiefs of Staff (JCS) directive 1067 of April 1945, which initially applied to the British and French zones as well and strongly influenced the decisions of the Potsdam Conference and the Allied Control Council. The core of the purging measures undertaken in the first weeks of the occupation was the dismissal of former members of the National Socialist German Workers' Party

---

[1] Anna J. Merritt and Richard L. Merritt, *Public Opinion in Occupied Germany: The OMGUS Surveys, 1945–1949* (Urbana, Ill., 1970), 35–6, 63.

[2] Lutz Niethammer, "Alliierte Internierungslager in Deutschland nach 1945," in Christian Jansen, Lutz Niethammer, and Bernd Weisbrod, eds., *Von der Aufgabe der Freiheit: Politische Verantwortung und bürgerliche Gesellschaft im 19. und 20. Jahrhundert: Festschrift für Hans Mommsen zum 5. November 1995* (Berlin, 1995), 474. Whereas in the first nine months of the occupation 1 out of every 142 inhabitants in the American zone was interned, it was 1 out of every 144 in the Soviet zone, 1 out of every 263 in the French zone, and 1 out of every 284 in the British zone.

[3] Norbert Frei, *Vergangenheitspolitik: Die Anfänge der Bundesrepublik und die NS-Vergangenheit* (Munich, 1996), 54–69.

[4] Lutz Niethammer, *Die Mitläuferfabrik: Die Entnazifizierung am Beispiel Bayerns* (Berlin, 1982), 11; this first appeared under the title *Entnazifizierung in Bayern: Säuberung und Rehabilitierung unter amerikanischer Besatzung* (Frankfurt am Main, 1972).

(*Nationalsozialistische Deutsche Arbeiterpartei*, or NSDAP) as well as all "active supporters of Nazism or militarism."[5] In addition, provisions were made for the arrest and trial of war criminals and the internment of officials of the Nazi regime. The rigorous conditions for dismissal clearly betrayed the influence of Vansittartism, which saw in National Socialism the criminal outgrowth of a specifically German mentality that had developed over time. This fundamentalist concept, largely impervious to subtler distinctions, aimed not at replacing officials in key positions but at punishing as many as possible of those who had been involved with the National Socialist regime. As a result, the guidelines for dismissal were applied in none of the Western zones as extensively as in the American zone. More arrests were also made in the American zone than in any of the other three.[6]

On July 7, 1945, detailed regulations for the implementation of JCS 1067 arrived at the U.S. headquarters. They stated that any persons who had been more than "nominal party members" were to be dismissed from key positions in public life. Those affected had no right of appeal, and along with their occupational and social positions they also lost any claim to pensions from their employer. Their assets were frozen. The political past of all those involved was to be recorded and systematically evaluated using a 131-point questionnaire that demanded information on formal incriminating factors such as party and organizational membership and party functions. The group of those subject to dismissal was precisely defined using 125 formal criteria. It included practically all members of the NSDAP who had joined the party prior to May 1, 1937 (Reich Civil Service Law), and all NSDAP officials, including those in subsidiary organizations, as well as all officers of SS and

Storm Troopers (*Sturm-Abteilung*, or SA) down to the rank of noncommissioned officer. Moreover, all higher officials of the Reich, the states, and municipalities, regardless of any party function or membership, were to be dismissed, including police lieutenants on ordinary duty and mayors of small towns. A comparable procedure based on individual incriminating factors was recommended for the military and economic elite of the Third Reich, but it was not compulsory.

As a reaction to public sentiment in the United States that the military government's denazification policy was too lax, Military Law No. 8, directed at the economy, was issued at the end of September 1945. It barred all members of the NSDAP and associated organizations from managerial or supervisory positions in the private sector. This directive, aimed at small companies and nominal members of the NSDAP, marked the abandonment of a *political* purge dedicated to replacing key personnel within the state and society. The desire for a settling of moral accounts with the former Nazis had gained the upper hand over rational calculation in American strategy and led to an overextension of the purging policy.

Yet, could these measures be effective in the long run? If they had been applied consistently, the American guidelines for dismissal would have necessarily led to the collapse of public life, for they failed to grasp the social reality of the Third Reich.[7] A few statistics illustrate this. In 1945, at least every fifth adult male in Germany was a "Pg." (i.e., a *Parteigenosse*, or party member). In the younger age groups, the proportion was distinctly higher. The middle class was strongly overrepresented among NSDAP party members. The *Dienstklasse* (service class), as Niethammer has called it, was particularly conspicuous for its organizational closeness to the regime. For example, by 1937 63 percent of the civil service had joined the NSDAP. Many

[5] JCS 1067, reprinted in Beate Ruhm von Oppen, ed., *Documents on Germany under Occupation, 1945–1954* (London, 1955), 17. See also Tom Bower, *The Pledge Betrayed: America and Britain and the Denazification of Postwar Germany* (Garden City, N.Y., 1982); James F. Tent, *Mission on the Rhine: Reeducation and Denazification in American-Occupied Germany* (Chicago, 1982).

[6] Cornelia Rauh-Kühne, "Die Entnazifizierung und die deutsche Gesellschaft," *Archiv für Sozialgeschichte* 35 (1995): 35–70.

[7] Hermann Lübbe, in a philosophical essay that has attracted much attention, was the first to raise the question of the "continuity of the nation" as a problem in "the mastering of the past"; see Hermann Lübbe, "Der Nationalsozialismus im deutschen Nachkriegsbewusstsein," *Historische Zeitschrift* 236 (1983): 579–99.

party members were more than just "nominal" members, for National Socialism, with its grotesquely over-bureaucratized organizational structure, had turned the Germans into a "nation of Führers." Toward the end of National Socialist rule, the total number of political "leadership positions" was about two million and, again, the middle class, especially the civil service, was disproportionately represented in relation to the total population. The proportion of workers was also remarkably high.[8]

On the other hand, it was by no means the case that an individual's willingness to cooperate in attaining the goals of the National Socialist regime necessarily took the form of party membership or acceptance of party office. In particular, the representatives of the economic elite, who kept the armaments machinery and the managerial mechanisms of the economy running so efficiently, seem often to have distanced themselves from the NSDAP.[9]

German opponents of National Socialism, therefore, saw the main difficulty with denazification in distinguishing "real Nazis" from mere fellow travelers. To avoid placing too much emphasis on formal criteria, the denazification process had to include participation by those Germans who had the necessary inside information. New injustice must not be heaped upon old injustice.

However, this criticism raises the question of whether, in the framework of a purging concept originally aimed at key positions in society, there could be meaningful alternatives to the military government acting on its own. A purging policy supported by Germans would have to honor the sense of justice of those involved if it were not to lose credibility in the eyes of the German public. However, a denazification policy committed

to the principle of justice would have led to insoluble conflicts with the structural requirements of personnel replacement, which could not be carried out without individual hardship. The tribunal (Spruchkammer) procedure later introduced in the American zone offers just as many examples of this dilemma as the purging practices in the French and Soviet zones, where Germans had already been involved in the denazification process from the early phase of the occupation.[10]

FROM RIGOROUS PURGES TO MASS REHABILITATION

The dismissals carried out by the Americans in the course of 1945 led to the collapse of many branches of government; the economy seems to have been hard hit as well, though there are still no specific studies of this subject. By the end of March 1946, close to 340,000 persons in the American zone had been directly affected by the directives governing dismissals. Of those, 56 percent were in the civil service. Despite the general confusion, that was only a small percentage of party members and, presumably, did not even include all those who had held party office. Clearly, the guidelines had not been strictly applied. The pragmatism and desire for efficiency among many technical officers of the military government, as well as the delaying tactics of German leaders in government and industry, had managed to prevent a "worse" outcome. Nevertheless, in many places the dismissals brought public life to a standstill. There were large firms in which the management had to be completely replaced and rural communities that had no teachers and no local police, where grocery stores were closed and the only veterinarian for miles around had been

---

[8] Lothar Kettenacker, "Sozialpsychologische Aspekte der Führer-Herrschaft," in Karl Dietrich and Manfred Funke, eds., Nationalsozialistische Diktatur 1933–1945: Eine Bilanz (Düsseldorf, 1983), 118.

[9] Cornelia Rauh-Kühne, "Die Unternehmer und die Entnazifizierung der Wirtschaft in Württemberg-Hohenzollern," in Cornelia Rauh-Kühne and Michael Ruck, eds., Regionale Eliten zwischen Diktatur und Demokratie (Munich, 1993), 320; Michael H. Kater, The Nazi Party: A Social Profile of Members and Leaders, 1919–1945 (Oxford, 1983), 160–1.

[10] Rainer Möhler, Entnazifizierung in Rheinland-Pfalz und im Saarland unter französischer Besatzung von 1945 bis 1952 (Mainz, 1992); Helga A. Welsh, "Antifaschistisch-demokratische Umwälzung und politische Säuberung in der sowjetischen Besatzungszone Deutschlands," in Klaus-Dietmar Henke and Hans Woller, eds., Politische Säuberung in Europa: Die Abrechnung mit Faschismus und Kollaboration nach dem Zweiten Weltkrieg (Munich, 1991), 84–107.

denied permission to practice.[11] Although many of those dismissed were not considered Nazis by their neighbors, the same could not be said of some of those spared.

The military government was apparently just as surprised at the scope and one-sided social impact of its regulations as at the resistance its policies encountered in the ranks of former opponents of National Socialism. Only later was it recognized that the functional elites of German society had been organizationally co-opted by National Socialism to such an extent that, after the purges, the replacement personnel ran into insurmountable problems. As a result, the denazification policy the Americans had pursued on their own initiative had reached a dead end by the end of 1945. When they decided, for that reason, to turn denazification over to the German authorities, it was clear that many dismissals had to be reversed and that many merely nominal adherents of National Socialism had to be rehabilitated.

The Americans and ultimately their Western allies, therefore, began to adopt the approach to denazification that both opponents and former followers of the National Socialist regime supported. This approach claimed to mete out "justice" and judged individuals on a case-by-case basis according to their political behavior. With the "Law for Liberation from National Socialism and Militarism" (the so-called *Befreiungsgesetz*, or Liberation Law), which took effect on March 5, 1946, the tribunal system was first introduced in the American zone. It placed denazification in the hands of lay legal panels, which functioned like courts of assessors and consisted of delegates from the political parties in the cities and rural districts. In many cases, the panels were composed entirely of people with no prior legal training. In procedures resembling those of courts of justice, the tribunals reached decisions about the culpability and "measures of atonement" of the accused. Their decisions were reviewed by the military government and could be appealed; this was usually the practice, which created a flood of review proceedings. The basic

change from the previous denazification directives of the military government was expressed in Article 2 of the Liberation Law, according to which each individual case was to be judged "by justly weighing individual responsibility and actual overall behavior."[12]

Although the military government accepted this provision of the German law, which aimed at the rehabilitation of many who had been unjustly dismissed, it also insisted – with one eye on the American public – on the adoption of the 125 formal incriminating factors established in July 1945. As a consequence, the political past of all Germans older than eighteen and residing in the American zone was reviewed by means of a questionnaire. Those who were affected by the Liberation Law – about 30 percent – were then divided into five categories by the "Public Prosecutor" based on their incriminating factors: (1) "major offenders" (*Hauptschuldige*); (2) "incriminated persons" (*Belastete*); (3) "less incriminated persons" (*Minderbelastete*); (4) "fellow travelers" (*Mitläufer*); and (5) "non-incriminated persons" (*Entlastete*). The assignment to a category of culpability by a purely systematic classification – contrary to legal traditions – constituted a legal presumption of guilt. The burden was on the accused to refute it.

This reversal of the burden of proof could not help but create an attitude of self-justification highly detrimental to the political morality of postwar society. The classification system adopted for the Liberation Law from the American denazification guidelines was also fraught with consequences for the reputation of the tribunals. Perhaps the most fateful repercussions resulted from the mandatory provision that a fixed and detailed "measure of atonement" be assigned to each formal incriminating factor, such as membership in an organization or holding party office. This provision was irreconcilable with the requirement of "weighing individual responsibility." As presumably "incriminated persons" (category 2), the millions of former office holders, SA and SS members, and nominal party members who had fortified

[11] See, e.g., Elmar Ettle, *Die Entnazifizierung in Eichstätt: Probleme der politischen Säuberung nach 1945* (Frankfurt am Main, 1985), 95.

[12] Erich Schullze, ed., *Gesetz zur Befreiung von Nationalsozialismus und Militarismus vom 5. März 1946*, 3d ed. (Munich, 1948), 8.

the ranks of the NSDAP prior to 1937 were threatened with a labor-camp sentence as well as complete, or at least partial, expropriation of property and the loss of their right to social welfare or pensions. Finally, they were to be excluded for five years from any occupational activity with the exception of ordinary labor for hire.

Article 58 of the Liberation Law hindered the progress of denazification by stipulating that all those who had been provisionally assigned to categories 1 or 2 were allowed until the conclusion of their cases to engage only in "ordinary labor." As a result, the tribunals were "torn back and forth between the two equally pressing obligations of freeing the little Nazis from discrimination at the hands of the law and punishing the big Nazis as quickly as possible."[13]

In view of the crimes committed under National Socialist rule, the measures of atonement were certainly not extreme. However, their categorical application in no way took account of the various kinds of individual responsibility that had existed under the circumstances of government in the Third Reich. It was predictable that the wholesale presumption of guilt in the Liberation Law would not last long. The tribunals felt compelled by individual justice to reassign the accused to a lower category, particularly because those persons assigned to categories 1 or 2 by the excessive formal criteria had in many cases already suffered serious injury, be it by internment, occupational prohibitions, freezing of assets, or requisitioning.

Niethammer pointed out in 1972 that "the overwhelming ... majority of tribunal members [were] far removed from consciously subverting the Liberation Law in a pro-Nazi sense"; recent regional studies have confirmed this. The tribunals set to work with considerable energy – as did the German purging committees of the French zone. But they were confronted with an impossible task.[14]

By August 1949, the tribunals' activity in the American zone amounted to about 950,000 cases, completed for the most part in writing, of which more than half ended in a determination of fellow-traveler status and a small fine. For each person whose case had been brought to completion, there were three whose cases were dismissed. The tribunals dealt neither with younger persons nor with those in the lower income groups that had been granted general amnesty in 1946. Thus, if denazification before a tribunal remained an experience of the middle class, affecting more than half of all civil servants but only 3 percent of workers,[15] this may represent the willingness of the "service class" to accommodate itself to the National Socialist regime, but it is hardly an adequate reflection of the relatively significant number of members of the working class among the "political leaders" of the NSDAP and the officer corps of the Waffen-SS.

Although the process of granting amnesty favored the lower classes, the tribunals often showed leniency when reaching decisions on suspects in prominent positions. The higher the social status of the person affected, the more favorable the course of his denazification and the more impressive the series of advocates who appeared on his behalf. These prominent citizens evidently had a network of neighborhood and occupational contacts that made a particularly trustworthy impression.

All in all, in the American zone, 1,654 persons (0.17 percent) were classified and sentenced as "major offenders" in category 1; 22,122 (2.33 percent) emerged from their trials as "incriminated persons"; and 106,422 (11.2 percent) were deemed "less incriminated persons," who likewise could receive occupational sanctions of limited duration. The system had "run the sea through a sieve ... in order to catch a couple of fish."[16]

[13] Justus Fürstenau, *Entnazifizierung: Ein Kapitel deutscher Nachkriegsgeschichte* (Neuwied, 1969), 72.

[14] Niethammer, *Mitläuferfabrik*, 393–4; Hans Woller, *Gesellschaft und Politik in der Amerikanischen Besatzungszone. Die Region Ansbach-Fürth* (Munich, 1986), 127.

[15] Niethammer, *Mitläuferfabrik*, 551; see also the results of polls from the year 1953 on the way in which specific classes were subjectively affected by denazification, in Clemens Vollnhals, *Entnazifizierung: Politische Säuberung und Rehabilitierung in den vier Besatzungszonen, 1945–1949* (Munich, 1991), doc. no. 100, 335–8.

[16] Fürstenau, *Entnazifizierung*, 122 (quotation), 228.

The trifling scope of the measures of atonement made a mockery of the intimate connections between the National Socialist leadership
and society. The measures made it clear that
those who had wanted to turn denazification
into a court for punishment of the nation had
failed just as badly as those who had wanted
to replace the incumbents in all key positions.
In the face of the tribunals, the personnel of the
National Socialist dictatorship had "more or less
dissolved into thin air."[17] More dubious than
this result, however, was the way it had come
about and the effect it had of discrediting denazification in the eyes of the German public.[18]
With the American public in mind, OMGUS
tried to maintain the appearance of a rigorous
and unwavering purge. The tribunals, which in
the beginning turned out fellow-traveler ver-
dicts almost exclusively, were criticized for allegedly lacking the necessary enthusiasm for the
job of purging. "That mysterious mechanism"[19]
by which whole ranks of former activists mu-
tated into "fellow travelers" was not, however,
set into motion by the tribunals but by another
change of American policy that benefited the
National Socialist political elite rather than the
army of fellow travelers.

After the attitude in the United States
changed in favor of the Germans in the wake of
the emerging conflict between East and West,
the American government was willing to use
almost any means to bring denazification to an
end as quickly as possible. When the Soviets
announced the end of denazification in their
zone in August 1947, the situation became more
critical. After earlier amnesties for young people (those born 1920 and later) and for low-
income wage earners, the military government
agreed in October 1947 to an amendment of

the Liberation Law that made it possible to classify even suspected National Socialist activists as
fellow travelers. While the tribunals were working at top speed and were finally able to turn
their attention to the difficult cases, decision
makers in Washington were considering the idea
of a general amnesty. It was dropped after the intervention of the military governor, Lucius D.
Clay. But on March 25, 1948 – at about the
same time that the purges ended in the Soviet
occupation zone – the second amendment to
the Liberation Law went into effect. From now
on, culpable persons could be classified as fellow
travelers by means of an accelerated procedure
with no review by the military government,
which now withdrew completely from the process of denazification. Those most favored by
this "procedural simplification" were the highly
culpable. This policy had a devastating effect,
reducing different levels of responsibility to a
common denominator and thus creating a spirit
of solidarity among the accused. It robbed the
denazification project, which had at first been
supported by many Germans, of all credibility.
Neither the criterion of "individual responsibility and actual overall behavior," as provided
in the Liberation Law, nor formal incriminating factors were crucial for determining classification and atonement measures, but rather
when the case was heard. Life rewarded the late-
comers.

The most conspicuous victims of this development were those Germans who had taken
upon themselves the thankless task of denazification. Maligned as befoulers of their own nest,
the full-time employees of the tribunals often
had great difficulty finding new positions after
the tribunals were closed.

CONSEQUENCES OF DENAZIFICATION FOR WEST GERMAN SOCIETY

The political purges had no effect on the
social structure of the Federal Republic. Beginning in early 1947, the managers and civil
servants who had previously been dismissed en
masse as "fellow travelers" returned one by
one to their old positions. Soon the boards of

---

[17] Vollnhals, *Entnazifizierung*, 23.

[18] Polls conducted by OMGUS in March 1946 on the
implementation of denazification in the American zone
still showed the approval of 57 percent of those surveyed.
After that, the approval rate sank steadily. In September
1947, it was 32 percent; in May 1949, only 17 percent
(Merritt and Merritt, *Public Opinion*, 304–5).

[19] Ralph Giordano, *Die zweite Schuld, oder Von der Last
Deutscher zu sein* (Hamburg, 1987), 89.

directors; boards of supervisors; agencies of city, district, and state governments; and even the newly created federal administration were being filled with experienced old-timers. Opponents of National Socialism believed they were witnessing "renazification" on a broad scale, and observers in all the military governments were just as surprised at the extent of the rehabilitation as they were in 1945 by the effects of the dismissals they had ordered. One exception to the nearly ubiquitous impression of continuity was the new political leadership that had been put in place in 1945–6 by the military government. It had been recruited to a considerable extent from politicians who had earned their spurs during the Weimar Republic. In other areas, however, the people moving back into jobs and positions of rank were the same people on whom the tribunals had imposed long-term occupational bans. With the amnesty and integration of even unabashed National Socialist criminals during the early Adenauer years, any further prosecution of National Socialist crimes had lost its public legitimacy. This also encouraged the quasi-rehabilitation of war criminals,[20] which might not have occurred without the earlier disavowal of denazification policy and the resulting sense of solidarity on the part of those who were its targets. Under the circumstances of the Cold War, the renewed budding of nationalism, and the increasing sense that Germany had paid its dues, even highly culpable top-level officials of the National Socialist regime were able to resume their places among their former colleagues. Not a few were successful in continuing to advance their careers. This was even true for the National Socialist elite in the stricter sense – high functionaries of the NSDAP and of its organizations and units. Even for officers of the Gestapo and the SS, there were no insurmountable obstacles to re-entry or advancement. The young, ambitious, middle- or upper-class person with an academic background[21] – a type well

represented in the leadership positions of the SS and Security Service (*Sicherheitsdienst*, or SD) – was to prove indispensable for leadership tasks in the society of the Federal Republic as well. The presence of these individuals among the personnel of the Federal Republic was without a doubt detrimental to its reputation abroad, particularly because the GDR understood so well how to use it for propaganda purposes, but it never brought Bonn substantial disadvantages, such as a threat to Western integration. The conflict between the Western and communist worlds allowed no room for such "personnel issues."

In retrospect, one can say that West German democracy brought favorable social opportunities even to the former elite of the NSDAP. After a temporary interruption of their careers, most succeeded in regaining positions consistent with their social background and education, which they presumably would have also attained without National Socialism and denazification.[22]

This underscores the fact that the restructuring of personnel in the society of the Federal Republic, once a cornerstone of American occupation policy, was a failure. There are many reasons for this. It is difficult to say how mistaken approaches could have been avoided. The interwoven character of National Socialist rule and German society forced the occupation powers into a profound dilemma. In essence, it made a policy of *political* purges concentrating on key positions just as questionable as the approach of "mastering the past" (*Vergangenheitsbewältigung*) through judicial procedures addressing the individual's political behavior, a policy that became reality in the form of the tribunal system. Finally, the absence of a "substitute elite" that was politically acceptable to the occupation forces made the failure of personnel replacement in the Western zones inevitable. This distinguished the Western situation from that of the Soviet occupation zone, where it was possible to draw on

---

[20] Ulrich Brochhagen, *Nach Nürnberg: Vergangenheitsbewältigung und Westintegration in der Ära Adenauer* (Hamburg, 1994).

[21] Norbert Frei, *Der Führerstaat: Nationalsozialistische Herrschaft 1933 bis 1945* (Munich, 1987), 129, 171–2.

[22] Ulrich Herbert, "Rückkehr in die Bürgerlichkeit? NS-Eliten in der Bundesrepublik," in Bernd Weisbrod, ed., *Rechtsradikalismus und politische Kultur: Die verzögerte Normalisierung in Niedersachsen in der Nachkriegszeit* (Hannover, 1995), 157–73.

a pool of politically untainted adherents of the left who in many cases had proven themselves in the resistance movement.[23] It will be a matter for future research to reveal, however, whether the continuity of the nation, which was common to both parts of Germany, was also "mastered" as effortlessly and rigorously in the East as it has appeared up to now.

American policymakers recognized the problematic nature of their own concept of denazification only after the directives for purging had already set into motion what Niethammer calls *Gleichschaltung* (leveling), which indiscriminately exposed activists and mere conformists – indeed, even opponents of National Socialism – to political defamation and existential insecurity. When the tribunals then assumed the responsibility for denazification as a German endeavor, they were forced to accept the role of unwilling administrators of a policy based on fundamentally flawed premises. The image of "fellow-traveler factories" (*Mitläuferfabriken*) in no way does justice to the difficult work of the tribunals, which often required a great deal of self-sacrifice. After the Soviets ended denazification in their zone and the Americans had diametrically shifted their attitude toward denazification overnight, it was not surprising that there was a lack of enthusiasm for purges in West German society. Only then did the tribunals begin to adapt to the growing trend toward broad-based amnesty. This set the stage for the social

reintegration of even the National Socialist elite.

Nevertheless, the "renazification" of West German politics and society feared by observers of these developments both in Germany and abroad did not occur. Despite the foregoing argument, denazification was partly responsible for that. Along with automatic arrest, internment, and civil and military criminal trials, denazification helped keep the National Socialist elite out of political life in West Germany for years and enabled a new political class to take root, at first on the lowest level of the rural districts and towns, and then in the states and on the federal level. As a result, a large-scale *political* comeback of former prominent Nazis occurred nowhere – with the significant exception of the judiciary.

The fact that denazification made the "German catastrophe" a personal debacle as well, if only temporarily, for broad segments of the social elite certainly helped to discredit the National Socialist regime after 1945 among large numbers of its once-faithful adherents. In this sense, denazification was, despite its undeniable deficiencies, a significant success and an indispensable element of American occupation policy.

In view of its quantitative scope and the fluid boundaries between National Socialist functionaries and functional elites, the social reintegration of the numerous National Socialist elite as well as the mass of fellow travelers was probably not only a political necessity but also the price an open society with a still unsteady democracy had to pay for political stabilization.

[23] Helga A. Welsh, *Revolutionärer Wandel auf Befehl? Entnazifizierungs-und Personalpolitik in Thüringen und Sachsen (1945–1948)* (Munich, 1989), 29–30, 41.

CHAPTER FIVE

The Marshall Plan and the Origins of the Cold War

Michael Wala

Translated by Andrew Long

The Marshall Plan was one of the most influential foreign policy programs of the postwar era. It signaled the end of American attempts to forge a joint policy with the Soviet Union on Europe and Germany. By spring 1947, it had become clear that the United States and the Soviet Union held conflicting views about how best to deal with their former enemy economically and in terms of security issues. Western Europe and Germany were central to the American planning that led to a politically motivated economic aid program. The Marshall Plan was to become the cornerstone of the United States' dual containment policy toward the USSR and Germany.

The Soviet Union wanted to support its own economic recovery through reparations paid out of Germany's current industrial production. At the same time, it sought to secure political and military control of Germany by taking part in the monitoring of the Ruhr region, Germany's industrial heartland. American foreign policy experts recognized that the result of such a policy would be a German economy geared almost exclusively to the needs of the USSR. Germany's neighbors, it was thought, would inevitably suffer heavily, making rapid economic recovery in Western Europe extremely difficult to achieve. This view, held by many expert observers and by members of the American military government in Germany, was also shared by prominent Republicans, including former president Herbert Hoover. Hoover led a commission on economic conditions in Germany

and Europe that had been created by President Harry S. Truman, and he confirmed this assessment in a report of March 1947:

The whole economy of Europe is interlinked with the German economy through the exchange of raw material and manufactured goods. The productivity of Europe cannot be restored without the restoration of Germany as a contributor to that productivity.[1]

A further injection of American financial aid also had become necessary to avert the risk that communist parties and organizations would gain in popularity, take power in West European countries (France and Italy appeared to be particularly vulnerable), and perhaps even bring the whole of Western Europe under the political influence of the USSR. By spring 1947, $9 billion in aid had already been poured into regions laid waste by the war, without producing the desired results.

Truman's foreign policy was supported by influential Republicans, such as Senator Arthur H. Vandenberg (R-Mich.), but Congress, which the Republicans had controlled since the midterm elections of 1946, was pushing for tax cuts and a reduction in spending. Thus, without a convincing overall plan for European economic recovery, any attempt to secure further costly

---

[1] The President's Economic Mission to Germany and Austria, Report no. 3, Mar. 18, 1947, in Herbert Hoover, *Addresses upon the American Road, 1945–1948* (New York, 1949), 84.

support for individual countries could expect to encounter substantial congressional opposition.

At the Council of Foreign Ministers meeting held in Moscow in March and April 1947, George C. Marshall, who had taken over as secretary of state in January, made a last attempt to win Soviet backing for a joint policy on Germany's four zones of occupation. His efforts, however, were to no avail. Each side, Soviet and American, feared that the other was seeking to gain a dominant position in Europe, lure Germany over to its side, and win control of the region. In Washington, politicians were hoping that the USSR would seize this last chance for cooperation. Stalin and Foreign Minister Viacheslav Molotov, however, stuck firmly to their demands and played for time. Visibly disappointed, Secretary Marshall returned to the United States and began to lay the foundations for a new American policy toward Europe without Soviet agreement.

Immediately after his return on April 28, the State Department began frantic attempts to prepare the public for the imminent changes in foreign policy, to secure House and Senate support for the inevitably high relief spending it would entail, and to begin making plans for a massive economic aid program.[2] The offer to provide aid to Greece and Turkey, announced in the Truman Doctrine of March 12, had generally been considered insufficient, while the broad promise of the Doctrine, that the United States would rush to the aid of *all* subjugated peoples, had been regarded as unrealistic. On May 8, 1947, Undersecretary of State Dean Acheson set out the new foreign policy in a speech before the Delta Council, an alliance of farmers and businessmen concerned with international issues based in the Mississippi Valley. He linked the economic recovery of Europe and Asia to

the reconstruction of the German and Japanese economies and called for renewed efforts to turn around the economies of those countries – if necessary, without unanimous Allied approval.[3]

In early May, Secretary Marshall instructed George F. Kennan and his State Department Policy Planning Staff (PPS) to draw up a general framework for an economic aid program. Kennan's tendency to interpret international relations in psychological terms was reflected in a preliminary report of May 23 that predicted that the American offer of assistance would, in itself, contribute greatly toward the restoration of morale in Europe. Kennan saw the aid program as "political economy in the literal sense of that term." He wanted the United States to be regarded as a generous donor, which would indeed offer help but would leave the implementation and distribution of aid to the countries concerned:

The formal initiative must come from Europe.... The role of this country should consist of friendly aid in the drafting of a European program and of later support of such a program by financial and other means, at European request.[4]

This memorandum received confirmation and support in reports issued by other branches of the administration.[5] The direct catalyst for Marshall's remarkable speech of June 5, 1947, in which he announced the aid program, was

---

[2] Forrest C. Pogue, *George C. Marshall: Statesman, 1945–1959* (New York, 1987), 197–217. See also the important book by Michael J. Hogan, *The Marshall Plan: America, Britain, and the Reconstruction of Western Europe, 1947–1952* (Cambridge, 1987). For an insight into contemporary thinking by an advocate of the Marshall Plan, see Allen W. Dulles, *The Marshall Plan*, ed. and with an introduction by Michael Wala (Providence, R.I., and Oxford, 1993).

[3] U.S. Department of State, *Bulletin*, May 18, 1947, 991–4. Acheson's summary of events leading up to the speech may be found in Acheson to Jonathan Daniels, Sept. 9, 1949, in Acheson Papers, box 29, Harry S. Truman Library, Independence, Mo.

[4] The Director of the Policy Planning Staff (Kennan) to the Undersecretary of State (Acheson), May 23, 1947, in U.S. Department of State, *Foreign Relations of the United States* (hereafter *FRUS*), 1947, 3:224–30. The quoted passage was later directly incorporated into the text of the speech announcing the Marshall Plan. The PPS reports for this period were published in U.S. Department of State, Policy Planning Staff, *The State Department Policy Planning Papers*, 3 vols. (New York, 1983).

[5] Report of the Special ad hoc Committee to the SWNCC, Apr. 21, 1947, *FRUS*, 1947, 3:204–19; United States Assistance to Other Countries from the Standpoint of National Security, Report by the Joint Strategic Survey Committee, Apr. 29, 1947, *FRUS*, 1947, 1:736–50.

provided by Undersecretary for Economic Affairs William L. Clayton. After returning from a trip to Europe in May 1947, visibly affected by the destruction he had seen there, Clayton wrote to Secretary Marshall on May 27: "Without further prompt and substantial aid from the United States, economic, social, and political disintegration will overwhelm Europe." Beyond the implications of such a development for future world peace and security, Clayton also stressed the direct impact on the United States' domestic economy: Export markets for surplus domestic production would disappear, leading to unemployment, economic crisis, and massive budget deficits on top of a mountain of war loans.[6]

By the time Marshall, Acheson, Clayton, Kennan, and other State Department officials assembled for a meeting on May 28, 1947, they had essentially decided to take the initiative to stabilize the European political situation through economic measures. A central topic at their meeting was the question of whether the countries of Eastern Europe should be included. After some discussion, they agreed to put forward a plan that would include these countries, "provided the countries would abandon near-exclusive Soviet orientation of their economies."[7]

Whether the USSR and the countries of Eastern Europe should participate or be excluded was the most significant political issue affecting the planning of the aid program. On the one hand, the planners feared that exclusion of these countries would further exacerbate tensions between the USSR and the United States, lay the responsibility for the seemingly inevitable division of Germany and Europe on the United States, and antagonize the (politically important) communist and socialist parties of Western Europe. The cooperation of France and Italy, both led by socialist governments, would be jeopardized.

State Department officials, on the other hand, hoped to use the economic aid program to pry Poland, Czechoslovakia, and possibly other Eastern European countries out of their close relationship with the USSR. And yet it was hardly likely that sums of $10 to $20 billion would be forthcoming from a Congress that two and a half months earlier had needed to be cajoled, with barely concealed anti-Soviet rhetoric, into approving the comparatively meager sum of $400 million for Greece and Turkey. In view of this dilemma, it was decided to invite the USSR; the terms, however, would make it impossible for the Soviet leadership to accept.[8]

Just a few days later, the opportunity arose for Marshall to make the American initiative public: He had been invited to give a speech at the Harvard University commencement ceremonies. Marshall did not offer a finished plan on June 5, 1947 – only an American promise to support Europe. Neither the USSR nor the countries of Eastern Europe were mentioned in direct terms, and all European nations were invited to participate. And yet it was quite obvious that the United States was attaching conditions to its offer. Marshall declared that the goal of the American offer was "the revival of a working economy in the world so as to permit the emergence of political and social conditions in which free institutions can exist." The secretary of state – who just a short while before had strongly denounced the USSR's unwillingness to participate in the reconstruction of Europe – then expressed himself in even plainer terms, warning governments, political parties, and political groups that the United States would respond to any attempt on their part to exploit human suffering for their own ends.[9]

[6] Memorandum of the Undersecretary of State for Economic Affairs (Clayton), May 27, 1947, FRUS, 1947, 3:230–2.

[7] Summary of the Discussions on Problems of Relief, Rehabilitation, and Reconstruction of Europe, May 29, 1947, FRUS, 1947, 3:234–6.

[8] Joseph M. Jones, The Fifteen Weeks (February 21-June 5, 1947) (New York, 1955), 253. On June 6, 1947, the day after Marshall's speech, Kennan and Bohlen once more assured the worried secretary of state of their confidence that there was no danger that the USSR would actually take up the offer. See Charles E. Bohlen, Witness to History, 1929–1969 (New York, 1973), 263–5.

[9] Memorandum by Charles P. Kindleberger, July 22, 1948, FRUS, 1947, 3:241–7; Charles E. Bohlen, The Transformation of American Foreign Policy (New York,

The Harvard University commencement ceremonies were clearly not the appropriate occasion to announce an initiative of such global significance. But the secretary of state wanted to attract the attention of the Europeans while avoiding any potential outcry from the isolationist press and from representatives and senators who were committed to budget cuts. It was, therefore, several days before the British and French foreign ministers reacted. Ernest Bevin and Georges Bidault met in mid-June for preliminary talks. They told the State Department that they welcomed Washington's offer, and invited the Soviet foreign minister to Paris for talks on how best to proceed. Both had hoped that the USSR would decide not to take part and, indeed, it does appear that no one in Moscow was quite sure how to respond to Marshall's speech – whether to see it as an offer or a threat.[10] The Soviet ambassadors in Warsaw, Prague, and Belgrade were informed that Moscow thought it would be advantageous if its allies were to express their interest in accepting the American aid offer. At the same time, however, the Soviet leadership was discussing how it might prevent the United States from using Marshall's offer as a way of achieving the political goals of the Truman Doctrine.[11]

William Clayton attended a first round of talks in London on June 24 and, three days later, the Soviet, French, and British foreign ministers held a meeting in Paris. Molotov suspected that the French and the British had already taken far-reaching decisions in consultation with the Americans, but nonetheless consented to join the talks. As had been the case with Soviet loan requests in the past, he wanted it understood that the United States was to act only as financier and would have no right to influence or examine the economies of beneficiary countries. The Soviet foreign minister also objected strongly to Germany's participation in the planned reconstruction program for fear that German reparations payments to the USSR would dwindle. For the three Western Allies, however, Germany's participation and an increase in its industrial capacity (especially its coal production) were central and indispensable prerequisites for the economic recovery of Europe as a whole.

During the Paris negotiations, it quickly became apparent that the aid program involved more than just a friendly helping hand extended to equal partners. The Americans made it clear that they were not willing to relinquish control over the resources they were offering. For the United States, access to participating countries' internal economic data and influence over the distribution of the resources were preconditions of the aid program. The economic recovery of Western Europe was to take priority, and Eastern European countries were to support this recovery by supplying the necessary raw materials. All participating economies would need to be closely integrated, which meant that an East European economic orientation toward the USSR was out of the question.

Molotov could not and would not accept such a plan. He quit the talks after the fifth session on July 2, but not before accusing the British and the French of having plotted, together with the Americans, the political and economic subjugation of Europe. Shortly afterward, Bevin and Bidault invited all European nations – with the exception of fascist Spain and the USSR – to a July 12 conference to determine where American aid would be needed and how it should be distributed.

1969), 88–90. The text of the speech is printed in *FRUS, 1947*, 3:237–9.

[10] A number of archives and holdings of the former USSR have already been opened to historical research, but a final assessment will probably be possible only after all archives have been made public. An important insight into Soviet thinking based on available materials may be found in Scott D. Parrish, "The Turn Toward Confrontation: The Soviet Reaction to the Marshall Plan, 1947," in Scott D. Parrish and Mikhail M. Narinsky, *New Evidence on the Soviet Rejection of the Marshall Plan, 1947: Two Reports*, Woodrow Wilson International Center for Scholars, Cold War International History Project, Working Paper 9 (Washington, D.C., 1994), 1–40.

[11] Mikhail M. Narinsky, "The Soviet Union and the Marshall Plan," in Parrish and Narinsky, *New Evidence on the Soviet Rejection of the Marshall Plan*, 42–3. See also Vladislav Zubok, "Stalin's Plans and Russian Archives," *Diplomatic History* 21 (1997): 299–300; and Vladislav M. Zubok and Constantine Pleshakov, *Inside the Kremlin's Cold War: From Stalin to Khrushchev* (Cambridge, Mass., 1996).

At Molotov's suggestion, Czechoslovakia and Poland had first accepted the invitation to the conference, but then declined on July 9 and 10 under heavy pressure from Moscow. Two and a half months later, the organization Cominform was established to consolidate the USSR's influence in Eastern Europe and to counter the threat, political and economic, posed by the Marshall Plan. By the end of the year, the USSR had signed a series of trade contracts with Eastern European countries designed in particular to compensate Czechoslovakia and Poland for the advantages they had foregone by not joining the Marshall Plan. The USSR's reaction to the Marshall Plan and its consequences thus led to a hardening of the Soviet attitude toward the Western powers, especially the United States. After some initial hesitation, Molotov and Stalin introduced a bloc policy, with the result that Europe and the world were split into two hostile camps.

Even as Molotov was leaving Paris, William Clayton – aided by the American ambassadors in Paris and London, Jefferson Caffery and Lewis W. Douglas – pressed the representatives of the sixteen nations gathered in Paris to form a joint organization and to agree to work together closely. In his memorandum of May 1947, Clayton had referred to the urgent necessity for economic cooperation among European countries like that already in place between Belgium, the Netherlands, and Luxembourg (Benelux). He left the Europeans in no doubt that they would have to do without American economic aid if they were not prepared to grant America's wishes. It was not in the United States' interest to function merely as financial sponsor and provider of goods to individual countries. The Committee of European Economic Cooperation (CEEC) was duly founded and was swiftly labeled by the Soviets as a tool of American imperialism and a threat to the sovereignty of European nations.

The final CEEC report was ready on September 22, 1947. Marshall and Truman feared that the political and economic situation could deteriorate dramatically within a short time. On November 17, at a special session of Congress, the president therefore requested provisional aid of $597 million for Italy, France, Austria, and China. The communist coup in Czechoslovakia, at the end of February 1948, accelerated the political debate in the United States. On March 13, 1949, the bill authorizing the European Recovery Program, as the Marshall Plan was officially named, was passed in the Senate by 69 votes to 17. The House of Representatives, after voting to cut the sum authorized for the first year, followed suit on March 31, by 329 votes to 74. Of the requested $17 billion, over $12 billion was approved for the planned four-year reconstruction program.[12]

A sum of approximately $1.3 billion was made available to West Germany under the Marshall Plan, representing about 10 percent of total funds paid out. Far more important for the Germans, however, was that the Marshall Plan gave them the chance to take responsibility for their own future and to become members of the community of nations again.

In April 1948, the Organization for European Economic Cooperation (OEEC) emerged out of the CEEC to coordinate the aid program with America's Economic Cooperation Administration and to oversee the distribution of funds to the participating nations. The Federal Republic of Germany was founded in May 1949 and joined the OEEC in October the same year. The OEEC laid one of the cornerstones for European unification.

[12] U.S. House Committee on Foreign Affairs, *Hearings on Emergency Aid* and *Hearings on United States Foreign Policy for a Post-War Recovery Program*, 80th Cong., 1st sess., 1949; also U.S. Senate, *Hearings on United States Assistance to European Economic Recovery*, 3 pts., 80th Cong., 2d sess., 1949.

CHAPTER SIX

Winning the Peace

The United States, Western Germany, and the Ambiguities of "Dual Containment," 1945–1950

Ruud van Dijk

The Cold War ended where it began: in Eastern and Central Europe and in Germany. In 1989, the Soviet leadership ended the East-West stand-off by consciously failing to enforce its power monopoly in the region. The following year, Mikhail S. Gorbachev agreed to German unification and NATO membership for an enlarged Federal Republic. In doing so, the leader of the sinking Soviet empire gave in to Western maximum demands dating back to the early years of the East-West conflict. Although internal causes drove the Soviet surrender, Western policies contributed significantly to bringing it about. In any case, the Cold War's resolution resembled the forecast included in the most famous Western policy formulation since 1945: George F. Kennan's strategy of containment. In an article published in 1947, Kennan, then the head of the State Department's Policy Planning Staff, advocated a policy "designed to confront the Russians with unalterable counterforce at every point where they show signs of encroaching upon the interests of a peaceful and stable world." In addition, Kennan wrote, "the United States has it in its power to increase enormously the strains under which Soviet policy must operate, to force upon the Kremlin a far greater degree of moderation and circumspection than it has had to observe in recent years, and in this way to promote tendencies which must eventually find their outlet in either the breakup or

the gradual mellowing of Soviet power."[1] Kennan may not have been its "inventor," and the policy was implemented in ways the author of the "X" article soon began to criticize, but containment did succeed in preventing the spread of Soviet influence across Western and Southern Europe. It also kept a large part of Germany out of Moscow's reach.[2]

For the latter accomplishment, the contribution of West Germans was crucial. For the entire duration of the Cold War, they chose participation in Western political, economic, and military organizations over neutrality or alignment with Moscow, and the Federal Republic of Germany was one of the Western alliance's mainstays. However, Germany's role was quite different in the immediate postwar years, when the Cold War and the division of Europe were taking shape. Germans were more vanquished foes than Cold War allies at this time. That the first postwar years became a period of rapid change in U.S. foreign policy, accompanied by

[1] George F. Kennan, "The Sources of Soviet Conduct," *Foreign Affairs* 25 (July 1947): 566–82; 581, 582 (quotations).
[2] For the point that containment was in place well before Kennan invented it, see Melvyn P. Leffler, *A Preponderance of Power: National Security, the Truman Administration, and the Cold War* (Stanford, Calif., 1992), 60, 61.

a rush toward West German rehabilitation, was due mainly to the Soviet challenge. And although the Federal Republic eventually joined containment, the United States and its partners remained ambivalent. First, World War II was not forgotten. Second, Germany had been divided by the Cold War; hopes of reunification, the West feared, might keep the West Germans from cooperating wholeheartedly with Western policies. For their part, West Germans could not avoid the uncomfortable realization that while they were teaming up with the West, their compatriots in the Soviet zone were at the mercy of Joseph Stalin and his German puppets. This gave German participation in containment an ambivalence that tended to confirm Western concerns.

SWITCHING ENEMIES

At the end of the war, U.S. policymakers were determined to eliminate its causes, many of which they traced back to the aftermath of World War I. They were particularly concerned about three factors: European recovery and independence, Germany's political and economic make-up and international status, and the policies of the Soviet Union. All were connected because of Germany's political and economic centrality on the Continent and the Allied occupation of Germany. Most important, each factor had the potential to affect, once more, American interests negatively. Washington policymakers concluded that their country should contribute to a European order where peace would be safe from the ambitions of revisionist or revolutionary powers. The United States should not withdraw politically from Europe, as it had done after World War I, but neither should it again foot a large part of the bill for German and European economic recovery and political stabilization. A key factor for success in Europe, these officials believed, was whether the United States could and should cooperate with the one remaining great power on the Continent,

Stalin's Soviet Union. A critical test case was the joint occupation of Germany and the determination of this country's national and international identity.

Within months after Germany's surrender, it became clear to the U.S. government that relations with Moscow would be competitive rather than cooperative. Moscow appeared intent on spreading its influence across western and southern Europe, including Germany, by exploiting the economic hardship and political disillusionment that prevailed there. Starting in early 1946, therefore, most senior American officials became convinced that a common approach to current and future challenges in Europe or Germany was impossible with Stalin, and that a continued stalemate would perpetuate Europe's instability and encourage the growth of communist power. This not entirely unanticipated but nonetheless unwelcome reality confronted Washington with some momentous policy choices.

The policy concept Washington eventually adopted during the acrimonious tug-of-war with Moscow became known as "containment" only later. In practice, it had already emerged at the Allied meeting at Potsdam in July–August 1945. After it received its first internal expert justification in the form of Kennan's "Long Telegram" from Moscow in 1946,[3] it became the foundation of U.S. foreign policy and was officially announced[4] and implemented in the first half of 1947. At its core, containment aimed to prevent the further spread of Soviet influence in Europe and elsewhere. Although during these years the United States remained committed to checking Germany's ambitions, the Cold

[3] The Chargé in the Soviet Union (Kennan) to the Secretary of State, Feb. 22, 1946, U.S. Department of State, *Foreign Relations of the United States, 1946,* 6:696–709.

[4] The official announcement of containment occurred by means of President Harry S. Truman's proclamation of the so-called Truman Doctrine on Mar. 12, 1947.

War – as the contest with the Soviet Union became known – became the defining characteristic of the postwar era.

One of the driving forces behind the rise of the Cold War was East-West discord over Germany. Disagreement over war reparations precluded treatment of the country as an economic unit, which in turn hindered the development of other nationwide institutions. Denying the other side a share from or a voice in its own zone rapidly became more important than the joint administration of Germany. More than merely a vanquished foe, Germany soon became a major bone of contention – first between the four occupying powers, then between East and West.

The question of how much Germany should pay in reparations, especially in the form of payments from the Western occupation zones to the Soviet Union, forced the U.S. government to make fundamental policy decisions as soon as the war ended and the occupation began. Washington had to grapple with the pressing problems of administering a devastated country, but was also determined to avoid incurring burdens like those of the 1920s. It, therefore, decided to revive, to a certain extent, Germany's own capabilities and to limit, at least for the time being, its reparation burdens. Reviving the German economy would not only help the Germans help themselves and keep occupation costs down: American officials also believed such a revival to be essential for West European economic reconstruction as a whole.[5] What had been fundamental assumptions in 1945 became American policy by mid-1946.

The change consisted of three parts. First, in May, the head of the American occupation regime, General Lucius D. Clay, stopped reparation extractions from the American zone for the benefit of other zones (particularly the French and Russian).[6] Second, Secretary of State James F. Byrnes announced in September – after the Soviets rejected his proposal for a twenty-five-year demilitarization of Germany – that American troops would not leave Germany as long as other countries maintained occupation forces there. Both Clay's action and Byrnes's speech were also early indications of the American conviction that the struggle over Germany required the support of the Germans themselves. As a third step in the Western policy transition, the United States and Britain announced and began working toward a merger of their zones of occupation, "Bizonia."

The developments of 1946, both in and around Germany and in U.S. policy, moved matters a good deal closer to the official and public adoption of containment. The actual turning point, however, did not occur until the famous "fifteen weeks" (February 21–June 5) of the following year.[7] In mid-1947, the Truman government completed the transformation of President Franklin D. Roosevelt's optimistic, conciliatory policies of the war years into an anti-Soviet line of action. The change had begun as early as Roosevelt's final weeks, and the United States' attitude toward Moscow continued to harden after spring 1947, but it was during the "fifteen weeks" that the central lessons of the war's aftermath were turned into policy and sold to Congress and the public.

Nevertheless, an anti-Soviet line of action was in itself not sufficient to accomplish Washington's primary goal at the time: the reconstruction of Europe. This also happened to be the goal most immediately threatened by Stalin's apparent objectives on the Continent. As part of the process that finalized the adoption of the policy, therefore, a West European recovery program, better known as the Marshall Plan, became containment's first project. Its makers envisioned Western Germany's inclusion. When Soviet Foreign Minister Viacheslav M. Molotov walked out of the preliminary discussions of the plan in July and Moscow forced its East European clients to do the same, containment had scored its first victory. Moscow would not be involved with what was to become a major

[5] For the early development of U.S. policy, see Leffler, *Preponderance of Power,* chaps. 1–3.

[6] On Clay, see Wolfgang Krieger, *General Lucius D. Clay und die amerikanische Deutschlandpolitik 1945–1949* (Stuttgart, 1987), chap. 4.

[7] Joseph M. Jones, *The Fifteen Weeks (February 21–June 5, 1947)* (New York, 1955).

effort at West European economic reconstruction that included Western Germany. In response, the Soviet Union began to consolidate its sphere of influence in Europe, thus demonstrating containment's trade-off: Western Europe might become more secure; what lay east of the Iron Curtain awaited Stalinization.[8]

Although containment did not cause the division of Germany or Europe – the policy was rather a response to this trend – and the new American commitment to the independence and recovery of Western Europe probably prevented a bad situation from turning worse, the deepening divisions in Europe would soon create doubts about the wisdom of the policy. These doubts would persist as long as containment's ultimate promise of a mellowing or collapse of Soviet power remained unfulfilled. For West Germans, containment's unfulfilled promise would be a sore point. As long as the Soviet Union existed, it appeared, there would be Germans living under communism, and the longer this went on, the farther East and West Germans would drift apart.

PARTNERSHIP

Like its emergence, the implementation of containment would be a process. How far and in what way Washington would be able to implement a program like the Marshall Plan depended on the policies of the Soviet Union as well as those of France, Britain, and other Western countries. Furthermore, there was no telling what would be next: more economic programs, peace, or perhaps programs of a different nature such as military cooperation. This, too, it would turn out, depended heavily on the Soviets and the Europeans. Finally, almost all economic and political details of Western Germany's contribution to the reconstruction of Western Europe remained unresolved in mid-1947. One thing did seem certain: The contest with Moscow, as George Kennan had written, was a political

contest, a struggle of ideas and ideals rather than a military affair. The United States had to convince enough Europeans, including Germans, that the West had better answers to the postwar crisis than Stalin; that for an independent and prosperous future, the Europeans could rely on their own strengths and traditions instead of turning east. As expressed in the initial offer of Marshall aid, Washington also wanted the Europeans to make a joint effort so that in the long run they would not have to depend on the United States, either. Guided by their strategy of supporting the revival, independent from Soviet influence, of the major industrial areas around the world, American officials hoped that such cooperation among the states of Western Europe could be the beginning of a process of European integration.[9]

But regardless of whether European integration would be an instant success, American officials would now pay close attention to the needs and desires of the population of the Western occupation zones in Germany. This, in their eyes, was the way to deny Moscow any influence beyond its own zone. It was also the way to shape a future German role in a new Europe. Thus, Western Germany was to benefit from Marshall aid. Also, Western Germans received more political responsibilities. In all this, however, the Germans from the Western zones were not yet participants in containment. Although they were becoming contributors, in 1947 and 1948 their main role was still primarily that of object or target. Furthermore, in their willingness to envision Germany's rehabilitation, the Americans were well ahead of most Europeans, who certainly until early 1948 feared a revival of German militarism as much as Soviet expansionism.

Once initiated, containment took on a life of its own and assumed an increasingly military

---

[8] See Vojtech Mastny, *The Cold War and Soviet Insecurity: The Stalin Years* (New York, 1996), chaps. 1 and 2.

[9] For analyses of Kennan's view of containment and of the policy's evolution, see John Lewis Gaddis, *Strategies of Containment: A Critical Appraisal of Postwar American National Security Policy* (New York, 1982), chaps. 1–4, esp. 2; and Wilson D. Miscamble, C.S.C., *George F. Kennan and the Making of American Foreign Policy, 1947–1950* (Princeton, 1992).

character. This was caused primarily by growing international tensions after 1947, but also by the imprecise and over-ambitious language with which the Truman administration had publicized the policy. Among themselves, leading government officials saw the Soviet threat as political and the task as enabling the Europeans to regain faith in their own strength, but the sweeping language of the Truman Doctrine and George Kennan's "X" article conveyed the image of a relentlessly hostile Soviet Union and implied a military-style conflict. In 1948, the internal nuances lost out against public apprehension over apparent Soviet aggression in Czechoslovakia and Berlin. Containment also changed, finally, because European views on the immediate future of the Continent turned out to be rather different from those of the American government. The Europeans did not succeed in producing a joint plan for the European Recovery Program, nor did they particularly relish the prospect of (re)integrating Western Germany or facing down communism alone without American security guarantees.

Ironically, the success of containment, already apparent in 1947, propelled its transformation. As soon as the Truman administration made the strategy public, Moscow implemented a series of measures to secure its claims and consolidate its holdings in Europe. Stalin was regrouping and reevaluating his strategy. The communist parties in Hungary and Czechoslovakia established and consolidated a near-exclusive hold on power, Moscow banned dissent or semi-independence ("National Roads to Socialism" as well as "Titoism") in the communist world, and the Kremlin tightened its control over the communist parties of Europe through the founding of the Cominform. Even though most of these steps reflected Soviet insecurity, this was not how many West Europeans understood them. Where they should have felt more secure in the face of what was mostly a Soviet circling of the wagons, the West Europeans drew the opposite conclusion and began to ask Washington for a military alliance. Faced with the fact that Europe's self-confidence had not yet been sufficiently restored, American officials felt they could not turn down these

entreaties. The signals from Moscow were in any case mixed. The stage was set for the militarization of containment and the emergence of NATO.[10]

Developments in the Western zones of occupation in Germany became intertwined with these international developments, particularly after the communist coup in Czechoslovakia of February 1948. If Western Germany's contribution was crucial for Western Europe's revival, and communism should fail there, the Germans had to be offered a real future with the West. Most of all, they should be given the chance to govern themselves. This had been the American view for some time, but now the British and the French came to believe it too. Between March and June 1948, therefore, Germany's Western occupiers, led by the United States, began preparations for the founding of a West German state consisting of all three Western occupation zones. This started another escalation when Stalin responded by erecting the Berlin Blockade. Stalin's move proved detrimental to his own aims. Although intended to force the West back to the negotiating table, the Blockade reinforced Western impressions of a recklessly and irreconcilably expansionist Soviet Union. Instead of renewing the old stalemate in Germany, it furthered the creation of a West German state while creating a climate in which the U.S. Congress could be persuaded to support American membership in NATO. Finally, it helped ease West European concerns about Germany's rehabilitation. These changes contributed to the founding of the Federal Republic of Germany in 1949.

Just as his policies had inspired the policy of containment, the Marshall Plan, NATO, and the founding of the Federal Republic, Stalin eased West Germany's transition from occupied former enemy to ally of the West by giving the starting signal for the Korean War. Although the Federal Republic's economic integration with Western Europe had recently been advanced by France's announcement of the Schuman Plan (May 1950), it was the communist offensive in

---

[10] See, e.g., Alan Bullock, *Ernest Bevin: Foreign Secretary 1945–1951* (New York, 1983), pts. 3 and 4.

Korea that greatly accelerated West Germany's acceptance as a member of the Western Alliance. With fears of war on the rise in Europe and NATO troop levels lagging far behind Moscow's, Washington quickly came to view a West German military as the linchpin of containment in Europe.[11] Although they remained more hesitant than the Americans, Germany's neighbors could not really argue with this conclusion.

Those who were suspicious of German intentions and German power, or just anxious about German anxieties, regarded the prospect of West German rearmament as a new danger. In the face of these persistent doubts and the acute military needs of the West, the only way to realize a German contribution to the Western alliance was to integrate the Federal Republic with Western political, economic, and military structures on the basis of equality. The only way to have the Germans help against the Russians was by embracing them, but for this they had to be wooed with what they wanted most: equality and independence. Under the influence of the Korean War, West Germany fully joined containment and became a partner of the West, not just a former foe. The rehabilitation process was a difficult one and would not be completed until 1955. Even then, World War II remained a powerful memory. Where memories of the war did fade, new uncertainties about German division took their place. Containment, therefore, retained a double or "dual" meaning: With the help of Germany, the policy sought to contain Soviet expansionism; with the integration of Germany, it sought to contain German power and possible German revisionism.[12]

---

[11] For U.S. policy toward Germany after 1949, see Hermann-Josef Rupieper, *Der besetzte Verbündete: Die amerikanische Deutschlandpolitik 1949–1955* (Opladen, 1991), esp. chap. 2.

[12] For the phrase "double containment," see Wolfram Hanrieder, *Germany, America, Europe: Forty Years of German Foreign Policy* (New Haven, Conn., 1989). Thomas A. Schwartz argues for using "dual containment," as this captures better the connection between the two policies. See Thomas Alan Schwartz, *America's Germany: John J. McCloy and the Federal Republic of Germany* (Cambridge, Mass., 1991), 299, 391.

PERSISTING DOUBTS

Inevitably, West Germany's participation in containment was ambivalent from the outset. Whereas the policy's anti-Soviet line was fairly unproblematic, Western integration was not. Germany's division, after all, was integrally linked to the East-West contest, and Western policies had contributed as much as anything to the emergence of the two-state reality. Although supportive of the goal of unification, neither the West German government of Konrad Adenauer nor the West as a whole had an active strategy for its realization. In fact, the strategy of containment was essentially passive. It had emerged in response to the East-West deadlock responsible for Germany's division and had served to confirm the status quo. Thus, by joining the Western side in the Cold War and pursuing containment, West Germans appeared to opt against dealing actively with their national division and seemed even to deepen it. After 1950, neither the Federal Republic's relations with the West nor its Ostpolitik ever managed to get out from under the dark shadow cast by German division.

The ultimate promise of containment, that this "policy of strength" would eventually cause the Soviet Union to give in, struck many West Germans as too abstract. Western integration seemed to go against the German national interest. Many Germans believed that if opposing the Soviet Union deepened the division of their country, perhaps talking to the Russians should be tried instead or alongside of containing them. Maybe negotiations, concessions, and compromises were inevitable after all – with or without the Western Allies. Although there never was a majority of West Germans in support of this idea, ambivalence in the Federal Republic toward the price of Western integration and containment sufficed to make the success of the Western program appear uncertain to West German leaders and their American partners. The Soviet leadership was well aware of these German national anxieties and, along with its East German helpers, rarely missed an opportunity to exploit them, particularly during the early 1950s, when West Germany was not yet a member of the Western alliance.

After the Federal Republic's entry into NATO brought about a certain stabilization of the Cold War, East and West did cautiously begin to explore ways to make their rivalry less dangerous. But neither the tenuous "détente" of the mid-1950s nor the more substantial accommodation that began a decade later turned the Federal Republic into a normal, self-assured participant in containment. West Germans were hardly encouraged by the fact that relaxation of East-West tensions, far from bringing reunification closer, seemed to depend on recognizing the two-state reality in Germany. The anxieties and ambivalence in Bonn and Washington about West Germany's role in the Cold War, therefore, remained. With Germany no longer central to every East-West discussion, would West Germans keep faith in their allies' ability or willingness to further the German national interest against Moscow's determination to gain Western recognition of the status quo? And what if Bonn itself, in an effort to keep the German question alive and open, tried to talk to the Soviet leadership about reunification? The Kremlin would always try to drive a wedge between Washington and its most important European ally. What would be left of the Western alliance if it succeeded; and what of the effort after World War II to ensure a different, more benign German role in European politics? Even responsible, pro-Western West German leaders could not be expected to control a process of accommodation with the East once it was underway.

Although Washington's and Bonn's policies of détente of the late 1960s and early 1970s went far in providing reassuring answers to most of these questions, they could not take the place of reunification. Germany's Western integration, therefore, remained fundamentally problematic as long as containment's ultimate promise appeared hollow. Only in 1989, when the peace was definitively won, did this situation change.

CHAPTER SEVEN

The United States and the Founding of the Federal Republic, 1948–1949

Hermann-Josef Rupieper

Translated by Sally Robertson

The decisive phase in the history of the establishment of the Federal Republic began at the end of the conference of Allied foreign ministers in London in December 1947. The latest attempt to negotiate a joint solution to the German problem had failed. The United States was determined to reorient its policies in West Germany to complete the stabilization of Western Europe that it had begun with the Truman Doctrine and the Marshall Plan.

While still in London, American and British diplomats and representatives of the military governments discussed the formation of a provisional government for "Bizonia," which the French zone could join. The bizonal administrations were to be restructured as effective political institutions with expanded responsibilities. The first meetings between the American and British military governors, the minister presidents of the *Länder* (states) in the unified economic zone, and representatives of the bizonal administrations took place on January 7–8 in Frankfurt am Main, the seat of the American military government. The outcome was the creation of a new organizational form consisting of a parliamentary body, the Economic Council, the *Länder* Council, and an Administrative Council with executive responsibilities.[1]

However, this did not yet constitute a political structure for a future West German government. The American military governor, General Lucius D. Clay, emphasized that the new institution would be responsible only for economic and financial matters. The Americans and British did not want to be accused of being responsible for the division of Germany. The degree to which this concern was justified became evident on January 24, 1948, when the French military government protested the reorganization of Bizonia and spoke out decisively against any centralizing tendencies toward creation of a unified German state. The criticism from the minister presidents in Bizonia was of a different nature. Whereas they applauded the economic aspects of the reorganization as a welcome chance to promote reconstruction, they stressed that the reorganization threatened the unity of the nation. They pushed for restoration of German unity – backed up by the United States and Great Britain and based on free elections in all four zones. This established the basic positions, which were to remain unchanged for the time being.[2]

For U.S. Secretary of State George Marshall, the division of Germany had in essence already

[1] Bettina Blank, *Die westdeutschen Länder und die Entstehung der Bundesrepublik: Zur Auseinandersetzung um die Frankfurter Dokumente vom Juli 1948* (Munich, 1995), 27–33; Gerd Wehner, *Die Westalliierten und das Grundgesetz 1948–1949: Die Londoner Sechsmächtekonferenz* (Freiburg im Breisgau, 1994), 17–64.

[2] Karl-Ulrich Gelberg, *Hans Ehard: Die föderalistische Politik des bayerischen Ministerpräsidenten 1946–1954* (Düsseldorf, 1992), 104–8.

been accomplished by the Soviet Union, and he argued on February 20, 1948, in his negotiating directives before the London conference that the Western powers had "no alternative except to undertake to integrate both economy and political life of Western Germany with Western Europe."[3] He acknowledged the desire of the German people for a unified Germany, but at the same time made it clear that the time for waiting had passed and that inaction in West Germany would threaten the security of the Western democracies. Soviet control over future developments in Germany could not be tolerated, he declared.

At the urging of the United States, a six-power conference took place in London from February 23 to March 6 and from April 20 to June 2, 1948. At this conference, the United States, Great Britain, France, and the Benelux countries agreed upon a uniform plan for the economic and political future of the three Western zones of occupation. The final document consisted of three parts: the call for development of a constitution for a West German state, the call for reform of *Länder* boundaries, and the basic outline of an occupation statute to regulate relations between a future German government and the Allied authorities. The documents were a compromise between the extremely federalist concept favored by the French for security reasons and the more moderate federalism of the United States, which sought a reasonable division of powers between the *Länder* and the central government. Great Britain was largely on the side of the United States.[4]

Those most affected – the German people – were not involved in this planning until spring 1948. The West German minister presidents, who had taken on the role of authorized negotiators for the Germans by virtue of their sub-ordination to and increasing cooperation with the military governments,[5] were not officially informed of the London six-power conference until its results were announced in Frankfurt on July 1, 1948. (Unofficially, the minister presidents of Bizonia had been notified on May 14, 1948.)

The minister presidents felt overwhelmed by all three assignments imposed by the occupation powers, particularly the task of convening a constituent assembly within two months. In view of the serious consequences such a step would have for German unity, they first asked for time to consider the plans and to discuss the Frankfurt documents in their cabinets and *Landtage* (state parliaments). To distribute the responsibility for the decision as widely as possible, they also maintained close contact with the leaders of the Christian Democratic Union (*Christlich-Demokratische Union*, or CDU), Christian Social Union (*Christlich-Soziale Union*, or CSU), Free Democratic Party (*Freie Demokratische Partei*, or FDP), and the Social Democratic Party (*Sozialdemokratische Partei Deutschlands*, or SPD) while retaining their own decision-making authority.

This was perfectly agreeable to Clay, who could not understand why party leaders should influence the positions of the elected minister presidents. However, close contact with the parties was imperative because party leaders such as Kurt Schumacher (SPD) disputed, among other things, the minister presidents' right to make decisions on a constituent assembly. Although counterproposals were made (much to the vexation of the Allies), the attitude of the minister presidents and party leaders after three years of occupation and in light of developments in the Soviet zone of occupation was decidedly pro-Western. Fear of the Soviet Union ensured that there was no thought of neutrality or other plans involving the Soviet zone. As demonstrated by

---

[3] The Secretary of State to the Embassy in the United Kingdom, Feb. 20, 1948, in U.S. Department of State, *Foreign Relations of the United States* (hereafter *FRUS*), *1948*, 2:72.

[4] Johannes Volker Wagner, ed., *Der Parlamentarische Rat 1948–1949: Akten und Protokolle*, vol. 1: *Vorgeschichte* (Boppard am Rhein, 1975), 1–17, with the final communiqué.

[5] On the development of the relationships between the minister presidents and the American military administration, see James K. Pollock, *Besatzung und Staatsaufbau nach 1945: Occupation Diary and Private Correspondence 1945–1948*, ed. Ingrid Krüger-Bulcke (Munich, 1994).

the discussions of the minister presidents and party leaders on July 8–10, 1948, at the Rittersturz hunting lodge near Koblenz, the ideas of the Western powers enjoyed majority support, despite concerns about constitutional policies that might threaten German unity. Even more important was the fact that all party representatives, even those of the hesitant and splintered SPD, declared themselves willing to cooperate with the military governors. However, they did not want to assume responsibility for establishing a West German state. Therefore, they persisted in their demand for an "organized provisional government" and creation of a "Basic Law" rather than a constitution. They also attempted to portray enactment of the occupation statute as an Allied measure rather than an act of free self-determination by the German people.[6]

The Allies had only themselves to blame for this reaction by the minister presidents; their communications with the German representatives had been inadequate and typical of the relationship of victors to occupied peoples. The minister presidents proceeded on the assumption that the London decisions represented a starting point for discussion rather than binding dictates. The attitude of the minister presidents particularly aggravated Clay, who had hoped to bring matters to a close as quickly as possible. Now the minister presidents of Bizonia were endangering the painstakingly negotiated Allied compromise and offering the French new opportunities for intervention and obstruction. The agreement of the minister presidents to begin discussions on establishing a West German state was considerably facilitated, however, by the positive attitude of West Berlin politicians such as Ernst Reuter and Otto Suhr. These men urged that West Berlin, threatened by the Soviet blockade, which had begun on June 18, 1948, be integrated into a federal state. This persuaded the initially hesitant minister presidents of the Western zones to favor the American plan by

the time they met at the Niederwald conference on July 15–16, 1948.[7]

However, the minister presidents had quite different views regarding the basic problem of federalism. While the southern German minister presidents, led by Hans Ehard (CSU) of Bavaria, supported a strengthening of the *Länder* and a weak central authority, others, primarily the *Länder* ruled by the SPD, argued for strong central powers. During this time, German politicians on various levels sought contact with the different military governments and considerably increased their meager store of information on Allied objectives. It was for this reason that Ehard, who as a proponent of the federalism concept had particularly close contact with the American occupation authorities, called another conference at Herrenchiemsee (August 10–23, 1948). The constitutional convention at Herrenchiemsee discussed the decisive constitutional questions: regulation of the federal financial system, establishment of the *Bundesrat* (upper house of parliament), and a site for a constituent assembly. However, it was not able to present the constitutional commission report in the form of a binding government bill to the Parliamentary Council, which met in Bonn from September 1, 1948 to May 23, 1949. Increasingly, the party delegates sent by the individual *Landtage* began to take control of the political process.[8]

The three military governments established offices for liaison with the Parliamentary Council and continued their attempts to influence developments and to bring Allied constitutional policies to fruition, both through personal contacts and through unofficial meetings with the minister presidents and leading politicians. This led to difficult negotiations, as federalist positions varied both among the West

---

[6] Gelberg, *Hans Ehard*, 123–30; Udo Wengst, *Staatsaufbau und Regierungspraxis 1948–1953: Zur Geschichte der Verfassungsorgane der Bundesrepublik Deutschland* (Düsseldorf, 1985), 46–53.

[7] Gelberg, *Hans Ehard*, 130–48; Blank, *Die westdeutschen Länder*, 36–49; Eberhard Pikart and Wolfram Werner, eds., *Der Parlamentarische Rat 1948–1949: Akten und Protokolle*, vol. 5, pt. 1, *Ausschuss für Grundsatzfragen* (Boppard am Rhein, 1993), 233–52, 271, 299–303.

[8] Rudolf Morsey, "Entscheidung für den Westen. Die Rolle der Ministerpräsidenten in den drei Westzonen im Vorfeld der Bundesrepublik Deutschland 1947–1949," *Westfälische Forschungen* 26 (1974): 1–21.

German parties and among the Allied powers. Because cooperation of the two big parties, the CDU/CSU and SPD, was necessary in order to approve a constitution and because failure would have served no one, a compromise was finally reached. Other constellations would have been possible, such as cooperation between the CDU/CSU and the FDP, but collaboration of the two large parties prevented any party from being denounced as an agent of the Allies. At this point, the British military government attempted to mediate between the Parliamentary Council and the American and French military governments, who were pushing for greater independence and autonomy of the individual states. A breakdown in negotiations would have postponed the integration of Western Europe; an imposed constitution would have been the worst conceivable foundation for cooperation between the Allies and the Germans. The situation was further complicated by the fact that the responsibility for occupation policy was beginning to shift in Washington, and the State Department was pushing harder than it had before for a compromise between the West German parties and the Allies. Therefore, the complex negotiations regarding the draft constitution, agreement on the occupation statute among the three Western powers, and the associated problems of reparations and control of the Ruhr region dragged on until early 1949.[9]

At this point, in a surprise development much to the dismay of Clay, the Germany experts in Washington appeared again to throw the establishment of a West German state into question. The new secretary of state, Dean Acheson, could not understand the situation. He "indicated that he did not understand either how we ever arrived at the decision to see established a Western German government or State. He wondered whether this had not rather been the brainchild of General Clay and not a govern-

mental decision."[10] There were several factors underlying this sudden hesitation on the part of Washington: the insistence of Western German politicians that the constitution be only provisional; uncertainty whether a West German state alongside a "rump Germany" (*Restdeutschland*) made sense; concern about ending the Berlin Blockade, which would mean renewed discussion with the Soviet Union about Germany; and the wavering attitude of the French government, which had informed the administration in Washington that it had not yet made a final decision to favor the creation of a West German state and reject another attempt at reaching an all-German solution with the Soviet Union.[11]

Even more serious was the fact that the State Department's Policy Planning Staff under its director, George Kennan, released a "Program A" on August 12, 1948, in the middle of this difficult phase of decision making, which called all previous plans into question and was so explosive that it posed at least a temporary threat to their implementation.[12] The core points of this program for new Four Power negotiations were installation of a provisional all-German government; free elections on all levels under United Nations supervision; creation of a German constitution; establishment of an Allied commission for monitoring Germany and protecting the rights of the Allies; withdrawal of occupation troops or retreat of remaining contingents to enclaves; demilitarization of Germany based on the Byrnes Plan of 1946; accelerated completion of reparations payments; and appointment of a Ruhr authority without American or Soviet involvement.

It is unnecessary to explain the problems and weaknesses of this controversial proposal, which

---

[9] On this point, see Adolf M. Birke, "Grossbritannien und der Parlamentarische Rat," *Vierteljahrshefte für Zeitgeschichte* 42 (1994): 313–59; Hans-Jürgen Grabbe, "Die deutsch-alliierte Kontroverse um den Grundgesetzentwurf im Frühjahr 1949," *Vierteljahrshefte für Zeitgeschichte* 26 (1978): 393–418.

[10] Memorandum of Conversation by the Acting Director of the Office of German and Austrian Affairs (Murphy), Mar. 9, 1949, *FRUS, 1949*, 3:102.

[11] On the changes in French policy toward Germany, for which the blockade of Berlin was a catalyst, see Cyril Buffet, *Mourir pour Berlin? La France et l'Allemagne 1945–1949* (Paris, 1991).

[12] Axel Frohn, *Neutralisierung als Alternative zur Westintegration: Die Deutschlandpolitik der Vereinigten Staaten von Amerika 1945–1949* (Frankfurt am Main, 1985).

would have meant new Four Power negotiations with an uncertain outcome. However, the rise of Kennan, the influential Russia and Germany expert, demonstrates the degree to which Washington's German policy was in flux and the fact that positions were put forward there that, if implemented, would not necessarily have led to the division of Germany.[13] As late as the end of March 1949, even Clay believed that the time-consuming negotiations in the Parliamentary Council and continuing disagreement among the three powers would prevent establishment of a West German state: "Recent events convince me that West German Government will not result. French delaying tactics have won and sentiment has now strongly turned against West German Government. This stems largely from failure to develop Tripartite common policy."[14]

The West finally reached agreement at the meeting of foreign ministers of the three Western powers in Washington on April 6–8, 1949. With the signing of the occupation statute, the agreement on a modified federalist concept that addressed French demands, French entry into Bizonia, and the preparations for negotiations on Germany with the Soviet Union after the end of the blockade, the path was finally clear for establishment of the Federal Republic of Germany. Another contributing factor was the signing, on April 4, 1949, of the Atlantic Treaty, which offered Europe protection from the Soviet Union and strengthened the negotiating position of the West. Just as important, however, was the fact that the representatives of the West German parties in the Parliamentary Council, with the exception of those of the German Communist Party (*Kommunistische Partei Deutschlands*, or KPD), had fundamentally agreed on the establishment of the Federal Republic, and that the conflicts over the content of the Basic Law and the specific form of federalism were of secondary significance. They also did not rule out a later entry of the Soviet zone of occupation into the Western state, although this was founded on wishful thinking. In light of the East-West conflict and Soviet policy, which was regarded as a threat to the Western democracies, the great majority sought peace, freedom, security, and economic prosperity in an integrated Western Europe backed by the dominant Atlantic power, the United States. On May 8, 1949, the Parliamentary Council approved the draft of the Basic Law by a vote of fifty-three to twelve. Allied approval came four days later with presentation of the Occupation Statute. The constitutional decisions necessary for establishment of the Federal Republic had been made. Despite repeated intervention by the Western powers,[15] the Basic Law had remained in the tradition of German federalism. On the other hand, stabilization would hardly have been possible at the time if the German adherents of federalism had not received the support of the American military government.

---

[13] This needs to be stated, in light of the debate newly reopened by Carolyn Eisenberg, *Drawing the Line: The American Decision to Divide Germany* (New York, 1996).

[14] Clay to Vorhees, Mar. 25, 1949, in Jean Edward Smith, ed., *The Papers of General Lucius D. Clay: Germany 1945–1949* (Bloomington, Ind., 1974), 2:1061.

[15] See Edmund Spevak, *Allied Control and German Freedom: American Political and Ideological Influences on the Framing of the West German Basic Law (Grundgesetz)* (Münster, 2001).

CHAPTER EIGHT

From Occupation to Alliance

German-American Relations, 1949–1955

Frank Schumacher

Translated by Richard Sharp

At noon on May 5, 1955, the Federal Republic of Germany became a sovereign state. As the flag was raised at the Schaumburg Palace, Chancellor Konrad Adenauer, who would have preferred to mark the occasion with a ceremony in the Bundestag, said: "We stand as free men among free men, as partners of our former occupiers.... There is only one place for us in this world: on the side of the free peoples."[1]

This article examines the amazing transformation of the Federal Republic of Germany between 1949 and 1955: from occupied nation to ally of the West and of the West's dominant power, the United States. This metamorphosis has been described, with good reason, as one of the greatest successes of American foreign policy.[2] The present account first considers the most important stages of this process of change, then goes on to examine the mechanisms and instruments that brought it about, of which the most important was the determination of the United States to win the confidence of the West German people.

---

[1] Hans-Peter Schwarz, *Adenauer*, vol. 2: *Der Staatsmann 1952–1967* (Munich, 1994), 176.

[2] Hans-Jürgen Schröder, "USA und westdeutscher Wiederaufstieg (1945–1952)," in Klaus Larres and Thorsten Oppelland, eds., *Deutschland und die USA im 20. Jahrhundert: Geschichte der politischen Beziehungen* (Darmstadt, 1997), 108; Thomas A. Schwartz, "The United States and Germany after 1945: Alliances, Transnational Relations, and the Legacy of the Cold War," *Diplomatic History* 19 (1995): 549–68, esp. 554.

ENEMIES BECOME FRIENDS: THE UNITED STATES AND THE FEDERAL REPUBLIC, 1949–1955

German-American relations in the years 1949–55 passed through two stages of development. The first, which must also be seen as the key phase in the transition from occupation to alliance, lasted from the foundation of the Federal Republic of Germany in May 1949 to the signing of the General Treaty and the treaty establishing the European Defense Community (EDC) in May 1952. The second stage, comprising the years 1953–5, was most notable for the unusually close personal cooperation between Adenauer, the new American president Dwight D. Eisenhower, and his secretary of state, John Foster Dulles. This phase, during which the Federal Republic enjoyed a limited form of sovereignty, ended with the failure of the EDC and West Germany's admission to NATO. At the same time, the Federal Republic achieved almost complete national sovereignty.

The conversion of the Allied military governments to civilian high commissions when the Federal Republic was founded in May 1949 ended the period of direct occupation and signaled a new beginning in relations between the Germans and the victorious powers.

Although the early years of the partially sovereign Bonn Republic were still characterized by widespread mistrust on the part of West

Germany's neighbors and the United States,[3] by April 1949 the Allied High Commission had already announced, in a revision clause of the Occupation Statute, a review, and a possible further reduction, of the authority of the victorious Allies over the new Western state.

Just two months after the Occupation Statute had come into force, it underwent its first revision in the Petersberg Agreement of November 22, 1949. The dismantling of German industrial plants was restricted, and the Federal Republic was conceded the right to establish consular relations with foreign countries and to join international organizations. At the same time, it was to conclude a bilateral economic agreement with the United States on Marshall Plan aid and join the Council of Europe as an associate member.

At the end of October 1949, the Federal Republic of Germany had become a member of the Organization for European Economic Cooperation (OEEC). The Marshall Plan agreement between Germany and America was signed on December 15, and on April 1, 1950, West Germany was invited to join the Council of Europe, an invitation it accepted on July 1.[4] A comprehensive revision of the Occupation Statute, effective from March 6, 1951, not only brought virtually complete internal self-government but also permitted the establishment of a foreign ministry, which duly came into existence on March 15. In addition, the Federal Republic was one of the six founding states of the European Coal and Steel Community (ECSC), established in Paris on April 18, 1951.

At this time, sovereignty already seemed to be within the West Germans' grasp. The main reason for this was the Korean War. North Korea's attack on the Republic of South Korea on June 25, 1950, had radically altered relations between the Western powers and the Federal Republic. The fear that now began to spread throughout Western Europe demonstrated to the Allies the urgent need for a West German contribution to European defense.[5] First, however, the fears aroused in Germany's West European neighbors, and in the United States as well, by the prospect of a rearmed Germany would have to be allayed. The American High Commission's director of public relations, Shepard Stone, who would do much to help consolidate relations between Germany and America over the next forty years, spoke for many when he warned against a hasty relaxation of control over the Federal Republic: "We should go very slow in announcing any revision of the Occupation Statute. . . . We should take all the time permitted us under the statute itself to make our 'reviews,' because change made in the atmosphere of the Korean and therefore the world situation could well be in error."[6]

From an early stage, military circles in America had been considering ways of exploiting Germany's potential. Yet, the rearming of the former enemy had, until the Korean War, been seen as one of the biggest threats to the security of the West. This view changed because of a number of factors, the Korean War acting merely as the catalyst. The USSR had itself possessed a nuclear capability since fall 1949, so that its superiority in conventional weapons in Europe was now seen as an even greater threat. The founding of NATO had brought no immediate improvement in the situation as far as the West was concerned, and the military now concluded that the imbalance could be redressed only with the aid of German divisions. Another factor in favor of rearmament was that it would ease the financial burden on the West European allies. The most compelling political argument, however, was that the complete integration of the Federal Republic into the Western alliance would prevent, once and for all, any return to

---

[3] See the chapter by Thomas Reuther, vol. 1, Society.
[4] See the chapter by Gerd Hardach, vol. 1, Economics.

[5] See the chapter by David Clay Large, vol. 1, Security.
[6] National Archives, RG 59, 611.62/8-250, quoted in Hermann-Josef Rupieper, *Der besetzte Verbündete: Die amerikanische Deutschlandpolitik 1949–1955* (Opladen, 1991), 77.

a German policy of walking the tightrope between East and West.

And so, from summer 1950, the question was no longer whether Germany would be rearmed but what form rearmament would take. The analogy between the Korean and German situations – a distorted analogy, yet suggestive – helped to reduce gradually the reluctance of the Western powers, and of public opinion within them, to accept a German defense contribution. The West German government, especially the chancellor, saw a unique opportunity under these circumstances to gain, through a defense contribution, sovereignty and the standing of an equal partner within the Western community of nations considerably earlier than had been expected.

At first it appeared that the solution to the problem would be found within Europe. The French prime minister, René Pleven, put forward a plan in October 1950 in which a supranational organization, the EDC, would cushion the threat German rearmament posed to the West. The aim of the Pleven Plan was to enable German troops to be raised without creating a West German national army. The resulting negotiations were tough and protracted. The French, in particular, took a hostile position toward the idea of German troops that was overcome only by considerable pressure from Washington. Not until May 9, 1952, was a draft treaty finalized. The membership and organizational form of the EDC would make it a military counterpart of the ECSC. While this treaty was being negotiated, the occupying powers and the Federal Republic, whose policy naturally linked a defense contribution to the issue of sovereignty, drew up what later came to be known as the Paris Treaties, which provided for the end of the occupation and promised the West German state its sovereignty, apart from some residual Allied rights.[7]

However, the failure of the EDC also delayed the coming of West German sovereignty. The treaty establishing the EDC was signed by the foreign ministers of the participating states in Paris on May 27, 1952, but on August 30, 1954, the French National Assembly refused to ratify it. Two years of hard work, by Europeans and Americans alike, to create a European military force had come to nothing.[8] But just three months later, in October 1954, the NATO foreign ministers agreed to accept the Federal Republic as a member of the North Atlantic Treaty Organization. On May 5, 1955, the Paris Treaties, which included slight modifications to the 1952 agreements, came into force. The Bonn Republic was now a sovereign state and a member of NATO.

In a very few years, the Federal Republic of Germany had not only achieved sovereignty under international law but had also become a member of the Western alliance on almost equal terms. Although complete equality was to remain "an ultimately unfulfilled ambition" until 1991, the transition from occupied territory to ally marked a huge advance in Germany's return to the international community of nations.[9] Allied high commissioners had become ambassadors; occupying troops were now "guarantors of the alliance"; the West German missions in Washington, London, and Paris had acquired full diplomatic status.

This remarkable change in Germany's position within the international postwar system was mainly attributable to German-American relations and Washington's policy toward Europe in the context of the East-West confrontation. Principally, the upgrading of the Federal Republic from occupied to allied status was the logical outcome of America's strategy of containing its Soviet adversary by uniting the noncommunist world in a system of alliances under American hegemony. A geographical focus of this strategy was Western Europe, where Washington was confronted by a dual challenge. First, the Soviet Union had to be prevented from extending its dominion into Central and Western Europe. Second, Germany must never again be

---

[7] See the chapter by Richard Wiggers in this section.

[8] See also the chapter by David Clay Large, vol. 1, Security, and Thomas Schöttli, *USA und EVG: Truman, Eisenhower und die Europa-Armee* (Bern, 1994).

[9] Gregor Schöllgen, *Geschichte der Weltpolitik von Hitler bis Gorbatschow* (Munich, 1996), 106.

allowed to become a threat to world peace. The United States' plan for meeting this dual challenge was to integrate the Western European states: By increasing the economic and military strength of western Europe, integrating it politically and revitalizing it psychologically and ideologically, America hoped to prevent both the expansion of the USSR and the uncontrolled resurgence of Germany. This approach by Washington was assisted by the desire of many European governments to form part of a European economic and security system under U.S. leadership.[10]

At the point of intersection between the two plans – the strategy of integration and the policy of containment – lay the German question. America's policy toward Germany had two main objectives: protection against Germany and protection against the USSR. These aims were conceptually interwoven and formed the basis of an approach that is now called dual containment.[11] To prevent any resurgence of German militarism, West Germany was gradually but tightly integrated into the political, economic, and military structures of an emerging North Atlantic community under the leadership of the United States. At the same time, however, the integration of the young Federal Republic also served to contain the USSR. The economic and military potential of West Germany was to give the ailing western half of Europe a shot in the arm to bolster its defenses. Wolfram Hanrieder has neatly described this dual strategic approach as "the containment of the Soviet Union at arm's length and of West Germany with an embrace."[12]

For its strategy to succeed, America needed reliable allies[13] – all the more so as, ultimately, it could not ensure the cohesion of the system within its own camp without doing severe damage to the credibility of the American alternative to the USSR's totalitarian and imperialistic concept of leadership.[14] The United States interpreted the possibility of the collapse of the anticommunist consensus and rising neutralism among its allies as serious threats to its own national security. NSC-68, the now famous directive on national security, emphasized these concerns:

Strength at the center, in the United States, is only the first of two essential elements. The second is that our allies and potential allies do not as a result of a sense of frustration or of Soviet intimidation drift into a course of neutrality eventually leading to Soviet domination. If this were to happen in Germany, the effect upon Western Europe and eventually upon us might be catastrophic.[15]

The transformation of the Federal Republic from occupied territory to ally was thus built into the conceptual framework of America's containment strategy. The fact that the change took place in a relatively short period was attributable to the American interests embodied in that strategy and to the increasing polarization of the international system from 1950 onward; but it was also due to the efforts of certain outstanding figures and, especially, the United States' unceasing endeavors to gain the

---

[10] Geir Lundestad, "Empire by Invitation? The United States and Western Europe, 1945–1952," *Journal of Peace Research* 23 (1986): 263–77; Geir Lundestad, *"Empire" by Integration: The United States and European Integration, 1945–1997* (Oxford, 1998).

[11] Wilfried Loth, "Die doppelte Eindämmung: Überlegungen zur Genesis des Kalten Krieges 1945–1947," *Historische Zeitschrift* 238 (1984): 611–31; Thomas A. Schwartz, "Dual Containment: John J. McCloy, the American High Commission and European Integration, 1949–52," in Francis Heller and John R. Gillingham, eds., *NATO: The Founding of the Atlantic Alliance and the Integration of Europe* (New York, 1992), 193–212; Wolfram F. Hanrieder, *Germany, America, Europe: Forty Years of German Foreign Policy* (New Haven, Conn., 1989); Rolf Steininger et al., eds., *Die doppelte Eindämmung: Europäische Sicherheit und deutsche Frage in den Fünfzigern* (Munich, 1993).

[12] Wolfram F. Hanrieder, "The FRG and NATO: Between Security Dependence and Security Partnership," in Emil Kirchner and James Sperling, eds., *The Federal Republic of Germany and NATO* (New York, 1992), 195.

[13] Stephen Walt, *The Origins of Alliances* (Ithaca, N.Y., 1987), 3.

[14] Robert J. McMahon, "Credibility and World Power: Exploring the Psychological Dimension in Postwar American Diplomacy," *Diplomatic History* 15 (1991): 455–571.

[15] Reprint of NSC-68 in Ernest R. May, ed., *American Cold War Strategy: Interpreting NSC-68* (Boston, 1993), 26.

confidence of the West German people and so secure the country's psychological and ideological allegiance to the West.

FRIENDSHIP THROUGH INTEGRATION: LEADERS AND THE TRANSNATIONAL PUBLIC

In Chancellor Adenauer the Americans found a steadfast partner and guarantor against what they (and he) regarded as the dangerous German policy of swinging between East and West.[16] The chancellor made complete integration with the West a cornerstone of policy and rejected all Soviet blandishments about reunification. In addition, the "Old Man" personified the spirit of European integration, pursuing reconciliation with France and lending his support to the plans for an EDC. Adenauer's close ties with the United States, the leading power of the West, gave him a steadily growing influence on American policy during the 1950s. Relations between the two governments were particularly close in the years 1953–5.[17] The very friendly personal relationship between the chancellor and Secretary of State Dulles also contributed to the close cooperation between the two countries during this period.[18]

Unsurprisingly, therefore, the American government also supported the German chancellor in domestic politics, especially during the 1953 federal election campaign.[19] The doubts about the stability of German postwar democracy so often voiced by the Americans were in many ways allayed by the chancellor's reelection in September 1953. As long as Adenauer held the reins of government, Washington felt there was no danger of a resurgence of revanchism or of a German policy of seesawing between East and West.

In addition to Adenauer and Dulles, two other central figures in the shaping of postwar German-American relations – the high commissioner John J. McCloy and his successor James Conant – have been the subjects of extensive research.[20] However, there is still a shortage of studies on the development of a transatlantic elite in postwar Germany and on the important contributions made by such individuals as Shepard Stone, Henry Kellermann, and Henry Byroade to the development and shaping of American policy toward Germany.

Beyond the diplomatic scene, there is also room for further coverage of relations between the two peoples, and especially the attitude of the West German public to the United States. In particular, there is still no comprehensive study of transnational relations between the two

[16] Hans-Jürgen Schröder, "Chancellor of the Allies? The Significance of the United States in Adenauer's Foreign Policy," in David E. Barclay and Elizabeth Glaser-Schmidt, eds., *Transatlantic Images and Perceptions: Germany and America Since 1776* (New York, 1997), 309–31; Klaus Schwabe, ed., *Adenauer und die USA* (Bonn, 1994); Klaus Larres, "Germany and the West: The 'Rapallo Factor' in German Foreign Policy from the 1950s to the 1990s," in Klaus Larres and Penikos Penayi, eds., *The Federal Republic of Germany Since 1949: Politics, Society, and Economy Before and After Reunification* (London, 1996), 278–326.

[17] Klaus Larres, "Eisenhower, Dulles und Adenauer: Bündnis des Vertrauens oder Allianz des Misstrauens (1953–1961)," in Klaus Larres and Thorsten Oppelland, eds., *Deutschland und die USA im 20. Jahrhundert: Geschichte der politischen Beziehungen* (Darmstadt, 1997), 119–50.

[18] Manfred Görtemaker, "John Foster Dulles und die Westintegration der Bundesrepublik Deutschland," in Rolf Steininger et al., eds., *Die doppelte Eindämmung: Europäische Sicherheit und deutsche Frage in den Fünfzigern* (Munich, 1993), 9–38; Hans-Jürgen Grabbe, "Konrad

Adenauer, John Foster Dulles, and West German-American Relations," in Richard H. Immermann, ed., *John Foster Dulles and the Diplomacy of the Cold War* (Princeton, N.J., 1990), 109–32; Detlef Felken, *Dulles und Deutschland: Die amerikanische Deutschlandpolitik 1953–1959* (Bonn, 1993).

[19] See the chapter by Ronald J. Granieri in this section.

[20] Thomas A. Schwartz, *America's Germany: John J. McCloy and the Federal Republic of Germany* (Cambridge, Mass., 1991); Kai Bird, *The Chairman: John J. McCloy and the Making of the American Establishment* (New York, 1992); Klaus Schwabe, "Fürsprecher Frankreichs? John J. McCloy und die Integration der Bundesrepublik," in Ludolf Herbst, Werner Bührer, and Hanno Sowade, eds., *Vom Marshallplan zur EVG: Die Eingliederung der Bundesrepublik Deutschland in die westliche Welt* (Munich, 1990), 517–33; James G. Hershberg, *James B. Conant: Harvard to Hiroshima and the Making of the Nuclear Age* (New York, 1993).

countries in the years 1945–55.[21] The American government's wooing of public opinion in the Federal Republic, too, has so far received no more than rudimentary coverage.[22] Yet, it was precisely this endeavor by the United States to win over the West German public that not only helped the policy of democratization to succeed but also expedited the conversion from occupation to alliance by underpinning Germany's psychological and ideological commitment to the West.

The foundations of this German-American success story had been laid earlier with the end of the war and the events of the early postwar years. The Americans were seen to be magnanimous in victory, an image far removed from that portrayed in National Socialist propaganda. The Germans, hungry and defeated, soon came to trust the GIs, whose behavior was far different from the excesses of the Red Army.[23] These early impressions, encouraging for the most part, were then further strengthened by the massive economic aid provided under the Marshall Plan.[24]

From the outset, the functional integration of the Federal Republic into the political, economic, and military structures of the Western world went hand in hand with ideological integration. The main instrument of this intellectual reorientation was a comprehensive program of democratization beginning in 1946–7: Yesterday's enemy was now to be transformed into an allied democracy on the Western model. Thus, the objective of social reform was another integral part of the strategy of dual containment. From the American point of view, it was important for the sake of a stable international system – and hence for the sake of America's own national security – that Germany should be welcomed back into the fold of the Western democracies.

America, therefore, addressed the West German people directly, encouraging them to commit themselves to the West without reservation. One reason for this direct approach was that the American government was often unsure about the West German people's basic attitude to foreign policy. The major West German controversies of the 1950s – rearmament, neutrality, integration with the West, and reunification – confronted the United States with the dilemma that the newborn spirit of democracy might seriously jeopardize the strategy of dual containment. The gradual relaxing of the Western Allies' control over the Federal Republic between 1949 and 1955 and the subversive and propagandistic activities of the USSR in West Germany deepened the concerns of America's leaders. They reacted to this challenge with a massive propaganda offensive designed to boost the political, economic, and military integration of West Germany. This public-relations effort by the United States thus helped bring about the controlled transformation of West Germany from occupied territory to ally.[25]

The various American public-relations programs concentrated on encouraging West European integration, bringing about a West German defense contribution, ensuring close links between the Federal Republic and the United States (by establishing friendly and cooperative

[21] For coverage of some aspects, see Werner Link, *Deutsche und amerikanische Gewerkschaften und Geschäftsleute 1945–1975* (Düsseldorf, 1978); Hermann-Josef Rupieper, *Die Wurzeln der westdeutschen Nachkriegsdemokratie: Der amerikanische Beitrag 1945–1952* (Opladen, 1993), 26; Schwartz, "The United States and Germany."

[22] Marita Hein-Kremer, *Die amerikanische Kulturoffensive: Gründung und Entwicklung der Information Centers in Westdeutschland und Westberlin (1945–1955)* (Cologne, 1996); Frank Schumacher, "Democratization and Hegemonic Control: American Propaganda and the West German Public's Foreign Policy Orientation, 1949–55," in Knud Krakau, ed., *The American Nation, National Identity, Nationalism* (Münster, 1997), 285–315.

[23] See the chapter by Klaus-Dietmar Henke, vol. 1, Society.

[24] Klaus Schönberger, "'Hier half der Marshallplan': Werbung für das europäische Wiederaufbauprogramm zwischen Propaganda und Public Relations," in Gerald Diesener and Rainer Gries, eds., *Propaganda in Deutschland: Zur Geschichte der politischen Massebeeinflussung im 20. Jahrhundert* (Darmstadt, 1996), 193–212.

[25] See Frank Schumacher, "Kalter Krieg und Propaganda: Die USA, der Kampf um die Weltmeinung und die ideelle Westbindung der Bundesrepublik Deutschland, 1945–1955," Ph.D. diss., University of Cologne, 1997.

relations), countering disruptive communist propaganda, relieving the collective fears of war, and supporting the government in Bonn.

In its promotion of European integration, American propaganda focused on establishing a causal relationship between German unity and European unification. Intensive individual campaigns stressing the economic, security, and cultural aspects of integration were intended to defuse the reunification dilemma as a potential disruptive force in German-American relations. Enthusiasm for Europe, it was hoped, would provide the public with a psychological substitute for the deep-seated desire for national unity. As was logical, then, the Americans also supported Konrad Adenauer who, like them, rejected any notions of neutrality and was committed to the wholehearted allegiance of Germany to the Western powers. The Eisenhower administration intervened in various ways in the 1953 Bundestag election campaign to improve the chancellor's prospects. At the same time, an extensive advertising campaign to promote the peaceful use of nuclear energy was designed to establish the United States in the public mind as a force for peace, relieve the widespread fears of war, and neutralize criticism of Washington's security policy. A similar purpose was served by the deliberate contrasting of the American and Soviet models of society, which stressed the fundamental community of interests of the "free world" and left no doubt as to the superiority of its moral values and concept of civilization over those of communism.

In one way or the other, most West German citizens experienced American propaganda during the 1950s – through exhibitions, books, radio broadcasts, posters, or leaflets. Regular surveys designed to monitor the effect on public opinion kept the American government informed of the progress of its program for Germany. The Truman and Eisenhower administrations both believed that American political propaganda in the Federal Republic played a substantial part in bringing the West German public onto the side of the West and keeping it there. The active public-relations campaign pursued by the Americans, the broad concurrence of interests between Bonn and Washington, the polarization of the international system, the activities of outstanding figures on both sides, and the United States' strategic interest in raising the status of the Federal Republic of Germany – all these factors combined to transform the country, within a very few years, from occupied territory to ally and so laid the foundation for more than fifty years of German-American cooperation.

CHAPTER NINE

Rollback

An Offensive Strategy for the Cold War

Bernd Stöver

Translated by Jeremiah M. Riemer

Although the intellectual foundations of rollback date back to the nineteenth century, the emergence of the concept as a political strategy during the Cold War is inseparably bound up with the conceptual development of containment. Rollback emerged as the Republican Party's direct counterpart to the Democrats' containment model, especially as developed by George F. Kennan after 1946.[1] Behind the new strategy stood the idea of taking the offensive to push communism back rather than just defensively containing it. Open and covert measures would preoccupy and weaken communist power by stirring up problems within its sphere, preventing its further expansion and ultimately forcing it to relinquish control over individual states.[2] It was here that the proponents of rollback saw a crucial difference with the policy of containment, which, although it fought communist influence outside the East bloc by supporting endangered governments with financial and military aid, did not aim at actively liberating those peoples already "imprisoned" by communist regimes. The concepts *rollback* and *liberation* thus described the same thing.

The crucial initiator of the policy of rollback was John Foster Dulles,[3] the integrative figure for the Republican Party. From 1947 on, he advocated rollback in numerous speeches and articles, especially during the election campaign of 1948 and in his 1950 book *War or Peace*: "It is time to think of taking the offensive in the world struggle for freedom and of rolling back the engulfing tide of despotism."[4]

In retrospect, the election campaign of 1952 appears a decisive year for heightening the rhetoric of rollback. Numerous "hawks" picked up the theme and, at the cost of the nuances the concept once had, turned it into a slogan that the media reported worldwide. By contrast, Averell Harriman, who had been the U.S. ambassador in Moscow until 1946 and spoke on the Democrats' behalf, came to the defense of containment's offensive aspects: "The policy of the administration . . . has been an affirmative policy. . . . In 1946 Iran, in Greece in 1947 the Communists' financed and inspired civil war has

---

[1] See the chapter by Ruud van Dijk in this section.

[2] Bennet Kovrig, *The Myth of Liberation: East Central Europe in U.S. Diplomacy and Politics Since 1941* (Baltimore, 1973); John J. Yurechko, "From Containment to Counteroffensive: Soviet Vulnerabilities and American Policy Planning, 1946–1953," Ph.D. diss., University of California at Berkeley, 1980; Martin Beglinger, *"Containment" im Wandel: Die amerikanische Aussen- und Sicherheitspolitik im Übergang von Truman zu Eisenhower* (Stuttgart, 1988).

[3] Ronald W. Pruessen, *John Foster Dulles: The Road to Power* (New York, 1982); Mark G. Toulouse, *The Transformation of John Foster Dulles: From Prophet of Realism to Priest of Nationalism* (Macon, Ga., 1985); Richard Immerman, ed., *John Foster Dulles and the Diplomacy of the Cold War* (Princeton, N.J., 1990); Frederick W. Marks III, *Power and Peace: The Diplomacy of John Foster Dulles* (Westport, Conn., 1993).

[4] John Foster Dulles, *War or Peace* (New York, 1950), 175.

been rolled back . . . "[5] However, this conceptual adoption did not succeed in erasing the impression among the public, created by the new strategy's proponents, that much more might be at stake for them, and that the liberation of Eastern Europe was a fixed postulate of American foreign policy. "We should make it clear to the tens of millions of restive subject people in Eastern Europe and Asia," said Dulles in December 1949, "that we do not accept the status quo of servitude that aggressive Soviet Communism has imposed on them, and that eventual liberation is an essential and enduring part of our foreign policy."[6]

Many voices calling for a moderately offensive posture toward the USSR were drowned out in a climate characterized by the political culture's overall shift to the right and by a fear of communism sometimes bordering on hysteria. In July 1952, the Republicans' campaign platform adopted, nearly word for word, Dulles's demand to liberate Eastern Europe: "It will be made clear, on the highest authority of the President and the Congress, that United States policy, as one of its peaceful purposes, looks happily forward to the genuine independence of those captive peoples . . . [This program] will mark the end of the negative, futile and immoral policy of 'containment' which abandons countless human beings to a despotism and Godless terrorism, which in turn enables the rulers to forge the captives into a weapon for our destruction."[7]

Through its lack of clarity, the new concept let loose an avalanche of hopes and expectations in Europe and the United States, all the more so when its "inventor" Dulles became secretary of state in the Eisenhower administration. But it was also important that other authors picked up and elaborated the theme. Above all, James Burnham deserves mention.[8] Another representative of the ideology of liberation who could hardly be overestimated for his impact on Eastern Europe was Charles Douglas Jackson, who was briefly vice president of Time, Inc., the head of Radio Free Europe, and an adviser to Eisenhower. Unofficial groups in the United States and Europe also lent the policy of rollback a decisive dynamism all its own by promoting the liberation of Eastern Europe when official policy, for diplomatic reasons, had to express itself in far more differentiated terms.[9]

In practice, the policy of rollback relied overwhelmingly on classical "open" propaganda. For countries on the other side of the "Iron Curtain," leaflets were printed, radio programs broadcast, and mailings organized. Economic assistance (e.g., to the German Democratic Republic after the uprising of June 17, 1953, or to Poland in 1957) and cultural exchange were also seen as components of this policy. These measures were flanked by aid to allies on the basis of the Marshall Plan or the Mutual Security Act. In addition, "covert operations" got an early start. Along with classical espionage and sabotage, these activities included support for resistance groups in the Eastern bloc as well as direct attempts at overthrowing governments, as in Albania after 1949.[10] The Americans deliberately recruited émigrés for deployment in communist countries. In scope and effectiveness, however, these covert actions, planned and implemented

---

[8] James Burnham, *The Coming Defeat of Communism* (New York, 1950).

[9] James D. Marchio, "Rhetoric and Reality: The Eisenhower Administration and Unrest in Eastern Europe, 1953–1959," Ph.D. diss., The American University, 1990.

[10] Beatrice Heuser, "Subversive Operationen im Dienste der 'Roll Back'-Politik 1948–1953," *Vierteljahrshefte für Zeitgeschichte* 37 (1989): 279–97; John Prados, *Presidents' Secret Wars: CIA and Pentagon Covert Operations Since World War II* (New York, 1986); Harry Rositzke, *The CIA's Secret Operations: Espionage, Counter-Espionage, and Covert Action* (New York, 1977). For an overview of the older literature, see Myron J. Smith, *The Secret Wars: A Guide to Sources in English*, vol. 2, *Intelligence, Propaganda and Psychological Warfare, Covert Operations, 1945–1980* (Santa Barbara, Calif., 1981).

---

[5] Harriman on CBS-TV, Aug. 28, 1952, Mudd Library, Princeton, John Foster Dulles Papers, Selected Correspondence (hereafter JFDP/SC), box 63, folder: Re Republican Presidential Campaign.

[6] The Pursuit of Liberty, Dec. 13, 1949, 8, JFDP/SC, box 42, folder: Re Liberation Policy.

[7] 1952 Republican Platform, July 10, 1952, 5, JFDP/SC, box 63, folder: Re Republican Presidential Campaign.

for the most part by the CIA, lagged far behind measures undertaken out in the open. Covert actions were severely restricted in the late 1950s after their poor results and enormous political complications were made public.

The first shift from the policy of containment to the "war of liberation" took place not in a politically explosive and heavily armed Europe, but in Asia.[11] On October 1, 1950, American troops under UN command crossed the border to communist North Korea after the North Korean attack earlier in the year had been driven back to its starting point. To be sure, the official rationale for the American-UN action was that this was merely the pursuit of an aggressor. Simultaneously, however, it was emphasized that the Thirty-eighth Parallel could not be recognized, neither de jure nor de facto, as the border between North and South Korea – a clear reference to the intention of liberating North Korea. The intervention of Chinese "volunteers" – along with military defeats ultimately culminating in calls for the deployment of atomic weapons – then became the reason for accepting the original solution of partition after all. In Korea, the offensive policy of liberation ran up against its limits when the conflict threatened to get out of control and turn into a nuclear war. The United States encountered this very same obstacle in Europe as well.

In general, the focal point of the policy of rollback from the start was Germany, not Asia.[12] The Federal Republic became a center of coordination for the rollback strategy in Europe by virtue of its geographic position, and the GDR and Eastern Europe were the central targets.[13] West Germany was where the majority of leafleting actions started, the broadcast center for Radio Free Europe/Radio Liberty was there, and it was also where the East European émigré organizations were established as the most important unofficial propagandists for the idea of liberation. West Berlin was an ideal location for rollback activities directed against the GDR. RIAS, the main Western broadcaster accessible in East Germany, was located there, and Western secret intelligence services cooperated there with the most important German anticommunist organizations, like the militant "*Kampfgruppe gegen Unmenschlichkeit*" (KgU, or "Combat Group Against Inhumanity"), which undertook sabotage actions on its own inside the GDR. Chancellor Konrad Adenauer advocated a "policy of strength" vis-à-vis the East but nonetheless supported, like President Dwight Eisenhower, a moderate version of rollback.

The first major test of the rollback strategy also occurred in Germany. The uprising in the GDR of June 17, 1953, showed for the first time – and much to the Americans' surprise – how strongly people in communist countries had perceived the rhetoric of liberation as a promise of support.[14] As early as June 16, insurgents from East Berlin were broadcasting their demands over RIAS. In this case, too, Washington's ultimate response followed a familiar pattern. The danger that Western help could turn the East German conflict into a military confrontation with the Soviet Union precluded any additional support beyond general expressions of sympathy. Eisenhower categorically rejected deploying volunteers or giving military aid.

Scholarly research has almost uniformly assessed the behavior of the United States during the uprising in the GDR, like the failure to intervene in Hungary in 1956, as an

---

[11] David Horowitz, *Kalter Krieg: Hintergründe der US-Politik von Jalta bis Vietnam* (Berlin, 1969).

[12] Manfred Görtemaker, "John Foster Dulles und die amerikanische Deutschlandpolitik 1953–1954," Habilitationsschrift, Berlin, 1990; Detlef Felken, *Dulles und Deutschland: Die amerikanische Deutschlandpolitik 1953–1959* (Bonn, 1993).

[13] See Bernd Stöver, "Liberation Policy. Entstehung, Karriere, Wahrnehmung und Wirkungen eines offensiven aussenpolitischen Konzepts im Kalten Krieg 1947 bis 1991," Habilitationsschrift, Potsdam, 2001.

[14] Christian Ostermann, "Keeping the Pot Simmering: The United States and the East German Uprising of 1953," *German Studies Review* 19, no. 1 (Feb. 1996): 39–61; Christian Ostermann, *The United States, the East German Uprising of 1953, and the Limits of Rollback*, Woodrow Wilson International Center for Scholars, Cold War International History Project, Working Paper 11 (Washington, D.C., 1994); Valur Ingimundarson, "The Eisenhower Administration, the Adenauer Government, and the Political Uses of the East German Uprising in 1953," *Diplomatic History* 20 (1996): 381–409.

instance where the policy of rollback and liberation amounted to nothing more than lip service. Even if this view is not correct and rollback really was understood as a concrete political strategy, Washington's passive behavior was nonetheless decisive, especially for public opinion. There was considerable criticism even from Western allies, especially the Federal Republic. As a result, the official rhetoric of rollback abated after the uprising.

In the American administration, however, the uprising was deemed a success; it demonstrated how strong measures were capable of destabilizing communist rule from within: "We have powerful instruments in the form of RIAS, the Free Jurists, the *Kampfgruppe* [*gegen Unmenschlichkeit*] and the CDU and SPD Ost-Buro, to feed and nurture the spirit of revolt among the people of the Soviet Zone of Germany, who tasted blood June 16–17 and have not yet been brought fully under control."[15] After the uprising, therefore, the rollback model was not just retained; in light of recent developments, it was expanded. Along with NSC Strategy Paper 158 (June 29, 1953),[16] NSC Papers 174 (December 1953) and 5608 (July 1956) also banked on exploiting the Eastern bloc's problems more consistently.[17] Characteristically, immediately after the uprising, in summer 1953, a broadly conceived "psychological offensive" clearly designed to throw those wielding power in the East further on the defensive was launched. It included, among other provisions, a food drive for the GDR. James Conant, the American High Commissioner for Germany, described its purpose: "Moreover, the program has given East Germans contacts with the West and has made it once more a real, vital force in their lives. They know that the West ex-

ists, thinks about them and hopes some day that the East will be free. To people, many of whom have not seen the West for years, this physical contact is all important."[18]

It was the uprising in Hungary, which was much bloodier than that in the GDR, that precipitated a real crisis for the rollback model. Accusations that the United States had also incited this uprising by its promises of assistance led to hearings in Congress and the Bundestag as well as to fierce criticism among the American public. Testimony also made clear that nonofficial broadcasters had promised military aid.[19]

Morally, the policy of rollback and liberation was largely discredited after 1956. The beginnings of rapprochement between the blocs, together with the death of John Foster Dulles in 1959, caused the once dominant orientation of rollback policy toward Eastern Europe and the GDR to all but disappear.

The decisive shift became evident in 1961 during the crisis over the construction of the Berlin Wall, when the danger of military confrontation between the superpowers reemerged as a threat. While the center of gravity for rollback policy moved to the Third World, where Cuba and Vietnam stood out as potential areas of conflict, in Europe the United States shifted to a policy of maintaining the status quo. President John F. Kennedy's famous letter to Willy Brandt in August 1961 made it especially clear to the West Germans that Washington, for the sake of détente in its relationship with the USSR, was ready to put aside its offensive rollback policy and accept the existence of two German states.[20] The impetus for what later became détente and Ostpolitik was, therefore, provided by Kennedy, who had already expressed an extremely critical position on the rollback policy in the 1960

---

[15] Working Paper Prepared in the Eastern Affairs Division, Berlin Element, HICOG, June 25, 1953, HICOG, in U.S. Department of State, *Foreign Relations of the United States* (hereafter *FRUS*), *1952–1954*, vol. 7, pt. 2:1594–9, 1597.

[16] Reprinted in Christian Ostermann, "Implementing 'Roll Back': NSC 158," *SHAFR Newsletter*, Sept. 1996, 1–7.

[17] National Archives, RG 273, Policy Papers, NSC 174, Annex to NSC 5608.

[18] The United States High Commissioner for Germany (Conant) to the Department of State, July 31, 1953, *FRUS, 1952–1954*, vol. 7, pt. 2:1633–9, 1635.

[19] See Christopher Simpson, *Der amerikanische Bumerang: NS-Kriegsverbrecher im Sold der USA* (Vienna, 1988), 317.

[20] Diethelm Prowe, "Der Brief Kennedys an Brandt vom 18.8.1961: Eine zentrale Quelle zur Berliner Mauer und der Entstehung der Brandtschen Ostpolitik," *Vierteljahrshefte für Zeitgeschichte* 33 (1985): 373–83.

election campaign.[21] In 1963, when Egon Bahr (then head of the Berlin Senate's press office) couched future policy toward the GDR in the formula "change through rapprochement" and pleaded for "putting aside previous notions of liberation," he explicitly referred to Kennedy's "strategy of peace."[22]

Strong hopes were still placed on American liberation policy in 1961, especially among West Germans. But on September 21, 1961, just weeks after the Berlin Wall went up, the Cologne business paper *Industriekurier* provided one example of a more resigned attitude when it asserted that the Wall had definitely pushed liberation of the GDR into the distant future. "Reunification of the kind that every German patriot has dreamed of – a reunification with garlands and flag-waving and the Bundeswehr marching triumphantly through the Brandenburg Gate – there won't be this kind of reunification for the foreseeable future." That became clear on August 13, when the Western powers restricted themselves to renewing only their existing guarantees for West Berlin. Now one would "have to reconcile oneself to the *coexistence* of two German states for a long time to come."[23]

When one looks at actual policy in Europe following the building of the Wall, it is striking how it distanced itself from offensive conceptions of rollback. Economic and cultural relations were upgraded, and when the Warsaw Pact violently suppressed the reform movement in Czechoslovakia in 1968, the United States basically limited itself to protestations.

From the end of the 1950s onward, especially in Southeast Asia and Cuba, it was becoming evident how the Third World was moving into

the foreground in the same measure as Eastern Europe was fading from rollback's field of view. In particular, the first offensive measures undertaken against Cuba following the revolution displayed all the features of a classic rollback strategy. The failed invasion attempt at the Bay of Pigs in April 1961 characteristically included the help of anticommunist émigrés and had Kennedy's explicit approval; it clearly aimed to eliminate the government of Fidel Castro. There is some indication that the Cuban Missile Crisis of 1962 was also seen as a way of furthering this goal: Immediately after the solution to the crisis, presidential adviser Walt Rostow's long-term strategy for Cuba, as well as the CIA's plans, explicitly envisioned a "liberation" of the island.[24]

But Cuba was a special case. To be sure, American policy toward Vietnam also possessed elements of rollback, but toppling the North Vietnamese government was not among America's immediate goals. President Lyndon Johnson, in keeping with the strategy of containment, always pointed out that the only goal was to force Hanoi to cancel its support for the revolution in the south. However, beginning in 1964 with the "34-A Operations," the United States did carry out large-scale covert action in North Vietnam that in part went beyond this limited goal. The massive "counterinsurgency" program in Vietnam, correctly designated as a central element of the "Kennedy Doctrine," also had many points in common with the strategy of rollback.[25] The impossibility of winning a jungle war by conventional means and the massive domestic pressure in the United States to end the conflict ultimately caused a shift toward a solution based on partition, as in Germany and Korea. Like these precedents, however, such a partition did not entirely rule out "liberation" of the communist-ruled section.

---

[21] See Kennedy's Senate speech of June 14, 1960, reprinted in Klaus Schoenthal, ed., *Der neue Kurs: Amerikas Aussenpolitik unter Kennedy 1961–1963* (Munich, 1964), 18–27, 24.

[22] Vortrag des Leiters des Presse- und Informationsamtes des Landes Berlin, Bahr, in der Evangelischen Akademie Tutzing, in Bundesministerium für Innerdeutsche Beziehungen, *Dokumente zur Deutschlandpolitik*, ser. 4, vol. 9 (Frankfurt am Main, 1978), 572–5, 575, 572.

[23] "Wo stehen wir?" *Industriekurier*, Sept. 2, 1961, 1.

[24] Bernd Greiner, *Kuba-Krise: 13 Tage im Oktober: Analysen, Dokumente, Zeitzeugen*, 2d ed. (Hamburg, 1988); Ernest R. May and Philip D. Zelikow, eds., *The Kennedy Tapes: Inside the White House During the Cuban Missile Crisis* (Cambridge, Mass., 1997).

[25] Louise FitzSimmons, *The Kennedy Doctrine* (New York, 1972).

The year 1968 was not a watershed for the policy of rollback. In Europe, the offensive strategy had been gradually abandoned in favor of a policy of détente in the years following the building of the Wall. In the Third World as well, the failed invasion of Cuba in 1961 and the Cuba crisis of 1962 revealed the limits of an offensive rollback policy. In Vietnam, unlike in Korea, this prevented the definitive shift toward a war of liberation. Ultimately, despite all the rhetoric, the danger of stumbling into a nuclear war over a local conflict was the decisive reason for seeking an "evolutionary solution" in practice. In retrospect, one can, therefore, argue that the policy of containment remained the definitive basic program throughout the Cold War.[26] However, starting in 1981 under the Reagan administration, and especially as a result of setbacks to the policy of détente that were severely criticized in the United States, the concept of rollback experienced a renaissance that went beyond rhetoric and displayed numerous parallels to the 1950s. The renewed proclamation of the "policy of strength" was now paired with the outright promotion of anticommunist and anti-Soviet organizations, especially in South and Central America, but also in Afghanistan. Starting in 1983, the right-wing "Contras" were supported in their struggle against the socialist Sandinistas in Nicaragua, with the CIA again providing armed assistance. The intervention in Grenada, also following a left-wing coup, was interpreted in America as a classic action for rolling back communism. The "Reagan Doctrine" behind this policy, as announced by the president before the Senate in 1986, was a classic statement of rollback and the policy of liberation. The doctrine called for pushing back "communist tyranny" by means both direct and indirect, military and economic.[27]

It remains controversial to what extent the West's offensive rollback policy of the 1980s promoted the collapse of the USSR and helped bring about the end of the Cold War.[28] It seems indisputable that the Western armament effort and the Soviet attempt to keep up with it pushed the entire Soviet economy into a desperate situation. On the other hand, its seems rather less likely that this led inevitably to the collapse of the Soviet Union and the liberation of Eastern Europe.

[26] John Lewis Gaddis, *Strategies of Containment: A Critical Appraisal of Postwar American National Security Policy* (New York, 1982).

[27] U.S. Policy Information and Texts, no. 39, Mar. 17, 1986, 9–21.

[28] Günther Schild, "Wer gewann den Kalten Krieg? Reflexionen in der amerikanischen Literatur," *Zeitschrift für Geschichtswissenschaft* 43 (1955): 149–58.

CHAPTER TEN

From Supreme Authority to Reserved Rights and Responsibilities

The International Legal Basis of German–American Relations

Richard Wiggers

Two contrasting traditions have governed the relationship between American diplomacy and international law. In one, the United States acts as the principal upholder of global law and morality. In the other, national interests reign supreme, and international law merely sanctions and ennobles the foreign policies of the strong. These contradictory impulses were nowhere more apparent than in the United States' postwar relations with Germany.

In 1945, the United States and its allies assumed "supreme authority" over the defeated foe and implemented numerous occupation measures that violated the spirit, if not the word, of international law. Several years later, American officials seemed to rediscover their respect for that body of law as they began to construct a postwar European order. They championed German recovery, granted sovereign rights to an emerging Federal Republic of Germany, and defended their new ally against challenges from Moscow and the rival German Democratic Republic (GDR). Not only was the framework created in 1945 unique in the history of diplomacy and international law,[1] the expansion of

the web of contractual relationships between the Federal Republic, the GDR, and the Four Powers also coincided with the ebb and flow of the Cold War, with the United States playing a prominent role throughout.

SUPREME AUTHORITY

The military occupation of German territory began in September 1944 when units of Supreme Headquarters Allied Expeditionary Forces (SHAEF) crossed the frontier and assumed supreme legislative, judicial, and executive authority over the territories under their military control.[2] At the time, Articles 42–56 of the 1907 Hague Regulations entitled SHAEF to establish a "belligerent occupation" of enemy territory and maintain public order.[3] Yet, the United States and its allies sought much broader powers that would permit them to transform postwar German society and political structures. President Franklin Roosevelt's insistence on Germany's unconditional surrender was partly motivated by his desire for a legal carte blanche unencumbered by the Hague Regulations

---

[1] Günther Doeker and Jens A. Brückner, eds., *The Federal Republic of Germany and the German Democratic Republic in International Relations*, vol. 1: *Confrontation and Cooperation* (Dobbs Ferry, N.Y., 1979); Günther Doeker and Lukas H. Meyer, eds., *The Federal Republic of Germany and the German Democratic Republic in International Relations: Second Series: From Cooperation to Unification*, 3 vols. (Dobbs Ferry, N.Y., 1991–2).

[2] Military Government (SHAEF), Proclamation No. 1, Sept. 18, 1944, quoted in M. E. Bathurst and J. L. Simpson, *Germany and the North Atlantic Community: A Legal Survey* (London, 1956), 3.

[3] For the text, see U.S. Department of the Air Force, *Treaties Governing Land Warfare* (Washington, D.C., 1958), 15–17.

and the Geneva Convention of 1929. The European Advisory Commission (EAC), established in London to coordinate planning among the Big Three, also intended to assume extraordinary powers when it formulated a surrender instrument, joint administrative machinery, and zones of occupation in 1944–5.[4]

The victors began to assert those extraordinary powers even before hostilities ended. In the United Nations (UN) Charter, Articles 107 ("Enemy States Clause") and 53 exempted Allied occupation rights in postwar Germany from UN jurisdiction.[5] Coinciding with the surrender, the United States and its allies also directed foreign governments to withdraw their diplomatic representatives from Germany, and the Swiss government was removed as Geneva Convention Protecting Power over German POWs.[6]

Germany never signed a capitulation document.[7] The final instruments of surrender of May 7–8, 1945, were exclusively military in character and constituted only a general armistice.[8] However, they did contain a clause that anticipated the imposition of more sweeping conditions. This expanded assertion of occupation rights accompanied the Declaration of Berlin of June 5, in which the Allies assumed "supreme authority with respect to Germany, including all the powers possessed by the German Government, the High Command, and any state, municipal or local government or authority."[9]

At the time, some legal scholars, especially in America, argued that the defeat and unconditional surrender of Germany's armed forces and the assumption of Allied supreme authority led to the extinction of the German state.[10] This theory of *debellatio* seemed to be confirmed by the emergence of two rival republics in 1949 and their admission to the UN in 1972. Despite this de facto dismemberment, however, Germany was never formally dissolved after World War II and continued to fulfill some of the minimum requirements of statehood, including a national people and territory. The victors rejected any attempt to annex Germany and saw their exercise of supreme authority as exceptional and temporary.[11] Most postwar states and courts also recognized that Germany never ceased to exist as a legal entity, even though it lacked central state organs and the capacity to act internationally.

Some scholars have also argued that the state of war with Germany ended in 1945 because the Allies could not continue to be at war with a country whose government functions they had assumed. Yet, at Potsdam, the Big Three acknowledged that a formal end to the war and to the military occupation of German territory would have to await the emergence of a restored government capable of freely signing a peace settlement. Even when the United

---

[4] The relevant documents are reprinted in U.S. Department of State, *Documents on Germany, 1944–1985* (hereafter *DG*) (Washington, D.C., 1985), 1–9, 12–13.

[5] Dieter Blumenwitz, "Enemy States Clause in the United Nations Charter," in Rudolf Bernhardt, ed., *Encyclopedia of Public International Law* (hereafter *EPIL*)(Amsterdam, 1995), 2:90–5.

[6] Telegram from Secretary of State, May 13, 1945, National Archives (hereafter NA), RG 332, European Theater of Operations, file 383.6/10; Note for Judge Advocate (JA), G-1 Communications Zone, June 17, 1945, NA, RG 332, European Theater of Operations, file 383.6.

[7] Hereafter, *Germany* refers to *Germany as a whole*, a legal term that describes the territories and populations of the Reich within its 1937 borders.

[8] Burkhard Schöbener, *Die amerikanische Besatzungspolitik und das Völkerrecht* (Frankfurt am Main, 1991).

[9] For the text of the Berlin Declaration, see *DG*, 33–40.

[10] Hans Kelsen, "The International Legal Status of Germany to Be Established Immediately Upon Termination of the War," *American Journal of International Law* 38 (1944): 689–94; Hans Kelsen, "The International Legal Status of Germany According to the Declaration of Berlin," *American Journal of International Law* 39 (1945): 518–26; Karl-Ulrich Meyn, "Debellatio," *EPIL*, 1:969–71.

[11] Friedrich Frhr. Waitz von Eschen, *Die völkerrechtliche Kompetenz der Vier Mächte zur Gestaltung der Rechtslage Deutschlands nach dem Abschluss der Ostvertragspolitik* (Frankfurt am Main, 1988), 1–73; Georg Wilhelm Prinz von Hannover, *Die völkerrechtliche Stellung Deutschlands nach der Kapitulation* (Cologne, 1984), 8–54; Theodor Schweisfurth, "Germany, Occupation After World War II," *EPIL*, 2:582–90.

States unilaterally ended the state of war in the sense of municipal and domestic law in 1951 (through domestic legislation intended to normalize commercial and diplomatic relations),[12] a formal state of war persisted in international law until 1990. Given this unprecedented legal framework, it is hardly surprising that Allied occupation policies were initially formulated with little regard for international law or German sovereignty. A study conducted by American officials in 1946 acknowledged that "many acts of the four Powers, the Control Council and of Military Government in the United States zone of occupation are incompatible with the theory of belligerent occupation under the provisions of the Hague Regulations."[13] Yet, numerous postwar courts and scholars confirmed the validity of Allied policies. They asserted that earlier treaty framers had not envisioned the situation facing the Allies in 1945 and that total warfare and Germany's utter destruction required developments in international law "to meet a new situation."[14] Even American scholars argued that "it would be foolish to let legalistic considerations tie our hands" in dealing with postwar Germany.[15]

One of the first decisions concerned the territorial boundaries. The Big Three decided the occupation would be based on Germany's

national frontiers and *Land* (state) borders of December 1937; changes after that date were rendered void. The annexation of Austria was annulled; the acquisition of the Sudetenland under the Munich Agreement was declared invalidated by the 1939 invasion of Czechoslovakia; Alsace-Lorraine and Eupen-et-Malmedy, illegally incorporated by Nazi Germany in 1940, were returned. The Saar region, which the French had tried to appropriate after 1945, was restored to Germany in 1957. Minor adjustments to the western frontiers were settled in other agreements.[16]

The territorial transfers in the East were more controversial. Although Germany was not dismembered as many had hoped, it was reduced in size. At Potsdam, the Big Three transferred Königsberg and the surrounding region to Soviet administration and approved de facto Polish control over the remaining German lands east of the Oder and Neisse Rivers. This amounted to nearly a fourth of all German territory within the borders of 1937. The Allies also approved the "orderly transfer" of German-speaking populations from those regions, as well as from Hungary and Czechoslovakia.

Allied legal authority for these territorial revisions was dubious at best and barely sufficed to mask the brutality of the mass expulsions and property expropriations that ensued. Yet, legal title over Germany's eastern provinces was never officially transferred to the Polish or Soviet governments. The status of these lands remained indeterminate despite the GDR's acceptance of the Oder-Neisse frontier in a 1950 treaty with Poland and the Federal Republic's similar guarantees under Ostpolitik.[17] Definitive changes to the 1937 frontiers, particularly in the East, still required a peace treaty with Germany.

With the onset of Cold War tensions, the Council of Foreign Ministers (CFM) and the

---

[12] For the relevant documents, see Doeker and Brückner, *Confrontation and Co-Operation*, 106; and *DG*, 356, 443–4. See also Quincy Wright, "The Status of Germany and the Peace Proclamation," *American Journal of International Law* 46 (1952): 299–308.

[13] Major G. B. Crook, Civil Affairs Division (CAD), and Major W. G. Downey, Judge Advocate General (JAG) to the JAG, Present Applicability of Hague and Geneva Conventions in Germany, NA, RG 389, Provost Marshal General, Historical File, 1941–1958, box 35, 1946.

[14] Lieutenant Colonel Howe, Legal Consequence of Unconditional Surrender (draft), Jan. 13, 1945, NA, RG 107, Assistant Secretary of War, file 387.4; William Malkin, Memorandum on the Position if There Is no "Instrument of Surrender," Jan. 18, 1945, Charles Fahy Papers, box 65, Franklin D. Roosevelt Library, Hyde Park, N.Y.

[15] Ernst H. Feilchenfeld et al., "Status of Germany," in *World Polity: A Yearbook of Studies in International Law and Organization* (Washington, D.C., 1957), 1:181–4, 192, 202–3.

[16] The relevant documents are reprinted in *DG*, 208–9; Hans-Dietrich Treviranus, "Boundary Settlements Between Germany and her Western Neighbour States After World War II," *EPIL*, 1:475–8.

[17] For the text of the Poland-GDR agreement and the "Warsaw Treaty" between Poland and the Federal Republic, see *DG*, 310–13, 1125–7.

Allied Control Council proved unable to decide on a peace settlement and common occupation policies for Germany.[18] Although the principle of Four Power rule was never officially abandoned, until 1990 the joint military missions located in each of the original zones were the only institution outside of Greater Berlin where cooperation continued. This breakdown of joint occupation set the stage for the first major revision of the legal structure of quadripartite rule.

"RESERVED RIGHTS AND RESPONSIBILITIES"

As East-West tensions intensified, U.S. officials pressed for the economic recovery and integration of Western Europe. To facilitate that effort, they took the lead in revising the legal framework governing the Western zones.[19] The military governors had already signed the Convention for European Economic Cooperation and the American-sponsored European Recovery Program (ERP) on behalf of the Western zones. Now they sought a representative and indigenous central government to work with them and encouraged delegates from the *Land* governments to establish a parliamentary council and draft a constitution. The name of the resulting document, Basic Law (*Grundgesetz*), implied its provisional nature pending the unification of Germany. It was ratified by most of the state legislatures in May 1949, and in August the Federal Republic elected its first parliament.

Simultaneously, the British-American zone (Bizonia) was merged with the French zone in April 1949, and the defunct quadripartite Control Council was transformed into a tripartite civilian High Commission. With passage of a revised Occupation Statute and a new High Commission Charter, the first and most onerous phase of the occupation ended. Allied supreme authority was now redefined in less objectionable terms as "reserved rights and responsibilities," and the newly elected Bonn government now assumed "full legislative, executive, and judicial powers" from the occupation authorities.[20] Increasingly, relations between it and the three Western Powers were based on contractual obligations among allies rather than the occupation rights of victors.

As the Federal Republic assumed more diplomatic responsibility, it was allowed to negotiate and conclude trade and financial agreements, albeit under continued supervision by the High Commission. The Petersberg Protocol of 1949 ended industrial dismantling in exchange for the Federal Republic's acceptance of an International Ruhr Authority and authorized Bonn to exchange consular and commercial representatives with the Western Powers.[21] In 1951, the Federal Republic established a foreign ministry and joined the European Coal and Steel Community, the Council of Europe, and a number of specialized UN agencies.

Arguing that the Western Allies had unilaterally breached Four Power agreements with these measures, the Soviets promoted the emergence of a rival German successor state. But the quadripartite occupation regime remained in place, and both successor states continued to derive their semisovereign powers from the allies governing their territory. In the Federal Republic, the High Commission continued to review all federal and state laws and regulations, and the "reserved rights and responsibilities" could be exercised at any time to revoke the Occupation Statute and restore military government.

THE BONN AND PARIS AGREEMENTS

The Korean War of 1950–3 increased American determination to include a rearmed Federal Republic in an expanded European security organization. Washington now helped formulate an even more drastic transformation of the legal framework of quadripartite control to reconcile American and German national aims with European security concerns.

---

[18] See the chapters by Edmund Spevack and Gunther Mai in this section.

[19] See the chapter by Hermann-Josef Rupieper in this section.

[20] The relevant documents are reprinted in *DG*, 212–74, quotes: 213–17.

[21] The Petersberg Protocol is reprinted in ibid., 310–13.

Chancellor Konrad Adenauer was willing to accept de facto partition of Germany as long as the door was left open to eventual unification. He was sensitive to the security concerns of Germany's neighbors, but sought reconstruction and rearmament for the fledgling West German state. He was also willing to embed the Federal Republic firmly within Western European and multilateral structures but insisted on relative equality and diplomatic freedom of maneuver for Bonn in return. The Bonn and Paris Agreements of 1952–4 were a complex network of treaties, letters, and conventions that attempted to accomplish many of these diverse goals.[22] In fulfillment of American aims, the Federal Republic was permitted to rearm and contribute to the common defense of Western Europe. To allay the security concerns of its neighbors, Bonn renounced atomic, biological, and chemical weapons; its armed forces were firmly embedded in the Brussels Pact and the North Atlantic Treaty Organization (NATO).[23] In turn, the United States and the other Western allies recognized the Federal Republic as the sole legitimate representative of all Germans. They also committed themselves to seeking a final peace treaty and reunification, maintaining troops in West Berlin, and consulting Bonn on the exercise of their remaining rights and responsibilities in Germany.

Adenauer, always fearful that Four Power authority might be restored in the event of reunification, proposed an additional clause that would have bound the Allies to grant a reunified Germany no fewer rights than the agreements currently being negotiated would grant the Federal Republic. In turn, a unified Germany would be bound to the goal of West European integration contained in the Bonn and Paris Treaties.[24]

This "binding clause" (*Bindungsklausel*) aroused considerable opposition in Adenauer's own government because it seemed to preclude any negotiations with the Soviet Union on German reunification; after the failure of the European Defense Community (EDC) in 1954 forced a renegotiation of the agreements, the *Bindungsklausel* was dropped altogether. Nevertheless, the episode demonstrated Adenauer's fear of arbitrary decisions by the Allies (*Potsdam-Komplex*) and his deep distrust of his own people: Both he and the Western Powers tried to secure the Federal Republic's permanent tie to the West (*Westbindung*) while arguing to the East that only a reunified Germany could enter into binding agreements.

The Bonn and Paris Agreements brought an official end to Four Power control. The Occupation Statute was revoked, the High Commission and its subordinate offices were abolished, and the Allied High Commissioners were transformed into ambassadors. Most importantly, the Federal Republic was granted full authority of a sovereign state over its internal and external affairs.

But the official termination of Four Power occupation still did not signify complete freedom of maneuver for Bonn in foreign affairs. Until a peace settlement was concluded, the Western Powers continued to use the occupation regime to maintain their rights and responsibilities in Greater Berlin, their right to station troops on German territory and ensure the security of their forces, and their final authority over reunification and territorial revisions. Although these residual Allied rights seldom infringed directly on Bonn's sovereignty, they restricted its practical exercise and gave troops of the Western Powers privileges beyond those of other NATO forces stationed in the Federal Republic. All subsequent governments in Bonn accepted this semisovereign status because all of them realized that the position of the Western Allies was in West Germany's own interest. Allied residual

---

[22] The relevant documents for the Bonn and Paris Agreements are reprinted in *DG*, 424–38. See also Wilhelm A. Kewenig, "Bonn and Paris Agreements on Germany (1952 and 1954)," *EPIL*, 1:422–32.

[23] The protocol on the Federal Republic's accession to NATO is reprinted in *DG*, 432–4.

[24] Walter Schwengler, "Der doppelte Anspruch: Souveränität und Sicherheit: Zur Entwicklung des völkerrechtlichen Status der Bundesrepublik Deutschland 1949 bis 1955," in Militärgeschichtliches Forschungsamt, ed., *Anfänge westdeutscher Sicherheitspoli-*

tik 1945–1956 (Munich, 1997), 4:270–7, 328–30; see also Hans-Peter Schwarz, *Konrad Adenauer: A German Politician and Statesman in a Period of War, Revolution and Reconstruction* (Providence, R.I., 1995), 1:635–6, 664–87.

rights formed a framework that prevented the different parts of Germany from drifting farther apart: They could be invoked against the secessionist claims of the East German regime,[25] and they secured the freedom of West Berlin.

Berlin had formed a special administrative area within the Soviet zone since 1945.[26] The Allies divided its districts among the four sectors, and in February 1947 the state of Prussia was formally dissolved and Greater Berlin elevated from a municipality to a *Land*. As in the CFM and the Allied Control Council, disputes escalated in the quadripartite *Kommandatura*, which administered Greater Berlin, and the Soviets withdrew from this body in 1948.

At first, American policymakers did not consider the Western sectors vital to their interests. It was only during the Berlin Blockade that the city gained great importance in U.S. policy as a symbol of Western fortitude. Thereafter, the Western Allies would persistently invoke their legal rights – rooted in the original occupation of postwar Germany – to defend their position in Greater Berlin.

The Jessup-Malik Agreement of May 4, 1949,[27] and the Quadripartite Agreement of 1971 seemed to confirm Allied occupation rights. But the Soviet Union and the GDR continued to argue that only West Berlin remained subject to quadripartite authority or that it constituted a completely separate political entity. The status of the Western sectors remained a source of dispute, and Greater Berlin became an important political and legal battleground for Cold War confrontations between the Western Powers and the Federal Republic on the one side and the Soviet Union and the GDR on the other. Although Bonn feared any accommodation that would divide Berlin or Germany permanently, it had no choice but to rely on the Western Allies and their retained occupation rights to guarantee the independence of the Western sectors. Bonn was concerned with the establishment of new legal precedents, whereas the Western Allies had to defend the security and accessibility of their sectors with anachronistic legal formulas dating back to 1945.

To maintain a semblance of continued Four Power control over Greater Berlin, the Western Allies asserted their access rights in the Eastern sector with daily "flag patrols." The Soviets responded by maintaining a guard detachment at the War Memorial in the British sector and retaining their special rights over railway, canal, and lock properties in the Western sectors. The Air Safety Center in the American sector was also run on a quadripartite basis, monitoring air traffic over Greater Berlin until 1990. Spandau Prison was administered jointly until it was demolished after the death of Rudolf Hess in 1987. The Soviets tried to undermine the quadripartite status of the city by delegating duties to GDR authorities, but the Western Powers refused to discharge the Soviets from ultimate responsibility for their own sector and the transportation routes to the city.

The administrative consolidation of the Western sectors of Greater Berlin generally followed the pattern of the zones. After the failure of the Blockade and the establishment of a rival city assembly, magistrate, and other organs in the Soviet sector, the Western sectors were merged to form West Berlin. The Kommandatura continued to operate, but as a tripartite body with jurisdiction restricted largely to the Western sectors. Greater self-government was granted in 1949 with the "Little Occupation

---

[25] Jochen Abr. Frowein, "Die Rechtslage Deutschlands und der Status Berlins," in Ernst Benda, Werner Maihofer, and Hans-Jochen Vogel, eds., *Handbuch des Verfassungsrechts der Bundesrepublik Deutschland*, 2d ed. (Berlin and New York, 1994), 48.

[26] See the chapter by Diethelm Prowe in this section; *Dokumente zur Berlin-Frage 1944–1966* (Munich, 1987); I. D. Hendry and M. C. Wood, *The Legal Status of Berlin* (Cambridge, 1987); Ernst R. Zivier, *The Legal Status of the Land Berlin: A Survey After the Quadripartite Agreement* (Berlin, 1980); Udo Wetzlaugk, *Berlin und die deutsche Frage* (Cologne, 1985).

[27] For the text, see Editorial Note, in U.S. Department of State, *Foreign Relations of the United States, 1949*, 3:751.

Statute," which remained in effect until 1955.[28] After passage of the Basic Law, West Berlin was regarded as a *Land* and territorial component, but still not a sovereign unit or legal part, of the Federal Republic.[29]

A "covering law," or *Mantelgesetz*, permitted federal legislation to apply to West Berlin, subject to Kommandatura approval. The West Berlin government was also given expanded jurisdiction, and decisions were increasingly made in consultation with it. West Berlin was incorporated into the European Communities, and the federal government was permitted to represent it in various international agreements. But the occupation status of the city was never terminated, nor was sovereignty transferred to the West Berlin government or to federal organs. To protect the quadripartite status of Greater Berlin, the commandants of the Western Powers retained final authority over legislative issues and circumscribed the political links between the Federal Republic and West Berlin. Allied military control was more extensive in West Berlin than in the Federal Republic proper; military personnel remained responsible for freedom and security but exempt from most local jurisdiction. Occupation laws continued to override local ones, especially in areas of civil aviation, demilitarization, federal court jurisdiction, and control of the police.

After another series of crises that began in 1958, the construction of the Berlin Wall in 1961 marked a major shift. By enhancing the viability of the GDR, the Wall forced many in the Federal Republic to accept the long-term partition of Germany. Similarly, the United States and the other Western allies could do little more than attempt to defend the status quo. Indeed, many Western officials were relieved that the Wall had stabilized the volatile Berlin issue. As President John F. Kennedy told one of his aides: "It seems silly for us to be facing an atomic war over a treaty preserving Berlin as the future capital of a reunited Germany when all of us know that Germany will probably never be reunited."[30]

CONCLUSION

In international law, the Germany of 1937 and a formal state of war continued to exist throughout the Cold War era. It is debatable whether the Allies' unilateral assumption of supreme authority in 1945 was sufficiently grounded in international law to legitimate the full range of measures taken in postwar Germany and the maintenance of Four Power control for forty-five years thereafter. Subsequent developments in international law certainly eliminated many technical loopholes that had been used to assert supreme authority in 1945. Yet, both the Federal Republic and the GDR recognized Four Power rights and responsibilities in successive treaties and agreements. Although Germany remained divided and under Four Power supervision, the Federal Republic was guaranteed that there would be no unilateral changes in the status of West Berlin or Germany as a whole.

The United States played a prominent role in the evolution of the legal framework that determined Germany's status. In 1945, American officials helped engineer the unconditional surrender of German armed forces and the unilateral assumption of Allied supreme authority. From 1949 on, the United States led the Western Allies in remodeling the failed legal framework of Four Power control, remaking postwar German society, and orchestrating the establishment of the Federal Republic. The new ally became a vital part of the broader reconstruction of Western European economic and military might, while the assertion of Four Power control in Greater Berlin and the retention of rights over some aspects of German affairs reflected Washington's determination to remain involved in the future of Germany.

By 1968, a number of developments had reopened many of the issues covered by the Paris

---

[28] See the relevant documents reprinted in *DG*, 262–4, and in Doeker and Brückner, *Confrontation and Co-Operation*, 1:231–2.

[29] The relevant documents are reprinted in *DG*, 262–73, 322–41.

[30] Quoted in Ernest R. May, "America's Berlin: Heart of the Cold War," *Foreign Affairs* 77, no. 4 (1998): 148–60, 158.

and Bonn agreements more than ten years earlier. One of these developments involved the
right of the Western Allies to declare a state of
emergency – and wield commensurate powers –
in the Federal Republic. In the Bonn and Paris
agreements, the Allies had agreed to rescind this
right as soon the Federal Republic included its
own emergency provisions in the Basic Law.
However, efforts of successive Bonn governments to do so had provoked strong domestic
opposition and were one of the main targets
of the protests in the 1960s. The Grand Coalition of 1966–9 finally passed the Emergency
Laws (*Notstandsgesetze*), which removed one of
the more glaring strictures on West German
sovereignty. Another provision of the 1952–4
agreements, Adenauer's unilateral renunciation

of atomic weapons, gained new significance
with the German-American controversy over
the Non-Proliferation Treaty.[31] Meanwhile, the
GDR introduced a revised constitution and definition of citizenship, and imposed additional
restrictions on the access routes to West Berlin.
Finally, superpower détente encouraged a new
generation of leaders in Bonn to pursue a revamped Ostpolitik. Although the Federal Republic seemed to accept its semisovereignty, by
the end of 1968 it was following the lead of the
United States in seeking a new basis for its foreign relations.

[31] See the chapter by Erhard Forndran, vol. 1, Security.

CHAPTER ELEVEN

Germany Between the Superpowers, 1948–1968

Manfred Görtemaker

Translated by Terence M. Coe

Following the unconditional surrender of German forces on May 8–9, 1945, and military occupation by the Allies, the victors of World War II officially assumed "supreme authority" in Germany on June 5, 1945. It was above all the United States and the Soviet Union, newly emerged from the war as "superpowers," that determined the basic direction of Germany in international politics for almost half a century until the revolution of 1989 and Germany's reunification on October 3, 1990. Germany was caught in the center of the tensions produced by the East-West conflict. Particularly in the period from 1945 to 1968, this meant a high degree of dependency until détente and a new policy toward the East changed the underlying conditions and created greater freedom of action for the Federal Republic of Germany and the German Democratic Republic (GDR).[1]

FROM FOUR POWER CONTROL TO PARTITION

The beginning of the postwar period in Germany was completely overshadowed by Allied Four Power control.[2] Plans for partition that had been considered during the war initially played no part following the Yalta Conference in February 1945. The victors were unable to agree on a partition strategy because the expert commissions from the United States and Great Britain, in the course of their planning for Germany in 1943–4, had come to the conclusion that breaking up Germany would have serious disadvantages for the reintroduction of economic and political stability in postwar Europe.[3] At the last wartime conference of the Big Three, from July 17 to August 2, 1945, in Potsdam, an express agreement was made "to treat Germany as a single economic unit" and to set up central administrative units that could serve as the core of a new all-German government.[4]

The Allies were also in agreement in early 1945 on the need for a rigid occupation policy. The Germans were to be punished for the crimes of the Nazi regime and subjected to strict Allied control. Thus, for example, the Joint

---

[1] See Gregor Schöllgen, *Geschichte der Weltpolitik von Hitler bis Gorbatschow 1941–1991* (Munich, 1996).

[2] See Michael Balfour and John Mair, *Four-Power Control in Germany and Austria, 1945–1946* (London, 1956).

[3] See Hermann Graml, *Die Alliierten und die Teilung Deutschlands: Konflikte und Entscheidungen 1941–1948* (Frankfurt am Main, 1985), 31–61. This view has recently been challenged by Carolyn W. Eisenberg, who claims that the United States had opted early for a partition of Germany, primarily in order to be able to assert its economic interests in Western Europe; see Carolyn Eisenberg, *Drawing the Line: The American Decision to Divide Germany, 1944–1949* (New York, 1996).

[4] U.S. Department of State, *Documents on Germany, 1944–1985* (Washington, D.C., 1985), 58–9. The complete German and English text of the negotiation protocol of August 2, 1945, which is also called the "Potsdam Agreement," is in Bundesminister des Innern, *Dokumente zur Deutschlandpolitik*, ser. 2, vol. 1, pt. 3: *Die Konferenz von Potsdam* (Frankfurt am Main, 1992), 2149–73.

Chiefs of Staff stated in their directive JCS 1067 of April 26, 1945, that Germany would "not be occupied for the purpose of liberation but as a defeated enemy nation." It must be made clear "that the Germans cannot escape responsibility for what they have brought upon themselves."[5] The Potsdam Conference participants also decided upon an internal reorganization of Germany, with the goal of democratization, decentralization, demilitarization, and denazification.

Nevertheless, it remained unclear how these concepts were to be implemented in practice. The lines of division did not run simply between the Soviet Union and the Western powers.[6] In the beginning, at least, the largest source of trouble was France, which did not participate in the wartime conferences. The authorities in Paris continued to desire corrections to the borders and even the dismembering of Germany. On September 14, 1945, France therefore made its consent for the creation of German central administrative units expressly contingent upon having the territories west of the Rhine as well as the Ruhr region separated from Germany. It consequently used the Control Council, in which decisions could only be made unanimously, to block the creation of central administrative units.[7]

The Soviet Union also followed its own course in policy toward Germany. Long-term preparations for this course had been made through the intensive training of exiled German communists in Moscow.[8] Fundamental systemic changes were introduced in Eastern Germany in September 1945, with land reform, nationalization of heavy and key industries, and a restructuring of the educational system. This also meant a structural isolation of the Soviet zones vis-à-vis the Western zones, even though the bureaucratic execution of this policy in detail was not always as coherent as has long been assumed in the West.[9] With the forced merging of the Social Democratic Party (Sozialdemokratische Partei Deutschlands, or SPD) and the Communist Party (Kommunistische Partei Deutschlands, or KPD) into the Socialist Unity Party (Sozialistische Einheitspartei Deutschlands, or SED) in April 1946, it also became clear that, despite all assertions of a "popular democratic path," there was a de facto concentration of political power in the hands of a monopoly party based on the Soviet model.[10] The "uniformity of procedure by the supreme commanders in their respective zones of occupation" as agreed to in 1944 within the European Advisory Commission (EAC) could, therefore, no longer be maintained. Germany became a test case for the impending East-West conflict.[11]

George F. Kennan, envoy at the American embassy in Moscow since July 1944, had

---

the Soviet Union; see Vladislav Zubok and Constantin Pleshakov, *Inside the Kremlin's Cold War: From Stalin to Khrushchev* (Cambridge, Mass., 1996). See also Richard C. Raack, *Stalin's Drive to the West, 1938–1945: The Origins of the Cold War* (Stanford, Calif., 1995); Vojtech Mastny, *The Cold War and Soviet Insecurity: The Stalin Years* (New York, 1996).

[9] See Norman M. Naimark, *The Russians in Germany: A History of the Soviet Zone of Occupation, 1945–1949* (Cambridge, Mass., 1995).

[10] Hermann-Josef Rupieper, ed., *Die Zwangsvereinigung von KPD und SPD: Einige ausgewählte Dokumente der SMAD 16.1.1946–7.6.1946* (Halle, 1997). On the role of the Soviet military administration, particularly in 1946, see Stefan Creuzberger, *Die sowjetische Besatzungsmacht und das politische System der SBZ*, Schriften des Hannah-Arendt-Instituts für Totalitarismusforschung, vol. 3 (Weimar, 1996).

[11] See Lothar Kettenacker, "Die anglo-amerikanischen Planungen für die Kontrolle Deutschlands," in Josef Foschepoth, ed., *Kalter Krieg und Deutsche Frage: Deutschland in Widerstreit der Mächte 1945–1952*, Veröffentlichungen des Deutschen Historischen Instituts London, vol. 16 (Göttingen, 1985).

---

[5] Directive to Commander in Chief of United States Forces of Occupation Regarding the Military Government of Germany, Apr. 26, 1945, in U.S. Department of State, *Foreign Relations of the United States* (hereafter *FRUS*), 1945, 3:487.

[6] See Melvyn P. Leffler, *The Struggle for Germany and the Origins of the Cold War*, German Historical Institute, Occasional Paper 16 (Washington, D.C., 1996).

[7] See F. Roy Willis, *The French in Germany, 1945–1949* (Stanford, Calif., 1962); and Wolfgang Marienfeld, *Konferenzen über Deutschland: Die alliierte Deutschlandplanung und -politik 1941–49* (Hannover, 1962), esp. 308. See also the chapter by Gunther Mai in this section.

[8] See Alexander Fischer, *Sowjetische Deutschlandpolitik im Zweiten Weltkrieg 1941–1945* (Stuttgart, 1975), 83–119. Apparently Stalin's objective was to create a demilitarized, united Germany that would be friendly to

foreseen this development some time earlier. In a letter to Charles Bohlen, a member of the American delegation in Yalta, he proposed as early as January 1945 that cooperation with the Soviet Union be abandoned and that Europe be divided between the Soviets and the Americans.[12] Kennan's opinions at first received little attention in Washington. Secretary of State James F. Byrnes was particularly hesitant to embark on a collision course with the Soviet Union. Speaking to his French colleague, Georges Bidault, before the start of the Paris foreign ministers conference in May 1946, Byrnes claimed that he "had been subjected to considerable criticism for 'appeasing' Russia and yielding too much." This period, however, had passed.[13]

Byrnes then announced, in a policy speech in Stuttgart on September 6, 1946, the economic merging of the American and British zones into "Bizonia" as of January 1, 1947. He advocated the speedy formation of a provisional German government in order to create the necessary national prerequisites for economic stabilization.[14] As the Western Powers began implementing their plans to establish a West German state, however, the Soviet Union attempted to prevent this, first by withdrawing their representatives from the Allied Control Council and the Allied military headquarters on March 20, 1948, and ultimately by instituting a blockade of the land and water routes to West Berlin at the end of June and beginning of July 1948.[15] Moscow apparently still adhered to Four Power control in Germany while not yet giving up the hope of ultimately exerting its own control over all of Germany. At the same time, however, a "People's Congress movement," instigated by the SED in December 1947, introduced steps for the formation of an East German state.

Nevertheless, the blockade of Berlin only increased solidarity in the West and above all increased American willingness to become involved in Germany. In addition, the supplying of Berlin through the airlift initiated by General Lucius D. Clay was so successful that the Soviet Union finally had to lift the restrictions in May 1949. Moscow was forced to submit to this show of resolution by the West, especially to the power that the United States had increasingly exercised in the European arena since 1946.[16]

THE INTEGRATION OF THE SUCCESSOR STATES

For Konrad Adenauer, the first chancellor of the Federal Republic of Germany, the division of Germany was no longer an imminent danger in April 1948 but already a fact. It was caused by the East, he declared in the *Kölnische Rundschau*, and must now be rectified through the reestablishment of German unity by the West.[17] In his view, the measures that had been taken were not Western decisions against reunification but inevitable consequences of the development of Soviet policy, which had as its goal the control of Eastern and Central Europe up to the borders defined by the advance of the Red Army. Even before his election as head of government, Adenauer confirmed that in the area of foreign policy, his politics would be "primarily [aimed at] creating a close relationship with neighboring countries in the Western world, particularly the United States."[18] The western portion of

[12] Charles E. Bohlen, *Witness to History, 1929–1969* (New York, 1973), 175. See also George F. Kennan, *Memoirs, 1925–1950* (Boston, 1967), 258.

[13] Memorandum of Conversation by the Director of the Office of European Affairs (Matthews), May 1, 1946, *FRUS, 1946*, 2:204. See also James F. Byrnes, *Speaking Frankly* (New York, 1947), 123–37.

[14] Byrnes thus followed a suggestion that Lucius D. Clay, the U.S. military governor in Germany, had made in Paris, "recognizing fully the political implications of such a merger" (Lucius D. Clay, *Decision in Germany* [Garden City, N.Y., 1950], 78).

[15] For the motives and strategies of Soviet policy in the Cold War, see Caroline Kennedy-Pipe, *Stalin's Cold War: Soviet Strategies in Europe, 1943–1956* (Manchester, 1995).

[16] See Avi Shlaim, *The United States and the Berlin Blockade, 1948–1949: A Study in Crisis Decision-Making* (Berkeley, Calif., 1983), 388.

[17] "Deutsche Einheit vom Westen her," *Kölnische Rundschau*, Apr. 3, 1948.

[18] Adenauer to Helene Wessel, Aug. 27, 1949, in Konrad Adenauer, *Briefe 1949–1951*, ed. Hans Peter Mensing, Adenauer Rhöndorfer Ausgabe, ed. Rudolf Morsey and Hans-Peter Schwarz (Berlin, 1985), 97.

Germany should be solidly integrated into the Western community to be able to strive for reunification from a position of strength. Without a secure connection to the West, reunification would be possible only at the price of the Sovietization of all Germany.

By joining the Organization for European Economic Cooperation (OEEC) on October 31, 1949,[19] and the Council of Europe on July 8, 1950, the Federal Republic of Germany took the first steps toward its institutional incorporation into Western organizations. The Schuman Plan of May 1950, which led to the creation of the European Coal and Steel Community (ECSC) on April 18, 1950, was also hailed by Adenauer as a step toward European integration. When the outbreak of the Korean War in June 1950 stirred Western interest in a military contribution by West Germany within the context of a European Defense Community (EDC), the chancellor exploited this opportunity to improve West Germany's political and military position.[20] Although the EDC failed in the French National Assembly in August 1954, a substitute solution was found in the Paris Treaties of October 1954 and West Germany's entry into NATO in May 1955. These events established West Germany's integration into the West as envisioned by Adenauer. The last step in this direction was the establishment of the European Economic Community (EEC) through the Treaty of Rome on March 25, 1957. With the signing of this treaty, the Federal Republic of Germany finally became a partner of the Western Powers in the reconstruction of Europe.

Adenauer still had problems implementing this policy against significant internal political resistance because it carried a high price: renunciation of reunification in the near future and a deepening of German division. Even against the background of the Cold War, many West German citizens, not least those who had been driven from Germany's former eastern territories, had difficulty giving up the idea of a unified German state.

The situation was no different in East Germany. Proponents of a "bridge function" for Germany between the East and West, such as Jakob Kaiser in the newly founded Ost-CDU (the Christian Democratic Union in the East), called for upholding the commitment to reunification as much as did proponents of a communist regime for all of Germany. Even Stalin's offer of March 10, 1952, to reunify Germany and simultaneously make it neutral was genuine in this context – even though it was also intended to drive Adenauer out of power and create a people's front government, with the ultimate aim of a reunified Germany friendly to the Soviet Union.[21] Beginning as early as summer 1945, the Soviet occupation zone and later the GDR were closely interwoven with Soviet power structures.[22] This also meant from the Eastern side that the division of Germany intensified in relation to the unfolding of the Cold War after 1946. The incorporation of East Germany into the Soviet empire was already a fact in 1945 and could no longer be seriously doubted after the founding of the GDR in 1949.[23]

In contrast to West Germany, where integration into the West was carried out with the approval of a majority of the population (aside from many opponents of the Adenauer policy, who saw in this a deepening of German division), people in the East felt that developments there were a political catastrophe. Valentin Falin, one of the Kremlin's leading experts on

---

[19] See the chapter by Werner Bührer, vol. 1, Economics.

[20] See the chapter by David Clay Large, vol. 1, Security.

[21] See Gerhard Wettig, "Die Deutschland-Note vom 10. März 1952 auf der Basis der diplomatischen Akten des russischen Aussenministeriums," *Deutschland Archiv* 26 (1993): 786–805, as well as the controversy between Wettig and Wilfried Loth in *Deutschland Archiv* 28 (1995): 290–8, 743–50. See also Hannes Adomeit, *Imperial Overstretch. Germany in Soviet Policy from Stalin to Gorbachev: An Analysis Based on New Archival Evidence, Memoirs, and Interviews*, Internationale Politik und Sicherheit, vol. 48 (Baden-Baden, 1998).

[22] See Erich W. Gniffke, *Jahre mit Ulbricht* (Cologne, 1966), 93–171.

[23] See above all Mary Fulbrook, *The Divided Nation: A History of Germany, 1918–1990* (Oxford, 1992); Christoph Klessmann, *Die doppelte Staatsgründung: Deutsche Geschichte 1945–1955* (Göttingen, 1982). For the problems involved in this approach, see Mary Fulbrook, *The Two Germanies, 1945–1990: Problems of Interpretation* (London, 1992).

Germany, commented on this after the fall of the GDR in a conversation with Markus Wolf, the former head of East German foreign espionage: "The number of those who supported the regime in the GDR was never higher than 30 percent, and usually lower. As a result, the question arose at some point as to whether we should dissolve the GDR or else institute measures at the border with West Germany to prevent people from leaving the country."[24]

EASING TENSIONS

The complete sealing off of the GDR mentioned by Falin began only in 1961 with the building of the Berlin Wall. Following Stalin's death in March 1953, Chancellor Adenauer at first feared that the death of the Soviet dictator would lead to a weakening of the front lines of the Cold War. If the Western Powers considered making a compromise with the Soviet Union within the context of a policy of détente, thought Adenauer, this could easily work to Germany's disadvantage. He commented on this in an interview with Ernst Friedländer in June 1953:

Bismarck spoke of his great nightmare of coalitions against Germany. I also have my nightmare: It's called Potsdam. The danger of a common policy by the big powers that would damage Germany has existed since 1945, and continued to exist even after the founding of West Germany. Thus, the goal of West Germany's foreign policy was to extricate itself from this danger zone. Germany must not fall between the two millstones, because then it would be lost.[25]

Until the end of the 1950s, however, such a danger was minimal. The period of experiments in German policy had been over since the debates about Stalin's notes.[26] Because

reunification could not be achieved under acceptable conditions – that is, on the basis of free all-German elections – the priority now was to consolidate the German position in the West and bring about economic and social reconstruction. As Adenauer explained in a briefing with two British journalists, the time to begin negotiations with the Soviet Union would come only when "in the face of the West's strength, Russia begins to consider its own internal political problems" and thus to turn inward. According to Adenauer, Germany was only one link in the great chain of the global East-West conflict.[27]

Adenauer was, therefore, by no means a "monomaniac for reunification." For him, this goal was bound up with a "bevy of other goals, which included the freedom and security of the Federal Republic and a reunified Germany as well as the securing of peace in Europe and Germany's permanent integration into the Western democracies."[28] For that reason, it was only after West Germany had been accepted into NATO and its integration in the West was no longer in doubt that Adenauer could undertake the 1955 visit to Moscow that led to the initiation of diplomatic relations between the Federal Republic and the Soviet Union and the return of the last German prisoners of war from the USSR.

---

[24] Markus Wolf, *Spionagechef im geheimen Krieg: Erinnerungen* (Munich, 1997), 132–3.

[25] Interview with Ernst Friedlander, June 13, 1953, in Presse- und Informationsamt der Bundesregierung, *Bulletin* 109 (June 13, 1953): 926.

[26] In a 1952 exchange of notes between the Soviet Union and the Western occupation powers, Stalin proposed new negotiations for a peace treaty in which German unification would be coupled with German neutrality and the withdrawal of all foreign troops from

German territory. Adenauer declined to pursue this offer. There has a heated debate among German historians on the sincerity of Stalin's offer and the question of whether the offer was a missed chance for German reunification. On this subject, see Ruud van Dijk, *The 1952 Stalin Note Debate: Myth or Missed Opportunity for German Reunification*, Woodrow Wilson International Center for Scholars, Cold War International History Project, Working Paper 15 (Washington, D.C., 1996) (http://cwihp.si.edu/pdf/Wp14.pdf); Torsten Ripper, "Die Stalin-Note vom 10. März 1952: Die Entwicklung der wissenschaftlichen Debatte," *Zeitgeschichte* 26/2 (1999): 372–96.

[27] Discussion on June 3, 1952 (transcription of June 4, 1952), printed in Konrad Adenauer, *Teegespräche 1950–1954*, Hanns Jürgen Küsters, Adenauer Rhöndorfer Ausgabe, Rudolf Morsey, and Hans-Peter Schwarz, eds. (Berlin, 1984), 301.

[28] Hans-Peter Schwarz, "Die deutschlandpolitischen Vorstellungen Konrad Adenauers 1955–1958," in Hans-Peter Schwarz, ed., *Entspannung und Wiedervereinigung*, Rhöndorfer Gespräche, vol. 2 (Stuttgart, 1979), 15.

A fundamental change in this situation occurred only as a result of Nikita Khrushchev's ultimatum in November 1958, in which the Soviet party chairman and head of state demanded that West Berlin be transformed into a "free city" – that is, that Allied troops be withdrawn. In response, the United States indicated that it might be prepared to retreat from its previous policy of strength in the interest of Soviet-American relations. When John Foster Dulles was then forced to resign as secretary of state in early 1959 for health reasons, Adenauer's "Potsdam complex" was reawakened. His feelings of mistrust increased still more when President Dwight Eisenhower received Khrushchev at Camp David during the Soviet leader's visit to the United States from September 15 to 27, 1959. Agreement between the superpowers at Germany's expense once again appeared possible.[29]

The change finally became clear with the beginning of the Kennedy administration in January 1961. Although the crises in Berlin and Cuba in 1961 and 1962 initially delayed Soviet-American rapprochement, they could not stop it.[30] President John F. Kennedy's resolve to end the arms race in order to avert an imminent nuclear war required a stabilization of the status quo and, thus, the de facto recognition of German division. If the Federal Republic were to oppose this trend toward relaxation of tensions, it would be threatened with international isolation. Adenauer, therefore, turned to France in order to find support from President Charles de Gaulle, who had returned to power in 1958 and who had acted decisively to maintain a Western presence in Berlin following Khrushchev's ultimatum. For his part, de Gaulle wanted the West German chancellor to support his own European policy, which was strongly colored by

anti-American sentiment.[31] The result was the Élysée Treaty of January 22, 1963, which established a new Franco-German relationship and immediately triggered fears in Washington of an independent Franco-German position.[32] Former secretary of state Dean Acheson declared that for him, as one of the "most reliable friends of Germany," the signing of this agreement was "one of the darkest days of the postwar era."[33] Kennedy's undersecretary of state George Ball saw the agreement as part of a Franco-German conspiracy.[34] President Kennedy himself sent word through Ambassador Walter Dowling that the mood among the American public could cause the United States to withdraw from Europe.[35]

These initial reactions were, in fact, highly exaggerated. In reality, the United States had absolutely no intention of sacrificing Germany and Europe.[36] Washington even continued to support, in principle, the German demand for reunification. Nevertheless, the need for a reconciliation with the Soviet Union had pushed the German question toward the bottom of the American policy agenda. As throughout the Cold War, Germany's development now depended upon the overall structure of relationships between the superpowers. But whereas this structure had worked in favor of Adenauer's policy in the 1940s and 1950s, the chancellor

---

[29] See Felix von Eckardt, *Ein unordentliches Leben: Lebenserinnerungen* (Düsseldorf, 1962), 614.

[30] On the Berlin Crisis of 1958–1961, see Hope Harrison, "Ulbricht, Khrushchev, and the Berlin Wall, 1958–1961: New Archival Evidence from Moscow and Berlin," in Gustav Schmidt, ed., *Ost-West-Beziehungen: Konfrontation und Détente 1945–1989* (Bochum, 1993), 2:333–48.

[31] See the essay by Eckart Conze in vol. 2, Politics.

[32] See Wilhelm G. Grewe, *Rückblenden 1976–1951* (Frankfurt am Main, 1979), 463.

[33] Acheson as quoted by Ambassador Karl-Heinrich Knappstein in a telegram to Konrad Adenauer, Jan. 30, 1963, Stiftung-Bundeskanzler-Adenauer-Haus, Rhöndorf (hereafter StBKAH), III/7, Geheim.

[34] George W. Ball, *The Past Has Another Pattern: Memoirs* (New York, 1982), 271.

[35] Conversation between Konrad Adenauer and Walter Dowling, Feb. 4, 1963, StBKAH, III/62, Geheim. See also Horst Osterheld, *"Ich gehe nicht leichten Herzens . . ." Adenauers letzte Kanzlerjahre: Ein dokumentarischer Bericht* (Mainz, 1986), 199–200. For the current status of research, see Hanns Jürgen Küsters, "Adenauers Deutschland- und Nuklearpolitik in der Berlin-Krise 1958–1962," in Guido Müller, ed., *Deutschland und der Westen: Festschrift für Klaus Schwabe* (Stuttgart, 1998), 270–87.

[36] See Pascaline Winand, *Eisenhower, Kennedy, and the United States of Europe* (New York, 1993), 336–40.

now became an irritant in the Soviet-American rapprochement. His resignation in the fall of 1963, occurring almost simultaneously with the assassination of President Kennedy, gave his successors the opportunity for a new orientation in East-West relations. Despite initial relaxation of tensions, they were able to keep the German question open, at least in principle. In the final analysis, the Germans were not to become, as Adenauer feared and as Heinrich Krone noted in his diary at the peak of the controversy surrounding the Nuclear Test-Ban Treaty in 1963, "the victim of American détente policy."[37]

With the building of the Berlin Wall on August 13, 1961, however, the situation within Germany had changed as well. Willy Brandt remarked on this event in his memoirs:

... in August 1961 a curtain was drawn aside to reveal an empty stage. To put it more bluntly, we lost certain illusions that had outlived the hopes underlying them – illusions that clung to something which no longer existed in fact. ... My political thinking in the years that followed was substantially influenced by this day's experience, and it was against this background that my so-called Ostpolitik – the beginning of détente – was formed.[38]

The imminent collapse of the GDR, an eventuality that had motivated Adenauer and Dulles in formulating their "policy of strength," now appeared quite improbable. After August 13, events seemed to indicate that the GDR was undergoing an internal stabilization and would, therefore, endure in the foreseeable future. The building of the Wall was, therefore, the starting point for a new Ostpolitik that could make German division more bearable; overcoming that division was at most a long-term perspective. In a speech on the German question on July 15, 1963, at the Evangelical Academy in Tutzing, Egon Bahr, then press spokesman for West Berlin Mayor Willy Brandt, justified this new strategy:

We have said that the Wall is a symbol of weakness. One could also say that it is a symbol of anxiety and of the communist regime's instinct for self-preservation. The question is whether there exists the possibility of gradually alleviating these entirely justified concerns of the regime to such an extent that a loosening up of the borders and the Wall become more practical because the risk is bearable. This is a policy that one could describe as "change through rapprochement."[39]

During the Vietnam War, which led to a "global political detour" (Richard Löwenthal) between the United States and the Soviet Union and to a delay in détente, no great progress could be made in policy toward Germany. A comprehensive dialogue with the Soviet Union was made possible only by the fundamental change in the East-West climate that occurred after President Richard M. Nixon and his security adviser, Henry Kissinger, assumed office on January 20, 1969. By that time, the Federal Republic was also prepared for such a dialogue. Willy Brandt had served as foreign minister in Bonn during the Grand Coalition of the CDU/CSU and SPD beginning in December 1966; Egon Bahr had assumed leadership of the political planning staff in the Foreign Ministry, where with the support of the ministry he had conceived the details of the new Ostpolitik.[40] The fundamental pattern of world politics had changed, and the freedom of action for German foreign policy increased significantly after 1969. Nevertheless, Germany now inserted itself into the new structure of détente just as it had previously done within the structure of the Cold War.

---

[37] Heinrich Krone, diary entry, Aug. 4–5, 1963, Archiv für Christlich-Demokratische Politik, St. Augustin.

[38] Willy Brandt, *People and Politics: The Years 1960–1975* (Boston, 1978), 20.

[39] For the text, see Vortrag des Leiters des Presse- und Informationsamtes des Landes Berlin, Bahr, in der Evangelischen Akademie Tutzing, in Bundesministerium für innerdeutsche Beziehungen, *Dokumente zur Deutschlandpolitik*, ser. 4, vol. 9 (Frankfurt am Main, 1978), 572–5.

[40] See Egon Bahr, *Zu meiner Zeit* (Munich, 1996), 194–220. See also Andreas Vogtmeier, *Egon Bahr und die deutsche Frage: Zur Entwicklung der sozialdemokratischen Ost- und Deutschlandpolitik vom Kriegsende bis zur Vereinigung* (Bonn, 1996); Peter Bender, *Die "Neue Ostpolitik" und ihre Folgen: Vom Mauerbau bis zur Vereinigung*, 3d rev. and exp. ed. (Munich, 1995), 118–38.

CHAPTER TWELVE

The United States and the German Question, 1949–1968

Frank A. Ninkovich

For the United States, "the German question" between 1949 and 1968 was actually a cluster of interrelated problems. First and foremost, American policymakers worked to integrate the newly created Federal Republic of Germany into a Western European community and, more loosely, into a world community of democratic, market-oriented nations. Economic integration was quickly followed up with an urgent push to include a rearmed Germany into an undermanned Western alliance system. "Double containment," as this intricate multipronged approach has since been called, was designed both to stave off the Soviet threat and to clip the wings of German nationalism. It was, however, more complicated than that. Despite its essentially supranational and international thrust, this policy of integration also sought to make use of nationalist sentiment by dangling the lure of unity before the German people.

Policymakers in Washington played to nationalist feeling even though they approached German questions from a global perspective in which the Soviet Union had assumed Germany's former role as the chief threat to the integrity of an open world system. With global issues uppermost in American minds, reunification was not high on Washington's list of priorities. In contrast, Germans tended to focus more narrowly on local problems, oscillating between a desire to become part of the West and a conflicting urge to see their nation reunified. Although Americans thought this preoccupation

with national identity was neurotic, they also felt they had to address it in some way lest a deeply rooted German nationalism once again unleash the furies of particularism throughout Europe.

The contrast between American and West German views on reunification generated a built-in tension between the United States and West Germany and sowed the seeds for some notable Cold War crises with the Soviet Union. Although American policymakers never considered reunification an urgent matter, they were compelled to pay more than lip service to it in the interest of attaining other, more important foreign policy goals. America's credibility on the reunification issue and on the related problem of Berlin's status was crucial to mollifying the West German people, whose support was essential for the stability of Western Europe. For a time, it was also the key to sustaining America's global position in the Cold War.

In spring 1949, during his first months as President Harry Truman's new secretary of state, Dean Acheson had to decide on the future of the Western occupation zones in Germany. The inclusion of the Western zones in the Marshall Plan and the convocation of a parliamentary council to draft a constitution for a new West German state had already generated powerful institutional momentum. George Kennan, the influential chief of the State Department Policy Planning Staff, believed that the integration of the Western zones into Western Europe – besides setting the stage for a revival of German nationalism – would harden the lines of division in Europe and make a negotiated end to the Cold War impossible. A more stable long-term solution, Kennan thought, would emerge from a mutual disengagement of Soviet and American power from Europe, which would create the political space for a united Germany within a European federation.

After hearing Kennan out, Acheson decided that "there would be fewer and less painful difficulties by going ahead with the West German government than by attempting to unite Germany first."[1] Striking out on Kennan's proposed course seemed risky, whereas the Western option, despite its problems, could be more readily controlled and was more likely to produce economic success. Opinion in Europe favored this course, too, as the overwhelmingly hostile reaction to a leaked version of Kennan's proposals indicated. Thus, by year's end, the Federal Republic of Germany had been founded and the Soviet zone had been similarly transformed into the German Democratic Republic (GDR).

The problem of integration became more complex in 1950 when, following the outbreak of the Korean War, American policymakers determined that Europe's defenses needed to be strengthened. The recently created NATO alliance was at that time a political deterrent only, and the Korean conflict had shown how words could be misinterpreted. The only way of markedly upgrading European security was to rearm Germany, an idea only recently taboo. Only German manpower could add the needed deterrent force, and only the Federal Republic's territory could provide a defense in depth. Although Truman was unenthusiastic about this departure, it is testimony to the fear evoked by Korea that the United States decided to take this controversial step.

The prospect of German rearmament also created a stir among America's European allies and, quite disturbingly, upset the West Germans themselves. The question of German reunification, which heretofore had been lurking in the background, now became more urgent. This is not to say that reunification emerged on the horizon of political possibility. For all the talk of reunification and the many proposals floated afterward, it is likely that by this time the political point of no return had already been passed. Acheson was already confiding to a Senate committee that "at the present time there is a line drawn across Europe which, so far as we can see, looks as though it were permanent."[2]

Naturally, this hardening of partition distressed many within the newly created Federal Republic. Reunification was a basic goal of the new West German state and was enshrined in the preamble to its "Basic Law" (*Grundgesetz*), which called for "the unity and freedom of Germany." The Basic Law was itself supposed to be only temporary, for it anticipated that a permanent constitution (*Verfassung*) would be adopted at the time of reunification. The party politics of the new state amplified these concerns and gave them the status of doctrine. The Social Democrats (*Sozialdemokratische Partei Deutschlands*, or SPD), the opposition party in what was then a nearly evenly divided electorate, made reunification a basic plank of their party platform. Under the formidable leadership of Kurt Schumacher, the SPD was determined to avoid Western integration, all the better to steer a neutralist course in the Cold War which, it believed, would expedite the achievement of German unity. Apart from trading in reunification sentiment, the SPD took advantage of an understandable reluctance on the part of many Germans, given the recent military disaster under Hitler, to put on uniforms once again.

The reluctance of ordinary Germans to march in step with the West pointed to yet another dimension of the German problem in the Cold War: German nationalism. The problem

---

[1] Acheson to Truman, May 18, 1949, PSF-NSC Meetings, Summaries, box 220, Truman Library, Independence, Mo.

[2] Acheson testimony of Jan. 10, 1950, in Senate Committee on Foreign Relations, *Reviews of the World Situation: 1949–1950: Hearings Held in Executive Session Before the Committee on Foreign Relations*, 81st Cong., 2d sess., Historical Series (Washington, D.C., 1974), 114.

of German national character, Acheson recalled, "was central to everything that everyone was talking about, but nobody could speak about it."[3] Neutrality, with its emphasis on "unification first," was symptomatic of the "lone wolf" or outcast mentality that had come to be symbolized by the notorious 1922 German-Soviet Treaty of Rapallo. No one was suggesting, at least openly, that the Germans were bent on resuming an adventurist course. But a neutralist nationalism – pacifistic for the moment, to be sure – evoked the dangerous possibility of a Germany swinging between East and West. By auctioning its services to the highest bidder, such a Germany would make the institutionalization of the Cold War impossible.

During World War II, American opinion had been torn between the hope of integrating Germany into the world community and the desire to pursue a punitive policy of "control." Postwar policy depended on successfully blending these two elements, minus the Morgenthauist connotation. An additional advantage of integration was the positive broadening effect that membership in a larger European community would have on the German national character: Germans could gradually be transformed into good Europeans. Neutralism would have jeopardized all these objectives.

The solution to the many dimensions of the German problem took on a personal aspect in the figure of Konrad Adenauer, the Christian Democratic chancellor of the new Federal Republic. It is fashionable among historians nowadays to downgrade the "great man" theory of history, yet Adenauer provides an example of how a single individual could have an extraordinary impact on the outcome of the Cold War. He was a believer in a Europe whose greatness was supranational. He was also a pronounced anticommunist and Cold Warrior who had foreseen the East-West conflict earlier than most Americans. He gravitated naturally to the solution reached in 1949 and 1950. In the absence of

a pro-Western consensus in the Federal Republic, Adenauer was able to steer it into Western Europe and into the Western alliance while appeasing nationalist sentiment among his countrymen. American policymakers fully realized that having Adenauer on their side was "a remarkable stroke of luck in history."[4]

A masterful politician, Adenauer knew he would have to appeal to the widespread desire for unification. He adopted the slogan of "reunification through strength," which argued that the creation of an economically prosperous and militarily powerful Western Europe, made possible in large measure by the Federal Republic's membership, was the best way of ending the division of Germany and of Europe. This argument paralleled the American "magnet theory" for ending the Cold War. For example, an important 1953 document insisted that a united Western Europe would "exert a strong and increasing attraction on Eastern Europe, thus weakening the Soviet position there and accelerating Soviet withdrawal from that area."[5]

For many, this argument reeked of cynicism and condescension. It did not require great political insight for skeptics to realize that the more the Federal Republic leaned toward the West, the more tenaciously the Soviets were likely to hang onto East Germany. That was the logic of realism. But it would be unfair to judge Adenauer from a realist standpoint. After all, his outlook paralleled the long-range historical framework from which Americans approached the Cold War. Adenauer's approach also had an enormous short-term political advantage. The occupation was not yet over, but had been merely "civilized" by substituting civilian high commissioners for the military governors. Adenauer realized that his indispensability to the West would allow him quickly to secure a status of relative equality for the Federal Republic within the alliance. Thus, in

---

[3] Princeton Seminar transcripts, Oct. 10–11, 1953, Acheson papers, box 79, Truman Library.

[4] Henry Byroade oral history, Truman Library, 74–5.
[5] NSC 160/1, United States Position with Respect to Germany, Aug. 17, 1953, NSC Series, Policy Papers Subseries, Eisenhower Papers, Eisenhower Presidential Library, Abilene, Kans.

return for membership in the common army of the European Defense Community (EDC), Adenauer adroitly negotiated a new set of contractual agreements to replace the occupation statute.

The EDC project crashed in August 1954 when the French National Assembly voted against ratification. However, the United States quickly shifted its efforts to gaining admission for the Federal Republic into NATO. The French were in no position to resist, even though NATO membership entailed the creation of a discrete German army. "We could get along without France but not without Germany," said President Dwight D. Eisenhower.[6] The supranational controls exercised by the West European Union, the assurance of watchful American leadership, and the absence of any need to submerge French sovereignty in the new arrangement contributed to this turnabout.

With German membership in NATO bringing an end to the occupation and conferring equal status on the Federal Republic, "double containment" was finally in place. However, as part of the bargain, reunification was made a regular topic of discussion on the superpower diplomatic agenda. What realistic chances of success these East-West exchanges may have had is another matter. The Western formula for German reunification called first of all for free elections in East Germany, a proposal Western policymakers knew that Moscow could not possibly accept. For their part, the Soviets envisioned a merger of the two Germanies in which Eastern institutions, by being melded into a new whole, would be in a position to exert substantial influence in the reunified state.

The Western Powers had already used free elections to derail a 1952 reunification proposal put forward by Stalin in the hope of forestalling the Federal Republic's membership in the EDC. Elections were a useful ploy because the Soviet proposal was so "shrewdly drafted" that

Acheson believed the United States "would be ill-advised in the circumstances to turn it down out of hand."[7] Historians have long bewailed this "lost chance" for reunification, but this presupposes doing what was, at the time, impossible: changing the American view of Germany and of the Cold War as a whole. Acheson was dead set against it from the moment it was proposed, viewing it as a transparent attempt to sow discord in the Western alliance, which it most definitely was.

In addition, the Americans insisted that a united Germany should be free to join NATO if it wished to do so. NATO was a defensive alliance, they argued, whose control mechanisms made it impossible for Germany to break away. Continued division, they suggested, was more likely to stimulate aggressive nationalism. But this line of argument was wholly unacceptable to the Soviets, who were willing to entertain German unity only if NATO were *dissolved*. With the GDR's entry into the Warsaw Pact in May 1955 and the USSR's diplomatic recognition of the Federal Republic later in the year, the postwar issue was settled: There were two Germanies as far as Moscow was concerned. Thereafter, a negotiated unification, always a long shot under Cold War conditions, became virtually impossible.

From the mid-1950s onward, the cluster of problems associated with Germany entered a new phase. With respect to economic and military integration, the issue shifted from ends to deciding the best means of achieving them. Economically, integration developed an unstoppable momentum with the creation of the European Economic Community in 1958. The German economic miracle exceeded the wildest expectations of policymakers as the Federal Republic played a major role in pulling the rest of

---

[6] Quoted in John Foster Dulles, memorandum of conversation with Eisenhower, Dec. 14, 1954, John Foster Dulles papers, White House Memoranda series, box 1, Princeton University.

[7] Acheson to Truman, Mar. 11, 1952, PSF: Subject: Cabinet, box 159, Truman Library. The 1952 note has generated much debate within Germany about a "lost chance" for reunification. For a recent example of the extended scholarly argument, see Rolf Steininger, *The German Question: The Stalin Note of 1952 and the Problem of Reunification*, trans. Jane T. Hedges (New York, 1990).

Western Europe into a historically unparalleled period of sustained prosperity.

Militarily, the story was less encouraging. Like many of its allies, the Federal Republic failed to meet the force projections of the Lisbon Program of 1952. With conventional forces unable to provide a sufficiently credible deterrent, NATO adopted a nuclear strategy. This added new complexities to the relationship. Being on the nuclear frontlines exacerbated popular fears within the Federal Republic that the country would become a potential nuclear battleground in an atomic war while other countries survived relatively unscathed. In addition, the emergence of a nuclear stalemate in the 1950s gave an increasingly hollow ring to the slogan of "reunification through strength."[8]

As the 1950s drew to a close, the relationship between reunification and global Cold War issues took a dramatic turn. Ironically, reunification alone was of little interest to the United States. American policymakers, like many Europeans, were not wholly displeased by the de facto partition that emerged in the aftermath of World War II. Nevertheless, this view could not be expressed publicly for fear of upsetting the Germans and subverting an American Cold War strategy based on world public opinion. The fidelity of the Federal Republic was central not only to the continued existence of NATO, the linchpin of American policy in Europe but also to the effectiveness of Cold War policy as a whole. Disappointing the Germans would raise the question of general credibility.

This global aspect of the German problem became most evident in the Berlin Crisis, which ran from 1958 through at least 1961. With the two-Germanies solution all but irreversible, the status of Berlin as an occupied city became more and more anomalous. As a convenient escape hatch for refugees from the German Democratic Republic, a divided Berlin hindered the establishment of a stable socialist regime in the East. In fall 1958, in response to GDR leader Walter Ulbricht's nagging, and

perhaps to express displeasure over the Federal Republic's desire for nuclear weapons, Soviet leader Nikita Khrushchev announced his intention to end once and for all Berlin's abnormal status. If some satisfactory agreement were not reached, Khrushchev proposed to sign a peace treaty with the GDR. With that, the occupation would end, Berlin would become the property of the East German communist regime, and the Western Powers would be forced to depart.

Khrushchev's initiative caused nightmares in Washington. The Soviets could not be allowed to have their way on Berlin, Washington believed, because the demoralizing effect on the Germans and on Europe as a whole would eviscerate NATO. A communist takeover or neutralization of Berlin, the symbolic capital of Germany, would quash reunification hopes and take away the incentive for Germans to remain faithful to the alliance. Globally, by backing down in Berlin the United States would give a green light to the communists to chip away with impunity at the free world's defenses. Fully conversant with the reigning creed, the West German foreign minister threw Cold War dogma into the faces of the Americans in the hope of stiffening their spines. "Any concessions to the GDR ... will start an avalanche which nothing can stop and which will have catastrophic consequences," he warned.[9]

Publicly, the Western Powers in Berlin proclaimed their refusal to be evicted. They insisted on maintaining their occupation rights as victors, pending the conclusion of a peace treaty for Germany as a whole. But behind the bold public stance, Washington had nagging doubts about the prudence of such a hard line. In traditional strategic terms, Berlin itself was of little importance; indeed, it was a military liability. Moreover, there was something definitely odd about basing American global policy on an atavistic German nationalism that had to be constantly propitiated. If the Germans were indeed good citizens of the West, presumably there would be

---

[8] On NATO strategy as a part of the German-American relationship, see the chapter by Kori Schake, vol. 1, Security.

[9] Briefing on the Status of Berlin, Nov. 25, 1958, Eisenhower Papers, White House Office, Office of the Staff Secretary, International Series, box 6, Eisenhower Presidential Library.

no need for the United States to make these kinds of sacrifices to the archaic god of nationalism.

Furthermore, in an era of nuclear parity, it was doubtful whether this issue merited the risk of nuclear annihilation; indeed, it was increasingly questionable whether *any* issue merited such a risk. American strategic thinking was already beginning to take a significant turn toward downgrading nuclear weapons in favor of conventional military options. However, according to the logic of this policy of "flexible response," soon to be adopted by the Kennedy administration in place of the outdated "massive retaliation" of the Eisenhower years, it made little sense to take a stand in a place like Berlin, where the conventional military deck was stacked against the United States.

The crisis was an on-again, off-again affair, with Khrushchev setting and withdrawing deadlines as well as heightening and deflating tensions to suit his convenience. Finally, in summer 1961, the issue came to a head. Following the contentious Vienna summit meeting with Kennedy in June, the Soviet leader decided to act. In a surprise maneuver, the East Germans began erecting a wall around the Western sectors of Berlin. Although this fait accompli effectively achieved Khrushchev's minimum ends by closing the escape hatch for refugees, Moscow continued to pressure the West in Berlin. Washington viewed the episode as a foreign policy victory for Khrushchev. The global denouement to the Berlin affair occurred in the Cuban Missile Crisis of October 1962. Following that confrontation, there was a visible relaxation of tension between the two superpowers on all matters that might lead to another showdown.

In the wake of Berlin and Cuba, perceptions and positions within the United States and Germany evolved in the direction of greater honesty. Increasingly, the American government made known its preference for the two-Germanies status quo. One of the ironies of the situation is that Kennedy, who was accorded a hero's welcome during a 1963 visit for his stirring rhetorical defense of Berlin, was simultaneously suggesting that the Germans had better get used to the idea of division as a fact of life for the foreseeable future.[10] Following Kennedy's death in November 1963, President Lyndon Johnson went even farther down that road. In 1966, he made clear that a restored Germany could "only be accomplished through a growing reconciliation. There is no shortcut."[11]

Such a volte-face could not have occurred without a corresponding change of opinion within the Federal Republic. The Berlin Crisis may have exploded Adenauer's doctrine of reunification through strength, but it also exposed the hollowness of the Social Democratic vision of a neutral and demilitarized Germany living placidly between the two superpowers. Ultimately, it was the Social Democrats' recognition that their policies were barren that made a change possible. Harbingers had come as early as 1959, when the SPD dropped Marxism as its official philosophy. The Berlin Crisis generated a similar transformation of the party's foreign policy outlook.

The mayor of West Berlin during the crisis was Willy Brandt, who took away from the affair the realization that the United States, far from being devoted to German concerns, was committed to a larger global agenda in which reunification was put on the shelf. It was not long before Brandt was calling reunification "at present and for an immeasurable time to come, a hopeless issue."[12] In 1962, the SPD abandoned its outworn advocacy of neutrality as a solution to reunification. The new outlook was fully articulated in 1963 and formalized under the slogan of "change through rapprochement." By the mid-1960s, the SPD was the party urging acceptance of the two-Germanies status quo. That did not mean abandoning the goal of unity, but it did mean accepting a new timetable of history and a new strategy for keeping the political possibility of reunification alive for when the historic moment did come.

[10] See the chapter by David Posner, vol. 1, Society.

[11] James MacGregor Burns, ed., *To Heal and to Build* (New York, 1968), 142.

[12] Quoted in Wolfram Hanrieder, *West German Foreign Policy, 1949–1963* (Stanford, Calif., 1967), 226.

The Christian Democrats, meanwhile, in the aftermath of Adenauer's retirement in 1963, continued to adhere to their old formulas. Adenauer, formerly an indispensable figure, was now perceived by Kennedy as an obstacle to desirable change. This forsaking of the grand old man was not a matter of personalities or differences attributable to age; American policy tolerated the crankiest and most bizarre leaders when it had to. Rather, Adenauer's declining stature in the eyes of Americans was the consequence of the perceived need for changes in the Federal Republic's self-deceiving and dangerous insistence on unification.

Residual issues related to European integration continued to rile the Alliance throughout the 1960s. Most important was the smoldering question of nuclear weaponry, a problem that reemerged thanks to French president Charles de Gaulle's announced intention to create an independent nuclear deterrent, or *force de frappe*. That announcement, combined with the surprising signature of a Franco-German treaty between Adenauer and de Gaulle in early 1963, led to fears that the Federal Republic would soon start down the path of nuclear independence. That obviously would have been disastrous for NATO, but it also would have short-circuited a growing understanding between the United States and the Soviet Union on the need to close the door to nuclear proliferation. In an attempt to keep the genie of nuclear nationalism within the bottle, the Kennedy administration proposed a scheme for nuclear sharing known as the multilateral force. But this died of neglect a few years later.[13]

By the end of the 1960s, the German problem in its main dimensions had been normalized. Many of the disputes between the United States and the Federal Republic, like the issue of offset payments to cover the cost of keeping American troops in Germany,[14] were in retrospect nuts-and-bolts matters of alliance management and not fundamental disagreements. There would be some tension in the late 1960s and early 1970s as Brandt implemented his Ostpolitik[15] but that, too, despite some hand-wringing by Henry Kissinger in Washington, involved no basic difference of perspective. In all, the stage was set for policies that would successfully end the Cold War.

Over the course of twenty years, the mixture of elements that formed the German problem became much more stable. As in the process of vitrification that transforms hazardous nuclear materials into glass, the problem had been rendered inert. The Federal Republic was successfully integrated, economically and militarily, into Western Europe. The crises centering on credibility and reunification were surmounted. Germans displayed a readiness to accept the reality of division, and Americans, at least in Europe, became less obsessed with asserting their credibility.

The problem of nationalism as part of the German national character or culture seemed also to have lost its urgency as the Federal Republic entered a period in which the tension between being a good German and being a good European dissolved. Of course, the speed of this cultural transformation raises the question of whether there was, in fact, a cultural problem to begin with. Those who remained unconvinced would continue to wonder about flaws in the German national character, although to less and less effect. However deep the change, there is little question that West Germans felt increasingly comfortable, ideologically and culturally, in their new Western home.

---

[13] See the chapters by Erhard Forndran and Kori Schake, vol. 1, Security.

[14] See the chapter by Hubert Zimmermann, vol. 1, Economics.

[15] See the chapters by Christian Hacke and Werner Link, vol. 1, Politics.

CHAPTER THIRTEEN

Divided Loyalties in Transatlantic Policy Toward Europe

Manfred Knapp

Translated by Andrew Long

Manfred Knapp

Translated by Andrew Long

THE UNITED STATES, EUROPE, AND
GERMANY: THE FUNDAMENTAL
LINK BETWEEN EUROPEAN AND
GERMAN POLICY

Between the end of World War II and the end of the 1960s (and even later), both the United States and the Federal Republic of Germany perceived their respective European and German policies as intimately connected. Finding a solution to the German question was a central issue in America's policy toward Europe, a problem that, in the American view, should be resolved by the creation of a close (West) European association of nations. For West Germany, the notion of Europe represented both a central guiding concept and an ideal for a new frame of reference in its foreign policy. It promised speedy economic recovery, political rehabilitation, and a means to overcome foreign policy isolation by voluntary integration into the Western world just beyond the Federal Republic's borders. In both Bonn and Washington, the link between European policy and *Deutschlandpolitik* (policy toward the future of Germany as a whole) underwent significant changes that would frequently become a source of irritations and problems in the German–American relationship.[1]

It is remarkable that neither the United States nor the Federal Republic had any clearer notion about the likely form or institutional structure of an "integrated" or "unified" Europe. When addressing this issue, Washington politicians would talk of how the United States should serve as a model and an example for Europe. America generally welcomed moves toward European unity, provided that those moves accepted the need for continued American leadership in Europe. For the Federal Republic, official ideas about Europe were mostly associated with notions of creating a federal, supranational community of nations, even if by no means all German foreign policy experts had completely renounced their faith in the organizing principles of the nation-state. These often subliminal uncertainties about the respective policies being pursued toward Europe felt on both sides of the Atlantic sometimes seriously impeded mutual

---

[1] The following works offer useful introductions to this subject: Wolfram F. Hanrieder, ed., *The United States and Western Europe: Political, Economic, and Strategic Perspectives* (Cambridge, Mass., 1974); Pierre Melandri, *Les États-Unis face à l'unification de l'Europe 1945–1954* (Paris, 1980); Erhard Forndran, *Die Vereinigten Staaten von Amerika und Europa: Erfahrungen und Perspektiven transatlantischer Beziehungen seit dem Ersten Weltkrieg* (Baden-Baden, 1991); Geir Lundestad, *"Empire" by Integration: The United States and European Integration, 1945–1997* (Oxford, 1998); Manfred Knapp et al., *Die USA und Deutschland 1918–1975: Deutsch-amerikanische Beziehungen zwischen Rivalität und Partnerschaft* (Munich, 1978); Wolfram F. Hanrieder, *Germany, America, Europe: Forty Years of German Foreign Policy* (New Haven, Conn., 1989); Klaus Larres and Torsten Oppelland, eds., *Deutschland und die USA im 20. Jahrhundert: Geschichte der politischen Beziehungen* (Darmstadt, 1997).

endeavors to construct a postwar European order.

After the United States had emerged from World War II as the most powerful of the allied nations, the Truman administration (1945–53) was determined to play the role of leading power in postwar Europe. American foreign policy sought to establish conditions in Europe that would allow for the creation and development of a global economic and trade regime founded on liberal and multilateral principles and under American leadership. Further, after the defeat of Nazi Germany, there could be no question of allowing any European power (whether an old and now recovered power or a new one) to dominate a postwar European order.

The increasingly evident political and ideological conflict with the Soviet Union meant that the original design for America's European policy had to be amended shortly after the end of the war. However, the foreign policy decision makers of the Truman administration saw an indissoluble link between policy toward Germany and toward Europe. The desired economic recovery and return to political stability in Europe could be achieved only by means of a virtually parallel economic and political recovery in Germany.

The increasingly clear linkage between the Truman administration's policies toward Germany and Europe during the immediate postwar years initially became less of a problem for German-American relations and much more a point of contention in America's relations with some of Germany's western neighbors. The American administration needed to put a great deal of persuasion and effort into making it clear that the desired return to stability in Europe presupposed both the controlled harnessing of Germany's available industrial and economic potential and a functioning German state. From 1947 onward, American occupation policy in Germany was first and foremost a policy of integration.[2] The most significant instrument linking U.S. policy on Germany and Europe in the immediate postwar era was the Marshall Plan, in which Western Germany was included from the start.[3]

America's strategy of integration, which began with the Marshall Plan, made the German question a European question. As the East-West conflict intensified, this strategy was further consolidated by the gradual integration of the Federal Republic into the West on the basis of military and political alliances. After the failure of the European Defense Community (EDC), the Federal Republic was finally accepted directly into NATO in 1955.[4] In the early 1950s, the United States had welcomed the fact that France – with the Schuman Plan of May 1950 and the founding of the European Coal and Steel Community (ECSC) in cooperation with the Federal Republic, Italy, and the Benelux countries – had actively adopted the integrationist course set by Washington.

With the further development of the West European integration process, which received strong initial support from the United States, a problem that had already been apparent in the early 1950s became a persistent factor in German-American (and European-American) relations. For the Federal Republic, cooperation in security policy was organized under the auspices of NATO – a transatlantic grouping – while cooperation in economic policy was conducted primarily within the framework of the three West European integration communities: the ECSC, the European Economic Community (EEC), and the European Atomic Energy Community (Euratom). Because of this dichotomy in the structure of the two countries' security and economic relations, tensions, and differences of interest began to emerge in the German-American relationship after the early 1960s.

die Deutsche Frage 1945–1990 (Frankfurt am Main, 1991), 105–28. See also Lundestad, *"Empire" by Integration*.

[3] See the chapters by Gerd Hardach, vol. 1, Economics, and Michael Wala, vol. 1, Politics.

[4] See the chapter by Frank Schumacher, vol. 1, Politics.

[2] Klaus Schwabe, "Deutschlandpolitik als Integrationspolitik: Die USA und die Deutsche Frage 1945–1954," in Wolfgang-Uwe Friedrich, ed., *Die USA und*

The United States repeatedly tried to use its close relationship with the Federal Republic to influence both the West European integration process and the policies of the European Community (EC). Ever since the founding of the Federal Republic, Washington had seen the West German state as a dependent partner that would also allow itself to be used as an operational basis not only for America's all-important European policy but also for its global economic goals.

The situation that had prevailed until the mid-1950s was an exceptional one, defined by the East-West conflict, Germany's lingering economic weakness, and the occupation regime that remained in force until May 1955. Thereafter, however, the Federal Republic developed into a more independent foreign policy player. The differences that had been an occasional feature of German-American relations since the mid-1950s could no longer be so easily overcome. Bonn found it increasingly difficult to live with the contradiction between the demands of transatlantic security policy and the loyalty its West European integration partners expected.

THE PERIOD OF MILITARY OCCUPATION (1945–1949)

As the chief victor and occupying power in postwar Germany, the United States was from the start faced with the task of striking a balance between its policy of occupation and its general policies toward Europe. After a contradictory and indecisive experimental phase within the framework of the Four Power administration agreed upon at the Potsdam Conference,[5] Washington policymakers became convinced, in 1947, that America's policies toward Germany and Europe should be linked in a constructive manner. The integration of West Germany into the matrix of West European industrial nations had two goals: first, to control Germany, and second, to be able to harness its potential to help bring about the economic recovery of

Europe. Only with such an integration strategy for Western Europe, the Truman administration believed, could the United States realize its goals of economic and political stability within the context of a European postwar order. This combined American strategy toward Germany and Europe gained momentum from the intensification of both the East-West conflict and the political power struggle with the Soviet Union.

The basic concept of the Marshall Plan, which was developed in 1947–8, corresponded precisely with America's integrationist strategy toward Western Europe.[6] This strategy saw the association of states promoted by the European Economic Recovery Program – which for the time being loosely formed the Organization for European Economic Cooperation (OEEC) – as a crucial factor in European economic and political stability and as the basis for the Western alliance now emerging as part of the East-West conflict.

The tenets of these closely interwoven American strategies toward Germany and Europe were established as early as mid-1948, as a key State Department document shows:

The fundamental objective of the United States with respect to Germany is to insure that Germany does not again menace the peace of the world and makes a vital contribution to the economic rehabilitation and political security of Europe.... No ideal solution embracing the whole of Germany is at present possible. German policy is of necessity influenced by overriding policy with respect to western Europe. Such policy dictates that Germany must not be drawn into the Soviet orbit or reconstructed as a political instrument of Soviet policy. It requires that Germany be brought into close association with the democratic states of western Europe and that it be enabled to contribute to and participate in European economic recovery.[7]

An American strategy toward Europe that included West Germany was, of course, bound to find great favor with the architects of Germany's

---

[5] See the chapters by Edmund Spevack and Gunther Mai, vol. 1, Politics.

[6] Compare in this context the chapters by Gerd Hardach, vol. 1, Economics, and Michael Wala, vol. 1, Politics.

[7] Department of State Policy Statement, Aug. 26, 1948, in U.S. Department of State, *Foreign Relations of the United States, 1948*, 2:1297, 1317.

early postwar policy. West German politicians were quick to see the opportunities offered by Washington's policy of integration, which not only gave West Germany the chance for rapid economic recovery but also cleared the way for the country to rejoin the community of nations. As the Cold War intensified, turning toward Europe for support represented, for the western part of postwar Germany, both an element of security in its new beginning and a newly won identity – even if Europe itself was divided.

West Germany derived support from the European strategy Washington advocated so forcefully, and even in the earliest days of the Federal Republic there was considerable similarity between it and the European ideas cultivated by the West Germans. When Konrad Adenauer became chancellor in fall 1949, the basic consensus on European policy between the United States and West Germany was, within the context of the predominant East-West conflict, a factor upon which he could immediately start building his policy of integration with the West. The considerable convergence between Washington and Bonn's European policies was an important foundation for the emerging German-American relationship.

THE 1950S

The broad complementarity between American and German policies toward Europe in the early years of the Federal Republic continued throughout the first half of the 1950s. The Americans supported Western Europe's integration process enthusiastically and welcomed the founding of the ECSC, which the Adenauer government (1949–63) also perceived as the start of an equal partnership within the framework of a supranational unification of Western Europe. In June 1950, after the outbreak of the Korean War, leaders of joint Western institutions were called upon to consider the rearming of West Germany. France opposed the September 1950 proposal of then Secretary of State Dean Acheson that a West German defense contribution be set up within the framework of the

North Atlantic alliance, and countered with its Pleven Plan for the creation of a supranational European Defense Community (EDC). Both the Truman administration and its successor, the Eisenhower administration (1953–61), were prepared to accept the EDC as a way of strengthening the West's Cold War position and securing the military and political participation of the Federal Republic.[8]

Washington and Bonn's European policy goals still appeared to be very much in harmony when, after the failure of the EDC in 1954, the six partners in the European integration process attempted to extend their cooperation to the sphere of economics by setting up a common market. After their strenuous efforts to influence the EDC ratification process had failed, the Eisenhower administration – Secretary of State John Foster Dulles in particular – officially maintained a more reserved position during the signing of the Treaty of Rome (March 1957), which established the EEC and Euratom.[9]

The United States essentially supported the continued European integration engendered by the founding of the two European communities. The deepening of the West European integration process seemed to offer good prospects for renewed strengthening of the Western camp. If successful, this process could create a new European entity, or "third force," that could reduce the global political burden of the United States and whose anti-Soviet, Western orientation was beyond doubt.[10]

The United States believed that the continued European integration process offered its new West German ally in particular a basis on which to build a forward-looking foreign policy and foster a new identity. The 1955 Geneva

---

[8] See the chapter by David Clay Large, vol. 1, Security, as well as Thomas U. Schöttli, *USA und EVG: Truman, Eisenhower und die Europa-Armee* (Bern, 1994).

[9] Brian R. Duchin, "The 'Agonizing Reappraisal': Eisenhower, Dulles, and the European Defense Community," *Diplomatic History* 16 (1992): 201–21. See also Pascaline Winand, *Eisenhower, Kennedy, and the United States of Europe* (New York, 1993).

[10] Detlef Felken, *Dulles und Deutschland: Die amerikanische Deutschlandpolitik 1953–1959* (Bonn, 1993): 404–8.

conferences (i.e., summit conference and council of foreign ministers conference) had demonstrated that the Western concept of German reunification was out of the question for the foreseeable future. Washington, therefore, thought it all the more important that the Federal Republic be tied still closer to the West; the structures of West European integration could serve this end. On the other hand, the Adenauer government was keenly interested in the expansion of the functions and institutions of the West European community, for it continued to see Western integration – which showed clear promise of success – as the basic concept of its entire foreign policy and of its policy toward the future of Germany as a whole.

Until the mid-1950s, German-American relations were not unduly troubled by the two countries' respective European policies. As the EEC took shape, however, the first signs of trouble began to appear. The first phase of the European customs union had been burdened by Great Britain's alternative suggestion of a free-trade zone, an idea that also had its supporters in the Adenauer government. During this time, Adenauer began to see that he could count on only limited support from the three Western Powers for his basic policy positions on the future of Germany as a whole. By the end of his term in office, the chancellor could no longer rid himself of the fear that the Americans and the Soviets might one day reach a broader disarmament agreement based on a tacit acceptance of the territorial status quo in Europe and on the de facto recognition of a divided Germany. As early as the late 1950s, it seemed in Bonn's interest at least to consider whether this trend from Washington might be countered by the establishment of an economic community of nations in continental Europe – a community that was also political in character and could later be expanded.

THE 1960S

The new difficulties in European policy that had begun to reveal themselves in the German-American relationship in the late 1950s became the focus of the differences between Bonn and Washington during the Kennedy administration (1961–3). At first, however, the attention of both allies was occupied by Communist Party chief and Soviet premier Nikita Khrushchev's November 1958 ultimatum and the ensuing second great Berlin Crisis. The Americans' response to the crisis, which culminated in the building of the Berlin Wall in August 1961, clearly demonstrated that Kennedy was determined to defend to the utmost the West's position in West Berlin, but also that he saw a relaxation of tensions in America's relationship with the Soviet Union as a primary foreign policy objective, even if simultaneous improvement of the situation in divided Germany was not possible. The dangerous events of the October 1962 Cuban Missile Crisis strengthened the Kennedy administration's commitment to these foreign policy priorities.

Disappointed by this clear setback to his *Deutschlandpolitik*, Adenauer drew closer to France during the final years of his government. Since 1958, however, France had been led by Charles de Gaulle, a politician who not only had other ideas than Adenauer about the nature of West European integration but also tried to use the EC to play a role in international relations markedly more independent from the United States.[11]

Despite these differences between German and French policies toward Europe, Adenauer was prepared to sign the Franco-German friendship treaty with de Gaulle in January 1963. Just a few days before the signing of the Élysée Treaty, the French president had flatly rejected Great Britain's application to join the EEC, which Washington had strongly supported, thereby preventing the economic community from assuming a more transatlantic character. Washington had consequently become all the more suspicious of closer Franco-German cooperation. Although the preamble to the German act of ratification gave the bilateral Paris treaties

[11] Eckart Conze, "Hegemonie durch Integration? Die amerikanische Europapolitik und ihre Herausforderung durch de Gaulle," *Vierteljahrshefte für Zeitgeschichte* 43 (1995): 297–340.

a more conciliatory gloss by highlighting the importance of German-American relations, it became obvious that, since the early 1960s at the latest, the European policies of the United States and Germany were no longer compatible in all respects.

This was already evident, for example, in Germany's position on the Kennedy administration's "Grand Design" for the future course of transatlantic relations. Washington's concept foresaw the building of an Atlantic community between the United States and a unified Western Europe. For the West European states, it was clear that such a concept would inevitably lead to tensions between the equal partnership granted by the United States in economic matters and the European NATO allies' continued dependence on the United States in security matters.[12] Of all EC members, the Federal Republic was the most dependent on the United States in security policy, but it was also beginning to take a leading role in the EC. The Federal Republic would, therefore, be the most closely affected by the increasing tensions in the years to come.

Chancellor Ludwig Erhard, who had succeeded Adenauer in late 1963, and his foreign minister, Gerhard Schröder, at first tried to defuse these tensions by conducting a distinctly pro-Atlantic foreign policy but this inevitably brought them into conflict with their French partner in European integration. The disputes within the Federal Republic over how to resolve or at least minimize the tensions arising from the conflict between the country's duties under the transatlantic alliance with the United States and its obligations toward its West European partners (especially France) would long fuel the disputes between German "Atlanticists" and "Gaullists."

For the Erhard government (1963–6), this foreign policy dilemma was further complicated by the fact that, by the mid-1960s, both the EEC integration process and the joint security policy within NATO were in crisis.[13] With its "empty

chair" policy, France blocked any progress by the Council of Ministers of the EEC for months; it resumed cooperation only after its demands had been substantially met. After the two superpowers had attained strategic nuclear parity, considerable uncertainty had arisen within NATO as to the credibility of the American nuclear guarantee for Europe. This uncertainty had been increased by the earlier controversy over plans for a multilateral nuclear force (MLF) abandoned in 1965.[14] And the Johnson administration (1963–9) appeared to alienate its European allies still further with its escalation of the Vietnam War.[15] France had already pulled out of the NATO integrated military command in 1966, signaling a growing distance from the Alliance's leading power. Moreover, with the inflexible nature of its policies toward the East and toward the German question, the Federal Republic had increasingly isolated itself from its allies, and was seen as delaying the now desired relaxation of East-West tensions.

The government of the CDU-SPD "Grand Coalition" (1966–9) under Chancellor Kurt Georg Kiesinger (CDU) and Foreign Minister Willy Brandt (SPD) (1966–9) had the daunting task of bridging the differences between Western Europe and the United States while catching up with the détente process. During the 1960s, the EC had turned itself into a preferred zone for American direct investment, but it had also become a more independent player in world trade, as demonstrated in the Kennedy Round (1964–7) of GATT and on other occasions.[16] With its protectionist agricultural policy

[12] George M. Taber, *John F. Kennedy and a Uniting Europe: The Politics of Partnership* (Bruges, 1969).

[13] Hans von der Groeben, *Aufbaujahre der Europäischen Gemeinschaft: Das Ringen um den gemeinsamen Markt und*

die Politische Union (1958–1966) (Baden-Baden, 1982); David Calleo, *The Atlantic Fantasy: The U.S., NATO, and Europe* (Baltimore, 1970); Helga Haftendorn, *NATO and the Nuclear Revolution: A Crisis of Credibility, 1966–1967* (Oxford, 1996).

[14] Henry A. Kissinger, *The Troubled Partnership: A Reappraisal of the Atlantic Alliance* (Garden City, N.Y., 1966), 129–61. See also the chapters by Kori Schake and Erhard Forndran, vol. 1, Security.

[15] See the chapter by T. Michael Ruddy, vol. 2, Security.

[16] Andrew Shonfield, ed., *International Economic Relations of the Western World, 1959–1971*, vol. 1: *Politics and Trade* (London, 1976); Norbert Welter, "Die Kennedy-Runde," in Karl Carstens et al., eds., *Die*

and the preferential agreements it had reached with third states, the EC had also emerged as an unwelcome competitor to American exports.

The Federal Republic attempted to play the role of mediator in trade conflicts between America and Europe. In the 1960s, Bonn was also ready to support the old Bretton Woods currency system of fixed exchange rates in favor of the United States, which frequently provoked criticism from its EC partners. In 1967, the North Atlantic alliance had implemented the change of strategy toward "flexible response" imposed by Washington; with the conclusion of the Harmel Report, which accorded NATO the dual function of providing military security and promoting détente, the alliance had made important adjustments that reflected the changed European security situation. Nevertheless, Bonn's European policy frequently presented a challenge for German-American relations.

EFFORTS TO FORGE A TRANSATLANTIC
CONSENSUS

A brief summary of the changing relationships between the United States, (Western) Europe, and West Germany during the first two and a half decades after the end of World War II shows that a remarkable transformation occurred – one that effectively turned "Europe" into a "problem" for the German-American relationship.

In the immediate postwar period – during the military occupation of Germany and in the early years of the Federal Republic – the United States saw the use of Germany, and in particular the constructive use of German economic potential for an integrated reconstruction of Europe, as a primary factor in the construction of a European postwar political order. In this way, Germany was to become firmly and perma-

nently linked with the Western community of nations and thereby controlled. American policy toward Germany was thus an integral part of American policy toward Europe. For the United States, an integrated Germany – which because of the East-West conflict meant only West Germany – was an object of its integration plans, a basis of operations, and soon also a reliable partner in America's policy efforts to construct a stable Europe.

From the perspective of West Germany and the Adenauer government, this integrated American policy toward Germany and Europe in the early postwar years closely reflected its own foreign policy goals. Adenauer saw Germany's participation in West European unification – which he could achieve with the ideological and material assistance of the United States – as the essence of a new, reformed German foreign policy. In the first decade after the war and under the overriding constraints of the East-West conflict, both the West European and the transatlantic elements of his Western integration policy were so closely interwoven that no irreconcilable differences could arise between them.

This changed from the late 1950s onward and became a persistent problem for German-American relations in the following decade. The construction of the EC brought the emergence of a six-state partnership capable of competing with the United States. The "chicken war" that broke out in the early 1960s between America and the EEC was to be only a harbinger of the transatlantic trade conflicts to follow. Moreover, as the general relaxation of East-West tensions continued, reflected particularly in the conclusion of the Limited Test Ban Treaty (1963) and the nuclear Non-Proliferation Treaty (1968), America's influence on its allies' security policies declined. This was all the more evident as the Johnson administration, entangled in Vietnam, appeared increasingly to distance itself from the needs of its European allies. The doubts about America's ability to uphold the nuclear guarantee, which had been generated by the loss of America's strategic nuclear superiority over the Soviet Union, could no longer be entirely overcome. Furthermore,

Internationale Politik 1966–1967 (Munich, 1973), 405–25. See also the chapters by Hans-Eckart Scharrer and Kerstin Müller-Neuhof, vol. 1, Economics, and Monika Medick-Krakau, vol. 2, Economics.

successive governments in Bonn had come to
a dead end with their inherited *Deutschland-*
politik.

The combination of all the above factors
meant that the Federal Republic under Adenauer and his successors had to decide how to
link transatlantic security policy on the basis
of close German-American relations with West
European integration policy within the framework of the EC and the close Franco-German

relationship.[17] This inevitably led to differences,
even conflicts. The Federal Republic was, however, consistently aware of the boundaries of the
resulting German-American disputes and always
strove to maintain a transatlantic consensus.

[17] Werner Link, "Adenauer, Amerika und die
deutsche Nachwelt," in Klaus Schwabe, ed., *Adenauer*
und die USA: Rhöndorfer Gespräche, vol. 14 (Bonn, 1994),
133, 148.

CHAPTER FOURTEEN

The U.S. Congress and German-American Relations

Steven J. Brady

In studies of German-American relations, the role of the American Congress has received comparatively little attention. This comes as no surprise because even many legislators accepted the primacy of the executive in foreign policy until America's involvement in Vietnam provoked a reassertion of congressional prerogatives. A 1962 study of Congress's role in foreign policymaking concluded that legislative influence was "primarily (and increasingly) one of legitimating and amending policies initiated by the executive to deal with problems usually identified by the executive."[1] Or, in Robert Dahl's words, "the President proposes, the Congress disposes."[2]

Although America's policy toward Germany has tended to confirm Congress's deference to the White House, one cannot say that congressional leaders "shied away from foreign policy issues,"[3] even if they did shy away from forcing policy changes. Legislators grappled with many of the most important issues in postwar German-American relations, and rarely could the president – or the government in Bonn – simply ignore congressional opinion. Understanding Congress's role is, therefore, vital to understanding the postwar German-American relationship.

As World War II drew to a close, Congress generally reflected the nation's attitudes toward Germany. Legislators were particularly interested in seeing that those responsible for war crimes be punished. Prior to Germany's collapse, the House Committee on Foreign Affairs considered resolutions defining American policy toward war criminals. Executive and legislature generally agreed on this important issue. Both the State Department and the committee, for instance, rejected House Joint Resolution 93, which called for a commission to set plans for dealing with war criminals. Although a postwar House subcommittee questioned the efficacy of divided Four Power administration of occupied Germany, the primary concern of the representatives was the Germans themselves, whom they found to possess "an arrogance of spirit," even in defeat.[4]

However, members of Congress did not want America to be seen as responsible for starvation in its zone of occupation, and the administration soon faced calls from Congress for a *less* vindictive occupation policy. On January 18, 1946, thirty-four senators petitioned President Harry S. Truman to "take immediate steps" to relieve famine in Germany, noting that America "did not fight the war to exterminate the German

[1] James A. Robinson, *Congress and Foreign Policy-Making: A Study in Legislative Influence and Initiative* (Homewood, Ill., 1962), v.

[2] Robert Dahl, *Congress and Foreign Policy* (New York, 1950), 58.

[3] James M. Lindsay, *Congress and the Politics of U.S. Foreign Policy* (Baltimore, 1994), 70.

[4] See U.S. House, *Problems of World War II and Its Aftermath* (Washington, D.C., 1976), pt. 2:413–30, 439–41, 467.

people, but to destroy forever the criminal Nazi leadership and their war machine."[5] The petition was echoed by other calls for a less punitive German policy.

Similarly, throughout 1946, the revival of the American zone became the focus of administration policy toward Germany. In that year, the American and British zones were merged into "Bizonia." Senator Arthur Vandenberg (R-Mich.) noted the importance of the new "economic unit" in Western Germany. The arrangement, meant to facilitate economic revitalization of Germany, was "indispensable," not only for saving Germany from an "economic tragedy but also to relieve our own responsibilities, and above all, to stabilize Europe."[6] Senate Foreign Relations Committee chairman Tom Connally (D-Tex.) expressed similar views.

But occupation paired with economic revival would cost money, and the Republicans who seized control of Congress in fall 1946 had run on a platform of government economy. Although the Eightieth Congress proved surprisingly willing to cooperate in the creation of a bipartisan foreign policy, its control of the purse strings would give it considerable leverage over European policy in the coming years. With the cost of German occupation and the frustration with postwar Soviet actions increasing, Congress acted in 1947 to make its weight felt. In January, Vandenberg associated himself with a proposal made by John Foster Dulles calling for the integration of Western Germany's industrial potential into Western Europe's economy. Vandenberg, Dulles, and other supporters of the plan had come to favor the economic revitalization of Germany as a solution to the dual problems of the cost of occupation and the containment of Soviet expansion.

Although the mainstream of congressional opinion was moving toward German economic revival, critics of foreign aid – most famously Senator Robert Taft (R-Ohio) – continued to link criticisms of Truman's German policy with discussions of the Marshall Plan, a massive in-fusion of American aid into postwar Europe.[7] Taft accused the administration of hampering Germany's and Europe's economic recovery by continuing to dismantle German industry. If the administration was correct in its portrayal of the European Recovery Program (ERP) as a way to stem the spread of Soviet-sponsored communism, Taft asked, then why was it necessary to dismantle German factories?

The issue came to a head in late 1947. Certain legislators, frustrated with the cost of occupation and the practice of shipping German industrial plant eastward in accordance with the Potsdam agreements, sought to force a change in administration policy. On December 18, House Foreign Affairs Committee member John Vorys (R-Ohio) reported Resolution 365, which called upon the secretaries of state and defense to give the House answers to eleven questions about the dismantling of German industries. Among other things, these inquiries sought to establish whether dismantled plant could have contributed to European recovery; how much it was costing America to "make up for" lost German production; and why the administration had not temporarily halted dismantling until Congress was able to assess its impact on European recovery.[8] On the following day, Styles Bridges (R-N.H.) of the Senate Appropriations Committee introduced an amendment to prevent supplemental appropriations from being used to finance dismantlement. This was strong stuff: Had the amendment passed, the Senate would have forced an end to dismantlement. Vandenberg quickly intervened, promising to investigate the matter when his Foreign Relations Committee held hearings on ERP aid. Bridges then withdrew his amendment, and Congress stopped short of forcing the president's hand.

But the Bridges amendment and Resolution 365 had sent a signal to the administration: Congress could not be counted on to keep appropriating money for a German policy that seemed at odds with itself. Nor was it only the

[5] *Congressional Record* (hereafter *Cong. Rec.*), 79th Cong., 2d sess., 92, pt. 1:121.

[6] *New York Times*, Oct. 20, 1946, 50.

[7] See the chapter by Michael Wala, vol. 1, Politics.

[8] *Cong. Rec.*, 80th Cong., 1st sess., 93, pt. 9:11636.

Republicans who desired a revival of the German economy. Democrats like Connally and his colleagues Walter George (D-Ga.) and Richard Russell (D-Ga.) had all come to believe that European recovery was impossible without German recovery.[9] By early 1948, concerns about congressional attitudes had become a factor in the administration's thinking on German policy. In its response to the House inquiry on January 24, 1948, the administration defended dismantlements and transshipments while indicating that shipments from the American occupied zone to the Soviets should soon cease, pending East-West agreement on other economic questions.[10] The administration never lost sight of the need to placate Congress on this issue. In its contacts with the British and French, the administration warned of the possible effects of Allied action on congressional opinion, leading British foreign secretary Ernest Bevin to ask if Vandenberg's committee was "the sole arbiter of what happens in Germany."[11] It was not. But Congress clearly could not be ignored as it pressed to hasten the revival of the Western German economy.

Influential members of Congress viewed German recovery as vital to the success of the ERP. During a hearing on the ERP bill on February 12, 1948, Vandenberg summed up the attitude of the Foreign Relations Committee: "We all recognize the fact that Western Germany is the key, finally, to the whole show."[12] The committee expressed its commitment to the revival of Germany's economy in its final report on the ERP bill (Senate Bill 2202). With regard to the Bridges amendment, the committee was satisfied that administration policies were not undermining the goals of the ERP. Bipar-

tisanship had prevailed, thanks in large part to Vandenberg.

Secretary of State Dean Acheson nevertheless continued to keep one eye on Congress when formulating occupation policy. In telegrams to the American embassy in London on March 11, 1949 – in the midst of tripartite talks on the occupation statute – the secretary indicated his concern for congressional opinion. The United States would have to retain the "principal voice in economic policies" in the trizonal area. Only thus could appropriations be guaranteed. He also informed London that the administration was reluctant to commit to long-term restrictions on German industry, noting that "we cannot contemplate a repetition of our experience with Congress on reparations."[13] Congressional opinion did not end dismantlement, but it had certainly limited the flexibility of the Truman administration in negotiations with London and Paris.

After the Soviets closed access to West Berlin in June 1948, Vandenberg and other Republicans called for unity in dealing with the challenge. The establishment of a West German government also enjoyed broad consensus. West German rearmament, however, was made politically feasible only by the Korean War.[14] This shift in congressional opinion guaranteed both the Truman and the Eisenhower administrations overwhelming legislative support for a policy of German rearmament. In the weeks following the outbreak of hostilities in Korea, a number of influential senators spoke out in favor of efforts to arm West Germany. Acheson and the new secretary of defense, George C. Marshall, made ample use of congressional opinion and congressional control of military assistance funds to pressure the recalcitrant French into accepting German rearmament.[15] In a November 3 telegram to the French embassy, Acheson

[9] For comments by Connally, see remarks in ibid., 11692; for George's remarks, see ibid., 11436; on Russell's views, see Gilbert C. Fite, *Richard B. Russell, Jr.: Senator From Georgia* (Chapel Hill, N.C., 1991), 219.

[10] U.S. Department of State, *Bulletin*, Feb. 8, 1948, 185–91.

[11] Memorandum of Conversation, in U.S. Department of State, *Foreign Relations of the United States* (hereafter *FRUS*), *1948*, 2:820.

[12] U.S. Senate Committee on Foreign Relations, *Foreign Relief Assistance Act of 1948* (New York, 1979), 194–5.

[13] See Acheson's telegrams to the embassy in the United Kingdom in *FRUS, 1949*, 3:50–1, 560–1.

[14] On the Korean invasion's impact on America's German and NATO policy, see Thomas A. Schwartz, *America's Germany: John J. McCloy and the Federal Republic of Germany* (Cambridge, Mass., 1991), 124–35.

[15] See *FRUS, 1950*, 3:315, 341, 342–3, 353, 1392.

maintained that the American delegation to the tripartite talks had "conscientiously" avoided linking of military assistance funds to French pliability on the German rearmament issue. They nevertheless had to make it clear to Paris that Congress expected a guarantee that Military Assistance Program appropriations were "based on a mil[itarily] realistic plan."[16]

On April 14, 1951, the Senate passed Senate Resolution 99 approving the dispatch of American troops to Europe and declaring that consideration "should be given as soon as possible" to provide for the "utilization on a voluntary basis of the military and other resources of West Germany."[17] Truman agreed. The president submitted the Bonn Contractual Accords to the Senate for ratification on June 3, 1952. The Contractuals would restore West German sovereignty and extend Atlantic Pact security guarantees to the Federal Republic. Part of these agreements was the treaty establishing the European Defense Community (EDC). Although the United States was not a signatory to this treaty, by agreeing to the Contractuals, the Senate gave its consent to the rearming of West Germany in the context of a European army. Support for the Contractuals in the Senate was bipartisan and exceptionally strong; on July 1, the Senate ratified them by overwhelming margins.

As Congress grew more committed to German rearmament, its leaders grew more interested in maintaining West German chancellor Konrad Adenauer in office. In February 1952, Senate Foreign Relations Committee chairman Alexander Wiley (R–Wisc.) expressed his concern to Acheson about Adenauer's "tenuous hold" on power. The secretary noted the connection between the success of the European army and the chancellor's prospects in the 1953 elections.[18] In that election year, Congress sought to bolster Adenauer's standing in West Germany. Wiley invited Adenauer to appear before the Foreign Relations Committee during his first visit to the United States in April 1953.[19] Adenauer declared that he was "deeply impressed" by the importance attached to his appearance before the committee.[20] No doubt he hoped that the West German voter would be equally impressed. After the June uprisings in East Germany, Congress acted quickly to voice its support for the East German people and for Adenauer. On July 2, the Senate passed a resolution expressing its sense that the German people had the right "to be a unified nation."[21] Making no effort to hide his committee's preferences in German politics, Wiley stated publicly that the resolution "will be helpful from the standpoint of Adenauer's coming election test."[22]

The Senate also sought to help the Contractuals and the EDC along. In July 1954, the Foreign Relations Committee reported a resolution expressing the sense of the Senate that "if future developments" made it desirable, the president "should take such steps as he deems appropriate and as are consistent with United States constitutional process to restore sovereignty to the Germany [sic] and to enable her to contribute to the maintenance of international peace and security." By clearly hinting at unilateral American action to implement the major clauses of the Contractuals if France failed to ratify, the resolution reveals the high degree of legislative-executive agreement on the issue of restoring sovereignty to, and rearming, the Federal Republic.[23]

After the French National Assembly rejected the EDC, Wiley denounced the French government but ruled out action along the lines of the resolution his committee had drafted in July: There would be no solution at France's expense, and the defense of the West required

---

[16] Ibid., 429–30.

[17] *Cong. Rec.*, 82d Cong., 1st sess., 97, pt. 3:3282–3.

[18] U.S. Senate Committee on Foreign Relations, *Executive Session Hearings of the Senate Foreign Relations Committee*, Historical Series (Washington, D.C., 1976), 4:178.

[19] See U.S. Senate Committee on Foreign Relations, *Chancellor Konrad Adenauer* (Washington, D.C., 1953).

[20] Konrad Adenauer, *Erinnerungen 1945–1953* (Stuttgart, 1965), 586.

[21] *Cong. Rec.*, 83d Cong., 1st sess., 99, pt. 6:7458.

[22] *New York Times*, July 3, 1953, 4.

[23] U.S. Senate Committee on Foreign Relations, *Executive Session of the Senate Foreign Relations Committee*, Historical Series (Washington, D.C., 1977) 6:659–81, 687–705.

Franco-German cooperation.[24] Congress remained skeptical of French intentions, however, and delayed consideration of the Paris agreements – which would bring West Germany into NATO as a full-fledged partner – until after the Europeans had ratified them. Following brief hearings in late March 1955, the Foreign Relations Committee ratified the agreements by the overwhelming vote of seventy-six to two.[25]

Coinciding roughly with the Democrats' success in regaining the majority in both houses of Congress in 1954, the Paris agreements represented the high tide of congressional acquiescence in administration policy toward Germany and Europe. From mid-decade on, however, Democrats such as Mike Mansfield, Hubert Humphrey, and John F. Kennedy raised questions about the Eisenhower administration's allegedly hard line on European defense issues and its commitment to Adenauer. In June 1955, Mansfield questioned the advisability of allowing America's German policy to rest on the shoulders of one man, namely Adenauer, and suggested that the size of West Germany's contribution to NATO could be a topic for negotiation with the USSR. He also suggested that West and East Germany should discuss the topic of reunification among themselves.[26] Humphrey, chairman of the Senate's Subcommittee on Disarmament, pressed for more flexibility on European issues. In December 1956, he suggested the possibility of creating a "zone in which military equipment and manpower would be kept in a prescribed limit." A "redeployment" of American troops from Germany might be part of such an arrangement.[27]

Proposals for Bonn to negotiate with East Berlin ran up against the Adenauer government's claim to be the sole representative of all Germans. The suggestion of a demilitarized zone in central Europe was unacceptable to a government that sought to garner influence in the West by contributing to the Western defense effort. And any mention of American "redeployment" was bound to cause anxiety for a chancellor who already worried that East-West rapprochement could undermine his government's foreign policy.[28] Such proposals eventually failed while leaving the issue of Europe's division unresolved.

In these circumstances, on November 10, 1958, Nikita Khrushchev reopened the Berlin issue, setting a six-month deadline for the West to negotiate with the East German regime. The announcement stirred up a beehive of activity in the Senate. But the responses and proposals of the senators were so diverse – often urging the administration to work in opposite directions – that the Senate was not able to provide policy leadership.

In February 1959, Mansfield proposed a flexible Western policy toward Berlin, and he repeated his call for negotiations on West German rearmament. He also raised a number of other possibilities: a unified, neutralized Germany, Bonn's recognition of East Germany, a multilateral withdrawal from Germany, and a demilitarized zone. The West would also have to give up on the idea of reunification through free elections.[29] The plan differed substantially from the administration's position that the West, although professing willingness to negotiate, would not compromise on its rights in Berlin.[30] Bonn immediately attacked Mansfield's plan. On February 19, fearing that Mansfield's comments could let America appear divided at a critical time,

---

[24] *New York Times*, Sept. 4, 1954, 1; *U.S. News and World Report*, Sept. 24, 1954, 40.

[25] See U.S. Senate Committee on Foreign Relations, *Protocol on the Termination of the Occupation Regime in the Federal Republic of Germany and Protocol to the North Atlantic Treaty on the Accession of the Federal Republic of Germany* (Washington, D.C., 1955); *Cong. Rec.*, 84th Cong., 1st sess., 101, pt. 3:4233.

[26] *Cong. Rec.*, 84th Cong., 1st sess., 101, pt. 7:9079–81.

[27] U.S. Senate Committee on Foreign Relations, Subcommittee on Disarmament, *Control and Reduction of Armaments: Disarmament and Security in Europe* (Wash-

ington, D.C., 1956), vi; *Cong. Rec.*, 85th Cong., 1st sess., 103, pt. 2:1663–7.

[28] See Konrad Adenauer, *Erinnerungen 1955–1959* (Stuttgart, 1967), 203, 284–8.

[29] *Cong. Rec.*, 86th Cong., 1st sess., 105, pt. 2:2242–8.

[30] For Eisenhower's statement of this basic policy to leading members of Congress, see *FRUS, 1958–1960*, 8:428.

Senators Thomas Dodd (D-Conn.) and Jacob Javits (R-N.Y. and until then an opponent of West German rearmament) introduced Resolution 82, which strongly differed with many of Mansfield's proposals.

But even as the administration was under attack for the rigidity of its policy, other weighty voices in the Senate used the Berlin crisis to continue to attack Eisenhower for military weakness at a time of crisis. Particularly vocal was Stuart Symington of Missouri, but the sentiment was shared even by liberals like Humphrey and Paul Douglas (D-Ill.). Fulbright asked Acting Secretary of State Christian Herter whether it was not "very poor psychology" for the administration to carry out a planned troop cut of 30,000 during the Berlin crisis.[31] Eisenhower ridiculed congressional calls for a conventional force buildup and continued to act as if there were no crisis.[32]

The suggestions from Congress – including Fulbright's call for a bilateral pullback – had little impact on administration thinking. Herter went to the Geneva foreign ministers conference determined to discuss Berlin only in the larger context of German unification. The Western powers also categorically rejected German neutrality.[33] But if the talks achieved little of substance, they at least reduced tensions; the flow of congressional proposals abated for a time.

The Berlin Crisis heated up again in 1961, as Khrushchev hammered away at a stunned President John F. Kennedy in Vienna. The administration's hard-line response found support on both sides of the aisle in the Senate, notably from Russell and Wiley. Mansfield, however, called for all of Berlin to be declared a free city until such time as it could be the capital of a united Germany. The proposal brought forth

objections both from Bonn and from Republican senators Bridges, Hugh Scott, and Javits, who suggested passing a resolution in support of the president.

The debate was not reassuring to Adenauer. Although Kennedy had stood firm, particularly in his July 25 address to the nation, Mansfield's suggestions had to be reckoned with. In late July, Fulbright weighed in on the side of a free-city agreement.[34] Adenauer complained to Secretary of State Dean Rusk in August that America was presenting a confused face to the world. According to the chancellor, statements by Fulbright, Mansfield, and Humphrey threatened to undo the benefits of Kennedy's "splendid" speech.[35] Most galling of all for Adenauer must have been Fulbright's statement at the end of July that he did not "understand why the East Germans don't close their border because I think they have a right to close it."[36] The Soviets must have been asking themselves the same question; on August 13, they began building a barrier between the two halves of the city. Although the Berlin Wall did not silence debate in Congress about the city's future, it rendered initiatives like Mansfield's academic.

By the mid-1960s, congressional enthusiasm for German policy and for European policy in general had reached low ebb. As the Berlin Crisis faded into memory and contacts between East and West increased, military confrontation in Europe appeared increasingly unlikely. In Asia, by contrast, America found itself deeply involved in the costly war in Vietnam. Moreover, France's departure from NATO's military command and the failure of other NATO allies to meet agreed force levels led many in Congress to wonder exactly why the United States paid

---

[31] *Cong. Rec.*, 86th Cong., 1st sess., 105, pt. 3:3507, 3799; U.S. Senate Committee on Foreign Relations, *Executive Sessions of the Senate Foreign Relations Committee, Historical Series* (Washington, D.C., 1982), 11:222–3.

[32] See Stephen E. Ambrose, *Eisenhower: The President* (New York, 1984), 517–19.

[33] See G. Bernard Noble, *Christian A. Herter* (New York, 1970), 43.

[34] Randall Bennett Woods, *Fulbright: A Biography* (New York, 1995), 315.

[35] Hans-Peter Schwarz, *Adenauer*, vol. 2: *Der Staatsmann 1952–1967* (Stuttgart, 1991), 656.

[36] Woods, *Fulbright*, 315; *New York Times*, Aug. 3, 1961, 2. For Adenauer's response to Fulbright's comments, see Adenauer, Kanzler-Tee, Aug. 17, 1961, in Konrad Adenauer, *Teegespräche 1959–1961*, ed. Hanns Jürgen Küsters, Adenauer Rhöndorfer Ausgabe, ed. Rudolf Morsey and Hans-Peter Schwarz (Berlin, 1988), 544.

such a heavy price to defend allies who did not seem to feel threatened.

Mansfield posed this question on August 31, 1966, in the form of Senate Resolution 300. The "Mansfield Resolution" expressed the sense of the Senate that "a substantial reduction of U.S. forces permanently stationed in Europe can be made without adversely affecting either our resolve or ability to meet our commitment under the North Atlantic Treaty." The resolution was predicated upon the reduction in tension between East and West that had occurred since the early 1950s. Mansfield also pointed to the high costs of maintaining existing force levels in Europe.[37] The senator – who would reintroduce the amendment the following January – garnered significant support for his resolution: Within a month, forty-four cosponsors had signed on.

As opponents of the resolution were quick to point out, the vast majority of any force reductions would inevitably be redeployed from West German territory. Javits worried in January 1967 that the Federal Republic was "in a terrible state of flux and ambivalence," feeling pulls toward the East as well as the West. He raised the specter of "neo-Nazism" on the rise in West Germany and suggested that unilateral American withdrawals might cause the West Germans to ask "whether they had better make a deal with the East, or be left high and dry."[38] In congressional hearings that spring, Mansfield's detractors highlighted the impact of withdrawals on West Germany and her neighbors. Acting Secretary of State Nicholas Katzenbach echoed Javits's warnings about Bonn's fears of abandonment while voicing a new concern: If the United States made "major withdrawals" from Europe, America's allies would "doubt America's commitment to Europe" and resort to "new and essentially nationalistic answers" to the question of European security. The result would be a "much greater fear of Germany . . . both in the east and I would think in the west as well." Henry "Scoop" Jackson (D-

Wash.) likewise worried that if the United States let West Germany make "too large a contribution of forces in Central Europe," it would jeopardize "the opportunity of improving relations with Eastern Europe" and harm chances for reunification.[39] It was to be an enduring irony of the Federal Republic's postwar status that advocates of a position that helped the Bonn government should have to play upon the fear of Germany.

This effort to play the German card did not convince the resolution's proponents. Mansfield used the announcement of further West German defense budget cuts to argue that America should not "be more militant about the defense of Germany than the Germans themselves."[40] It was, instead, the Soviet invasion of Czechoslovakia in August 1968 that killed the Mansfield Resolution. Opponents of the measure had objected that a unilateral force reduction would send the wrong signal to Moscow and perhaps encourage Soviet probing in Europe. In September, Mansfield himself acknowledged the risk of "misinterpretation" of an American troop withdrawal and suggested deferment of the issue. The Senate forced no major redeployments.

The episode illustrates the difficulty in assessing the impact of Congress on America's German policy from 1945 to 1968. The period that James M. Lindsay has labeled "the golden era of bipartisanship," when "party leaders saw their duty as supporting the president in foreign affairs," was not yet at an end, although the war in Vietnam would hasten its demise.[41] Congress still tended to defer to the executive in matters of foreign policy, a reality even the Mansfield Resolution reflected. The resolution merely expressed the "sense of the

---

[37] *Cong. Rec.*, 89th Cong., 2d sess., 112, pt. 16:21442–3.

[38] *Cong. Rec.*, 90th Cong., 1st sess., 113, pt. 1:1005.

[39] U.S. Senate, Combined Subcommittee of Foreign Relations and Armed Services Committees, *United States Troops in Europe* (Washington, D.C., 1967), 46, 75.

[40] *Cong. Rec.*, 90th Cong., 1st sess., 113, pt. 1:1199. On West German awareness of the effects of troop cuts on support for the Mansfield resolution, see Karl Dietrich Bracher et al., eds., *Geschichte der Bundesrepublik Deutschland*, 5 vols. (Stuttgart, 1984): Klaus Hildebrand, *Von Erhard zur Grossen Koalition 1963–1969*, 4:292–3.

[41] Lindsay, *Congress and U.S. Foreign Policy*, 70.

Senate"; had it passed, it would have imposed no legal obligation to comply. Congress did possess the "power of the purse," which it had threatened to use in the late 1940s. Yet, even Mansfield questioned an attempt by Symington in April 1968 to limit appropriations to support a force in Europe of only 50,000. The Senate refused to use its most powerful tool for compelling executive compliance with legislative wishes.

That exercise of power would come later, but would compel troop withdrawals from Indochina, not Europe. Until then, Congress's role in shaping German policy in the first quarter-century of the Cold War was limited. Congress tended to support major executive decisions; when legislators disagreed with administration policy, or wished to advance new policy options, they faced huge difficulties in moving the legislature, as a body, to impose its will on the executive. Congress was a factor to be reckoned with, sometimes supporting, often questioning, but never determining administration policy.

CHAPTER FIFTEEN

Political Parties and German-American Relations

Politics Beyond the Water's Edge

Ronald J. Granieri

Perhaps the most cherished cliché of American political discourse is that politics "ends at the water's edge," that domestic partisan battles should be put aside when dealing with important international questions. This principle, however, is honored more in the breach than in the observance. Despite such lofty sentiments, foreign policymaking in democracies remains intensely political. The study of relations between democracies, therefore, cannot ignore domestic politics or the essential domestic actors, political parties.

The alliance between the Federal Republic of Germany and the United States of America has been one of the keys to the postwar international system. Although both partners recognize its "existential" significance, the details of the alliance have been subject to constant negotiation, with political parties in the center. In both the Federal Republic and the United States, structures and practices have favored the executive in foreign affairs. In the United States, the "imperial Presidency," exercising the expanded powers that came with the New Deal and World War II, sought maximum freedom from legislative interference.[1] In the Federal Republic, Chancellor Konrad Adenauer quickly established his semiauthoritarian "chancellor democracy" (*Kanzlerdemokratie*).[2] This did not mean,

however, that legislatures became irrelevant. Although it was possible to make initial decisions without legislative consent, it remained necessary to defend those decisions before the electorate. To make their case, governments relied on political parties to frame the issues and garner public support.

Both German and American parties assumed positions that reflected their domestic situation: While in opposition, they criticized the structure of the alliance; when in power, they supported it – in each case hoping to gain partisan advantage. In the Federal Republic, once voters accepted the fundamental importance of the German-American alliance for the Federal Republic's future, a party's attitude toward the United States would help determine its domestic political success.[3] The existential nature of the German-American alliance did not insulate the alliance from politics but rather made everything about it political.

The role of political parties in German-American relations was closely related to the postwar American and German party systems. In the United States, the two-party system was well established. It united the moderate majority of both major parties and provided broad

---

[1] Arthur M. Schlesinger Jr., *The Imperial Presidency* (Boston, 1973).

[2] Arnulf Baring, *Aussenpolitik in Adenauers Kanzlerdemokratie: Bonns Beitrag zur Europäischen Verteidigungs-* *gemeinschaft* (Munich, 1969); Karlheinz Niclauss, *Kanzlerdemokratie: Bonner Regierungspraxis von Konrad Adenauer bis Helmut Kohl* (Stuttgart, 1988).

[3] Hans-Jürgen Grabbe, *Unionsparteien, Sozialdemokratie und Vereinigte Staaten von Amerika 1945–1966* (Düsseldorf, 1983).

support for such important initiatives as the Marshall Plan and NATO. In Germany, the tradition of strongly ideological or regional parties and the immediate totalitarian past meant that such a system had to be created. In the western occupation zones, only the Social Democratic Party (*Sozialdemokratische Partei Deutschlands*, or SPD) under the centralized leadership of Kurt Schumacher could claim a respectable democratic pedigree. The rest of the political spectrum was in shambles, the former bourgeois parties discredited by their general lack of resistance to the régime and, in some cases, their active collaboration with the National Socialists. This political imbalance worried the Western Allies, especially the Americans, who sought to develop a stable multiparty system.[4]

Balance was eventually secured through the creation of the Christian Democratic Union/Christian Social Union (*Christlich-Demokratische Union/Christlich-Soziale Union*, or CDU/CSU). Building on the traditions of the Center (*Zentrum*), the Bavarian People's Party (*Bayerische Volkspartei*), and a variety of smaller groups, the Union represented both the culmination of a long-held dream of uniting Catholic and Protestant Germans in a single "Christian" party and the emergence of a new force in German politics, the centrist "people's party" (*Volkspartei*). The Union's heterogeneity reflected its origins in divided Germany. In contrast to the centralized SPD, the Union was the product of regionally distinct movements that converged in the immediate aftermath of the German surrender.[5] Beyond an informal "working group" (*Arbeitsgemeinschaft*), no formal national organization existed until October 1950, when Konrad Adenauer was elected national chairman. The Bavarian CSU remained

formally separate from its larger sister, allying with the CDU at the national level to form a common Bundestag parliamentary group (*Fraktion*). The bond between these diverse elements was the Union's self-image as a Christian party, which allowed it to share in a rich German political tradition while distancing itself from the "materialist" ideologies of socialism, communism, and especially National Socialism.[6] The Union's development followed a common pattern in postwar Europe as bourgeois political forces turned to the ideology of Christian Democracy to compete with Democratic Socialism.[7] The Union thus contributed to the (re-) construction of a stable West German democracy, uniting an electorate that had splintered in Weimar.

Especially in foreign policy, the political history of the Federal Republic's first decades is the history of the struggle between the Union and the SPD. Although the liberal Free Democratic Party (*Frei Demokratische Partei*, or FDP) was a member, in coalitions with the Union, of most West German governments between 1949 and 1966, it did not control high-level positions in foreign affairs until Walter Scheel became foreign minister in 1969 and the FDP subsequently "colonized" the Foreign Office. Nevertheless, the FDP was a vocal, if sometimes erratic, contributor to the foreign policy debates of the Federal Republic's early years.[8]

These debates split the FDP into two wings, hindering efforts to maintain a steady political course. One wing, led by President Theodor Heuss and Minister for the Marshall Plan Franz Blücher, supported the Union's firm commitment to the German–American alliance; the more nationalist wing, represented especially by Justice Minister Thomas Dehler, emphasized

---

[4] Daniel E. Rogers, *Politics After Hitler: The Western Allies and the German Party System* (New York, 1995).

[5] See Hans-Otto Kleinmann, *Geschichte der CDU* (Stuttgart, 1993), and Alf Mintzel, *Geschichte der CSU* (Opladen, 1977). Useful studies in English include Geoffrey Pridham, *Christian Democracy in Western Germany* (New York, 1977); Noel D. Cary, *The Path to Christian Democracy: German Catholics and the Party System from Windhorst to Adenauer* (Cambridge, Mass., 1996).

[6] Maria Mitchell, "Materialism and Secularism: CDU Politicians and National Socialism, 1945–1949," *Journal of Modern History* 67, no. 2 (June 1995): 278–308.

[7] David W. Ellwood, *Rebuilding Europe: Western Europe, America, and Postwar Reconstruction* (London, 1992), 42–4. See also Stathis N. Kalyvas, *The Rise of Christian Democracy in Europe* (Ithaca, N.Y., 1997).

[8] See Erich Mende, *Die FDP: Daten, Fakten, Hintergründe* (Stuttgart, 1972).

reunification, even if that meant neutrality in the Cold War. Dehler's positions ultimately led to his exclusion from the cabinet and his emergence as Konrad Adenauer's most bitter and vocal critic. His election as party chairman in 1954 caused a crisis that led to the fragmentation of the FDP two years later: In 1956, a small group of deputies remained with the government while the rest of the party followed Dehler into opposition. The FDP resumed cooperation with the Union in 1961 under the leadership of Erich Mende, but remained unstable. The party did not resolve its conflict until Walter Scheel became chairman in 1967. Scheel pursued a leftward course, determined to build a coalition with the SPD in a common commitment to détente with the East, a goal that he and Willy Brandt achieved in the historic *Machtwechsel* (change of power) of 1969.[9]

It is easy, but inaccurate, to draw parallels between the Union and SPD on one side and the Republicans and Democrats on the other, and then assume that relative ideological affinity between the parties explains their political behavior. Ideology matters, but it has not always been the determining factor. The Union, for example, enjoyed profitable cooperation with a Democratic administration from 1949 to 1953, and the SPD was able to cooperate with Republican administrations in the 1970s. What facilitated such cooperation and, indeed, underlay the entire German-American alliance during the Cold War was not merely ideology but the recognition of common political interests.

During the immediate postwar years, it was difficult to predict which of the two major German parties would most likely support an alliance with the United States. Both advocated cooperation with the liberal democracies of the West, but neither specified the nature of that cooperation. Schumacher and the SPD engaged in heated public disputes with the American military governor General Lucius

Clay, who distrusted their socialist economic plans. Recent research has suggested, however, that SPD attitudes toward the Americans were more complex. Respect for American democratic ideals, and a shared distaste for communism, encouraged Social Democrats such as the mayor of West Berlin, Ernst Reuter, to advocate cooperation with the United States. Similarly, many Americans, despite their worries about the SPD's Marxism, respected the Social Democrats as important partners in building a democratic German state.[10] At the same time, the Union, though anticommunist and committed to the American-style neoliberal economics of Ludwig Erhard, was also ambivalent about the United States. The Union's "antimaterialist" self-image included traditional conservative German distaste for American society. For Konrad Adenauer and many others in the Union, American culture remained "basically foreign" ("*im Grunde fremd*").[11] The Union's conception of the Federal Republic's role in the Western community also emphasized continental European integration as an end in itself, leaving open the question of Germany's and Europe's ultimate relationship with the United States.[12]

Either the SPD or the Union could have been an acceptable partner for the United States. The shape of the German-American alliance would ultimately be determined by practical negotiation and the results of the first Bundestag election in 1949. The Union's narrow victory made Konrad Adenauer, not Kurt Schumacher, the

---

[9] Arnulf Baring, *Machtwechsel: Die Ära Brandt-Scheel* (Stuttgart, 1982).

[10] Dietrich Orlow, "Ambivalence and Attraction: The German Social Democrats and the United States, 1945–1974," in Reiner Pommerin, ed., *The American Impact on Postwar Germany* (Providence, R.I., 1995), 35–51.
[11] Grabbe, *Unionsparteien, Sozialdemokratie und Vereinigte Staaten*, 25–50; the quotation is on 41. See also Klaus Dohrn, "Das Amerikabild Adenauers," in Dieter Blumenwitz et al., eds., *Konrad Adenauer und seine Zeit*, 2 vols. (Stuttgart, 1976), 1:510–23.
[12] Ronald J. Granieri, "America's Germany, Germany's Europe: Konrad Adenauer, the CDU/CSU, and the Politics of German Westbindung, 1949–1963," (Ph.D. diss., University of Chicago, 1996).

first chancellor, with important historical consequences. To the surprise of many, the seventy-
three-year-old former mayor of Cologne would
lead the Federal Republic for the next fourteen
years, placing his stamp on both the Union and
the German-American alliance.

Once in power, Adenauer and the Union began with a general commitment to integrating
the Federal Republic into the West. In his first
policy statement before the Bundestag, Adenauer expressed German gratitude for American
aid, but phrased his policy in the most pragmatic
terms. "The only way to freedom," Adenauer
declared, "is that we try, in close cooperation
with the Allied High Commission, to expand
our freedoms and our responsibilities piece by
piece."[13] Adenauer's decision to cooperate with
the Western Allies while attempting to expand
the autonomy of both his government and the
Federal Republic, a policy summarized as *Westbindung*, was born as much of political necessity
as ideological preference. Instead of insisting
upon fixed principles, which would perhaps
have led to confrontation and deadlock, Adenauer chose to be flexible in building a sovereign
Federal Republic within the West. This willingness to work within Allied limits corresponded
to U.S. policy and helped create a mutually profitable relationship among Adenauer, his party,
and the Americans.[14]

As Adenauer and the Union deepened their
commitment to the German-American alliance,
the SPD moved in the opposite direction. Although the Social Democrats remained committed to the democratic values of the West,
the exigencies of opposition forced them to reject Adenauer's version of *Westbindung*. Determined to make the SPD the standard-bearer
of German reunification, Schumacher violently
attacked Adenauer's government for betraying

national interests. These attacks reached dramatic heights on November 25, 1949, during
the pivotal Bundestag debate on the Petersberg Protocols, in which Schumacher labeled
Adenauer "the chancellor of the Allies."[15] Such
strident rhetoric alienated the Americans. After meeting Schumacher in 1949, Secretary of
State Dean Acheson labeled him "a fanatic
of a dangerous and pure type" and believed
that "as long as he was in command of the
[SPD] it was going to be hopeless."[16] Acheson's assessment symbolized the estrangement
between the SPD and the United States that
lasted through the 1950s. As the SPD sought alternatives to *Westbindung*, it became isolated and
vulnerable to charges that it sought to detach
the Federal Republic from the West altogether.
Despite its commitment to Western democracy, the SPD could not build an acceptable
relationship with the Americans, while Adenauer and the Union worked ever closer with
Washington.

On the American side, attitudes toward the
German-American alliance were also determined more by political calculation than by
ideological affinity. The initial steps toward a
close German-American alliance were taken by
the Democratic Truman administration, which
quickly overcame its doubts about the "archconservative" Adenauer. Meanwhile, the Republicans were locked in an increasingly bitter
intraparty dispute, with neo-isolationists led
by Senator Robert Taft criticizing the American commitment to Europe and advocating
a stronger focus on Asia. These isolationist
tendencies inhibited closer ties between the
Republicans and the Union. Adenauer exemplified Union fears about the Republicans when
he pronounced himself "horrified" by early
signs that Taft might win their 1952 presidential nomination, warning that any change in
American policy would mean "an extremely

[13] Klaus A. Maier and Bruno Thoss, eds., *Westintegration, Sicherheit und deutsche Frage: Quellen zur Aussenpolitik
in der Ära Adenauer* (Darmstadt, 1994), 15–21; the quotation is on 20.
[14] Hans-Jürgen Schröder, "Kanzler der Alliierten?
Die Bedeutung der USA für die Aussenpolitik Adenauers," in Josef Foschepoth, ed., *Adenauer und die
deutsche Frage* (Göttingen, 1988), 118–45.

[15] *Verhandlungen des deutschen Bundestages*, 1. Wahlperiode, 18. Sitzung, 449–527; Schumacher's quotation is
on 525.
[16] Acheson quoted in Thomas A. Schwartz, *America's
Germany: John J. McCloy and the Federal Republic of Germany* (Cambridge, Mass., 1991), 80.

dangerous time" for Europe.[17] As the election approached, the Union leadership continued to worry, even after the more pro-European Dwight D. Eisenhower defeated Taft.

Remembering Adenauer's comments places the following years in an ironic light. Neither Adenauer nor his party were happy to see Truman and Acheson go. They worried that the Republicans, even under Eisenhower, would be less reliable partners. Events would prove these worries unfounded. Historians consider the Eisenhower era the "golden years" of the German-American alliance, primarily due to the close relations between Adenauer and Secretary of State John Foster Dulles.[18] Despite initial concerns on both sides, the two Cold Warriors' shared political convictions encouraged closer German-American relations.

Adenauer's collaboration with Dulles also brought domestic benefits. On the eve of the 1953 German elections, Dulles courted controversy when he told reporters that a Union defeat would be "disastrous to Germany."[19] This electoral intervention prompted protests from the SPD but did nothing to harm the Union's image. On the contrary, Adenauer and the Union consistently exploited their relationship with the Americans for domestic political gain. Adenauer's tour of the United States in April 1953, especially his emotional visit to the Tomb of the Unknown Soldier at Arlington National Cemetery, figured prominently in Union election propaganda, for example. This willingness to use American electoral aid was so great that some Union members feared alienating the Federal Republic's European allies. Adenauer's response revealed the eminently political nature

of his choices. While agreeing that it would be foolish to base the entire campaign on American help, Adenauer asked one critic "also to consider that the Americans are right now our only friends, and that we will not give up our friends, who hold decisive power in their hands, just to please Britain and France."[20] As long as the "American card" paid political dividends, Adenauer was determined to play it.

Adenauer's willingness to trade on his ties to Eisenhower and Dulles cemented the Union's domestic position throughout the 1950s and made the German-American alliance appear to be the private preserve of the Union and the Republicans. This forced opposition parties on both sides of the Atlantic to modify their positions. By 1957, another election year, the SPD borrowed from Adenauer's strategy when party chairman and chancellor candidate Erich Ollenhauer made his own "pilgrimage" to Washington. Although Ollenhauer failed to win support for his plan to replace NATO with a European security system, his visit signaled the SPD's new willingness to court the Americans and to recognize the centrality of the German-American alliance in German politics.[21]

As the SPD groped for a more constructive relationship with Washington, the American opposition also challenged the Adenauer-Dulles orthodoxy. In a widely read article in the influential journal *Foreign Affairs*, a rising young senator from Massachusetts, John F. Kennedy, led the charge. "The Age of Adenauer is over," Kennedy declared, asserting that the Eisenhower administration, "like its Democratic predecessor, [had] riveted its policy and favor exclusively on one leader and party and made pariahs of the opposition."[22] Kennedy and other Senate

---

[17] Adenauer, Presse-Tee, Apr. 2, 1952, in Konrad Adenauer, *Teegespräche 1950–1954*, ed. Hanns Jürgen Küsters, Adenauer Rhöndorfer Ausgabe, ed. Rudolf Morsey and Hans-Peter Schwarz (Berlin, 1984), 226.

[18] See Hans-Jürgen Grabbe, "Konrad Adenauer, John Foster Dulles, and West German–American Relations," in Richard H. Immerman, ed., *John Foster Dulles and the Diplomacy of the Cold War* (Princeton, N.J., 1990), 109–32; Detlef Felken, *Dulles und Deutschland: Die Amerikanische Deutschlandpolitik 1953–1959* (Bonn, 1993).

[19] "Dulles Pins Blame for Split Germany as Soviet Policies," *New York Times*, Sept. 4, 1953, 1.

[20] Adenauer to Erik Blumenfeld, Aug. 4, 1953, in Konrad Adenauer, *Briefe 1951–1953*, ed. Hans-Peter Mensing, Adenauer Rhöndorfer Ausgabe, ed. Rudolf Morsey and Hans-Peter Schwarz (Berlin, 1987), 419–20.

[21] Memorandum of Conversation between Ollenhauer and Eisenhower, Feb. 28, 1957, in U.S. Department of State, *Foreign Relations of the United States, 1955–1957*, 26:201–2.

[22] John F. Kennedy, "A Democrat Looks at Foreign Policy," *Foreign Affairs* 36, no. 1 (1957): 49. See also Frank

Democrats, including Hubert Humphrey, Mike Mansfield, and William Fulbright, developed an alternative vision of the alliance, exploring the possibility of détente with the Soviets and American troop reductions in Germany and considering a more constructive relationship with the SPD.

Kennedy's bold prediction of Adenauer's impending departure appeared rather premature in 1957, when the Union became the first and thus far only party in German parliamentary history to win an absolute majority of votes cast in a democratic election. Nevertheless, subsequent political developments made Kennedy's statements appear prophetic. The Cold War entered a new phase in the shadow of the Soviet ultimatum on Berlin. The death of John Foster Dulles in May 1959 was a sign that old ideas and old leaders were on the way out. Both Soviet and American leaders began to speak hopefully about the chances for détente, especially after Nikita Khrushchev's 1959 visit to the United States. Meanwhile, the SPD, after suffering devastating electoral defeats trying to formulate alternatives to the Union's foreign and domestic policies, undertook a historic change of direction. At their 1959 Bad Godesberg Party Conference, the Social Democrats rejected Marxism and embraced most of the Union's domestic agenda. The SPD also abandoned its opposition to *Westbindung*. In a historic Bundestag speech on June 30, 1960, Herbert Wehner announced his party's decision to embrace West German rearmament and membership in NATO. Thus began the SPD's policy of "commonality" (*Gemeinsamkeit*) with the Union, which was aimed at making the SPD an acceptable partner in a national coalition. Along with Wehner, the young SPD leadership, especially Willy Brandt, Helmut Schmidt, and Fritz Erler, presented a new and more acceptable face of the party to both the West German electorate and the Americans.[23]

These developments led to a crisis of confidence within the Union. Unnerved by SPD attempts to co-opt Union positions, Adenauer was further disturbed by signs that, with Dulles gone, American policy was changing. In search of greater security, Adenauer began to rely more heavily on European cooperation, developing a closer relationship with President Charles de Gaulle of France. Cooperation with de Gaulle both reflected and intensified Adenauer's suspicion of the Americans, culminating in the Élysée Treaty of January 1963. Many within the Union, however, were uncomfortable with de Gaulle's European vision, which they considered too anti-American. Disagreement over the proper balance between the Federal Republic's European and Atlantic commitments led to intraparty conflict between "Gaullists" such as Adenauer and Defense Minister Franz-Josef Strauss and "Atlanticists" such as Ludwig Erhard and Foreign Minister Gerhard Schröder – a conflict the Americans observed with mounting concern.[24] This programmatic dispute also had a personal side. Fearing that Erhard would succeed him as chancellor, Adenauer sought to limit Erhard's influence in the party and government. Their rivalry would further divide the Union during Adenauer's final years in office.[25]

John F. Kennedy's 1960 election to the presidency was a decisive moment in German-American relations. Echoing his *Foreign Affairs* article, Kennedy advocated a more flexible approach to European and German problems and sought new German allies. These calls for new thinking – and the age difference between Kennedy and Adenauer – brought the SPD and the Americans closer to one another. The Berlin Wall crisis revealed how much had changed. Responding to German criticisms of American passivity, Kennedy sent Vice President

A. Mayer, *Adenauer and Kennedy: A Study in German-American Relations, 1961–1963* (New York, 1996).

[23] Beatrix W. Bouvier, *Zwischen Godesberg und Grosser Koalition: Der Weg der SPD in die Regierungsverantwortung 1960–1966* (Berlin, 1990). See also Kurt Klotzbach, *Der*

Weg zur Staatspartei: Programmatik, praktische Politik und Organisation der deutschen Sozialdemokratie 1945 bis 1965 (Berlin, 1982).

[24] Eckart Conze, *Die Gaullistische Herausforderung: Die deutsch-französische Beziehungen in der amerikanischen Europapolitik 1958–1963* (Munich, 1995).

[25] Daniel Koerfer, *Kampf ums Kanzleramt: Erhard und Adenauer* (Stuttgart, 1987).

Lyndon Johnson to Bonn and Berlin. Johnson provided a welcome boost of morale but little help to Adenauer's embattled government, which was in the midst of another national election. Remembering previous campaign help, Adenauer's aides suggested that the chancellor accompany Johnson to Berlin, both to symbolize continued German-American cooperation and give Adenauer a crucial photo opportunity. The Americans demurred, claiming they did not want to get involved in German politics. Instead, Johnson toured West Berlin with the city's mayor, who also happened to be the SPD's chancellor candidate, Willy Brandt. The significance of this choice was not lost on Adenauer or his party.[26] American sympathy for the young and energetic – some would say Kennedyesque – Brandt signaled a shift in German-American relations. Although he survived the 1961 election, the end of the Adenauer era was at hand.

After Adenauer retired in October 1963, replaced despite his intense misgivings by Ludwig Erhard, divisions within the Union deepened. The struggle between Gaullists and Atlanticists disrupted the party and hampered Erhard's efforts at repairing relations with Washington.[27] Although the Atlanticists, led by Erhard and Schröder, controlled official policy, Union Gaullists occupied visible and influential positions. Adenauer himself remained chairman of the CDU until 1966, while Strauss led the CSU. From these positions, Adenauer and Strauss commanded the respect and loyalty of a sizable minority and could pour heavy fire on their Atlanticist colleagues. Although they could not make policy, they could and did make plenty of trouble for the new chancellor.

Although Erhard hoped to use his friendship with the Americans to master his domestic problems, it was the Americans who delivered one of the death blows to his administration.

In autumn 1966, in the midst of a recession, Erhard traveled to Washington to negotiate a compromise over the costs of stationing American troops in the Federal Republic. The Johnson administration, facing its own budgetary and diplomatic problems, was neither willing nor able to oblige. When Erhard returned empty-handed, he had no further defense against his Gaullist critics and within weeks was forced to resign.

The Union's inability to reach a consensus on foreign affairs hastened the collapse of Erhard's government and allowed the SPD to gain the political respectability it had sought since 1959. Erhard's fall led in December 1966 to the formation of a "Grand Coalition" of the SPD and the Union. This new government, though a marriage of political convenience, was a historic turning point in German politics. Whereas the SPD was now a participant in national government for the first time since Weimar, the Union had to part with its dominance of foreign affairs and surrender the Foreign Office to Willy Brandt. The Union had proved too divided to offer consistent foreign policy leadership. By contrast, the SPD had remained largely immune to the Gaullist temptation and in Brandt offered a guarantor of the Atlanticist thinking the Americans favored.[28] During the Grand Coalition, Brandt also began to experiment with new ideas for détente with the East, which would flower into Ostpolitik when he became chancellor in 1969.[29] By the time the new SPD-FDP coalition assumed power that autumn, the Republican Nixon administration in Washington had its own plans for détente. The SPD soon emerged as the preferred partner in that common effort.

The role of political parties in the German-American alliance between 1945 and 1968 illustrates the relationship between international relations and domestic politics in democracies. The need to garner support for foreign policy positions can often force a reconsideration

[26] Horst Osterheld, *"Ich gehe nicht leichten Herzens . . ." Adenauers letzte Kanzlerjahre: Ein dokumentarischer Bericht* (Mainz, 1986), 62–3.

[27] Horst Osterheld, *Aussenpolitik unter Bundeskanzler Ludwig Erhard 1963–1966: Ein dokumentarischer Bericht aus dem Kanzleramt* (Düsseldorf, 1992); Klaus Hildebrand, *Von Erhard zur Grossen Koalition* (Stuttgart, 1984).

[28] Reiner Marcowitz, *Option für Paris? Unionsparteien, SPD und Charles de Gaulle 1959–1969* (Munich, 1996).

[29] Reinhard Schmoeckel and Bruno Kaiser, *Die vergessene Regierung: Die grosse Koalition 1966–1969 und ihre langfristigen Wirkungen* (Bonn, 1991).

of the ideological principles on which they are based. In the 1950s, the SPD's principled commitment to national reunification and rejection of *Westbindung* earned it neither friends nor national power. Once it became clear that opposition had led to a dead end and that *Westbindung* was a practical reality, the party reconsidered its principles. Changes in the SPD coincided with changes in American policy to bring the Social Democrats closer to the United States. As a result, the SPD was able to gain the trust of a new administration in Washington and pull itself out of the political wilderness at home. The Union, on the other hand, had become so deeply divided by the late 1960s that it lost its privileged place in West German politics. It would need its own thirteen-year sojourn in the wilderness before it could return to its former dominance.

For the Federal Republic of Germany, especially in questions about the German-American alliance, politics never stopped at the water's edge. On the contrary, for a state whose existence depended on close cooperation with its allies, the domestic political balance was inseparable from international relations. Mastering this double challenge was the key to success in the Bonn Republic.

CHAPTER SIXTEEN

Personalities and Politics

The American Ambassadors to the Federal Republic

Suzanne Brown-Fleming

In late September 1959, Chancellor Konrad Adenauer of West Germany asked Ambassador David Bruce of the United States to pay him a "personal" visit. "He told me," recalled Bruce, "[that] he wanted to talk to me as his friend Mr. Bruce and not as ambassador." Bruce knew what such a request really meant: Adenauer needed to "express [certain] fears about U.S. government policy [or] some individuals connected with it." At Adenauer's request, Bruce treated these conversations as private and thus used great discretion when reporting to his superiors.[1] Particularly during the Adenauer governments, this ritual was crucial for healthy German-American relations; it allowed the chancellor to express his deepest concerns and, presumably, to have them swiftly conveyed to Washington. By 1968, however, this ritual had lost its substance.

Washington expected the American ambassador to keep his ear to the ground, maintain a loose leash on the chancellor, and faithfully report his observations on the latest developments. Each of the ambassadors to Germany between 1955 and 1968 attempted to go beyond these duties and make policy recommendations. Unless they already matched current thinking in the American administration, however, these efforts were ignored. The ambassadors' power, then, lay in their ability not to advise, but to listen

and observe. This function depended on maintaining a close relationship with the chancellor; the ambassadors' effectiveness must, therefore, be measured by this standard. Four men served as ambassadors to the Federal Republic of Germany between 1955 and 1968. The first, James Conant, was the least successful.

JAMES BRYANT CONANT
(MAY 1955–FEBRUARY 1957)

James Bryant Conant learned to admire Germany as an undergraduate studying chemistry at Harvard University. Born in 1893 to "hard working, middle income parents" of the Boston suburb of Dorchester, Conant became president of Harvard University at the tender age of forty. He gained far more notoriety, however, from his leadership in the Office of Scientific Research and Development (OSRD) S-1 section, which was responsible for building the atomic bomb. This brought him to the attention of the Truman and Eisenhower administrations and, in 1953, President Harry S. Truman asked him to become high commissioner to Germany. He served in this prestigious post from March 1953 until May 1955, when he became the first U.S. ambassador to the Federal Republic.[2]

---

[1] Diary Entry by the Ambassador to Germany, Sept. 30, 1959, in U.S. Department of State, *Foreign Relations of the United States* (hereafter *FRUS*), *1958–1960*, 9:55.

[2] James G. Hershberg, *James B. Conant: Harvard to Hiroshima and the Making of the Nuclear Age* (New York, 1993), 61. Secretary of State John Foster Dulles chose Conant on the advice of the current high commissioner,

More a scholar than a statesman,[3] Conant was singularly unsuccessful as ambassador. One of Conant's favorite activities during his posting was to visit German universities in a private train previously owned by Hermann Göring. He often spoke at graduation ceremonies, in fluent German, and relished "spirited conversations on deep, scholarly subjects" with German students and professors.[4] Conant could not develop as good a rapport, however, with the most important figure in the Federal Republic, Chancellor Konrad Adenauer. Adenauer, who enjoyed the staunch support of President Dwight Eisenhower and Secretary of State John Foster Dulles, disliked Conant. Worse, Adenauer recognized that Dulles placed significant limits on Conant's ability to shape American policy in Bonn. Although this is partly attributable to Dulles's general reluctance to delegate power to his diplomats abroad, it also reflects the fact that Conant's own skills as a diplomat did not nearly match his abilities as a scientist and administrator. Adenauer, therefore, repeatedly bypassed the high commissioner's office and dealt directly with Dulles or his advisers.[5]

On July 13, 1956, in the midst of the intense debate in the Bundestag over conscription legislation, the *New York Times* reported the possibility of a major reduction in U.S. ground troops stationed in the Federal Republic. The story echoed the claims of the opposition Social Democratic Party (*Sozialdemokratische Partei Deutschlands*, or SPD) and infuriated Adenauer.[6] Neither Eisenhower nor Dulles had hinted of any such reduction during Adenauer's visit to Washington the previous month. Adenauer, who knew that Washington bypassed its own ambassador at times, used the crisis to highlight

the incompetence of Conant. What good, argued the chancellor, was an ambassador who could not properly inform him of possible troop reductions?[7] Adenauer "could neither confide in nor trust" him. Even the local press referred to Conant as "Bubble-head."[8] Three days later, at Adenauer's request and with the approval of Eisenhower and Dulles, Conant was quietly offered the ambassadorship to India. His effectiveness as ambassador, already long questioned on account of his poor relations with the chancellor, had ended. Conant left the Bonn post in February 1957, departing on a "slightly sour note."[9] It was with great relief that Adenauer received his replacement, David Bruce.

DAVID K. E. BRUCE
(APRIL 1957–OCTOBER 1959)

Described by biographer Nelson Lankford as the "last American aristocrat,"[10] David Bruce was born in 1898 to a wealthy southern Virginia planter family; in 1925, he married the daughter of Secretary of the Treasury Andrew Mellon. Like Conant before him and George McGhee after him, Bruce had his first taste of a career in the Foreign Service during World War II when, as head of the European Theater of Operations, Office of Strategic Services (OSS), he witnessed the Blitz of London, D-Day, and the liberation of Paris. The war instilled in Bruce a lifelong distaste for Germans.

In 1957, Bruce became ambassador to a nation he disliked, but not before having registered a decade of distinguished service in West European foreign affairs. He was the head of the Economic Cooperation Administration (Marshall

John J. McCloy. See Thomas A. Schwartz, *America's Germany: John J. McCloy and the Federal Republic of Germany* (Cambridge, Mass., 1991), 280.

[3] See Hugh Appling, interview by Charles Stuart Kennedy, CD-ROM, June 26, 1990, Foreign Affairs Oral History Project (hereafter FAOH), National Foreign Affairs Training Center Arlington, Va.

[4] James Bahti, interview by Charles Stuart Kennedy, Mar. 26, 1990, FAOH.

[5] Hershberg, *James B. Conant*, 668.

[6] Ibid., 694.

[7] Adenauer insisted that the American ambassador inform him *directly* of important developments. When the chancellor heard an erroneous report that Ambassador Walter Dowling might be leaving, Adenauer reminded Dowling that "if and when the ambassador was to leave, he should come and tell the chancellor about it" (memorandum of conversation, Apr. 13, 1962, *FRUS, 1961–1963*, 15:104).

[8] Hershberg, *James B. Conant*, 688.

[9] Ibid., 703.

[10] Nelson Lankford, *The Last American Aristocrat: The Biography of David K. E. Bruce, 1898–1977* (Boston, 1996).

Plan) mission to France in 1948, ambassador to France in 1949–52, undersecretary of state in 1952, and special envoy to the European Defense Committee (EDC) talks from February 25, 1953, to December 19, 1954. Eisenhower, already sensing his mistake in appointing Conant high commissioner, offered Bruce a position in Bonn in October 1954. Bruce at first declined, telling Dulles to "send someone to Bonn who could speak German."[11] In truth, Bruce regretted that his mission, to rearm Germany within a supranational European organization (the EDC), had failed and found the prospects in the West German capital rather less grand than those of his previous assignments. Disappointed, he returned to Washington. Over the next three years, however, Bruce grew bored with private life and keenly aware of his awkward status as a prominent Democrat among the mostly Republican diplomats of the Eisenhower administration. Bonn offered Bruce the opportunity to maintain his membership in the foreign policy elite until a more attractive opportunity arose, and he accepted the posting in 1957.[12]

Bruce's diary entries revealed his dissatisfaction with his new surroundings: "I motored over to the East Sector [of Berlin, which] looked as dreary as ever, and the banal Stalinallee buildings dull as ditchwater. The people are, we are told, healthy and well-fed, but they must be unspeakably bored with their drab lives."[13] Bruce nevertheless cultivated an extremely strong relationship with Adenauer, whom he knew well from having worked with him on European integration alongside Jean Monnet, the chief economic adviser to France after World War II. Bruce spoke highly of Adenauer, noting that he contributed the "strongest and most consistent singular support for Monnet's European idea" and demonstrated "high political courage and deep moral sensibility in providing reparations to Israel." Best of all, added the francophile Bruce, was Adenauer's "passionate belief in the

merit of encasing Germany in a veritable Western European straitjacket."[14]

The greatest challenge to the Bonn embassy during Bruce's tenure was the second Berlin Crisis of November 1958. Using a carrot-and-stick approach, Soviet premier Nikita Khrushchev threatened to sign a separate peace treaty with the German Democratic Republic and grant the East Germans control over access to Berlin unless the Western Powers signed a "suitable" accord within six months.[15] Bruce immediately advocated a forceful response. Within a week after Khrushchev's note, Bruce advised the State Department to "say nothing which might lead [the Soviets] to infer that we would not use force to maintain our land and air access."[16] Although Dulles agreed with Bruce's hard line,[17] the Eisenhower administration showed a clear reluctance to use force. Bruce reacted with disdain: "Flexibility as an end in itself appears to me singularly dangerous; it is not a policy."[18] Furthermore, insisted Bruce, Americans were bound by "honor" to support West Berlin, even if this pledge meant nuclear war with the Soviets "if all else failed."[19]

Bruce submitted his resignation in fall 1959, a decision Adenauer regretted. The chancellor jokingly told Eisenhower that Bruce should

---

[14] Telegram From the Embassy in Germany to the Department of State, Feb. 17, 1959, *FRUS, 1958–1959*, 8:375.

[15] Frank A. Ninkovich, *Germany and the United States: The Transformation of the German Question Since 1945*, 2d ed. (New York, 1995), 117.

[16] Telegram from the Mission to the North Atlantic Treaty Organization and European Regional Organizations to the Department of State, Nov. 26, 1958, *FRUS, 1958–1959*, 8:130.

[17] Earlier that week, Dulles pronounced to Bruce "American readiness, if necessary, to resort to a general war in the face of aggression." Diary Entry by the Ambassador to Germany, Dec. 19, 1958, *FRUS, 1958–1959*, 8:220. For Dulles's impact on Germany policy generally, see Detlef Felken, *Dulles und Deutschland: Die amerikanishe Deutschlandspolitik 1953–1959* (Berlin, 1993).

[18] Telegram from the Embassy in Germany to the Department of State, Feb. 16, 1959, *FRUS, 1958–1959*, 8:361.

[19] Telegram from the Embassy in Germany to the Department of State, Mar. 2, 1959, *FRUS, 1958–1959*, 8:406–7.

---

[11] Ibid., 268.

[12] Ibid., 275–6, 293–4.

[13] Diary Entry by the Ambassador to Germany, Dec. 27, 1958, *FRUS, 1958–1959*, 8:223.

not be permitted to resign but should remain in Germany indefinitely. Bruce recalled that he "got out of that one" by saying that he had been happy in Germany but "simply had to return home."[20] Washington apparently lost its charm rapidly, for Bruce returned to Europe less than two years later, this time to London, where he served as ambassador until 1969. To his successor in Bonn, Walter Dowling, he left the inheritance of the ongoing Berlin Crisis.

WALTER CECIL DOWLING
(NOVEMBER 1959–APRIL 1963)

Walter Dowling came to the Bonn mission with much experience in European diplomatic affairs. He had served on the U.S. Advisory Council for Italy (1944), as assistant chief of the Division of Southwest European Affairs (1947), and later, as acting chief of that division (1949). He had also been deputy U.S. high commissioner for Austria in 1952 and then deputy high commissioner in Germany the following year. He replaced Bruce as ambassador in November 1959.[21] Embassy employee Emerson M. Brown has described Dowling as "very low profile, vis-à-vis the Germans."[22] He was the "consummate traditional diplomat."[23] Embassy official Joseph Greene provided a fuller sketch of Dowling, whom he called "very resourceful and intelligent, a professional officer who was wise in his ways without being too clever or too narrow-minded."[24] Like Bruce, Dowling enjoyed the close relationship with Adenauer that had so eluded Conant.[25] However, his reception

in Washington was lukewarm at best, especially during the administration of John F. Kennedy, who thought Dowling "reflected Bonn opinion too much to be the man to bend it."[26]

Dowling's tenure was dominated by growing Franco-German rapprochement and the Berlin Crisis. The Franco-German treaty of 1963 seemed to have the potential to "break up the dominant position the United States held in postwar West Germany."[27] Even more problematic was the issue of Berlin. By summer 1961, the status of Berlin still remained unresolved and the flow of refugees from east to west had reached intolerable proportions. In late July, the State Department warned the Bonn embassy that there "might be serious disorders in the [Eastern] Zone unless the East Germans took steps to control the flow of refugees to the west." Dowling could also "foresee [a] real possibility of explosion," but replied that "it [was] of course somewhat early to forecast [the] trend of events in [the] Soviet Zone."[28] When the GDR began to erect a barbed-wire fence around the periphery of West Berlin on August 13, Dowling was in Bad Godesberg watching a Sunday afternoon Little League baseball tournament. The U.S. mission in Berlin sent urgent telegrams to its Bonn counterpart, but the duty officer at the embassy did not see fit to inform Dowling. Instead, the ambassador received the news from a correspondent in Berlin several hours after the Wall was already under construction. Caught in this embarrassing situation, Dowling was

---

[20] Diary Entry by the Ambassador to Germany, Sept. 30, 1959, FRUS, 1958–1960, 9:56.

[21] U.S. Department of State, Biographic Register of 1961–1962, s.v. "Dowling, Walter Cecil."

[22] Emerson M. Brown, interview by Charles Stuart Kennedy, Feb. 2, 1990, FAOH.

[23] Thomas J. Dunnigan, interview by Charles Stuart Kennedy, Sept. 7, 1990, FAOH.

[24] Joseph N. Greene Jr., interview by Charles Stuart Kennedy, Mar. 12, 1993, FAOH.

[25] The sense of trust and frankness between the two men is evident in many of Dowling's reports to the State

Department. See FRUS, 1961–1963, 15:101–5, 276–7, and 13:269–72.

[26] Memorandum from President Kennedy to Secretary of State Rusk, Sept. 12, 1961, FRUS, 1961–1963, 14:402.

[27] Brown, interview. For Dowling's assessment of Bonn's position vis-à-vis France, see Adrian W. Schertz, Die Deutschlandpolitik Kennedys und Johnsons: Unterschiedliche Ansätze innerhalb der amerikanischen Regierung (Cologne, 1992), 156–7. See also the chapter by Eckart Conze, vol. 2, Politics.

[28] Telegram from the Embassy in Germany to the Department of State, July 12, 1961, FRUS, 1961–1963, 14:191; Frank A. Mayer, Adenauer and Kennedy: A Study in German-American Relations, 1961–1963 (New York, 1996), 35.

"absolutely livid," recalled embassy officer Elizabeth Brown.[29]

Dowling joined the Bonn embassy at a time of profound transformation in the German-American partnership. As he noted in March 1960, "we are rapidly approaching an end to that era of complete dependence of the Germans upon us, [a change] which some of us have affected to deplore." Dowling respected German strength, predicting that the Federal Republic would fast become a power to reckon with: "I have stressed in previous messages my belief that the Federal Republic must be firmly cemented into the fabric of the West as an *equal* ally, and that we must continue to support legitimate aspirations of the German people, including reunification." If the United States did not guide the Federal Republic toward American interests, its newfound independence might, noted Dowling, "contain elements of grave danger."[30] He believed it healthful, rather than merely preventive, for Germany to become a full and capable Western partner. Others in the administration, however, still had long memories of Germany's troubled past, including President Eisenhower himself. When Dowling urged the president not to abandon West Berlin, reminding him that it contained a population equal to that of Norway, Eisenhower fired back that "the Norwegians had not brought this on themselves by initiating an aggressive war."[31]

The German-American relationship was to become increasingly troubled throughout the next decade. "Double containment," the American policy created during the 1950s to counter the threat to world peace posed by Germany and Russia, ceased to be appropriate. During the 1960s, the United States sought détente with the Soviets, a shift that the German chancellery found difficult to accept. The demise of double containment raised another issue: Should Germany still be viewed as a threat, or truly accepted as an ally?[32] Dowling warned his superiors of impatience among Germans, "only beginning to be audible," with the fact that despite their attachment to the United States and the Atlantic community for the last fifteen years, they were still regarded as "second-class members" of the West.[33] Whereas Dowling rode out the peaks and valleys of changing relations, his successor, George McGhee, witnessed the decline – though one could also say the maturation – of the German-American partnership.

GEORGE CREWS MCGHEE
(MAY 1963–MAY 1968)

George McGhee accepted President John F. Kennedy's offer to become the fourth U.S. ambassador to the Federal Republic after nearly two decades of service in the State Department. McGhee was born in 1912 in Waco, Texas, to parents of modest means. A Rhodes scholar, McGhee earned a Ph.D. at Oxford University and became a geologist. A combination of sharp business acumen and an advantageous marriage into a wealthy Dallas oil family allowed McGhee to become an oil millionaire before he was thirty. What he called his "financial independence"[34] allowed him to pursue a career in the State Department. He took up his first appointment in January 1946, and by the time of his May 1963 assignment to the Bonn embassy, he had served as coordinator for Greek-Turkish Aid (1947–9), ambassador to Turkey (1951–3), and undersecretary for political affairs (1961–3).

[29] Elizabeth Ann Brown, interview by Thomas Dunnigan, May 30, 1995, FAOH.

[30] Telegram from the Embassy in Germany to the Department of State, Mar. 11, 1960, *FRUS, 1958–1960*, 9:217 (italics mine).

[31] Memorandum of Conference with President Eisenhower, Mar. 14, 1960, *FRUS, 1958–1960*, 9: 219–20.

[32] Ninkovich, *Germany and the United States*, 74–5, 135–6.

[33] Telegram from the Embassy in Germany to the Department of State, Mar. 11, 1960, *FRUS, 1958–1960*, 9:217.

[34] George McGhee, "Oxford Letters: The Transformation of a Texan," manuscript, The Ambassador George C. McGhee Library, Georgetown University School of Foreign Service, Washington, D.C., June 1991, 260.

McGhee's tenure as ambassador from 1963 to 1968 was characterized by what he called a "clearer separation, but not necessarily a divergence," of West German economic and political policy from that of the United States, especially after the fall of the Erhard government in late 1966.[35] The Federal Republic loosened its ties to "the American Protecting Power" and the Germans' "most important guarantor,"[36] strengthening instead its economic and political ties to France and the Eastern bloc countries. McGhee fit the pattern set by his two predecessors: He built a good relationship with Chancellors Ludwig Erhard and Kurt Georg Kiesinger and supported German interests faithfully, but Washington rarely accepted his policy suggestions. Three issues illustrate the frustrations McGhee faced in trying to further West German interests that diverged from the reigning outlook in the Oval Office: first, the responsibility for the cost of U.S. troops and supplies in West Germany, an increasingly divisive issue because of America's growing commitment to South Vietnam; second, West German access to nuclear power; and third, the beginnings of a new Ostpolitik under the Grand Coalition government (1966–9) of Chancellor Kiesinger and his foreign minister, Willy Brandt.

McGhee believed President Lyndon Johnson's stubborn stance on the issue of paying for American troops in Germany led to the so-called offset-payments crisis that contributed to the collapse of the Erhard government in 1966.[37] In late summer 1966, Erhard visited Johnson in Washington, seeking an extension on West German payments for U.S. military equipment and services (offset payments), which under the current agreement were due in full by June 1967. McGhee, who enjoyed a close relationship with Erhard and was privy to the chancellor's intentions, became "increasingly apprehensive" about this meeting. He wanted to speak to Johnson personally, but the president was vacationing at his ranch. McGhee instead drafted a memorandum to Johnson, urging him to "take into account Erhard's weakened political position [in that] an obvious failure for Erhard in the talks could bring down his government ... we should be prepared without sacrificing vital interests to make accommodation with him."[38] Johnson ignored McGhee's cable, demanding that Erhard pay in full by June 1967. In Johnson's view, the relative strength of the German mark against the American dollar and the British pound left the Germans in the best position to "pay up." The alternative, a reduction of troops stationed in West Germany, was "out of the question" because it might weaken the NATO alliance.[39] Forced to propose an unpopular tax increase in order to meet the offset payment, Erhard watched his cabinet collapse and announced his resignation on November 2, 1966.

Parallel to the offset-payments crisis, the Federal Republic's nuclear status became another major issue in German-American relations during McGhee's mission. The Federal Republic's dependence on the United States for nuclear protection was increasingly unacceptable to German leadership. Germany saw its chance for nuclear participation in the multilateral force (MLF), the concept of a NATO-controlled fleet that would allow West Germany (and other NATO allies) to participate meaningfully in the control of NATO nuclear weapons. More important to the United States was that the MLF would inhibit "purely national nuclear weapons programs."[40] The MLF, however, had many enemies, including the British, the

---

[35] George McGhee, *At the Creation of a New Germany: From Adenauer to Brandt, An Ambassador's Account* (New Haven, Conn., 1989), 229.

[36] Willy Brandt, *People and Politics: The Years 1960 to 1975* (Boston, 1976), 318.

[37] McGhee, *At the Creation of a New Germany*, 182; Thomas A. Schwartz, "Victories and Defeats in the Long Twilight Struggle: The United States and Western Europe in the 1960s," in Diane B. Kunz, ed., *The Diplomacy of the Crucial Decade: American Foreign Relations During the 1960s* (New York, 1994), 138–40. See also the chapter by Hubert Zimmermann, vol. 1, Economics.

[38] George McGhee, *On the Frontline in the Cold War: An Ambassador Reports* (Westport, Conn., 1997), 175–6.

[39] Lyndon Baines Johnson, *The Vantage Point: Perspectives of the Presidency, 1963–1969* (New York, 1971), 306.

[40] Memorandum to All NATO Capitals from Secretary of State Rusk, Feb. 15, 1964, fiche 8: George McGhee files, U.S. Department of State.

Italians, and especially the French, who sponsored instead their *force de frappe*, an independent nuclear arsenal under national control. Johnson abandoned the MLF in December 1964 without informing Erhard.[41] McGhee cabled Johnson in September 1966 to remind him that "it would be wise to inform Erhard confidentially that we [the United States] regard the MLF as unlikely of achievement." With such a warning, Erhard could prepare himself for the criticism Adenauer's "Gaullist" camp would level at him when hearing the Federal Republic remained excluded from nuclear control.[42] Just as he ignored McGhee's warnings with regard to the offset issue, Johnson disregarded the ambassador's advice.

The question of West Germany's nuclear status continued to burden German-American relations after the Kiesinger-Brandt coalition took office in 1966. The Non-Proliferation Treaty (NPT), signed in July 1968 by the Soviet Union, the United Kingdom, the United States, and more than fifty other countries, barred states without nuclear weapons from constructing or purchasing them in the future. The West German government, McGhee informed Johnson, objected to the treaty on the grounds that it would "forever deprive Germany of the ultimate means of self-defense" and "lock [Germany] into a position of permanent inferiority."[43] West Germany signed the treaty a year later, but the damage to German-American relations had been done. Just as America's increasing commitment to Vietnam prevailed over Erhard's plea that Johnson reduce the ceiling on offset payments, Soviet-American interests took precedence over the German-American partnership in the area of nuclear weapons. In both cases, McGhee tried to reduce the damage to diplomatic relations by encouraging Johnson to be flexible and frank with his German counterparts, but he was ignored. McGhee himself eventually paid the price: After Kiesinger complained that McGhee was not providing the Germans with enough information, McGhee "became something of a *persona non grata* in Bonn."[44]

McGhee's failure to persuade the Oval Office to share his faith in Germany was poignantly demonstrated by the effects of West Germany's new Ostpolitik on German-American relations. As Ostpolitik began to take shape under the Grand Coalition, Washington worried that the policy would make West Germany more susceptible to Soviet pressure and influence. These concerns would later intensify under the administration of Richard Nixon after Brandt became chancellor in 1969 and Ostpolitik entered its most active phase.[45] McGhee did not share these fears; instead, he found the Federal Republic's new political independence "refreshing and healthy."[46] When what McGhee called a "wave of anxiety" over Ostpolitik hit Washington in October 1967, he told Assistant Secretary of State for European Affairs John M. Leddy that "the West German effort toward a better relationship with the Soviet Union was fully consonant with Western interests [and] American interests."[47]

CONCLUSION

The personal style of the American ambassador in Bonn and his relationship with the chancellor

[41] Ninkovich, *Germany and the United States*, 134; Frank Costigliola, "Lyndon B. Johnson, Germany, and 'the End of the Cold War,'" in Warren I. Cohen and Nancy Bernkopf Tucker, eds., *Lyndon Johnson Confronts the World: American Foreign Policy, 1963–1968* (New York, 1994), 190. See also the chapter by Erhard Forndran, Junker, vol. 1, Security section.

[42] Memorandum from Ambassador McGhee to President Johnson, Sept. 22, 1966, fiche 14: George McGhee files, U.S. Department of State.

[43] Memorandum from Ambassador McGhee to President Johnson, Apr. 25, 1967, fiche 18: George McGhee files, U.S. Department of State.

[44] Gregory F. Treverton, *The Dollar Drain and American Forces in Germany* (Athens, Ohio, 1978), 90.

[45] McGhee, *At the Creation of a New Germany*, 242; Brandt, *People and Politics*, 288.

[46] George McGhee, interview by author, tape recording, Washington, D.C., Dec. 3, 1992.

[47] Memorandum from Ambassador McGhee to the Assistant Secretary of State for European Affairs (Leddy), Oct. 12, 1967, fiche 7: George McGhee files, U.S. Department of State.

were especially important in the early years of the Adenauer government. Adenauer's close ties with Secretary of State John Foster Dulles highlighted his inability to confide in Conant. Adenauer insisted on expressing his concerns to a trusted medium that had enough influence to convey them directly to the Oval Office. This was not particularly difficult during the 1950s, when American policy toward Germany complemented containment of the Soviet threat. The common Soviet enemy made a close German-American partnership essential. As superpower détente began to emerge in the 1960s, however, the Federal Republic's position on the American agenda changed. The ambassadors could no longer provide the chancellor with a direct link to makers of foreign policy in Washington. Adenauer had noticed already in the late 1950s that communication was beginning to deteriorate, and he reminded Dowling that changes in leadership of the Bonn embassy should be discussed directly with the chancellor. Erhard, like his predecessor, confided in McGhee and expected his concerns to be transmitted directly to the president. McGhee faithfully complied, only to be ignored in Washington. The power of the U.S. ambassadors never lay in their ability to influence policy but in their skill at cultivating a close relationship with the chancellor and managing the flow of information between the chancellery and the Oval Office. By the mid-1960s, however, these functions had become all but irrelevant: No matter how close the relationship between the ambassador and the chancellor, the goals of Washington and Bonn now diverged.

CHAPTER SEVENTEEN

The Ambassadors of the Federal Republic of Germany in Washington, 1955–1968

Rainer A. Blasius

Translated by Sally E. Robertson

Ambassadors oversee official communications and business between governments and ordinarily reside in the capital of their host country. Such obvious facts are worth remembering when we look at relations between the United States and the Federal Republic of Germany between 1955 and 1968 (and during the period before the opening of diplomatic relations on May 6, 1955) from the perspective of the head of the West German diplomatic mission. The character of international relations with the Germans was an open question following Germany's unconditional surrender in May 1945 and the revelation of the crimes against humanity committed during the era of the Third Reich. Accordingly, the new beginning of bilateral relations in June 1950 started on an extremely modest basis.

HEINZ L. KREKELER (1950–8)

The first representative of the Federal Republic sent to the United States was of necessity a man with as few ties as possible to "Wilhelmstrasse," the old Foreign Office in Berlin. A Foreign Ministry in Bonn did not as yet exist. Instead, an "Office for Foreign Affairs in the Federal Chancellery," established on June 7, 1950, maintained missions abroad to represent the Federal Republic in consular and economic matters. These offices were designated as Consulates General or, simply, Consulates.

At the express wish of Chancellor Adenauer, Heinz L. Krekeler was named General Con-

sul in New York, notably not in Washington, but with executive authority for the consular district of the United States of America. The chemist and cofounder of the Free Democratic Party (*Freie Demokratische Partei*, or FDP) took up his office in New York on June 28, 1950. His job was not to conduct business with the American government; Adenauer himself performed this function via the high commissioner in Bonn. Rather, Krekeler concentrated on a very successful, intensive travel and lecture program aimed at building confidence in the young Federal Republic among the American people.

Exactly one year later, after the Foreign Office had been reestablished as a federal ministry on March 15, 1951, Krekeler became chargé d'affaires and head of the "Diplomatic Delegation of the Federal Republic of Germany" in Washington. After the Federal Republic gained its sovereignty in May 1955, he also became its first ambassador to the United States.

Krekeler felt that one of the most dramatic periods during his mission was the sequence of events surrounding the Radford Plan in July 1956. This plan made it seem conceivable that the Federal Republic would be "liberated" from advancing Soviet troops by atomic annihilation, the result of massive American retaliatory attacks.[1]

---

[1] Werner Abelshauser and Walter Schwengler, *Wirtschaft und Rüstung: Souveränität und Sicherheit* (Munich, 1997), 39. See also the chapter by Kori Schake, vol. 1, Security.

The furor unleashed by this horrifying scenario was so great that Krekeler was immediately summoned to Bonn to make a report. On July 24, 1956, the chancellor instructed him to draft a letter to U.S. Secretary of State John Foster Dulles. Adenauer himself then reworked the draft thoroughly, attempting to make a forceful appeal to Dulles's conscience. The chancellor declared that "no one whose behavior is determined by Christian faith and Christian ethics can justify such a development before God or his own conscience." The letter closed with the admonition, "I pray to God that He will guide and direct you."[2]

Further investigation in Washington revealed that the Radford Plan had merely been a preliminary draft written by a policy expert. The skeptical Adenauer's reluctance to accept his diplomats' conclusion about the document contributed significantly – in the opinion of the embassy – to a deterioration in German-American relations. Envoy Albrecht von Kessel pointed out that Secretary of State Dulles, Admiral Arthur Radford, and James B. Conant, who represented the United States in the Federal Republic as ambassador from 1955 to 1957,[3] must therefore have "felt that the Chancellor was branding them as outright or reckless liars."[4]

The relationship between the West German government and its diplomatic representatives in Washington had its share of friction during 1956 and 1957. Bonn accused the embassy of making incomplete reports on various occasions. In response, Kessel complained to Georg von Lilienfeld, director of the American desk at the Foreign Ministry and later ambassador to Washington: "Without instructions, [the German embassy] is not in a position to represent the policies of the Federal Republic. We are

instead forced to pursue an independent policy. It is a miracle that it has been possible to maintain both of these policies up to now."[5]

Such admonishments even show through to some degree in the résumé report that Ambassador Krekeler wrote for Foreign Minister Heinrich von Brentano at the end of his mission after Adenauer offered him a high position in the European Atomic Energy Community (EURATOM) in December 1957. The ambassador sharply warned against "suggesting [to the Americans] that their foreign policy ideas are primitive" and recommended that "the foundation of trust in the alliance be maintained at all costs."[6]

WILHELM G. GREWE (1958–62)

The position of ambassador to the United States subsequently went to Wilhelm G. Grewe, who for many years had served as director of the legal and political divisions of the Foreign Ministry. On February 26, 1958, the international law professor and former adviser to Adenauer assumed leadership of the embassy in the American capital.

During his first two years in office, Grewe enjoyed the full support of Bonn, demonstrated not least by the fact that he was assigned to lead the German delegation to the Four-Power Conference of Foreign Ministers in Geneva in 1959. Not until the beginning of the Kennedy administration was the ambassador discredited both at home and at his Washington base of operations.

At first Grewe felt that the Kennedy administration offered "far greater opportunities for close contact than its predecessor ... given the type and generation of the new people."[7] The first shadow fell across Grewe's enthusiasm for Kennedy during Adenauer's visit on April 12–13, 1961. The ambassador took offense at

[2] Heinz L. Krekeler, *Meine Mission in den Vereinigten Staaten von Amerika* (typed manuscript, 1979), 285, ED 15/173, Institut für Zeitgeschichte, Munich.

[3] Prior to his appointment as ambassador, Conant had served two years as U.S. high commissioner to Germany. See the chapter by Suzanne Brown-Fleming in this section.

[4] Kessel to Brentano (draft), Nov. 23, 1956, Kessel Estate, vol. 7, Politisches Archiv des Auswärtigen Amts, Bonn (hereafter PA/AA).

[5] Kessel to Lilienfeld, Nov. 3, 1956, ibid.

[6] Carbon copy of a fifteen-page typed manuscript (hand-dated February 1958), ED 135/48, Institut für Zeitgeschichte, Munich.

[7] Grewe to Carstens (carbon copy), Nov. 27, 1960, Grewe Estate, vol. 82, PA/AA.

the fact that the joint communiqué contained merely an acknowledgment of the Germans' right to self-determination and a reaffirmation of the promise "to preserve the freedom of the population of West Berlin." For the first time, an American president referred to "West Berlin" rather than "Berlin," a shift that displeased the attentive international law expert.[8]

In June 1961, the Foreign Ministry in Bonn took exception to Grewe's increasingly negative reporting on the Kennedy administration.[9] Adenauer himself initiated this rebuke. In a letter to Brentano on May 31, 1961, he described Grewe's detailed analysis of the new president as "incorrect" and Kennedy as an "intelligent man of vision." Adenauer thus suggested that the minister should consider transferring Grewe at an early opportunity because the ambassador did not currently possess "all the qualities required for this important post" in the United States.[10]

No action was taken on the chancellor's devastating evaluation, and developments in summer 1961 would overtake it. In a television address to the American people on July 25, Kennedy announced (or "reduced," according to Grewe) the basic guidelines for his Berlin policy. The remaining three essentials were the presence of Western troops, unimpeded access to and from Berlin, and the security and freedom of the population. From the perspective of the ambassador, the Americans had at least demonstrated their resolve to defend (West) Berlin. However, none of this deterred the German Democratic Republic (GDR) from erecting the Wall along the Western sectors of Berlin with Soviet support and fortifying its border with the Federal Republic.

The reaction of Western governments and the German federal government to the building of the Wall was notoriously weak, all the more so because Kennedy continued discussions with the Soviet Union through Secretary of State Dean Rusk. The ambassador also felt hindered by the "leadership gap in Bonn" that existed prior to the Bundestag elections and even more so after the loss of the Christian Democrats' absolute majority on September 17, 1961. For weeks, uncertainty existed about whether Adenauer would lead the government for the fourth time. Grewe quickly gained the impression that Bonn's foreign policy "needed to offer an interpretative framework, initiative, articulation, and public clarification with greater frequency and intensity than in normal times."[11]

The first of Grewe's outspoken remarks occurred during a radio interview on September 10, 1961, in which he called Berlin the symbol of national unity and stated that negotiations should not be conducted about Berlin in isolation but only in the context of European security and perhaps general disarmament.[12] This clear message was only the prelude to his first stunning television appearance on September 22, 1961, in which he declared that it was "not a good policy to answer maximum demands from the Eastern side with maximum concessions from the Western side." He argued that the principles of the joint Western policy had, since 1954, consisted of "non-recognition of the present frontiers of Germany" and "non-recognition of East Germany as a separate state."[13]

On October 8, 1961, two days after a high-profile meeting in the White House between Kennedy and Soviet Foreign Minister Andrei Gromyko, Grewe made his last major television appearance in the United States. By the time of the broadcast, the German diplomat had still received no official information from the State Department regarding the meeting. Thus, based on press reports, he condemned

[8] Wilhelm G. Grewe, *Rückblenden 1976–1951* (Frankfurt am Main, 1979), 462–4.

[9] Carstens to Grewe, June 15, 1961, Grewe Papers, vol. 82, PA/AA.

[10] Adenauer to Brentano, May 31, 1961, in Arnulf Baring, *Sehr verehrter Herr Bundeskanzler! Heinrich von Brentano im Briefwechsel mit Konrad Adenauer 1949–1964* (Hamburg, 1974), 316.

[11] Grewe, *Rückblenden*, 492.

[12] News from the German Embassy, Sept. 23, 1961, Grewe Estate, vol. 82, PA/AA.

[13] Federal Ambassador to the U.S. on the Free World's Tactics, in Press and Information Office of the German Federal Government, *The Bulletin* 10 (Oct. 3, 1961): 5.

the Kennedy-Gromyko meeting in Washington as a "step backwards" compared to the Rusk-Gromyko talks in New York in September. He said that the "unsettling thing is that the conclusion of these talks was more negative than the beginning, which is not very encouraging." His public relations effort was unusual for a diplomat; after reprimanding the American administration for its handling of the negotiations, Grewe forcefully warned that the vital interests of Berlin needed to be taken into consideration in future negotiations.[14]

Kennedy's willingness in April 1962 to officially discuss with the Soviet Union the idea of setting up an international agency to govern access to the divided Berlin triggered the most serious crisis of confidence between Washington and Bonn since the Radford Plan. On April 9, 1962, the American recommendations, or Draft Principles, went to the ambassador of the Federal Republic. The proposed negotiating package included not only the question of a special authority for controlling access to Berlin but also an agreement on such issues as nonproliferation of nuclear weapons and use of technical commissions composed of representatives of the Federal Republic and the GDR to oversee cultural contacts and promote economic exchange. Because Rusk wanted to negotiate all these points with Soviet Ambassador Anatoly Dobrynin just a few days later, the Federal Republic was given a period of just forty-eight hours to respond. Grewe immediately transmitted the Draft Principles to Adenauer. Because the deadline was issued in the manner of an ultimatum and because of the content of the negotiating paper, Bonn began to fear that recognition of the GDR was on the agenda. The West German government went into alarm mode. Politicians from all the parties sitting in the

Bundestag were called together for a cross-party crisis session on the afternoon of April 12. At the same time, the first details of the negotiating proposals aired on German radio and appeared in some newspapers. The *New York Times* and *Washington Post* picked up the reports the next day. Confidence was on the verge of collapse. That same evening, April 13, an incensed Foy Kohler of the State Department called Grewe to vent the outrage of the American government. The next morning, Grewe had to account for the incident. Kohler traced the press reports back to official sources in Bonn. "Ambassador Grewe said he failed to see what the Germans could have hoped to gain from a leak. It would not, after all, improve the Ambassador's position, and that is well known in Bonn."[15] Soon thereafter, Grewe discovered how right he was when a widely read and well-connected columnist wrote: "The White House has long believed that Ambassador Wilhelm Grewe in Washington has been a primary instigator of the leak system and President Kennedy has frequently expressed in private his annoyance at what he regarded as Grewe's violation of the canons of diplomacy."[16] With this assessment, the ambassador became fair game.

Researchers no longer rule out the possibility that Adenauer may have been the source of this perhaps unintentional but probably deliberate indiscretion.[17] Nevertheless, the chancellor ended the ambassadorial crisis in his own pragmatic way. At a press conference in Berlin on May 7, 1962, he first expressed his opposition to the proposal of a special authority for controlling access roads to Berlin as a first step toward international legal recognition of the GDR. Then, without missing a beat, he suddenly announced that he was recalling Grewe from Washington

---

[14] Interview of the ambassador of the Federal Republic in Washington, Grewe, for the television program *Issues and Answers* of the American Broadcasting Company, Oct. 8, 1961, in *Dokumente zur Deutschlandpolitik*, ed. Bundesministerium für Innerdeutsche Beziehungen, series 4, vol. 7 (Frankfurt am Main, 1976), 678–86, quotations on 679.

[15] Memorandum of conversation, Apr. 14, 1962, in U.S. Department of State, *Foreign Relations of the United States* (hereafter FRUS), 1961–1963, 15:110.

[16] Marquis W. Childs, "Bonn's Use of Leaks Is Making Allied Unity More of a Problem than East-West Differences," *St. Louis Post Dispatch*, Apr. 17, 1962, C-1.

[17] Henning Köhler, *Adenauer: Eine politische Biographie* (Frankfurt am Main, 1994), 593.

with the words: "When complications arise, the innocent always have to suffer!"[18]

KARL HEINRICH KNAPPSTEIN (1962–8)

Grewe's succession was handled quickly and pragmatically. After the obligatory preliminaries, President Kennedy granted official recognition on June 6, 1962, to the next ambassador, Karl Heinrich Knappstein, who had served as the Federal Republic's observer at the United Nations in New York. Knappstein had been an economic policy editor for the *Frankfurter Zeitung* prior to 1945. He arrived in Washington on September 10, 1962. Just two months later, from November 13 to 15, 1962, Adenauer's last visit to Washington was staged as a thoroughly harmonious summit meeting between the countries. However, this momentary high was followed by a low point never seen before.

On January 14, 1963, U.S. Undersecretary of State George Ball presented a proposal in Bonn to include the Federal Republic in the planned multilateral nuclear force (MLF).[19] The chancellor responded positively from Paris a short time later, on January 22, 1963, and also gave notice that the treaty on German-French cooperation was about to be signed. Knappstein had to deliver this letter to the president in person on January 23, 1963. But in their thirty-five-minute conversation, Kennedy expressed annoyance at the Paris treaty and concern "that the Germans and French want to form a *force within a force*." He considered it possible "that Bonn might in the future support Paris in its anti-Americanism," with catastrophic consequences for NATO and "the fight against Communist expansion in all parts of the world."[20]

From February 4 to 7, 1963, Undersecretary Karl Carstens was dispatched to the U.S. capital at Knappstein's request to support him in conducting a total of fifteen conversations with more than ninety interlocutors on the matter. From that point on, both the undersecretary and Foreign Minister Gerhard Schröder endorsed a resolution by the Bundestag that put the emphasis on NATO and the United States and that, after much domestic debate, resulted in the preamble to the law ratifying the French-German Treaty adopted on May 16, 1963. On the first anniversary of the treaty, Knappstein offered a precise description of the difference between Washington's relationships with Paris and with Bonn: "The French-American relationship is 'poor' but firm, solidly founded and apparently unshakable. The German-American relationship is 'good' but superficial and easily damaged."[21] Adenauer's successor, Ludwig Erhard, and Foreign Minister Schröder ignored this apt assessment. Both believed that they could use their resentments toward French President Charles de Gaulle to curry favor with Kennedy's successor, Lyndon B. Johnson, and thus move the United States toward a joint anti-French policy.

Beginning in fall 1963, considerable problems arose between Bonn, Paris, and Washington during the preliminary negotiations over an MLF. De Gaulle and the German "Gaullists," particularly former Chancellor Adenauer, did everything to prevent the MLF and its proponents from being publicly discredited at the very outset. By contrast, the "Atlanticists" in Bonn surrounding Chancellor Erhard clung to the hope that a corresponding treaty could be signed, sealed, and delivered by the end of 1964. American and British efforts to achieve an agreement with the Soviets on nuclear nonproliferation foiled this wishful thinking.

---

[18] Quoted in Hans-Peter Schwarz, *Adenauer: Der Staatsmann, 1952–1967* (Stuttgart, 1991), 749.

[19] On the MLF, see the chapter by Erhard Forndran, vol. 1, Security.

[20] Ambassador Knappstein, Washington, to Foreign Minister Schröder, Jan. 23, 1963, in Hanz-Peter Schwarz, ed., in cooperation with the Foreign Office and the Institut für Zeitgeschichte, *Akten zur Auswärtigen*

Politik der Bundesrepublik Deutschland 1963 (hereafter *AAPD*), 1:163–5, quotations on 164.

[21] Ambassador Knappstein, Washington, to the Foreign Ministry, Jan. 22, 1964, *AAPD* 1964, 1:114. On this triangle of relationships, see the chapter by Eckart Conze, vol. 2, Politics.

To escape the muddled situation, Erhard even proposed to Johnson on September 30, 1964, that as a first step, Bonn and Washington should sign the MLF charter alone. At the end of 1964, the recently elected Johnson reacted with what Knappstein called the soft approach to alliance policy. He left the Europeans alone to see, first, if they could agree on the nuclear defense of Europe without American pressure.[22]

In November 1964, Knappstein first noticed a possible shift in the direction of White House policy on MLF and reported it. On November 21, 1964, he told Foreign Minister Schröder, upon the arrival of the latter in Washington: "The status of MLF is very tricky here. The government, particularly the State Department, stands very firm on MLF and is encouraging us to stand firm. But we have observed a growing resistance on the part of the press, particularly leading journalists and the major newspapers. I fear that the president will not be immune to the pressure." Despite this, the minister instructed the embassy to make the positive stance of the German federal government on MLF "forcefully clear" in Washington. In December 1964, at the last cabinet meeting of the year, Schröder was accused in Bonn of pushing the issue of the MLF too hard and pursuing it even "when it was already dead and buried in Washington." In response and against his better judgment, he named a scapegoat in front of a sizable audience. Ambassador Knappstein was a "completely unsuitable man," Schröder declared, who belonged to the "sad legacy" that he had been forced to adopt from his predecessor Brentano; he had "kept the Foreign Ministry only poorly or belatedly informed, if at all." Federal Minister Heinrich Krone informed Knappstein of Schröder's tirade and declared, to the contrary, that it was much too easy to blame "inadequate reporting by the ambassador" for how discussion in the United States had developed and the Federal Republic's reaction to it.[23]

Krone knew all too well that it had been a long time since foreign policy business with major powers and significant allies could simply be conducted through correspondence with a diplomatic delegation or oral status reports made by an ambassador. Another issue was the position of Ambassador George McGhee in Bonn. Between May 16, 1963, and May 21, 1968, McGhee had by his own reckoning

participated in 344 meetings with senior West German officials, including 24 with President Lübke, and 96 with the three chancellors, including 14 with Adenauer, 65 with Erhard, and 15 with Kiesinger. I held 39 meetings with Foreign Minister Brandt and 29 with Foreign Minister Schröder, 64 with Undersecretary Carstens, and 117 with other ministers and their subordinates.[24]

Such a successful record for a diplomat, impressively confirmed by reading minutes from meetings in the Foreign Ministry and the Chancellery, illustrates the extent to which Knappstein was at a disadvantage in Washington. He was acutely conscious of his "lack of contact with Johnson."[25] Whereas McGhee more or less came and went as he pleased in the German Foreign Ministry and the Chancellery, the same was unthinkable for a German ambassador in Washington.

In the negotiations in subsequent years over a say in nuclear policy, foreign-exchange settlements,[26] nonproliferation agreements,[27] support for the United States in the Vietnam War,[28] and stationing of U.S. troops in the Federal Republic, the embassy primarily had an

---

[22] Ambassador Knappstein, Washington, to the Foreign Ministry, Dec. 30, 1964, *AAPD* 1964, 2:1570–77.

[23] The following according to correspondence of Knappstein with Federal Minister Heinrich Krone: Knappstein to Krone, Jan. 13, 1965 (letter is erroneously dated 1964 by Knappstein), and Krone to Knappstein, Feb. 4, 1965, Krone Estate, I-028–005/4, Archiv für Christlich-Demokratische Politik, St. Augustin (hereafter ACDP).

[24] George McGhee, *At the Creation of a New Germany: From Adenauer to Brandt: An Ambassador's Account* (New Haven, Conn., 1989), 268.

[25] Knappstein to Krone, Jan. 13, 1965, Krone Estate, I-028–005/4, ACDP.

[26] See the chapter by Hubert Zimmermann, vol. 1, Economics.

[27] See the chapter by Matthias Dembinski, vol. 2, Security.

[28] See the chapter by T. Michael Ruddy, vol. 2, Security.

observer function. This was not least of all because special emissaries such as Rainer Barzel,
Kurt Birrenbach, Georg Ferdinand Duckwitz,
Karl Theodor Freiherr von und zu Gutten-
berg, Helmut Schmidt, and many others were
constantly coming and going in Washington.
Therefore, before going into early retirement
at the end of the Johnson administration on
December 20, 1968, Knappstein stepped into
the spotlight once more on January 30, 1968,
to issue a major cable on "The American Attitude Toward Our Eastern Europe Policy,"
which had become a substantial issue since
the formation of the "Grand Coalition" under Kurt Georg Kiesinger (CDU) and Willy
Brandt (SPD). Knappstein described the growing impression held in the United States about
the West German government's policies: "We
could ultimately be compelled to recognize the
'GDR' without actually gaining any concessions for the population there." Washington, he
stated, was not ruling out the possibility "that
the Germans might go their own dangerous way
to achieve unification through direct negotiations with Moscow. If Germans go their own
way, they might go over into the other camp."
Like his two predecessors, Knappstein thus recommended extremely close consultations with
the United States.[29]

CONCLUSION

The age of influential and worldly super-
ambassadors had ended by the beginning of the
second half of the twentieth century. In the wake
of the travel and summit diplomacy that had
been common since the 1940s, official diplomatic delegations abroad were now responsible
more for cultivating personal contacts and conducting day-to-day political business than for
helping to craft major policy decisions.[30] Modern transportation and communications tech-

nology contributed decisively to this transformation. These benefited a range of competitors
who were gradually emerging and threatened
ambassadors' claim to be the sole representatives of their countries' interests. Ambassadors
now faced the claims of representatives from political parties, banks, industry, and foundations,
not to mention the influence of their counterparts in regional and international organizations
and other governmental bodies. Nevertheless,
the overall political responsibility for relations
with the host country, at least in theory, remained (and remains) that of the ambassadors.
The fact that the leader of the diplomatic delegation was completely dependent on the policies of his own government was the common
experience of Heinz L. Krekeler, Wilhelm G.
Grewe, and Karl Heinrich Knappstein, even as
their individual experiences of the position varied. The three ambassadors were appointed from
outside Bonn's foreign-service ranks and were,
therefore, not burdened by the "Wilhelmstrasse
mark" of the old Foreign Office in Berlin.[31]

Krekeler was in Washington at a time when
Chancellor Adenauer monopolized foreign policy in general and German-American relations
in particular, conducting them by means of summit diplomacy and contacts with the high commissioner or, later, with the U.S. ambassador in
Bonn. Diplomatic representatives abroad were
largely left to fend for themselves.

Grewe represented the Federal Republic at a
time when the old formula of the Western Powers, "according to which global détente could be
only achieved by reunification, was being firmly
[pushed] aside."[32] The new trend amounted to
a reversal: first détente, then reunification. The
ambassador fought this on his own initiative
and with great passion in fall 1961. It was the
downfall of Grewe, who had also made himself

---

[29] Ambassador Knappstein, Washington, to the Foreign Ministry, Jan. 30, 1968, *AAPD* 1968, 1:117–20,
here: 120.

[30] Gordon A. Craig and Francis Loewenheim, eds.,
The Diplomats 1939–1979 (Princeton, N.J., 1994), 5–7.

[31] On the ambassadors who held the post in Washington, see also Frank Lambach, *Der Draht nach Washington: Von den ersten preussischen Ministerresidenten bis zu
den Botschaftern der Bundesrepublik Deutschland* (Cologne,
1976).

[32] Klaus Hildebrand, *Integration und Souveränität: Die
Aussenpolitik der Bundesrepublik Deutschland 1949–1982*
(Bonn, 1991), 54.

unpopular in the State Department and White House with his public appearances and pedantic style. Though completely blameless, he had to bear the consequences of indiscretions at the same time that Adenauer managed to achieve a temporary victory over the "reincarnation of the American appeasement line."[33]

Knappstein occupied his post in Washington in what was certainly the most difficult period of German-American relations. He put all his energy into overcoming the serious crisis of confidence that arose in spring 1962 and eradicating any further suspicion of a "great leak" in the embassy. As Adenauer turned partially away from the United States and began cautiously concentrating on France, as Erhard returned the focus completely to the United States, and as Kiesinger turned cautiously back toward France (and focused on a new Ostpolitik, set in motion together with Brandt), Knappstein worked around the many special emissaries from Bonn and strove, with patience and skill, to explain Germany to Washington.

[33] Schwarz, *Adenauer*, 743.

CHAPTER EIGHTEEN

Berlin

Catalyst and Fault Line of German–American Relations in the Cold War

Diethelm Prowe

Throughout the Cold War, Berlin played a pivotal role in German-American relations. The American defense and material support of the Western sectors of the old German capital against the most unremitting Soviet assaults at the front lines of the Cold War forged the earliest and strongest bonds between Americans and Germans. These battles also created a strong American identification with West Berlin, which weakened isolationist tendencies in the United States. The severest of the Berlin crises even contributed significantly to a reshaping of American policies toward Germany and Europe. Yet, the city also put a burden on German-American relations. During the peak years of the Cold War, the Berlin issue was more vulnerable than any other to a creeping mistrust and divergence of interests that could not be allowed to break into the open because both the Americans and the West Germans had too much invested in Berlin as a symbol – of their Cold War leadership for the former and of their exclusive claim of national representation for the latter.

Even though the Soviet and American World War II allies clashed first in Berlin, the basic shift in postwar American policy toward Germany was not *caused* by the confrontation in that city.[1] But it was in Berlin that a deeper sense of common purpose was built, which became essential for the German-American relationship. Here, the Cold War first became a concrete reality for American administrators, as the confrontation lines within the Four Power Allied Control Council for Germany and the Berlin Kommandatura increasingly ran between the Soviets on one side and the three Western Powers on the other. The earliest local frictions between American and Soviet authorities involved troop movements, access routes, and military quarters. This soured the atmosphere among the Allies without as yet affecting the relationship with the Berlin population. But when the Soviets moved against basic democratic freedoms of Berliners, the fundamental principles of the American occupation government's democratization mission for Germany were challenged. Even though the Allies remained determined to prevent the defeated Germans from driving wedges between them, an increasing number of American officials found it difficult to refuse support to Berliners wishing to exercise their most basic rights of political expression.

The first such occasion that stirred American political officers into action was the effort of the Soviets' German communist agents between November 1945 and March 1946 to force Social Democrats to merge with the Communist Party by preventing or manipulating a membership referendum in the Western sectors of Berlin. The fact that the U.S. City Commandant publicly promised enforcement

[1] For an analysis of the causes, see the chapters by Manfred Görtemaker and Frank Schumacher in this section.

of valid balloting procedures and, with the British and French, posted control officers at the voting booths demonstrated a common front with democratic Germans against the Soviets.[2] It suggested for the first time the emergence of a German-American democratic partnership in the Four Power city of Berlin. This local Berlin experience moved Deputy U.S. Military Governor Lucius D. Clay, despite his ongoing commitment to Four Power cooperation, to recommend that Germans be accepted into a democratic state system. U.S. Secretary of State James F. Byrnes delivered Clay's recommendation almost verbatim in his epochal September 1946 speech, promising to help Germans gain economic and political-democratic recovery.

By spring 1947, when students protested arbitrary exclusion of noncommunists at the venerable Berlin (Humboldt) University in the Soviet sector, the American military government supported the rebels openly by granting them a license to publish in West Berlin. One year later, they gained Clay's support to establish the Free University in the American sector. Founded in December 1948 at the height of the Berlin Blockade, the Free University came to symbolize the cultural bond between West Berlin and America. On its American-style campus, built with major support of the Ford Foundation, American-style social sciences first triumphed in Germany. Many German emigrants to America returned to teach there, and a few young American scholars settled in Berlin. Until a new wave of student activism opened a crevice of anti-Americanism in the later 1960s, the Free University stood as the loftiest symbol of the Cold War defense of American and Western values against communism in Germany. Many American visitors, including President John F. Kennedy, came to speak in the university's Henry Ford Building.[3]

When the Soviets closed all ground access to the city in the Berlin Blockade of June 1948–May 1949, the American-led airlift kept West Berliners fed, warm, and free.[4] This event consolidated the close German-American Cold War relationship, creating a sense of trust and shared political values that found concrete expression in the copy of the Liberty Bell, financed by private American donations, that Blockade hero General Clay presented to Berliners in October 1950 at West Berlin's Schöneberg City Hall. With this act, Clay symbolically extended the American spiritual nation to West Berlin, just as President Kennedy would thrill another crowd with his famous declaration *"ich bin ein Berliner"* at the same spot in 1963. This enthusiasm for an American-German bond – a welcome reassurance to Americans amidst the Korean War – was echoed four months after the presentation of the Liberty Bell duplicate by the overwhelmingly positive reception West Berlin Mayor Ernst Reuter received on what was the first visit by a postwar German leader to the United States. This link to Berlin was forged well before West German chancellor Konrad Adenauer earned his reputation among Americans as the guarantor of a new, reliable, and democratic Germany. Even in 1953, when both Adenauer and Reuter visited the United States, the *Voice of America* described Reuter as the most important German visitor that year.[5]

In the wake of the Blockade victory, Americans came to see West Berlin as living proof and a showcase of the superiority of American democracy and the free market. The city

---

[2] General Ray W. Barker in a declaration of Mar. 29, 1946, and General Lucius D. Clay, press conferences, Mar. 23, 1946, both in Berliner Senat, *Berlin: Kampf um Freiheit und Selbstverwaltung 1945–1946*, Schriftenreihe zur Berliner Zeitgeschichte, vol. 1 (Berlin, 1961), 393, 401. See also Harold Hurwitz, *Die Anfänge des Widerstandes*, pt. 2, *Zwischen Selbsttäuschung und Zivilcourage: Der Fusionskampf* (Cologne, 1990), 1180–94.

[3] Cf. James F. Tent, *The Free University of Berlin: A Political History* (Bloomington, Ind., 1988); Siegward Lönnendonker, *Freie Universität Berlin: Gründung einer politischen Universität* (Berlin, 1988).

[4] Cf. W. Phillips Davison, *The Berlin Blockade: A Study in Cold War Politics* (Princeton, N.J., 1958); Ann Tusa and John Tusa, *The Berlin Airlift* (New York, 1988); Avi Shlaim, *The United States and the Berlin Blockade, 1948–1949* (Berkeley, Calif., 1983).

[5] Report by David Berger, *Voice of America*, Mar. 25, 1953, Ernst-Reuter-Archiv, vol. 107, Landesarchiv Berlin.

gained a special place in the American public consciousness and became a favorite destination for U.S. leaders as well as tourists. A broad-based, largely private Berlin lobby emerged in the United States that in the following decades promoted a number of highly visible projects beyond the Free University. Dubbed "Club of Berliners," this group included former diplomats, officials, and journalists with Berlin experience, including Clay, diplomat Robert Murphy, banker Benjamin Buttenwieser, Auto Workers chief Walter Reuther, former U.S. High Commission for Germany (HICOG) administrator Shepard Stone, and, above all, Eleanor Dulles, the sister of Secretary of State John Foster Dulles and longtime head of the State Department's Berlin Desk. Through this network, the American presence found many cultural and economic expressions in Berlin. Notable examples are the ultramodern Congress Hall, nicknamed "Dulleseum" for Eleanor Dulles's role; the American participation in the 1957 international architectural exhibition to rebuild the Hansaviertel district; and, somewhat later, the Berlin Aspen Institute long headed by Shepard Stone.

This German-American solidarity in Berlin also increasingly blurred natural differences in German and American interests. Among Berliners, it fed the illusion that long-term American goals were identical to their own. Although Americans and West Germans were, in fact, in full harmony on the protection of West Berlin, there were significant differences in their long-term perspectives. Americans defined their goals both more narrowly and more flexibly. On one hand, they insisted that American responsibility was limited to the American sector or, in cooperation with the British and French, to *West* Berlin. They were committed to defending Allied territorial rights in West Berlin, including free access and the economic viability of their sectors. In return for this commitment, they expected ideological loyalty and were particularly irritated by neutralist tendencies. On the other hand, the unity of the city and German reunification could not be primary or immediate goals for the United States. On the contrary, it had to be in the interest of the

American superpower to reduce its risks without weakening its position vis-à-vis the Soviet Union. Throughout the Cold War, American governments, therefore, looked for interim solutions that might help stabilize Berlin. Especially during the greatest Soviet threats, this made Germans fearful that their interests might be sacrificed on the altar of an American-Soviet settlement. The major Berlin crises were thus not only the moments when Americans and Germans closed ranks most tightly but also when serious irritations in the German-American relationship broke into the open for brief moments before the necessity of cooperation moved both sides to close any rifts again.

In the post-Blockade years, American assurances of support thus left Berliners with a deep faith that the United States was unconditionally committed to their cause. The 1950 International Congress for Cultural Freedom in Berlin buttressed this belief by marking the city as the outpost for the American-led Western struggle against communist tyranny. However, the East German uprising of June 17, 1953, and its violent suppression by the Soviets momentarily exposed cracks in the perceived unity of interests in Berlin.[6] The crisis tore away the illusion that the United States identified with the freedom struggle in the East. In the face of the spreading rebellion, American authorities hastened to contain potentially uncontrollable German actions. Radio in the American Sector (RIAS) was barred from broadcasting Eastern strike calls, barricades were erected at the sector borders to keep West Berlin supporters from crossing over, and American officials delayed flying the charismatic Mayor Reuter back from Vienna. Only Eleanor Dulles, who happened to be in the city, approached the young rebels

---

[6] Cf. Arnulf Baring, *Der 17. Juni 1953* (Stuttgart, 1983); Gerhard Beier, *Wir wollen freie Menschen sein: Der 17. Juni 1953: Bauleute gingen voran* (Cologne, 1993); Manfred Hagen, *DDR: Juni '53: Die erste Volkserhebung im Stalinismus* (Stuttgart, 1992); Torsten Diedrich, *Der 17. Juni 1953 in der DDR: Bewaffnete Gewalt gegen das Volk* (Berlin, 1991); Ilko-Sascha Kowalczuk, Armin Mitter, and Stefan Wolle, eds., *Der Tag X: 17. Juni 1953* (Berlin, 1995).

at the sector border and tried to calm them, to explain the situation, and to give them hope.

Yet, the American reaction to June 1953 did not leave the deep scars in confidence that the Wall did later. As Willy Brandt would do in 1961, Reuter urgently called for Western action, but the anti-American resentment was short-lived in 1953. The Soviet suppression of the uprising and East German secret-police actions against anticommunist leaders in West Berlin were so brutal that West Berliners anxiously sought the reassuring protection of the United States. Moreover, an American food-parcel program for East Germans offered a show of responsibility for the victims of communism after the uprising. The spectacle of the Four Power Conference on the German Question in Berlin six months later even appeared to reaffirm open sector borders and the goal of reunification.

Most importantly, the events of June 1953 solidified the German-American alliance by providing the most dramatic proof of the communist threat and showing the clear commitment of post-Nazi Germans to democracy. This general German allegiance to American-style democratic freedoms was demonstrated most sharply in Berlin, where East and West Germans could still meet and where young Easterners deeply impressed Eleanor Dulles with their desire for freedom. Berlin's majestic central boulevard leading straight to the Soviet sector border was renamed in honor of June 17, the date that also became West Germany's national holiday until reunification. Such symbols not only marked Germans as the staunchest members of the anticommunist Western alliance, they also acknowledged West Berlin as the "capital" of a whole democratic and anticommunist Germany – long before the West German parliament officially designated Berlin "the German capital" in February 1957.

Confronted almost daily with Cold War tensions, West Berliners developed a unique political culture. The city became intensely political, and well over half its citizens regularly turned out to mass rallies. Visitors from satiated West Germany and abroad were struck with the political electricity in the air and felt their Cold War commitments renewed. The crowds that came out to cheer the American troops at the parades were clearly important in maintaining the commitment of the United States and defeating moves in Congress to reduce the American military presence in Germany. This intense political consciousness became a source of local pride, endowing West Berliners with a global importance that made up for the dependence and powerlessness of their tiny island in the roaring ocean of the Cold War. Yet, this political intensity was also highly volatile and could turn from adulation to injured rage. The demonstrations against the building of the Wall, for example, were directed as much against Americans as against the East. In the Vietnam War years, the anti-American demonstrations at times overshadowed the gratitude and loyalty that normally prevailed in the media.

Even in the years after June 1953, when West Berliners felt securely sheltered in the close German-American relationship, this proud political consciousness spawned two independent-minded initiatives beyond the city's assigned place as a *Frontstadt* (frontline city). Both were based on alternative identities of the city and were potentially divisive in the German-American alignment: Berlin as the true German capital and as a bridge between East and West. The former briefly blossomed into a drive to make West Berlin the capital of (West) Germany in a wave of national enthusiasm during the Cold War thaw of the "Spirit of Geneva" that accompanied the 1955 Four Power summit conference and the Austrian State Treaty.[7] This campaign, which was headed off with the 1957 formal designation of Berlin as the "German capital," aroused considerable Allied opposition because it violated the city's Four Power status. It would remain a recurring irritant and be the last remaining bone of contention after the 1972 Quadripartite Agreement. The same 1950s Cold War thaw also emboldened a number of local political operatives to forge contacts with Soviet counterparts in East Berlin in hopes of repairing the municipal division and perhaps

---

[7] Willy Brandt, *Von Bonn nach Berlin: Eine Dokumentation zur Hauptstadtfrage* (Berlin, 1957).

exploring reunification along the lines of the Austrian State Treaty.

Soviet leader Nikita Khrushchev intended to appeal precisely to such hopes for easing the crisis and partition when he demanded the creation of a "Free City" in West Berlin in his ultimatum of November 1958.[8] Although this threat precipitated a deep East-West crisis, it was directed at *West* Berlin and, therefore, did not expose German-American differences. When the Soviet leader threatened to sign a peace treaty with East Germany unless the Western Allies withdrew their forces from the city, he called Western access to West Berlin into question but not the unity of the city. He thus attacked the very place where German-American agreement was closest: the protection of *West* Berlin. A disagreement did emerge briefly when Dulles suggested that deputized East German officials might be acceptable on the access routes. For the Americans, this seemed like a logical compromise that would reduce risk while protecting Western access. West Germans and Berliners, however, feared that it would lead to recognition of the East German state and the division of Germany. Dulles repudiated the scheme ten days later, but his musings betrayed Americans' lukewarm commitment to German unity despite their public assurances.

The deepest crisis in German-American Cold War relations occurred with the building of the Berlin Wall on August 13, 1961. Despite continued claims of international law and commitments of the Western Allies to German unity, the Wall destroyed the last bit of national unity in the everyday lives of East and West Berliners. At this most traumatic moment for the city since the Blockade, President Kennedy breathed a sigh of relief and, like the other Western leaders, continued to enjoy his summer vacation.

The feared access crisis over Berlin, with which Khrushchev had threatened the young president in Vienna only ten weeks before, had not come to pass. In fact, the Soviets had surrendered immediate claims to West Berlin by building a wall around it, and they had studiously respected the access routes. The West, in turn, eschewed an overly belligerent response to the Wall for fear that the Soviets would restrict access to the city. Berliners nonetheless felt abandoned in the face of this brutal attack against their city, which destroyed a living urban community and cut all personal human as well as economic and cultural links between its two halves. Yet, the United States had never explicitly promised to protect the rights of East Berliners or *German* access to the Soviet sector under the Four Power Status. The Kennedy administration's guarantees had consistently targeted only *West* Berlin. Neither American nor German leaders had cared to make a point of this, and wishful thinking had made citizens in the old German capital close their eyes to this reality. As Willy Brandt, West Berlin's mayor at the time, later recalled, "a curtain was drawn aside to reveal an empty stage."[9]

The shock of the Wall was so severe that the sense of crisis rose to a new pitch. This surprised Western leaders, who had assumed that the insulating barrier of the Wall would make West Berlin and access to it safer by reducing communist resentment of West Berlin as the haven for swelling streams of East German refugees. Yet, the crisis of confidence in Berlin compelled Kennedy to make a dramatic Cold War gesture by sending Vice President Lyndon B. Johnson and Blockade hero Clay along with troop reinforcements to reassure the population of America's determination to protect West Berlin. Meanwhile, Khrushchev and the East German leadership indulged in cries of triumph and militant bullying to vent their long frustration over their inability to neutralize West Berlin. This unleashed a new round of Cold War provocations, which reached their climax in the rather theatrical showdown face-off of Soviet

---

[8] For the most important analyses of the 1958–62 crises, see John C. Ausland, *Kennedy, Khrushchev, and the Berlin-Cuba Crisis, 1961–1964* (Oslo, 1996); Frank A. Mayer, *Adenauer and Kennedy: A Study in German-American Relations, 1961–1963* (New York, 1996); Robert M. Slusser, *The Berlin Crisis of 1961: Soviet-American Relations and the Struggle for Power in the Kremlin, June–November 1961* (Baltimore, 1973).

[9] Willy Brandt, *People and Politics: The Years 1960–1975* (Boston, 1978), 20.

and American tanks, barrel to barrel, at Check-point Charlie. East and West fired at one another across the Wall with gas grenades and wa-ter cannons. The exploratory détente talks be-tween foreign ministers Dean Rusk and Andrei Gromyko and the ambassadorial negotiations in Moscow collapsed as the Soviets returned to their "Free City" demands and challenged the access routes. Finally, the Cuban Missile Crisis of October 1962 echoed strongly in West Berlin with fears of a Soviet counterstrike.[10]

Although West Berliners clung to the protec-tive American alliance during these prolonged crises, the Wall left gnawing doubts about the re-lationship. A year after the building of the Wall, incensed crowds went on an anti-American rampage when the eighteen-year-old East Ger-man Peter Fechter was killed at the sector line as he tried to escape. The shock reverberated all over Germany. For years, claims circulated that Americans had known the Wall would be built and perhaps even encouraged it. The experi-ence left the younger generation more cynical toward America and may have made it more vulnerable to the anti-Americanism of the late 1960s in Berlin.

Yet, the Wall also led to a maturation of the German-American Cold War relationship. It re-moved illusions on both sides – about reunifi-cation and real American interests for Germans, and on the limits of the much-praised spirit of Berliners for Americans. In Berlin, the Brandt government adjusted to the need to work for in-terim solutions, just as Kennedy had prescribed in his retort to Brandt's anguished letter under the first shock of the Wall.[11] Kennedy, mean-while, learned to respect the real pain and mo-bilizing power of the Cold War division in the daily lives of Berliners. Both the Cold War con-frontation and the need to find interim solu-tions to reduce East-West tensions were nec-essary foundations for a successful common German-American policy. The most eloquent articulation of this fact occurred one memorable afternoon on June 26, 1963, when Kennedy first roused the fullest support of Berliners by pro-claiming *"ich bin ein Berliner"* in the name of the Cold War ideological community, only to lay out, a little later at the Free University, the path toward an interim solution with the East. Cold War diplomacy required both, and both had to be at the basis of a healthy German-American relationship at the front lines of the Cold War.

The Kennedy speeches, which recognized the long-term reality of the Wall while affirming West Berliners' pain and anger over it, allowed a specific post-1961 West Berlin identity to sta-bilize and evolve in the following decades even as Cold War provocations and incidents con-tinued. East Germany naturally experienced a gradual stabilization because, in the wake of the Wall, it left its population no other choice. For West Berlin, however, the defining elements of this emerging political-cultural identity, which also distinguished it from West Germany, were a much clearer contrast with East Berlin and an intense, complex association with America and its culture. The Wall and the grim com-munist checkpoints not only insulated East and West Berliners almost totally from each other, but West Berliners also defined themselves pri-marily against "the other," the gray, old, dimly lit, and cowed East Berlin in contrast to their own supercolorful, hypermodern, dazzling, re-bellious city. This sense of "the other" became so deeply ingrained that it would last at least a generation after reunification.

The zealous identification with Americans and Americana was based on this Cold War identity. West Berlin wanted to become more modern and more American than any other place in Germany, Europe, or the world. Amer-icans, therefore, also felt a special bond to West Berlin. Yet, the combination of high political-cultural intensity and the close links to American pop and youth cultures also brought Vietnam-era protests and anti-Americanism first and most violently to this city. The most radical

---

[10] See Ernest R. May and Philip D. Zelikow, eds., *The Kennedy Tapes: Inside the White House During the Cuban Missile Crisis* (Cambridge, Mass., 1997).

[11] Diethelm Prowe, "Der Brief Kennedys an Brandt vom 18. August 1961: Eine zentrale Quelle zur Berliner Mauer und der Entstehung der Brandtschen Ostpolitik," *Vierteljahrshefte für Zeitgeschichte* 33 (1985): 373–83.

neo-Marxist demonstrations took place at the Free University, not least because of its American, Cold War origins. This anti-Americanism lasted longer than anywhere else in Germany or Western Europe.

Another American presidential visit to the city, Richard Nixon's in 1969, provided a critical impulse toward a formal interim solution that would allow West Berlin's intense political culture to endure for nearly three decades. In contrast to Kennedy six years earlier, Nixon could already witness the characteristic love-hate relationship toward America that was central to West Berlin's culture. The welcome for the American president was still overwhelming, but the police had to keep sizable anti-American demonstrations in check. Much like Kennedy, Nixon combined the Cold War reassurance to his audience, that all people of the "Free World" were "truly Berliners," with an even more urgent call for an interim solution. With a stabilized East just as eager as Vietnam-era America to reduce unpredictable international risk, and with West German–Berlin public opinion now favorable toward an interim solution, this appeal was well received. A last major access crisis over the election of the West German president in Berlin drove home the urgency for a settlement. After nearly two years of hard negotiations, the 1971 Quadripartite Agreement on Berlin was the result. The first Four Power settlement shaped with decisive West German–Berlin participation and endorsement, the Quadripartite Agreement formed the peak of a genuine German-American consensus.

Once the chronic crisis situation in Berlin had been alleviated, the city's pivotal role diminished. Still, the direct Allied responsibility required close German-American cooperation and reminded West Germans of the limits of their sovereignty. The remarkably secure East-West stability after 1968 was underscored by President Ronald Reagan's second Berlin visit in 1987, where he openly challenged Soviet leader Mikhail Gorbachev to tear down the Wall. In Kennedy's time, such aggressive Cold War tones would have risked provoking the crowds to storm the Wall. Reagan's call has been seen as a first decisive strike against the communist empire, but at the time it was no more than a propaganda ploy that lacked the substance of Kennedy's or Nixon's dual initiatives for negotiation behind the shield of a Western Cold War consensus.

With the American departure from the city after German reunification, the centrality of Berlin in the German-American relationship has all but vanished. Yet, traces remain that will blend uniquely into the new capital. Among the many reminders are Eleanor Dulles's Congress Hall, the Free University's Henry Ford Building, the Berlin Aspen Institute, and the American Academy in Berlin. These symbols will provide continuing bonds in the German-American alliance for decades to come. President Bill Clinton's Kennedyesque visit in July 1994 suggested such a link in his fluent German words: *Amerika steht an ihrer Seite, jetzt und für immer* – America will stand by your side, now and forever.[12]

---

[12] Remarks by President Clinton and Chancellor Kohl in Address to the People of Berlin, July 12, 1994, The White House, Office of the Press Secretary (Berlin).

CHAPTER NINETEEN

"Little Room for Maneuver"

Relations Between the United States and the GDR

Christian F. Ostermann

Translated by Richard Sharp

The founding of the German Democratic Republic (GDR) in October 1949 came as no surprise to the administration of President Harry S. Truman. The resolution adopted at Potsdam to set up centralized institutions in Germany had come to nothing;[1] in summer 1947 the Russians had created the German Economic Commission in their zone, a body that wielded quasi-governmental powers in many areas; and at the Six Power conference in London in 1948, the Western Allies had resolved to create a West German state.[2] In light of these developments, the American government fully expected the creation of a new state in the eastern part of Germany. Unclear, however, were Soviet dictator Joseph Stalin's objectives in choosing to establish a German government in the Soviet occupation zone. Whereas some observers within the American military government interpreted the founding of the GDR as the start of a radical transformation of the Soviet zone into a "German people's republic," there were others who warned that Stalin was still pursuing ambitions for Germany as a whole, that his sights were still set on the Western occupation zones with their greater economic value, and that he would use the new GDR merely as a pawn in future negotiations on German unity. The greatest fear of the American government was that Moscow might manage to establish a noncommunist yet pro-Moscow government with aspirations for all of Germany that would extend Soviet influence to encompass the entire country.[3]

A few days after the founding of the GDR, the Allied High Commission also stated its position: "The so-called government of the German Democratic Republic is an artificial creation ... which is devoid of any legal basis and has determined to evade an appeal to the electorate, [it] has no title to represent Eastern Germany. It has an even smaller claim to speak in the name of Germany as a whole."[4] Consequently, the American government refused to recognize the regime in the Soviet zone under international law. During their talks in Paris in November 1949, the foreign ministers of Britain, France, and the United States agreed to refrain from any steps that even might imply de facto recognition. In matters relating to East Germany, they intended to continue dealing with the Soviet Control Commission. Trade relations with East Germany were to be conducted through low-level official channels or private bodies such as chambers of commerce. The United States was particularly emphatic in urging this strict policy of nonrecognition on its

---

[1] See the chapter by Gunther Mai in this section.

[2] See the chapter by Hermann-Josef Rupieper in this section.

[3] See Hermann-Josef Rupieper, "Die Reaktion der USA auf die Gründung der DDR," in Elke Scherstjanoi, ed., *Provisorium für längstens ein Jahr: Die Gründung der DDR* (Berlin, 1993), 59–66.

[4] Editorial Note, in U.S. Department of State, *Foreign Relations of the United States* (hereafter *FRUS*), *1949*, 3:532.

allies. It sometimes met considerable resistance, as in the case, for example, of the Scandinavian states, which had a traditionally strong interest in trade with eastern Germany. Until the early 1970s, the GDR remained largely isolated internationally.

As the gulf dividing the country deepened with the creation of the two German states, American fears grew that a Soviet-backed "National Front" government of the aligned parties might be able to trade on the sense of national unity among many Germans and the potential for opposition in the Federal Republic. With Berlin as a capital city and prospects of trade with Eastern Europe, the GDR could offer incentives that could exercise the same kind of attraction as was expected of the economically prosperous and democratic Federal Republic. As a defensive measure against the East's propaganda in favor of national unity, the Americans felt it necessary to "bring the West Germans more on the offensive vis-à-vis the East Germans."[5] In February 1950, therefore, a committee was set up within the American High Commissioner's office (HICOG) with the task of planning and coordinating political and propaganda activities against the GDR and against Soviet policy toward Germany. By the end of February 1950, High Commissioner John McCloy had already taken the political offensive by declaring the willingness of the United States to organize free elections for the whole of Germany. A few weeks later, he proposed elections throughout Berlin as a first step toward reuniting the divided city. In calling for free elections, McCloy had hit upon a formula that was widely popular in the GDR, unacceptable to the ruling German Socialist Unity Party (*Sozialistische Einheitspartei Deutschlands*, or SED), effective for propaganda purposes, and in line with Western security interests.

In the months that followed, the American government made an effort to increase the consistency and intensity of activities directed against the GDR and against Soviet policy toward Germany. In April 1950, the Propaganda Committee, set up for this specific purpose, was provided with a program whose aims were to sustain passive resistance to communist ideology, Soviet propaganda, and the strengthening of totalitarian rule; to help bring about the collapse of the Soviet power base in Germany; and to slow the sovietization of East Germany. Further reflection at the State Department and HICOG led, in December 1950, to the report *Psychological Warfare in Germany* written by two HICOG advisers, the social scientist Hans Speier and the journalist Wallace Carroll. The report called for action "to destroy the Soviet power in Germany" and urged that the full arsenal of weapons of political and economic warfare should be deployed to that end, from trade restrictions against the GDR to the recruitment of leading East German experts in economic and technical fields and Western military demonstrations. Carroll and Speier also recommended establishing a strong and centrally controlled resistance movement in the Soviet zone, supported by American government departments, with a program ranging from information and propaganda activities through the infiltration of selected organizations in the zone (e.g., the emergency services and the state police) to sabotage, kidnapping, and "direct actions against highly placed officials."[6]

The aggressive line adopted by the Carroll-Speier report prompted discussions within the Truman administration. Against the background of growing controversy regarding the integration of the Federal Republic into the Western world and the "Stalin note" of August 1952, these discussions led to a new strategy paper. The resulting directive authorized political and subversive action aimed at the "reduction of Soviet potential in Eastern Germany" and laid particular emphasis on the favorable location of West Berlin as a base for psychological operations against the GDR and other satellite

[5] Thomas A. Schwartz, *America's Germany: John J. McCloy and the Federal Republic of Germany* (Cambridge, Mass., 1991), 89.

[6] Wallace Carroll and Hans Speier, *Psychological Warfare in Germany: A Report to the United States High Commissioner for Germany and the Department of State*, Dec. 1, 1950, released by the U.S. Department of State at the author's request.

regimes.[7] The objective of American policy was "controlled preparation for more active resistance."[8]

An extremely important tool for informing and influencing the population of East Germany was the American radio station in Berlin, RIAS. Because of Berlin's central position within the GDR, the signal could be picked up anywhere in the country, and American estimates suggested that the RIAS broadcasts were very popular in the "Zone," with 70 to 80 percent of all East Germans regularly tuning in to this "spiritual and psychological center of resistance in a Communist-dominated, blacked-out area."[9]

HICOG was extremely well informed about the critical political and economic situation in East Germany during the early 1950s, partly through secret-service sources but also through contacts with numerous anticommunist groups like the Campaign Against Inhumanity and the Free Lawyers' Investigatory Committee. Even so, the new Republican administration under President Dwight D. Eisenhower took a somewhat pessimistic view of the prospects of destabilizing the GDR. The feeling in Washington was that the SED regime and the Soviet occupying power had the situation under firm control despite increasing public discontent. The American government underestimated the hopes raised among the East German population after Stalin's death (March 5, 1953) by the announcement of the "rollback" policy by Eisenhower and his secretary of state, John Foster Dulles.[10] When demonstrations began in East Berlin on June 16, 1953, the strikers expected support from RIAS, which since the spring had been conducting a targeted campaign against the increased work quotas in the GDR. During the day, however, the RIAS

management received orders "to do nothing that could provoke the Soviets"[11] and instructed its editorial staff to stick to "factual reporting." Despite these restrictions, RIAS reports and commentaries took the side of the demonstrators; in the early hours of June 17, the station called on the East German population to support the demonstrators in East Berlin. The RIAS broadcasts made a major contribution to the rapid spread of the strikes and demonstrations from East Berlin to the whole territory of the GDR. Only after the intervention of the Russian armed forces and the declaration of a state of emergency by the Soviet occupying power on June 17 did the reporting become more restrained.

Washington was swift to recognize the excellent propaganda potential of the uprising.[12] Internal discussions, in which the option of military intervention on the side of the insurgents was rapidly discarded, resulted in the adoption in late June of National Security Council (NSC) directive 158 on the exploitation of unrest in Soviet satellite states. NSC 158 laid down a dual strategy. For public consumption, the emphasis was to be on efforts to restore German unity on the basis of free elections and to arrange Four Power talks. Behind the scenes, meanwhile, plans were laid for a wide variety of propaganda and subversion tactics designed "to nourish resistance to communist oppression throughout satellite Europe, short of mass rebellion in areas under Soviet military control, and without compromising its spontaneous nature."[13] The foreseen measures included setting up subversive radio stations, systematic propaganda operations, and assistance with the "elimination" of East German politicians. But the centerpiece of American reaction to the unrest was an ambitious program of food aid for the East German population, designed to express American

[7] Paper prepared by the Psychological Strategy Board, Oct. 9, 1952, *FRUS, 1952–1954*, vol. 7, pt. 1:370–80; Boerner to Kellermann, Feb. 20, 1953, National Archives (hereafter NA), Record Group (hereafter RG) 59, 511.62A/2-2053.

[8] HICOG Bonn to Department of State, June 3, 1953, NA, RG 59, 511.62A/6-353.

[9] McCloy to Secretary of State Dean Acheson, Aug. 24, 1950, NA, RG 59, 511.62B4/8-2450.

[10] See the chapter by Bernd Stöver in this section.

[11] Quoted in Manfred Hagen, *DDR – Juni 1953: Die erste Volkserhebung im Stalinismus* (Stuttgart, 1992), 97.

[12] State Department to HICOG Bonn, June 17, 1953, NA, RG 59, 762B.00/6-1753.

[13] Interim U.S. Psychological Strategy Plan for Exploitation of Unrest in Satellite Europe (PSB D-45), July 1, 1953, NA, RG 273, NSC 158 series.

sympathy for their situation, force the Soviets onto the defensive, and dramatize the antagonism between population and government. The parcel campaign – which supplied more than 5.5 million parcels to residents of the zone between late July and early October through distribution points in West Berlin – in fact proved effective not only in the East but also in the West, where it contributed to Adenauer's victory in the elections of September 1953.[14]

Nevertheless, the uprising in the GDR also exposed the dangers of an offensive rollback policy. In late September, the State Department warned that, although it might be possible to sustain a "psychological climate of resistance," any attempts to roll back the Soviet power in the GDR would always have to be measured in terms of their impact on efforts to integrate the Federal Republic with the West: "We do not want to risk precipitating prematurely a mass, open rebellion and then incur blame for the consequences."[15]

Discussions within the American government about the events of June 17, 1953, resulted in the adoption of directive NSC 174 in December of that year. This directive was the first to refer to the GDR as a Soviet satellite state and to treat it in the context of America's policy toward Eastern Europe, although emphasizing that the GDR had "specific features . . . by which [it is] differentiated in important ways from the other satellites." NSC 174 stressed that East Germany was causing more serious problems for the Soviet Union than the other satellite states. Because the majority of the German people in the Federal Republic had made steady progress toward freedom and economic

prosperity, while West Berlin presented an opportunity for contact with the free world, hope of escape from Soviet dominion remained alive. Even so, "the detachment of any major European satellite from the Soviet bloc" appeared to the National Security Council "not . . . feasible, except by Soviet acquiescence or by war." Although "feasible political, economic, propaganda, and covert measures" should be adopted "to create and exploit troublesome problems for the USSR," any "incitement to premature revolt" was to be avoided.[16]

This basic statement of policy toward Eastern Europe and the GDR did not, of course, silence dissenting voices within the American government. The Central Intelligence Agency (CIA) was particularly critical of the "soft approach," and its director, Allan Dulles, cautioned the government against subsiding into a "do-nothing policy." The supporters of psychological warfare also argued in favor of a more provocative line. They saw the GDR as "the only satellite which now lends itself to possible detachment" and recommended a "concentration of political, economic, and psychological measures . . . with East Germany as a target."[17] However, the State Department was quick to block such proposals.[18] The department had long feared that provocative action against the GDR might have a negative impact on America's policy toward Germany, particularly at a time when the military integration of the Federal Republic into the Western alliance was entering a critical phase. After the Soviet Union had used military force to put down the Hungarian uprising in November 1956, it became

[14] See Christian F. Ostermann, "Keeping the Pot Simmering: The United States and the East German Uprising of 1953," *German Studies Review* 19 (1996): 61–89; Valur Ingimundarson, "The Eisenhower Administration, the Adenauer Government, and the Political Uses of the East German Uprising in 1953," *Diplomatic History* 20 (1996): 381–409; James G. Hershberg, *James B. Conant: Harvard to Hiroshima and the Making of the Nuclear Age* (New York, 1993), 659–65.

[15] Department of State Circular Airgram, U.S. Policy on Unrest in Soviet Occupied Germany, Sept. 30, 1953, NA, RG 59, 762B.00/9-3053.

[16] A Report to the National Security Council by the NSC Planning Board on United States Policy Toward the Soviet Satellites in Eastern Europe, Dec. 11, 1953, reprinted in Christian F. Ostermann, ed., *The Post-Stalin Succession Struggle and the 17 June 1953 Uprising in East Germany: The Hidden History* (Washington, D.C., 1996).

[17] Paper Prepared by the Operations Coordinating Board Working Group on NSC 174, Dec. 30, 1954. *FRUS, 1952–1954*, 8:142–57, esp. 153.

[18] See the comments by the representative of the State Department in the Minutes of the Meeting of the Operations Coordinating Board, Jan. 5, 1955, *FRUS, 1954–1955*, 8:157–9, esp. 158.

clear that recognition of the realities of power politics in Eastern Europe offered the only hope of persuading the Russians to loosen their grip, both there and in East Germany.

As far as East Germany was concerned, it was significant that the changing political strategy of the Eisenhower administration toward Eastern Europe was being matched by a more flexible attitude in its political stance on Germany. Admittedly, the Western Powers supported the Hallstein doctrine, postulated by the West German government following the establishment of diplomatic relations with the Soviet Union and maintaining the Federal Republic's sole right of representation in relations with other countries. However, this could not conceal the fact that their commitment to reunification became weaker in the years that followed while their interest in agreeing upon a policy of détente with the Soviet Union grew stronger. The Americans were increasingly prepared to abandon their traditional demand that German reunification take precedence over the creation of a European security system urged by the Russians. Progress on arms control was no longer to be made conditional on steps toward resolving the reunification issue.

Such shifts of emphasis in American policy on Germany were carefully noted by the East German leadership. More nuanced – though still ideologically oriented – internal analyses of American policy gradually softened the completely stereotyped and distorted portrayal of the United States as the dominant power of "international monopoly capitalism." Since 1949, East German propaganda – fluctuating from day to day in its political line between emphasis on "national" interests and a determination to distance East Germany from the Federal Republic – had highlighted either the "colonial policy of suppression and exploitation of American, British, and French imperialism" or the role of the "reactionary" Adenauer government. Ideological blinders were also apparent in the emphasis on the "contradictions" between the Western Allies and the West German government that were often conjured up in both internal analyses and official propaganda.

Foreign Minister Georg Dertinger told Minister President Otto Grotewohl as early as June 1950 that "the igniting spark originally expected from the Marshall Plan . . . has not materialized. The social impact of Marshall aid has been nonexistent." The Western Powers were trying "to project the image of a boom with an expanded armaments industry." By deciding in favor of the military integration of the Federal Republic, he said, America and the West had "torn up the Potsdam Statute" and involved the Federal Republic in "active collaboration and in assisting the aggressive preparations by the Western Powers against the USSR."[19] From the standpoint of the SED, the uprising of June 17, 1953, confirmed that Western intelligence teams were working to undermine the GDR. However, American policy directed against the GDR was not regarded as materially significant until the mid-1950s. Careful watch was kept on the activities of "realists" within the United States, a definition that now included the founding father of containment, George F. Kennan.

The Americans began to attach more importance to the GDR from the mid-1950s, not just as an element in an apparently solidifying European status quo but, above all, in light of America's position in Berlin. The sovereignty agreement between the USSR and the GDR concluded in 1955 and the Bolz-Zorin correspondence (September 1955) resulted in new tensions over the control of the Allied lines of access to Berlin. With a view to enhancing the status of the GDR, Moscow had officially declared the SED regime "master of the roads"[20] and threatened to have both West German and Allied transit traffic stopped and searched by the East German police. Although disputes arose repeatedly about rights of access to Berlin, the Soviet Union refrained until 1958 from

---

[19] Dertinger to Grotewohl, June 2, 1950, Stiftung Archiv der Parteien und Massenorganisationen der DDR im Bundesarchiv, Berlin (hereafter SAPMO/BArch), NY 90/463.
[20] Letter from the Ambassador in Germany (Conant) to the Secretary of State, May 21, 1955, *FRUS, 1955–1957*, 26:376–81, esp. 377.

questioning the Four Power status of the city – and the responsibility of the occupying powers for Germany as a whole. Efforts by the SED leadership to compel diplomatic recognition of East Germany by measures such as compulsory visas for U.S. diplomats or "steps to eliminate the travel board pass" (required by East German residents for travel to the West) were, therefore, strictly limited. When an American army helicopter crash-landed in East Germany in early June 1958, the GDR leaders tried to exploit the negotiations over the return of the interned American service personnel to force formal recognition; ultimately, they had to make do with a protocol from representatives of the Red Cross.[21]

The ambivalence of the Americans' attitude toward the issue of recognition became obvious in the Berlin Crisis of 1958–62. Secretary of State John Foster Dulles first resorted to the "agent theory," based on an Allied idea of August 1954 whereby the GDR frontier guards posted on the approaches to Berlin were to be regarded merely as Soviet lackeys. However, the ground was pulled out from under the agent theory on November 27, 1958, when the Soviets sent a note to the Western Powers repudiating the Four Power agreements over Berlin, proposing the conversion of West Berlin into a demilitarized and independent "Free City," and backing these proposals with an ultimatum to the effect that, if the West refused, East Germany would be given full control over its territory by treaty within six months. Following protests by Adenauer, Washington began after December 1958 to adopt a tougher stance on East German border controls. The GDR did, of course, greatly enhance its international status by participating in the conference called in Geneva to resolve the crisis in summer 1959 (at which the Federal Republic was also represented).

Whereas Eisenhower and Dulles had categorically ruled out recognition of East Germany, not least out of loyalty to Adenauer,

John F. Kennedy felt no obligation either toward the German chancellor or toward the traditional code of principles governing policy on Germany. Even more than Eisenhower, the new president was interested in finding a modus vivendi with the Soviet Union. The new American administration had scarcely taken office when Soviet premier Nikita Khrushchev presented another ultimatum on Berlin, repeated at the Vienna summit conference in June 1961. Kennedy's response showed he was not prepared to offer any guarantees for the liberty of the population of East Berlin and East Germany. By the end of July 1961, the president had given his approval to acceptance of the stamping of American military documents by the East German frontier authorities. When border guards sealed off West Berlin from the eastern sector of the city, and from East Germany itself, in August 1961 to stem the flood of refugees, the American government reacted with great caution. Just a few weeks after the building of the Berlin Wall, internal preparations for talks with the Soviet Union on Berlin indicated willingness to accept de facto recognition of the GDR and talks between the two Germanys under the auspices of a "Joint West-East German Commission."[22] Even separate peace treaties with the two German states were considered. The proposal aired in April 1962 – that an international control authority be established to regulate Allied access to Berlin – also implicitly raised the status of the GDR.

The more flexible stance of the Kennedy administration was immediately noted in East Berlin. Although a study carried out in January 1961 by the foreign ministry for the SED leadership regarded Kennedy's victory in the elections as the result of the "degeneracy of capitalism in the heartland of modern imperialism," it also suggested that the new president could be expected to be "more realistic in judgment and

---

[21] The negotiations are documented in SAPMO/BArch, NY 4182/1323.

[22] Thomas A. Schwartz, "Victories and Defeats in the Long Twilight Struggle: The United States and Western Europe in the 1960s," in Diane B. Kunz, ed., *The Diplomacy of the Crucial Decade: American Foreign Relations During the 1960s* (New York, 1994), 125.

positive in action" while still "pursuing the im-perialistic aims of a more flexible and probably more skillful policy." Overall, however, there would be "virtually no change in the foreseeable future . . . in the basic stance adopted by govern-ing circles in the USA toward the GDR." The report, therefore, recommended that the GDR should "stand by its basic position on the con-clusion of the peace treaty and the resolution of the Berlin Wall issue . . . but not [take] any steps in the immediate future that might prompt the United States and West Germany to heighten the tensions or block any trend or moves to-ward a degree of willingness to compromise." The ministry recommended that the country should "look toward the forces of liberalism" and so "weaken the United States' support for the Hallstein doctrine." In addition, a wide-ranging propaganda offensive should include "a special plan to ensure that every possible effort is made to exert a direct influence that will give Americans an idea of the GDR and its achieve-ments."[23]

In view of the Wall and other human-rights violations, image-boosting tactics of this kind were unlikely to enjoy much success. In the second half of the 1960s, therefore, East Berlin switched the main focus of its strat-egy to strengthening economic ties with the United States. From 1965 onward, more Amer-ican companies participated in the Leipzig trade fair, and from March 31 to April 15, 1966, an East German foreign-trade delegation visited the United States and held meetings with leading American businessmen. East Berlin also hoped to profit from problems in relations between the United States and the Federal Republic. In a gross overassessment of East Germany's impor-tance, an internal SED memo to party leader Walter Ulbricht in April 1966 observed that "the United States government . . . [is] clearly interested in using the GDR as an important political and economic factor in implementing

its European policy and as a means of exerting political influence on the West German govern-ment."[24]

However, neither the GDR nor the United States had any room for maneuver in the in-terest of a more intensive bilateral relationship. Narrow boundaries were imposed by the raison d'être of the GDR – its dependence on and subordination to Moscow. It was swiftly rec-ognized in East Berlin that the policy of dif-ferentiation toward Eastern Europe initiated by Kennedy's successor Lyndon B. Johnson posed a threat to the GDR: Washington was trying to capitalize on nationalistic tendencies in some Eastern European countries and, by means of a differentiated dismantling of trade barriers, "to bring about 'change through rapprochement,' in other words a softening of the socialist sys-tem, in those countries and undermine their close cooperation with other socialist states, es-pecially the USSR."[25] Arrests of American cit-izens in Berlin and East Germany reinforced the negative image of the GDR in the eyes of many Americans, and economically the coun-try had virtually nothing to offer the United States.

American policy, too, was confined within narrow limits. In the mid-1960s, the GDR was the only Warsaw Pact state that showed no signs of internal liberalization. "The Ul-bricht regime," noted the United States Mission in Berlin early in 1964, "continues unprogres-sive, even Stalinist, and remains subservient to Moscow to a very high degree."[26] Policy as-sessments in subsequent years also called for the GDR to remain excluded from Washington's policy of "peaceful engagement" toward East-ern Europe. Most of all, however, the priorities of U.S. policy toward Germany – strengthen-ing the alliance with Bonn in the medium term and reunifying Germany in the long term – left

[23] Winzer (East German Foreign Ministry) to Ul-bricht, Einschätzung der künftigen Politik der Regier-ung Kennedy, Jan. 10, 1961, SAPMO/BArch, NY 4182/1323.

[24] W. Jarowinsky to Ulbricht, Apr. 29, 1966, SAPMO/BArch, NY 4182/1323.
[25] Study (1964), SAPMO/BArch, NY 4182/1323.
[26] United States Mission in Berlin to Department of State, Jan. 30, 1964, NA, RG 59, Central Foreign Policy Files, 1964–1968, box 2201.

little room for maneuver. Policy on the GDR, according to American diplomats in Berlin as late as the beginning of 1968, was "a function of our relations with the FRG, which is at least as interested as the US in preventing any further institutionalization of the division of Germany." However interested the Americans might have been in the liberalization of the GDR and the enlightenment of the East German people about the United States (through increased cultural exchanges, for example), Washington was prepared to "concede the primacy of Bonn's responsibility in this area."[27] Politically, economically, and culturally, the American government and people perceived the GDR as entirely "in the shadow of the Federal Republic."[28]

[27] United States Mission in Berlin to Department of State, Jan. 30, 1968, NA, RG 59, Central Foreign Policy Files, 1967–1969, box 2098.

[28] R. Gerald Livingston, "Ganz im Schatten der Bundesrepublik," *Die Zeit*, Sept. 30, 1988.

SECURITY

Security Through Deterrence?

German–American Security Relations, 1945–1968

Wolfgang Krieger

Translated by Sally E. Robertson

During the four decades between 1950 and 1990, the United States maintained approximately 320,000 to 350,000 troops in Europe, more than two-thirds of them in Germany. This presence was unique in both American and European history. Although the U.S. military presence extended to numerous bases and installations in Western and Southern Europe and over large parts of the Middle East and North Atlantic regions, this transatlantic involvement of the United States affected the Federal Republic of Germany more than any other nation in Europe.[1]

The Federal Republic occupied the central place in the hegemonic position of the United States in Europe and, therefore, in its role in shaping world politics. A special German–American relationship developed, its origins and substance based on security policy. For precisely this reason, that relationship ceased to exist following the international political revolution of 1989–91. Although the extensive military withdrawal of the United States from German soil may at first seem to have been largely a matter of troop counts and weapons systems, in reality it represented a fundamental shift in foreign policy. The foreign and security policies of unified Germany will most likely remain largely

limited to the framework set by the European Union (EU). Little scope will be left for a special relationship with the United States.

Two reasons existed for the Atlantic orientation of the old Federal Republic and its close ties to the United States, and both have disappeared since 1990. The first was the Soviet threat to the existence of the West German state and social system, a threat for which the nations of Western Europe could not compensate militarily. The second reason was that the United States was the most willing of the three Western Allies to support a German policy of reunification. Bonn, of course, often doubted the force of Washington's conviction on this area, most seriously during the administrations of John F. Kennedy and Lyndon B. Johnson from 1961 to 1969. Still, unlike London and Paris, Washington explicitly adhered to the principle of German unity. The degree to which the United States differed from Great Britain and France in this question became briefly but abundantly clear when the Berlin Wall fell.

Security was the priority shaping German–American relations. Yet, American policy was always concerned with Europe (and the neighboring regions), never with Germany alone. It treated Western and Central Europe as more important than the much less developed Eastern Europe. There was never a time after 1939

[1] Simon W. Duke and Wolfgang Krieger, *U.S. Military Forces in Europe: The Early Years, 1945–1970* (Boulder, Colo., 1993).

when American policy on Germany abandoned this broader geostrategic perspective.

Washington's perspective naturally led to tensions with German interests, for every chancellor (even Konrad Adenauer, who is often criticized, completely unjustifiably, on this point) had two objectives. These goals did not necessarily coincide with American interests in Europe: a Germany with equal rights in the international community (to the extent possible) and a unified Germany.

For its part, the United States could have easily tolerated a unified Germany with equal rights. However, Washington found it difficult to convince the prominent political forces in Europe that such a Germany – back to "normal" – was desirable. Therefore, the central task and major source of legitimation for American hegemony in Europe became to prevent Germany from becoming a disruptive force or even gaining the capacity to become such a force again.

The crowning achievement of West German foreign policy was to cleverly restrain itself by accepting this fact, thus keeping the path open for a European consensus on German unification. This feat was accomplished with exceptional diplomatic skill in 1989–90.[2] It was only logical that the United States played a key role in this development, given American policy on Germany since 1943. It nonetheless represented a remarkable act of well-calculated hegemonic politics.

THE AMERICAN–SOVIET CONTEXT

The degree to which German–American security policy was subject to the influence of third parties is demonstrated primarily and most intricately by the example of the Soviet Union. It was not the mere existence of the Soviet Union, but rather the particular policy it promulgated soon after 1945 that triggered the onset of the Cold War. This assessment is important because Western revisionists interpret the course followed by Stalin largely as a reaction to a fundamentally hostile policy pursued by the Western powers.[3] In light of recently uncovered sources on both sides, these assumptions now seem insupportable.[4]

Not the mere existence of the Soviet Union as a major power, but its stationing of troops in large numbers west of the Soviet border and up to the Elbe River caused increasing mistrust in the West. These troops remained in place despite the fact that Germany had been completely disarmed and Anglo-American military forces had largely withdrawn from the European continent by mid-1946.[5] Moscow was clearly pursuing a dual objective. First, its forces in Central Europe served the purpose of intimidation. Second, they were an instrument of a power politics that sought to restructure the eastern half of Europe, leaving Central Europe hanging in the balance for the time being. The presence of the Red Army made political, economic, and ideological control of Eastern Europe as well as Soviet policy toward Germany since 1948–9 possible. Soviet rule over Eastern Europe, including the German Democratic Republic (GDR), encompassed all imaginable areas of public life – indeed, many areas of private life as well – but this military presence constituted

---

[2] See the chapter by Stephen Szabo, vol. 2, Politics, and the chapter by Karl Kaiser, vol. 2, Security.

[3] Gabriel Kolko, *The Politics of War: The World and United States Foreign Policy, 1943–1945* (New York, 1968); Walter LaFeber, *America, Russia, and the Cold War*, 8th ed. (New York, 1996); Melvyn P. Leffler, *A Preponderance of Power: National Security, the Truman Administration, and the Cold War* (Stanford, Calif., 1993); Carolyn Eisenberg, *Drawing the Line: The American Decision to Divide Germany, 1944–1949* (New York, 1996).

[4] See John Lewis Gaddis, *We Now Know: Rethinking Cold War History* (Oxford, 1997); Norman M. Naimark, *The Russians in Germany: A History of the Soviet Zone of Occupation, 1945–1949* (Cambridge, Mass., 1995); Vojtech Mastny, *The Cold War and Soviet Insecurity: The Stalin Years* (New York, 1996).

[5] John Erickson, ed., *Soviet Military Power and Performance* (Hamden, Conn., 1979); J. M. Macintosh, *Strategy and Tactics of Soviet Foreign Policy* (Oxford, 1962); William T. Lee and Richard F. Staar, *Soviet Military Policy Since World War II* (Stanford, Calif., 1986); Hannes Adomeit et al., eds., *Die Sowjetunion als Militärmacht* (Stuttgart, 1987); Uwe Nerlich and Falk Bomsdorf, eds., *Sowjetische Macht und westliche Verhandlungspolitik im Wandel militärischer Kräfteverhältnisse* (Baden-Baden, 1982).

the central element of the Soviet satellite system. The upheaval of 1989 provided inescapable proof. Once Moscow became willing to withdraw its military, none of the other instruments of its rule – not even all of them in combination – could stop the collapse of the Soviet empire.[6]

The Soviet threat was completely different from the German threat. For this reason, the term *double containment* is so misleading that it should be completely discarded.[7] Of course, the concept of containment does describe the core of American efforts since 1945: Soviet power was not to extend beyond the Iron Curtain.[8] However, this also meant that the problem posed by the Soviet Union – namely, the existence of a totalitarian great power, later a superpower – was considered insoluble. Without much exaggeration, one can thus describe the policy of the West toward the Soviets as appeasement; this description seems appropriate, even though the policy of the West toward National Socialist Germany in the years between 1933 and 1941 is not entirely comparable.

The fundamental difference between U.S. policy toward Germany and U.S. policy toward Moscow was that after 1945, Washington not only considered the German problem to be soluble but in fact did solve it. The solution consisted of subjecting Germany to strict supervision of unspecified duration and permitting its reascendance only if *all* the important political forces and nations in Europe agreed, including the Soviet Union. This constellation could not be achieved until 1990. Even then, the international treaties on German unification set a

limit of unspecified duration on the country's sovereignty in the area of security policy, requiring Germany's unconditional renunciation of atomic, biological, and chemical weapons; continued German membership in NATO; a relatively low upper limit on conventional forces (370,000 troops); renunciation of any kind of territorial expansion; and, finally, close integration of Germany in the EU.[9] This solution of the German problem, one fundamentally focused on security policy and as much in effect between 1945 and 1990 as after reunification, was quite different from the containment of Soviet power. American security policy toward Germany from 1945 to 1989–90 can thus be seen as a solution to the German problem because it bound Germany to a European order from which it could not break free and that did not depend on Germany's voluntary subordination. This solution was temporary only in the sense that it took several decades for the Soviet Union to accept it.

The United States, in contrast, could not solve the Soviet problem unless it wanted to risk a nuclear war. Whether the gamble of tolerating and containing a totalitarian world power would succeed was an open question and the subject of ongoing skepticism. Throughout the Cold War, fear ran through both Western and Eastern Europe (and particularly Germany) that the two superpowers would reach an overall solution – or at least a mutually tolerable European solution – to the detriment of European interests. The fear also existed that the two powers had perhaps already done so quietly – namely, by accepting the status quo of a divided Europe and Germany.

These doubts about containment policy surfaced, for example, in Bonn's criticism of American arms-control policies. Although they reduced the threat of war, they might also have led to a "solution" of the East-West conflict forced jointly on Europe by the superpowers,

[6] William E. Odom, *The Collapse of the Soviet Military* (New Haven, Conn., 1998).

[7] Wilfried Loth, "Die doppelte Eindämmung: Überlegungen zur Genesis des Kalten Krieges 1945–1947," *Historische Zeitschrift* 238 (1984): 611–31; Wolfram F. Hanrieder, "The FRG and NATO. Between Security Dependence and Security Partnership," in Emil Kirchner and James Sperling, eds., *The Federal Republic of Germany and NATO* (New York, 1992), 194–220; Rolf Steininger, ed., *Die doppelte Eindämmung: Europäische Sicherheit und Deutsche Frage in den Fünfzigern* (Munich, 1993).

[8] See the chapter by Ruud Van Dijk, vol. 1, Politics.

[9] Vertrag über die abschliessende Regelung in bezug auf Deutschland vom 12.9.1990 [Treaty on the Final Provisions Regarding Germany of September 12, 1990], in Ingo von Münch, ed., *Die Verträge zur Einheit Deutschlands* (Munich, 1991), 29–34.

thereby cementing the division of Germany.[10] It is no wonder, then, that both the periodic intensification of the Cold War and the American-Soviet policy of détente led to increased tensions within the Western alliance.

THE INFORMATION FACTOR

It is difficult to decipher the signs of these tensions because much material remains classified. Thanks to the relatively generous release of files on the American side, the first two postwar decades can be considered fairly well researched, but significant gaps still exist for the later period. Overall, the diplomatic dimension of the German-American relationship remains much better documented than its military history. Access to information for research purposes is poorer in all areas on the German side.

The role of the intelligence services in security policy remains one gap that is particularly difficult to fill. "We do not know how much we do not know," warns Christopher Andrew, the leading British historian of intelligence services.[11] Aside from individual episodes that can be reconstructed from Western archives or, more recently, from former Soviet archives, only a few general conclusions are possible.

First, we now know that the Soviet leadership had access to practically all important NATO documents and data on the structure of forces in addition to an abundance of American and West German classified documents. The West German security agencies in particular, but also those in the United States and Western Europe, were infiltrated to a massive degree by the East.[12] This meant that secrecy functioned much better

against the public in the West than against the West's actual strategic opponent.

Second, it can be assumed, although only partially substantiated, that the high expenditures of the United States on its intelligence agencies yielded considerably more information on the Soviet Union and particularly on Soviet security policy than has been officially admitted up to now. For instance, not until the mid-1990s were at least some of the results of American deciphering of Soviet documents declassified, but only for the period of World War II.[13] Virtually nothing about this domain has been released for the postwar period.[14]

THE TECHNOLOGY FACTOR

Alongside the information factor, the technology factor holds special significance for security policy. Military technology has always been of historical importance, but in very different ways. The two world wars offer a comparison. In World War I, the new technologies, particularly machine guns and mobile artillery, made a major contribution to the stalemate on the western front. The few airplanes and tanks on hand did little to alter the situation, and the large British and German battleship fleets turned out to be ineffectual. In contrast, the highly technical weapons systems in World War II had a very different effect. They often compensated when the enemy held a numerical advantage. High technology accelerated the Allied victory considerably. Aircraft carriers, long-range bombers, radar, signals intelligence, and, ultimately, atomic weapons contributed decisively to this end.

Particularly in the United States, this gave rise to a powerful mythology about advances

---

[10] On this point, see the chapter by Erhard Forndran in this section.

[11] Christopher Andrew, "Nachrichtendienste im Kalten Krieg: Probleme und Perspektiven," in Wolfgang Krieger and Jürgen Weber, eds., *Spionage für den Frieden? Nachrichtendienste in Deutschland während des Kalten Krieges* (Munich, 1997), 23–48.

[12] See Udo Ulfkotte, *Verschlussache BND* (Munich, 1998).

[13] Robert L. Benson and Michael Warner, eds., *VENONA: Soviet Espionage and the American Response, 1939–1957* (Washington, D.C., 1996).

[14] James Bamford, *The Puzzle Palace* (Boston, 1982); David E. Murphy, Sergei A. Kondrashev, and George Bailey, *Battleground Berlin: CIA vs. KGB in the Cold War* (New Haven, 1997); and see the chapter by Wesley Wark in this section.

in weapons technology that would permit war to be waged with minimal loss of human life. The economic and geostrategic dominance of the United States very soon turned into dominance in practically all technologies with military applications, even in sectors of the industry in which Germany had taken the lead prior to 1945, such as the construction of missiles and submarines.

Another new development was the increasing overlap between military and civilian technology, which gave the United States a considerable and commercially exploitable lead, for example, in aircraft construction and computer technology. Two factors bear emphasis. First, the state funded a majority of research and development costs, which was novel in American history and was presumably made possible on this scale only because of Cold War conditions. Second, this technological and associated economic dominance led to considerable tensions within the Western camp, and talk of an "American threat" came into circulation.[15] Fears in Western Europe about high-tech American international conglomerates became an important stimulus for creating a European counterweight through the tool of European integration. With the current pressure of globalization, this factor is again playing an important role in the policies of the EU.[16]

The purchase of large American weapons systems played a dominant role in the initial phase of building the Bundeswehr, the West German army. In a second phase, the Germans attempted to have their own armaments industry build American products under license and thereby catch up to American technology. The Starfighter F-104G was an important example. If the Germans had chosen the French Mirage in the late 1950s instead of deciding to build the Starfighter under license, and if closer cooperation around armaments had existed among the European NATO members, it would have been easier to eventually achieve a "European defense identity" and to limit American dominance within NATO. Current NATO reforms and discussions of the future of security arrangements for the EU still reflect the consequences of this choice. The weapons procurement practices of the Bundeswehr bore a clear American stamp, however, and continued to do so for a long time. Not until a third phase of armament policy in the Federal Republic did domestic products became available that, in turn, acted as a German or Western European challenge to the global, omnipresent U.S. armaments industry.[17] Western European Tornado fighter planes, German frigates and submarines, and the Leopard tank are hallmarks of this third phase.

Careful investigation is still required to determine how far the technology race, including the arms race, was a reaction to the Soviet threat and how far this competition itself contributed to the escalation of the Cold War. Presumably, both factors were involved, but the current state of historical research does not permit a conclusive answer.[18] It is fairly certain, although the details have barely been uncovered to date, that American high technology was a significant factor in the Soviet swing toward reform in 1985 and, ultimately, the collapse of the Soviet bloc. In particular, the program launched in 1983 to build a space-based defense against intercontinental missiles – the Strategic Defense Initiative (SDI) – triggered a deep insecurity among Soviet political, economic, and military leaders. It also unsettled the West Europeans to such a degree that they responded with the EUREKA program of the EC.

The Soviet Union did, in fact, do a remarkable job of closing the technological gap created by the United States in the first half of the Cold War. The Soviet Union either matched

[15] Jean-Jacques Servan-Schreiber, *Le défi américain* (Paris, 1967), German edition of 1968 with foreword by Franz-Josef Strauss.

[16] The primary civilian examples are the major technological projects to develop the Airbus, Concorde, and Ariane.

[17] See the chapter by Michael Neufeld, vol. 1, Security, and Joachim Rohde, vol. 2, Security.

[18] Few Soviet primary sources on this subject have been released to date. See Matthew Evangelista, *Innovation and the Arms Race: How the United States and the Soviet Union Develop Military Technologies* (Ithaca, N.Y., 1988).

the Americans in certain key areas, such as nuclear warheads and missiles, or undermined the American lead by producing weapons in larger numbers and with greater destructive power or by deploying them in more favorable geostrategic locations. The United States did not rely on advantages in their weapons technology but opted for symmetrical responses. It built up its network of overseas bases from World War II in order to protect its allies and interests on the periphery of the regions controlled by the Soviet Union and China. It also stationed large numbers of troops and weapons systems in these locations. Thus, the security empire of the United States manifested itself not only in technological and economic superiority but also in a massive global military presence. All three factors – technological superiority, a global presence, and large numbers of military personnel and weapons – were completely new in the history of American foreign and security policy.

DEFEATED GERMANY AS A SECURITY PROBLEM (1945–50)

The first phase of American security policy in Europe is the most difficult to reduce to a common denominator because it contained many a conceptual about-face.[19] When the German high command capitulated on May 8–9, 1945, three assumptions that had served as U.S. planning principles had already proven untenable. A German government or a central administrative structure that could be subordinated to an occupying regime no longer existed. The number of U.S. troops to be deployed for a military administration, therefore, had to be much greater than originally planned. They had to create German administrative bodies themselves, and they had to be active in many areas for which they had made few preparations. U.S. officials considered the example of the Rhineland occupation – which the United States had participated

in during the 1920s – but decided it offered no useful guidance.[20]

The task of setting up an occupation became easier, however, when fears that the German "werewolves" might engage in fanatical guerrilla warfare turned out to be unfounded. American troops received a mainly friendly reception from a population worn down by the war but, in part, hopeful. Many Germans felt they had been liberated by the Americans. The American troops, for their part, maintained an amazing degree of discipline, and misconduct was kept to a minimum. (Red Army troops, by contrast, terrorized the German civilian population and commited many rapes and other abuses.) Millions of first encounters between GIs and German civilians laid the foundation for later German-American friendship.[21]

This disposed with the need for most of the precautions taken by the American side – for example, the bomber squadrons intended for deployment against nests of German guerrillas. The unexpected readiness of the Germans for peace made it possible to prepare enormous troop contingents for transport to the Asian theater of war immediately after the end of hostilities in Europe. This plan for shifting troops was never implemented because the atomic bombs dropped on Japan on August 6 and 9, 1945, ended the war much more quickly than expected.

American military leaders now sought to implement the security policy they had been planning for the postwar period since 1941, a policy that rested on four pillars.[22] First, it foresaw maintaining universal military training on a

---

[19] See the chapter by Steven Rearden in this section.

[20] Earl Ziemke, *The U.S. Army in the Occupation of Germany, 1944–1946* (Washington, D.C., 1975); Wolfgang Krieger, *General Lucius D. Clay und die amerikanische Deutschlandpolitik 1945–1949* (Stuttgart, 1987).

[21] See the chapter by Klaus-Dietmar Henke, vol. 1, Society.

[22] Michael Sherry, *Preparing for the Next War: American Plans for Postwar Defense, 1941–1945* (New Haven, 1977); Wolfgang Krieger, "American Security Policy in Europe Before NATO," in Francis H. Heller and John Gillingham, eds., *NATO, the Founding of the Atlantic Alliance, and the Integration of Europe* (New York, 1992), 99–128.

permanent basis, thereby reintroducing a piece of military reform that had gone by the wayside after the end of World War I. Second, it provided a means for overcoming the fragmentation of military organization and command structures by creating a single department of the Department of War and the Department of the Navy. Much progress had been made toward unifying command during the war, but legislation was necessary to prevent a return to the old conditions of separate command centers for the different branches of the military. Third, the plan called for keeping expenditures for weapons research at a high level in order to maintain and extend the technological lead that the United States had achieved during the war. Finally, the fourth envisioned pillar of U.S. defense policy for the postwar period was to be a global American presence operating under the umbrella of the United Nations (UN); this presence would rely in particular on the American fleet of long-range bombers and the existing worldwide network of American bases. At the center of these plans was the idea that a continuation of the wartime coalition with Great Britain and the Soviet Union would make possible a new kind of security structure that could defeat an aggressor anywhere on earth. The United States would thereby offer the UN Security Council, primarily its five permanent members, a powerful military tool for controlling aggressors. President Franklin D. Roosevelt's concept of the "four (world) policemen"[23] (France was to be included) would have become a powerful instrument of a completely new type of order for international peace.

For a variety of reasons, putting more than a greatly reduced version of this four-part plan into practice was not possible. Congress, which the Republicans controlled after the elections in fall 1946, demanded such a modest

military budget that universal military training in peacetime was out of the question.[24] Reform efforts for greater integration of the formerly largely autonomous branches of the military met with stiff resistance from the U.S. Navy. The National Security Act of 1947 eventually brought some progress in this initiative. A common Department of Defense and a common Joint Chiefs of Staff were established, although the authority and personnel of both institutions were severely limited. Further progress toward integration was drawn out over a period of decades, and in the case of the Joint Chiefs of Staff, it was only achieved in the 1990s.

The third reform measure – continuation of weapons research and development at a high level of funding – could only be partially carried out in the years immediately following the war. For example, soon only vestiges of the Manhattan Project remained.[25] Most researchers returned to their universities because the GI Bill had triggered an enormous increase in higher education jobs. Ongoing weapons research also remained severely limited. In addition, the Navy and Air Force were locked in a fierce debate over procurement priorities. The great issue was the choice between aircraft carriers and bomber fleets, because it appeared there was not adequate funding for both.

A new UN security system, conceived at least partially as legitimation for a continued global military presence of the United States, also proved infeasible. The institutions and practices provided for in Chapter VII of the UN Charter remained empty phrases because the Soviet Union was not willing to participate in or permit a global intervention system for enforcing peace. It was not possible to provide the Security Council with either the military contingents called for in Article 43 or the "immediately available national air-force contingents for combined international enforcement

[23] Detlef Junker, *Franklin D. Roosevelt: Macht und Vision. Präsident in Krisenzeiten*, 2d ed. (Göttingen, 1989), 142–3; Robert Dallek, *Franklin D. Roosevelt and American Foreign Policy, 1932–1945*, 2d ed. (New York, 1995), 434–5; Townsend Hoopes and Douglas Brinkley, *FDR and the Creation of the UN* (New Haven, Conn., 1997).

[24] C. Joseph Bernardo and Eugene H. Bacon, *American Military Policy: Its Development Since 1775*, 2d ed. (Westport, Conn., 1974), 445–52.

[25] Vincent C. Jones, *Manhattan: The Army and the Atomic Bomb* (Washington, D.C., 1985), 579–601.

action" called for in Article 45. Nor was the Military Staff Committee cited in Articles 26, 46, and 47 established. The committee would have consisted of the military chiefs of staff of the permanent members of the Security Council; that is, the five world policemen.

As the private papers of General Dwight D. Eisenhower make clear, the American military leadership seriously attempted to implement this part of the UN charter.[26] High-level Air Force generals such as George Kenney and Joseph McNarney stood at the ready for this task. In the fierce clashes over budget allocations, primarily between the Navy and the Air Force, this UN assignment would have redounded to the benefit of the Air Force. Because the British had far fewer long-range bombers and the Soviet Union possessed hardly any, the leadership role within the UN would have fallen naturally to the United States. Above all, however, it was atomic weapons in combination with American long-range bombers – particularly the newest model, the B-29, deployed in Hiroshima and Nagasaki – that would have given the Americans a global leadership role. This was presumably an important reason for the Soviets' boycott of these sections of the UN Charter.

In this context, it must be noted that the American military would have been entirely ready to pursue a nuclear weapons ban within the framework of the UN, as the Truman administration had proposed in the Baruch plan of 1946. The Navy leadership was already opposed to concentrating resources on nuclear weapons because aircraft carriers were not yet able to launch nuclear weapons. The Army, too, could have passed up nuclearization, given the state of technical development at the time. However, it became more and more difficult to continue negotiations with Moscow in light of Soviet policies of violence and stiff demands in Eastern and Central Europe. In addition, we now know from Soviet documents that Stalin was not interested in negotiating an international ban on nuclear weapons until the Soviet Union itself was in complete possession of that technology.[27]

THE SHIFT IN DEFENSE POLICY OF 1950

Toward the end of the 1940s, a new concept in security policy emerged that replaced the failed initial plan in large part. But it was the outbreak of the Korean War that created the financial latitude necessary for Americans' global military policy to operate; it would remain in effect for the entire remainder of the Cold War and, to a large extent, through to the present day. It was during this period as well that the United States decided to be involved in security policy in Western Europe on a large scale and to station large numbers of troops there. This policy included arming the Federal Republic of Germany, thereby launching a German-American security partnership.

Of course, this dramatic turnaround in American security policy did not come entirely unexpectedly. As early as 1946, when Soviet intentions in Eastern Europe became apparent, Washington began to draft the strategy that later became known as the policy of containment. This policy aimed to use political and economic tools to prevent further expansion of Soviet political power. Early on, however, Army and Air Force staffs began to consider the consequences of Soviet policies for Western defense. This included intensification of intelligence activity in order to determine any possible preparations for military aggression.[28]

Emergency plans were also prepared, including the plan, often mentioned in later publications, for an American withdrawal across the English Channel and behind the Pyrenees.[29]

---

[26] Alfred D. Chandler and Louis Galambos, eds., *The Papers of Dwight D. Eisenhower*, 17 vols. (Baltimore, 1970–96).

[27] David Holloway, *Stalin and the Bomb: The Soviet Union and Atomic Energy, 1939–1956* (New Haven, Conn., 1994).

[28] Phillip A. Karber and Jerald A. Combs, "The United States, NATO, and the Soviet Threat to Western Europe. Military Estimates and Policy Options, 1945–1963," *Diplomatic History* 22 (1998): 399–429.

[29] John L. Gaddis, *Strategies of Containment: A Critical Appraisal of American National Security Policy* (New York, 1982).

That was a worst-case secenario based on on the low number of available troops in Europe. Such plans did not indicate anything about the possible deployment of the main body of troops stationed in the United States or the will of the United States to wage total war.

Political and military leaders of the United States at the time did not anticipate a major Soviet attack. At most, they expected local conflicts and Soviet gestures designed to intimidate. It was primarily with such scenarios in mind that the United States intensified its military cooperation with Great Britain and France during the Berlin Crisis of 1948–9. The French chiefs of staff took the initiative in this direction in October 1947.[30] The United States at first merely kept a watchful eye on military planning by the Brussels Pact, which had been established in March 1948.

A year later, the North Atlantic Treaty of April 4, 1949, and the associated Military Assistance Act formalized this cooperation and an American security guarantee reinforced it. Internal U.S. government documents make clear that Washington linked these treaties with the hope that most of the troops remaining in Western Europe could soon be brought home. Since the North Atlantic Treaty was expressly declared to be a regional security alliance in the sense of Article 52 of the UN Charter, one can see here a conceptual link to the original American security plan, which had been strongly oriented toward the UN.

The idea of a German military contribution to the West occurred early in planning execises on the threat of war with the Soviet Union. Not only U.S. but also British and French military files offer evidence for this.[31] Viewed from a strictly military point of view, defending Western Europe without the involvement of German

soldiers appeared absurd, even impossible. Politically, however, this idea was still taboo.

Progress toward a common Western defense strategy was achieved early in the area of logistics. In the event of a Soviet advance across the north German plains, supply lines to American troops through Bremerhaven would be seriously threatened. Therefore, U.S. Army planners began to plan a second route in 1949 for supplies from Bordeaux across France. At the same time, the U.S. Air Force secretly stockpiled fuel supplies in eastern France, using the American Graves Registration Command as a front. All of these measures were politically sensitive. The ongoing presence of American troops in France became increasingly controversial among French political parties. The communists and nationalists (Gaullists) saw them as posing a grievous limitation on French sovereignty. Not until early June 1950 could official government negotiations begin, leading in November to a treaty concluded for an initial five-year period. Soon thereafter, the NATO Status of Forces Agreement of June 1951 would offer a viable legal foundation through which U.S. troops could be stationed in or remain in France and certain other member nations of the alliance. However, it was primarily the dispatch of four additional American divisions to Europe that created a completely new NATO, with a high-level U.S. officer as NATO supreme commander and a staff and planning organization that took the place of the military institutions of the Brussels Pact.

In 1949, the United States began the search for an effective response to the first Soviet atomic test and the communist victory in the Chinese civil war. A summary of the ideas and plans developed in this search came in the National Security Council study written primarily by Paul Nitze that was presented to President Truman in April 1950 (NSC-68).[32] It had already been decided a few months earlier to increase nuclear weapons production capacity greatly. In summer 1949, the United States had

---

[30] Wolfgang Krieger, "Die Ursprünge der langfristigen Stationierung amerikanischer Streitkräfte in Europa, 1945–1951," in Ludolf Herbst, ed., *Vom Marshallplan zur EWG: Die Eingliederung der Bundesrepublik in die westliche Welt* (Munich, 1990), 373–98.

[31] See Militärgeschichtliches Forschungsamt, ed., *Anfänge westdeutscher Sicherheitspolitik 1945–1956*, 4 vols. (Munich, 1982–97).

[32] Ernest R. May, ed., *American Cold War Strategy: Interpreting NSC-68* (Boston, 1993).

"only" about 100 nuclear weapons; in January 1950, the decision was made to build the hydrogen bomb.[33] These decisions cleared the way politically for the rapid development of new types of nuclear weapons and for the production of previously unimaginable stockpiles with an equally unimaginable destructive potential.

The Korean War was decisive in sweeping away the political barriers to these developments and in spurring massive arms buildups in Great Britain, France, and the Benelux nations. It became possible to push through a completely new defense policy in Congress with nearly four times the price tag of the old one. Without much exaggeration, one can argue that until 1989, U.S. troop strength and the U.S. military budget remained at the level brought about by the shock of the Korean War.

GLOBAL READINESS FOR WAR IN PEACETIME
(1950–61)

The subsequent epoch was characterized, first, by the buildup of the Western military arsenal that was the determining factor of German-American security relations for the duration of the Cold War and, second, by the process of defining the role that the Federal Republic of Germany would play in security policy.[34] The basic decision in fall 1950 to arm West Germany triggered a long-lasting debate that affected not only the Western powers and Germany itself but the Soviet Union as well.[35] The results included several NATO and Bundeswehr crises, as well as the second Berlin Crisis (1958–62). Not until the late 1960s were the core issues of the West German defense contribution resolved. Through its membership in NATO's Nuclear Planning Group, Bonn gained a limited voice at the nuclear table. In addition, the Non-Proliferation Treaty (NPT) permanently excluded the Federal Republic from possession of nuclear weapons. This represented an unacknowledged gesture of appeasement toward the Soviet Union that, in turn, constituted an important prerequisite for Chancellor Willy Brandt's Ostpolitik. The German Social Democrats finally gave up their opposition to the Bundeswehr and, for the first time since 1920, put forward a defense minister from their ranks, Helmut Schmidt. Now the Bundeswehr was able to "produce" markedly more Western security than it had "cost" during the preceding crises.

The integration of the Federal Republic into the security structure of the Western military bloc demanded a large measure of diplomatic skill from the United States. France in particular, but also Great Britain and the other NATO members, set more and more conditions for their assent. It thus took four years to establish even the external political framework. Significantly, during this phase the Federal Republic was able to attach its defense contribution to major political demands on the Western allies and thereby undertook its first independent foreign policy initiatives. The Federal Republic succeeded in rejecting the first proposal for integration – namely, the French Pleven Plan of 1951 – and acted as an important negotiating partner in pushing through its own ideas on the second plan, the European Defense Community (EDC) of 1952.

These two integration models initially met with American skepticism because they ruled out German membership in NATO and would lead to French domination of Germany in the area of military policy; France would have gained this position despite the fact that it was suffering a severe breakdown in domestic policy at the time and was militarily weak. Not until the French parliament rejected the EDC's "small European" army in August 1954 did Germany join NATO. This paved the way for Germany to become a full and equal participant in the Western bloc. However, Germany was a special case militarily because, unlike the other NATO

[33] Richard Rhodes, *Dark Sun: The Making of the Hydrogen Bomb* (New York, 1995), esp. 363, 374.
[34] Marc Trachtenberg, *A Constructed Peace: The Making of the European Settlement, 1945–1963* (Princeton, N.J., 1999).
[35] See the chapter by David Clay Large in this section.

states, not only certain units but virtually the entire Bundeswehr was subordinated to NATO's Supreme Command.

In terms of military and weapons technology, the establishment and arming of the Bundeswehr in 1956 must be seen in the larger context of the West European arms buildup at the time that led to massive expansion in the West European armaments industry. The Federal Republic had to decide to what extent it wanted to build up its own weapons research and armaments industry. Although the initial supply of large weapons came from existing American stockpiles, medium-term possibilities under consideration included domestic production and cooperation in the context of NATO. This was driven in part by the desire not to be just "kitchen boys" to the alliance (in the words of Franz Josef Strauss) but come as close as possible to being a full military partner. Developing an armaments industry also offered an opportunity to support economically weak regions of the Federal Republic.

The issue of the nuclear armament of the Bundeswehr played a special role. Bonn had, from the outset, renounced a national nuclear weapons capability comparable to that of the United States, Britain, or, later, France. But for more than a decade after Germany had joined the alliance, it remained unresolved how the Federal Republic might participate in NATO nuclear forces, whether it would be allowed to participate, or if it even wanted to. The question ignited fierce foreign and domestic policy debates over the quality of Germany's NATO membership. Essentially, three models came under discussion, each of which had many possible variations: participation in the American, the French, or a future European nuclear force within the framework of NATO.

The first model foresaw a limited nuclear role for the Federal Republic in which the Bundeswehr, under the supervision of the United States, would be equipped with nuclear delivery systems (i.e., howitzers, bombers, missiles) and, in the event of war, would be supplied with American nuclear warheads. Because other non-nuclear NATO nations could also partake

of this pool, it prevented establishment of nuclear-free zones or sections on NATO's central frontline that might have been attractive targets for Soviet tank offensives. The United States had already begun in 1954 to arm its forces stationed in the Federal Republic with nuclear weapons – more precisely, with tactical nuclear weapons for battlefield use. It seemed logical to arm most of the American troops and some of the European NATO troops with these weapons.

Both the new German defense minister, Franz Josef Strauss, and Chancellor Konrad Adenauer favored the creation of this arsenal of "state-of-the-art weaponry," as it was called at the time. Strauss was determined to stop the perpetuation of old ideas about military engagement that many high-level officers of the Bundeswehr were using in an attempt to preserve "proven" methods of German warfare from World War II. In contrast, a strategy that was at least partially nuclear represented completely new ground, even for German career officers, and thus signaled a break with tradition. And, not least, it signalled the primacy of political over military leadership that Strauss was advocating. Adenauer, meanwhile, saw nuclear weapons primarily as a means of binding the United States to Germany and as a political lever with which Germany could gain political and international equality with the other mid-sized powers, at least in the long term.

After the United States proposed this weapons pool for European NATO members in 1956, France countered with a Western European nuclear plan that provided for involvement of the Federal Republic, Italy, and possibly other NATO states under French leadership, a sort of nuclear EDC. Research on this puzzling episode has recently made great advances. The French initiative seems to have originated with the simple assumption that nuclear weapons would soon become "normal" weapons that would be found in the arsenals of every highly industrialized nation in the foreseeable future. From the French point of view, it would be best if the Federal Republic took this step under the supervision of Paris and contributed significantly to the funding of the French nuclear program.[36] Bonn would simultaneously purchase large quantities of French armaments, including Mirage bombers.

Recent research has made it increasingly clear that it was not until much later that Paris began to pursue plans for a strictly national *force-de-frappe* (nuclear force). Initially, it sought an internal NATO option that would strengthen French influence within the alliance. This line continued under General Charles de Gaulle, who returned to power in summer 1958, until France withdrew from NATO's integrated military command in 1967.[37]

In 1956, Adenauer and Strauss showed great interest but had to be extremely cautious before the German public. The U.S. government, in communication with Bonn, assumed a wait-and-see attitude. In December 1957, the NATO Council finally accepted the weapons pool concept proposed by the United States. It was uncertain, however, how long the United States would maintain a massive military presence in Europe that had been expressly conceived as a stopgap arrangement until the West Europeans could defend themselves. Being dependent on Washington without having full information about – much less a say in – the stationing, arming, command, or target planning of nuclear units was thus wholly unsatisfactory to the Federal Republic.[38]

The plan presented by the United States in 1960 for a NATO nuclear force was intended to address Germany's frequently voiced concerns. It called for formation of a "multilateral force" (MLF) from the European member states, with the United States contributing nuclear weapons and delivery systems. The British nuclear force would be subordinated to this structure, as would a French nuclear force, which was expected to emerge in the foreseeable future.

Contemporary nuclear-policy debates often referred with exaggerated polemics to the "German finger on the nuclear trigger," even though Bonn was actually more concerned with having a finger on the nuclear safety catch. This triggered much unrest among the public in the West. The leadership in Moscow presumably also viewed further expansion of NATO nuclear forces with concern and instrumentalized German participation to particularly effective political ends. Nikita Khrushchev's policy regarding Berlin at the time was probably guided to some degree by those nuclear-policy debates, although this cannot be definitely proven.[39] Moscow had already used the entry of the Federal Republic into NATO to force the Eastern European satellite states into the rigid confines of the Warsaw Pact and to accelerate the previously concealed arms buildup of the GDR. In November 1958, Khrushchev threatened to "solve" the German question through a unilateral peace treaty with the GDR and thereby terminate the Four-Power status of Berlin as well.

In hindsight, we recognize that Moscow was primarily interested in solving the economic crisis of the GDR and halting the flow of refugees through West Berlin. However, the Berlin Crisis, with the aggressive act of building the Berlin Wall in summer 1961, was a menacing violation of international law on the part of the Soviet Union and the GDR. It could easily have led to military conflict even if that was not Moscow's intent.

The Soviet Union was alone, however, in using the East-West confrontation to its political advantage. The Kennedy administration, which had come into office in early 1961, considered the situation so dangerous that it was prepared to make political concessions and now demanded practical and political guarantees from Moscow for West Berlin alone. This constituted the de facto surrender of Four-Power responsibility

---

[36] Maurice Vaïsse, *La France et l'atome* (Brussels, 1994).

[37] Georges-Henri Soutou, *L'alliance incertaine: Les rapports politico-stratégiques franco-allemands 1954–1996* (Paris, 1996); Maurice Vaïsse, *La grandeur: La politique étrangère du général de Gaulle 1958–1969* (Paris, 1998).

[38] Wolfgang Krieger, *The Germans and the Nuclear Question*, German Historical Institute, Occasional Paper 14 (Washington, D.C., 1995); Matthias Künzel, *Bonn und die Bombe: Deutsche Atomwaffenpolitik von Adenauer bis Brandt* (Frankfurt am Main, 1992).

[39] Vladislav M. Zubok and Constantine Pleshakov, *Inside the Kremlin's Cold War: From Stalin to Khrushchev* (Cambridge, Mass., 1996).

for East Berlin.[40] Security and stability replaced Western political principles with respect to Germany, indeed, the maxims of Washington security policy in Europe.

Adenauer's policies on Germany and security became dangerously exposed. Although he had for years attempted to explain that the integration of the Federal Republic into NATO and the close ties of Bonn to Washington in the area of security policy would bring German unity closer, it was now clear that Western security policy aimed increasingly at stability – in other words, at an appeasement policy toward Moscow. The German question in particular could no longer be advanced because it was supposedly the greatest threat to this stability. The Western alliance threatened to become a virtual guarantee *against* a solution to the German question, and the recently created Bundeswehr would quite possibly be forced to keep watch over this cementing of the division of Germany.

THE KENNEDY AND JOHNSON ERA (1961–8)

The fact that this abrupt change in German-American security relations had taken place mainly over questions of nuclear policy made it particularly difficult for Bonn to present its position to the public in an acceptable and comprehensible way. It was impossible to communicate to the public within Germany itself or in the allied countries that greater German participation in NATO nuclear matters would lead to a security gain for the West as a whole. It stood to reason that a strong, conventionally armed Bundeswehr would make a Soviet surprise attack against Western Europe less likely and allow Paris, Amsterdam, and London to breathe a little easier. But did the same principle apply to a greater nuclear role for the government in Bonn? At least psychologically, that seemed difficult to imagine. If nuclear deterrence was a necessity, then it seemed more desirable for the "button" to be located in Washington rather than in Bonn or, worse yet, in Berlin.

The Kennedy administration took advantage of this attitude as it affected a turnaround in nuclear policy and thus in transatlantic security policy as a whole.[41] President Eisenhower had been entirely ready to cooperate closely and possibly even as a partner on nuclear policy with European allies (including the Federal Republic). But Kennedy insisted on U.S. leadership. Eisenhower's offer of nuclear participation, co-determination, and co-ownership, perhaps in an MLF under the command of the European NATO partners, ran completely contrary to the efforts of the Kennedy administration to concentrate the nuclear command structure of the alliance and the American military more fully under the control of the president and his closest advisers.

Sheltered in the political lee of Kennedy's policies, Great Britain saw a chance to emphasize its nuclear partnership with the United States, which it had enjoyed since World War II, thus blocking France from an equal leadership position in NATO and keeping the Federal Republic completely out of this nuclear-policy group.[42] This was the actual message of the British-American agreement in Nassau in December 1962, to which the Federal Republic and France responded with their defiant Élysée Treaty of January 1963. Great Britain received intercontinental Polaris missiles with nuclear capability from Washington, while the United States continued its policy of hostility toward French nuclear-arms development and forced the Federal Republic to place its signature on the American-British-Soviet test ban treaty along with the GDR government.

In this situation, the only possibility remaining for Bonn appeared to be a close alliance with France. However, this last grand gesture of the Adenauer government presented a number of serious problems. Would the United States seize the opportunity to reduce its military

---

[40] See the chapter by Diethelm Prowe, vol. 1, Politics.

[41] See the chapter by Kori N. Schake in this section.

[42] John Baylis, *Ambiguity and Deterrence: British Nuclear Strategy, 1945–1964* (Oxford, 1995), and Susanna Schrafstetter, *Die dritte Atommacht: britische Nichtverbreitungspolitik im Dienst von Statussicherung und Deutschlandpolitik 1952–1968* (Munich, 1999).

commitment in Central Europe? Would France be able or willing to spread its incipient nuclear capacity as a protective shield over the Federal Republic? Would Paris really be more willing than Washington to offer the Germans a partnership in questions of nuclear deterrence?

There was no prospect that any of these questions would be answered affirmatively. Thus, the treaty between Germany and France did not at first lead to closer ties between the two states. Instead, it produced, on the one hand, a recognition of the indispensable German-American security alliance and, on the other, a cautious opening toward the East. The former became apparent in the preamble to the German ratifying law for the Élysée Treaty, which referred to the common defense in the context of the North Atlantic alliance and the integration of the military forces of the nations united in this alliance.[43] This formula was tantamount to a fundamental rejection of French policy on NATO. The tenuous beginnings that became the new Ostpolitik of the social democratic-liberal coalition in 1969 followed the example of the United States, which sought, initially through arms-control agreements and later on account of the situation in Vietnam, a stability-oriented relationship with Moscow.[44] At the same time, the departure of France from the NATO military command brought an end to the continual NATO crises. The year 1967 saw not only a new NATO strategy (flexible response) and formation of a NATO committee for nuclear consultation (the Nuclear Planning Group) that permitted German participation without German co-ownership. It was also the year that the Harmel Report affirmed the compatibility of détente and nuclear deterrence, so that both the arms-control negotiations of the United States begun in 1967 and the new German Ostpolitik – underway even before the arrival of

the social democratic-liberal coalition – could be declared compatible with NATO.[45]

This finally broke the old linkage between the German question and European security. Bonn had to admit that security without a solution to the German question was clearly possible and, indeed, desirable to many Europeans. While arms races continued at breakneck speed, only a vague hope remained that there could be what Egon Bahr called "*Wandel durch Annäherung*" (change through rapprochement) in East Germany. This concept presupposed an inner democratization in the Soviet Union and a fundamental change in foreign and military policy, developments that did not appear on the horizon for another two decades. Many in the West quite happily suppressed thoughts about the internal situation in the Soviet Union, its politics, and its armaments.

This situation led to the rise of the "strategy intellectuals." They emerged in the United States in the 1950s and in the Federal Republic much later and in much smaller numbers. The German public surrendered (quite understandably) to a yearning for peace that clearly privileged an orderly coexistence with the East, particularly the GDR, over the old policy of intimidation and the old legal positions on the German question. The American public became more and more agitated over the Vietnam War and hardly took an interest in European issues, not to mention German ones. Thus, an era in German-American security relationships came to an end on both sides of the Atlantic in 1967–8.

SUGGESTIONS FOR FURTHER READING

Still indispensable for a comprehensive look into this subject are the standard work by Helga Haftendorn, *Sicherheit und Entspannung. Zur Aussenpolitik der Bundesrepublik Deutschland 1955–1982*,

---

[43] See U.S. Department of State, *Documents on Germany, 1944–1985* (Washington, D.C., 1989), 847.

[44] See the chapter by Werner Link, vol. 2, Politics.

[45] Helga Haftendorn, *Sicherheit und Entspannung: Zur Außenpolitik der Bundesrepublik Deutschland 1955–1982*, 2d ed. (Baden-Baden, 1986); Helga Haftendorn, *NATO and the Nuclear Revolution: A Crisis of Credibility, 1966–1967* (Oxford, 1996).

2d ed. (Baden-Baden, 1986) and the volumes of the yearbook established by Wilhelm Cornides, *Die Internationale Politik* (later *Jahrbuch Internationale Politik*), which have been published since 1955 and contain important ongoing analysis of German-America security policy. A synopsis appears in Wolfram Hanrieder, *Germany, America, Europe: Forty Years of German Foreign Policy* (New Haven, Conn., 1989) and in the related chapters of the five-volume *Geschichte der Bundesrepublik Deutschland* (Stuttgart, 1983–7), edited by Karl Dietrich Bracher. The two-volume edition *Sicherheitspolitik der Bundesrepublik Deutschland 1945–1977* (Cologne, 1978–9), edited by Klaus von Schubert, offers a useful collection of primary documents.

Wolfgang Krieger's *General Lucius D. Clay und die amerikanische Deutschlandpolitik* (Stuttgart, 1987) addresses security relationships during the occupation. The prehistory and early history of German rearmament are detailed in the four-volume *Anfänge westdeutscher Sicherheitspolitik 1945–1956* (Munich, 1982–97), published by the Militärgeschichtliche Forschungsamt. David C. Large's *Germans to the Front: West German Rearmament in the Adenauer Era* (Chapel Hill, N.C., 1996) offers a more readable account. The two-volume biography *Adenauer* (Stuttgart, 1986–91) by Hans-Peter Schwarz is the definitive work on Adenauer's foreign and security policies. Among the earlier literature, Hans-Gert Pöttering's *Adenauers Sicherheitspolitik 1955–1963: Ein Beitrag zum deutsch-amerikanischen Verhältnis*, 2d ed. (Düsseldorf, 1976) remains useful.

No history of the Bundeswehr and the armament policies of the Federal Republic has been published to date. The government publication *Verteidigung im Bündnis: Planung, Aufbau und Bewährung der Bundeswehr 1950–1972* (Munich, 1975), published by the Militärgeschichtliches Forschungsamt, may serve as an introduction to the subject. Alternative interpretations of German defense policy were developed by Bogislav von Bonin, whose papers have been edited by Heinz Brill: *Opposition gegen Adenauers Sicherheitspolitik: Eine Dokumentation* (Hamburg, 1976). Lothar Wilker's *Die Sicherheitspolitik der SPD, 1956–1966: Zwischen Wiedervereinigungs-* *und Bündnisorientierung* (Bonn, 1977) investigates the incremental convergence of the SPD with Adenauer's NATO policy. Thomas Enders, *Die SPD und die äussre Sicherheit 1966–1982* (Melle, 1987), addresses subsequent developments in defense policy when the party was in power. For the liberal party, see Dietrich Wagner, *FDP und Wiederbewaffnung: Die wehrpolitische Orientierung der Liberalen in der Bundesrepublik Deutschland 1949–1955* (Boppard am Rhein, 1978).

No standard work exists on the security policy of the United States toward Europe or Germany. Readers may gain some sense of the issues from Kevin R. Byrne, ed., *A Handbook of American Military History: From the Revolutionary War to the Present* (Boulder, Colo., 1996); Warren W. Hassler, *With Shield and Sword: American Military Affairs, Colonial Times to the Present* (Ames, Iowa, 1982); Allan R. Millett and Peter Maslowski, *For the Common Defense: A Military History of the United States of America*, rev. ed. (New York, 1994); Hans-Jürgen Schraut, *Vom Besatzer zum Beschützer: Der Wandel der Militärstrategie der USA und die Präsenz amerikanischer Streitkräfte in Deutschland 1945–1953* (Neuried, 1994); John L. Gaddis, *Strategies of Containment* (New York, 1982); McGeorge Bundy, *Danger and Survival: Choices about the Bomb in the First Fifty Years* (New York, 1988); Saki Dockrill, ed., *Controversy and Compromise: Alliance Politics Between Great Britain, the Federal Republic of Germany, and the United States of America, 1945–1967* (Bodenheim, 1998); Lawrence Freedman, *Kennedy's Wars: Berlin, Cuba, Laos, and Vietnam* (New York, 2000). Marc Trachtenberg's *A Constructed Peace: The Making of the European Settlement, 1945–1963* (Princeton, N.J., 1999) is particularly important for its picture of the Eisenhower and Kennedy administrations.

The classic study of nuclear issues, still largely valid, is Catherine MacArdle Kelleher, *Germany and the Politics of Nuclear Weapons* (New York, 1975). Of continuing importance is also Dieter Mahnke, *Nukleare Mitwirkung: Die Bundesrepublik Deutschland in der Atlantischen Allianz 1954–1970* (Berlin, 1972). Detlef Bald, *Die Atombewaffnung der Bundeswehr. Militär, Öffentlichkeit und Politik in der Ära Adenauer* (Bremen, 1994)

traces public reactions. A useful English treatment is Marc Cioc, *Pax Atomica: The Nuclear Defense Debate in West Germany During the Adenauer
Era* (New York, 1988). The following studies
produced in the context of the Nuclear History Program are based on access to extensive
sources: Johannes Steinhoff and Reiner Pommerin, *Strategiewechsel: Bundesrepublik und Nuk-*

learstrategie in der Ära Adenauer-Kennedy (Baden-
Baden, 1992); Christoph Hoppe, *Zwischen Teil-
habe und Mitsprache: Die Nuklearfrage in der
Allianzpolitik Deutschlands 1959–1966* (Baden-
Baden, 1993); Axel Gablik, *Strategische Planun-
gen in der Bundesrepublik 1955–1967. Politische
Kontrolle oder militärische Notwendigkeit?* (Baden-
Baden, 1996).

CHAPTER ONE

Overcast, Paperclip, Osoaviakhim
Looting and the Transfer of German Military Technology

Michael J. Neufeld

World War II was a war of science and technology. By 1944 that truth was recognized by almost everyone, and certainly by leading officers in the U.S. armed forces. The spectacular mid-1944 debut of Germany's "vengeance weapons" – the jet-powered V-1 cruise missile and the rocket-powered V-2 ballistic missile – drove home that point even more firmly. Although ultimately ineffective, those weapons also raised the specter of a future "push-button" war fought over enormous distances – a specter even more real to the handful of decision makers who knew of the Manhattan Project to build an atomic bomb.

On August 21, 1944, the Anglo-American Combined Chiefs of Staff created the Combined Intelligence Objectives Subcommittee (CIOS), a joint operation, to coordinate the seizure of German weapons and technology by special "T-Forces" accompanying the ground units then breaking out from Normandy. However, the first technical intelligence team to enter Paris a few days later had already been formed in 1943. Major General Leslie Groves, head of the Manhattan Project, had created the Operation Alsos to seek out evidence of a German atomic bomb. Other American teams and organizations soon arose in imitation of Alsos and CIOS, or in response to the vision of farsighted military leaders like General Henry H. "Hap" Arnold, commander of the U.S. Army Air Forces (USAAF), who formed a "Scientific Advisory Group" in fall 1944 to investigate

the advanced technologies needed to maintain American air superiority in the postwar era.[1]

Out of these organizations, and others on the British, Soviet, and French sides, emerged one of the most remarkable instances of plunder in world history – one with profound effects on the Cold War and German-American relations. Although plunder has been a feature of war since time immemorial, no earlier war, including World War I, had ended with the massive seizure of the defeated power's science and technology – not just weapons, but laboratories, patents, people, equipment, even whole factories and organizations.[2]

The centrality of science and engineering to the war was one major factor behind these massive operations. Equally important were the utter totality of Germany's defeat and the essential technological equality among the warring sides in Europe. Although the seizure of German technology by the Allies – popularly symbolized by the American "Project Paperclip" that emerged in 1945–6 – led to postwar myths of German technical superiority, in fact the Third Reich only led in some areas, such as missiles,

[1] John Gimbel, *Science, Technology, and Reparations* (Stanford, Calif., 1990), 3–10; Samuel Goudsmit, *Alsos* (New York, 1947); Michael H. Gorn, *The Universal Man* (Washington, D.C., 1992), 96–110.

[2] Jörg Fisch, "Reparations and Intellectual Property," in Matthias Judt and Burghard Ciesla, eds., *Technology Transfer Out of Germany After 1945* (Amsterdam, 1996).

jet aircraft, submarines, and chemical weapons.[3] Yet, even in areas where the Allies (particularly the Western Allies) were ahead, such as radar, conventional aircraft, and atomic weapons, there was almost always something to be learned from Nazi Germany's successes and failures. By contrast, Japan's technology was closely evaluated after its defeat but aside from a few areas like biological warfare, little effort was made to export Japanese scientific and technical knowledge and resources.

The liberation of occupied territories in Western Europe in 1944 produced some successes for technical intelligence. Most notably, there was fairly conclusive proof that the German nuclear, weapons project had not gotten very far. But only the final collapse of the Reich in April–May 1945 produced the actual race to seize and export German assets and weapons. Competition was embedded in the process from the outset. One of the earliest harbingers of the Cold War was the mutual suspicion and lack of cooperation between Soviet and Anglo-American intelligence forces in the seizure of key technical facilities and personnel in spring 1945. But even among the Western Allies there was rivalry and confusion. The joint structures of the Anglo-American alliance created some cooperation between the British and United States forces, but both thought the Free French were little better than the Soviets. British and American groups nevertheless sometimes fought bureaucratic battles with one another, which were compounded by a profusion of competing CIOS teams, leading some to nickname the organization "Chaos." Even inside the American forces, differing service interests were a factor. Army Ordnance formed "Special Mission V-2," the Navy the "Naval Technical Mission in Europe," and the USAAF "Operation Lusty."

The forces of competition were no more clearly displayed than in the race to seize the fruits of the German rocket program. At the end of March, the Western Allies broke through the Rhine barrier. The U.S. Army soon found itself deep within Saxony and Thuringia, the future Soviet zone of occupation. On April 11, American units overran the underground Mittelwerk complex near Nordhausen, which used concentration-camp labor from the Mittelbau-Dora camp to produce operational V-2s, V-1s, and other weapons. Many engineers evacuated from the German Army rocket center in Peenemünde were still in the region. "Special Mission V-2" under Colonel Holger Toftoy immediately began the seizure of 100 V-2s or parts for same, plus relevant personnel and equipment, before the Soviets could move into their zone. Intelligence officers also ferreted out the location of the central cache of Peenemünde documents and whisked fourteen tons of paper out of a mine in the future British zone, allegedly just as the British Army was setting up checkpoints. Earlier in May, the core leadership from Peenemünde, headed by Dr. Wernher von Braun and General Walter Dornberger, had surrendered to American units in the Alps.[4]

The Peenemünde group quickly became an important factor in American postwar policy, as Toftoy and Army Ordnance wanted to bring a large number of them to the United States in order to acquire their knowledge of rocketry. Toftoy's initiative and that of others in the Navy and Air Forces led to the formal creation of "Project Overcast" by the U.S. Joint Chiefs of Staff in July 1945. This project's mandate was to bring 350 "chosen, rare minds" from Germany to help the war effort against Japan. The sudden end of that war the next month did not stop the program, however, as the Pacific war had been in part a convenient excuse to bring German scientists and engineers to America or at least deny them to the Soviets and other powers. Toftoy was allotted 100 slots for the Peenemünde group, although ultimately more than 120 came. Friction arose with the

[3] One of the most influential journalistic accounts, Tom Bower's *The Paperclip Conspiracy: The Battle for the Spoils and Secrets of Nazi Germany* (London, 1987), unfortunately upholds the myth of German superiority.

[4] James McGovern, *Crossbow and Overcast* (New York, 1964); Michael J. Neufeld, *The Rocket and the Reich* (New York, 1995).

British over some of the rocket experts, but ultimately the disagreements were minor. London had made a fundamental decision that it could not afford a major ballistic-missile program and was thus uninterested in competing with the United States.[5]

With the Soviet Union, the situation was far different. Soviet forces had captured Peenemünde in May, but found it stripped by the Germans, and occupied the Mittelwerk on July 5, only to find it partly stripped by the Americans, who had also taken with them hundreds of other German scientists and engineers from key laboratories and industries in Saxony and Thuringia – not always voluntarily.[6] There were, nonetheless, large quantities of production equipment and missile parts in the Mittelwerk and many second-rank rocket engineers and technicians still in the area. Frustrated at their inability to get Wernher von Braun, the Soviets still managed to lure Helmut Gröttrup, the deputy chief of guidance in Peenemünde, over to their side to lead a German rocket group. (The French also began to hire German engineers away from the American zone, many of whom laid the foundation for the French missiles and space program.) The Soviets used equipment from the Mittelwerk to restart limited rocket production. A year later, on October 22, 1946, Soviet troops suddenly rounded up and forcibly deported to the USSR the whole rocket organization in Thuringia, along with thousands of other "specialists" and their families from the Soviet zone. This coordinated action, code-named "Osoaviakhim," exacerbated the tensions already building between East and West over German occupation policy and many other issues.[7]

Although the V-2 program ironically proved to be a military boondoggle that damaged the German war effort, it clearly demonstrated the missile's feasibility and potential, especially if combined with the atomic bomb that suddenly arrived on the world scene with the Hiroshima attack of August 6, 1945. Thus, the centrality of missile technology to postwar Allied rivalry over German technical resources is not surprising. Yet, the prominence of the large von Braun group in Overcast and its successor, "Project Paperclip," has misled many. That group represented only a minority of those brought to the United States, and the same was true of the rocket engineers among the "specialists" sent to the USSR.

In both countries and probably in Britain and France too, aviation experts predominated. The USAAF and its successor, the U.S. Air Force (USAF) formed in 1947, took more than 700 German scientists and engineers under Overcast/Paperclip by 1952, somewhat more than the Army and more than twice as many as the Navy. Of the at least 3,500 "specialists" sent to the Soviet Union (many more were technicians and skilled workers than in the West), 35 percent are estimated to have come from aviation, about twice as many as from rocketry.[8]

For the United States, the Luftwaffe's massive investment in transonic and supersonic aerodynamic research was particularly attractive. Allied technical officers and experts were amazed at the lavish facilities and advanced wind tunnels captured by the Allies; in the British zone, it was the huge Luftwaffe research complex at Braunschweig-Völkenrode that stunned British

---

[5] Clarence Lasby, *Project Paperclip* (New York, 1971), 66–143; John Gimbel, "Project Paperclip," *Diplomatic History* 14 (1990): 343–65; Stephen Robert Twigge, *The Early Development of Guided Weapons in the United Kingdom, 1940–1960* (Chur, 1993), 185–7.

[6] John Gimbel, "U.S. Policy and German Scientists: The Early Cold War," *Political Science Quarterly* 101 (1986): 433–51.

[7] Ulrich Albert, Andreas Heinemann-Grüder, and Arend Wellmann, *Die Spezialisten* (Berlin, 1992);

Norman M. Naimark, *The Russians in Germany: A History of the Soviet Zone of Occupation, 1945–1949* (Cambridge, Mass., 1995), chap. 4; Steven J. Zaloga, *Target America* (Novato, Calif., 1993).

[8] See Burghard Ciesla, "German High Velocity Aerodynamics and Their Significance for the U.S. Air Force 1945–1952," in Matthias Judt and Burghard Ciesla, eds., *Technology Transfer Out of Germany After 1945* (Amsterdam, 1996), 93–106; Albert, Heinemann-Grüder, and Wellmann, *Die Spezialisten*, 176–80. Systematic studies of French and British postwar exploitation of German science and technology are much needed.

and American visitors; in the Bavarian Alps, it was the evacuated Peenemünde wind tunnels at Kochel. The U.S. Navy eventually sent the Kochel tunnels to the new Naval Ordnance Laboratory outside Washington, D.C., along with nine leading members of the institute. The USAF got the institute director, Dr. Rudolph Hermann, plus wind tunnels and many more experts from Braunschweig and other places. Once again, as in the case of the V-2, it was the victors who benefited from Germany's extravagant misdirection of its research resources.[9]

Certain results from German aerodynamic research proved to be of immediate value. The theory first formulated by Dr. Adolf Busemann in Germany, that swept rather than straight wings would improve lift and drag around and above the speed of sound, had been independently discovered in America, but German wind-tunnel data provided the needed confirmation. This data led to the redesign of important, early USAF jets such as the F-86 fighter and the B-47 nuclear bomber. But the USAF, the Navy, and the aircraft firms also benefited from a panoply of other German developments in areas such as turbojet engines, aircraft structures, ejection seats, and exotic designs. In many cases, notably in jet engines, the German lead over Britain and the United States was small but still of interest. (The Soviets, on the other hand, had no significant jet programs and thus gained proportionately more from the seizure of aircraft industries and experts in their zone.) Another area where the United States made significant gain from German research was in aerospace medicine – the study of special stresses on the human body such as high altitude and speed, and the development of equipment to ensure the survival of pilots and their ability to function effectively.

On the Navy side, there were further important gains beyond the application of aeronautics to sea power. German submarine technology,

much of it undeployed at the end of the war, opened new vistas on undersea performance. In the waning days of the war, a joint British-American team seized the Kiel firm of legendary inventor Professor Hellmuth Walter. The team members already knew about his experimental use of hydrogen peroxide as a propellant for high-speed submarines, as well as the widespread application of the substance to German rocket aircraft and missiles. They found further evidence of his innovations, including a revolutionary rounded hull shape already tested in 1939 and other means of increasing underwater speed and endurance, such as greatly enlarged battery packs. Some of these innovations had been incorporated into the conventional diesel-electric Type XXI U-boats just deployed at the end of the war. Walter and his associates were extensively debriefed and later brought to Britain and the United States.[10]

Walter's innovations raised the possibility that the submarine could remain submerged for long periods of time and have the speed to outrun surface sub-hunting ships. As relations with the USSR deteriorated, this possibility became both alluring and frightening for American naval officers: If the Soviets could manufacture large numbers of Type XXI U-boats, the antisubmarine warfare technology of the Western Allies would be worthless. The Navy brought German experts to America under Paperclip, started at least three hydrogen-peroxide projects, launched experimental programs in submarine design, investigated German advances in sonar, and pursued the already existing American lead in oceanography as applied to submarine concealment and detection. Ultimately, it would be nuclear power, developed entirely at home, that would make virtually unlimited underwater performance possible, but German advances played a crucial role in initiating a revolution in submarine design. Certain experiments with launching rockets from U-boats also influenced the emergence of the ballistic-missile submarine in the 1950s.[11]

[9] Ciesla, "German High Velocity Aerodynamics"; Peter Wegener, *The Peenemünde Wind Tunnels* (New Haven, Conn., 1996), 103–34; Helmuth Trischler, *Luft- und Raumfahrtforschung in Deutschland 1900–1970* (Frankfurt am Main, 1992).

[10] Gary E. Weir, *Forged in War* (Washington, D.C., 1993), 68–79.

[11] Ibid., 115–47, 228–73.

The arrival of so many scientists and engineers in America from an often hated enemy inevitably created controversy. From the outset, the American military chose to carry out Overcast and Paperclip in secret but, by late 1946, the presence of the Wernher von Braun group in Texas and many others elsewhere was so well known that carefully controlled public relations efforts were necessary. This sparked a brief round of protest in early 1947 from left-wing scientists and Jewish groups, but the Cold War soon made it difficult to question the presence of "Nazi scientists" in the United States. Opponents were further hampered by the military's deliberate cover-up of the questionable records of a number of Paperclip Germans, such as von Braun's associate Arthur Rudolph, who had been production manager in the underground slave-labor plant, and Dr. Hubertus Strughold, a leader in aerospace medicine who had knowledge of if not direct involvement in gruesome experiments on concentration-camp prisoners at Dachau. Only in the 1980s did many of Paperclip's scandals come to light.[12]

Even inside the U.S. government there was conflict over the Germans and their records. From the beginning of Overcast in mid-1945, State Department officials created roadblocks, if only because the Germans were brought overseas under military custody, circumventing regular immigration procedures. Moreover, Overcast and Paperclip implicitly contradicted State Department programs to prevent the exodus of Nazis abroad to restart weapons production in third countries, as after World War I. But in 1946–7, the dubious records of some of those imported under Paperclip also became an issue between military and State Department officials, leading to the rewriting of the security files of von Braun and others to evade the restrictions against importing "ardent Nazis." Some journalists have detected a conscious

mid-level conspiracy in the Pentagon to violate President Harry Truman's policy as laid down in the March 4, 1946, directive creating Project Paperclip. Yet, these evasions of the law appear to have been approved by the Cabinet and probably Truman himself. Pragmatism ruled, not principle; Paperclip was designed first to benefit American military and industrial power, second to deny German technology to other countries – at first, almost everyone; later, the USSR in particular.[13]

Inevitably, this pragmatic and at times cynical policy also conflicted with occupation policy in Germany. In July 1945, CIOS disappeared along with the joint military command; the American deputy military governor, General Lucius Clay, created the Field Information Agency, Technical (FIAT) on July 14 to coordinate the exploitation of German technology and industry in the American zone. FIAT oversaw a massive program of plunder, not just of military technology and laboratories but also of industry. American teams, many of them consisting of corporate executives in uniform, went through German industry seizing machines, documents, and patents. Some of this material, such as that relating to synthetic rubber and gasoline, had direct relevance to military technology, but the long-term value of this program, particularly its civilian side, is unclear, and it certainly did not cripple German industry as some feared.

One of the side effects of this wholesale technology transfer was the undermining of denazification policy. Almost all of the engineers and scientists sent to America under Overcast and Paperclip were taken without having gone through denazification trials, and many other examples of the evasion of these laws became known under FIAT. Reinforced by the imminent Cold War, the exploitation of German science and industry generated further cynicism in Germany about denazification. At the same time, the value of German technology to the Allies contributed, at least in a small way, to the revival of German national pride and to respect

[12] Linda Hunt, "U.S. Coverup of Nazi Scientists," *Bulletin of the Atomic Scientists* (Apr. 1985): 16–24; and Linda Hunt, *Secret Agenda: The United States Government, Nazi Scientists, and Project Paperclip, 1945 to 1990* (New York, 1991); Bower, *Paperclip Conspiracy*; Christopher Simpson, *Blowback* (New York, 1988).

[13] John Gimbel, "German Scientists, United States Denazification Policy, and the 'Paperclip Conspiracy,'" *International History Review* 12 (1990): 441–65.

for Germany in the West. In view of the equally cynical but much more harshly applied policies of plunder, dismantling, and exploitation by the Soviet occupation forces in the East, the policies of the United States, Britain, and France ultimately did not look so bad to the Germans. Even more important, these policies ironically helped integrate West German industry with the West because using German patents and processes often meant reestablishing contacts to get the necessary "know-how."[14]

FIAT was abolished in July 1947, in large part because its industrial program apparently conflicted with the policy of reviving German industry. But Project Paperclip continued unabated into the early 1950s and, under various cover names, for twenty years thereafter. Even so, it is clear that the great bulk of the transfer of military science and technology from Germany to the United States took place between 1945 and 1950. Once the Bundeswehr was formed and armed in the late 1950s, some technology was reexported to Germany – or at least the flow of military technology equalized and then reversed. A noteworthy example is the license production of the Lockheed F-104 Starfighter by the German aircraft industry beginning around 1961, which helped build and modernize that industry. In small part, this represented the reexport of German high-speed aerodynamic and jet-engine research to its country of origin.

With the transition to the Cold War in 1947–8, the United States transferred another form of military knowledge as well: the strategic, tactical, and practical experience of German officers, particularly in waging war with the USSR. For the U.S. Army, this transfer evolved from the massive interrogation program of the Historical Division of the Army in Europe. Thousands of German officers and general officers in prisoner-of-war camps were interviewed or paid to write studies for official histories of U.S.

Army campaigns. In 1947, as tensions rose in Germany, some former officers were asked to write about the Eastern Front and German experiences fighting the Soviets. After 1948, most were released and were paid to write at home; by the mid-1950s, some two thousand reports and interrogations had been done. A few studies, such as those on cold-weather fighting or Soviet tactics, were issued as pamphlets to American troops. Seeing the success of this program, the USAF launched a more limited effort at Karlsruhe in 1952, leading to about twenty monographs by former Luftwaffe officers, mostly on the air war in the East. This material, like some of that written for the Army, helped educate American forces regarding Soviet tactics and doctrine and brought German and American officers closer together. The cost was the all-too-ready acceptance of the apologia of former Wehrmacht officers for their role in the genocidal, racist campaign in the East and their corresponding underestimation of their former enemy.[15]

All in all, the transfer of military technology and knowledge after 1945 had profound effects on German-American relations. Despite its origins in the outright plunder of the defeated Reich, under the pressure of Cold War conditions this transfer aided the cooperation between the United States and the later Federal Republic. German scientists and engineers were incorporated into the American defense establishment and industries, while German and American officers cultivated closer relations. Those German industries most damaged by American and Allied exploitation, the aircraft and armament industries, were also those the Germans had the least desire to revive in the 1940s and 1950s. In other cases, the seizure of German patents and processes helped revive industrial contacts over the long run. The value of German technology

[14] See Raymond G. Stokes, "Assessing the Damages: Forced Technology Transfer and the German Chemical Industry," in Judt and Ciesla, eds., *Technology Transfer*, 81–91.

[15] United States Army Headquarters, Europe, Historical Division, *Guide to Foreign Military Studies* (Karlsruhe, 1954); Telford Taylor, "Introduction to the Series," in Richard Suchenwirth, ed., *Historical Turning Points in the German Air Force War Effort* (1959; reprint, New York, 1968).

to the Allies also contributed to national pride and respect for Germany, in part by fostering myths of German technological superiority.

The impact on this transfer on the Cold War was equally profound. The seizure of German science and technology helped speed the Cold War's coming by fueling the mutual suspicion and incipient arms race between East and West. Most notably, the German rocket program and its exploitation by both sides accelerated the appearance of the nuclear-armed ballistic missile by as much as a decade, with destabilizing effects on the arms race. Both sides gained much from German aeronautics and submarine technology as well, and both acquired the nerve gases Tabun and Sarin, which had been secretly invented in Germany but fortunately never used. In absolute terms, the United States gained most from the transfer of German technology and knowledge; it acquired the best people and the best selection of patents, equipment, and weapons. Yet – in another irony – in relative terms, Stalin's Soviet Union gained more from the plunder of the Third Reich because it was behind the West in aviation, nuclear, naval, and radar technology and because it moved more energetically to build a rocket program after the war. The USSR became a global military threat to the Western alliance sooner because of what it gained from the Germans. Thus, the transfer of German military knowledge and technology contributed much to the security of America and the West after the war – but, unavoidably perhaps, much to their insecurity as well.

CHAPTER TWO

The Dilemmas of Dual Containment

Germany as a Security Problem, 1945–1950

Steven L. Rearden

When Allied armies overran Hitler's Third Reich in 1945, it appeared unlikely that Germany would ever again play a major role in European security. Yet, within a few years, the onset of the Cold War, by producing sharp friction and deepening divisions between East and West, had changed this outlook. The result by 1950 was a wholly different European security system than anyone had envisioned just five years earlier. All the more remarkable was the emergence of two competing German states: a communist-dominated satellite of the Soviet Union in the East and a liberal democracy in the West aligned with France, Britain, and the United States. Although both seemed to experience a steady recovery of power and influence, the government in the West, the Federal Republic, by virtue of its population and resources, appeared destined to have the most impact on European security.

That a German state should do so represented a wholesale reversal of Allied expectations as World War II drew to a close. Among the members of the victorious Allied coalition, it was practically an article of faith that postwar Germany should undergo sweeping reforms and be subjected to radical reductions in its power and territory. A leading advocate of this approach was U.S. Treasury Secretary Henry Morgenthau Jr., whose name became almost synonymous with imposing a draconian peace settlement through deindustrialization. A close friend of President Franklin D. Roosevelt's, Morgenthau interjected himself personally in the

planning process for postwar Germany and, at the second Quebec Conference (September 1944), he obtained an agreement in principle from Roosevelt and British Prime Minister Winston S. Churchill to support a plan for turning Germany into "a country primarily agricultural and pastoral in its character."[1] Despite a good deal of skepticism among American and British technical advisers, the so-called Morgenthau Plan became one of the basic tenets of Joint Chiefs of Staff directive 1067, the U.S. occupation directive in the immediate postwar period.[2]

Meeting at Yalta in February 1945 and again at Potsdam that summer, the Western Allies and the Soviet Union tried to go beyond generalities to fashion a new security regime that would permanently curb German power and influence. As agreed at the Yalta Conference, Germany would be stripped of its sovereignty, have its borders redrawn, and be subjected to an indefinite period of political, economic, and social reform to eliminate all vestiges of National Socialism

---

[1] Memorandum Initialed by President Roosevelt and Prime Minister Churchill, Sept. 15, 1944, in U.S. Department of State, Foreign Relations of the United States (hereafter FRUS), The Conference at Quebec, 1944, 467.

[2] See Steven L. Rearden, "American Policy Toward Germany, 1944–1946," (Ph.D. diss., Harvard Unversity, 1975); Paul Y. Hammond, "Directives for the Occupation of Germany: The Washington Controversy," in Harold Stein, ed., American Civil-Military Decisions: A Book of Case Studies (Birmingham, Ala., 1963), 311–464.

and militarism. To guarantee that the reforms took place, military forces drawn from Britain, the United States, the Soviet Union, and, later, France would administer the country from separate occupation zones and coordinate their efforts through an Allied Control Council. However, by the time the Allied leaders reconvened at Potsdam, it was evident that emerging schisms within their ranks would make it exceedingly difficult for them to adhere to a unified policy on Germany. A major source of contention was the Soviet Union's demand for substantial reparations; the Western Powers were reluctant to agree for fear of being saddled with heavy costs for subsidizing the German economy. The upshot was a complicated and conditional reparations agreement that proved ultimately unworkable and fatally divisive to quadripartite control.

Despite emerging differences among the wartime Allies, all still saw it in their common interest to impose restraints that would eliminate once and for all the threat of German aggression. As World War II ended, Soviet premier Joseph Stalin predicted that, without permanent checks on its power, Germany would undergo a full revival in fifteen to twenty years.[3] Similar worries haunted the French as well. To help assuage their fears, U.S. Secretary of State James F. Byrnes offered a twenty-five-year disarmament treaty in summer 1946. The Soviets, all but ignoring the offer, implied that it was insufficient and that there was nothing to back it up but empty promises. Completing the delivery of reparations, they insisted, should come first. For the British and French, a main concern was that the United States would again retreat into isolation, withdraw its forces, and leave Europe facing either a resurgent Germany or Soviet hegemony. Looking to themselves for protection, Britain and France in March 1947 signed the Treaty of Dunkirk, a mutual security agreement aimed ostensibly at Germany but with anti-Soviet overtones.[4]

Meanwhile, defense planning in the West took less and less note of Germany as a possible threat to future peace and stability. With Germany disarmed and prostrate and under Four-Power military control, an early repetition of the recent conflict seemed inconceivable to Western strategic planners. As a result, defense planning in Britain and the United States immediately after the war rarely mentioned Germany; instead, it focused on such matters as demobilization of wartime forces, the allocation of shrinking postwar resources, and the assignment of service roles and missions. The potential long-term threat causing the most worry in the West was not a renascent Germany but an expansionist Soviet Union. It was with this threat in mind that American and British defense planners looked to the future.

As the Cold War intensified, it led gradually to a rethinking of Germany's role in Western strategy and postwar European security. Two key developments were the abandonment by the Western Powers of any further pretense at quadripartite control following the abortive Moscow foreign ministers conference of early 1947 and the announcement that June of the Marshall Plan to rehabilitate Europe. The inclusion of the American, British, and French zones of Germany under the Marshall Plan ended any further pretense of adherence to the Morgenthau Plan. Although it was by no means a foregone conclusion, Germany's participation had a certain logic that Western policymakers found irresistible. As the U.S. military governor in Germany, General Lucius D. Clay, described it, "42 million Germans in the British and American zones represent today the strongest outpost against Communist penetration that exists anywhere."[5] It did not take much imagination to see that if Germany could serve as a political

[3] Vladislav Zubok and Constantine Pleshakov, *Inside the Kremlin's Cold War* (Cambridge, Mass., 1996), 47.

[4] Anne Deighton, *The Impossible Peace: Britain, the Division of Germany and the Origins of the Cold War* (Oxford, 1990), 38–9; John Baylis, "Britain and the Dunkirk Treaty: The Origins of NATO," *Journal of Strategic Studies* 5 (1982): 236–47. On the evolution of U.S. policy, see Carolyn W. Eisenberg, *Drawing the Line: The American Decision to Divide Germany, 1944–1949* (New York, 1996).

[5] Clay to Draper, Nov. 3, 1947, in Jean Edward Smith, ed., *The Papers of General Lucius D. Clay: Germany, 1945–1949* (Bloomington, Ind., 1974), 1:478.

and economic bulwark against communism, it might eventually serve as a military one as well.

Nonetheless, the experiences of the recent war were still too fresh for the Western Allies to contemplate any significant departure from their policy of keeping Germany disarmed and demilitarized. Indeed, despite worsening relations with Russia, the Western Powers continued to practice what has been aptly described as a strategy of "dual containment" designed to keep both Germany and the Soviet Union from establishing hegemony in postwar Europe.[6] Although welcomed into the Marshall Plan to help further Europe's recovery, Western Germany's participation was on a clearly limited basis, with no promise or immediate expectation that it would result in anything other than improved economic conditions and the gradual restoration of more self-government.

Thus, while the Western Powers set about improving Germany's economic and political conditions, they also maintained close control of internal security functions. Routine police duties, though performed largely by Germans, fell under the strict supervision of the military authorities. The only weapons allowed the police, except in unusual circumstances, were side arms and carbines. Towns and cities with populations over 5,000 had to have independent police forces, towns with under 5,000 could contract for state protection. Anyone applying for a job with the police faced a thorough background check; those with even a hint of a Nazi past could expect to be summarily rejected.[7] Regulations adopted at the outset of the quadripartite occupation prohibiting such activities as fencing clubs (deemed "paramilitary organizations" by the Allies) and the ownership or manufacture of sporting guns remained in effect for the most part until 1950, when the Allied High Commission began to repeal them on a case-by-case basis. Although perhaps excessive and even unnecessary in some cases, these laws stayed on the books as long as they did because of continuing concern among American, British, and French authorities over whether Germany was as yet fully reformed.[8]

The Berlin Blockade of 1948–9 was a turning point in the West's attitude toward German security. This crisis led not only to closer ties between the Western Allies and the German people but also to the creation in April 1949 of the North Atlantic Treaty Organization (NATO). Obviously, with its economic potential, strategic location, and large population, West Germany was a logical candidate for NATO membership. But the subject remained off-limits for political reasons. Not only did the European members of NATO generally oppose adding Germany but there was scant popular support in the United States as well. Indeed, in presenting the North Atlantic Treaty to Congress, Secretary of State Dean Acheson went out of his way to reassure legislators that prohibitions on militarily significant industries would continue to be "complete and absolute" and that "discussion of including western Germany in the pact is not possible."[9]

A year later, the administration's official position remained the same, reinforced by adverse public reactions to West German chancellor Konrad Adenauer's interview of December 1949 with the *Cleveland Plain Dealer*, in which he discussed the role of the recently created Federal Republic of Germany in its own security affairs. Although he clearly was against rearmament, Adenauer emphasized the Allies' responsibility to protect the Federal Republic or, alternatively, to make arrangements for it to protect itself, possibly through a European army with a West German contingent.[10]

Adenauer's interview caused sharp public controversy, but it also brought discussion of German rearmament to the fore just as policy elites and military planners in the West were

---

[6] Thomas Alan Schwartz, *America's Germany: John J. McCloy and the Federal Republic of Germany* (Cambridge, Mass., 1991), 299.

[7] Lucius D. Clay, *Decision in Germany* (New York, 1950), 255–7.

[8] *Kessing's Contemporary Archives*, Apr. 22–9, 1950, 10663; June 24–30, 1950, 10796.

[9] U.S. Senate Committee on Foreign Relations, *Hearings: North Atlantic Treaty*, 81st Cong., 1st sess., 1949, 57, 61.

[10] Konrad Adenauer, *Memoirs, 1945–53* (Chicago, 1965), 267–8.

starting to have serious second thoughts about keeping the Federal Republic permanently disarmed and demilitarized. The discovery in September 1949 that the Soviet Union had acquired atomic capability, followed shortly by the consolidation of communist power in China, had provided the impetus in Washington for a long overdue reassessment of basic national security policy. The resulting report (NSC 68), tentatively approved by President Harry S. Truman in April 1950, saw major shifts in the balance of power and warned of dire consequences for the West if the United States and its allies did not reorder their priorities and devote significantly greater resources to strengthening their military posture. This effort should include a more open attitude toward the once-taboo subject of German rearmament. As the paper put it, the time had come to contemplate "separate arrangements" with the former Axis powers in order to "enlist the energies and resources" they could bring to bear as members of the free-world coalition.[11] The report did not specifically endorse German rearmament, but it was hard to draw any other conclusion.

By spring 1950, most American and British defense planners were convinced that a German military contribution to NATO would be a welcome addition, especially in view of recent Soviet efforts to organize an East German police force, a development suspected in the West as the prelude to the creation of an East German army under Soviet control. Elaborating on the themes in NSC 68, the U.S. Joint Chiefs of Staff in May 1950 endorsed "the appropriate and early rearming of Western Germany" as being of "fundamental importance to the defense of Western Europe against the USSR."[12] British defense planners shared this view and advised the Foreign Office "that Western Europe is indefensible without German manpower."[13] The plan then favored in London and Washington foresaw the creation of a small gendarmerie followed by the gradual formation of larger units. The consensus among American and British defense planners was that these units should not be independent national forces but rather subject to NATO or some other form of multilateral control.

Yet, even if rearming West Germany may have made sense militarily, it still faced enormous political, diplomatic, and emotional hurdles. Not the least of these was overcoming resistance from the French and other European NATO members who remembered all too vividly the atrocities of the German occupation in World War II. Moreover, British policymakers were concerned that if NATO went ahead with the rearmament of Germany, it would establish a strong competing claim on outside resources (i.e., American military aid) and eventually give the United States an excuse for withdrawing its forces from Europe. Weighing the pros and cons, the Foreign Office concluded that it would be "undesirable at present" and serve "no useful purpose" for Britain to come out in favor of German rearmament.[14]

As with so many other issues confronting Europe after World War II, the United States seemed to hold the deciding vote. Despite repeated urgings from the Joint Chiefs, Acheson elected not to press the issue of German rearmament with the NATO allies, a decision driven as much by personal uncertainties as by his worry that a debate over German rearmament could undermine NATO's still fragile unity. Rather than focusing on rebuilding Germany's military potential, Acheson welcomed political and economic initiatives, starting with West German membership in the Council of Europe and

[11] United States Objectives and Programs for National Security [NSC 68], Apr. 7, 1950, *FRUS, 1950*, 1:275.

[12] Memo, Chairman JCS to Sec. of Defense, May 2, 1950, National Archives, RG 330, CD 9-4-29; also quoted in Report to the National Security Council by the Secretary of Defense (Johnson) [NSC 71], June 8, 1950, *FRUS, 1950*, 4:686–7, 687.

[13] C.O.S. (50)108, Apr. 3, 1950, Military Aspects of United Kingdom Policy Towards Germany, doc. no. 38i, microfiche supplement to Roger Bullen, ed., *Documents on British Policy Overseas* (London, 1987), ser. 2, vol. 2.

[14] Brief for UK Delegation, Apr. 26, 1950, sub: Reestablishment of German Armed Forces, in Roger Bullen, ed., *Documents on British Policy Overseas* (London, 1987), ser. 2, vol. 2, 138–40.

participation in the European Coal and Steel Community (the Schuman Plan), that would improve trust and cooperation between the Federal Republic and its neighbors. In time, this might create a more favorable climate in which alliance members could consider the more sensitive issue of rearming Germany. Although he was aware of the strategic advantages of a German military contribution, Acheson felt that NATO was not yet mature enough to give objective consideration to a subject as potentially divisive as German rearmament. Nor was he convinced that German militarism ceased to pose a threat. Even the idea of a small West German gendarmerie left him uneasy. Handwritten notes by Truman suggest that he shared Acheson's reservations. In short, the philosophy of dual containment still prevailed.[15]

The most accurate and telling gauge of Allied sentiment toward Germany on the eve of the Korean War were the results of the May 1950 North Atlantic Council meeting in London. In private preliminary sessions, the foreign ministers of France, Britain, and the United States agreed the time was not yet ripe for a decision on German rearmament. In a public statement, they offered instead to work toward the Federal Republic's full integration into "the community of free peoples of Europe."[16] Noting West Germany's concern for its security, they also gave assurances that an attack on Allied occupation forces still in the Federal Republic would constitute an attack on NATO, a loose though not altogether unrealistic reading of the North Atlantic Treaty.[17] Relying heavily on American air power, NATO strategy included no commitment to respond to enemy aggression at the point of attack, and with only garrison troops

left in Germany it was hard to tell how much actual protection NATO's guarantee offered. Still, it was a first move toward incorporating the Federal Republic in the alliance structure.

Attitudes changed quickly with the outbreak of the Korean War in June 1950. Fearing that the conflict in Asia might spread to Europe, NATO leaders now felt compelled, despite their misgivings, to accept the Federal Republic's material help in bolstering the alliance. Owing chiefly to stubborn French resistance, it would still be several years before the allies could agree on a formula for including German troops in NATO. But as the deliberations prior to the Korean invasion make clear, a rearmed West Germany linked one way or another to the North Atlantic alliance was only a matter of time; the Korean War simply hastened events.

From 1945 to 1950, Germany seemed to come almost full circle. Defeated in World War II, it reemerged as a pivotal part of the European security system. Deteriorating relations between Russia and the West provided the catalyst for redefining Germany's role and made it difficult for both sides in the Cold War to exclude Germany from their strategic calculations. For the Western Powers, these developments initially led to a strategy of dual containment designed to prevent either Germany or the Soviet Union from dominating Europe. But as Cold War tensions mounted, it became increasingly difficult for Western policymakers to deny Germany the status of a potential military partner. Incorporating the Federal Republic into NATO seemed the logical solution and represented the most practical safeguard against possible misuse of the military power Germany would reacquire. But despite the apparent eagerness of military planners to see Germany rearmed, Western political leaders approached this step with great caution; they finally felt forced to take it by the outbreak of hostilities in Korea. German rearmament would follow in due course but at a rate that would continue to reflect lingering hostility and distrust of German intentions.

[15] See Schwartz, *America's Germany*, 121–2; Robert H. Ferrell, *Harry S. Truman: A Life* (Columbia, Mo., 1994), 357.

[16] Joint Declaration on Germany, May 14, 1950, U.S. Department of State, *Bulletin*, May 22, 1950, 787.

[17] Dean Acheson, *Present at the Creation* (New York, 1969), 395.

CHAPTER THREE

Partners in Defense

America, West Germany, and the Security of Europe, 1950–1968

David Clay Large

When Nazi Germany was defeated in 1945, the United States, like the other victorious Allied powers, embarked on a demilitarization campaign designed to keep the Germans totally disarmed for the foreseeable future. Yet, a few years later, in the wake of the collapse of the wartime alliance and Germany's division along the Iron Curtain, America began urging the new West German state to contribute to the military defense of Western Europe. During the next five years, the United States took the lead among the occupation powers in the protracted diplomatic efforts to rearm the Germans. When the Bundeswehr finally appeared in 1956, it was widely seen as a child of the Cold War coupling between Washington and Bonn. As the young West German army struggled in subsequent years to become a viable military organization and to make its mark in NATO, America continued to play a critical nurturing role. However, from the very beginning of the rearmament process to the emergence of the Bundeswehr, Bonn did not simply cower in the shadow of its powerful new ally, nor was the Bundeswehr a clone of the U.S. Army. America and the Federal Republic became firm partners in the arena of European security, but their military partnership, like all genuinely sound marriages, was never without its creative tensions.[1]

THE REARMAMENT CALCULUS

In 1948, American military planners concerned with defending the European continent against Soviet expansionism developed a strategic concept that called for the "holding of a line containing the Western Europe complex preferably no farther to the West than the Rhine."[2] Upon further consideration, however, this goal seemed unrealistic given the Soviets' clear superiority in land forces over the Western Powers. Budgetary considerations and political realities in the Western democracies spoke against sending reinforcements to Central Europe so soon after large numbers of troops had been demobilized. In this context, some American strategists began to argue that there was no alternative but to rearm the Germans. More specifically, the Western Powers should put as many of "their" Germans in uniform as necessary to make a defense of Western Europe viable.

In addition to military necessity, the American strategists were animated by an admiration

---

[1] Among the many studies dealing with America's role in rearming West Germany, see esp. Laurence W. Martin, "The American Decision to Rearm Germany," in Harold Stein, ed., *American Civil-Military Decisions: A* Book of Case Studies (Birmingham, Ala., 1963); Robert McGeehan, *The German Rearmament Question: American Diplomacy and European Defense After World War II* (Urbana, Ill., 1971); Thomas Alan Schwartz, *America's Germany: John J. McCloy and the Federal Republic of Germany* (Cambridge, Mass., 1991); David Clay Large, *Germans to the Front: West German Rearmament in the Adenauer Era* (Chapel Hill, N.C., 1996).

[2] Quoted in Melvyn P. Leffler, *A Preponderance of Power: National Security, the Truman Administration, and the Cold War* (Stanford, Calif., 1992), 273.

for the fighting qualities the German soldiers had so amply demonstrated in the war. General Matthew Ridgway argued that it would be impossible to stop a Soviet attack without "the best infantry in Europe." Pentagon analysts concurred that the martial skills of the "German male" were among "the highest in the world."[3] Yet, it was precisely because the Germans made such competent and zealous soldiers that they would have to be rearmed with extreme caution. Instead of creating an independent army, German soldiers would be attached to Allied forces and operate exclusively under Allied command.

The American strategists who hoped to rush the West Germans to the Cold War front imagined that their former enemies would be eager to cooperate: Were they not, after all, militarists at heart? The majority of Germans, however, turned out to be anything but enthusiastic about fielding a new military force, in whatever form. They claimed to have learned (in the words of one journalist) that "As soon as Germany has soldiers, there will be war."[4] Moreover, many Germans believed that because the Western Allies had insisted upon total German disarmament, it was up to them to defend Europe. Finally, West Germans understandably worried that any steps toward rearmament would harden the division between East and West, undermining possibilities for German reunification.

The new West German government under Chancellor Konrad Adenauer did not share this popular reluctance. On the contrary, Adenauer publicly offered to make a military contribution to Western defense. He believed that this was necessary not only to enhance Bonn's security but also to cement the new state firmly in the Western camp. However, he hedged his offer

with various conditions, including the gradual attainment of political sovereignty and "military equality" for the German forces.[5] Bonn displayed a surprising measure of independent thinking, and its insistence on military equality was a consistent theme in the rearmament discussions.

The outbreak of the Korean War in 1950 gave added urgency to considerations about German rearmament. As General Omar Bradley, chairman of the Joint Chiefs of Staff, declared: "Communism is willing to use arms to gain its ends. This is a fundamental change and it has forced a change in our estimate of the military needs of the United States."[6] Now more than ever, the Pentagon concluded, America needed German troops on the Cold War front.

The Korean War provoked panic in West Germany. Many citizens were convinced that the conflict presaged a similar fate for Germany, which was also divided into pro-Soviet and pro-Western spheres. Chancellor Adenauer ordered his first security adviser, Count Gerhard Schwerin, to conduct secret talks on emergency security measures with General George P. Hays, deputy to American High Commissioner John J. McCloy. The chancellor also repeated his offer of a West German defense force, which he said must be armed by America and integrated into the Western alliance. Significantly, he coupled his offer with a formal call for revisions of the Occupation Statute governing Bonn's relations with the Western Powers.

In October 1950, a group of former Wehrmacht officers and other security experts met secretly at the Himmerod Cloister in the Eifel Mountains to discuss arrangements for a possible West German defense contribution. They produced a document that has justly been called the "magna carta for the Bundeswehr."[7]

---

[3] See U.S. Policy Respecting the Disarmament and Demilitarization of the Federal German Republic, Jan. 23, 1950, G3 091 Germany TS (Section 1), Cases 1–20, Plans and Operations Division, National Archives, RG 319, box 538.

[4] Eugen Kogon quoted in Ernst Nolte, *Deutschland und der Kalte Krieg* (Munich, 1974), 291.

[5] On Adenauer's offer, see Large, *Germans to the Front*, 51–6.

[6] Quoted in Martin, "American Decision," 651.

[7] It was so labeled by Count Schwerin in Militärgeschichtliches Forschungsamt, *Aspekte der deutschen Wiederbewaffnung bis 1955* (Boppard, 1975), 142.

It insisted that the Germans have considerable latitude in devising the kind of army they would field. More specifically, it proposed a force of twelve fully equipped tank divisions, a modern airforce, and a navy capable of contending with the Soviets in the Baltic. In terms of "internal structure" – the intricate web of disciplinary rules, motivational ideals, and leadership principles that help determine an army's battleworthiness and relationship to civilian society – the memo called for a compromise between the traditions of the German military and the new directions an altered political landscape demanded. The military had to be subordinate to the civilian authorities but remain "above parties"; combine loyalty to the "new ideas of Europe" with a "healthy love for the German fatherland"; and eschew caste arrogance while recovering "the soldiers' traditional position of prestige in German society."[8] This was a very tall order, and the military apparatus outlined at Himmerod went well beyond what Germany's future security partners, including the United States, had in mind at the time.

FROM THE EUROPEAN DEFENSE COMMUNITY TO THE "NATO SOLUTION"

The discrepancy between Bonn's ambitions and the security role the occupation powers envisaged for West Germany became evident in the four-year struggle over the abortive European Defense Community (EDC). The EDC was an outgrowth of the Pleven Plan, a scheme put forth by Prime Minister René Pleven of France to arm West Germany within the framework of a common European army.[9] France would

have preferred to avoid German rearmament entirely, but because American pressure made this impossible, it advanced the European army plan as a means to circumscribe and control the German contingent. The project called for the integration of national army units at the lowest possible level (namely, battalions) and the creation of a common defense budget, arms-procurement agency, and defense administration responsible to a European parliament. These institutions would be in place *before* any troops were assembled. The plan discriminated against the Federal Republic because it alone would have to keep all its troops under the European command. Moreover, for the time being, West Germany could deploy no air or naval forces and it would not belong directly to NATO.

Although it welcomed France's apparent willingness to see Bonn armed, Washington opposed many provisions of the Pleven Plan, especially the insistence on battalion-level military integration and postponement of deployment until common political structures were in place. America proposed a complicated compromise that allowed for somewhat larger national contingents and an earlier start to actual deployment.

Bonn was not enthusiastic about either the Pleven Plan or the American compromise; Adenauer complained that the project envisioned "second-class" troops for Germany. But the chancellor soon concluded that some form of integrated European army, provided it could be further modified in Bonn's favor, was the safest and fastest route to German rearmament. Over the course of the EDC negotiations in Paris, Bonn's delegation, led by Adenauer's new security adviser, Theodor Blank, presented a rearmament plan based on the Himmerod blueprint. On the all-important question of military organization, it stressed the need for fully operational armored divisions supported by tactical and coastal defense units. In making this

---

[8] Hans-Jürgen Rautenberg and Norbert Wiggershaus, "Die Himmeroder Denkschrift von Oktober 1950," *Militärgeschichtliche Mitteilungen* 21 (1977), 262–6.

[9] On the Pleven Plan, see Schwartz, *America's Germany*, 141–4; Gerhard Wettig, *Entmilitarisierung und Wiederbewaffnung in Deutschland, 1943–1955* (Munich, 1967), 363–9; David Clay Large, "Grand Illusions: The United States, the Federal Republic of Germany, and the European Defense Community, 1950–1954," in

Jeffry M. Diefendorf, Axel Frohn, and Hermann-Josef Rupieper, eds., *American Policy and the Reconstruction of West Germany, 1945–1955* (New York, 1993), 376–80.

argument, the Germans drew on their unique experience fighting the Russians as well as on their knowledge of the U.S. Army *Field Manual*, which stated that "the only unit organized to act independently is a division."[10] Blank also insisted that Bonn must have a ministry of defense, for only this arrangement was compatible with the new state's democratic structure. With the support of the United States, which put pressure on the European partners from the sidelines, Bonn was able to eliminate some of the anti-German features of the draft EDC treaty.

Bonn was less successful in gaining support from its future European partners for a progressive set of "internal structure" principles that had been worked out by a group of reformers in the Federal Republic's military planning agency under Blank. Early on in the EDC negotiations, France presented a *discipline général*, which Blank described as "worse than anything the Nazis had tried to do." Hoping to create regulations that were faithful to the "advanced technological requirements of modern military forces" and to the need for "individual personal development and self-expression" in a democratic society, the German delegation advanced a program that minimized the traditional distinctions between military and civilian life. But they quickly ran into opposition from the other powers, especially the French, who, according to one German delegate, were "very reluctant" to adopt new forms, always putting "the national before the European."[11]

In the area of military reform, the Germans received no support from the United States. General Hays rejected a request from Blank to give Bonn advice on how to create a "democratic army." The Americans, in any event, understood "democracy" in military organization to mean little more than guaranteeing promotion by merit and securing the soldiers' constitutional rights. The American military

establishment's lingering admiration for the Wehrmacht also played a role here. At that moment, the U.S. Army was remodeling its own forces according to lessons learned from the Germans in World War II. When American officers became aware of the scope of the German reform plans, they worried, as General Alfred Gruenther put it in 1954, that "the quality of the soldiers of the new German army would not be as high as those of the Second or Third Reich."[12]

The overall German success in modifying the EDC plan lessened its attractiveness to France, which still had grave reservations about German rearmament in any form and questioned the prudence of sacrificing part of its own national sovereignty on the altar of European military integration. Paris, therefore, failed to ratify the EDC treaty in August 1954 and the project died.

The death of the EDC did not derail German rearmament because the Western Allies, again led by Washington, immediately substituted NATO as the framework for Bonn's military integration into the Western community. The Paris Treaties, authorizing the creation of a West German military contribution to NATO, were ratified by all the member states by March 1955. The top brass at Supreme Headquarters Allied Powers Europe (SHAPE) were pleased by this turn of events, for they had always harbored doubts about the military viability of a common European army and believed NATO offered better prospects for the utilization of German manpower.[13]

BIRTH OF THE BUNDESWEHR

The period of the Bundeswehr's initial deployment, which began with the commissioning of officers in November 1955 and the creation of training cadres in January 1956, offered considerable opportunity for cooperation with the

---

[10] Quoted in The United States Deputy High Commissioner for Germany (Hays) to the Secretary of State, Jan. 27, 1951, in U.S. Department of State, *Foreign Relations of the United States* (hereafter *FRUS*), 1951, vol. 3, pt. 1:996–1001, 999.

[11] Quoted in Large, "Grand Illusions," 388–9.

[12] "Gruenther Takes Precautions," *Foreign Report*, Oct. 21, 1954, 4–5.

[13] "SHAPE Prepares for Germans," *Foreign Report*, Oct. 8, 1954, 6–7.

U.S. Army because Bonn's nascent military was heavily dependent on the Americans for organizational, logistical, and financial support. In many ways, the Bundeswehr looked like an offspring of its powerful American counterpart. Its uniforms and helmets followed American designs and most of its weaponry was made in the United States. The various service branches were integrated under a general inspector (similar to the chairman of the Joint Chiefs of Staff) who reported directly to the minister of defense. The Bundestag Security Committee, like America's House and Senate Armed Services Committees, closely monitored developments in the new military. Bundeswehr officers traveled frequently to America for training and orientation courses.

Nonetheless, the unique conditions under which West Germany was rearmed and the Germans' determination to learn from the mistakes of their own military past ensured that the Bundeswehr was an organization *sui generis*, differing significantly from previous German armies as well as from those of its new security partners. By treaty, all the Federal Republic's forces (twelve divisions with a maximum of 500,000 troops) would operate under NATO command. Bonn formally renounced atomic, bacteriological, and chemical weapons. Supreme command was divided among the defense minister, who held the reins during peacetime; the chancellor, who took control during time of war or national emergency; and the president, who exercised ceremonial functions. A military commissioner of the Bundestag watched over the political and civil rights of the soldiers. The Bundeswehr maintained no separate military-justice system because of the abuse of such arrangements under the Third Reich. For similar reasons, draftees did not swear a formal oath of allegiance when joining the service. Initially, the period of conscription was only twelve months, and the provisions for conscientious objection were exceptionally liberal.

Observers of the young Bundeswehr were often struck by how different it seemed in spirit and deportment from previous German armies, especially the Wehrmacht. Charles Thayer, an aide to McCloy, was surprised upon visiting a

Bundeswehr training facility in 1956 to find the soldiers' rooms and lockers arranged to individual taste, with civilian clothes hanging next to uniforms and underwear piled every which way. As a graduate of West Point and descendant of that institution's founder, he concluded that the American academy, not the new German army, was "the last stronghold of Frederick's [the Great's] Prussian discipline."[14]

Although America and West Germany forged close military ties in the mid- and late 1950s, differing conceptions of how best to contend with the Soviet threat occasioned some genuine conflict. The Bundeswehr was born at a moment when America and NATO were shifting to an emphasis on strategic nuclear defense – "massive retaliation." The so-called Radford Plan, leaked to the press in July 1956, proposed that America's nuclear-strike capacity, augmented by hydrogen bombs, would allow Washington to pull some 800,000 troops out of Europe in the next few years.[15] Although the troop withdrawal was not implemented, it seemed evident that Washington perceived West Germany as little more than a protective "shield," behind which American air power could extend its nuclear "sword." The thicker the shield and the longer the sword, the faster America might be able to reduce its troop strength in Europe. But the Germans had always seen their willingness to rearm as a means of securing the American presence and gaining stature as an equal in the Western community.

The Adenauer government – more specifically, its pugnacious new defense minister, Franz Josef Strauss – unilaterally decided to scale back the Bundeswehr's buildup from 500,000 men in three years to 350,000 over five years. Strauss insisted that this was as much as the Federal Republic could manage without jeopardizing its social and economic health. (In fact, full employment was making it difficult to recruit the hoped-for number of volunteers, and employers

[14] Charles Thayer, *The Unquiet Germans* (New York, 1957), 243–7.
[15] On the Radford Plan, see Hans-Georg Pöttering, *Adenauers Sicherheitspolitik 1955–1963: Ein Beitrag zum deutsch-amerikanischen Verhältnis* (Düsseldorf, 1975), 62–4.

did not want to sacrifice valuable labor to conscription.) He also claimed to be putting "quality before quantity."[16] The Americans saw this as a dangerous display of backsliding and assertiveness. Speaking for the Eisenhower administration, Secretary of State John Foster Dulles declared that America was getting a "raw deal" from its newest partner, and questioned whether the "large effort that the U.S. is making [in Germany] is justified."[17]

BONN AS NATO'S CONTINENTAL ANCHOR

Given NATO's emphasis on a nuclear deterrent, Bonn questioned the logic of fielding an army that had no nuclear weapons. Sounding the old theme of military equality, Strauss demanded that the Bundeswehr be equipped with "the most modern weapons" (meaning nuclear arms); otherwise, the German forces would be nothing but "expensive cannon-fodder."[18] At the very least, he added, the Germans must have access to tactical nuclear arms through NATO and be outfitted with the hardware (i.e., missiles, aircraft, and artillery) necessary to deliver them.

Washington, anxious to see its continental European partners capable of waging tactical atomic warfare, persuaded the NATO Council in late 1956 to approve a "New Look" for Europe that included equipping Bonn's divisions for nuclear combat. In April 1957, the Council refined this decision by drafting a "two-key" system, whereby the U.S. Army would retain custody over the atomic warheads on European soil while the European powers, including West Germany, would control the necessary "atomic carriers."[19]

Once they became known in Germany, these decisions generated a fierce public battle that revived all the passions of the original rearmament debate. Adenauer poured fuel on the flames by declaring that tactical atomic weapons were "nothing but the further development of artillery" and that Germany must possess such "practically normal weapons."[20]

While controversy still swirled around the Bundeswehr's armaments program, NATO slowly abandoned its strategy of "massive retaliation" in favor of "flexible response" – the doctrine that Western armies should be able to respond to an attack either by conventional or nuclear means, or a combination of both. Although this doctrine helped to legitimize the conventionally armed Bundeswehr, it infuriated Strauss, who saw it as renewed "discrimination" against the Germans, who would now be frozen in their status as a non-nuclear power. His press secretary fired off an article dismissing the doctrine of limited conventional warfare as "military alchemy."[21] But flexible response was also alarming because it revived the old specter of America's possible "decoupling" from Europe in a time of emergency. Would the United States be willing to come to Europe's defense if this risked the safety of American cities?

Apart from feeling left out of the atomic loop, Bonn's new soldiers were often dissatisfied with the conventional arms at their disposal. Wehrmacht veterans complained that some of their American-made weapons were inferior to those they had used in the last war. Their new machine guns did not fire as quickly as the old German models, and their gas-powered M-47 tanks were less efficient than the old German diesels. It would be some time, however, before Bonn could extensively supply its troops with weapons and equipment made in Germany. Most German firms with the capacity

---

[16] Catherine Kelleher, *Germany and the Politics of Nuclear Weapons* (New York, 1975), 61–88; Mark Cioc, *Pax Atomica: The Nuclear Defense Debate in West Germany During the Adenauer Era* (New York, 1988), 34–5.

[17] Memorandum of a Conversation, Paris, Dec. 11, 1956, *FRUS, 1955–1957,* 4:123–33, 126.

[18] Franz Josef Strauss, *Die Erinnerungen* (Berlin, 1989), 320.

[19] Harald Schneider, "Sicherheitspartner: Die Bundeswehr im NATO-Bündnis," in Franz H. U. Borken-

hagen, ed., *Bundeswehr: Demokratie in Oliv?* (Bonn, 1986), 71.

[20] Karl Dietrich Bracher et al., eds., *Geschichte der Bundesrepublik Deutschland,* 5 vols. (Stuttgart, 1981–1987), 2:359.

[21] "Sie kamen bei Nacht und Nebel," *Die Zeit,* Oct. 20, 1982.

to produce weapons preferred to concentrate on the civilian market, which was beginning to boom. Yet, Bonn's civilian and military leaders believed that a national arms industry was important to the country's status within NATO and could eventually play a significant role in the domestic economy. The Adenauer government, therefore, began promoting domestic weapons manufacturing wherever it could.

At first, the focus was on small arms and munitions up to 40 millimeters. To promote the construction of larger weapons systems at home, Strauss pursued license agreements with Bonn's NATO allies. For example, half of West Germany's French-designed Hotchkiss light tanks were built in the Federal Republic. To help revive Germany's aircraft industry, the defense ministry encouraged partnerships between manufacturers like Messerschmitt, Heinkel, and Dornier, which then landed contracts to maintain and refurbish airplanes that the NATO powers had given or sold to the Federal Republic.[22]

Bonn's strong military connection with the United States was exemplified by its decision in 1958 to purchase the Lockheed F-104G Starfighter, the Luftwaffe's first truly modern aircraft. Strauss had originally favored the French Mirage III, but the Luftwaffe pushed for the Starfighter, which had a longer range and better electronics.[23] However, because the Luftwaffe planned to use the aircraft as an all-weather fighter-bomber, which it was not designed to be, the Starfighter had to be reconfigured in a way that added substantially to its weight. It crashed so often that it soon became known as the "flying coffin."

The Starfighter was not the only problem that plagued the young Bundeswehr. It continued to have difficulty meeting its manpower goals, especially at the NCO and junior-officer level. Its poor performance in NATO's fall maneuvers in 1962 was leaked to the magazine *Der Spiegel*, which published a devastating critique, concluding: "After nearly seven years of

rearmament, and after six years of Strauss's leadership, today's German army still gets the lowest note on NATOs' report card: 'conditionally prepared for defense.'"[24] The government reacted by ordering the arrest of the article's author and the magazine's publisher, tactics that recalled an earlier era. The ensuing scandal forced Strauss to resign as defense minister.

In the wake of the *Spiegel* affair, the Bundeswehr leadership stepped up efforts to correct the inadequacies that had been so painfully revealed. By 1965, the West German military managed to reach the manpower goals set out for it ten years earlier. The Bundeswehr was now NATO's largest conventional force in Europe, a status that became more significant in 1966 when France, anxious to pursue an independent nuclear strategy, pulled out of the NATO command. The German army improved its combat-readiness after 1965 by adopting a longer and more thorough training program. It also significantly modernized its weaponry, 45 percent of which was now produced at home.[25] Perhaps the most notable weapons acquisition was the domestically produced Leopard tank, which reestablished Germany's reputation for excellence in armor. Bonn's importance within the Atlantic alliance was acknowledged by appointments of Germans to high posts in the bureaucratic and military-command structure of the organization.[26]

Bonn had reason to be proud of these achievements, and Washington duly appreciated their significance, not the least because they helped overcome the doubts that many ordinary Americans had harbored about the wisdom of bringing this erstwhile enemy into the Atlantic alliance and giving it access to (although not control over) tactical nuclear weapons. At the time of German rearmament, the American press had been deeply divided on these issues, but the successful integration of the Bundeswehr

[22] Manfred Behrend, *Franz Josef Strauss: Eine politische Biographie* (Cologne, 1995), 37.

[23] Strauss, *Erinnerungen*, 315.

[24] "Bedingt abwehrbereit," *Der Spiegel* 16 (Oct. 10, 1962): 33, as quoted in Cioc, *Pax Atomica*, 183.

[25] Militärgeschichtliches Forschungsamt, *Verteidigung im Bündnis: Planung, Aufbau und Bewährung der Bundeswehr 1950–1972* (Munich, 1975), 205–7.

[26] Schneider, "Sicherheitspartner," 74.

into the new German democracy and the NATO alliance helped assuage lingering fears. In fact, once its growing pains had receded, the West German army received little attention in the American press or in domestic debates about foreign affairs. No doubt some Bundeswehr officers would have preferred to establish a higher profile for their institution on the other side of the Atlantic, but the fact that the Bundeswehr did not loom large in the American consciousness was itself a sign of its remarkable political success.

CHAPTER FOUR

Variable Architectures for War and Peace

U.S. Force Structure and Basing in Germany, 1945–1990[1]

Bryan T. van Sweringen

Viewed as part of security policy, the structure and basing of U.S. forces in Germany between 1945 and 1990 might appear somewhat static. However, although Germany literally held center stage, American forces and installations stationed there were always part of larger forward-deployed military commands with land, sea, and air components throughout Western Europe. Their numbers, therefore, continually varied in response to changes in the larger postwar security environment and in the United States' commitment to Europe.

REDEPLOYMENT AND REORGANIZATION: 1945–50

At the end of World War II, the sinews of American military power stretched from the continental United States across the Atlantic Ocean to the heart of Central Europe. U.S. forces in the European Theater of Operations were under the command of the combined British-American Supreme Headquarters, Allied Expeditionary Force (SHAEF) for operations, and the Headquarters, European Theater of Operations United States Army-Communications Zone (ETOUSA-COMZ) for administration and supply. In addition to the COMZ, ETOUSA commands included the Twelfth Army Group, the Sixth Army Group, the U.S. Strategic Air Force in Europe (USSTAF), and the United States Naval Forces in France.[2] General Dwight D. Eisenhower, U.S. Army, commanded SHAEF and ETOUSA.

Within Germany, U.S. ground forces included the First, Third, Ninth, and Fifteenth Armies of the Twelfth Army Group, and the Seventh Army of the Sixth Army Group.[3] Following the unconditional surrender of the German armed forces on May 8, 1945, these units began to prepare for the occupation of Germany and immediate redeployment to the Pacific Theater of Operations. The reorganization of the European Theater followed. Headquarters ETOUSA was located with SHAEF at the IG Farben Building in Frankfurt am Main.[4] On July 1, 1945, General Eisenhower redesignated ETOUSA as U.S. Forces European Theater (USFET) and dissolved SHAEF two weeks later.

The number of U.S. tactical units in Germany was rapidly reduced. With the deactivation of the Sixth and then the Twelfth Army Group, operational control of all U.S. forces in theater

---

[1] This essay is dedicated to the memory of Colonel Samuel Nelson Drew, United States Air Force: Würzburg, February 25, 1948 – Mt. Igman, August 19, 1995.

[2] Oliver J. Frederiksen, *The American Military Occupation of Germany, 1945–1953* (Darmstadt, 1953), 19.

[3] Ibid., 3.

[4] Bruce Saunders, *A Brief History of the U.S. Army Europe (USAREUR)* (Heidelberg, 1994), 1–2.

passed to USFET at the end of July 1945.[5] By mid-March 1947, all tactical Army headquarters had been deactivated or transferred from Germany.

Although approximately 90 percent of the occupation forces were ground forces, it is important to note that USFET major commands in Germany also included air and sea forces. On July 24, 1945, USFET reorganized the U.S. Strategic Air Force in Europe as the U.S. Air Forces in Europe (USAFE) with headquarters in Wiesbaden. The Headquarters of the U.S. Naval Forces in France accompanied SHAEF to Germany. Originally located in Frankfurt, U.S. Naval Forces in Germany (NAVFORGER) moved to Bremen when Headquarters, U.S. Naval Forces Europe (NAVEUR) relocated there from London.

Theater reorganization included the rapid reduction in American troop strength, from 3,069,310 on V-E Day to 135,000 on July 1, 1947.[6] The 1947 figure remained fairly constant until the European augmentation in 1951–2. The U.S. Air Forces in Europe were demobilized at an equally dramatic rate. Whereas on V-E Day USSTAF had controlled more than 17,000 aircraft and more than 450,000 officers and airmen, by the end of 1947, 458 planes and 18,120 people in uniform were all that remained.[7] Within Germany, combat aircraft were based at Neubiberg and Fürstenfeldbruck.[8] Other USAFE air bases were at Tempelhof (Berlin), Wiesbaden, Rhein-Main, Erlangen, Giebelstadt, Erding, Landsberg, and Munich.

U.S. forces assumed control of the American zone proper (Hesse, Württemberg-Baden, and Bavaria) and the Bremen Enclave (Bremerhaven-Bremen) in July 1945. Supplies from Bremerhaven, the sole port of entry under American authority, were stored in the "supply triangle" (an area bounded by Giessen, Frankfurt, and Hanau) and from there distributed throughout the American zone.

By mid-1946, forces assigned to USFET were primarily performing either military government or occupation duties. The U.S. Constabulary, established to maintain security within the American zone, moved to Heidelberg on July 1, 1946. Composed of approximately 30,000 troops, it was essentially a police force capable of limited defensive operations.

The mission of Commander, U.S. Naval Forces, Germany (COMNAVFORGER) initially included force redeployment and occupation, in addition to conducting port operations at the Naval Advanced Base, Bremerhaven. COMNAVFORGER established the Rhine River Patrol on December 23, 1948.[9] The patrol was headquartered on the Rhine at Schierstein with bases at Mannheim and Karlsruhe. Jointly manned by navy and constabulary personnel, it reported navigational hazards on the Rhine River between Bingen and Karlsruhe.[10]

The European Command (EUCOM) replaced USFET on March 15, 1947. As a "unified" command, EUCOM consisted of subordinate commands: the U.S. Army, Europe (USAREUR), the USAFE, the U.S. Forces in Austria (USFA), and the USNAVEUR. The Commander in Chief, European Command (CINCEUR) also served as the military governor and as a member of the Allied Control Council.

The economic fusion of the American and British zones into "Bizonia" took place on January 1, 1947. Following the establishment of the "bizonal capital" at Frankfurt in 1948, space requirements necessitated the relocation of EUCOM headquarters to Heidelberg; the constabulary headquarters moved to Stuttgart.

[5] Frederiksen, *American Military Occupation*, 29–30.

[6] Ibid., 30.

[7] Thomas S. Snyder and Daniel F. Harrington, *Historical Highlights: United States Air Forces in Europe, 1942–1997* (Ramstein, 1997), 8.

[8] USAFE Office of History, *Valor and Vigilance: A Brief History of United States Air Forces in Europe* (Ramstein, 1994).

[9] Frederiksen, *American Military Occupation*, 196.

[10] Following the admission of the Federal Republic of Germany into NATO, the U.S. Navy Rhine River Patrol and the U.S. Naval Facility at Schierstein were used to train members of the Labor Service for induction into the German navy. Both ships and installations were transferred to the German government in 1958.

Following the founding of the Federal Republic of Germany on May 23, 1949, the Office of Military Government and the position of military governor were dissolved. All remaining governmental responsibilities were transferred to the Office of the High Commissioner for Germany (HICOG).

WAR IN KOREA AND AUGMENTATION
IN EUROPE

Although the North Atlantic Treaty was signed in April 1949, NATO remained largely a paper construct until the invasion of South Korea on June 25, 1950. Meeting in New York from September 15 to 18, NATO's North Atlantic Council (NAC) recommended the establishment of an "integrated force under a centralized command, adequate to deter aggression and ensure the defense of Western Europe."[11] On December 18, 1950, the NAC requested that General Eisenhower be appointed the first Supreme Allied Commander, Europe (SACEUR). General Eisenhower activated Allied Command Europe (ACE) and established the Supreme Headquarters, Atlantic Powers in Europe (SHAPE) at Roquencourt near Paris on April 2, 1951.[12] Given General Eisenhower's wartime experience as commander of both SHAEF and ETOUSA-COMZ, it is not surprising that EUCOM was quickly drawn into a close relationship with SHAPE/ACE.

NATO commands were subdivided into northern, central, and southern European regional commands, and thereunder by service. Most of the American forces marked for Germany were to be deployed to the central region. Because a support of the NATO commands became a primary mission of the European Command, each EUCOM commander was given additional NATO command responsibilities. For example, the commander in chief of the U.S. Army Europe (CINCUSAREUR)

was "dual-hatted" as the Commander of the Central Army Group (COMCENTAG), a subordinate command of Allied Land Forces Central Europe (ALFCE). The CENTAG headquarters was co-located with the army headquarters in Heidelberg. The commander of U.S. Air Forces in Europe was "dual-hatted" as the Commander in Chief of the Allied Air Forces Central Europe (AAFCE) with headquarters at Fontainebleau.[13] The European headquarters of the U.S. Naval Forces moved from Bremen to Naples, where its commander assumed the additional NATO duty of Commander in Chief, Allied Forces Southern Europe (CINCSOUTH).[14]

When the transition from combat to occupation forces was complete, European Command ground forces consisted of the headquarters and two tactical units: the constabulary and the First Infantry Division (The Big Red One), which had remained in Germany after World War II.[15] The EUCOM Troop Augmentation Program called for a total of 260,000 army and 50,000 air force personnel to be stationed in Germany by July 1, 1952. The Seventh Army was reactivated at Stuttgart on November 24, 1950, absorbing the constabulary and the First Infantry Division. Arriving in Germany in early 1951, the Fourth Infantry Division (Ivy Division) was the first new unit to augment Seventh Army.[16] The Fifth Corps deployed from Fort Bragg, North Carolina, to Bad Nauheim and was assigned to Seventh Army. The Seventh Corps, activated at Fort George G. Meade, Maryland, in 1951, deployed to Stuttgart and was also assigned to Seventh Army. By the end of 1951, the two corps contained five divisions: the First, with headquarters at Würzburg; the Fourth, with headquarters at Frankfurt; the Twenty-eighth;

---

[13] Patricia Parrish, *Forty-Five Years of Vigilance for Freedom: United States Air Forces in Europe, 1942–1987* (Ramstein, 1987), 39.

[14] United States European Command, Office of the Command Historian, *History of Headquarters, U.S. Naval Forces, Europe (USNAVEUR)* (Stuttgart, n.d.), 1.

[15] Saunders, *Brief History*, 2.

[16] HQ Seventh Army, Historical Section, *Seventh Army: Freedom's Pyramid of Power in Europe* (n.p., 1954), 39.

---

[11] Hastings Lionel Ismay, *NATO: The First Five Years, 1949–1954* (Utrecht, 1955), 32.

[12] *Allied* was later substituted for *Atlantic*.

the Forty-third; and the Second Armored Division (Hell On Wheels), with headquarters at Bad Kreuznach.[17] Also of significance for future developments in Germany was the activation of the European Command Communications Zone (COM-Z) at Orleans, France.

Following the Berlin airlift, the USAFE mission began to shift from occupational operations to tactical support. The Twelfth Air Force, activated at Wiesbaden on January 21, 1951, assumed control of all units assigned to USAFE in the Federal Republic of Germany. In 1950, USAFE consisted of 4 wings of 371 aircraft stationed at 8 bases. By 1954, it had increased in size to 16 wings of more than 2,100 aircraft stationed at 33 bases.[18] USAFE units were integral parts of NATO's Second and Fourth Allied Tactical Air Forces (headquartered at Mönchengladbach and Ramstein, respectively).[19]

In July 1952, the headquarters of the newly organized U.S. Naval Forces, Eastern Atlantic and Mediterranean, was established in London. On June 1, 1957, its commander in chief assumed direct command of U.S. Naval Forces in Germany.

The three European commands (U.S. Naval Forces, Eastern Atlantic and Mediterranean; USAFE; and EUCOM) were combined under a "new" joint headquarters, the U.S. European Command (USEUCOM) on August 1, 1952. The former EUCOM Headquarters at Heidelberg was redesignated Headquarters, U.S. Army Europe (USAREUR). Originally established at the I.G. Farben Building in Frankfurt, HQ USEUCOM moved to Camp-des-Loges in the forest of St. Germain-en-Laye, near SHAPE, in May 1954.

Noting the vulnerability of the Bremen Enclave to Soviet forces stationed in the German Democratic Republic, American military planners devised lines of communication (LOC) extending across France to West Germany. The new defensive mission of American forces in Germany mandated that depots in the American zone be transferred to a secure area west of the Rhine and that reserves be located in France. The northern enclave of the French zone (Rhineland-Palatinate) was the logical area for storing supplies and stationing troops. On August 30, 1950, the Joint Chiefs of Staff authorized the relocation of EUCOM's peacetime supplies to the west of the Rhine. Together with the theater reserve supplies to be stored in France, the stocks in the Rhine General Depot (established in 1949) would constitute a reserve stored in LOC facilities, which, as noted previously, would reach from the Atlantic coast to the Rhine.

At the September 1950 Council of Foreign Ministers conference in New York, French foreign minister Robert Schuman proposed an exchange of areas and facilities within existing zonal boundaries. The final agreement on the exchange of areas was signed by the high commissioners and commanders in chief at Remagen on March 2, 1951.[20] In addition to five major army technical service depots, air force installations were also to be relocated to the French Northern Enclave.

As in the case of the Bremen Enclave, American planners determined that air combat and logistical support units should be relocated west of the Rhine. Negotiations with the French resulted in their agreement to design and contract for the construction (from war reparations payments) of air bases at Bitburg, Hahn, Landstuhl, Sembach, and Spangdahlem, all within the French zone. Construction began in 1951. In April, the Fourth Allied Tactical Air Force (ATAF) was organized at Landstuhl. In June 1952, the CINCEUR signed an agreement for the use of the bases with the commander of the French occupation forces in Germany. On September 1, USAFE officially established air bases at Bitburg, Hahn, Sembach, and Spangdahlem. In April 1953, a tract of land near the

[17] The names and locations of divisions stationed in Germany would change over the next thirty-nine years. See ibid., 40–2.

[18] USAFE, *Valor and Vigilance*, 11.

[19] NATO Information Service, *NATO Facts and Figures* (Brussels, 1969), 169.

[20] HQUSAREUR, Historical Division, *Exchange of Troops and Facilities: United States and French Zones, 1950–1957* (Heidelberg, 1952), 9. Reference used is unclassified.

Landstuhl Air Base was designated the Ramstein Air Base. Also in April, the Fourth ATAF moved from Landstuhl to Trier Air Base, and the HQ Twelfth Air Force consolidated at Ramstein. The USAFE Combat Operations Center was established near Kaiserslautern in the "Kindsbach Cave" in August 1953. In the event of war in Central Europe, it was to serve as the command control center for the USAFE tactical force and the tactical wings of the Fourth Allied Tactical Air Force. In November 1953, the major functions of HQ USAFE and Twelfth Air Force were consolidated. Ramstein Air Base became the USAFE advance headquarters. In November 1959, the Seventeenth Air Force assumed control of all USAFE tactical units in Germany, where it became the major USAFE subordinate command.

CONVENTIONAL FORCES AND UNCONVENTIONAL WEAPONS

Following the 1952 presidential elections, financial considerations prompted the Eisenhower administration to take a "New Look" at the expensive buildup of conventional forces in Europe.[21] As a consequence, U.S. and NATO planners turned to strategic and tactical nuclear weapons as a less costly alternative.[22] In Europe, the air force provided USAFE with nuclear-capable delivery systems. USAFE's first missile unit, the First Pilotless Bomber Squadron, Light, transferred to Bitburg Air Base in March 1953. It was assigned the first American surface-to-surface guided missile, the Matador (TM-61). The first missile wing in the air force, the 701st Tactical Missile Wing, was established at Hahn Air Base on September 15, 1956. Matador squadrons at Hahn, Bitburg, and Sembach were assigned to this new wing. The Matador was replaced by the Mace missile (TM-76) in 1959. As intended, USAFE conventional forces became a casualty of the New Look: USAFE personnel

strength declined from a high of 136,475 in 1955 to less than 88,000 by the end of the decade.[23]

As a consequence of disagreements with the French government over the storage of nuclear weapons, USAFE redeployed the atomic-capable Forty-ninth Tactical Fighter Wing to Spangdahlem and the Fiftieth Tactical Fighter Wing to Hahn. The last Mace unit assigned to USAFE, the Seventy-first Tactical Missile Wing, was deactivated at Bitburg Air Base on April 30, 1969. On April 5, 1985, HQ USAFE activated a ground-launched cruise missile (GLCM) unit, the Thirty-eighth Tactical Missile Wing, at Wüschheim Air Station.[24]

Concerned about the implications of the air force's inventory of strategic and tactical atomic weapons, the army had developed tactical battlefield weapons in 1951. In fall 1953, a 280-millimeter "atomic gun" capable of delivering conventional and atomic munitions was deployed to U.S. artillery units in the Federal Republic.[25] Atom Annie was followed by Honest John, the first genuine tactical nuclear system, the following year.[26] The Federal Republic of Germany agreed to accept atomic weapons in March 1958. It is interesting to note that the Soviet fear of the "nuclearization" of the Bundeswehr may have been a primary reason for the Berlin Crises of 1958 and 1961, which, in turn, prompted the United States to increase its conventional forces in Europe.[27] By 1963, the arsenal of the Seventh Army Artillery included the Sergeant, Corporal, Redstone, and La Crosse missiles as well as the Honest John. In 1964, the nuclear-capable Pershing missile, with a range of

---

[21] I am greatly indebted to Daniel Harrington, Carol Parks, and Thomas Snyder at the Office of History, USAFE, Ramstein Air Base, for their assistance.

[22] See the chapter by Kori Schake in this section.

[23] *A Brief History of the United States Air Forces in Europe: 50th Anniversary Issue*, USAFE Pamphlet 210–1 (Ramstein, 1992), 5.

[24] Snyder and Harrington, *Historical Highlights*, 98, 128.

[25] Andreas Förestel, *Chronik 1953: Tag für Tag in Wort und Bild* (Dortmund, 1993), 174.

[26] Hans-Jürgen Schraut, "U.S. Forces in Germany, 1945–1955," in Simon W. Duke and Wolfgang Krieger, eds., *U.S. Military Forces in Europe: The Early Years, 1945–1970* (Boulder, Colo., 1993), 179.

[27] Vladislav M. Zubok, *Khrushchev and the Berlin Crisis (1958–1962)*, Woodrow Wilson International Center for Scholars, Cold War International History Project, Working Paper 6 (Washington, D.C., 1993), 3–4.

400 miles, was deployed to Europe to replace the obsolete Redstone.[28] Pershing II missiles, together with the GLCMs, were deployed to Germany in the 1980s. All Pershing missiles in Europe were the responsibility of the Fifty-sixth Artillery Group.

REINFORCEMENT AND RELOCATION

Two events in the early to mid-1960s severely tested the ability of U.S. forces to respond rapidly to changes in the security environment: the Berlin Crisis of 1961 and the withdrawal of France from NATO's integrated military command.

On June 15, 1961, Soviet premier Nikita Khrushchev renewed his threat, first made in 1958, to sign a separate peace treaty with the German Democratic Republic, which would have effectively terminated the access rights of the Western Allies to Berlin. President John F. Kennedy had already called for an increase in conventional forces as part of the new strategy of "flexible response."[29] As a consequence, the Third Armored Cavalry Regiment deployed to Germany. For the next three and a half years, infantry battle groups were rotated into Berlin every ninety days. In June 1962, the total strength of the USAREUR force reached 277,342 troops, the highest number since the end of World War II.[30] The 1961 Berlin Crisis also catalyzed the largest overseas deployment of U.S. Air Force units since the end of World War II. Under Operation Stair Step, eleven Air National Guard squadrons were deployed to deactivated USAFE air bases in France. These squadrons returned to the United States in summer 1962.[31]

The United States faced another logistical challenge on March 6, 1966, when President Charles de Gaulle announced that France would withdraw from NATO's integrated military command. At the end of the month, France informed NATO that all allied headquarters and forces located in France were to leave by April 1, 1967. The SHAPE relocated from Paris to Mons, Belgium. Headquarters, U.S. EUCOM relocated from Camp-des-Loges to Stuttgart, displacing Seventh Army Headquarters, which combined with USAREUR at Heidelberg in December 1966.

Although USAFE was required to give up nine air bases, tactical units had already redeployed from France during Project Red Richard. Whereas most went to the United Kingdom, the headquarters of the HQ 26 Tactical Reconnaissance Wing moved to Ramstein Air Base. Remaining units redeployed to the United States under the concept of dual basing discussed in the next subsection.

USAREUR was faced with the Herculean task of relocating 813,000 tons of material and 69,000 people to the United Kingdom and Germany. Once the planning was complete, the fast relocation (FRELOC) of American forces began. The Headquarters of the USACOMZEUR was moved from Orleans to Worms, where it was combined with Headquarters, United States Army Area Command (USAACOM) to become the Theater Army Support Command (TASCOM). At the conclusion of FRELOC, the majority of army installations were located in the Federal Republic. Ultimately, USAREUR would have to develop new LOC north of France, running from the ports of Belgium and the Netherlands through Luxembourg and into Germany.

---

[28] Major Theodore Shoemaker, "Sunday Punch for the Army," in *Army in Europe*, DA Pamphlet 360-1-19, June 1968, 7–10.

[29] *NATO Facts and Figures*, 49. See also the chapter by Frank Ninkovich, vol. 1, Politics.

[30] Saunders, *Brief History*, 3.

[31] Parrish, *Forty-Five Years of Vigilance*, 109, 114–7.

DECLINING DOLLARS AND DUAL BASING:
1966–9

During the mid- to late 1960s, American forces in Germany began to feel financial constraints imposed by the war in Southeast Asia and an unfavorable balance of payments in Europe. In May 1967, the United States announced its intention to withdraw 35,000 military personnel from the Federal Republic.[32] Approximately 80 percent of the personnel were to come from USAREUR, which consequently conducted the first "Redeployment of Forces *From* Germany" exercise in 1968. Under dual basing, the 28,000 troops withdrawn remained assigned to the U.S. EUCOM. Approximately 12,000 were redeployed to Germany during the "Return of Forces *To* Germany" (REFORGER) exercise the following year.

Another consequence of dual basing was the Prepositioning of Material Configured to Unit Sets (POMCUS). In 1962–3, equipment required for an infantry division, an armored division, and ten supporting units was "prepositioned" in the Federal Republic. This concept, developed and tested through the REFORGER exercise, was intended to save both time and the "lift" required for rapid deployment to Germany.

As the war in Southeast Asia drew to a close, forces began to return to USAREUR. The first significant increase in U.S. combat forces since the EUCOM Augmentation Plan occurred with the deployment of the Third Brigade of the Second Armored Division from the United States to Bremerhaven in the mid-1970s.

During Operation Crested Cap in 1967, the USAFE relocated units to New Mexico and Idaho.[33] The Forty-ninth Tactical Fighter Wing, for example, which had moved from Etain-Rouvres Air Base in France to Spangdahlem under Project Red Richard, returned to Holloman Air Force Base in New Mexico.[34] The reduction of U.S. forces in Germany was temporarily halted in August 1968, when the Warsaw Pact invaded Czechoslovakia.

THE WAR IN SOUTHWEST ASIA AND THE END OF THE COLD WAR

In September 1989, 248,621 U.S. military personnel were stationed in the Federal Republic of Germany.[35] The majority, 208,142, were assigned to the USAREUR and the Seventh Army. The headquarters of the Fifth and Seventh Corps were located in Frankfurt and Stuttgart, respectively. Forces assigned to Fifth Corps included the Third Armored Division, with headquarters at Frankfurt; the Eighth Infantry Division, with headquarters at Bad Kreuznach; and the Eleventh Armored Cavalry Regiment (Blackhorse Regiment), with headquarters at Fulda. Forces assigned to Seventh Corps included the First Armored Division (Old Ironsides), with headquarters at Ansbach; the Third Infantry Division, with headquarters at Würzburg; the First Infantry Division (Forward), with headquarters at Göppingen; and the Second Armored Cavalry Regiment, with headquarters at Nuremberg. The separate Second Armored Division (Forward), with headquarters at Garlstedt, was assigned to USAREUR. Other USAREUR commands in Germany included U.S. Army Berlin; Thirty-second Army Air Defense Command, with headquarters at Darmstadt; Twenty-first Theater Army Area Command, with headquarters at Kaiserslautern; Seventh Medical Command, with headquarters at Heidelberg; Eighteenth Engineer Brigade; Fifty-sixth Field Artillery Brigade, with headquarters at Schwäbisch Gmünd; Fifty-ninth Ordnance Brigade, with headquarters at Pirmasens; and the Fourth Transportation Command.[36] In accordance with the NATO General

[32] The following description of dual basing is based on Saunders, *Brief History*, 3–4.

[33] Parrish, *Forty-Five Years of Vigilance*, 139.

[34] David A. Levin, *History of the 52 FW and Spangdahlem Air Base* (Spangdahlem, 1993), 8.

[35] U.S. European Command Public Affairs Directorate, Public Information Division, *Headquarters United States European Command Fact Book 1990* (Stuttgart, n.d.), 7.

[36] Ibid., 12.

Defense Plan, the mission of the USAREUR commands was "to hold off an attack from the East until reinforcements could arrive from the United States."[37]

Also in September 1989, there were 40,031 USAFE personnel stationed in Germany. In addition to USAFE headquarters at Ramstein, one of its three numbered air forces, the Seventeenth Air Force, was located at Sembach Air Base. Major USAFE units in Germany were stationed at Bitburg, Hahn (Lautzenhausen), Lindsey (Wiesbaden), Rhein-Main (Frankfurt), Spangdahlem, Hessisch-Oldendorf, Zweibrücken, and Tempelhof (Berlin). Other forces stationed in Germany included the 340 sailors and 108 Marines assigned to NAVEUR.[38]

All these force structures would be radically altered by the fall of the Berlin Wall only two months later and the "velvet revolution" in Central Europe. On January 29, 1990, U.S. Secretary of Defense Richard Cheney announced the first of a series of annual base closures in Europe. Planning for the drawdown of U.S. forces began that spring. Chemical weapons were removed from Germany in the joint German-American operation Steel Box (July 26–September 22, 1990). Intermediate nuclear weapons were also removed from Germany.

The withdrawal of American forces from Germany was delayed by Operation Desert Shield, which began five days after the Iraqi invasion of Kuwait on August 2, 1990. The Cold War REFORGER Exercise became a model for the DEFORGER deployment of U.S. and coalition forces from the European Theater to Southwest Asia. On November 8, 1990, President George Bush announced that Seventh Corps would deploy to Southwest Asia from Germany. The First and Third Armored Divisions, the Second Armored Division (Forward), and the Second Armored Cavalry Regiment also deployed from Germany. At the end of hostilities, Seventh Corps returned to Stuttgart for a dramatic farewell before returning to the United States for deactivation. Other units to depart a reunified Germany included the Third Armored Division, the Eighth Infantry Division, the Second Armored Cavalry Regiment, and the Eleventh Armored Cavalry Regiment.[39]

Aircraft assigned to the USAFE began to deploy to Southwest Asia in early August 1990. The deactivation of Thirty-eighth Tactical Missile Wing (GLCMs) on August 22 at Wüschheim Air Station, therefore, went largely unnoticed.[40] The drawdown of USAFE units, including the Seventeenth Air Force – the major USAFE subordinate command stationed in Germany – also resumed following the Gulf War.

CONCLUSION

The structure and basing of U.S. forces in Germany from 1945 to 1990 varied in response to changes in the larger international security and economic environments. Rapid demobilization of American forces in Germany following World War II left only the small residual force necessary for demobilization, military government, and internal security. Wartime experience provided a useful model for the equally rapid augmentation of American forces in Europe that followed the outbreak of the Korean War in 1950. Although the "Fast Relocation" from France in 1966–7 initially increased the military presence of the United States in Germany, economic considerations prompted a reduction in this presence; dual basing was intended to manage this shift. A major reduction of American forces in Germany began in the "year of unification" that followed the dramatic events of 1989. Temporarily postponed by the Gulf War, the drawdown would continue on into the 1990s, reducing American forces and installations in Germany to their smallest size in forty-five years.

---

[37] Stephen P. Gehring, *From the Fulda Gap to Kuwait: U.S. Army, Europe and the Gulf War* (Washington, D.C., 1998), 18.

[38] Ibid., 16.

[39] Saunders, *Brief History*, 5.

[40] Snyder and Harrington, *Historical Highlights*, 138.

CHAPTER FIVE

The Shifting Military Balance in Central Europe

Frederick Zilian Jr.

After the onset of the Cold War, Western force deployments in Central Europe shifted not simply because of perceived changes in the Soviet military threat but also because of technological developments, changes of political leadership, budgetary constraints, and the granting of sovereignty to the Federal Republic of Germany in 1955. On the Eastern side, shifts in military formations and technologies stemmed from changes in the Soviet political leadership and from Soviet military policy, strategy, and doctrine, which called for the Soviet armed forces not only to maintain their superiority in conventional combat power but to attain nuclear superiority as well.

The German-American security relationship remained relatively constant from 1945 to 1968. The Western occupation zones of Germany and, after 1949, the Federal Republic were dependent on NATO and, therefore, ultimately on the United States for their fundamental security. Continuity was also ensured, despite inevitable frictions, by the tenure of Konrad Adenauer, who served as chancellor from September 1949 to October 1963. But even during the government of Ludwig Erhard (1963–6) and the Christian Democratic-Social Democratic "Grand Coalition" under Kurt Georg Kiesinger (1966–9), there was no genuine alternative to alignment with the West under the leadership of the United States.[1]

THE GLARING CONVENTIONAL MILITARY WEAKNESS OF THE WEST

After the end of the war in Europe in May 1945, the military balance between the future protagonists of the Cold War quickly shifted as the United States began to withdraw its forces. By the end of the year, the West had a mere dozen under-strength divisions in Europe, whereas the Soviet Union maintained twenty-five fully armed divisions in Central Europe with 140 to 175 divisions at battle strength, supplemented by the armed forces of the Soviet-dominated states of Eastern Europe. In 1948, the United States had a total ground reserve force of only two and one-third divisions. To send more than a division anywhere would have required a partial mobilization.[2] The rapid demobilization left American forces in Europe militarily

---

[1] For an analysis of the German-American security partnership, see the chapter by David Clay Large in this section.

[2] Robert E. Osgood, *NATO: The Entangling Alliance* (Chicago, 1962), 29.

insignificant, poorly equipped, and with poor morale.[3]

As the hopes for cooperative leadership by the Four Powers faded, antagonistic military measures increased. The first such measure by the United States came in November 1946, when six B-29 bombers from Arizona were deployed for twelve days to Rhein-Main Airfield in Frankfurt. In March 1947, the U.S. European Command (EUCOM) was formed, headed by General Lucius D. Clay, the military governor of Germany. Clay assigned his deputy, General Clarence R. Huebner, the mission of restoring the combat readiness of all tactical forces in Germany. Huebner's first step was to reopen the Grafenwoehr military training area in May 1947. In that same month, the Strategic Air Command (SAC) of the United States directed that its units begin thirty-day rotations (later shortened to ten-day). Nevertheless, Western ground forces still remained pitifully weak throughout 1947. By the end of the year, the U.S. Army in Germany could point to only one regiment, the Twenty-sixth Regimental Combat Team, with about 3,000 men, as fully combat ready.[4]

Even more so than the communist-inspired coup in Czechoslovakia, the Berlin Blockade by the Soviet Union made 1948 a pivotal year for the military balance in Central Europe. Coupled with the already ongoing efforts of Generals Clay and Huebner, the Blockade spurred the return of American forces to combat readiness. The Western response to the Blockade, the Berlin airlift from June 1948 to May 1949, dramatically illustrated the logistical capability of U.S. and British forces. In addition, President Harry S. Truman decided in 1948 to send two bomber groups to Europe. After the success of the airlift and after almost two years of enhanced training activities, U.S. military leaders in Europe considered their forces no longer a

symbolic deterrent but a vital component of West European defense.[5]

The Berlin airlift led to a much more positive relationship between the United States and the people of Berlin and Western Germany.[6] Before the airlift, American forces had been viewed principally as victors and occupiers; after 276,926 flights had delivered 2.3 million tons of supplies to Berlin, they were seen more as protectors. This dramatic episode in which Allied, but principally American, forces maintained aerial lifelines to the people of beleaguered Berlin may be considered the beginning of the German-American alliance.

THE MILITARIZATION OF NATO

In June 1950, Secretary of State Dean Acheson admitted that NATO defenses were "totally inadequate" while underlining the continued commitment of the United States to a demilitarized Germany. This attitude changed after North Korea attacked South Korea that same month. The Korean War not only generated large increases in the U.S. defense budget, it also had an immediate and fundamental impact on NATO's military posture. The commitment of the United States to the defense of Europe now developed into full-blown military force, conventional as well as nuclear, and the alliance began its evolution into a highly sophisticated and differentiated military organization. By the end of 1950, General Dwight D. Eisenhower had become the first Supreme Allied Commander, Europe (SACEUR), with American and French troops under his command. The United States pledged to maintain at least six divisions in Europe, called for greater contributions by the

---

[3] Hans-Jürgen Schraut, "U.S. Forces in Germany, 1945–1955," in Simon W. Duke and Wolfgang Krieger, eds., *U.S. Military Forces in Europe* (Boulder, Colo., 1993), 153.

[4] Ibid., 161–3.

[5] Ibid., 172. For a detailed analysis of the overestimation of Soviet capabilities before 1948 and the underestimation thereafter, see Phillip A. Karber and Jerald A. Combs, "The United States, NATO, and the Soviet Threat to Western Europe: Military Estimates and Policy Options, 1945–1963," *Diplomatic History* 22 (1998): 399–429.

[6] See the chapter by Diethelm Prowe, vol. 1, Politics.

British and French, and now supported German rearmament. "Forward defense" had arrived.[7]

In September 1950, President Truman announced the reinforcement with four more divisions of the single U.S. Army division in Germany. The Seventh Army and Twelfth Air Force were activated in Germany, and support lines of communication were established running through France. A combined exercise was conducted including EUCOM and French and British air and ground units. The strength of U.S. troops in EUCOM increased from about 80,000 in 1950 to more than 255,000 in 1952.[8] In summer 1952, all five U.S. combat divisions were assigned to NATO's central command, and in the fall of that year the first NATO maneuvers (Exercise Rosebush) were held on German soil, including more than 75,000 U.S. and French troops. By the end of 1952, the West's conventional combat power, though still dwarfed by Soviet capabilities, had significantly improved.[9]

This combat power was boosted in the mid-1950s by the establishment of the German armed forces, the Bundeswehr. With the deepening of the Cold War, the Allies increasingly viewed the Federal Republic as a potentially vital component of Western defense. The initial planning for the West German armed forces had begun in 1950 with a view toward shaping a German contribution to the European Defense Community. Following the failure of this plan, efforts were directed toward organizing forces that would serve under NATO's integrated military command. In May 1955, the Western Allies recognized German sovereignty, ended their occupation regime, and admitted the Federal Republic as a member of NATO.[10]

On January 20, 1956, Chancellor Adenauer greeted the first 1,500 Bundeswehr volunteers and called on them to work with Germany's allies to ensure peace: "The single goal of German rearmament is to contribute to the maintenance of peace."[11] That very same year, German officers were assigned to important positions in the NATO integrated command staffs.[12] From its inception, the German army, the land-forces component of the Bundeswehr, had a target force structure of twelve divisions, to be integrated into the military structure of NATO. From its initial strength of about 1,000 men in January 1956, it grew within a year to 55,000, 100,000 in 1958, 159,000 in 1960, and 252,000 in 1962.[13] By 1965, the activation and outfitting of the twelve German divisions were complete and the units were assigned to NATO.[14]

WESTERN RELIANCE ON NUCLEAR WEAPONS

When Dwight D. Eisenhower was elected president in November 1952, American strategy underwent a revision. Under Eisenhower's "New Look," conventional defense along the lines of the 1952 Lisbon force goals was judged to be simply too expensive. U.S. strategy, therefore, began to rely more heavily on nuclear weapons, to which the doctrine of massive retaliation assigned a tactical as well as strategic role in deterrence.[15]

---

[7] Robert Jervis, "The Impact of the Korean War on the Cold War," *Journal of Conflict Resolution* 24 (1980): 569–81.

[8] Schraut, "U.S. Forces in Germany," 173–4; Daniel J. Nelson, *A History of U.S. Forces in Germany* (Boulder, Colo., 1987), 45.

[9] Schraut, "U.S. Forces in Germany," 176–7.

[10] John A. Reed Jr., *Germany and NATO* (Washington, D.C., 1987), 58–9. For a comprehensive discussion, see Donald Abenheim, *Reforging the Iron Cross: The Search*

for Tradition in the West German Armed Forces (Princeton, N.J., 1988), chaps. 3–5.

[11] Militärgeschichtliches Forschungsamt, ed., *30 Jahre Bundeswehr 1955–1985: Friedenssicherung im Bündnis* (Mainz, 1985), 54; Eric Waldman, *The Goose Step Is Verboten: The German Army Today* (New York, 1964), 97.

[12] Waldman, *Goose Step*, 98.

[13] *30 Jahre Bundeswehr*, 82–6.

[14] Reed, *Germany and NATO*, 61. See Waldman, *Goose Step*, 96, for chronologies of major events in German rearmament and the buildup of the Bundeswehr.

[15] Catherine M. Kelleher, *Germany and the Politics of Nuclear Weapons* (New York, 1975), 16; William P. Mako, *U.S. Ground Forces and the Defense of Central Europe* (Washington, D.C., 1983), 13–6; see also the chapter by Kori Schake in this section.

The deployment of nuclear delivery systems began in 1953 and eventually included more than 7,000 tactical nuclear weapons. In July, artillery units with the dual-capable 8-inch/280-mm "atomic gun" arrived. In September, NATO conducted its first field exercise with simulated tactical nuclear weapons. The following month, Washington announced that tactical nuclear weapons would be used in any major military conflict in Europe. Following the American lead, the North Atlantic Council authorized its military commanders to plan to use tactical nuclear weapons in the event of attack. By year's end, five battalions with a total of twenty guns were deployed in EUCOM, and in spring 1954, the first special-weapons unit designated to maintain control of nuclear warheads arrived in Germany. By summer 1955, six 8-inch battalions and one Corporal battalion, the latter with a range of seventy-five miles and carrying a nuclear warhead with a yield of 20 KT, were assigned to U.S. forces in Europe. In addition, six battalions of Honest John, a low-yield surface-to-surface missile, were deployed in the middle of 1954. In January 1954, SACEUR General Alfred M. Gruenther declared: "We can now use atomic weapons against an aggressor, delivered not only by long-range aircraft but also by the use of shorter range planes, and by 280-mm artillery."[16]

The first clear indication that nuclear weapons were included in NATO's defense of Germany emerged in June 1955 in exercise Carte Blanche. The exercise assumed that 300 to 400 tactical nuclear weapons had exploded between Hamburg and Munich, killing 1.7 million Germans and wounding another 3.5 million. This ignited a tremendous political uproar in Germany. Pacifist and antinuclear groups formed, and the opposition Social Democratic Party argued that Adenauer's policies would lead to nuclear destruction. Nonetheless, Adenauer continued his policy of close ties to the West and to the United States, building the Bundeswehr and supporting U.S. tactical nuclear forces for

the defense of Germany.[17] From this crisis on, two issues would dominate German-American strategic discussions: the ability of Germany to participate in its own nuclear defense and the credibility of the U.S. nuclear guarantee to defend Germany against Soviet attack.

In 1957–60, NATO made itself entirely dependent on the early use of nuclear weapons by thoroughly equipping shield forces with nuclear-capable armament. Germany became fully engaged in this "equipment revolution" as increasingly large portions of the defense budget were devoted to nuclear-capable equipment such as nuclear-strike aircraft, short-range nuclear artillery, and intermediate-range missiles. By 1960, Germany had a high stake in acquiring what would eventually become the second-largest capability in the West for delivering nuclear warheads.[18]

In 1959, the United States began to install Thor and Jupiter missiles in Great Britain, Italy, and Turkey. Capable of striking the Soviet Union from European bases, these intermediate-range ballistic missiles (IRBMs) added another factor to the nuclear debate. Even before initial deployment of Thors and Jupiters was completed, Washington announced that it was reevaluating the original IRBM program; ultimately, the program was canceled altogether because of rapid technological advances in intercontinental ballistic missiles (ICBMs). These developments generated concern in Bonn that the United States would withdraw to North America and barricade itself behind its intercontinental arsenal. In 1960, SACEUR General Lauris Norstad revised plans for Thors and

---

[16] Schraut, "U.S. Forces in Germany," 178–9; William Park, *Defending the West: A History of NATO* (Boulder, Colo., 1986), 30.

[17] Nelson, *History of U.S. Forces in Germany*, 65–6; Kelleher, *Germany and Nuclear Weapons*, 35–43; Schraut, "U.S. Forces in Germany," 179–80. This was followed by a crisis in July 1956 generated by reports that Chairman of the Joint Chiefs Admiral Arthur Radford had called for major changes in U.S. strategic planning that would lead to reliance on the U.S. *strategic* retaliatory capability by the mid-1960s and the reduction of all other forces. As a result, West Germany, although it had renounced the production of nuclear weapons in 1954, now called for NATO to place atomic weapons at Germany's disposal. Kelleher, *Germany and Nuclear Weapons*, 43–8.

[18] Kelleher, *Germany and Nuclear Weapons*, 89.

Jupiters. They would be replaced in 1960–5 with 300 to 600 more modern missiles, fulfilling SACEUR's requirements for medium-range ballistic forces.[19]

These improvements in nuclear capabilities, however, were accompanied by a decline in conventional forces. With France's transfer of four divisions from the Continent to Algeria beginning in 1954 and Great Britain's withdrawal of two divisions following its decision to develop an independent nuclear force, the West had fewer than twenty effective divisions in Europe. By 1958, NATO estimates indicated that the Soviets had 175 divisions, 140 standing divisions (22 in East Germany and Poland and about 80 in the rest of Eastern Europe and western Russia) with a capability of mobilizing 400 divisions in thirty days. Even taking into account the smaller size of the Soviet divisions, the military balance was dramatically unfavorable.[20]

SOVIET MILITARY POWER UNDER STALIN AND KHRUSHCHEV

During the period up to 1953, Stalin and the Soviet military leadership maintained and improved the dramatic conventional superiority of the Soviet military forces in Central Europe. The vanguard of these forces was the thirty Soviet divisions in high readiness deployed in the countries of Eastern Europe, including twenty-two in East Germany (i.e., ten mechanized, eight tank, and four motorized rifle). The Soviet forces in East Germany (Group of Soviet Forces Germany, or GSFG) consisted of six field armies with the supporting Twenty-fourth Air Army and had a strength of about 400,000 men. Behind these, an estimated fifty to sixty divisions stood ready in the western military districts of the Soviet Union. Under Stalin, the firepower and battlefield mobility of divisions had been increased through motorization and reinforcement of their armored elements. The T–52 tank appeared in late 1952, replacing World War

II–vintage tanks. At same time, early-generation jet aircraft were introduced into the Twenty-fourth Air Army in East Germany; by the end of 1952, the 1,700 aircraft in this unit included some 500 MIG-15 jet fighters and 211 IL-28 jet light bombers. The MIG-17, the successor to the MIG-15, was introduced the following year. Similar changes in equipment and training took place in smaller groups of Soviet forces in Poland, Hungary, and Romania.[21]

After the Soviets exploded their first atomic bomb in 1949, most of their efforts to fashion a delivery capability went into systems for Eurasian rather than intercontinental missions. These systems included IL-28 jet light bombers in tactical aviation units, the TU-4 piston medium bombers (copied from the B-29), and later the TU-16 Badger jet medium bomber in long-range aviation units. At the same time, the Soviet Union was developing and deploying medium-range missiles (MRBMs) and IRBMs, suitable primarily for coverage of targets in the NATO European area.

In 1949, the Soviet Union began a military rehabilitation program of the armed forces of East European countries. This involved reorganization along the lines of Soviet doctrine, personnel purges, large infusions of Soviet military officers, and sizable quantities of Soviet arms and equipment. By 1953, these forces numbered around 1.5 million men, or an estimated sixty-five to eighty divisions. Although these changes would later lead to substantial accumulation of military power under Khrushchev, perhaps less than half of the East European forces were good enough to be significant militarily. Until the end of Stalin's reign, the Soviet Union essentially relied on its own forces to carry the burden of defense against the West.

From 1955 to 1964, the Soviet Union undertook four troop reductions to ease tensions, reduce military spending, and free manpower for the Soviet economy. Overall military manpower in the Soviet armed forces dropped from 5.7 million to around 3 million. Nevertheless,

[19] Ibid., 135; Nelson, *History of U.S. Forces in Germany*, 67.

[20] Osgood, *NATO*, 118.

[21] This and the following analysis are based on Thomas F. Wolfe, *Soviet Power and Europe, 1945–1970* (Baltimore, 1970), 39–44, 164–77.

at the outset of the Khrushchev period, the strength of Soviet forces in Europe remained at about 500,000 men. In 1955, Western sources estimated that the entire Soviet ground force numbered 2.5 million, or 175 divisions. Of these, twenty-eight to thirty divisions were believed to be deployed in Eastern Europe, facing NATO forces of less than twenty divisions on the central front. Behind these stood an estimated sixty to seventy divisions in western Russia. About 2,500 tactical aircraft were available in Eastern Europe for support.

By the end of the Khrushchev period in 1964, the overall strength of Soviet forces was estimated to be between 3.1 million and 3.3 million, about 2 million in ground forces, or about 140 divisions, but there was no agreement among Western analysts on how many of these were at full strength. Based on the same three categories of readiness the Soviets used to describe these divisions, Western sources placed about sixty to seventy in the first category (at or near full combat strength), forty to fifty in the second category, and the rest in the category of low-strength cadres. Tactical air estimates were also reduced to 4,000, from around 10,000 in the mid-1950s. A large part of the reduction apparently stemmed from Khrushchev's major military policy shift toward reliance on tactical and medium-range missiles. By 1964, tactical air in East Germany and Poland had fallen to about 1,200.

Numerically, the new estimates presented a military balance not as drastically unfavorable to the West as had been earlier believed. Although in overall manpower the Warsaw Pact's 3 million men outnumbered NATO's 2.2 million, the figure for the Warsaw Pact drops to 1.5 million if one counts only Soviet forces in Eastern Europe. The balance in divisions also looked less discouraging for NATO in 1964. In Central and Northern Europe, NATO had the equivalent of about twenty-five compared to the Soviet Union's twenty-six (i.e., twenty in East Germany, four in Hungary, and two in Poland). Thus, there was relative parity of NATO and Soviet combat-ready divisions in Europe. However, Soviet forces in Eastern Europe were backed up by sixty East European

divisions, of varying loyalty and readiness, and about sixty Soviet divisions in western Russia.

The principal innovation in firepower under Khrushchev was the integration of tactical nuclear weapons within the theater forces down to division level. Delivery systems were mainly rockets and tactical missiles, but also tactical air power, with ranges of 10 to 300 miles. Tanks and armored personnel carriers increased the mobility of divisions. The new T-62 medium tank appeared in 1963, replacing the T-54. The modernization during this period left GSFG with improved combat capabilities as well as shortcomings. At the end of the Khrushchev era in 1964, the GSFG had twenty divisions: ten tank and ten motorized rifle. Critics in the Soviet military argued, however, that the streamlining of these forces for faster operation in a nuclear environment came at the expense of staying power, a potential problem in a protracted campaign.

WESTERN "FLEXIBLE RESPONSE"

After John F. Kennedy's election as president of the United States, the New Look strategy of massive retaliation and the reliance on tactical nuclear weapons for the defense of Europe were replaced with the strategy of "flexible response." In his address to NATO's Military Committee in April 1961, Kennedy said that NATO needed not a new strategy but the achievement of previously determined goals in conventional as well as nuclear strategy. This speech marked the beginning of a six-year debate between the United States on one side and Germany and NATO on the other, culminating in the NATO Defense Planning Committee's adoption of flexible response in 1967.[22]

While publicly supportive, in private almost all German political and military leaders questioned the need for and consequences of the American push for improved conventional capabilities. The Germans resisted, in most cases

[22] Kelleher, *Germany and Nuclear Weapons*, 158; Mako, *U.S. Ground Forces*, 16–20; see the chapter by Kori Schake in this section.

reacting with confusion and bafflement. While criticizing Washington's plans, the Federal Republic did increase the term of conscription from twelve to eighteen months, called up more recruits and reservists, and returned the overall force goal to the original 500,000.[23]

After the public German-American confrontations of 1961–2, the period 1963–6 was marked more by conciliation and reaffirmation. Political and military contacts and consultations increased and were formalized. In September 1963, NATO formally acknowledged the inter-German border as the alliance's first line of defense. Supreme Headquarters, Atlantic Powers in Europe (SHAPE) held that the minimum force needed for this was thirty divisions, equipped with both conventional and nuclear weapons. This estimate was valid only under the assumption that tactical nuclear weapons would be used immediately; a purely conventional defense would require thirty-five to forty divisions.[24]

The changes in strategy during this period were reflected in changes in U.S. conventional troop strength. EUCOM had 323,000 military personnel in 1960, more than 370,000 in 1962, and then only 304,000 in 1967. Of these personnel, 242,000 were stationed on German soil in 1960; the figure reached 280,000 in 1962 and receded to 210,000 by 1968.[25]

In the early 1960s, the Kennedy administration began to consider "dual-basing" military units. Under this concept, units in the United States would reinforce Europe on short notice by means of a massive airlift. The first such exercise, "Big Lift," took place in 1963 and involved 14,983 men and 116 tons of equipment transported to Europe in 63 hours. This demonstration of American technology and commitment to Europe at once boosted German morale but also made Germans wonder whether such operations would be used to justify the redeployment of American forces from Germany to the United States.[26]

With the burdens of the Vietnam War and balance-of-payments problems increasing in the mid-1960s, calls in the United States for a reduction of its forces in Europe grew louder. The first Mansfield Resolution calling for reductions was introduced in the Senate in August 1966, the second in January 1967. On May 2, 1967, after talks among the United States, Great Britain, and West Germany, it was announced that, beginning in early 1968, some 35,000 American troops and four fighter squadrons would be returned to the United States on the dual-basing plan. This was expected to reduce the balance-of-payments deficit by about $75 million annually. Joining with the United States, Britain and France each redeployed 5,000 from Germany.[27]

SOVIET–WARSAW PACT MILITARY POWER
UNDER BREZHNEV–KOSYGIN

Despite important geopolitical factors such as the Vietnam War and Soviet-Chinese tensions, Soviet power in Europe kept its traditional primacy throughout the period of "collective leadership" that began under Leonid Brezhnev and Aleksey Kosygin in 1964. Not only were there large combined arms formations in Eastern Europe but there was also a large Soviet MRBM-IRBM force targeted on NATO Europe, continuing the Pact's redundant capabilities.[28]

In 1964–8, steps were taken to restore general-purpose theater forces to the stature and role they had occupied in the Soviet military before Khrushchev. In 1967, the separate command for ground forces was restored and a new military service law increased the number of youths inducted annually by 30 to 40 percent. The theater Soviet ground strength was 2 million, with 140 divisions, and theater tactical air strength remained constant at 4,000 aircraft. Theater forces in Eastern Europe remained more or less constant from the end of

[23] Kelleher, *Germany and Nuclear Weapons*, 165–6, 168, 172, 174.

[24] Ibid., 203–10.

[25] Nelson, *History of U.S. Forces in Germany*, 81.

[26] Ibid., 69.

[27] Wolfe, *Soviet Power and Europe*, 462; Institute for Strategic Studies, *Strategic Survey, 1968* (London, 1969), 11; see the chapter by Bryan T. van Sweringen in this section.

[28] Wolfe, *Soviet Power and Europe*, 459.

the Khrushchev period in 1964 to the onset of the Czechoslovakia crisis in August 1968. Twenty-six Soviet divisions were outside the Soviet Union, supported by 1,200 tactical aircraft. Most of these – twenty divisions and about 800 aircraft – were stationed in East Germany, the rest in Hungary and Poland. Western sources estimated sixty Soviet divisions in the European Soviet Union, of which twenty-five were considered capable of operations in Europe within two weeks of outbreak of war. The level of MRBM/IRBM launchers remained stable at about 700 in fixed sites.[29]

During this period, the Soviet Union called on the Warsaw Pact to fulfill two roles: first, to assist the Soviet Union in countering NATO militarily; second, to promote and, if necessary, enforce cohesion within the bloc. A very significant feature of Soviet military policy under Brezhnev/Kosygin was the conduct of multinational field training exercises, with at least one major and one lesser exercise each year. After Khrushchev's removal and until the Czech crisis, there were about seventeen joint theater exercises, compared to nine during the entire Khrushchev period.[30]

THE SITUATION IN 1968

On August 21, 1968, the Soviet Union and its allies invaded Czechoslovakia with an estimated twenty to thirty-five divisions, the majority of which were Soviet, assisted by two to four Polish divisions, elements of two to three East German divisions, and less-than-division-size contingents from Hungary and Bulgaria. These ground forces were supported by 400 to 700 tactical and 250 transport aircraft.[31] NATO closely observed the buildup but, seeing no direct threat, adopted no alert measures and flew in no reinforcements. The speed and suc-

cess of the Soviet invasion brought into question NATO's ability to reinforce its forward-deployed forces in Central Europe before they were overwhelmed.

Whether the Soviets had changed the military balance in Europe was hotly debated. At the November 1968 meeting of the NATO Defense Planning Committee, some countries announced nominal measures in response to the Soviet invasion. For example, West Germany agreed to increase its 1969, defense spending by 5.2 percent, and Britain decided to order an extra squadron of Harrier aircraft. However, the meeting produced no significant strengthening of forces.[32] By early 1969, it appeared that the Soviets had withdrawn all but four to five of the divisions that had taken part in the invasion.[33]

As the 1960s drew to a close, a major external factor affected the strategic picture, mental energies, and budget of the United States – the Vietnam War. At the beginning of 1968, the Vietcong and the North Vietnamese launched the Tet Offensive. U.S. troop strength in Vietnam would reach 540,000 troops by year's end, whereas American troop strength in Germany declined to 210,000, the lowest since 1953. The United States' growing involvement in Vietnam exerted a major influence not only on its deployments in Central Europe but more so on the quality and operational readiness of its units, testing the German-American security relationship.[34]

Finally, by late 1968, it was generally recognized that the Soviet Union had reached rough numerical parity in ICBMs with the United States.[35] This fundamental change in the strategic environment raised questions about the commitment of the United States to the defense of Germany and drew more attention to the shortcomings of the West's defensive capabilities in Central Europe.

---

[29] Ibid., 464–8; John Erickson, *Soviet Military Power* (London, 1971), 47.

[30] Wolfe, *Soviet Power and Europe*, 477.

[31] Ibid., 468.

[32] *Strategic Survey, 1968*, 12.

[33] Wolfe, *Soviet Power and Europe*, 468.

[34] See the chapter by T. Michael Ruddy, vol. 2, Security.

[35] *Strategic Survey, 1968*, 1; Erickson, *Soviet Military Power*, 44.

CHAPTER SIX

NATO Strategy and the German–American Relationship

Kori N. Schake

The relationship between the Federal Republic of Germany and the United States was the most important security commitment either state had in the Cold War. This symbiosis was due in large part to the hard facts of the Cold War: The United States was the Western "superpower," whereas Germany was the Western state most exposed to Soviet power and, because of armament restrictions imposed by its allies, unable to defend itself. Neither state could meet its security goals without the other.

This security interdependence was managed primarily within the North Atlantic Treaty Organization (NATO). NATO strategy represented the consensus between the Federal Republic and the United States on the requirements of Western defense. The central strategic questions for NATO from 1945 to 1968 were where to defend Germany, what means to use, and Germany's role in that defense. America's answers to these questions determined in large part the nature of the German–American relationship.

From about the end of World War II until the administration of John F. Kennedy began its new approach in 1961, NATO strategy was responsive to and even driven by German interests. The policies of presidents Harry S. Truman and Dwight D. Eisenhower were designed to revitalize Germany, incorporate it firmly into Western political and military structures, and prevent neutrality from becoming the preferred political option for the West German leadership. Concern that Germany remain voluntarily allied with the West gave the Federal Republic great leverage over NATO strategy, which from 1949 to 1961 aimed to defend Germany as far east as possible and with as much German participation as Chancellor Konrad Adenauer would support.

The Kennedy administration and its successor under Lyndon Johnson, by contrast, took for granted that West Germany's best option was strong defense embedded in Western institutions; they were less willing than previous administrations to allow the Federal Republic to determine the terms and pace of NATO's strategic evolution. Neither the Adenauer government nor its successor under Ludwig Erhard was able to reverse this tide, and the Federal Republic's disappointed expectations created friction in the German-American relationship.

The 1961 Berlin Crisis occasioned a major disagreement over how much NATO should rely on conventional forces to defend Europe. This dispute was not resolved until 1967, and then only uneasily. The Kennedy administration argued that an extended phase of conventional war was necessary to convince the Soviet Union that NATO would escalate to nuclear war. The United States advocated a strategy in which West Germany would be defended only with conventional weapons and with increased German participation, which would require combat throughout German territory. The Federal Republic believed this approach would make war more likely and rightly saw it as a retreat from the commitments of previous administrations influenced by a desire to limit damage to the United States even at increased risk to Germany.

Although the Federal Republic achieved important modifications to the strategy of flexible response, it could not reconcile the divergent positions of France and America. Intransigence over strategy in the 1960s strained the German-American relationship as the Federal Republic tried to avoid choosing between its goals of maintaining the American security commitment and building a European order on the basis of Franco-German cooperation. The United States eventually gained NATO acceptance of flexible response in 1967, but at the cost of West German confidence that a strong defense in NATO alone could make Germany secure.

THE ORIGINAL BARGAIN: FORWARD DEFENSE

The collapse of the 1947 Four-Power foreign ministers' meeting, the 1948 Communist coup in Prague, and the 1948 Soviet blockade of Berlin highlighted the vulnerability of Western Europe to Soviet aggression and the need for an American security commitment. The original NATO bargain was that the United States would remain committed to the defense of Europe and the Europeans would cooperate with each other and develop forms of organization to contribute to their own security.

The U.S. military advocated German rearmament as part of the deal, but Secretary of State Dean Acheson, and even Adenauer, considered it politically impossible in 1949. With European societies still recovering from wartime devastation and Western occupation forces providing the only combat power in the Western sectors of Germany, a territorial defense of Western Europe against the Soviet army was impossible. NATO's first strategy was near-complete reliance on U.S. strategic forces, with Europeans providing "the hard core of ground forces" and tactical aviation.[1] Agreement on this strategy reinforced the German-American relationship

even though the newly formed Federal Republic of Germany played no role in its own defense.

Even before the Korean War, NATO defense planners advocated forward defense and large conventional forces in order to prevent the Warsaw Pact from rapidly overrunning Germany.[2] The first detailed military planning for defense of the NATO area, approved in March 1950, outlined the requirement to "hold the enemy as far to the east in Germany as possible, and by using all offensive and defensive means available." It considered allied airpower, both strategic and tactical, to be "the most efficient offensive means likely to be available at the outbreak of the war." The Federal Republic was seen as "sympathetic towards the allies, but their strategic or political situation will be precarious and their resources may not be available." The plans called for a major expansion of allied military capabilities by 1954 to 90 armored, infantry, and airborne divisions; 8,004 land-based fighter, bomber, and reconnaissance aircraft; 3,264 naval aircraft; 982 major surface combatants; and 107 submarines.[3]

Because NATO members were nowhere near to having these capabilities, the short-term plan traded space for time: NATO troops were to fall back farther into Germany to organize their defenses if they could not hold their positions. In practice, the Federal Republic would not just be a frontline state, it also would be the battlefield for the West's defense or, worse yet, the path of retreat to the Pyrenees for Western forces.

The Korean War highlighted the dangerous gap between NATO capabilities and plans as well as the absence of a structure for defense

---

[1] Defense Committee (hereafter DC) 6/1, The Strategic Concept for the Defense of the North Atlantic Area, Jan. 6, 1950, in North Atlantic Treaty

Organization, *NATO Strategy Documents* (Brussels, 1997) (hereafter *NSD*), 52.

[2] Greg Pedlow, The Evolution of NATO Strategy, 1949–1969, *NSD*, xiv; see also Military Committee (hereafter MC) 14, Strategic Guidance for North Atlantic Regional Planning, Mar. 3, 1950, *NSD*, 69; Christian Greiner, "Die alliierten militärischen Planungen zur Verteidigung Westeuropas 1947–1950," in Militärgeschichtliches Forschungsamt, ed., *Anfänge westdeutscher Sicherheitspolitik 1945–1956*, vol. 1: *Von der Kapitulation bis zum Pleven-Plan* (Munich, 1982), 119–323.

[3] DC 13, North Atlantic Treaty Organization Medium Term Plan, *NSD*, 108, 90, 124.

coordination. In Lisbon in 1952, NATO leaders established a permanent consultative body (the North Atlantic Council), created the post of secretary general, admitted Greece and Turkey as members, and created a standing integrated military command that could collect national forces into a multinational defense. NATO also adopted short-term force goals of 50 combat-ready divisions, 4,000 aircraft, and 704 major naval combat ships. At that time, the alliance countries had only twenty-six divisions; to meet the Lisbon force goals, they would have to nearly double their defense effort.[4] Unquestionably, this would require German rearmament.

Strategically, German rearmament was a welcome development; politically, it remained exceedingly difficult.[5] Some allies were suspicious of American intentions, believing (rightly) that the United States sought to transfer the burden of defending Europe to Germany. European allies wanted German troops without German influence in either the military or the political structures governing their use. The European Defense Community (EDC), which had been developed in 1954 as an independent structure to avoid bringing Germany into NATO, was rejected by the French government because of "a greater fear that the U.S. might in some way back the irredentist aspirations of Germany."[6] The German threat, and the possibility of German-American collusion, remained more salient to some Europeans than the Soviet threat in 1954.

Ironically, the EDC defeat accelerated German rearmament and accession to NATO membership because the Eisenhower administration made continued American participation contingent on a central German role.[7] The London and Paris Agreements ended Germany's occupation and admitted it to NATO. Restrictions on German weapons, with the Brussels Treaty powers as monitors, were carried over from the EDC, clearing the way for German rearmament. With American support, the Federal Republic made a voluntary pledge not to produce nuclear, chemical, or biological weapons. Although there is dispute over Adenauer's assertion that the German pledge was *rebus sic stantibus*, meaning it could be revoked if the circumstances changed, both the Eisenhower and Kennedy administrations understood the German "nonproduction pledge" to be dependent on circumstances. For example, in 1961, Adenauer told Kennedy that a dilution of the U.S. nuclear guarantee to NATO would lead to national nuclear programs, including a German one.[8]

The Adenauer government agreed to raise twelve divisions for the NATO effort, arguing to its wary public that the only way to gain Soviet acquiescence to German unification on Western terms was for the Federal Republic to be a strong and integral member of the West. For aligning the Federal Republic with the West, rearming under its auspices, and restricting its own weapons production, Adenauer gained the long-term presence of American forces, support from the NATO allies for reunification, equal treatment in the alliance, and the West's solidarity in refusing to recognize the German Democratic Republic. American support for Germany created goodwill between the two countries and reflected their similar assessments of European security and military strategy.

[4] The twenty-six-division count does not include Greek and Turkish forces; however, the Lisbon force goals did not account for defending Greek or Turkish territory. See North Atlantic Treaty Organization, *Facts and Figures* (Brussels, 1984), 30.

[5] See the chapter by David Clay Large in this section.

[6] Memorandum by the Second Secretary of the Embassy in France (Herz), Post-Mortem on the Rejection of the EDC Treaty, Sept. 16, 1954, in U.S. Department of State, *Foreign Relations of the United States* (hereafter *FRUS*), *1952–1954*, 5:1094–113, 1112.

[7] Statement by the Secretary of State, Aug. 31, 1954, *FRUS, 1952–1954*, 5:1120–2; Bruno Thoss, "Der Beitritt der Bundesrepublik Deutschland zur WEU und NATO im Spannungsfeld von Blockbildung und Entspannung (1954–1956)," in Militärgeschichtliches Forschungsamt, ed., *Anfänge westdeutscher Sicherheitspolitik 1945–1956*, vol. 3: *Die NATO-Option* (Munich 1993), 1–134; Ernest R. May, "The American Commitment to Germany, 1949–55," *Diplomatic History* 13 (1984): 431–60.

[8] Chancellor Adenauer's visit, Apr. 12–13, 1961, Truman Library, Acheson papers, box 85, State Department and White House Advisor, Apr.-June 1961.

A SWORD/SHIELD STRATEGY

As NATO and the Adenauer government were planning German rearmament, the Eisenhower administration was adjusting U.S. strategy to rely more heavily on nuclear weapons in order to reduce the burden on military forces. This "New Look" extended the division of labor implicit in the original bargain: The Europeans would provide most of the conventional forces, whereas the United States would provide strategic nuclear forces and arm both American and allied forces with substrategic nuclear weapons.[9] Giving nuclear capability to NATO allies made extended deterrence more credible by reducing their dependence on America to cross the nuclear threshold.

In December 1954, NATO approved Military Committee (MC) 48, "The Most Effective Pattern of Military Strength for the Next Few Years," which brought NATO strategy into alignment with American thinking. By incorporating nuclear weapons into NATO military operations, MC 48 intended to provide the military effect of the Lisbon force goals without increasing NATO's conventional forces. Nuclear capability within ground combat units could deter the Warsaw Pact from massing forces for a breakthrough attack by threatening its forces, radar, airfields, ports, and key transshipment points. MC 48 concluded that "the advent of new weapons, *plus* a German contribution . . . will for the first time enable NATO to adopt a real forward strategy with a main line of defense well to the East of the Rhine-Ijssel."[10]

The Supreme Allied Commander in Europe (SACEUR), General Alfred Gruenther, conducted "New Approach" studies to establish the supporting force requirements. He concluded that forward defense required a "shield" of only thirty divisions supported by substrategic nuclear weapons until the United States employed its "sword" of strategic nuclear forces. This would dramatically reduce the forces required by Defense Committee (DC) 6/1 and the Lisbon force goals.[11]

Even as NATO validated the continuing need for German rearmament, two developments almost derailed the process: Carte Blanche and the Radford Plan. Carte Blanche was a NATO exercise designed to test the sword/shield strategy and force structure. It envisioned using 355 nuclear weapons on West German territory to thwart an attack, at the cost of five million casualties. The Radford Plan was an American proposal that used the increased firepower provided by nuclear forces as a way to reduce the personnel of American combat units. Both Carte Blanche and the Radford Plan were reported in the German press and exploited by opponents of Adenauer's policy of strength.[12] As a result, although Adenauer managed to secure Bundestag support for rearmament, the government reduced the size and conscription period for German forces.

Other allies argued for carrying the New Look to its logical conclusion: a "trip wire" or "plate glass window" strategy in which NATO would retain few conventional forces and quickly escalate to nuclear war. The Adenauer government strongly objected to this approach, believing that Germany might be abandoned if the strategy were not carried out, and destroyed if it were. Because Germany had no good choices for strategy in the nuclear age, the Adenauer government stressed deterrence over war fighting. Eisenhower rejected proposals for a new strategy and disengagement of NATO and Warsaw Pact forces on the same grounds — namely, "the effect on Germany and on our

[9] Saki Dockrill, *Eisenhower's "New Look" National Security Policy, 1953–61* (New York, 1996).

[10] MC 48, The Most Effective Pattern of NATO Military Strength for the Next Few Years, *NSD*, 171. See also Klaus A. Maier, "The Federal Republic of Germany as a 'Battlefield' in American Nuclear Strategy, 1953–1955," in Jeffry M. Diefendorf, Axel Frohn, and Hermann-Josef Rupieper, eds., *American Policy and the Reconstruction of West Germany, 1945–1955* (New York, 1993), 395–409.

[11] DEFE 6/26, JP(54)99 (final), Dec. 2, 1954, Public Record Office, London.

[12] David N. Schwartz, *NATO's Nuclear Dilemmas* (Washington, D.C., 1983), 42; Hans-Peter Schwarz, *Adenauer: Der Staatsmann 1952–1967* (Stuttgart, 1991), 290–6; Axel F. Gablik, *Strategische Planungen in der Bundesrepublik Deutschland 1955–1967: Politische Kontrolle oder militärische Notwendigkeit?* (Baden-Baden, 1996), 86–94, 103–6.

friend Adenauer."[13] The United States allowed the Federal Republic to set important parameters for Western strategy, even if they were contrary to American preferences.

THE PAUSE CONCEPT, THE BERLIN CRISIS, AND FLEXIBLE RESPONSE

One of Adenauer's chief concerns was that NATO strategy did not distinguish between local incidents and general war. In 1957, the SACEUR, General Lauris Norstad, adapted NATO strategy to take account of this concern. Norstad's "pause" concept would respond to local incidents with conventional forces, conduct a "brief holding action" with conventional forces to determine Soviet intentions, employ substrategic nuclear capabilities only if necessary to prevent defeat of Western forces, preclude a "limited war" or extended conventional war in Europe, and, for cases of large-scale aggression, retain the integrated conventional/nuclear operations and rapid escalation to strategic nuclear war from the sword/shield strategy.

By defining military responses for a broader range of contingencies, the pause concept introduced the idea of a flexible response to aggression. It restricted conventional operations to responding to local incursions; if the aggressor moved to reinforce, NATO would use substrategic nuclear weapons as part of the shield force. This approach was included in NATO's 1956 political directive guiding military planning, MC 14/2, NATO's overall strategy, and the MC 48 military measures supporting that strategy (which entailed no modification of the levels established by the New Approach studies).[14]

To reinforce the bond between the members of the alliance, the Eisenhower administration in 1957 offered them medium-range ballistic missiles, air-delivered bombs, and nuclear artillery; in 1959, it offered participation in a multilateral nuclear force under SACEUR's control.[15] The Federal Republic accepted deployment of bombs and artillery with the Bundeswehr and participation in the multilateral force. The administration's offers, made to West Germany no differently than to other NATO allies, further reinforced the German-American relationship. Adenauer gained support in the Bundestag with the argument that the Federal Republic needed to be armed with the most modern equipment in order to be an equal partner. NATO strategy was now to defend the Federal Republic at its eastern border using conventional forces if possible but nuclear forces if necessary, with full West German participation in both the conventional and nuclear aspects of alliance defense.

The Kennedy administration's response to the Berlin Crisis established how NATO would conduct the strategy of flexible response for the next six years.[16] The United States embarked on a conventional buildup for Berlin, removed planning authority from SACEUR to civilian analysts in the Defense Department, and stressed an escalating series of conventional responses to Soviet attempts to hinder Western access. Planning envisioned a conventional war involving seven Western divisions – about 140,000 troops – without nuclear weapons.[17] In the course of its planning for Berlin, the Kennedy administration developed the tenets of flexible response: graduated escalation, an expanded range of conventional operations, a clear firebreak between conventional and nuclear action, and centralized political control of military operations.

---

[13] Eisenhower to Anthony Eden, July 27, 1956, as quoted in *FRUS, 1952–1954*, 4:92–3n.7.

[14] C-M(56)138 (final), Directive to the NATO Military Authorities From the North Atlantic Council, Dec. 13, 1956, *NSD*, 198; MC 14/2, Overall Strategic Concept for the Defense of the North Atlantic Treaty Organization Area, *NSD*, 206; MC 48/2, Measures to Implement the Strategic Concept, *NSD*, 230–8. See also Robert Wampler, "Eisenhower, NATO, and Nuclear Weapons: The Strategy and Political Economy of Alliance Security," in Günter Bischof and Stephen E.

Ambrose, eds., *Eisenhower: A Centenary Assessment* (Baton Rouge, La., 1995), 162–90.

[15] Lawrence S. Kaplan, *NATO and the United States* (New York, 1994), 92.

[16] Marc Trachtenberg, *History and Strategy* (Princeton, N.J., 1991), 215–34.

[17] Memorandum from Secretary of Defense McNamara to President Kennedy, Subject: Military Planning for a Possible Berlin Crisis, May 5, 1961, *FRUS, 1961–1963*, 14:61–3.

The NATO allies considered this approach more provocative to the Soviets and less able to protect Western interests.[18] They were never convinced that the Soviet Union, when engaged with more than a hundred thousand troops in a war they had initiated, would accept defeat rather than escalate. The Allies thought the administration's unwillingness to cross the nuclear threshold would limit damage to America while increasing the risk of war and destruction in Europe. They also feared that graduated escalation and removing authority from military commanders would lead to a catastrophic failure of political will in a crisis. They fundamentally did not believe that the approach created a broader range of political choices during a conflict, as the Kennedy administration had claimed. The new strategy seemed to disregard the political implications of Soviet behavior and the difficulty of holding NATO together in crisis and war.

European concerns about the United States seemed justified when the Berlin Wall was constructed in August 1961. The Kennedy administration did not consult with NATO allies on a course of action, but instead sought accommodation with the Soviet Union. The administration's actions during the crisis undercut Adenauer's support and strengthened the claim of the opposition Social Democratic Party (*Sozialdemokratische Partei Deutschlands*, or SPD) that the policy of strength could not make Germany secure.[19]

The Kennedy administration used Berlin as the primary example of the need to change NATO strategy in accord with American thinking. It considered NATO strategy "dangerously rigid," too dependent on the threat of nuclear war, and too responsive to European interests.[20] Contrary to the SACEUR's assessment, the administration believed that the thirty-division sword/shield force could fight a Warsaw Pact force for several weeks without recourse to nuclear weapons and that NATO should develop the capability to fight an even longer conventional war.[21]

The European allies did not support an extended phase of conventional war or the administration's assessment of Soviet and NATO capabilities. The Adenauer government feared the strategy "would convince the Soviets that the United States is afraid of nuclear war and encourage them to engage in limited conventional warfare."[22] From the German perspective, flexible response could produce the worst possible outcome: war in Germany, surrender of territory to the Warsaw Pact, and abandonment by allies unwilling to escalate in a crisis.

Although the Kennedy and Johnson administrations more than doubled the number of tactical nuclear weapons in the NATO inventory, they did not provide a framework for integrating the use of those weapons into NATO operations. The United States canceled programs for sharing control of NATO nuclear forces through the multilateral force and the SACEUR intermediate-range ballistic missile force, withdrew nuclear units along the inner-German border (to increase the survivability of the forces), and introduced locks requiring enabling codes from Washington for American nuclear weapons assigned to NATO. These actions aggravated NATO allies by highlighting their subordinate role in decisions over the use of nuclear weapons stationed on their territory.[23]

Throughout the 1960s, the Kennedy and Johnson administrations pressed European allies to build larger and better-equipped conventional forces so that NATO would not need to

---

[18] Memorandum of Conversation, Subject: Tripartite Meeting on Berlin and Germany, Aug. 5, 1961, *FRUS, 1961–1962*, 14:269–80.

[19] Current Intelligence Weekly Summary, in National Security Archive, ed., *The Berlin Crisis, 1958–1962* (Alexandria, VA., 1991), doc. 02328, Aug. 17, 1961.

[20] Arthur Schlesinger Jr., *A Thousand Days* (Boston, 1965), 382.

[21] Dean Acheson, Review of North Atlantic Problems for the Future, Mar. 1961, John F. Kennedy Library, National Security Files, Regional Security, NATO, box 220.

[22] German defense minister Franz Josef Strauss, quoted in July 12, 1961, Current Intelligence Weekly Summary, in National Security Archive, ed., *The Berlin Crisis, 1958–1962* (Alexandria, VA., 1991), doc. 2139.

[23] Christoph Hoppe, *Zwischen Teilhabe und Mitsprache: Die Nuklearfrage in der Allianzpolitik 1959–1966* (Baden-Baden, 1993).

use nuclear weapons in its defense. The Federal Republic was the only NATO ally that substantially increased its forces, up to the originally planned level of 500,000 troops. The Erhard government wanted to avoid excessive reliance on nuclear forces but also any suggestion that NATO would accept conventional defeat rather than use nuclear weapons in its defense. The Defense Department under Robert McNamara advocated the use of nuclear weapons only "as late as possible," which was unacceptable to many allies, especially France. The Erhard government, seeking middle ground between the Federal Republic's two major allies, succeeded in committing NATO also to the use of nuclear weapons "as early as necessary."[24]

Whereas French-American differences remained intractable and France withdrew from NATO's command structures in 1966, the German changes to flexible response gave enough latitude for other allies to accept the strategy. Even after NATO's adoption of the new strategy in 1967, European governments continued to support the early use of substrategic nuclear weapons and rapid escalation to general war as both the best deterrent to Soviet aggression and the best approach to fighting a war in Europe.

As Europe accepted the inevitability of bringing NATO strategy into line with American thinking, the Federal Republic led efforts to limit the damage of disagreement over strategy and create structures to foster political discourse within NATO. The Germans successfully negotiated for a Nuclear Planning Group, which routinely informed the European allies on United States nuclear forces and strategy.[25] Most importantly, the Federal Republic advocated a review of NATO's future tasks to accompany adoption of the new strategy. The review resulted in the Harmel Report, which established NATO's responsibility for détente as well as deterrence. The Harmel Report restored consensus on NATO's purposes and provided the basis for the alliance's approach to arms control and defense until the end of the Cold War.

The United States' approach to NATO strategy created a major fissure in the German-American relationship that persisted through 1968. The duration and intensity of debate over the strategy of flexible response signaled a transatlantic crisis of confidence. European concerns about military strategy reflected European mistrust of America's political judgment. After the supportive relationship during the Eisenhower years, the approach of the Kennedy and Johnson administrations was a disappointment to the Adenauer and Erhard governments, and the United States never fully regained the Federal Republic's confidence.

[24] Catherine M. Kelleher, *Germany and the Politics of Nuclear Weapons* (New York, 1975), 142.

[25] Helga Haftendorn, *NATO and the Nuclear Revolution: A Crisis of Credibility, 1966–1967* (Oxford, 1996).

CHAPTER SEVEN

German–American Disagreements over Arms-Control Policy

Erhard Forndran

Translated by Richard Sharp

ARMS CONTROL AS AN ELEMENT OF INTERNATIONAL POLITICS

Underlying the concept of disarmament is the notion that the partial or complete elimination of existing or planned arms and armed forces, unilaterally or by treaty, will bring security and peace. Serious doubts have been raised about this optimistic idea.[1] It is impossible for a disarmament treaty to encompass the extremely wide range of military capabilities, the counterargument runs, and monitoring compliance is very difficult. The disarmament process carries an inherent risk of instability, and a disarmed world would not necessarily be a peaceful world. Morover, states' insistence on their sovereignty makes it unlikely that measures restricting their control of their military options – including the decision between war and peace – could be achieved.

It was criticisms like these, in conjunction with attempts to prevent surprise attacks, that gave rise to the concept of arms control.[2] Arms

control is based on the assumption that peace can be safeguarded not by eliminating arms but by controlling them in the interests of stability. Control in this sense means not just ensuring the maintenance of certain previously agreed arrangements but rather dynamically influencing the whole armament process and military and security policy. This approach may well favor disarmament concepts, but it may equally well recommend the acquisition or upgrading of arms – for example, the development of a credible second-strike capability to deter potential surprise attacks. Arms control, then, may not only contribute to the reduction of armaments and armed forces but may also influence the development and production of weaponry and the makeup, geographical distribution, and intended deployment of troops. Arms control involves far more specific fields of policy than disarmament while pursuing a more modest aim: namely, stability.

A necessary consequence of this understanding of arms control is that any analysis of the disagreements between Germany and America in this field must always take account not only of the efforts to bring about disarmament but also of the evolution of military strategy, security policy, and détente. Moreover, Germany's striving for equality, sovereignty, and

[1] Donald G. Brennan, ed., *Arms Control, Disarmament and National Security* (New York, 1961).
[2] For a definition, see Erhard Forndran, "Abrüstung und Rüstungskontrolle," in Karl Dietrich Bracher and Ernst Fraenkel, eds., *Internationale Beziehungen* (Frankfurt am Main, 1969), 9–27; see also Erhard Forndran, *Rüstungskontrolle: Friedenssicherung zwischen Abschreckung und Abrüstung* (Düsseldorf, 1970). For the earlier history, see Bernhard G. Bechhoefer, *Postwar Negotiations for Arms Control* (Washington, D.C., 1961); John W. Spanier and

Joseph L. Nogee, *The Politics of Disarmament* (New York, 1962).

unity often influenced the arms-control policy it pursued.

PROTECTION FROM GERMANY THROUGH COMPLETE DISARMAMENT

One of the central aims of American foreign policy after 1945 was protection against Germany in the future. An important means to this end, set out in the Potsdam Agreement of August 1945,[3] was the "complete disarmament and demilitarisation of Germany and the elimination or control of all German industry that could be used for military production." The United States initially stood by this aim despite its growing irritation at Soviet conduct. In spring 1946, Secretary of State James Byrnes proposed to the Soviet Union and Britain a security pact, to which the United States would also be a party, that would guarantee the disarmament of Germany for twenty-five years.[4] This offer was intended to allay the fears of Germany's neighbors for their safety and, at the same time, to consolidate the power the United States had acquired in continental Europe.[5]

The growing differences with the Soviet Union, which refused Byrnes's offer, changed the United States' position on Germany.[6] The effect was to transform relations between Germany and the United States from hostile confrontation into an unusually close although not entirely conflict-free alliance in just a few years. The subjects of disarmament and arms control were soon to display their potential as sources of conflict. The parallel courses of the different lines of development can be seen in the fact that the offer of an anti-German security pact was still on the table as George F. Kennan's "long telegram" from Moscow in February 1946 and Winston Churchill's speech at Fulton the following month were signaling a fundamental change in East-West relations. With a speech by Byrnes in Stuttgart that September, the United States gave official notice of the reconstruction of the Western zones of Germany. German disarmament moved steadily further down on the list of American objectives.

SECURITY WITH AND FROM GERMANY: ARMS CONTROL THROUGH INTEGRATION

Rapidly deteriorating relations with the Soviet Union soon raised the question of whether the security of the West could be guaranteed without drawing on Germany's military potential. The United States thus faced a policy dilemma. Due allowance for French security concerns,[7] which the United States acknowledged, required careful control over German rearmament. To rule out the possibility of independent Geman military action, accordingly, Germany was to be integrated within the West and was to contribute to the West's military capability. The idea of the complete disarmament of Germany gave way to a plan for integrating its armed forces and militarily important industries. The various integration proposals put forward by France were made only in response to American demands.

[3] The English and Russian versions of the communiqué, each with a German translation, can be found in Bundesminister des Innern, *Dokumente zur Deutschlandpolitik*, ser. 2, vol. 1, pt.3, *Die Konferenz von Potsdam* (Frankfurt am Main, 1992), 2106–7, and, for the Russian text, 2131.

[4] See Proposal by the United States Delegation at the Council of Foreign Ministers, Apr. 30, 1946, in U.S. Department of State, *Foreign Relations of the United States, 1946*, 2:190–3.

[5] See Ernst-Otto Czempiel, *Das amerikanische Sicherheitssystem 1945–1949* (Berlin, 1966).

[6] Hans-Peter Schwarz, *Vom Reich zur Bundesrepublik: Deutschland im Widerstreit der aussenpolitischen Konzeptionen in den Jahren der Besatzungsherrschaft 1945–1949*, 2d ed. (Stuttgart, 1980); Wolfgang Krieger, "Die Deutschlandpolitik der amerikanischen Besatzungsmacht 1943–1949," in Wolfgang-Uwe Friedrich, ed., *Die USA und die Deutsche Frage 1945–1990* (Frankfurt am Main, 1991), 79–104.

[7] See Thomas A. Schwartz, *America's Germany: John J. McCloy and the Federal Republic of Germany* (Cambridge, Mass., 1991), 84–155.

The Petersberg Agreement of November 1949[8] and the founding of the European Coal and Steel Community in April 1951 were manifestations of this form of arms-control policy toward Germany. French fears focused on Germany's heavy industry, which France regarded as the key to the possible rebirth of the German military arsenal. At the same time, though, France recognized that American policy called for Germany to be integrated into the Western community; thus, that old-fashioned power politics geared exclusively to national interest was no longer practicable toward Germany. The new response lay in arms control through political and economic integration, which the United States advocated and Chancellor Konrad Adenauer accepted as a stepping stone toward equality.[9]

This concept also became the foundation of policy on German rearmament.[10] American politicians were concerned about the possible effects on France of German rearmament and, therefore, hesitated to recommend such a step. Nor did they pursue the idea of West German accession to NATO at this time because of French opposition. In July 1950, President Harry S. Truman asked his secretary of state, Dean Acheson, "How can German manpower be used without establishing a German Army?"[11] The answer was provided in October 1950 by the Pleven Plan. The plan, in keeping with the idea of integration, envisioned the creation of a European Defense Community (EDC), and by mid-1951 it had the backing of the American leadership.

GERMANY'S ACCESSION TO NATO AND THE WESTERN INTEREST IN DÉTENTE

After the French National Assembly rejected the EDC Treaty in August 1954, the United States pressed for the early acceptance of the Federal Republic as a member of NATO. Although all members of NATO have equal status, this step, too, was accompanied by arms-control policy measures imposed on the new recruit. The German armed forces were to be fully integrated under the direct control of NATO's decision-making bodies. German accession to the Western European Union (WEU) meant that German rearmament would be strictly monitored to ensure compliance with the ban on producing atomic, biological, and chemical weapons and the restriction on certain types of conventional weapon systems, giving Germany a special status for the purposes of arms control.[12]

With the admission of the Federal Republic to NATO in May 1955, the political landscape underwent a substantial change. The Federal Republic achieved its sovereignty, subject to continuing reserved rights of the Four Powers regarding Germany as a whole. It was, however, allowed freedom of action in foreign policy only within this integrated structure. That freedom was further restricted by the fact that West Germany's security was guaranteed by its allies, especially the United States. For the Western Allies, German reunification ceased to be a central issue now that West Germany's military

---

[8] Horst Lademacher and Walter Mühlhausen, eds., *Sicherheit, Kontrolle, Souveränität: Das Petersberger Abkommen vom 22. November 1949: Eine Dokumentation* (Melsungen, 1985).

[9] See Wolfram Hanrieder, *Die stabile Krise: Ziele und Entscheidungen der bundesrepublikanischen Aussenpolitik 1949–1969* (Düsseldorf, 1971).

[10] Klaus A. Maier, "Die internationalen Auseindandersetzungen um die Westintegration der Bundesrepublik Deutschland und um ihre Bewaffnung im Rahmen der Europäischen Verteidigungsgemeinschaft," in Militärgeschichtliches Forschungsamt, ed., *Anfänge westdeutscher Sicherheitspolitik 1945–1956*, vol. 2: *Die EVG-Phase* (Munich, 1990), 1–234; see also the chapter by David Clay Large in this section.

[11] Schwartz, *America's Germany*, 129; see also Paul Noack, *Deutsche Aussenpolitik seit 1945* (Stuttgart, 1972), 36.

[12] See Aufzeichnung des Amtes Blank, Abt. 2, Nov. 9, 1954, in Klaus A. Maier and Bruno Thoss, eds., *Westintegration, Sicherheit und deutsche Frage: Quellen zur Aussenpolitik in der Ära Adenauer 1949–1963* (Darmstadt, 1994) [hereafter *WSDF*], 155–9; Bruno Thoss, "Der Beitritt der Bundesrepublik Deutschland zur WEU und NATO im Spannungsfeld von Blockbildung und Entspannung (1954–1956)," in Militärgeschichtliches Forschungsamt, ed., *Anfänge westdeutscher Sicherheitspolitik*, vol. 3: *Die NATO-Option*, 1–234.

potential was securely in the hands of NATO. Gradually, they grew more interested in stable relations with the Soviet Union. In this first phase of the policy of détente, it became clear what sorts of shared interests and limited co-operation would be possible between the two superpowers in the future despite their continuing hostility. Arms-control policy became increasingly important. This trend was of consequence for German–American relations because in Bonn's view, the issues of Germany's standing as an equal within the Western community, German security, and reunification had to take precedence over or at least remain closely linked to the policies of détente and disarmament. The result was that disagreements between Washington and Bonn extended into the field of arms control.

The Western interest in détente was already apparent in the invitations to attend the 1955 summit. The German question was no longer mentioned. More disturbing still to the German leadership were the Western arms-control proposals because they seemed to jeopardize Germany's security and affiliation with the West. Among the proposals was the Eden Plan,[13] which in its revised form assumed the unity of Germany but cast doubt on its newly achieved integration by suggesting a demilitarized zone between East and West. Adenauer was particularly alarmed when the American president referred to the possibility of a neutral *cordon sanitaire* including Germany.[14] This opened the way to the disengagement controversy of the years that followed.

In addition to this issue, the question of Germany's future civilian and military uses of nuclear power also played an important part.[15] The Germans saw the peaceful use of atomic energy as indispensable not only on account of their economic and technological interests but also, in the longer term, for reasons of security policy. The German renunciation of national nuclear weapons, both in the context of the EDC agreements and in Adenauer's declaration in the negotiations with the Western powers in 1954, was not voluntary and never unambiguously represented total abandonment of a German nuclear option. Nuclear weapons under German control were, of course, incompatible with the allies' notions of stability. A German share in the West's nuclear weapons and voice in decisions on their use were, on the other hand, conceivable.[16]

THE DEBATE ON MILITARY STRATEGY AND DISENGAGEMENT

As American policy sought a change in military strategy and the composition of the armed forces,[17] German misgivings deepened. What was known as the Radford Plan[18] envisaged a dramatic reduction in the United States' conventional armed forces in favor of an increased nuclear strike force and signaled the transition from defense to deterrence. The plan had an arms-control dimension: Its aim was deterrence by means of a new deployment of weapons. It did not, however, address the question of how modern conventional weapons – in particular those of the Bundeswehr, the Federal Republic's new army – and the integration of nuclear weapons into the existing military structures and strategic planning could effectively be

Küntzel, *Bonn und die Bombe: Deutsche Atompolitik von Adenauer bis Brandt* (Frankfurt am Main, 1992).

[13] See Hermann Volle and Claus Jürgen Duisburg, *Probleme der internationalen Abrüstung: die Bemühungen der Vereinten Nationen um internationale Abrüstung und Sicherheit 1945–1961*, 2 vols. (Frankfurt am Main, 1964), 1:101–3.

[14] See Konrad Adenauer, *Erinnerungen 1953–1955* (Frankfurt am Main, 1968), 445–50.

[15] See Peter Fischer, *Atomenergie und staatliches Interesse: Die Anfänge der Atompolitik in der Bundesrepublik Deutschland 1949–1955* (Baden-Baden, 1994); Matthias

[16] See Peter Fischer, "Das Projekt einer trilateralen Nuklearkooperation: Französisch-deutsch-italienische Geheimverhandlungen 1957–1958," *Historisches Jahrbuch der Görres-Gesellschaft* 112 (1992): 143–56; Hans-Peter Schwarz, "Adenauer und die Kernwaffen," *Vierteljahrshefte für Zeitgeschichte* 37 (1989): 567–95.

[17] See the chapter by Kori Schake in this section.

[18] For Adenauer's evaluation of the plan, see Protokoll des CDU-Bundesvorstandes, Sept. 20, 1956, *WSDF*, 230–1.

combined.[19] The need for stability played an even more fundamental role because the credibility of the American guarantee of German security was open to question. In the event of war, American policy had to view any form of containment as desirable, even the use of nuclear weapons on German soil. But the Germans could accept the theory of massive retaliation only if war could be completely excluded. This dilemma was to influence German opinions on Western arms-control policy repeatedly. The Radford Plan carried the threat, in Adenauer's view, of a security policy that would isolate Germany, and it revived German interest in a military nuclear option. During the administrations of John F. Kennedy and Lyndon B. Johnson, this interest would lead to the project for a multilateral nuclear force.

The disengagement debate took place parallel to this controversy among the Western nations. It centered on the idea of dissolving the alliances and creating a nuclear weapon-free zone that would include Germany. For Adenauer, these ideas amounted to a revised version of the neutralization proposals based on the status quo, an impediment to Germany's equal standing within the Western camp, and a dangerous reduction in German security.[20] His position clearly reflected a dilemma faced by German policy. Unification could be achieved only amid a general détente and hence an agreed arms-control policy between the two blocs. That carried the danger that the victorious powers would strike a balance of interests at the expense of the Federal Republic. On the other hand, Germany could not oppose Western proposals for disarmament or arms control without raising the specter of isolation.[21] German policy had to attempt to influence the arms-control proposals in a way that took due account of the Federal Republic's own security and efforts for reunification. But because

these aims were at odds with arms control, Adenauer had to decide in favor of one or the other. He rejected the various disengagement proposals – such as the Rapacki Plan for a nuclear weapons-free zone in Central Europe[22] – while the question being discussed in the Western capitals was whether disengagement might not indeed offer a way of loosening Moscow's control over the Eastern European states and ultimately of changing the situation in Central Europe. Because of Adenauer's dismissive attitude toward these proposals, shared by the American secretary of state, and ultimately because of the renewed escalation of the East-West conflict, nothing came of them.

THE CHANGE IN AMERICAN STRATEGY AND
THE POLICY OF DÉTENTE

When the Kennedy administration took office, arms-control theory was recognized by policymakers for the first time as an essential foundation of foreign policy. Conscious application of arms-control theory had a direct effect on German-American relations in several instances.[23] The starting point for the realignment of American policy was the understanding of the nuclear stalemate that had arisen between East and West: The United States, too, had now become vulnerable, especially because current strategy meant that in the event of even a limited attack from the East, American presidents would face the unattractive choice between capitulation and the use of nuclear weapons.[24] Under President Kennedy, therefore, the United States moved away from the concept of massive retaliation in favor of the strategy of

---

[19] Christian Greiner, "Die militärische Eingliederung der Bundesrepublik Deutschland in die WEU und die NATO 1954–1957," in Militärgeschichtliches Forschungsamt, ed., Anfänge westdeutscher Sicherheitspolitik, vol. 3: Die NATO-Option, 561–850.

[20] See Stellungnahme Adenauers vor dem CDU-Bundesvorstand, June 3, 1955, WSDF, 192–4.

[21] See Schreiben von Brentanos an den Bundeskanzler, Mar. 28, 1956, WSDF, 228.

[22] See Volle and Duisburg, Probleme der internationalen Abrüstung, 1:201–2, 2:644–51.

[23] For a general account of this period, see Ernst-Otto Czempiel, "Auf der Suche nach neuen Wegen: Die deutsch-amerikanischen Beziehungen 1961–1969," in Wolfgang-Uwe Friedrich, ed., Die USA und die Deutsche Frage 1945–1990 (Frankfurt am Main, 1991), 167–93, esp. 177–93.

[24] This was particularly emphasized by Maxwell D. Taylor, The Uncertain Trumpet (New York, 1960); see also Henry Kissinger, The Troubled Partnership (New York, 1965).

flexible response, which depended less on nuclear weapons and more on the reinforcement of the West's conventional capabilities. This undermined the credibility of the American deterrent all the more, however, because it strongly suggested to the Europeans that the United States had abandoned its automatic nuclear defense of Western Europe.

The German government rejected the change of strategy.[25] The lines of argument adopted in the disagreement over the Radford Plan had now been reversed. Kennedy pointed out that, on the basis of stability criteria, a deterrent based entirely on nuclear weapons was of questionable credibility despite the simultaneous move to develop a second-strike capability and that conventional armament was unavoidable. To the Germans, this meant that a war waged with conventional weapons was once again becoming more likely. This was a logical dilemma of applied arms-control policy.

Arms-control policy affected a second area of German-American relations in the early 1960s. Kennedy was striving for constructive relations between East and West; arms control offered one possible way of achieving them. The Kennedy administration assumed that a policy of détente that might eventually pave the way to a change in the situation in Central Europe would only be possible on the basis of recognition of the status quo in Europe – and, therefore, at least temporary recognition of the division of Germany as well. Adenauer opposed this view because he assumed that the German question would become a secondary issue. In fact, the Kennedy administration considered any progress on this issue to be impossible for the present; its aim for the time being, therefore, was to prevent any deterioration in the status quo. Confronted by this attitude on the part of the Americans, the Germans increasingly came to fear that the Soviet Union would be given greater freedom to intervene in the affairs of the Western alliance. Adenauer thus continued to have considerable reservations about arms-control policy. There were, however, some in the Christian Democratic Party

(including Foreign Minister Gerhard Schröder), the Free Democratic Party, and the opposition Social Democratic Party who went over to the American line.[26]

German policy was also caught between differing American and French policy positions. President Charles de Gaulle of France rejected Washington's renewed claim to leadership and argued that only a national nuclear option could guarantee a credible nuclear deterrent. This argument had serious consequences for Germany. One was that Germany's call for nuclear weapons of its own now seemed justified. This fact caused friction in the area of arms control. The 1963 Nuclear Test Ban Treaty – which affected the Federal Republic only indirectly in that East Germany's standing was enhanced by having signed – made clear the dilemma of West Germany's position between France, which rejected the treaty, and the United States, which wanted the Federal Republic to sign. On the other hand, the conflict between French and American policy caused Washington to worry that the Federal Republic might side with France. The American government, therefore, could not simply disregard Germany's interests. The result of Germany's intervention, then, was that Washington did not go along with Moscow's desire to conclude a nonaggression pact between East and West at the same time as the test ban treaty.

THE MLF PROJECT AND THE NATO CRISIS

Arms control influenced German-American relations in a third instance during this period. The Kennedy administration tried to meet German demands for a more credible nuclear shield by proposing the concept of a sea-based multilateral force (MLF), an idea that had been advanced under President Dwight D. Eisenhower in the form of a land-based European nuclear force. The MLF was primarily a political instrument for the integration of the Western

---

[25] See Konrad Adenauer, *Erinnerungen 1959–1963: Fragmente* (Frankfurt am Main, 1970), 90–8.

[26] See Waldemar Besson, *Die Aussenpolitik der Bundesrepublik: Erfahrung und Massstäbe* (Munich, 1970), 296–303.

European Union.[27] It was a response to the French criticism of the American deterrent guarantee and the French attempts to establish a nuclear triumvirate consisting of the United States, Britain, and France. That idea would have allowed a European defense structure as a counterweight to the United States. It was not, however, in Germany's interest because it compromised West Germany's equal status and security by excluding it from the "nuclear club." Despite all their criticisms of Kennedy's policy, therefore, German policymakers endorsed the MLF project.[28] In theory, the participants were to be equal partners of the United States but in practice, the Americans were unwilling to relinquish their powers of decision. The plan, therefore, offered little beyond a "more acceptable form of American nuclear hegemony."[29] What is not clear in this context is whether Adenauer and his defense minister, Franz Josef Strauss, committed themselves to this project in order to secure German access to nuclear weapons.

The MLF plan ultimately came to nothing because of a conflict of aims within American arms-control policy. Since taking office, the Kennedy administration had tried to reach an agreement with the Soviet Union on the nonproliferation of nuclear weapons. The MLF plan ran counter to this aim. When the Soviet Union indicated it was prepared to negotiate seriously on nonproliferation, President Johnson let the MLF project drop in December 1964.[30] The aim of nonproliferation, rooted in arms-control policy, required an agreement with the Soviet Union even at the cost of an abrupt snub to the Federal Republic.

As an alternative, U.S. Secretary of Defense Robert McNamara proposed to his NATO colleagues in May 1965 the formation of a consultative committee that would keep the partners in the alliance informed of and involved in planning for nuclear deployment, including the deployment of strategic nuclear weapons.[31] The hope was that increased European involvement in the nuclear decision process, especially in the planning of targets and deployment, would counteract the efforts of other European states to acquire their own nuclear weapons. In 1966, after difficult negotiations – which eventually led to a major conflict with France – these proposals resulted in the Nuclear Planning Group (NPG). There were seven member states: four permanent members (the United States, Britain, Germany, and Italy) and three members chosen in rotation from the other interested allies. Although the NPG has often been regarded only as a watered-down substitute for the MLF or national control over nuclear weapons, it nevertheless developed into a body in which the differences between the strategic concepts of the United States and those of its European allies were gradually smoothed over.

For the Federal Republic, the alliance's adoption of the flexible-response strategy,[32] which was decided on in 1967 and was partly justified by arms-control policy, posed a further challenge to security policy. The new strategy conflicted with Germany's desire for a clear-cut automatic mechanism of escalation in response to an attack. Here, the interests of the United States and the Federal Republic failed to coincide. Even arms control was unable to solve the alliance's nuclear problem.

THE NONPROLIFERATION OF NUCLEAR WEAPONS

American interest in the nonproliferation of nuclear weapons became a central point of conflict

[27] See Christoph Hoppe, *Zwischen Teilhabe und Mitsprache: Die Nuklearfrage in der Allianzpolitik 1959–1966* (Baden-Baden, 1993); see also Catherine M. Kelleher, *Germany and the Politics of Nuclear Weapons* (New York, 1975); Dieter Mahncke, *Nukleare Mitwirkung* (Berlin, 1972).

[28] See Presseerklärung des Staatssekretärs von Hase, Jan. 14, 1963, *WSDF*, 312–13.

[29] Besson, *Aussenpolitik der Bundesrepublik*, 319.

[30] For background, see Hanrieder, *Stabile Krise*, 39.

[31] See Helga Haftendorn, *NATO and the Nuclear Revolution: A Crisis of Credibility, 1966–1967* (Oxford and New York, 1996).

[32] See Helga Haftendorn, "Entstehung und Bedeutung des Harmel-Berichtes der NATO von 1967," *Vierteljahrshefte für Zeitgeschichte* 40 (1992): 169–221.

in German-American relations. In 1965, negotiations began on a treaty that would require the Federal Republic to renounce nuclear weapons conclusively.[33] The Soviet Union used these negotiations as an opportunity to depict the Federal Republic as the major troublemaker in East-West relations. As the negotiations progressed, the United States did steadily less to defend its ally against these charges.[34] Germany seemed in danger of isolation. The Americans hardly informed Bonn on the progress of the negotiations, which created the impression in Germany that the Federal Republic would be forced to sign as result of American-Soviet collusion. Moreover, the first drafts of the agreement made it clear just how great the imbalance would be between the obligations of those states that had nuclear weapons and those that did not. Criticism from Germany did persuade the Americans in spring 1967 to adjourn the negotiations and consult with their allies, especially on the planned control mechanisms, but that did nothing to change the demand that Bonn renounce a military nuclear capability. For the Federal Republic, there was even more at stake: Arms-control policy clearly showed that the two superpowers were interested in a cooperative arrangement that would affect German reunification, equality, and sovereignty.

Faced with this situation, the government of Ludwig Erhard set itself four objectives: German renunciation of nuclear weapons must bring progress toward reunification, allow for German participation in any future multilateral nuclear force, involve Germany more deeply in the alliance's nuclear planning, and keep open the option of a European nuclear force.[35] The Christian Democratic–Social Democratic Grand Coalition government under Erhard's successor, Kurt Georg Kiesinger, had to abandon the first two of these objectives because, first, the linking of reunification to arms control had ceased to enjoy American support since the late 1950s and, second, there could be no reviving of the MLF. On the other two issues, however, the Grand Coalition aligned itself with a phalanx of other non-nuclear states that wanted to reduce existing nuclear capabilities, ensure the future of nuclear energy for peaceful purposes, and maintain due regard for existing control mechanisms. This aided Bonn vis-à-vis Washington. As a result, the inspection issue was ultimately resolved as Germany had wished: The European Atomic Energy Community (EURATOM) was empowered to inspect its own members. The "European" nuclear option, including German participation, was also kept open.[36] Nonetheless, the Federal Republic had to develop a new policy position of its own as a medium-sized state without nuclear ambitions if it did not want to cut itself off from the further development of détente. This view remained highly controversial in domestic politics during the period of the Grand Coalition,[37] and only when the Social-Liberal coalition under Willy Brandt came to power did West Germany sign the Nonproliferation Treaty. By doing so, Germany succeeded in relieving the strain arms control had imposed on German-American relations during the 1960s. The Federal Republic fell into line with both détente and arms-control policy.

---

[33] See Erwin Häckel, *Die Bundesrepublik Deutschland und der Atomwaffensperrvertrag* (Bonn, 1989); Beate Kohler, *Der Vertrag über die Nichtverbreitung von Kernwaffen und das Problem der Sicherheitsgarantien* (Frankfurt am Main, 1972); Johannes Preisinger, *Deutschland und die nukleare Nichtverbreitung: Zwischenbilanz und Ausblick* (Bonn, 1993); Glenn T. Seaborg and Benjamin Loeb, *Stemming the Tide: Arms Control in the Johnson Years* (Lexington, Mass., 1989); Mohamed J. Shaker, *The Nuclear Nonproliferation Treaty: Origin and Implementation, 1959–1979* (London, 1980).

[34] See Erhard Forndran, *Probleme der internationalen Abrüstung* (Frankfurt am Main, 1970), 183–5, 257–86.

[35] See Theo Sommer, "Bonn Changes Course," *Foreign Affairs* 45 (1967): 477–91, esp. 482–6.

[36] See Küntzel, *Bonn und die Bombe*, 214–17, 240–2, 250–2.

[37] Klaus Hildebrand, *Von Erhard zur Grossen Koalition 1963–1969* (Stuttgart, 1984), 310–14.

CHAPTER EIGHT

The Origins of Intelligence Cooperation Between the United States and West Germany

Wesley K. Wark

The nature of intelligence cooperation between nation-states remains one of the most closely guarded of secrets. Nevertheless, the secret underside of alliance systems bears study for what it reveals of common perceptions of threats, degrees of mutual trust and confidence, the development of mechanisms for information exchange, and the status of intelligence within the partner states. Despite the secrecy that surrounds the subject, inspection of the inner workings of intelligence relationships can provide insight into broader patterns of cooperation.

Intelligence alliances were a prominent feature of the Cold War and the "wrestler's embrace" between the United States and the Soviet Union.[1] Such alliances reached paradigmatic status in the British-American "special relationship," which provided for a wide-ranging and institutionalized exchange of even the most secret and sensitive data.[2] But the British-American intelligence alliance was forged in the fires of World War II and functioned within a shared Atlanticist culture. By contrast, intelligence cooperation between the United States and Germany had very different origins; its history testifies to the chemistry of accident and necessity.

When American occupation forces began their work amidst the ruins of the Third Reich

in May 1945, the idea of future cooperation between the intelligence services of the United States and a restored German government was unimagined and unimaginable. The intelligence agencies of the Third Reich lay, like the system they served, in ruins. Apart from being ground under by military defeat, Nazi intelligence had suffered from intense internecine warfare, which peaked in the final year of the conflict. Victory by the SS in this internal struggle had only intensified the collapse of the Reich's intelligence function.[3]

The situation was little better in the United States, although for quite different reasons. The United States was unique among twentieth-century great powers in having no real tradition of peacetime intelligence-gathering. Under the pressures of budgetary rollback, demobilization, and public unease about the maintenance of an "American Gestapo," President Harry S. Truman in September 1945 authorized the wholesale dismantling of the Office of Strategic Services (OSS).[4] The OSS had been one of the pillars of American wartime intelligence and its

---

[1] Thomas Powers, "The Truth About the CIA," *New York Review of Books*, May 13, 1995, 55.

[2] Jeffrey T. Richelson and Desmond Ball, *The Ties that Bind*, 2d ed. (Boston, 1990).

[3] David Kahn, *Hitler's Spies: German Military Intelligence in World War Two* (New York, 1978), 61–2. For a brilliant analysis of the structures of German intelligence on the eve of World War II, see Michael Geyer, "National Socialist Germany: The Politics of Information," in Ernest R. May, ed., *Knowing One's Enemies: Intelligence Assessment Before the Two World Wars* (Princeton, N.J., 1984), 310–46.

[4] For a comprehensive study of the demise of the OSS, see Thomas Troy, *Donovan and the CIA: A History of the*

chief, General William Donovan, had argued relentlessly for the agency's survival as the nucleus of a peacetime intelligence community in the United States.

The dissolution of the OSS also meant the departure from the scene, at least temporarily, of one of America's few intelligence professionals at the time: Allen Dulles. Dulles had been at the forefront of wartime OSS intelligence-gathering on Germany from his outpost in Bern, Switzerland. He was the natural choice to head the OSS's postwar "German unit." But Dulles had only three short months to build up a postwar intelligence system in occupied Germany before the OSS was dissolved and he headed back to his law practice.[5]

Seen, then, from the vantage point of late 1945, there was simply no reason to give any consideration to the prospect of future German-American cooperation in the field of intelligence. Soon after 1945, however, two circumstances quickly emerged that forced a process of imagining the unimaginable. One was the growing American apprehension about Soviet policies and aims in Europe and elsewhere. The other was the self-proclaimed mission of a dedicated German intelligence professional, General Reinhard Gehlen.

The emerging Cold War proved fertile ground for Gehlen, the former chief of *Fremde Heere Ost* (FHO), the German army's intelligence operations on the Eastern front. More than any other individual, Gehlen shaped the postwar fortunes of German intelligence and its relations with the United States. He also attempted to shape the historical portrayal of his achievements.[6]

Gehlen tells his story dramatically and with overtones of classical myth. He appears as a kind of prophet or magical figure who descends from his mountain stronghold at the end of the war to offer his unique wisdom and insight into the realities of Soviet power. He told his American captors that he had kept a nucleus of his intelligence staff alive and together and that they had stashed away in the Bavarian Alps an important archive of intelligence documents on the fighting in the East. Gehlen laced this information with his own political reading of the current situation facing the Americans. He emphasized that "the collapse of the East-West alliance could only be a matter of time; a conflict of interests was bound to break out between East and West and this would jeopardize the safety of Europe and of the United States."[7]

Gehlen's message fell on fertile ground. The U.S. Army agreed to collect his staff together, bring in the stashed material, and send the Germans and their documents to Washington for detailed debriefing and study. Gehlen's small group (five former FHO officers, including himself) was kept in conditions of semicaptivity at Fort Hunt, Virginia, from September 1945 to June 1946. Much of that time was taken up with detailed debriefings, then with research work directed by U.S. military intelligence and using the Gehlen team's analysis of captured documents.[8]

At the same time, Soviet-American relations were cooling rapidly after the public confrontation in March 1946 over the Soviet presence in Iran[9] and the war scare over Turkey later the

Establishment of the Central Intelligence Agency (Frederick, Md., 1981).

[5] Neal H. Petersen, "From Hitler's Doorstep: Allen Dulles and the Penetration of Germany," in George C. Chalou, ed., *The Secrets War: The Office of Strategic Services in World War II* (Washington, D.C., 1992); Peter Grose, *Gentleman Spy: The Life of Allen Dulles* (Boston, 1994); Christof Mauch, *Schattenkrieg gegen Hitler: Das Dritte Reich im Visier der amerikanischen Geheimdienste* (Stuttgart, 1999).

[6] The major sources for this story are Reinhard Gehlen, *The Service: The Memoirs of General Reinhard*

Gehlen, trans. David Irving (New York, 1972); Heinz Hohne and Hermann Zolling, *Network: The Truth About General Gehlen and His Spy Ring* (London, 1972); Zachary Karabell, "Die frühen Jahre der CIA in Deutschland," in Wolfgang Krieger and Jürgen Weber, eds., *Spionage für den Frieden? Nachrichtendienste in Deutschland während des Kalten Krieges* (Munich, 1997), 71–86; Mary Ellen Reese, *General Reinhard Gehlen: The CIA Connection* (Fairfax, Va., 1990).

[7] Gehlen, *The Service*, 9.

[8] Hohne and Zolling, *Network*, 62–3.

[9] Bruce Robert Kuniholm, *The Origins of the Cold War in the Near East* (Princeton, N.J., 1980), chap. 5.

same year.[10] These regional tensions rebounded on the situation in Central Europe. The Gehlen group soon became part of the United States' re-mobilized intelligence effort against the Soviet Union.[11] The American initiatives were driven by need and opportunism. There was, in the be-ginning, no long-range plan, no grand strategy for an intelligence contest with the Soviets, and very few resources. The Gehlen group was now available to fill the vacuum left by the end of the Allen Dulles operation in fall 1945. And so the inmates of Fort Hunt were returned to Ger-many in June 1946 and established under U.S. Army control at Camp King in Oberusel.

For a period of ten years (June 1946–March 1956), the Gehlen organization, as it came to be called, operated under the direct con-trol of the U.S. authorities – first the army and then, after 1949, the Central Intelligence Agency (CIA). Expansion was rapid, marked by a move to larger, self-contained premises at Pullach, Bavaria, in December 1947. The Gehlen organization soon began to take on operational intelligence-gathering and counter-espionage missions. Its most significant oper-ation was probably Hermes, which involved a massive effort to collect and collate intelli-gence from the debriefing of former German POWs and refugees returning from the So-viet Union and Eastern Europe.[12] The potential of the Gehlen organization to provide insights into the intelligence services of the Soviet-bloc countries was demonstrated by Operation Bo-hemia in 1949, which managed the defection of two senior Czech intelligence officers to West Germany.[13] This led to the destruction of a Czech spy ring operating in West Germany and was the Gehlen organization's first demonstrable counter-intelligence success.

Incorporating the Gehlen organization into the architecture of American Cold War intelli-gence led to inevitable friction. On the German side, the early priorities for the Gehlen organi-zation were fiscal stability and a maximum of operational authority and independence. Such goals clashed with American imperatives, which were to extract maximum value for money, to ensure a monopoly over the uses of the acquired intelligence, and to certify the security and gen-uineness of German intelligence-gathering op-erations. American officials, therefore, resisted any efforts by Gehlen to erect a wall of secrecy between German intelligence and themselves. Struggle over this issue reached a peak when the CIA began to assume responsibility for the Gehlen organization in 1949. The first chief of the CIA's liaison staff at Pullach, James Critch-field, drove a hard bargain, insisting on full access to the operational details of the Gehlen organi-zation's spy networks. Eventually, a compromise was reached in which the CIA was given access to the names of the top 150 agents employed by Gehlen. In addition, the CIA would receive all reports prepared by the German service, and CIA officers would act as liaisons to each of the Gehlen organization's main departments.[14] In bringing this arrangement to pass, the CIA quite openly deployed the power of the purse.

The CIA maintained budgetary and opera-tional control over the Gehlen organization un-til April 1, 1956, when the organization was transferred to the control of the federal govern-ment of West Germany and renamed the *Bun-desnachrichtendienst* (BND, Federal Intelligence Service). The transfer of authority profoundly changed the nature of the intelligence link-ages between postwar Germany and the United States. Up to that point, the semisovereign status of the new German state had dictated the sub-ordination of German intelligence to American control. After joining NATO in 1955, however,

---

[10] Eduard Mark, "The War Scare of 1946 and Its Con-sequences," *Diplomatic History* 21 (1997): 383–415.

[11] On the origins of U.S. intelligence in the early Cold War period, see Christopher Andrew, *For the Pres-ident's Eyes Only: Secret Intelligence and the American Presi-dency from Washington to Bush* (New York, 1995), chap. 5; Trevor Barnes, "The Secret Cold War: The C.I.A. and American Foreign Policy in Europe, 1946–1956," pts. 1 and 2, *Historical Journal* 24 (1981): 399–415; 25 (1982): 649–70. See also Rhodri Jeffreys-Jones, "Why Was the CIA Established in 1947?" *Intelligence and National Secu-rity* 12 (1997): 21–40.

[12] For brief accounts of Operation Hermes, see Hohne and Zolling, *Network*, 77; and Karabell, *Die frühen Jahre*, 73–4.

[13] Gehlen, *The Service*, 142.

[14] Reese, *General Reinhard Gehlen*, 108–11.

the Federal Republic was able to strengthen its sovereignty; accordingly, the BND now reported not to the CIA but to the federal chancellor. Although the intelligence relationship with the United States remained a top priority for the German service, it was diffused through the integration of the BND into the NATO intelligence system. To mark its sovereign status and increasing interest in global issues beyond the East German frontier, the BND also began to develop its own bilateral relationships with a number of other foreign intelligence services, including those of Switzerland, Israel, and Egypt.[15]

A noticeable veil conceals the subject of the German-American intelligence partnership after 1956. As one American scholar has noted, the centrality of intelligence liaisons in American intelligence "has been matched only by the effectiveness with which that key role has been kept secret, during the Cold War and since."[16] Gehlen's memoirs are full of details about his relationship with the American authorities prior to 1956 but are extremely guarded about the new landscape of intelligence sharing thereafter. Instead, he offers a sugary maxim:

Since late 1950 the attitude of our American friends towards the future of the Gehlen organization had undergone a remarkable change.... By various means they [the CIA] prevailed on their other allies to accept at government level what had formerly been an American-controlled agency. The expectation was that my organization would continue to work in close collaboration with the Western Allies; and the CIA was convinced that this helpfulness on their part would pay for itself later in cementing the future political partnership between Bonn and the Western Allies. In this they were not disappointed. The lasting comradeship and trust that was born then has since profited everybody concerned.[17]

Yet, anecdotal evidence suggests that after 1956, the BND became less rather than more

important for U.S. foreign intelligence. One (anonymous) former senior CIA official argued that the Gehlen organization made a distinct contribution in the early days but that its production was eventually undermined by tighter Soviet security and an excessive reliance on clandestine collection. According to this source, there was a good deal of disenchantment with the Gehlen organization by the mid-1950s, but a need, in American eyes, to remain close to the German service: "We were in bed with them and wanted to stay there. They were the intelligence service of one of our most powerful allies. . . . But in practice – they faithfully sent us *Die Übersicht* (The Overview), we got it every week, and nobody ever used it."[18]

German-American intelligence relations after 1956 were also troubled by continual security breaches and sensations. The Gehlen organization and the BND suffered from aggressive targeting of their agents and operations by both the KGB and the East German Ministry for State Security. Insider's memoirs published after the end of the Cold War have lent support to the legend that the Soviet-bloc services won the battle of penetration.[19] Certainly, there were numerous penetrations of the Gehlen organization and the BND, some highly publicized. Perhaps the most embarrassing case was that of Heinz Felfe, the West German equivalent of Kim Philby. Felfe was a double agent who operated for a decade since 1951 and rose, like Philby, to dominate the BND's Soviet counterintelligence operations. A recent authoritative account stresses that Felfe "caused considerable damage to BND and to West German and Allied security until his arrest in November 1961."[20]

Security breaches on a scale of the Felfe case pose the ultimate challenge to intelligence alliances by calling into question one of their underlying maxims: Intelligence alliances are

[15] See Hohne and Zolling, *Network*, 174–5, 239–41.

[16] H. Bradford Westerfield, "America and the World of Intelligence Liaison," *Intelligence and National Security* 11 (1996): 526. The chapter on liaison arrangements was excised from the published version of an important CIA official history. See Ludwell Lee Montague, *General Walter Bedell Smith as Director of Central Intelligence: October 1950–February 1953* (Philadelphia, 1992).

[17] Gehlen, *The Service*, 195–6.

[18] Source quoted in Reese, *General Reinhard Gehlen*, 176.

[19] See, e.g., Markus Wolf, *Man Without a Face: The Autobiography of Communism's Greatest Spymaster* (New York, 1997).

[20] David E. Murphy, Sergei A. Kondrashev, and George Bailey, *Battleground Berlin: CIA vs. KGB in the Cold War* (New Haven, Conn., 1997), 430.

designed to enhance, not undermine, security by providing insights and a degree of watchfulness over the operations of a friendly intelligence service. One retired CIA official, William Johnson, put this maxim more bluntly: "It used to be standard folklore that the primary and ultimate purpose of all liaison was penetration. Services were supposed to exchange information and their officers to socialize primarily for the purpose of recruiting one another."[21]

The idea that intelligence alliances serve to facilitate "penetration" of a friendly intelligence service need not be taken in quite the literal or Machiavellian sense that Johnson conveys. But it points to some general truths applicable to the post-1956 relationship between German and U.S. intelligence. Intelligence alliances between sovereign states function in a quasi-commercial way; they are properly seen as "trading" relationships, or what Michael Herman astutely calls "professional bargains."[22] The commodity being traded has, however, its unique attributes. It is secret information in a narrow sense or, more broadly, knowledge of how another state perceives the world and its troubles. Trading information can also influence perceptions and even shape policy, as each partner tests its information, assumptions, and conclusions about the state of world politics against the views of its ally. It is impossible to determine, on present evidence, precisely how the intelligence relationship between the United States and the Federal Republic influenced the policies of either state during the Cold War. Some have charged that the influence has been profoundly negative, arguing that the Gehlen organization exaggerated the Soviet menace, but there is no evidence for such an assertion.[23] More likely is that the sharing of intelligence between the

United States and Germany helped reassure each state about the reliability of the other as an ally. This was particularly important for Germany's integration into NATO, which inevitably raised historical concerns about a revived German military.

Paradoxically, the direct exchange of intelligence between the United States and Germany may have become less important for their alliance in the tense Cold War decades of the 1950s and 1960s. Two other features of intelligence alliances came increasingly to the fore: burden sharing and forward basing.

The resources to mount a global watch are beyond the capacity of even the largest intelligence services. Alliance burden-sharing is a way to sustain coverage of intelligence targets while operating within budget and resource constraints. For the BND after 1956, the value of the alliance with the United States was the access it provided to the American intelligence community's vastly greater resources and geographic reach. Although the relationship was less significant for the CIA, it offered a way to verify American intelligence on Soviet-bloc activities in Europe as well as information about areas where the United States found it difficult to operate (for example, Egypt and sub-Saharan Africa).

The provision of forward bases for U.S. intelligence operations was another important element of the German-American intelligence relationship between 1956 and 1968. The agent operations beyond the Iron Curtain and the Berlin Wall, though often celebrated in spy novels, were only one example of how West German geography benefited American intelligence. The Federal Republic was also a base for major U.S. reconnaissance operations. These ranged from Operation Moby Dick, an early Cold War project that collected aerial photos of the Soviet Union with gigantic cameras attached to high-altitude weather balloons, to the U-2 spy plane, which truly revolutionized the collection of intelligence on Soviet strategic nuclear forces. The very first U-2 flight over Soviet territory, which penetrated as far as Moscow, was launched from Wiesbaden on July 4, 1956. The condition for the use of German bases was that the German chancellor, Konrad

---

[21] Quoted in Westerfield, "America and the World of Liaison," 539. See also Martin Alexander, "Introduction: Knowing Your Friends, Assessing Your Allies: Perspectives on Intra-Alliance Intelligence," *Intelligence and National Security* 13 (1998): 8.

[22] Michael Herman, *Intelligence Power in Peace and War* (Cambridge, 1996), 218.

[23] This argument is advanced by Christopher Simpson, *Blowback: America's Recruitment of Nazis and Its Effects on the Cold War* (New York, 1988), 63–5.

Adenauer, together with BND president Reinhard Gehlen, be briefed on the results of the U-2 intelligence. On viewing one set of U-2 photographs, the phlegmatic Adenauer was reported to have exclaimed, "*Fabelhaft! Fabelhaft!* [fabulous, fabulous]."[24]

Other exotic aircraft also operated from bases in Germany and were designed to monitor various types of Warsaw Pact communications, from radar emissions to radio and voice transmissions sent by the Soviet air defense system. These "ferret" missions were dangerous, not least because the aircraft, often modified Hercules transport planes, were easy targets for interception. Designed to operate just on the edges of Soviet airspace, ferret missions required delicate navigation. One such mission flown from Germany in 1958 went off course and strayed over Soviet territory, where it was shot down with the loss of all seventeen crew members.[25]

Less dangerous and less provocative, though operating in the same spectrum of signals intelligence (SIGINT), were the American ground stations located in West Germany. These installations remained highly secret during the Cold War and little is known of them even today. One source suggests that the National Security Agency had tactical and strategic SIGINT facilities at at least three sites in Germany: Berlin, Augsburg, and Bad Aibling.[26] The trade-off for base facilities for SIGINT stations in West Germany may well have been modest access, as a "third party," to the close signals intelligence alliance known as UKUSA, which linked the United States, Britain, Canada, Australia, and New Zealand.[27]

The most sensational SIGINT operation on West German territory during the early Cold War was code-named Operation Gold.[28] This joint British-American effort involved building a tunnel from the American zone in West Berlin to allow engineers to tap a major Soviet phone cable network. Work on the tunnel, ingeniously disguised, began in late 1954 and was completed in spring 1955. Thereafter, Operation Gold collected a staggering amount of intercepted phone communications, until the Soviet command in East Berlin uncovered the tunnel in April 1956 and displayed the find to journalists. Although British double agent George Blake had revealed the existence of the tunnel to the KGB, the operation still managed to produce useful intelligence. Despite the claim made by one of Gehlen's biographers, there is no evidence that the Gehlen organization played any role in or had knowledge of Operation Gold.[29] This information blackout most likely stemmed from security concerns.

While U.S. intelligence used bases and platforms on German territory to monitor Soviet-bloc communications, it also made an effort to communicate via radio with populations living behind the Iron Curtain. The two most important radio stations to function in this war of words were Radio Liberty and Radio Free Europe (RFE); both were based in Germany and both were funded clandestinely by the CIA. RFE began broadcasting on July 4, 1950, from a shortwave transmitter in Lamperheim. Radio Liberty came on the air in 1953 and was designed to reach into the Soviet Union. Both initiatives were the brainchild of Frank Wisner, the first head of the CIA's covert action arm, the Office of Policy Coordination. Wisner liked to refer to the stations as his "Mighty

[24] Dino Brugioni, *Eyeball to Eyeball: The Inside Story of the Cuban Missile Crisis* (New York, 1991), 36.

[25] Paul Lashmar, *Spy Flights of the Cold War* (Annapolis, Md., 1996), 170; see also William E. Burrows, *Deep Black: Space Espionage and National Security* (New York, 1986).

[26] Jeffrey Richelson, *The U.S. Intelligence Community*, 3d ed. (Boulder, Colo., 1995), 190. For a general history of the American signals intelligence agency, the National Security Agency, see James Bamford, *The Puzzle Palace: A Rreport on America's Most Secret Agency* (Boston, 1982).

[27] Richelson, *The U.S. Intelligence Community*, 277.

[28] The best treatment of Operation Gold is found in Murphy, Kondrashev, and Bailey, *Battleground Berlin*, chap. 11, also app. 5 and 9.

[29] The claim about Gehlen's role as the originator of the idea for the tunnel is made by Hermann Zolling, "The Affair of the CIA Tunnel," app. B of Hohne and Zolling, *Network*. The claim is refuted authoritatively in Murphy, Kondrashev, and Bailey, *Battleground Berlin*, 206.

Wurlitzers."[30] The content of broadcasts from both stations was to prove controversial, especially during the Hungarian uprising of 1956. RFE added to the passions of the crisis by re-broadcasting local messages from Hungarian stations. This created the enduring impression that the United States had helped incite the uprising, only to leave the Hungarians to their own devices once they had to face the Soviet tanks. In the aftermath of the crisis, the West German government, at the direct instigation of Konrad Adenauer, insisted on an investigation of RFE policy. RFE was cleared of charges that it had attempted to incite an anti-Soviet coup, but caution prevailed thereafter, especially during the events of 1968 in Czechoslovakia.[31]

By the time Reinhard Gehlen retired as chief of the BND in 1968, the architecture of the intelligence relationship between Germany and the United States that he had helped to build had fundamentally changed. Gehlen had imagined a close relationship between the American authorities and a tightly controlled, unified German intelligence system under his direct command. At the heart of this relationship would be a German espionage apparatus collecting clandestine intelligence to influence American perceptions of the Soviet threat and to help create and sustain a sovereign West German government.

By 1968, however, the intelligence link between Germany and the United States looked far different from Gehlen's vision. Intelligence was only a thread in the complex web of relations between Bonn and Washington, and the BND, the outgrowth of the Gehlen organization, was only one component in the German-American intelligence relationship. Since the 1950s, the Federal Internal Security Office (*Bundesamt für Verfassungsschutz*), the Military Security Service (*Militärischer Abschirmdienst*), and the military intelligence branch of the reborn German army had all developed their own relationships with their American counterparts. In any case, the value of the intelligence relationships had shifted from the direct feeding of information from German sources into the American system to the implicit set of bargains represented by access to German geography and burden-sharing. The Federal Republic now operated within the NATO intelligence model and had acquired some, though certainly not all, of the qualities of the British-American special relationship. Given the tangled origins of the intelligence relationship between the United States and Germany, this was a considerable achievement.

---

[30] Evan Thomas, *The Very Best Men: Four Who Dared: The Early Years of the CIA* (New York, 1995). This book contains an extended portrait of Frank Wisner, based in part on his CIA personnel file.

[31] John Ranelagh, *The Agency: The Rise and Decline of the CIA* (New York, 1986), 308–9. Cord Meyer was in charge of the radios as head of the CIA's International Division in the mid-1950s, and he gives a valuable account of this period in his memoirs: Cord Meyer, *Facing Reality: From World Federalism to the CIA* (New York, 1980), 110–38.

ECONOMICS

From Enlightened Hegemony to Partnership

The United States and West Germany in the World Economy, 1945–1968

Christoph Buchheim

Translated by Richard Sharp

The United States was the dominant political and economic power in the Western world in the postwar years. The states of Western Europe were dependent upon it. One example of this dependence was the "dollar gap" that forced them to rely on American aid to finance indispensable imports. For Western Germany as an occupied territory, dependence in this case meant being at the mercy of the occupying powers, and the United States soon set the tone among those powers.

As is always the case in such situations, the United States took advantage of this position of dominance to achieve objectives of its own. It was in the Americans' interest to eliminate discrimination against their exports and establish a liberal, multilateral world economy. It was thus necessary from the American perspective that an economically strong West Germany be integrated within that economy. Marshall Plan aid was one of the levers used by the United States to set the process in motion. By means of that lever, the United States set Western Europe moving toward liberalization and persuaded France to accept the creation of a Western state on German soil that would grow in economic strength. In Western Germany itself, the United States also made an effort toward the permanent reduction of concentrations of economic power by insisting that competition and market mechanisms be strengthened. In this way, the United States laid the essential foundations of the social market economy in the Federal Republic.

The realization of these American goals was in large part responsible for the boom in economic growth after World War II. West Germany was a main beneficiary. U.S. policy was undeniably driven by self-interest, yet was also in the collective economic interest of the West, so it seems appropriate to speak not of American hegemony but rather of "enlightened hegemony" in the first phase of the postwar period. This relationship gave way to something much more like a partnership in the 1960s.

GROWTH OF THE WESTERN WORLD ECONOMY

For more than twenty years after the end of World War II, the economic power of the Western industrialized nations grew at a pace unmatched before or since. Western Europe's gross domestic product (GDP) in real terms rose by an average of more than 4 percent per year from 1949, when it once again reached its prewar level, until 1968, when it stood at more than double the 1938 figure (see Table 1).[1] Living standards improved accordingly. A new age of mass consumerism dawned, which led, for example, to ever more electrical appliances in Western homes, mass motorization, and mass tourism.

[1] These figures and those that follow are based on Angus Maddison, *Monitoring the World Economy, 1820–1992* (Paris, 1995), 194–7, 228.

Table 1. *Growth of Per Capita National Product in Real Terms (percent per year)*

	1913–49	1949–68
United States	1.5	2.7
Western Europe	0.7	4.1

Source: Angus Maddison, *Monitoring the World Economy, 1820–1992* (Paris, 1995), 194–7, 228.

By the early 1950s, the United States had already reached the average per capita GDP that Western Europe would attain in 1968. The age of mass consumption had begun there in the interwar years. But in the United States, too, economic growth was much faster than it had been previously; the per capita GDP increased by an average of 2.7 percent per year from 1949 to 1968, as compared with no more than 1.5 percent per year from 1913 to 1949.

Great as this difference in economic growth between the periods 1913–49 and 1949–68 was in the United States, it was far greater in Western Europe, where the increase in the per capita GDP in the former period had averaged only 0.7 percent. In these countries, however, unlike the United States, the national income fell fairly sharply during both wars. If we discount this effect and consider only growth between 1924, the first year in which the 1913 level was slightly exceeded, and 1938, the last full year before the outbreak of World War II, the figure, 1.6 percent, is very much in line with the American one. Nonetheless, the difference between the American and Western European per capita GDPs – which, according to the available figures, had been about 40 percent even in 1913 – had widened to more than 80 percent by 1949. Only after that date did it begin to narrow again, returning to approximately 40 percent in 1968.

Because these differences in growth between the periods before and after 1949 were a phenomenon that affected Western economies in general, it seems reasonable to suppose that there were no specific national reasons for them but, rather, a general cause. And there was: the degree of liberalization of world trade. The interwar period was one of rampant protectionism.

Already in the 1920s, the import restrictions many countries imposed were higher than they had been before World War I; in many cases, restrictions were imposed as a reaction to the political and economic consequences of the war. Protectionism increased greatly during the international economic crisis: Customs duties, import quotas, discrimination, foreign exchange control, and bilateralism were universal features of the 1930s. Overall, the level of protectionism between the two world wars was much higher than it had been before or would be later.[2]

It is, therefore, not surprising that world trade grew more slowly than world production in the interwar years – even though, as noted, production also increased relatively slowly. Precisely the opposite situation prevailed in the years before 1913 and after 1949. After World War II, world trade was the vital engine of growth for all Western industrialized countries. Whereas export quotas (individual countries' exports as a percentage of their net national products) were often lower during the 1920s than they had been in 1913 and decreased further during the 1930s, they rose far beyond the pre-1913 level after World War II.[3] In particular, there was an enormous increase in intra-industry trade, which became the most important factor in world trade and the main force behind its dynamic expansion.

Whereas industrialized countries before World War II had focused their foreign trade mainly on the exchange of industrial goods for raw materials and food, industrial goods made up a growing portion of their imports after 1949. Increasingly, industrial goods were traded for other industrial goods, even in the same product

---

[2] Forrest Capie, "Protectionism in Europe Before 1939," in Richard Tilly and Paul J. J. Welfens, eds., *European Economic Integration as a Challenge to Industry and Government: Contemporary and Historical Perspectives on International Economic Dynamics* (Berlin, 1996), 181–206; Wolfram Fischer, "Wirtschaft, Gesellschaft und Staat in Europa 1914–1980," in Wolfram Fischer et al., eds., *Handbuch der europäischen Wirtschafts- und Sozialgeschichte*, 6 vols. (Stuttgart, 1987), 6:178–9.

[3] Maddison, *Monitoring the World Economy*, 38.

categories.[4] For example, industrial products accounted for two-thirds of West Germany's exports in 1949 but for only about 17 percent of its imports. The figures had risen to 90 percent and more than 50 percent, respectively, by 1968 and stood at 90 percent and 75 percent in 1990.[5] These figures show that the foreign-trade structure of the Federal Republic in 1968 hardly marked the end of the trend in which the industrialized countries became each other's most important trading partners. By 1968, though, the fundamental change vis-à-vis 1949, which was occurring everywhere, was clearly evident.

Unlike trade that made use of comparative cost advantages, intra-industry trade rarely resulted in the eclipse of whole sectors of industry in the countries concerned. Instead, companies reacted to the inevitable competition by differentiating their products, specializing in particular lines, and looking more and more to a worldwide market. In principle, this process opened up growth opportunities for the industries in all countries, which reduced resistance to trade liberalization and encouraged investment. Investment, in turn, spurred swift deployment of technological advances, in the form of new machinery and plant, thereby contributing to the rapid increase in productivity and high growth. Germany provides a typical example of these interactions. Under the Weimar Republic, export activity was relatively weak, the investment rate remained on average far lower than it had been before World War I, and gains in productivity remained modest. After World War II, by contrast, rapidly rising exports and investment provided the most important sources of growth during the 1950s and 1960s. The dismantling of the severe protectionism of the interwar years and the liberalization and multilateralization of world trade – which had found institutional expression in the International

Monetary Fund (IMF) and the General Agreement on Tariffs and Trade (GATT) – proved to be greatly beneficial for growth not only in West Germany but also, as the figures show, for Europe as a whole and the United States.

One development that needs to be explained is the very considerable gap between the average growth rates in the United States and Western Europe during this period. Not only was per capita income initially far higher in America than in Western Europe after World War II but labor productivity was higher as well. Even in 1913 there had been a considerable difference; subsequently, as in the case of the GDPs, the gap widened further.[6] After World War II, however, this huge gap in productivity also offered an enormous potential for accelerated growth in Western Europe once the far more productive American technologies could be imported and imitated. Two factors determined the extent to which this occurred.

First, the efficient use of high-technology plant required an appropriately skilled workforce. It can be assumed that the necessary broad base of human capital had long existed in Western Europe – unlike in many developing countries – and, far from being eroded by the temporary economic weakness and the effects of the war, had probably been strengthened.

Second, to ensure that the American technologies took hold quickly, substantial investment was needed. As noted previously, improved productivity is often linked to the installation of new equipment. This was exactly what had been lacking between the wars. A radical transformation took place after World War II, however, caused by a profound change in the institutional framework of the international economy.

As a result, productivity in Western Europe rose at an extraordinary rate during the postwar period. This was possible only because Europeans could adopt technologies that had already been introduced in the United States rather than

[4] On the subject of intra-industry trade, see also the chapter by Lutz Frühbrodt in this section.

[5] Christoph Buchheim, *Die Wiedereingliederung Westdeutschlands in die Weltwirtschaft 1945–1958* (Munich, 1990), 186–7. Statistisches Bundesamt, *Statistisches Jahrbuch für die Bundesrepublik Deutschland*, 1969:294; 1991:290.

[6] S. N. Broadberry, "Convergence: What the Historical Record Shows," in Bart van Ark and Nicholas Crafts, eds., *Quantitative Aspects of Post-War European Economic Growth* (Cambridge, 1996), 327–46.

rely on the much slower course of innovation.[7] Many industries, in fact, provide examples of how the adoption of American technologies resulted in rapid growth.[8] As the country generally at the leading edge of technology, however, the United States could not employ such a strategy to the same extent. This helps to explain why the growth of the American economy in the period under review was slower than that of the West European countries. The result was a convergence, though not a complete equalization, of productivity levels and living standards between the United States and Western Europe.[9]

THE WEST GERMAN ECONOMY AND AMERICAN OCCUPATION

A powerful economic upturn began in Western Europe immediately after the end of the war as there had been after World War I. By 1947, industrial production in many countries had returned or come close to the level of 1937. In contrast to the period after World War I, this postwar boom was not immediately followed by a severe depression. There was, rather, an almost seamless transition into the long-lasting period of prosperity just described.[10] Defeated Germany was an exception. By spring 1948, production in Western Germany had still not reached half its 1937 level, and the Soviet zone of occupation fared little better.[11] Even three

years after the end of the war, the economic position was catastrophic.

The reasons for the stark contrast between development in Western Germany and the rest of Western Europe appeared obvious enough. There was, for one, the massive destruction caused by bombing. Many of Germany's cities lay in ruins, as did much of its industry. That was not all. What had remained intact of German industry was dismantled. The implementation of the 1946 level-of-industry plan would certainly have caused drastic losses in production capacity; the plan was not, however, carried out. Nevertheless, what was indeed dismantled was still very substantial, according to informed German calculations at the time.[12]

Initially, not just Allied reparations policy but occupation policy in general seemed to emphasize destruction rather than reconstruction. The spirit of U.S. Treasury Secretary Henry J. Morgenthau's ideas clearly lived on in a good many phrases of the Joint Chief of Staff's interim directive for the postsurrender period (JCS 1067), which, among other things, prohibited the military government from doing anything at all to promote Germany's economic recovery. Many passages of the Potsdam Agreement were similarly discouraging. Harsh programs of deconcentration and decartelization soon followed, and foreign trade, which had been completely removed from the control of German companies, shriveled. The Allies did nothing to remedy the grotesque monetary situation. As if that were not enough, they imposed huge burdens on their respective zones to finance the cost of the occupation.[13] That, at least, was how public opinion at the time saw matters – a view that is also reflected in the scholarly literature.[14]

---

[7] See also, with a different emphasis, the chapter by Raymond G. Stokes in this section.

[8] For examples, see Johannes Bähr and Dietmar Petzina, *Innovationsverhalten und Entscheidungsstrukturen: Vergleichende Studien zur wirtschaftlichen Entwicklung im geteilten Deutschland 1945–1990* (Berlin, 1996); see in general Ludger Lindlar, *Das missverstandene Wirtschaftswunder: Westdeutschland und die westeuropäische Nachkriegsprosperität* (Tübingen, 1997).

[9] Nicholas Crafts and Gianni Toniolo, "Postwar Growth: An Overview," in Nicholas Crafts and Gianni Toniolo, eds., *Economic Growth in Europe Since 1945* (Cambridge, 1996), 1–37.

[10] Alan S. Milward, *The Reconstruction of Western Europe, 1945–51* (London, 1984), 1–13.

[11] For the official industrial production figures for 1945–8, see the chapter by Wilfried Mausbach in this

section; for the prewar period, see Walther G. Hoffmann, *Das Wachstum der deutschen Wirtschaft seit der Mitte des 19. Jahrhunderts* (Berlin, 1965), 390–5.

[12] See Gustav W. Harmssen, *Am Abend der Demontage: Sechs Jahre Reparationspolitik* (Bremen, 1951).

[13] Institut für Besatzungsfragen, *Sechs Jahre Besatzungslasten: Eine Untersuchung des Problems der Besatzungskosten in den drei Westzonen und in Westberlin 1945–1950* (Tübingen, 1951).

[14] Kurt Häuser, "Die Teilung Deutschlands," in Gustav Stolper, Kurt Häuser, and Knut Borchardt, *Deutsche*

The end of hopelessness, the start of the upturn, and the possibility of escape from misery and hardship took visible form with the currency reform of June 20, 1948. Overnight, store windows filled and the black market disappeared. Money was worth something once more and, therefore, worth working for. Production rose steeply. The currency reform marked the beginning of the economic miracle[15] and became the founding myth of the Federal Republic in the public mind. In this capacity, it was joined, especially in the minds of economists,[16] by the social market economy (*soziale Marktwirtschaft*). Whereas the currency reform was an Allied undertaking, the social market economy is seen as a German contribution to the growth boom and the critical factor behind its long duration. Ludwig Erhard, then director of the bizonal economic administration, is regarded as having taken the first courageous stride toward the introduction of this new order with the economic reform based on the *Leitsätzegesetz* (Law on the Principles of Economic Controls and Price Policy after the Currency Reform)

undertaken in conjunction with the currency reform.[17]

Essential aspects of this view of events were called into question by Werner Abelshauser in the mid-1970s.[18] Abelshauser showed that the effects of war damage and dismantlement on industrial capital stock were much less serious than generally assumed. Despite these losses, capital stock in 1948 was not only larger but also more modern than it had been in 1936 or 1937, primarily as a result of investments that had continued well into the war years. In making this point, Abelshauser tended in fact to overestimate the effects of industrial dismantling.[19] At least in the immediate postwar years, German industry had considerable excess capacity when measured against its low productivity. Contrary to popular opinion, it cannot generally be said that there was a shortage of production plant after 1945 – a fact that well-informed observers recognized at that time.[20] Because the labor force, too, had grown from its prewar level as a result of the influx of refugees and expellees, and because it cannot be said that there was a general decline in workers' qualifications, the postwar conditions for industrial production were, on the whole, very favorable. In addition, as Abelshauser also explained in detail, the American and British occupation authorities constructively supported

Wirtschaft seit 1870, 2d ed. (Tübingen, 1966), 209–41; but see also non-German authors: Nicholas Balabkins, *Germany Under Direct Controls: Economic Aspects of Industrial Disarmament, 1945–1948* (New Brunswick, N.J., 1964), 207–12; André Piettre, *L'économie allemande comtemporaine (Allemagne occidentale) 1945–1952* (Paris, 1952) refers on page 89 to the first phase of occupation as the *"phase punitive."* Only recently, the same view was given further weight in an important book written by economists on the economic history of the Federal Republic: Herbert Giersch, Karl-Heinz Paqué, and Holger Schmieding, *The Fading Miracle: Four Decades of Market Economy in Germany* (Cambridge, 1992), 18–19. The opposite opinion, however, was already argued at a relatively early stage by John H. Backer, *Priming the German Economy: American Occupational Policies, 1945–1948* (Durham, N.C., 1971).

[15] See also, from the earlier literature, Piettre, *L'économie allemande*, 207; Henry C. Wallich, Mainsprings of the German Revival (New Haven, Conn., 1955) 69; Balabkins, *Germany Under Direct Controls*, ix.

[16] Giersch, Paqué, and Schmieding, *The Fading Miracle*, 26–38; Rainer Klump, *Wirtschaftsgeschichte der Bundesrepublik Deutschland: Zur Kritik neuerer wirtschaftshistorischer Interpretationen aus ordnungspolitischer Sicht* (Stuttgart, 1985), 51–71.

[17] Gerold Ambrosius, *Die Durchsetzung der Sozialen Marktwirtschaft in Westdeutschland 1945–1949* (Stuttgart, 1977); Christoph Klessmann, *Die doppelte Staatsgründung: Deutsche Geschichte 1945–1955*, 5th ed. (Göttingen, 1991), 190–1.

[18] Werner Abelshauser, *Wirtschaft in Westdeutschland 1945–1948: Rekonstruktion und Wachstumsbedingungen in der amerikanischen und britischen Zone* (Stuttgart, 1975); see also Werner Abelshauser, *Wirtschaftsgeschichte der Bundesrepublik Deutschland 1945–1980* (Frankfurt am Main, 1983).

[19] Alan Kramer, *Die britische Demontagepolitik am Beispiel Hamburgs 1945–1950* (Hamburg, 1991), 440–5.

[20] See a memorandum written by Ludwig Erhard on the instructions of the military government in May 1945, when he was head of the Economic Office in Fürth, described in Hans Woller, *Gesellschaft und Politik in der amerikanischen Besatzungszone: Die Region Ansbach und Fürth* (Munich, 1986), 240–1. For the way steel companies saw their situation, see Klaus-Dietmar Henke, *Die amerikanische Besetzung Deutschlands* (Munich, 1995), 533–45.

West German economic policy in the important and largely successful effort to eliminate bottlenecks in transport, coal mining, and food distribution. On the other hand, Abelshauser also emphasized the burdens imposed on the German economy by the occupying powers. Those burdens stemmed less from the dismantling of industrial plant than from quasi-reparations, in the form of vastly undervalued forced exports of coal and other raw materials, and the high costs of occupation. Even so, these losses were offset "at least to some extent by aid consignments and dollar credits."[21]

Abelshauser drew two important conclusions from his analysis. First, "from the very beginning...all the necessary prerequisites were in place that *had* to enable the West German economy to return swiftly to its historical path of growth."[22] Abelshauser thus assumed that, given the positive contribution of occupation policy to the relaunching of the economy,[23] the upturn was to a certain extent inevitable. Second, Abelshauser's view of the role of the American and British occupying powers in the early occupation period was less negative than had long been customary. Nevertheless, after offsetting foreign aid against the one-sided burdens imposed,[24] he concluded that Western Germany was largely dependent on its own efforts to reconstruct its economy until well into 1948.[25]

The first of Abelshauser's conclusions triggered a lively debate among historians and economists.[26] The outcome of this debate was a consensus that although postwar conditions in West Germany were in fact favorable to growth, it was only with the currency reform and other

economic controls serving as a catalyst that they were able to have an effect.

This conclusion immediately poses a challenge to Abelshauser's second conclusion – that West Germany had to rely largely on its own efforts to trigger the growth boom. If we understand "efforts" as meaning not just tangible resources but also intangible concepts, then it becomes clear that the Allies, by carrying out the currency reform themselves, did make a very important contribution to the favorable conditions for growth in West Germany. The reduction of the money supply through the currency reform, which followed the American conception set out in the Colm-Dodge-Goldsmith plan, was sharp and irrevocable. It amounted to a sweeping act of expropriation and was initially perceived as such by the population. For that very reason, it gave rise to ideal monetary conditions for a rapid upturn by maximizing incentives for work and production. This was clearly demonstrated when industrial production in Bizonia rose by more than 50 percent in the second half of 1948.

By contrast, the Homburg Plan, the official currency reform proposal worked out by the Sonderstelle Geld und Kredit,[27] had contained no provision for the permanent elimination of the glut of money: Like the Reich debt instruments, this glut was instead to be converted into so-called Reichsmark liquidation certificates. It was left open when and on what terms it would be possible to convert those certificates into new currency. Moreover, because the equalization of burdens (*Lastenausgleich*) was directly linked

---

[21] Abelshauser, *Wirtschaftsgeschichte der Bundesrepublik*, 32.

[22] Abelshauser, *Wirtschaft in Westdeutschland*, 169 (emphasis added).

[23] Ibid., 89–90, where Abelshauser expressly distances himself from the widespread view to the contrary (see previous note).

[24] Ibid., 160.

[25] Abelshauser, *Wirtschaftsgeschichte der Bundesrepublik*, 32.

[26] See the suggestions for further reading at the end of this chapter.

[27] The Sonderstelle Geld und Kredit was a special agency created by the Economc Council of the Combined Economic Area (Wirtschaftsrat des Vereinigten Wirtschaftsgebietes) to make recommendations on monetary and financial issues. The Homburg Plan is reprinted in Horst Möller, ed., *Zur Vorgeschichte der Deutschen Mark: Die Währungsreformpläne 1945–1948* (Basel, 1961), 477–503; a new study offering an interpretation that differs from my own is Arne Weick, *Homburger Plan und Währungsreform: Kritische Analyse des Währungsreformplans der Sonderstelle Geld und Kredit und seiner Bedeutung für die westdeutsche Währungsreform von 1948* (St. Katharinen, 1998).

to this arrangement, sustained and bitter arguments would have likely ensued over the release of individual tranches of the reichsmark liquidation certificates. As in the case of the revaluation debate during the Weimar Republic, these conflicts would have poisoned the political atmosphere, and arguments about distribution would have had an adverse effect on growth. In this sense, then, the undisturbed exploitation of the existing growth potential was in no small measure because the currency reform was an Allied imposition that needed to take no account of German public opinion.

The Allies also provided enormous material assistance to the German economy.[28] Contrary to Abelshauser's view, the one-sided burdens imposed on Western Germany by the occupying powers did not offset this aid. The great majority of raw-materials exports were paid for at realistic prices and, therefore, cannot be regarded as concealed reparations payments. Anything else would not have made sense in any case because it was the declared aim of the Americans and British to minimize the burden imposed by the occupation on the budgets and payments balances of their German states. That was precisely why they had battled successfully for the first-charge principle and the dollar clause. These held, respectively, that no reparations should be paid from current production until Western Germany's essential imports had been covered and that German exports must be paid for in dollars. For the same reasons, far from trying to impose artificial restrictions on exports, the occupying powers were soon pursuing an active export-promotion policy. Its success was very limited as long as the money surplus and the price freeze strangled virtually any incentive for German industry to export. Understandably, therefore, there was no upturn in exports of industrial goods until after the currency reform, the implementation of which was long delayed by the efforts of the Western Allies to reach agreement with the Soviets on a quadrizonal

procedure. But even the elimination of other one-sided burdens on West Germany – industrial dismantling, occupation costs, and the brain drain – would have done little to help generate a swift and decisive increase in exports and the resulting influx of foreign currency. That meant Western Germany would in any case have been dependent on large-scale foreign food-aid shipments. Had no such aid been forthcoming, had Morgenthau – who proclaimed that he had no interest in the fate of the German population – been taken seriously, there would certainly have been a great many deaths from starvation and epidemics.[29]

Reviewing once again, against this background, the measures taken by the military government, which were always regarded as clearly burdensome and often also played a major part in the negotiations of the Control Council,[30] we can see that their negative effects were often less serious than commonly believed and were sometimes accompanied – or even more than offset – by positive ones. The dismantling of industrial plant had little impact on the revival of the economy, especially as plans were gradually scaled back. As a result of the first-charge principle and the dollar clause, the reparations burden on current production was very light. Even the compulsory transfer of German technological know-how was evidently not as significant as has sometimes been assumed.[31]

The burdens of occupation have also been reassessed. The sums demanded of the Western

[28] See the chapter by Wilfried Mausbach in this section.

[29] Buchheim, *Wiedereingliederung Westdeutschlands*; John E. Farquharson, *The Western Allies and the Politics of Food: Agrarian Management in Postwar Germany* (Leamington Spa, 1985); Günter J. Trittel, *Hunger und Politik: Die Ernährungskrise in der Bizone (1945–1949)* (Frankfurt am Main, 1990).

[30] Wilfried Mausbach, *Zwischen Morgenthau und Marshall: Das wirtschaftspolitische Deutschlandkonzept der USA 1944–1947* (Düsseldorf, 1996); Gunther Mai, *Der Alliierte Kontrollrat in Deutschland 1945–1948: Alliierte Einheit – deutsche Teilung?* (Munich, 1995).

[31] John Gimbel, *Science, Technology and Reparations: Exploitation and Plunder in Postwar Germany* (Stanford, Calif., 1990); but see also Mathias Judt and Burghard Ciesla, eds., *Technology Transfer Out of Germany After 1945* (Amsterdam, 1996).

zones fell far short of covering the occupation costs the Allies incurred. Contrary to the view Germans expressed at the time, the occupiers would have had every right to demand even higher payments from Western Germany. In addition, the costs of occupation in Western Germany were used to finance important administrative services provided by the foreign military powers.[32]

The question now arises of how to classify Allied measures that affected the Western German economic system. The Americans in particular thought that certain features peculiar to the German economic order had contributed to National Socialist aggression.[33] These features included a high level of concentration of economic power, especially in the steel and chemical industries and in the banking system; a strong tendency to form cartels; and highly protectionist trade policies geared toward autarchy.

Even before the war ended, the United States was planning a radical liberalization of Germany's foreign trade and the full integration of Germany into a new multilateral world economy. This would not only make Germany more economically vulnerable but also would obtain the maximum benefit for other countries from Germany's great economic potential. The United States turned intention into action after the war. In the face of strong resistance, the United States stood by the dollar clause introduced in 1945 to prevent the uncontrolled outflow of resources from the occupied zones even after that threat had ceased to exist. By doing so, the United States effectively prevented the incorporation of West Germany into the strongly bilateralist European trade system.

It was not until summer 1949, in a trade agreement with Switzerland, that a principle inherent to the dollar clause – that all imports had to be certified as absolutely essential – was abandoned. However, because the same agreement largely exempted West Germany's Swiss imports from all quotas, it was not so much

a conventionally bilateral document as a step toward liberalization. A series of similar agreements with other countries were quickly concluded in the following months, all still under the aegis of the American-dominated Joint Export-Import Agency (JEIA), the foreign trade office of the Western zones. At the same time, under heavy pressure from the United States, liberalization began within the framework of the Organization for European Economic Cooperation (OEEC).[34] It is fair to say, then, that the United States was the dominant force in ensuring that postwar Germany turned definitively toward a liberal foreign-trade system.[35]

The demand for a prohibition of cartels and of what was seen as excessive industrial concentration was made in both JCS 1067 and the Potsdam Agreement. Consequently, cartels were banned in the three Western zones in 1947.[36] The ban remained in force until the *Gesetz gegen Wettbewerbsbeschränkungen* (GWB, or anti-cartel law) was passed in 1957. The fact that this act included a ban on cartels, though diluted by many exceptions, must be regarded as a triumph for Ludwig Erhard and his competition-oriented economic policy. The Federal Association of German Industry (*Bundesverband der Deutschen Industrie*) and the German Chamber of Industry and Commerce (*Deutscher Industrie- und Handelstag*) had rejected the GWB and given their approval only to a toothless supervisory mechanism of the type that had already existed in the Weimar Republic. Industry's position enjoyed widespread support among the Union parties (Christian Democratic Union and Christian Social Union). In view of this resistance, it seems reasonable to assume that the GWB would never have come about but for the Allied prohibition of cartels and the repeated urgings of the Allied High Commission that a similar ban should be included in the German legislation on

[32] See the chapter by Hubert Zimmermann in this section.

[33] Regina Ursula Gramer considers this in detail elsewhere in this section.

[34] See the chapter by Werner Bührer in this section.

[35] Buchheim, *Wiedereingliederung Westdeutschlands,* 42–9, 119–25; Werner Bührer, *Westdeutschland in der OEEC: Eingliederung, Krise, Bewährung 1947–1961* (Munich, 1997), 137–41.

[36] For additional background, see the chapter by Regina Ursula Gramer in this section.

competition.[37] With hindsight, the establishment of a cartel office and the principle of prohibition that was eventually enshrined in the GWB can be seen as the start of an increasingly tough competition policy that was manifested in later amendments to the law. The practical application of competition policy during the growth boom then brought about a change of heart within German industry, which from the 1960s onward expressed no further serious misgivings about this policy.[38]

The American plans for the deconcentration and decartelization of German industry, even in their watered-down form, were largely unsuccessful, however. An exception was the breaking up of the I.G. Farben group, which especially benefited the West German chemical industry. The three big, dynamic companies that succeeded I.G. Farben were able to conquer international markets once again.[39] The steel industry, by contrast, saw a move back toward concentration, though the pre-1945 structure was never fully restored.[40] The big banks, formally broken down into independent regional banks, were even able to reestablish themselves in their previous forms in 1957–8.[41] The former Reichsbank, however, had been liquidated for good. The military government replaced it in 1948 with a two-tier central banking system for West Germany in which independent central banks in each state controlled a subsidiary institution, the *Bank deutscher Länder* (or BdL; Länder Union-Bank). However, the BdL soon gained precedence, and the Bundesbank Act of 1957 drew the logical conclusion by converting the state central banks into administrative units of the German Bundesbank.

Another principle enshrined by the occupying powers in the act establishing the BdL, evidently in the face of German opposition, nonetheless did become a permanent and central constituent of the German monetary and economic systems: the political independence of the central bank. A provision to that effect had been approved in 1922 during the Weimar Republic only because of pressure exerted by the Allied reparations creditors. In 1924, it was incorporated into the new Reichsbank Act, which, as part of the Dawes Plan, had to be approved by the Reparations Commission. But in 1939, the Reichsbank was once again put under the authority of the government, that is, Hitler.

The principle of the independence of Germany's central bank has, therefore, been imposed twice by outside pressure during periods of restricted national sovereignty. The central bank defended this principle against attacks by the federal government during the 1950s, and an increasingly aware public was sympathetic to the bank's position. Like the cartel ban, the political independence of the central bank can be described as an act by the military government that proved to be a decisive turning point in the evolution of Germany's economic order.[42]

Competition is the heart of the market economy. Neoliberal economists, however, clearly perceived that in a purely laissez-faire economy such competition is increasingly restricted by the accumulation of market power in private hands. In their view, it was thus an essential feature of the social market economy that the state should act to preserve competition. Leonhard Miksch, a close colleague of Ludwig Erhard,

[37] Volker R. Berghahn, *The Americanization of West German Industry, 1945–1973* (Leamington Spa and New York, 1985), 155–81; Peter Hüttenberger, "Zur Kartellgesetzgebung der Bundesrepublik 1949–1957," *Vierteljahrshefte für Zeitgeschichte* 24 (1976): 287–307.

[38] Anthony J. Nicholls, *Freedom with Responsibility: The Social Market Economy in Germany, 1918–1963* (Oxford, 1994), 336–8.

[39] Raymond G. Stokes, *Divide and Prosper: The Heirs of I. G. Farben Under Allied Authority, 1945–1951* (Berkeley, 1988).

[40] John Gillingham, *Coal, Steel, and the Rebirth of Europe, 1945–1955: The Germans and French from Ruhr Conflict to Economic Community* (Cambridge, 1991), 352–5.

[41] Theo Horstmann, *Die Alliierten und die deutschen Grossbanken: Bankenpolitik nach dem Zweiten Weltkrieg in Westdeutschland* (Bonn, 1991); Carl-Ludwig Holtfrerich, "Die Deutsche Bank vom Zweiten Weltkrieg über die Besatzungsherrschaft zur Rekonstruktion 1945–1947," in Lothar Gall et al., *Die Deutsche Bank 1870–1955* (Munich, 1995), 409–578.

[42] Christoph Buchheim, "The Establishment of the Bank deutscher Länder and the West German Currency Reform," in Deutsche Bundesbank, ed., *Fifty Years of the Deutsche Mark: Central Bank and the Currency in Germany Since 1948* (Oxford, 1999), 77.

referred to the market economy as a "governmental institution." In addition, to ensure undistorted competition, relative price stability came to be seen as the second essential pillar of the social market economy.[43]

All this suggests the following conclusion, though further research is needed to substantiate it: The social market economy was a term and concept of German origin, but its realization – contrary to what the existing literature might suggest – was essentially the result of Allied prescriptions. These prescriptions aimed to avert a renewed concentration of economic power along traditional German lines. Decartelization and the integration of Germany into the world economy through a liberalization of its foreign-trade system served this goal. Allied policy also secured the long-term future of competition based on market forces, though economic performance also benefited from the failure of radical plans for deconcentration. Moreover, the drastic and permanent reduction of the money supply brought about by the currency reform and the incorporation of the principle of political independence in the central bank legislation – again by the military government – created a solid basis for a high degree of price stability in the Federal Republic. Thus, two pillars of neoliberal regulatory policy, which their supporters viewed as essential parts of the social market economy, were erected primarily by the American occupying power even before Erhard's economic reforms and in the face of German resistance.

The argument, popular in the 1970s, that U.S. policies effectively blocked a thorough reorganization of West Germany thus does not stand up to scrutiny. To a certain degree, one can speak of a capitalism "imposed" by the United States.[44] But the imposition of this capitalism, which was at odds with German tradition, was an essential precondition for the boom that followed. To put it provocatively: The "enlightened hegemony"

of the United States after World War II, the effects of which were particularly pronounced in West Germany because of the occupation and political control of the country, was in economic terms a great – some would say unmerited – boon for the Federal Republic.

THE MARSHALL PLAN AS A LEVER

There were indications of a serious balance of payments crisis in Western Europe in 1947. The dollar gap was considerably wider than in 1946. America was the only country able to supply substantial quantities of food, important raw materials, and capital goods. All were in extremely short supply in Western Europe, yet they were indispensable if the already low living standards in most West European countries were not to deteriorate further and if a rapid economic reconstruction were not to be endangered.[45] Striving to raise living standards and push ahead with reconstruction, the governments of the affected states regarded further dollar aid essential.

This explains why the United States was able to impose strict conditions on the provision of further dollar aid and why the European recipient countries accepted them, although with audible gnashing of teeth in some cases. Herein lay the essential difference between the funds provided under the Marshall Plan and most earlier forms of aid: The new grants were not unconditional. The criticism directed at the formerly widespread overestimation of the direct contribution to reconstruction and growth made by the Marshall Plan is certainly justified.[46] But it is important here not to throw the baby out with the bathwater.[47] The Marshall Plan dollars, because they met an overpowering West European need, provided the United States with a lever with which to enforce acceptance of many of its ideas. As soon became apparent, however,

---

[43] See Nicholls, *Freedom with Responsibility*, 136–50.

[44] Eberhard Schmidt, *Die verhinderte Neuordnung 1945–1952* (Frankfurt am Main, 1970); Ute Schmidt and Tilman Fichter, *Der erzwungene Kapitalismus: Klassenkämpfe in den Westzonen 1945–1948* (Berlin, 1971).

[45] Milward, *Reconstruction of Western Europe*, 19–55.

[46] See the suggestions for further reading at the end of this chapter.

[47] See Michael J. Hogan, *The Marshall Plan: America, Britain, and the Reconstruction of Western Europe, 1947–1952* (Cambridge, 1987), 430–2.

the results were in everyone's best interests. This can, therefore, be seen as another example of "enlightened hegemony."[48]

Although the institutions that were supposed to form the foundation of the new international economic order, the IMF and GATT, had already existed for two years after the war's end,[49] a liberal international economy was still far from being a reality in 1947. Many countries, not least in Western Europe, regulated their foreign trade by bilateral agreements. The Marshall Plan can thus be understood as a device the United States used to achieve its aim of a multilateral international economy by an indirect route. To stimulate growth and improve living standards, productivity was to be increased by close cooperation between the European countries and the integration of their markets. This would also create the necessary conditions for political stabilization and, because increased production would reduce dependence on imports from the dollar area, promote the incorporation of Europe into the liberal world economy.

The Foreign Assistance Act, the legislative basis of the Marshall Plan, made aid conditional upon a "continuous effort of the participating countries to accomplish a joint recovery program through multilateral undertakings and the establishment of a permanent organization for this purpose."[50] This "permanent organization" (OEEC) now became the framework within which, with constant urging from the United States, the liberalization of intra-European trade took place. In 1950, after much resistance had been overcome, the European Payments Union (EPU) was founded as a suborganization of the OEEC.[51] To encourage this development, the United States repeatedly exerted leverage through Marshall aid. The United States regularly threatened to reduce aid unless it saw the kind of progress it wanted. Second, it used Marshall Plan dollars to provide material backing for the liberalization plans; for example, in financing the operating capital of the EPU.

As a consequence, trade between the OEEC countries, including their overseas currency areas, increased strongly, and dependence on supplies from the United States was reduced. In effect, European foreign trade was Europeanized. The liberalization of imports eliminated many shortages. Competition from foreign companies led to efficiency improvements and increased productivity in the participating countries. The competitiveness of West European economies in the world market improved, as reflected, for instance, in the increase in their exports to the United States. Accordingly, imports from the dollar area could gradually be freed from quantitative restrictions and, at the end of 1958, most West European currencies made the transition to full convertibility.[52] The United States had thus achieved its aim of a liberal international economy, and the IMF and GATT were able to become fully operational.

The Americans had foreseen that the inclusion of West Germany in the Marshall Plan would be essential to its success, and this was precisely why the United States had made German inclusion the second central condition for the granting of aid.[53] Germany had been the principal supplier of capital goods to many European countries before the war. Once Germany became unable to play this part, only the United States could step in, and that, in turn, decisively widened the dollar gap. Germany's involvement in the advancing integration of Europe meant that it could once again take on its former role. As a result, the demand for the dollar abated. Because West Germany was a much better customer for European products than the

[48] Buchheim, *Wiedereingliederung Westdeutschlands*, 99–107.

[49] An overview of this, still useful today, is William A. Brown Jr., *The United States and the Restoration of World Trade* (Washington, D.C., 1950); see also Harold James, *International Monetary Cooperation Since Bretton Woods* (Oxford, 1996).

[50] *U.S. Statutes at Large* 62 (1948): pt. 1, 157.

[51] Jacob J. Kaplan and Gunther Schleiminger, *The European Payments Union: Financial Diplomacy in the 1950s* (Oxford, 1989).

[52] Monika Dickhaus, *Die Bundesbank im westeuropäischen Wiederaufbau: Die internationale Währungspolitik der Bundesrepublik Deutschland 1948 bis 1958* (Munich, 1996).

[53] Bührer, *Westdeutschland in der OEEC*, 37–71.

United States, no "deutschmark gap" comparable to the dollar gap opened up. It could even be said that the reintegration of West Germany into the European and world economies helped to make the reestablishment of those economies possible.[54]

To involve West Germany fully in the Marshall Plan, however, the Americans again had to use dollar aid as both carrot and stick.[55] France resisted, prompted by considerations of both security policy and economics. The American plan meant the unification of the French zone with Bizonia, the abandonment of the French objective of internationalizing the Ruhr, a considerable increase in the level of German industrial production allowed, and, ultimately, the creation of a West German state.[56] France had to adapt to this program in the end, and one scholar has gone so far as to write of "blackmail by the Americans."[57] France was nevertheless able to push through the creation of the International Ruhr Authority to monitor the coal and steel industries. In sum, it can be said that the Marshall Plan was of very special importance to Germany because it was very closely linked to the creation of the West German state, negotiated at the Six-Power conference in London in 1948.

France reacted constructively to this turn of events brought about by the Marshall Plan. With the awareness that a Ruhr authority discriminating against West Germany would not be sustainable in the long term, work began immediately after the London conference on a project that eventually resulted in the Schuman Plan in May 1950.[58] Roughly a year later, after protracted negotiations, the treaty establishing the European Coal and Steel Community (ECSC) – the predecessor of the European Economic Community (EEC) – was signed by France, Germany, Italy, and the Benelux countries. This not only dispensed with the need for the unilateral renunciation of sovereignty that the Ruhr authority represented for the Federal Republic, it also meant that the supervision of the Ruhr's industry need not be placed solely in German hands because heavy industry in all ECSC member states was placed under a joint supranational authority.

In this way, the reconstruction of an economically strong West German state – a goal of the Marshall Plan and an economic necessity for Western Europe – was made politically acceptable. This paved the way for the establishment of a liberal world economic order and, ultimately, the enduring growth boom after World War II.

THE FEDERAL REPUBLIC'S PATH TOWARD ECONOMIC EQUALITY

By 1968, the Federal Republic had made good progress toward closing the economic gap that separated it from the United States. This is clearly apparent from a comparison of per capita GDPs. In 1949, the figures were roughly $9,000 in the United States, but only $3,600 in West Germany. By 1968, they stood at $14,700 and $10,800.[59] The levels of labor productivity had followed a similar pattern of change.

Foreign trade between the two countries returned to normal. In 1948–9, the United States accounted for 45 percent of West German imports, but it was an insignificant customer for German products, purchasing only 4 percent of all West German exports. In 1950, the Federal Republic's dependence on American imports

---

[54] Buchheim, *Wiedereingliederung Westdeutschlands*, 171–81.

[55] John Gimbel went so far as to see this as the prime original motive for Marshall Aid, though other authors have not followed his lead. See John Gimbel, *The Origins of the Marshall Plan* (Stanford, Calif., 1976).

[56] Hogan, *Marshall Plan*, 128–33.

[57] Raymond Poidevin, "Ambiguous Partnership: France, the Marshall Plan and the Problem of Germany," in Charles S. Maier and Günter Bischof, eds., *The Marshall Plan and Germany: West German Development Within the Framework of the European Recovery Program* (New York and Oxford, 1991), 331–59.

[58] Milward, *Reconstruction of Western Europe*, 126–67; Poidevin, "Ambiguous Partnership," 358–9.

[59] These figures are in 1990 prices, calculated with purchasing power parities; see Maddison, *Monitoring the World Economy*, 194–7.

Table 2. *Structure of Foreign Trade Between the Federal Republic and the United States, 1968 (billions of dollars)*

	Exports	Imports
Food and Beverages	43.4	332.9
Raw Materials and Fuels	16.8	461.1
Manufactured Goods Including:	2,621.4	1,155.2
Chemical Products	164.6	249.2
Machinery and Vehicles	1,585.2	535.4
Including: Motorized Vehicles	1,043.9	12.3
Total (including types of goods not listed separately)	2,709.9	2,212.1

Source: Statistisches Bundesamt, Fachserie G, ser. 5, Special Trade According to the Classification for Statistics and Tariffs (CST), 1968(2).

dropped abruptly to only 16 percent. This development clearly reflected the steps toward intra-European liberalization taken under the auspices of the OEEC.

German exports to the United States picked up during the 1950s. By 1958, America was purchasing 7 percent of all German exports. The car industry played a critical part in this increase. The Volkswagen Beetle was then beginning its triumphal progress through the United States, and it became Germany's biggest export success. Germany's trade deficit with the United States was reduced, though even in 1958 it was still DM 1.5 billion. But this was no longer a problem because after 1952–3, Germany's trade deficit with the United States had been largely offset by the so-called troop dollars spent by the American military in the Federal Republic.[60] As a consequence, from 1954 onward, dollar imports were also liberalized in a rapid succession of measures.[61] In the second half of the 1960s, the balance of trade between the two countries finally reached parity and, indeed, the Federal Republic was now achieving occasional surpluses. After glancing at the foreign-trade structure, one might even have the impression that Germany had now become the dominant economic partner (see Table 2).

This impression is deceptive, however. The high proportion of food and raw materials among German imports reflects the fact that the United States, though an industrial nation, was highly competitive in these products as well; in the late 1940s, they had accounted for a still higher proportion of American imports to Germany. And the fact that Germany exported far more machinery and motor vehicles to the United States than it imported from there was attributable to the special situation in the car market mentioned previously. It should also be recalled that direct American investment in West Germany had increased considerably during the 1960s, much of it targeted toward manufacturing.[62] Consequently, industrial exports from the United States were at least partially replaced by American production abroad.

Direct American investment was also a major vehicle for technology transfer, which was still playing an important role in the German economy. In 1968, the level of American investment was still incomparably higher than that of German direct investment in the United States, and that remained the case until the mid-1970s. Germany's overall balance of capital transactions with the United States, however, remained negative at the end of the 1960s – in other words, the Federal Republic was exporting more capital to the United States than it was receiving in return.

[60] See the chapter by Hubert Zimmermann in this section.

[61] Buchheim, *Wiedereingliederung Westdeutschlands*, 148–52, 186–7.

[62] See the chapter by Hans-Eckart Scharrer and Kerstin Müller-Neuhof in this section.

Two decades after the end of the war, West Germany was becoming an increasingly important exporter of capital, a natural consequence of its enormous current account surplus.[63] At about the same time, the United States' current account balance became negative, and the country became an importer of capital. The situation that existed in the immediate postwar years had thus been reversed. At that time, the United States had been the world's biggest exporter of capital, and the dollar gap was omnipresent. West Germany had been extremely weak as an exporter and largely reliant on American aid to finance essential imports. By the late 1960s, the Federal Republic had become a dynamic exporter of products and capital. The dollar gap had been replaced by a dollar glut, which in later years would result in the collapse of the fixed-exchange-rate system. In 1969, the Deutsche Mark was revalued against the dollar for the second time. It had obviously become the world's second-most important reserve currency, behind the dollar but ahead of the pound sterling.[64] Among investors, the Deutsche Mark was the most trusted currency of all, which was why, as soon became apparent, every flight from the dollar resulted in a rush to the mark.

One should be wary, however, of interpreting the situation at the end of the 1960s as an indication that the American economy was in decline. In fact, there was no basis for this notion, as the continuing upward curve of American economic growth shows. Nonetheless, America's worldwide security policy and military commitments, including its deep embroilment in the Vietnam War, were such exceptionally heavy burdens that they threatened to overtax even America's economic potential. The situation in the late 1960s also resulted from the boom in the Federal Republic and throughout Western

Europe, which had greatly narrowed the gap between them and the United States. Western Europe had won its economic emancipation, thanks in no small part to American aid and the implementation of the reforms necessary to a liberal world economy.

This final point is also reflected in the fact that the United States in the 1960s had lost its position as chief architect of the international economic system. For example, the founding of the EEC brought a radical change for the GATT. The multilateral approach formerly pursued by this organization had been strongly affected by the polarization between the United States and the EEC. The GATT Kennedy Round on the lowering of customs duties in the mid-1960s illustrated this clearly. The talks were strongly influenced by the negotiations between the two dominant economic powers on global reciprocal reductions in customs duties, because GATT had previously been left with no alternative but to accept the EEC despite that organization's many violations of GATT rules.[65]

In the course of the 1960s, the United States, the EEC, and the larger states of Western Europe, including the Federal Republic, had become independent players on the economic stage. As a consequence of liberalization, they had formed among themselves an intensive and now multilateral network of trade and capital relations that was one of the most important motors of world economic growth. Technological styles became increasingly similar due largely to the adoption of American technologies. As a result, productivity in Western Europe increased rapidly. The continuing development of the liberal world economic order became a common purpose. There were indications that, in the future, the internal economic policies of the various partners would also have to be more closely coordinated.

[63] Deutsche Bundesbank, *40 Jahre Deutsche Mark: Monetäre Statistiken 1948–1987* (Frankfurt am Main, 1988).

[64] "Die längerfristige Entwicklung der Weltwährungsreserven," *Monatsberichte der Deutschen Bundesbank* (Jan. 1990): 41–2; see also the chapter by Harold James, vol. 2, Economics.

[65] Robert E. Hudec, *The GATT Legal System and World Trade Diplomacy* (New York, 1975); Thomas W. Zeiler, *Free Trade, Free World: The Advent of GATT* (Chapel Hill, N.C., 1999).

SUGGESTIONS FOR FURTHER READING

The growth of the world economy is described in long-term perspective in Angus Maddison, *Monitoring the World Economy, 1820–1992* (Paris, 1995). In the interest of comparability, Maddison converted the individual data into dollars at 1990 prices with the aid of purchasing-power parities. Reconstruction and growth in Europe is the subject of three recently published collections: Barry Eichengreen, ed., *Europe's Post-War Recovery* (Cambridge, 1995); Bart van Ark and Nicholas Crafts, eds., *Quantitative Aspects of Post-War European Economic Growth* (Cambridge, 1996); and Nicholas Crafts and Gianni Toniolo, eds., *Economic Growth in Europe Since 1945* (Cambridge, 1996).

An interesting, though not uncontroversial, treatment of economic reconstruction as a European political problem can be found in Alan S. Milward, *The Reconstruction of Western Europe, 1945–51* (London, 1984). Milward deals at length with the Marshall Plan in this context. A more balanced account is Michael J. Hogan, *The Marshall Plan: America, Britain, and the Reconstruction of Western Europe, 1947–1952* (Cambridge, 1987), the standard work on the subject. Only the economic aspects of the plan are addressed by Immanuel Wexler, *The Marshall Plan Revisited: The European Recovery Program in Economic Perspective* (Westport, Conn., 1983). On the role of the Marshall Plan in West Germany, a valuable collection is Charles S. Maier and Günter Bischof, eds., *The Marshall Plan and Germany: West German Development Within the Framework of the European Recovery Program* (New York, 1991). The wide-ranging academic controversy over the Plan is documented in Hans-Jürgen Schröder, ed., *Marshallplan und westdeutscher Wiederaufstieg: Positionen – Kontroversen* (Stuttgart, 1990). The decisive significance of the Marshall Plan for the reintegration of West Germany into the world economy is expounded in the study by Christoph Buchheim, *Die Wiedereingliederung Westdeutschlands in die Weltwirtschaft 1945–1958* (Munich, 1990). The OEEC, created to implement the Marshall Plan, was the first international stage on which West Germany was able to appear as an independent player, as shown by Werner Bührer, *Westdeutschland in der OEEC: Eingliederung, Krise, Bewährung 1947–1961* (Munich, 1997).

An important contribution to the interpretation of the economic history of West Germany during the occupation was made by Werner Abelshauser with *Wirtschaft in Westdeutschland 1945–1948: Rekonstruktions- und Wachstumsbedingungen in der amerikanischen und britischen Zone* (Stuttgart, 1975). He took up the theme again in *Wirtschaftsgeschichte der Bundesrepublik Deutschland (1945–1980)* (Frankfurt am Main, 1983), and many of his ideas have also been expounded upon in Alan Kramer's *The West German Economy, 1945–1955* (New York, 1991). A central issue in Abelshauser's argument was his correction of the official index of bizonal industrial production through reference to power consumption, where he assumed constant productivity in the power industry. The resulting picture is one of relatively constant growth in West Germany from autumn 1947, which caused Abelshauser to see the importance of the currency reform in very relative terms. This judgment was largely endorsed by subsequent writers.

In the mid-1980s, this thesis became the subject of debate (for a summary, see Rudolf Morsey, *Die Bundesrepublik Deutschland: Entstehung und Entwicklung bis 1969*, 4th ed. [Munich, 1999], 158–60). First, Albrecht Ritschl ("Die Währungsreform von 1948 und der Wiederaufstieg der westdeutschen Industrie: zu den Thesen von Mathias Manz und Werner Abelshauser über die Produktionswirkungen der Währungsreform," *Vierteljahrshefte für Zeitgeschichte* 33 [1985]) pointed out that Abelshauser's assumption regarding constant electrical productivity was untenable. This seemed to rehabilitate the official figures. Instead of finished products, company owners before the currency and economic reforms appear mainly to have stockpiled raw materials and semifinished goods, as Christoph Buchheim explains in "The Currency Reform in West Germany in 1948," in *German Yearbook on Business History, 1989–92*. Rainer Klump,

Wirtschaftsgeschichte der Bundesrepublik Deutschland: Zur Kritik neuerer wirtschaftshistorischer Interpretationen aus ordnungspolitischer Sicht (Stuttgart, 1985) criticized Abelshauser for underestimating the importance of the free-market framework for the boom in growth. Finally, Bernd Klemm and Günter J. Trittel, "Vor dem 'Wirtschaftswunder': Durchbruch zum Wachstum oder Lähmungskrise? Eine Auseinandersetzung mit Werner Abelshausers Interpretation der Wirtschaftsentwicklung 1945–1948," *Vierteljahrshefte für Zeitgeschichte* 35 (1987), accuse Abelshauser of determinism.

The debate has since died down. There seems to be a broad consensus that the sound potential for reconstruction rightly diagnosed by Abelshauser, contrary to earlier opinions, was an important factor in the sustained postwar boom. Even so, it could not become properly effective until after the currency reform because, without it, the threat of loss of real assets, high costs, and the impossibility of calculating profits realistically made production and market sales unattractive to most private businesses.

A recent overview of West Germany's economic history has been drawn by three liberal economists: Herbert Giersch, Karl-Heinz Paqué, and Holger Schmieding, *The Fading Miracle: Four Decades of Market Economy in Germany* (Cambridge, 1992). As the title alone implies, they also look at the slowdown of growth in the Federal Republic, which they attribute in part to the failings of regulatory policy.

The origin and substance of the concept of the social market economy have been recently and knowledgeably described by Anthony J. Nicholls, *Freedom with Responsibility: The Social Market Economy in Germany, 1918–1963* (Oxford, 1994). For two primary-source collections on this, see Wolfgang Stützel et al., eds., *Standard Texts on the Social Market Economy: Two Centuries of Discussion* (New York, 1982), and Alan Peacock and Hans Willgerodt, *Germany's Social Market Economy: Origins and Evolution* (London, 1989). The way in which this concept was implemented has not yet been the subject of a comprehensive study; but for individual aspects, such as the prohibition of cartels and the liberalization of imports, see Volker Berghahn, *The Americanisation of West German Industry 1945–1973* (Leamington Spa, 1985); Buchheim, *Die Wiedereingliederung Westdeutschlands* (mentioned previously); and Christoph Buchheim, "Die Unabhängigkeit der Bundesbank: Folge eines amerikanischen Oktrois?" *Vierteljahreshefte für Zeitgeschichte* 49 (2001): 1–30. The West German system of financial compensation for losses suffered in the World War II is discussed in conjunction with the currency reform and the new social market economy by Michael L. Hughes, *Shouldering the Burdens of Defeat: West Germany and the Reconstruction of Social Justice* (Chapel Hill, N.C., 1999).

CHAPTER ONE

From Weakening an Enemy to Strengthening an Ally
The United States and German Reparations

Jörg Fisch

Translated by Sally E. Robertson

PLANNING AND DECISIONS BY THE
VICTORIOUS POWERS, 1941–7

German reparations were one of the major economic and political problems that poisoned the international atmosphere during the period between the world wars. Nevertheless, it was undisputed among the Allies during and after World War II that Germany and its allies would again have to pay reparations.[1] That was a consequence of, among other things, Article 231 of the Treaty of Versailles. The Allies had consistently defended the idea they found in (or at least read into) the treaty that the Germans were obligated to make reparations because they were to blame for the war. If they had dispensed with reparations in 1945, it would have meant that they felt Germany was less to blame this time than it had been in 1914.

However, there was not much discussion of reparations during the war. In the United States, only lower-level agencies were working on the issue prior to 1945. They made extravagent estimates of the German capacity to pay reparations. One committee within the State Department named sums between $10 billion and $50 billion. In fall 1944, the Foreign Economic Administration even considered it possible that Germany could make payments of well over $200 billion.[2]

Reparations did not become a major policy item until the Soviets presented the outline of a concrete plan at Yalta. Germany was to pay reparations in the amount of $20 billion, of which the Soviet Union would receive half, because it had sustained by far the greatest damage. Ten billion dollars would be taken from the German economy in the form of dismantling and other reductions in assets, the rest from current production.[3] The Americans cautiously accepted the plan as a basis for discussion in a reparations commission yet to be established. Their own internal discussions had assumed a significantly higher reparations capacity on the part of Germany, and they did not want to endanger a possible agreement before negotiations began.

---

[1] For a general overview with extensive bibliography, see Jörg Fisch, *Reparationen nach dem Zweiten Weltkrieg* (Munich, 1992). The results with regard to Germany are summarized in Jörg Fisch, "Die deutschen Reparationen und die Teilung Europas," in Wilfried Loth, ed., *Die deutsche Frage in der Nachkriegszeit* (Berlin, 1994), 67–101. For the baseline conditions and economic background, see Friedrich Jerchow, *Deutschland in der Weltwirtschaft 1944–1947: Alliierte Deutschland- und Reparationspolitik und die Anfänge der westdeutschen Aussenwirtschaft* (Düsseldorf, 1978).

[2] Otto Nübel, *Die amerikanische Reparationspolitik gegenüber Deutschland 1941–1945* (Frankfurt am Main, 1980), 25, 128; Philip Andrew Baggaley, "Reparations, Security, and the Industrial Disarmament of Germany: Origins of the Potsdam Decisions" (Ph.D. diss., Yale University, 1980), 102, 294.

[3] Second Plenary Meeting, Feb. 5, 1945, 4 p.m., Livadia Palace, in U.S. Department of State, *Foreign Relations of the United States* (hereafter *FRUS*), *The Conferences of Malta and Yalta, 1945*, 611–33, esp. 620–1 and 630–1.

The British, meanwhile, resolutely refused to settle on any kind of figures.[4]

In the following months, the American position rapidly neared that of the British, not because of any bilateral agreements but because of conflicts within the American administration. The idea now was to keep reparations to a minimum and give preference to industrial dismantling. This new position was related not only to the growing mistrust of the Soviet Union but, more important, to a crystallization of attitudes about how to deal with Germany. The ideas of Secretary of the Treasury Henry Morgenthau began to gain influence, though they did not entirely carry the day.[5] If the goal was the destruction or at least a considerable reduction of German economic potential, one could not simultaneously use that potential to produce reparations. Consequently, the United States was no longer willing to name a fixed sum. Invoking the experience of the interwar period, the Americans argued that absolute priority should be given to achieving a German balance of trade before taking reparations from current production. Otherwise, they feared, the United States would end up footing the bill for reparations in the form of loans.[6]

Such attitudes almost inevitably led to conflict with the Soviet Union, which had high expectations for reparations. At first, the Western Powers delayed the start of the reparations commission's work, then they refused to talk about concrete numbers. As a result, the Allies were farther from reaching a solution in Potsdam than they had been at Yalta.[7] The outcome of Potsdam was essentially no solution either, at least not a mutual one, but rather a division of Germany and Europe for purposes of reparations policy between the Soviets on the one side and the British and Americans on the other. From its zone, the Soviet Union had to settle only its own claims and those of Poland, whereas the three Western occupation powers were jointly responsible for all the other victorious nations. In addition, the Soviets were to be allowed to compensate for their losses with German property in the former German satellite states of Finland, Hungary, Romania, Bulgaria, and in the Soviet zone in Austria, whereas German assets in the rest of the world were reserved for the Western Powers.

The initiative for this division came from the United States. The British were skeptical, while the Soviets, who wanted to share in the potential of the Western zones, protested long and hard. The central point of contention was reparations from current production. More important politically, however, was the fact that the Soviets lost all opportunity to influence the West German economy. The provision that the Soviet Union should receive 25 percent of the proceeds from dismantlings in the Western zones did little to change this arrangement. In practice, the provision proved almost meaningless. For the Western Powers, the political price was the de facto acceptance of the Oder-Neisse line as the future eastern boundary of Germany.

Although relations with the Soviet Union were rapidly deteriorating in this period, the Americans did not view the Potsdam decision so much as a blow against the Soviets as the expression of their own plan for weakening Germany.[8]

The division of Germany for purposes of reparations was also motivated on the Western

---

[4] Alec Cairncross, *The Price of War: British Policy on German Reparations, 1941–1949* (Oxford, 1986); John Farquharson, "Grossbritannien und die deutschen Reparationen nach dem Zweiten Weltkrieg," *Vierteljahrshefte für Zeitgeschichte* 46 (1998): 43–67.

[5] Of fundamental importance for the period up to 1947 is the recent work of Wilfried Mausbach, *Zwischen Morgenthau und Marshall: Das wirtschaftspolitische Deutschlandkonzept der USA 1944–1947* (Düsseldorf, 1996).

[6] John H. Backer, *The Decision to Divide Germany: American Foreign Policy in Transition* (Durham, N.C., 1978), 46–60.

[7] See *FRUS, The Conference of Berlin (Potsdam), 1945*, 2 vols.; *Documents on British Policy Overseas*, ser. 1, vol. 1; Ministry of Foreign Affairs of the USSR, *Die Sowjet-*

union auf internationalen Konferenzen während des Grossen Vaterländischen Krieges 1941–1945, vol. 6: *Die Potsdamer (Berliner) Konferenz der höchsten Repräsentanten der drei alliierten Mächte – UdSSR, USA und Grossbritannien (17. Juli–2. August 1945): Dokumentensammlung* (Moscow, 1986).

[8] Revisionist research maintains otherwise; e.g., Bruce Kuklick, *American Policy and the Division of Germany: The Clash with Russia over Reparations* (Ithaca, N.Y., 1972).

side by a further fundamental decision of a defensive nature. The fear that the Soviets would use reparations claims to expand their influence in West Germany was greater than the hope of augmenting Western influence in East Germany and Eastern Europe in the event a cooperative solution could be found. Although it had been agreed in Potsdam that Germany would be treated as a single economic unit, the division of Germany for the purpose of reparations rendered that agreement meaningless.

In the following years, the U.S. government firmly held the line against internal attempts – for example, by the military governor of the American zone, General Lucius D. Clay – to reach a mutually agreeable all-German solution on reparations. The American policy was increasingly supported by the British but not by the French, who viewed reparations much more positively.[9]

REPARATIONS POLICY IN WEST GERMANY, 1945–53

The three Western occupation forces were now jointly responsible for the reparations claims of all victorious powers except the Soviet Union and Poland. In December 1945 in Paris, eighteen nations established the Inter-Allied Reparation Agency (IARA) to allocate German payments.[10] At the very outset, the British and Americans, against the will of the continental European nations in particular, pushed through the principle that reparations from current production were out of the question, at least for the time being.[11]

There remained, therefore, only two significant reparations sources for the IARA: dismantlings and expropriation of Germany's foreign assets. The latter was a matter for the IARA only in theory because each member state could proceed as it saw fit in this regard. The three occupation powers had complete discretion over dismantlings, however.[12] At least for the Americans, the primary concern was not to obtain reparations but to destroy a significant portion of German industrial potential. If certain facilities slated for dismantling could be put to profitable use, that was welcome; otherwise, they had to be destroyed. The results of this policy fell far short of the expectations of the IARA, which lodged repeated protests, especially against the United States, which was the first of the Allies to restrict dismantling. Beginning in 1946, the United States also began to use dismantling as a tool to pressure France and the Soviet Union to accept American ideas on Germany policy. As the East-West conflict emerged, the goal of weakening German potential faded into the background, and the view that the (West) German economy was indispensable for reconstructing (Western) Europe and strengthening it vis-à-vis the Soviet Union became more and more accepted. Although individual dismantlings could still be justified within the framework of such a plan – for example, to eliminate excess capacity or the forbidden armaments industry – it hardly made sense to further weaken an economy through dismantling that was supposed to be rebuilt as quickly as possible. By the time of the Petersberg Protocol of November 22, 1949, dismantling was no longer an issue. The practice did not stop entirely, however, until 1951. As consistent as this policy might have been in subordinating everything to the new political situation presented by the East-West conflict, it was not popular in the countries that Germany

---

[9] Marie-Thérèse Bitsch, "Un rêve français: Le désarmement économique de L'Allemagne (1944–1947)," *Relations Internationales* 51 (1987): 313–29.

[10] Inter-Allied Reparation Agency, *Report of the Assembly to its Member Governments* (Brussels, 1951).

[11] U.S. Department of State, *United States Economic Policy Toward Germany*, Dept. of State Publication 2630 (Washington, D.C., 1946), 124–5.

[12] For contemporary sources on dismantlings, see, in particular, Gustav W. Harmssen, *Reparationen, Sozialprodukt, Lebensstandard: Versuch einer Wirtschaftsbilanz*, 4 vols. (Bremen, 1948); Gustav W. Harmssen, *Am Abend der Demontage: Sechs Jahre Reparationspolitik* (Bremen, 1951). Later studies include Wilhelm Treue, *Die Demontagepolitik der Westmächte nach dem Zweiten Weltkrieg: Unter besonderer Berücksichtigung ihrer Wirkung auf die Wirtschaft in Niedersachsen* (Göttingen, 1967); Alan Kramer, *Die britische Demontagepolitik am Beispiel Hamburgs 1945–1950* (Hamburg, 1991).

had just destroyed, particularly because the British and Americans continued to rule out reparations from current production by arguing now that such payments would weaken vital German economic strength. Given the uncooperative attitude of the United States in the matter of reparations, other forms of compensation became almost unavoidable. The Marshall Plan took on this function, among others.[13]

The American position remained unchanged even after the West German economy continued to improve, and the reparations issue was put on the back burner. The Transition Agreement of 1952, which did not take effect until 1955, states: "The question of reparations will be . . . regulated by the peace treaty."[14] The 1953 London Agreement on German External Debts postponed a final decision on the reparations issue indefinitely.[15] In the Treaty on the Final Settlement with Respect to Germany between the occupation forces and the two German states on September 12, 1990, it was not even mentioned and thus tacitly abandoned. The Soviet Union had already relinquished all further claims to reparations from East Germany in 1953.

REPARATIONS, INDIVIDUAL COMPENSATION, AND RESTITUTION SINCE 1953

After 1945, ever-increasing numbers of individual claims for restitution were filed in the countries occupied by Germany during World War II. According to the existing legal position, injured parties had to petition their own government, which could then attempt to obtain reparations from Germany. However, in the negotiations for the London debt agreement, the three occupation powers and the Federal Republic rejected a petition from the Netherlands that individual claims for restitution not fall under the reparations postponement.[16] The

countries affected by this decision attempted to plead their case by arguing that this was not reparation for war damages but restitution for National Socialist injustices unrelated to the war. They met with only modest success. Between 1959 and 1961, the Federal Republic concluded lump-sum compensation agreements with eight West European countries totaling only DM 825 million.[17] The countries on the other side of the Iron Curtain received nothing, although their claims (with the exception of Poland) were also the responsibility of the Western occupation powers.

The Jews were in a unique position with regard to the reparations issue. Because they did not make up their own state during the war, they could register their claims only as citizens of other states, not as Jews. For the same reason, however, their claims did not fall under governmental renunciation of reparations. The same was true for the state of Israel, which took up these claims in 1951 and managed to receive a total of DM 3.45 billion from the Federal Republic in a compensation agreement on September 10, 1952.[18] The United States was skeptical about these negotiations because it feared for West Germany's economic viability.

The one really relevant exception resulted from domestic West German legislation on compensation. This was first tackled in the various zones and *Länder* (federal states), largely under pressure from the occupation powers. After further pressure from the Allies, and especially after a promise made by the government of the Federal Republic to the Conference on Jewish Material Claims Against Germany in a special protocol to the 1952 treaty with Israel, a German federal law was passed in 1953 and later

---

[13] See the chapters by Gerd Hardach in this section and by Michael Wala, vol. 1, Politics.

[14] *Bundesgesetzblatt*, 1955/2, 439.

[15] Ibid., 1953/2, 340.

[16] Ulrich Herbert, "Nicht entschädigungsfähig? Die Wiedergutmachungsansprüche der Ausländer," in Lu-

dolf Herbst and Constantin Goschler, eds., *Wiedergutmachung in der Bundesrepublik Deutschland* (Munich, 1989), 280.

[17] See Ernst Féaux de la Croix and Helmut Rumpf, *Der Werdegang des Entschädigungsrechts unter national- und völkerrechtlichem und politologischem Aspekt* (Munich, 1985), 201–76, 333–5.

[18] *Bundesgesetzblatt*, 1953/2:37–97. See also Nicholas Balabkins, *West German Reparations to Israel* (New Brunswick, N.J., 1971), and Herbst and Goschler, *Wiedergutmachung*, for further details.

repeatedly amended.[19] Technically, this law did not amount to reparations. Rather, it involved domestic compensation for damage sustained by persons who had lived within the boundaries of the German Reich and been connected to it in some way. However, 80 percent of those persons, predominantly Jews, now lived abroad, so that the payments became de facto reparations – not to foreign states but to their citizens. Because an entirely different basis was used for calculating these payments, they reached an extraordinarily large sum compared to actual reparations by West Germany: Between 1954 and 1994, about DM 65 billion flowed out of the Federal Republic in this manner.[20]

ECONOMIC INTERESTS OF THE UNITED STATES: REPARATIONS AND DEBT REPAYMENT

The picture painted so far of an American policy consistently aimed at minimizing German reparations is indeed too one-sided. That aim generally conformed to the overriding political interests of the United States. But it only partially coincided with American economic interests where, within the prescribed political limits, clear distinctions were made from case to case

based on the possible benefits. Edwin W. Pauley, the American delegate to the Reparations Commission, succinctly stated American interests in June 1945: "We cannot use plants, machinery and labor. But we can take and should assert to the fullest extent our demand for gold currencies, foreign assets, patents, processes, technical know-how of every type."[21]

These guidelines were indeed followed. It had been taken for granted from the beginning that the foreign holdings of the defeated nations would be confiscated around the world, even in the neutral countries, although this, like the dismantlings, represented a reduction in the assets of the German economy. The same applied to the appropriation of intellectual property in the broadest sense, such as patents, construction documentation, and technical know-how.[22] The United States combed through the industry in its zone (and even in the parts of the Soviet zone it occupied in spring 1945) no less thoroughly than the other occupation powers. Finally, German solvency was also constrained by the extraordinarily high costs of occupation.[23]

Any attempt to weigh the relative significance of the economic and political factors in American policy must go beyond actual reparations payments. Reparations are generally defined as restitution for damage and losses suffered by the recipient at the hands of the debtor nation in the course of war. However, the economic resources needed to pay these reparations can be used, instead, for entirely different types of payments. The British were the first, at Yalta, to clearly demonstrate such an interest. One of the

---

[19] *Bundesgesetzblatt*, 1953/2:85–94, 1953/1:1387–1408, 1956/1:559–96, 1965/1:1315–40; Ronald W. Zweig, *German Reparations and the Jewish World: A History of the Claims Conference* (Boulder, Colo., 1987). On the attitude of the other German state, see Angelika Timm, *Alles umsonst? Verhandlungen zwischen der Claims Conference und der DDR über "Wiedergutmachung" und Entschädigung* (Berlin, 1996).

[20] Cornelius Pawlita, *"Wiedergutmachung" als Rechtsfrage? Die politische und juristische Auseinandersetzung um Entschädigung für die Opfer nationalsozialistischer Verfolgung (1945 bis 1990)* (Frankfurt am Main, 1993); German Bundestag, *Bericht der Bundesregierung über Wiedergutmachung vom 31.10.1986*, 10. Wahlperiode, Drucksache 10/6287; Constantin Goschler, *Wiedergutmachung: Westdeutschland und die Verfolgten des Naziregimes 1945–1954* (Munich, 1992); and the large compilation Bundesminister der Finanzen, with Walter Schwarz, eds., *Die Wiedergutmachung nationalsozialistischen Unrechts durch die Bundesrepublik Deutschland*, 6 vols. (Munich, 1974–87). The most recent overview is Hermann-Josef Brodesser et al., *Wiedergutmachung und Kriegsfolgenliquidation. Geschichte – Regelungen – Zahlungen* (Munich, 2000).

[21] The Representative on the Allied Commission for Reparations (Pauley) to the Secretary of State, June 19, 1945, *FRUS, The Conference of Berlin (Potsdam), 1945*, 1:511.

[22] For fundamental information in this regard, see John Gimbel, *Science, Technology, and Reparations: Exploitation and Plunder in Postwar Germany* (Stanford, Calif., 1990). See also Jörg Fisch, "Reparations and Intellectual Property," in Matthias Judt and Burghard Ciesla, eds., *Technology Transfer out of Germany After 1945* (Amsterdam, 1996), 11–26.

[23] See the chapter by Hubert Zimmermann in this section.

reasons they rejected the Soviet proposal on reparations was that they first wanted to see the Germans pay off their prewar debts.[24] Such claims had to be deferred for the time being, however, because reparations in the form of cash payments had been ruled out for economic reasons. If the Germans had been permitted to repay debts in cash, it would have been difficult to justify why reparations could not also be paid in cash. Nevertheless, the fundamental priority of debt repayment was also anchored in the IARA treaty.[25]

In the early 1950s, after the West German economy had revived, pre- and postwar financial claims unrelated to reparations were brought forward and regulated in the London Agreement on German External Debts of February 27, 1953. In that agreement, the Federal Republic pledged to repay 56 percent of prewar debt and 44 percent of postwar debt (in particular, credits given in connection with the Marshall Plan) by 1994, a total of DM 14.5 billion.[26] German solvency was, therefore, used to benefit the money lenders rather than the victims of war. The associated "restoration of German credit"[27] could probably have been achieved just as well with reparations payments as without if the United States had supported reparations as strongly as it did the debt agreement.

THE SCOPE OF WEST GERMAN PAYMENTS

Precise details on the amount and economic significance of reparations during the early years are more difficult to obtain for West Germany than for the Soviet zone/German Democratic

Republic.[28] The occupation powers generally made available to the IARA only that matériel that was of little interest to them. The IARA gave an exceptionally low appraisal to the goods it distributed, particularly the dismantlings, and the individual countries generally credited only symbolic sums for the German property they confiscated. The IARA statement of accounts of May 15, 1951, ran to approximately $151 million (in 1938 dollars) for dismantlings, around $295 million for foreign assets, and $44 million for the German merchant marine.[29] Later estimates were much higher; dismantlings, for example, were calculated at $500 million to $1.2 billion in 1938 dollars. The reduction in capacity has been estimated at 3 to 5 percent. Data on the value of foreign assets (which represented an all-German reparations payment) show an even greater discrepancy, from a few billion to 30 billion marks.[30]

That was not much compared to the payments made by the Soviet zone/GDR from 1945 to 1953, especially considering the considerably greater potential of the Western zones. This is illustrated by looking at reparations as a percentage of gross national product (GNP). They probably amounted to between 18 and 33 percent in the Soviet zone/GDR between 1945 and 1953, compared to only 8 to 13 percent in West Germany.[31] Intellectual property is not included in these figures because meaningful estimates are virtually impossible. Labor is also not

[24] British Proposal on Reparations, Feb. 10, 1945, *FRUS, The Conferences of Malta and Yalta, 1945*, 885.

[25] IARA Treaty of Dec. 21, 1945, pt. 1, art. 2C, printed in *United Nations Treaty Series*, 55:70–108.

[26] *Bundesgesetzblatt*, 1953/2, 336–485. See Christoph Buchheim, "Das Londoner Abkommen," in Ludolf Herbst, ed., *Westdeutschland 1945–1955: Unterwerfung, Kontrolle, Integration* (Munich, 1986), 219–29.

[27] Hans-Peter Schwarz, ed., *Die Wiederherstellung des deutschen Kredits: Das Londoner Schuldenabkommen* (Stuttgart, 1982).

[28] For information on the GDR, see Rainer Karlsch, *Allein bezahlt? Die Reparationsleistungen der SBZ/DDR 1945–1953* (Berlin, 1993), and Rainer Karlsch, Jochen Laufer, and Friederike Sattler, eds., *Sowjetische Demotagen in Deutschland 1944–1949. Hintergründe, Ziele und Wirkungen* (Berlin, 2002).

[29] Inter-Allied Reparation Agency, *Report of the Assembly*, schedule 1 and 2(a).

[30] Overviews of the various data in Fisch, *Reparationen*, 204–10, and Christoph Buchheim, *Die Wiedereingliederung Westdeutschlands in die Weltwirtschaft 1945–1958* (Munich, 1990), 77–95.

[31] Fisch, *Reparationen*, 199, 217. Karlsch, *Allein bezahlt?*, 234, reports that reparations encompassed as much as 50 percent of the gross national product in the Soviet zone/GDR in 1945–6, and were still 12.9 percent in 1953; his figures for the Western zones are 14.6 percent for 1946 and 3.8 percent for 1953.

considered because attempts to credit it run up against nearly insurmountable difficulties.

In the 1950s and 1960s, payments based on the London debt agreement, the Israel treaty, the agreement with the Western European countries, and the compensation legislation came to approximately DM 2 to 3 billion per year. They declined gradually to around DM 1.5 billion in the 1970s and 1980s. The burden on the GNP was never much more than 1 percent.[32]

The relatively restrained reparations policy, therefore, paid off for the recipients as well. Ultimately, considerable sums had been extracted from West Germany. The fact that those most damaged by German aggression were not necessarily the ones who received the most in the end is another matter.

In light of the poor experience with reparations in the period between the world wars, the victorious powers at first agreed to demand payments only in kind and not in cash. Nevertheless, West Germany (unlike East Germany) ended up making the lion's share of its payments in cash. A separate study would be required to determine whether this was possible only on the foundation of a more or less functional liberal and multilateral international economy.

A central argument in the American policy against reparations was that large payments would ultimately have to be made by the United States via loans to the countries that owed reparations, as had been the case in the interwar period. This argument was consistently used to reject claims, especially those of the Soviet Union. Nevertheless, the procedure was practiced where it was politically desirable: in the case of Italy and Austria, for example, and in particular with the Marshall Plan as a substitute for German reparations payments. On the other hand, the repayment of loans granted to

West Germany under the Marshall Plan showed that the United States, despite initial loans, did not automatically have to finance all reparations over the long term.

AMERICAN REPARATIONS POLICY:
SOME CONCLUSIONS

Based on the results, the American policy on reparations can be judged to have been quite successful. By offering relative leniency to the Western zones, it facilitated a more rapid economic recovery. This guaranteed West Germany a significant head start over East Germany, from which the Soviet Union extracted considerably greater payments. At the same time, it ensured West Germany's capacity to make hefty payments at a later date. The ruinous consequences feared on account of interwar experience did not materialize. Of course, only in a qualified sense was this positive outcome the result of a consistent policy. It was not compatible with the initial intention of weakening defeated Germany in order to eliminate its potential for aggression permanently. Only in connection with the emerging Cold War was that policy abandoned for one of consistent lenience so that West German economic potential could be harnessed for the western half of Europe. This leniency, moreover, did not apply to all reparations, but only to those in which the United States was not interested.

Ultimately, the issue of reparations, for all its economic significance, became a turning point in the emerging Cold War. Within the reparations framework, the United States was able to exploit its superior economic power for its political aims against the Soviet Union. By the time of Potsdam at the latest, the United States did so not to penetrate the Soviet sphere of influence but to insulate Western Europe from it.

---

[32] Fisch, *Reparationen*, 219–24.

CHAPTER TWO

Restructuring and Support

Beginnings of American Economic Policy in Occupied Germany

Wilfried Mausbach

Translated by Richard Sharp

The economic policy the United States pursued in occupied Germany combined politically motivated security considerations with the provision of humanitarian aid. This duality accounted for its often striking inconsistency. Both aspects, however, had evolved unavoidably from a single cause: Hitler's aggression. That seemed to have stemmed from a peculiarly German mind-set and a corresponding set of political, social, and economic conditions that had to be fundamentally changed if mankind were to be spared yet another outbreak of German aggression. At the same time, the war Hitler unleashed had recoiled on Germany itself, leaving the country in ruins and inhabited by a population incapable of supporting itself. The Allies, therefore, confronted the problem of having to provide the German people with the means of subsistence while destroying the economic base of Germany's potential for war. The Americans, moreover, were determined not to let either of these imperatives become a long-term obstacle to the liberalization of world trade, the foundations of which were laid at Bretton Woods in 1944.[1]

FROM EUROPEAN ECONOMIC REVOLUTION TO THE RECONSTRUCTION OF TRADITIONAL TRADE PATTERNS

Germany was nonetheless the principal reason for the initial failure of American plans for a multilateral world economic system. Before the war, Germany had been the workshop of Europe, exporting finished products and capital goods while providing a market for food, raw materials, and semifinished products from other European countries. In 1938, 69.7 percent of all German exports went to other European countries, which in turn supplied 54.5 percent of Germany's imports.[2] Even after the aggressive intentions of Hitler's Germany had long been apparent, Western Europeans were still spending twice as much on capital goods from Germany as from the United States. American postwar planners initially hesitated to tamper with these traditional flows of trade – which, indeed, they regarded as an important prerequisite for a swift reconstruction of Europe.

From the outset, a central theme of America's postwar security policy and economic planning was that the peace conditions imposed on Germany should be tailored to the requirements of a liberal world trade system. The reparations

[1] Diane B. Kunz, *Butter and Guns: America's Cold War Economic Diplomacy* (New York, 1997), 6–13; Harold James, *International Monetary Policy Since Bretton Woods* (Washington, D.C., 1996), 27–57; Richard N. Gardner, *Sterling-Dollar Diplomacy: The Origins and Prospects of Our International Economic Order*, 3d ed. (New York, 1980). See also the chapter by Werner Bührer in this section.

[2] Statistisches Bundesamt, *Bevölkerung und Wirtschaft 1872–1972* (Stuttgart, 1972), 199, 201.

issue, which had been so damaging after World War I, was now viewed not as a matter of punishment for the past but as a means of advancing the cause of multilateralism in the future.[3] Economic disarmament – insofar as it went beyond actual armaments – was to affect not machinery but mechanisms: the autarkic National Socialist economic order, discriminatory trade practices, German agricultural protectionism, and the cartel system.[4] German industry was to be harnessed for the benefit of European reconstruction, and a moderate system of reparations levied on current production was to ensure that it was harmed as little as possible.[5]

In late summer 1944, Henry Morgenthau Jr. threw these plans into disarray. Popular legend notwithstanding, Morgenthau's intervention never led to serious considerations of turning Germany into a purely agricultural country. Morgenthau did, however, manage to subordinate American postwar planning to security concerns that now encompassed machinery as well as mechanisms.[6] The Foreign Economic Administration (FEA) took up this idea in 1945 and turned it into a comprehensive disarmament plan. Its core assumption read: "Although Germany is a militarily defeated nation, the economic base of her aggression – the resources, the capacity, the organizing institutions – is still available or can be reconstituted, unless appropriate measures are taken to alter fundamentally the base and orientation of the German war

economy."[7] Industrial sectors that were important to the war economy were to be drastically cut back, whereas the production of consumer goods was to be encouraged. The main instrument of this policy was to be a wide-ranging transfer of dismantled plant that would move the center of Europe's heavy industry away from Germany.

The Potsdam Protocol reflected these ideas. It conceived of demilitarization as affecting German society as a whole and used only a vague notion of peacetime German industry as the basis for guaranteeing a minimum level of subsistence. Meanwhile, the removal of "surplus capacities" in Germany's heavy industry was intended to satisfy the victorious powers' demands for reparations. These decisions were given concrete form in the Allied level-of-industry plan of March 28, 1946, whose provisions stood the structure of German foreign trade on its head.[8]

The level-of-industry plan never became a reality; its long-term objective to revolutionize European economic life proved impractical. This was mainly the result of political developments: the onset of the Cold War and its crippling effect on the Allied Control Council's ability to function.[9] The United States became increasingly aware that German exports were essential to European reconstruction. Economic security considerations à la Morgenthau came under increasingly harsh criticism.[10] The gradual recovery of Western Europe demanded capital goods and, as the situation then stood, these

---

[3] U.S. Proposal with Regard to Questions of Reparations, n.d., in U.S. Department of State, *Foreign Relations of the United States* (hereafter *FRUS*), *1943*, 1:740–1; Economic Aspects of German Reparations (Interim Draft) by Howard Ellis, Federal Reserve Board of Governors, Dec. 2, 1943, National Archives (hereafter NA), RG 59, Notter file, box 49.

[4] See the chapter by Regina Ursula Gramer in this section.

[5] Otto Nübel, *Die amerikanische Reparationspolitik gegenüber Deutschland 1941–1945* (Frankfurt am Main, 1980), 81–3.

[6] Wilfried Mausbach, *Zwischen Morgenthau und Marshall: Das wirtschaftspolitische Deutschlandkonzept der USA 1944–1947* (Düsseldorf, 1996).

[7] The FEA Disarmament Plan II, Aug. 6, 1945, NA, RG 59, lot M-17/18, box 13. As yet, there has been no study of this agency and its role in American economic warfare.

[8] Text in OMGUS, *A Year of Potsdam: The German Economy Since the Surrender: A Report Prepared by the Economics Division*, OMGUS (Berlin, 1946); Benjamin U. Ratchford and Ward D. Ross, *Berlin Reparations Assignment: Round One of the German Peace Settlement* (Chapel Hill, N.C., 1947).

[9] See the chapters by Edmund Spevack and Gunther Mai, vol. 1, Politics.

[10] See the chapter by Michael Wala, vol. 1, Politics.

could be procured only in the United States. Lacking the required dollar reserves, European countries pleaded endlessly for American foreign aid, while trade within Europe threatened to degenerate into a system of bilateral barter.[11] Increasingly, therefore, American policy toward Germany began to focus on Europe's economic needs. At the Moscow Council of Foreign Ministers conference in 1947, U.S. Secretary of State George Marshall tried to have these needs – ignored at Potsdam – introduced into Allied policy.[12] After the failure of the conference, the issue then became the key to the formulation of a revised, bizonal level-of-industry plan. By the time Bizonia was ready to be incorporated into the Marshall Plan, economic revolutions had disappeared from the agenda. Beyond purely humanitarian aims, the purpose of American foreign aid now was to restore the European trade flows of the prewar years and, by implication, the traditional German industrial structure. This was the only way to bring about economic and political stability in Europe, close the dollar gap, and bring a multilateral world economic order into being.[13]

PLANS AND REALITIES

The temporary effort to redesign Germany's industrial structure was one of several elements of security policy that became long-term headaches for the Office of Military Government United States (OMGUS), which had an essentially constructive attitude. If its fear that such efforts would "become the tail that wags the dog"[14] proved unfounded, the reason

was that OMGUS cherished no illusions about the order in which its tasks had to be performed: "The task for the interim period is to get enough production going to avoid chaos, while developing long-range policy to prevent the revival of war production."[15] Early on, plans hatched on the Potomac became a side issue in Germany. In any case, the broad discretionary power that had been built into occupation directive JCS 1067 at the urging of the Pentagon paid off.[16] With its stipulation that disease and civil unrest were to be avoided at all cost, it allowed the American commander-in-chief, General Dwight D. Eisenhower, to postpone the most restrictive terms of the directive and institute constructive measures immediately.[17]

One week after the German surrender, the commanders of the occupying troops received instructions to maintain supplies of food, medical equipment, soap, lubricants, fertilizers, fuels, insecticides, and textiles using the existing production capacities and to produce materials needed for the maintenance of infrastructure. This list could be lengthened on request, and local commanders seem to have readily done so.[18] They were able to draw upon a capital stock that was in fact larger than it had been in 1936.[19] Compared with the damage bombing had inflicted on the inner cities and infrastructure, the stock of machinery had escaped

[11] William Diebold Jr., *Trade and Payments in Western Europe: A Study in Economic Cooperation 1947–51* (New York, 1952), 15–21; Alan S. Milward, *The Reconstruction of Western Europe, 1945–51* (London, 1984).

[12] Statement by Secretary Marshall, Moscow Session of Council of Foreign Ministers, Apr. 3, 1947, in U.S. Department of State, *Germany, 1947–1949: The Story in Documents* (Washington, D.C., 1950), 410.

[13] Christoph Buchheim, *Die Wiedereingliederung Westdeutschlands in die Weltwirtschaft 1945–1958* (Munich, 1990).

[14] Murphy to Despres, May 3, 1945, Bundesarchiv Koblenz, Z 45 F, POLAD 737/26.

[15] Staff Meeting US Group CC, May 26, 1945, Institut für Zeitgeschichte, Munich, Fg 12/1.

[16] John H. Backer, *Priming the German Economy: American Occupational Policies, 1945–1948* (Durham, N.C., 1971); Paul Y. Hammond, "Directives for the Occupation of Germany: The Washington Controversy," in Harold Stein, ed., *American Civil-Military Decisions* (Birmingham, Ala., 1963), 311–464.

[17] Klaus-Dietmar Henke, *Die amerikanische Besetzung Deutschlands* (Munich, 1995).

[18] For an example of the necessary reappraisal of these local activities, see Reinhold Billstein, "'Was machen wir mit der Kölner Industrie?' Bestandsaufnahme und Weichenstellungen unter amerikanischer Kontrolle im Frühjahr 1945," in Jost Dülffer, ed., *"Wir haben schwere Zeiten hinter uns": Die Kölner Region zwischen Krieg und Nachkriegszeit* (Vierow, 1996), 267–93.

[19] Werner Abelshauser, *Wirtschaft in Westdeutschland 1945–1948: Rekonstruktion und Wachstumsbedingungen in der amerikanischen und britischen Zone* (Stuttgart, 1975), 14–30.

Table 1. *Index of Industrial Production in Occupied Germany (1936 = 100)*

Year	U.S. Zone	U.K. Zone	French Zone	Soviet Zone
1945 (4th quarter)	19	22	—	22
1946	41	34	36	44
1947	Bizonia 44		42	54
1948	63		56	60

Sources: Werner Abelshauser, *Wirtschaftsgeschichte der Bundesrepublik Deutschland* (Frankfurt am Main, 1983), 34; Albrecht Ritschl, "Die Währungsreform von 1948 und der Wiederaufstieg der westdeutschen Industrie: Zu den Thesen von Mathias Manz und Werner Abelshauser über die Produktionswirkungen der Währungsreform," *Vierteljahrshefte für Zeitgeschichte* 33 (1985): 136–65; Wolfgang Zank, *Wirtschaft und Arbeit in Ostdeutschland 1945–1949: Probleme des Wiederaufbaus in der Sowjetischen Besatzungszone Deutschlands* (Munich, 1987), 192–4.

relatively intact, so that production was able to resume rather quickly.

The year-by-year data conceal, however, the repeated fluctuations in the rate of economic development (see Table 1). These fluctuations were caused by a number of interrelated bottlenecks, especially shortages of raw materials, food, and transport facilities.

In 1945–6, many companies still had considerable stocks of raw materials; in fact, raw material shortages of the time might be summed up in a single word – coal. Coal was by far the most important source of energy and, as early as spring 1945, the British-American Potter-Hyndley report had contained a worrying prediction that it would be in short supply in postwar Europe.[20] The coal directive promptly issued by President Harry Truman gave the supplying of the liberated areas priority over German domestic consumption.[21] The envisioned distribution of European coal by the European Coal Organization was frustrated in Germany's case by Soviet veto. It was, therefore, left to the Control Council to determine Germany's internal coal requirements, and the deadlock in the

council soon made this the responsibility of the commanders in the individual zones. In Bizonia, the distribution of coal became the most important means of controlling the economy.[22] Increased food rations, wage raises, improved living conditions, the reintroduction of the miners' guild pension, and a variety of point systems – all these incentives were to be used to spur the miners on to maximum productivity.[23] Contrary to widespread rumors, coal was not being taken away in bulk to pay for reparations. Indeed, according to Allied figures, the proportion of total production exported was well below the prewar figure, and the sale of coal by the occupying powers below the world market price caused less of a loss than is usually assumed (see Table 2).[24]

The supply of coal was nonetheless far from adequate to meet demand. Not only were productivity levels still too low, but – as evidenced by the occasional accumulation of substantial coal stockpiles – there were also transport problems. By the end of the war, Germany's

[20] Bericht über die Kohlesituation in Nordwesteuropa, June 7, 1945, in Bundesminister des Innern, *Dokumente zur Deutschlandpolitik,* ser. 2, vol. 1, pt. 1: *Die Konferenz von Potsdam* (Frankfurt am Main, 1992), 481–8; John Gimbel, *The American Occupation of Germany: Politics and the Military, 1945–1949* (Stanford, Calif., 1968), 9–10.

[21] Text in U.S. Department of State, *United States Economic Policy Toward Germany* (Washington, D.C., 1946), 76–7.

[22] Wolfgang Krumbein, *Wirtschaftssteuerung in Westdeutschland 1945–1949: Organisationsformen und Steuerungsmethoden am Beispiel der Eisen- und Stahlindustrie in der britischen/Bi-Zone* (Stuttgart, 1989).

[23] Werner Abelshauser, *Der Ruhrkohlenbergbau seit 1945: Wiederaufbau, Krise, Anpassung* (Munich, 1984), 36–49.

[24] Christoph Buchheim, "Kriegsschäden, Demontagen, Reparationen: Deutschland nach dem Zweiten Weltkrieg," in Deutscher Bundestag, *Materialien der Enquete-Kommission "Aufarbeitung von Geschichte und Folgen der SED -Diktatur in Deutschland"* (Baden-Baden, 1995), 2, pt. 2:1030–69, esp. 1059.

Table 2. *Production, Stocks, and Exports of Solid Fuels, Bizonal Area, 1936 and 1945–8*
(in Thousands of Metric Tons)

Period	Hard Coal	Pitch Coal	Raw Brown Coal	Stocks at Mines	Exports
1936	116,963	1,443	56,829	N/A	31,378
1945	35,484	1,215	24,248	5,649	N/A
1946	53,946	1,317	51,590	582	12,023
1947	71,124	1,410	58,725	1,701	10,822
1948	87,033	1,381	64,856	311	17,824

Source: OMGUS, Report of the Military Governor, Statistical Annex, July 1949, 174, 178–9.

transport system had been brought to a virtual standstill: 90 percent of the country's railroad network was either blocked by wrecked rolling stock or unusable because of bomb damage to track systems. All major bridges had been destroyed, and river and canal navigation channels were impassable because of bridge debris and sunken wrecks.[25]

Although the situation soon improved perceptibly, with considerable assistance from Allied engineer units, the transport system was in no condition to meet the revived industrial sector's increasing demand for raw materials and intermediate goods. The Americans estimated that by June 1945 only 75,000 of the prewar stock of 600,000 freight cars were still usable.[26] The Hitler regime's cannibalization of infrastructure and equipment in the last years of the war meant that more and more rolling stock had to be taken away to the repair yards, where the steel shortage was preventing maintenance work.

Regular setbacks in coal production were usually associated with general reductions in food rations, which indicates that production levels and absenteeism were determined not by the increased rations given to the miners but by the undernourishment of their families. Originally, the United States had no reser-

vation in expecting the Germans to subsist on short rations; President Franklin Roosevelt made the oft-quoted remark that they could receive three helpings of soup per day from the field kitchens.[27] However, the supply crisis proved so serious that soon substantial quantities of goods from army supplies were being issued to civilians. Then, contrary to initial plans, the occupiers also began to bring food supplies into Germany specifically for the civilian population; by summer 1946, the U.S. Department of the Army had opened a special budget line for these supplies (Government Aid and Relief in Occupied Areas, or GARIOA). By 1948, the Americans and British between them had spent more than $2 billion on GARIOA aid.[28] Yet, many Germans soon came to interpret the undeniably short rations as an instrument of vengeance. Confronted with 100 million starving people in Europe, failed harvests throughout the world, and the loss of the surplus production from areas of Central and Eastern Europe destroyed by Hitler's war, Washington had to impose priorities on exports of American food stocks, even if this repeatedly strained the fragile threads of trust between occupiers and occupied.[29] Not until 1947 was there any

[25] Report to Committee of European Economic Cooperation, Combined U.S./British Zones of Germany, Transport (Aug. 3, 1947), NA, RG 260, Records of the Transportation Division, box 21, Marshall Plan folder.

[26] SHAEF, G-4 (Mov and Tn), Transportation in Germany, May 16, 1945, NA, RG 260, Office Records of Lewis A. Douglas, box 47.

[27] Memorandum by President Roosevelt to the Secretary of War, Aug. 26, 1944, *FRUS, 1944,* 1:544.

[28] OMGUS, Economics Division, Supply Accounting Branch, Report of Issues of CA/MG Supplies to the German Economy for the Period from Occupation to 31 December 1946, Oct. 1947; Deutsche Bundesbank, *Deutsches Geld- und Bankwesen in Zahlen* (Frankfurt am Main, 1976), 341.

[29] John E. Farquharson, *The Western Allies and the Politics of Food: Agrarian Management in Postwar Germany*

awareness of the industrial-policy aspect of what had previously been purely emergency aid supplies, and this realization was reflected – with the help of better harvests – in a considerable increase in food imports. Overall, there is no doubt that the Allied aid shipments alone prevented widespread starvation in Germany after 1945, but the American dogma of political decentralization may also have been partly responsible for a defective system of registration and distribution.[30]

In the meantime, this aid was devouring more and more American tax revenue even though the United States had tried at an early stage to erect safeguards at the level of the Allies against such a development. The most important was known as the first-charge principle, whereby proceeds from exports of German goods were to be offset against the costs of imports until the German balance of payments was restored. Only then would goods from current production be used for reparations purposes. In addition, Washington demanded that German exports be paid for entirely in U.S. dollars. The first-charge principle and the dollar clause certainly prevented a massive hemorrhaging of German resources, but they also stymied bilateral German trade with other European countries, which served the American multilateral agenda.[31]

In the face of strenuous Soviet resistance, U.S. Secretary of State James Byrnes abandoned the first-charge principle at Potsdam as a concept for the whole of Germany in favor of a zonal arrangement.[32] In doing so, he simultaneously thwarted another prerequisite for minimizing American aid shipments: German economic unity. Allied inability to achieve the overall eco-

Table 3. *Bizonal Area, Exports and Imports, Aug. 1, 1945–Dec. 31, 1948 (in Millions of Dollars)*

Period	Export Deliveries	Import Arrivals
1945 (Aug.–Dec.)	20	96
1946	148	643
1947	225	734
1948	653	1,353

Source: Monatsberichte der Bank Deutscher Länder, Jan. 1949, 8.

nomic settlement envisioned at Potsdam and the problems of interzonal trade were disadvantageous to the structurally imbalanced Western zones.[33] A quarter of the food imports into Bizonia could have been dispensed with, according to OMGUS estimates, if surplus production from the East had been available.[34]

In this respect, Bizonia was a withdrawal to the second line of defense, though it fell far short of reducing imports to a level for which the ailing exports could have earned the necessary foreign exchange (see Table 3).

The situation was particularly precarious in the American zone, where exports from August 1945 through April 1946 earned only $3.8 million, and the cost of imports over the same period amounted to $91 million, food alone accounting for $72 million.[35] It is hardly surprising, then, that as early as fall 1945, OMGUS had come to an agreement to pool exports with the British zone, whose substantial coal exports promised to bring in foreign exchange. Nor is it surprising that the British were very soon trying to balance this "subsidy" by pooling the finance of imports, too.

(Leamington Spa, 1985), 95–7; Wolfgang Krieger, *General Lucius D. Clay und die amerikanische Deutschlandpolitik 1945–1949* (Stuttgart, 1987), 166–72.

[30] Günter J. Trittel, *Hunger und Politik: Die Ernährungskrise in der Bizone (1945–1949)* (Frankfurt am Main, 1990).

[31] Buchheim, *Wiedereingliederung*, 6–14.

[32] Gunther Mai, *Der Alliierte Kontrollrat in Deutschland 1945–1948: Alliierte Einheit – deutsche Teilung?* (Munich, 1995), 204–9.

[33] OMGUS, *Economic Data on Potsdam Germany: Special Report of the Military Governor*, Sept. 1947, 12–29.

[34] OMGUS, *Economic Policies, Programs and Requirements in Occupied Germany: Answers to Questions Submitted by Members of the Select Committee on Foreign Aid, House of Representatives*, Sept. 1947, 156.

[35] SE and I/P (46)4(Rev1) Annex to DECO/P/ (46)220, May 22, 1946, NA, RG 260, Records of the Economics Division, Industry Branch, OMGUS, box 30, 211 Exports (Policy).

FOREIGN TRADE IN A STRAITJACKET

The American occupiers made countless attempts to stimulate Germany's foreign trade.
However, OMGUS, appointed by Military
Government Laws 53 and 161 to keep watch
over foreign trade and foreign exchange transactions, soon began to feel the impact of the
numerous unmanageable trade restrictions that
had been imposed on the German economy
for reasons of security. At an early stage, in
any case, export orders issued showed a massive
imbalance to the detriment of traditional German exports.[36] In the first year of occupation,
only 4 percent of the American zone's export
proceeds came from finished and semifinished
products; hops, potash, salt, and lumber made up
the whole of the remainder.[37] Even with the addition of the British zone, with its concentration
of heavy industry, this pattern was by no means
reversed. Overall, though, the capital goods sector as a whole (iron and steel, nonferrous metals,
and construction materials) achieved a very notable recovery, far outstripping the performance
of the consumer goods sector (see Table 4).[38]

An export structure diametrically opposed to
the needs of postwar Europe was far from being the only obstacle to foreign trade, however.
The occupation had also severed all contacts of
any kind between German businessmen and the
outside world. This isolation was intended to
prevent the migration of German capital assets
into foreign holdings that might be used to finance possible resistance or to prepare for a further outbreak of aggression.[39]

Table 4. *Leading Export Goods, Bizonal Area*
(Monthly Average, Jan.–May 1947, in
Thousands of Dollars)

Coal	7,223
Forest Products	1,673
Iron and Iron Alloys	379
Salt	278
Vehicles	123
Machinery	110
Potash	77
Electric Power	64
Dyes	59

Source: OMGUS, Report of the Military Governor, Statistical Annex, Jan. 1948, 64.

Foreign businessmen could visit Germany
only at great inconvenience, and Germans were
forbidden to travel abroad altogether. German
companies were not allowed to place or receive
international telephone calls; there was no air-
mail service; and sending out samples, invoices,
and transport documents was prohibited. Instead, contacts had to be arranged through the
trade attachés at U.S. embassies. Similarly, cum-
bersome diplomatic channels were then used to
determine whether prospective trading partners
were acceptable or had previously maintained
cartel relations with German firms.[40] There
was no improvement until after the Anglo-
American Joint Export-Import Agency (JEIA)
had taken over responsibility for foreign trade
in Bizonia. The export/import departments of
the regional occupation authorities were converted to decentralized JEIA branch offices and
they, too, could now grant export licenses. Germans were once again allowed to establish foreign business contacts and were even permitted

[36] Friedrich Jerchow, *Deutschland in der Weltwirtschaft
1944–1947: Allierte Deutschland- und Reparationspolitik und
die Anfänge der westdeutschen Aussenwirtschaft* (Düsseldorf,
1978), 350–427.

[37] DeWilde to Ripman, Aug. 22, 1946, NA, RG 59,
600.62/8–2246; Nicholas Balabkins, *Germany Under Direct Controls: Economic Aspects of Industrial Disarmament
1945–1948* (New Brunswick, N.J., 1964), 30.

[38] Abelshauser, *Wirtschaft in Westdeutschland*, 32–42.

[39] As yet there has been no comprehensive study
of the Safehaven Program for the liquidation of
German assets abroad. There is now an excellent
opportunity for this to be remedied: A preliminary
study produced in the United States in connection
with the Swiss bank affair and made available on

the Internet includes a provisional list of the relevant
material in the National Archives: William Z. Slany,
"U.S. and Allied Efforts to Recover and Restore
Gold and Other Assets Stolen or Hidden by Germany
During World War II," May 1997, and appendix:
"Finding Aid to Records at the National Archives at
College Park," Internet: http://www.state.gov/www/
regions/eur/rpt_9705_ng_links.html (last accessed
March 18, 2003).

[40] Salant to Baker et al., Screening Out of Undesirable
Consignees for German Exports, Oct. 1, 1946, NA, RG
59, 600.629/10–146.

before long to travel abroad again, though only after going through a Kafkaesque clearance procedure. On November 5, 1947, the first five German businessmen left the country, bound for the United States.[41]

The JEIA faced an unenviable dual task: to eliminate restrictions on trade while maintaining tight control over the conduct of German business. "That unhappy agency, whose efforts in the face of impossible odds deserve greater recognition than they have received, found itself cast in the role of an export monopoly for an economy that had neither the means nor the incentives to export."[42] German businesses had to export at prices specified by the Allies, which were often unattractive, as domestic and foreign prices had ceased to be linked since the National Socialist price freeze order of November 26, 1936. In the period that followed, a system of pent-up inflation had developed, under which (rationed) goods could be purchased only with a combination of cash and coupons. All the cash that could not be spent because of a lack of coupons formed a reserve of purchasing power for which, even after 1945, there was no sufficient outlet.[43] Allied attempts to drain the cash surplus with a series of drastic tax increases came to nothing because the additional revenue was immediately reabsorbed by the costs resulting from the war. The dubious value of the Reichsmark made material assets all the more attractive. Exporters, who in any case received only the Reichsmark equivalent of the foreign exchange proceeds credited to the

accounts of the occupying powers, were therefore often only willing to produce goods for export if they received payment in raw materials. The JEIA tried to solve this problem by offering a variety of foreign-currency bonuses but, anticipating a currency reform, German companies also hoarded the raw materials and semifinished products received under these schemes. As a result, a rising tide of barter transactions began to replace market-oriented business activity.[44]

In the face of this trend, the occupying powers' program, geared to the absolute minimization of imports, became increasingly difficult to apply. For that reason, the United States had already begun looking for new ways of securing the supply of raw materials by 1946. A pilot project in which cotton had been provided for the production of textiles for export was followed by the approval of imports of raw materials for five export programs, involving products ranging from pharmaceuticals and colorants to window and door frames, from furnishings and prefabricated houses to cameras, bicycles, and toys.[45] In Bizonia, imports were then divided into two categories: Category A comprised food, seed, fertilizers, medical supplies, and fuel, the financing of which was taken over by the Americans and British; Category B imports were industrial raw materials and semifinished products, which were to be financed from the proceeds of German exports. Approval of Category B imports was the responsibility of the JEIA, and every German importer first had to prove to the JEIA that the exported goods produced using the imports would earn at least three times as much foreign exchange as their procurement had cost. Because imports, unlike exports, remained until August 1947 a

[41] JEIA, An Analysis of Its Progress, Problems and Plans, Nov. 21, 1947, NA, RG 260, Records of the Executive Committee, Control Office, box 514, JEIA memos.

[42] Henry C. Wallich, *Mainsprings of the German Revival* (New Haven, Conn., 1955), 230–1; see also Alan Kramer, *The West German Economy, 1945–1955* (New York, 1991), 106–9, which emphasizes the need for a systematic study of the JEIA.

[43] Karl-Heinrich Hansmeyer and Rolf Caesar, "Kriegswirtschaft und Inflation (1936–1948)," in Deutsche Bundesbank, *Währung und Wirtschaft in Deutschland 1876–1975* (Frankfurt am Main, 1976), 367–429; Willi A. Boelcke, *Die Kosten von Hitlers Krieg: Kriegsfinanzierung und finanzielles Kriegserbe in Deutschland 1933–1948* (Paderborn, 1985).

[44] Eduard Wolf, "Geld- und Finanzprobleme der deutschen Nachkriegswirtschaft," in Deutsches Institut für Wirtschaftsforschung, *Die deutsche Wirtschaft zwei Jahre nach dem Zusammenbruch: Tatsachen und Probleme* (Berlin, 1947), 195–262.

[45] Economics Division Memorandum No. 57, Verantwortlichkeiten nach dem Abkommen zwischen OMGUS und U.S. Commercial Company über Warenvorschüsse für Ausfuhrprogramme, Dec. 26, 1946, Bundesarchiv Koblenz, Z1/740.

monopoly of the JEIA headquarters in Minden, which was entirely unable to concern itself with all the special goods needed for export production, there was at first little movement on the export side.

An additional factor may have been that Bizonia, in its early stages, also had to struggle with the task of converting the centralized planning and administration system of the British zone to a decentralized structure like that in the American zone. Not until May 1947 did a new administrative structure do away with these difficulties.[46] The American military government took advantage of this multistage reshuffle to clamp down on efforts at socialization in the British zone, following the prevention of similar moves in Hesse.[47] As time passed, the Allies were eventually able to overcome the bottlenecks in the iron and steel industry and the transport system by the consistent establishment of a series of priorities and a transition from producer to consumer quotas.

This concentration on a small number of bottlenecks consolidated, however, the neglect of the consumer goods industries. In the original restructuring plans, exports by those industries had figured as the chief means to restore the German balance of payments. However, not only did exports remain at a thin trickle but also domestic demand could hardly be satisfied. Even a "penny article program" – matches, sewing thread, and the like – brought no relief to Bizonia. In figures submitted to Congress, the American military government calculated that the American zone had been able to produce only one shirt per person between July 1946 and June 1947 and that with the current distribution quotas, it would take twenty years before every citizen could be provided with one new coat.[48]

A postwar German government could scarcely have sustained such stringent rationing and a price freeze for as long as the Allies did. Given their inability to agree among themselves, the Allies' adherence to the Nazi regime's rationing schemes initially enabled them to postpone fundamental structural decisions. At the same time, however, the occupying powers protected the Reichsmark against national and international speculation, which had led to hyperinflation after World War I, and the Western powers also ensured that the inevitable currency cut was covered from the supply side.[49] Until that time, however, many people relied on the black market, where cigarettes constituted a universal currency that was also notably resistant to inflation. Although inexhaustible supplies of cigarettes were poured into the market, the quantity in circulation remained relatively stable, because this currency, having done its job, disappeared in a puff of smoke.

---

[46] Werner Plumpe, *Vom Plan zum Markt: Wirtschaftsverwaltung und Unternehmerverbände in der britischen Zone* (Düsseldorf, 1987); Gerold Ambrosius, *Die Durchsetzung der Sozialen Marktwirtschaft in Westdeutschland 1945–1949* (Stuttgart, 1977), 54–61.

[47] Dörte Winkler, "Die amerikanische Sozialisierungspolitik in Deutschland 1945–1948," in Heinrich August Winkler, ed., *Politische Weichenstellungen im Nachkriegsdeutschland 1945–1953* (Göttingen, 1979), 88–110; Rolf Steininger, "Reform und Realität: Ruhrfrage und Sozialisierung in der anglo-amerikanischen Deutschlandpolitik 1947–1948," *Vierteljahrshefte für Zeitgeschichte* 27 (1979): 167–240.

[48] OMGUS, *Economic Policies*, 3–4.

[49] Horst Mendershausen, *Two Postwar Recoveries of the German Economy* (Amsterdam, 1955), 30–6. See also the chapter by Werner Plumpe in this section.

CHAPTER THREE

From Decartelization to Reconcentration

The Mixed Legacy of American-Led Corporate Reconstruction in Germany

Regina Ursula Gramer

The liberalization of international trade and the creation of an open world economic order were principal objectives of U.S. foreign policy after 1945. A consistent but often overlooked facet of the American attempt to restructure the global economy was the demand for international control of private cartel agreements.[1] Cartels are defined as "agreements between firms in the same branch of trade limiting the freedom of these firms in the production and marketing of their products."[2] Ranging in form from centralized purchasing and distribution organizations to informal gentlemen's agreements, cartels aim to restrict output, allocate market shares, and fix product prices. According to various estimates, on the eve of World War II, international cartels controlled 30 to 50 percent of world trade, and American businesses participated in 107 out of 179 international cartels. Even though cartels were especially pronounced in sectors such as raw materials, chemicals, pharmaceu-

ticals, and electrical equipment, they "reached into practically every branch of the modern economy."[3]

The impetus for global decartelization after World War II originated in the American antitrust tradition and the New Deal. In the United States, corporate mergers had been the characteristic form of market regulation and economic concentration, in contrast to Britain and continental Europe, where industrial combinations traditionally had taken the form of syndicates and cartels. Although the Sherman Act of 1890 prohibited monopolization and collusion in restraint of trade, the Clayton Act of 1914 forbade price discrimination, tying contracts, and certain types of intercorporate concentration only in cases where anticompetitive or monopolistic effects could be demonstrated. Because American antitrust legislation mediated the formation of corporate consolidations while banning horizontal agreements – a legal tradition unknown in Europe – the Sherman Act in effect functioned as anticartel law.[4] Until

---

[1] Graham D. Taylor, "Debate in the United States over the Control of International Cartels, 1942–1950," *International History Review* 3 (1981): 385–98.

[2] Edward S. Mason, "The Future of International Cartels," *Foreign Affairs* 22 (1944): 604–15. For more extensive discussions of various cartel definitions, see Karl Pribram, *Cartel Problems: An Analysis of Collective Monopolies in Europe with American Application* (Washington, D.C., 1935); Fritz Machlup, "The Nature of the International Cartel Problem," in Corwin D. Edwards et al., *A Cartel Policy for the United Nations* (New York, 1945), 1–24; and Ervin Hexner, *International Cartels* (Chapel Hill, N.C., 1945).

[3] James A. Rahl, "International Cartels and Their Regulation," in Oscar Schachter and Robert Hellawell, eds., *Competition in International Business: Law and Policy on Restrictive Practices* (New York, 1981), 244–5; George W. Stocking and Myron W. Watkins, *Cartels or Competition? The Economics of International Controls by Business and Government* (New York, 1948), 68–98, 92.

[4] Martin J. Sklar, *The Corporate Reconstruction of American Capitalism, 1890–1916: The Market, the Law, and Politics* (Cambridge, Mass., 1988), 106, 154–66, 330–1, 381; Morton Keller, "Regulation of Large Enterprise: The

the 1950s, populist resentment of the reported economic injustice and political corruption of monopolies fueled the American drive against restrictive business practices and distinguished its reformist intent: to provide a "comprehensive charter of economic liberty" imbued with preserving "democratic, political, and social institutions."[5]

By April 1938, during the New Deal, President Franklin D. Roosevelt launched "the most intensive antitrust campaign in American history," targeting domestic monopolies and the "concealed cartel system."[6] In September 1944, he officially proclaimed the development of a joint international policy for curbing cartel practices. Within two weeks, the interdepartmental Executive Committee on Economic Foreign Policy, under the aegis of the State Department, provided a program for an international convention to eliminate restrictive cartel practices along the lines of U.S. domestic antitrust measures.[7] The American proposal was inserted into the abortive Havana Charter for an International Trade Organization of 1948, reappeared in 1953 in a rejected Report on Restrictive Business Practices by the United Nations Economic and Social Council, and eventually found its way, if only fragmentarily, into the European Economic Community's

1962 regulation on restrictive trade practices.[8] The immediate cause for President Roosevelt's decartelization and deconcentration initiative of September 1944 was the unresolved controversy in Washington over the treatment of Germany. Seizing on I.G. Farben as a ready example of the political and economic abuses of concentrated power in the form of domestic monopolies and international cartels, President Roosevelt remarked that "the history of the use of the I.G. Farben trust by the Nazis reads like a detective story," and declared that the "defeat of the Nazi armies will have to be followed by the eradication of these weapons of economic warfare."[9]

By the late 1930s, American liberals had come to view fascism as an expression of monopolistic economic tendencies, and Germany represented the "classic land of cartels."[10] With the dramatic growth in its number of industrial cartels from an estimated 673 in 1910 to 3,000 in 1930 – promoted by governmental competition policy and cartel-friendly courts – Germany had become the most highly cartelized country in the world even before the National Socialist takeover. The National Socialist enactment of unlimited compulsory cartelization on July 15, 1933, resulted in 1,600 new cartel agreements by December 1936, which increased the overall share of cartelized industrial production to about 46 percent in the years 1935–7.[11] From an American

United States Experience in Comparative Perspective," in Alfred D. Chandler Jr. and Herman Daems, eds., *Managerial Hierarchies: Comparative Perspectives on the Rise of Modern Industrial Enterprise* (Cambridge, 1980), 161–81.

[5] Robert T. Jones, "American Anti-Trust and EEC Competition Law in Comparative Perspective," *Law Quarterly Review* 90 (1974): 192. See also Richard Hofstadter, "What Happened to the Antitrust Movement? Notes on the Evolution of an American Creed," in Earl F. Cheit, ed., *The Business Establishment* (New York, 1964), 114–51.

[6] Ellis W. Hawley, *The New Deal and the Problem of Monopoly: A Study in Economic Ambivalence* (Princeton, N.J., 1966), 412, 421.

[7] Memorandum D-53, A Tentative Program for Dealing with International Cartels, Sept. 15, 1944, National Archives, RG 59, Harley Notter Files, box 42, folder: Central Minutes. The final revision of memo D-53 was Memorandum D-40, Program for Dealing with Restrictive Agreements and Practices of International Cartels and Combines, Mar. 9, 1945, ibid., box 35, folder: Cartel Memos.

[8] Taylor, "Control of International Cartels," 386; William Adams Brown Jr., *The United States and the Restoration of World Trade: An Analysis and Appraisal of the ITO Charter and the General Agreement on Tariffs and Trade* (Washington, D.C., 1950), 125–31, 222–6.

[9] Roosevelt to Cordell Hull, Sept. 6, 1944, in Samuel I. Rosenman, ed., *The Public Papers and Addresses of Franklin D. Roosevelt*, vol. 13: *Victory and the Threshold of Peace, 1944–1945* (New York, 1950), 255–9.

[10] Louis Domeratzky, "Cartels and the Business Crisis," *Foreign Affairs* 10 (1931): 34–53, 37; Charles S. Maier, "The Politics of Productivity: Foundations of American International Economic Policy After World War II," *International Organization* 31 (1977): 607–33.

[11] Heinz König, "Kartelle und Konzentration," in Helmut Arndt, ed., *Die Konzentration in der Wirtschaft* (Berlin, 1960), 1:304; Harm G. Schröter, "Kartellierung und Dekartellierung 1890–1990," *Vierteljahrschrift für Sozial- und Wirtschaftsgeschichte* 81 (1994): 457–83; Wilfried Feldenkirchen, "Concentration in German

perspective, the international activities of German cartels, which were controlled by the Nazi state, appeared even more perilous. They threatened to divide the world into commercial blocks and challenged in particular U.S. trade predominance in Latin America. As congressional committee hearings during World War II revealed, the dangers German cartels posed to U.S. national security were considered even more important than their political and economic effects. Most hearings prominently figured the allegations of the Justice Department's Antitrust Division against the largest German corporate giant, I.G. Farben, charging the chemical trust with hampering U.S. war production and military preparedness by conspiring with Standard Oil of New Jersey to suppress the development of synthetic rubber.[12]

The deconcentration as well as decartelization of German industry were, therefore, key objectives of the American effort to reconstruct postwar Germany – in addition to the stated goals of demilitarization, denazification, and democratization. Article 36 of the Joint Chiefs of Staff Directive 1067 of May 1945 ordered the U.S. High Command in occupied Germany to "prohibit all cartels or other private business arrangements and cartel-like organizations."[13] Furthermore, Article 12 of the Potsdam Agreement of August 1945 committed Great Britain and the Soviet Union to the American decartelization objective: "At the earliest practicable date, the German economy shall be decentralized for the purpose of eliminating the present excessive concentration of economic power as exemplified in particular by cartels, syndicates, trusts, and other monopolistic arrangements."[14] But although there existed consensus regarding the aim of decartelization, both the purpose of deconcentration and the implementation of both policies proved to be most controversial.

Differences over the thorny issue of whether cartels served as source or tool of National Socialist aggression had cropped up throughout the war. Decartelization emerged as an uneasy and confusing compromise between conflicting policy prescriptions. Whereas antitrusters used decartelization to promote deconcentration, free-traders accepted reconcentration in pursuit of decartelization. With the onset of the Cold War, the advocates of the so-called soft line (mainly located in the State Department and the Council on Foreign Relations), who pushed for a fast (West) German recovery and reintegration into a liberal world economy, won the upper hand over the proponents of far-reaching German reforms and restructuring (mainly located in the Justice and Treasury Departments and the Foreign Economic Administration).[15] In 1950, James Stewart Martin, former first chief of the Decartelization Branch of the Office of Military Government United States (OMGUS) in Germany, published detailed charges against U.S. big-business interests at large – and against certain officials, such as Brigadier General William Draper, head of the Economic Division at OMGUS – for having purposefully obstructed the German decartelization and deconcentration program. Draper's close connections to the investment banking firm Dillon, Read and Co. and, through his collaborators, to Republic Steel, General Motors, AT&T, and ITT seemed to provide a ready explanation for his advocacy of a soft line toward German industry.[16]

No significant steps toward deconcentration or decartelization were taken by February 1947. Once the decentralization of I.G. Farben had

---

Industry, 1870–1939," in Hans Pohl, ed., *The Concentration Process in the Entrepreneurial Economy Since the Late 19th Century* (Stuttgart, 1988), 118–19.

[12] Wendell Berge, *Cartels: Challenge to a Free World* (Washington, D.C., 1944); Joseph Borkin and Charles A. Welsh, *Germany's Master Plan: The Story of Industrial Offensive* (New York, 1943).

[13] U.S. Department of State, *Germany, 1947–1949: The Story in Documents* (Washington, D.C., 1950), 21–3, 29–30.

[14] Protocol of the Proceedings of the Berlin Conference, Aug. 1, 1945, in U.S. Department of State, *Foreign Relations of the United States, The Conference of Berlin (Potsdam), 1945*, 2:1478–85, 1483–4.

[15] Regina Ursula Gramer, "Reconstructing Germany, 1938–1949: United States Foreign Policy and the Cartel Question," (Ph.D. diss., Rutgers State University of New Jersey, 1992), chaps. 3–4.

[16] James Stewart Martin, *All Honorable Men* (Boston, 1950).

begun, it was not broken up into fifty-two
components as originally intended, but rather
into three large companies: Bayer, Hoechst, and
BASF. Even though the German banks were
dissolved, the so-called Big Three (Deutsche
Bank, Dresdner Bank, and Commerzbank) regained their leading positions in the 1950s. The
German electrical engineering giants Bosch and
Siemens underwent only slight restructuring.
The steel industry was reorganized into twenty-
six companies. However, most of the ties between the coal and steel producers were broken.
The degree of deconcentration that eventually was established in the Federal Republic of
Germany turned out to be much more favorable to West German industry preferences than
had been conceived in 1945. Allied deconcentration policies were, in the long run, nevertheless successful in that they helped to stir the
reconcentration of West German industries after
1955 along oligopolistic rather than monopolistic lines.[17]

In the short run, the Allies differences over
the course of German economic reconstruction certainly hampered their deconcentration
and decartelization efforts. Using company size
as the sole criterion for deconcentration, the
Soviets proposed to restructure categorically all
enterprises with more than 3,000 employees
and a 1938 annual sales volume of 25 million
Reichsmark. The British opposed the Russian
motion and suggested, instead, the creation of a
Four-Power commission that would proceed on
a case-by-case basis and operate by unanimous
accord. The American draft of a decartelization
law, however, resembled the Soviet proposal in
its provision for mandatory action against firms
of a certain size. Nevertheless, the British refusal
to accept the Soviet definition of excessive concentration led to the suspension of Allied talks
in fall 1945.[18] The three Western Allies, therefore, began to enact separate, albeit similar, de-

cartelization laws in their respective occupation
zones. Law 56 in the American zone and Law
78 in the British zone, both issued on February 10, 1947, prohibited cartels and comparable
agreements in restraint of trade for the first time
in Germany even though the Americans ended
up conceding to the British that only companies
with more than ten thousand employees qualified, prima facie, as examination cases of excessive concentration. Furthermore, Ordinance 96
in the French zone, issued on June 9, 1947, did
not prohibit price arrangements per se. Despite
these inconsistencies, the Allied Laws 56, 78,
and 96 remained in force until January 1958 –
well after the official termination of the occupation regime in May 1955.[19]

Independent of the divergent Allied occupation programs, postwar German decartelization
efforts were also shaped by home-grown developments. In the 1930s and early 1940s, a circle
of liberal economists and jurists known as the
Freiburg School had formulated the concept of
"ordoliberalism," which gave the state the decisive role in maintaining perfect competition.
However, the ordoliberal draft of a cartel law, the
so-called Josten Bill of 1949 – which included
an absolute ban on cartels and provided for the
control of mergers and the deconcentration of
groups and consortia – was rejected despite support from Economics Minister Ludwig Erhard.
In addition, opposition from the Federal Association of German Industry (*Bundesverband der
Deutschen Industrie*, or BDI) stalemated the 1951
government draft of a law prohibiting cartels.
Following years of intense controversy concerning the principles of cartel prohibition versus
cartel control, the Law Against Restraints on
Competition was finally passed on July 27, 1957.
The Cartel Law of 1957 still forbade cartels but
granted numerous exceptions for the banking,

---

[17] Volker R. Berghahn, *The Americanisation of West
German Industry, 1945–1973* (Leamington Spa, 1986), 90–
110, 283–304.

[18] Graham D. Taylor, "The Rise and Fall of Antitrust
in Occupied Germany, 1945–1948," *Prologue* 11 (1979):
23–39.

[19] J. F. J. Gillen, *Deconcentration and Decartelization
in West Germany, 1945–1953* (n.p., 1953), 25–6; Ivo E.
Schwartz, "Antitrust Legislation and Policy in Germany:
A Comparative Study," *University of Pennsylvania Law Review* 105 (1957): 643–8; Günther Schulz, "Die Entflech-
tungsmassnahmen und ihre wirtschaftliche Bedeutung,"
in Hans Pohl, ed., *Kartelle und Kartellgesetzgebung in Praxis
und Rechtsprechung vom 19. Jahrhundert bis zur Gegenwart*
(Stuttgart, 1985), 210–22.

transport, insurance, agriculture, and utilities industries; it contained no provisions for merger control or deconcentration. Neoliberalism, the theoretical underpinning of the Federal Republic's *soziale Marktwirtschaft* (social market economy), had thus supplanted ordoliberalism: Instead of attempting to create perfect competition, it limited the cartel legislation to preventing restraints on competition. Neoliberal competition laws were detached from the broader functions of social policy and limited to achieving formal rather than material justice. The official number of German cartels, as registered by the Federal Cartel Office, fell dramatically to 266 in 1978 and to 241 in 1985.[20]

The Allied decartelization and deconcentration program was a fundamental intervention into the structure of the West German economy and has been characterized as one of the "greatest experiments in modern economic organization and economic history."[21] It is, therefore, curious that historians of the occupation period have tended either to downplay the subject or dismiss the Allied restructuring of German industry as a punitive and naive reform effort.[22] Recent scholarship argues that Allied

decartelization and deconcentration did not hamper economic recovery and deemphasizes the role of the Cold War in the retreat from reformism. Rather, the focus is on long-term changes in the mentality of West German industrialists and the emergence of Keynesian thinking and growth politics on both sides of the Atlantic. Long-term assessments of Allied decartelization and deconcentration largely depend on whether they take account of the shift in U.S. policy aims from economic restructuring and the elimination of Germany's war potential to aiding West German recovery.[23] One interesting question for future research is whether the changing American attitudes toward Germany in 1946–7 did in fact trigger the relative abatement of American efforts toward decartelization in other areas of the world.

The enforcement and internationalization of American antitrust laws were undoubtedly the main causes of the demise of cartelization after World War II. The Justice Department had filed about sixty antitrust cases concerning international cartels in the 1940s and, by 1973, at least twenty-eight nations had adopted antitrust laws inspired by American principles. Until the 1960s, decartelization, upheld by sustained economic growth as well as American pressure, progressed faster and more effectively in West Germany than in any other European country.[24] The increasing globalization of competition after the mid-1970s presented new challenges for antitrust laws and their enforcement. The 1980s probably witnessed the fastest period of growth for world foreign direct investment and

[20] Theodore F. Marburg, "Government and Business in Germany: Public Policy Toward Cartels," *Business History Review* 38 (1964): 88–93; Rüdiger Robert, *Konzentrationspolitik in der Bundesrepublik: Das Beispiel der Entstehung des Gesetzes gegen Wettbewerbsbeschränkungen* (Berlin, 1976), 102–343; Reinhard Blum, *Soziale Marktwirtschaft: Wirtschaftspolitik zwischen Neoliberalismus und Ordoliberalismus* (Tübingen, 1969), 38–142; Peter Hüttenberger, "Wirtschaftsordnung und Interessenpolitik in der Kartellgesetzgebung der Bundesrepublik," *Vierteljahrshefte für Zeitgeschichte* 24 (1976): 287–307; A. J. Nicholls, *Freedom with Responsibility: The Social Market Economy in Germany, 1918–1963* (Oxford, 1994), 325–38.

[21] Heinrich K. Bock and Hans Korsch, "Kartellauflösung und Konzernentflechtung in der westdeutschen Wirtschaft seit 1945," *Wirtschaft und Wettbewerb* 7 (1957): 411–37.

[22] John H. Backer, *Priming the German Economy: American Occupational Policies, 1945–1948* (Durham, N.C., 1971); Nicholas Balabkins, *Germany Under Direct Controls: Economic Aspects of Industrial Disarmament, 1945–1948* (New Brunswick, N.J., 1964); John Gimbel, *The American Occupation of Germany: Politics and the Military, 1945–1949* (Stanford, Calif., 1968); John D. Montgomery,

Forced to Be Free: The Artificial Revolution in Germany and Japan (Chicago, 1957).

[23] Werner Abelshauser, *Wirtschaftsgeschichte der Bundesrepublik Deutschland, 1945–1980* (Frankfurt am Main, 1983); Berghahn, *Americanisation of West German Industry*; Marie-Laure Djelic, *Exporting the American Model: The Postwar Transformation of European Business* (Oxford, 1998).

[24] James A. Rahl, "International Application of American Antitrust Laws: Issues and Proposals," *Northwestern Journal of International Law and Business* 2 (1980): 336–64, 353; Harm G. Schröter, "Cartelization and Decartelization in Europe, 1870–1995: Rise and Decline of an Economic Institution," *Journal of European Economic History* 25 (1996): 129–53.

the most frenetic wave of merger consolidations in the United States since the late nineteenth century. The overall level of concentration in the European Community, which had leveled out in the mid-1970s, began to rise slowly following the recession of the early 1980s. Even more pronounced was the rapid rise in merger and takeover activity in all European countries after 1982. The structures of multinational enterprises loosened as they entered into frequently fluctuating multifirm alliances and acquired greater geographic flexibility in the interest of global competitiveness.[25] Such fluid internationalization impaired unilateral antitrust regulation.

In response to these new problems, policymakers and lawyers in the European Community and the United States reinvigorated foreign antitrust enforcement in order to protect domestic antitrust achievements. They also recognized the need to harmonize the various national antitrust regimes. Already in June 1976, the United States and the Federal Republic of Germany had formally agreed to cooperate in the application of their competition laws to international business; the European Community signed its first cooperation agreement with the United States in September 1991. Since the early 1990s, German officials have pushed for the establishment of a European Cartel Office that would reproduce the German model of competition policy at the European level.[26]

In contrast to Germany, where the application of antitrust law has remained strictly legalistic, the European Community pursued diverse, if not contradictory, competition policy goals. In particular, since 1984 the Commission of the European Community has utilized the anticartel and antimonopoly clauses of the Treaty of Rome (Articles 85 and 86) primarily to shape single-market integration, and only secondarily to eliminate restrictive business practices. From the perspective of the German Federal Cartel Office, the European Merger Control Regulation of December 1989 and the European Union Treaty of February 1992 completed the unwise triumph of industrial policy over competition policy. The BDI, on the other hand, has recommended that Germany adapt to the European model, arguing that the strict cartel ban impeded the international competitiveness of German industry.[27] This renewed debate over European competition laws reveals lasting differences among various national approaches to antitrust policies, such as the French view of competition law as "an instrument of state economic control" versus the German insistence on keeping industrial policy and enforcement of competition law separate. It confirms the differences over whether merger-induced concentration would stimulate new international cartels or greater global competitiveness.[28]

---

[25] David J. Gerber, "Antitrust and the Challenge of Internationalization," *Chicago-Kent Law Review* 64 (1988): 689–709; Geoffrey Jones, *The Evolution of International Business: An Introduction* (London, 1996), 52, 56; Walter Adams and James W. Brock, "Revitalizing a Structural Antitrust Policy," *Antitrust Bulletin* 39 (Spring 1994): 235–71; Henk Wouter de Jong, "Market Structures in the European Economic Community," in Henk Wouter de Jong, ed., *The Structure of European Industry*, 2d ed. (Dordrecht, 1988), 4–5, 37–8.

[26] Joseph P. Griffin, "EC and U.S. Extraterritoriality: Activism and Cooperation," in Barry E. Hawk, ed., *Antitrust in a Global Economy: Annual Proceedings of the Fordham Corporate Law Institute* (New York, 1994), 43–78; Barry E. Hawk, "EEC and U.S. Competition Policies – Contrast and Convergence," in Frederick M. Rowe, Francis G. Jacobs, and Mark R. Joelson, eds.,

Enterprise Law of the 80s: European and American Perspectives on Competition and Industrial Organization (Luxembourg, 1980), 39–62; Stephen Wilks and Lee McGowan, "Disarming the Commission: The Debate over a European Cartel Office," *Journal of Common Market Studies* 32 (1995): 259–73.

[27] André R. Fiebig, "The German Federal Cartel Office and the Application of Competition Law in Reunified Germany," *University of Pennsylvania Journal of International Business Law* 14 (1993): 373–407; Silke Hossenfelder, Martina Müller, and Susanne Parlasca, "Das Kartellverbot und seine Ausnahmen: Unternehmenskooperationen im Spannungsfeld zwischen nationalem und europäischem Wettbewerbsrecht," *Zeitschrift für das gesamte Handelsrecht und Wirtschaftsrecht* 160 (1996): 1–30.

[28] Barry E. Hawk, "The American (Anti-trust) Revolution: Lessons for the EEC?" *European Competition Law Review* 9 (1988): 53–87.

CHAPTER FOUR

Opting for the Structural Break

The West German Currency Reform and Its Consequences

Werner Plumpe

Translated by Richard Sharp

INTRODUCTION

When the National Socialist regime collapsed in May 1945, the war had left behind not only human suffering and destruction but also a massive financial burden. The indebtedness of the Reich alone has been estimated at more than 400 billion reichsmark, more than four times the prewar national income.

Although the greatly inflated money supply did not have a direct effect on demand (pent-up inflation) on account of the price and wage freezes still in effect at the end of the war, it nonetheless hung like the sword of Damocles over Germany's economic and financial development. Moreover, despite officially controlled prices, the fall in the value of money was obvious – not least on the black market. Until a solution could be found to the financial consequences of the war, it would be impossible for Germany to return to normal economic (and political) conditions and thus come to terms with the other burdens left by the war. If no solution were forthcoming or if it were to be long delayed, creeping economic paralysis threatened to develop into a full-scale disaster. It is not surprising, then, that the "money question" had become prominent in both German[1] and Allied[2] minds even before the war ended. It soon became apparent, of course, that this was not a purely technical issue of finance: Important political decisions had to be made before the financial consequences of the war could be dealt with. Most important of all, a successful reduction in the money supply presupposed an agreement on the political fate of Germany and fundamental decisions on *Ordnungspolitik* (regulatory policy). These decisions were eventually taken in spring 1948 in favor of a division of the country and the establishment of a free market economy in the Western zones of occupation. At that point, a currency reform in the Western zones was not just politically possible, it was also the indispensable key to the successful restoration of market-economy conditions and thus, ultimately, to the successful creation of the West German state.[3]

---

[1] Michael Brackmann, *Vom totalen Krieg zum Wirtschaftswunder: Die Vorgeschichte der westdeutschen Währungsreform 1948* (Essen, 1993).

[2] See in particular John H. Backer, *The Decision to Divide Germany: American Foreign Policy in Transition* (Durham, N.C., 1978); and, more recently, Wilfried Mausbach, *Zwischen Morgenthau und Marshall: Das wirtschaftspolitische Deutschlandkonzept der USA 1944–1947* (Düsseldorf, 1996). Important American sources can be found in U.S. Department of State, *Foreign Relations of the United States, 1944*, vol. 2; *1945*, vols. 3 and 5; *1946*, vol. 2; *1947*, vol. 2; and *1948*, vol. 2; see also Jean Edward Smith, ed., *The Papers of General Lucius D. Clay*, 2 vols. (Bloomington, Ind., 1974). For the British view, see Ian Turner, "Great Britain and the Post-War German Currency Reform," *Historical Journal* 30 (1987): 685–708.

[3] Christoph Buchheim, "Die Notwendigkeit einer durchgreifenden Wirtschaftsreform zur Ankurbelung

Against this background, the action taken in June 1948 has proven – after the fact – to be exceptionally fortunate, though at the time it was more than risky, because the currency reform implied the almost total expropriation of people's cash assets without suggesting any scheme to equalize the burdens thus imposed. This article traces the successful course of this German-American "joint venture" in currency reform.[4]

des westdeutschen Wirtschaftswachstums in den 1940er Jahren," in Dietmar Petzina, ed., *Ordnungspolitische Weichenstellungen nach dem Zweiten Weltkrieg* (Berlin, 1991), 55–65.

[4] The historical literature on the currency reform has grown considerably in recent years, following a long period in which eyewitness accounts were the dominant source. See Hans Möller, ed., *Zur Vorgeschichte der Deutschen Mark: Die Währungsreformpläne 1945–1948* (Tübingen, 1961); Hans Möller "Die westdeutsche Währungsreform von 1948," in Deutsche Bundesbank, ed., *Währung und Wirtschaft in Deutschland 1876–1975* (Frankfurt am Main, 1976), 433–83; Manuel Gottlieb, "Failure of Quadripartite Monetary Reform, 1945–1947," *Finanzarchiv* 17 (1956): 398–417. For a more recent survey, see Christoph Buchheim, "Die Währungsreform 1948 in Westdeutschland," *Vierteljahrshefte für Zeitgeschichte* 36 (1988): 189–232; idem, "Marshall Plan and Currency Reform," in Jeffrey M. Diefendorf, Axel Frohn, and Hermann-Josef Rupieper, eds., *American Policy and the Reconstruction of West Germany, 1945–1955* (Cambridge, 1993), 69–83. The economic significance of the monetary reform was first called into question by Werner Abelshauser, *Wirtschaft in Westdeutschland 1945–1948: Rekonstruktion und Wachstumsbedingungen in der britischen und amerikanischen Zone* (Stuttgart, 1975); see also Werner Abelshauser "Wiederaufbau vor dem Marshallplan: Westeuropas Wachstumschancen und die Wirtschaftsordnungspolitik in der zweiten Hälfte der 1940er Jahre," *Vierteljahrshefte für Zeitgeschichte* 29 (1981): 545–78; for a critical view of this, see Albrecht Ritschl, "Die Währungsreform von 1948 und der Wiederaufstieg der westdeutschen Industrie," *Vierteljahrshefte für Zeitgeschichte* 33 (1985): 136–65; also Bernd Klemm and Günter J. Trittel, "Vor dem 'Wirtschaftswunder': Durchbruch zum Wachstum oder Lähmungskrise? Eine Auseinandersetzung mit Werner Abelshausers Interpretation der Wirtschaftsentwicklung 1945–1948," *Vierteljahrshefte für Zeitgeschichte* 35 (1987): 571–624. A mixture of contemporary and expert comments with the results of academic research can be found in Peter Hampe, ed., *Währungsreform und Soziale Marktwirtschaft: Rückblicke und Ausblicke* (Munich, 1989).

THE ANTECEDENTS OF THE CURRENCY REFORM

The lead-up to the currency reform is essentially identical to the history of occupation policy as a whole, because a currency reform was a necessary expression of the way in which Germany's political and economic future was to be shaped. In 1944–5, the victorious powers were still making a common effort to come to terms with the financial and monetary consequences of the war, but differences of opinion were apparent from an early stage. Whereas France opposed everything that seemed to favor the centralization of Germany and to hinder the economic exploitation of its occupation zone, the British were less interested in a radical cut in the money supply than in controlled inflation, which they believed would provide a better route to the goals of their occupation policy. For the Russians, the currency issue was hardly a priority because they had destroyed the banking system early on and brought it under their complete control, so that the excess money supply in the Soviet zone had been wiped out as early as 1945.[5] The Soviets' main concern was that steps taken to reform the currency should not jeopardize Germany's reparations payments. The Americans, too, were initially not interested in swift action, because the "ambivalent nature of American postwar policies" made it seem inadvisable, at least to the military government in Germany, to add "the difficult and controversial currency question" to the agenda.[6] In the context of this confusion of divergent interests – complicated further by conflicts that put Washington and London at odds with their respective military governments in Germany – it is hardly surprising that there was no quick agreement. By spring 1946, the

[5] Theo Horstmann, "Die Angst vor dem finanziellen Kollaps: Banken- und Kreditpolitik in der britischen Zone zwischen 1945 und 1948," in Dietmar Petzina and Walter Euchner, eds., *Wirtschaftspolitik im britischen Besatzungsgebiet 1945–1949* (Düsseldorf, 1984), 215–34; Jochen Laufer, "Die UdSSR und die deutsche Währungsfrage 1944–1949," *Vierteljahreshefte für Zeitgeschichte* 46 (1998): 455–85.

[6] Backer, *Decision to Divide Germany*, 118.

negotiations between the Allies on this subject had reached a dead end.

It was the Americans, prompted by the deteriorating economic situation in the winter of 1945–6, who made a move toward ending the stalemate on the currency issue by appointing a team of experts. In spring 1946, Gerhard Colm, Joseph M. Dodge, and Raymond W. Goldsmith held numerous discussions with the responsible officers of the occupying forces and undertook a comprehensive information program in all four zones. On May 20, 1946, they presented their "Plan for the Liquidation of War Finance and the Financial Rehabilitation of Germany" (known as the CDG plan) to the American deputy military governor, General Lucius D. Clay. After intensive scrutiny in Washington, copies of the plan for the currency reform were also passed to the other three occupying powers. The plan envisaged eliminating 90 percent of the surplus money supply, without compensation, by exchanging ten old Reichsmark for one new Deutsche Mark (DM) and canceling the Reich debt. The capital-market institutions affected by the debt cancellation (e.g., financial institutions, insurance companies, and savings banks) were to receive sufficient compensation in new bonds to enable them to meet their commitments. Prices, wages, incomes, and taxes were to be converted on a one-to-one basis. As part of a *Lastenausgleich* (equalization of burdens), a 50 percent land charge was initially to be imposed on real estate and industrial plant, and, eventually, there was to be a property levy of 10 to 90 percent of the net assets concerned. Colm, Dodge, and Goldsmith also gave their views on the economic and political requirements, conditions, and consequences of a currency reform. Although deferring a radical cut in the money supply was indeed possible, they observed, there was a danger of a gradual deterioration in the economic situation, with adverse consequences for occupation policy. The existing veil of money was preventing any kind of normal economic activity and encouraging a shadow economy that, sooner or later, would paralyze political control over the economy, quite apart from the social and moral

repercussions of the fact that one cigarette could fetch more than could be earned by a full day's work. In brief, they said, if economic stability was to be restored in Germany, the currency cut could not be too long delayed.

The Russians indicated their consent to the CDG plan, provided that it did not result in any cut in Germany's reparations payments, but the British and French were more critical. Whereas the British still favored the idea of gradual controlled inflation, the French thought the American plan too generous. They feared that a reform along these lines would enable Germany to recover too quickly and so they, like the British, initially rejected the plan. For a while, there did seem to be a realistic prospect that a decision could be reached in principle in favor of a four-zone currency reform based on a modified version of the CDG plan, but agreement was initially obstructed by a side issue and eventually – against a background of new conflicts – prevented altogether.

The CDG plan envisaged not only a cut in the money supply but also the introduction of a completely new currency. Even the technicalities of its production were not a simple matter and, ultimately, the decisive conflict was sparked by the question of where it was to be printed. Whereas the Americans proposed that the new bills should be produced by the Reich printing works in the American sector of Berlin, the Russians wanted one set of the plates to be handed over to them so that new bills could also be printed in Leipzig. The British and French were initially prepared to accommodate this demand, but the Americans rejected it out of hand partly because Soviet-American relations were already beginning to deteriorate by the second half of 1946. As this deterioration continued throughout 1947, agreement became more and more improbable. The controversy over printing the bills now proved to be a matter of tactical maneuver. Russia eventually gave way on the issue, but the Americans were unmoved, which indicates that by early 1948 at the latest, the United States was no longer in real agreement with the Soviet Union. At any rate, this was the view of the British representative on the Finance

Directorate, Paul Chambers, who wrote in the journal *International Affairs* in 1948, "It would be wrong to assume that a technicality of this kind was all that separated the representatives of the four occupying powers. Behind this disagreement on the technicality lay fundamental differences in objectives."[7]

It was these "fundamental differences" that defined the initial positions in the Cold War, the context in which the United States fundamentally changed its policy on Germany and Europe.[8] Instead of suppression and supervision for Germany, there was to be a controlled reconstruction within the West European community; this policy concept found its practical expression in the Marshall Plan.[9] This policy called for the formation of a West German state; the success and political legitimacy of that state – and, obviously, its value to Western Europe – would depend on its economic viability. Because the Soviet Union could not accept this plan – to do so would be to accept a liberal world economic order under American hegemony – the decision for a separate currency reform in Western Germany was almost inevitable. In September 1947, therefore, the Americans decided unilaterally and in the strictest secrecy to have the new banknotes printed in America. Early in 1948, again secretly, the notes were shipped to Germany and initially "hidden" in the former Reichsbank buildings in Frankfurt.[10]

The technical groundwork for a separate currency reform had thus been laid. The final political decisions were also taken during spring 1948. The green light for a separate money supply cut came, above all, at the six-power conference in London, where the West Europeans and the Americans agreed on the establishment of a

West German state[11] and, in effect as a consequence, the Russians withdrew from the Control Council. In April 1948, the representatives of the three Western occupying powers agreed that the cut should be swift and radical. After internal disagreements, it was decided that the *Lastenausgleich* should be treated separately from the currency reform and with special German legislation.[12]

Once these decisions had been made, everything was dependent on the technical implementation of the currency reform. The Western powers entrusted this task to a German working group, which began its work at the top-secret Rothwesten Conclave in April 1948.[13] The substance of the German working group's mandate was clear: First, 70 percent of existing credit balances were to be written off, 20 percent blocked, and 10 percent converted to the new currency; second, the Reich debt was to be canceled and *Land* bonds issued to the capital market institutions; and third, the *Lastenausgleich* legislation was to be transferred to German responsibility.[14] Apart from the separate treatment of equalization, these provisions basically followed the CDG plan. They also made it apparent that the Allies would not accept the German currency reform plan that had been submitted to them in April 1948, the so-called Homburg plan.

In the breathing space provided by the conflicts between the Allies, the Frankfurt Economic Council had initiated currency reform plans of its own by setting up a special institution in Homburg, the Sonderstelle Geld und Kredit, which quickly set to work in fall 1947 under the direction of Ludwig Erhard. Although there were no formal contacts between the Homburg office and the occupying powers, there was a great deal of unofficial interest in its activities. The currency reform plan the Homburg office presented in April 1948, drawing on German discussions of currency reform dating back to

---

[7] Quoted in ibid., 132.

[8] John Gimbel, *The American Occupation of Germany: Politics and the Military, 1945–1949* (Stanford, Calif., 1968).

[9] See the chapter by Gerd Hardach in this section and the chapter by Michael Wala, vol. 1, Politics.

[10] Eckhard Wandel, "Zur Vorgeschichte der Währungsreform von 1948," in Peter Hampe, ed., *Währungsreform und soziale Marktwirtschaft: Rückblicke und Ausblicke* (Munich, 1989), 45.

[11] See the chapter by Hermann-Josef Rupieper, vol. 1, Politics.

[12] Brackmann, *Vom totalen Krieg zum Wirtschaftswunder*, 242.

[13] Möller, *Die westdeutsche Währungsreform*, 445–51.

[14] Buchheim, *Die Währungsreform 1948*, 212.

1943, envisaged a drastic cut in the money supply, certification of pre-reform debts, and a *Lastenausgleich* that would have no effect on assets. It was thus inevitable that there would be conflicts with the Allies who, at the same time, had decided to separate *Lastenausgleich* from currency reform and who must have viewed the certification of existing debts with no clear prospects for financing them as an incalculable risk.

In giving their instructions to the conclave, therefore, the military governors made it clear from the outset that the Germans would have no room for maneuver on these issues (*Lastenausgleich*, cancellation of pre-reform debts) but would merely be required to implement the Allied plan.[15] However, the Economic Council did instruct the German experts of the conclave to take the Homburg plan into account. But, in view of the justified Allied criticism of the unclear certification of existing debts, the Germans could produce no convincing alternative to the Allied requirements. Conflict on these matters within the conclave was, therefore, limited even though the Germans continued to reject the cancellation of private debts. On other issues, in any case, opinions did not differ so widely. The major disagreements were no longer over the approach to reform but over its financial format. The main areas of contention concerned the envisioned allowance per person and the ration of frozen and ready assets. The Germans argued for generous per capita sums (DM 50 instead of the proposed DM 25), but lower quotas for ready and frozen assets (5 percent and 15 percent, respectively). After protracted argument, agreement was reached in late May 1948 that 80 percent of monetary holdings should be neutralized, 10 percent converted, and 10 percent frozen in deposit accounts; in addition, the per capita sum was to be DM 50. Then finally, shortly before the cutoff date, the following quotas were established: DM 60 per capita, plus 15 percent frozen and 5 percent ready, against which the per capita amount was to be set off.[16]

[15] Brackmann, *Vom totalen Krieg zum Wirtschaftswunder*, 247–60.
[16] On this and following points, see Buchheim, *Die Währungsreform 1948*, 217–19.

THE CURRENCY REFORM

On June 20, 1948, the era of the reichsmark came to an end. Three laws enacted by the Allies first made the Deutsche Mark the sole legal tender as of June 21, 1948 (*Währungsgesetz*), regulated the issuance of the Deutsche Mark by the *Bank Deutscher Länder* (*Emissionsgesetz*), and eliminated the glut of money (*Umstellungsgesetz*). Later, the *Festkontogesetz* of October 4, 1948, set out the rules governing frozen assets. The *Umstellungsgesetz* was the core of the currency reform. Section 1 extinguished all existing corporate and institutional Reichsmark assets and converted all other credit balances at 10 to 1; half of the resulting sum was credited to a ready deutschmark account and the other half to a frozen deposit account (allowance being made for the sum of DM 60 for each individual and the initial allocation of DM 60 per employee for companies). The *Festkontogesetz* slashed another two-thirds of the frozen assets so that, in effect, larger credit balances were converted at a rate of 100 to 6.5. Section 2 of the *Umstellungsgesetz* dealt with debit balances in reichsmarks: The debts of the Reich, the Reich authorities, the National Socialist Party, and similar institutions were frozen. They were not expunged nor were they mobilizable. They were not finally settled until the late 1950s, although capital-market institutions had previously been granted what were referred to as *Ausgleichsforderungen* ("equalization claims") to enable them to balance their liabilities. Liabilities between financial institutions were written off, and recurrent liabilities such as rents, wages, and salaries were converted at 1 to 1; all other reichsmark debit balances were discounted by 10 to 1. Other laws, including those dealing with deutschmark balance sheets, pension adjustment, and the *Lastenausgleich*, followed subsequently, but these in no way changed the substantive provisions of the currency reform.

This core legislation on the currency reform, which in effect expropriated Germans' monetary assets without compensation, was supplemented by a radical reform of the economic system. The act laying down the tenets of economic policy after the currency reform abolished in principle the existing system of rationing and the rules governing it, though direct measures of control and distribution remained in force. In conjunction with changes to the tax system (e.g., lower direct taxation, more opportunities for equity formation), the economic reform linked to the currency reform signaled a distinct preference for a supply-side policy with a strong emphasis on the production of consumer goods.[17]

The immediate effect of the currency reform was phenomenal. The postwar misery seemed to vanish overnight; the store windows were full again. Within a few days, the bureaucratically manipulated goods shortage had given way to a self-regulating currency shortage, controlled by markets and prices and monitored by an independent central bank. Although the shortage of currency did not entirely eliminate the shortage of goods, it did impose a specific structure on it.[18] "Money worries" rather than scarcity of goods would henceforth determine Germans' perceptions of everyday existence. Until June 1948, according to opinion surveys conducted by the occupying powers, the picture had been dominated by worries about food and clothing, which were mentioned by between 40 and 55 percent of those questioned. After that time, these preoccupations suddenly fell to below 10 percent, while general money problems soared from 10 percent to nearly 70 percent. From June 1948, therefore, the availability of money dominated the everyday lives of an expropriated population, for whom there was only one way to gain access to money: work.

THE CONSEQUENCES OF THE
CURRENCY REFORM

The consequences of the currency reform and the legislation associated with it were com-

plex. To record them all is hardly feasible because identifying the currency reform as the cause of any subsequent development is always somewhat arbitrary. Even so, there are some effects – short, medium, and long term – that can confidently be attributed to it, although the importance of the currency reform naturally becomes more diffuse as the reform itself becomes more remote in time.[19]

The immediate consequence of the currency reform and the removal of many rationing restrictions was the abrupt restoration of a market economy through the creation and institutional maintenance of a cash squeeze – by means, indeed, of mass expropriation. The result was to change the incentives of economic behavior, which now shifted toward acquiring money and monitoring market prices. As a consequence of the mass expropriation, the need to acquire money meant a de facto imperative to find work, which for the great majority of the population was the only means available to continue to meet financial obligations. For business, it was imperative to produce and market goods. Although some reserve stocks of products and raw materials existed, they were entirely insufficient to sustain solvency. If a company wanted to continue paying its bills, it had to produce and sell products – and keep a sharp eye on market prices because the policy of price increases that some companies first thought of trying was very swiftly thwarted by the intervention of the central bank. Production and labor productivity thus rose immediately and sharply as a result of the currency reform.[20]

Along with the restoration of market-economy conditions and the payment imperatives thus created, economic and fiscal legislation was decisive in determining the

---

[17] Werner Plumpe, *Vom Plan zum Markt: Wirtschaftsverwaltung und Unternehmerverbände in der britischen Zone* (Düsseldorf, 1987), 277–88.

[18] For the fundamentals of this, see Niklas Luhmann, *Die Wirtschaft der Gesellschaft*, 2d ed. (Frankfurt am Main, 1989), 177–271.

[19] Christoph Klessmann, *Die doppelte Staatsgründung: Deutsche Geschichte 1945–1955* (Göttingen, 1982), 376.

[20] For the controversy on the immediate economic impact of the currency reform, see Rainer Klump, "40 Jahre Deutsche Mark: Diskussionsschwerpunkte und Ergebnisse der Währungsreformforschung," in Rainer Klump, ed., *40 Jahre Deutsche Mark: Die politische und ökonomische Bedeutung der westdeutschen Währungsreform von 1948* (Wiesbaden, 1989), 51–68.

medium-term effect of the currency reform – the *Wirtschaftswunder*, the economic miracle. Legislation strengthened the orientation of the economy toward production. The currency reform had already produced direct and sweeping "supply policy" effects. The subsequent economic and fiscal policies encouraged the formation of private capital for production purposes, thus further strengthening German industry's elasticity on the supply side, which was already relatively high thanks to the favorable factor endowment.[21] The 1950s thus saw the start of a period of high and noninflationary economic growth, not least because of the determination of the country's politicians to press ahead with reintegration into the world market.[22] Politically, the success of the currency reform helped to produce a stable center-right majority in government, which strove to consolidate the favorable economic conditions in West Germany. The implementation and consolidation of a political and economic model that favored production over distribution can thus also be seen to have its origins in the course set by the currency reform.

This relationship applies only very indirectly to the long-term consequences of the currency reform and the economic miracle. The currency reform made possible and encouraged the economic miracle, which, in turn, contributed considerably to the acceleration of social change in the Federal Republic – a change that began with the sectoral structure and regional mobility, then extended to the qualifications acquired by the workforce and vertical social mobility. Whereas the structure of West German society in the early 1950s still closely resembled that of Germany between the wars, the picture had changed radically by the late 1960s, if not before, as the greatly increased pace of social mobility changed traditional attitudes. In short, the currency reform and the stable economic development it made possible brought a new dynamic

to social change.[23] The revolt of 1968 was the result of this new dynamic. Although its protagonists saw it as a rebellion against the 1950s, it was the events of those years that had made the rebellion possible in the first place. The shift now taking place in economic and social policy, away from production and toward reallocation, conceived as a process of settling scores with the "injustice of the restoration years," also marked the end of the economic dynamic – at least in the eyes of free-market advocates.[24]

THE CURRENCY REFORM AS MYTH

The economic and political significance of the currency reform, still undisputed in the 1960s, has since been called into question by the work of Werner Abelshauser. In view of the favorable initial conditions prevailing in Germany, Abelshauser argued, the reform had much less real economic significance than had been uncritically assumed for many years. Reconstruction had begun more than a year before the currency reform, and the ostensible successes of the latter were largely the result of inadequate analysis of production statistics in the reichsmark period.[25] These suggestions have certainly played an important part in demonstrating that the economic miracle was not solely the result of smart decisions but was equally dependent on existing potentials. In the heat of debate, this has sometimes been presented as a dichotomy, as if either the political decisions or the existing economic potential determined the subsequent course of economic events. It would be more logical to argue that both potential and decisions were equally indispensable for bringing about the economic miracle; it, therefore, makes

---

[21] Abelshauser, *Wirtschaft in Westdeutschland*.

[22] Christoph Buchheim, *Die Wiedereingliederung Westdeutschlands in die Weltwirtschaft 1945–1958* (Munich, 1990); see also the chapter by Werner Bührer in this section.

[23] Hartmut Kaelble, ed., *Der Boom 1948–1973: Gesellschaftliche und wirtschaftliche Folgen in der Bundesrepublik Deutschland und Europa* (Opladen, 1992).

[24] Herbert Giersch, Karl-Heinz Paqué, and Holger Schmieding, *The Fading Miracle: Four Decades of Market Economy in Germany* (Cambridge, 1994).

[25] Wolfram Fischer, ed., *Währungsreform und Soziale Marktwirtschaft: Erfahrungen und Perspektiven nach 40 Jahren* (Berlin, 1989).

little sense to give one factor preference over the other.

Yet, those factors, it should be emphasized, were different in nature. Although the availability of Western Germany's human and material resources after 1945 was to some extent predetermined, the question of how economic decisions would turn out was very much open. In the struggle to come to terms with the economic and financial consequences of the war, there was no certainty that a neoliberal course would prevail, given that public opinion seemed more inclined to favor a third way between Moscow and Washington. Nor could it be taken for granted that the de facto expropriation of the monetary assets of much of the population would be accepted without protest. The decision to go ahead with the currency reform in the form it actually took was thus as risky as it was unlikely. It came about because of a combination of factors. The German "experts" were firmly resolved to switch the economic system from distribution to production and, in doing so, not just to accept the resulting high social costs but even deliberately to exploit the performance incentives those costs generated.

Another factor was the legitimacy of the actions, particularly of the American occupiers, which German social critics were unable to call into question. Partly because of their promised reconstruction aid, the Americans made it possible in the first place to carry through a radical currency reform without a *Lastenausgleich* motivated by reallocation concerns. This constellation of factors made it possible to break with the Weimar tradition of democracy based on distribution and the National Socialist obsession with control (which was being continued, in rather different form, in the Soviet occupation zone). The radicalism of this break and the unconditional new beginning after the currency reform became central elements of the currency-reform myth, which itself eventually constituted one of the driving forces of the economic miracle. However much one may argue about the details of the economic significance of the currency reform, its importance to the (economic) policy underlying the economic miracle cannot be overestimated. Seen in this way, that the currency reform became a myth was almost a blessing, which no one could have anticipated before June 20, 1948.

CHAPTER FIVE

The Marshall Plan

Gerd Hardach

Translated by Terence M. Coe

THE HISTORICAL SIGNIFICANCE OF THE
MARSHALL PLAN

The European Recovery Program (ERP) was proposed in 1947 by U.S. Secretary of State George C. Marshall and was implemented from 1948 through 1952.[1] The Marshall Plan, as the program was soon generally known in honor of its originator, was at the time the largest project for international economic cooperation ever to be organized during peacetime. The United States and sixteen European countries participated in the recovery program from 1948 through 1952: Austria, Belgium, Denmark, France, (West) Germany, Great Britain, Greece, Iceland, Ireland, Italy, Luxembourg, The Netherlands, Norway, Portugal, Sweden, and Turkey. The financial volume of the program was $14 billion. This was a considerable sum for that time; according to various estimates, this expenditure in current prices would equal approximately $70 billion to 90 billion.[2] Since then, there have been larger multinational

economic projects, but none has attained the prestige of the Marshall Plan. In economic crisis situations, there have been and are frequent calls for a replay of the successful Marshall Plan scenario. A Marshall Plan for the Third World has been proposed as well as a Marshall Plan for Eastern Europe.

In Germany, the Marshall Plan has a political symbolic value far exceeding its economic importance. It was a sign that the Western occupying powers, after two years of economic stagnation and fruitless controversies among the former allies, had decided to dedicate themselves to the political and economic reconstruction of Germany. The change from controlling to reconstructing Germany was attributed above all to the United States, although Great Britain and France also supported this policy. Even in its own time, therefore, the Marshall Plan was greeted as a turning point in German-American relations and as the beginning of a transatlantic partnership between Germany and the United States. Although the ERP soon came under the influence of the Cold War and sharpened the division of Germany, the large majority of West Germans accepted this as an inevitable side effect of reconstruction and integration with the West.[3]

---

[1] Michael Hogan, *The Marshall Plan: America, Britain, and the Reconstruction of Western Europe, 1947–1952* (Cambridge, 1987); Imanuel Wexler, *The Marshall Plan Revisited: The European Recovery Program in Economic Perspective* (Westport, Conn., 1983).

[2] The lower estimate according to Bart Le Blanc, "Fifty Years' Marshall Plan: Building on Atlantic Solidarity," in Hans H. J. Labohm, ed., *The Fiftieth Anniversary of the Marshall Plan: In Retrospect and Prospect* (The Hague, 1997), 82; the upper estimate according to Curt Tarnoff, "The Marshall Plan: Design, Accomplishments, and Relevance to the Present," Library Of

Congress, Congressional Research Service, Report for Congress, Jan. 6, 1997, 1.

[3] Gerd Hardach, *Der Marshallplan: Auslandshilfe und Wiederaufbau in Westdeutschland 1948–1952* (Munich, 1994); Charles Maier and Günter Bischof, *The Marshall*

THE OBJECTIVES

According to Marshall's own account, the impetus for the plans that led to the European Recovery Program was the Moscow Conference of
Foreign Ministers from March 10 to April 24,
1947, from which the American government
expected a decision on the economic stabilization and future political order in Germany.[4]
Two years after the end of the war, the German
economy remained mired in a severe crisis.[5]
When it became apparent during the Moscow
conference that no agreement could be found
on a common policy, Secretary of State Marshall and his British colleague Ernest Bevin decided in April 1947 to introduce an independent
stabilization policy in the British-American
zone. They expected that France and possibly the Soviet Union would later join in this
policy.[6]

From the very start, American policy proceeded from the assumption that the German
economy could be stabilized only within a
broader European context. Because Germany's
economy had been closely interlinked with its
neighbors' prior to the autarchic policies of the
National Socialists, a plan that included European cooperation was in the interest not only
of Germany but also of all of Europe. Once
President Harry S. Truman had promised in the
so-called Truman Doctrine of March 1947 to
protect the free peoples of the world from totalitarian regimes, the economic stabilization of
Europe also gained in political importance.[7] As
early as May 1947, Undersecretary of State Dean

Acheson had prepared the public for a change
in the course of American policy toward its former enemies. He described Germany and Japan
as "workshops of Europe and Asia" that had to
be rapidly rebuilt and reintegrated into the international division of labor.[8] On June 5, 1947,
Secretary of State Marshall made his first public
proposal for a European recovery program. He
emphasized that the countries of Europe should
cooperate economically in order to overcome
the postwar crisis and accelerate recovery in Europe. He stated that the United States was ready
to act in an advisory capacity to plan the program and support its implementation through
foreign aid. Marshall directed his proposal to all
European countries that were ready to cooperate, including the Soviet Union.[9] Marshall felt
that the ideological demarcation line Truman
had drawn in March 1947 should not prevent
economic cooperation with the Soviet Union.

Nevertheless, the Paris Conference of June
27–July 2, 1947, at which the foreign ministers
of the three major European powers negotiated
a common response to Marshall's speech, clearly
revealed the irreconcilable differences between
the United States and its Western European
partners on the one side, and the Soviet Union
on the other. Although the Soviet government
was interested in American foreign aid, it refused
the multinational cooperation that the Americans viewed as an essential condition of the
program for European reconstruction, claiming
that such cooperation was a restriction of Soviet sovereignty.[10] The Soviet Union's refusal
to participate also extended to the Eastern European states under its influence, as well as to
neutral Finland. The dispute over the program

Plan and Germany: West German Development Within the
Framework of the European Recovery Program (New York,
1991).

[4] See the chapter by Michael Wala, vol. 1, Politics.

[5] See the chapter by Wilfried Mausbach in this section.

[6] Marshall, Memorandum of Conservation, Apr. 8,
1947, in U.S. Department of State, Foreign Relations of
the United States (hereafter FRUS), 1947, 2:315–7.

[7] Recommendations on Greece and Turkey (Truman
Doctrine): Message of the President to the Congress,
Mar. 12, 1947, in U.S. Senate Committee on Foreign
Relations, A Decade of American Foreign Policy: Basic Doc-
uments, 1941–1949: Prepared at the Request of the Senate
Committee on Foreign Relations by the Staff of the Committee

and the Department of State (hereafter DAFP) (Washington, D.C., 1950), 1253–7.

[8] U.S. Department of State, Bulletin, May 18, 1947,
991; Dean Acheson, Present at the Creation (New York,
1969), 227–30.

[9] Remarks by the Honorable George C. Marshall,
secretary of state, at Harvard University on June 5, 1947,
FRUS, 1947, 3:237–8.

[10] Ministère des Affaires Etrangères, Documents de la
Conférence des Ministres des Affaires Etrangères de la France,
du Royaume Uni et de l' URSS tenue à Paris du 27 juin au
3 juillet 1947 (Paris, 1947).

increased tensions between the United States and the Soviet Union, which at this time began to be described as a "Cold War."[11]

From July 12 through September 22, 1947, sixteen European states negotiated in the Committee of European Economic Cooperation (CEEC) to set up a European Recovery Program (ERP) in response to Marshall's initiative. The participating states were Austria, Belgium, Denmark, France, Great Britain, Greece, Iceland, Ireland, Italy, Luxembourg, The Netherlands, Norway, Portugal, Sweden, Switzerland, and Turkey. The United States was represented through observers, who increasingly intervened in the consultations to ensure that the European Recovery Program would correspond to the American proposal. In America's view, which was formulated in August 1947 as a recommendation to the CEEC, Western Europe's goal must be to break out of the crippling cycle of low production, government budget deficits, inflation, and foreign-trade isolation. According to the American position, an increase in production, combined with fiscal and monetary stability, would permit the West European economies to bring their balance of payments into equilibrium and open their borders to neighboring countries. Regional integration, by expanding markets and increasing competition, was supposed to increase productivity so that Europeans in a second phase could open themselves to the dollar area and to the overall global market. The United States would support the integration process, which was proposed for a period of four years, by providing foreign aid to eliminate bottlenecks in production and reduce risks to the balance of payments.[12]

From a European perspective, the economic situation in Western Europe was much more stable than the American observers assumed. Reconstruction made rapid progress, and employment and production increased steadily. In 1947, industrial production in the future member states of the Organization for European Economic Cooperation (OEEC), not including West Germany, was already 7 percent above the prewar level of 1938.[13] Most of the European countries pursued a Keynesian economic policy, in which the promotion of employment and production took priority over price stability and foreign-trade equilibrium. To limit inflation, price controls and rationing were applied with varying degrees of success. In terms of foreign trade, economic recovery was assured through currency controls and import restrictions. European foreign trade was based largely on bilateral agreements.[14]

The reconstruction of foreign trade lagged behind the rapid increases in production. Imports by West European countries in 1947 reached 95 percent of the 1938 level in real terms, while exports reached only 76 percent.[15] According to an estimate by the International Monetary Fund, in 1947 the future OEEC member states had a deficit totaling $7.5 billion vis-à-vis the dollar area and from dollar transactions with other regions.[16] This dollar gap was balanced out primarily through American credits and transfer payments. Without American foreign aid, Western Europe faced a major crisis in its balance of payments. The Europeans, therefore, expected that the ERP would above all be a continuation of American foreign aid, but considered an opening of borders as recommended by the United States premature. Finally, the Europeans agreed in September 1947 on an ERP that accepted the American recommendations but without obligating the participants to concrete economic policy measures. The objectives specified in the agreement were balance-of-trade equilibrium, stabilization of currencies and finances, and an increase in production.

[11] Eric Frederic Goldman, The Crucial Decade (New York, 1956), 60.

[12] The Acting Secretary of State to the Embassy in France, Aug. 26, 1947, FRUS, 1947, 3:383–9.

[13] Organisation für Europäische Wirtschaftszusammenarbeit, Europäisches Wiederaufbauprogramm: Zweiter Bericht der Organisation für europäische wirtschaftliche Zusammenarbeit (OEEC) (Bad Godesberg, 1950), 174.

[14] Alan S. Milward, The Reconstruction of Western Europe, 1945–51 (London, 1984).

[15] Der Europäische Wirtschaftsrat in Paris (OEEC), Fünfter Bericht: Fortschritt und Probleme der europäischen Wirtschaft (Bad Godesberg, 1954), 363.

[16] International Monetary Fund, annual report, 1951, 5.

West Germany, which was not yet represented at this conference, was to be included.[17]

At this time, however, it was by no means certain that the U.S. Congress would give its consent to such a massive foreign-aid program for Europe. Parallel to the negotiations with the CEEC, therefore, President Truman began to pave the way for the European program domestically through negotiations with influential congressmen and senators, the creation of expert commissions to examine all important aspects of the program, and an intensive public-relations campaign. Because the American government felt that time was of the essence, an Interim Aid Program was introduced in December 1947 for Austria, France, and Italy.[18] A short time later, Truman introduced the ERP to Congress. The president emphasized the political importance of the program, which had come to be seen as part of the new policy of containment, along with its economic goals.[19] The program was to begin in April 1948 and to last for four years. Total costs were estimated at $17 billion.[20] Although the debate on the ERP was increasingly colored by the Cold War, Congress underscored the economic policy objectives. In early April 1948, the House of Representatives drafted a formal resolution stating that the recovery program was "primarily an economic undertaking although political and other gains will be the byproducts."[21]

THE IMPLEMENTATION OF THE EUROPEAN RECOVERY PROGRAM

The ERP came into effect in April 1948. The purpose of the program was to establish economic equilibrium in Europe within four years. The objectives for economic policy recom-

mended to the participating European countries were currency stabilization, the balancing of public budgets, promotion of international trade, and an increase in production.[22]

To carry out the Marshall Plan, the American government set up the Economic Cooperation Administration (ECA) as an independent cabinet-level agency. Truman appointed the entrepreneur Paul Hoffman as its first director. The OEEC was founded in April 1948, with headquarters in Paris, to represent the participating European countries. West Germany was also included in this group. Because of its close economic links with neighboring European countries, Switzerland became a member of the OEEC, although it did not otherwise participate in the Marshall Plan. In the convention on European economic cooperation in April 1948, the OEEC members updated and expanded the CEEC's ERP of September 1947. The objectives were (1) to increase production; (2) to promote economic cooperation, create a multilateral system of payments, and remove restrictions in payments and trade; (3) to examine the possibility of customs unions or similar arrangements, such as free-trade zones; (4) to reduce customs duties and other trade restrictions; (5) to stabilize currencies and public finances and establish appropriate rates of exchange; and (6) to make comprehensive and effective use of manpower resources.[23] The group was unable to come to a binding agreement on objectives and strategies, and thus the Marshall Plan gradually took shape only in the negotiations between the United States and the participating European countries.

In addition to executing the ERP, the ECA also had a political mission from the very start. Beginning in April 1948, it organized support for the Chinese national government and, in August 1948, it was drawn into the American embargo policy against the communist countries. It also participated in the Mutual Defense Assistance Program beginning in 1949.

[17] Committee of European Economic Cooperation, General Report, Washington, D.C., Sept. 1947.

[18] Foreign Aid (Interim) Act of 1947, *DAFP*, 1278–83.

[19] See the chapter by Ruud Van Dijk, vol. 1, Politics.

[20] *Public Papers of Presidents of the United States: Harry S. Truman, 1947* (Washington, D.C., 1963), 525–9.

[21] *Congressional Record*, 80th Cong., 2d sess., 94, pt. 3:4061.

[22] Economic Cooperation Act, Apr. 4, 1948, *DAFP*, 1299–1321.

[23] Economic Cooperation Administration, *First Report to Congress: Supplement* (Washington, D.C., 1948).

Following the outbreak of the Korean War in June 1950, rearmament took priority over reconstruction. In 1951, the Marshall Plan was integrated into the new Mutual Security Program, an umbrella program intended to coordinate economic and military foreign aid. The ECA was dissolved in December 1951, and the ERP was administered by the new Mutual Security Agency (MSA) for the remainder of its duration through the end of 1952.[24] The Marshall Plan essentially lasted only two years in its original incarnation as a program for European recovery, even though its effects extended far beyond this period.

The ERP's activities emphasized foreign aid, European integration, and the reorientation of the individual participants' economic policies. Foreign aid, in the form of preferential credits, transfer payments, or payments in kind, had been an important instrument of American foreign policy even prior to the Marshall Plan. Important programs included the GARIOA program (Government Aid and Relief in Occupied Areas) for the occupied countries, the UNRRA aid from the United Nations (United Nations Relief and Rehabilitation Administration), the British-American finance agreement of 1946, and the Interim Aid Program of December 1947. From the end of World War II until the beginning of the ERP, the United States granted a total of $15 billion of foreign aid around the world in various programs.[25]

From April 1948 to June 1949, the ERP had a volume of $6 billion. In the second annual program of 1949–50, Congress had already made clear that the increasing economic independence of the Europeans had reduced the need for foreign aid; it, therefore, reduced the volume of aid to $3.5 billion. The third annual program of 1950–1 was reduced to $2.4 billion and the fourth annual program of 1951–2 was for an amount of $1.9 billion, including several transfers in the second half of 1952.[26] Although

public programs in general tend to exceed their proposed costs, the Marshall Plan, with a volume of $14 billion, remained far below the early estimates. In real terms, the recipients had received a total of $13 billion in the form of goods and services by the end of 1952.

Great Britain received the largest portion of foreign aid, 25 percent of the total volume, followed by France at 20 percent, Italy at 11 percent, West Germany at 10 percent, and The Netherlands at 7 percent. Austria, Belgium, Denmark, Greece, Iceland, Ireland, Luxembourg, Norway, Portugal, Sweden, and Turkey together received 27 percent of foreign aid.

West Germany received a total of $1.6 billion in American foreign aid within the scope of the GARIOA program from 1946 to 1950, and another $1.6 billion within the scope of the Marshall Plan from 1948 to 1952. In the London Agreement on German External Debts of 1953, American foreign aid was valued at a total of $3 billion, following several deductions. Of this amount, two-thirds were granted as a gift, and the Federal Republic of Germany was obligated to repay $1 billion.[27]

The most important contribution of the Marshall Plan to the recovery lay in stabilizing the balance of payments. Thanks to foreign aid, West Germany could import additional food for its undernourished populace as well as urgently needed raw materials for industry. Above all, in the difficult first years of the social market economy from 1948 to 1950, the Marshall Plan made significant contributions to the stabilization of West Germany's foreign-trade balance. After this time, economic growth and the successful reintegration of the West German economy into the international division of labor[28] reduced the significance of foreign aid. Overall, 22 percent of West German imports from 1948 to 1952 were financed by foreign aid; the Marshall Plan alone

[24] Hardach, Der Marshallplan, 123–34.
[25] National Planning Association, The Foreign Aid Programs and the United States Economy (Washington, D.C., 1957), 56–7.
[26] These and the following data from Mutual Security Agency, European Program: Procurement Authorizations

and Allotments (Washington, D.C., 1953), 4, and Mutual Security Agency, European Program: Paid Shipments (Washington, D.C., 1953), 2.
[27] Auslandsschulden-Abkommen, Feb. 27, 1953, Verhandlungen des Bundestages, 1. Wahlperiode, Drucksache 4260, Bundesgesetzblatt 1953, 2:331–511.
[28] See the chapter by Werner Bührer in this section.

contributed 14 percent.[29] It was quite clear to politicians and experts, despite frequent public overestimates of the Marshall Plan's importance, that foreign aid could contribute to overcoming bottlenecks but could have no great influence on the overall supply of goods and services. Total foreign aid provided from 1948 to 1952 corresponded to an average of 2.3 percent of West Germany's net national product.[30]

In Germany, the counterpart funds to be paid by domestic importers for the deliveries from the ERP were consolidated into a central investment fund. The *Kreditanstalt für Wiederaufbau* (Reconstruction Loan Corporation), founded in 1948, was created to guide these funds into economically important investment projects at favorable terms. From 1949 through 1952, a total of DM 5.5 billion was invested from the counterpart funds of the GARIOA program and the Marshall Plan. Of this amount, DM 3.4 billion was invested through the Reconstruction Loan Corporation.[31] The repayment of foreign aid agreed to in the London debt treaty was made not from separate funds but from the general budget. The ERP investment fund, therefore, remained intact as a special fund of the German government beyond the end of the Marshall Plan and grew significantly over the course of time through the accumulation of interest. In 1996, the ERP special fund was valued at DM 23 billion.[32]

The aim of the ERP was to use foreign aid as an instrument to promote a multilateral trade and payment system in Western Europe and prepare for the integration of the European states into the Bretton Woods currency system and the

liberal trade system of the General Agreement on Tariffs and Trade (GATT). Even before the start of the Marshall Plan, several West European countries entered into the Agreement on Multilateral Monetary Compensation in November 1947. This clearing agreement, however, had little effect because of the small number of participants. In October 1948, the OEEC approved a European payments agreement, which applied retroactively to July 1, 1948, and lasted until June 30, 1949. The European payments agreement, with the consent of the ECA, used a portion of the American foreign aid to promote intra-European trade. The participating countries were to estimate in advance their trade with all other OEEC countries. If a bilateral export surplus was expected, the exporting country was to grant "drawing rights" to the importing country and waive any payment up to this amount. The exporting countries were to receive compensation for this amount out of funds from the Marshall Plan, granted as "conditional aid." Because the drawing rights were negotiated concurrently with the distribution of the foreign aid, it was almost impossible to determine whether the countries who were strong exporters were actually compensated through additional funds from the Marshall Plan or whether they were themselves providing intra-European foreign aid to those countries with weak exports. For this reason, there was little willingness to grant drawing rights. In September 1949, the European payments agreement was extended for the period of July 1, 1949, through June 30, 1950.[33] Overall, in the two years from July 1948 to June 1950, 32 percent of the balances in intra-European trade were financed through the drawing rights of the two payment agreements.[34]

---

[29] Bundesministerium für den Marshallplan, *Wiederaufbau im Zeichen des Marshallplanes 1948–1952* (Bonn, 1953), 23–4, 83, 209; Koordinierungsausschuss für die deutschen Marshallplan-Arbeiten, Die Wirtschaft der französischen Besatzungszone im ersten Marshallplan-Jahr, Aug. 1949, Bundesarchiv Koblenz (hereafter BK), B 146/227.

[30] Bundesministerium für den Marshallplan, *Wiederaufbau*, 23–4.

[31] Manfred Pohl, *Wiederaufbau: Kunst und Technik der Finanzierung 1947–1953* (Frankfurt am Main, 1973).

[32] Kreditanstalt für Wiederaufbau, *Die KfW von 1948 bis heute* (Frankfurt am Main, 1997).

[33] Bank for International Settlements, 19th annual report, 1948–9, 217–20; and 20th annual report, 1949– 50, 234; Werner Abelshauser, "Der kleine Marshallplan: Handelsintegration durch innereuropäische Wirtschaftshilfe 1948–1950," in Helmut Berding, ed., *Wirtschaftliche und politische Integration in Europa im 19. und 20. Jahrhundert* (Göttingen, 1984), 212–24.

[34] Organization for European Economic Cooperation (OEEC), *Die Wirtschaftslage Westeuropas: Fortschritte und Probleme. Dritter Bericht* (Bonn, 1951), 136.

Concurrently with the European payments agreement, the OEEC in July 1949 voted on a program for the liberalization of intra-European trade. In this agreement, the member states obligated themselves to a gradual removal of quantitative import restrictions and the elimination of most of these restrictions by 1951.[35] Paul Hoffman recommended in October 1949 that the Europeans continue to expand their liberalization policy to form a common market. His goal was "a single large market within which quantitative restrictions on the movements of goods, monetary barriers to flow of payments and eventually all tariffs are permanently swept away."[36] This vision went too far for the Europeans, but the removal of quantitative trade restrictions was in fact introduced in November 1950.[37]

The European payments agreement and a liberalization program by the OEEC prepared the way for the European Payments Union (EPU), which was founded in September 1950 and applied retroactively to July 1, 1950. Intra-European convertibility of currencies was established at fixed exchange rates within the EPU. The Bank for International Settlements (BIS) in Basel assumed the function of a clearing house. Member countries who had import surpluses could claim credit from the EPU, whereas on the other side, countries with an export surplus were to credit a percentage of their claims. The EPU was initially established for a period of only two years, but was extended a number of times until it was replaced by the European Monetary Agreement in 1958, following the introduction of convertibility for the most important member currencies.[38]

The West European countries opened themselves to the global as well as the European market; the European protectionism feared by many critics of block integration did not materialize. In the first round of multilateral negotiations from 1947 to 1951 in Geneva, Annecy, and Torquay, the GATT achieved impressive reductions in customs duties. The devaluation of the British pound, the Deutsche Mark, and other European currencies in September 1949 created realistic exchange rates, which prepared the way for achieving a foreign-trade balance. Overcoming the dollar gap, however, took longer than expected. When the Marshall Plan ended in 1952, the member states still had significant trade deficits with the United States. It was not until 1958 that convertibility against the dollar was introduced for the most important European currencies.[39]

If the West European nations wanted to open themselves to the global marketplace, their economic policies needed to place a high priority on price stability, balancing government budgets, and equilibrium in balance of payments. According to the monetarist view on which the ERP was based, this policy should not act to the detriment of production and employment, but instead promote economic growth over the long term. Many European governments, however, feared the negative consequences for employment and production and, therefore, hesitated to follow American recommendations and give up their Keynesian economic policies, which were predicated on the goal of full employment. For this reason, the ECA assumed the right to influence the economic policy of the individual participant countries in order to lead the Europeans in the right direction. Richard Bissell, one of Hoffman's most important colleagues,

[35] OEEC, Council Decision on the Liberalization of Intra-European Trade, July 4, 1949, BK, Z 14/48.

[36] Statement of Paul G. Hoffman, Economic Cooperation Administrator, before OEEC, Oct. 31, 1949, National Archives (hereafter NA), Record Group (hereafter RG) 469, Hoffman speeches, box 1.

[37] Beschluss des Rates der OEEC über weitere Massnahmen der wirtschaftlichen Zusammenarbeit, Nov. 2, 1949, BK, Z 14/165 a.

[38] William Diebold, *Trade and Payments in Western Europe: A Study in Economic Cooperation, 1947–51* (New York, 1952); Barry Eichengreen, *Reconstructing Europe's*

Trade and Payments (Manchester, 1993); Sandra Hartig, *Die westeuropäische Zahlungsunion: Ein Vorbild für Osteuropa?* (Marburg, 1996); Jacob J. Kaplan and Günther Schleiminger, *The European Payments Union: Financial Diplomacy in the 1950s* (Oxford, 1989).

[39] Monika Dickhaus, *Die Bundesbank im westeuropäischen Wiederaufbau: Die internationale Währungspolitik der Bundesrepublik Deutschland 1948–1958* (Munich, 1996).

emphasized in June 1948 that the ECA must not only restrict itself to foreign aid and balances of payments but must also guide the recovery in Europe.[40]

In West Germany, the currency and economic reform of June 1948 replaced the planned economy of the early postwar years with a market economy. Since 1949, this has been known as the social market economy.[41] According to the intent of the ERP, the commitment to a market economy was to be supplemented by a liberal foreign-trade policy. Hermann Pünder, the head of the Economic Council in Frankfurt, advised the future federal government in August 1949 that for political and economic reasons, West Germany must become a "pioneering proponent of the American view on the elimination of trade restrictions."[42] Despite this agreement, there were repeated controversies between German politicians and their American advisers on the correct course of economic policy, for example, in the inflationary period following the currency reform of June 1948, during the labor market crisis of 1949–50, and during the balance of payments crisis of 1950–1. The policy of the Economic Council and the German federal government were at first disputed within Germany as well, for although an economic upswing followed the currency reform, there was also a marked increase in unemployment. In February 1950, the labor market crisis reached its highest level since the end of the war, with at least 2.3 million unemployed in West Germany and West Berlin.[43]

Not only in West Germany but also in the other participating European countries, a reorientation of economic policy took place to support the opening of borders begun with the Marshall Plan. Nevertheless, the individual OEEC countries had different areas of emphasis in their economic, currency, and financial policies. Richard Bissell confirmed in 1950 that the ECA was unable to implement a uniform stabilization policy in Europe.[44] What the West European countries had in common during the long economic upswing of the 1950s and 1960s was a mixed economic system in which the market was supplemented to a greater or lesser extent by governmental economic and social policies. Using Herman van der Wee's model, one can distinguish three models within the spectrum: a "neoliberal" variant in West Germany; a "neocollectivist" variant in France, Great Britain, and Italy: and, between these two poles, a "social partnership" variant in Austria, the Benelux countries, and Scandinavia.[45]

THE EFFECTS OF THE MARSHALL PLAN

The importance of the ERP lay above all in opening the West European countries to the global market. The reconstruction of the international division of labor created favorable conditions for economic development in all of the participating countries. The Marshall Plan's transfer payments received a great deal of attention at the time and are often emphasized in historical accounts. Despite their importance, however, they did not have the same effect as the reorganization of international economic relationships.[46] The Marshall Plan helped enable the recovery of the late 1940s to develop without interruption into the long growth phase

[40] Administrator's staff meeting, June 30, 1948, NA, RG 469, Deputy Administrator, subject files, box 1.

[41] Gerold Ambrosius, *Die Durchsetzung der Sozialen Markwirtschaft in Westdeutschland 1945–1949* (Stuttgart, 1977); see the chapter by Werner Plumpe in this section.

[42] Pünder to Ludwig Erhard, Aug. 30, 1949, BK, Z 6/175.

[43] *Zweiter Bericht der Bundesregierung über die Durchführung des Marshallplanes, 1.1.1950 bis 31.3.1950* (Bonn, 1950), 46.

[44] Bissell to Hoffman and Foster, Jan. 22, 1950, NA, RG 469, Administrator, Inter-Office Memorandums, box 3.

[45] Herman Van der Wee, *Der gebremste Wohlstand: Wiederaufbau, Wachstum und Strukturwandel der Weltwirtschaft seit 1945* (Munich, 1984), 317–88.

[46] For a discussion of the effect of the Marshall Plan, see also the introductory essay by Christoph Buchheim in this section.

of the 1950s and 1960s. In West Germany, the real net national product per capita exceeded the prewar level of 1938 for the first time in 1953.[47] The unemployment level of 9.5 percent in 1953 was still very high, but gradually decreased in the following years. After overcoming the balance-of-payments crisis in 1950–1,

the West German economy achieved regular export surpluses.[48] Population growth, technology transfer from the United States, and successful integration into the global market created the basis both in West Germany and in other West European countries for a rare combination of economic growth, full employment, price stability, and foreign trade equilibrium.

[47] Walther G. Hoffmann, Franz Grumbach, and Helmut Hesse, *Das Wachstum der deutschen Wirtschaft seit der Mitte des 19. Jahrhunderts* (Berlin, 1965), 172–4, 827–8.

[48] Statistisches Bundesamt, *Bevölkerung und Wirtschaft 1872–1972* (Stuttgart, 1972), 148, 270.

CHAPTER SIX

Protégé and Partner

The United States and the Return of West Germany to the Liberal World Economic System

Werner Bührer

Translated by Richard Sharp

The creation of a liberal world economic system organized on multilateral lines was one of the economic and political priorities of both the United States and West Germany after World War II, though for different reasons. In the United States, besides short-term and long-term economic aims – smoothing the transition from wartime to peacetime production, reconstruction of a world economy still suffering from the effects of the global economic crisis and the disintegration that followed, stability and prosperity based on free world trade – political and strategic considerations linked to the systemic conflict against communism were decisive from 1946–7 onward. In West Germany, the primary concern was the dependence on exports, which had become even more severe after Germany's division. Although the pre-1914 era was often evoked as a desirable model, American politicians and experts in particular were determined that this time the liberal order would be achieved by political means and secured for the long term by institutional means. In contrast to the situation after World War I, the United States was now prepared to take on the leading role its economic standing warranted. The Federal Republic rapidly progressed to become the junior partner of the United States and the more or less willing pacesetter for liberalization in Western Europe, thus restoring Germany's traditional status as a major trading power.

The United States' gradual turn away from the protectionism it practiced between the wars can be traced back to 1934. The Reciprocal Trade Agreement Act, which allowed customs duties to be reduced on a reciprocal basis, was of limited practical significance, however. The corresponding passage in the Atlantic Charter of 1941, too, was still couched in quite vague terms. But greater commitment could be found in the 1942 Lend-Lease agreement with Britain, in which the parties undertook to refrain from any form of discrimination and to dismantle all trade barriers. Other milestones in America's campaign for a liberal world economic order were the Bretton Woods Agreement of July 1944, with its commitment to a liberal world economy and multilateral free trade, and the negotiations on the formation of an International Trade Organization (ITO), which continued until 1948. The General Agreement on Tariffs and Trade (GATT) of October 1947 marked a modest partial success. In accordance with the GATT, a trade charter that took most-favored-nation treatment, the reduction of customs duties and quotas, and the elimination of preference zones as its guiding principles, was signed in Havana in March 1948; only two of the original signatory states ratified the charter, however, and it thus never entered into force.

In addition to these endeavors, the American government, influenced by the emerging Cold War, had decided to embark on the

Marshall Plan, a program of regional reconstruction and liberalization limited to Western Europe.[1] Although such a regional association was contrary to the aim of global free trade, it made a great deal of sense as a pragmatic interim step, all the more so as the importance of the West European states in international trade destined them to play a critical part in the creation of the sought-after liberal world economy. In the negotiations on the European Recovery Program (ERP), therefore, the Americans demanded from the outset that the participating states should take "concerted steps to facilitate the greatest practicable interchange of goods and services among themselves, adopting definitive measures directed toward the progressive reduction and eventual elimination of barriers to trade within the area in accordance with the principles of the ITO Charter."[2] Such appeals were by no means unnecessary because those responsible for trade policy in Western Europe initially showed little inclination to depart from the bilateral agreements and trading practices that had been customary in the immediate postwar years. And, although they were not yet officially approved, the ITO principles were already the guidelines of American trade policy.

The pressure brought to bear by the Marshall Plan proved effective. In the convention establishing the Organization for European Economic Cooperation (OEEC) of April 1948, the member states undertook "to continue the efforts already initiated to achieve as soon as possible a multilateral system of payments among themselves, and [to] co-operate in relaxing restrictions on trade and payments between one another, with the object of abolishing as soon as possible those restrictions which at present

hamper such trade and payments."[3] The American planners were convinced that West Germany could and should play a critical part in bringing this project to fruition.

In the period under consideration, the initially very one-sided cooperation to create a liberal, multilateral world economy – which began with the decision to bring the Western zones of Germany within the ERP – can be subdivided into three main phases. Until 1951, the priority for the United States was the creation of the institutional structure, whereas West Germany strove, step by step, to achieve autonomy in matters of trade policy. The next turning point came in 1958 with the return of most European currencies to convertibility, an essential condition for unimpeded trade relations and payment transactions, and the launch of the European Economic Community (EEC). In the following decade, securing the successes achieved on the transatlantic and European level and pressing ahead with the worldwide opening-up of markets within the framework of the GATT were the main concerns.

WEST GERMAN CONTRIBUTIONS TO
THE INSTITUTIONAL FOUNDATION OF
THE LIBERAL WORLD ECONOMIC
SYSTEM, 1947–51

"There have been important changes in world trade policy since Germany was cut off from overseas trade by the last world war," according to a report from spring 1948 produced by the Bizonal Economic Administration, the precursor of the West German Ministry of Trade and Commerce. Although one can only wonder at the casual attempt to gloss over the isolationist trade policy of the Third Reich, this document's listing of significant events – the Atlantic Charter, GATT, ITO, and the Marshall Plan – should

---

[1] See the chapter by Gerd Hardach in this section.

[2] The Acting Secretary of State to Diplomatic Representatives Accredited to Countries Participating in the Conference of European Economic Cooperation and to the United States Political Adviser for Germany (Murphy), Sept. 7, 1947 in U.S. Department of State, *Foreign Relations of the United States, 1947* (Washington, D.C., 1972), 3:412–5, 415.

[3] Convention for European Economic Co-Operation, Paris, 16 April 1948, in Documents on International Affairs 1947–1948. Selected and edited by Margaret Carlyle (London, 1952), 178–86, 179–80.

be indisputable. Although Germans had been excluded from the negotiations on these agreements, they were pleased with the results. Especially well received was the procedure used to reach agreement on the GATT treaty complex: an initial round of bilateral negotiations followed by the bundling of the individual treaties into a single multilateral agreement.[4]

The first German statements on the multilateral approach to liberalization were skeptical. Even Ludwig Erhard, who later reveled in his role as the pacemaker of liberalization, called for "temporary solutions" for West Germany, although he conceded that the "multilateral exchange of goods" was a "more mature form" of foreign trade than bilateral agreements; only at a later time would "the ideal become practicable," he said.[5] In stating the case for bilateralism, the German experts, of course, could base their arguments on the contemporary practice of concluding bilateral agreements on goods and payments as did the Joint Export-Import Agency, the Anglo-American office responsible for the foreign trade of Bizonia. This is to say nothing of the fact that for most Germans, "liberalization" meant first and foremost the dismantling of Allied trade restrictions.

There was more behind the widespread bilateralism in Western Europe after the war than the conviction that national trade interests could be more effectively pursued in direct, head-to-head negotiations, however. Above all, there was the "dollar gap," the sharp disparity between the limited dollar reserves held by individual European countries and the massive demand for food, raw materials, and capital goods from the United States.[6] To ensure that their precious dollars were used as efficiently as possible, most European governments adopted rigid foreign-exchange controls – a practice that imposed tight limits on trade expansion. West Ger-

many suffered particularly from this situation on account of the "dollar clause" adopted by the United States and Britain, whereby imports from the American and British zones of occupation always had to be paid for in dollars.

The progress made along bilateral lines toward the intensification of trade within Europe did not satisfy the Americans. In the American view, bilateralism was a trade obstacle to be overcome. The United States pressed the OEEC to take energetic steps toward the liberalization of trade, above all through the Economic Cooperation Administration (ECA) entrusted with the development of the ERP. The OEEC responded with a step-by-step program to remove quantitive restrictions from private trade among the member states. In the first stage of this program, 50 percent of private imports were to be liberalized by October 1, 1949.[7] The ECA had envisaged a leading role for West Germany in this process, and one of its staff encouraged the federal government, which had just taken office, to demonstrate "that the new Republic is prepared to take the initiative in working for the benefit of all Europe in an open international economy."[8] The Federal Republic was predestined for this role for two reasons: first, the considerable influence wielded by the United States as an occupying power, which allowed the Americans to exert a measure of control; and second, the importance of West Germany's economic potential.

In the past, Germany had supplied a large proportion of its European neighbors' capital goods; it ceased to serve that function after World War II, with the consequences mentioned previously. "The size of Western Europe's dollar deficits over the period 1945–1948 was directly related to the absence of German exports of capital goods."[9] If what was, in effect,

[4] Aufzeichnung, Hauptabteilung V, Apr. 7, 1948, Parlamentsarchiv, Bonn, Bestand 2/597.

[5] Address by Erhard, May 1948, quoted in *Aussenhandel* 1 (1948): 4–7, esp. 6.

[6] See Christoph Buchheim, *Die Wiedereingliederung Westdeutschlands in die Weltwirtschaft 1945–1958* (Munich, 1990), esp. 111–19.

[7] See Werner Bührer, *Westdeutschland in der OEEC: Eingliederung, Krise, Bewährung 1947–1961* (Munich, 1997), 137–44, 179–88.

[8] Proposal for German Trade Liberalization, Nov. 5, 1949, National Archives, RG 469, FOA, Special Representative for Europe, Program Division, West Germany 1949–1952, box 9.

[9] Alan S. Milward, "The Marshall Plan and German Foreign Trade," in Charles S. Maier, ed., *The Marshall*

Europe's leading economy could be brought on course for liberalization, this would undoubtedly have an impact on the trade policies of the other West European countries. Before the government could establish this course, it had to overcome a good deal of domestic resistance and, in spring 1951, a looming balance-of-payments crisis.[10] In all fairness, however, it must be recalled that the American government's commitment to a liberal world economic order provoked opposition even within the United States. With the aid of protectionist forces in Congress, certain agricultural and industrial interests were able to dilute America's liberal trade policy through numerous exceptions favorable to themselves.[11]

In the field of customs policy, too, the West German government had the opportunity to show whether it was willing to take on the leading role expected of it in the construction of a liberal world economy. After a number of GATT member states had, on the initiative of the United States, already granted reciprocal most-favored-nation treatment to the Western zones of occupation in 1948, German accession to GATT was to be finalized at a conference planned for Torquay in 1950–1. First, though, the current customs tariffs would have to be revised and brought into line with the changed circumstances. The draft produced by the West German government fell far short of the expectations of the Allied High Commission, however. In order not to jeopardize German accession, the Allies eventually settled for a few somewhat insignificant concessions. Following the negotiations in Torquay, highly successful from the German view, the Federal Republic officially acceded to GATT on October 1, 1951; it thereby achieved "sovereignty in trade and customs policy" six and a half years after the end of the war.[12] The United States could now count on an increasingly independent and confident ally in its efforts to bring about a liberal and multilateral world economy.

TOWARD THE EURO-ATLANTIC WORLD ECONOMY, 1951–8

Two important and somewhat contradictory trends dominated events in the 1950s. On one hand, liberalization of trade under the auspices of the OEEC made further progress as the leading member states made the transition to a convertible currency. On the other, France, the Federal Republic, the Benelux states, and Italy forged ahead toward European integration with the founding of the European Coal and Steel Community (ECSC) in 1951 and the EEC in 1957. Reconciling these two trends – the global opening of markets and the creation of a West European bloc – sometimes proved difficult.

Having overcome the balance-of-payments crisis of early 1951, the West German government was finally able to slide into the role of liberalization trailblazer envisioned for it by the ECA.[13] Although West Germany had by no means achieved its full potential, it was still able to place in the top rank. Whereas by January 1952, only 57 percent of private imports – compared with the reference year of 1949 – had been liberalized, by April 1953, the quota had risen to 90 percent. It initially became bogged down around this mark before rising further to 91.5 percent in September 1956 and 94 percent in June 1958.[14] The government thus failed to meet persistent foreign demands for complete liberalization, though many American and European experts believed that doing so would not have required intolerable sacrifices. Instead,

Plan and Germany: West German Development Within the Framework of the European Recovery Program (New York, 1991), 452–87, 453.

[10] See Bührer, *Westdeutschland in der OEEC*, esp. 198–229.

[11] See Herman van der Wee, *Der gebremste Wohlstand: Wiederaufbau, Wachstum und Strukturwandel der Weltwirtschaft seit 1945* (Munich, 1984), 428–30.

[12] See Friedrich Jerchow, "Aussenhandel im Widerstreit: Die Bundesrepublik auf dem Weg in das GATT 1949–1951," in Heinrich August Winkler, ed., *Politische Weichenstellungen im Nachkriegsdeutschland 1945–1953* (Göttingen, 1979), 281.

[13] See Bührer, *Westdeutschland in der OEEC*, 284–97.

[14] See Herbert Giersch, Karl-Heinz Paqué, and Holger Schmieding, *The Fading Miracle: Four Decades of Market Economy in Germany* (Cambridge, 1994), 10.

Bonn concentrated on tightening the OEEC rules of liberalization and thereby helped ensure that the other member states did not slacken in their efforts to reduce trade barriers. The West German government also began to liberalize dollar imports following a massive increase in West German dollar reserves that was partly attributable to the surpluses achieved within the European Payments Union (EPU). The United States was a particular beneficiary of this measure because American goods still accounted for some 85 percent of these imports.[15]

The West German government attached even greater importance to the problem of convertibility, without which global free trade was inconceivable. Because the first attempt at convertibility by a European country after the war – the floating of the pound against the dollar – failed within a few weeks, potential imitators proceeded with extreme caution. Neither Britain nor the Federal Republic, though they were the only two serious candidates for such a step, was willing to risk another attempt to go it alone, and finding partners proved difficult. Appeals to the United States to support an Anglo-German initiative did not meet with a positive response. The West German government, despite Erhard's constant appeals to risk the leap to convertibility, instead pursued "cooperative gradualism" within the EPU. This did not succeed until the end of 1958, when the EEC states, Britain, Denmark, Norway, and Sweden introduced convertibility of their currencies for nonresidents. Having done its job, the EPU was dissolved and, as agreed in 1955, replaced by the European Monetary Agreement. This move away from foreign-exchange controls in Europe meant that the Bretton Woods Agreement came into force, de facto, more than fourteen years after it was concluded, delivering the International Monetary Fund from its heretofore shadowy existence.[16]

In the 1950s, in contrast to the preceding period, the United States intervened only intermittently in the process of liberalization within the OEEC framework. Evidently, the Americans generally approved of the gradual creation of a regional free trade system. On the other hand, the process of European integration, which had begun with the founding of the ECSC, caused concern on the trade-policy front. Whether the ECSC conformed to the principles of a liberal world economy was a matter of debate among contemporary economics experts and academics and remains so today in research on the history of integration. There are convincing grounds, however, for believing that the ECSC was "not a foreign body in the multilateral world economy represented by GATT" but became an integral part of it and actively supported the efforts at the time to liberalize trade.[17]

The situation with the EEC was different, not because it adopted a less cooperative attitude toward GATT than the ECSC but because its establishment created what appeared to be an ominous trade-policy split in Western Europe. There was broad opposition in the Federal Republic to continuing the supranational integration of the Six. Liberal economists such as Wilhelm Röpke as well as Economics Minister Erhard, the German Federation of Trade Unions, and the Federation of German Industry (*Bundesverband der deutschen Industrie*, or BDI) joined in this opposition. Ultimately, the critics could achieve nothing against Konrad Adenauer's politically motivated decision to go along with the founding of the Common Market and the European Atomic Energy Community. The warnings about protectionism and interventionism, tirelessly repeated by Erhard and the BDI in particular, proved far less prophetic than had been feared. The Federal Republic had most to lose by the disintegration of the OEEC because of its close trade relations with countries like Austria, Switzerland, Denmark, and Sweden, which shortly afterward

[15] See Buchheim, *Wiedereingliederung Westdeutschlands*, 148–52; Vermerk über Besprechung mit HICOG- and FOA-Vertretern, Apr. 6, 1954, Bundesarchiv, Koblenz, B 102/11579.

[16] See Bührer, *Westdeutschland in der OEEC*, 310–25, 381–93; Buchheim, *Wiedereingliederung Westdeutschlands*, 170; van der Wee, *Der gebremste Wohlstand*, 505–9.

[17] Christoph Buchheim, "Schuman-Plan und liberale Weltwirtschaft (GATT)," in Klaus Schwabe, ed., *Die Anfänge des Schuman-Plans 1950/51* (Baden-Baden, 1988), 161–70, 169.

combined to form the European Free Trade Association (EFTA), but "this relapse into narrowly limited regionalism did not represent a serious break with West Germany's successful policy of liberalization during the 1950s, since there was no threat to the substance of the advances achieved by the OEEC/EPU system."[18] Germany's return to the world market, ceaselessly announced by Erhard, thus focused in the 1950s on familiar territory: "The real money was being made in Western Europe in the more protectionist framework which the Marshall Plan had created."[19] In 1955, 64.8 percent of exports went to Western Europe; in 1960, the figure was still 63.5 percent; before World War II it had been "merely" 52 percent. Only exports to the United States had more than doubled since 1937, from 4.1 to 9 percent by 1960, whereas the combined share of the remaining countries (excluding Eastern Europe) fell from 27.7 to 25.6 percent.[20]

THE 1960S: FROM THE MULTILATERAL TO THE BIPOLAR WORLD ECONOMY?

The efforts of the United States and the Federal Republic in foreign economic and trade policy during the 1960s concentrated mainly on consolidating the successes achieved during the previous decade in constructing a liberal world economy. First and foremost, relations between the United States and the EEC had to be restructured.

The first "victim" of these efforts was the OEEC. Whereas the United States wanted future transatlantic cooperation to concentrate more on the coordination of economic policy and the harmonization of development aid,[21] the Federal Republic was keenly interested in preserving the "existing OEEC system of cooperation," especially the instruments of liberal-ization.[22] In the negotiations, the United States, supported by France and Britain, ultimately had its way in its desire for a "more outward looking organization." Although the members of the new Organization for Economic Cooperation and Development (OECD), founded in late September 1961, undertook "to contribute to the expansion of world trade on a multilateral non-discriminatory basis in accordance with international obligation,"[23] the OECD lacked the resources to put this commitment into practice. It metamorphosed into a study center for issues concerning the Western world's economic, monetary, and trade policies, a kind of moral arbiter of international economic policy.

Did the founding of the OECD mark the end of Western European dependence on the United States and the start of an era of interdependence, as the Americans claimed? There is no doubt that relations had changed noticeably; the economic resurgence of Western Europe had transformed the former recipients of aid into serious competitors. The United States observed the dynamic progress of the EEC with mixed feelings, detecting a possible threat to its position of economic dominance. But a genuinely equal partnership was still out of the question. The negotiations on the reorganization of the OEEC had themselves shown that the Europeans were more heavily reliant on the United States than vice versa.[24]

What institutional supports for a consistent policy of liberalization still remained after the disappearance of the OEEC? There was indeed progress in dismantling trade barriers within the EEC, and the first steps had also been taken toward the free movement of labor and capital. The customs union became a reality even earlier than expected. At the same time, though, efforts at liberalization in the services sector bogged down; so-called nontariff trade

---

[18] Giersch, Paqué, and Schmieding, *Fading Miracle*, 123–4.

[19] Milward, *Marshall Plan*, 476.

[20] Giersch, Paqué, and Schmieding, *Fading Miracle*, 91. See also the chapter by Lutz Frühbrodt in this section.

[21] See the chapter by Marten Pereboom, vol. 2, Economics.

[22] Resortbesprechung, Feb. 5, 1960, Politisches Archiv Auswärtiges Amt, Bonn, Abt. 4/401, vol. 326.

[23] Communiqué Issued at Paris by Ministerial Meeting of Members and Associates of the OEEC, Dec. 13, 1960, in U.S. Department of State, Historical Office, *American Foreign Policy: Current Documents, 1960* (Washington, D.C., 1964), 334.

[24] See Bührer, *Westdeutschland in der OEEC*, 400–16.

barriers became more important; and there were noticeable signs of protectionist tendencies toward countries outside the EEC.[25] The EEC retreated as a champion of free, multilateral world trade.

However, there remained GATT, which devoted two series of conferences – the Dillon Round of 1961–2 and the Kennedy Round of 1964–7 – to efforts to reduce customs duties. Whereas the first round produced modest results, the second did see a reduction of as much as 35 to 40 percent in tariffs on industrial goods. Even so, the Kennedy Round had certain anachronistic features, as the loss of customs protection was now compensated for in the Western economies by "new, completely equivalent protective measures," specifically the nontariff trade barriers mentioned previously. "As a result, the further lowering of the tariffs assumed a trade structure that by the end of the 1960s had largely been overtaken by world economic events."[26] It was unmistakable, however, that world economic events were essentially being shaped by two centers: the United States and the EEC. And both sides in the 1960s demonstrated little interest in pressing on resolutely with the establishment of a liberal world economy.

CONCLUSION

Measured against the lofty proclamations about free trade, the actual results were mixed. Both in the United States and in the Federal Republic, protectionist tendencies increased during the 1960s. Even so, it is fair to say that, "Despite all the problems and partial obstacles, the basic decision taken in 1944 to reestablish a free worldwide system of trade . . . was largely adhered to outside the Eastern Bloc."[27] This was partly attributable to the various institutional safeguards that characterized the world economy after 1945 – in contrast to the period before 1914 – and also, in particular, to the United States and its junior partner, the Federal Republic of Germany.

---

[25] Giersch, Paqué, and Schmieding, *Fading Miracle*, 167–8.

[26] Van der Wee, *Der gebremste Wohlstand*, 433.

[27] Wolfram Fischer, "Die Entwicklung der Weltwirtschaft seit 1945 im historischen Vergleich," in Herbert Giersch, ed., *Probleme und Perspektiven der weltwirtschaftlichen Entwicklung* (Berlin, 1985), 26.

CHAPTER SEVEN

American and German Trade Relations

Lutz Frühbrodt

Translated by Richard Sharp

The United States and the Federal Republic of Germany were leading players in world trade between 1945 and 1968. This article first analyzes the two countries' trade balances and a few other key trade figures. A discussion of bilateral trade relations is then followed by a brief overview of East-West trade, which took on a special significance in the context of the Cold War.

THE "WORLD EXPORTS CHAMPION" AND THE "RUNNER-UP"

The United States emerged from World War II not just as the dominant political and military force in the Western world but also as the world's foremost and, for the moment, unchallenged economic power. It dominated world trade consistently over the period 1950–70 even though it lost a little ground during the 1960s (see Table 1). Germany, defeated in war, began the postwar period in a comparatively weak position because of the destruction of much of its industry and the restrictions on economic policy imposed by the Allied occupation. Seen in this light, the Federal Republic's dazzling leap from 3 percent share of world trade in 1950 to 9 percent share in 1960 seems all the more remarkable (see Table 2). West Germany supplanted Great Britain, once the world's trade leader, in second place and, during the 1960s, closed in on the United States. Japan's ascent as an exporter also began during this period and, by 1970, it had,

with a 6 percent market share, pulled even with Britain.

Apart from the first two years after its founding, the Federal Republic achieved a positive trade balance throughout the period ending in 1970. The United States also recorded a trade surplus during this period. Both countries were primarily involved in intra-industry trade, though with subtle differences. This exchange of similar industrial goods between equally advanced economies became the dominant structural characteristic of trade policy in all Western industrialized countries. In 1970, machinery, motor vehicles, and other industrial goods (especially steel and metal products) made up about 60 percent of the United States' imports and exports alike. This high proportion was the result of the massive decline in the importance of agricultural products, raw materials, and producer goods in American foreign trade since the 1950s. Agricultural imports, for example, declined from 31.2 percent of total American imports in 1950 to 15.6 percent in 1970.[1] The makeup of West Germany's foreign trade underwent a similar though less dramatic change. It is striking, however, that the Federal Republic's total imports included a comparatively high proportion (30 percent) of primary products and producer goods – an indicator of West Germany's dependence on foreign raw

[1] U.S. Department of Commerce, Bureau of the Census, *Statistical Abstract of the United States*, 1951, 835–40; 1971, 773–4.

Table 1. *U.S. International Trade Indicators*

	1950	1960	1970
Balance on Current Account (DM billion)	−2.1	1.8	0.4
Trade Balance (DM billion)	1.1	4.9	2.2
Share of World Exports (percent)	16.0	16.0	14.0
Foreign Trade Quota (percent)	6.7	7.1	8.5
Regional Breakdown of Exports (percent)			
North America[a]	24.5	22.5	24.9
South and Central America	22.3	14.3	11.2
Europe	29.5	36.4	34.7
EEC[b]	15.8	19.3	19.5
FRG	4.3	6.2	6.3
East European State-Trading Countries			
USSR	x	0.2	0.3
GDR	no data	x	0.1
other COMECON	1.1	1.1	0.9
Asia	14.4	20.3	23.2
Others	9.7	6.4	6.5
Regional Breakdown of Imports (percent)			
North America[a]	25.7	22.8	30.9
South and Central America	31.5	24.0	11.6
Europe	16.6	29.4	28.7
EEC[b]	6.4	15.4	16.5
FRG	1.2	6.1	7.8
East European State-Trading Countries			
USSR	0.4	0.2	0.2
GDR	no data	x	x
other COMECON	0.7	0.7	0.6
Asia	18.5	18.6	24.1
Others	8.0	5.4	5.0

[a] Canada, Mexico.
[b] France, Italy, Benelux.
x Figure below 0.1 percent.
COMECON: Council of Mutual Economic Aid
Sources: U.S. Department of Commerce, Bureau of the Census, *Statistical Abstract of the United States,* 1960: 886–90, 1975: 814–7; author's calculations.

materials. Exports, as in the case of the United States, were very much dominated by capital goods, especially machinery and motor vehicles, which accounted for 55 percent of the total.[2]

The trade ratio – the cumulative share of gross domestic product composed of imports and exports – is an indicator of the degree of an economy's international integration. The figures show that the Federal Republic moved decisively toward integration into the world market in the 1950s. The West German trade ratio more than doubled between 1950 and 1970, rising from 15.5 to 34.7 percent. These high figures indicate the enormous importance of foreign trade to the West German economy: Every boom before 1970 was export driven.

The American economy followed a course toward international integration that paralleled the Federal Republic's, though much less dramatically. The trade ratio rose between 1950 and 1970 by just under a quarter, from 6.7 to 8.5

[2] Jerold Blümle and Rainer Feninger, "Die Entwicklung des Aussenhandels der Bundesrepublik nach dem Zweiten Weltkrieg," in Theodor Dams and Kunihiro Jojima, eds., *Internationale Wirtschaftsbeziehungen: Japan – Europäische Gemeinschaften – Bundesrepublik Deutschland* (Berlin, 1983), 36.

Table 2. *West German International Trade Indicators*

	1950	1960	1970
Balance on Current Account (DM billion)	−0.3	5.6	4.7
Trade Balance (DM billion)	−2.3	8.2	20.8
Share of World Exports (percent)	3.0	9.0	11.0
Foreign Trade Quota (percent)	18.9	29.9	34.7
Regional Breakdown of Exports (percent)			
North America	6.1	9.5	10.3
United States	5.1	7.8	8.9
South and Central America	7.5	6.0	3.4
Europe	77.6	69.0	74.8
EEC[1]	35.2	29.7	39.4
East European State-Trading Countries			
USSR	x	1.5	1.0
GDR	no data	2.0	1.9
other COMECON	3.7	2.0	2.3
Asia	5.5	8.8	6.5
Others	5.2	7.8	6.7
Regional Breakdown of Imports (percent)			
North America	19.5	17.7	14.2
United States	19.3	15.9	12.9
South and Central America	3.5	6.1	3.1
Europe	71.8	68.9	74.6
EEC[a]	32.3	31.6	44.5
East European State-Trading Countries			
USSR	x	1.1	0.9
GDR	2.5	2.3	2.4
other COMECON	2.1	3.0	4.2
Asia	2.1	3.0	4.2
Others	4.0	5.0	4.7

[a] France, Italy, Benelux.

x Figure below 0.1 percent.

Sources: Deutsche Bundesbank, ed., *40 Jahre D-Mark: Monetäre Statistiken* (Frankfurt am Main, 1988), 5, 254; Statistisches Bundesamt, ed., *Der Aussenhandel der Bundesrepublik Deutschland*, pt. 1, *Zusammenfassende Übersichten* (Stuttgart), 1951: 46–7, 1961: 36–7, 1972: 46–7; author's calculations.

percent. The low figure, compared to that for the Federal Republic, is partly attributable to America's much larger domestic market. Moreover, the trade ratio obscures the fact that the United States was increasingly involved in the international economy in this period through direct foreign investment, particularly in Western Europe (Britain and West Germany).[3] The profits that flowed back to the United States from these investments were by far the largest credit item in the country's services account and helped keep the invisible balance, like the current account balance as a whole, in surplus throughout the 1960s. The heaviest debit item in the services account was the cost of stationing and deploying American troops abroad (direct military expenditures).[4] By contrast, the Federal Republic's net services figure was negative during the 1960s, largely owing to the tourism services foreign countries recorded as a result

---

[3] See the chapter by Hans-Eckart Scharrer and Kerstin Müller-Neuhof in this section.

[4] See the chapter by Hubert Zimmermann in this section.

of West Germans' enthusiasm for travel. Similarly, the German balance-on-transfer account showed a sharply rising deficit in the 1960s that was caused primarily by private transfers arranged by the fast-growing population of foreign "guest workers" (about 2 million individuals in 1970) sending money home, above all to Turkey. Until the mid-1960s, the main transfer payments were those made to Israel toward Holocaust compensation.[5] However, the large surpluses in trade in goods resulted in a generally positive West German current account balance; the years 1949, 1950, 1962, and 1965 were the exceptions. The large American balance-of-transfers deficit between 1950 and 1970 was a result mainly of government payments to international organizations (e.g., the UN, the World Bank, NATO) and economic and military aid to other countries, usually of strategic importance.

What was the regional orientation of the American and West German economies, and how did they change between 1950 and 1970? The immediately striking feature of West German foreign trade, both exports and imports, is the predominance of the European – especially Western European – countries, which accounted for between two-thirds and three-fourths of all transactions. After an initial period in which West German foreign trade diversified in the direction of the Americas, Asia, and Africa, the focus increasingly shifted during the 1960s toward West Germany's fellow member states of the European Economic Community (EEC). In 1970, nearly 40 percent of West German exports went to France, Italy, and the Benelux states, which in turn provided between them nearly 45 percent of the Federal Republic's imports.

The regional breakdown of American foreign trade presented a much more uniform overall picture than that of West Germany. There was a high degree of continuity in the United States' trade with its neighbors: Canada and Mexico accounted for about a fourth of U.S. exports and imports throughout the period 1950–70. The Latin American countries became far less

important, especially on the import side. Their share of all U.S. imports fell from 31.5 percent in 1950 to 11.6 percent in 1970. At the same time, the United States stepped up its trade relations with the Asian countries, most notably Japan, and Western Europe, especially the EEC. The EEC states' share of U.S. imports soared from 6.4 percent in 1950 to 16.5 percent in 1970 at the same time that their share of U.S. exports grew comparatively slowly, from 15.8 to 19.5 percent.

BILATERAL TRADE RELATIONS: A PROCESS OF
GERMAN EMANCIPATION

Bilateral West German–American trade relations reflected the changing pattern of EEC–United States trade. West German exports to the United States increased after 1950 and accounted for 9 percent of the Federal Republic's exports by 1970. The development on the import side was more marked: The United States' share of West German imports fell from nearly 20 percent (a very high level for a single country) to about 13 percent. In the first twenty years after the war, the United States was the Federal Republic's main export market but, in 1968, France and The Netherlands permanently ousted it from that position. Although the Federal Republic's share of all U.S. exports in the period 1950–70 rose from 4.3 to 6.3 percent, its contribution to imports grew much faster, from 1.2 to 7.8 percent.

The structure of the bilateral balance of trade also underwent radical long-term changes. The chronic trade surplus the United States had built up in its trade with the Federal Republic during the late 1940s and the 1950s melted away in the first half of the 1960s and gave way to a deficit from 1966 onward. At the same time, although the United States was able to preserve its structural surplus in trade with the EEC as a whole, there were signs of a move toward equilibrium. The change in the pattern of transatlantic trade flows to the detriment of the United States created tensions in its economic relations with the Federal Republic. In the bilateral context, of course, these tensions

---

[5] See the chapter by Jörg Fisch in this section.

were increasingly overshadowed by America's balance-of-payments problems arising from the outflow of dollars to Britain and the Federal Republic for imports, direct foreign investment, venture capital, and the cost of stationing troops. Washington repeatedly pressured Bonn to "correct" this trend by exporting more capital.[6]

There have been several attempts to explain the change in German-American trade relations. Although they are at odds to some extent, these explanations are, for the most part, complementary.

The Protectionism Thesis

In the early postwar years, close economic links were forged between (West) Germany and the United States as a result of the policies enacted by the Allies during the occupation. The "dollar clause," which compelled West Germany to invoice all its export transactions in U.S. dollars between 1945 and 1949, initially caused trade discrimination against the other countries of Western Europe. Moreover, those countries' currencies were overvalued, so American imports were generally cheaper for West Germany.[7]

In the second half of the occupation period and during the early years of the Federal Republic, Washington gave Bonn substantial political support with its economic and institutional integration into the world economy.[8] Institutionally, the final step was taken in 1951 with West Germany's accession to the General Agreement on Tariffs and Trade (GATT), which, together with the introduction of Deutsche Mark convertibility in 1954–8, was the basis of the country's liberal foreign-trade system. This development and the close political ties between Bonn and Washington resulted in intensive German-

American trade relations in the 1950s. The U.S. government realized at an early stage that free trade *within* Europe was a necessary detour on the way to multilateral free trade. Consequently, the Marshall Plan made intra-Europe cooperation a condition for the provision of aid.[9] With the founding of the European Payments Union (EPU) in September 1950, economic relations within Europe, in which the Federal Republic increasingly participated, became even closer.[10]

As a founding member of the European Economic Community (EEC), the Federal Republic concentrated its foreign-trade relations on Western Europe from 1957 on. The relative regionalization of German foreign trade in the late 1950s and the 1960s strongly suggests that the formation of the European customs union had the effect of diverting trade from other countries, to the disadvantage of the United States. To put it another way, the Federal Republic's liberal foreign-trade system took on protectionist features as a result of the country's incorporation into EEC structures.

The percentage growth rates for EEC imports both for the EEC countries as a whole (total growth 1958–72: 51.7 percent) and for the Federal Republic (55.8 percent) were in fact considerably higher than those for imports from non-EEC countries (29.2 and 30.4 percent, respectively). Over the course of time, however, the differential between the EEC and nonmember states did not become any greater, even after the finalization of the European customs union in mid-1968. In any event, the United States benefited more than the average non-EEC country from the increase in imports by the EEC and West Germany in the period 1958–62 and, to a noticeably lesser degree, thereafter. Here again, however, there is no clear correlation in time with the customs union. Thomas Vajna has pointed out that growth rates in U.S. trade with other Western industrialized countries that were not EEC members at the time (e.g., Britain, Denmark, and Ireland) followed a largely identical pattern. This indicates that

---

[6] Manfred Knapp et al., *Die USA und Deutschland 1918–1975: Deutsch-Amerikanische Beziehungen zwischen Rivalität und Partnerschaft* (Munich, 1978), 198–210.

[7] Christoph Buchheim, "Die Bundesrepublik in der Weltwirtschaft," in Wolfgang Benz, ed., *Die Geschichte der Bundesrepublik Deutschland* (Frankfurt am Main, 1989), 172–4.

[8] See the chapter by Werner Bührer in this section.

[9] See the chapter by Gerd Hardach in this section.

[10] Frank D. Weiss et al., *Trade Policy in West Germany* (Tübingen, 1988), 103–8.

the relative downturn in trade suffered by the United States was clearly not the result of protectionist barriers erected by the EEC.[11] The EEC's foreign-trade system did take an undeniably protectionist turn in 1965 with the introduction of the Common Agricultural Policy. In the case of the Federal Republic, however, this was of little relevance because, in the 1960s, America's share of total West German imports of agricultural goods was only 2 percent. Spectacular trade disputes in the agricultural sector, such as the "chicken war" of the early 1960s, were certainly the exception in trade relations between Germany and the United States.[12]

The Reconstruction Thesis

The reconstruction of industrial capacity in Japan and Western Europe resulted in increased competition for the United States. The reconstruction thesis, as it has been called by William Branson and others, assumes that the United States experienced an artificial economic dominance, resulting from political and military events, after World War II and that realistic economic power relationships were restored in the 1950s and 1960s. One manifestation of this process was the gradual evening-out of differences in productivity among the Western industrialized nations; another was the growing similarity between their production and foreign-trade structures, which became increasingly intra-industrial.[13]

This was especially the case in West German–American trade relations. In 1970, for example, 60 percent of West German imports from the United States were in the machinery and motor vehicles sector. The fact that intra-industry exchanges tended to be more advantageous to the Federal Republic than to the United States cannot, however, be attributed solely to the German process of recovery. Clearly, West German exporters were able to assemble a more attractive array of offerings than their American competitors. This was also apparent in dealings with other markets: German exports achieved growth precisely where there was a lasting rise in world demand for imports. The fact that West Germany's exporters had become very much more competitive – especially in factors not related to price, such as the skill of the workforce and the capacity for innovation – was also apparent from the fact that in some segments of the world market (machinery and motor vehicles, chemical products), Germany was able to challenge the United States' share of the export market.

The Monetary Thesis

Changes in the two countries' economic strength and international competitiveness called for corresponding adjustments in currency parities. In Germany's case, however, it was apparent that the revaluations of the Deutsche Mark in 1961 and 1969 could do nothing to slow the trend unfavorable to the United States. The Bretton Woods system of fixed exchange rates contained a critical structural flaw: The United States was the only member that could not unilaterally adjust the value of its currency. Its trading partners consequently tried to delay revaluation of their currencies for as long as possible. It could be argued that the revaluations of the mark came too late and, at 5 percent and about 9 percent, were an insufficient reflection of the change in the economic performance of the two countries. The United States was not able to secure a radical realignment of exchange rates until the Smithsonian Agreement of 1971. Overall, however, a pivotal role cannot be ascribed to monetary policy, especially because the pressure to revalue the Deutsche Mark was caused in large part by the influx of venture capital into the German capital markets.

[11] Thomas Vajna, *Die Handelsbeziehungen zwischen USA und EG* (Cologne, 1973), 8–9, 18, 24.

[12] Ross B. Talbot, *The Chicken War: An International Trade Conflict Between the United States and the European Economic Community, 1961–1964* (Ames, Iowa, 1978).

[13] William H. Branson, *Trends in U.S. International Trade and Investment Since World War II* (Cambridge, Mass., 1980); see also Ludger Lindlar, *Das missverstandene Wirtschaftswunder: Westdeutschland und die westeuropäische Nachkriegsprosperität* (Tübingen, 1997).

The Direct Investment Thesis

Although the strong dollar tended to inhibit American exports, it offered advantages for investment in Western Europe. There is no denying that some American exports to the EEC were replaced by direct "on-the-spot" American investment.[14] There is, however, no firm consensus on the extent to which direct investment not only replaced American exports but also actually expanded them.[15] But, as Manfred Knapp has shown, if the American multinationals' sales in the Federal Republic had been added to exports (and German sales resulting from investments in the United States were likewise added to German exports), the Americans would have been more than able to make good their trade deficit with the Federal Republic from the second half of the 1960s onward.[16]

IDEOLOGY AND ECONOMICS: EAST-WEST TRADE

Trade between the Western industrialized countries and the state-controlled economies of Eastern Europe suffered greatly from the political and ideological confrontation between the two blocs. As a consequence, the full economic potential of trade relations between East and West never came close to being realized.

The greatest economic barriers to a flourishing East-West trade were the economic weakness of the Central and Eastern European countries and their limited ability to compete in the world market – both the result of inefficient central planning. Another hindrance was a Soviet-ordered export policy oriented toward political geography rather than markets. The reason for this was that the economic planning of the Council of Mutual Economic Aid (COMECON), founded on Moscow's initiative in 1949, aimed in the long run at economic self-sufficiency for its socialist member states.

However, this strategy met with only limited success. At the end of the 1960s, the "intrabloc trade" of the Eastern European states accounted for two-thirds of their total foreign trade, which was still far lower than the percentage the Western industrialized nations traded with each other (about three-fourths). East-West trade was more important for the Central and Eastern European countries, accounting for about a fourth of their foreign trade, than it was for the Western industrial nations (less than 4 percent).[17]

The total volume of East-West trade increased from just less than $1.3 billion in 1950 to more than $9.5 billion in 1969.[18] With its traditionally good trade relations with the East and advantageous geographical position, the Federal Republic was the main trading partner of the Eastern bloc countries. Nevertheless, as is apparent from Table 2, exports to Eastern Europe (excluding East Germany) accounted for about only 3.5 percent of West Germany's total exports and declined slightly between 1950 and 1970. Eastern Europe's share of West German imports was around 3 percent. West Germany's main trading partners in the East were the Soviet Union, Czechoslovakia, Romania, and Poland.[19] The Federal Republic had a structural trade surplus with the great majority of the Eastern bloc states aside from the Soviet Union. This was primarily a result of the goods that comprised West German trade with the East. Whereas West Germany's main exports to the Eastern bloc states were finished industrial goods, chemicals, and iron and steel products (especially machinery), its main imports from the region were raw materials (timber and oil), semifinished products (iron, steel, and nonferrous metals), and agricultural produce.

---

[14] See the chapter by Hans-Eckart Scharrer and Kerstin Müller-Neuhof in this section.

[15] On this point, see Vajna, *Handelsbeziehungen*, 30–6.

[16] Knapp et al., *USA und Deutschland*, 192.

[17] Klaus-Heinrich Standke, *Der Handel mit dem Osten: Die Wirtschaftsbedingungen mit den Staatshandelsländern*, 2d ed. (Baden-Baden, 1972), 34–5.

[18] Claus-Dieter Rohleder, *Die Osthandelspolitik der EWG Mitgliedstaaten, Grossbritanniens und der USA gegenüber den Staatshandelsländern Südeuropas* (Munich, 1969).

[19] Yugoslavia, excluded in 1948 from the Kremlin-controlled COMINFORM (Communist Information Bureau), occupied a special position, pursuing a largely autonomous socialist policy.

However, the agricultural export base of the COMECON states continued to shrink as a result of their ambitious programs of industrialization begun in the mid-1950s, which shifted the weight of their internal economic resources toward the secondary sector.[20]

On the Western side, political reservations – especially security concerns – were the major hindrance in trade with the East.[21] In 1949, all NATO members (except Iceland) and Japan ratified the "COCOM List" (COCOM: Coordinating Committee for Multilateral Export Controls) of strategically important goods such as arms, high technology, and the associated know-how that could not be supplied, directly or indirectly, to Eastern bloc states. Additional national rules often created further obstacles to trade with the East. In the second half of the 1960s, however, the Federal Republic introduced a number of liberalizing measures that might be interpreted as economic harbingers of the policy of détente toward the East.[22]

Economic relations between the two German states took on special political significance. From the West German standpoint, "interzonal trade" was "primarily conceived as a way of preserving one of the last links between the two parts of Germany."[23] The volume of trade between West and East Germany rose from DM 400 million in 1952 (the first year for which records were kept) to DM 4.4 billion in 1970. This represented 2 to 3 percent of West Germany's total exports and imports. The equivalent figures for East Germany, about 8 percent in each case, reflected the greater economic dependence of the East on the West. Along with coal, the major imports from East Germany included footwear, food, clothing, and textiles. West Germany's

main exports to the East were chemicals, machinery, animal feeds, and iron and steel products. From 1966 onward, the Federal Republic recorded an almost continuous surplus in trade with the German Democratic Republic.

Measured by export sales, the Federal Republic ranked well ahead of Britain and Japan as the main Western trading partner of the Eastern bloc states by the end of the 1960s, and the United States occupied only sixth place. The United States' trade with the East showed a uniformly positive balance between 1950 and 1970. Its relative unimportance for American foreign trade as a whole is apparent, though, from the fact that the COMECON's share of all U.S. exports and imports over the entire period 1950–70 never exceeded 1 percent and, indeed, was well below that most of the time (see Table 1). The United States' most important trading partner in the East was Poland, followed by Czechoslovakia. In the 1960s, economic relations with the Soviet Union also became more important, especially as a result of large U.S. grain sales. The main American imports from the Soviet Union were high-grade industrial raw materials such as palladium, diamonds, and chromium ore. Otherwise, there was little consistency to the makeup of U.S. trade with Eastern and Central Europe, though the exchange of agricultural goods played a dominant part.[24]

The United States found itself facing much greater structural obstacles to its trade with the East than did the Federal Republic and the other West European allies. The economic base for intensive trade relations with the East did not exist because most of the goods exported from the East were available within the United States itself or could be procured from its more favorably located neighbor, Canada. The biggest political brake on trade with the East was applied by the Export Control Act of 1949: Its "positive list" was very much longer than the COCOM list, initially placing an embargo on 1,800 items (reduced to about 800 by 1969). However, the larger American companies, at least, could

---

[20] Reinhold Biskup, "Einflüsse auf die Entwicklung des Aussenhandels in beiden Teilen Deutschlands seit dem Zweiten Weltkrieg," *Wirtschaftswissenschaftliches Studium* 15 (1986): 327–32.

[21] Gary K. Bertsch, ed., *Controlling East-West Trade and Technology Transfer: Power, Politics, and Policies* (Durham, N.C., 1988).

[22] Robert Mark Spaulding, *Osthandel and Ostpolitik: German Foreign Trade Policies in Eastern Europe from Bismarck to Adenauer* (Providence, R.I., 1997).

[23] Standke, *Der Handel mit dem Osten*, 227.

[24] Ibid., 285–8.

circumvent the Export Control Act by routing their trade with the Eastern bloc through Western European subsidiaries.[25]

CONCLUSION

Both the United States and the Federal Republic had structural foreign-trade surpluses. That the relative size of the American surplus decreased while that of the Federal Republic rose reflected the changing position of each country in world trade. Although the United States clearly dominated world trade between 1945 and 1970, its lead over the second-largest exporter, West Germany, shrank.

The West German economy was heavily dependent on exports as well as on imports of raw materials. As a result, West Germany was quickly integrated into the international market in 1950s. The United States, with its large domestic market, was not as dependent on foreign trade, although in the 1960s it did turn increasingly toward the world market. Growing international interdependence did not bypass the United States and was manifested in increased direct investment by American multinationals, especially in Western Europe. The profits that flowed back to the United States were the largest item in the American services account during the 1950s and 1960s. Otherwise, the trade in services had not yet become a major factor for the two countries in the 1950s and 1960s, and intra-industry trade still clearly predominated.

American foreign trade was fairly evenly distributed across the globe, although with an increasing emphasis on Asia and Western Europe. The proportion of imports originating in the EEC increased significantly during the 1960s. To the detriment of the United States, especially on the import side, the Federal Republic also began to focus more on its EEC partners. At the same time, the United States' initially high surpluses in its trade with West Germany declined and gave way to deficits from 1966 on. The primary cause of this development was not incorporation of the liberal West German economy in the allegedly protectionist EEC foreign trade system. More important were the economic recovery of the Federal Republic relative to the United States since World War II and the fact that some West German industries had become more competitive than their American counterparts. The change in the economic balance of power was only belatedly reflected in exchange rates, although the United States was able to compensate for its trade losses by way of direct investment.

In East-West trade, ideological and strategic factors were more important than economic ones. Many politically motivated restrictions ensured that the economic potential of trade between the Western industrialized nations and the state-controlled economies of Eastern Europe remained far from being realized. These restrictions were greater in the United States than in the Federal Republic.[26]

---

[25] Roland Schönfeld, "The U.S.A. in Economic Relations Between East and West," *Soviet and Eastern European Foreign Trade* 10 (1974): 3–18.

[26] Hélène Seppain, *Contrasting U.S. and German Attitudes to Soviet Trade, 1917–1991: Politics by Economic Means* (New York, 1992).

CHAPTER EIGHT

Technology and the Construction of the Alliance

Technology Transfer, the Cold War, and German-American Relations

Raymond G. Stokes

It is well known that industrial nations have one another as their biggest trading partners and that their exchange consists of a high proportion of manufactured goods. What is less commonly recognized is that technology is one of the key commodities they trade. Transfer of technology is especially intensive between partners of roughly similar levels of industrial development. New machines, new systems, and new ideas about their organization and deployment – elements of what is known as "international technological best practice" – tend to flow rapidly between highly industrialized countries, primarily through contact between particular individuals and their firms.

Applying this observation to the German-American situation following World War II might seem problematic, given West Germany's undeniable junior status in technology. Still, it is crucial to keep in mind that, despite the evident inequalities between them, West Germany and the United States had many technological and scientific capabilities in common after 1945, especially when compared to virtually any other country in the world.

Indeed, an interpretation of technology transfer in the postwar period based on notions of uniformly superior American technology and unidirectional transfer from the United States to West Germany would be wildly inaccurate, though such an interpretation is implicit in many economic histories of West Germany

in the postwar period.[1] The story of technology transfer between the United States and the Federal Republic of Germany is, in fact, much richer than that, and recent research indicates that it was central to the development of the postwar German-American relationship.

This article examines some of the most important findings on this subject and argues that (1) West Germany's offerings – as well as its acquisitions – in international technology transfer markets were a crucial factor in its rapid recovery from the war and its continued success in international markets after 1945, and (2) the mutual invigoration of technology among the nations of the West created a Western, capitalist, liberal-democratic technological "style" that helped to cement the alliance among Western industrialized nations while distinguishing it from its rival, the Eastern bloc.[2]

---

[1] Some of the key literature is reviewed in Rolf Dumke, "Reassessing the *Wirtschaftswunder*: Reconstruction and Postwar Growth in West Germany in an International Context," *Oxford Bulletin of Economics and Statistics* 52 (1990): 451–91.

[2] On technological style generally, see Thomas Parke Hughes, *Networks of Power* (Baltimore, 1983). On technology in the Eastern bloc, see Paul R. Josephson, "'Projects of the Century' in Soviet History: Large-Scale Technologies from Lenin to Gorbachev," *Technology and Culture* 36 (1995): 519–59; Raymond G. Stokes, "In Search of the Socialist Artefact: Technology and Ideology in East Germany, 1945–1962," *German History* 15 (1997): 221–37.

In other words, the transfer of technology was also a way to transfer values and institutions. Some might see this as the "Americanization" of West German industry,[3] but such a view risks overlooking key characteristics of technology transfer. The Americans, after all, although the dominant players in most technological markets, were not the only ones. Indeed, the Americans were almost as likely as anyone else to be affected by trends in international technological best practice. The process might, therefore, better be termed "internationalization," both of technological systems and of the organizational and management systems that made them work. Each capitalist country retained aspects of its traditions and values in these areas, but all converged to some extent through participation in increasingly freer international trade in goods and technology.

This article is presented thematically in three main periods: 1945–7/8, 1947/8–55, and 1955–68. The final section briefly develops some of the larger implications of the story of technology transfer. In the case of the Federal Republic, the creation of a relatively unified Western capitalist technological style can best be seen in contrast to developments in the communist German Democratic Republic (GDR).[4] Although it is not possible to examine this in detail, a few illustrative comments are made in the course of this article.

tion: from Germany to the former Allies, including the United States.

We now know just how massive the transfers to the United States were.[5] American technical investigations went far beyond the frequently cited seizure of the aeronautical engineers who would later form the core of the U.S. space program. The effort also included interviews of German engineers and scientists; seizure of machinery, blueprints, and technical documentation from German firms and government laboratories; and publication of overviews of key developments in prewar and wartime German technology.

The Americans were not alone in their seizure of "intellectual reparations," nor were they necessarily the most active. The Soviets especially, but also the French and the British, joined the Americans in seizing the scientific and technological spoils of war.[6]

What effects did the transfer of German machines and information have on American and other Allied industry? The transfers appear to have affected the trajectory of military technology,[7] but their purpose extended also to the civilian sphere. The literature on the development of the American petrochemical and magnetic-tape industries claims that, at least in specific areas, the information collected in Germany was extremely important.[8] However, the sole study to tackle this question on the basis

TECHNOLOGY AS A SPOIL OF WAR: 1945–7/8

Technology transfer immediately after 1945 was simple: When it occurred, it was in one direc-

---

[3] Volker R. Berghahn, *The Americanisation of West German Industry, 1945–1973* (New York, 1986); Christian Kleinschmidt, *Der produktive Blick: Wahrnehmung amerikanischer und japanischer Management- und Produktionsmethoden durch deutsche Unternehmer 1950–1985* (Berlin, 2002).

[4] Johannes Bähr and Dietmar Petzina, eds., *Innovationsverhalten und Entscheidungsstrukturen: Vergleichende Studien zur wirtschaftlichen Entwicklung im geteilten Deutschland 1945–1990* (Berlin, 1996).

[5] John Gimbel, *Science, Technology, and Reparations: Exploitation and Plunder in Postwar Germany* (Stanford, Calif., 1990).

[6] Rainer Karlsch, *Allein bezahlt? Die Reparationsleistungen der SBZ/DDR 1945–53* (Berlin, 1993); Ulrich Albrecht, Andreas Heinemann-Grüder, and Arend Wellmann, *Die Spezialisten: Deutsche Naturwissenschaftler und Techniker in der Sowjetunion nach 1945* (Berlin, 1992). On intellectual reparations in general, see Matthias Judt and Burghard Ciesla, eds., *Technology Transfer out of Germany After World War II* (Amsterdam, 1996).

[7] See the chapter by Michael Neufeld, vol. 1, Security. On the impact of transfers on the Soviet Union's military technology, see Ulrich Albrecht and Randolph Nikutta, *Die sowjetische Rüstungsindustrie* (Opladen, 1989).

[8] See, for example, Peter Spitz, *Petrochemicals: The Rise of an Industry* (New York, 1988), 176, 329–31; David L. Morton, "'The Rusty Ribbon': John Herbert Orr and

of archival sources and for specific companies concludes that the seizures of German technical information and machines had only limited impact on the development of American synthetic-rubber and magnetic-tape technologies.[9] Despite these findings, more work is needed before the full story of the impact of technology transfer from Germany to the United States in the immediate postwar period can be known.

A variety of factors motivated the Allied effort to investigate German science and technology in the immediate aftermath of the war. At first, the continuing war against Japan was the major justification. Thereafter, commercial considerations, which had always been part of the motivation behind the investigations, took on greater importance. Throughout these shifts, there were tensions among the former Allies generated by the clear association between science and technology on one hand and military and economic power on the other. At first these tensions characterized relations not just between the Soviet Union and the United States but among all the former Allies. However, the emerging Cold War soon had an impact: By June 1947, intellectual reparations officially ended in the Western zones of occupation, in part because of the desire to avoid sharing the information with the Soviets, in part to promote the recovery of West German industry. In the Soviet zone/GDR, seizures of intellectual property remained in force until the early 1950s, including the forcible removal of specially trained personnel to the Soviet Union.

The evidence on the long-term consequences of intellectual reparations indicates that their negative impact on West Germany (and concomitant positive impact on the Allies) was not nearly as substantial as the Germans feared (or the Allies hoped). Indeed, intellectual reparations arguably helped in the long run to integrate West Germany into American-dominated

Western technological culture after 1945. The technical investigation missions promoted both renewed awareness of German technological capabilities on the part of Allied industry and renewed contact between German and Allied engineers and managers. This function of establishing a "conveyor-belt for future business connections" between representatives of the formerly warring nations may have been the most enduring legacy of intellectual reparations.[10]

REBUILDING TECHNOLOGICAL RELATIONSHIPS: 1947/8–55

Following the official end to seizure of reparations, technological relations between the Federal Republic and the Western Allies – between firms as well as governments – gradually normalized from 1947/8 to 1955. Led by the Americans, the Western Allies slowly removed restrictions on research and development at German laboratories. The West Germans also reinstated patent protection during this time, providing an impetus to innovation.

The West Germans benefited, as did other Europeans, from technical-assistance missions organized under the auspices of the European Recovery Program (ERP) and the Organization for European Economic Cooperation (OEEC). These missions involved visits by European experts to the United States or by American experts to Europe. Their avowed purpose was to promote organizational and technological change in European countries by allowing them to learn directly from American developments, although the emphasis was primarily on management techniques and industrial relations rather than machines and their deployment. These missions may have aided in the transfer of American technological best practice to Europe, but they formed a relatively small

the Making of the Magnetic Recording Industry, 1945–1960," *Business History Review* 67 (1993): 589–622.

[9] Peter J. T. Morris and Mark Clark, "Worthless Plunder? Allied Intelligence Operations and the German Synthetic Rubber and Magnetic Recording Industries, 1939–1950," *Technology and Culture* (forthcoming).

[10] This argument is elaborated in Raymond G. Stokes, "Forced Technology Transfer and European Integration," in Francis Heller and John Gillingham, eds., *The United States and the Integration of Europe: Legacies of the Postwar Era* (New York, 1996), 281–8.

proportion of Marshall Plan aid. Total aid to all European countries under the Marshall Plan through 1951 was \$12 billion, of which just \$30 million was earmarked for technical assistance. Most of that portion was expended in the eighteen months between the outbreak of the Korean War in June 1950 and the end of 1951.[11]

At the same time that the West German and Western Allied governments normalized technological relations to allow freer and easier transfer of technology, additional restrictions were placed on such transfers to the GDR. CO-COM (Coordinating Committee), formed in 1949 by capitalist countries under the leadership of the United States, was responsible throughout its existence for developing lists of high-technology items for which trade or technical cooperation between the capitalist West and the socialist East was prohibited.[12]

Deficiencies in the planning system ultimately accounted for the GDR's inability to innovate effectively during the postwar period, but COCOM restrictions probably had a substantial impact as well. High-technology industries were most likely to come under COCOM regulations. They are also industries requiring rapid technological development in the form of either technology transfer or independent research. By delaying transfer of critical technologies, COCOM may have hindered such development. This helps explain the fact that, although the GDR began independent development of new technologies at virtually the same time as West Germany, their full-scale application frequently occurred eight to ten years later than in the West.[13]

Governments could promote or hinder technology transfer through various means. But many economists and economic historians fail to recognize that, in capitalist countries especially (and even in socialist ones), the transfer process was located not so much at the governmental or the macroeconomic level but at the level of the industrial firm.

Economic histories of postwar Germany, to the extent that they mention technology transfer, emphasize that West Germany imported not only labor but also technical (and organizational) know-how. The source of such imports is generally assumed to be the United States, the clear technological leader through much of the postwar period. Evidence for these contentions comes primarily from West Germany's global technological balance of payments, which measures the difference between payments for and receipts from patents, licenses, and know-how transfers between countries. Karl Hardach, for example, notes a steady technological balance-of-payments deficit through the mid-1950s, which increased through the late 1960s as "German industry tried to regain the general standard in conventional technology which had been lost during the war and the immediate postwar years."[14] He essentially argues, then, that there was a "technological gap" between West Germany and the United States during this period.[15]

Steuerung von Werkzeugmaschinen," *Technikgeschichte* 60 (1993): 307–19.

[14] Karl Hardach, *The Political Economy of Germany in the Twentieth Century* (Berkeley, Calif., 1980), 195–6 (quotations). Dumke, in "Reassessing the *Wirtschaftswunder*," reviews and elaborates on many of the key arguments regarding convergence of productivity toward the American standard by means of technology transfer in the postwar period, although he, like most other economic historians, treats the transfer process in very general terms.

[15] On the debate about the "technological gap," see, for example, Jean Servan-Schreiber, *The American Challenge* (London, 1968); OECD, *Gaps in Technology: Comparisons Between Member Countries* (Paris, 1970); Stanley Woods, *Western Europe: Technology and the Future* (London, 1987); Helge Majer, *Die "technologische Lücke" zwischen der Bundesrepublik Deutschland und den Vereinigten Staaten* (Tübingen, 1973). Dumke, "Reassessing

[11] See Michael J. Hogan, *The Marshall Plan: America, Britain, and the Reconstruction of Western Europe, 1947–1952* (Cambridge, 1987), 142–3, 415–22; OECD, *The European Reconstruction: A Bibliography* (Paris, 1996), esp. 86–7.

[12] Robert W. Dean, *West German Trade with the East: The Political Dimension* (New York, 1974), 103–4.

[13] See, e.g., Raymond G. Stokes, "Autarky, Ideology, and Technological Lag: The Case of the East German Chemical Industry, 1945–1964," *Central European History* 28 (1995): 29–45; André Steiner, "Technikgenese in der DDR am Beispiel der Entwicklung der numerischen

This appears to be a plausible argument, but closer analysis of the evidence reveals a much more ambiguous picture. During the period in which Hardach notes substantial technological balance-of-payments deficits, West Germany's share in world industrial production rose from 4.2 percent in 1948 to 9.4 percent in 1969.[16] West German productivity increased during approximately the same period from about one-third of that of the United States in 1950 to about 71 percent in 1973.[17] These figures suggest impressive growth in West German technological capability relative to that of the United States during the 1950s and 1960s, a convergence in productivity that indicates the development of a Western capitalist technological style. The figures certainly do *not* indicate irredeemable deficiencies in this area.

Other evidence confirms that the putative "technological gap" between West Germany and the United States in the 1950s and 1960s is a problematic concept. Hardach implicitly posits an association between West Germany's technological balance-of-payments deficit through the late 1960s and recovery and reconstruction from the war and occupation. We would thus expect that the deficit would turn into a surplus – or at least a balance – following recovery and reconstruction. Yet, West Germany ran a technological balance-of-payments deficit through at least 1993. Indeed, every major industrial country, with the exception of the United States (with extremely large surpluses) and the United Kingdom (with relatively modest surpluses), ran such deficits into the early 1990s.[18] The statistic may, then, not be so much an indicator of

technology gaps as of gaps in certain technologies only: namely, those expensive, extremely advanced technologies, especially electronics, in which the United States was the unquestioned world leader for the entire postwar period. In fact, the figures may indicate advanced technological capability more than backwardness. After all, only West Germany and other highly industrialized states that had such capability would benefit from extensive purchase of licenses and know-how from abroad.

Another set of figures confirms this impression of West German technological prowess. For selected years between 1900 and 1938, Germany accounted for the lion's share of all foreign patents registered in the United States, between 30 and 38 percent. This figure dropped to 0.57 percent in 1950 but, by 1958, West Germany had regained the premier position in foreign patent registrations in the United States and continued to hold this position until Japan overtook it in the late 1970s. The Federal Republic's share of all registrations, about a fourth, never matched that of pre-World War II Germany, but the rapid growth after 1950 confirms that German technology had returned to a high standard that was recognized in the United States.[19]

In view of the ambiguity in these aggregate national figures on transfer of technology and technological capability, other approaches are needed. One way is to proceed from the assumption that technology transfer takes place on the level of individual firms and then to examine case studies of negotiations between particular firms with regard to particular technologies.

It is clear that cooperative technological development between American and West German companies occurred through various means, including joint ventures, licensing, purchase of machines and/or know-how, and copying and industrial espionage. Although the only extensive historical treatments of technology transfer between specific firms deal with the chemical and the tire industries,[20] their findings

the *Wirtschaftswunder*," surveys related economic literature on the "productivity gap"; see esp. 452, 456, 470–4.

[16] Jeremy Leaman, *The Political Economy of West Germany* (London, 1988), 93.

[17] Giovanni Dosi, Keith Pavit, and Luc Soete, *The Economics of Technical Change and International Trade* (New York, 1990), 52.

[18] OECD, *Basic Science and Technology Statistics* (Paris, 1995); German figures for 1976–93 are on 62. Compare figures for the United States (453), the UK (440), Italy (238), France (143), and Japan (259). Japan is the only country with a long-running deficit that ran into surplus, but this began only in 1992.

[19] Dosi, Pavit, and Soete, *Technical Change and International Trade*, 43.

[20] Raymond G. Stokes, *Opting for Oil: The Political Economy of Technological Change in the West German*

can show how West German firms in other industries parlayed early foreign-trade successes, which were based primarily on prewar and wartime technology, into self-sustaining competitive capabilities.

The case of the chemical industry provides a number of starting points for examining other industries. First, technology transfer was not exclusively from the United States to West Germany, even in the petrochemical industry, where American firms had a clear head start on their German counterparts. Instead, there was true exchange between the two; already in the early 1950s, West German firms were offering expertise and know-how to American firms, which were impressed with – and in need of – key aspects of German chemical technology. The West Germans used their technological capabilities and their reputations to obtain access and funding with which to purchase American, British, and Dutch petrochemical technology. In other words, the development of this crucial industry depended as much on West German *offerings* as it did on *acquisitions* of technology and know-how on the international market.

Second, the study of the chemical industry sheds light on the issue of Americanization versus internationalization of West German industry. American firms were not the only ones to transfer world-class chemical technology to West Germany. In fact, West German firms in the petrochemical industry had broadly based cooperative agreements and conducted joint ventures not with their American counterparts, but with the British and the Dutch. Petrochemical technology was becoming international, not American, and the West Germans contributed substantially to this internationalization.

The third point highlighted by the postwar history of the chemical industry concerns its long-term impact: The petrochemicals industry is a key example of the gradual emergence of a Western, capitalist, liberal-democratic technological style. High-tech and capital-intensive, the petrochemicals industry required extensive international cooperation, access to cheap oil, mass motorization, and a mass-consumption society for its development and expansion. An American-led international trade and security structure provided these conditions; based on them, all major Western industrialized countries developed petrochemicals industries by the 1960s. The Eastern bloc lagged far behind the West in this respect, maintaining a backwardness that formed a crucial part of the contrasting socialist technological style.[21]

<h3 style="text-align:center">PARTNERS IN TECHNOLOGY AND ALLIANCE: 1955–68</h3>

Historians have only begun to scratch the surface in exploring technology transfer during the late 1950s and the 1960s. Certainly, the formal end of the occupation of West Germany and the regaining of full political sovereignty ushered in a new era by allowing reinstitution of a fully normalized framework for international transfer of technology. The founding of the European Economic Community shortly thereafter may well also have had an effect on technological relations with the United States, although the evidence on technological balance of payments indicates that the United States remained the largest supplier of patents, licenses, and know-how to all highly industrialized countries, including West Germany.

Continued export and general economic success for the Federal Republic during the late 1950s and early 1960s meant that there was no pressing need to inquire into the state of German science and technology.[22] The economic

Chemical Industry (New York, 1994), esp. chap. 4; Paul Erker, "The Long Shadow of Americanization: The Rubber Industry and the Radial Tire Revolution" (paper presented at conference on The Americanization of Western European Economy, Isegran, Norway, Aug. 22, 1997); see also Paul Erker, *Competition and Growth: The Continental AG Story* (Düsseldorf, 1996), 45–7.

[21] See Stokes, "Autarky, Ideology, and Technological Lag," for more on the East German petrochemical industry; see Stokes, "In Search of the Socialist Artefact," for more on the technological style of the Eastern bloc.
[22] Reinhard Neebe, "Technologietransfer und Aussenhandel in den Anfangsjahren der Bundesrepublik

slowdown of the mid-1960s, however, called into question the technological basis of the economic miracle. In this climate, French journalist Jean Servan-Schreiber's best-selling book *The American Challenge*, published in French in 1967 and in English and German in 1968, struck a chord with its talk of a "technology gap" between the United States and European countries.

Statistics from the Organization for Economic Cooperation and Development (OECD) can help clarify the ambiguous notion of a technological gap. In 1964, the year for which the available data are most detailed, West Germany relied on foreign imports of patents, licenses, and know-how in every major industry group. Its "coverage ratio,"[23] the ratio between what West Germany paid for technology and what it received from it, was 30 to 40 percent in most areas. Even in chemicals and allied products, for which the Germans were highly regarded, receipts from technological transfers covered only 60 percent of West Germany's payments.

In 1964, West Germany paid $150.9 million to the top 11 industrialized countries for foreign patents, licenses, and know-how. Of this, 43 percent flowed to the United States, followed by Switzerland (28.3 percent), the United Kingdom (11.3 percent), and The Netherlands (7.4 percent). The United States purchased foreign technology to a much lesser degree. Of the $87.8 million it paid to foreign countries for patents, licenses, and know-how in 1964, the lion's share went to Canada (42.8 percent), followed by Britain (23.9 percent). The other two major partners for the United States were France (13.3 percent) and West Germany (12.3 percent).[24]

West Germany was clearly the junior partner in this relationship, but the substantial disparities between it and the United States should not obscure two facts. First, the United States was a net technological exporter to all other countries during this period. Second, both were among the very small number of nations who traded sophisticated technologies with one another. This second point indicates an important characteristic common to both countries: Both were vigorous participants in the unfolding of a Western technological style that contrasted sharply with the one emerging at the same time in the Eastern bloc.

CONCLUSION

Although much more research needs to be done on the history of German-American technology transfer, especially for the period after 1955, it is clear that the United States and West Germany were partners in technological development in the postwar period. The United States was obviously the senior partner in this relationship, but just as obvious is West Germany's capability of utilizing the knowledge attained from the more "advanced" Americans and supplying them with know-how.

Technological *exchange*, then, was the watchword in the relationship between the Federal Republic and the United States. This exchange allowed them to share in each other's technology and provided concrete links that strengthened their political and economic alliance.

Deutschland," *Vierteljahrschrift für Sozial- und Wirtschaftsgeschichte* 76 (1989): 49–75, esp. 72.

[23] The concept of the coverage ratio comes from Woods, *Western Europe*, 32. A ratio of 1.0 would indicate equivalence of payments and receipts. Less than 1 indicates a deficit; greater than 1 indicates a surplus.

[24] OECD, *Gaps in Technology*, 201, 203.

CHAPTER NINE

Occupation Costs, Stationing Costs, Offset Payments

The Conflict over the Burdens of the Cold War

Hubert Zimmermann

Translated by Robert Kimber and Rita Kimber

Germany was the focal point of the Cold War; perhaps that is the very reason why armed conflict never broke out there. The major weapons employed in the Cold War were propagandistic and economic in nature. The latter proved decisive in the end. Soon after the end of World War II, American planners recognized the importance of West Germany's economic potential in the growing contest with the Soviet Union, and this realization was a crucial motivating factor behind the rapid incorporation of the Federal Republic into the Western community of nations. As a consequence, the sacrifices West Germany was called on to make during the Cold War were primarily financial. In the years 1950 to 1968, appropriations for defense ate up between 20 and 38 percent of the Federal Republic's budget.[1] Because the Federal Republic had neither the military nor economic means to provide for its own security, its incorporation into the Western defense system was vitally important. The military presence of West Germany's most important allies – of American troops in particular – thus became an integral part of German defense policy. Moreover, the presence of foreign troops stood as a symbol of Germany's membership in the Western defense community and as a prerequisite for the Western nations' acceptance of German recovery in Europe.

Occupation costs, stationing costs, and offset payments constituted the price the Federal Republic had to pay for its dependence on its Western allies, and those costs, therefore, have to be regarded as part of the German defense burden during the Cold War. Just how high those costs were to be remained a source of conflict in German-American relations for forty years, and at the heart of this conflict was the question of how the burdens of the Cold War were to be distributed. How much the Federal Republic had to pay for the troops stationed on its territory was determined in difficult negotiations with its allies and depended on a number of factors, such as the intensity of the Cold War, current military strategy, the economic policies of the countries involved, and the situation in the international monetary system. This article, therefore, treats troop costs as a major element in the political economy of the Cold War.

OCCUPATION COSTS

Between 1945 and 1955, the Western zones of occupation and the Federal Republic paid about DM 53.36 billion in occupation costs to the three Western Powers, DM 22.17 billion of which went to the United States.[2] Occupation

---

[1] Bundesministerium der Finanzen, *Finanzbericht 1969*, 446–9.

[2] There were additional costs to German budgets as a result of occupation (*Besatzungsfolgekosten*). These included payments that the occupying powers did not treat as occupation costs as well as occupation costs in Berlin.

costs was one of the matters reserved to the control of the occupying powers. They explicitly reiterated this reservation in the Occupation Statute of 1949. The Allied powers also determined the amount to be paid.[3] At times, the payments absorbed as much as 15 percent of German national income. On average, they accounted for 35 percent of the budgets of the Western zones and, later, of the Federal Republic.[4] From the outset, one of the most important aims of German authorities was to reduce this burden, which in fact exceeded the cost of overall social welfare payments. However, it was next to impossible for the state (*Länder*) governments, which were responsible for meeting these costs in the first postwar years, to lower the Allied demands.

After 1949, the federal government assumed responsibility for the payment of occupation costs. But because of the increasing tension in the East-West confrontation, the significance of the costs changed. The occupying forces became protectors, and the federal budget for 1950 took this fact into account by declaring that the occupation costs were from now on a defense contribution. The decision to rearm Germany added another dimension to the debate over the amount of occupation costs the Federal Republic should pay in the future. Led by its minister of finance, Fritz Schäffer, who soon became notorious among the Allies for his stubbornness, the West German government announced that it simply could not afford to rearm while continuing to support the Allied forces at the

previously established level. However, the Western Powers strongly objected to the suggestion of a rapid end to the German payments. Because of the strain on its own currency, Great Britain was particularly reluctant to raise the foreign exchange needed to fund its troops.

The United States took a compromise position. On the one hand, the Eisenhower administration did not want to let occupation costs stand in the way of German rearmament;[5] but, on the other, the U.S. Senate made the stationing of additional troops in Europe dependent on the Europeans themselves assuming the greater part of the burden for their own defense. And in no case could the Federal Republic of Germany, which had experienced a spectacular economic recovery in the years following the Korean War, be let entirely off the hook, especially if it was relieved of occupation costs while German rearmament was increasingly delayed.

Uncertainty bred by the seemingly endless discussions on the establishment of the European Defense Community (EDC) complicated in turn the decision on how much West Germany should contribute to European defense and how much of that sum would be allotted to the allied troops. During the EDC debate, the West German government tried in vain to shake off the yoke of occupation costs, claiming that its defense contribution alone was already excessive. Finally, in February 1952, after long and difficult negotiations, it was agreed that until the EDC agreement went into effect, the Federal Republic would provide a maximum of DM 850 million monthly for its own *and* foreign forces, of which up to DM 600 million could be used for allied troops.[6] Despite renegotiations each year, this figure remained

---

The Federal Republic was obliged to carry these latter costs until reunification because in Berlin the Occupation Statute remained the legal basis for the stationing of troops there. Helmut Rocke, "Leistungen der Bundesrepublik für die ausländischen Streitkräfte," in Presse- und Informationsamt der Bundesregierung, *Bulletin* (hereafter *BPI*) 24 (Feb. 3, 1961): 221–2.

[3] The occupying powers demanded compensation for costs incurred in German currency for the maintenance of their forces – for example, salaries for German civilian employees, goods provided by German producers, and costs for quartering troops – but also for a large number of other deutschmark expenses incurred by the occupation authorities that had little to do with the troops.

[4] Jörg Fisch, *Reparationen nach dem Zweiten Weltkrieg* (Munich, 1992), 218.

[5] United States Delegation Minutes of the Fourth Meeting of the Foreign Ministers of the United States, United Kingdom, and France Held at Washington, Sept. 13, 1951, in U.S. Department of State, *Foreign Relations of the United States* (hereafter *FRUS*), *1951*, 3:1272–8. On the debate over German rearmament, see the chapter by David Clay Large, vol. 1, Security.

[6] Werner Abelshauser, "Wirtschaft und Rüstung in den fünfziger Jahren," in Militärgeschichtliches Forschungsamt, ed., *Anfänge westdeutscher Sicherheitspolitik 1945–1956*, 4 vols. (Munich, 1997), 4:1–185.

unchanged until the Federal Republic joined NATO. Because the EDC collapsed in the interim, these payments did not differ significantly from West Germany's defense costs before 1955. Funds appropriated for German forces were not used and, together with monies not withdrawn for the allied forces, produced a large surplus in the federal budget, the so-called *Juliusturm*. The surplus took this name from the tower in the Berlin-Spandau citadel where the German Reich had kept French reparation payments after the war of 1870–1.

The struggle over West Germany's contribution to defense shows clearly that the actual goal of the rearmament debate – namely, the creation of West German armed forces – was not the Bonn government's top priority and would in no way be allowed to hamper economic growth. It was, after all, the United States' nuclear deterrent and the presence of allied troops that guaranteed West Germany's safety, not her own newly formed military forces. But as the following years would demonstrate, due to these circumstances, the Allies argued that the Federal Republic had a lasting obligation to help share the financial burdens of Western defense.

In a sense, however, the problem of occupation costs proved beneficial to the rearmament of the Federal Republic. Because the costs of the arms buildup initially remained below those of occupation, and because cash reserves were still available in the *Juliusturm*, rearmament could be financed without a major increase in taxes or a curtailment of expenditures for social benefits. Given the hard-fought debate within Germany over rearmament, this fact was very important.

Very little research has been done to date on the issue of occupation costs. The most detailed studies undertaken in the 1950s had the explicit purpose of demonstrating how unreasonable Allied demands were.[7] Recent research has dealt hardly at all with the political and economic

consequences of the occupation costs. The same can be said of the economic impact of the occupation forces themselves, which remained the largest employer in the Federal Republic into the early 1950s. Nor do we have the slightest idea yet about how those enormous sums of money were spent, sums over which the German authorities had no control. Both regionally and throughout West Germany, the occupation expenditures may well have had the effect of a reflationary program. But in the absence of detailed research into these aspects of postwar economic history, we cannot yet determine the specific effects of such Allied spending.

STATIONING COSTS, 1955–8

Even after the Federal Republic joined NATO, the relationship between occupation costs and West Germany's defense budget remained controversial. Arguing that some time would have to pass before German troops would be available in significant numbers and that the Allies would, therefore, have to continue to bear the major part of the defense burden, the Western Powers managed once again to secure a continuation of occupation payments.[8] Indeed, German rearmament was proceeding slowly. The presence of allied troops meant that the Federal Republic did not have to curtail economic development in order to finance rearmament.

At the NATO Council meeting in December 1955, the Western Allies presented Schäffer and Defense Minister Theodor Blank with demands for a direct contribution to the support of foreign forces stationed in Germany.[9] Both ministers rejected these demands as discriminatory. As a sovereign state, they asserted, the Federal

---

[7] See Institut für Besatzungsfragen, *6 Jahre Besatzungslasten* (Tübingen, 1951). For a brief summary, see Christoph Buchheim, *Die Wiedereingliederung Westdeutschlands in die Weltwirtschaft 1945–1958* (Munich, 1990), 88–93. For further references, see Daniel Hof-

mann, *Truppenstationierung in der Bundesrepublik Deutschland* (Munich, 1997).

[8] Final Report of the Working Party on the Termination of the Occupation, Oct. 2, 1954, *FRUS, 1952–1954*, vol. 5, pt. 2:1339–44, esp. 1342–3 (Finance Convention). In the period from May 1955 to May 1956, the Germans were to pay DM 3.2 billion.

[9] Telegram from the U.S. Delegation at the North Atlantic Council Ministerial Meeting to the Department of State, Feb. 17, 1955, *FRUS, 1955–1957*, 4:44–9.

Republic was no longer willing to pay occupation costs. To do so would violate West Germany's political equality in NATO because no
payments had been demanded of other countries where NATO troops were stationed. This
question quickly prompted bitter public debate.[10] At issue for the West German government was how much it was willing to pay to
maintain allied troops at their present level and,
more important, to maintain harmonious relations with its key allies. The factors that spoke
against continuing payments were economic
considerations, the struggle to achieve equal status, and the public's increasing objection to the
payments. But, in the end, the importance of
retaining the allied presence tipped the balance
in favor of continuing payments, although at a
reduced level.

In the late 1950s, the conflict over troop costs,
which focused increasingly on the foreign-
exchange expenditures of the allied forces,
took place primarily between West Germany
and Great Britain. Germany's payments to the
United States decreased[11] and, in 1958, Washington even provided financial support to Great
Britain to allay the Anglo-German conflict. The
Americans were content to receive an early partial payment of $150 million on Germany's post-
war debt. This payment presented no problem
for the Federal Republic because in these same
years, the Deutsche Mark had become the most
stable currency in the Western world. Foreign
troops had had no small part in bringing that
about. The Bundesbank calculated that despite
stationing and occupation costs, West Germany
took in from the allied forces between 1950 and
1959 foreign-exchange earnings of about DM
16.5 billion ($3,926 million).[12] American forces

accounted for 87 percent of that amount. Thus,
the strength of the Deutsche Mark in the 1950s
was due in large part to the national security
environment created by the Cold War; monetary policy and defense policy were inextricably
linked. This would become eminently clear in
the 1960s, as the example of the negotiations on
offset payments will show.

NEGOTIATIONS ON OFFSET PAYMENTS

The expense of maintaining American troops
in Germany became a central issue in German-
American relations during the 1960s. The precipitating factor was the large deficits in the
American balance of payments starting in 1958.
The resulting pressure on the dollar led to an
alarming reduction of America's gold reserves,
as the role of the dollar as reserve currency
was supported by the U.S. government's guaranteed exchange rate of an ounce of gold for
$35. Since the end of World War II, the United
States, relying on the role of the dollar and on
high demand for American goods, had been
able to pursue a policy of worldwide engagement on all conceivable fronts without having
to worry about its balance of payments. Among
these expensive ventures was the stationing of
troops throughout the world, the contingent in
Germany being by far the largest. Once the
Federal Republic stopped making occupation
payments, the foreign-exchange expenditures
for American forces produced a balance-of-
payments deficit of $600 million per month.
The U.S. government was no longer willing to
absorb these losses.

During the years 1958–60, intense debates
about a possible reduction of forces in Europe
took place within the American administration.
But only in the course of 1960 did the pressure
on the dollar become so great that the Eisenhower administration felt forced to act. A high-
ranking American delegation led by Secretary

---

[10] Hubert Zimmermann, *Money and Security: Troops
and Monetary Policy, and West Germany's Relations with
the United States and Britain, 1950–1971* (Cambridge and
Washington, D.C., 2002).

[11] In 1956–7, the United States received DM 650 million; in the following year, only half that amount. *Bundesgesetzblatt*, 1959/2, 410–2.

[12] The German export surplus in this same period amounted to $5,095 million. See Vermerk: Die
Bedeutung der Deviseneinnahmen von fremden Trup-
pen für die Entwicklung der Zahlungsbilanz und der

Währungsreserven, Dec. 4, 1959, Bundesbankarchiv,
B330/10161; Deutsche Bundesbank, *40 Jahre DM:
Monetäre Statistiken 1948–87* (Frankfurt am Main, 1988),
5.

of the Treasury Robert Anderson and Under-secretary of State Douglas Dillon demanded a payment of $650 million per year from Bonn to cover the foreign-exchange expenditures of U.S. forces in Germany. An unveiled threat to withdraw American troops lent emphasis to this demand. Realizing that the imminent change of government significantly undercut the American delegation's authority, the Germans categorically refused to "resurrect occupation payments."[13] However, if the Germans thought that President John F. Kennedy would apply less pressure, they quickly learned otherwise. The new administration instituted a strategy of flexible response, which required stronger conventional forces, and the Americans were not willing to bear the associated costs alone. Furthermore, the balance-of-payments problem was a chief concern in Kennedy's thinking. The administration saw itself faced with a dilemma that would determine American foreign policy throughout the 1960s: How could the United States maintain a credible deterrent without at the same time undermining the strength of the dollar?

Consequently, the first German-American disagreement of the Kennedy era focused on troop costs. Kennedy immediately rejected as inadequate the proposals of the German government in response to the Anderson-Dillon delegation.[14] Contrary to Bonn's view, Washington considered the balance-of-payments difficulties a structural problem that was closely linked to the costs of defending the free world. The Americans, therefore, expected the country with the largest balance-of-payments surpluses to take lasting corrective measures.[15] At the same time, they abandoned their demand for direct payments as no longer politically feasible. The search for ways to return to the United States the dollars from American forces that were accumulating in the Bundesbank soon focused on the one area in which German compensatory payments could at least begin to approach American demands: German purchases of military hardware from the United States.

The West German Defense Ministry, which was charged with the task of conducting these negotiations, quickly realized that the difficult position of the United States offered the Federal Republic an opportunity to further its interests. In exchange for German help in ridding the Americans of their balance-of-payments deficit, the German negotiators expected American cooperation on a diverse array of military and security matters, some of which had been on the German agenda for a long time.[16] But, despite these mutual interests and heavy pressure from the American side, these negotiations could not be concluded until after the building of the Berlin Wall. The increased defense expenditures that followed that event allowed the Federal Republic's defense ministry to make weapons purchases at the level desired by the Americans. In October 1961, Undersecretary of Defense Roswell Gilpatric and German Defense Minister Franz Josef Strauss signed a protocol stating West Germany's intention to compensate the foreign-exchange expenditures of American forces in Germany by purchasing weapons from the United States. Limited to two years, this Offset Agreement was renewed for a further two years in 1962 and 1964.[17]

[13] Erika Donfried, "The Political Economy of Alliance: Issue Linkage in the West-German American Relationship," (Ph.D. diss., Tufts University, Fletcher School of Law, 1991); Horst Mendershausen, *Troop-Stationing in Germany: Value and Cost* (Santa Monica, Calif., 1968).

[14] *BPI* 29 (Feb. 10, 1961): 258; *BPI* 37 (Feb. 23, 1961): 332.

[15] Memorandum for the President by Dean Rusk, German Balance of Payments Proposals, Feb. 15, 1961, John F. Kennedy Library, President's Office File, Countries: Germany, box 117.

[16] Among the concessions Defense Minister Franz Josef Strauss was able to win were the acquisition of highly sophisticated missile systems, greater influence on strategy debate within the alliance, the incorporation of the Bundeswehr into the logistical structure of the U.S. Army in Europe, as well as the training of German soldiers on American bases and the relinquishment of certain areas for conducting maneuvers; see Conversation between Undersecretary Gilpatric and Minister Strauss, Oct. 24, 1961, National Archives (hereafter NA), RG 84, Bonn Embassy 1959–1961, box 26.

[17] Texts of these agreements in *FRUS, 1961–1963*, 9:132–3; Institut für Zeitgeschichte, ed., *Akten zur*

The agreement had major military and economic consequences as well as significant implications for policy within the alliance. In the
military realm, it brought about an ever closer
cooperation between German and American
forces. The United States thus became the preferred supplier to the Bundeswehr, especially in
the area of high-tech weaponry.[18] A third of
the rapidly increasing American weapons exports in the 1960s went to the Federal Republic.
A further consequence of the Strauss-Gilpatric
protocol was the extensive incorporation of the
Bundeswehr into the logistical system of the
American forces in Europe. The agreement
amounted to an explicit choice of military cooperation with the United States, and this meant
in turn that the opportunities for developing
common weapons systems with other countries,
France in particular, were severely limited.

The most important component in this offset
arrangement remained, however, the balance-
of-payments issue. Because arms sales to Germany appeared on the credit side in the
military balance of payments, the Kennedy administration was able to achieve at least a limited
reduction of the deficit. From this point on,
the Treasury Department regarded the Offset
Agreement as a key element of monetary policy,
thus determining Washington's position for the
rest of the decade.[19] Furthermore, ongoing debate in Congress about troop reductions[20] made
it clear that the Offset Agreements were essential
to the continuing presence of American troops

in Germany, as German defense minister Kai-
Uwe von Hassel learned in no uncertain terms:

[United States Secretary of Defense Robert
McNamara] wished to make clear that he was making
no threats, but it would be absolutely impossible for
the United States to accept the gold drain caused by
the U.S. forces in Germany, if Germany did not assist
through continuation of the Offset Agreement.[21]

The Offset Agreements had major significance for the foreign policy of both sides. Retention of existing American troop strength
became a major constant in the foreign policy of Chancellor Ludwig Erhard in response
to massive criticism from members of his own
party who looked more to France as an ally
and objected to his strong orientation toward
the United States. For the Americans, the
agreements were the most important means of
reconciling the dual goals of maintaining a massive presence in Europe while maintaining the
stability of the international monetary system.
But the contradictions between these goals became increasingly difficult to reconcile. Despite the Offset Agreements and a number of
other monetary initiatives, the U.S. government
was not able to reduce its deficit significantly.
The burdens of the Vietnam War placed the
American balance of payments under increased
pressure, while the relaxation of East-West
tensions following the Cuban Missile Crisis lessened the importance of troops stationed in Europe. Also, the successful incorporation of the
Federal Republic into the Western defense system made any "control" American forces might
have exerted over the Germans increasingly
obsolete.

Nevertheless, the Erhard government continued to insist on an unreduced American military presence. It closed its eyes to the fact
that maintaining that presence ultimately depended on the Federal Republic's willingness to
provide additional offset funds. In 1965–6, the

Auswärtigen Politik der Bundesrepublik Deutschland 1964
(Munich, 1965) (hereafter *AAPD*), 1:526.

[18] A large number of the German purchases provided for in the agreements comprised modern missiles like the Pershing and the Nike; see Nuclear History
Project, Lehrstuhl Hans-Peter Schwarz, Politisches Seminar, Universität Bonn, Deklassifizierte Akten aus dem
Verteidigungsministerium, Sprechzettel für Ministerbe-
such in den USA, Nov. 13, 1961.

[19] Douglas Dillon to George Ball, May 31, 1963, NA,
RG 59, SF 1963, box 3455, FN 12 WGER; Telegram
from the Department of State to the Embassy in Germany, July 11, 1963, *FRUS, 1961–1963*, 9:176.

[20] Phil Williams, *The Senate and U.S. Troops in Europe*
(New York, 1985).

[21] McNamara–von Hassel talks, May 11, 1964, Declassified Documents Reference System, Washington,
D.C., 1995/3179; see also Aufzeichnung des Vortragen-
den Legationsratres I. Klasse, Graf von Hardenberg, May
11, 1964, *AAPD 1964*, 1:526–7.

Federal Republic's budget went awry, and the government was soon forced to realize that it could no longer meet the terms of the Offset Agreement.[22] In addition, the Bundeswehr arsenals were full, and pressure from German weapons suppliers was increasing. Under heavy political attack at home, Erhard made a personal appeal to President Lyndon Johnson for a moratorium on payments. However, the chancellor's visit to the United States in September 1966 turned into a fiasco.[23] German payments had already been calculated into McNamara's defense budget and into the Treasury Department's projections.[24] The U.S. administration insisted that West Germany fulfill its obligations under the agreement. The chancellor's failure to alter the American position contributed significantly to his downfall a few weeks later.

The offset solution, which had spared the United States from having to reform the international monetary system and had allowed the Germans to maintain the defense structure of the 1950s, had outlived its usefulness. Now the so-called trilateral negotiations of 1966–7 had to determine whether far-reaching monetary reform and/or American and British troop withdrawals would be implemented, or whether still another interim solution could be found that would spare both the United States and the Federal Republic a policy shift in these crucial areas.[25] Perhaps the most important

outcome of these negotiations was the formalization of what had been the Federal Republic's previously unarticulated willingness to be accommodating on matters of monetary policy in exchange for maintenance of the existing security structure in Europe. Decisive here was a letter of March 30, 1967, from Karl Blessing, the president of the Bundesbank, in which the bank explicitly promised a policy of continuing cooperation on monetary issues, pledging in particular to refrain from exchanging its dollar reserves for American gold.[26] In taking this step, the Federal Republic supported a monetary policy of questionable rationality for the sake of defense objectives and goals within the alliance. That the Bundesbank had to yield to government pressure and back off from its principles in the field of monetary policy indicates how closely linked monetary and defense policy had become in the 1960s.

In exchange, the American government maintained its massive troop presence and also succeeded in dissuading the British from making any large withdrawals. But, in the following years, pressure for troop withdrawals became increasingly strong in the U.S. Senate. The subsequent Offset Agreements were shaped by the administration's efforts to frustrate the Senate's initiatives.[27] However, as a consequence of the turbulence in money markets after 1967, offset had already lost much of its significance as a corrective to the balance of payments. The Blessing letter was a major step away from the dollar-gold standard and toward a pure dollar standard. In

[22] Auszug aus dem Protokoll der 20. Kabinettssitzung, Mar. 25, 1966, Bundesarchiv Koblenz, B136/3135.

[23] For documentation on Erhard's talks in Washington, see *FRUS 1964–1968*, 13:471–7 and 15:413–37 as well as the Editorial Note in *FRUS 1964–1968* 8:303–4. A detailed account of this visit is also contained in George McGhee, *At the Creation of a New Germany: From Adenauer to Brandt* (New Haven, Conn., 1989).

[24] Treasury Paper, Trilateral Talks, Oct. 24, 1966, Lyndon B. Johnson Library, Henry Fowler papers, box 69.

[25] Georg F. Duckwitz, "Truppenstationierung und Devisenausgleich," *Aussenpolitik* 18 (1967): 471–5; Helga Haftendorn, *NATO and the Nuclear Revolution: A Crisis of Credibility, 1966–1967* (Oxford, 1996); Gregory F. Treverton, *The Dollar-Drain and American Forces in Germany: Managing the Political Economics of the Alliance* (Athens, Ga., 1978); David Wightman, "Money

and Security: Financing American Troops in Germany and the Trilateral Negotiations of 1966/67," *Rivista di Storia Economica* 1 (1988): 26–77; Hubert Zimmermann, "'. . . They've got to put something in the family pot': The Burden Sharing Problem in German-American Relations, 1960–67," *German History* 14 (1996): 325–46.

[26] In addition, the Bundesbank invested $500 million in medium-term U.S. Treasury papers.

[27] Elke Thiel, *Dollar-Dominanz, Lastenteilung und amerikanische Truppenpräsenz in Europa* (Baden-Baden, 1979), 67, provides a summary of the agreements, which were cobbled together out of monetary measures, arms purchases, and German investments in the United States.

August 1971, President Richard Nixon took a long overdue step by officially cutting the dollar loose from the gold standard. The introduction of flexible exchange rates in 1973 deprived offset almost entirely of its rationale. Increasing opposition in the Federal Republic to this "camouflage of occupation costs" (Helmut Schmidt) finally won the day. In a joint declaration of 1976, the two governments put a definitive end to the practice of offset payments.

CHAPTER TEN

From Reconstruction Aid to Capital Interlocking

Direct and Portfolio Investments

Hans-Eckart Scharrer and Kerstin Müller-Neuhof

Translated by Tradukas

LONG-TERM CAPITAL EXPORTS
AS AN ELEMENT OF INTERNATIONAL
ECONOMIC INTEGRATION

World War II left Germany and the rest of Europe in ruins, uprooted millions of people, and destroyed most of the continent's national economies. The war wrecked a substantial portion of private and state-owned production capacity. Private savings were rendered all but worthless and gold and foreign currency reserves exhausted. The initial impetus for the reconstruction and reintegration of the European and international economies could only come from the United States: through governmental transfers of capital ("reconstruction aid") and the opening of the high-income American market to exports from Europe and the rest of the world.

Providing aid for the reconstruction of Europe was in the economic and political interests of the United States.[1] The creation of export markets for American companies and the containment of communism presupposed a flourishing Western European economy that was organized according to free-enterprise principles. With the Marshall Plan, the United States not only made (public) start-up capital available to Europeans for reconstruction, it also helped to relieve the acute shortage of foreign currency, inaugurated the revival of international trade that had been sluggish since the Great Depression, and created the basis for a gradual, multilateral liberalization of trade.[2] Not private but state-sponsored international capital transactions initially stood at the center of political and economic action. The primary objective was to revive international trade and production.

This dual objective was served by the U.S.-backed founding of new international financial institutions: the International Monetary Fund (IMF), the International Bank for Reconstruction and Development (World Bank), and the European Payments Union (EPU). It was not until a decade after the end of the war, with the revival of the European economy and the gradual lifting of currency restrictions, that private international capital transactions gained momentum again. Direct investment by companies played a central role in this development and in bilateral West German-American capital interlocking. Forms of direct investment included the founding and capitalization of subsidiary corporations as well as the acquisition of companies or equity participation in companies abroad with the goal of exerting long-term entrepreneurial influence over them. Portfolio capital transactions – the acquisition of foreign stocks and bonds in order to generate returns

---

[1] Joyce Kolko and Gabriel Kolko, *The Limits of Power: The World and United States Foreign Policy, 1945–54* (New York, 1972).

[2] On this issue, see the chapters by Gerd Hardach and Werner Bührer in this section.

(rather than to exercise control) and the issuing of stocks and bonds on foreign capital markets – became important only in later years.

PRECONDITIONS FOR THE RESUMPTION OF DIRICT INVESTMENT AFTER WORLD WAR II

Formidable restrictions at first hindered the rebuilding of German industrial property abroad. Allied Control Council Law No. 5, promulgated on October 30, 1945, subjected all German external assets to Allied control. The United States also passed the War Claims Act of July 3, 1948, thus creating the legal basis for the uncompensated confiscation of German (and Japanese) private assets in America. It was not until April 17, 1953, that an order to halt all confiscations came into effect and put an end to the legal uncertainty that had stood in the way of new investments in the United States.

By that time, 469 German companies – 10 of them valued at more than $10 million – as well as more than 45,000 patents and 375 trademarks had been confiscated. The chemicals industry in particular had made large investments in the United States before the war. For many companies, the loss of their trademarks created a greater disadvantage than the loss of assets. American buyers, often competitor firms, had acquired "4711," "Löwenbräu," "Bayer," "Aspirin," and other internationally established brand names and trademarks from the Office of Alien Property. At a considerable cost in "good will," the affected German firms thus had to start over with new brand names in the American market (and in some other foreign markets as well) in competition with the new brand-owners; another, usually costly, alternative was to buy the brand or trademark back.[3]

In the early postwar years, Germans were prohibited from investing abroad entirely. The Allies began granting permission on a case-by-case basis in 1952, and approval was given only for investments that would earn or save foreign exchange immediately and on a sustained basis. The London Agreement on German External Debt of 1953 lifted further limitations in the settlement on German foreign debt and, in 1956, general authorization replaced compulsory individual authorization. The remaining restrictions were then completely removed by the end of 1958.[4] Apart from these limitations, the shortage of capital and foreign exchange stood in the way of German direct investment; the scarce capital available was needed above all for domestic reconstruction efforts.[5]

Three developments in external trade relations made the rapid German liberalization of capital possible. First, the Organization for European Economic Cooperation (OEEC), founded in 1948, and its partner organization, the EPU, provided an effective institutional framework for overcoming European bilateralism, liberalizing the flow of trade and payment transactions, and reintegrating the national economies of the Western industrialized countries.

Second, the successful conclusion of the London Conference on External Debts in 1953 prevented a decades-long encumbrance on the German balance of payments, as had happened after World War I. The final settlement of Germany's prewar foreign debt, along with the debts from economic aid after the war, contributed decisively to restoring the international creditworthiness of the Federal Republic.[6]

---

[3] Hans-Dieter Kreikamp, *Deutsches Vermögen in den Vereinigten Staaten: Die Auseinandersetzung um seine Rückführung als Aspekt der deutsch-amerikanischen Beziehungen 1952–1962* (Stuttgart, 1979), 31–42.

[4] Hubertus Seifert, *Die deutschen Direktinvestitionen im Ausland: Ihre statistische Erfassung als Instrument der internationalen technisch-wirtschaftlichen Zusammenarbeit* (Cologne, 1967), 45–9; Deutsche Bundesbank, "Zur Freizügigkeit im Kapitalverkehr der Bundesrepublik mit dem Ausland," in *Monatsberichte der Deutschen Bundesbank* 37 (July 1985): 13–24.

[5] Henry Krägenau, "Entwicklung und Förderung der deutschen Direktinvestitionen," in Hans-Eckart Scharrer, ed., *Förderung privater Direktinvestitionen: Eine Untersuchung der Massnahmen bedeutender Industrieländer* (Hamburg, 1972), 492.

[6] The London Agreement on German External Debts is the most significant instrument for international debt settlement ever devised in German economic history. The overall sum of prewar and postwar debts subject to the settlement was estimated at DM 14.5 billion.

Finally, from 1951 on, West Germany had a large and growing current account surplus (1951: DM 2.3 billion; 1958: DM 6.0 billion). This ultimately put the Federal Republic in an economic position not only to rebuild its official gold and foreign currency reserves but also to remove further barriers to private capital exports.

American direct investment in Germany encountered major hurdles in the early postwar years. As in the case of German capital exports, capital imports were initially also subject to foreign-exchange controls. Because new investments of foreign capital would have further increased Germany's foreign debt, Allied regulations generally prohibited them until June 1950. Afterward, first the *Sperrmark*[7] and later the liberalized *Kapitalmark*[8] were approved for investment purposes. As of 1955, there were three basic possibilities for making foreign investments in Germany: using liberalized capital assets, making contributions in kind, and bringing in foreign exchange.[9] It was not until

the transition to full convertibility of the Deutsche Mark in 1958 that foreign investment in the Federal Republic was fully liberalized.

In the 1960s, long after restrictions had been lifted, American investors ran into a rather different kind of problem: fears that the European economy was in danger of falling under the control of the United States. French author Jean-Jacques Servan-Schreiber voiced this concern most memorably by suggesting, "Fifteen years from now it is quite possible that the world's third greatest industrial power, just after the United States and Russia, will be not Europe, but American industry in Europe."[10] His predictions had somewhat less resonance in Germany than in some countries. The Germans had always placed emphasis on the positive effects of foreign investment, including American investment, on employment and economic growth. The discussion in West Germany at the time focused on the argument, put forward above all by business, that the country had to catch up in foreign investment; this argument was coupled with a call for policy measures to stimulate capital exports.[11]

From the very beginning of the Cold War, the American government encouraged long-term capital exports, first to Europe and later to developing countries. Direct investment was expected to accelerate the economic development of these countries, support the market economy, and open up export opportunities for American business. The major turning point came in 1965, when the increasing balance-of-payments deficit and rising long-term capital exports forced the American government to introduce foreign-exchange restrictions, the so-called Balance of Payments Programs.[12]

See Ernst Taubner, "Schuldenabkommen," in *Enzyklopädisches Lexikon für das Geld-, Bank- und Börsenwesen*, 2 vols. (Frankfurt am Main, 1957), 2:1384–92. See also the chapter by Jörg Fisch in this section.

[7] The limitations on the right of nonresidents to dispose of German capital assets – already introduced in 1931 – were continued after the war in modified form. Thus, nonresidents could essentially only use their assets in Deutsche Mark in domestic bank accounts (*Sperrmark*) for acquiring domestic investments, but not for paying for export deliveries or transfers abroad. Nonresidents were allowed to trade in *Sperrmark* assets with other nonresidents. See Rudolf Kühne, "Sperrmarkguthaben," in *Enzyklopädisches Lexikon für das Geld-, Bank- und Börsenwesen*, 3d ed., 2 vols. (Frankfurt am Main, 1967–8), 2:1537–8.

[8] Liberalized capital assets were introduced in September 1954, when the framework of payment agreements permitted (limited) transfers abroad for *Sperrmark* assets. At the same time, limitations on the right to utilize *Sperrmarks*, which had applied to the purchaser (in contrast to the initial owner), were lifted. Until 1958, making foreign investments in the Federal Republic remained in practice dependent on having sums of liberalized *Kapitalmarks* at one's disposal that could be freely traded abroad. See Rudolf Kühne, "Liberalisierte Kapitalguthaben," in ibid., 2:1119–20.

[9] "Ausländische Investitionen in der Bundesrepublik Deutschland," in ibid., 1:95–6.

[10] Jean-Jacques Servan-Schreiber, *The American Challenge* (New York, 1968), 3 (emphasis in original).

[11] Scharrer, ed., *Förderung privater Direktinvestitionen*, i–iii.

[12] The program, which was initially voluntary, called on private enterprise to make a contribution toward improving the balance-of-payments situation. It was made compulsory in 1968 after being extended twice (in 1966 and 1967). At this date, it included the following provisions: a limitation on direct investments abroad, regulations on the remittance of profits made abroad, as

DEVELOPMENT AND DETERMINANTS OF
DIRECT INVESTMENT BETWEEN THE UNITED
STATES AND GERMANY

The volume of direct investment between Germany and the United States in the initial postwar decades seems very small measured by today's standards (see Table 1).[13] However, what was remarkable was their dynamic nature, which of course varied in intensity on the two sides of the Atlantic. Given the scarce financial resources of German companies, restoration of their domestic production facilities initially had priority over investment abroad. This was particularly true because with the exchange rate of DM 4.00 to the dollar (which reigned until 1969), exports from Germany could also serve the American market. At the same time, the high value of the dollar made direct investment in the United States relatively expensive. No comparable restrictions existed for American companies. The favorable conditions prevailing in the Federal Republic induced many of them to choose Germany for their Western European investments. As a result of these different strategies and benchmark data, American investment in Germany in 1970 was ten times that of German companies in the United States.

The chemical industry held the leading position among German investors in the United States (1964: DM 162.5 million), reestablishing the strong presence that it had enjoyed in the American market before the war. The capital goods industry (DM 74.4 million) and the insurance business (DM 73 million) followed,

albeit on a much more modest scale.[14] A fundamental motive behind German investments in the United States was the size of the American market. Exports alone could only open up this market to a limited extent; a growing number of companies thus considered local production in the United States a necessity. German companies' need to buy back the German subsidiaries that Allied authorities had seized also played a significant role in these decisions.[15]

U.S. direct investment in West Germany during the 1950s was still limited because of the administrative limitations mentioned previously; this, incidentally, was also the case in all European countries except Great Britain. In the 1960s, Europe attracted more American direct investment then any other region of the world; within Europe, only Great Britain surpassed the Federal Republic as a destination of American investment.[16] The largest direct investments in Europe were made in the chemical, mechanical engineering, metal, and motor vehicle industries, all of them growth industries with rapidly expanding markets.[17]

American investors reacted positively to the rapid improvement of the economic situation in Germany and Europe. The Marshall Plan guaranteed security, restored faith in the future, and thus helped remove psychological barriers to investment in West Germany.[18] The early move to

[14] Deutsche Bundesbank, "Die deutschen Direktinvestitionen im Ausland," *Monatsberichte der Deutschen Bundesbank* (Dec. 17, 1965): 24–5.

[15] Gerd Tacke, "Kapitalexport durch industrielle Direktinvestitionen," *Zeitschrift für das gesamte Kreditwesen* 22 (1969): 1160–2.

[16] In 1970, American investments in Europe reached a value of $24.5 billion, or 31.4 percent, of all American direct investments ($78.2 billion); $8 billion of this sum was invested in Great Britain. See Krägenau, *Internationale Direktinvestitionen*, 87.

[17] Haubold, *Entwicklung und Förderung der amerikanischen Direktinvestitionen*, 106–7.

[18] Frohmund Grünärml, "Ursprung und Entwicklungstendenz der 'internationalen Produktion': dargestellt unter besonderer Berücksichtigung amerikanischer auswärtiger Direktinvestitionen," *Jahrbücher für Nationalökonomie und Statistik* 191 (1976): 135–6; Volker Berghahn, "Wiederaufbau und Umbau der westdeutschen Industrie nach dem Zweiten Weltkrieg," *Tel*

well as the reduction and repatriation of the short-term, liquid assets of American companies operating abroad. See Dietmar Haubold, "Entwicklung und Förderung der amerikanischen Direktinvestitionen," in ibid., esp. 108–21; Dominique G. Carreau, "The U.S. Balance of Payments Program: New Development in the American Regulations of Capital Movements," *Journal of World Trade Law* 6 (1968): 601–55.

[13] The German statistics, in contrast to the American figures, do not take account of reinvested profits. The statistical data thus underestimated the actual investments of German assets abroad. See Henry Krägenau, *Internationale Direktinvestitionen 1950–1973: Vergleichende Untersuchung und statistische Materialien* (Hamburg, 1975), 31.

Table 1. *Net Holdings of German and U.S. Direct Investments (DI), and the Proportion of Overall Direct Investments This Represented in the Period 1950–70 (in Millions of U.S. Dollars; Proportions in Percent)*

Year	Net Holdings of German DI in the United States	Proportion of Overall German DI	Net Holdings of U.S. DI in Germany	Proportion of Overall U.S. DI
1950	—	—	204	1.7
1955	27.7[a]	26.3[a]	347	1.8
1960	84.0[b]	8.7[b]	1,006	3.1
1965	133.5	6.4	2,431	4.9
1970	448.9	8.5	4,597	5.9

[a] For the period to 1960, data is only available for North America.
[b] 1961.

Source: For the United States, 1950–60: U.S. Department of Commerce, *Balance of Payments, Statistical Supplement*, rev. ed., 1963; 1961–70: U.S. Department of Commerce, *Survey of Current Business*, various years; for Germany: *Monatsberichte der Deutschen Bundesbank*, Dec. 1965, 26, and details from the Federal Ministry of Economics.

Deutsche Mark convertibility created a further incentive. The liberalization of monetary transactions in connection with the fixed exchange rates established by the Bretton Woods agreement allowed investors to transfer profits to the United States at any time with only a minimal exchange rate and transfer risks.

The founding of the European Economic Community (EEC) in 1957 also saw the emergence of a market comparable in size and potential to the U.S. market. The EEC's common external tariff, initially high, often made it seem more advantageous to set up production facilities in the EEC than to export to it. The Federal Republic was viewed as a preferred European location for investment because of its liberal economic policy, skilled labor force, and the wage restraint practiced by its trade unions.

THE DEVELOPMENT OF PORTFOLIO CAPITAL FLOW BETWEEN GERMANY AND THE UNITED STATES

Whereas much of the revived international flow of capital immediately after the war took the form of direct investment, international capital transfer before World War I and during the

interwar period had been dominated by portfolio capital investment. International portfolio investments are defined as acquisitions of foreign stocks and bonds (i.e., stocks, fixed-interest securities, and mixed securities) by domestic investors, whose decisions are based on the difference in the rate of return in individual national economies. It is unimportant whether foreign stocks and bonds are acquired on the domestic or the foreign-capital market. The international procurement of portfolio capital consists of the issue of securities on foreign-capital markets.[19]

Postwar portfolio capital transactions did not start picking up again until the late 1950s, and for a long time they were of little significance. This was also true in the bilateral relationship between West Germany and the United States. Three stages of development can be discerned here. In the first phase, from 1945 through 1958, foreign currency controls were in force in most countries of the world, with the exception of the United States and Switzerland, and domestic issue of securities and lending was also subject to control almost everywhere. Germany was no exception in this respect: international capital transactions were long subject to restrictive

Aviver Jahrbuch für deutsche Geschichte 19 (1990): 261–82; see also the chapter by Gerd Hardach in this section.

[19] Helmut Lipfert, *Internationale Finanzmärkte: Probleme und Entwicklungen eines Jahrzehnts* (Frankfurt am Main, 1964), 490.

regulations. Liberalization began with the grad-ual lifting of the exchange restrictions for for-eigners (nonresident convertibility).[20] Only as a second step was convertibility also reestablished for domestic residents; that is, they were now allowed to transfer foreign currency freely to acquire foreign assets (e.g., securities). In some countries, the process of introducing domes-tic convertibility took several decades. Inter-national capital flow in the first years after the war was thus limited on the whole to the post-war economic aid provided by the United States (unilateral transfers as well as loans).

It was not until the transition to nonresi-dent convertibility toward the end of the 1950s that efforts were made in Germany to rein-tegrate capital transactions. Private individuals were also permitted to acquire foreign securities as of 1956. The first foreign stocks were intro-duced on the stock exchange in May 1958. In the fall of the same year, the first foreign bond in deutschmarks appeared on the German capital market.

In the second phase, from 1959 through 1963–4, foreign issuers had completely free ac-cess to the German capital market, but high in-terest rates lessened its attractiveness. The other costs of issuance – including the tax on securi-ties – were high in comparison with other coun-tries. With the exception of 1959, when foreign bonds to the value of $81.5 million were issued in Germany, the total volume of securities is-sued annually was below $25 million.[21] Thus, although West Germany was initially of no sig-nificance on the international financial map, it did increasingly become a favored destination for foreign investors, Americans included.

Long-term net U.S. capital exports rose from $1.6 billion to $4.5 billion between 1959 and 1964. High economic growth rates made invest-ment in Europe particularly attractive.[22] This also applied to Germany. Although high Ger-man interest rates and the expected revaluation

of the Deutsche Mark[23] initially attracted Amer-ican money to the Federal Republic, a range of other factors also bespoke favorable prospects for investment. These included the growth dynamic, the free-enterprise orientation of eco-nomic policy, and the social harmony reigning in the Federal Republic. Also attractive was the monetary policy of the (independent) Bundes-bank, which was directed toward maintaining the value of the currency. Indeed, restrictive financial and borrowing policies pushed Ger-man companies to tap into foreign sources of capital themselves. Their demand for cap-ital found a ready supply in these sources.[24]

The United States' rising net-capital exports and the growing import of foreign capital into the Federal Republic in the third phase (1963–4 through 1968) induced both governments to take drastic measures. From the end of the 1950s onward, net-capital exports from the United States increased to such an extent[25] that the cur-rent account surplus was no longer sufficient to finance it. Considerable balance-of-payment deficits developed. In July 1963, the American authorities thus introduced an "interest equal-ization tax"[26] on foreign bonds on the American capital market applicable to issuers from indus-trialized countries.[27] American acquisitions of foreign securities then fell off significantly.

---

[20] Harald Joerges, "Devisenbewirtschaftung," *Enzyk-lopädisches Lexikon*, 1:442.

[21] Hans Wielens, *Die Emission von Auslandsanleihen* (Wiesbaden, 1968), 198–200.

[22] Bank für Internationalen Zahlungsausgleich (here-after BIZ), *39. Jahresbericht* (Basel, 1969), 87–9.

[23] The Deutsche Mark was revalued upward against the dollar by 5 percent on March 6, 1961.

[24] *Sachverständigenrat zur Begutachtung der gesam-twirtschaftlichen Entwicklung, Stabiles Geld – stetiges Wachs-tum: Jahresgutachten 1964/65* (Stuttgart, 1965), 109–11; Deutsche Bundesbank, "Änderung des Wechselkurses der DM," *Monatsberichte der Deutschen Bundesbank* 13 (Mar. 1961): 3.

[25] This was caused both by the sharp rise in the issue of securities by foreign issuers in the United States and the extensive acquisitions by foreign securities then in circulation by American investors. See Wielens, *Emission von Auslandsanleihen*, 204.

[26] Richard N. Cooper, "The Interest Equalization Tax: An Experiment in the Separation of Capital Mar-kets," *Finanzarchiv*, n.s., 24 (1965): 447–71.

[27] In February 1965, the foreign lending of banks and nonbanks was also subjected to the tax and a quantita-tive restriction was introduced for new foreign credits. This was necessary because the introduction of the inter-est equalization tax encouraged the reallocation of for-eigners' borrowing in the United States from the stock markets to the banks. BIZ, *39. Jahresbericht*, 90.

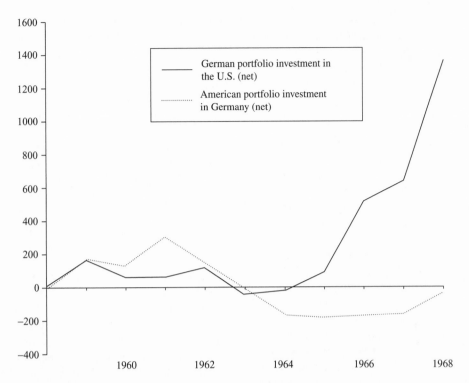

Source: Deutsche Bundesbank

Graph 1. German and American Portfolio Investments in Bilateral Transactions 1958–68 (in millions of DM); German Portfolio Investments in the United States (net); United States Portfolio Investments in Germany (net)

Because of the continuous high net capital imports, in March 1964 the German government announced a 25 percent withholding or coupon tax (*Kuponsteuer*) on the interest earnings of fixed-interest German securities owned by nonresidents; one year later, the tax went into law.[28] As a result of this announcement and the introduction of the interest equalization tax in the United States, the issuing of foreign stocks and bonds on the German capital market increased markedly.[29] Since 1965, there has been extensive capital flow out of the Federal Republic.

Although the United States had already become an importer of capital from the Federal

Republic in 1964, the world's largest exporter of private capital did not turn into a capital-import country on a global scale until 1968. One factor behind this reversal was that American companies no longer financed their expansion abroad with capital exports from the United States owing to the capital export restrictions; instead, they underwrote expansion by issuing bonds and taking up credits in Europe.[30] The value of dollar bonds issued on European capital markets nearly quadrupled between 1964 and 1967, rising from $456 to 1,589 million.[31] At the same time, the flow of foreign capital into the United States also increased substantially; this was especially true of German portfolio investments, which had grown considerably since 1966 (see Graph 1). The growing demand abroad for American

[28] Siegfried Menrad, "Die Auswirkungen der Kuponsteuer," *Schmollers Jahrbuch für Gesetzgebung, Verwaltung und Volkswirtschaft* 86 (1966): 301–33.

[29] Deutsche Bundesbank, "Die Emission ausländischer Anleihen in der Bundesrepublik," *Monatsberichte der Deutschen Bundesbank* 20 (Apr. 1968): 6.

[30] BIZ, *39. Jahresbericht*, 90–1.

[31] Deutsche Bundesbank, "Emission ausländischer Anleihen," 7.

securities in particular had its roots in the acceleration of economic growth in the United States beginning in 1965 and the rising profits that resulted. Investors' security worries after the Warsaw Pact's invasion of Czechoslovakia in 1968 also played a role.[32]

CONCLUSION

The initially very one-sided flow of capital from the United States to Germany and Europe gave way in the 1960s to vigorous private capital transactions in both directions. The basis for this shift was the rapid surmounting of the consequences of the war in Western Europe, the energetic economic revival in the Federal Republic within the framework of a market economy, and the process of European integration (the future direction of which was signaled by the founding of the EEC in 1957). Already in the second half of the 1950s, favorable prospects for growth and locational advantages prompted American companies to increase their direct investment in Germany. By contrast, German companies long

hesitated before setting up production facilities of their own in the United States on account of their narrow capital bases, the competitive advantages they enjoyed at home, and the business risks involved. At the end of the period considered here, American direct investment in Germany exceeded German companies' investment in the United States by a factor of ten.

Portfolio capital transactions were a different matter. German capital exports to the United States grew quickly from 1965 on; private investments outstripped direct investment by German companies, whereas American capital flows toward Germany stopped. German portfolio investment in the United States was driven by economic factors – in particular, the size and transparency of the U.S. securities market – as well as by state intervention, on both sides of the Atlantic, in international capital transactions. At the same time, the German capital market developed into an important source of finance for direct investments by American companies.

Compared with the frenzied expansion in the decades that followed, the bilateral integration of capital and international capital transactions generally were still limited in this period. Nevertheless, these years marked the start of the financial reintegration of the world economy as well as an ever closer economic and financial intermeshing of Germany and the United States.

---

[32] Wilfried Guth, "Die amerikanische Herausforderung: Wandlungen im internationalen Kapitalverkehr," *Zeitschrift für das gesamte Kreditwesen* 22 (1969): 770–3.

CHAPTER ELEVEN

German and American Economic and Monetary Policy

Monika Dickhaus

Translated by Richard Sharp

INTRODUCTION

In the large body of literature that now exists on American and German economic policy since World War II, two apparently contradictory viewpoints constantly recur. One holds that the two countries' economic policies were quite different in nature, that there was "no place for Keynesianism" in the Federal Republic of Germany, and that German economic policy pursued a neoliberal line of its own with the concept of the social market economy. The other school of thought maintains that in the postwar period, the Federal Republic – more than other states – was linked by a special relationship to the United States, was receptive to American influences, and exhibited similarities and parallels with the United States that led to an extensive process of Americanization.[1]

This apparent contradiction is examined here by considering the statements of the aims and concepts of economic policy, and of *Ordnungspolitik* (neoliberal regulatory policy) and *Prozesspolitik* (regulatory process policy) on each side of the Atlantic. The main emphasis is on financial and monetary policies. These were seen

as the central branches of governmental economic policy following the Great Depression and in keeping with the ideas of John Maynard Keynes and are, therefore, a suitable starting point for a comparison.

ECONOMIC TRENDS, 1945–68

After 1945, Germany and the United States faced enormous challenges in economic policy. Both countries had to solve the problems created by the financing of the war effort, switch their industries to peacetime production, and integrate their demobilized troops into the production process. There were, however, differences as well: In Germany, securing basic needs and reconstruction were necessarily the overriding aims, whereas the infrastructure of production in the United States had been spared the destructive effects of war. In Germany, heavy capital investment and measures to stimulate new capital formation were needed. Moreover, Germany had to restore its international competitiveness, build up its foreign-currency reserves, and reconstruct its shattered foreign-trade relations.

The way in which these problems were solved is an unparalleled success story. This period was marked by unexpected stability, the absence of major crises, and high growth rates. It is often referred to today as a "golden age" or, in the case

[1] See Werner Abelshauser, *Wirtschaftsgeschichte der Bundesrepublik Deutschland 1945–1980* (Frankfurt am Main, 1983), 106–11; Bent Hansen, *Fiscal Policy in Seven Countries, 1955–65* (Paris, 1969), 481; Volker R. Berghahn, *The Americanization of West German Industry 1945–1973* (Leamington Spa, 1985).

Table 1.

	Unemployment		Price Change		Growth		Gold Reserves	
	USA (percent)	FRG (percent)	USA (percent)	FRG (percent)	USA (percent)	FRG (percent)	USA (bil. US$)	FRG (bil. DM)
1948	3.8		7.8		4.5		23.51	
1949	5.9		-1.0	-1.2	0.1		24.43	
1950	5.3	11.0	1.0	-6.3	9.6		23.91	
1951	3.3	10.4	7.9	7.8	7.9	10.4	22.03	0.12
1952	3.0	9.5	2.2	2.1	3.1	8.9	23.25	0.59
1953	2.9	8.4	0.8	-1.8	4.5	8.2	22.42	1.37
1954	5.5	7.6	0.5	0.2	-1.4	7.4	21.89	2.63
1955	4.4	5.6	-0.4	1.7	7.6	12.0	21.69	3.86
1956	4.1	4.4	1.5	2.6	1.8	7.3	21.81	6.23
1957	4.3	3.7	3.6	2.0	1.4	5.7	22.49	10.60
1958	6.8	3.7	2.7	2.2	-1.1	3.7	21.57	10.96
1959	5.5	2.6	0.8	1.0	6.4	7.3	19.95	10.93
1960	5.5	1.3	1.6	1.5	2.5	9.0	19.01	12.29
1961	6.7	0.8	1.0	2.3	1.9	5.4	17.38	14.43
1962	5.5	0.7	1.1	3.0	6.6	4.0	16.36	14.49
1963	5.7	0.8	1.2	3.0	4.0	3.4	15.74	15.14
1964	5.2	0.8	1.3	2.3	5.5	6.7	15.46	16.73
1965	4.5	0.7	1.7	3.4	6.3	5.5	14.26	17.37
1966	3.8	0.7	2.9	3.5	6.5	2.9	13.46	16.91
1967	3.8	2.1	2.9	1.4	2.6	-0.2	13.02	16.65
1968	3.6	1.5	4.2	1.5	4.7	7.3	10.71	17.88

Sources: Author's calculations; U.S. Department of Commerce, Bureau of the Census, ed., *Historical Statistics of the United States: Colonial Times to 1970* (Washington, DC, 1975), 135, 210, 224, 992; Statistisches Bundesamt, *Bevölkerung und Wirtschaft 1872–1972* (Stuttgart, 1972), 148, 211, 247, 260–1.

Source: Author's depiction based on data from Table 1.

Graph 1. Growth Rates

of West Germany, as an "economic miracle."[2] The data in Table 1 show what was achieved.

Economic growth as a whole was above average; negative growth occurred only in 1954 and 1958 in the United States and in 1966 in the Federal Republic. Initial fears of a major depression, especially in the United States, proved unfounded. Even so, the picture was not uniformly positive. First of all, actual output fell short of potential output, as was noted with increasing criticism, especially in the United States, during the 1960s. Second, economic growth was generally slower in the United States than in

West Germany and numerous other countries. Finally – as Graph 1 shows – there were cyclical fluctuations.

Both the United States and West Germany did well in curbing unemployment, which had reached traumatic levels in the early 1930s. Unemployment averaged 4.7 percent in the United States and 4.0 percent in West Germany during the period under consideration. There was no long-term mass unemployment, though there were certainly some difficult periods. In the United States, unemployment rose slowly toward the end of the 1950s and hovered around 5 percent at the end of the decade. The more or less unanimous view, therefore, was that the target of "full employment" had been missed. In the Federal Republic, unemployment was worryingly high in the early years of the country's history but fell steadily over the remainder of the period despite the massive tide of refugees and considerable immigration. By the mid-1950s, indeed, West Germany had not just full employment but also a manpower shortage, so that efforts were made to attract foreign workers.

Prices followed a similarly satisfactory pattern. The United States, to be sure, saw prices

[2] See Angus Maddison, *Dynamic Forces in Capitalist Development: A Long-Run Comparative View* (Oxford, 1991); Herbert Giersch, Karl-Heinz Paqué, and Holger Schmieding, *The Fading Miracle: Four Decades of Market Economy in Germany* (Cambridge, 1994); Rolf H. Dumke, "Reassessing the 'Wirtschaftswunder': Reconstruction and Postwar Growth in West Germany in an Economic Context," *Oxford Bulletin of Economics and Statistics* 52 (1990): 451–91; Rainer Klump, "Wirtschaftsordnung und Wirtschaftspolitik in der Bundesrepublik Deutschland 1949–1990," in Wolfgang Harbrecht and Jürgen Schneider, eds., *Wirtschaftsordnung und Wirtschaftspolitik in Deutschland 1933–1993* (Stuttgart, 1996), 397–414.

rise by 7.9 percent in 1948 after the abolition of price controls and again by 7.8 percent in the Korean War boom of 1951. Further significant rates of increase occurred in the late 1960s. Nevertheless, prices in the United States can be generally regarded as stable, with an average increase of 2.2 percent over the period. Here, too, the Federal Republic did better than the United States, with an average price increase rate of 1.6 percent.

Only the fourth side of the "magic square," foreign-trade equilibrium – for which I use gold reserves as a rough measure – presented difficulties. West Germany initially had little or nothing in the way of gold reserves, but it succeeded over the years in amassing a gold hoard of DM 18 billion. The United States' gold reserves, on the other hand, steadily melted away. This pattern of events had certain consequences for American and German economic policy. At times, the changes in the balance of payments caused considerable pressure on the dollar, cramping the United States' freedom of action in economic policy. But German economic policy, too, was constricted, because the pegging of exchange rates under the Bretton Woods system meant that balance-of-payments surpluses inevitably resulted in inflationary pressure.

CONCEPTS AND AIMS OF ECONOMIC POLICY

For victors and vanquished alike, the end of the war made many forms of state intervention in the economic process and the control mechanisms needed in wartime obsolete. The organization of the economic system had to be reconsidered along with the aims and functions of government economic policy. The Great Depression had shown that the capitalist, free-market economic system had its drawbacks; that state intervention in the economy could create problems also became clear, however, over time.

In the United States, the controls introduced to run the war economy were quickly dismantled. The wage freeze was lifted in August 1945, and price controls ended in June of the following year. These decisions restored prices as a control mechanism, and so they remained except during

a few periods of crisis (i.e., Korea 1951, Vietnam 1971). During the 1960s, however, government economic policy played a part in determining prices by way of what were known as wage-price guideposts, which in some ways amounted to voluntary price and wage controls.[3]

Prices were not given free rein in Western Germany until summer 1948. Prior to that time, National Socialist price and wage controls remained in place. It was only in conjunction with the currency reform of June 20, 1948, that Ludwig Erhard, economics director of the Combined Economic Area, was able to revoke many price-control regulations.[4]

Erhard's measures amounted to the establishment of a liberal economy and, in later years, the currency reform was duly hailed as the beginning of the social market economy or seen as setting the economic policy course that the soon-to-be established West German state would follow. Although the *Grundgesetz* (Basic Law) of 1949 was neutral in regard to economic policy, the reforms of June 1948 in fact committed the Federal Republic to a free-market economy.[5]

Erhard's arrangements were by no means uncontested. Although no one mourned the passing of the price controls and rationing measures installed by the National Socialists, many in the early postwar years favored an economic system with a substantial element of planning. Laissez-faire economies, relying on price alone as the mechanism of control, were usually thought of as inadequate and regarded with keen skepticism. Accordingly, a neoliberal program was implemented only slowly and with difficulty. Not only the Communist Party (*Kommunistische Partei Deutschlands*, or KPD), the Social Democratic Party (*Sozialdemokratische Partei Deutschlands*, or SPD), and the labor unions but even

---

[3] See *Economic Report of the President* (Washington, D.C., 1962), 185–9; John Sheahan, *The Wage-Price Guideposts* (Washington, D.C., 1967); Hugh Rockoff, *Drastic Measures: A History of Wage and Price Controls in the United States* (Cambridge, 1984), 177–233.

[4] See the chapters by Wilfried Mausbach and Werner Plumpe in this section.

[5] See Theodor Eschenburg, *Jahre der Besatzung 1945–1949* (Stuttgart, 1983), 504.

sections of the Christian Democratic Union (*Christlich-Demokratische Union*, or CDU) and the occupying powers criticized this course, in some cases bitterly,[6] particularly because its positive effect (increased production) had to be weighed against negative ones (rising unemployment, credit shortage, and higher prices).[7] Nevertheless, after the Korean crisis of 1951 – widely viewed as an important "test of *Ordnungspolitik*" – had been overcome, the neoliberal progam could generally be regarded as the firmly established doctrine of the Federal Republic's economic policy.[8]

The concept of the social market economy is rooted in ordoliberalism, and both are generally regarded as specifically German developments. As a neoliberal concept, the social market economy is based on market control of economic processes. Its aim, however, is not merely a return to laissez-faire capitalism. According to Alfred Müller-Armack, who coined the term, the social market economy aims more for a "new type of synthesis," a combination of the principles of market economics with social equilibrium (*sozialer Ausgleich*). The precise meaning of "social equilibrium" was, however, vague and open to interpretation. Nor was it clear how much importance was to be attached to the social aspect.[9] The concept was also unclear about interference by economic policy with the economic process. Some adherents of the social market economy accepted such interference; they saw it as a possibility or, in some cases, even a necessity, but they insisted that all action must conform to the rules of the market. Other supporters of the social market economy categorically rejected measures to steady the course of economic events, regarding them as entirely unnecessary if not actually destabilizing. In their view, establishing an economic framework and maintaining competition were of the highest priority; these measures, combined with a consistent economic policy, would make it possible to avoid policy blunders and crises.[10]

Thus, the first responsibility the social market economy assigned to governmental economic policy was to establish and maintain a system for economic competition. The other goals of economic policy – stabilization of the economic process and combating unemployment – were considered secondary and were not directly stated. Further responsibilities were added later. Since 1963, the *Sachverständigenrat* (council of expert economic experts) has reported each year on the general economic situation and the government's policy in light of the aims of the "magic square." The requirement

---

[6] See Gerold Ambrosius, *Die Durchsetzung der Sozialen Marktwirtschaft in Westdeutschland 1945–1949* (Stuttgart, 1977); Georg Müller, *Die Grundlegung der westdeutschen Wirtschaftsordnung im Frankfurter Wirtschaftsrat 1947–1949* (Frankfurt am Main, 1982).

[7] For the effects of the currency reform, see Werner Abelshauser, *Wirtschaft in Westdeutschland 1945–1948: Rekonstruktion und Wachstumsbedingungen in der amerikanischen und britischen Zone* (Stuttgart, 1975); Christoph Buchheim, "Die Währungsreform 1948 in Westdeutschland," *Vierteljahrshefte für Zeitgeschichte* 36 (1988): 189–231; idem, "Marshall Plan and Currency Reform," in Jeffrey M. Diefendorf, Axel Frohn, and Hermann-Josef Rupieper, eds., *American Policy and the Reconstruction of West Germany, 1945–1955* (Cambridge and Washington, D.C., 1993), 69–82; Rainer Klump, *Wirtschaftsgeschichte der Bundesrepublik Deutschland* (Stuttgart, 1985).

[8] Ludwig Erhard Foundation, *Die Korea-Krise als ordnungspolitische Herausforderung der deutschen Wirtschaftspolitik* (Stuttgart, 1986); Werner Abelshauser, "Ansätze 'Korporativer Marktwirtschaft' in der Korea-Krise der frühen fünfziger Jahre: Ein Briefwechsel zwischen dem Hohen Kommissar John McCloy und Bundeskanzler Konrad Adenauer," *Vierteljahrshefte für Zeitgeschichte* 30 (1982): 715–56.

[9] Alfred Müller-Armack, "Soziale Marktwirtschaft," in Erwin von Beckerath et al., eds., *Handwörterbuch der Sozialwissenschaften* (Göttingen, 1956), 9:390–2. For a comprehensive and traditional account, see Reinhard Blum, *Soziale Marktwirtschaft: Wirtschaftspolitik zwischen Neoliberalismus und Ordoliberalismus* (Tübingen, 1969); for a more recent brief introduction, see Karl-Georg Zinn, *Soziale Marktwirtschaft: Idee, Entwicklung und Politik der bundesdeutschen Wirtschaftsordnung* (Mannheim, 1992); for a historical perspective, see Anthony J. Nicholls, *Freedom with Responsibility: The Social Market Economy in Germany, 1918–63* (Oxford, 1994).

[10] See Alfred Müller-Armack, "Wirtschaftslenkung und Marktwirtschaft," in Alfred Müller-Armack, ed., *Wirtschaftsordnung und Wirtschaftspolitik* (Freiburg im Breisgau, 1966), 51–5, 159–67; Walter Eucken, *Grundsätze der Wirtschaftspolitik*, ed. Edith Eucken and Karl P. Hensel, 6th ed. (Tübingen, 1990), 308–12.

that the government respond to the council's report gave additional incentive to observe those aims even though it was not explicitly obliged to do so until 1967.[11] The 1967 *Stabilitätsgesetz* (Stability Act), an initiative of Social Democratic Economics Minister Karl Schiller, stipulated that the government was required to "have due regard for the requirements of overall economic equilibrium in implementing its economic and financial policies," in other words, to pursue the aims of the "magic square."[12] Thus, as Schiller himself put it, the social market economy became an "enlightened" market economy.[13]

Whereas West German economic policy was explicitly required to pursue economic equilibrium, price stability, high employment, external equilibrium, and steady growth, a similar list of policy goals had been laid down for the U.S. government as early as 1946. The Employment Act of 1946 emphasized "that it is the continuing policy and responsibility of the federal government to use all practicable means . . . to promote maximum employment, production and purchasing power."[14] New institutions were set up to achieve these aims and to monitor the efforts of the government. A Council of Economic Advisers (CEA) was established within the administration to advise the president, and a Joint Economic Committee (JEC) was to function as a congressional watchdog. The president

was also obliged to present an annual economic report.[15]

The Employment Act, which the CEA described as the economic constitution of the United States,[16] thus made promoting growth and employment the central elements of American economic policy. This represented a radical difference between the goals and tasks addressed by German and American economic policy, and the outlooks behind the governments' economic policies differed accordingly. It has often been stressed that the United States had absorbed the ideas of Keynes at an early stage and that economic policy there had accepted its new responsibilities and thus took account of the Keynesian revolution. By contrast, the argument runs, German economic policy had distanced itself from Keynesianism and from employment policy. Although there is some truth to this argument, it must also be qualified. The basis of the Employment Act was free competitive enterprise, and it became abundantly clear in the course of the legislative process that there were also many in the United States who opposed government responsibility for full employment and stability. Thus, the Full Employment Act of 1945 became the less ambitious Employment Act of 1946; moreover, many of its provisions were necessarily vague, ambivalent, and inconsistent.[17] Finally, as is demonstrated, neither the United States nor the Federal Republic followed its statements of aims and functions fully and consistently.

ORDNUNGSPOLITIK

The aim of *Ordnungspolitik* is to give legal and organizational shape to the economic system. It should be understood as including measures to

---

[11] For a comparison between the *Sachverständigenrat* and its American counterpart, see Henry C. Wallich, "The American Council of Economic Advisers and the German 'Sachverständigenrat': A Study in the Economics of Advice," *Quarterly Journal of Economics* 82 (1968): 349–79.

[12] The obligation also extended to the *Land* governments. Article 109 of the *Grundgesetz*, which laid down the financial autonomy of the *Länder*, was amended; see Fünfzehntes Gesetz zur Änderung des Grundgesetzes vom 8. Juni 1967, *Bundesgesetzblatt*, 1967, pt. 1, 581.

[13] Karl Schiller, "Das Stabilitäts- und Wachstumsgesetz und die Globalsteuerung," in Uwe Jens and Georg Kurlbaum, eds., *Beiträge zur sozialdemokratischen Wirtschaftspolitik* (Bonn, 1983), 81.

[14] See Public Law 304, reprinted in *U.S. Code, Congressional Service, Laws of the 79th Congress, 2nd session* (New York, 1946), 20–3, esp. 20.

[15] See Silvio Borner, *Die amerikanische Stabilitätspolitik seit 1946* (Bern, 1977).

[16] Council of Economic Advisers, *First Annual Report to the President* (Washington, D.C., 1946), 2–3.

[17] See Stephen Kemp Bailey, *Congress Makes a Law: The Story Behind the Employment Act of 1946* (New York, 1950); Louis Galambos and Joseph Pratt, *The Rise of the Corporate Commonwealth: U.S. Business and Public Policy in the Twentieth Century* (New York, 1988), 133.

control production patterns, the structure of the market, and the monetary and financial system. In the period 1945–68, *Ordnungspolitik* measures were especially important in West Germany. New institutions had to be set up and new legal bases created. But American economic policy, too, became active in the area of *Ordnungspolitik* to adapt the economic system to economic developments.

Ordnungspolitik measures in the United States primarily concerned the issues of currency and competition. The independence of the American Federal Reserve system had steadily eroded since the mid-1930s. Financing the war and supporting the value of government bonds after the war made an independent monetary policy impossible. The Federal Reserve System was not able to take effective action to curb inflationary tendencies again until the Treasury Department released it from its obligation to support bond values during the Korean War boom of 1951. In this respect, a new central bank system was created in that year.[18]

Safeguarding competition also received attention in the United States. For example, the Celler-Kefauver Anti-Merger Act of 1950 closed loopholes in existing legislation. A revision of the antitrust laws was also undertaken. The recommendations submitted by a commission of inquiry in 1955 were regarded as inadequate because they called only for "a stricter enforcement of the laws" but not for fundamental reform.[19] In the following years, however, a number of spectacular precedents were set on the basis of these recommendations. Interest in

competition policy also revived. Although the antitrust laws are often criticized as inadequate, they have, on the whole, been effective. The period 1948–68 has even been described as a renaissance in American antitrust law.[20] As in the United States, *Ordnungspolitik* in Germany dealt primarily with competition and the monetary and central bank systems.

Ordoliberal recommendations envisaging an automatically functioning monetary system and a strictly independent central bank were realized to a large degree during the 1950s. The independence of the central bank had been laid down in a transitional act in 1951. The act provided that the government could only defer decisions by the central bank, not overrule them. Nor did the government have a voice in the committee that decided on monetary policy. However, because these rules were only temporary, the bank's position remained vulnerable until the Bundesbank Act of 1957 placed its independence on a secure legal footing.[21] The dissolution just a year later of the European Payments Union (EPU), the European soft-currency bloc set up in 1950, also compelled the government to react far more than it had in the past to changes in the balance of payments. It did so in accordance with the automatic mechanism of the dollar-gold standard, now internationally established, even though this kind of automatic mechanism had in a sense existed previously, and the German mark had been regarded, de facto, as a convertible currency since 1954.[22]

[18] See Richard Sylla, "The Autonomy of Monetary Authorities: The Case of the U.S. Federal Reserve System," in Gianni Toniolo, ed., *Central Banks' Independence in Historical Perspective* (Berlin, 1988), 31–2. For a detailed account of events, see Marriner S. Eccles, *Beckoning Frontiers: Public and Personal Recollections* (New York, 1951), 479–91; A. Jerome Clifford, *The Independence of the Federal Reserve System* (Philadelphia, 1965), 230–51; G. L. Bach, *Making Monetary and Fiscal Policy* (Washington, D.C., 1971), 78–85.

[19] See Theodore P. Kovaleff, "The Antitrust Record of the Eisenhower Administration," *Antitrust Bulletin* 21 (1976): 592; Estes Kefauver, *In a Few Hands: Monopoly Power in America* (New York, 1965).

[20] Tony Freyer, *Regulating Big Business: Antitrust in Great Britain and America, 1880–1990* (Cambridge, 1992), 298–310; for a more skeptical note, see Galambos and Pratt, *Rise of Corporate Commonwealth*, 153–4; for the degree of concentration, see Robert C. Puth, *American Economic History* (Chicago, 1982), 434.

[21] See Volker Hentschel, "Die Entstehung des Bundesbankgesetzes 1949–1957," *Bankhistorisches Archiv* 14 (1988): 3–31, 79–115; Carl-Ludwig Holtfrerich, "Relations Between Monetary Authorities and Governmental Institutions: The Case of Germany from the 19th Century to the Present," in Toniolo, ed., *Central Banks' Independence*, 139–50.

[22] For details of the EPU and the long road to convertibility, see Monika Dickhaus, *Die Bundesbank im westeuropäischen Wiederaufbau* (Munich, 1996); Monika Dickhaus, "'It Is Only the Provisional That Lasts': The

By the end of the 1950s, an *Ordnungspolitik* framework had been created for monetary policy in the Federal Republic. Two points should be kept in mind, however. First, the Federal Republic had an extremely comfortable foreign currency cushion by the end of 1958, so that the "automatic mechanism" that was now in place could not, for the moment, compel the application of a restrictive monetary policy.[23] Second, the independence of a central bank is by no means determined by its legal position alone.[24]

Ordoliberalism regarded a strict law on competition as essential for ending the German cartel tradition and preventing the abuse of economic power. Indeed, Erhard described such a law as the "heart of the social market economy."[25] After strenuous disagreements, since analyzed in detail, between Erhard, the industrial policy associations, and Chancellor Konrad Adenauer, the anticartel law (*Gesetz gegen Wettbewerbsbeschränkungen*, or GWB) was passed in 1957.[26] It did not, however, satisfy ordoliberal principles. Although it did prohibit cartel arrangements in principle, that principle, vehemently attacked by industry, was vitiated by numerous rules specifying exceptions. The position of the newly established *Bundeskartellamt* (Federal Cartel Office), too, was weak. In view of these defects, there were still demands for

competition to be strengthened, and there were efforts at reform in subsequent years. It was not until 1973, however, that the second *Kartellnovelle* (amendment to the Cartels Act) established merger control and the abolition of resale price maintenance.[27]

In the ordoliberal view, the economic order should not only limit economic power but also guarantee that neither individual enterprises nor self-regulating business associations should have disproportionate influence. Although critics complain that business associations were often able to exert a substantial influence on the legislative process and achieved positions of such strength during the Korean crisis that the social market economy had virtually been transformed into a "corporatist" market economy,[28] others point out that the restoration of certain characteristic corporatist elements is not sufficient to justify such a comment on the Federal Republic's economic order as a whole.[29]

PROZESSPOLITIK

Prozesspolitik is the German term for measures of economic policy intended to influence the overall course of economic events: measures of regulatory policy, foreign-trade policy, budgetary

---

European Payments Union, 1950–1958," in Richard T. Griffiths, ed., *Explorations in OEEC History* (Paris, 1997), 183–200.

[23] It should also be borne in mind that "automatic" rules are never automatic in the sense that they are never definitive but can always be amended and repealed, depending on the market position.

[24] See Roland Vaubel, "Eine Public-Choice-Analyse der Deutschen Bundesbank und ihre Implikationen für die Europäische Währungsunion," in Dieter Duwendag and Jürgen Siebke, eds., *Europa vor dem Eintritt in die Wirtschafts- und Währungsunion* (Berlin, 1993), 23–79; Helge Berger, "The Bundesbank's Path to Independence: Evidence from the 1950s," *Public Choice* 93 (1997): 427–53.

[25] See Ludwig Erhard, *Deutsche Wirtschaftspolitik* (Frankfurt am Main, 1962), 151.

[26] See Peter Hüttenberger, "Wirtschaftsordnung und Interessenpolitik in der Kartellgesetzgebung der Bundesrepublik Deutschland 1948–1957," *Vierteljahrshefte für Zeitgeschichte* 24 (1976): 287–307; Rüdiger Robert, *Konzentrationspolitik in der Bundesrepublik* (Berlin, 1976).

[27] See Zweites Gesetz zur Änderung des Gesetzes gegen Wettbewerbsbeschränkungen vom 3. August 1973, *Bundesgesetzblatt*, 1973, pt. 1, 917–29. See also Werner Jäckering, *Die politischen Auseindandersetzungen um die Novellierung des Gesetzes gegen Wettbewerbsbeschränkungen (GWB)* (Berlin, 1977).

[28] See Werner Abelshauser, "The First Post-Liberal Nation," *European History Quarterly* 114 (1984): 305; Abelshauser, *Wirtschaftsgeschichte der Bundesrepublik*, 76–84, 113–16; Abelshauser, "Ansätze 'Korporativer Marktwirtschaft.'" Olson's thesis that the economic performance of the Federal Republic was partly attributable to the destruction of the associations after the war is generally rejected; see Mancur Olson, *The Rise and Decline of Nations: Economic Growth, Stagflation and Social Rigidities* (London, 1982); Simon Reich, *Fruits of Fascism: Postwar Prosperity in Historical Perspective* (Ithaca, N.Y., 1990).

[29] See Nicholls, *Freedom with Responsibility*, 8; Berghahn, *Unternehmer und Politik*, 230–7; Hans Jaeger, *Geschichte der Wirtschaftsordnung in Deutschland* (Frankfurt am Main, 1988), 223–33; Peter J. Katzenstein, ed., *Industry and Politics in West Germany* (Ithaca, N.Y., 1989).

and fiscal policy, monetary and credit policy, and, in general, policy on the economic cycle and stability. In addition to reconstruction, the main priorities of the period 1945–68 were the control of the economic process, the achievement of economic stability, and the attainment of growth generated by the tools of fiscal and monetary policy. This analysis, therefore, focuses on these policies; they are of additional interest because it was at this time that the debate on the pros and cons of monetary and/or fiscal policy began.

Fiscal policy encompasses public revenues, debt, and expenditures. It involves not only questions of taxation and subsidies but also measures designed to influence demand and stabilize the economic process.

In the early years of the West German state, the main priority was not the stability of the economic cycle but reconstruction, in which fiscal policy played a direct part in the form of government investment in housing and infrastructure. More important, however, was the indirect contribution by way of tax incentives that virtually compelled the reinvestment of profits. Even though the capital market in the early 1950s lacked absorptive capacity, substantial investments were set in train by these incentives for self-financing.[30] Overall, German fiscal policy, having fostered growth without inflation, has been considered very successful in regard to reconstruction.[31] However, such concomitant effects as social injustice and unequal distribution of income and property cannot be passed over in silence.[32]

The stabilization of the course of the West German economy was only an implicit aim of fiscal policy. Here again, there was discussion of fiscal policy measures that did serve that aim, but the philosophy of balancing the budget was still widely accepted and led to caution and skepticism. A particularly vehement proponent of this philosophy in the early years of the Federal Republic was Fritz Schäffer, finance minister from 1949 to 1957. He opposed virtually every increase in spending and always came out firmly against deficit spending, frequently referring to the *Grundgesetz* and the narrow limits that the Federal Republic had imposed on itself. But however rigid the *Grundgesetz* may appear at first glance, there is a broad consensus that it certainly does allow scope for a discretionary fiscal policy. Nevertheless, Schäffer kept a tight rein on spending increases and borrowing and carried forward unexpended appropriations and accumulated substantial credit balances. As a result, the federal government's indebtedness fell almost continuously during his tenure.[33]

Schäffer has often been portrayed as a "thrifty housekeeper." This verdict should not be seen as an unqualified compliment, however; it also refers to an outdated position that Schäffer defended with dogmatic rigidity.[34] In 1949–50, he opposed measures to promote employment. In the years between 1952 and 1956, he accumulated considerable budgetary surpluses that were supposed to finance defense spending; he thereby dampened growth, and when he did eventually release this hoard – in the form of electoral favors shortly before the 1957 Bundestag election – it was at an inappropriate phase of the economic cycle.[35]

---

[30] See Alfred Boss, *Incentives und Wirtschaftswachstum* (Kiel, 1987); Zoltán Jákli, *Vom Marshallplan zum Kohlepfennig: Grundrisse der Subventionspolitik in der Bundesrepublik Deutschland 1948–1982* (Opladen, 1990). On housing, see Georg Müller, *Sozialstaat gegen Wohnungsnot: Wohnraumbewirtschaftung und sozialer Wohnungsbau im Bund und in Nordrhein-Westfalen 1950–1970* (Paderborn, 1995).

[31] Frederick G. Reuss, *Fiscal Policy for Growth Without Inflation: The German Experiment* (Baltimore, 1963).

[32] See Hans-Hermann Hartwich, *Sozialstaatspostulaat und gesellschaftlicher Status Quo*, 4th ed. (Opladen, 1977).

[33] See Wilhelmine Dreissig, "Zur Entwicklung der öffentlichen Finanzwirtschaft seit dem Jahre 1950," in Deutsche Bundesbank, ed., *Währung und Wirtschaft in Deutschland 1876–1976* (Frankfurt am Main, 1976), 738–9; Helge Berger, *Konjunkturpolitik im Wirtschaftswunder: Handlungsspielräume und Verhaltensmuster von Bundesbank und Regierung in den 1950er Jahren* (Tübingen, 1997).

[34] See Dieter Grosser, "Die Rolle Fritz Schäffers als Finanzminister in den ersten beiden Kabinetten Konrad Adenauers," in Wolfgang Mückl, ed., *Föderalismus und Finanzpolitik* (Paderborn, 1990), 67; Bundesministerium für Finanzen, *Haushaltsreden: Die Ära Schäffer 1949–1957* (Bonn, 1992).

[35] See Volker Hentschel, *Geschichte der deutschen Sozialpolitik 1880–1980* (Frankfurt am Main, 1983);

Schäffer's departure in 1957 marked a change in the Federal Republic's fiscal policy. The new finance minister, Franz Etzel, was certainly not a committed adherent to a Keynesian fiscal policy, but nor did he show his predecessor's rigidity in insisting on a strictly balanced budget.[36] The scope for fiscal policy activities broadened accordingly and, in 1962, the *Gesetz zur Einschränkung der Bautätigkeit* (Act Restricting Construction Work) marked the first hesitant moves toward deliberate countercyclical policy measures.[37] Even so, in 1965–6, the *Sachverständigenrat* criticized what it saw as a destabilizing fiscal policy, for which it principally blamed the lack of coordination among the responsible institutions and the fiscal autonomy of federal government and *Länder* arising from West Germany's federal structure. Schiller's economic reforms attempted to eliminate these weaknesses: the *Stabilitätsgesetz* provided economic policy with a few new instruments, such as the business-cycle reserve, and ways of intervening in the budgetary economics of the regional and local authorities.[38]

For American economic policymakers, the emphasis was not on reconstruction but on stabilization of the economic process. This meant that demand management was able to play a more dominant part in the United States. The war had increased the importance of the federal budget, and the state was now able to call upon an "enormously powerful new revenue-raising machinery."[39] As far as fiscal policy was concerned, the period 1945–68 is commonly subdivided into two phases, with the year 1961 seen as the turning point between them.[40]

The recession of 1948–9, which saw unemployment rise to 5.9 percent, was an occasion for government intervention, but the government did little. Although the deficit that developed over the course of the crisis on account of the automatic stabilizers was still accepted, Congress refused to increase spending further. President Harry Truman, too, was in favor of a balanced budget.[41] This was no less true of his successor, and continuing mistrust of discretionary measures resulted in a repeat of the 1948–9 scenario in the 1953–5 recession.[42]

Based on limited anticyclical action and no longer focused on balancing the budget by force, this fiscal policy differed considerably from traditional budget management. Yet, it is still not accurate to speak of a genuine revolution in fiscal policy, given the continued veneration of a "budget-balancing religion."[43] Not until the Kennedy administration did the "new

---

Hans-Günter Hockerts, *Sozialpolitische Entscheidungen in Nachkriegsdeutschland: Alliierte und deutsche Sozialversicherungspolitik 1945 bis 1957* (Stuttgart, 1980); Joachim Scheide, "Die deutsche Konjunkturpolitik in den fünfziger Jahren: Beginn der Globalsteuerung?" *Konjunkturpolitik* 33 (1987): 243–67; Joachim Scheide, *Der Beitrag der Konjunkturpolitik zum deutschen Wirtschaftswunder nach der Währungsreform* (Bergisch-Gladbach, 1995); Brigitte Schenkluhn, *Konjunkturpolitik und Wahlen: Eine fallanalytische Langzeituntersuchung der konjunkturpolitischen Regierungsentscheidungen in 7 Wahlperioden (1949–1976)* (Bergisch-Gladbach, 1985).

[36] See Bundesministerium der Finanzen, *Haushaltsreden: Franz Etzel: 1957 bis 1961* (Bonn, 1994).

[37] See, for example, Werner Ehrlicher, "Finanzwirtschaft, öffentliche, II: Die Finanzwirtschaft der Bundesrepublik Deutschland," in Willi Albers et al., eds., *Handwörterbuch der Wirtschaftswissenschaften* (Stuttgart, 1981), 3:190. But see also Dreissig, "Entwicklung der öffentlichen Finanzwirtschaft," 738–9.

[38] See Sachverständigenrat, *Jahresgutachten 1965–66* (Stuttgart, 1966), 96; Lieselotte Klein, *Finanzpolitische Instrumente der Konjunkturpolitik: Institutionelle Möglichkeiten und Grenzen ihrer Anwendung in Deutschland und Frankreich* (Berlin, 1963); Egbert Osterwald, *Die Entstehung des Stabilitätsgesetzes* (Frankfurt am Main, 1982), 59–99.

[39] Herbert Stein, *Presidential Economics: The Making of Economic Policy from Roosevelt to Reagan and Beyond* (New York, 1984), 68.

[40] See Nicolas Spulber, *Managing the American Economy from Roosevelt to Reagan* (Bloomington, Ind., 1989).

[41] See Francis H. Heller, ed., *Economics and the Truman Administration* (Lawrence, Kans., 1981), 119; A. E. Holmans, *United States Fiscal Policy 1945–59: Its Contribution to Economic Stability* (Oxford, 1961); Bach, *Monetary and Fiscal Policy.*

[42] See Stephen E. Ambrose, *Eisenhower: The President* (London, 1984), 158; *Economic Report of the President* (Washington, D.C., 1959).

[43] Herbert Stein, *The Fiscal Revolution in America* (Chicago, 1969), 319, 374; Hansen, *Fiscal Policy,* 482.

economics" usher in a "dramatic period in the history of American macroeconomic policy."[44]

The focus of U.S. fiscal policy shifted in the early 1960s in response to the persistence of a relatively high level of unemployment and the considerable gap between actual and potential output.[45] The built-in stabilizers were perceived as inadequate; discretionary action now became more important.

The major fiscal policy measure undertaken under the Kennedy and Johnson administrations was the 1964 tax cut, which was enacted despite a budget deficit. The intention was to increase demand, give a boost to the economy, and reduce unemployment. The budget would then later be balanced in a second stage. The tax cut could thus be seen as the "completion of the Keynesian Revolution"; after twenty years of hesitation, the obligations imposed by the Employment Act had finally been acknowledged.[46] But this Keynesian revolution was very tame: an attempt to influence demand by means of a tax cut, not an increase in expenditure.[47]

The fiscal policy of the 1960s has been vehemently criticized, even deemed a failure. Critics have claimed that the inflationary tendencies were not identified in 1966 and that taxes were not increased despite the burdens of the Vietnam War and the cost of the Great Society; as a result, fiscal policy had become a destabilizing element.[48] These charges also bespeak a new shift in economic policy. Since the late 1940s, Milton Friedman had been stressing that fiscal

policy was being expected to achieve too much and monetary policy too little. His views, which had received a very reserved response at the beginning of the period considered here, gradually attracted support. The shortcomings of existing policy and long debate brought about a gradual yet steady swing of opinion on both fiscal and monetary policy.[49]

MONETARY POLICY

When the Federal Reserve Board was released from the responsibility of supporting the Treasury Department in 1951, it was once again able to deploy its instruments effectively and to pursue an anticyclical monetary policy.[50] In the years that followed, known as the Post-Accord Era, the discount rate – as Graph 2 shows – again became subject to sharp changes. The Fed cut it in the recession periods of 1954 and 1957–9, for example. In general, the focus of monetary policy shifted back to controlling inflation. Richard Timberlake has described the Fed's monetary policy as "decidedly conservative."[51]

Monetary policy nonetheless remained of secondary concern during the first half of the 1960s.[52] Even the changes in the balance of payments, which called for measures to prevent the outflow of capital from the country (i.e., appropriately high interest rates), did not lead to a restrictive approach. Instead, the Federal Reserve launched Operation Twist in 1961, an attempt to introduce different rates of interest for different maturity periods. This had some initial success, although in summer 1963, the

---

[44] Robert Aaron Gordon, *Economic Instability and Growth: The American Record* (New York, 1974), 137.

[45] Accordingly, this policy is described as "growth-oriented" as opposed to "counter-cyclical." See Arthur F. Burns and Paul A. Samuelson, *Full Employment, Guideposts and Economic Stability* (Washington, D.C., 1967), 31–2; Spulber, *Managing the American Economy*.

[46] See Walter W. Heller, *New Dimensions of Political Economics* (Cambridge, Mass., 1966), 1–2.

[47] See Stein, *Presidential Economics*, 107.

[48] See Robert J. Gordon, "Postwar Macroeconomics: The Evolution of Events and Ideas," in Martin Feldstein, ed., *The American Economy in Transition* (Chicago, 1980), 121; Charles E. McLure Jr., "Fiscal Failure: Lessons of the Sixties," in Phillip Cagan, ed., *Economic Policy and Inflation in the Sixties* (Washington, D.C., 1972).

[49] See Milton Friedman, "A Monetary and Fiscal Framework for Economic Stability," *American Economic Review* 38 (1948): 245–64; for a climax of the debate, see Milton Friedman and Walter W. Heller, *Monetary vs. Fiscal Policy: A Dialogue* (New York, 1969).

[50] See Milton Friedman and Anna J. Schwartz, *A Monetary History of the United States, 1867–1960* (Princeton, N.J., 1963), 591–638.

[51] Richard H. Timberlake, *Monetary Policy in the United States: An Intellectual and Institutional History* (Chicago, 1993), 327.

[52] Bach, *Monetary and Fiscal Policy*, 113, 119.

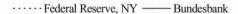

····· Federal Reserve, NY ——— Bundesbank

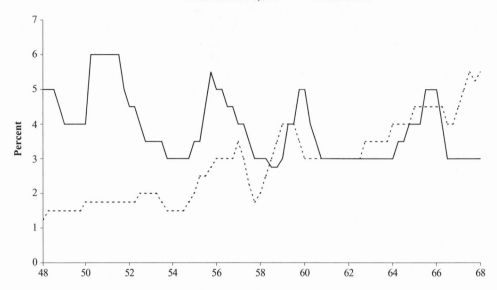

Sources: Bundesbank, annual reports, various years; Board of the Governors of the Federal Reserve System, *Federal Reserve Bulletin*, various years.

Graph 2. Discount Rates

Federal Reserve had to react to the balance-of-payments trend by raising the discount rate.[53] In 1965, the Fed, unimpressed by Johnson's intervention, raised the rate again, to 4.5 percent in response to increased inflationary pressure. When it became apparent in 1966 that taxation would not be increased, the Fed took a clearly more restrictive approach with the "credit crunch."[54]

The United States was not the only country to undergo a shift in monetary policy in the early 1950s. In other countries as well, the days of a Keynesian cheap-money policy were over. Only West Germany seems to have stood apart from this development. A cheap-money policy had clearly found little favor there from the outset, and the relatively high discount rate of 1948 (5 percent), the raising of the discount rate during the Korean crisis, and the reputation the

Bundesbank had earned during the 1950s with its conservative policies suggest that this attitude continued to hold sway.[55]

In recent years, however, archival records have shown that in West Germany, too, there were misgivings early on about variations in the discount rate and that selective credit controls were preferred. Despite the rejection of measures to alleviate unemployment, there was certainly concern for "legitimate borrowing requirements" and reluctance to disregard those requirements with a blanket increase in the discount rate.[56] Not until 1950, during the acute balance-of-payments crisis, did the *Zentralbankrat* (Central Bank Council) reluctantly raise the discount rate and thereby deploy the "classical" instrument of monetary policy. The prospect of an EPU balance-of-payments credit

[53] See Gordon, *Economic Instability and Growth*, 154, 158.

[54] See Bach, *Monetary and Fiscal Policy*, 120–32; Phillip Cagan, "Monetary Policy," in Phillip Cagan, ed., *Economic Policy and Inflation in the Sixties* (Washington, D.C., 1972), 96–109.

[55] See Rudolf Stucken, *Deutsche Geld- und Kreditpolitik 1914–1963*, 3d ed. (Tübingen, 1964); Ernst Dürr, *Wirkungsanalyse der monetären Konjunkturpolitik* (Frankfurt am Main, 1966); Heinz Müller, *Die Politik der deutschen Zentralbank 1948–1967* (Tübingen, 1967); Deutsche Bundesbank, *Währung und Wirtschaft*.

[56] See Dickhaus, *Die Bundesbank*, 65–9.

played an important part in this decision.[57] As a result, in 1950–1, a shift in monetary policy took place in the Federal Republic as well. In subsequent years, the Bundesbank, like the Federal Reserve, pursued an anticyclical policy: It put the brakes on in boom periods and kept interest rates low during downturns. This occasionally caused friction with West Germany's trading partners, which often regarded German monetary policy as too restrictive.

The most recent studies also confirm that monetary policy was certainly dependent on factors other than price stability. At the start of the period, the exchange rate of the Deutsche Mark and trends in foreign trade were also extremely important. The policies pursued by other central banks also seem to have been important from the outset. Although this is not reflected in source material on the 1950s, a cor-

relation analysis does show that "instead of responding to domestic variables, the bank seems to have shadowed the Fed's policy."[58]

CONCLUSION

This comparison of West German and American economic policy between 1945 and 1968 shows that there were considerable differences in both the concepts and aims of economic policy. However, it is also clear that many of these differences arose inevitably because the two countries started from different situations and confronted different problems. A simple juxtaposition of cyclical and stabilization policy on the one hand and a neoliberal market economy on the other is too crude. Keeping in mind the particulars of their policies, it should rather be emphasized that the Federal Republic did not withdraw from economic and cyclical policy to the extent that was for many years said to be the case and that the Employment Act in the United States certainly did not lead directly to stringent demand management.

[57] See Till Geiger and Duncan M. Ross, "Banks, Institutional Constraints and the Limits of Central Banking: Monetary Policy in Britain and West Germany, 1950–2," *Business History* 33 (1991): 138–56; Volker Hentschel, "Die Europäische Zahlungsunion und die deutschen Devisenkrisen 1950/51," *Vierteljahrshefte für Zeitgeschichte* 37 (1989): 715–58.

[58] Berger, *Bundesbank's Path to Independence*, 429.

CHAPTER TWELVE

The Influence of the United States on German Economic Thought

Harald Hagemann

Translated by Terence M. Coe

THE AMERICANIZATION OF ECONOMICS

The growth of economics as an academic discipline following World War II was marked by an increasing internationalization that was simultaneously in large part a process of Americanization.[1] Richard Portes has even asked "whether there is now any economics outside and independent of the United States. All the data confirm American leadership."[2] Although one could still speak of an Anglo-American leadership position for the period up to the end of the 1960s because of the enormous influence of John Maynard Keynes, post-Keynesian economists such as Roy Harrod and Nicolas Kaldor, as well as other English economists such as Sir John Hicks, James Meade, and Richard Stone, the influence of British economists has since shrunk to such an extent that America's leadership in economics is now beyond debate. The Nobel Prize for Economics, which has existed since 1969, has been awarded to American economists in twenty-eight out of forty-two cases. Recently, this has raised questions about the independence of European economic thought as well as about the similarities and differences between American and European economics.[3]

Both continents experienced an increasing "economization" of public life during the historically unmatched growth of the 1950s and 1960s, a period that also saw a noteworthy expansion in academic positions in economics. In a process of continuing professionalization during the postwar period, the number and importance of economists, economics institutions, and economics publications increased dramatically in the United States as well as in Germany and other Western European countries. Trained economists played a role in the central banks, as policy advisers, and as leading politicians, especially Ludwig Erhard (1897–1977) and Karl Schiller (1911–94) in West Germany. The increasing internationalization of economics was accompanied by an internationalization of economics. This was largely a convergence process associated with the creation of commonly recognized analytical and methodological standards. It led to a "professional 'Gleichschaltung,'"[4] or coordination, characterized by the growing importance of mathematical economics as well as statistical and

[1] A. W. Bob Coats, ed., *The Post-1945 Internationalization of Economics* (Durham, N.C., 1997).

[2] Richard Portes, "Economics in Europe," *European Economic Review* 31 (1987): 1330.

[3] See the results of the symposium edited by Bruno S. Frey and Rene L. Frey, "Is There a European Economics?" *Kyklos* 48 (1995): 185–311.

[4] See Alan Peacock, "Professional 'Gleichschaltung': A Historical Perspective," *Kyklos* 48 (1995): 267–71.

econometric methods in empirical analysis. This methodological revolution detached economics from the humanities and social sciences, in which it had been embedded by the Historical School of German economics.

The triumphant ascent of American economics after World War II is not merely the consequence of the United States' political and economic leadership role and the pragmatic and technological orientation of the Americans. It also reflects a national style of economic research characterized by a high degree of specialization and applied work. Graduate education in the leading universities played a decisive role in this process by giving students the necessary mathematical and econometric tools. Harry Johnson sees this as the decisive reason for the increasing significance of American economics, not only in contrast to countries such as France and Italy but even in comparison with the Oxbridge tradition, which concentrated more strongly on educating politicians and bureaucrats than on producing scholars. With the rise of America's international leadership, these features of American economics have established themselves as the decisive characteristics of modern economic thought.[5] Nevertheless, many economists who had fled the totalitarian dictatorships in Europe made significant contributions to America's predominance in economic theory.

EUROPEAN BRAIN DRAIN AND AMERICAN INNOVATION

The dismissal of scientists and scholars from German universities under the Restoration of Professional Public Service Act (*Gesetz zur Wiederherstellung des Berufsbeamtentums*) promulgated by the National Socialists on April 7, 1933, and the expulsion of academics from Germany, and, beginning in 1938, Austria and other European countries, interrupted or cut short promising developments in economics as well as in other areas.[6] Because of the caesura of 1933, German economics fell behind internationally; after 1945, it had to undergo a laborious catching-up process without being able to compensate fully in the following decades for the loss of qualified personnel. By contrast, the economists who had been driven out of Germany not only enriched the growth of their specializations in their host countries but also influenced the direction of research internationally. This was especially true for the United States, which was the direct or indirect destination for some two-thirds of German-speaking émigré economists.[7]

This enormous shift, due not least to emigration from fascist and Stalinist European countries to the United States, can also be put in figures. Whereas the Soviet Union lost 24 of its 36 most outstanding economists and the successor states of the Austro-Hungarian Empire lost 36 of 50, the United States gained a total of 161 through immigration. This figure was equivalent to 30 percent of those economists born in the United States. In contrast, the percentage of leading economists worldwide from the German-speaking countries decreased from 15 to 3 percent.[8]

The long-term shift of intellectual resources to the United States was reinforced by the influx of leading scholars from Great Britain at the beginning of World War II. These included, for example, Adolph Lowe and Jacob Marschak, whom the Rockefeller Foundation regularly consulted to evaluate the academic

[5] Harry G. Johnson, "National Styles in Economic Research: The United States, the United Kingdom, Canada and Various European Countries," *Daedalus* 102 (1973): 65–74; Harry G. Johnson, "The American Tradition in Economics," *Nebraska Journal of Economics and Business* 16 (1977): 17–26.

[6] Paul A. Samuelson, "The Passing of the Guard in Economics," *Eastern Economic Journal* 14 (1988): 319.

[7] See the chapters in Harald Hagemann, ed., *Zur deutschsprachigen wirtschaftswissenschaftlichen Emigration nach 1933* (Marburg, 1997).

[8] Bruno S. Frey and Werner W. Pommerehne, "The American Domination Among Eminent Economists," *Scientometrics* 14 (1988): 97–110.

qualifications of émigré or refugee economists and other social scientists. Initially, both taught at the same American university, the New School for Social Research in New York. The New School's graduate faculty was founded by Alvin Johnson in 1933 as the "University in Exile" and became the most significant sanctuary for émigré economists.[9]

The unique atmosphere at the New School, with its intensive interdisciplinary discourse, was very similar to the atmosphere of close cooperation in the academic and social sciences that had prevailed during the era of the Weimar Republic, primarily at the Institute for Social Policy and Political Economy (*Institut für Sozial- und Staatswissenschaften*) in Heidelberg, the reform-oriented Goethe University in Frankfurt, and the Institute of World Economics (*Weltwirtschaftsinstitut*) in Kiel. Even the seminar conducted by Ludwig von Mises at New York University had largely the character of his former "private seminar" in Vienna. Through his students, who included Israel M. Kirzner and Murray N. Rothbard, Mises's influence grew considerably, and the ideas of "Austrian economics" in the United States have come to form a significant part of the heterodox approach in economics that maintains a critical distance from the more mathematical focus of the neoclassical mainstream.[10]

Apart from Mises and the economists of the New School, who exerted their greatest influence during the period of President Franklin Roosevelt's New Deal and in the first years after the war, the economists who maintained their specifically European approaches had, however, little influence on American economics in the long term.[11]

Many American universities were nonetheless forced to rely on European immigrants, who not only made outstanding graduate programs possible but also introduced a number of innovations. In the postwar years, these were often transferred back to Germany and Europe after some delay and were, therefore, considered "American" influences. Among the more significant of these innovations were the following:

1. The development of modern public finance by Richard Musgrave, who emigrated to the United States in fall 1933 after graduating from the University of Heidelberg;

2. Economic-development theory, which evolved in Great Britain and, in the United States, at the embryonic United Nations and its ancillary organizations after the war, with outstanding contributions provided by émigrés such as Alexander Gerschenkron, Albert O. Hirschman, Paul N. Rosenstein-Rodan, Sir Hans Singer, and Paul Streeten;

3. The long sought-after cooperation between Oskar Morgenstern, who had been Friedrich August Hayek's successor as director of the Austrian Institute for Business Cycle Research (*Institut für Konjunkturforschung*) in Vienna from 1931 through 1938, and the Budapest-born mathematician John von Neumann. This cooperation first occurred in 1939–43 at the Institute for Advanced Study in Princeton and culminated in *Theory of Games and Economic Behavior* (1944), which formed the basis for game theory;[12]

4. The "mathematization" of economics and the triumphant advance of econometrics, for which the work of the Cowles Commission had been of decisive importance after 1943, following Marschak's departure from the New School for the University of Chicago, where he became

[9] Claus-Dieter Krohn, *Intellectuals in Exile: Refugee Scholars and the New School for Social Research* (Amherst, Mass., 1993).

[10] Stephen Littlechild, ed., *Austrian Economics*, 3 vols. (Aldershot, 1990); Karen I. Vaughn, *Austrian Economics in America: The Migration of a Tradition* (New York, 1994).

[11] Earlene Craver and Axel Leijonhufvud, "Economics in America: The Continental Influence," *History of Political Economy* 19 (1987): 175; Lewis A. Coser,

Refugee Scholars in America: Their Impact and Their Experiences (New Haven, Conn., 1984).

[12] The award of the Nobel Prize in 1994 demonstrated the strongly increased importance of game theory in modern economics. Characteristically, the three award winners included the American John F. Nash (Princeton); John C. Harsanyi (Berkeley), a native Hungarian; and Reinhard Selten (Bonn), a German economist.

the Commission's new research director. The Econometric Society had been founded in 1930, with Yale economist Irving Fisher as its first president. Its most outstanding representatives – Ragnar Frisch in Norway and Jan Tinbergen in the Netherlands (who jointly won the first Nobel Prize for Economics in 1969) – had, however, remained in their German-occupied home countries. Many European-born economists nonetheless played a substantial role in the econometric revolution. Foremost among them were the Dutchman Tjalling Koopmans and the Norwegian Trygve Haavelmo, who had studied under Frisch. Haavelmo's early works from the years 1943–4 on the modeling of a system of simultaneous equations and the probability approach in econometrics laid the foundations for what was to become the trademark of the Cowles Commission. Koopmans and Haavelmo also received the Nobel Prize later, as did many younger economists who had worked on the Cowles Commission: the Americans Kenneth Arrow, Lawrence Klein, Harry Markowitz, and Herbert Simon; the Italian-born Franco Modigliani; and the French-born Gerard Debreu. The pioneering work of the Cowles Commission led to the institutionalization of a new field of research. Through research visits abroad by promising young European economists, these modern developments in economics were eventually brought to Europe. One example in Germany is Wilhelm Krelle. For a long period, Krelle had directed the *Deutsche Forschunggemeinschaft's* Collaborative Research Center in econometrics and mathematical economic theory at the University of Bonn, where Marschak had also been a visiting scholar in 1973–4 as a prize recipient of the Alexander von Humboldt Foundation.

ORDOLIBERALISM AND THE SOCIAL MARKET ECONOMY

The extensive isolation of Germany from international developments and debates during the period of National Socialist rule was all the more fateful because of the great strides in economic

research during these years.[13] As noted previously, émigré economists made significant contributions to the development of international research that German economists had to catch up with after 1948. Compensating for the lost years was made even more difficult by the fact that only very few of the exiled scholars returned to Germany or Austria.

The field of economics in Germany also suffered as a result of the early deaths of August Lösch (1945), Heinrich von Stackelberg (1946), and Walter Eucken (1950).[14] After Thünen's pioneering analysis of the spatial distribution of economic activities, spatial economics became one of the areas where German economics made an internationally important contribution to the field. This was true later for Wilhelm Launhardt and Alfred Weber but even in the National Socialist period for the research of Walter Christaller (1933) and, above all, the work of August Lösch (1940), who applied the general equilibrium theory to spatial economics and developed a new economics of location.[15] After 1945, thanks to Wolfgang F. Stolper, these works became familiar in the United States, where they were largely absorbed into the modern regional sciences through the work of Walter Isard.[16] From there, they later returned to Germany in part as a reimport. The great theoretical achievements of Stackelberg in capital theory, price theory, and general equilibrium theory are undisputed today, but because of his initial association with the National Socialist party and the fact that even his most important work[17] has not

[13] G. L. S. Shackle, *The Years of High Theory: Invention and Tradition in Economic Thought, 1926–1939* (Cambridge, 1967).

[14] Ernst Heuss, "Die theoretische Nationalökonomie im deutschsprachigem Raum vor und nach 1945," in Bertram Schefold, ed., *Deutsche Nationalökonomie in der Zwischenkriegszeit* (Berlin, 1989), 63–74.

[15] Walter Christaller, *Central Places in Southern Germany* (Englewood Cliffs, N.J., 1966); August Lösch, *The Economics of Location* (New Haven, Conn., 1954).

[16] Walter Isard, *Location in Space Economy* (New York, 1956).

[17] Heinrich von Stackelberg, *Marktform und Gleichgewicht* (Vienna, 1934).

yet been translated into English, Stackelberg's work has had little influence on the longer-term development of international research.

Conversely, the Americans had a decisive influence on the West German currency reform of June 20, 1948, and thus on a key aspect of the long-term growth process.[18] Their influence on the predominant conception in economic policy after 1945, the social market economy, however, was quite minor. On the contrary, the fundamental ideas of ordoliberalism, above all those of the Freiburg School under Walter Eucken, originated in the years 1938–45 in opposition to National Socialism and on the basis of Christian convictions.[19] Eucken's theoretical magnum opus, *Die Grundlagen der Nationalökonomie*,[20] had been published in 1940. In the competitive order he conceived, the state plays a substantially stronger role than in the Anglo-American perspective. This is especially visible in the "regulating principles" (i.e., monopoly control, social policy, correction of external effects) that supplement the "constituting principles" of the market economy (i.e., private ownership, competition in open markets, freedom of contract, as well as a functional pricing mechanism, monetary stability, and consistency in economic policy). Although Eucken was a well-known critic of the Historical School, his taxonomic concept, which focuses on reconciling economic factors with legal, institutional, and social factors, is evidence of the German tradition of political economy, or *Staatswissenschaften*. In the Anglo-Saxon tradition of "pure" economic theory, by contrast, social and political factors are more likely to be excluded. The Historical School lost its once-dominant position in Germany after World War I, and no other approach was able to establish

itself among the many different trends in the period between the wars. Nonetheless, even after 1945, various trends in economics still existed within the German historical tradition, some of which remained active in research and teaching even into the 1960s.[21] They were, by nature, as resistant to American influences as were the economists in the German Democratic Republic from 1945 through 1989, who represented another German *Sonderweg*.

THE INFLUENCE OF THE NEOCLASSICAL
SYNTHESIS IN GERMANY

Erich Schneider (1900–70), who accepted a professorship at the University of Kiel in early 1946 and returned from Aarhus to Germany, is generally credited with reestablishing the connection to international developments in economics, particularly to Anglo-American mainstream economics. His three-volume *Einführung in die Wirtschaftstheorie*[22] encompassed national accounting as well as micro- and macroeconomic theory. With this work, Schneider created a link to the "neoclassical synthesis" that Hicks had introduced in 1937. Beginning in the 1940s and through the towering influence of Paul Samuelson, the neoclassical synthesis grew to become the dominant school in economic theory in the United States and thus internationally. It combined macroeconomic Keynesian considerations with the classical teachings and more microeconomically oriented optimization calculations of neoclassical economic theory and remained predominant until 1968. During this period, entire generations of students were influenced in their economic thinking by Schneider's textbooks, each of which reached double-digit editions.

Another economist worthy of note in this context is Andreas Paulsen, whose *Neue Wirtschaftslehre* (*New Economics*, 1950) not only made this label of Keynesianism popular in

---

[18] See the chapter by Werner Plumpe in this section.
[19] Christian Watrin, "The Principles of the Social Market Economy: Its Origins and Early History," *Zeitschrift für die gesamte Staatswissenschaft* 135 (1979): 405–25; Heinz Rieter and Matthias Schmolz, "The Ideas of German Ordoliberalism: Pointing the Way to a New Economic Order," *European Journal of the History of Economic Thought* 1 (1993): 87–114.
[20] Walter Eucken, *The Foundations of Economics* (London, 1950).

[21] See the overview in Rieter and Schmolz, "Ideas of German Ordoliberalism," 90.
[22] Erich Schneider, *Einführung in die Wirtschaftstheorie*, 3 vols. (Tübingen, 1946–52).

Germany but also contributed significantly to the dissemination of this doctrine. His work clearly shows the influence of Alvin Hansen who, during his professorship at Harvard University (1937–55), became the leading American Keynesian and whose teachings, such as the emphasis on fiscal-policy measures during recessions, also had a certain influence in Germany.

The most successful economics textbook of all time, Samuelson's *Economics*, appeared in 1948 and was translated into forty-one languages; fifteen editions have so far sold more than four million copies. The work was translated into German[23] as early as January 1952 by Bund-Verlag, which published a number of revised editions and sold several tens of thousands of copies. Samuelson's influence diminished somewhat in Germany only after the monetarist (counter) revolution initiated by Milton Friedman in the early 1970s. This loss of influence was only relative, however; the textbooks by Schneider and Paulsen, by contrast, disappeared almost completely from German universities.

Richard Musgrave's work on public finance has remained highly influential. It connects the Anglo-Saxon concept of public finance, which is more strongly theoretical and borrows heavily from general economics, with the continental European-German tradition, which gives greater emphasis to legal, sociological, and historical aspects.[24] Musgrave's excellent knowledge of the German literature stood him in good stead. Of particular importance for Musgrave was Knut Wicksell's *Finanztheoretische Untersuchungen* (1896), with its contribution to the modern theory of public goods. Wicksell's studies also inspired James Buchanan and the public choice approach, which has strongly influenced German public finance since the 1970s. Musgrave also drew on the more strongly

theoretical fiscal analysis at the end of the Weimar Republic, such as Gerhard Colm's systematic study of the effects on the economic cycle of changes in government expenditures,[25] that was close to the Anglo-Saxon tradition. Musgrave's *The Theory of Public Finance* (1959) remained the standard text on public finance for more than twenty years, was very successful in its German translation,[26] and was used in almost every university. Musgrave's differentiation between the allocation, distribution, and stabilization aspects of the public budget has shaped the thinking of entire generations of students, just as discussions of his multiple theory of public budget based on existing interdependencies have influenced research up to the present.

"WE ARE ALL KEYNESIANS NOW"

In terms of economic policy, Keynesianism had its breakthrough in the United States with the Employment Act of 1946, which established the Council of Economic Advisers to the President and specified for the first time an obligation by the federal government to strive for the economic goal of "maximum" employment, production, and purchasing power.[27] Keynesianism was in full bloom in the years of the Kennedy administration, and in 1966 Alvin Hansen was able to announce emphatically, "We are all Keynesians now."[28] Shortly thereafter, Keynesianism gained a relatively late entry into Germany's economic policy with the Stability and Growth Act (*Stabilitäts- und Wachstumsgesetz*) ratified by the Grand Coalition on June 8, 1967, as a reaction to the recession of 1966–7.[29]

[25] Gerhard Colm, *Volkswirtschaftliche Theorie der Staatsausgaben: Ein Beitrag zur Finanztheorie* (Tübingen, 1927).
[26] Richard A. Musgrave, *Finanztheorie* (Tübingen, 1966).
[27] See the chapter by Monika Dickhaus in this section.
[28] Alvin H. Hansen, "Keynes After Thirty Years (with Special Reference to the United States)," *Weltwirtschaftliches Archiv* 97 (1966): 213–31.
[29] Peter Hall, ed., *The Political Power of Economic Ideas: Keynesianism Across Nations* (Princeton, N.J., 1989); Luigi L. Pasinetti and Bertram Schefold, eds., *The Impact of Keynes on Economics in the 20th Century* (Cheltenham,

[23] Paul A. Samuelson, *Volkswirtschaftslehre: Grundlagen der Makro- und Mikroökonomie* (Cologne, 1952).
[24] Richard A. Musgrave, "Public Finance and Finanzwissenschaft Traditions Compared," *Finanzarchiv* 53 (1996): 145–93; Richard A. Musgrave, "Crossing Traditions," in Harald Hagemann, ed., *Zur deutschsprachigen wirtschaftswissenschaftlichen Emigration nach 1933* (Marburg, 1997), 63–79.

A law creating a council of experts to assess overall economic development had, though, already been ratified on August 14, 1963, at the initiative of Ludwig Erhard. The German council of economic experts (*Sachverständigenrat zur Begutachtung der gesamtwirtschaftlichen Entwicklung*) consists of five members and has presented its annual report since fall 1964. Despite comparable objectives, it differs from the American model in that it is not part of the government, but rather an external and independent committee for policy consulting.[30] Its purpose is to "investigate how it may be possible within the scope of a market economy to simultaneously achieve stability of the price level, a high level of employment, and external equilibrium together with steady and appropriate growth" (Article 2). By law, the council is not to make any recommendations for economic policy. In practice, however, the explicit mission to present the overall economic situation and its foreseeable development, to identify possible problems and indicate options for avoiding or eliminating them, does imply an advisory role. This has also led to several conflicts with the government, unions, and employer associations over the decades.

Karl Schiller's term of office as Germany's finance minister from the end of 1966 through summer 1972 can be seen as the heyday of Keynesian economic policy in Germany. Nevertheless, it should not be overlooked that Schiller's motto of "competition to the extent possible, planning to the extent necessary" – with "planning" understood in the sense of Keynesian demand management – joined the "Freiburg imperative" with the "Keynesian message" and thus did homage to Eucken as well as Keynes.[31] For all its Anglo-American influences, this approach has a distinct German accent. Influenced by Milton Friedman, Schiller and a majority of the council under the direction of Herbert Giersch advocated flexible exchange rates, and thus a de facto revaluation of the German mark, in order to eliminate an imbalance in foreign trade and payments and dampen inflation at the end of the 1960s. Schiller also contributed to efforts to reorganize the international currency system, such as the ratification of the Smithsonian Agreement in December 1971.[32]

OUTLOOK

With the inflationary developments of the 1970s – with the stagflation following the first oil crisis at the latest – Keynesian considerations lost ground against monetarist ideas. This "monetarist counterrevolution" was inspired in the United States primarily by Milton Friedman in the 1950s and later by Karl Brunner and Allan H. Meltzer as well. In Germany, it began to find favor in the late 1960s and made its first appearance in economic policy in December 1974, when the Bundesbank formulated a money supply target for the first time.

Friedman's statements on the role of monetary policy before the American Economic Association on December 29, 1967,[33] were one of those rare contributions that strongly influenced the thinking of economists and economic policymakers alike, in Germany and elsewhere. This applies in particular to the concept of the "natural unemployment rate" and the related criticism of the "Phillips Curve"; that is, the trade-off between unemployment and inflation, which had dominated the more strongly Keynesian thinking of the 1960s. Friedman's position was that there was no conflict in objectives between full employment and price-level stability and that the Phillips Curve runs vertically in the long run. At the same time, he stated, gains in employment could be achieved over the short term only through unexpected and accelerating

---

1999); Gottfried Bombach et al., eds., *Der Keynesianismus*, 5 vols. (Berlin, 1976–84).

[30] Henry C. Wallich, "The German Council of Economic Advisers in an American Perspective," *Journal of Institutional and Theoretical Economics* 140 (1984): 355–63.

[31] Karl Schiller, "Wirtschaftspolitik," in *Handwörterbuch der Sozialwissenschaften*, 12 vols. (Stuttgart, 1962), 12:210–31.

[32] See the chapter by Harold James, vol. 2, Economics.

[33] Milton Friedman, "The Role of Monetary Policy," *American Economic Review* 58 (1968): 1–17.

inflation. These ideas gained an increasing number of adherents. Nevertheless, the well-known slogan by Helmut Schmidt, then Germany's minister for economics and finance, during the campaign of 1972, "better 5 percent inflation than 5 percent unemployment," clearly demonstrated that there was significant resistance to the implementation of monetarist ideas.

In the academic realm, the Constance Seminar on Monetary Theory and Policy initiated by Karl Brunner was the primary vehicle for helping theoretical concepts of monetarism achieve a breakthrough in Germany as well.[34] Held for the first time in June 1970 and regularly each summer since then, this international symposium concentrated from the very beginning on the analysis not only of monetary theory but also of German monetary policy. The objective of the Constance Seminar was to inform Germans about dynamic developments in the fields of monetary theory and policy in the United States and, ultimately, to influence German economic theory and policy. Accordingly, the participants consisted primarily of leading American monetarists, economists from German universities and independent research in-

stitutes, and executives from the Bundesbank and commercial banks. The monetarist example clearly shows that, compared to the period 1945–68, the international dominance of American-influenced economic theory has led to an increasing influence of the United States on German economic thought since 1968.

Growth theory also provides an excellent illustration of this point. Whereas the fundamental model of neoclassical growth theory developed in the United States by Robert M. Solow was still the main rival to the post-Keynesian approaches coming primarily from Great Britain from the mid-1950s until the early 1970s, American economists such as Robert J. Barro, Robert E. Lucas, and Paul M. Romer dominated the New Growth Theory of the 1980s. In their core models, based on the notion of learning by doing[35] formulated by Kenneth J. Arrow, endogenous growth in per capita income is possible through the introduction of externalities in the accumulation of real and human capital. This is of essential importance both for the explanation of empirical growth processes and for the theoretical foundation of a long-term growth policy.

[34] Karl Brunner, Hans G. Monissen, and Manfred J. M. Neumann, eds., *Geldtheorie* (Cologne, 1974).

[35] Kenneth J. Arrow, "The Economic Integration of Learning by Doing," *Review of Economic Studies* 29 (1962): 155–73.

CULTURE

A New Start and Old Prejudices

The Cold War and German-American Cultural Relations, 1945–1968

Frank Trommler

Translated by Tradukas

Frank Trommler

Translated by Tradukas

THE COLD WAR AS CULTURE

Despite conflicts between East and West over cultural policy, the Cold War was not a clash of cultures. Rather, it developed a cultural dynamic of its own. The culture of propaganda developed during World War II had suffused word and image with confrontation across the globe. The Cold War became a new and fertile field for this confrontational language, and both sides had few qualms about reviving it. The Cold War produced its own heroes and provided the opportunity for a globally recognized power of violence and rhetoric of violence to enliven a gray political reality. The Cold War gave birth to its own issues, made careers, and allowed politicians and the military to define and dominate the language used to discuss contemporary problems. Finally, the Cold War had such an influence on cultural developments originating in the social and technical modernization of the 1920s and 1930s that it is not always easy now to distinguish clearly between forces pushing forward (mostly in the West) and forces exerting a backward pull (mostly in the East).

The Cold War overcame centuries of cultural polarity between Europe and America. At least, that is what politicians liked to proclaim. It does not matter how culture was understood: European-American and German-American relations were permanently changed by the general consensus that culture could be defined politically and by the sense of proximity, rather than a customary distance, that came with transatlantic communication. But it is less certain whether the process of cultural rapprochement was as rapid as has often been claimed since the 1950s. The following overview devotes particular attention to this issue.

In 1961, the cultural critic Jean Améry closed his brilliant essay *Preface to the Future* (*Geburt der Gegenwart*) with the provocative words: "Euro-American civilization, as seen at the end of the destiny-laden decade of 1950–1960, had only one point of reference – consumption. The rest is illusion."[1] Améry saw the coming together of the West as a result of consumer society. Because the West lacked a truly overarching idea, Améry wrote, this society was also endangered by the anarchy of the capitalist economy. For most of his contemporaries, the consumer society criticized by Améry was a great achievement. With the building of the Berlin Wall in the same year, 1961, the need for a common Western ideal also became less urgent. A more direct and convincing way of creating a sense of common identity could not have existed than rejection of that monstrosity.

What Améry called "Euro-American civilization" truly seemed to have become reality. Alongside politicians, sociologists in particular regularly produced new arguments for this view, and the perspective on the modern industrial society put forward by scholars such as

---

[1] Jean Améry, *Preface to the Future: Culture in a Consumer Society* (Olten, 1961; New York, 1964), 298.

371

David Riesman[2] and Daniel Bell[3] was applied to the German situation as well. The wish to leave behind the legacies of Weimar and Hitler motivated German adoption of these interpretations and readings of the Western situation.[4] But American interest in German acceptance of these ideas was no less politically motivated: They represented a transatlantic intellectual triumph, extending the American claims to leadership into the cultural sphere. In addition, the United States was proud to have led its former enemy Germany along the American – that is, the economic – path to rebirth.

Only under the conditions of the Cold War could such an ideology that harmonized through its consumer orientation become so broadly established as a surrogate for Western culture. A similar process took hold in the East, where Soviet Communism took on the role of an ideology of harmony and concealed the cultural differences between the different societies in the Eastern bloc until its final demise. On both sides, creative potential, particularly in the cultural sphere, was sacrificed, although in the West this did not lead to the subjugation and destruction of a whole class of artists and intellectuals. But the United States also experienced the infamous blacklisting of artists, scientists, and film and theater directors under Joseph McCarthy. And in assessing American literature, Jean Améry was not the only critic to attribute a decline in creativity since the 1930s to the conformism and the debilitating effects of the Cold War.[5] The apparently unpolitical promotion of mass culture, by which the consensus of consumerism was spread around the world, certainly constituted a major component of the politics of confrontation.

The Cold War also produced a debilitating kind of conformism in Germany, even if it cannot be held entirely responsible for the barren intellectual climate after 1945 in East and West. The Cold War contributed little toward making discussion and debate on National Socialism the basis of a new culture. Initially, East-West confrontations diverted both attention and moral energy from a discussion of Germans' common responsibility for the past. The Cold War marginalized the public debate on the persecution and extermination of the Jews, a debate that Eugen Kogon had initiated in his book *Der SS-Staat* (*The Theory and Practice of Hell*) at the time of the Nuremberg trials.[6] (At the time, the word "Auschwitz" denoted this history, while the term "Holocaust" was not widely used until the late 1970s.)

A more positive conclusion about the effects of the Cold War is possible if we examine the way in which each culture evaluated the other across the Atlantic (although East Germany was largely ignored by the Americans). Americans relinquished the association with arrogance and imperiousness that, in World War I, they had learned to link with the once-admired German concept of Culture with a capital "C." The Germans revised their deeply internalized view of American culture as anticulture and of the Americanization of German culture as a destruction of German culture. This kind of rethinking was not immune to fluctuation and relapse. But it proved to be enduring and was accompanied by an attempt to stop using the idea of culture polemically.

Both views were colored by traditions of appropriating or rejecting the other culture. In America, German language and literature had been introduced into university education in the nineteenth century and remained a respected subject in the middle of the twentieth century. In Germany, neither American history nor American culture had been taught, which allowed the broad education and literature program of the occupying power to assume a central

---

[2] David Riesman, with Reuel Denney and Nathan Glazer, *The Lonely Crowd: A Study of the Changing American Character* (New Haven, Conn., 1950).

[3] Daniel Bell, *The End of Ideology: On the Exhaustion of Political Ideas in the Fifties* (Glencoe, Ill., 1960).

[4] See the chapter by Uta Poiger in this section.

[5] Améry, *Preface to the Future*, 96–101.

[6] Eugen Kogon, *The Theory and Practice of Hell: The German Concentration Camps and the System Behind Them* (Frankfurt am Main, 1946; New York, 1950). See the chapter by Alan Steinweis in this section, which shows how difficult it was for this subject to break through the culture of consensus in the United States.

position. Like the Americans themselves, Germans looked to Great Britain for determining the quality and weight of English-language literature and culture. Americans saw German culture as a well-known feature of the modern world that Wilhelm II and Hitler had abused. Germans, by contrast, concealed their ignorance by according a low value to American culture and history. Culture was seen as a tool whose representational quality was as important as its usefulness for understanding others. After 1945, Germany underwent a process of catching up, in which the occupying power played a part in the spheres of literature and theater with some success.[7] German readers and audiences felt that American literature could help them to reconnect with the present. Yet, at the same time, they cultivated a certain remove from the present, which they were inclined to see as a kind of corrective to occupation policies. Americans had learned to understand the culture of Goethe, Beethoven, and Thomas Mann as a way of moving beyond German politics under Hitler. Germans, and particularly Germans of the younger generation, readily came to see the new terrain of American literature as a corrective to traditional cultural identities.

Both sides appeared to be out of step with political developments. But with growing social and economic stability in the 1950s, politics no longer enjoyed absolute primacy. In the 1960s, after Cold War politics had become a rigid defense of the status quo, the cultural realm gained in significance because it was a place where new experiences and change were possible.

REEDUCATION AND THE GERMAN INTELLECTUALS

The Allied armies had come to defeat, not to educate Germany. The harsh program of the Psychological Warfare Division, which was set forth in Joint Chiefs of Staff (JCS) Directive 1067, left little room for compassion. JCS 1067 stipu-

lated that the Germans would have to endure the chaos and suffering for which they themselves were ultimately responsible on account of their brutal practices in war.[8] The Potsdam Conference specified that the German educational system would be restructured, but the American military administration gave reeducation specialists only a marginal role in the division for education and religious affairs. The sociologist Hans Speier, who worked for the American government for some time, pointed out in 1947 that while the American public supported the concept of reeducation, it seemed either too ambitious to become reality or its implementation was not actually seriously planned.[9] What in fact took place was limited from the outset by extreme financial constraints and could not be compared to the educational initiatives undertaken by the Russians and the French. In the much-discussed case of the reform of the Bavarian educational system, American suggestions were only successful where the Germans were themselves willing to engage in reform.[10]

Exerting influence on the popular press and radio programming, magazine and book production, film, theater, and music was more successful. Responsibility for this work lay in the hands of the Information Control Division (ICD), which was initially separate from the American Military Government (OMGUS) but later integrated into it.[11] Although American efforts to reform the German mass media have long been recognized, responses to the reeducation of the Germans have always been ambivalent. In retrospect, the growing demand for the production of anticommunist journalism, which began with the Cold War in 1947–8 and was seen as propaganda, took priority over the subtler impulses of antifascist education, which

---

[7] See the chapters by Martin Meyer and Andreas Höfele in this section.

[8] U.S. Department of State, Office for Public Affairs, *Germany 1947–1949: The Story in Documents* (Washington, D.C., 1950), 21–33.

[9] Hans Speier, "'Reeducation' – The U.S. Policy (1947)," in *Social Order and the Risks of War: Papers in Political Sociology* (New York, 1952; Cambridge, Mass., 1969), 397–414.

[10] See the chapter by James Tent in this section.

[11] See the chapter by Rebecca Boehling in this section.

doubtlessly also existed.[12] The new East-West opposition meant that it did not take long for democracy to become equated with praise of the American way of life and for Nazism to be seen as a form of totalitarianism akin to communism. In spite of the enormous amount of mostly negative publicity that the American concept of reeducation received, Speier's résumé of the first phase is worth recalling: "The story of the American reeducation effort is but an anecdote in the larger context of U.S. foreign policy in Europe."[13]

Although he had his doubts about the ability of administrative intervention to initiate intellectual creativity, Speier later concluded that appeals to the Germans' great respect for culture should have been made:

For several years, no attempt approaching in scope that of the French or the Russians or even that of the British was made in the American Zone to bring German intellectual leaders, artists, writers and musicians in contact with outstanding Americans who shared their interests and equaled or surpassed their talent.[14]

In other words, American officials who believed in German collective guilt and the rules against American-German fraternization harbored no great hopes that the instrumentalization of culture could be used to reach the German elites and win their loyalty. And yet, theater, film, and lectures broke down these barriers on a local level. As part of a culturally enriched, at times critical self-representation of the United States, the Amerika Haus institutions were particularly successful and represented an important factor in German democratic reorientation at the beginning of the 1950s.[15] The Russians, in contrast, were able to involve German intellectuals and artists in their program of a socialist renewal in the early postwar years because they promoted the Germans' own initiatives through the Cultural Association for Democratic Renewal in Germany (Kulturbund zur demokratischen Erneuerung Deutschlands). The French succeeded in revitalizing long-established cultural relations through traditional cultural programs and used them for their educational aims.[16]

The much-cited exception in American occupation policy was the superbly produced newspaper Die Neue Zeitung, which had a circulation of well over a million and was, along with the Tägliche Rundschau in the Russian zone, the most widely read paper of these years. It is characteristic that Die Neue Zeitung was managed by two emigrants – Hans Habe and, from summer 1946, Hans Wallenberg – and was intended as a forum for Germans and Americans, emigrants and Germans who had stayed, a policy that met with some official disapproval.[17] This "American newspaper for the German population" (as the subtitle read) included a feature section under the guiding hand of Erich Kästner that provided a public forum for such talents as Friedrich Luft (theater), Hans Heinz Stuckenschmidt (music), and Werner Haftmann (art). Unlike other mostly locally licensed newspapers, Die Neue Zeitung was able to overcome the notorious isolation and provincialism of these years with its Munich flair. Later, the Süddeutsche Zeitung would successfully continue the project. How seriously the occupying power took supervision of the media was made evident not only by Habe's dismissal in 1946[18] but also by the withdrawal of licenses for the journals Der Ruf (1947) and Ende und Anfang (1948), both of which campaigned for European socialism as an alternative to American capitalism and Soviet communism. Alfred Andersch and Hans Werner Richter, editors of Der Ruf, had not forgotten what they had learned as prisoners of war in American camps. Their biographies

---

[12] Harry Hartenian, "The Role of Media in Democratizing Germany: United States Occupation Policy 1945–1949," *Central European History* 20 (1987): 145–90.

[13] Speier, *Social Order*, 414.

[14] Ibid., 408.

[15] See the chapter by Axel Schildt, vol. 1, Society.

[16] Stefan Zauner, *Erziehung und Kulturmission: Frankreichs Bildungspolitik in Deutschland 1945–1949* (Munich, 1994), 270–318.

[17] Friedrich Prinz, ed., *Trümmerzeit in München: Kultur und Gesellschaft einer deutschen Grossstadt im Aufbruch 1945–1949* (Munich, 1984), 211–4, 252–60.

[18] Hans Habe, *Im Jahre Null: Ein Beitrag zur Geschichte der deutschen Presse* (Munich, 1966), 103–40.

reveal both the influence and limitations of American democratization campaigns, which became evident when they ran up against the occupiers' efforts to control the media.

This control over the press clearly showed the ambivalence of American cultural policy toward the Germans. From the very beginning, a contradiction was apparent between the desire to fulfill a moral and cultural mission in Germany and the traditional American mistrust of any form of state intervention in cultural affairs. This mistrust had only once been overcome in America, and then only reluctantly, in the state-funded projects for artists and writers during the New Deal. There was also a divide between the desire to claim cultural superiority as the victor over fascism and savior of Europe on the one hand and, on the other, the deep-seated recognition of European culture among the American cultural elite that forced them to promote the equality of American (high) culture after 1945. The Germans noticed these contradictions, and that resulted in equally ambivalent reactions. They could easily combine a growing interest in American literature and drama with an impassioned rejection of American forms of reeducation. What made the plays of Thornton Wilder, William Saroyan, and Arthur Miller and the novels and stories of Ernest Hemingway, William Faulkner, and Thomas Wolfe so successful was less their inherent critique of America than their rather poetic and distanced diagnosis of the chaotic times. Yet, Germans took precisely the criticism of the American way of life offered by these authors[19] as a sign that American literature possessed depth and authenticity.

German intellectuals came to appreciate the unfamiliar and yet sudden and direct provocation of this culture. It enabled up-and-coming writers to find their own voices but was not suited to enrich the literary life halted by National Socialism with new modes of cultural engagement. Still, culture offered the key to a new beginning after the self-destruction of German politics. The French were much more successful in many ways in incorporating the experience of war, collaboration, and resistance into their intellectual reconstruction program. Alfred Andersch, for instance, summed up his time as a volunteer at *Die Neue Zeitung* with the comment: "The instinctive rejection of Sartre by *Die Neue Zeitung* was instructive for me. The fronts were becoming clear very early on."[20] The socialist-European line taken by Andersch and Richter in *Der Ruf* was in fact much closer to Sartre's combining of existentialism and Marxism than to the American occupiers' anticommunist propaganda of democracy. At this time, *Frankfurter Hefte* was probably the most influential cultural journal alongside the East Berlin *Aufbau*. Edited by Eugen Kogon and Walter Dirks, *Frankfurter Hefte* advocated a policy of a third way for Germany firmly aimed toward European integration. This policy had roots that reached back before 1933 and was still influential among intellectuals when the Federal Republic was founded and accepted into the Western alliance as a partner, albeit a junior partner.

The swing to the left that spread through European societies after the Nazis' regime of terror was also initially evident in Germany. The National Socialists had weakened the left and its cultural initiatives – ranging from the *Weltbühne* to Bertolt Brecht, from the working-class culture of the Social Democratic Party (*Sozialdemokratische Partei Deutschlands*, or SPD) and the Communist Party (*Kommunistische Partei Deutschlands*, or KPD) to the Frankfurt Institute for Social Research – to such a degree that after 1945, the left did not have the resources for a genuine renewal. Antifascists who worked toward a new beginning and sought an independent "German" way soon found their efforts thwarted by the American-Soviet confrontation. Certainly, by the time that the Soviets blockaded Berlin in 1948–9, no room for maneuver remained. The oft-noted depolitization of the German intelligentsia, together with its relatively weak national and international

---

[19] Lary May, ed., *Recasting America: Culture and Politics in the Age of the Cold War* (Chicago, 1989).

[20] Alfred Andersch, "Der Seesack: Aus einer Autobiographie," *Literaturmagazin* 7, "Nachkriegsliteratur" (1977): 130.

standing, was directly tied to the division of the country and the hardening of ideological camps in East and West. The German literary intelligentsia became a factor on the international stage only when writers began to address the subject of the Nazi past as part of political and economical renewal.[21] Antifascism, which was used as an excuse for domination in the Soviet sphere of influence, was not helpful here. Nor was the American cultural policy initiative of interesting German elites in the United States in the name of democratization.[22] Along with the culture of protest and confrontation of the 1960s, it was above all the work of emigrants who had returned to Germany that was significant here. The population did not like them, but their presence represented an encounter with the past wrought from personal stories and experiences.[23] Their controversial role in Germany became evident in the figure of Willy Brandt during the electoral battles of this decade.

EMIGRANTS AS MEDIATORS

Contemporary German developments played only a minor role in American intellectuals' debates on the relationship between American and European culture in the first postwar decade. Although Western journalists reported widely on political events in Central Europe, particularly after 1948 in Berlin, Germany had largely disappeared as a subject of intellectual discussions on cultural policy. A page of history had been turned and not much interest existed in turning back. It was mostly due to the insistence of refugees from German-speaking countries that an ongoing intellectual dialogue about German developments was maintained. The administration of the occupied territories certainly required American personnel, whose presence was followed by large numbers of troops

stationed over several decades as the Cold War intensified. But these events only rarely provided any momentum that had an impact on the cultural scene in the United States. Guest tours by American artists, musicians, and intellectuals in ravaged postwar Europe may have left deep impressions on the individuals involved, but they mostly followed a predetermined program, one dominated by ideological confrontations with communism in the 1950s.

The importance of the culture that Hitler had driven out or destroyed – the culture that had decisively pushed Germany into modernity in the 1920s – grew in proportion to the apparent insignificance of postwar German culture. The shock of Nazism, terror and war, and the horrific persecution of the Jews shaped cultural life forcefully and led to a far more positive appraisal of the culture of "classical" modernity than had been the case during the Weimar Republic. Postwar developments were thus evaluated even more negatively than they deserved. Such views were particularly widespread among emigrants. Yet, emigrants made up a large proportion of those mediators without whom the reintegration of German art, culture, and science into the international arena would have taken much longer. A Jew in Washington or New York needed to be extremely magnanimous, or have a great need for recognition, or exceptionally high hopes for links between Europe and America to work on plans to help with the reconstruction of Germany, or even to work actively for this goal in Berlin and Frankfurt.

The fact that refugees dealt with a significant part of all practical relations involving Germany gave rise, however, to mistrust and suspicions that they might attempt to undermine American interests. During a series of lectures held by prominent immigrants in Philadelphia in 1952, which was actually intended to counter this mistrust, none other than the European star of Romance languages and literature at Yale University, Henri Peyre, proclaimed:

A sad gap in American leadership was revealed during World War II when this country had to resort liberally to German-born and German-trained specialists when it had to organize military government,

---

[21] Jeffrey Herf, *Divided Memory: The Nazi Past in the Two Germanys* (Cambridge, Mass., 1997).

[22] See the chapter by Willi Paul Adams, vol. 2, Culture.

[23] See the chapter by Claus-Dieter Krohn, vol. 1, Society.

economic assistance, and cultural propaganda in Germany. The devotion of those anti-Nazi German specialists to their adopted country in the New World was beyond question. But American prestige would have been far better served by an able group of specialists of Germany (and other countries of Europe and Asia) who would have been Americans looking at foreign problems with a keener awareness of the American scene and of American moods and needs.[24]

If the history of cultural transfer should be written one day, this statement could be seen as a classic example for the fact that homogeneous cultural perceptions are ill-suited to defining concrete forms of engagement with other societies in times of war and peace. The American government's hesitation in admitting Jewish refugees from Nazi Germany in the 1930s and 1940s did not mean that the experience of refugees was not used extensively for political purposes, as the work of Herbert Marcuse, Hajo Holborn, and Franz Neumann in the State Department, the Office of Strategic Services, the Office of War Information, and other government institutions showed.[25] Without emigrants, it would hardly have been possible to meet the tasks of an occupying power so effectively. Involvement in Europe, which many Americans felt to be forced and alien to them, was carried out in large proportion by Europeans. These Europeans thus also actively participated in the process of answering the old question of what America really was and who Americans really were.

The debates of the postwar years showed that addressing this question was not solely a matter of the continuous assertion of an American identity vis-à-vis Europe (and later communism), as Daniel Boorstin suggested in his famous essay *America and the Image of Europe*.[26] The

energy of a group of migrants, uprooted through the events of world history, also helped to solve the problem of American identity. Searching for new identities, this class drew on the cultural elites of both continents. America's entry into World War I in 1917 set into motion a period of self-discovery for the elites on both sides of the Atlantic that did not merely consist in replaying the old dichotomies of Old and New World, culture and anticulture. For European artists and intellectuals who could no longer be sure of their role as national interlocutors, the American "project" of making a whole from many parts and constituent cultures – as in the motto *e pluribus unum* – held a practical and not just utopian attraction. For American artistic elites, European respect for art and high culture remained very attractive. Europe even supplied important means for making America more "cultured" in its ascendancy as a world power. When the art critics Clement Greenberg and Harold Rosenberg, along with New York art dealers, enthroned Abstract Expressionism as the new avant-garde in the 1940s, it became the yardstick of the cultural emancipation of America. Greenberg and Rosenberg made increasing claims to American leadership in intellectual and commercial competition with Europe, especially Paris; with Jackson Pollock as a hero of the American avant-garde and the technique of elevating ever newer styles to authentic representations of modernity, the Americans pulled clearly into the lead.[27]

Declaring artistic independence from Europe also had its downside for American artistic and intellectual elites. This is demonstrated by what was probably the most important contemporary documentation of national convictions, the 1952 symposium "Our Country and Our Culture" organized by the most highly respected cultural journal of the time, *Partisan Review*. The editors asked well-known writers and intellectuals such as Reinhold Niebuhr, Lionel Trilling, David Riesman, Joseph Frank, Sidney Hook, Philip Rahv, and Leslie Fiedler to comment on

---

[24] Henri Peyre, "The Study of Literature," in Franz L. Neumann et al., eds., *The Cultural Migration: The European Scholar in America* (Philadelphia, 1953), 52.

[25] Alfons Söllner, "Vom Staatsrecht zur 'political science'? Die Emigration deutscher Wissenschaftler nach 1933, ihr Einfluss auf die Transformation einer Disziplin," *Politische Vierteljahresschrift* 31 (1990): 627–54.

[26] Daniel J. Boorstin, *America and the Image of Europe: Reflections on American Thought* (Gloucester, Mass., 1960). The essay was published under the title "Amerika und

das Bild Europas" in the American cultural journal for German readers *Perspektiven*, no. 14 (1956): 83–98.

[27] See the chapter by Sigrid Ruby in this section.

the fact that American intellectuals had turned away from Europe and now felt new, closer ties to America, a country that had formerly been seen as hostile to art and culture. Most of the contributors hesitantly agreed with this diagnosis, although Norman Mailer lodged a strong protest against this public conversion and open embrace of American ideals. Mailer argued that it was impossible to discuss democracy and mass culture in the United States without acknowledging restrictions on the freedom of speech, a clear reference to McCarthy's intimidation tactics. By asking for suggestions for what could take over the European role of a defender of the artistic mission in the face of mass culture, the editors managed to reveal the problem underlying their "declaration of independence": Abandoning Europe, the home of high culture, made American elites vulnerable to mass culture and required new strategies of legitimization. Since World War I at the latest, Europe had offered sanctuary and support for American intellectuals and outsiders. But now Europe's role as a bastion against American mass culture became less significant. The contributors to "Our Country and Our Culture" did not conceal their discomfort at having to accept a culture that was dominated by Hollywood. Some of them joined Sydney Hook in arguing that the front against Hollywood should not be allowed to harden. Hollywood did not necessarily stand in the way of high culture.[28] In his oft-cited 1962 volume, *Against the American Grain*, Dwight Macdonald, once a spokesman of popular culture, summarized the strategies of defense against "Masscult" and "Midcult."[29]

This criticism of the downside to American culture bore a European, even German, imprint. In the face of fascist manipulation of the masses, any hopes for Marxist instrumentalization of mass culture had already given way to deep skepticism in the 1930s in Germany. In *Dialectic of Enlightenment* (*Dialektik der Aufklärung*, 1944),

Theodor W. Adorno and Max Horkheimer had developed this skepticism into a comparative condemnation of fascist and capitalist forms of manipulation.[30] *Dialektik* became a central text for the German student rebellions in the 1960s, but it was only later translated into English. But other publications from the Frankfurt Institute of Social Research circle, which included Herbert Marcuse and Leo Löwenthal, had an effect on the American debate.[31] Without this influence, criticism of mass culture – initially a favorite activity of conservative thinkers from José Ortega y Gasset to T. S. Eliot – would hardly have become a genre within sociology with broad resonance on the left.[32] Unlike conservative critics, Adorno saw higher culture less under threat from democratic leveling tendencies than from commercialization, which registered its first substantial triumphs in the American postwar boom and cheapened every cultural product by turning it into a commodity. The commercialization theory also retained a central position in discussions about art and culture even after the return of the Frankfurt School to Germany. But this thesis was so close to traditional stereotypes about America and its materialism that its supporters often simply seemed to be anti-American. Adorno was, however, sensitive to the antidemocratic elements in this position and attempted to counter German cultural self-righteousness in the 1950s.[33]

Adorno's and Horkheimer's decision to return to Germany – despite the Germans' resistance to intellectual change – may have been partly motivated by the belief that remnants

[30] Theodor W. Adorno and Max Horkheimer, *Dialectic of Enlightenment* (New York, 1972), esp. the chapter "The Culture Industry: Enlightenment as Mass Deception."

[31] Anson Rabinbach, "German-Jewish Connections: The New York Intellectuals and the Frankfurt School in Exile," *German Politics and Society* 13, no. 3 (1995): 108–29.

[32] Christopher Brookeman, *American Culture and Society Since the 1930s* (New York, 1984).

[33] Kaspar Maase, "A Taste of Honey: Adorno's Reading of American Mass Culture," in John Dean and Jean-Paul Gabilliet, eds., *European Readings of American Popular Culture* (Westport, Conn., 1996), 201–11.

[28] Newton Arvin et al., "Our Country and Our Culture: A Symposium," *Partisan Review* 19 (1952): 282–326, 420–50, 562–97.

[29] Dwight Macdonald, *Against the American Grain* (New York, 1962).

of German humanist culture had survived National Socialism and could be revived. Hannah Arendt wrote a highly critical report of her experiences as a visitor to Germany in 1950. Only the people of Berlin escaped her verdict that the Germans were detached from reality, shied away from responsibility, and were intransigent.[34] By contrast, Adorno lent an optimistic tone to his critical report on his first semester in Frankfurt, "Auferstehung der Kultur in Deutschland?" ("A Resurrection of Culture in Germany?"). Culture "in the traditional sense" had indeed become anachronistic,[35] but the fact that it was outmoded also represented the possibility of a new start that could be directed against both totalitarian barbarity and crass commercialism. The anachronistic preference for intellectual pursuits and culture that he observed among his students, Adorno argued, should be channeled into a politically and socially constructive awareness so that National Socialism would not in the end triumph.

CULTURAL POLICY DURING THE COLD WAR

With the public acclaim that his wartime readings received in the United States, Thomas Mann had helped to prevent the National Socialists from completely usurping the traditional image of German culture. He ensured that educated Americans more readily thought of Faust and Mephistopheles when they thought of German culture than of Hitler. Both his speech at the Library of Congress in 1945, "Germany and the Germans," and his 1947 novel *Doctor Faustus* were seen as attempts to comprehend Germany's barbaric aberration through aesthetic and psychological categories. This approach seemed closely attuned to the predominantly psychological and anthropological analyses that treated Germany as a patient, thereby offering some

popular justification for the American reeducation programs.[36]

The idea of Germany as a traditional and romantic country remained a commonplace in the German departments of U.S. universities until well into the postwar era. The fact that the Americans occupied the less-industrialized parts of southern Germany, in particular Bavaria, unintentionally confirmed this impression. More than five million Americans spent several years of their lives in Germany as part of the occupation. Growing sympathy for Germany in the 1950s and 1960s rested to a considerable degree on the stereotypes of this cultural romanticism, ensuring a steady stream of tourists searching for inspiration in the Neuschwanstein castle.

Thomas Mann was the most famous German emigrant after Albert Einstein, and when he returned to Europe in 1952, he did not do so out of interest for his former fatherland, which had rejected him. Mann was the uncrowned king of the refugees from Hitler and had been Franklin Roosevelt's guest in the White House on several occasions. As in the case of Charlie Chaplin, Mann's departure was seen as a form of turning his back on an America, an America that was in danger of betraying its democratic mission in the name of the struggle against communism. Mann may not have been summoned before a congressional investigative committee like Bertolt Brecht was in 1947, but he faced strong public accusations of being a communist or communist sympathizer, which he countered courageously and unambiguously. Other emigrants such as Lion Feuchtwanger and Stefan Heym expressed their disappointment with the McCarthy era in their novels.[37] Heym, who moved to the German Democratic Republic, dealt with the problems of American policy in Germany in his 1948 novel *The Crusaders* (*Der bittere Lorbeer*), which was written in English and portrayed the first signs of the anticommunist crusade.

---

[34] Hannah Arendt, "The Aftermath of Nazi Rule: Report from Germany," *Commentary* (Oct. 10, 1950): 342–53.

[35] Theodor W. Adorno, "Auferstehung der Kultur in Deutschland?" *Frankfurter Hefte* 5 (1950): 471.

[36] Richard Brickner, *Is Germany Incurable?* (Philadelphia, 1943).

[37] Hans-Bernhard Moeller, "Deutsche und amerikanische Intellektuelle zur Zeit McCarthys," *Neue Deutsche Hefte* 23 (1976): 544–63.

To better understand the differing experiences of the Cold War in America and Germany, it is necessary to remember that Germans only rarely conceived of this confrontation in terms of individuals and their potential influence. It was quite different for Americans, for whom the confrontation was linked to individuals through the notion of the "McCarthy era" and the blacklists of leading scientists, artists, and intellectuals. As a result of losing the war, Germans had lost any thoughts of actively seeking influence on the world stage. Germans learned to see themselves as the objects of history and the confrontation with the Soviet Union as a phenomenon that derived from an inaccessible play of abstract forces and ideologies, with the threat of nuclear world war reawakening visions of apocalypse. The censorship practiced by McCarthy extended as far as the Amerika-Haus centers in Germany,[38] but Germans did not see it as a violation of the individual: Rather, it became a feature of total ideological control, which was commonly associated with the Soviet Union. The Congress for Cultural Freedom formed as a large association of prominent intellectuals in Berlin in 1950 and aimed for intellectual mobilization of the West, but only a few German intellectuals felt willing to commit themselves to its mission. Because the congress sought to lead the left away from communism and toward a commitment to Western democracy, it only appealed to those intellectuals who were willing to recognize democratic politics as a part of cultural practice. Karl Jaspers, Carlo Schmid, Willy Brandt, Rudolf Pechel, Ludwig Rosenberg, Theodor W. Adorno, Rudolf Hagelstange, and others understood it this way. The journal *Der Monat*, which was supported by the Congress for Cultural Freedom, also took this view. Founded in 1948 by Melvin Lasky, *Der Monat* became the most significant publication of left-wing supporters of the transatlantic relationship. Not until the late 1950s did younger intellectuals in business and in the universities gain sufficient practical understanding of American thought and behavior and begin to see this relationship as more than political

opportunism.[39] The single-most successful American cultural initiative alongside establishment of the Amerika Haus program was the Fulbright Program, which provided an institutional basis for visits and exchanges across the Atlantic and made a decisive contribution to the process of democratic acculturation.[40]

Although this process has been understood as a political aspect of West German democracy, it has not yet been investigated as a contribution to changing the mind-sets of leading literary figures and scholars in Germany. The strong continuing influence of a national culture was not only demonstrated by the disinterest displayed toward America at traditional universities and in literature and theater but also in the fact that literary and cultural historians have clearly appraised the achievements of these years within a German frame of reference. The discussion of the Americanization of everyday life and consumer culture has been the only exception to this rule so far. This discussion has, though, found it difficult to acknowledge properly the continuing influence of German modernism, which had developed since the 1920s, without notable breaks, throughout and beyond the Third Reich.[41]

It was the official American stance to view national cultures as lesser matters, unless they interfered with the goal of democratization, as they had in Germany or Japan. Cultural relations were primarily intellectual or, rather, ideational relations, which did not refer to higher culture.[42] Even when American cultural policy was freed from its function as "the occupiers' agenda," it adhered to its mission to educate and move individuals through ideas. The 1950 Campaign for Truth, one feature of the Cold War, had to bear the double burden of offering an ideological defense of the West and serving

---

[38] See the chapter by Jessica C. E. Gienow-Hecht in this section.

[39] See Michael Hochgeschwender, *Freiheit in der Offensive: Der Kongress für kulturelle Freiheit und die Deutschen* (Munich, 1998).

[40] See the chapter by Karl-Heinz Füssl in this section.

[41] Uta Poiger discusses this problem in her chapter in this section. See also the chapter by Raimund Lammersdorf, vol. 1, Society.

[42] Frank A. Ninkovich, *The Diplomacy of Ideas: U.S. Foreign Policy and Cultural Relations, 1938–1950* (New York, 1981), 181.

as a source of information on the United States. Without this double mission, the United States Information Agency (USIA), founded in 1953, would not have been able to survive over several decades as a channel for American cultural policy.[43] It was not able to justify its existence by offering up American art and (higher) culture alone. From 1947 onward, any combination of Europe, culture, and left-wing politics lay open to the accusation of being subversive or communist. Offerings of modern American art and literature regularly provoked negative reactions in conservative circles in the United States, ironically leading to a backlash against the otherwise successful plan of improving American cultural prestige in Europe. Even if President John F. Kennedy supported efforts to raise the image of American art overseas, his main interest was still so-called information policy. The revelation in 1967 that the Central Intelligence Agency (CIA) had given support to the West European left provoked some outrage; those in the know realized, however, that the CIA had more freedom to maneuver, because Congress did not control its expenditures as strictly as was the case for USIA.

The fact that during the Cold War higher culture had a representative role in the service of freedom (to use a common oxymoron of the time) can be seen as an American concession to Europe or to European heritage in America. America's major contribution to cultural understanding after World War II was linked to the information policies of the Cold War, however; these policies expanded the way in which (Western) culture could and should be defined beyond the sphere of high culture. Culture included forms of communication and conflict mediation, as well as democratic and economic traditions, technical superiority, and models of cooperation between employers and the workforce.[44] In the 1950s and 1960s, this concept of culture was systematized and broadened out

to include all aspects of society and cannot be sufficiently explained in terms of the burgeoning ideology of consumer society of the time. It drew significant momentum from Western information policy against the communist enemy and the intellectually calcified and materially backward communist world.

It was not until 1970 that – following a proposal put forward by Ralf Dahrendorf – the Germans officially spoke of a broader concept of culture that could serve as a guideline for West German cultural policy abroad and particularly for the newly founded Goethe Institutes. Up to that point, West Germany had concentrated on presenting the traditional image of German achievements in culture and art, from Mozart and Beethoven to Goethe, Thomas Mann, and Günter Grass. West Germany's cultural initiatives abroad initially concentrated on its West European neighbors and approached the United States only very cautiously. The founding of a Goethe House in New York in 1957 involved complicated diplomatic maneuvering between the embassy and leading Americans, such as the former High Commissioner John McCloy, former ambassador James Conant, General Lucius Clay, and Eric Warburg, in order to hold anti-German feelings and memories of National Socialist propaganda about America at bay.[45] In 1967, there were still only three Goethe Institutes in the United States. And cultural activity in the United States organized by the German Foreign Ministry concentrated on classical music and culture rather than contemporary German culture. This confirmed the prejudice that contemporary Germany did not have much to offer.[46]

A QUESTIONABLE PARTNERSHIP

In 1952, H. Stuart Hughes, the eminent historian of transatlantic cultural and scientific relations, offered a description of the cultural relations running between Europe and America,

[43] See the chapter by Jessica C. E. Gienow-Hecht in this section.
[44] Richard Pells, "American Culture Abroad: The European Experience Since 1945," in Rob Kroes, R. W. Rydell, and D. F. J. Bosscher, eds., *Cultural Transmissions and Receptions: American Mass Culture in Europe* (Amsterdam, 1993), 67–83.

[45] Manuela Aguilar, *Cultural Diplomacy and Foreign Policy: German-American Relations, 1955–1968* (New York, 1996), 144–52.
[46] Ibid., 156.

warning against overestimating contemporary American culture. Europeans tended to overrate mediocre writers because they wrote forcefully and in a typically American way, he asserted. "The American suspects that his European friends have mistaken an admittedly impressive quantity of intellectual activity for a kind of cultural renaissance."[47] Hughes attributed this to the fact that systematic research on aesthetics and aesthetic values had only begun to make real progress in the United States as of the 1930s.[48] Hughes pointed out that American universities had now gained a considerable academic advantage over European universities. These were indeed important preconditions for exceptionally influential American achievements in Europe. Backed up by broad developments in the social sciences, researchers and intellectuals such as David Riesman, C. Wright Mills, John Kenneth Galbraith, Talcott Parsons, Edward Shils, and Daniel Bell set new standards for discussion on the state of modern society. They had a decisive influence in helping to overcome a revived rhetoric of cultural pessimism in Germany after 1945.[49] Their books, which were based on empirical findings and freed of the traditional weight of academic arrogance, provided the intellectual foundation for a budding democracy such as the Federal Republic. Although they were tied into strategies of the Cold War, American social scientists – with their new, sober discourse – made a contribution to overcoming the intellectual isolation of analyses of the present based on nationalism and cultural pessimism. They voiced their views in cultural journals ranging from *Der Monat* to *Merkur*, in the cultural sections of the press, and in the evening programs of radio stations.

This did not mean, however, that the United States influenced cultural life wherever literary and artistic talent won new independence and recognition. Apart from the Soviet zone, France was from the beginning far more influential in this realm. German intellectuals were familiar with the central ideas of existentialism and the Résistance as formulated in the plays and essays of Jean Paul Sartre and Albert Camus; it was also important for them that Paris was a culturally vibrant capital city. In view of the isolated geographical position of Berlin, it became a substitute metropolis for many Germans. France, like Germany, also used the concept of culture as a public space in which the proving ground of intellect and imagination creates community, even if this was a community full of contradictions and bickering. This explains why Paris long held such an extraordinary attraction for American artists and writers, and why it was an exception to their declared cultural independence from Europe.

The lion's share of West German cultural foreign policy was directed toward France, while Bonn showed more reserve toward the United States. Any developments in relations with America that involved the question of reconciliation were tied up with National Socialist crimes against the Jews, as General Lucius D. Clay and High Commissioner John McCloy insisted from the outset. They argued that generous compensation for the large proportion of Jewish refugees who had become residents in the United States was a precondition for the Germans' moral rehabilitation.

Only two transatlantic initiatives that received official support matched the Fulbright Program in importance. The first was the return of the *Institut für Sozialforschung* (Institute of Social Research) to Frankfurt, which McCloy supported;[50] the second was the return of the Bauhaus, supported both by McCloy and the West German government, which was symbolically staged in 1955 with the founding of the design school in Ulm, the *Hochschule für Gestaltung*. Walter Gropius had harshly criticized the first attempts to reestablish links back to the

---

[47] H. Stuart Hughes, "Second Thoughts on an Old Relationship," *Confluence* 1, no. 2 (1952): 25.

[48] In her chapter in this section, Pamela Potter gives both insight into musical influences from Germany and general information on the flourishing of the classical music scene in the United States since the 1930s.

[49] See the chapter by Philipp Gassert, vol. 1, Society.

[50] Martin Jay, *The Dialectical Imagination: A History of the Frankfurt School and the Institute of Social Research, 1923–1950* (Boston, 1973), 281–3.

pre-1933 years in Germany, but he nonetheless delivered the inaugural speech.[51] For both sides, Gropius represented an ideal mediating figure for the common project that was modern industrial culture. At the end of the 1950s, Bauhaus culture, which had already shaped the appearance of American cities, became a kind of representative culture for the new sober and modest German democracy.[52] The Cold War ensured that the discrepancies in this common architectural ground with America remained largely out of view.

In each of these cases, the United States was a channel through which pre-1933 German contributions to modern culture and science could live on; this was far more conspicuous in the case of scholarship and science, for America had taken in many experts, mainly Jewish, who had been driven out of Germany. On the one hand, America's mediating role also served its ambitions to become the leading Western force in these fields; on the other, many Germans ultimately felt that what had come into being was not a new culture but a mix of German-European talent and American drive. From the very beginning of the postwar period, a common view saw Americans and Russians making use of German researchers, engineers, and patents to fight the Cold War and even conquer the moon. Project Paperclip and the work of Wernher von Braun seemed to confirm this view, and recognition of American hegemony was accompanied by an ironic sense of satisfaction that the Germans themselves had made an important contribution.[53] Instead of regretting the loss of creative potential that had resulted from the forced exile of artists and scientists after 1933, there developed a compensatory notion of partnership that long concealed the actual losses incurred by German culture and science. It was

no coincidence that Germans woke up to this fact in the years when America itself, shocked by the launch of Sputnik, began to restructure its educational system under Kennedy and Johnson and to take seriously public responsibility for culture. Georg Picht set the tone for the Federal Republic with a series of articles entitled "*Die deutsche Bildungskatastrophe*" ("The German Education Catastrophe") in which he drew on the American idea of the economics of education and predicted that a crisis in education would amount to a crisis for the economy. The German parliaments and education ministries now underwent their own Sputnik shock.[54]

The compensatory partnership idea was a contributing factor to the continuing cultural provincialism during the Cold War that lasted until the 1960s – a provincialism unaffected by the American entertainment industry's expanded dominance in the area of popular culture. Hollywood had begun to establish its dominance immediately after the end of the war, although it would take until the 1970s before the German film industry was forced to accept its inexorable control.[55] During the 1950s, pop music ousted German popular music (*Schlagermusik*) little by little.[56] Jazz first established an artistic aura imbued with a certain exclusivity, but rock 'n' roll then began to offer youth a new sense of independence, one that transcended the much-discussed phenomenon of the *Halbstarken* (young rowdies) and created a singular sense of solidarity for a younger generation. West German leaders, particularly the "Cold War liberals,"[57] found a way of defusing this socially explosive phenomenon. They declared this music and the behavior associated with it to be a natural part of growing up and an apolitical development. Overuse of the term "Americanization" appears to have defeated its challenge to

---

[51] See the chapter by Werner Durth in this section.

[52] Paul Betts, "Die Bauhaus-Legende: Amerikanisch-Deutsches Joint Venture des Kalten Kriegs," in Alf Lüdtke, Inge Marssolek, and Adelheid von Saldern, eds., *Amerikanisierung: Traum und Alptraum im Deutschland des 20. Jahrhunderts* (Stuttgart, 1996), 270–90.

[53] See the chapter by Michael Neufeld, vol. 1, Security.

[54] Georg Picht, *Die deutsche Bildungskatastrophe: Analysen und Dokumentation* (Freiburg im Breisgau, 1964).

[55] As shown by Daniel J. Leab in his chapter in this section. See also the chapters by Anton Kaes and Thomas Koebner, vol. 2, Culture.

[56] Edward Larkey deals with this and gives many examples in his chapter in this section.

[57] See the chapter by Uta Poiger in this section.

the dominant notion of culture. As long as the definition of "Americanization" remained confined to the traditional prejudices about consumer society and the loss of values and materialism, and as long as it thereby reproduced the dichotomy of high and low culture, its challenge remained within familiar, manageable parameters. Only when the dichotomy was being diminished and the social relevance of the institution of culture was called into question did people feel alarmed. American influences contributed to this during the 1960s[58] in a process of internal social confrontation during which America itself became a target as the leading Cold War power.

THE 1960S

If the cultural distinctiveness of the Cold War is defined as the overshadowing of every aspect of life with a self-regulating confrontational ideology, then one can understand both the ideology of harmony of the 1950s and the protests and rebellion of individual intellectuals and artists in East and West in the 1960s. But this confrontational ideology was no more than a starting point: It did not produce any sustainable system, no political or philosophical platform, even if it was directly instrumentalized under communism to legitimize party and state. In the East, this ideology developed a dynamic of its own, but the building of the Berlin Wall in 1961 proved that it ultimately only embellished preconceived political and military structures. As soon as this barrier between East and West had been erected, the cultural presence of the Cold War was reduced to images of nocturnal chase scenes in English and American spy films set in rain-drenched Berlin streets. The cultural transformation of the 1960s in the United States and Western Europe derived its energy from the younger generation's creation of its own non-official confrontational thinking. The Wall not only cut off East from West and West from East, it also cut off the younger generation from experiencing the Cold War as a continuation of the earlier actual war.

Even Kennedy's enormous popularity in Germany was based on more than just the governor-cum-protector role of someone such as Eisenhower. It resulted from the understanding that the United States was not granted its dominant position by God himself but had earned it by seriously grappling with the country's founding ideas and allowing others to participate in the process. This also applied to the spheres of art and culture. Under Kennedy, it became increasingly clear that American culture's new self-exultation as a culture of the victors was now truly proving its innovative potential in partnership with Europe. After 1960, Americans managed to emerge from the intense cultural insularity of the 1950s, and Western Europeans, now growing together economically and gaining in self-confidence because of their increased prosperity, embarked on a hitherto unknown level of transatlantic communication. Architecture, design, and painting became important catalysts of an increasingly visual and representational culture. German artists were stimulated by American pop art, which was internationally marketed as art had never been before. Pop enthusiasm opened up new markets for art. The encounter with pop art, more than contact with France, helped artists in the Federal Republic to free themselves from their increasingly noncommittal abstractionism and to learn to incorporate everyday life, consumer society, and protest into their works. The increased radicalism of Jackson Pollock and other artists of the New York School had now clearly outstripped the innovations of the École de Paris and paved the way for the explosive banal realism of pop art.[59] For American painters such as Robert Rauschenberg and Roy Lichtenstein, recognition in Europe brought the final breakthrough to world fame.

[58] Bernd Greiner gives a critical overview, "'Test the West': Über die 'Amerikanisierung' der Bundesrepublik Deutschland," in Heinz Bude and Bernd Greiner, eds., Westbindungen: Amerika in der Bundesrepublik (Hamburg, 1999), 16–54.

[59] Günter H. Lenz, "Refractions of Modernity – Reconstituting Modernism in West Germany after World War II: Jackson Pollock, Ezra Pound, and Charlie Parker," in Christina Giorcelli and Rob Kroes, eds., Living with America, 1946–1996 (Amsterdam, 1997), 163–74.

German-American encounters failed to have a similarly inspirational effect in literature.[60] National differences in readership played a role. Here, one can see the influence of different national literary canons. Americans had mainly read the classic authors of their student days, which only sometimes included such authors as Thomas Mann, Lion Feuchtwanger, and Franz Werfel; Germans' prewar encounter with Ernest Hemingway and Theodor Dreiser as well as Louis Bromfield and Margaret Mitchell's huge bestseller *Gone With the Wind* had been significant.[61] American literature made its strongest effect in Europe immediately after the war. New German literature gained a constant but limited readership with war novels, the works of Max Frisch and Friedrich Dürrenmatt, and later, of Heinrich Böll and Günter Grass. In the 1960s, the two most prominent German bestselling authors, Hermann Hesse and Günter Grass, became popular icons of the new American counterculture, as did the Volkswagen "Beetle."[62]

The fact that the Hesse cult was particularly centered on *Steppenwolf* was probably inspired by the traditional way of looking at European classics. The hero Harry Haller brought to life Goethe's and Mozart's world of high culture in a magic theater under the influence of hashish. Young Americans who were open to new encounters with European culture wanted it to be adapted to their own requirements. After becoming acquainted with a newly thriving Western Europe in their travels, Americans brought home forms of European *savoir vivre*, technological design, consumer behavior and intellectual fashions, and a particular urban lifestyle. Thus, they made an important contribution to transforming the traditions of an insular, consensus-oriented American society. Any analysis of the creation of "Euro-American civilization" in the second half of the twentieth century will need to take account of both the enormous influence of American counterculture in Europe and the varied effects that the European way of life had on the United States. Richard Pells has used the concept of "transatlantic counterculture" to explain the intertwining of Americanization and Europeanization between the 1960s and the 1980s.[63]

This intertwining was never particularly harmonious, neither with France, which certainly did not wish to renounce its own claim to cultural hegemony, nor with Germany, where the consensus of the 1950s ended with the Berlin Crisis and the building of the Berlin Wall, as well as with the anti-Semitic graffiti of 1959 and the Eichmann trial in 1961. It was because of these events that William L. Shirer's book, *The Rise and Fall of the Third Reich* (1960), provoked such overwhelming interest in the United States.[64] This book rekindled the old fears, repressed in the meantime, of the potential for terror in Germany. In a depressing portrait of contemporary Germany published in *Die Zeit* in 1965, the American journalist Joseph Kraft went so far as to write: "In practice the American image of Germany is a blank."[65] This ran completely counter to the intense interest in America shown by a German public. But familiarity with events in the United States at the time of President Kennedy's assassination or familiarity with racial clashes, street protests, as well as the escalating Vietnam War, in no way guaranteed a less critical view of America. The young generation in Germany had learned to expect to identify with America, especially with its music and film idols. That precisely this generation developed a new form of anti-Americanism has been the subject of extensive speculation and only seems paradoxical on the

---

[60] This is reflected in the chapters by Sigrid Bauschinger and Martin Meyer, this section, on Germans' and Americans' responses to each other's literature.

[61] Birgit Bödeker, *Amerikanische Zeitschriften in deutscher Sprache 1945–1952: Ein Beitrag zur Literatur und Publizistik im Nachkriegsdeutschland* (Frankfurt am Main, 1993), 190–9.

[62] See the chapter by Sigrid Bauschinger in this section.

[63] Richard Pells, *Not Like Us: How Europeans Have Loved, Hated, and Transformed American Culture Since World War II* (New York, 1997), 283.

[64] Gavriel D. Rosenfeld, "The Reception of William L. Shirer's *The Rise and Fall of the Third Reich* in the United States and West Germany, 1960–62," *Journal of Contemporary History* 29 (1994): 95–128.

[65] Joseph Kraft, "Deutschland – ein weisser Fleck: Wie uns die Amerikaner sehen," *Die Zeit*, Feb. 19, 1965, 3.

surface. On both sides, writers and intellectuals in particular proved deeply suspicious, as their unflattering literary portraits of the other society reveal.

Nonetheless, the move away from reviving or setting up new hierarchies of culture in the 1950s to a new, more open, and less status-conscious culture was irreversible in both societies. The old project that authors such as Brecht had already formulated in the 1920s, bringing art, literature, and theater closer to everyday life, to youth and popular taste – making them catalysts in modern life – now broke through the parameters of much-cherished national traditions. Staging this breakthrough was part of this new culture, and Americans could draw on their long experience in creating such moments.

SUGGESTIONS FOR FURTHER READING

There is not yet a comprehensive overview of German-American cultural relations since 1945 such as those for the areas of political, economic, and security ties. Culture is the one field that most strongly resists scholarly narratives of "progress." It provides the least material for dismantling confrontational traditions, as can be seen in the ongoing interest in Germany in Adolf Halfeld's influential book *Amerika und der Amerikanismus* (Jena, 1927), which the author followed with the similarly critical volume *USA greift in die Welt* (Hamburg, 1941). The essay collection *The German-American Encounter: Conflict and Cooperation Between Two Cultures, 1800-2000*, Frank Trommler and Elliott Shore, eds. (New York, 2001) offers a broad historical assessment and gives particular attention to the postwar period.

The most important accounts of reeducation policy have emerged from political history, including Herman-Josef Rupieper's impressive *Die Wurzeln der westdeutschen Nachkriegsdemokratie: Der amerikanische Beitrag 1945–1952* (Opladen, 1993). Karl-Ernst Bungenstab first covered the subject in *Umerziehung zur Demokratie? Re-education-Politik im Bildungswesen der U.S.-Zone 1945–1949* (Düsseldorf, 1970), followed by James F. Tent in *Mission on the Rhine:*

"Reeducation" and Denazification in American-Occupied Germany (Chicago, 1982). More recent investigations use new archive material and offer further important insights. They include Winfried Müller, *Schulpolitik in Bayern im Spannungsfeld von Kultusbürokratie und Besatzungsmacht 1945–1949* (Munich, 1995) and Rebecca L. Boehling, *A Question of Priorities. Democratic Reform and Economic Recovery in Postwar Germany: Frankfurt, Munich, and Stuttgart under U.S. Occupation, 1945/1949* (Providence, R.I., 1996).

Early overviews of the cultural policies of the occupying power in the context of American cultural policy abroad were provided by Henry J. Kellermann, *Cultural Relations as an Instrument of U.S. Foreign Policy: The Educational Exchange Program Between the United States and Germany, 1945–1954* (Washington, D.C., 1978) and Frank A. Ninkovich, *The Diplomacy of Ideas: U.S. Foreign Policy and Cultural Relations, 1938–1950* (New York, 1981). Analyses of nongovernment initiatives in this area appear in Kathleen D. McCarthy, "From Cold War to Cultural Development: The International Cultural Activities of the Ford Foundation, 1950–1980," *Daedalus* 116, no. 1 (1987) and Giuliana Gemelli, ed., *The Ford Foundation and Europe, 1950s-1970s: Cross-Fertilization of Learning in Social Science and Management* (Brussels, 1998). The most thorough works on official German-American cultural relations are Maritta Hein-Kremer's *Die amerikanische Kulturoffensive: Gründung und Entwicklung der amerikanischen Information Centers in Westdeutschland und Westberlin 1945–1955* (Cologne, 1996) and Manuela Aguilar's *Cultural Diplomacy and Foreign Policy: German-American Relations, 1955–1968* (New York, 1996).

For the role of culture in the Cold War, see Peter Coleman, *The Liberal Conspiracy: The Congress for Cultural Freedom and the Struggle for the Mind of Postwar Europe* (New York, 1989); Stephen J. Whitfield, *The Culture of the Cold War* (Baltimore, 1991); Peter Duignan and L. H. Gann, *The Rebirth of the West: The Americanization of the Democratic World, 1945–1958* (Oxford, 1992); and Michael Hochgeschwender, *Freiheit in der Offensive? Der Kongress für kulturelle Freiheit und die Deutschen* (Munich, 1998). Volker R. Berghahn illuminates an important chapter in the history of American cultural policy during the Cold War in his study, *America and the Intellectual Cold Wars in Europe: Shepherd Stone: Between Philanthropy, Academy, and Diplomacy* (Princeton, 2001).

With historians' increasing interest in the culture of everyday life and the investigations of mass culture (partly inspired by the Frankfurt School), the influence of American consumer and popular culture on West German society has become a major area since the 1980s. However, the popular concept of Americanization seems not to have offered an adequate scholarly framework for investigations into cultural relations and interactions, even when social scientists have theorized about them as a form of modernization. The limits of this approach are apparent in Ralph Willet's *The Americanization of Germany, 1945–1949* (London, 1989). By contrast, the collection of essays edited by Alf Lüdtke, Inge Marssolek, and Adelheit von Saldern, *Amerikanisierung: Traum und Alptraum im Deutschland des 20. Jahrhunderts* (Stuttgart, 1996), reflects on the limitations of the concept. In his book, *Moderne Zeiten: Freiheit, Massenmedien und "Zeitgeist" in der Bundesrepublik der 50er Jahre* (Hamburg, 1995), Axel Schildt includes a helpful overview in his chapter entitled "Zur Orientierung an den USA und zum Stellenwert der 'Amerikanisierung,'" which draws on opinion polls. Arnold Sywottek challenges the trend in studies on Americanization to overestimate American influence in his article, "The Americanization of Everyday Life? Early Trends in Consumer and Leisure-Time Behavior," in Michael Ermarth, ed., *America and the Shaping of German Society, 1945–1955* (Providence, R.I., 1993). Bernd Greiner offers a similarly critical view in his "'Test the West': Über die 'Amerikanisierung' der Bundesrepublik Deutschland," in Heinz Bude and Bernd Greiner, eds., *Westbindungen: Amerika in der Bundesrepublik* (Hamburg, 1999), 16–54.

These studies generally operate with the expanded concept of culture predominant since the 1960s, but few systematically investigate the reciprocal relationship between high and popular culture, which has long been closely entwined with the study of European and American culture. Despite important contributions from critical American studies in Germany, Manfred Henningsen's provocative book, *Der Fall Amerika: Zur Sozialgeschichte einer Verdrängung. Das Amerika der Europäer* (Munich, 1974) did not inspire further comparable analyses in Germany. In the United States, Daniel Boorstin gave an apt characterization of America's tense cultural relationship with Europe into the 1950s in his book, *America and the Image of Europe* (Gloucester, Mass., 1960), but did not follow up on his compact treatment of the subject. Two helpful volumes on American cultural policy toward France and Austria have appeared: Richard F. Kuisel's *Seducing the French: The Dilemma of Americanization* (Berkeley, 1993) and Reinhold Wagnleitner's *Coca-Colonization and the Cold War: The Cultural Mission of the United States in Austria After the Second World War* (Chapel Hill, N.C., 1994). The volumes edited by Rob Kroes at the America Institute in Amsterdam, among them *Cultural Transmissions and Receptions: American Mass Culture in Europe* (Amsterdam, 1993), cover related questions.

Comparative studies are probably best suited to cover the complex reciprocal relationship between America and Europe since World War II. A good example is *Amerikanisierung und Sowjetisierung in Deutschland 1945–1970* (Frankfurt am Main, 1997), edited by Konrad Jarausch and Hannes Siegrist. Recently, more interest has emerged in placing studies devoted to one country into a European context. A good and very readable example is by Richard Pells, *Not Like Us: How Europeans Have Loved, Hated, and Transformed American Culture Since World War II* (New York, 1997).

CHAPTER ONE

U.S. Cultural Policy and German Culture During the American Occupation

Rebecca Boehling

Any analysis of American cultural policy toward occupied Germany needs to take into account the occupiers' motives and goals and the events affecting those goals over time. Because cultural policy, even in an occupation setting, involves interactions and transactions, each group's understanding of its own as well as the other's culture must be considered. Germans differentiate between *Bildung* as the transmission of culture in a historical value-oriented context and *Erziehung* as intentional, structured learning by the individual. But whereas Germans tend to stress education and culture within the context of *Bildung*, Americans are prone to regard both as aspects of socialization.

American cultural policy in occupied Germany was based initially on the premise that German culture – elite, popular, and political – was complicit in the militarism that led to two world wars and in the failure of German democracy to prevent the rise of Nazism. The American planners of cultural policy were primarily education experts[1] who took on what they saw as the task of socializing postwar Germans in order "to provide long-range protection against a recurrence of aggression." This specific form of socialization was called "reeducation" and was meant to build "a psychological foundation on which political and economic reform could rest."[2] The term reeducation was initially used to characterize all the plans in the American zone intended to reverse the Nazis' regimentation of cultural life (*Gleichschaltung*) as well as any authoritarian social and political traditions from German history before 1933.

Reeducation involved indoctrination, licensing, and censorship of the means of mass communication, as well as numerous measures to democratize the German education system and reorient various areas of German cultural life. The State Department, which did not have jurisdiction over occupation policy until the civilian High Commission for Germany replaced the Office of Military Government, United States Zone (OMGUS) in 1949, had had numerous American education experts begin work on reeducation in 1943 and had formulated a "Long-Range Policy Statement for German Reeducation" in May 1945.[3] But the primary directive that actually governed American occupation policy in Germany from October 1945

---

[1] Manfred Strack, "Amerikanische Kulturbeziehungen zu (West-) Deutschland 1945–1955," *Zeitschrift für Kulturaustausch* 37, no. 2 (1987): 288.

[2] Henry J. Kellermann, *Cultural Relations as an Instrument of U.S. Foreign Policy: The Educational Exchange Program Between the United States and Germany, 1945–1954*, U.S. Department of State Publication 8931 (Washington, D.C., 1978), 22.

[3] SWNCC [State-War-Navy Coordinating Committee] Directive 269/5 in U.S. Department of State, *Germany, 1947–1949: The Story in Documents*, Publication 3556 (Washington, D.C., 1950), 541–2.

until July 1947, JCS 1067,[4] did not provide explicitly for any cultural policy or reeducation. It was not until July 1947 that the replacement directive for JCS 1067 concretely connected reeducation to democracy: "the re-education of the German people is an integral part of policies intended to help develop a democratic form of government."[5]

The implementation of reeducation and cultural policy was assigned to two U.S. occupation agencies, the Information Control Division (ICD) and the Education and Religious Affairs Branch. They failed to coordinate reeducation tasks because their structural organization was not designed to facilitate direct communication. The lack of official policy directives and of systematic coordination between agencies limited the potential of a strong, effective cultural program of reeducation.[6]

The ICD was supposed to denazify the information media, build up a German information service, and oversee the reawakening of public life.[7] The ICD exercised considerable authority via licensing and censorship, especially early on. Whereas the ICD created or imported into Germany many forms of popular media to denazify and democratize the Germans, Germans themselves took most initiatives in areas of elite culture such as music and art. The ICD, therefore, had little influence over German cultural and nonpolitical public life beyond its mass-media focus. This was due largely to its unclear mandate in relation to the other agency involved in implementing cultural policy, the Education and Religious Affairs Branch.

Originally composed of ten American educational experts, the Education and Religious Affairs Branch of OMGUS considered its primary concern to be denazifying and democratizing the education system. Its preoccupation with education and its shifting location within low-priority agencies, such as OMGUS's Public Health and Welfare Division, limited its influence on other aspects of German culture. By the time the Education and Religious Affairs Branch acquired division status in 1948, U.S. cultural policy had moved away from reeducation and become a less ambitious plan of "reorientation" toward anticommunism, consumerism, capitalist reconstruction, and Western-style parliamentary government. Unlike reeducation, this reorientation was devoid of any aspects of the denazification program, which had been abandoned as the Cold War heated up and anticommunism became a higher priority than anti-Nazism.[8]

The intensification of the Cold War brought about a more efficient organizational structure for the implementation of U.S. cultural policy. Operation Backtalk, intended to build up resistance against communism and support for capitalism and Western-style democracy, was instituted in the American zone in mid-1947 in response to propaganda in the Soviet zone against the Western Allies. The operation coincided with heightened tensions in East-West relations as a result of growing Soviet political intervention in Eastern Europe, the formation of Bizonia, and the announcement of the Truman Doctrine and the Marshall Plan earlier that year.[9] It also signaled a more ideologically politicized emphasis on reeducation. Within months, OMGUS made ICD responsible for the "creation, operation and maintenance of libraries and information centers" as part of the democratic reorientation and

---

[4] JCS 1067 reprinted in Beate Ruhm von Oppen, ed., *Documents on Germany Under Occupation, 1945–54* (London, 1955), 13–27.

[5] U.S. Department of State, *Germany, 1947–1949*, 40–1.

[6] OMGUS differentiated between democratization in a political-structural sense and reeducation in a cultural and intellectual sense, with the former falling under the jurisdiction of the large and powerful Civil Administration Division. See Christoph Weisz, ed., *OMGUS-Handbuch: Die amerikanische Militärregierung in Deutschland 1945–1949* (Munich, 1994), 110–2.

[7] Edward C. Breitenkamp, *The U.S. Information Control Division and Its Effect on German Publishers and Writers, 1945 to 1949* (Grand Forks, N.D., 1953), 6–7.

[8] See the chapter by Cornelia Rauh-Kühne, vol. 1, Politics.

[9] See the chapters by Michael Wala and Manfred Görtemaker, vol. 1, Politics.

"assimilation of the German people into the society of peaceful nations through the revival of
international cultural relations."[10] It is no coincidence that seven new U.S. information centers
were set to open at the same time as Operation Backtalk began. As early as 1945, information centers, lending libraries, and reading
rooms opened in the American zone under private auspices to disseminate information about
the outside world, especially the United States.
Dubbed Amerika-Häuser by the Germans, they
were not explicitly recognized by OMGUS
until 1947, when anticommunist information
became their focal point. Until then, books
about Russian history had been among the most
popular among German visitors to the
Amerika-Häuser. Then, after the Amerika-
Häuser sponsored a growing number of lectures and discussions with German groups and
institutions on American history, society, law,
and comparative German-American topics, the
number of American history books checked out
grew at the expense of Russian history.[11]

In many ways, the Amerika-Häuser were the
most successful aspect of the reeducation program; as a "window to the West,"[12] they had an
impact that went far beyond anticommunism.
The purpose of the information centers was to
provide Germans with a picture of the United
States and acquaint them with democratic ideas
and "classics" in order to counteract twelve years
of isolation and propaganda. At their peak in
1950 there were twenty-seven Amerika-Häuser
in major West German cities and 135 affiliated

reading rooms in smaller towns. They attracted
14 million German visitors per year in the early
1950s. The libraries contained an average of
16,000 books, of which one-fourth were in
German, and collectively they possessed close
to 4,000 films.[13] Besides U.S. publications, these
libraries made available European books that
had been banned by the Nazis. The open-shelf
system was extremely popular among Germans
accustomed to closed stacks. Most of the sponsored discussions, exhibits, debates, and lectures
were by Germans.

The Amerika-Häuser spawned a series of
German-American institutes founded by Germans to cultivate relations with the United
States. Many of the information centers were ultimately converted into such institutes or other
German-run structures in the 1950s. The Americans judged this cultural program to have been
"more extensive, more dynamic, and on the
whole perhaps more effective than the corresponding programs in other countries." Although the information centers were aimed
at the general public, they "probably attracted
the attention of more serious-minded Germans than any other single undertaking" of
the OMGUS and the U.S. High Commission
for Germany (HICOG) occupation periods.[14]
Eventually, the information centers fell under
the purview of the U.S. Information Agency
and became part of the broader American diplomatic effort in international cultural relations.[15]

This experiment in U.S. cultural policy was
not imposed on the Germans. Rather, the discussions, forums, and reading circles encouraged
German participation by providing a welcoming
arena for cultural exchange, especially for young
Germans who had not yet formed ideological
positions. All the Allies established agencies to
promote their cultures, but the Americans had
the distinct financial advantage and could offer to an exhausted, disillusioned people participation in an appealing culture that conflated

[10] Office of Military Government (U.S. Zone), *Military Government Regulations*, no. 21–800, Sept. 17, 1947.
[11] Karl-Ernst Bungenstab, "Entstehung, Bedeutungs-
und Funktionswandel der Amerika-Häuser," *Jahrbuch
für Amerika-Studien* 16 (1971): 198. See also Axel
Schildt, "Die USA als 'Kulturnation': Zur Bedeutung der Amerikahäuser in den 1950er Jahren," in Alf
Lüdtke, Inge Marssolek, and Adelheid von Saldern, eds.,
*Amerikanisierung: Traum und Alptraum im Deutschland des
20. Jahrhunderts* (Stuttgart, 1996).
[12] This was the name of the privately funded library,
considered the forerunner of the Amerika-Haus, opened
at the University of Marburg in 1945. See Henry P. Pilgert, *The History of the Development of the Information Services Through Information Centers and Documentary Films*
(Mehlem, 1951), 7.

[13] Strack, "Amerikanische Kulturbeziehungen," 290,
297–8.
[14] Pilgert, *Development of the Information Services*, 39, 5.
[15] See the chapter by Jessica C. E. Gienow-Hecht in
this section.

consumption with happiness.[16] Although the information centers certainly were intended to promote the American model of capitalist democracy, they also exposed Germans to other, less consumer-oriented aspects of American culture, both political and elite, as well as to a more democratic style of discussion and intellectual exchange.

Reeducation was most successful in its goal of democratization when it provided a framework for cultural tolerance and political openness. However, various reeducation and reorientation projects initiated in or after 1948 to make German ideas and attitudes more compatible with American policy showed less regard for German traditions and circumstances and, therefore, found little resonance among the German population.

One example of this change in approach is the Women's Affairs Section. OMGUS established the section in March 1948 for the democratization of women, who made up the majority of the electorate and were needed in the economy. American women journalists and political and civic leaders had tried to pressure OMGUS into taking the specific problems of German women seriously and into forming a special women's organization as early as 1946, but this did not happen until OMGUS began to fear women's susceptibility to communism, particularly in the form of the Democratic Women's League of Germany (*Demokratischer Frauenbund Deutschlands*, or DFD), which had been founded in the Soviet zone but was attracting supporters in the Western zones as well.[17]

Although a number of quite capable American women specialists in journalism, politics, labor, and law served intermittently as visiting experts in projects sponsored by the Women's Affairs Section, the section itself focused on shaping German women's organizations along the lines of American middle- and upper-class women's civic and charity clubs. Through the influence of such clubs, German women were to be restored to what was believed to be their inherently morally superior position of influence in the family; from there, they would be expected to extend their cultural and "civilizing" role into the public sphere. This emphasis on volunteerism and civic service failed to resonate with the German women's organizations, which by 1948 tended to be more professionally or vocationally oriented or affiliated with political parties. The large number of German women who no longer lived in traditional families could not identify with the section's strong emphasis on women's family roles and its idealization of maternal traits.[18] By the last year of its existence, 1952, the Women's Affairs Section thought it had found a way out of this dilemma: "to create a politically educated group of German leaders [among single women] as a bulwark against communist infiltration and pernicious communist propaganda."[19] The U.S. policy of women's reeducation to democracy had become another means to the end of anticommunism.

Another less-than-successful cultural policy was the use by the Economic Construction Administration of Marshall Plan funds in the early 1950s to subsidize the construction of single-family homes and promote private property ownership. Whereas the Women's Affairs Section relied on the concept of republican motherhood for the woman's role in the family and society, the Economic Construction Administration used the patriarchal model to appeal to (male) individualism and the maintenance of the traditional nuclear family. Although this policy resembled the program for housing construction adopted by the German Christian Democratic Party in 1949, it was clearly influenced

---

[16] Reinhold Wagnleitner, "Propagating the American Dream: Cultural Policies as Means of Integration," *American Studies International*, Apr. 1986, 67.

[17] Archiv des Instituts für Zeitgeschichte, Munich, OMGUS, ECR 5/297-1/1 (1 of 4).

[18] See Rebecca Boehling, *U.S. Democratization Plans, Gender Politics, and the Revival of German Self-Government in Postwar Germany*, Volkswagen Foundation Program in Postwar German History, the American Institute for Contemporary German Studies and the German Historical Institute, Working Paper 3 (Washington, D.C., 1995), 5–7.

[19] Sophia Smith Collection, Smith College, Ruth F. Woodsmall papers, box 57, folder 1, HICOG Cultural and Exchange Program, Program Area no. 525, Women's Affairs.

by the American ideal of owning one's own home.[20] By building settlements in northwestern industrial areas for working-class buyers, the Economic Construction Administration sought to counter trade union and left-wing support of land reform and nationalization with the American conception of personal freedom as private property ownership. However, half the miners for whom houses were built with American capital preferred to rent rather than buy these homes, and those German workers who chose to buy often found themselves with less mobility and freedom than those who rented.[21] German residential property ownership patterns diverged considerably from the American norm of frequent turnover and geographical mobility, with the result that Germans felt tied down by having to make forty to fifty years of payments before they could own the settlement homes.

American cultural policy was ultimately most successful when it exposed Germans to international literature and information and involved them in cultural exchange without an explicit ideological agenda. Such policy probably had the most impact on up-and-coming young German intellectuals who were completing their studies at or shortly after the end of the war.[22] They belonged to the oldest generation that reeducation policymakers seriously targeted and were dealing with precisely some of the same

concerns that had been the impetus behind the early reeducation program, like the legacy of authoritarianism in German political and social culture. By contrast, debates and discussions among representatives of the older generation of the intellectual elite, though reported in newspapers in the American zone, were not sponsored by American cultural policy. Exiles such as Hans Habe and Hans Wallenberg did play a direct part in American cultural and political reeducation in their role as editors of the *Neue Zeitung*, which was published directly by the American military government. But many Germans who had remained in the country saw them as they saw most exiles: as no longer "real Germans" or out of touch with Germans' wartime experiences.[23]

Between these two aforementioned generations were some politically untainted intellectuals who were in their thirties when the war ended. Their first contact with the American military government often was when it licensed or censored their publications. Such was the case with Alfred Andersch and Hans Werner Richter, the editors of the short-lived antifascist political periodical *Der Ruf*.[24] *Der Ruf*'s editorials mirrored the search of young intellectuals for their generation's cultural and national identity. After pinpointing some of the mistakes of the older generation and rejecting a clear-cut choice between an American capitalist or a Soviet communist "way," Andersch and Richter had their license revoked by the U.S. military government in 1947. A few months thereafter, they founded the less overtly political, literary *Gruppe 47*. By the late 1940s, Andersch and Richter, together with many other left-oriented writers and poets associated with *Gruppe 47*, began to publish works filled once again with strong democratic themes and socially critical messages. They tried to come to terms with the past while critiquing authoritarian and fascist continuities in the present. However, by this time much of the West German public was more

---

[20] Hans H. Hanke, "Eigenheime – bewohnte Bollwerke der Demokratie," in Gabriele Clemens, ed., *Kulturpolitik im besetzten Deutschland 1945–1949* (Stuttgart, 1994), 14.

[21] Ibid., 14.

[22] For example, Hildegard Hamm-Brücher was born in 1921, studied chemistry in Munich from 1940 to 1945, worked with the U.S. military government newspaper *Die Neue Zeitung*, contributed to the short-lived *Der Ruf*, and then in 1949–50, while a city councilwoman in Munich, participated in an academic exchange with Harvard University. Her commitment to educational and political reform as well as to free speech and her steady contact with the United States attest to the influence that certain aspects of American culture had on her intellectual development. See Rebecca Boehling, "Symbols of Continuity and Change in Postwar German Liberalism: Wolfgang Haussman and Hildegard Hamm-Brücher," in Konrad Jarausch and Larry E. Jones, eds., *In Search of a Liberal Germany: Studies in the History of German Liberalism from 1789 to the Present* (Providence, R.I., 1990), 361–87.

[23] See Hermann Glaser, *The Rubble Years: The Cultural Roots of Postwar Germany* (New York, 1986), 118–20. See also the chapter by Claus-Dieter Krohn, vol. 1, Society.

[24] See Hans Schwab-Felisch, ed., *Der Ruf* (Munich, 1962).

attracted to the popular and consumer-culture elements of the American dream than to any painful soul-searching about the Third Reich and its legacies.

Nevertheless, by banning the publication of *Der Ruf* and causing its contributors to find other arenas for expression, the military government unintentionally contributed to the formation of *Gruppe 47* and the critical jumpstart it gave to the careers of the major novelists and poets of the Federal Republic. *Gruppe 47* provided a place for the youngest writers and intellectuals, whom American cultural policy had targeted, to meet with and have their work critiqued by their slightly senior German colleagues. Future cultural critics who benefited from this opportunity included Ilse Aichinger, Ingeborg Bachmann, Heinrich Böll, Hans Magnus Enzensberger, Günter Grass, and Martin Walser.[25]

[25] Peter Demetz, *Postwar German Literature* (New York, 1970), 54–5.

This group of young intellectuals of the 1950s would eventually influence the next generation of West Germans who indeed did push for and eventually accomplish more political and social democratization of German society beginning in the late 1960s.

The political culture of the early Federal Republic combined American ideas about political freedom, democracy, capitalism, and free trade with older German political and social structures and traditions. However, it was the American example of consumerism and anticommunism, rather than American ideas about democracy, that had the strongest impact on West German popular culture and everyday life. Germans grew to accept *Amerika* in the culture of the new Federal Republic not while they were being "reeducated" to democracy in the "Rubble Years" immediately after the war, but while they were experiencing the reconstruction, material prosperity, and Cold War tensions of the 1950s.

CHAPTER TWO

American Influences on the German Educational System

James F. Tent

Traditionally, American and German educational systems have shown more contrasts than similarities. This was the case in 1945 and, despite some changes, it still holds true today at all levels. Nevertheless, during the occupation, American officials sought earnestly to alter German education, especially elementary and secondary education, under the banner of democratization. The American reformers concluded that Germany's multitrack schools separated a small elite from the main school-age population and gave them a superior secondary education in the advanced-level high schools (*Gymnasien*), which in turn gave them a virtual monopoly on securing a university education. Seeing education as a kind of "pressure point" that could aid in the formation of a more democratic society in Germany, American officials adopted public school restructuring as part of their "reeducation" program. This reform effort continued until the conflicting pressures of the Cold War directed the occupiers' chief concerns elsewhere.[1]

A CONFUSED START

In the immediate aftermath of the war against National Socialism, American reformers were concerned with forging tools of democracy. In education, that translated into three basic goals: to increase the number of school years of primary education that all pupils shared in common; to upgrade the professional status of all primary and secondary teachers by providing university training for both groups rather than for secondary teachers alone; and to end tuition for pupils in primary and secondary education. Although they were successful in securing this last goal, reform measures failed to achieve the first and second.

This failure stemmed from the ambiguous and shifting aims of American occupational policy in general. For any ambitious plan to have succeeded, it would have had to be in place and functioning at Germany's *Stunde Null*, its Zero Hour, on May 8, 1945. An occupying power should have formulated concrete plans in advance and had a large, trained occupation force that could identify German traditions and German organizations willing to work for meaningful reform.[2]

---

[1] Major works on postwar German education reform in the American zone include Karl-Ernst Bungenstab, *Umerziehung zur Demokratie? Re-education-Politik im Bildungswesen der U.S. Zone* (Düsseldorf, 1970); Jutta B. Lange-Quassowski, *Neuordnung oder Restauration? Das Demokratiekonzept der amerikanischen Besatzungsmacht und die politische Sozialisation der Westdeutschen: Wirtschaftsordnung – Schulstruktur – Politische Bildung* (Opladen, 1979); Hans-Joachim Thron, "Schulreform im besiegten Deutschland: Die Bildungspolitik der amerikanischen

Militärregierung nach dem Zweiten Weltkrieg," (Ph.D. diss., University of Munich, 1972).

[2] See James F. Tent, *Mission on the Rhine: Reeducation and Denazification in American-Occupied Germany* (Chicago, 1982), 312–8.

This was simply not the case for the Americans when they established their Office of Military Government (OMGUS) at the end of the war. Handicapped by uncertainties at the highest levels of the U.S. government, OMGUS wavered between the desire to punish and the need to reconstruct Germany. Moreover, OMGUS was a comparatively small organization with only a minuscule unit in charge of education, its Education and Religious Affairs (E&RA) branch. Most of its personnel were ignorant of German educational reform traditions onto which they might have grafted their own plans. They were also uninformed about those institutions or persons who might have aided in the implementation of reforms. Finally, they had given almost no thought to changes in higher education.

Desultory discussions on "reeducation" programs and possible changes in German education had taken place at the State Department in 1944 and 1945 under the leadership of Undersecretary Archibald MacLeish and to a lesser degree in the Pentagon's Civil Affairs Division (CAD). The State Department concluded that lasting reforms in Germany would have to be based on German traditions. However, in 1945, the Pentagon eclipsed the State Department. The CAD was virtually silent on the subject of education, so that its field agency, OMGUS, was largely unaware of the State Department's cogent conclusions.[3]

The handful of Americans who constituted E&RA at OMGUS headquarters were mostly secondary-school administrators – volunteers in uniform drawn from American public-school systems. At that time, the influence of educator John Dewey on how Americans thought about public schools was particularly strong. Dewey's followers took his ideas to mean that schools serve a profound social as well as educational purpose. Their ideal was that children from all religious, social, and ethnic groups should learn together. In short, America's public schools taught "democratic living." In the context of the American occupation, Dewey's ideas held special meaning because they supported the notion of schools as an instrument of democratization. As up-to-date school administrators, the E&RA officials shared a "one best school mentality," to use the phrase of education historian David Tyack. Those same officials translated Dewey's ideas into German and distributed them throughout the American zone.[4]

Although it was not apparent at first, this American reform effort ultimately fell on deaf ears. Stunned by defeat and initially deferential, German educational authorities worked alongside the newly arrived Americans to stem the effects of widespread physical destruction and social chaos. E&RA officials searched for trustworthy Germans to help with denazification; with help from the U.S. Army's military government teams, they vetted teachers, school administrators, and education ministries. They also located emergency buildings to replace damaged or destroyed schools. Alerted during wartime to the pervasiveness of Nazi ideology in schoolbooks, they replaced them with Weimar-era reprints. OMGUS leaders viewed the problem of education in the simplest terms in 1945: Get the children off the streets. The E&RA staff comprised only a dozen officials in 1945, the most senior of whom was only a captain. That they accomplished anything during the chaos of defeat was little short of miraculous. Their lack of early commitment to specific changes at war's end ensured that American reform proposals were not discussed until 1946–7.

As much as the chaos would allow, education had to resume in accordance with the normal rhythm of the school year. Consequently, elementary schools reopened in September 1945, secondary schools in November, and the universities sporadically throughout that autumn and winter. Significantly, the reopenings took place along traditional structural lines. The multitrack system remained solidly in place, and the

---

[3] Ibid., 17–23, 29–39.

[4] See Wade Jacoby, "The Politics of Institutional Transfer: Two Postwar Reconstructions in Germany, 1945–1995," (Ph.D. diss., Duke University, 1996), 156–7.

institutional features of the schools through-out the American zone paralleled those of the Weimar Republic. This held true for all states (*Länder*) in the American zone: Bavaria, Hesse, Baden and Württemberg, Bremen, and the American sector of Berlin. However, if the Americans had been prepared to impose signif-icant structural changes in Germany, then they could have justified merging the schools as a way of achieving savings in plant, tuition, texts, and teacher training amid the shortages in these ar-eas after the war. That window of opportunity closed in fall 1945, never to reopen.[5]

If little planning had occurred for elementary and secondary education, none had occurred for the universities. By happy coincidence, Edward Y. Hartshorne, a Harvard sociologist and prewar expert on German universities un-der National Socialism, entered Germany in 1945 with psychological-warfare experts from Supreme Headquarters, Allied Expeditionary Force (SHAEF). A chance meeting with old ac-quaintances at the University of Marburg con-vinced him that the army was likely to close the universities for two years. On his own ini-tiative, Hartshorne transferred to the nascent E&RA staff and established the procedures and directives for a rapid reopening of the univer-sities. Because of his efforts, the universities in the American zone established their own com-mittees to draw up new constitutions and to denazify faculties, staff, and curricula. For hu-manitarian reasons, the American authorities re-opened the Medical School at Heidelberg in August 1945 to accelerate training of physicians. Hartshorne used this as an opportunity to re-vive the other faculties. Nevertheless, despite his initiatives, the universities reopened largely along pre-1933 lines. Hartshorne's directives ac-centuated student governance, introduced new learning materials and international contacts, produced interzonal university forums, and at-tracted émigré scholars back to Germany. How-ever, his was almost a one-man crusade, and his untimely death in August 1946 removed the only influential American voice in German

university affairs. American policymaking re-turned to dormancy again at OMGUS head-quarters.[6]

A "ONE BEST SYSTEM" MENTALITY

As the educational systems began functioning along older lines, E&RA strength rose to forty officials by mid-1946. Because of its lowly sta-tus within the military government, E&RA was unable to attract a prominent American educa-tion expert to lead it. Military Governor Lucius D. Clay was, therefore, forced to appoint his un-known section chief, John W. Taylor, who had a doctorate in education from Columbia Teach-ers College. Taylor then enlisted his old mentor, Richard Thomas Alexander, as his adviser. Both were well acquainted with prewar German ed-ucation. An outspoken critic of the traditional multitrack system, Alexander enlisted German reformers, such as the Prussian education expert Erich Hylla, in his cause. Paramount in Alexan-der's thinking was the need to create six-year *Volksschulen*, or common schools, with a max-imum of educational opportunity for school-age children of all classes. In his view, the elite *Gymnasien* were antidemocratic and had to be abolished.[7]

Alexander was hardly alone in his rejection of the multitrack system. There had long been a reform tradition in Germany that aimed at altering the elementary/secondary system to al-low gifted pupils of any social class to transfer more easily from one school to another. The So-cial Democratic Party (*Sozialdemokratische Partei Deutschlands*, or SPD) naturally had endorsed this distinctive reform tradition, though it

[5] Ibid., 182.

[6] See James F. Tent, "Denazification in the Ameri-can Zone: E. Y. Hartshorne and the Cleansing of the German Universities," in Werner F. Ebke and Detlev F. Vagts, eds., *Democracy, Market Economy, and the Law* (Heidelberg, 1995), 157–76.

[7] See Thomas Alexander and Beryl Parker, *The New Education in the German Republic* (New York, 1929), 368–72. This was Alexander's only published statement about German elementary and secondary education. He issued no further publications on the subject either during or after the occupation.

conceded that educational systems must recognize differences of ability as part of human nature. In any event, the Social Democrats were distracted by more immediate needs in the postwar years, when entire industries lay crushed, unemployment was rampant, and misery among the working classes was universal. The urge for educational restructuring was far less noticeable in the Christian Democratic Union (*Christlich-Demokratische Union*, or CDU), although some groups within it also wanted a more flexible system. What is significant is the fact that neither Taylor nor Alexander targeted German political allies in their quest for educational reform. Instead, they ignored party politics and chose their counterparts in Germany, the school administrators, as their negotiating partners. Internal discussions between these two groups of professional colleagues would decide the issue – or so the Americans thought.

As an American Southerner, General Clay despised the notion of carpetbaggers. He, therefore, encouraged the rapid reestablishment of local and regional government in the American zone and intended to downsize OMGUS as soon as possible in favor of indigenous German bureaucracies. Such a position naturally militated against ambitious plans for changes by a foreign occupation force.

External to Clay's considerations was an event that took place halfway around the globe. With the cooperation of General Douglas MacArthur in Tokyo, a U.S. education mission visited Japan and issued an ambitious plan for educational reform. Always interested in what MacArthur was doing, Clay accepted a similar mission to Germany in 1946. It called for a radical reordering of German schools. Echoing Dewey's ideas, the plan called for the establishment of six-year elementary schools. Secondary schools would be under the same roof but would have three tracks. Because the members of the education mission were also school administrators, led by Dr. George F. Zook, the main features of the plan resembled the American system. Clay accepted the "Zook Report" uncritically; in a circular of January 10, 1947, addressed to each *Land*, he called for six-year elementary schools and multifaceted secondary schools, preferably under one roof. In addition, the Zook Report demanded that tuition and textbooks should be free and that all teachers, both elementary and secondary, should receive university-level training. Children of all classes would receive education equal to their abilities. Public education would be truly free, and all teachers would receive training of uniform quality.[8]

Simultaneously, Taylor and Alexander toured the American zone, urging the cultural ministries of each *Land* to submit concrete plans that included the same reforms. Thus prodded, the respective cultural ministries submitted various plans in October 1947. Greater Hesse and Bremen Enclave came closest to accepting the American goals, Württemberg-Baden far less so, and Bavaria not at all. The reason for the latter's intransigence was no mystery. Bavaria's minister for education and the arts (*Kultusminister*), Alois Hundhammer, was a highly conservative official in the Bavarian affiliate of the CDU, the Christian Social Union (*Christlich-Soziale Union*, or CSU), and he did not hesitate to condemn the Americans' reform plans. Incarcerated briefly by the Nazis in 1933 for his political views, Hundhammer held impeccable anti-Nazi credentials in 1945 and was a powerful political force in postwar Bavaria. Moreover, he represented an influential segment of German public opinion that categorically rejected American school reforms. Convinced that humans possess differing levels of ability, the mainstream CDU/CSU, the Catholic Church, and the Protestant Church concluded that one-track school systems lowered educational standards. Arguments about democratization carried no weight with them. No longer as acquiescent as in the period immediately following Germany's defeat, they began to fight tenaciously against American educational reform proposals. Because of Hundhammer's unassailable position in the CSU, he became the central figure in the campaign to derail American reform proposals.

Encouraged by Hundhammer's intransigence, other *Land* ministries took heart and

[8] See Jacoby, "Politics of Institutional Transfer," 184–6.

began to alter or rescind reform proposals made earlier that year. Officials like Bremen senator Christian Paulmann or Hessian Kultusminister Erwin Stein distanced themselves from Clay's reforms. Faced with this declining support, American E&RA officials, most notably R. T. Alexander (Taylor had already left OMGUS), held fast to their position and demanded compliance with American reform proposals.

By 1948, weaknesses in the E&RA organization had become apparent. Although knowledgeable about German education, Alexander was the most influential figure at E&RA headquarters only by default. He certainly was not the ideal figure to negotiate the increasingly politicized issues of school reform. Harboring unfortunate prejudices against Bavaria and the Roman Catholic Church, Alexander chose a former priest, Charles Falk, to be the chief American negotiator in talks with the feisty Dr. Hundhammer over school reform. Falk's past effectively undermined the American negotiating position. Within a short time, Hundhammer also acquired a powerful new ally against American school reform efforts: Cardinal Faulhaber of Bavaria.

As attitudes hardened in 1948, Hundhammer finally asked his American opposites if they were merely suggesting school reforms or ordering them. The reply was that OMGUS expected compliance. "Ah," Hundhammer replied, "I am a soldier. I know how to take orders."[9] He promptly introduced a school reform bill into the Bavarian Landtag that reflected all that Alexander had been demanding. Hundhammer then launched a skilled public-relations campaign to defeat the very bill he had just introduced. Having made no effort to court political allies, the American negotiators faced an impossible political situation.[10]

Stung by this impending public-relations disaster, Clay effected a face-saving compromise with Bavaria's minister president, CSU leader Hans Ehard. In exchange for the Americans' agreement to drop their plans for school restructuring, the more moderate Ehard acceded to a bill eliminating tuition and textbook fees for pupils. Multitrack education in the fourth school year remained in place, as did the *Gymnasien*. Taking their lead from Bavaria, the other *Länder* backpedaled. When the Federal Republic of Germany came into existence in 1949, school restructuring was a dead issue. French and British authorities had never attempted a radical restructuring, and the Soviet zone remained isolated. As a result, the school systems in the West German *Länder* standardized their features to accommodate national school norms.[11]

Discredited, Alexander left the military government in September 1948. His replacements were Indiana University president Herman Wells, who became Clay's cultural adviser, and Alonzo Grace, a school administrator from Connecticut. Simultaneously, E&RA was upgraded to the Education and Cultural Relations Division at OMGUS. Wells's appointment was especially significant: He was one of the most celebrated educational administrators of his generation.

FROM REEDUCATION TO REORIENTATION

Wells and Grace abandoned school restructuring and concentrated on more positive "reorientation" programs that reflected the reconstructionist policy America began to adopt toward Germany amid the onset of the Cold War and the Marshall Plan. New programs included "visiting experts" from the United States to advise at all levels of education. Some of those experts were school administrators and continued without success to advocate American models. Others, however, including celebrated German émigrés such as Sigmund Neumann and noted American educators such as University of Chicago president Robert Hutchins, exercised considerable influence at the universities. Wells also encouraged American public and private funding to provide much-needed

---

[9] See Tent, *Mission on the Rhine*, 142.
[10] Ibid., 110–63.

[11] Ibid., 164–253.

international scholarly holdings in public and university libraries. Even more influential was a highly popular cultural exchange program designed to bring Germans with leadership potential to the United States to observe democracy firsthand. Starting in 1948, when German resources could not support such undertakings, thousands of young Germans traveled abroad at American expense. No reliable figures on the effectiveness of the cultural-exchange programs exist. However, they helped end the German cultural isolation that had prevailed since 1933.[12] One beneficiary of the cultural exchanges was an impoverished law student from Berlin's Free University who studied at the University of Wisconsin. Ernst Benda eventually rose to the rank of minister of the interior for the Federal Republic in 1968–9 and ended his distinguished career as president of the Constitutional Court.

State Department officials had announced in 1945 that reforms, if they were to last, must come from German initiatives. That maxim proved itself in Berlin in 1948 when German students responded to Communist control of the old Berlin University by creating their own university. American authorities made common cause with the students, providing financial resources and the protection of a great power. The result was the Free University of Berlin, which became a new type of university and demonstrated positive results in an area where Americans had had little success since the loss of E. Y. Hartshorne in 1946. The Free University won a reputation as a reform university with strong student self-governance and an openness to new academic disciplines. American public and private organizations such as the Ford Foundation continued to nurture the Free University during its first decades until German resources could mobilize adequate support. In fact, American public and private resources continued to fund a wide variety of German educational institutions after the occupation years, phasing out only as the fruits of Germany's economic miracle permitted funding from indigenous sources.[13]

At times, other trends in American higher education produced equally unintended consequences in Germany. In the late 1950s and early 1960s, student activism began in modest fashion, taking as a point of departure the Beat Generation's revolt against social conformity. The activists soon moved on to antinuclear protests that merged into demonstrations against the U.S. Congress's controversial House Committee on Un-American Activities. The trend gathered momentum with the Berkeley free-speech movement, then moved on to the much larger civil rights movement, and culminated in mass student protests against the Vietnam War. This activist fever spread quickly to German universities, where the baby-boom generation was already inclined toward major social and political change.

Starting in 1965 at the Free University of Berlin, pioneering student protesters within the student government (*Allgemeiner Studentenausschuss*, *AStA*) and the Socialist German Students' Organization (*Sozialistischer Deutscher Studentenbund*, or SDS) began organized protests over a wide variety of issues, including free speech. The activism of students such as Wolfgang Lèfevre and Ekkehart Krippendorff generated violent protests against an unwritten ban on the teaching of Marxist theories. But they were only part of a larger revolt by West Germany's youth against what was seen to be a stuffy, self-satisfied, and hypocritical older generation. The stage was set for a profound generational conflict. The ripple effect of the "sixty-eighters" in German society was felt for decades. It produced demands for an unvarnished examination of the National Socialist era in secondary-school curricula; for school reorganization and the creation of comprehensive schools (*Gesamtschulen*); for greater citizen political participation through class-action suits, public resolutions, and voter propositions; and for far greater attention to

---

[12] On the origins of cultural exchanges, see Henry J. Kellermann, *Cultural Relations as an Instrument of U.S. Foreign Policy: The Educational Exchange Program Between the United States and Germany* (Washington, D.C., 1978). On reorientation programs in general, see Tent, *Mission on the Rhine*, chap. 6.

[13] See James F. Tent, *The Free University of Berlin: A Political History* (Bloomington, Ind., 1988), chaps. 1–3.

environmental issues. The latter offshoot led directly to the founding of the environmentalist Green Party. Although German activism had parted company with the American initiatives of the 1960s, no one doubted that those same initiatives had exerted a strong influence on their German counterparts.[14]

CONCLUSION

On balance, direct American influences on the German educational system after World War II were limited. By failing to assess German reform traditions adequately, by not installing a knowledgeable bureaucracy in a timely fashion, and by allowing the reopening of existing educational structures in 1945, OMGUS lost its best chance at instituting reforms. By treating ambitious school restructuring as an internal issue for professional educational administrators, the Americans placed themselves in a vulnerable position. German politicians, led by Alois Hundhammer, chose to fight them in the court of public opinion, a court reopened by the Americans once they decided on an early reactivation of local government and local elections.

[14] For a detailed documentation of the student protests in Berlin, see Tilman Fichter and Siegwart Lönnendonker, eds., *Freie Universität Dokumentation*, vols. 1–4 (Berlin, 1973–83); Uwe Schlicht, *Vom Burschenschafter bis zum Sponti: Studentische Opposition gestern und heute* (Berlin, 1980); see also Tent, *Free University of Berlin*, 286–335.

However, by recognizing in 1948 that long-lasting reforms would have to come from German initiatives, the Americans recorded some significant gains. Although exact measurements are lacking, American cultural-exchange programs undoubtedly had some impact on the thinking of the next generation of German political and educational leadership. American officials wielded some local influence by supporting Berlin students in their efforts to found a university with strong student governance, although that experiment was not typical for Germany as a whole.

Other forces, therefore, may have played a more profound role in influencing German education than efforts specifically directed at institutional changes. The increasing pervasiveness of American popular culture and the dramatic increase of English as a global language continue to have an impact that no one in the postwar years could have foreseen. The cultural exchanges of the 1940s and 1950s later led to tens of thousands of German high-school pupils annually attending American high schools during their eleventh school year in order to consolidate their English language proficiency. Finally, student activism by the baby boomers in both countries generated profound generational conflict and initiated major changes in social attitudes that mirrored the aims of the sixty-eighters. These dimensions are essential to understanding the American influence on German education not only during the occupation period but also in the following decades.

CHAPTER THREE

American Cultural Policy in the Federal Republic of Germany, 1949–1968

Jessica C. E. Gienow-Hecht

Translation by Robert Kimber and Rita Kimber

The United States never pursued a cultural policy in Germany simply for its own sake.[1] Rather, its efforts in this area were, from the outset, a reaction against the propaganda of the Third Reich and, later, the German Democratic Republic (GDR) and Soviet Union.[2] Already during the final phase of World War II, Anglo-American military forces began informing their enemies about American culture as part of their psychological-warfare offensive to correct misconceptions that prevailed in the Third Reich.[3] This idea of "setting the record straight" formed the underlying basis for the reeducation program pursued by American occupation forces after 1945 in Germany and remained central to U.S. cultural policy. This chapter focuses on cultural policy planning in Washington and how it was implemented, taking the Amerika-Häuser and media policy as examples.[4]

PLANNING IN WASHINGTON

The reeducation program of the postwar period was initially planned as only a temporary measure during the War Department-run military occupation. However, it was not only because of the anti-American propaganda that the Socialist Unity Party (SED) began disseminating in 1946 and the Berlin Blockade but also American uncertainty about the viability of democracy in West Germany that resulted in the creation of a permanent cultural program controlled by the U.S. State Department.[5] Aimed at providing Germany and the world with a "full and fair picture" of the United States, the Smith-Mund Act of 1948 enabled the administration to implement a worldwide, peacetime cultural and information program. This law authorized creation of an overseas information service and an exchange service.

The budget approved by Congress in 1949 set out the goals of U.S. cultural policy: to counter propaganda from both the Left and the Right, to explain U.S. policy, and to create better understanding between the United States and the

[1] I thank Hans Tuch, Frank Trommler, Maritta Hein-Kremer, Christiane Eisenberg, Arpád von Klimó, Georg Goes, Karsten Timmer, Henrike Fehsenfeld, and Heiko Hecht for their comments on this study.
[2] For background, see Emily Rosenberg, *Spreading the American Dream: American Economic and Cultural Expansion, 1890–1945* (New York, 1982); J. Manuel Espinosa, *Inter-American Beginnings of U.S. Cultural Diplomacy, 1936–1948* (Washington, D.C., 1976).
[3] The constant use of terms such as "truth" and "facts," "objectivity" and "factual" document how intent the American planners were on portraying only "the truth" and on disassociating themselves from the propaganda of the Third Reich.
[4] On cultural political influence, see the chapters by James F. Tent, Uta Poiger, Karl-Heinz Füssl, Martin

Meyer, Edward Larkey, Daniel J. Leab, Andreas Höfele, and Werner Durth in this section; see also the chapter by Willi Paul Adams, vol. 2, Culture.
[5] Gary E. Kraske, *Missionaries of the Book: The American Library Profession and the Origins of United States Cultural Diplomacy* (Westport, Conn., 1985), 225–6.

Federal Republic.[6] A "truth campaign" developed in 1950 in response to the invasion of South Korea laid the ground for a psychological offensive against the Soviet Union. This campaign targeted opinion makers such as journalists and politicians, and its organizers selected exhibitions and programs on the basis of how effectively they could represent the "American way of life" to audiences abroad. The State Department distributed, for example, about two million copies of American literary classics in translation overseas.[7] These efforts served the project of democratic reeducation in Germany, but they were also a response to similar initiatives that had cropped up in the GDR and the Soviet Union, where culture and education served as major vehicles for communist propaganda.[8]

Whereas education and exchange remained the responsibility of the State Department, the United States Information Agency (USIA), under the direction of Theodor Streibert, took over information policy in August 1953. Implementation of the agency's programs abroad fell to the United States Information Service (USIS).[9] From Washington's point of view,

the mission of the USIA was to convince other countries that the policies of the United States promoted freedom, progress, and peace across the globe.[10] Consequently, the USIA programs focused on topics that American strategists thought were not only characteristic of the United States but would also waken the empathy and sympathies of foreign audiences. Freedom, tolerance, and individualism were, according to the USIA, Americans' most important ideals. Stressing America's high standard of living, bountiful range of consumer goods, and the advantages of a market economy, the USIA programs painted a picture of a country that promised progress and prosperity for everyone. The USIA's foreign audiences in the 1950s learned less, however, about the other side of America: its racism, economic inequality, and crime rate.[11]

The 1950s were important for the development of American cultural policy in Germany: An official cultural program was established during these years,[12] although its operation initially remained somewhat erratic. The goals pursued through its information and propaganda

[6] Henry J. Kellermann, *Cultural Relations as an Instrument of U.S. Foreign Policy: The Educational Exchange Program Between the United States and Germany* (Washington, D.C., 1978), 83; John W. Henderson, *The United States Information Agency* (Washington, D.C., 1969), 64–5.

[7] Howland H. Sargeant, "Information and Cultural Representation Overseas," in the American Assembly Graduate School of Business, ed., *The Representation of the United States Abroad* (New York, 1956), 73–4; Hansjörg Gehring, *Amerikanische Literaturpolitik in Deutschland 1945–1953: Ein Aspekt des Re-Education-Programms* (Stuttgart, 1976), 93, 112; Shawn J. Parry-Giles, "Exporting America's Cold War Message: The Debate over America's First Peacetime Propaganda Program, 1947–1953," (Ph.D. diss., University of Indiana, 1992).

[8] D. G. White, *U.S. Military Government in Germany: Radio Reorientation* (Karlsruhe, 1950), 114–7; Peter Grothe, *To Win the Minds of Men: The Story of the Communist Propaganda War in East Germany* (Palo Alto, Calif., 1958), 123–47; Charles A. Thomson and Walter H. C. Laves, *Cultural Relations and U.S. Foreign Policy* (Bloomington, Ind., 1963), 126–9.

[9] In addition, Eisenhower's President's Emergency Fund for Participation in International Affairs made

available $5 million annually from 1954 on to support the overseas tours of about 60 musical and theatrical programs. Thomas Klöckner, *Public Diplomacy: Auswärtige Informations- und Kulturpolitik der USA: Strukturanalyse der Organisation und Strategien der United States Information Agency und des United States Information Service in Deutschland* (Baden-Baden, 1993), 82–9; Thomas C. Sorensen, *The Word War: The Story of American Propaganda* (New York, 1968), 47; Hans Tuch, *Communicating with the World: U.S. Diplomacy Overseas* (New York, 1990), 14–21. See also John Harper Taylor, "Ambassadors of the Arts: An Analysis of the Eisenhower Administration's Incorporation of 'Porgy and Bess' into Its Cold War Foreign Policy," (Ph.D. diss., Ohio State University, 1994).

[10] Klöckner, *Public Diplomacy*, 82–9; Sorensen, *Word War*, 47.

[11] See Laura A. Belmonte, "Defending a Way of Life: American Propaganda and the Cold War," (Ph.D. diss., University of Virginia, 1996); Walter A. Hixson, *Parting the Curtain: American Propaganda in the Era of the Cold War* (New York, 1997).

[12] Randolph Wieck, *Ignorance Abroad: American Educational and Cultural Foreign Policy and the Office of Assistant Secretary of State* (Westport, Conn., 1992), 18–20.

offerings shifted frequently, and vacillating congressional support made it difficult to formulate consistent, long-term policy. Officials responsible for cultural affairs were constantly obliged to redefine their goals and defend their programs against budget cuts and political enemies, especially in Congress. Moreover, experts disagreed about how the United States should present itself overseas. Should the country's social problems be addressed or should only its positive side be portrayed? Toward the end of the 1950s, some noted intellectuals and political observers criticized government cultural policy, charging that the government's programs presented an unfavorable picture of the United States and were not active enough in promoting cultural activities abroad.[13]

These discussions led to a reorientation of American overseas cultural policy in the 1960s. Long-term plans for cultivating international understanding through education replaced short-lived informational programs. Measures in West Germany included greater emphasis on instruction in English and, in 1961, an expansion of the Fulbright Program.[14] The Kennedy era saw the USIA also become more strongly identified with the administration and its political goals. The USIA's mission was no longer limited to the dissemination of information but was now officially declared to be "influencing" public opinion overseas. Kennedy wanted to develop close cooperation with the USIA, which was to advise the administration in planning ways of influencing public opinion abroad. According to former USIA employees, however, cooperation of this sort rarely occurred.[15]

IMPLEMENTATION IN GERMANY

Three factors shaped U.S. cultural policy in West Germany: a genuine commitment to reconstructing a democratic society, the Cold War and the division of Germany, and the interaction between Germans and Americans. The thousands of Americans who aided in the reconstruction of Germany and the many Germans who, in the first two decades after the founding of the Federal Republic, traveled to the United States established a network of German-American contacts. Antitotalitarianism and the democratization of Germany, promotion of the Western alliance, and the confrontation with communism determined the rhetoric of the program.

The Federal Republic was both a model and an exception in American cultural policy abroad. On the one hand, the intentions of American cultural strategists were clearer in Germany than in any other country. On the other hand, as a victor in World War II, the United States wielded more authority in the sections of West Germany and West Berlin under its administration than in any other country, with the possible exception of Japan. Nowhere else was the United States determined to bring about such profound changes as in Germany. Nowhere else did the United States invest as much money in its cultural programs. The Federal Republic received a fully developed program, specifically tailored to its needs – as determined by the Americans – that included numerous exhibits, concerts, and theater performances. In addition, up to 1952, the U.S. government even made DM 52.7 million available to German institutions outside the territory administered by the U.S. High Commission in Germany (HICOG) for educational purposes.[16]

Over and above these official measures, Washington's cultural emissaries displayed a personal interest that went far beyond professional

---

[13] John Boardman Whitton, ed., *Propaganda and the Cold War: A Princeton University Symposium* (Washington, D.C., 1963); W. Phillips Davison, *International Political Communication* (New York, 1965), 3–10; Franz M. Joseph and Raymond Aron, eds., *As Others See Us: The United States Through Foreign Eyes* (Princeton, N.J., 1959); William J. Lederer, *The Ugly American* (New York, 1958).

[14] See the chapter by Karl-Heinz Füssl in this section.

[15] Manuela Aguilar, *Cultural Diplomacy and Foreign Policy: German-American Relations, 1955–1968* (New York, 1996), 118.

[16] See Dewey A. Browder, *Americans in Post-World War II Germany: Teachers, Tinkers, Neighbors and Nuisances* (Lewiston, N.Y., 1998).

obligation and duty. This kind of commitment was evident not only among the numerous emigrants who returned to Germany from the United States to help with reconstruction but also among many other American officials. Moreover, numerous individual American citizens and independent organizations contributed to the rebuilding effort on a voluntary basis. American military authorities and the High Commission were dependent on private organizations such as women's clubs and unions, particularly in the first postwar decades. Between 1948 and 1954, roughly 11,000 German high school and university students, professors, and professionals visited the United States. During the same period, about 1,600 American consultants and lecturers traveled to the Federal Republic, where they worked in the fields of education, health care, welfare services, and municipal government. These programs were often funded by HICOG but sometimes in part by private sources as well. All of these efforts contributed to conveying a sense of American values.[17]

Just as German-American relations evolved from being unilateral to bilateral, so American cultural policy came to reflect the transition of West Germany and West Berlin from a defeated and occupied country into an independent republic. These changes could be seen in a series of agreements for cultural exchanges and transatlantic visits.[18]

With the end of the HICOG period in 1955, bilateral cultural relations replaced what had been a unilateral American program in Germany. The founding of the Federal Republic as an ally made the United States' one-sided financial support for a cultural program seem unnecessary, and American cultural policy consequently became less important. America's

attention was now also gradually focusing more on the Third World.[19] In response to German requests, some of the American cultural programs continued, including the Amerika-Häuser. On the whole, however, Germany began to assume a larger role in the two-way cultural exchange with the United States.

AMERIKA-HÄUSER

When a reading room originally set up in Bad Homburg by the Psychological Warfare Division was relocated to Frankfurt am Main in 1946, the first fully equipped Amerika-Haus in Germany was launched. A little less than five years later, twenty seven Amerika-Häuser had been established in West German cities and Berlin, along with 135 affiliated reading rooms in smaller towns. The Amerika-Häuser had reading rooms and offered art exhibits, films, concerts, lectures, conferences, American studies seminars, language courses in English, theatrical productions, discussions, films for children, special women's programs, and meetings for parents. A range of interest groups and opinion makers took advantage of these offerings.[20] The libraries played a particularly important role by supplying books that had been banned in the Third Reich or that offered a complex and varied picture of the United States. Library visitors had access to works, in both English and German translation, in fields such as contemporary literature, politics, psychology, education,

---

[17] See the chapter by Karl-Heinz Füssl in this section.

[18] Wolfgang Dexheimer, "Die deutsch-amerikanischen Kulturbeziehungen seit den zwanziger Jahren," in Kurt Düwell and Werner Link, eds., *Deutsche auswärtige Kulturpolitik seit 1871* (Cologne, 1981), 140; William J. Weissman, *Kultur- und Informationsaktivitäten der USA in der Bundesrepublik während der Amtszeiten Carter und Reagan* (Pfaffenweiler, 1990), 63.

[19] Philip H. Coombs, *The Fourth Dimension of Foreign Policy: Educational and Cultural Affairs* (New York, 1964), 101–2; Aguilar, *Cultural Diplomacy*, 127.

[20] Karl-Ernst Bugenstab, "Entstehung, Bedeutungs- und Funktionswandel der Amerika Häuser: Ein Beitrag zur Geschichte der amerikanischen Auslandsinformation nach dem 2. Weltkrieg," *Jahrbuch für Amerikastudien* 16 (1971): 189–203; Maritta Hein-Kremer, *Die amerikanische Kulturoffensive 1945–1955: Gründung und Entwicklung der amerikanischen Information Centers in Westdeutschland und Westberlin 1945–1955* (Cologne, 1996), 198–241; Axel Schildt, "Die USA als 'Kulturnation': Zur Bedeutung der Amerikahäuser in den 1950er Jahren," in Alf Lüdtke, Inge Marssolek, and Adelheid von Saldern, eds., *Amerikanisierung: Traum und Alptraum in Deutschland des 20. Jahrhunderts* (Stuttgart, 1996).

art, economics, and history. Acquisitions were funded in part by private donations from the United States.

This book program in fact precipitated a major crisis for the Amerika-Häuser in 1953. In connection with its "campaign for truth," the U.S. government had internally redesignated the Amerika-Häuser as information centers and integrated them more closely into its political propaganda activities. This shift caught the attention of the interest of Senator Joseph McCarthy, who claimed that seventy-five of the authors represented all over the world through the information centers were known to be procommunist agitators. A directive in February 1953 banned all works by communists and communist sympathizers from American libraries in Germany. That same year, McCarthy dispatched his two staffers, Roy Cohn and Gerard D. Schine, to inspect Amerika-Häuser in Germany. As a result of their tour, J. M. Franckenstein, director of the American news service, and Theodore Kaghan, the deputy director of the Public Affairs Office, were both fired. In addition, Cohn and Schine determined that 30,000 books contained communist material. Their visit created mistrust among German observers and fear among Amerika-Haus employees. Some USIS employees removed standard works of American literature, culture, and history from the bookshelves, among them the work of John Dos Passos, Reinhold Niebuhr, and Frank Lloyd Wright. There were even reports of book burnings at two centers.[21]

Despite this unhappy interlude, the growing partnership between the United States and the Federal Republic resulted in a new Amerika-Haus policy after the HICOG period ended. The goal of this policy was to promote a German-American dialogue that would not shy away from controversial subjects. As German public libraries and adult-education institutions resumed their work, HICOG began cutting back on the number of Amerika-Häuser after

1951. The cutbacks eliminated independent orchestras and theater troupes from the program, and a diplomatic agreement between the United States and the Federal Republic transformed the Amerika-Häuser in Darmstadt, Mannheim, Marburg, Regensburg, and Tübingen into German-American institutes.[22]

MEDIA

Once all restrictions on German publishing houses were lifted after 1949, U.S. officials attempted to use the news service "Amerika-Dienst" to inject American cultural content into the German media. German publishers could reprint articles at no cost from more than one hundred American magazines, including *The Atlantic Monthly, The Saturday Evening Post*, and *The New York Times Magazine*. The Book Translating Unit, originally part of the military government, had translated more than 340 American books into German by March 1953. A monthly information bulletin, *Bücher aus Amerika*, gave advice regarding translation rights to German publishers and made suggestions for publications. Interested publishers received large shipments of paper for their editions, which the American authorities then bought up at a discount for distribution among the German reading public. Until 1950, German publishers imported about 800,000 volumes per year and by 1970 that number had risen into the millions.[23]

Even though German publishers no longer needed a special license to operate, HICOG continued to issue its own publications, among them *Die Neue Zeitung*, which appeared throughout the Federal Republic until 1953 and in Berlin until 1955. Its purpose was to offer

[21] Sorensen, *Word War*, 35; Gehring, *Amerikanische Literaturpolitik*, 94–101; Marion Gräfin Dönhoff, *Amerikanische Wechselbäder: Beobachtungen und Kommentare aus vier Jahrzehnten* (Stuttgart, 1983), 37–40.

[22] Thomas Pilz, ed., *Zweihundert Jahre deutsch-amerikanische Beziehungen 1776–1976* (Munich, 1975), 106; Manfred Strack, "Amerikanische Kulturbeziehungen zu (West-) Deutschland 1945–1955," *Zeitschrift für Kulturaustausch* 37, no. 1 (1987): 290–1.

[23] Daniel Haufler, "Amerika, Du hast es besser? Zur deutschen Buchkultur nach 1945," in Konrad H. Jarausch and Hannes Siegrist, eds., *Amerikanisierung und Sovjetisierung in Deutschland 1945–1970* (Frankfurt am Main, 1996), 387–408.

insight into American perspectives, culture, and politics. Edited by returned Jewish emigrants, *Die Neue Zeitung* became an important forum for German intellectuals debating the future of German culture. The sophisticated journal *Der Monat*, under the anticommunist editorship of Melvyn Laski from 1948 to 1955, assumed an equally significant role. Through contributions from well-known intellectuals, it formed a kind of "cultural airlift" between European and American culture.[24]

In radio broadcasting, the American authorities continued to act as programming advisers for a long time as well. By 1956, they had seen to it that individual stations were organized as public broadcasters limited to particular regions. The members of broadcasters' boards of directors were encouraged to take courses in "democratic radio management." In summer 1952, the Federal Republic and the United States had also signed an agreement on the operation of independent American radio stations within Germany. The Americans hoped to use these stations to extend the reach of their information programs into the German Democratic Republic and other Eastern bloc countries. American Forces Network (AFN), the English-language broadcaster created to entertain American forces in Germany, attracted a large audience among German listeners with its music programming. The German-language station Radio in the American Sector (RIAS), established in 1946, provided the population of Berlin and the Soviet occupation zone with music, news, and educational programs centered on political themes. Until the end of the 1960s, the U.S. government provided financial support for RIAS, whose German staff had ever-increasing responsibility.[25] The American authorities provided German schools with radios so that school children would get some exposure to American programs. As late as the early 1960s, about 60 percent of all schools in the former American occupation zone still included American radio shows in their curriculum.[26]

CONCLUSION

American cultural policy in Germany from 1949 onward operated with the principle of "assist and advise." American cultural officials did not seek to impose their ideas with a heavy hand but instead preferred to take the role of observers and consultants. As the example of the Amerika-Häuser demonstrates, American policy did not reach out to the population at large, but relied on the multiplier effect: It targeted key individuals who, it was hoped, would absorb the offerings and then pass on to a broader public what they had learned. American cultural strategists expanded their initial focus on antitotalitarian programs into a long-term policy for education and international understanding. A point worth noting here is that up to the end of the 1960s, American cultural programs consisted primarily of offerings from the domain of high, not popular culture; they sought to demonstrate to the Germans and Europeans that the United States was their cultural equal.

The major problem that American cultural policy in Germany encountered originated not in Germany but in Washington, where the USIA came under constant pressure to justify its existence. Because it did not operate within the United States, the USIA lacked a lobby to speak on its behalf in congressional budget debates. Moreover, the government in the United States

[24] Jessica C. E. Gienow-Hecht, *Transmission Impossible: American Journalism as Cultural Diplomacy in Postwar Germany, 1945–1955* (Baton Rouge, La., 1999); Kenan Holger Irmak, "Die westdeutsche Nachkriegsgesellschaft im Spiegel der Zeitschrift 'Der Monat' 1948–1955" (M.A. thesis, University of Marburg, 1993), 19.

[25] Ralph Willett, "America in Germany: The Post-War Period," *Contributions to American Studies* 18 (1990):

236–49; Herbert Kundler, *Rias Berlin: Eine Radio-Station in einer geteilten Stadt* (Berlin, 1994).

[26] Apart from pursuing their educational goals, the various American radio stations exercised an influence on the development of musical culture in the postwar period that can hardly be overestimated. Hermann Glaser, "1945 – Cultural Beginnings: Continuity and Discontinuity," in Reiner Pommerin, ed., *Culture in the Federal Republic of Germany, 1945–1995* (Oxford, 1996), 26–7.

had a long-standing tradition of not supporting cultural activities financially. In a certain sense, the internal contradiction that plagued American cultural diplomacy was that its mission was to combat precisely something that it was producing itself – namely, government-controlled culture.[27] Thus, Joseph McCarthy's relentless attacks on the State Department and American information campaigns abroad were really no more than extreme expressions of a widely held attitude.

Furthermore, USIA officials found it difficult to agree on a canon of values and characteristics that was representative of the American way of life. Their internal conflicts reflected the diversity of American life and culture, but they failed as a concept of diplomacy. The only point of agreement was anticommunism: American culture defined itself by the very values that the Soviet Union rejected. But in taking this position, America's cultural emissaries locked themselves into a negative view of their opponent that, in the eyes of some USIA staffers, seriously limited the flexibility of their program.[28]

Gauging the success of American cultural policy in Germany will need to assume a different form than the present study. Here we can ask, however, what American planners knew about German responses to their programs. Best documented so far are German assessments of the Amerika-Häuser, which "probably attracted the attention of more serious-minded Germans than any other single undertaking."[29] In 1954, about half the German population was familiar with Amerika-Häuser and, of that group, about 84 percent knew in detail what the Amerika-Häuser offered. When the U.S. government radically reduced the number of Amerika-Häuser

in 1951, the German population registered a strong protest.[30]

American experts on public opinion were certain that most West Germans held a positive view of the United States during the 1950s. In 1953, about half the visitors to Amerika-Häuser stated that the U.S. information centers had changed their opinion about the American political system; about one-third said the same thing about American culture. In January 1957, 37 percent of all those questioned said that they viewed Americans favorably, whereas seven years later 58 percent felt that way. In this same period, the number of those who admitted to "not liking America" dropped from 24 to 19 percent.[31]

By the end of the 1960s, the cultural honeymoon between the United States and the Federal Republic was over. For many West Germans, especially young ones, the Vietnam War and America's racial problems had undermined America's credibility; they now tended to see the United States as imperialistic and materialistic. "My entire liberal education began in the Amerika-Haus, where I studied the American Declaration of Independence," a young left-liberal German said. "What is happening now is a clear violation of those ideals."[32] This dissociation had an almost emancipatory character: In liberating themselves from their identification with the American model, West Germans asserted their own identity.

PROSPECTS FOR FURTHER RESEARCH

Research on American cultural policy in Germany is still in its early stages, in large part

---

[27] W. Howard Adams, "Public Aid for the Arts: A Change of Heart," in Stephen A. Greyser, ed., *Cultural Policy and Arts Administration* (Cambridge, Mass., 1973), 1–5; Michael Kammen, "Culture and the State in America," *Journal of American History* 83 (1996): 791–814.

[28] Sorensen, *Word War*, 304.

[29] Henry P. Pilgert, *The History of the Development of Information Services Through Information Centers and Documentary Films* (Mehlem, 1951), 5.

[30] Office of the High Commissioner in Germany, "The Amerika Haus Evaluated: A Study of the Effectiveness of the U.S. Information Center in West-Germany," report no. 181 (n.p., July 17, 1953).

[31] Elisabeth Noelle and Peter Neumann, eds., *The Germans: Public Opinion Polls, 1947–1966* (Allensbach, 1967), 543; see the chapter by Knud Krakau, vol. 1, Society.

[32] As quoted in Weissman, *Kultur- und Informationsaktivitäten*, 66.

because many historians still doubt that analysis of culture as an instrument of foreign policy
is a respectable scholarly enterprise. The official
American sources for the 1960s and beyond also
remain in part unavailable; consequently, most
studies have thus far focused primarily on the
period between 1945 and 1955. We still have no
comprehensive study of American cultural policy in Germany after 1955. Declarations about
the goals or the development of programs have
to date attracted more interest than the question of how well those programs were implemented, or what German reactions to them
were. Analyses of this kind still lack a compelling theoretical basis. Advocates of the view
that America engaged in cultural imperialism
claim that after World War II, the United States
attempted – through cultural expansion – to secure for itself the ideological loyalty, markets,
and raw materials of other less aggressive countries.[33] More recent studies dealing with the
influence of American cultural policy abroad
maintain that reactions to it were more nuanced, involving elements of both resistance and
acceptance.[34]

Further questions have surfaced in the field
of social history. Since the fall of the Berlin
Wall, intellectuals on both sides of the Atlantic
have begun to discuss what role cultural influence plays in a society's identity. A comparison of American cultural policy in postwar
Germany and social and cultural change in the
new states of the reunited Germany brings out
not only interesting parallels but also possibilities for developing sound policy and avoiding conflict in the future. Finally, analysis of
German-American cultural relations provides
cultural historians with a vantage point from
which to research American identity. The concept of multiculturalism has replaced the old
synthetic "melting pot" view of American culture. According to this newer concept, no unified American culture exists, only a number
of coexisting, independent cultures. However,
the study of official American cultural policy
shows how American experts, whose primary
task was to scrutinize representations of their
country abroad, also perceived their own culture and wanted others to perceive it. Analysis
of this American self-perception offers a promising entry point for further study of U.S. cultural
diplomacy in Germany.

[33] Wolfgang Kreuter and Joachim Oltmann,
"Coca-Cola statt Apfelmost: Kalter Krieg und Amerika-
nisierung westdeutscher Lebensweise," *Englisch–
Amerikanische Studien* 6 (1984): 22–35; Ralph Willett,
The Americanization of Germany, 1945–1949 (London,
1989).
[34] Rob Kroes, Robert W. Rydell, and Doeko F. J.
Bosscher, eds., *Cultural Transmissions and Receptions:
American Mass Culture in Europe* (Amsterdam, 1993);

Reinhold Wagnleitner, *Coca-Colonization and the Cold
War: The Cultural Mission of the United States in Austria
After the Second World War* (Chapel Hill, N.C., 1994);
Richard Pells, *Not Like Us: How Europeans Have Loved,
Hated, and Transformed American Culture Since World War
II* (New York, 1997).

CHAPTER FOUR

Between Elitism and Educational Reform

German-American Exchange Programs, 1945–1970

Karl-Heinz Füssl

Translated by Sally E. Robertson

Germans and Americans could look back in 1945 to a long tradition of cultural exchange. Germany's intellectual life and renowned universities had drawn nearly 10,000 American students to the country in the second half of the nineteenth century.[1] The German-American exchange of professors between Harvard and Columbia and the Friedrich-Wilhelm University of Berlin from 1904 to the outbreak of World War I was an important element of cultural and educational policy.[2] The exchange of professors attests to the German Empire's rather late start in the field of international cultural and educational policy. At the same time, it illustrates the tendency in the period before World War I to use international academic ties as political instruments for cultural self-representation, active cultural propaganda, and international understanding.[3]

In 1930, the Academic Exchange Service (*Akademische Austauschdienst*, founded 1923–4), the Alexander von Humboldt Foundation (founded 1925), and the German Academic Foreign Office of the Association of German Universities (*Deutsche Akademische Auslandsstelle des Verbandes der deutschen Hochschulen*, founded 1927) united to form the German Academic Exchange Service (*Deutscher Akademischer Austauschdienst*, or DAAD). Together with the Institute of International Education, founded in New York in 1919, DAAD organized a German-American student exchange during the Weimar era. The collaboration, based on the principle of reciprocity, was continued during the Third Reich. However, the modest number of handpicked German exchange students sent to the United States (150 between 1925 and 1930) shows that the exchange was aimed at increasing German prestige abroad and was guided by the principle that international cultural policy serves diplomatic as well as scholarly and educational objectives.[4]

---

[1] Winfried Herget, "'Overcoming the Mortifying Distance': American Impressions of German Universities in the Nineteenth and Early Twentieth Centuries," in Dieter Gutzen, Winfried Herget, and Hans-Adolf Jacobsen, eds., *Transatlantische Partnerschaft: Kulturelle Aspekte der deutsch-amerikanischen Beziehungen* (Bonn, 1992), 195–208.

[2] Bernhard vom Brocke, "Der deutsch-amerikanische Professorenaustausch: Preussische Wissenschaftspolitik, internationale Wissenschaftsbeziehungen und die Anfänge einer deutschen auswärtigen Kulturpolitik vor dem Ersten Weltkrieg," *Zeitschrift für Kulturaustausch* 31 (1981): 128–82.

[3] Rüdiger vom Bruch, "Gesellschaftliche Initiativen in den auswärtigen Kulturbeziehungen Deutschlands vor

1914: Der Beitrag des deutschen Bildungsbürgertums," *Zeitschrift für Kulturaustausch* 31 (1981): 43–66.

[4] Volkhard Laitenberger, *Akademischer Austausch und auswärtige Kulturpolitik d.dt. Akademischer Austauschdienst (DAAD) 1923–1945* (Göttingen, 1976); Barthold C. Witte, "Deutsche Kulturpolitik im Ausland: Ziele, Chancen, Grenzen," in Karl Dietrich Bracher, Manfred Funke and Hans-Peter Schwarz, eds., *Deutschland zwischen Krieg und Frieden: Beiträge zur Politik and Kultur im 20. Jahrhundert* (Düsseldorf, 1991), 371–93.

After 1945, the United States seized the initiative with a plan that broke radically with the past and placed cultural relations with the American zone of occupation and the Federal Republic of Germany on a completely new foundation. The creation, development, and effects of the exchange program initiated by the United States between 1945 and 1955 are the focus of this article. It also discusses developments through the end of the 1960s and an attempt to summarize the benefits and value of the original American intentions for the development of cultural and educational relations between the two countries.

CREATION

In the mid-1930s, the United States developed a cultural foreign policy aimed initially at Latin America, where it was intended to counter the effects of National Socialist propaganda.[5] The cultural and educational policy of the postwar period built upon these earlier experiences. The impetus, however, came from the Conference of Allied Ministers of Education (CAME), which had been meeting in London since 1943 to discuss problems related to the intellectual and material aftermath of National Socialism in Europe. CAME called for a constructive program to address the decimation of intellectual life, the disappearance of cultural treasures, and the loss of traditional values. The U.S. Department of State lent its support to this idea in early 1944.[6] In spring 1944, the State Department sent a delegation headed by future senator J. William Fulbright to London to study the political, social, and economic instability that was expected on the European continent in the wake of the war and to plan an aid program with a comprehensive catalog of measures, including the training of teachers in the United States.

Germany, the wartime adversary, played a special role in the growing American involvement in Europe. The reeducation policy conceived for Germany by the State Department in 1945 was intended to bring about a fundamental change in the German character. It was to eradicate militarism, chauvinism, and National Socialist thinking as well as promote the development of democratic principles. It was to be made clear to the Germans that they had lost the war and would be held responsible for the crimes of National Socialism. Reeducation was to be accompanied by a transformation in the social structure that would facilitate this democratic change. The goal was a pluralistic democracy committed to maintaining peace. The exchange program with Germany gained a position of central importance in the work toward this goal, though few measures were implemented in the first years of the occupation. In the early 1950s, however, after the occupation ended, the exchange program with Germany developed into the largest program the United States had ever implemented with another country. A 1956 review showed that the United States had sent more than 14,000 people on exchange programs to Germany; more than 12,000 Germans had visited the United States for periods ranging from a month to a year.[7]

IMPLEMENTATION

The U.S. military government intended that exchange programs should contribute to the democratization of German society. After 1949, the misleading expression *reeducation* was replaced with the term *reorientation*, which

5 Manuel Espinosa, *Inter-American Beginnings of U.S. Cultural Diplomacy, 1936–1948* (Washington, D.C., 1976); Sharon Mueller Norton, "The United States Department of State International Visitor Program: A Conceptual Framework for Evaluation," (Ph.D. diss., Tufts University, 1977); Jürgen Müller, *Nationalsozialismus in Lateinamerika: Die Auslandsorganisationen der NSDAP in Argentinien, Brasilien, Chile und Mexico 1933–1945* (Stuttgart, 1997).

6 Karl-Heinz Füssl, "Restauration und Neubeginn: Gesellschaftliche, Kulturelle und Reformpädagogische Ziele der amerikanischen 'Re-education' Politik nach 1945," *Aus Politik und Zeitgeschichte* B 6/97 (1997): 3–14.

7 Henry J. Kellermann, *Cultural Relations as an Instrument of U.S. Foreign Policy: The Educational Exchange Program Between the United States and Germany, 1945–1954* (Washington, D.C., 1978).

referred to indirect methods of educational influence through participation in democratic processes, assumption of responsibility, and education in principles of humanity and tolerance. These efforts were aimed primarily at members of the younger generation, who were to be trained as democrats through extended sojourns in the United States.

On August 1, 1945, President Harry S. Truman signed the Surplus Property Act Fulbright had initiated; the act provided for an exchange program to be funded through the sale of surplus military supplies and equipment. After Congress took further steps toward a worldwide cultural and educational program with the Smith-Mund Act in 1948, the German exchange began in earnest. The resident officers in the countries had a particularly important role. They were responsible for establishing commissions in each German state (*Land*) for selecting exchange candidates. The commissions had German members and were chaired by Americans. The criteria for selecting candidates included not only educational qualifications but also a strong personality, flexibility, English-language skills, and an untainted past. The primary concern, however, was that the exchange candidate would use and disseminate the experience gained in America upon his or her return. The Cold War also had an effect on the selection process. The Internal Security Act of 1950 and the Immigration and Nationality Act of 1952 prohibited all persons with past or present ties to communist organizations from entering the United States.[8]

Administratively, the exchange program was part of the Education and Cultural Relations Division of the military government. Its autonomy increased in 1948 when it became the Interdivisional Reorientation Committee (IRC). In the State Department in Washington, the program was administered by the Area Division for Occupied Areas, where Henry J. Kellermann headed the Office of German and Austrian Public Affairs (GAI). In fall 1948, a permanent advisory commission was added under the auspices of the American Council on Education. This Commission on the Occupied Areas (COA) had the job of supporting and coordinating the program, negotiating with private organizations, and recruiting qualified American personnel. The commission was chaired by Hermann B. Wells; its director was Harold E. Snyder. Beginning in fall 1949, responsibility in the State Department fell to the Bureau of Public Affairs, International Educational Exchange Service, under the direction of James W. Riddleberger, and in Germany to the Office of Public Affairs under Ralph Nicholson and later under Shepard Stone.[9]

In keeping with the intention of the program to contribute to German educational reform through direct experience in the United States, the projects for 1949 listed subjects such as "School Administration and Organization," "Parent-Teacher Associations," "Instructional Materials and Testing Procedures," "Student Organizations and Recreational Activities," "Social Sciences and Social Work," and "Municipal Administration and Public Relations." In the 1950 exchange year, a total of 241 projects were carried out, from kindergarten teaching to continuing education for journalists, involving 1,255 Germans from the fields of social work, childcare, and education.[10] In addition to these projects, which were open to politicians or other public figures, there were programs for university students and trainees, including young trade unionists and those working toward a career in law (3,700 participants between 1949 and 1955), as well as programs for secondary school students (2,283 participants between 1949 and

---

[8] Institute of International Education, *Leaders for a Free World: Report on the National Conference on Exchange of Persons*, Feb. 23–5, 1955.

[9] Harold E. Snyder and George E. Beauchamp, eds., *Responsibilities of Voluntary Agencies in Occupied Areas: A Report of the Second National Conference on the Occupied Countries Held Under the Auspices of the Commission on the Occupied Areas of the American Council on Education in Cooperation with the Department of State and the Department of the Army, Washington, D.C., November 30 and December 1, 1950* (Washington, D.C., Feb. 1951).

[10] Henry J. Kellerman, Exchange Program for Germany FY-51, July 11, 1950, Review of FY-51 Exchange Program, July 10, 1950, National Archives, RG 59, lot 52–367, B153.

1956). There were a number of nongovernmental organizations in the United States responsible for the on-site care of secondary school students between the ages of sixteen and eighteen: the American Friends Service Committee, Rotary International and National Grange, the 4-H Foundation, the National Conference of Christians and Jews, and the American Field Service. Particularly in the case of these younger students, it became clear how fine the line was between success and failure. Parts of this program were taken over by the National Catholic Welfare Conference after a surprising number of youths housed with families belonging to the Church of the Brethren were converted to that teaching.[11] The young were particularly fascinated by the prospect of a stay in the United States. This is illustrated by the fact that in 1953 the commissions could select from a pool of 18,000 applications to fill 414 spots. The high point of the program was from 1951 to 1953, when approximately 6,500 people took part in the transatlantic exchange. The majority were Germans visiting the United States. During the same period, about 600 American specialists traveled to Germany to undertake studies on behalf of the High Commission, to teach at universities, or to contribute to the development of new curricula.

The design of the exchange program reveals that its American administrators effectively ignored the German intermediary organizations that had been reestablished on the Weimar model. The Fulbright Agreement signed on July 18, 1952, by Chancellor Konrad Adenauer and High Commissioner John McCloy succeeded in relaxing the dominance of American cultural and educational policy. Despite the German-American parity on the Fulbright Commission, however, the funding continued to come exclusively from American sources until 1962. The Fulbright Program, in worldwide operation since 1946, comprised twenty-four countries by 1952, including ten in Western Europe. Beginning in 1946, the Board of Foreign Scholarships oversaw the program, and the International Educational Exchange Service (IEES) within the State Department also contracted with nongovernmental organizations that were responsible for the various divisions of the Fulbright Program: teaching and research on the university level (Conference Board of Associated Research Councils), graduate students (Institute of International Education), and public school students (U.S. Office of Education).[12]

The Fulbright Program absorbed most of the academic components of the HICOG program as of 1953–4 and established a roughly balanced exchange (235 Germans and 239 Americans in 1953). Although the program approximated German traditions in its exchange of academic elites and foreign-language teachers, it also set a new tone by emphasizing the social sciences and empirical research methods and by generously supporting American studies programs at German universities.[13] Another new element was the fact that the exchange of graduate students, who made up the majority of participants in the Fulbright Program, was bringing American university students back to Germany for the first time since 1945. The situation was difficult for American undergraduates, however, because the German institutions felt that their status corresponded only to the upper level of the German advanced-level high school (*Gymnasium*). Some American universities, therefore, decided to establish their own satellite programs overseas. For example, the German campus of Stanford University in Beutelsbach recruited mostly first-semester students under the Junior Year Abroad program and enabled students to integrate their German study into the curriculum at the California campus. However, such arrangements

---

[11] Memo from McManus to Hochwalt, Foreign High School Student Program, July 10, 1957, Catholic University of America, National Catholic Welfare Conference, numerical files, 258 B, box 34.

[12] U.S. International Educational Exchange Service, *Swords into Plowshares: A New Venture in International Understanding: The Story of the Educational Exchange Program Authorized by the Fulbright Act of 1946* (Washington, D.C., 1956); Walter Johnson and Francis J. Colligan, *The Fulbright Program: A History*, with a foreword by J. W. Fulbright (Chicago, 1965).

[13] See the chapter by Willi Paul Adams, vol. 2, Culture.

isolated students not only from the German educational system but also from the German population. Even more problematic for international exchange was the widespread attitude among American students that they could learn nothing meaningful in Europe, especially Germany, because the social sciences were so underdeveloped there.[14]

After the exchange program gradually came to a close with the end of the American High Commission in Germany in 1955, the traditional intermediary organizations continued transatlantic exchange on a markedly lower level on the basis of the principle of reciprocity. In the United States, the cultural-policy offensive of the immediate postwar period led to a dramatic increase in the number of foreign students. In 1923–4, for example, only 6,700 foreign students studied in the United States. The figure remained more or less constant through the end of World War II. In 1946–7, the number of foreign students in the United States was 14,900; it climbed steadily to 30,400 by 1951–2 and set a temporary record of 47,000 in 1960.[15] By 1960, Europe accounted for the largest share in the exchange program, with Germany in first place until 1955. Those responsible for the exchange programs were engaged in a continual effort to steer them clear of the counteroffensive to communist propaganda that the United States Information Agency (USIA) had been operating since the Campaign of Truth in April 1950.[16] This effort was rewarded with some success when the USIA was institutionally separated from the State Department in April 1953. However, the exchange programs could not be entirely insulated from the Cold War, as public affairs officers and cultural attachés responsible for the programs overseas were also employees of the USIA.[17]

IMPACT

Between 1950 and 1960, the Department of State issued some thirty contracts to various research institutes to study the results of the U.S. exchange program. The significance of the German program is underscored by the fact that fourteen of these studies targeted the German participants alone. Two main questions stood behind these studies. First, the State Department wanted to know whether and in what way the exchange program contributed to the adoption, dissemination, and reinforcement of positive attitudes toward the United States. Second, the studies were supposed to determine the extent of the influence of returning exchange participants in their native land.

The studies generally were based on surveys of program participants collected at the beginning and end of their stays in the United States. The socioeconomic level of exchange participants was slightly above average, their educational level markedly above average; most were males. The university exchange students had high expectations of the program, most of which were fulfilled.[18] Upon arrival in the United States, most of the participants named promotion of international understanding as the primary purpose of the exchange program; at the end of their stays, they defined the goal as improved understanding of democracy. Over time, there was a marked drop in the number of participants who responded that the main benefit was personal and professional gain. The secondary school students had difficulty adjusting to social conditions and family life in the United

[14] John A. Garraty and Walter Adams, *From Main Street to the Left Bank: Students and Scholars Abroad* (East Lansing, Mich., 1959), 198.

[15] Claire Selltitz et al., *Attitudes and Social Relations of Foreign Students in the United States* (Minneapolis, 1963); Institute of International Education, *Education for One World: Annual Census of Foreign Students in the U.S., 1951–1952* (New York, 1952).

[16] See the chapter by Jessica C. E. Gienow-Hecht in this section.

[17] Hans N. Tuch, *Communicating with the World: U.S. Public Diplomacy Overseas* (New York, 1990); Maritta Hein-Kremer, *Die amerikanische Kulturoffensive: Gründung und Entwicklung der amerikanischen Information Centers in Westdeutschland und West-Berlin* (Cologne, 1996).

[18] Bureau of Social Science Research, *An Analysis of Attitude Change Among German Exchangees* (Washington, D.C., Aug. 1951).

States. The overwhelming majority said they were particularly impressed with the human qualities of Americans. Thirty-nine percent of the public figures, 17 percent of university students, and only 8 percent of secondary school students criticized the practice of racial separation in the United States. The university students were least impressed with American democracy (29 percent, compared to 45 percent of secondary school students). The greatest difference between arrival and departure was in the attitude toward American education, to which 33 percent of university students and 41 percent of secondary school students attributed materialistic aims (compared to 14 percent and 4 percent, respectively, upon arrival). Despite these individual negative findings, the exchange program brought about lasting attitudinal changes in five different areas: It sensitized the participants to the achievements of other countries, particularly the United States; it contributed to the belief that Germany could learn from the United States, particularly in the areas of education and policy toward trade unions; it promoted the acceptance of democratic values; it reinforced the positive image of America; and it fostered openness to international cooperation.[19]

Time in the United States left a particularly strong impression on the secondary school students. They returned more mature and self-confident, friends and relatives reported, and they probably brought back a more positive image of America than any other group of exchange participants. The Germany to which they returned now seemed overcrowded and run-down to them.[20] They found the attitudes of those who had stayed home to be narrow-minded or even militaristic. More than half reported serious problems in readjusting to their old environment and social conditions. The democratic student-teacher relationship in the United States encouraged many of them to work actively toward developing student participation in Germany. Quite a number of them expressed the desire to go into teaching as a profession so that they could put into practice the experiences they had gained from the exchange program. The desire to emigrate to the United States if possible was expressed more often by the secondary school students than by any other group.

It can be concluded from these studies that the German exchangees returning from the United States had considerable influence on West German society. In early 1952, when more than 4,000 Germans had participated in exchange programs, the American High Commission ordered a representative study of 1,200 adult Germans. Those surveyed were asked about their degree of familiarity with and reactions to the exchange program. The opinion researchers also wanted to learn how the Germans had received the exchange program as a whole. Eight percent of those surveyed reported having received new ideas and stimuli from returning exchangees. Extrapolation of these data led to the conclusion that, at the time of the survey, between 900,000 and 1.6 million Germans had been exposed to the multiplier effect of the exchange program. The extrapolation also showed that each of the returning exchangees had spoken with 150 to 300 other Germans about his or her stay in the United States. This figure is based on a relatively conservative method of assessment, because the data do not take into account how long the exchangee had been back in Germany and how much his or her possibilities for contact and influence may have expanded in that time. A study carried out two years later confirmed these findings and concluded additionally that the participants' experiences with the American educational system were of the most interest to other Germans upon their return.[21] The opinion

[19] International Public Opinion Research, Inc., *German Exchangees: A Study in Attitude Change* (New York, Aug. 1953).

[20] International Public Opinion Research, Inc., *A Follow-Up Study of German Teenager Exchangees* (New York, Feb. 1954).

[21] West German Receptivity and Reactions to the Exchange of Persons Program, Aug. 1952, and Dissemination Record of Exchangee Categories for Significant Areas of American Life, June 1954, The United States High Commissioner for Germany, Office of Public Affairs, Bonn.

researchers certified the program as a notable success that had surpassed all expectations.

OUTLOOK

The Weimar traditions of support for the intellectual elite were taken up again by the reestablished DAAD (1950) and Alexander von Humboldt Foundation (1953) in association with the German Research Foundation (*Deutsche Forschungsgemeinschaft*), the Max Planck Society (1951), the West German Conference of University Presidents and Ministers of Culture, Education, and Church Affairs (*Westdeutsche Rektoren- und Kultusministerkonferenz*, 1949), and the cultural section of what was then the Office for Foreign Affairs (*Dienststelle für Auswärtige Angelegenheiten*). These traditions were revived, however, in the context of a complete reorientation of German foreign policy and the rapid reintegration of the Federal Republic into the international community. German-American exchange – with the exception of the Fulbright Program, almost entirely in American hands – hardly figured, quantitatively, in the activities of the traditional intermediary institutions until the mid-1950s. After the American program expired, the traditional organizations continued the exchange, though at a markedly reduced rate. In 1957, as an expression of gratitude for the Marshall Plan, DAAD established a scholarship program that encompassed about 100 Americans per year and, beginning in 1960, a comparable number of Germans. A change in foreign cultural and educational policy took shape in the mid-1960s against the backdrop of the rapid expansion and reform of the West German educational system. The opening up of *Gymnasien* and universities to all social classes and the accompanying expansion of the educational system laid the groundwork for bringing new groups into the international exchange. Between 1963 and 1972, the number of applicants for study in the United States quadrupled, and German-American exchanges took second place behind German-Japanese exchanges. The figures for academic exchange show that, by the late 1970s, between 4,000 and

5,000 Germans and Americans were living in the partner country. A parallel development can be seen in the Foreign Ministry's culture and education budget. In 1952, it was DM 2.8 million, but by 1966 it had grown to DM 215.2 million.[22] The approach associated with Ralf Dahrendorf, the undersecretary for foreign affairs (1969–70), attempted to make both academic cooperation and broad social interaction essential elements of the exchange programs.

Private organizations also made a significant contribution to German-American exchange. In 1951, the Carl Duisberg Society reestablished its relationships from the Weimar era. In 1952, *Atlantik-Brücke* (Atlantic Bridge) was founded under the chairmanship of Ernst Friedlaender. The German Society for American Studies (*Deutsche Gesellschaft für Amerikastudien*) was organized in 1953. By the early 1960s, sixty-four organizations dedicated to exchange with the United States had been established. The remarkable increase in private initiatives compared to the Weimar Republic reflects not only the growth in interest but also the common practice in the United States.

The massive expansion of American cultural and educational policy after 1945 has given rise to accusations that liberal intellectuals and the educational system were instrumentalized for the Cold War and, consequently, that the original goal of democratization was forgotten.[23] This argument is not valid at least for the exchange programs, as the firsthand information and direct, on-site experience with American democracy cast a rather different light on the intentions behind the exchange programs. Moreover, the hoped-for educational and social reform in Germany implied almost necessarily that democratic developments would be promoted and totalitarian efforts forestalled.

This raises the question of the significance and long-term effects of the exchange programs.

---

[22] Ulrich Littmann, *German-American Exchanges: A Report on Facts and Developments* (Bonn, 1980).
[23] Ralph Willett, *The Americanization of Germany, 1945–49* (London, 1989); Frank A. Ninkovich, *The Diplomacy of Ideas: U.S. Foreign Policy and Cultural Relations, 1938–50* (Cambridge, Mass., 1981).

To what extent did German-American exchange contribute to the educational reform
of the 1960s, a watershed for social change
in the Federal Republic? Although there has
been no systematic investigation of these questions, initial research indicates that the effects
are greater than previously assumed.[24] In youth
services and social work, American theories of
group education, remedial assistance, and community work clearly had found their way into
the instructional programs of the newly established educational institutions in the Federal Republic. Contrary to the assumption that
traditional values dominated developments in
Germany, the history of the Federal Republic
confirms that new, open forms of youth services, youth social work, and leisure-time instruction were adopted relatively readily. The
reception of American methods had a lasting
effect on education and career training and led
to new forms of practice. This process was aided
by the increasingly academic approach to education, which led to the relocation of teacher
training or programs for social work from the
advanced vocational schools (*Höhere Fachschulen*)

to the newly founded academic institutions
(*Fachhochschulen, Pädagogische Hochschulen*). Participants in the exchange programs performed
decisive functions in these areas of training
and practice. One example of the relationship
between exchange programs and educational
reform initiatives is the Bergstrasse school village in Hessen, which was modeled after an
American community school. Clear connections between transatlantic exchange and educational reform can be seen in the work of
Göttingen education reformer Heinrich Roth,
who had participated in the exchange program
for teachers in the United States in 1950–1.
In the German Educational Council (*Deutscher
Bildungsrat*, established 1965), Roth vehemently
advocated mobilizing talent reserves and opening upper-level educational institutions to a
broad spectrum of society. His concept of a realistic pedagogical science, with the introduction
of empirical research methods, abandonment of
a static concept of talent, and efforts to exert
practical and political influence, had a profound
influence on the discussion of educational reform.[25]

---

[24] Interim report on the project "Professionalisierung
und Modernisierung" conducted at the Humboldt Universität in Berlin under the auspices of the German Research Foundation, July 30, 1997.

[25] Dietrich Hoffmann, *Heinrich Roth oder Die andere
Seite der Pädagogik: Erziehungswissenschaft in der Epoche der
Bildungsreform* (Weinheim, 1996).

CHAPTER FIVE

Science and Scientific Exchange in the German-American Relationship

Mitchell G. Ash

The history of German-American scientific relations after 1945 has a special place in the complex story of the de- and reinternationalization of science in the twentieth century. In one sense, developments after 1945 are comparable with the realignment of international scientific research and communication networks following World War I. In both cases, involvement of German and Allied scientists in military and other government projects contributed, along with wider political factors, to an atmosphere of competition, mutual isolation, and mistrust that inhibited postwar cooperation at first. However, the realignment of international scientific relations during the Cold War was far more drastic than that which followed World War I. As a result, new frameworks for cooperation emerged while older ones were revitalized. At the same time, new political, social, and cultural realities affected German scientific research.

In the early postwar years, German-American relations in the sciences and technology were dominated by Allied exploitation of human and physical resources and by Allied efforts to control or redirect research in the occupation zones. During the first years of the chancellorship of Konrad Adenauer, a significant recirculation of scientific elites occurred; younger German scientists emigrated to the United States largely for economic reasons, while a number of scholars and scientists who had fled from Hitler returned to the Federal Republic. In strong interaction with this trend, a formal framework of scientific and cultural relations gradually emerged,

the newest aspect of which was the Fulbright Program. Adenauer-era science and technology policies reflected an uneasy mix of cooperation and rivalry with the United States, while West German social scientists introduced research methods imported largely from that country – an effort hotly contested as "Americanization."

THE IMMEDIATE POSTWAR PERIOD: EXPLOITATION AND CONTROL

As soon as Allied troops entered Germany, an immense transfer of human resources and apparatus began to transform Germany's scientific landscape.[1] In the physical sciences and technology, Allied intelligence missions focused initially on preventing further military research and gathering intelligence on weapons-related projects for use against Japan. Important examples were the ALSOS mission, which captured ten leading nuclear scientists, including Nobel Prize winners Otto Hahn, Werner Heisenberg, and Max von Laue, and brought them to

---

[1] John Gimbel, *Science, Technology, and Reparations: Exploitation and Plunder in Postwar Germany* (Stanford, Calif., 1990); Matthias Judt and Burghard Ciesla, eds., *Technology Transfer out of Germany After 1945* (Amsterdam, 1996); Ulrich Albrecht, Andreas Heinemann-Gruder, and Arend Wellmann, *Die Spezialisten: Deutsche Naturwissenschaftler und Techniker in der Sowjetunion nach 1945* (Berlin, 1992). For further discussion, see the chapter by Raymond Stokes, vol. 1, Economics.

England, where they were held for over a year, and the CIOS group, which concentrated on radar, synthetic fuels, torpedoes, and rockets. By spring 1945, however, Allied objectives had shifted to outright expropriation of the economic and military potential of German science and technology. In contrast to the British, the Americans appear not to have considered employing the scientific ethos as an aid to reeducation.[2] In connection with expropriation, all Allied forces attempted surveys of scientific and technological resources; the joint United States–British "Field Intelligence Agency, Technical" (FIAT) program established in May 1945 yielded the most comprehensive and detailed results.

In contrast to Soviet measures, which concentrated on the evacuation of entire research teams and the dismantling of production sites, the Americans and British, working from lists drawn up in advance, recruited selected leading scientists, who then organized their own research teams. Best known on the Western side, in addition to the ALSOS mission, were operations Overcast and Paperclip.[3] At the same time, other teams swept through the research departments and patent records of the German chemical industry. These actions were justified at the time as "intellectual reparations." However, aside from a vague statement in the Potsdam accords that allowed the removal of property as reparations by each of the Allied powers from its zone pending the conclusion of a final peace treaty, the legal basis of these expropriations remains unclear to this day.[4]

Two points about the impact of the removals of German scientists and equipment on later German-American scientific relations need emphasis here. First, the removals were largely limited to specific fields considered to be of military or commercial interest, such as chemical engineering, aerodynamics, and rocketry. Second, whereas the majority of German scientists and technicians in the Soviet Union were permitted to return to the GDR by the mid- to late 1950s, most of those in the United States chose to remain there.[5]

In addition to exploiting Germany's scientific manpower and research potential, a second objective of Allied policy was to control scientific research in Germany itself. As indicated in directive JCS 1076/6 of April 1945, the Americans initially sought to prohibit research altogether, whereas the British preferred to permit basic research while controlling its use. After difficult negotiations among the Allies, Allied Control Authority Law 25 of April 29, 1946, forbade military research in Germany, including basic science that could have military applications. A fundamental ambiguity in this law was the difficulty of establishing the boundary between basic and applied research. Thus, for example, construction plans for aircraft as well as airplane motors were included among the prohibitions, though basic research in aerodynamics was not possible without the latter. This ambiguity, along with a lack of enforcement personnel, made it possible for German scientists to circumvent the stricter provisions of the law.[6]

In any case, by the time Law 25 was promulgated, the emerging superpower conflict was

[2] Alan Beyerchen, "German Scientists and Research Institutions in Allied Occupation Policy," *History of Education Quarterly* 22 (1982): 289–99; David Cassidy, "Controlling German Science, I: U.S. and Allied Forces in Germany, 1945–1947," *Historical Studies in the Physical and Biological Sciences* 24 (1994): 197–235.

[3] See the chapter by Michael J. Neufeld, vol. 1, Security.

[4] Rainer Karlsch, *Allein bezahlt? Die Reparationsleistungen der SBZ/DDR 1945–1953* (Berlin, 1993); Burghard Ciesla, "'Intellektuelle Reparationen' der SBZ an die alliierten Siegermächte?" in Christoph Buchheim, ed., *Wirtschaftliche Folgelasten des Krieges in der SBZ/DDR* (Baden-Baden, 1995); Jörg Fisch, "Reparations and Intellectual Property," in Judt and Ciesla, eds., *Technology Transfer*, 11–26.

[5] On the return of German scientists from the Soviet Union to the GDR, see Burghard Ciesla, "Der Spezialistentransfer in die UdSSR und seine Auswirkungen in der SBZ und DDR," *Aus Politik und Zeitgeschichte* B 49–50/93 (1993): 24–31; André Steiner, "The Return of German 'Specialists' from the Soviet Union to the German Democratic Republic: Integration and Impact," in Judt and Ciesla, eds., *Technology Transfer*, 119–30.

[6] Maria Osietzky, *Wissenschaftsorganisation und Restauration: Der Aufbau ausseruniversitärer Forschungseinrichtungen und die Gründung des westdeutschen Staates 1945–1952* (Cologne, 1984), 95–7; Helmuth Trischler, *Luft- und Raumfahrtforschung in Deutschland 1900–1970: Politische Geschichte einer Wissenschaft* (Frankfurt am Main, 1992), 290.

already beginning to move Allied policy toward more cooperative measures aimed at rebuilding the economic base in the Western zones. Before the effects of that policy change can be assessed, it is necessary to consider briefly two further dimensions of elite circulation: the departure of younger German scientists for economic reasons and the return to Germany of émigré scientists and scholars from the Nazi era.

THE "BRAIN DRAIN" FROM GERMANY AND
THE IMPACT OF RETURNING ÉMIGRÉS

Due primarily to economic circumstances, an as yet uncounted number of younger German scientists in the late 1940s and early 1950s chose to leave the Western occupation zones, and later the Federal Republic, and go either to Great Britain or the United States for scientific training. Though little is known about this exodus, it seems reasonable to suppose that these economic emigrants became an important resource base for later German-American interactions. This was certainly true for German scientists brought to the United States by the military, most prominently rocket scientists Wernher von Braun and Bernhard Goetaert.[7]

More prominent at the time were émigrés who had been forced to leave Nazi Germany and chose to return either for brief visits or permanently during the Adenauer era. The number of returnees varies widely by discipline. Natural scientists were the fewest, understandably so in view of the resources available in the rapidly expanding American research network and the still desolate state of German facilities. Among émigré biologists, for example, only three university teachers who had gone to Turkey returned to Germany after 1945.[8] Among educationists, by contrast, nineteen of forty four (47.5 percent) of those who held academic positions before 1933 and were still alive after 1945

returned permanently.[9] Particularly significant among the numerous émigrés who returned temporarily were the economists and social scientists brought in as expert consultants by the Allies. One example was Gerhard Colm of the New School for Social Research, a coauthor of the Colm-Dodge-Goldsmith Plan, which, with significant changes, eventually became the basis of West German currency reform in 1948.[10]

Prominent social scientists who returned permanently to the Federal Republic include Ernst Fraenkel, Arnold Bergsträsser, and Erich Voegelin, who accepted professorships at the Free University of Berlin, Freiburg, and Munich, respectively, and played significant roles in the establishment of political science as a discipline in West Germany; sociologist Rene König, who accepted a professorship in Cologne and soon became a leader in his field; and the heads of the so-called Frankfurt School, Max Horkheimer and Theodor W. Adorno.[11] By contrast, Kurt Bondy, who accepted an appointment in Hamburg in 1950, was the only émigré psychologist who returned permanently to West Germany while still an active researcher. In the humanities, too, the returnees were few in number but high in impact. Examples include historian Hans Rothfels, first professor in Marburg and then founding director of the Institute for Contemporary History in Munich; Germanist Richard Alewyn, professor in Cologne; and Germanist Werner Richter, professor in Bonn and later president of the German Academic Exchange Service.[12]

[9] Klaus-Peter Horn and Heinz-Elmar Tenorth, "Remigration in der Erziehungswissenschaft," *Exilforschung* 9 (1991): 173.

[10] See the chapter by Werner Plumpe, vol. 1, Economics; Claus-Dieter Krohn, *Wissenschaft im Exil: Deutsche Sozial- und Wirtschaftswissenschaftler in den USA und die New School for Social Research* (Frankfurt am Main, 1987), 221–3.

[11] Alfons Söllner, *Deutsche Politikwissenschaftler in der Emigration: Studien zu ihrer Akkulturation und Wirkungsgeschichte* (Opladen, 1996), chap. 15; Rolf Wiggershaus, *Die Frankfurter Schule: Geschichte, theoretische Entwicklung, politische Bedeutung* (Munich, 1988), chap. 6.

[12] Winfried Schulze, "Refugee Historians and the German Historical Profession Between 1950 and 1970," in Hartmut Lehmann and James J. Sheehan, eds., *An*

[7] Johannes Weyer, *Akteurstrategien und strukturelle Eigendynamiken: Raumfahrt in Westdeutschland 1945–1965* (Göttingen, 1993), 59.

[8] Ute Deichmann, *Biologists Under Hitler* (Cambridge, Mass., 1996), 48–50.

These returned émigrés cannot be described as wholesale re-importers of American-style research. Rothfels, for example, was well received in large part precisely because his methodology was compatible with the version of historicism then predominant in West Germany. In another case, the pioneering research of social psychologist Kurt Lewin in the 1930s on the behavior of children's play groups organized on "authoritarian," "democratic," and "laissez faire" principles, his research paradigms and results were widely cited in the 1950s, though Lewin himself, who died in 1947, was no longer present to propagate them.

Most important, and sobering, is the contrast between hope and political reality reflected in the plans that émigré scholars developed during the war and occupation periods to restructure German society and reeducate Germans for democracy. These plans were based on an optimistic, one might almost say American, belief in the efficacy of science to produce social change; some of them were financed by the Office of Strategic Services (OSS) and the U.S. State Department.[13] Unfortunately, they had little relation to realities on the ground. The shock of widespread German self-absorption and indifference to the fate of the Jews, noted for example by Hannah Arendt in a 1950 report, ran deep.[14] Most bitter of all, perhaps, was the realization that denazification and reeducation could only have succeeded by employing the very dictatorial methods the émigrés had just

fought to defeat.[15] Instead, German academics used the autonomy granted them by the Allies for practical reasons to rehire dismissed Nazi colleagues and reconstruct the rigidly hierarchical universities of the pre-Nazi era.

Nonetheless, émigré scholars' views on Germany in the early years of the Federal Republic show a mix of skepticism and optimism. Social theorist Franz Neumann dismissed the Federal Republic's Basic Law as "constitutional fetishism" at work; by this, he meant the problematic belief that the forms of the legal state alone would guarantee democratic government.[16] Returnees Ernst Fraenkel and Arnold Bergsträsser, on the other hand, both supported the emerging Atlantic partnership, although for different reasons. Fraenkel saw in the NATO alliance an embodiment of "the principles of democracy, individual freedom and the rule of law," while Bergsträsser saw a convergence of "western natural law and German humanism" in the face of a common totalitarian threat.[17]

GERMAN–AMERICAN RELATIONS AND ADENAUER-ERA SCIENCE POLICY: BETWEEN COOPERATION AND RIVALRY

Scientific relations between the Federal Republic and the United States in the 1950s were governed by two countervailing forces: efforts to establish new bases for expanded cooperation

Interrupted Past: German-Speaking Refugee Historians in the United States After 1933 (New York, 1991), 206–25; Regina Weber, "Zur Remigration des Germanisten Richard Alewyn," in Herbert A. Strauss, ed., *Die Emigration der Wissenschaften nach 1933: Disziplingeschichtliche Studien* (Munich, 1991), 235–56. For a discussion of the general situation of returned émigrés, see Claus-Dieter Krohn et al., eds., *Handbuch der deutschsprachigen Emigration 1933–1945* (Darmstadt, 1998), pt. 6

[13] Thomas Koebner et al., eds., *Deutschland nach Hitler: Zukunftspläne im Exil und aus der Besatzungszeit 1939–1949* (Opladen, 1987); Gerhard Paul, "Deutschland nach Hitler: Neuordungspläne im deutschen Exil," in Krohn et al., *Handbuch der deutschsprachigen Emigration*, 638–60.

[14] Hannah Arendt, "The Aftermath of the Nazi-Rule: Report from Germany," *Commentary* 10 (1950).

[15] See, for example, "The Progress of Reeducation in Germany: Office of Intelligence Research Report 4237, 3 June 1947," in Alfons Söllner, ed., *Zur Archäologie der Demokratie in Deutschland* (Frankfurt am Main, 1986), 2:177–216. For nuanced analyses of this dilemma, see Jürgen C. Hess, Hartmut Lehmann, and Volker Sellin, eds., *Heidelberg 1945* (Stuttgart, 1996), esp. pts. 1 and 2.

[16] Neumann, quoted in Alfons Söllner, "Zwischen totalitärer Vergangenheit und demokratischer Zukunft: Emigranten beurteilen die deutsche Entwicklung nach 1945," *Exilforschung* 9 (1991): 147.

[17] Ernst Fraenkel, *Deutschland und die westlichen Demokratien*, 6th ed. (Stuttgart, 1964; reprint, 1974), 7; Bergsträsser quoted in Axel Schildt, "Reise zurück aus der Zukunft: Beiträge von intellektuellen USA-Remigranten zur atlantischen Allianz, zum westdeutschen Amerikabild und zur 'Amerikanisierung' in den funfziger Jahren," *Exilforschung* 9 (1991): 30–1.

on the one hand, and to ignore, evade, or undermine restrictions on research and development on the other. The most prominent story of cooperation is that of the Fulbright Program. Bilateral exchanges under the Fulbright-Hays Act of 1946 began as early as 1947, despite the absence of a German national entity; a formal exchange agreement was reached in 1952. Article 4 of that document set a precedent by prescribing equal German and American membership in the commission that administered the program.[18] The number of scientists and scholars involved in this and other formal exchange programs was quite small at first. In the first decade after the refounding of the Alexander von Humboldt Foundation in 1953, for example, the United States ranked tenth in total grantees with 47, compared with 235 from Japan.[19] In specific cases, however, these programs were of strategic importance in science transfer. An example from the social sciences is the Fulbright exchange agreement between the universities of Chicago and Frankfurt, which was earmarked for work in that field.

The tension between cooperation and rivalry was most evident in the fields of nuclear research, aerodynamics, rocketry, and space science – the very areas that had been most strongly affected by Allied expropriation and control measures during the occupation. When they learned of the atomic-bomb explosion over Hiroshima in August 1945, the German physicists interned at Farm Hall reacted at first with shock and disbelief, then realized the extent to which they had relinquished world leadership in their field to the United States.[20] Werner Heisenberg

and others explicitly justified their subsequent efforts to restructure science policy in the Federal Republic by the need to recover Germany's scientific standing.[21] They also presented scientific leadership as compensation for lost political power. A 1953 memorandum on the establishment of a federal German Research Council (Deutsche Forschungsrat), for example, quotes physicist Max von Laue as saying that "scientific research is today virtually the only form in which Germany can still conduct foreign policy."[22] However, this initiative failed due to resistance from universities and state governments.

West German policy from the mid-1950s onward, spearheaded by conservative modernizers like "Atom-Minister" Franz Josef Strauss, saw science and technology as routes to renewed self-assertion. This policy shift posed both problems and opportunities for American–West German relations. In nuclear physics, the European Defense Community agreement of 1952 had allowed the Federal Republic only a single research reactor with limited capacity; by 1957, membership in the European Atomic Community and the European Council for Nuclear Research provided a framework that allowed the Federal Republic to expand its research programs while also receiving fissionable material from the United States as part of the "Atoms for Peace" program.[23] In aerodynamics and space research, the participation of the Federal Republic in the International Geophysical Year (1957–8) provided opportunities to use international cooperation involving the United States as an aid in overcoming deficits caused by earlier research controls. The Committee on

---

[18] Ulrich Littmann, Gute Partner – Schwierige Partner: Anmerkungen zur akademischen Mobilität zwischen Deutschland und den Vereinigten Staaten von Amerika (1923–1993) (Bonn, 1996), 106–8, 112; Henry J. Kellermann, Cultural Relations as an Instrument of United States Foreign Policy: The Educational Exchange Programs Between the United States and Germany, 1945–1954 (Washington, D.C., 1978). For further discussion, see the chapter by Karl-Heinz Füssl in this section.

[19] Heinrich Pfeiffer, ed., Alexander von Humboldt Foundation, 1953–1983 (Bonn, 1984), 80; see also Littmann, Gute Partner – Schwierige Partner, 99–101.

[20] Operation Epsilon: The Farm Hall Transcripts (London, 1993), report 4 (Aug. 6–7, 1945).

[21] Helmut Eickemeyer, ed., Abschlussbericht des Deutschen Forschungsrates über seine Tätigkeit von seiner Gründung am 9.3.1949 bis zum 15.8.1951 (Munich, 1953), preface.

[22] Eickemeyer, Abschlussbericht, 66.

[23] Michael Eckert, "Kernenergie und Westintegration: Die Zähmung des westdeutschen Nuklearnationalismus," in Ludolf Herbst, Werner Bührer, and Hanno Sowade, eds., Vom Marshallplan zur EWG: Die Eingliederung der Bundesrepublik Deutschland in die westliche Welt (Munich, 1990), 313–34; Maria Osietzky and Michael Eckert, Wissenschaft für Macht und Markt: Kernforschung und Mikroelektronik in der Bundesrepublik Deutschland (Munich, 1989), 56–8.

Space Research (COSPAR) program established in 1958 gave German scientists an opportunity to restart a rocketry program under nonmilitary auspices; in December 1959, however, a NATO committee approved a bilateral agreement with the United States that had the effect of containing such efforts by allowing the Germans to lease American equipment.[24]

In the biological sciences, especially in human genetics, criticisms by American and other scientists concerned by the renewed prominence of geneticists who had been supporters of the Third Reich inhibited the reintegration of German scientists into international networks. As late as 1963, the site of the International Genetics Congress and the Congress on Human Genetics had to be moved from the Federal Republic, in part because Israeli, American, and European geneticists objected to the participation of Otmar von Verschuer in the proceedings.[25] In any case, the tendency of senior German scientists in biology and other fields to continue research programs begun long before 1945 had the effect of distancing German research still further from international trends.

IMPACT ON SCIENCE AND CULTURE:
FROM REEDUCATION TO CONTESTED
AMERICANIZATION IN THE SOCIAL SCIENCES

An impressive aspect of German-American scientific relations during the Adenauer era was the widespread effort to transform previously established theoretical traditions and research practices with the help of techniques imported from the United States. These efforts were most obvious, effective, and hotly debated in psychology and the social sciences. The extent to which Allied reeducation programs were directly responsible for such efforts is debatable. Psychological and sociological analyses of Nazism were circulated as part of American reeducation programs. Later, both the social sciences, "with emphasis on training in empirical research methods rather than pure theory," and "human relations" fields such as psychology were specifically listed among the fields to be supported by the Fulbright Program.[26] The impact of exchange visits on science in specific cases is undoubted. Helmut Becker, for example, stated that the idea of founding the Max Planck Institute for Educational Research in Berlin was a result of his visit to the United States after the war.[27]

However, in the social sciences, the trends were much wider and their impacts far deeper than could be attributed to any single Allied program. The case of psychology exemplifies both the fundamental reorientation of scientific and professional practices that was at work and its social roots. With the emergence of a social market economy accompanied by a welfare state in the Federal Republic, demand for psychological diagnostics increased in labor and welfare offices as well as schools. Initially, this demand was satisfied by drawing on techniques already developed in Germany during the 1920s and 1930s, such as handwriting analysis. But the emphasis on trained intuition that had seemed so well suited to the selection of elites, such as officer candidates and business managers, was less adapted to the needs of state administrations and corporations in the 1950s. American-style intelligence, aptitude, and personality testing, backed by sophisticated multivariate statistics, appeared to fit the new situation better.[28] Counterparts to these trends in basic research were increasing use of intelligence and personality tests as research tools as well as attention to individual differences in subjects' responses and to statistical significance-testing of results. American human-relations research in industrial and social psychology was so popular that even East

---

[24] Weyer, *Akteurstrategien*, 220–2; see also Trischler, *Luft- und Raumfahrtforschung*, 397–8.

[25] Deichmann, *Biologists Under Hitler*, 309–10; Ute Deichmann, "Auswirkungen des Nationalsozialismus auf die genetische Forschung in Deutschland," *Biologisches Zentralblatt* 115 (1996): 153–61.

[26] Littmann, *Gute Partner – Schwierige Partner*, 114.

[27] Kellermann, *Cultural Relations*, 181.

[28] For the following, see Peter Mattes, "Psychologie im westlichen Nachkriegsdeutschland: Fachliche Kontinuität und gesellschaftliche Restauration," in Mitchell G. Ash and Ulfried Geuter, eds., *Geschichte der deutschen Psychologie im 20. Jahrhundert* (Opladen, 1985), 201–24.

German psychologists attempted to use it in studies of worker cooperation in factories in the late 1950s, on the premise that such "bourgeois" science, in proper hands, could be useful to socialist reconstruction.[29]

However, the senior West German professoriat, nearly all of whom had been trained in the 1920s, had a vested interest in the older methods. The resulting debate over methods (*Methodenstreit*) began when Hamburg professor Peter Hofstätter, who had learned factor analysis and other statistical techniques in the United States, condemned qualitative methods and ideal-typical interpretations in 1953 as "speculative psychology." In reply, Mainz professor Albert Wellek argued that quantitative methods had their place but should not be used everywhere for the sake of "pseudo-American" appearances. The battle ended by the 1960s in more or less complete victory for the "Americanizers"; the younger generation of researchers and practitioners saw the modernizing potential of American methods and had little sympathy with the antitechnological views of their teachers.[30] A comparable trend appears to have occurred in sociology, where the increasing use of survey research techniques and statistical methods – vigorously supported by returned émigré Rene König in Cologne, among others – was equated, not entirely correctly, with "Americanization." However, older theoretical traditions, represented most prominently by König's rival Helmut Schelsky, persisted longer in this discipline than in psychology.[31]

The case of Theodor Adorno is a good example of the ambivalence with which Americanization in the social sciences could be viewed. After his work on the "authoritarian personality" in Berkeley in the late 1940s, Adorno helped to plan a major conference sponsored in part by the Allied High Commission in Germany on public opinion research in Frankfurt in December 1951. At that time, he plainly had hopes for the democratic potential of a method in which one person's opinion is as good as another. After his permanent return to Frankfurt in 1953, however, he eventually decided that the gains of "teamwork" and standardized procedures in empirical social research were achieved at the expense of theory – for him, too high a price.[32] Adorno's critique of the American culture industry also helped to form the views of the New Left, some of whom came to study with him in Frankfurt.[33]

Less publicly debated but nonetheless significant in the long term were transformations in the structure of training in both the natural and the social sciences. By the 1960s, the trend on the part of younger West German scientists toward doing at least some postdoctoral research at American laboratories had become so strong that many jokingly referred to the need for a fourth degree – the IAG, for *in Amerika gewesen* (been in America). The number of scientists who actually took this step is not known, and the concrete impact of this structural shift on topic or theory choice and research design also remains to be studied. One suggestive example of influence in the other direction is the impact of visits to the Institute for Genetics in Cologne by Max Delbrück, the German biophysicist and

[29] Hans-Dieter Schmidt, "Bedingungsgrundlagen der sozialen Betriebsatmosphäre und Probleme der innerbetrieblichen Kooperation," *Zeitschrift für Psychologie* 163 (1959): 157.

[30] See Alexandre Métraux, "Der Methodenstreit und die Amerikanisierung der Psychologie in der Bundesrepublik," in Mitchell G. Ash and Ulfried Geuter, eds., *Geschichte der deutschen Psychologie im 20. Jahrhundert* (Opladen, 1985), 225–51; Michael Grossheim, "Die westdeutsche Psychologie nach 1945 – amerikanistische Mode oder exakte Wissenschaft?" in Rainer Zitelmann, Karlheinz Weissmann, and Michael Grossheim, eds., *Westbindung: Chancen und Risiken für Deutschland* (Berlin, 1996), 391–419.

[31] See Karl-Siegbert Rehberg, "Auch keine Stunde Null: Westdeutsche Soziologie nach 1945," in Walter

H. Pehle and Peter Sillem, eds., *Wissenschaft im geteilten Deutschland: Restauration oder Neubeginn nach 1945?* (Frankfurt am Main, 1992), 26–44, and the sources cited there.

[32] Theodor W. Adorno, "Teamwork in der Sozialforschung" (1957), in Theodor W. Adorno, *Gesammelte Schriften* (Frankfurt am Main, 1972), 8:409–10; see also Wiggershaus, *Die Frankfurter Schule,* 551–3.

[33] Martin Jay, "Adorno in America," in Martin Jay, *Permanent Exiles: Essays on the Intellectual Migration from Germany to America* (New York, 1986), 125–6.

cofounder of molecular biology who had emigrated to the United States in the 1930s.

CONCLUSION: THE SITUATION IN THE 1960S

In the 1960s, the number of American participants in DAAD, Fulbright, and other exchange
programs began to grow rapidly; the United
States ranked second in the number of Humboldt Fellowships by 1973 and passed Japan to
take first place the following decade.[34] Scientists from both countries who made research
visits without direct support from one of these

programs far outnumbered those in formal programs. An infrastructure for scientific and educational cooperation was, therefore, firmly in
place by 1970 that would become the basis
for a new "normality" in German-American
scientific relations for the next twenty years.

The extent to which this increasingly
intensive internationalization also led to "Americanization" in the sciences remains to be determined. In psychology and the social sciences,
the transformation of scientific cultures was too
obvious to ignore. Nonetheless, traditional German organizational forms and intellectual traditions persisted, and German attitudes toward
American science, like those toward American
culture in general, remained ambivalent.

---

[34] Pfeiffer, *Alexander von Humboldt Foundation*, 80.

American Literature in Germany and Its Reception in the Political Context of the Postwar Years

Martin Meyer

Translated by Sally E. Robertson

Even before World War II had ended, Americans were preparing to popularize ideas that had been suppressed during National Socialist rule and were to be used after the war, particularly in Germany, to link up with international intellectual developments. They created book programs under the auspices of the Psychological Warfare Branch with the objective of transmitting American ways of thinking. American literature also served this purpose. As early as 1943, American soldiers were outfitted with millions of paperback books, as virtual staples in their kits. These Armed Services Editions (with a print run of 123 million) were followed in early 1945 by Overseas Editions in a similar format (3.6 million printed), which were made specially available to the population in the occupied areas in English and sometimes in the local language. One example is Alfred Kazin's *On Native Grounds*. Kazin's book on modern American prose, which originally appeared in 1942, came out in 1945 as an Overseas Edition in both the original language and a German translation by Hans Sahl. Beginning in 1947, significant works of intellectual history that were available in regular editions in American bookstores were also published in Germany. "No book was too thick to be translated," Hans-Joachim Lang later

observed, adding: "And the selection must be described as excellent."[1]

It is usually assumed that censorship in Nazi Germany prevented publication of many authors, including American ones. Works such as Sinclair Lewis's *It Can't Happen Here* (1935) were clearly banned because they exposed mechanisms on which the regime was based. In addition, the drop in book production in Germany between 1927 (31,000 books) and 1939 (20,000 books) must also have had an effect on titles from the United States. However, literature from abroad was by no means completely unknown. Birgit Bödeker has pointed out that the German public learned about newly published foreign works through short reviews until 1939 and that publishers in Austria and Switzerland managed to "provide an almost uninterrupted

---

[1] Preface, in Horst Frenz and Hans-Joachim Lang, eds., *Nordamerikanische Literatur im deutschen Sprachraum seit 1945: Beiträge zu ihrer Rezeption* (Munich, 1973), 106. Also noteworthy on the history of American literature in Germany are Harold Jantz, "Amerika im deutschen Dichten und Denken," in Wolfgang Stammler, ed., *Deutsche Philologie im Aufriss*, 2d ed., 3 vols. (Berlin, 1952), 3:361–9; and Lawrence Marsden Price, *The Reception of United States Literature in Germany* (Chapel Hill, N.C., 1966) (with an extensive bibliography). The political implications are the subject of Hansjörg Gehring, *Amerikanische Literaturpolitik in Deutschland 1945–1953: Ein Aspekt des Re-Education Programms* (Stuttgart, 1976).

supply of translations to the German Reich."[2] This situation changed when the war began. In 1942, the list of banned English and North American writers contained more than 1,500 names, including John Dos Passos, Willa Cather, Ernest Hemingway, and Upton Sinclair.[3] Still, the twelve years from 1933 to 1945 no more represented a complete vacuum of American literature in Germany than May 1945 constituted an all-out "zero hour," no matter how often this has been claimed. Research in this area remains in its infancy.

In 1945 alone, more than fifteen million copies of the Armed Services Editions were issued to American soldiers in Europe. Many of these paperbacks found eager readers among the Germans as well, which was hardly surprising considering the meager supply of books available; the printing industry had largely been destroyed. In 1945 and 1946, a total of only about 2,400 titles appeared on the German book market. The figure reached 8,900 in 1947 and approximately 13,400 in 1948. Under these circumstances, the strategy of printing contemporary world literature on rotary presses proved to be a success, and many of the titles were by American authors. This process, which had proven useful in the production of Armed Services and Overseas Editions, was appropriated (probably at the suggestion of the Americans) by the German publishing company Rowohlt, which printed entire novels on newsprint and delivered them in newspaper format. Between 1946 and 1949, Rowohlt printed approximately three million *Rotations-Romane* (rotary novels).

Paperback series such as the *Universum-Sprachen-Bibliothek* edited by Arthur Seiffhart in 1946 at Berlin's Axel-Juncker publishing house met with more modest success, and only 5,000

copies of each volume were printed. Nevertheless, this run signaled a return to the tradition of original English-language literature in Germany that Tauchnitz in Leipzig had established in the nineteenth century and Albatross in Hamburg carried on in 1932. There were similar efforts in the German Democratic Republic (GDR), where the private Paul List publishing house in Leipzig brought out paperback books in their original language (Panther Books, 1953–7). Beginning in 1957, this series continued in East Berlin as the Seven Seas Books imprint, which also served as a forum for publishing East German writings in English translation.

The Soviet side had also prepared to shape cultural policy in Germany after the capitulation. Early on, in August 1945, the Soviet military administration issued a publishing license to the Aufbau publishing house of Berlin. The journal *Aufbau: Kulturpolitische Monatsschrift* appeared the following month, published by the *Kulturbund zur demokratischen Erneuerung Deutschlands* (Cultural League for the Democratic Renewal of Germany). The president of the *Kulturbund*, Johannes R. Becher, had gone into exile in Moscow in 1933 as a communist, and in 1935 organized the First International Congress of Writers for the Defense of Culture in Paris.[4] After the war, the *Kulturbund* became the "center of cultural life in Berlin" within just a few months "and a trend-setter, through Aufbau-Verlag, the first publishing house after the war that was able to provide the public with a relatively substantial book production."[5] In the opinion of politician and writer Ernst Niekisch,

---

[2] Birgit Bödeker, *Amerikanische Zeitschriften in deutscher Sprache, 1945–1952: Ein Beitrag zur Literatur und Publizistik im Nachkriegsdeutschland* (Frankfurt am Main, 1993), 192.

[3] See Erich Leitel, "Die Aufnahme der amerikanischen Literatur in Deutschland: Übersetzungen der Jahre 1914–1944 mit einer Bibliographie" (Ph.D. diss., Friedrich Schiller University, Jena, 1958), 99–102, which gives the total number of titles banned during Nazi rule as 5,485.

[4] Participants included André Gide, André Malraux, E[dward] M[organ] Forster, Aldous Huxley, Bertolt Brecht, Heinrich Mann, Boris Pasternak, and Theodore Dreiser. Peter Coleman expressed a critical opinion of Becher's role in Paris in his book, *The Liberal Conspiracy: The Congress for Cultural Freedom and the Struggle for the Mind of Postwar Europe* (New York, 1989), 3–4. Horst Haase's book, by contrast, offers praise for Becher's central role in Paris: *Johannes R. Becher: Leben und Werk*, 2d ed. (Berlin, 1987), 116–7.

[5] Horst Engelbach and Konrad Krauss, "Der Kulturbund und seine Zeitschrift Aufbau in der SBZ," in Gerhard Hay, ed., *Zur literarischen Situation 1945–1949* (Kronberg, Taunus, 1977), 177.

the Soviet side was making a bid to "win over middle-class intellectuals."[6]

Given this background, it is not surprising to learn that between the end of the war and 1967, more than 1,000 books were published around the world with the support of the U.S. Central Intelligence Agency (CIA).[7] Cultural institutions that received support from the CIA published many of these books. There was apparently some direct collaboration between authors and the CIA, but most book authors did not know that the CIA was facilitating publication of their books, as a report to the U.S. Senate emphasized. This development went back to 1947, when the covert subsidy of publications was categorized in-house under "psychological operations." Leading cultural journals throughout the world, including *Der Monat* (established October 1948 in Berlin) and *Encounter* (established October 1953 in London), received funds from the United States as well. The West had clearly also targeted intellectuals.

The U.S. intelligence agency underwrote a significant international conference as well, the Congress for Cultural Freedom, which convened in West Berlin from June 26 to 30, 1950, at the time when North Korean troops were marching into South Korea.[8] Many prominent personalities took part in the congress, including Dolf Sternberger, Golo Mann, Arthur Schlesinger Jr., Hugh Trevor-Roper, James T. Farrell, Arthur Koestler, Theodor Plievier, and Ignazio Silone. Arthur Koestler issued a manifesto at the event that described intellectual freedom as an inalienable human right and demanded the free expression of opinions, "even

when they deviate from the opinions of the authorities," as an individual human right. At the Second German Writers' Congress, which took place a week later in East Berlin (July 4–6, 1950), Johannes R. Becher took a stand on the manifesto. He described the participants in the Congress for Cultural Freedom as "stooges of the warmongers" and "gangsters in literary guise" and spoke of them as a "criminal clique," emphasizing that they were not only "hated," but regarded with "aversion and disgust as an anti-Bolshevist mob."[9] Tensions in world politics during these years had reached into the realm of literature in East and West.

A steady supply of literature emerged in the first postwar years under the control of the occupation forces. The American authorities established a translation unit in Bad Nauheim that commissioned translations of works from English into German and acquired the rights to books produced abroad (by authors in exile). This demonstrates the value placed on belles lettres. The authorities believed that after twelve years of National Socialist rule, the populace would be more receptive to literature than to propagandistic texts. In the selection of this literature, books that conveyed an impression of the "American way of life" received particular consideration.

Between 1945 and 1953, German publishers could select from translations of at least 341 titles; about a third of these were belles lettres and literary history, another 54 were dramas, and around 50 were biographies, along with a dozen volumes each of poetry anthologies and works on theory and criticism. The eagerness of German publishers to acquire translation rights (well over 300 had applied for a license by July 1946) stemmed from the monopoly position of the American authorities. Imports from abroad were banned, all rights existing prior to the war had been nullified, and publishers could only guarantee the paper for printing books they planned to publish through cooperation with the military government. At least until 1948,

---

[6] Ernst Niekisch, *Erinnerungen eines deutschen Revolutionärs*, 2 vols. (Cologne, 1974), 2:53.

[7] See Final Report of the U.S. Congress Senate Select Committee to Study Governmental Operations with Respect to Intelligence Activities, 94th Congress, 2d session, Senate Report 94–755, Book 1 (Washington, D.C., 1976), 193.

[8] The report on the congress is printed in *Der Monat* 2 (1950). (A detailed participant list appears on pp. 476–7; the manifesto mentioned here is on pp. 482–3.) Michael Hochgeschwender's *Freiheit in der Offensive? Der Kongress für kulturelle Freiheit und die Deutschen* (Munich, 1998) was published since this chapter was written.

[9] Cited in Bernhard Zeller, ed., *"Als der Krieg zu Ende war": Literarisch-politische Publizistik 1945–1950* (Munich, 1973), 550.

publishers benefited from the occupation authorities' occasional practice of acquiring certain quotas of books in order to distribute them
in the East.

Republication of certain works that the National Socialists had banned seemed particularly appealing, such as *A Farewell to Arms*
(Ernest Hemingway), *The Iron Heel* (Jack London), *Of Mice and Men* (John Steinbeck), and
others by John Dos Passos, Theodore Dreiser,
and Thomas Wolfe. Classical prose writers
(Nathaniel Hawthorne, O. Henry, Washington Irving, Herman Melville, Edgar Allan
Poe, Mark Twain), poets (Henry Wadsworth
Longfellow, Carl Sandburg, Walt Whitman),
and essayists (Ralph Waldo Emerson) also
attracted attention. Plays by Maxwell Anderson, Lillian Hellman, Clifford Odets, Eugene O'Neill, Thornton Wilder, and Tennessee
Williams were made available. Prose was the
best represented literary genre and poetry the
poorest.

The American occupation force had less tolerance for authors who were communists or
had a reputation of being communist sympathizers. When a Munich publisher wanted to
publish Howard Fast's *Freedom Road*, a title that
had been issued as an Armed Services Edition
in a large run in 1945 with public funds and
distributed to American soldiers, the authorities refused the request. Louis Adamic's work
also fell victim to this trend beginning in 1947.
His *The Native's Return* had appeared in the fall
of 1943 as an Armed Services Edition and *From
Many Lands* had still gone to press in 1946. But
in 1947, his work was denied further subsidies
from the translation program, as was Granville
Hicks's as well. A small controversy among a potential Berlin publisher, the American authorities, and author James T. Farrell flared up over
Farrell's *Studs Lonigan* trilogy, and the work remained untranslated in the end. Notable works
sometimes failed to reach Germany because the
incensed intervention of a single American citizen was enough to withhold a critical view of
the United States from the German public. This
was the case in 1947 with Arthur Miller's first
great success, *All My Sons*, a play focused on the
obsession with profits.

American literature also circulated in East
Germany, although to a much smaller extent
than in the West. By 1949, approximately fifty
different titles had appeared in the Soviet occupation zone. The Soviet authorities who oversaw literary works favored the classics (works
by Nathaniel Hawthorne, Edgar Allan Poe,
Henry David Thoreau, Walt Whitman, Herman
Melville, Mark Twain), authors who were on
the index during the Nazi era (Edward Bellamy,
Theodore Dreiser, Jack London, Upton Sinclair,
Agnes Smedley), anthologies of African American writers (William E. B. DuBois, Langston
Hughes, Lorraine Hansberry, James Baldwin),
and writers who illuminated the social and political condition of the United States from a
socialist – or, at least, a critical – perspective
(Howard Fast, Albert Maltz, John Steinbeck,
Sinclair Lewis). Upton Sinclair lost favor with
the powers that be when he criticized the Soviet Union, after which he counted as a "rene-
gade." Sinclair's books that had already been
published were no longer printed, and printed
copies were no longer distributed. Howard Fast
suffered the same fate after he withdrew from
the Communist Party. The Soviet occupation
force exerted direct influence through a cultural advisory board that it had created. No
book could be published without this board's
approval.[10]

In the course of 1947, the political climate
started to change, and this development had
its effect on policies concerning literature, too.
With campaigns such as Operation Backtalk, the
West began an anticommunist offensive in mid-
1947. For example, George Orwell's *Animal
Farm* was broadcast as a radio play in September of 1948 and printed in *Der Monat* (December issue), after having been confiscated
by the American side and turned over to the
Soviets for destruction the year before. In a
countermove, the other side removed Thornton Wilder's plays from East German playbills

[10] Karl-Heinz Schönfelder, "Amerikanische Literatur in der ehemaligen Sowjetischen Besatzungszone
Deutschlands (1945–1949)," *Wissenschaftliche Zeitschrift
der Karl-Marx-Universität Leipzig – Gesellschafts- und
Sprachwissenschaftliche Reihe* 11, no. 3 (1962): 640.

in September 1947, replacing them with plays by Clifford Odets, Albert Maltz, and Howard Fast.

A new ruling in September 1947 came into effect in the West that permitted free reprints from eighty-seven American magazines, including *The Atlantic Monthly* and *The Saturday Evening Post*. Previously, individual articles had to be licensed in a laborious, drawn-out process. Many of the nearly 600 journals licensed in the American zone took advantage of this ruling, especially those published in Germany under American direction, such as the *Amerikanische Rundschau, Heute, Neue Auslese*, and *Der Monat*. These four in particular "made an independent and previously unappreciated contribution to the German reception of American literature in the postwar period."[11] *The Amerikanische Rundschau* often reprinted short stories that the *New Yorker* had published first, and *Heute* often carried stories by authors that had appeared previously in Armed Services Editions.

Personal contacts between Americans working for the Psychological Warfare Division and Germans in the publishing industry appear to have facilitated the busy transatlantic transfer of literature that existed since the end of World War II. Further research is needed to determine who played what role in these transatlantic literary crossings, including the question of who functioned as a link between the American publishing world and authorities in Washington (e.g., Chester Kerr), or between the German and American literary scenes (including Alain Bosquet, Robert Creeley, Rainer Maria Gerhardt, Eugene Jolas, Alexander Koval, and Edouard Roditi). The connections running between the Office of War Information (OWI) and writers, both Germans in exile (e.g., Hans Sahl) and Americans (e.g., Kay Boyle), likewise merit further exploration. A biographical dictionary of American and German literary mediators, compiled jointly by scholars of American and German studies, would reveal a network of key figures who decisively influenced the face of American literature in Germany in the early postwar years.

AMERICAN LITERATURE IN GERMANY (1949–67)

The Occupation Statute of April 1949 laid out the rights of the Allies. It determined that the Americans no longer had any legal basis for directly interfering in Germany's cultural life. Between the early 1950s and the late 1960s, approximately 10,000 titles from the United States were published in German in the Federal Republic, about half of which were belles lettres.[12] A comparison with imports from Great Britain shows that the book market no longer had any detectable preferences for one or the other. A few more published translations came from Great Britain between 1955 and 1965 but more from the United States before and after that period. Together, they conquered a good 50 percent of the German translation market through the late 1960s. In light of this parity, it is surprising that British English remained the unchallenged standard in German schools during this period and literature from the United States was treated contemptuously.

In a strictly quantitative sense, light fiction held a premier position with the German public. Margaret Mitchell's *Gone With the Wind* (U.S. edition, 1936, and German edition, 1937) was popular even after the war with German readers, who also favored the novels of Pearl S. Buck and Louis Bromfield and appreciated the humor of James Thurber. With the exception of Thurber, these authors had already appeared in German in the 1930s, so they were able to reconnect with a tradition interrupted by the war. After the war, they remained well liked because the German public apparently remained responsive to their themes or because they offered diversion. American war novels were in high demand early on, particularly the books of Ernest Hemingway, Norman Mailer, and

---

[11] Bödeker, *Amerikanische Zeitschriften*, 308.

[12] These figures are taken from the Börsenverein des Deutschen Buchhandels (Association of the German Book Trade) and only take into account new licenses.

Irwin Shaw, understandably because readers in Germany were well familiar with the experience of having their lives disrupted and existence threatened. Hemingway was not only popular with the public at large but he also exercised a stylistic influence for a time on certain German writers who had lost their own domestic models. After twelve years of daily life permeated with pathos, his laconic style came as a relief to Germans, his sobriety seemed appropriate, and unadorned had become preferable to a more transcendent approach in literature. Colloquial language rendered in a paratactic style emphasized a certain unpretentiousness; Hemingway's dramatic dialogues left no room for moralistic commentary by the narrator. Readers were permitted to judge for themselves, a relief after twelve years of thinking in stereotypes and speaking a prefabricated language. Some readers discovered existentialism in Hemingway's books and others saw nihilism. Alfred Andersch, Heinrich Böll, Wolfgang Borchert, Stephan Hermlin, Wolfgang Koeppen, Hans Werner Richter, and Wolfdietrich Schnurre all knew his work. They were also familiar with Ambrose Bierce, O. Henry, William Faulkner, John Steinbeck, Thomas Wolfe, and Richard Wright. German writers were not exclusively on the receiving end of this exchange: Wolfgang Borchert's "*Generation ohne Abschied*" found an echo in the title of Kay Boyle's novel about Germany, *Generation Without Farewell* (1960).

The thriving magazine industry in the first years after the war ensured that the short story received special attention in Germany. Classic American masters of this genre – Poe, Irving, Hawthorne – and contemporary writers made an impression on both readers and authors. The great success of American literature can be explained by German readers' yearning for a sense of direction, which portions of the broad spectrum of American literature provided. American literature was also helped along by the political dominance of the American occupation forces and the organization of the magazine-dominated book market.

Among the classic authors, Poe was particularly important, but Irving, Hawthorne, Melville, Henry James, and Stephen Crane also found readers in Germany, and Thoreau was particularly popular among students in the 1960s. Benjamin Franklin, Henry Adams, Emerson, Whitman, and Emily Dickinson again became a focus of the university curriculum. Bret Harte, Mark Twain, and Jack London also found great popularity outside of the universities. New currents of contemporary authors representing various directions arrived in Germany in translation. Subjects included societal problems between blacks and whites (James Baldwin, Ralph Ellison, Richard Wright), voices of American Jews (Saul Bellow, Bernard Malamud, Philip Roth), erotic works (Mary McCarthy, Henry Miller, Vladimir Nabokov), authors of the beat generation (Jack Kerouac, Allen Ginsberg, Lawrence Ferlinghetti), representatives of the American South (William Faulkner, Truman Capote, Tennessee Williams), as well as numerous individualists (Paul Bowles, F. Scott Fitzgerald, Katherine Anne Porter, J. D. Salinger, William Saroyan, Thomas Wolfe). The German public was beginning to see a spectrum of works that, while distant, seemed to be moving closer, a spectrum that was fascinating but also a little shocking, one that existed in the present time at a remove, yet always retained the character of prophecy. America was the great model of modernization, and its literature displayed the social consequences of that process.

Of all the literary genres, prose dominated, and American short stories had a greater presence in Germany than did short prose from other countries. American poetry drew various kinds of responses. Young Germans read some poets enthusiastically, primarily in the journals *Das Lot* (1947–52) and *fragmente* (1949–52). This passionate interest stood in contrast to the professional, academic responses that took root in the 1950s. Klaus Martens sees Wallace Stevens as a counterpoint among young people to T. S. Eliot, who held sway in the academic milieu of the postwar years after Ernst Robert Curtius had introduced him to Germany in 1927. Martens described the role that the literary journal *Perspektiven* (1952–6) played in this process; it was edited by James Laughlin and published in several European countries with financing from the Ford Foundation.[13] The magazine gave a stage to Wallace Stevens, Marianne Moore, Robert Frost, Edward A. Robinson, Hart Crane, Archibald MacLeish, and e.e. cummings as well as to John Crowe Ransom and Allen Tate, representatives of the "New Criticism." Personal relationships were even more important vehicles in the transmission of poetry than in the other literary genres. Rainer M. Gerhardt and his journal *fragmente*, on which Robert Creeley and others collaborated, deserves special mention. Also noteworthy were Hans Magnus Enzensberger's contacts with William C. Williams and Allen Ginsberg; Walter Höllerer's relationship to Robert Creeley, Lawrence Ferlinghetti, and Charles Olson; and translator Eva Hesse's contact with Ezra Pound. American poetry did not gain much of a foothold in East Germany, with the exception of African American poetry and the work of Carl Sandburg.

CONCLUSION

American literature first came primarily to the American-occupied areas of destroyed Germany with the soldiers and found many eager readers there. After a short phase (1945–6) in which the Allies formulated denazification, reeducation, and democratization as goals, political changes after 1947 brought about a change in U.S. policy on literature in Germany. An anticommunist program made itself felt everywhere. After the Federal Republic was established in 1949, opportunities for direct influence by American authorities decreased. Indirect opportunities replaced them, for instance, through the editorship of journals (*Der Monat, Perspektiven*). In general, American literature in Germany after 1945 continued the trend that had emerged after World War I, when it experienced its first heyday in Germany. After World War II, a combination of a unique international political situation and an American sense of mission toward Europe ensured that American literature got a chance in Germany and took advantage of it. American literary works that corresponded to the mood in Germany met with an eager reception. In his first novel, *This Side of Paradise* (1919), F. Scott Fitzgerald had formulated the credo for his contemporaries after World War I. After World War II, there was a "lost generation" in Germany that could identify with Fitzgerald's hero, who concluded: "Here was a new generation, shouting the old cries, learning the old creeds . . . grown up to find all Gods dead, all wars fought, all faiths in man shaken."

[13] Klaus Martens, "Wege und Auswirkungen der übersetzerischen Vermittlung amerikanischer Lyrik in der Bundesrepublik Deutschland (1945–1956)," *Mitteilungen des Verbandes deutscher Anglisten* 3, no. 2 (Sept. 1992): 23.

CHAPTER SEVEN

The American Reception of Contemporary German Literature

Sigrid Bauschinger

Translated by Sally E. Robertson

THOMAS MANN AS A REPRESENTATIVE OF EXILE LITERATURE

During World War II, a significant portion of German literature was created in the United States. Bertolt Brecht's *Caucasian Chalk Circle* (*Der kaukasische Kreidekreis*), Carl Zuckmayer's *The Devil's General* (*Des Teufels General*), Hermann Broch's *The Death of Virgil* (*Der Tod des Vergil*), and Alfred Döblin's *Tales of a Long Night* (*Hamlet oder die lange Nacht nimmt ein Ende*) were all conceived and partly or entirely written in America.[1] This was also true of the prototypical work of exile literature, Thomas Mann's *Doctor Faustus* (*Doktor Faustus*).

Whereas the work of many exiled authors was never translated into English or was translated only much later, Thomas Mann had achieved fame in the United States beginning with the publication of *The Magic Mountain* (*Der Zauberberg*) in 1927. America was "the country with the second most translations after Sweden, and the country with the second most reviews of his work after Germany."[2] His extended lecture tours, radio addresses, and interviews made him the best known of German writers in exile. He spoke at the Library of Congress and at small colleges, wrote for large-circulation newspapers and the smallest of magazines, and communicated his conviction "that there are *not* two Germanys, a good and a bad one, but only one, whose best turned into evil through devilish cunning. Wicked Germany is merely good Germany gone astray, good Germany in misfortune, in guilt, and ruin."[3]

Thomas Mann stood at the center of American interest in contemporary German literature. His letter to Walter von Molo, "Why I Do Not Return to Germany," and the ensuing campaign against him by writers who had remained in Germany and considered themselves as part of an "inner emigration" were followed with interest in the United States. In his 1947 description of Thomas Mann's defense against his attackers, William Shirer called him "a great German soul crying out in the German wilderness."[4]

Mann's postwar books – from the biblical story *The Tables of the Law* (*Das Gesetz*, 1945) to his last work, *Confessions of Felix Krull, Confidence Man* (*Bekenntnisse des Hochstaplers Felix Krull*, 1954) – thus attracted considerable attention. In 1961, six years after his death, several books by or about Mann appeared within a period of just a few months, including his correspondence with Paul Amann, the

---

[1] See John Spalek and Joseph Strelka, eds., *Deutschsprachige Exilliteratur seit 1933*, vol. 1: *California*; vol. 2: *New York* (Bern, 1976 and 1989).

[2] Hans Wagener, "Thomas Mann in der amerikanischen Literaturkritik," in Helmut Koopman, ed., *Thomas-Mann-Handbuch* (Stuttgart, 1990), 925–39.

[3] Thomas Mann, *Addresses Delivered at the Library of Congress, 1942–1949* (Washington, D.C., 1963), 64.

[4] William Shirer, "End of a Berlin Diary," *Atlantic Monthly* (June 1947): 97–9.

autobiographical *A Sketch of My Life* (*Lebens-abriss*), *The Story of a Novel: The Genesis of Doctor Faustus* (*Die Entstehung des Doktor Faustus*), and his daughter Monika's memoirs. Thomas Mann was no longer simply the most respected representative of German literature; many considered him to be the greatest writer of his generation.[5]

Reviews in newspapers such as the influential literary supplement to the *New York Times* and magazines such as the widely read *Time* and the discriminating *New York Review of Books* played an influential role in shaping the tastes of the educated American public. My analysis here focuses on the critical reception accorded to German exile literature in these and similarly prominent publications, some of which no longer exist, such as the *New York Herald Tribune* and *Saturday Review*.

The critics reviewing Mann's late work in these publications were agreed: They lauded him as an essayist; as a novelist they did not always understand him. *Doctor Faustus* remained an impenetrable enigma for most American critics, but that did not keep it from becoming a Book-of-the-Month Club selection. Alfred Kazin heard "a great cry of love and despair over the country he fled" in the work.[6] And *Time*'s commentator wrote, "To those who look for it, it is a masterful explanation of those sides of the German character that welcomed Hitler."[7]

After the death of Franz Werfel in 1945, Lion Feuchtwanger was the second most successful writer in exile after Thomas Mann. He had achieved early fame for his historical novels. His *Proud Destiny* (*Waffen für Amerika*, also published under the title *Die Füchse im Weinberg*) appeared two years after the war, a novel about Benjamin Franklin's years in Paris. *This Is the Hour* (*Goya oder der arge Weg der Erkenntnis*) followed in 1951, and *T'is Folly to Be Wise or Death and Transfiguration of J. J. Rousseau* (*Narrenweisheit oder Tod und Verklärung des J. J. Rousseau*) in 1953. Feuchtwanger was also known for his *Stories from Far and Near* (1945), which contained six tales about the National Socialist era. These found an eager audience precisely because they convincingly depicted day-to-day life, with its bureaucratic tribulations, through small-scale, matter-of-fact tragedies. Feuchtwanger rendered these tales with cool detachment, even though the author had in fact suffered under the Nazi regime.

THE AMERICAN INTEREST IN PERSECUTION, RESISTANCE, AND WAR

The themes of persecution, resistance, and war preoccupied American readers intensely in the following decades. Alfred Neumann's 1945 work *Six of Them* (*Er waren ihrer sechs*) was one of the first books in which American readers learned of the German resistance, specifically the group known as the "White Rose." Despite its somewhat sentimental flavor, readers found *Six of Them* moving and honest. The case of Anna Seghers also merits mention in this context. In 1942, her resistance novel *The Seventh Cross* (*Das siebte Kreuz*) met with considerable success in America, and Fred Zinneman produced a film version of the book. However, American critics found more problematic the stereotyping in her collection of short stories, *The Dead Stay Young* (*Die Toten bleiben jung*), with its black-and-white characterizations of all Germans as either communists or Nazis.[8]

One of the first voices heard from Germany after the war was that of Ernst Wiechert, who came to the United States for a lecture tour in 1945. He could report from firsthand experience on life and persecution under the Nazi regime. His *Forest of the Dead* (*Der Totenwald*) appeared in 1947 and was followed by *Missa sine nomine* in 1954. Wiechert's books provoked

---

[5] For this reason, attempts by the FBI to discredit Thomas Mann as a representative of "premature antifascism" who played into the hands of the communists were doomed to fail. See Hans Vaget, "Hoover's Man: Gleanings from the FBI's Secret Files on Thomas Mann," in Wolfgang Elfe, James Hardin, and Gunther Holst, eds., *The Fortunes of German Writers in America* (Columbia, SC, 1992), 131–44.

[6] *New York Herald Tribune Book Review*, Oct. 31, 1948, 3.

[7] *Time*, Nov. 1, 1948, 1.

[8] *Chicago Sunday Times*, Aug. 6, 1950, 4; *Catholic World*, Oct. 1950, 74.

deeply emotional responses and won praise for their clear language. Yet, readers sensed that the author could not quite resist the temptation to portray himself as a martyr. Among the younger authors who dealt with the themes of resistance and persecution were Elisabeth Langgässer, in *The Quest* (*Märkische Argonautenfahrt*, 1954), and Alfred Andersch, in *Flight to Afar* (*Sansibar oder der letzte Grund, 1958*). Critics' interest in and goodwill toward work on this subject declined over time. Initially, books on resistance could count on at least a measure of critical regard, but that no longer held in the case of Ilse Aichinger's *Herod's Children* (*Die grössere Hoffnung*, 1963).

Unlike the plays of Bertolt Brecht, which were known in the United States mainly through performance, Rolf Hochhuth's *The Deputy* (*Der Stellvertreter*) had an audience of both theatergoers and readers. It was published in 1964 with a foreword by Albert Schweitzer. The critics displayed rare unanimity. None praised the implausible characters. None had good word for its pseudoclassical language and its heavy baggage of historical documentation. Theater scholar and director Robert Brustein called the play an "animal amphibium," neither good history nor good literature.[9] Susan Sontag felt that the play should not even be judged as a work of art but was nevertheless extremely important because it communicated truth.[10]

Rolf Hochhuth offered American readers a credible young voice. His actual subject, wrote Alfred Kazin in the *New York Review of Books*, was an attack on the intolerable moral callousness of German philistines, who were now enjoying both a new prosperity and the security of the free West. But even Kazin could not recognize *The Deputy* as a work of art. Hochhuth's mistake, he said, had been to believe that Auschwitz could be put on the stage. The victims had died a senseless death, and art cannot arise out of senselessness, argued Kazin.[11]

Between 1948 and 1968, many more German books about war appeared in the United States than books about Nazi persecution and anti-Nazi resistance. There was the "classic writer" Theodor Plivier's *Stalingrad* (1948), a gruesome and merciless depiction of the destruction of an army. The *New York Times* called his book the "most impressive novel of the second World War yet to appear in Europe."[12] It was followed by Erich Maria Remarque's *A Time to Love and a Time to Die* (*Zeit zu leben und Zeit zu sterben*) in 1954 and the *08/15* trilogy by Hans Hellmut Kirst, who won a firm place in the hearts of American readers and was taken very seriously by the literary establishment. Critics compared Kirst's novels featuring ordinary soldiers favorably with Erich Maria Remarque's books, whose characters often suffered from self-pity. Kirst's later books, such as *The Officer Factory* (*Fabrik der Offiziere*, 1963) or *The Night of the Generals* (*Die Nacht der Generäle*, 1964), were set in the postwar period and took aim at the Federal Republic during the period of the economic miracle. These works drew praise not only as thrillers but also for showing how detective stories could serve as a literary tool for laying bare a culture and society.[13]

Dieter Meichsner, Willi Heinrich, Heinrich Gerlach, Michael Horbach, Hans Wilhelm Pump, and many others also published war books. Not all garnered positive reviews, but there was enough reader interest that American publishers time and again published German books on the war and immediate postwar period.

HEINRICH BÖLL: "THE CONSCIENCE OF THE NATION"

This interest extended to the work of Heinrich Böll, an author who received high praise from the outset and whom American critics saw as the heir to Thomas Mann. When his first novel, *Acquainted with the Night* (*Und sagte kein einziges Wort*), appeared in 1954, the language caused

[9] *The New Republic*, Mar. 14, 1964, 23.

[10] *Book Week*, Mar. 1, 1964, 1.

[11] *New York Review of Books* (*NYRB*), Mar. 19, 1964, 1.

[12] *New York Times Book Review* (*NYTBR*), Oct. 17, 1948, 5.

[13] *NYTBR*, June 26, 1967, 18.

as much sensation as the plot. Reviews such as the one in *Time* made clear that the author had struck an American nerve. Böll, the magazine declared, "treats despair with that detailed evenness that the dullest of *The New Yorker* writers apply to domestic crises in suburban Connecticut."[14]

Many of Böll's short-story collections addressed the war theme or, more accurately, the antiwar theme. In the German postwar conditions that Böll criticized with a mixture of despair and irony, American readers discovered a materialistic mind-set similar to that prevalent in their own country. The Federal Republic and the United States had much in common during the 1950s. *Tomorrow and Yesterday* (*Haus ohne Hüter*, 1956) was the fourth of Böll's books to be published in the United States within a three-year period. *Time*'s reviewer considered the author the best contemporary German writer.[15] Early highpoints in Böll's critical reception came with the publication of his novels *Billiards at Half-Past Nine* (*Billard um Halbzehn*) in 1962 and *The Clown* (*Ansichten eines Clowns*) in 1965. The historical panorama that Böll depicted in *Billiards at Half-Past Nine* won him comparisons to Heinrich Mann. It also earned him a lengthy feature article in *Time* that has been called the most important review in the American reception of his work.[16] The feature not only placed Böll in the political context of West Germany but also compared him to Günter Grass and Uwe Johnson. The three became a veritable triumvirate of German postwar literature that American and German critics judged in very similar terms. *Time* praised Böll, Grass, and Johnson for the earnestness with which they devoted themselves to the overwhelming experiences of recent German history and for the parallels that they drew between the new West German materialism and resulting complacency on the one hand, and the Germans of the Nazi epoch on the other, those who were innocent in a legal sense but morally culpable.

The Clown, with its biting critique of society in the Federal Republic, also spoke to the American mind-set of the time. Hans Schnier was the German version of the dropouts who were surfacing in America and could soon be found from coast to coast as hippies and flower children. "In this bitter and brilliant book," wrote Daniel Stern in the *New York Times*, "an author who has the right to do so asks 'How can an honest man profess Christianity when Christian culture in the West failed to stem the rise of Nazism?'"[17]

Several reviewers drew a connection between Böll's clown and Pope John XXIII. Frank Warnke insisted in the pages of *New Republic* that the novel, despite its criticism of the church, was a deeply Catholic book.[18] The clown loved humanity with a hopeless love at the same time that he indicted it. Schnier was a holy fool, concluded George Steiner in the *Reporter*. Like Pope John, Schnier stood "for the possibilities of love in a world in which these possibilities are embarrassing or ludicrously unrealistic."[19]

For his American readers, Heinrich Böll had become the conscience of the German nation. That was the assessment of Leila Vennewitz, who translated *The Clown* and all of Böll's subsequent books. All were successful, with the exception of his *Irish Journal* (*Irisches Tagebuch*, 1967). Writing in the *New York Review of Books*, Conor Cruise O'Brien accused the book of an unacceptable idealization of poverty in Ireland. With his description of the contented Irish, O'Brien argued, Böll had wanted to set an example for his German countrymen. "In the most abominable passage of this ghastly little book, this man actually deplores the introduction of the 'pill' to Ireland," wrote a bitter O'Brien.[20] Böll's knowledge of Ireland, from which so many had had to emigrate to America, was quite limited, O'Brien charged. He had

[14] *Time*, Oct. 4, 1954, 106.

[15] *Time*, Oct. 21, 1957, 114.

[16] Ralph Ley, "Making It in the Big Apple: Heinrich Böll in the New York Press 1954–1988," in Wolfgang Elfe, James Hardin, and Gunther Holst, eds., *The Fortunes of German Writers in America: Studies in Literary Reception* (Columbia, S.C., 1992), 249–75.

[17] *NYTBR*, Jan. 24, 1965.

[18] *The New Republic*, Mar. 20, 1965.

[19] *The Reporter*, Feb. 25, 1965, 53.

[20] *NYRB*, Sept. 14, 1967, 10.

ventured onto terrain that was far more familiar in New York than in Cologne.

GÜNTER GRASS: THE BEST-KNOWN GERMAN AUTHOR IN THE UNITED STATES

Böll had encountered occasional criticism even earlier. For all the respect he was accorded, some critics saw a rather demoralizing undertow of guilt and inferiority in his books that could easily descend into self-pity. One work that remained safe from such accusations was a book that reached the American public in 1963, *The Tin Drum* (*Die Blechtrommel*) by Günter Grass. The book became the greatest success of German literature in America after World War II. On the *New York Times* best-seller list for three months, it sold 400,000 copies within a year. By 1970, Americans had bought a total of 600,000 copies of Grass's book. Volker Schlöndorff's adaptation of *The Tin Drum*, which won the Oscar for best foreign film in 1979, helped Grass become and remain the best-known contemporary German writer.

With *The Tin Drum*, a genuine storyteller took German history to task in a completely new language, one full of grotesque images and obscure symbols. The novel prompted a veritable flood of associations among American critics. They were reminded of Dante, Rabelais, Grimmelshausen, Voltaire, Goethe, Proust, Joyce, Faulkner, Ionesco, and Nabokov, and they described the book as romantic, expressionistic, grotesque, absurd, surrealistic, and even realistic.[21] Conservative critics, too, could not escape the powerful pull of this language. Hugh MacGovern called the novel a "long, crazy, unalleviated nightmare, void of any beauty . . . rotten with perverted eroticisms and . . . revolting in its numerous blasphemies of the Catholic Church." And yet, he concluded, the book conveyed "a burning horror and rage at the loathesomeness of the human condition."[22]

Some critics expressed regret over the fact that *Cat and Mouse* (*Katz und Maus*), which reached American readers in the same year, was so much shorter than *The Tin Drum*. Still, it met with nearly as much enthusiasm as the earlier book. Two years later, Grass's *Dog Years* (*Hundejahre*) appeared. This third volume in *The Danzig Trilogy* was again of reassuring epic length and was greeted as the work of a genius whose talent, wrote Paul West in *The Nation*, was so overwhelming that the reader must ration it.[23] With the verbal power of a James Joyce, said West, the book raised accusations that – although set in the context of German history – were nevertheless universal. Günter Grass also had the good fortune to find a congenial translator early on; Ralph Manheim, until his death, rendered all of the author's works into English, including *The Rat* (*Die Rättin*).

THE PARALLEL TASTES OF AMERICAN AND GERMAN READERS

No other German author, neither Böll nor Uwe Johnson, could hold his own in the United States against the dominance of Günter Grass. Johnson's *Speculations about Jakob* (*Mutmassungen über Jakob*) appeared in 1963 and gave America some of its first impressions of the division of Germany, a division that sat uneasily with the author, as *The Nation* reported.[24] Just as Johnson had moved from East to West so that he could live and write there, Jakob would have done the same had his character been developed logically. Johnson's *Two Views* (*Zwei Ansichten*) was read in 1967 as an accusation against both of the German political systems dividing humanity at the time. "The post-apocalyptic irresolution of *Two Views* may well be where European man, after history's extravagant demands, is glad to settle," wrote John Updike in *The New Yorker*.[25]

American readers did not initially see much of how the eastern part of Germany was reflected in its literature. They were not particularly

---

[21] See Sigrid Mayer, "Grüne Jahre für Grass: Die Rezeption in den Vereinigten Staaten," *text + kritik* 1, no. 1a (1978): 151–61.

[22] *America*, Mar. 9, 1963, 344.

[23] *The Nation*, Aug. 16, 1965, 81.

[24] *The Nation*, Apr. 6, 1963, 290.

[25] *The New Yorker*, Jan. 7, 1967, 92.

interested in works of socialist realism and, therefore, neither were the American publishers. However, those authors who indicated in their books that they had not completely adapted to their state's system, such as Manfred Bieler, were read with interest in the United States. Bieler's *The Sailor in the Bottle* (*Bonifaz oder der Matrose aus der Flasche*, 1966) was one of the first works of literature from the German Democratic Republic (GDR) to appear in the United States. Still, readers were on the lookout for traces of an Eastern bias. Readers, suggested the *Saturday Review*, "would have to hate the West Germans more than they deserve to be amused by this flat-footed diatribe."[26]

Many literary works written in German – by Swiss and Austrian authors as well as West and East Germans – were published in English translation in the United States during the quarter-century following the war. Max Frisch debuted in 1964 with *I'm Not Stiller* (*Stiller*). Friedrich Dürrenmatt, whose reputation – like that of Bertolt Brecht – was earned largely through performances of his works on stage, became known to U.S. audiences in 1959 through *The Pledge* (*Das Versprechen*), and Ingeborg Bachmann in 1964 with her short-story collection *The Thirtieth Year* (*Das dreissigste Jahr*). Poems by Wolf Biermann, Paul Celan, Hans Magnus Enzensberger, Karl Krolow, and Nelly Sachs appeared in magazines such as *The New Yorker, The Nation, Harper's*, and *Atlantic Monthly*, and a collection of selected poems by Günter Grass appeared in 1966.

The interest of American readers came to focus over the years on present-day Germany as reflected in narrative literature, including literature intended for sheer entertainment. Examples are Erich Kuby's *Rosemarie* (1960), a story based on the murder of a Frankfurt call girl that caused an uproar in the Federal Republic; Hans Scholz's *Through the Night* (*Am grünen Strand der Spree*), a Berlin *Decameron* about the war and postwar years that also appeared in 1960; and Rudolf Lorenzen's *Anything but a Hero* (*Alles andere als ein Held*), about a German "Everyman" of the period. In many cases, the tastes of German

and American readers coincided to a surprising degree, particularly in the realm of popular literature. Annemarie Selinko's *Desirée* was, for example, among these books most frequently borrowed from American public libraries in the 1950s.

"GERMANY 1967"

The more books by German authors of the younger generation that were published in the United States, the more complex Americans' image of the Federal Republic became. In 1966, Gruppe 47 met in Princeton. This loose-knit organization, with neither membership cards nor dues, had its beginnings in the United States, where Hans Werner Richter and Alfred Andersch had met in the prisoner-of-war camp at Fort Kearney, Rhode Island, and published the journal *Der Ruf* together with other writers, including Gustav René Hocke.

The critical reception of German literature in the first twenty-five years after the end of the war was certainly more lively and varied than in later decades. The two dominant figures were Günter Grass and the somewhat lesser-known Heinrich Böll, but the works of a variety of other German authors were also published in America in these years.

Toward the end of the period described here, a delegation of nine American intellectuals traveled to West Germany for two weeks to gain an impression of "Germany 1967" and to report on their observations in the *Atlantic Monthly*. Stanley Kauffmann was particularly interested in assessing the cultural situation.[27] He described, among other things, a discussion with Carl Friedrich von Weizsäcker in which the physicist-philosopher was asked how he explained the low level of intellectual and artistic achievement in Germany after 1945 compared to the creativity that followed World War I. Weizsäcker attributed this primarily to the "loss of intellectual substance." He estimated that about half of the significant German artists and intellectuals of his youth had been Jews. Others

---

[26] *Saturday Review*, Jan. 22, 1966, 42.

[27] Stanley Kauffmann, "Germany 1967," *Atlantic Monthly* (May 1967): 55–6.

who were interviewed, including film and theater people, cited even higher percentages in explaining the meager creative output in their fields. "The irony," remarked Kauffmann, "is that a small percentage of the population – half a million Jews in a pre-war Germany of 70 million – were persecuted as disproportionately influential, and now they are lamented, at least publicly, because their influence is lacking."[28] Kauffmann, a film and theater critic, found this deficiency particularly noticeable in the performing arts.

The loss of Jewish artists did not, however, completely explain the situation, he argued, for a curious contradiction was at work. Unlike film and theater, German postwar literature was important in a range of ways. German novelists, poets, essayists, and journalists were not only extremely productive, but they also showed the best and most progressive side of the German

spirit of the day. Kauffmann named Grass, Martin Walser, Günter Eich, Enzensberger, Böll, Wolfdietrich Schnurre, Ingeborg Bachmann, Marion Gräfin Dönhoff, and Wolfgang Leonhardt, who he said "form a collective voice: candid, critical, compassionate, and angry about Germany today."[29]

For Kauffmann and the other visitors, contemporary meant the Federal Republic of 1967. That was the year of Chancellor Kurt Georg Kiesinger's "Grand Coalition" and the year that saw a rise in support for the ultra-right-wing National Democratic Party (*Nationaldemokratische Partei Deutschlands*, or NPD), a party that would soon drop out of sight again. That is clear in many remarks of the American visitors, some of whom openly admitted that they had come to Germany in a state of alarm. However, the visit also showed how current events could affect responses to literature created earlier under entirely different circumstances.

[28] Ibid., 56.

[29] Ibid., 56.

CHAPTER EIGHT

Cold War Politics and American Popular Culture in Germany

Uta G. Poiger

In the aftermath of National Socialism and in the face of the Cold War, debates over American popular culture were central to (re)constructions of German identities on both sides of the Iron Curtain. American imports such as Hollywood movies, jazz, rock 'n' roll, and jeans were quite popular with German adolescents; as a result, they constituted some of the most controversial aspects of consumer culture in the two German states. In the 1950s and 1960s, East German authorities were more or less consistently hostile toward American imports. Many West German church leaders, politicians, and educators likewise attacked what they saw as cultural Americanization. By the late 1950s, however, an emerging Cold War liberal consensus made consumption, including the consumption of American popular culture, increasingly part of a new, liberal West German identity.[1]

After 1945, with the Allied occupation and the opening of its market, West Germany experienced an unprecedented influx of American products, from nylon stockings to popular music. The impact of these imports was by no means restricted to West Germany; it reached well beyond the Iron Curtain, especially via Berlin. East German authorities severely restricted American imports into their own territory and tried to prevent their population from consuming American movies, music, and fashions, but they could not control access. Until the construction of the Wall in 1961, a constant stream of people flowed back and forth between East and West Berlin. Large numbers of East Berliners and East Germans came to West Berlin to shop and enjoy themselves. Sometimes whole East Berlin school classes would cross into the Western sectors to watch movies. Many East Berlin boys and girls frequented West Berlin music halls, and young people from all over the German Democratic Republic (GDR) would go to West Berlin to buy jeans, leather jackets, or records, despite prohibitive exchange rates. At home, some of them would tune into Western radio stations, including the American Forces Network (AFN) and Radio Luxembourg, to listen to the latest American hits. Even after the Wall, radio, television, and visitors continued to bring American popular culture into

[1] On American popular culture in postwar Germany, see Heide Fehrenbach, *Cinema in Democratizing Germany: Reconstructing National Identity after Hitler* (Chapel Hill, N.C., 1995); Konrad H. Jarausch and Hannes Siegrist, eds., *Amerikanisierung und Sowjetisierung in Deutschland* (Frankfurt am Main, 1997); Kaspar Maase, *Bravo Amerika: Erkundigungen zur Jugendkultur der Bundesrepublik in den fünfziger Jahren* (Hamburg, 1992); Uta G. Poiger, "Rock 'n' Roll, Female Sexuality and the Cold War Battle over German Identities," *Journal of Modern History* 68 (1996): 577–616; Uta G. Poiger, *Jazz, Rock, and Rebels: Cold War Politics and American Culture in a Divided Germany* (Berkeley, Calif., 2000); Michael Rauhut, *Beat in der Grauzone: DDR-Rock 1964 bis 1972 – Politik und Alltag* (Berlin, 1993); Timothy Ryback, *Rock Around the Bloc: A History of Rock Music in Eastern Europe and the Soviet Union* (New York, 1990); see also the chapter by Axel Schildt, vol. 1, Society.

East Germany. Thus, whenever American music and fashions hit West Germany and West Berlin, their impact was felt in both German states.

EAST GERMAN HOSTILITIES

Beginning in the late 1940s, East German leaders described allegedly "decadent" and "degenerate" imports, like boogie-woogie, jazz, westerns, and jeans, as part of an "American cultural barbarism" that they saw at the root of American and West German imperialism. After the June 1953 uprising in East Germany, for example, the GDR press and politicians accused Americanized male adolescents in Texas pants and cowboy shirts of being responsible for instigating the revolt.[2]

Hostilities also became visible when rock 'n' roll music and dancing arrived in Germany in 1956 via American movies and numerous press reports about rock 'n' roll concerts. In December 1956, a cartoon in the East Berlin daily *Berliner Zeitung* showed a small, emaciated Elvis Presley performing under larger-than-life female legs in front of a crowd of girls much bigger than he was. The cartoon implied that female Presley fans were sexual aggressors who emasculated men: The girls were throwing off bras and garter belts and licking their lips in obvious sexual excitement. Their hairstyles marked some of these young women as possibly black (short curly dark hair) and others as white (blond ponytails) but, in portraying all of them with stereotypical "negroid" features (wide noses, thick lips), the cartoon labeled their behavior as typically black. The accompanying article claimed that young women were the main consumers of rock 'n' roll (described as American nonculture) and asserted that rock 'n' roll appealed to primitive humans. In such a depiction, allusions to gender upheaval and to alleged racial transgressions reinforced one another to portray rock as dangerous.[3] East German

adolescents encountered state sanctions for publicly expressing their preference for West European and American popular culture. These measures ranged from prohibitions of American music and "open" dancing to arrests for shouting "Ulbricht pfui, pfui, pfui – Elvis yes, yes, yes."[4]

The fact that many of the products of American culture were rooted in the culture of African Americans, whom communists recognized as an oppressed group, did not dissuade East German authorities from attacks on American music, dances, and especially jazz, boogie, and rock 'n' roll. Race played a complicated role in these attacks. It would seem that the racism apparent in East German charges of "decadence" and "primitivism" against American popular culture was clearly at odds with East Germany's public stance against racism in the United States. After all, East German papers in the mid-1950s reported extensively on efforts to integrate schools and public accommodations in the American South. However, East German visions of racial equality relied on ideals of male restraint and female respectability, including female sexual passivity, across races. This insistence on specific norms of male and female respectability found one of its most powerful articulations in official rejections of jazz as a music associated with gangsters and prostitutes. With such condemnations of jazz, which they saw as a black music, East German officials reasserted racial hierarchies in the realm of culture. Attacks on rock 'n' roll reinforced this. Even though highlighting American racism was one way to fight the Cold War against the United States and West Germany, East German authorities could not relinquish their own association between female sexual passivity, "civilization," and "whiteness."

However, throughout the 1950s, some voices in East Germany also argued that jazz was a protest music for African Americans (whom East German authorities recognized as an oppressed group); jazz could, therefore, be part of a new, "clean" German dance music. In brief periods of greater leniency, this view managed

---

[2] See Ausschuss für Deutsche Einheit, *Wer zog die Drähte? Der Juni-Putsch 1953 und seine Hintergrunde* (Berlin, 1954).

[3] "Appell an den Urmenschen," *Berliner Zeitung*, Dec. 13, 1956.

[4] See "Zuchthaus für Presley-Fans," *Depesche*, Nov. 3, 1959.

to gain acceptance: After the June 1953 uprising and again after Khrushchev's 1956 speech against Stalinism, jazz fans were able to found jazz clubs all over the GDR, usually connected to the communist state youth organization, the Free German Youth (*Freie Deutsche Jugend*, or FDJ).

Well aware of such arguments, East German authorities often walked a tightrope. When students at the Humboldt University tried to found a jazz club after the building of the Berlin Wall in 1961, East German officials were clearly alarmed but tried to avoid any public debates over jazz and American music. They suggested that jazz fans pursue their interests in authentic folk music in existing, carefully supervised dance and music groups, and urged local FDJ functionaries to be aware of "the political background of a strengthened jazz movement." Officials of the FDJ Central Committee claimed that such jazz associations were founded by West German agents. Present-day jazz, these officials said, was shaped by commercialism and imperialist ideas and was thus part of the "decadent trends of bourgeois ideology."[5] At the same time, the East German press and youth officials focused heavily on transforming the boys and girls who had frequented bars and dance halls in West Berlin and who had consumed, among other things, rock 'n' roll. Officials were satisfied when these adolescents no longer wore jeans. The official attention to the more conservative fashions of suits and dresses shows the importance of "proper" gender roles in the transformation process.[6] As throughout the 1950s, East German authorities viewed adolescent consumption of American-influenced popular culture as a potential political threat.

Authorities continued to waver in the 1960s, sometimes opening opportunities for adolescents to consume American influences. In 1963, they released an American western, *The Magnif-*

icent Seven; in 1964, the ruling Socialist Unity Party (*Sozialistische Einheitspartei Deutschlands*, or SED) promoted the Twist; and throughout the 1960s, authorities tried to channel adolescent energies into folk music, including some American compositions. However, the atmosphere remained mostly hostile: Authorities rallied against beat, arrested long-haired male beat fans, reported about cultural barbarism at West German rock concerts, and also blamed the Prague Spring of 1968 on such phenomena.[7]

WEST GERMAN HOSTILITIES

Until the second half of the 1950s, hostility also dominated West German commentaries on American popular culture. Similarities between reactions in the two German states were sometimes astounding: In vehement rejections of American imports, both sides conflated uncontrolled female sexuality, African American culture, and German lower-class culture, and linked all three to the threat of fascism. West Germans, especially conservatives – including intellectuals, church leaders, and politicians who promoted a "Christian West" – found themselves fighting on several fronts: against their fascist past, against the present Cold War enemy, and against the specter of an American-style consumer culture. In the early 1950s, West German educators and state officials attacked American dances like boogie-woogie as part of their youth-protection efforts. The supposed "primitivism" of faster-paced dances, like the boogie, signified the threat they posed to the gender roles so necessary to postwar West German identity. In West German discussions of dancing, concerns about premarital sex, especially by women, intersected with misgivings about working-class culture and a hostility toward black culture. Contemporaries cast working-class girls who hung out in the streets and who danced boogie-woogie as

---

[5] See Abt. Agit.-Prop., Einige Bemerkungen zu Frage des Jazz, Berlin, Nov. 29, 1961, and Unser Standpunkt zum Jazz, Berlin, Dec. 7, 1961, both in Jugendarchiv beim Institut für Zeitgeschichtliche Jugendforschung Berlin, AB547.

[6] Bericht über Jugendklubs, Nov. 11, 1962, Landesarchiv Berlin, Aussenstelle Breite Strasse, Rep. 121, No. 62.

[7] Dorothee Wierling, "Jugend als innerer Feind: Konflikte in der Erziehungsdiktatur der sechziger Jahre," in Hartmut Kälble, Jürgen Kocka, and Hartmut Zwahr, eds., *Sozialgeschichte der DDR* (Stuttgart, 1994), 404–25; Rauhut, *Beat in der Grauzone*. See also the chapter by Edward Larkey in this section.

potential sexual delinquents. A related attack was to point to the emasculating and feminizing effect of "sultry Negro songs" on boys.[8]

Such West German fears were exacerbated by the arrival of rock 'n' roll and by youth riots in the mid-1950s. West Germans connected what they saw as adolescent misbehavior to American influences. In 1956, for example, the West German youth magazine *Bravo* reported about male rioters who had roamed the streets in Britain after showings of the Bill Haley movie *Rock Around the Clock*. *Bravo* claimed that Bill Haley's music was rooted in the "ritual music of Africa's Negroes." Further, the magazine maintained that the influence of rock 'n' roll had turned "cool Englishmen" into "white Negroes" who rioted. *Bravo* thus labeled rioting a typically black behavior and warned against rock 'n' roll in racist terms; it also urged its German audience not to behave like the English. When it became clear that rock 'n' roll had many admirers in Germany and that German adolescents also took to the streets after showings of *Rock Around the Clock* (the German title was *Ausser Rand und Band*), another West German commentator worried about what he called "wild barbarians in ecstasy."[9] And, in 1957, the state-sponsored West German movie rating board demanded that scenes that allegedly showed the "aggressive flirting" of girls be cut from another rock 'n' roll movie because the film would otherwise foster the "materialist understanding of life" among adolescents.[10] Rock 'n' roll was so disturbing precisely because it seemed to undermine the ideal nuclear families of restrained male breadwinner protectors and asexual female

caretakers. The various reactions to rock 'n' roll show that many West Germans felt that American cultural influences led to transgressions of gender and indeed also of racial norms with potentially dire political consequences.

Despite many differences, West and East German authorities shared strong hostilities toward American popular culture. Both sides drew on a prewar tradition of cultural anti-Americanism,[11] but the Cold War battle added a new dimension. East German authorities time and again used images of Americanization in their propaganda, both against their own population and against the Cold War enemy to the West. In 1953, the East German press reported, for example, that West Germans were enslaved by American movies. Here and in many other instances, East German officials tried to exploit American cultural influences to attack West Germany's transformation into a capitalist liberal democracy and Bonn's growing military and political association with the United States.[12] Sometimes they indeed managed to put West German conservatives, who wondered whether adolescents were better protected in the East, on the defensive.

COLD WAR LIBERALISM

After the mid-1950s, West German leaders began to change their ideas about consumption and youthful rebellion. By the end of the decade, West German Cold War liberals increasingly replaced the religiously inspired conservatives, who had seen consumption as a terrible and, indeed, political threat. Ludwig Erhard's ascendancy to the chancellorship and the Social Democrats' rejection of Marxism were all part of this move toward Cold War liberalism. Cold War liberals were a loose conglomeration of intellectuals and politicians who began to transform the cultural conservatism of the first half

[8] A. Gügler, *Euer Sohn in der Entwicklungskrise* (Stuttgart, 1952), reprinted in Heinz-Hermann Krüger, ed., *"Die Elvistolle, die hatte ich mir unauffällig wachsen lassen": Lebensgeschichte und jugendliche Alltagskultur in den fünfziger Jahren* (Opladen, 1985), 50; Poiger, *Jazz, Rock, and Rebels*, chap. 1.
[9] "Die ganze Welt rockt und rollt," *Bravo*, Sept. 30, 1956; "Ausser Rand und Band," *Beratungsdienst Jugend und Film* 1 (Nov. 1956): B VII. See also Krüger, *Die Elvistolle*.
[10] Arbeitsausschuss der FSK, Jugendprotokoll: Ausser Rand und Band, II. Teil, Landesbildstelle Berlin, Pressearchiv.

[11] See the chapter by Philipp Gassert, vol. 1, Society.
[12] "Westfilm in amerikanischer Versklavung," *Der Morgen*, May 30, 1952. See also Poiger, *Jazz, Rock, and Rebels*, chap. 1.

of the 1950s. Among them were Erhard and social scientists like Helmut Schelsky and Curt Bondy. Cold War liberals widened the definitions of acceptable adolescent behavior; both male aggression and female sexual expressiveness became less threatening. For Cold War liberals, adolescent rebelliousness and the consumption of American popular culture were nonpolitical, psychological phenomena.

West German Cold War liberals confirmed the basic stability of a consumption-oriented society that had emerged in West Germany by the mid-1950s; they accepted, if not without some criticism, American David Riesman's conclusion in *The Lonely Crowd* (1950) that increased automation and increased leisure time leveled class distinctions. Schelsky and Erhard, for example, made consumption compatible with a new (West) German identity that they located beyond fascism and totalitarianism, indeed beyond all ideologies. In the late 1950s, West European and American intellectuals, among them Daniel Bell, were likewise propagating "the end of ideology" in the West. For West German Cold War liberals, much was at stake: They sought to disconnect themselves from Weimar and Nazism by erasing differences between West Germany and other Western societies and by fully integrating themselves into the fight against communism. They abandoned the fight for a third German way between consumerism in the West and communism in the East.[13]

Social scientists tried to render the German youth culture of the 1950s into a "private" matter. They stressed that adolescent rebelliousness, including listening to jazz or rock 'n' roll, was neither a political challenge nor a precursor of political challenges to come. The West German press and West German officials increasingly accepted these assessments. (This seems particularly ironic given the outrage that the student rebellion caused after 1966.) As part of reframing the youth rebellion as nonpolitical and psychological, West German sociologists and officials still tried to alter adolescent behav-

ior. Researchers described male aggression as a normal part of adolescence. Consumer culture could play a useful psychological role by helping to "release" normal male aggressions; for example, through the consumption of rock 'n' roll or westerns. According to researchers and the press, male rebelliousness disappeared altogether once boys became involved in stable, heterosexual relationships. The West German entertainment industry fostered this vision with images of wholesome German male and female teenagers dancing rock 'n' roll together. Rock 'n' roll and riots were, therefore, cultural styles whose threats could be resolved "privately."[14]

Nevertheless, Cold War liberals had an ambivalent relationship with consumer culture. Cultural goods associated with high modernism and "high" culture could help in redirecting adolescent behavior. Conservatives hardly championed expressionism or jazz, but by the late 1950s, Cold War liberals made modern art, modern architecture, and even jazz central to state efforts to portray West Germany as at once respectable, modern, and different from East Germany. As jazz became more respectable, West German jazz promoters, the press, and West German politicians portrayed both jazz musicians and fans as restrained and respectable; they also "whitened" the music by stressing that jazz had transcended its African American origins and by ignoring the Jewish background of many musicians.[15] In 1958, a state-funded film, *Why Are They Against Us?*, which was made specifically for schools and youth groups, made use of the new respectability of modern art and jazz in addressing problems of male rebelliousness. The working-class male hero rejected the "bad" girl, who danced to rock 'n' roll at the local soda fountain and who "came on" to boys, for a "good," restrained, middle-class girl who went to modern-art exhibits and attended jazz concerts. Like Erhard in his many public

---

[13] Ludwig Erhard, *Wohlstand für alle* (Düsseldorf, 1957); Helmut Schelsky, *Die skeptische Generation: Eine Soziologie der deutschen Jugend* (Cologne, 1957).

[14] See, for example, Curt Bondy et al., *Jugendliche stören die Ordnung: Bericht und Stellungnahme zu den Halbstarkenkrawallen* (Munich, 1957); Schelsky, *Die skeptische Generation*.

[15] See Dietrich Schulz-Köhn, "Der Jazz – Marotte oder Musik," *Kölnische Rundschau*, Dec. 14, 1958.

statements, the movie was critical of the middle-class father's prejudices against the working-class boy but, as part of legitimizing this critique, the moviemakers portrayed working-class cultural practices, "public" women, and the consumption of popular culture in negative terms. The working-class boy, the movie suggested, could raise his status by adopting a bourgeois style of cultural consumption. Thus, in this movie, liberalism with respect to class (promoted also by people like Schelsky and Erhard) rested explicitly on gender and cultural conservatism.[16] This also became evident when West Berlin officials after 1959 opened so-called jazz dance cafes in order to channel adolescent desires and successfully encouraged visitors to come in suits and skirts instead of jeans.

As West German authorities "depoliticized" consumption, it increasingly became a Cold War weapon. For example, West German officials made efforts to draw East Germans into the movie theaters on the Kurfürstendamm in the center of West Berlin. Here, East Germans were also exposed to West Berlin shop windows. And the jazz dance cafes fulfilled a dual function: They drew young people off the streets and displayed the openness of West German society – in pointed contrast to the ongoing repression of American cultural influences in East Germany. It would still be a few more years until West Berlin officials integrated rock 'n' roll into state-run youth programs but, in 1962, a review of an East German dictionary mocked the entry that described rock 'n' roll as a political threat.[17] For the West German authorities of the 1960s, leisure and pleasure were not what would destroy the West; they would actually be a key weapon against the East, exposing its economic inferiority and lack of democratic choice. West Germans successfully countered East German attacks that had mobilized the ambivalence and even hostility toward America that existed on both sides of the Wall. In this climate, consumption remained politicized, if on a different terrain.

This transformation laid one foundation for the anti-American and antiauthoritarian radical movements of the late 1960s. As in the United States, the 1950s youth cultures raised expectations for individual expression and sexual openness among many young men and women, and some of them expressed these expectations in explicitly political terms in the 1960s. Certainly, the rebellions of the late 1960s can be understood as a reaction against parental conservatism and the Cold War liberal consensus that emerged in the late 1950s and early 1960s in West Germany. Sixties radicals rejected a society focused on consumption but were often unaware how much their own expectations had been shaped by American-influenced consumer culture.[18]

In the 1950s and beyond, the German debates over American cultural influences were not simply about Germany becoming more American. Rather, in these conflicts over American imports, each state tried to lay claim to a German identity. East German authorities remained hostile toward American popular culture; West Germans began to draw on American styles and American ideas while trying to tame "excesses" of cultural Americanization. With East German authorities on the defensive, West Germans used the affluence and style of Americanized West German youth as a way to define the boundary between East and West. This dynamic would continue until the end of the Cold War.

---

[16] Siegfried Mohrhof, *Warum sind sie gegen uns?* (Seebruck/Chiemsee, 1958). In 1963, for example, Erhard reminded his fellow Germans that prosperity for all should not lead them to lose track of "Christian values." See "Politik der Mitte und der Verständigung," Oct. 18, 1963, in Karl Hohmann, ed., *Ludwig Erhard: Gedanken aus fünf Jahrzehnten* (Düsseldorf, 1988), 814–46.

[17] "'Krieg' mit Rock 'n' Roll," *Abend*, Aug. 16, 1962.

[18] See Richard McCormick, *Politics of the Self: Feminism and the Postmodern in West German Literature and Film* (Princeton, N.J., 1991).

CHAPTER NINE

Popular Music in Germany

The Genesis of a New Field of Discourse

Edward Larkey

The years 1945 to 1968 represent one of the most intense periods of diffusion of American and British popular music into Germany and the other German-speaking countries. A broad change in German popular-music traditions occurred, particularly in the commercial *Schlager* music, with which American and British music successfully competed. In the course of the diffusion, African American music elements were introduced through jazz, rock 'n' roll, and blues. The use of English lyrics by German vocal artists and musicians became standard procedure as well, and some German lyric writers and composers earned their livelihood by adapting lyrics and tunes from American or British pop stars. The diffusion also accompanied transformations in the music industry, which began to focus on changes in its audience and on the personality of the singer instead of on the song.[1] The German and international popular-music industry not only increased its production output many times over but, as a result of their emulation of American and British models, shifted its emphasis to youth and youth culture. The recording and broadcasting industries, which American capital interests had dominated ever since the mid-1920s, gradually replaced the music-publishing industry as the primary marketer of popular music.[2] The resulting profits were a driving force behind the introduction of the 45-rpm single, the 33-rpm long-playing record, high-fidelity and stereo recordings, and the increased utilization of the FM broadcasting band for popular music, which achieved undisputed dominance in radio and television programming. Concerts by American, British, and other foreign pop stars became a staple of German entertainment. The influence of the Beatles and the Rolling Stones in the 1960s launched a mass music-making movement by German teenagers striving to imitate their idols. Their efforts helped pave the way for the growth of new forms of German rock and pop music in the 1970s.

These influences provoked not only unabashed adulation and imitation but also resistance toward what was seen as the wholesale Americanization of German society and the advance of the commercial cultural industry at the expense of true culture, or *Kultur*.

JAZZ INFLUENCES

One of the first major developments in German popular music during the postwar period was the establishment of the American Army clubs, which offered live-performance opportunities

---

[1] See Matthias Bardong, Hermann Demmler, and Christian Pfarr, eds., *Das Lexikon des deutschen Schlagers* (Munich, 1993), 27–9. According to this account, the 1950s brought to the German *Schlager* "a new marketing strategy that was American."

[2] Dietrich Kayser, *Schlager – Das Lied als Ware: Untersuchungen zu einer Kategorie der Illusionsindustrie* (Stuttgart, 1975), 22.

for American and German jazz musicians. German musicians were able to play week-long gigs, which gave them a steady income and access to American GI audiences.[3] Thanks in part to this support, the German jazz scene, which had never been completely silenced in the years of Nazi repression,[4] rebounded in the postwar period. Jazz fan and impresario Horst Lippmann, who later became famous for organizing rock concerts in the 1970s, got his start by organizing Germany's first jazz festival in 1953, which featured jazz, blues, spiritual, and gospel music. American jazz musicians like Dizzie Gillespie, Louis Armstrong, Benny Goodman, Charlie Parker, and Coleman Hawkins undertook highly successful concert tours of Germany in the late 1940s. These efforts, after overcoming initial reservations of cultural bureaucrats and politicians in Washington, even garnered the sponsorship of the State Department.[5] This opened the way for broadcasting jazz music to Eastern Europe over the airwaves of American-owned or -operated radio networks like RIAS-Berlin, *Rot-Weiss-Rot* in Austria, the Voice of America, and Radio Free Europe.

The capital of German jazz until the 1960s was Frankfurt.[6] Here, the daily jazz scene took place in clubs such as the Hot Club, run by Lippmann and musician Carlo Bohländer. The Domicil du Jazz opened in 1952 and was one of a number of clubs in the city catering to jazz aficionados.[7] These clubs, however, mainly catered to the dyed-in-the-wool jazz enthusiasts, or *Jazzfreunde*, who considered themselves ideological nonconformists and opposed the so-called *Swingheinis*.[8] The "real jazz friends" were

horrified by the "endless drum solos, in which the drummer ultimately no longer drums on his instrument, but onto a horde of ecstatically screaming young people, driving them on with each beat to new gyrations of their bodies and to ever shriller screams."[9] The "true" jazz aficionados expected their existentialist-inclined, nonconformist audiences to sit reverently and listen to the newest jazz music. They had nothing but disdain for the more popular swing and traditional jazz varieties meant for dancing. The opposition to the *Swingheinis* was further nourished by boogie-woogie, precursor to rock 'n' roll, and reached its peak in the latter half of the 1950s with the advent of rock 'n' roll, the subculture of the *Halbstarken*. From 1956 to 1962, jazz competed with rock 'n' roll as an influential determinant of postwar German popular culture.

ROCK 'N' ROLL

The spread of rock 'n' roll to Germany represented a challenge to basic notions of German identity and respectability because many saw it "as a black or black-influenced music that undermined gender norms."[10] The provocative, rebellious behavior of youthful rock-'n'-roll fans (*Halbstarke*) at movies featuring Bill Haley and the Comets (*Blackboard Jungle* came to Germany in October 1955[11] and *Rock Around the Clock* in September 1956) was seen as proof of the intimate connection between youth-criminal deviance and rock 'n' roll. Countless German youths learned not only how to shake their bodies erotically but also how extensive sensationalist press reports provoked the disapproval of the older generations. Elvis Presley entered the U.S. Army in 1958 with a great deal of publicity and was stationed in Germany for the next two

---

[3] Werner Schwörer, *Jazzszene Frankfurt: Eine musiksoziologische Untersuchung zur Situation anfangs der achtziger Jahre* (Mainz, 1989), 41.

[4] See Michael H. Kater, *Different Drummers: Jazz in the Culture of Nazi Germany* (Oxford, 1995), 202–11.

[5] See Reinhold Wagnleitner, *Coca-Colonization and the Cold War: The Cultural Mission of the United States in Austria after the Second World War* (Chapel Hill, N.C., 1994), 210.

[6] Schwörer, *Jazzszene Frankfurt*, 43.

[7] Ibid., 43, 53–4.

[8] According to critic Joachim Ernst Berendt, *Swingheinis* have "hair that is longer and trousers that are shorter than usual, the jackets are too long, the shirts too colorful and the feet have striped socks" (Joachim

Ernst Berendt, *Das Jazzbuch: von Rag bis Rock* [Frankfurt am Main, 1953], 203).

[9] Ibid., 5.

[10] Uta Poiger, "Rock 'n' Roll, Female Sexuality, and the Cold War Battle of German Identities," *Journal of Modern History* 68 (1996): 582.

[11] See Jürgen Struck, *Rock Around the Cinema: Die Geschichte des Rockfilms* (Munich, 1979), 12.

years. Bill Haley and the Comets embarked on their first tour through Germany in the same year.[12] Concerts in Stuttgart, Essen, Berlin, and Hamburg ended in riots with the police, further reinforcing rock 'n' roll's image among conservatives as a devious attempt by an unscrupulous commercial industry to seduce Germany's youth.

In the wake of rock 'n' roll's notoriety, a series of clubs opened in Hamburg, including the Star Club on August 13, 1962, where the Beatles performed. The rock-'n'-roll enthusiasm was the musical accompaniment to the so-called *Halbstarken-Krawallen*, a series of youth riots and disturbances in urban centers between 1956 and 1958. Rock 'n' roll was a catalyst for these actions not only at the few concerts of the rock-'n'-roll stars but also at theaters showing rock-'n'-roll films, local festivals, and fairs, which played the latest tunes along with the rides and held rock-'n'-roll competitions.[13] The only other places to play rock 'n' roll were the American Armed Forces Network (AFN), Radio Luxembourg, and the new jukeboxes, because most of the German public radio stations boycotted the music.

The popularity of rock 'n' roll in Germany, and its challenge to both the liberal and conservative establishments, prompted the *Schlager* industry to harness the commercial benefits of rock 'n' roll while blunting its aggressiveness and its sexually and culturally transgressive aspects. Thus, it is not surprising that while English rock-'n'-roll and pop lyrics celebrated efforts to "flee the conventions of daily life, which are perceived to be constricting" and ignore "the ideal of the establishment for regulating intersexual relations," the German *Schlager* persisted in portraying marriage as the ideal form of relationship.[14]

Many *Schlager* vocalists, such as Peter Kraus, Ted Herold, and Werner Overheidt, were enlisted to sing versions of American pop tunes and rock-'n'-roll favorites. A few American pop singers achieved popularity on the German market, like Connie Francis, who sang her own tunes in German. Gus Backus and Bill Ramsey were two former GIs notorious for singing lyrics in German with thick American accents. They also were known for mixing German and English lyrics, such as in the 1962 tune by Backus, "No Bier, No Wein, No Schnaps," lyrics that were a horror for language purists and cultural critics. Many German *Schlager* singers gave themselves English-sounding names, and English words like "baby," "darling," "girls," and "boys" lent German *Schlager* lyrics an exotic touch.[15]

FOLK MUSIC

The revival of American and British folk music in the 1960s exerted a strong influence on popular music in Germany by helping to rehabilitate German folk traditions abused during the Nazi regime and exploited by the postwar commercial folk-music (*volkstümlich*) genre. American folk singers like Woody Guthrie and Pete Seeger were evidence of a more progressive folk-song tradition, which gradually gave rise to a domestic folk revival in Germany. Annual song festivals at the Burg Waldeck in the Hunsruck region of Rhineland-Palatinate began in 1964. These brought together a variety of folk singers, such as Phil Ochs, Los Paraguayos, and Odetta (South Africa), as well as German *Liedermacher* (singer-songwriters) who later became famous personalities. The festivals were modeled after those of French chansonniers and were designed to be an alternative to the commercial German *Schlager*.[16] A major contribution of the Burg Waldeck folk festivals was the development of politically engaged folksongs used in the

[12] See Peter Spengler, *Rockmusik und Jugend: Bedeutung und Funktion einer Musikkultur für die Identitätssuche im Jugendalter* (Frankfurt am Main, 1985), 38.

[13] See ibid., 38, 137–8.

[14] Helmut Schmiedt, *Ringo in Weimar: Begegnungen zwischen Hochliteratur und Popularkultur* (Würzburg, 1996), 20–1.

[15] See Elke Stölting, *Deutsche Schlager und Englische Popmusik in Deutschland: Ideologiekritische Untersuchung zweier Textstile während der Jahre 1960–1970* (Bonn, 1975), 42.

[16] See Florian Steinbiss, *Deutsch-Folk: Auf der Suche nach der verlorenen Tradition* (Frankfurt am Main, 1984), 33–4.

various actions of the Extraparliamentary Opposition (*Ausserparlamentarische Opposition*, or APO) in the late 1960s. Songs like Pete Seeger's "We Shall Overcome" and Bob Dylan's "Blowing in the Wind" became popular anthems.[17] Efforts to revive the German folk song along the lines of the folk revival in the United States or Great Britain were, however, a marginal phenomenon until the rise of the *kritische Liedermacher* in the 1970s.[18]

One influence of folk-inspired popular music was the increased importance accorded to the lyric content of songs. In contrast to the usual pop lyrics about love, personal relationships, or daily tribulations, the songs of Bob Dylan, Phil Ochs, Tom Paxton, and Joan Baez included political topics such as the threat of nuclear war, opposition to the war in Vietnam, and other "serious" topics. Bob Dylan was crucial in this development, not just for his lack of regard for meter and melodic song structures but also for his successful combination of rock music with folk at the Newport Folk Festival in 1965.[19] This blending of folk music with rock was to become a model for a distinctly German rock music in the late 1960s and early 1970s.

Some of the more commercial folk groups from the United States achieved popularity in Germany as well, such as Peter, Paul, and Mary and the Kingston Trio with their song "Tom Dooley," sung in both English and German by the Nilsen Brothers.[20] The song, which reinforced the romanticized image of America as a lawless land of opportunity, generated controversy in East Germany and Austria because it appeared to show sympathy for youthful rebellion and criminality. Nonetheless, the American and British folk revival laid the foundation for what was later called the *kritische Liedermacher* (a singer-songwriter who is also a social critic) in the Federal Republic, as well as the *Singebewegung* (singing movement) in the German

Democratic Republic (GDR) in the late 1960s. Whereas West German singers such as Franz Josef Degenhardt, Dieter Süverkrüp, Hannes Wader, and Reinhard Mey were instrumental in this revival, a Canadian émigré in the GDR, Perry Friedman, helped establish what was known as the *Hootenanny-Bewegung* (Hootenanny Movement) in 1959, which sought to incorporate progressive song traditions from all over the world. The Hootenanny Club was renamed *Oktoberklub* (for the 1917 revolution in Russia) in the wake of the Eleventh Plenum of the Socialist Unity Party (*Sozialistische Einheitspartei Deutschlands*, or SED). The *Oktoberklub* went on to become one of the most influential groups in the GDR during the transition from a folk-based to a rock-based youth music scene at the end of the 1960s.

The Hootenanny Movement in the GDR, which started as a spontaneous private effort on the part of a small group of dedicated enthusiasts, developed into the highly bureaucratized official *Singebewegung* of the *Freie Deutsche Jugend* (FDJ), the East German communist youth organization. It was designed to counteract the influence of the "beat" music popularized in the West by the Beatles and the Rolling Stones, and to form the musical and cultural basis for the noncommercial and socialist rejuvenation of GDR entertainment music. Selected amateur musicians were recruited into the ranks of grassroots political folk singers and groomed for entrance into the world of GDR professional entertainment.

BEAT MUSIC: THE ROOTS OF GERMAN ROCK MUSIC

The spread of British beat music to Germany in the mid-1960s is significant not only for the breadth of the amateur music-making stimulated by the commercial success of the Beatles and Rolling Stones (among others): It also helped to establish the supremacy of the English language as the language of popular music for many years. The popularity of rock music among Germans in the late 1960s also persuaded the major record firms to actively cultivate teenagers not just as customers but also

---

[17] See Albrecht Koch, *Angriff aufs Schlaraffenland: 20 Jahre deutschsprachige Popmusik* (Frankfurt am Main, 1987), 32.

[18] Steinbiss, *Deutsch-Folk*, 37.

[19] See Koch, *Angriff aufs Schlaraffenland*, 23–4.

[20] Günter Ehnert, *Hit Bilanz: Deutsche Chart Singles 1956–1981* (Hamburg, 1983), 360.

as employees and staff members, drawing on their aesthetic expertise with the new music and their connections to a scene that was independent of the old *Schlager* networks. American and British "beat bands" in the second half of the 1960s developed a new rock aesthetic using the newest electronic recording and sound production technologies from American music electronics firms. This music signaled a drastic break in generational experience and musical tradition. The new beat enthusiasts were adherents of a distinct youth culture, and German beat fans prided themselves on being the antithesis of the *Schlager* audience.

The musical influences of the Beatles can be traced not only to the rock 'n' roll of the 1950s, but also to its successor, skiffle music, a type of jazz-style folk music derived from African American forms and employing guitar, banjo, kazoo, washboard, and bass.[21] The main contribution of the music of the early Beatles and other British groups consisted in their collective manner of producing songs within but also beyond the influence of the established recording industry. In contrast to the artisanal manner of *Schlager* composing, whereby first the melody line, then the lyrics, and finally the arrangement are created, the British groups demonstrated to youths the viability and empowerment of writing their own tunes and attaining the same or greater levels of commercial success as the more established *Schlager* and pop musicians controlled by the commercial industry.

As in many other countries, the Beatles' popularity spawned prominent imitators. One of these was the Lords, formed as a skiffle band in 1959. At a contest underwritten by United Artists in 1964 entitled "Who Can Play Like the Beatles," the Lords won the chance to perform at Hamburg's Star Club. The band went on to release a series of hits on the German charts and, in 1966, toured Germany with the Beach Boys.[22]

The Rattles, originally formed in 1961, were the second prominent West German beat band. After an engagement at the Star Club in 1962, where it won a competition for the best beat band, the Rattles went on two tours of England in 1963. During the second tour, the group was able to perform with the British band Animals at the Cavern Club in Liverpool (where the Beatles had achieved early notoriety) and developed a small but enthusiastic following in Britain.[23] The band accompanied the Beatles on their tour through Germany in 1966.

BEAT IN THE GDR

After the Berlin Wall was built on August 13, 1961, the East German government sought to win back the loyalty of youth. A youth communiqué in 1963 signaled a more liberal climate toward youth culture in the GDR, but the period of liberalized cultural policies ended in December 1965 with the Eleventh Plenum of the SED. In 1964, on the occasion of the *Deutschlandtreffen der Jugend*, a youth festival in East Berlin that was to bring together thousands of youths from the East and more than 50,000 from the West, a new radio show was broadcast called *Jugendstudio DT64*, featuring, in addition to *Schlager* and folk, music called the *Guitarrensound*. Although it was viewed with great suspicion by most of the SED political leadership, the two-year period of liberalization provided enough opportunity for youths in the GDR to appropriate beat music.

To block the influx of Western popular music, a law enacted in 1958 stipulated that 60 percent of the repertoire of "dance music groups" and radio broadcasts was to be made up of songs from the socialist countries, with the remaining 40 percent from capitalist countries. Most youths, therefore, relied on the Western radio and television broadcasts for information about the new beat craze. Beat enthusiasm among GDR youths helped establish approximately 300 *Gitarrencombos* in East Berlin alone, mostly with English band names and English song lyrics learned

---

[21] Peter Wicke and Wieland Ziegenrücker, eds., *Rock-Pop-Jazz-Folk: Handbuch der populären Musik* (Leipzig, 1985), 468–9.

[22] Günter Ehnert, *Rock in Deutschland: Lexikon deutscher Rockgruppen und Interpreten* (Hamburg, 1979), 160–1.

[23] Ibid., 216.

from Western radio broadcasts, playing on self-made instruments and amplifiers. In April 1965, Amiga brought out a complete Beatles compilation LP. Several popular beat groups emerged, like the Theo Schumann Combo, the Butlers (the predecessor to the rock group Klaus Renft Combo popular in the 1970s), the Franke-Echo-Quintett, and the Sputniks. The music of Thomas Natschinski's band, Team 4, which later became the model for a modernized GDR pop music after the crackdown of 1965, also evolved from the Beatles.

After a Rolling Stones concert in the West Berlin Waldbühne on September 15, 1965, a riot broke out, causing almost DM 400,000 in damages; seventy-three people were injured.[24] The GDR media and SED government used the sensationalist reports of the West German newspapers to initiate a campaign against beat music, *Gitarrencombos*, and advocates of more liberal policies in the media and cultural life. Measures included forcing long-haired youths to have their hair cut, forcing the bands to change their English names to German ones, and revoking bands' performance licenses for noncompliance. English lyrics were prohibited in the officially authorized repertoire of the bands, who had to submit their lyrics to unsympathetic and ideologically blinkered editorial boards for approval before they were released for radio, recording, or live performance. Many beat bands were prosecuted for tax evasion and overcharging the venue managers. Amateur bands in need of gainful employment risked incrimination as *Asoziale* (antisocial), in the same manner as the *Halbstarke* in the 1950s had been branded as purveyors of Western imperialist culture. Although in the West bands like the Lords and Rattles were touring with British beat and rock groups, the GDR's communist youth organization, the FDJ, curtailed its support of the so-called *Gitarrenbewegung* under pressure from the SED. That move severely reduced the number of licensed beat groups and pressured the remaining ones to play more melodic, less rhythmic music and to distance themselves from Western youth culture.

The SED tried to develop a musical alternative to the beat movement by promoting the FDJ's *Singebewegung* as a source of musical innovation. Between 1966 and 1968, restrictions on the GDR rock bands gradually relaxed, and the Thomas Natschinski and Team 4 bands developed music that seemed to represent the syncretic alternative sought after by the cultural bureaucrats in the SED and FDJ. This music combined electric guitars and drums with German lyrics about topical events. However, it could not maintain the continual media presence necessary to compete with the Western music transmitted to the GDR from outside its borders.

The diffusion of popular music from the United States and, in the 1960s, Great Britain – jazz, rock 'n' roll, folk music, beat – accompanied the integration of the Federal Republic into the NATO alliance and the Cold War rivalry between the two German states. This music challenged conservative views on what it meant to be German and became one of the internationally available idioms for youth to articulate their identity within the framework of a commercialized consumer culture. The German popular-music traditions of *Schlager* and commercialized folk were profoundly altered as German youths shaped their music consumption, behaviors, and leisure activities according to models transmitted into the country by the electronic media. German bands and vocalists imitated the musical styles and incorporated African American elements into their repertoire. Use of English proliferated within German *Schlager* productions and competed for influence with German. German youths gained important creative experience with new music-making technologies such as phonographs, electric guitars, keyboard instruments, and recording and amplification equipment. Many were later recruited by the recording industry into its production and distribution apparatus as the new youth market revealed its potential. These developments paved the way for the burst of creativity by the so-called Kraut Rock and other groups moving into positions of influence within the German recording industry in the early 1970s.

[24] Ibid., 117.

CHAPTER TEN

German Musical Influences in the United States

Pamela M. Potter

In any discussion of German-American musical relations, it is important to bear in mind that any German influence on American musical life following World War II had a long prehistory. As early as the eighteenth century, American audiences were well acquainted with the works of German composers; at the turn of the nineteenth century, German immigrants started to establish symphonic and choral organizations; and the wave of German immigration beginning in 1848 brought a host of performers and educators, German music publishers, and German soloists and conductors who laid the foundations for conservatories, chamber-music performance, symphonic music, opera, and amateur choral activity.[1] A brief surge of nationalism during World War I focused new attention on American composers, and certain conductors made an effort to incorporate more American, French, and Russian art music into their programs, but works of the great German masters still constituted the standard repertoire. Even at the height of World War II, a music lover's

handbook published in New York in 1943 guided its readers toward understanding a concert repertoire dominated by the works of Beethoven, Haydn, Mozart, Schubert, Brahms, Wagner, and even Richard Strauss, at the time the most prominent living composer in Hitler's Germany.[2]

Because German conductors wielded much power over American concert life from its very beginnings, the flight of prominent conductors from Nazi Germany to the United States merely enhanced an already strong Austro-German presence in classical music. Among this group of refugees, Bruno Walter was noted for introducing the works of Bruckner and Mahler to a wide American public in his positions at the Metropolitan Opera and the New York Philharmonic. Similarly, Otto Klemperer, as chief conductor of the Los Angeles Philharmonic and founder of the Pittsburgh Symphony, promoted the works of modern German composers such as Arnold Schoenberg. Fritz Stiedry, who came to New York in 1937 to direct the New Friends of Music Orchestra and the Metropolitan Opera, specialized in Wagner and also promoted Schoenberg. Erich Leinsdorf, conducting at the Metropolitan Opera from 1938 to 1943, carried his symphonic mission to Cleveland and Rochester and promoted the operas of Wagner and Strauss. Finally, Wilhelm (William) Steinberg conducted the NBC

---

[1] Oscar Sonneck, "German Influence on the Musical Life of America," in William Lichtenwanger, ed., *Oscar Sonneck and American Music* (Urbana, Ill., 1983), 60–75; Nicholas Tawa, *The Coming of Age of American Art Music: New England's Classical Romanticists* (New York, 1991), 31–3, 35; Alan Levy, *Musical Nationalism: American Composers' Search for Identity* (Westport, Conn., 1983), 4, 8–10; Stanley Sadie, ed., *New Grove Dictionary of Music and Musicians*, 6th ed. (Washington, D.C., 1980), see entries on "Thomas, Theodore," "Philadelphia," "Boston," "New York," and "Cincinnati."

[2] Elie Siegmeister, ed., *The Music Lover's Handbook* (New York, 1943).

Orchestra in 1938 before moving on to Buffalo, Pittsburgh, and Boston. German performers with international reputations were similarly no strangers to the American public. When they arrived in the United States, they had no difficulties securing jobs in conservatories, many of which boasted long rosters of past and present faculty members of German origins. Artur Schnabel, Eduard Steuermann, and Rudolf Kolisch, to name only a few, were able to strengthen Germans' already firm position in America's music education and contribute to the proliferation of chamber music in the United States.[3]

Whereas the German presence in American concert activity experienced an enhancement of an already strong tradition, the influence of émigré composers and music educators was much more profound, entirely reshaping the postwar American musical landscape beyond the concert hall and conservatory. The unprecedented influx of composers, theorists, and musicologists in the late 1930s and 1940s resulted in fundamental changes that would serve to redefine the role of art music in postwar America. German émigré composers were instrumental in developing a culture that regarded composition as an elite, learned activity. The central figure in this transformation was Arnold Schoenberg, who came to the United States in 1933. Schoenberg's controversial approach to composition had brought him notoriety in the first decades of the century, when he attempted to replace the traditionally key-centered conventions of the eighteenth and nineteenth centuries with a sound complex that gave no priority to a particular key. Although Schoenberg's innovations were first received with great enthusiasm, his twelve-tone method, which structured compositions around a series of tones that incorporated all pitches of the chromatic scale, created works that sounded chaotic to the average listener. With the general call for composers to abandon their esoteric pursuits and meet the needs of the masses, Schoenberg's ideas were

starting to fall on deaf ears in Germany by the late 1920s. His work suffered an irreparable blow when Nazi ideologues condemned him and his teachings as "Jewish degeneracy."

Americans such as Roger Sessions had already begun to look closely at Schoenberg's controversial compositional techniques in the 1920s, and when Schoenberg arrived in the United States in 1933, he found several students eager to work with him. He made a home at the New School of Social Research in New York, which had already established itself as the creative center of the musical avant-garde.[4] After taking a teaching position at the University of California at Los Angeles in 1934, he received a steady flow of private students that even included film and popular-music composers.[5] Schoenberg's compositional approach, later expanded into what was known as serialism, would become the model for a large number of young American composers. Serialism was further promoted by other émigrés and, in the 1950s, it returned to Germany to become the standard for a new generation of composers disillusioned with the Nazi past and hungry for a new musical idiom free of ideological implications. With the help of Allied-controlled radio stations, composers of the Darmstadt school successfully resurrected and canonized Schoenberg and, especially, his student Anton Webern, both musical victims of National Socialism, and established a new musical idiom governed by serialism.[6] Serialism also acquired anticommunist connotations in the course of the Cold War. As the Soviets formulated a restrictive policy against musical "formalism" – that is, music not easily comprehended by the proletariat – serialism became an important means for American

[3] Hans Heinz Stuckenschmidt, "Deutsche Musik und deutsche Musiker in den USA," *Musica* 30 (1976): 381–2.

[4] Werner Grünzweig, "Vom 'Schenkerismus' zum 'Dahlhaus-Projekt,'" *Österreichische Musikzeitschrift* 48 (1993): 165–7.

[5] David Raskin, "Schönberg als Lehrer in Los Angeles," in Habakuk Traber and Elmar Weingarten, eds., *Verdrängte Musik: Berliner Komponisten im Exil* (Berlin, 1987), 129–39.

[6] Gesa Kordes, "Serialism as Political Reaction: The Darmstadt Avant-Garde, 1946–1960" (paper delivered at the Fifty-ninth Annual Meeting of the American Musicological Society, Montreal, Nov. 4, 1993).

composers to assert their anticommunist convictions. Aaron Copland, for example, adopted serialist technique in 1950 when he learned that he was under suspicion for communist leanings.[7]

American composers adopted not only Schoenberg's compositional methods but also his entire approach to the social function of contemporary composition. In Vienna after World War I, Schoenberg and his followers formed a Society for Private Musical Performance, in which works were premiered to select audiences without publicity, critics, or applause.[8] This assertion that the music of serious composers should not be subjected to the fickleness of the general public took hold in the United States as well, where an academic culture of composers was fostering the image of serious composition as an activity for specialists, to be created and re-created only within a rarefied intellectual setting. Milton Babbitt, the influential composition professor at Princeton University, not only adopted Schoenberg's serialism but also his attitudes toward the public. In his 1958 article, "Who Cares if You Listen?", Babbitt compared the mission of an academic composer to that of a scientist involved in basic research and the performance of a new work to a lecture on advanced mathematics.[9] This was a philosophy that came to dominate the growing number of composition departments at American universities in the 1950s and 1960s. It also helped solve a growing problem in American universities: The GI Bill had caused a huge increase in the student population and created an unforeseen demand

for teachers of basic music skills. For a time, lecturers could fill this need, but eventually more permanent academic posts had to be created. The solution came in the 1940s and 1950s with the proliferation of doctoral degree programs in music composition. This degree allowed teachers of musicianship to attain credentials acceptable for university employment. It also created a perceived need among them to validate their activities within a university setting, engendering a culture in which composition was regarded as a science and musical works enjoying mass appeal were deemed inferior.[10]

Several more European composers came to the United States to teach in universities, often harboring a rather contemptuous attitude toward the culture, education, and musical tastes of Americans. One such composer was Ernst Krenek, a onetime admirer of American jazz who fled Nazi-dominated Austria in 1938 and promoted serialism among his students in Minnesota and California.[11] Paul Hindemith taught at Yale University from 1940 to 1953 and also claimed to have found his American students seriously lacking in basic musical training. He set out to reconstruct the American music curriculum and greatly influenced those of his students who went on to teach.[12] The success of German composers in promoting their philosophies has been attributed to an elitism among American intellectuals disenchanted with popular culture and looking toward Europe for inspiration.[13] But America was ripe for any new ideas at this time, because the influx of German musicians fleeing Hitler coincided with a period of construction in American musical life that allowed émigrés to have a great impact on its development.[14]

---

[7] Jennifer DeLapp, "Of Politics and Style: Copland's Quartet for Piano and Strings" (paper delivered at the Sixty-second Annual Meeting of the American Musicological Society, Baltimore, Nov. 8, 1996).

[8] "Statement of Aims, Society for Private Musical Performance," in Nicholas Slonimsky, ed., *Music Since 1900*, 4th ed. (New York, 1971), 1307–8, reprinted in Piero Weiss and Richard Taruskin, eds., *Music in the Western World: A History in Documents* (New York, 1984), 431–2.

[9] Milton Babbitt, "Who Cares If You Listen?" *High Fidelity* 7, no. 2 (1958): 38–40, 126–7, reprinted in Piero Weiss and Richard Taruskin, eds., *Music in the Western World: A History in Documents* (New York, 1984), 529–34.

[10] Information from research by Patric Cohen for his doctoral dissertation in progress, "The American Composer and the Doctoral Degree: Case Histories of Doctoral Programs in Composition" (D.M.A., University of Illinois at Urbana-Champaign).

[11] John Rockwell, *All American Music: Composition in the Late Twentieth Century* (New York, 1983), 14–24.

[12] Geoffrey Skelton, *Paul Hindemith: The Man Behind the Music* (New York, 1975), 189–93.

[13] Rockwell, *All American Music*, 22–3.

[14] Grünzweig, "'Schenkerismus,'" 163–5.

454 Pamela M. Potter

The composers discussed here generally resisted conforming to American culture or, in the case of Hindemith, were attracted to certain aspects of American culture such as its literature[15] but held on to their German compositional principles. However, an equally important group of émigré composers gave full vent to their "American" impulses after arriving in the United States. The most prominent of these was Kurt Weill. Weill had worked with Bertolt Brecht in Germany toward transforming opera into a meaningful experience for a wide public and used American musical idioms in these works, the most successful of which was *The Threepenny Opera*. When he came to the United States, he directed this same reforming agenda toward Broadway with such works as *Lady in the Dark, One Touch of Venus, Down in the Valley, Street Scene*, and *Lost in the Stars*. Although condemned by compatriots and music scholars for "selling out," Weill displayed a consistency in his works composed in Germany and the United States, reaching out to as wide a public as possible and using musical theater to convey important messages.[16]

Alongside Weill were a substantial number of émigrés who found employment composing film music. Unlike the academic composers, film composers did not see themselves as "teaching the naive" but rather applied some of their own skills and learned new ones from their American colleagues. Some had already worked for film studios in Germany, such as Werner Richard Heymann, who composed for UFA studios and then scored such Hollywood films as *Bluebeard, Ninotchka*, and *To Be or Not To Be* – all in a very "non-German" style. Franz Waxman, composer for more than 200 films, including *Fury, Rear Window, Rebecca*, and *Dr. Jekyll and Mr. Hyde* (he won Oscars for the last two), managed to combine European and American styles, employing jazz instrumentation as well as Schoen-

bergian atonality. A few other émigré film composers brought more traditional European features into their film composition and could boast simultaneous successes in the concert and opera world. Karol Rathaus, Erich Korngold, and Ernst Toch all succeeded in Germany as symphonic and/or opera composers before arriving in the United States.[17] Toch went on to win a Pulitzer Prize for his Third Symphony, and in the 1950s he became a champion of such important avant-garde American composers as John Cage and Milton Babbitt.[18]

Besides composition, music theory and musicology in America were profoundly affected by the immigration of German intellectuals after World War II. Music theory developed as a new discipline more or less "invented" by German émigrés on American soil, while musicology already had developed a foundation among German-trained Americans before the refugees arrived. The ideas of Heinrich Schenker (a Viennese music teacher who developed innovative ways of looking at harmonic and contrapuntal relationships that could lead to an understanding of overall structures of large works) were promoted in the United States by his student Hans Weisse, who joined the faculty of the Mannes School of Music in New York in 1931 and transformed Schenker's often dogmatic ideas into a practical method. Weisse is credited with founding music theory as a distinct discipline, a field virtually unique to the United States and only recently established in a similar form in Britain. Weisse was joined by another Schenker student, Felix Salzer, in popularizing the application of Schenker's thought to musical analysis,[19] and Salzer's student Allen Forte established the first graduate degree in music theory at Yale University. To date, a separate discipline of music

[15] Kim Kowalke, "For Those We Love: Hindemith, Whitman, and 'An American Requiem,'" *Journal of the American Musicological Society* 50 (1997): 133–74.

[16] Kim Kowalke, "Looking Back: Toward a New Orpheus," in Kim Kowalke, ed., *A New Orpheus: Essays on Kurt Weill* (New Haven, Conn., 1986), 1–20.

[17] Habakuk Traber, "Dauernd da, doch meistens vergessen: Notizen über Filmmusik und Filmkomponisten," in Habakuk Traber and Elmar Weingarten, eds., *Verdrängte Musik: Berliner Komponisten im Exil* (Berlin, 1987), 195–204.

[18] Charlotte Erwin, "Toch in Amerika," in Habakuk Traber and Elmar Weingarten, eds., *Verdrängte Musik: Berliner Komponisten im Exil* (Berlin, 1987), 188–9.

[19] Grünzweig, "'Schenkerismus,'" 161–3.

theory exists in the United States but not in Germany, where Schenker's ideas are taken less seriously.[20]

In the area of musicology (i.e., the study of music history and non-Western musical cultures), American colleagues had long harbored a profound reverence for German scholarship even before the influx of refugees. Consisting of a small group of American-born scholars, most of them trained in Germany and Austria, American musicology eagerly adopted the practices of émigrés who arrived in the 1930s during the most significant growth spurt of the discipline in the United States.[21] Many émigrés singlehandedly established musicology departments that have since become the most important centers in this country. Edward Lowinsky arrived in 1940 and built a renowned research-oriented department at the University of Chicago; Manfred Bukofzer arrived in 1939 and accomplished similar feats at the University of California at Berkeley; Willi Apel came to America in 1936, occupying a position at Harvard and then building a department at Indiana University; Curt Sachs was appointed professor at New York University in 1937 and went on to become a leading scholar and organizer in American musicology; and Leo Schrade left his mark on the Yale musicology department from 1938 to 1958 before returning to Europe and taking a position in Basel.

The refugees arriving on American shores could be welcomed for renouncing the Germany of Hitler and be received as "good" Germans. But what of the "other" Germans, the collaborators? Following the shocking discoveries of genocide, how could Americans tolerate the knowledge that practitioners of one of the loftiest tasks – the creation of music – could have condoned the evils of Nazism by continuing to practice their art in Germany, some even collaborating with the barbarous regime? Should American musical life have obliterated all remnants of German music and its influence, save the labors of selected "good" Germans?

A wholesale purge of German music would have been virtually impossible, if not devastating for American musical culture. German music formed the basis of the classical music repertoire, the classical recording industry, and the entire approach to art music in the United States. Instead, the American music establishment was satisfied to single out a few prominent figures as Nazis, while ignoring the past of other Germans and carrying on fruitful collaborations with them. Wilhelm Furtwängler, for example, had had a volatile relationship with Nazi leaders. Named vice president of the newly established professional music organization, the Reich Music Chamber, in 1933, he publicly challenged the Nazis' intrusion of ideology in musical affairs on two occasions and was compelled to resign from his post. The fact that he remained in Nazi Germany until the end made him an object of postwar retribution. The Allied Information Control Division labeled him a Nazi tool and banned him from conducting in Berlin until he was acquitted by a German tribunal in April 1947; and in 1948, he was compelled to rescind his contract to conduct part time in Chicago after a large number of leading musicians refused to work with him.[22]

Having eased the American conscience with the selective branding of a few such individuals, the American musical establishment could resume normal relations with other prominent Germans. These were important figures in their profession, and there was no need to probe their pasts once a few outstanding "Nazis" had been identified. International stars such as Herbert von Karajan, who joined the Nazi party in Austria while it was still illegal and joined again in Germany, and Elisabeth Schwarzkopf,

[20] David Beach, "The Current State of Schenkerian Research," *Acta musicologica* 57 (1985): 276–81.

[21] Joseph Kerman, *Contemplating Music: Challenges to Musicology* (Cambridge, Mass., 1985), 26; Frank L. Harrison, "American Musicology and the European Tradition," in Frank L. Harrison, Mantle Hood, and Claude V. Palisca, *Musicology* (Englewood Cliffs, N.J., 1963), 56–7; Curt Efram Steinzor, ed., *American Musicologists, c. 1890–1945: A Bio-Bibliographical Sourcebook to the Formative Period*, Music Reference Collection no. 17 (New York, 1989).

[22] Daniel Gillis, *Furtwängler and America* (New York, 1970), 59–126.

a party member and officer in the Nazi Students' League, managed to avert inquiries into their pasts and pursued successful international careers.[23] It is also important to note that any anti-German reactions from the American public generally took the form of protests against artists rather than works. Although audiences picketed and heckled the appearances of Kirsten Flagstad from 1947 through 1950, no objections were raised to the performance of Wagner's *Ring* and *Parsifal* in 1949, for which Rudolf Bing had proposed Flagstad in the leading roles.[24] (The situation was different in Israel, where controversy raged for many years over the performance of works by Wagner, Orff, and Richard Strauss.) Statistics on symphonic repertoire similarly show that despite slight temporary declines during the two world wars, Austro-German music has always constituted more than half of the works performed by American orchestras.[25]

In the course of the 1950s, 1960s, and 1970s, peacetime and the expansion of travel, communications, and technology ushered in a new era of cooperation between two of the world's largest producers of classical music: West Germany and the United States. Although no statistics have been gathered and no research has yet explored the area systematically, it is safe to assume that the West German–American musical relationship has grown closer as the world has "become smaller." In 1969, the Boston Symphony Orchestra became the first American orchestra to record exclusively for Deutsche Grammophon, and American-German recording ventures have continued to grow since then. After the war, many American orchestras embarked on their first European tours, all of which included visits to the major concert halls in the Federal Republic (Berlin, Frankfurt,

Hannover, Hamburg, Bremen, and Munich). The Philadelphia Orchestra was the first to tour Europe after the war in 1949, followed by the Boston Symphony Orchestra in 1952, the New York Philharmonic in 1955 (it had toured Europe once before in 1930, with stops in Munich, Leipzig, Dresden, and Berlin), the Cleveland Orchestra in 1957, the Chicago Symphony in 1971, and the San Francisco Symphony in 1973. Although fewer German orchestras made the trip, the Berlin Philharmonic distinguished itself with frequent American tours (in 1955, 1956, 1961, 1965, and 1968).

These cultural exchanges notwithstanding, in the wide category known as classical or "serious" music, the German influence on America has traditionally outweighed the American influence on Germany and continues to do so (in contrast to the field of popular music, where American influences have permeated German culture to a remarkable degree[26]). A few notable exceptions can be found among avant-garde composers such as John Cage, but the wide acclaim in Germany of prominent Americans such as Leonard Bernstein must not be misunderstood as an American musical influence. Bernstein's main effect on classical music in Germany was to reinforce German repertoire and traditions, and even though in the 1980s he was considered to have "overtaken Karajan as the leading conductor in the German speaking world,"[27] he had always concentrated his conducting repertoire on Austro-German works and had begun to focus even more on the music of Brahms, Schumann, Mahler, and Wagner. As in the nineteenth century, when an American notion of high culture in music began to take shape under the influence of German immigrants, the United States in the postwar era has continued to turn to German prototypes, past and present, in setting its parameters for the preservation and proliferation of art music.

[23] Michael H. Kater, *The Twisted Muse: Musicians and Their Music in the Third Reich* (New York, 1997), 55–64.

[24] Robert Tuggle, "Clouds of War," *Opera News* 60, no. 1 (July 1995): 16–17.

[25] Philip Hart, *Orpheus in the New World: The Symphony Orchestra as an American Cultural Institution* (New York, 1973), 407.

[26] See the chapters by Edward Larkey in this section and in vol. 2, Culture.

[27] Humphrey Burton, *Leonard Bernstein* (New York, 1994), 484.

CHAPTER ELEVEN

Side by Side

Hollywood and German Film Culture

Daniel J. Leab

The United States played a very influential role in the film cultures of both East and West Germany from 1945 onward, both negatively and positively, both as an active force and one reacted against. Whatever the stated aims of the U.S. government with regard to a defeated, prostrate Nazi Germany at the end of World War II, these did not coincide with the much crasser intentions of the American film industry. Although it paid public lip service to official policies (the industry claimed to be "selling American democracy and the basis for a future peaceful and if possible better Germany"), Hollywood had more self-serving goals.[1] It intended to dominate a formidable international competitor and to capture German screens for its own product, using distribution channels under its commercial control.

With the collapse of the Nazi regime in May 1945, the German film industry simply evaporated. Its production facilities were destroyed and its personnel scattered, it had no means of distribution, and movie houses around the country had been bombed out. The debate over the issue of a *Stunde Null*, or zero hour, also applies to German film culture, which in most aspects proved to be not as transformed as had been thought.[2]

The American, British, French, and Soviet occupation authorities had dissimilar goals, a situation that hampered the resurrection of German film life on a national level. Each of the occupying powers recognized the value of motion pictures in rehabilitating and reeducating the defeated Germans. The American film policies ultimately had the greatest impact, but the Soviets acted first and managed to reestablish one vein of organized German filmmaking. As one historian has noted, "projectors, reels... and Soviet film classics were part of the Red Army's baggage."[3] Even before war's end, the Soviets began to show movies to an entertainment-starved populace in areas the Red Army controlled. Eventually, the films were dubbed into German; one of the first was Sergey Eisenstein's masterpiece *Ivan the Terrible*. Wolfgang Staudte, a Nazi-era journeyman actor and director, supervised

[1] OGMUS Berlin to Information Control Division, director, Jan. 16, 1946, quoted in H. Mark Woodward, "The Formulation and Implementation of U.S. Feature Film Policy in Occupied Germany, 1945–1948" (Ph.D. diss., University of Texas at Dallas, 1987), 183.

[2] See Jürgen Kocka, "Markets and Bureaucrats: The American Impact and Its Limits," *Zeitschrift für Kulturaustausch* 37, no. 2 (1987): 275. There is an excellent explication of various aspects of the *Stunde Null* debate in Geoffrey J. Giles, ed., *Stunde Null: The End and the Beginning Fifty Years Ago*, German Historical Institute, Occasional Paper 20 (Washington, D.C., 1997), therein esp. Konrad H. Jarausch, "1945 and the Continuities of German History: Reflections on Memory, Historiography, and Politics," 9–24.

[3] See R. C. Raack, *Stalin's Drive to the West: The Origins of the Cold War* (Stanford, Calif., 1996), 122.

the dubbing of this film in August 1945.[4] Subsequently, Staudte obtained a license from the Soviets and, under terrible working conditions, wrote and directed the first postwar German feature, *Die Mörder sind unter uns* (*The Murderers Are Among Us*). Premiering in October 1946, this gloomy examination of innocence and guilt was an overwhelming critical and commercial success that had enormous impact at home and abroad, and it remains a classic. Significantly, Staudte had first approached the Americans and other Western Allies for permission to shoot the film before finally getting a license from the Soviets.

Controlling more than 70 percent of Germany's once-magnificent movie facilities, the Soviets had the will and the means to shape the course of film in defeated Germany. Although war-ravaged (one cameraman recalled the streets of a Berlin movie lot as having "melted" because of the heavy bombing), these Soviet-controlled facilities included the largest copying plants, the only filmstock manufacturer, and much of the studio space.[5] Even before Hitler came to power in 1933, many of these facilities had been controlled by one huge concern, *Universum Film Aktiengesellschaft* (UFA). The Nazis used UFA to create a highly centralized state monopoly that by 1943 controlled just about every aspect of German film life. The Soviets followed this principle and on May 17, 1946, oversaw the formal organization of the *Deutsche Film Aktiengesellschaft* (DEFA). In one form or another, it remained a state monopoly under strict government control that closely regulated East Germany's film culture until the German Democratic Republic (GDR) dissolved in 1990.

Among DEFA's first activities was distribution of Staudte's film. The concern's initial

efforts, although frequently tinged with propaganda, often received well-deserved recognition outside the communist world. A good example was the 1947 film, *Ehe im Schatten* (*Marriage in the Shadows*), a moving version of a real-life 1930s tragedy – the joint suicide of a successful German film star and his Jewish wife as a result of Nazi pressure. But the Cold War impinged severely on DEFA, and didactic propaganda movies became the order of the day.[6] The foreign films imported by DEFA showed the dark side of capitalism, especially with regard to the United States. Only two American movies were distributed in the GDR during the 1950s: *Salt of the Earth*, a left-leaning film about striking Chicano miners in New Mexico and their newly militant wives; and *Marty*, which dealt with the depressing social life of a Bronx butcher and his friends.

The United States especially became a DEFA target. Again and again, DEFA productions attacked American "imperialism," the American character, and a West German leadership depicted as former Nazis subservient to their American capitalist masters. What the philosopher George Steiner called the GDR's "brutal parochialism" made itself felt in films like *Die Rat der Götter* (*The Council of the Gods*), a 1950 effort that emphasized I.G. Farben's Nazi past and the chemical cartel's ties to American capitalists; *Das verurteilte Dorf* (*The Condemned Village*), a 1952 movie dealing with the West Germans' supposed resistance to American bases in their midst; and *For Eyes Only/Streng Geheim*, a 1963 thriller extolling the GDR's counterespionage efforts against the plots of American agents.[7] Even one of DEFA's few international coproductions (with the French in the mid-1950s) was a filming of Arthur Miller's allegory, *The*

---

[4] With a few notable exceptions, the careers of Nazi-era film personnel outlived the Hitler era. Staudte is typical of what have been described as "the white-washed former Nazis" active in both postwar German states. Thomas Elsaesser, *New German Cinema: A History* (New Brunswick, N.J., 1989), 16.

[5] Günter Marczinkowsky, in Harry Blunck and Dirk Jungnickel, eds., *Filmland DDR: Ein Reader in Geschichte, Funktion und Wirkung des DEFA* (Cologne, 1990), 11.

[6] Government control was so restrictive that at one point in the early 1950s, feature-film production fell to six features annually, and an anonymous wit said that DEFA stood for "Das Ende für Autoren" (The End for Authors). See Thomas Heimann, *DEFA, Kunstler und SED Kultpolitik* (Berlin, 1994), 130.

[7] George Steiner, "Out of Central Europe," *Encounter* 22 (Apr. 1964): 112.

Crucible (*Die Hexen von Salem*), which used witch-hunting in seventeenth-century Massachusetts to allude to the McCarthyism of the 1950s.

Ultimately, the GDR's strict anti-Americanism fell victim to modern technology as moviegoers turned to television. Between 1957 and 1963, annual sales of cinema tickets fell from a peak of 316 million to about 99 million despite efforts by DEFA to be *Schauwert* (show-worthy); a significant percentage of East German TV viewers "emigrated" each night as they watched West German programs, including American movies. The anti-Americanism reflected in the East German film culture did find some echo among certain West German elites, who were aghast at what they perceived as a perversion of the "true" German culture and an unbridled consumerism inculcated by an imported American culture, especially movies.[8]

But these groups, for all their influence as critics, had little influence on West German filmmaking or moviegoing. There can be no doubt that "the Americanization of West German everyday life" took place.[9] Hollywood played a large part in the American conquest of the West German popular imagination, yet surprisingly (especially given the tens of thousands of GIs, their dependents, and American administrative personnel scattered across West Germany) substantial pockets of West German culture remained unaffected, including a significant part of movie life.

Certainly, American culture, as manifested by popular music, fashion, technology, and movies, had affected Germany for years before the Nazi takeover in 1933. Much of that influence survived the Nazi regimentation (*Gleichschaltung*) of German cultural life thereafter.[10] Moreover, the German film industry between 1933 and 1945 had never fulminated against the United States as it had against the British and Soviets, or as GDR filmmakers did during the 1950s and 1960s. Actively anti-American youth, certain critics, and members of the "chattering classes" have recognized and denigrated American influences.[11] But the overall impact on West German filmmaking and moviegoing may not have been as great as some thought from the 1950s onward.

Nothing like DEFA developed in the Western zones of occupation. As in the Soviet zone, there was an enormous hunger for movies: A British-zone businessman remembered that people were "crazy for movies."[12] The differing approaches taken by the Western Allies resulted in diverging policies. The Americans, initially committed to a stern policy of denazification,[13] at first wanted not only to vet the filmmakers at every level but also insisted on the licensing of theater operators. The British were more casual and proved less concerned about the content of Nazi-era nonpolitical movies. The French, much less devoted than either the Americans or the British to "sanitizing the German mind," allowed those who could to open movie houses for business with whatever films were on hand.[14]

Production in the three Western zones got underway slowly because of problems with licensing and funding such as those Staudte had faced. The Anglo-American newsreel, *Die Welt im Film*, which until 1949 had to be shown in all movie houses in the American and British zones, was initially prepared in London. The first British-licensed film premiered in 1946, only weeks after the first showings of Staudte's

---

[8] See the chapters by Philipp Gassert and Axel Schildt, vol. 1, Society.

[9] Ralph Willett, *The Americanization of Germany: The Inside Story of Nazi Radio Broadcasting and Propaganda Swing, 1945–1949* (New York, 1989), 112.

[10] See Horst J. P. Bergmeier and Rainer E. Lotz, *Hitler's Airwaves* (New Haven, Conn., 1997), 138–40.

[11] See Reinhold Wagnleitner, *Coca-Colonization and the Cold War: The Cultural Mission of the United States in Austria after the Second World War* (Chapel Hill, N.C., 1994).

[12] Claus Haas quoted in Ursula Besson, ed., *Trümmer und Träume: Nachkriegszeit und fünfziger Jahre auf Zelluloid: Deutsche Spielfilme als Zeugnisse ihrer Zeit: Eine Dokumentation* (Bochum, 1989), 27.

[13] See the chapter by Cornelia Rauh-Kühne, vol. 1, Politics.

[14] Earl F. Ziemke, *The U.S. Army in the Occupation of Germany, 1944–1946* (Washington, D.C., 1975), 376.

film, but much of *Sag die Wahrheit* (*Speak the Truth*, a simple-minded comedy about marriage) had been shot during the war's last weeks. Not until mid-1947 did two more British-licensed films debut. One was *In jenen Tagen* (*In Those Days*), a critical and commercially successful seven-episode film about life during the Nazi era. It was produced, directed, and cowritten by Helmut Käutner, whose directing career began in 1939. Also in mid-1947, the first French-licensed German feature appeared. At year's end, an American-licensed German feature film was finally premiered.

What happened in the American zone became increasingly important as international developments forced Britain and France to cede leadership in German affairs to the United States. It was under American aegis that the film policy of the three Western zones was harmonized, with vital consequences for West German film culture. Hollywood defeated the American zonal authority's efforts to aid the nascent West German film industry. Facing substantial economic problems domestically and increasingly dependent on revenues gained overseas, Hollywood acted tenaciously and successfully. It mounted a smear campaign against the returning émigré Erich Pommer; hailed as "the real genius of German cinema before 1933," as zone film officer he was constantly blocked in his attempts to achieve more unified production.[15] The efforts of Pommer and others to protect, encourage, and expand West German film production fell victim to Hollywood's efforts to stifle a serious former competitor. Efforts to stop Hollywood dumping its product failed in the early 1950s, when the U.S. high commissioner in Germany received orders that there should be no quota on the importation of American films.[16]

In the face of Hollywood's opposition, the initiatives of the Americans responsible for development of a West German film policy had

limited results. The holding company controlling UFA was never broken up, but its actions were so restricted that it proved ineffective. The concept of competition had led to the licensing of numerous undercapitalized companies; of the more than 150 licensed by 1950, fewer than 40 ever produced even one movie. Whereas West German filmmakers struggled to find financing, the American government not only compensated Hollywood for the costs accrued in the export of already amortized films but also guaranteed the industry approximately $25,000 in Marshall Plan funds for each film exported to participating countries like West Germany. Hollywood's moguls did not directly or totally take over the West German film industry but, certainly by the early 1950s, they had secured a privileged place in the West German film market.[17]

An attempt to ape the American film industry's self-regulation of film content failed relatively quickly; the industry's self-regulation body, the *Freiwillige Selbstkontrolle der Filmwirtschaft* (FSK) had to be modified because of the clamorous reaction in 1951 to *Die Sünderin* (*The Sinner*). An unabashed commercial success, the film contained the first postwar female nude scene and apotheosized the eponymous protagonist, who prostituted herself for love, committed suicide to prove her fidelity, and expired in the arms of her dying lover.[18] The film provoked religious and other groups concerned with bourgeois morality. As a result of the controversy, the FSK was revamped in a way that sharply reduced self-regulation and increased

---

[15] Paul Rotha quoted in Patrick McGilligan, *Fritz Lang: Nature of the Beast – A Biography* (New York, 1997), 45.

[16] Wagnleitner, *Coca-Colonization and the Cold War*, 244.

[17] Elsaesser, *New German Cinema*, 9–13; Thomas Guback, *The International Film Industry: Western Europe and American Film Since 1945* (Bloomington, Ind., 1969), 125–35; Woodward, "Formulation and Implementation of U.S. Feature Film Policy," 174–210; Johannes Hauser, *Neuaufbau der westdeutschen Filmwirtschaft 1945–1955 und der Einfluss der US-amerikanischen Filmpolitik: Vom reichseigenen Filmmonopolkonzern (UFI) zur privatwirtschaftlichen Konkurrenzwirtschaft* (Pfaffenweiler, 1989), 148–58.

[18] Heide Fehrenbach, "Cinema Spectatorship and the Problem of Postwar German Identity," in Reiner Pommerin, ed., *The American Impact on Postwar Germany* (Providence, R.I., 1995), 169.

the input from the state and procensorship groups.

West Germany may well have been "Hollywood's ideal overseas market,"[19] but the Federal Republic produced a film industry that retained a significant domestic market share into the 1960s. This domestic success was due partly to subventions by the federal government and the *Länder* (federal states) but also to an output that chilled intellectuals but attracted many West German moviegoers, who for much of the postwar period, as the occupation authorities found out early on, "preferred every kind of German film to the American."[20] Although Hollywood dominated for much of the 1950s and 1960s, until at least the early 1960s, the West German film industry held on to market share against "the Star-Spangled Octopus," as one European producer dubbed Hollywood.[21] And well into the decade, many more West German films than American ones ranked among the box office top ten.[22]

The domestic genres attracting moviegoers in the heyday of West Germany's postwar movie industry included "lederhosen and beer stein" comedies, musical revues, nostalgic war films, melodramas, and crime thrillers. The last form proved very viable even after film audiences began to shrink in the late 1950s. In 1959, the first of a series of thirty-two Edgar Wallace crime thrillers premiered, which by 1970, despite a limited marketplace and rapidly declining attendance, had earned over DM 140 million on a cost of DM 2.5 million. Even more successful was the *Heimat* film, well described

as "a dream world . . . of cliché-ridden, Agfa-colored . . . deceitful kitsch." More than 300 such films were made, mostly between 1951 and 1956, when this genre accounted for an estimated 20 percent of all West German film production. The industry also developed its own stars. West German moviegoers flocked to see lovely, engaging, teenaged Romy Schneider, especially in her charming performances of a young Austrian royal in the "Sissi" films of 1956–8. The capable comic actor Heinz Rühmann, whose career began in the 1920s, attracted legions of moviegoers for his portrayals of the title character in a variety of films, including *Charly's Tante* (*Charley's Aunt*) in 1955 and *Der brave Soldat Schwejk* (*The Good Soldier Schweik*) in 1960.[23]

Some West German films garnered international recognition during the 1950s and even obtained limited distribution in the United States: *Die letzte Brücke* (*The Last Bridge*), Helmut Käutner's moving antiwar statement, which won its lead player, Maria Schell, the award for best actress at the 1954 Cannes Film Festival; *Des Teufels General* (*The Devil's General*), a 1955 film about a general, splendidly portrayed by Curd Jürgens, who must come to terms with the realities of Nazi Germany; *Nachts, wenn der Teufel kam* (*The Devil Comes at Night*), one of émigré director Robert Siodmak's best projects after his return to Germany, which cleverly contrasted a German serial killer with the Nazi state and won an Oscar nomination for best foreign feature in 1957; *Die Brücke* (*The Bridge*), Bernhard Wicki's tough-minded, pacifist 1959 film, also nominated for an Oscar, about a group of German teenagers mindlessly defending to the death a nonstrategic bridge during the last days of World War II.

The American film industry had always cannibalized its foreign competition: "The food industry turned to Latin America for its bananas, the movie industry turned to Europe."[24] Postwar Germany was no exception. Hollywood

[19] Richard H. Pells, *Not Like Us: How Europeans Haved Love, Hated, and Transformed American Culture Since World War II* (New York, 1997), 216.

[20] Micaela Jary, *Traumfabriken Made in Germany: Die Geschichte des deutschen Nachkriegsfilms 1945–1960* (Berlin, 1993), 179.

[21] David Puttnam, *The Undeclared War: The Struggle for Control of the World's Film Industry* (London, 1997), 216.

[22] There is a breakdown by rank and nationality of top ten films in West Germany from 1950 to 1990 in Joseph Gamcasz, "Hollywood in Germany: Die Rolle des amerikanischen Films in Deutschland, 1925–1990," in Uli Jung, ed., *Der Deutsche Film: Aspekte seiner Geschichte von den Anfängen bis zur Gegenwart* (Trier, 1993), 200–13.

[23] Anton Kaes, *From Hitler to Heimat: The Return of History as Film* (Cambridge, Mass., 1989), 15.

[24] Robert Sklar, *Movie-Made America: A Social History of American Movies* (New York, 1975), 100.

brought to its studios stars like Jürgens, Rühmann, and Schneider, lesser players like Cornell Brochers, Paul Hubschmid (later Paul Christian), and Marianne Koch (later Marianne Cook), and directors like Käutner and Wicki. Some remained prominent internationally and in Germany, but the studios' attempt to shoehorn them into Hollywood's formulaic product failed.

The traffic was not one way. In addition to Siodmak, other émigré directors such as John Brahm, Fritz Lang, and Gerd Oswald directed West German films in the 1950s and 1960s, with mixed results. More successful artistically if not commercially had been the immediate postwar efforts of pre-Nazi German film personalities such as Peter Lorre (in his only stint as a director) and Fritz Kortner (whose writing, directing, and acting career extended into the 1960s). The West German film industry also proved hospitable to lesser Hollywood figures such as the actors George Nader, Sean Flynn, and Lex Barker. Hollywood also found the cheaper production costs and other benefits of filming in West Germany attractive, and both large and small studios filmed there in the 1950s and 1960s. Movies produced there included Twentieth Century Fox's 1954 Cold War anticommunist vehicle, *Night People*, which starred Gregory Peck, and the King Brothers' steamy romance, *Carnival Story*. A number of American stars like Peck who worked abroad for tax reasons made films in West Germany (e.g., Kirk Douglas in the 1961 courtroom drama *Town Without Pity*, which also showcased German starlet Christine Kaufman, who subsequently enjoyed a brief period of work in Hollywood).

As in America, television had an extremely deleterious impact on West German moviegoing. As one industry executive, Bernd Eichinger, later recalled, "Germans...just... didn't...go to the movies anymore."[25] Audiences shrank precipitously, revenues dried up,

and during the early 1960s many production, distribution, and exhibition companies failed; those that survived usually had American ties. A financially fraught industry faced a new, more affluent generation that wanted "a break with inherited cultural values and the cherished sense of community."[26] Where the traditional genre failed to attract, Hollywood professionalism succeeded. The quality of the failing industry's product has been vigorously debated. Industry insider Joe Hembus began his influential 1961 polemic, ironically titled *Der deutsche Film kann gar nicht besser sein* (*The German Film Could Not Be Better*), with the words *"er ist schlecht"* ("it is bad"). This belief overcame any argument, no matter how defensible, that the German film was not as bad as its reputation.[27]

Academics, critics, and intellectuals echoed Hembus's blast but were torn between their admiration for Hollywood's professionalism and their disgust at its content, especially the impact they thought it had on West Germans: "The people are fascinated by American life . . . , etc. That's box-office. This attitude is not shared by everyone."[28]

During the Oberhausen short-film festival in February 1962, this attitude manifested itself in a joint statement issued by twenty-six younger filmmakers proclaiming the West German film industry's "collapse," declaring the need for "a new cinema," and proposing "its artistic...and economic realization."[29] What came to be known as the New German Cinema set out to challenge Hollywood and, thanks to government subvention, produced a spate of films. Many of these films criticized Americanized West German society; some gained international recognition and made their creators

[26] Willett, *Americanization of Germany*, 126.

[27] Joe Hembus, *Der deutsche Film kann gar nicht besser sein: Ein Pamphlet von gestern, eine Abrechnung von heute* (Munich, 1981), 7.

[28] Reinhard Hauff and Peter Lillental, quoted in Alexander Kluge, ed., *Bestandsaufnahme, Utopie Film: Zwanzig Jahre neuer deutscher Film*, 2d ed. (Frankfurt am Main, 1983), 269.

[29] "The Oberhausen Manifesto" (1962), in Eric Rentschler, ed., *West German Filmmakers on Film: Visions and Voices* (New York, 1988), 2.

[25] Bernd Eichinger, "Some Thoughts on West German Cinema in the Eighties: An Interview with Bernd Eichinger," in Richard C. Helt and Marie E. Helt, eds., *West German Cinema Since 1945: A Reference Handbook* (Metuchen, N.J., 1987), 17.

famous (e.g., Volker Schlöndorff and Edgar Reitz). A few proved profitable, especially those with graphic sex scenes (thanks to relaxed censorship) or those that touched on taboo subjects such as abortion. But overall, the New German Cinema proved unable to challenge Hollywood.[30]

Moreover, a particular view of America continued to capture audiences. In the mid-1960s, movies based on Karl May's imaginative if wrongheaded novels about the American West dominated the box office top-ten list and also earned well in various export markets – though not in the United States. Starring a Frenchman (Pierre Brice) as the noble Apache Winnetou, with recycled Hollywood stars such as Lex Barker, Rod Cameron, and Stewart Granger as his frontiersman partner, the eleven-film

series garnered little acclaim from those touting New German Cinema, but the Western – even if produced by West Germans and Yugoslavs – remained a popular draw. As one exhibitor put it, "the critique is written at the box office."[31]

Josef Stalin once declared that "cinema is only illusion, but life dictates its rules."[32] Hollywood managed to have its own way much of the time in West Germany, even vis-à-vis the American government. But for all the impact of American culture generally and movies particularly, Hollywood never gained total control of West Germany's film culture, which retained a life of its own well into the 1960s.

---

[30] See the chapter by Anton Kaes, vol. 2, Culture.

[31] Ilse Kubaschewski quoted in Manfred Barthel, *So war es wirklich: Der deutsche Nachkriegsfilm* (Munich, 1986), 61.

[32] Stalin quoted in Robert Conquest, *Stalin: Breaker of Nations* (London, 1993), 129.

CHAPTER TWELVE

From Reeducation to Alternative Theater

German-American Theater Relations

Andreas Höfele

Translated by Sally E. Robertson

If you had opened the thin, six-page Satur-day edition of the *Rhein-Neckar Zeitung* on July 27, 1946, you would have first seen a full-page reprint of the closing statement made by the chief American prosecutor at Nuremberg, Robert H. Jackson: "The Prosecution Rests Its Case." The second page offered articles on a variety of current affairs: "Where Will We Put Refugees from the East?"; "Bread Ration Increased in French Zone"; and, in the feuilleton, a report on a "German Premiere in Esslingen am Neckar." The play under review was Eugene O'Neill's *Ah, Wilderness!*

Nothing could more clearly illustrate the at-mosphere of that time than this paradoxical – and entirely matter of fact – juxtaposition. Genocide, the crime to end all crimes, brushes up against the peaceful normalcy of an evening of theater in Esslingen am Neckar. One page announces that nothing will ever be the same. The other declares that life goes on; we've made it through again. The inconceivability of a re-turn to normalcy is contradicted by indications that normalcy had already returned. It could be found in the theater in Esslingen, for example, where the paper's reviewer saw "a piece of pop-ular theater with mildly ironic touches":

A benign wilderness infused with humanity, in which each person can prosper according to his own abilities and personality, as long as he respects his fellow hu-man beings and is just as respectful of their freedoms and choices as he is of his own. These themes are laid out by the case of the young Richard Miller, whose love life creates various complications that

bring him into conflict with God, humanity, and his family.... But, in the end, he stages a reconciliation and finds a place for himself in that inestimably happy 'wilderness'... [H]e will become a new citizen with new horizons stretching before him.

It almost sounds as though O'Neill wrote the play under contract to the Information Control Division (ICD),[1] the division of the American military government responsible for carrying out its reeducation program.[2] As the reviewer describes it, *Ah, Wilderness!* becomes a lesson in applied democracy, an American idyll that leaves its German audience with the joyous hope that once they have learned to respect the freedom of others, they too can ultimately "become new citizen[s] with new horizons" like the young Richard Miller.

Since the eighteenth century, since the era of Gottsched, Lessing, and Schiller, theater has probably been taken more seriously as a cultural institution in Germany than anywhere else in Europe. Because of this historical background, it was clear to reeducation planners that the-ater would have to play a significant role in the attempt to "reschool" Germans in democracy.

---

[1] "Ah, Wilderness!" was, in fact, written in 1933.

[2] On the organization and administrative structures of reeducation, see Hansjörg Gehring, *Amerikanische Literaturpolitik in Deutschland 1945–1953: Ein Aspekt des Re-Education-Programms* (Stuttgart, 1976); and Wigand Lange, *Theater in Deutschland nach 1945: Zur Theaterpoli-tik der amerikanischen Besatzungsbehörden* (Frankfurt am Main, 1980).

What they could hardly have anticipated, however, was the intensity of the theater boom that began immediately after the collapse of the Nazi regime. A September 1, 1944, order of Joseph Goebbels, General Plenipotentiary for Total War Measures, had officially suspended theater operations in the Reich. With the end of the regime, however, a veritable "theater frenzy,"[3] an irrepressible "stage hunger" broke out amid the rubble in the first months after the war.

Despite the destruction, "all state and municipal theaters in the territory held by the Reich in 1937 (except for those in Silesia, Pomerania, East Prussia)... resumed their work again in 1945 or 1946," either in their own often heavily damaged theater houses or in temporary quarters. In addition, a whole series of private theaters sprang up, including at least three dozen between 1945 and 1948 in Berlin alone.[4] More people were employed in theater work during the 1947–8 season in Germany than had been in the larger Reich in 1938–9.[5] By early February 1946, critic Friedrich Luft offered listeners to DIAS, an American sector radio station, the amazing statistic that theater was being performed "in nearly 200 locations" in Berlin.[6] And there was no shortage of theatergoers. The feverish enthusiasm for the theater begain to wane around the time of the postwar currency reform; this lends credence to the theory that theaters owed their high levels of attendance not only to "stage hunger" but also to the fact that little besides theater tickets could be purchased legally with Reichsmarks.

Those responsible for reeducation were well aware that mere decrees could not impart democratic attitudes and values with any lasting, deep-rooted effect. The German theater had

autonomy to the extent that the plays performed in the American zone did not have to be individually licensed. Instead, theater managers who received a license to produce plays simultaneously received the right to determine their own repertoire – as long as they did not produce plays of a militaristic, fascist, or subversive nature. Complaints were rare, and those that were made dealt with individual passages, not entire plays. There is no known case in which the American authorities stopped a production that had already opened. However, that may be due in part to the fact that, contrary to official pronouncements, a kind of unofficial preapproval did indeed operate. An anonymous black-list of the period certainly gives this impression, including not only such figures as, predictably, Hanns Johst and Erwin Guido Kolbenheyer but also Goethe's *Egmont* (with the explanatory comment: "opposition to foreign occupation forces") and Schiller's *Wilhelm Tell* (because "Gessler, for us Hitler, could be Eisenhower to Germans").[7]

Selecting the American plays that would be offered to German theaters for performance fell entirely into the hands of U.S. authorities. The theater department of the ICD functioned as the sole agent and also arranged for translation of plays deemed suitable for reeducation purposes. The criteria for suitability were never particularly clear and in some cases even contradictory. They called for an "undistorted" yet "favorable" portrayal of the United States. They favored plays that contributed "to the development of democratic and antimilitarist (later anticommunist) ideas by the Germans,"[8] as well as those of "intrinsic merit and value." More than half of the fifty-four American plays translated at the behest of the ICD essentially fell into the category of more sophisticated Broadway-style entertainment. Does this suggest that American theater policy, by encouraging escapism, failed in the goal of promoting democratization? Such a conclusion would be unjustified. It rests on the assumption that politicization of

---

[3] Hermann Glaser, *Kleine Kulturgeschichte der Bundesrepublik Deutschland 1945–1989* (Munich, 1991), 106.

[4] Henning Rischbieter, "Bühnenhunger," in Hermann Glaser, Lutz von Pufendorf, and Michael Schöneich, eds., *So viel Anfang war nie: Deutsche Städte 1945–1949* (Berlin, 1989), 226.

[5] Hans Daiber, *Deutsches Theater seit 1945* (Stuttgart, 1976), 26.

[6] Friedrich Luft, *Stimme der Kritik: Berliner Theater seit 1945* (Velber, 1965), 10–11.

[7] Lange, *Theater in Deutschland*, 322.

[8] Gehring, *Amerikanische Literaturpolitik*, 40.

the theater is the only legitimate norm by which the theater of the postwar years can be judged and would merely reproduce the extreme, far-reaching claims of pre-1945 totalitarian cultural policy, albeit from the opposite starting point. Even less convincing is Wigand Lange's charge that the American authorities "from the start blocked the majority of American dramas from reaching the German stage, in other words, pre-censored them."[9] This argument rests on the implicit premise that the political dramas of the 1930s, the so-called red decade, would have been the most suitable for instigating a truly democratic reeducation in Germany even though these works had, in fact, already by and large vanished from stages in their land of origin as well. The selection of dramas exported to Germany was, in fact, quite representative of American theater in the mid-1940s, reflecting Broadway's continued dominance. Certainly no systematic, preventive censorship of dramas destined for Germany existed, but certain "disagreeable" plays may well have been banned. In 1946, for example, the theater officer for Baden-Württemberg prevented a planned production of Steinbeck's *The Moon is Down* in Stuttgart, fearing that this play about a Norwegian city defending itself against German occupation might be interpreted as a call for resistance against the Americans. The banning of Arthur Miller's *All My Sons* the following year heralded all too clearly the spirit of the McCarthy era. The ban was triggered by a letter of complaint to the War Department, decrying Miller's portrait of a manufacturer who supplies the U.S. Air Force with defective airplane parts in pursuit of higher profits as communist "anti-business" propaganda: "Who is responsible for choosing Communist Miller's play? Some innocent in the Army? Or some Communist?"[10] The more emphatically the United States of the late 1940s represented itself as the bulwark of democratic freedoms, the more it proceeded to curtail them. Naturally, this political climate also affected reeducation programs. American

theater policy managed to maintain *one* fundamental liberal principle in that the German theaters actually did decide which of the plays offered by the ICD they would produce. Thus, such edifying patriotic-democratic pieces as Robert Sherwood's *Abe Lincoln in Illinois* were nonstarters, whereas the underside of the American dream could be viewed in stark and unvarnished form in Miller's *Death of a Salesman* or Steinbeck's *Of Mice and Men*. These choices were an amazing, politically instructive experience for an audience that had grown accustomed to the light, frothy comedies produced by the German UFA film studio in the last years of the war. The experience was by no means always perceived as a pleasant one, however, as one reviewer's enthusiasm over S. N. Behrman's Broadway comedy *Biography* demonstrated.

> The National Theater, with its selection of the charming comedy *Biography* by S. N. Behrman, has happily foregone the heavy fare typically presented by many American plays, always so unsettling for German audiences.... This appealing and entertaining ... story can be absorbed with ease and pleasure by the German theater audience without outside tutoring help.[11]

"Outside tutoring help" was exactly what the influx of modern theater from the outside world brought to Germany. If there was a breakthrough to modernity in German theater after 1945 despite all the continuity that existed – both aesthetically and in terms of personnel – then it consisted in large part of the encounter with modern dramatists from abroad. During the twelve years of Nazi dictatorship, Germans had been cut off from the work of Jean Anouilh, Jean Giraudoux, Jean-Paul Sartre, Albert Camus, T. S. Eliot, and the American playwrights Eugene O'Neill, Thornton Wilder, Arthur Miller, and Tennessee Williams.

Curiously, the reception of American drama began in the eastern sector of Berlin when Wilder's *Our Town* premiered at the Deutsche Theater on August 3, 1945. However, the play

[9] Lange, *Theater in Deutschland*, 326, 324.
[10] Gehring, *Amerikanische Literaturpolitik*, 70–1.

[11] Verlag Mannheimer Morgen, ed., *Theater in der Schauburg: Elf Jahre Nationaltheater Mannheim im Spiegel des "Mannheimer Morgen" 1945–56* (Mannheim, 1957), 7.

was cancelled after just one performance by order of the Soviet cultural officer, and Wilder's work was never performed on the stages of the German Democratic Republic (GDR). No other author defined the ideological fronts of the Cold War better. Whereas the Munich premiere of *Unsere kleine Stadt* (*Our Town*) was lauded as "the first really great theater evening of the season,"[12] the (East) Berlin *Weltbühne* responded to the (West) Berlin production of the play by jeering: "This ... American pound of schmalz.... A big nothing."[13] The fact that opinions differed so vehemently over Wilder's cosmic small-town idyll had less to do with aesthetics than with the worldview it embodied; after all, it gave critics in the eastern zone the opportunity to deride the triumph of the harmony of basic humanity over clashing social forces as mere "phony charm."[14]

Karl Heinz Stroux's stunning production of *The Skin of Our Teeth* proved even more resonant than *Our Town*. The production was first launched in Darmstadt on March 31, 1946, and then at Berlin's Hebbel Theater on July 4, 1946. The German title, *Wir sind noch einmal davon gekommen* – "We've Made It Through Again" – had a much more direct appeal than the English original, leaving no doubt that "we" could only mean the Germans. Wilder's epic revue of catastrophic events thus delivered a succinct formula to describe the state of a nation, a parable in which people in the bombed-out cities saw a reflection of their own experience shifted into an ultimately comforting mythical framework. Hans Egon Holthusen's portrayal of the appearance of the refugees in the first act of the Munich production conveys the poignant impression that the play made:

One of the most magnificent moments ... came when ... a horde of refugees, driven from the ice, pours into the four walls of the original human family ... people living an existence ... that was totally exposed and confronted with the extremes, seized by that weightless, feverish euphoria that the likes of us know here from the air raid shelters and being under siege. It was a breathtaking scene. It was humanity in our costume, now and here and always, the poetic unveiling of our fate: April 1945, world history as a last-minute reprieve.[15]

The emphasis on chance twists of fate in this rendering of world history, so highly praised in the West, was precisely what East German critics faulted. Wolfgang Harich was harsh: "What is the message behind Wilder's cosmic cabaret? The lie that war is a natural catastrophe."[16]

Program statistics give an inadequate picture of Wilder's extraordinary significance in German postwar theater. Performed far less often than Carl Zuckmayer's *Des Teufels General*, Wilder's work ranked behind not only the leading figure in French drama, Jean Anouilh, but also – at least until the third theater season after the war – behind John van Druten's touching romantic comedy *The Voice of the Turtle* (*Das Lied der Taube*), in which an unsuccessful young actress and a soldier on leave in New York find each other, and behind Robert Ardrey's now forgotten problem play *Thunder Rock* (*Leuchtfeuer*), which was even performed in the Soviet occupation zone at the time.

If Wilder was appreciated more in Germany than in the United States, Eugene O'Neill brought with him an esteem that could hardly be surpassed. Virtually all the early reviews paint O'Neill as the most important playwright in America. The author's work was actually returning to German stages because his early plays had been performed in the Germany of the 1920s.[17] After 1945, the magnum opus of his midcareer output, *Mourning Becomes Electra*, became the main discovery of German theater. This modern version of *The Oresteia* premiered almost simultaneously in the British zone

---

[12] Alfred Dahlmann, ed., *Der Theater-Almanach 1946/ 47: Kritisches Jahrbuch der Bühnenkunst* (Munich, 1946), 293.

[13] Max Berliner, "Babbit's fauler Zauber," *Die Weltbühne* 16 (1949): 557–8.

[14] Eberhard Brüning, *Das amerikanische Drama der dreißiger Jahre* (East Berlin, 1966), 69.

[15] Hans Egon Holthusen, "Der Mensch und die Katastrophe (1947)," in Hans Egon Holthusen, ed., *Der unbehauste Mensch: Motive und Probleme der modernen Literatur* (Munich, 1951), 126.

[16] *Die Weltbühne* 6 (1949): 217.

[17] See Ward B. Lewis, *Eugene O'Neill: The German Reception of America's First Dramatist* (New York, 1984).

(Hamburg, April 11, 1947) and the American zone (Frankfurt, April 12, 1947). The reviews spoke of the "most significant theatrical event of the postwar period."[18] It was also significant because of its controversial edge. The reviewer for Stuttgart's *Neues Vaterland* declared that it offered exactly the opposite "of what we need today."[19] Indeed, O'Neill's family tragedy, with its psychoanalytical version of the age-old battle of the sexes, offers little that might comfort or even prove edifying to audiences, and it was hardly a fitting advertisement for a democratic society. It fulfilled only one of the criteria of the reeducation program – "intrinsic merit" – but did so with exceptional force and became a prime example of American cultural achievement.

The two most important new American playwrights of the 1940s, Tennessee Williams and Arthur Miller, did not offer an optimistic picture of Americans to German audiences. On the contrary, they turned the American dream so nostalgically evoked in Wilder's town into a nightmare. The focus of their plays fell not on the realists who rolled up their sleeves and tackled problems but on the degraded, the failed, the disappointed, and the neurotic outsiders who fled into worlds of make-believe and lies, from a reality in which they could not hold their own: Laura in *The Glass Menagerie*, Blanche in *A Streetcar Named Desire*, Willy Loman in *Death of a Salesman*.

Statistics on works by American playwrights produced in Germany in the first decade after the war show the following: Miller holds first place right up to the end of the 1955–6 season, with a total of 129 productions, while Wilder had 118. This is due in part to the fact that *All My Sons*, with its German premiere at the National Theater in Weimar in January 1949, was produced no fewer than twenty-seven times in the Soviet occupation zone and the GDR by

the season of 1951–2, whereas Wilder was not produced in the East at all after August 1945.[20] Williams comes out fourth in these statistics, behind John Patrick, whose Broadway comedy *Teahouse of the August Moon* was produced in fifty theaters during the 1954–5 season alone; O'Neill tied for sixth with comic playwright Avery Hopwood (*Fair and Warmer*), coming in behind van Druten.

Further shifts are evident when we examine the long-term presence of American playwrights on West German stages. Statistics compiled by the *Deutsche Bühnenverein* (German Theater Association) from 1947 to 1975, which counted performances rather than productions, put Miller in twenty-second place, Williams twenty-third, O'Neill twenty-fifth, and Wilder twenty-ninth. John Patrick surpassed all of them; his durable *Teahouse* bumped him up to nineteenth place. The commentary that accompanied these figures remarked that although "the influence of American authors on German theater programs" began soon after 1945, "for the most part their plays were not performed here until the seasons between 1955 and 1965."[21] The success of certain long-running plays from the United States beginning in the mid-1950s affected this statistical development more than any other factor. For example, *The Diary of Anne Frank* (in the dramatization by Frances Goodrich and Albert Hackett) had more performances by far than any other play in the 1956–7 and 1957–8 seasons. *Twelve Angry Men* (Reginald Rose/Horst Budjuhn) reached second place in 1958–9 and took the top spot in 1959–60. Richard Nash's *Regenmacher* (*The*

---

[18] *Die Bühnenkritik: Ein monatlicher Sammelband von Aufführungsbesprechungen* 3 (1947): 1. Along these lines, see also Clemens Münster, "Theater unserer Tage," *Frankfurter Hefte* 7 (1947): 730–2; and Horst Frenz, "Eugene O'Neill in Deutschland," *Euphorion* 50 (1956): 307–27, 315.

[19] Quoted in Lange, *Theater in Deutschland*, 449.

[20] These figures are taken from the following master's thesis written under the direction of Henning Rischbieter: Sabine Hertwig and Heike Praetor, "Analyse der Spielpläne deutscher Schauspielbühnen zwischen 1945 und 1956" (M.A. thesis, Free University of Berlin, 1989), 220–4. "Alle meine Söhne" was produced some sixteen times in the western zones between 1949 and 1956, including in the American occupation zone.

[21] Dieter Hadamczik, Jochen Schmidt, and Werner Schulze-Reimpell, *Was spielten die Theater? Bilanz der Spielpläne in der Bundesrepublik Deutschland 1947–1975* (Cologne, 1978), 50. By comparison, Anouilh is in eighth place in these statistics, and Sartre in thirteenth.

Rainmaker) and Herman Wouk's *The Caine Mutiny* had similar successes. The story was different for the major representatives of American drama, however. *The Skin of Our Teeth* once again became a mirror of the times in the late 1950s, when the Germans of the "economic miracle" recognized themselves in the second act, with their "prosperity staring in the face of a constant threat of atomic war."[22] However, Wilder's fame had faded by the early 1960s. Tennessee Williams and Arthur Miller continued to be a presence with their new plays but never again achieved the success of *A Streetcar Named Desire* or *Death of a Salesman*. O'Neill was the only one to hold his own in German theater as a dramatist of undisputed world rank, an assessment due in part to significant productions of his late work. Oscar Fritz Schuh's production of *Long Day's Journey into Night*, for example, was celebrated as a high point of the 1956 Berlin theater festival, the *Festwochen*. O'Neill, one reviewer proclaimed, was "the playwright articulating a universal spirit of the times today."[23] It should be noted that this highly regarded author had already been dead for three years and that he had written the play in 1940–1. "Not much new from the United States" concluded the journal *Theater heute* in its summary of the 1961–2 season.[24] And this conclusion quite aptly characterized the condition of American drama at the end of a decade of declining creative energy.[25] The German reaction reflected this state of exhaustion. Marianne Kesting's assessment of the leading American playwrights in her 1962 overview of contemporary world drama is symptomatic of the change. She wrote that Arthur Miller, for example, "never fundamentally transcended Ibsen's dramaturgy . . . as has the European epic, poetic, and absurd theater" and that O'Neill was presented as an "executor

and shaper of European stimuli, while European theater has already long moved on to other terrain."[26] The tenor of these statements is clear. American playwrights, greeted just after 1945 as representatives of a hitherto suppressed modernity, appeared by 1960 to have been overtaken by more current strands of the modern associated with such names as Samuel Beckett, Eugène Ionesco, and Bertolt Brecht. Only Edward Albee, whose world debut took place in Germany with a production of *The Zoo Story* in Berlin's Schlosspark Theater in 1959, kept pace with the international avant-garde. In Europe, Kesting argued, he was essentially preaching to the converted with his violations of realist stage conventions, although such departures probably still counted as courageous in America. Albee's most successful and more conventionally realist play *Who's Afraid of Virginia Woolf?* came too late to be included in her assessment. It was this play that allowed the author, like Williams and Miller before him, to combine the claims of art and commerce into a major Broadway success and thus to present himself as a "new O'Neill."[27] The play's gripping depiction of the battle between the sexes became a much-discussed theatrical event in Germany as well. No American play since has resonated so much with both critics and the public in Germany.

In the same season (1964–5) in which *Who's Afraid of Virginia Woolf?* landed in second place in statistics on German productions, a German play was making a splash in New York: Peter Weiss's *Marat/Sade*, performed by the Royal Shakespeare Company under the direction of Peter Brook. The play received the two highest honors: the Tony Award and the New York Drama Critics Circle Award for best foreign play. It was a rare success that has never been achieved by any other German playwright on the American stage. And the exchange of dramatic literature between 1945 and 1968 remained one-sided. German and German-language playwrights played a much

---

[22] Rudolf Germer, "Wilder: The Skin of Our Teeth," in Paul Goetsch, ed., *Das amerikanische Drama* (Düsseldorf, 1974), 181.

[23] Willy H. Thiem in the *Frankfurter Abendpost*, Oct. 29, 1956.

[24] *Theater heute*, special ed., (1962): 110.

[25] C. W. E. Bigsby, *Tennessee Williams, Arthur Miller, Edward Albee*, vol. 2 of *A Critical Introduction to Twentieth-Century American Drama*, 3 vols. (Cambridge, 1982–85).

[26] Marianne Kesting, *Panorama des zeitgenössischen Theaters: 50 literarische Porträts* (Munich, 1962), 180, 53.

[27] *Der Spiegel* 43 (1963): 110.

smaller role in the United States than did American playwrights in Germany.[28] Several plays by Max Frisch and Friedrich Dürrenmatt were available in translation, but neither Frisch's *The Firebugs* (*Biedermann und die Brandstifter*), performed in 1963 in New York, nor his *Andorra* (1964) was very well received. Only the 1958 Peter Brook production of Dürrenmatt's *The Visit* (*Der Besuch der alten Dame*) achieved real critical acclaim, whereas the Broadway production of Rolf Hochhuth's *The Deputy* (*Der Stellvertreter*), which attracted much attention, drew more criticism than praise.

It would be a mistake, however, to take Broadway alone as a measure of success. As early as the 1950s, the more artistically challenging productions ran in Off-Broadway theaters and around 1960, small theaters and troupes of Off-Off-Broadway stages assumed their groundbreaking role. University theaters played a role in this story as well, for they took on the function of municipal theaters in many American cities. Brecht was, without a doubt, not only the most important German playwright for both academic and experimental Off-Off-Broadway theaters; as an author, theoretician, and director, he also served as the role model for an avant-garde in the 1960s that sought to combine aesthetic innovation and political activism. It is no coincidence that the *Tulane Drama Review*, situated at the intersection of theater studies and the theater avant-garde, devoted two theme issues to this German figure. The first, in September 1961, introduced Brecht the drama theoretician, apparently still largely unknown, and consisted primarily of texts by Brecht himself. The second, in fall 1967, investigated the forward-looking and now prominent leftist's relevance to the present, to a theater at odds with the American war in Vietnam. "In this country," Erika Munk wrote in her piece for the issue, "there are more Brechtians than there is Brecht, more essays than productions." Brecht's

ideology and style, she continued, were probably "largely irrelevant . . . to the American audience he might have wanted to reach: the disaffiliated poor, the hippies, the blacks, the young disgusted by lies and war." Perhaps, she concluded, one should deal with Brecht as he customarily dealt with other authors, namely "to produce him in a way that will make vivid again, for a new generation, the profound questions he raised for a past one."[29] A prime example of embracing Brecht in a way that goes far beyond Brecht himself appeared in the same issue. An interview with Judith Malina and Julian Beck, directors of the Living Theatre, focused on their ecstatic-ritualistic production of Brecht's *Antigone*: "Brecht used the practice known as alienation because he had faith in cool reason. In spite of the delights of cool reason, we realize it is not enough, and without the verification of the body nothing is really reasonable."[30]

The Living Theatre once again takes us back to Germany. It was the most famous of all theater communes and became a symbol of an alternative social model and a different way of life. At about the same time that the influence of most established American playwrights was decreasing noticeably in Germany, some more alert observers became aware of this American troupe. The Living Theatre had first given guest performances at Berlin's *Akademie der Künste* in 1961 with Jack Gelber's play about junkies, *The Connection*, and could be seen between 1964 and 1967 in other productions throughout Germany. This company was followed by other representatives of Off-Off-Broadway, such as La Mama or Joseph Chaikin's Open Theatre. Berlin became a center for these activities, as did Munich, with its annual theater workshop weeks beginning in 1967. Alternative theater in Germany – a landscape of independent troupes that emerged around the student movement and hippie culture – had its heyday in

---

[28] The discussion that follows draws on Manfred Durzak, "Die Rezeption der deutschen Literatur nach 1945 in den USA," in Manfred Durzak, ed., *Die deutsche Literatur der Gegenwart* (Stuttgart, 1971), 437–47.

[29] Erika Munk, "The Relevance of Brecht," *Tulane Drama Review* 12, no. 1 (1967): 20–1.

[30] Lyon Phelps, "Brecht's Antigone at the Living Theatre," *Tulane Drama Review* 12, no. 1 (1967): 129.

the 1970s and would have been inconceivable without the stimulus of these American role models.

In 1945, a victorious United States wanted to use theater to help put Germany on the path to democracy. In 1968, by contrast, the American theater practitioners who found an audience in Germany were those who declared that the official America and its promise of democracy were morally and ideologically bankrupt. Their ecstatic spectacles proclaimed that a radical counterculture could offer a real-life utopia.

This, too, was a reeducation but of a very different sort. Its motto could no doubt be found in the title of the most famous production of the Living Theatre: *Paradise Now!*[31]

---

[31] This production, which originated in France in 1968, was performed in January 1970 in Berlin at the Akademie der Künste. The author is grateful to Barbara Norminton, Wilfried Passow, Arno Paul, and Dirk Scheper for information on the influence of Off-Off-Broadway theater in Germany, which has received almost no scholarly attention to date.

CHAPTER THIRTEEN

Fascination, Ignorance, and Rejection

Changing Transatlantic Perspectives in the Visual Arts, 1945–1968

Sigrid Ruby

Translated by Edward Fichter

It seems to be assumed [in Europe] that since America has not yet produced anything very important in the way of art, there is little likelihood that it ever will.
— Clement Greenberg, 1950[1]

By 1960, when Pop Art first came out in New York, the art scene here had so much going for it that even all the stiff European types had to finally admit we were a part of world culture.
— Andy Warhol, 1980[2]

The special historical circumstances of the post-war period and the tenacity of century-old stereotypes in the evaluation of cultural production were ambivalent factors at work in the development of German-American relations in the art world after 1945. The powerful military, economic, and political presence of the American victor affected many segments of West German society. On the face of it, the occupation entailed a clearly defined relationship between ruler and ruled, of dominance and subordination. This relationship co-existed, however, with an assumption that European culture was superior, an idea that was the product of a long historical development and that had been internalized on both sides of the Atlantic. It had been a bedrock assumption for the "high" visual arts, a visible symbol of the Occidental intellectual tradition. Before 1945, artistic relations between

the old and new world had, without exception, flowed in only one direction: the significant developments in European painting and sculpture served as models both for mainstream artistic production and for its reception in American art circles.

With this tradition as a backdrop, the leading role claimed from the mid-1950s by American painting – in the form of abstract expressionism – constituted a radical reversal of the pre-existing relationship. The multiple influences of the United States in Western Europe during the Cold War gave powerful support to the thesis that a deliberate and politically motivated policy of American art cultural imperialism existed.[3] In retrospect, this interpretation of shifts in transatlantic influences in the arena of the visual arts remains premature and one-sided. Not enough empirical evidence speaks for this position and, in its narrow concentration on abstract expressionism, it fails to take into account the situation "after 1945" in all its complex historical and cultural dimensions. With different, primarily nationally defined traditions influencing the role and evaluation of art, the development of transatlantic cultural relations would take the

---

[1] Clement Greenberg, "The European View of American Art," *The Nation* (Nov. 25, 1950): 490.

[2] Andy Warhol and Pat Hackett, *POPism: The Warhol 1960s* (San Diego, 1960), 3.

[3] See Max Kozloff, "American Painting During the Cold War," *Artforum* 11, no. 9 (May 1973): 43–54; Eva Cockroft, "Abstract Expressionism: Weapon of the Cold War," *Artforum* 12, no. 10 (June 1974): 39–41; Serge Guilbaut, *How New York Stole the Idea of Modern Art: Abstract Expressionism, Freedom, and the Cold War* (Chicago, 1983).

form of a reciprocally driven process. An end result of this process was that the American avant-
garde received a place in the international artistic
landscape.

One cannot speak of any substantial art exchange between West Germany and the United
States until well into the 1950s. The exodus of
German avant-garde artists caused by National
Socialism, the "inner emigration" of numerous
German artists during Hitler's regime, German artists' isolation from international developments, and – not least – the crushing defeat
of the fascist state left an intellectually unsettled
and disoriented German society in its wake. At
first, no adequate way was found in the realm of
the visual arts to work through what had happened or to confront the present. Rather, artists
sought to escape from a narrow national context and to negate that which was "German."
In place of such a reckoning, the arts community
made a conscious attempt to revive and draw on
elements of classical modernism in order to be
accepted and to regain membership in the European cultural community. Orienting themselves
to the cultural standards of the 1920s, artists in
West Germany worked on developing an abstract formal language in which transcendence
of reality, dissociation from any practical political matters, and an allegedly universal validity
became the essential qualities of any modern
work of art that laid claim to excellence.[4] The
privileged position of abstraction,[5] which was
not entirely undisputed, offered a way for the
German art community to set itself off from the
works and propagandistic instrumentalization of
Nazi art production as well as from the vituper-
ative National Socialist campaign against modernism. Abstract art also offered a distinctive
visible alternative to the visual language pre-

scribed by the German Democratic Republic
(GDR) state, "socialist realism." By attempting
to be nonpolitical, mainstream art of the late
1940s and, especially, the 1950s thus remained
thoroughly politicized; it became the visual expression of a decision to forge ties to the Western
world, whose free and democratic institutions
would be the guarantors of the autonomy and
freedom of the arts and artistic expression.[6]

The United States served as a model of a
nation committed to freedom in the political,
economic, and social spheres and offered West
German society many opportunities to identify with its American counterpart. Still, Europe
remained the decisive frame of reference until
well into the 1950s, not only for visual artists
in the Federal Republic but also for their critics and patrons. The first *documenta* exhibition
in Kassel reflected this orientation by celebrat-
ing the reintegration of a style of German art
that was abstract in form and content into international, that is, European modernism. Art
coming out of the Federal Republic, which at
first primarily aimed at integration – although
perceived at home as thoroughly avant-garde –
did not attract much attention abroad. Compared to breakthrough artistic developments in
Paris and New York, this German work seemed
relatively uninteresting to American artists, critics, and curators.[7]

Why was no comprehensive attempt made
in West Germany until late in the 1950s to
critically assess contemporary American art, either by individuals or on the institutional level?
Long-lived and unexamined prejudices, ignorance, but also the absence of opportunities to
become better informed were in large measure responsible. For how could the artists who
had remained isolated in Germany for many
years have forged any personal ties to individuals
in the American art world? Where could they

[4] Bettina Ruhrberg and Karl Ruhrberg, "Im Zeichen der Abstraktion: Zur westdeutschen Kunst 1945
bis 1960," in Ferdinand Ullrich, ed., *Kunst des Westens:
Deutsche Kunst 1945–1960* (exhibition catalog) (Reckling-
hausen, 1996), 15–20.

[5] Falko Herlemann, "Zwischen unbedingter
Tradition und bedingungslosem Fortschritt: Zur
Auseinandersetzung um die moderne Kunst in der
Bundesrepublik Deutschland der 50er Jahre" (Ph.D.
diss., University of Bochum, 1989).

[6] See Martin Damus, *Kunst in der BRD 1945–1990*
(Reinbek bei Hamburg, 1995), 112–21.

[7] See Antje von Graevenitz, "Reservierter bis
schallender Applaus. Zur Resonanz der deutschen
Nachkriegskunst im Ausland," in Karl Ruhrberg, ed.,
Zeitzeichen (exhibition catalog) (Cologne, 1989), 436–
47.

have seen contemporary American works of art? Moreover, the United States had been first and foremost an importer of art from its founding, and its own artistic production had not been in high demand abroad.

As the occupation and Cold War drew the United States closer to Europe, the American desire for its culture to be widely and fundamentally identified with freedom and democracy became evident. Advocates for staging a comprehensive display of American art abroad cited various arguments: the opportunity to draw attention to long-neglected government promotion of the arts at home; the potential of an international cultural exchange that would link different peoples together and foster peace; competition with communism; and the perceived necessity of "reeducating" the West German population, including at the cultural level. In the face of the apparent "decline of the Occident" and the new international position of supremacy held by the United States, many believed that the time had come for America to conquer its long-standing cultural inferiority complex vis-à-vis Europe, and for Europe to finally accept America as a partner in a common Western cultural tradition.

The organization, overseas transport costs, and insurance required to realize a representative project proved to be a very expensive undertaking; the problem of putting together the financing turned out to be a substantial obstacle to the large-scale export of American art after World War II. Museums, art associations, and other private organizations at first found it impossible to bear the costs involved, and they repeatedly asked the American government for support.

In 1947, after several fierce and sometimes spectacular debates, the U.S. Congress voted against the use of tax monies for art exhibitions both at home and abroad. This delayed a long-term, government-funded program for art exhibitions for Europe until the late 1950s. Under the auspices of reeducation and reorientation policy and programs, the Department of Defense and later the State Department sent exhibitions of American crafts, consumer products, and Native American folk art to West Germany,

while ignoring other kinds of visual arts and contemporary American painting. Thus, one cannot really speak of an attempt to influence or control the German art scene during the occupation for imperialist, anticommunist, or any other motives by imposing a specifically "American" model.

Despite the ongoing refusal of the American government agencies to offer financing, a deeply committed art lobby – mainly in New York – succeeded in sending a small number of quite different exhibitions of contemporary American painting and sculpture privately or semi-officially to Europe, West Germany included. These exhibitions made no claims about the leading place of recent American art.[8] Rather, they sought a measure of acceptance: full membership in a world culture still largely defined by European criteria. Pluralism of style and individuality in artistic expression were presented as the hallmarks of the American nation and its free and democratic society, and they were thereby put forward as the opposite of a rigidly prescribed communist state culture. Abstract expressionism, later celebrated as the international avant-garde, was in the early 1950s itself the target of strong resistance; in the first American

---

[8] Exhibitions such as *Introduction à la peinture américaine, Amerikanische Malerei – Werden und Gegenwart, Zwölf amerikanische Maler und Bildhauer der Gegenwart*, and others presented different trends of contemporary American art side by side, on equal footing. Galerie Maeght in Paris showed "Introduction á la peinture américaine" in March–April 1947. The exhibit included works by artists attached to the Samuel Kootz Gallery, New York: Robert Motherwell, William Baziotes, Adolph Gottlieb, Carl Holty, Romare Bearden, and Byron Browne. *Amerikanische Malerei: Werden und Gegenwart* (Sept.– Dec. 1951) toured in Berlin, Vienna, and Munich. The exhibition included fifty paintings by twenty-five contemporary American painters employing very diverse styles – for example, Hyman Bloom, Edward Hopper, Stuart Davis, Loren MacIver, Ben Shahn, Jackson Pollock, and others. *Zwölf amerikanische Maler und Bildhauer der Gegenwart* (Apr. 1953–Mar. 1954) toured through Paris, Zürich, Düsseldorf, Stockholm, Helsinki, and Oslo. Along with sculptures by Theodore Roszak, Alexander Calder, and David Smith, works by Morris Graves, Arshile Gorky, Edward Hopper, John Marin, Jackson Pollock, Ben Shahn, John Kane, and Ivan Albright were exhibited.

exhibitions exported abroad, it appeared – if at all – as one extreme, yet tolerated artistic trend among many.

West Germans paid these early exhibits of contemporary art from the United States little attention. The works on display seemed to confirm a prejudice toward American culture as provincial and essentially derivative. The artistic or individual points of resonance remained hostage to a Eurocentric way of seeing.

In December 1952, the Zimmergalerie Franck in Frankfurt exhibited the work of four German painters deemed to be Neo-Expressionists. The works of Karl Otto Götz, Otto Greis, Heinz Kreutz, and Bernard Schultze signaled a movement against the carefully composed, highly formal, and increasingly decorative abstractions of West German postwar modernism. They treated the unformed, the processual, the not-yet-decided, the act of creation, and the uninhibited alienation as the major themes of painting, thereby suggesting strong parallels with the French *Informel* school. And, in fact, the four, who were later usually known by the group title of "Quadriga," had clearly and consciously made use of experiences they had gained in Paris and what they had seen in exhibitions at the city's galleries. These exhibits had included works of several American Abstract Expressionists, chiefly Jackson Pollock; the Parisian galleries gave them serious attention for the first time in 1951 and 1952. Thus, the only fruitful communication lines laid between the New York avant-garde scene and the studios of West Germany in this period took a detour and ran through the aesthetic filter of Paris. These contacts did not emerge directly through the art scene in West Germany, nor did West German artists take in this new work by visiting New York. The informal paintings of the Frankfurt Quadriga and of Gruppe 53 that was founded a little later in Düsseldorf, however, were not able to gain a following in the art world of the Federal Republic until the second half of the 1950s.[9] As a German variant

of the *Informel*, a movement that had gradually won critical acclaim, this style of painting became a fashionable model for portraying existential alienation and artists' creatively articulated posture of protest in an increasingly technically determined, standardized, and prefabricated world.[10] A long-delayed recognition for American abstract expressionism, including on the institutional and critical level, took place at the end of the 1950s in the framework of this interpretation and the needs to which it spoke.

Lawrence Alloway in London, Arnold Rüdlinger in Basel, Willem Sandberg in Amsterdam, and Michel Tapié in Paris had very early on identified an internationally significant avant-garde in the paintings of Jackson Pollock, Willem de Kooning, Franz Kline, Clyfford Still, and Mark Rothko and made efforts to organize European exhibitions of these painters. However, West German curators, museum directors, and gallery owners completely ignored this trend – no longer very new – until the second *documenta* of 1959. In the meantime, American exhibition organizers went on the offensive. Inspired and pressured by increased European interest, but also in light of the unmistakable fact that abstract expressionism had taken over a leading position on the New York art scene, the Museum of Modern Art in 1958 and 1959 sent "New American Painting" and "Jackson Pollock: 1912–1956" on tour through Western Europe, exhibitions that marked a turning point in the perception and understanding of American painting. With these two groundbreaking shows, the concept of a representative plurality of styles was abandoned in order to celebrate in its place abstract expressionism as the sole valid realization of the freedom of artistic expression, and to introduce it as not specifically American but international avant-garde art to the European public.

---

[9] Gruppe 53 was founded in 1953 to promote informal art in Germany as well. Among the first members were Gerhard Hoehme, Peter Brüning, Fritz Bierhoff,

Winfred Gaul, Egon Kalinowski, Friedrich Werthmann, and Peter Royen.

[10] On the *Informel*, see the exhibition catalog Städtisches Museum Schloss Morsbroich, Leverkusen, ed., *Thema: Informel. Teil 1. zur Struktur einer "anderen" Zeit* (exhibition catalog) (Berlin, 1973).

These two extraordinarily successful exhibitions prompted inclusion of a substantive American contribution to the *documenta II* in 1959. It was a last-minute addition on the part of the Kassel exhibition's organizers, and they borrowed from the other shows' conceptual apparatus almost to the point of plagiarism. Abstract expressionism was now accepted and celebrated as part of a "world language of abstraction." This became stylized as the quintessence of artistic and social freedom and thus the visual expression of a Western, mainly anticommunist, ideology. However, this process occurred without West Germans perceiving – or wanting to acknowledge – the fundamental differences between the European and American understanding of this style. In the West German interpretation of the late 1950s, Jackson Pollock, who died in an accident in 1956, emerged as a manic-depressive "titan of non-objectivity," as a "revolutionary," "subversive and new creator," whose "revolt of emotion" and "wild dreams"[11] made him the incarnation of the existentially uninhibited artist in an anonymous, atomized mass society and, consequently, a tragic hero of his age and country. The vitality and "barbaric force"[12] found in Pollock's paintings became keys to an understanding of an American art style whose primitivity, originality, and youthful openness were necessary components for establishing their avant-garde character in a comprehensive and acceptable way. Subsumed under a Eurocentric field of view, this one-sided interpretation of Pollock's work and hence of other abstract expressionists as well for a long time blocked – at least in terms of its institutionalized acceptance – a perception of the extraordinary materiality, of the entirely new treatment

of color, line, and canvas, and the retreat of the artistic subject that accompanied it. The ultimately depersonalized and objectified work of art was the genuine American contribution to modern painting, which from the 1950s on had been resolutely and to a large extent independently developed further in the works of Jasper Johns, Robert Rauschenberg, and then the Pop artists.[13] At first, the West German artists offered little that could compare with this new way of painting. Not until the early 1960s would an innovative and critical examination of American painting emerge that would also attract public interest.

Alongside painting, transatlantic contacts in other arts fields led to jointly organized events and projects. At the intersection of experimental music, theater, literature, and conceptual object art, a discussion of issues that had emerged on both sides of the Atlantic, more or less at the same time and on the same level, managed to neutralize the usual asymmetry in German-American relations. Already in the early 1950s, radical countermovements to the dominant abstract art and the bourgeois ideal of the autonomous work of art had developed in the form of European *Konkrete Kunst* (concrete art) and American "concretism." "Concrete artists," who did not limit themselves to the bounds of a single medium and advocated a strongly reduced role for the artist in the process of creation, one limited to its conceptual basis and leading to a work that as image, object, event, word, or sound, was to refer to nothing else but itself.

In the United States, the experimental composer John Cage assumed a decisive role in the formulation of this new vision of art. He conceived of music as an unrestricted sequence of sounds or noises and silence, not connected with any purpose and largely left to chance. Thus,

---

[11] See German press notices of the Jackson Pollock retrospective organized by the Museum of Modern Art, which could be seen in the *Kunsthalle* in Hamburg in summer 1958; for example, *Süddeutsche Zeitung*, Aug. 1, 1958; *Welt am Sonntag*, July 20, 1958; *Hannoversche Allgemeine Zeitung*, July 27, 1958; *Die Zeit*, July 25, 1958; *Deister- und Weserzeitung*, July 24, 1958; and *Weser-Kurier*, July 19, 1958.

[12] Werner Haftmann, "Einführung," in Harald Kimpel and Karin Stengel, eds., *II. documenta'59* (exhibition catalog) (Kassel, 1959), and "Malerei," ibid., 17.

[13] See Benjamin Buchoh, "Formalism and Historicity – Changing Concepts in American and European Art Since 1945," in the exhibition catalog *Europe in the 1970s: Aspects of Recent Art* (Chicago, 1977), 85; Hayden Herrera, "Besitzergreifen und Darstellen: europäische und amerikanische Malerei der Avantgarde 1945–1960," in *Europa/Amerika: Die Geschichte einer künstlerischen Faszination seit 1940* (exhibition catalog) (Cologne, 1986), 165–83.

every concert performance could turn into an audiovisual experience with action elements. Performances of this new music found a contemporary equivalent in the logic-defying, constantly shifting, and expandable happenings that Allan Kaprow, Claes Oldenburg, and Jim Dine had been staging since the end of the 1950s, primarily in New York. In the international summer courses devoted to new music that had been offered in Darmstadt since 1946, and in performances given by the studio for electronic music in Cologne, works by Cage, La Monte Young, and other experimental composers from the United States were performed at an early point in Germany as well. Personal contacts between European and American artists with similar interests and expectations intensified toward the end of the 1950s. It was primarily the studio of Mary Bauermeister and the Galerie Haro Lauhus in Cologne that between 1960 and 1962 created a forum – in the form of performances and exhibitions – for shared interests spanning the Atlantic.[14]

Against this background and as a conscious continuation of these growing bonds, the International Fluxus movement made its mark in Germany from 1961–2 onward under the vital direction of the American George Maciunas. A native of Lithuania, Maciunas had come to Germany in fall 1961 to propagate his ideas of an anti-institutional, emphatically anti-"serious" avant-garde. He had developed these conceptions in the fold of the progressive New York art scene and pursued them by attempting to put together a unified transatlantic front.[15] In the form of a now programmatically conceived Concretism, Maciunas propagated an anti-art that resisted the embrace of the establishment and whose spontaneity, unpredictability, and flexibility were supposed to

reflect or correspond to the banal reality of everyday life. In this regard, the contrasts between Europe and America initially revealed themselves as extraordinarily stimulating and productive. In the two international Fluxus Festivals organized by Maciunas in Düsseldorf (1962) and Wiesbaden (1963), the Bauermeister troupe, which concentrated on experimental music, intensified the activisim of its approach and expanded it to include elements of social criticism.[16] The Fluxus movement sought an increasingly politicized terrain beyond the traditional confines of art. Not only Maciunas but also Nam June Paik, Wolf Vostell, and Joseph Beuys endorsed and promoted this development through their "*Aktionen*"; however, this trend met with opposition from among American Fluxus artists. They ultimately distanced themselves from the events staged in Germany. As the international character of Fluxus fell away, so too did part of its provocative message.

The apparent transatlantic differences of artistic claims had their origin in the different traditions concerning the nature and uses made of art, as well as in the specific sociocultural conditions prevailing in West Germany in the early 1960s. The absence called for of any intrinsic purpose and intention in an artwork – a view propagated by John Cage, Allan Kaprow, and other American artists – arose from a rather formalistic conception of art. The historical or narrowly political dimension of an artwork was not considered particularly important. By contrast, at least since the emergence of Dada, Futurism, and the social-critical work of Kurt Schwitters, commentary on contemporary political matters had been part of the arsenal of artistic expression in Europe, especially in Germany. In the Federal Republic of the immediate postwar era, however, a kind of art had appeared that emphasized turning away from the world and concentrated on the self-expression of the artistic

[14] See Historisches Archiv der Stadt Köln, ed., *intermedial, kontrovers, experimentell: Das Atelier Mary Bauermeister 1960–62* (Cologne, 1993).

[15] See Ina Conzen, "Vom Manager der Avantgarde zum Fluxusdirigenten. George Maciunas in Deutschland," in Gabriele Knapstein and Carola Bodenmüller, eds., *Eine lange Geschichte mit vielen Knoten: Fluxus in Deutschland 1962–1994; Institut für Auslandsbeziehungen* (exhibition catalog) (Stuttgart, 1995), 18–31.

[16] Among the artists who worked in this often changing group were Dick Higgins, Alison Knowles, Benjamin Patterson, Emmet Williams, Nam June Paik, Wolf Vostell, Tomas Schmit, Addi Köpcke, Daniel Spoerri, Staffan Olzon, Frank Trowbridge, and Bendt af Klintberg.

ego; in the midst of West Germany's "economic miracle," this art had become firmly institution-alized. Confronting these trends, artists such as Wolf Vostell, Bazon Brock, and Joseph Beuys revived the potential of the European tradi-tion of modernism by using a comprehensive social criticism that encompassed both art and life to set radical new priorities.[17] Their works and efforts through Fluxus and beyond were a stimulating component of a wide-reaching so-cial protest movement that would eventually ex-plode violently in the second half of the 1960s.

The conflict between Germany and Amer-ica that had become evident in the collapse of Fluxus also characterized reactions to Pop Art during the 1960s. The art scene in the Federal Republic showed intense interest in this par-ticularly American cultural export item, an in-terest that demonstrated continuing fascination with the former occupying power and oscil-lated between rejection and identification. An increasing internationalization of the art mar-ket, the exhibition business, and the mass media in West Germany had also intensified transat-lantic exchange. An art "happening" staged by Gerhard Richter and Konrad Lueg, for instance, demonstrated the level of West Germans' fa-miliarity with current artistic developments in New York. In October 1963, the two men chose an unexceptional furniture store in Düsseldorf as the stage and context for their event "Liv-ing with Pop: A Demonstration for Capitalist Realism." The happening-like event "dis-played" the usual commodities of the furni-ture store, unpretentiously complemented by works by Lueg, Richter, and Beuys. The event also showcased its instigators as they "used" a living-room suite elevated on white pedestals. Lueg and Richter "promoted" their effort by invoking the pathbreaking "New Realists" ex-hibition of November 1962 at the Sidney Janis Gallery in New York and suggesting parallels

to their own work.[18] This carefully aimed and at the same time ironically inflected reference to American Pop Art created a transatlantic anal-ogy that not only defined but also legitimized German Pop Art. It did not set up the American counterpart as the determining model. Rather, Richter and Lueg, like their German colleagues Sigmar Polke and Manfred Kuttner, regarded Pop Art as an international art form whose com-mon roots they located in the very similar real-ities of late capitalist societies on both sides of the Atlantic.[19] By emphasizing common as well as independent elements, these self-designated "German pop artists"[20] deliberately laid claim to an equal place on the international art scene. And they lived up to this claim in the quality of their works and projects. Richter, Lueg, and Polke took full advantage of the visual and tech-nical resources of the mass media, like the Amer-ican Pop artists Andy Warhol, Roy Lichtenstein, James Rosenquist, Claes Oldenburg, Tom Wes-selman, and Robert Indiana. They, too, used ob-jects from everyday life, stereotype photographs and newspaper clippings along with materi-als and equipment of inferior quality for their works, whose conspicuous triviality taunted the traditional understanding of art and challenged the dominance of the increasingly smug abstract school.

The differences, however, remained just as clear. The very concept of "Capitalist Realism" draws attention to the inherently programmatic character of the German approach, a qual-ity absent from American Pop Art. Ironically

---

[18] Susanne Küper, Konrad Lueg, and Gerhard Richter, "Leben mit Pop – eine Demonstration für den Kapitalistischen Realismus," *Wallraf-Richartz-Jahrbuch* 53 (1992): 289–306.

[19] See the letter by Richter, Lueg, Polke, and Kutt-ner to the *Neue deutsche Wochenschau* (Apr. 29, 1963), reprinted in Hans-Ulrich Obrist, ed., *Gerhard Richter: Text, Schriften und Interviews* (Frankfurt a.M., 1993), 12.

[20] Richter and Lueg introduced themselves early in 1963 in the Paris galleries of Iris Clert and Ileana Sonnabend as "German pop artists." See Jürgen Harten, "Der romantische Wille zur Abstraktion," in Jürgen Harten, ed., *Gerhard Richter, Bilder/Paintings 1962–1985* (exhibition catalog) (Cologne, 1986), 16.

---

[17] See Friedrich Wolfram Heubach, "Die Kunst der 60er Jahre," in Wulf Herzogenrath and Gabriele Lueg, eds., *Die 60er Jahre: Kölns Weg zur Kunstmetropole; Vom Happening zum Kunstmarkt* (exhibition catalog) (Cologne, 1986), 112–6.

alluding to the "Socialist Realism" of GDR art, Lueg, Richter, and also Polke made fun of a Federal Republic saturated with the "economic miracle." "Not the appearance, but the social uses of goods"[21] are the subject of the German Pop Artists. Andy Warhol and Roy Lichtenstein chose to feature certain aspects of American everyday and popular culture in a "no comment" attitude and, by so doing, left the task of making sense of them largely up to the recipient. By contrast, the works of their German colleagues, because of their dialectical complexity and carefully introduced alienation effects, imply a certain degree of critical distance right from the beginning. A subversive potential is present in both cases, but in American Pop Art it was primarily aesthetically coded, and its activation rests on an always ambivalent decision to be made by the recipient.

German art criticism in the late 1960s believed that it had solved this problem of varying interpretations by adhering to unambiguous viewpoints. Whereas conservatives condemned Pop Art as "kitsch art" and as the "Coca-Colonization" of Western Europe, left-wing and more youthful critics saw it as a perfect example of art that criticized the system. The Left used a rhetoric of resistance whose antibourgeois, neo-Marxist impetus had its origins in the critical essays of Walter Benjamin and Herbert Marcuse; it interpreted Pop Art's straightforward integration of the ubiquitous and, therefore, theoretically available mass media and consumer products as a profoundly democratic act and at the same time as a cry of protest of the individual who is being destroyed in capitalism's apparatus of manipulation.[22] When being used for a political viewpoint or a critical position, the very ambiguity between affirmation and criticism that characterized American Pop Art naturally got lost.

The contradictory yet very intensive German involvement with Pop Art was conditioned by the massive presence of this art in the Federal Republic and the simultaneous expansion of a youthful protest movement. The commitment of gallery owners and collectors on both sides of the Atlantic brought a veritable flood of American Pop Art to West Germany, especially during the second half of the 1960s.[23] This "pop enthusiasm" took hold not only of the art scene, both established and in the making; it also took hold of a broad and especially youthful public that saw in the art of Warhol and Lichtenstein – as well as in rock music and beat culture – expressions of a new lifestyle and the opportunity to escape the stuffiness of an affluent bourgeois society.

People in the Federal Republic at the end of the 1960s thus experienced Pop Art as the evident conjunction of American consumer culture, popular culture, and high culture. It was a visible symbol of the New World that allowed for conservative rejection while also offering the liberating effects of identification. Internalized clichés and ideas about the "other" were confirmed in either case, and the joy of consumption could go on. Besides its critical dimension, many people simply found that an art whose "real," colorful images and symbols they could read and understand was fun. In any case, the dominance of American Pop Art at the fourth *documenta* in 1968 rendered it unmistakably clear that this art from the New World had finally achieved recognition.

---

[21] Stefan Germer, "Gekreuzte Blicke, verschobene Perspektiven: eine Skizze der deutsch-amerikanischen Kunstbeziehungen," in *Sammlungsblöcke: Stiftung Froehlich* (exhibition catalog) (Tübingen, 1996), 20.

[22] See Andreas Huyssen, "The Cultural Politics of Pop," in Stefan Germer, ed., *After the Great Divide: Mod-* *ernism, Mass Culture, Postmodernism* (Bloomington, Ind., 1986), 141–59.

[23] See Phyllis Tuchmann, "American Art in Germany: The History of a Phenomenon," in *Artforum* 9 (Nov. 1970): 55ff.

CHAPTER FOURTEEN

Architecture as Political Medium

Werner Durth

Translated by Tradukas

The world war unleashed by Germany turned back on the country in the middle of Europe with devasting, destructive force. Merciless bombing raids, fierce fighting by retreating German troops, and the Allies' advance transformed towns and cities into a landscape of ruins. In summer 1945, approximately five million of the nearly twenty million dwellings in Germany had either been destroyed or severely damaged. Air raids had killed more than 400,000 people and left approximately thirteen million homeless.[1]

In light of this daunting situation, many architects viewed rapid reconstruction as not only technically and economically unfeasible, but "morally impossible"[2] as well. Many of them expected that plans to dismantle industrial facilities would result in long-term impoverishment of the country. Consequently, beginning in spring 1945, they called for the agricultural resources and equipment necessary for future survival and for "reconstruction from the ground up."[3] Evacuees and refugees were urged to settle in rural areas,[4] while people who managed to maneuver around the restrictions on urban residency constructed makeshift dwellings in the cellars and ruins of German cities.

Despite the numerous plans drafted in both national and local institutions from the beginning of the air raids,[5] systematic reconstruction was initially out of the question. Not least among the reasons was that the Allies pursued differing policies in their respective occupation zones. In the Soviet zone, the redistribution of property following the October 1945 land reform became a high priority. Even the most urgent reconstruction efforts in cities failed because of a chronic shortage of materials. By contrast, French military authorities set up their own planning staffs; taking their cue from Le Corbusier, they envisioned a radically new pattern of settlement, with apartment towers set in spacious parks.[6] An early sign of the coming change in urban structure came on the initiative of the British occupation authorities; in 1946, they began construction of the steel-reinforced

---

[1] For detailed information on regional differences, see Uta Hohn, *Die Zerstörung deutscher Städte im Zweiten Weltkrieg* (Dortmund, 1991), 51.

[2] Otto Bartning, "Ketzerische Gedanken am Rande der Trümmerhaufen," *Frankfurter Hefte* 1 (1946): 63–72, 74.

[3] On this, see the editions of *Der Gärtnerhof*, published in the series *Neuaufbau vom Boden her*, ed. Franz Dreidax and Arved Gutschow (Hamburg, 1947).

[4] *Referate und Aussprachen der Kölner Arbeitstagung des Deutschen Verbandes für Wohnungswesen, Städtebau und Raumplanung* (Stuttgart, 1947).

[5] Werner Durth and Niels Gutschow, *Träume in Trümmern: Planungen zum Wiederaufbau zerstörter Städte im Westen Deutschlands*, 2 vols. (Braunschweig, 1988).

[6] On reconstruction planning in the various occupation zones, see Klaus von Beyme, *Der Wiederaufbau: Architektur und Städtebaupolitik in beiden deutschen Staaten* (Munich, 1987).

Grindelallee apartment complex on the ruins of an old neighborhood in the center of Hamburg.[7] There, as in other cities, strict controls on construction materials could be effectively deployed to block any improvised, ad hoc building projects. American occupation policies seem to have best met the pressing challenge of renovating destroyed or damaged buildings within the framework of existing property and ownership structures, even if Directive JCS 1067 – announcing the Morgenthau Plan – had caused Germans to fear the worst.

Lingering fear of the Morgenthau Plan confronted Walter Gropius, the originator of the internationally influential Bauhaus style, when he visited Germany in fall 1947. Gropius was returning to Germany for the first time since his emigration to the United States as a consultant to General Lucius D. Clay.[8] Germans responded to his lectures with clear distrust; when he presented his concept of restructuring urban residential areas into new "neighborhood units" of 5,000 to 8,000 residents, for example, some in his audiences suspected him of promoting yet another means of "keeping Germany down."[9] Still others saw similarities between his idea and the Third Reich's plans to transform postwar cities into spacious "urban landscapes" in which local Nazi party branches would be at the center of smaller housing developments.[10]

This model of opening up and restructuring the city – already envisioned during the war – could easily be reconciled with the Western Allies' proposals. Building on the concepts of 1920s urban planning, these models sought to dismantle the traditional layout of nineteenth-century cities, with their tenements, back courtyards, and narrow streets.

Reconstruction took a number of architectonic forms, varying according to local traditions and politics. At one end of the spectrum, some cities, such as Münster and Freudenstadt, opted to rebuild their destroyed centers in historical style. Other cities, such as Hamburg, Hannover, and Kassel, pursued radical modernization; after clearing away the ruins and rubble, they rebuilt entire districts along completely new lines. Local decision making and self-government grew stronger in western Germany as the influence of the English and French occupying powers declined. As a result, reconstruction was marked by a remarkable diversity of architectural forms unconstrained by either federal or state building restrictions.

The Western Allies had begun to promote their visions of an international modern style by staging exhibitions of model buildings as early as 1947.[11] Conservative architects in many places opposed the proponents of New Building or *Neues Bauen*. The latter, in conscious opposition to the historicizing and regional forms of "Third Reich architecture," sought connections to developments cut off by Nazi cultural policies after 1933. Walter Gropius's trip also encouraged the revival of the creative currents of the Weimar era. Through his recollections of the Bauhaus movement and an account of the work of German immigrants in the United States, Gropius sought to bring new life to architectural culture in Germany. However, upon his return to the United States, he remarked with dismay:

I was utterly disappointed. It is impossible for anyone who has not seen the current realities in Germany to understand just how profound the destruction is, both spiritual and physical. I found it particularly difficult to put myself into a frame of mind that would allow me to say something encouraging or positive. The only cause for optimism lies in the spirit of the older generation, those who finished school before Hitler came to power. Young people who grew up under Hitler are cynical and it is very difficult to deal with

---

[7] Axel Schildt, *Die Grindelhochhäuser: Eine Sozialgeschichte der ersten deutschen Wohnhochhausanlage* (Hamburg, 1988).

[8] Reginald R. Isaacs, *Walter Gropius: Der Mensch und sein Werk* (Berlin, 1984), 952–62.

[9] Ibid., 959.

[10] See Durth and Gutschow, *Träume in Trümmern*, 1:174–86; for a detailed overview of persons and concepts, see Werner Durth, *Deutsche Architekten: Biographische Verflechtungen 1900–1970* (Munich, 1992).

[11] For an overview, see Hartmut Frank, "Trümmer," in Bernhard Schulz, ed., *Katalog zur Ausstellung Grauzonen-Farbwelten* (Berlin, 1983), 66–8.

them, and this came out in the suggestions I made to General Clay.[12]

The public was able to read Gropius's recommendations in the December 1947 "Report on Urban Planning in Germany" published by the Department of the Army's press division. In this report, he called for more intense academic and cultural exchange between Germany and the United States as well as for a revival of the German *Werkbund*, the Bauhaus movement, and the German section of the *Congrès Internationaux d'Architecture Moderne* (CIAM). He also wanted German architects who had been active before 1933 to be able to resume participation in international professional gatherings.[13]

But without either a stable currency or a functioning construction industry, it was almost impossible to think in terms of systematic reconstruction. The debates between conservative and modern architects were initially without consequence. The chronic lack of building materials and dependence on the black market meant that little besides basic repair work was possible, and later the force of the status quo impeded broad planning. Not until the Marshall Plan and the June 1948 currency reform in the three Western zones did a solid basis for major construction work emerge. This basis was in turn strengthened by the founding of the Federal Republic of Germany in May 1949 and the housing construction law of April 1950. Diverse ways of life and housing styles could now be discussed more concretely. Exhibitions on model buildings in the United States stimulated a modernization of lifestyles and pointed to a new direction for architectural culture in Germany.[14]

In January 1948, a lavishly illustrated catalog of the 1944 Museum of Modern Art exhibition "Built in the U.S., 1932–1944" was published

in Germany.[15] The catalog documented the remarkable triumph of modern architecture on the other side of the Atlantic, showing picture upon picture of light-filled residences designed by figures such as Marcel Breuer, Walter Gropius, Philip Johnson, Richard Neutra, and Frank Lloyd Wright, and of institutional and professional buildings by Albert Kahn, Mies van der Rohe, and Skidmore, Owings & Merrill. In summer 1949, the exhibition on American lifestyles *"So wohnt Amerika"* ("How America Lives") showcased the advantages of mass-produced houses featuring the most up-to-date household technology; this exhibition offered visitors a glimpse of an almost utopian life far removed from actual conditions in the still heavily damaged cities of West Germany. An editorial in the conservative architectural journal *Der Baumeister* commented with irony and condescension, "We know how much childish enjoyment Americans have playing at home with their idol of technology, the more expensive, the better." Noting that Germans, with their cultural traditions, do not suffer from such weaknesses, the writer insisted: ". . . we do not – and in the Year of Goethe this goes almost without saying – waste our time on robots; we intend to remain real live human beings."[16]

Appealing to "Occidental values,"[17] conservative architects explicitly rejected the prospect of further modernization, of the automation of daily life, of a shift in design to reflect the advances brought by industrial production; implicitly, they thereby rejected modern architecture as well. American publications, on the other hand, encouraged those architects who hoped for a revival of the design principles, construction techniques, and attention to material aesthetics that had brought the *Neues Bauen* movement worldwide recognition in the 1920s.

[12] Gropius to Richard Paulick, Apr. 6–7, 1948, quoted in Isaacs, *Walter Gropius*, 964.

[13] Ibid., 960.

[14] Axel Schildt and Arnold Sywottek, eds., *Modernisierung im Wiederaufbau: Die Westdeutsche Gesellschaft der 1950er Jahre* (Bonn, 1993).

[15] Elisabeth Mock, ed., *In den USA erbaut 1932–1944* (Wiesbaden, n.d.).

[16] Rudolf Pfister, "So wohnt Amerika: Eine Betrachtung über das Fertighaus," *Der Baumeister* 10 (1949): 509.

[17] For details on this topos of cultural criticism, see Jost Hermand, *Kultur im Wiederaufbau: Die Bundesrepublik Deutschland 1945–1965* (Munich, 1986), esp. 77–8.

The catalog for the exhibition "Architektur der USA seit 1947"[18] presented examples of the newest architectural trends and provided models for many German architects:

This book's collection of materials demonstrates that American postwar architecture tends more and more toward a less rigid concept of floor plans, an emphasis on functional building components, and a blending of interior and exterior spaces. The latter might involve the incorporation of the surrounding landscape in the interior living areas by using big glass walls, or expansion of interior living areas to the exterior by adding porches, balconies, and outdoor sitting areas.[19]

A German construction publication noted with approval that this "American architecture" displayed clear European influences

because nothing specifically American can be found in this architecture. American influences on Europe in the 1920s and the flow of European emigrants to the United States in the 1930s have intensified mutual influence and cross-fertilization in such a way that one should rather speak of universal trends conforming to developments of the political economy.[20]

Although most state-supported single-family housing after 1950 largely followed German conventions in layout and appearance as they had been written into law during the 1930s, there were also increasing numbers of experiments in housing construction. These experiments employed a variety of floor plans and sought a stronger fusion of interior and exterior space. The 1950 housing construction law clarified the legal and financial framework, and a construction boom rapidly ensued, helped along by funding from the Marshall Plan's European Recovery Program (ERP). In 1951, a brochure published on behalf of the Federal Ministry for the Marshall Plan and the mission of the European Cooperation Administration (ECA) was distributed widely throughout Germany. The brochure pointed to the fact that 340,000 new

dwellings had been built in 1950, twice as many as had been built in 1929 in the area that later became the Federal Republic.[21] A special ERP program for refugee housing was also established. In summer 1951, the Federal Ministry of Housing and the ECA jointly publicized a nationwide competition to promote cost-saving and space-saving ideas for public housing; more than 700 architects participated.[22]

With pilot projects set up in fifteen cities, the ECA mission – using ERP monies – made DM 37.5 million available for experimental construction projects and financed the creation of 3,300 dwellings. Widespread publicity about these projects stimulated ideas for projects throughout West Germany.[23] The committee assessing these efforts, made up of well-known German architects and American experts, issued an interim report, *Kritik aus den USA* ("Criticism from the USA"). The report pointed out the failure of German housing construction and urban planning to adequately anticipate the push toward modernization. Pointing to the inflexible "schematism" in German housing development plans, they also forcefully criticized a "general failure to acknowledge the problems associated with the rapidly increasing motor vehicle traffic" in Germany. Moreover, they pointed to the lack of attention given to the "excellent opportunity to cast new plans for German city centers and also pass legislation needed for the redistribution of land." Even worse, the report argued, "owners of smaller lots were receiving permission to reconstruct their old dwellings, thus making replanning increasingly more difficult." [24]

German architects and planners, too, spoke of a "missed opportunity" for instigating a

---

[18] Cultural Institution Office of the Land Commissioner for Baden-Württemberg, ed., *Architektur der USA seit 1947* (Stuttgart, n.d.).

[19] Gerd Hatje, ed., *Amerikanische Architektur seit 1947* (Stuttgart, 1951), text from the cover.

[20] Bodo Remszhardt, "Neues Bauen in den USA," *Baukunst und Werkform* 7 (1951): 50–1.

[21] Details in the pamphlet *Nicht vergessen!*, ed. Bundesministerium für den Marshallplan und der ECA-Mission von Deutschland (Bonn, ca. 1951).

[22] See Hermann Wandersleb, ed., *Neuer Wohnbau: Neue Wege des Wohnungsbaues als Ergebnis der ECA-Ausschreibung* (Ravensburg, 1952).

[23] For detailed information, see Brigitte d'Ortschy and Georg Günthert, "Die 15 ECA-Siedlungen," in Hermann Wandersleb, ed., *Neuer Wohnungsbau*, 9–39.

[24] Donald Monson, "Städtebau," in Hermann Wandersleb, ed., *Neuer Wohnungsbau*, 129.

large-scale communal takeover of land. Guarantees for preexisting property ownership in the
Western occupation zones precluded the realization of comprehensive, modern urban planning concepts, including the separation of urban
functions and the construction of comprehensive transportation systems. At the end of the
1950s, a thoroughgoing reconstruction plan was
issued that included proposals for laying out
major traffic arteries; it was later criticized as
a second destruction of the cities.[25]

The impact of technology on urban development and the modernization of building production through use of prefabricated materials
had already gone too far for many architects.
Many Germans voiced their opposition to *Neues
Bauen* by still demanding customized, hand-
crafted production and design consistent with
traditional regional or national building styles.
Assimilation to the American way of life was
thus implicitly rejected. Many, including some
of the architects who had paved the way for
modernism, had second thoughts about the impact of the Bauhaus and the work of the architects who had emigrated to the United States.
In 1953, Rudolf Schwarz set off a heated debate
in the architectural world. Schwarz, a prominent architect since the Weimar period who had
not been politically compromised in the Third
Reich and who was mainly involved in the
construction of churches after 1945, launched
a damning critique of the Bauhaus movement
in the respected journal *Baukunst und Werkform*.
Of Gropius he wrote: "He obviously could not
think – I mean what is considered thinking in
the Occidental world."[26]

By setting up a polarity between "Occidental people" and the "agitated terrorists"[27] of

modernity – probably the proponents of the
Bauhaus style – Schwarz deepened the serious rift in the world of architects and divided
them into two hostile camps. His statements
reminded some contemporaries of the attacks
on the teachers and followers of the Bauhaus
movement by conservative architects in the late
1920s and the Nazis, attacks that became life
threatening after 1933. Gropius himself dismissed this polemic with the obsrvation that,
"in their crude and arrogant tone and their ignorance of the issues, these attacks are no different from the opponents of Bauhaus in the Hitler
era."[28]

By personalizing the problems of architectural culture and casting them in such an in-
sulting manner, Schwarz undermined his own
intention of "returning to the realm of a truly
grand historical tradition" and "instigating a
true dialogue" through a critique of the superficiality of modernism.[29] The 1953 "Bauhaus
Debate," as it was later called, was the last passionate public dispute among architects over the
choice between "Occidental" values and the
much criticized "materialism" of the postwar
period.[30] With the attacks against Schwarz and
the mid-1950s construction boom in the Federal
Republic, the call for alternatives to the moderate form of modernism in the architecture of
reconstruction died down. Arguments in favor
of taking the German "cultural heritage," with
its multiplicity of national and regional architectural traditions, into account were drowned
out by the German Democratic Republic's
(GDR) cultural propaganda. Complaining of
the "Americanization" of Germany cityscapes,
the GDR offered a historicizing, monumental official architecture as an alternative.[31] Both

[25] Deutscher Städtetag, ed., *Erneuerung unserer Städte:
Vorträge, Aussprachen und Ergebnisse der 11. Hauptversamm-
lung des deutschen Städtetages in Augsburg* (Stuttgart, 1960).

[26] Rudolf Schwarz, "Bilde Künstler, rede nicht,"
Baukunst und Werkform 1 (1953): 9–17.

[27] Ibid. See the reprint of Rudolf Schwarz's articles
and the controversy that they unleashed in Ulrich Con-
rads et al., eds., *Die Bauhaus Debatte 1953: Dokumente einer
verdrängten Kontroverse* (Braunschweig, 1994).

[28] Gropius to Richard Döcker, Mar. 14, 1953, in ibid.,
57.

[29] Schwarz, "Bilde Künstler, rede nicht," 17.

[30] For a discussion of the Bauhaus Debate, see also
Christian Borngräber, *Stil novo: Design in den 1950er Jahren*
(Frankfurt am Main, 1979).

[31] Edmund Collein, "Die Amerikanisierung des
Stadtbildes von Frankfurt am Main," *Deutsche Architektur*
4 (1952): 150–5.

architects and construction officials in the GDR made forceful appeals to their colleagues in the West to resist American "cultural barbarism" in modern architecture. These appeals had the unintended effect of stifling the call for a revival of the "truly grand tradition" in West Germany, and a superficial form of modernism increasingly began to shape the West German urban skyline.[32]

Although urban reconstruction in both western and eastern Germany was carried out according to the same model of "a structured and more spacious" city with buildings that were on a modest scale until 1949, an ideologically motivated reorientation took hold with the founding of the new state in the Soviet zone. GDR architecture, aspiring to forge a culture for Germany as a whole, looked for models among the great German architects of the nineteenth century. Under the motto "National in form, democratic in content!", architectural culture was thrust into the arena of foreign-policy propaganda.[33] In his programmatic speech of July 1950 entitled "The National Reconstruction Program and the Tasks of German Architecture," Walter Ulbricht, general secretary of the Socialist Unity Party (*Sozialistischen Einheitspartei Deutschlands*, or SED), denounced the division of Germany, declaring that it had led to a swift cultural decline in the West. He compared the "buildings of the Nazi government" with the new buildings of the "American and British occupying powers" and posed the polemical question: "Are these great boxes that dominate the landscape in parts of West Germany not the perfect expression of American interventionism and imperialism, which regard West Germany as its power base and do not respect the national culture of our people?" To regain national self-respect and with an eye to a reunited Germany, the task at hand was "to restore honor to architecture as a form of art and to develop German architecture

as the German art of building," in contrast to "the monotonous and culturally barren buildings" in the West.[34]

By winter 1949–50, the Central Committee of the SED had formulated a "Cultural Plan 1950." Aimed against Western "cosmopolitan" culture, it stated that all available resources should be utilized in an "uncompromising struggle . . . against the invasion of the cultural barbarism of American imperialism in West Germany."[35] Initially, this required that all proposed reconstruction plans that involved modern architecture or urban space in Eastern Germany had to be evaluated and redrafted in accordance with the new directives. Planning for greater Berlin, in the works since 1945, came under particularly close scrutiny. What officials in the West considered exemplary was held up as disastrous in the East. The spectrum of attacks on West German architectural work ranged from the charge that Bonn's austere parliament building was "un-German" architecture to the denunciation of the "Americanization of the cityscape of Frankfurt am Main,"[36] to comments on individual buildings.[37] Professional journals and photobooks showered praise on the GDR's first showcase buildings, such as apartment buildings in Berlin by the Weberwiese, and on plans for the future face of Stalinallee, lauding them as examples of a cultural standard for the whole of Germany.

Even after the death of Stalin in March 1953 and the June uprising, the construction of lavish, impressive-looking apartment complexes continued in major East German cities, especially

---

[32] See Klaus von Beyme et al., eds., *Neue Städte aus Ruinen: Deutscher Städtebau der Nachkriegszeit* (Munich, 1992), esp. introd., 9–30.

[33] See Jörn Düwel, *Baukunst voran! Architektur und Städtebau in der SBZ/DDR* (Berlin, 1995).

[34] Walter Ulbricht, *Das nationale Aufbauwerk und die Aufgaben der deutschen Architektur*, published by the Amt für Information der Regierung der DDR (Berlin, 1952), 6–8.

[35] "Verordnung zur Entwicklung einer fortschrittlichen demokratischen Kultur des deutschen Volkes und zur weiteren Verbesserung der Arbeits- und Lebensbedingungen der Intelligenz," published in *Gesetzblatt der DDR*, no. 28 (Mar. 3, 1950): 185–7.

[36] Collein, "Amerikanisierung des Stadtbildes."

[37] See Kurt Magritz, "Die Tragödie der westdeutschen Architektur," *Deutsche Architektur* 2 (1952): 57–65.

in the capital of the new state. In West Berlin, the International Exhibition of Building (*Internationale Bauausstellung*, or IBA) was organized with the cooperation of renowned architects from numerous Western countries. It opened in 1957 in the Hansaviertel, where a spacious parkland was built over the ruins of what had previously been a densely populated residential area at the edge of the Tiergarten. The high-rises and residential complexes built there, presented as the heralds of a bright new modern world, stood as proof that a plurality of lifestyles could coexist.[38]

As the double towers of the Frankfurter Tor on Stalinallee, with their echoes of the works of Berlin's Baroque master architects, were being completed in 1957, West German President Theodor Heuss spoke at the inauguration of the IBA in the Hansaviertel of a "surfeit of a historicizing 'cult of taste.'" Drawing a contrast to proclaimed nationalism in the East, Heuss praised the people of West Berlin "for their wonderful decision, made in freedom, to invite architects of other nationalities as well" to take part in the common Hansaviertel project. In a pointed remark against the showcase buildings in the eastern part of the city, Heuss added, "One thing is certain: whining for tradition falls on deaf ears, at least in the West."[39]

In contrast to historicizing buildings done up in the style of "national building traditions" that shaped the larger cities of East Germany, the centers of West German cities were defined by a form of vibrant modernity described, in the terminology of the time, as "organic."[40] In clear opposition to the monumental "Third Reich architecture" on the one hand and the monumental style of East Germany's Stalinist-era buildings on the other, even the most ambitious West German cultural and governmental buildings were distinguished by their simple formal language and functional architectural styles. All bombastic architectural elements were deliberately avoided in the parliament buildings in Bonn designed by Hans Schwippert in 1948–9, a starkly plain extension of the former Pedagogic Academy, and in subsequent projects.

At the 1958 World Exhibition in Brussels, Egon Eiermann and Sep Ruf won international recognition with their severely rational but also transparent and open-pavilion architecture. Eiermann also designed an elegant glass and steel building for the German Embassy chancellory in Washington, D.C. (1958–64). It was followed by the office tower for the members of the Bundestag in Bonn (1965) featuring an open-plan stacking of the stories. In the meantime, his colleague Sep Ruf designed the austere chancellor's bungalow, which was long featured in almost every television news broadcast as the unpretentious symbol of the Federal Republic's center of power. Germany was represented at the 1967 Montreal Expo in light, tentlike structures designed by Frei Otto and Rolf Gutbrod that drew woldwide attention. Günter Behnisch's similar designs on an even larger scale gave the 1972 Munich Olympic Games their reputation as the "bright games."

In prominent locations throughout the Federal Republic, a second modernism thus became evident. It both revived the *Neues Bauen* tradition interrupted by National Socialism and also self-consciously picked up on international trends in contemporary architecture. Elements of Bauhaus principles entered the curriculum and shaped a new generation of architects, more and more of whom were women. The Bauhaus architects came to be regarded as almost unequaled masters, particularly because their most recent buildings were still setting international standards. This was further confirmed by Walter Gropius's 1957 participation with The Architects Collaborative (TAC) at the IBA in Berlin, where he presented a large, slightly curved high-rise apartment building. His famous Pan Am Building was under construction in New York at that time. In addition, in 1962, he helped plan the Ruhr University in Bochum and, together with the TAC, he began work in 1960

[38] See also Internationale Bauausstellung Berlin GmbH, eds., *Interbau Berlin: Amtlicher Katalog der Internationalen Bauausstellung Berlin 1957* (Berlin, 1957).

[39] Preamble of the German Federal President, in ibid., 12–13.

[40] For reference to the diversity of architectural trends in the 1950s, see Werner Durth and Niels Gutschow, *Architektur und Städtebau der 1950er Jahre* (Bonn, 1987).

on the design of the large residential area in Berlin's Britz-Buckow-Rudow district that later became known as the "Gropiusstadt."[41]

Through his many publications, Ludwig Mies van der Rohe, the other grand master of the Bauhaus, came to be regarded as a major figure in modern architecture.[42] His work was considered as an enduring standard for future architecture, a standard even numerous American architects had adopted. His apartment buildings in Chicago and above all his office buildings, such as the Seagram Building in New York (completed 1959), served as models for an entire generation of younger architects working in the International Style. The steel-skeleton construction technique Mies van der Rohe perfected in the United States influenced office construction in the Federal Republic during the 1960s. Many German architects studied both his buildings and those of his students in the United States before they dared to tackle similar projects back home. Study trips to the United States became almost obligatory for young German architects.[43] Mies van der Rohe won widespread

recognition in 1968 with the opening of the New National Gallery in Berlin. This museum in the west of the city formed a fitting counterpart to Karl Friedrich Schinkel's Old Museum in East Berlin. Because of the cultural upheaval in the Federal Republic, 1968 was also the year that marked the end of the unquestioning adulation that classical modernism had hitherto enjoyed.

The enthusiasm for German-influenced American modernism reached its zenith during the 1960s German construction boom, particularly because prominent West German architects emulated American models. By continuing to teach architecture and the arts, former Bauhaus instructors such as Albers, Breuer, Gropius, and Mies van der Rohe still had widespread influence on architecture in the United States. They had overshadowed independent American traditions associated, for example, with Louis Sullivan, Henry Richardson, and Frank Lloyd Wright. But a younger generation of architects was now calling for a move away from rigid functionalism and purist modernism. In his 1966 *Complexity and Contradiction in Architecture*, Robert Venturi playfully turned Mies van der Rohe's famous maxim "less is more" into "less is a bore," hoping to incite the search for a more complex, formally richer, and picturesque architectural style.[44] His suggestions gained acceptance several years later in West Germany as well, at a time when the debate on "postmodern" architecture was beginning to react to structural transformations in architecture.

[41] Isaacs, *Walter Gropius*, 1061–95.

[42] Alfons Leitl, "Ludwig Mies van der Rohe: Bauten der letzten beiden Jahre," *Baukunst und Werkform* 5 (1951): 9–20, 11.

[43] Heinrich Klotz, *Architektur in der Bundesrepublik* (Frankfurt am Main, 1977); Helmut Hentrich, *Bauzeit* (Düsseldorf, 1995); Paul Betts, "Die Bauhaus-Legende: Amerikanisch-Deutsches *Joint Venture* des Kalten Krieges," in Alf Lüdtke, Inge Marsslock, and Adelheid von Saldern, eds., *Amerikanisierung: Traum und Alptraum im Deutschland des 20. Jahrhunderts* (Stuttgart, 1996), 270–90.

[44] Robert Venturi, *Complexity and Contradiction in Architecture* (New York, 1966).

CHAPTER FIFTEEN

The Legacy of the Holocaust in Germany and the United States

Alan E. Steinweis

The Nazi "Final Solution" was already under-way when the United States entered World War II in December 1941,[1] but it had been at most an indirect factor in America's decision. To be sure, news of Nazi violence against Jews had served to reinforce American fears of Nazism's threat to democracy and Western civilization. As the war continued, news of the mass murder leaked out of Nazi-occupied Europe and was reported widely in American newspapers. Several times between 1942 and 1945, the U.S. government declared its intention to punish Nazi war crimi-nals. Nonetheless, a wide discrepancy remained between official American rhetoric and actual American military and diplomatic efforts to in-tervene directly to stop the genocide.[2] Amer-ican moral repugnance at Germany's actions intensified in spring 1945 as American soldiers found mass graves, piles of bodies, and ema-ciated survivors at concentration camps such as Buchenwald and Dachau. Concrete evidence of German atrocities reinforced the conviction that the conflict against Nazi Germany had been a moral "crusade."[3]

An initial American postwar idealism mani-fested itself in war crimes prosecutions, a denaz-ification program,[4] an attempt at reeducation,[5] and refugee relief. The prosecution at the Inter-national Military Tribunal at Nuremberg, ad-ministered jointly by the United States, Britain, France, and the Soviet Union, attempted to show that the Nazi regime had engaged in a premeditated, centrally directed effort to exter-minate the Jews of Europe. Rising tensions be-tween the Western powers and the Soviet Union prevented further such international trials from taking place, but the United States, like many European states, moved forward with its own prosecutions. By 1949, the United States had held 12 highly publicized trials in Nuremberg, encompassing a total of 184 German govern-ment officials, business leaders, military officers, and members of the SS and related Nazi organi-zations. Nazi policy toward Jews figured promi-nently in several of the trials, particularly in the *Einsatzgruppen* case. American occupation

[1] I have relied on useful country-by-country surveys in David S. Wyman, ed., *The World Reacts to the Holo-caust* (Baltimore, 1996), particularly the articles by An-drei S. Markovits and Beth Simone Novick on West Germany (391–446), Jeffrey M. Peck on East Germany (447–72), and David S. Wyman on the United States (693–748).

[2] Deborah E. Lipstadt, *Beyond Belief: The American Press and the Coming of the Holocaust, 1933–1945* (New York, 1986).

[3] Note the title of Dwight D. Eisenhower's memoir of the war, *Crusade in Europe* (New York, 1948). On the liberation of the camps, see Robert H. Abzug, *In-side the Vicious Heart: Americans and the Liberation of Nazi Concentration Camps* (New York, 1985).

[4] See the chapter by Cornelia Rauh-Kühne, vol. 1, Politics.

[5] See the chapter by James F. Tent in this section.

authorities also conducted trials of more than 1,000 German concentration camp guards and officials.[6]

A broader program of denazification was supposed to remove from positions of influence Germans who had been personally involved in the Nazi movement.[7] But the escalation of Cold War tensions gradually eroded the crusading impulse behind the American occupation of Germany. American officials, anxious to rebuild the German economy and win the support of the German people in the Cold War, no longer wished to pursue policies that many Germans resented as heavy-handed interference by an occupying power. By the time the Federal Republic was founded in 1949, denazification, which had been implemented half-heartedly in the first place, had been abandoned, while reeducation had been transformed into a much softer policy of "reorientation."

Although the American occupation provided a protective umbrella under which a German democratic tradition could be revivified, it succeeded in nurturing only a negligible degree of German sympathy for the predicament of Europe's Jews. Opinion surveys conducted by the Americans in the late 1940s reflected the persistence of negative stereotypes about Jews, a lack of willingness to come to the assistance of Jewish survivors of German crimes, and even a propensity to shift some of the blame for the persecution and murder onto the Jews themselves. A 1946 survey found that more than 40 percent of the population refused to acknowledge that Germany had been responsible for widespread torture and mass murder in Europe during the war. Surveys conducted under West German auspices in the 1950s concluded that these attitudes persisted, and in some respects even hardened, after the end of the occupation. Levels of anti-Semitism remained between 30 and 40 percent, while even larger majorities, in some surveys approaching 70 percent, rejected the proposition that Germany bore the responsibility to compensate non-German victims of Nazism. The magnitude of the failure to recognize what had been perpetrated against the Jews was acutely reflected in a survey conducted in 1948, which not only found that 57 percent of Germans believed that "National Socialism was a good idea that was badly implemented" but also concluded that only about one-third of Germans so much as mentioned the persecution of the Jews when asked to think about the negative aspects of Nazism.[8]

The persistence of anti-Semitic attitudes in postwar Germany represented a continuity with past decades, but certain conditions specific to the immediate post-1945 period were also important. Many Germans understood themselves as victims of World War II rather than perpetrators of aggression and genocide. This self-perception hindered their ability to develop sympathy for the predicament of non-Germans. Related to this psychological dynamic were two specific conditions of the occupation. The first of these was the presence of tens of thousands of Jewish Displaced Persons (DPs) on German soil in the late 1940s. The mere presence of these Jewish DPs was a constant reminder of Germany's record as an oppressor. Compounding this psychologically disturbing factor was the refusal of the Jewish DPs to conform to a model of German middle-class "order" (*Ordnung*). Many were East European Jews of working-class origin who, in order to acquire adequate provisions, engaged in black-market commerce, an activity that reinforced long-held stereotypes about Jews among the German population. A second condition that exacerbated irritation stemmed from the implementation of property restitution procedures in the American zone in November 1947. Intended to compensate Jews whose property had been "Aryanized" during the Nazi regime, such measures generated further

---

[6] Adalbert Rückerl, *The Investigation of Nazi Crimes, 1945–1978* (Heidelberg, 1979).

[7] James F. Tent, *Mission on the Rhine: Reeducation and Denazification in American-Occupied Germany* (Chicago, 1982).

[8] Werner Bergmann and Rainer Erb, *Anti-Semitism in Germany: The Post-Nazi Epoch Since 1945* (New Brunswick, N.J., 1997), 1–2, 228, 247, 249.

resentment toward the occupation as well as to-ward the Jewish survivors.[9]

American policy at this time was not without its own contradictions. The strict immigration quotas of the 1930s remained in place after the war, forcing Jewish DPs who wished to emigrate to the United States to endure long delays. At the same time, the American government expe-dited the immigration of German scientists and engineers who had served the Nazi regime.[10] There was also collaboration between American intelligence units and known Nazi war crimi-nals, such as Klaus Barbie.[11] Although such cases were few in number, they were symptomatic of the radical shift in American attitudes toward Germany's recent Nazi past in the early phase of the Cold War.

Compared to later decades, the Holocaust received relatively little attention in either German state in the 1950s. Among West Germans who subscribed to the comforting notion of West German history beginning at a "zero hour" (*Stunde Null*), any preoccupation with the problematic recent past would have consti-tuted an obstacle to the immediate priorities of national reconstruction. East Germany, for its part, disclaimed any connection with the Nazi legacy. Communists (so went the official expla-nation) had been the victims of a fascist regime that had served the interests of the capitalist class. Whereas the capitalist-fascist tradition ostensibly had been preserved in West Germany, East Ger-many claimed to embody the humanistic, pro-gressive elements of German history. Like other communist states after 1945, East Germany did not acknowledge that the Nazi regime had tar-geted Jews as a group. Nazi racism made little sense when viewed through the lens of Marxist-Leninist ideology, which was better equipped to explain class oppression than ethnic prejudice.

Occasional confrontation with the Holocaust did indeed prove unavoidable for the West Ger-mans in the 1950s. To a limited degree, it was provoked by the efforts of intellectuals, such as Karl Jaspers, who recognized the need to work through this most problematic aspect of Ger-man history. The most unpleasant truths about the recent past were also brought to the surface as a result of the incomplete denazification pro-cess. Although few former Nazis occupied the key decision-making positions in the new Fed-eral Republic, they populated bureaucracies, technocracies, university faculties, and school systems. A controversy ensued in 1952 when a parliamentary investigation concluded that the Foreign Ministry had recruited into its ranks a disturbing number of formerly active Nazis (and not merely nominal party members), in-cluding several individuals who had helped implement the "Final Solution." The most con-troversial disclosure of this sort involved a state secretary in Konrad Adenauer's own chancery, Hans Globke, who in the Nazi period had writ-ten a legal commentary on the Nuremberg racial laws to facilitate their implementation. In the wake of such revelations, the Adenauer gov-ernment took steps to limit political damage to the Federal Republic's reputation. Despite broad-based rejection of the concept of "collec-tive guilt" within German society, for example, the government was reluctant to endorse grant-ing military pensions to former members of the Waffen SS because of possible negative reso-nance abroad.[12]

It was in the context of such controversies that West Germany negotiated and signed the Lux-embourg Agreement of 1952, which provided for West German compensation (*Wiedergut-machung*) to Jewish Holocaust survivors in Is-rael, the United States, and other countries. Konrad Adenauer had realized from fairly early on that the success of his project of tying the Federal Republic to the West (*Westbindung*) would require gestures of his country's readiness to assume responsibility for the Nazi regime's

[9] Angelika Königseder and Juliane Wetzel, *Lebens-mut im Wartesaal: Die jüdischen DPs (Displaced Persons) im Nachkriegsdeutschland* (Frankfurt am Main, 1994).

[10] See the chapter by Michael Neufeld, vol. 1, Secu-rity.

[11] Allan Ryan, *Klaus Barbie and the United States Gov-ernment: A Report to the Attorney General of the United States* (Washington, D.C., 1983); see also the chapter by Wesley K. Wark, vol. 1, Security.

[12] Wolfgang Benz, ed., *Die Bundesrepublik Deutsch-land: Geschichte in drei Bänden*, vol. 1: *Politik* (Frankfurt am Main, 1983), 16–21.

crimes against the Jews. Although the over-whelming majority of West German citizens were opposed to reparations payments to Jew-ish Holocaust survivors or to the state of Israel, Adenauer believed that such *Wiedergut-machung* was a morally appropriate policy that would benefit Germany's image, especially in the United States. Adenauer pushed the Luxem-bourg Agreement through the Bundestag de-spite the opposition of most of the delegates from his own Christian Democratic Party. The restitution agreement was a politically effective gesture of goodwill on the part of the Federal Republic. By assuming the moral responsibility for the deeds of the Nazi regime, which the Ger-man Democratic Republic (GDR) refused to do, the Federal Republic promoted its position as the legitimate successor state of the German Reich. Moreover, aside from its symbolic value, the agreement with Israel inaugurated a bilateral relationship that would prove beneficial to the economic and technological development of the Jewish state over the long term.[13] The United States, it should be noted, had played an impor-tant, albeit behind-the-scenes, role in bringing the Luxembourg Agreement to fruition.[14]

The attitude of the German Democratic Re-public toward reparations stood in marked con-trast to that of its Western counterpart. The communist regime had bestowed the status of "victims of fascism" onto its few Jewish citizens, entitling them to some material benefits. But the GDR rejected any responsibility to compensate Jews who lived elsewhere. Moreover, just as the details of the Luxembourg Agreement were be-ing ironed out, the Stalinist regimes of the So-viet bloc were implementing, under the guise of anti-Zionism, a vicious anti-Semitic campaign. A more tolerant atmosphere for Jews prevailed in the period of de-Stalinization after 1953, but a serious and sincere intellectual confrontation with German anti-Semitism and the Holocaust did not occur. Moreover, the GDR, like most

other communist states, persisted in its staunch hostility toward Zionism, even to the point that its Ministry for State Security (*Stasi*) provided training to Palestinian terrorists.[15]

In the Federal Republic of the 1950s, only a handful of historical publications dealt with anti-Semitism, the persecution of Jews in Ger-many in the 1930s, or the "Final Solution." No-table exceptions to this pattern were in most cases edited or written by Jews.[16] West German historians remained concerned primarily with the collapse of the Weimar Republic, the sys-tem of domestic terror under the Nazis, and elite resistance to Hitler within the military and the churches. The emphasis on domestic terror both reflected and reinforced the self-exculpatory notion that ordinary Germans in the Third Reich had little ability to dissent from or resist the regime whereas, paradoxically, em-phasis on singular acts of resistance, such as the attempt to assassinate Hitler on July 20, 1944, helped to salvage the nation's honor. Histor-ical studies produced in the German Demo-cratic Republic placed emphasis on the relation-ship between big business and the Nazi regime, as well as on the persecution of and resistance by communists. Although several "progressive" historians in the GDR had attempted to focus greater attention on the anti-Jewish dimension of Nazi policy, the first serious contribution to the study of the Holocaust by an East German scholar, Kurt Pätzold, would not appear until 1975.[17]

In the United States as well, only a few mainstream literary works, most notably *The Wall* (1950) by John Hersey, *The Diary of Anne Frank* (1952), and *Exodus* (1958) by Leon Uris, dealt with the Holocaust. The English

---

[13] Lily Gardner Feldman, *The Special Relationship Be-tween West Germany and Israel* (Boston, 1984).

[14] Thomas A. Schwartz, *America's Germany: John J. McCloy and the Federal Republic of Germany* (Cambridge, Mass., 1991).

[15] Markus Wolf, *The Man Without a Face* (New York, 1997).

[16] See, for example, Léon Poliakov and Joseph Wulf, eds., *Das Dritte Reich und die Juden* (Berlin, 1955); H. G. Adler, *Theresienstadt 1941–1945: Das Antlitz einer Zwangs-gemeinschaft* (Tübingen, 1955).

[17] Otto D. Kulka, "Major Trends and Tendencies in German Historiography on National Socialism and the 'Jewish Question,'" in Yisrael Gutman and Gideon Greif, eds., *The Historiography of the Holocaust Period* (Jerusalem, 1988), 1–51

translation of Elie Wiesel's *Night* appeared in 1960 but received very little notice. Scholarly studies about anti-Semitism and the Holocaust that appeared in the United States were, in most instances, produced by Jewish émigrés such as Eva Reichmann, Max Weinreich, Phillip Friedman, and Hannah Arendt.[18] So little attention was given to the Holocaust in mainstream American academic and intellectual life that Raul Hilberg, whose seminal work on the Nazi bureaucracies that implemented the Holocaust would later attain canonical status, struggled for years in the late 1950s to find a publisher for his book.[19] American historical scholarship was far more concerned with themes such as Prusso-German militarism and autocracy that were deemed directly relevant to explaining the failure of Germany to evolve into the sort of liberal democracy that Americans now envisaged for Germany's future.[20] The ascendancy of totalitarianism theory further contributed to the marginalization of the anti-Jewish dimension in the study of National Socialism. With a democratized West Germany as an ally against the Soviet Union, American scholars now sought to derive lessons from Germany's Nazi past that would be relevant for understanding, and containing, the Soviet Union. The attempt to stuff the Third Reich and the Soviet Union into a single paradigm of totalitarianism led scholars to emphasize comparable features of the two systems. Racially motivated genocidal anti-Semitism did not fit well into the paradigm and, therefore, received scant attention.[21]

Even in the American Jewish community, the Holocaust was not a major subject of discussion in the 1950s. Only a minority of American Jews has been directly affected by the Holocaust. Although anti-Semitism was a serious concern for the majority, in the postwar American context the preferred way to combat it was by advancing the project of assimilation. Future-oriented American Jews did not consider an intense interest in the recent victimization of European Jewry as a means to promote their own acceptance into the mainstream of American society. Moreover, with Germany now an important American ally against communism, American Jews may have been reluctant to dredge up disturbing aspects of the German past. And although their support of the new state of Israel and for the civil rights movement and other liberal causes in America was most definitely informed by a basic understanding of what had happened recently in Europe, it did not translate into an active historical curiosity about the Holocaust.[22]

If the 1950s had been a period of relative neglect of the Holocaust in both the United States and Germany, the 1960s was a period of transition to the far more active involvement with the subject that would characterize the subsequent decades. Events within Germany and abroad acted as catalysts to stimulate interest in the Holocaust. An epidemic of swastika graffiti in the Federal Republic in 1959–60 provoked discussions and introspection. The trial of Adolf Eichmann in Jerusalem in 1961 captured the attention of many Germans. Then, between 1963 and 1968, West Germany conducted a series of highly publicized trials of Germans who had worked at Auschwitz. These Auschwitz trials, although opposed by most West Germans, did much to direct further attention to the persecution and murder of the Jews. In 1964, during the trials, *Der Stellvertreter* (*The Deputy*), a controversial play by Rolf Hochhuth about the alleged inaction of Pope Pius XII during the Holocaust, premiered in the Federal Republic.

---

[18] Eva Reichmann, *Hostages of Civilization: The Social Sources of National Socialist Anti-Semitism* (London, 1950); Max Weinreich, *Hitler's Professors: The Part of Scholarship in Germany's Crimes Against the Jewish People* (New York, 1946); Philip Friedman, *Roads to Extinction: Essays on the Holocaust* (New York, 1980) (essays written before 1960); Hannah Arendt, *The Origins of Totalitarianism* (New York, 1951).

[19] Raul Hilberg, *The Politics of Memory: The Journey of a Holocaust Historian* (Chicago, 1996), 105–19.

[20] See, for example, Gordon Craig, *The Politics of the Prussian Army, 1640–1945* (Oxford, 1955).

[21] Carl J. Friedrich, ed., *Totalitarianism* (Cambridge, Mass., 1954).

[22] Deborah E. Lipstadt, "The Holocaust: Symbol and 'Myth' in American Jewish Life," *Forum on the Jewish People* 40 (1980–81): 77–88.

Of all the factors that contributed to the transformation of West German public attitudes toward the Holocaust in the 1960s, perhaps the most important was the so-called *Verjährungsdebatte* of 1965 – the debate over extending the statute of limitations on the prosecution of war crimes. Had the existing statute of limitations been allowed to expire, thousands of alleged war criminals would have been instantly placed beyond the reach of the West German legal system. The Bundestag voted overwhelmingly to extend the statute of limitations, but not before a lengthy, emotionally charged parliamentary debate that riveted much of the German public. The controversy resurfaced periodically after 1965 until the Bundestag abolished the relevant statute of limitations in 1979.

West German scholars displayed keener interest in the Holocaust, or at least Holocaust-related aspects of German history, during the 1960s. In 1963, Ernst Nolte published his pioneering work on fascism, in which Jew-hatred was treated as a core component of National Socialism.[23] Further works published by Andreas Hillgruber in 1965 and Hans-Adolf Jacobsen in 1968 linked anti-Semitism to the foreign policy and strategic doctrines of Nazi Germany.[24] Hans Mommsen's important study of the Nazi civil service (1966) devoted close attention to the dismissals of Jews from government positions.[25] Eberhard Jäckel's influential book on Hitler's worldview placed anti-Semitism at the very center of Nazi ideology.[26]

In the United States, it was during the 1960s that the term *Holocaust* came into regular use to describe the persecution and murder of the Jews by Nazi Germany. The Library of Congress added "Holocaust-Jewish, 1939–1945" to its subject classifications in 1968.[27] Early in the decade, the Eichmann trial captured public attention in America as it did in Germany. The trial coincided with the publication in 1961 of *The Destruction of the European Jews* by Raul Hilberg.[28] The book, which is now considered a standard work, received little attention from scholars or critics at the time of its publication. Some of Hilberg's conclusions about the Jewish response to Nazi policy were borrowed – and simplified almost beyond recognition – by Hannah Arendt, whose reports on the Eichmann trial appeared in *The New Yorker* and later in the widely discussed book *Eichmann in Jerusalem*. Also in 1961, the attention of the American public was focused on Nazi crimes (although not the Jewish Holocaust per se) by the film *Judgment at Nuremberg*.[29] Hochhuth's *Deputy* premiered on Broadway in 1964. Several books were published toward the end of the decade. *The Holocaust* by Nora Levin (1968), although deeply flawed as a work of scholarship, proved accessible to a wide readership in a way that Raul Hilberg's study had not.[30] Arthur Morse's *While Six Million Died* (1968) confronted readers with difficult questions about the failure of the outside world, including the United States, to come to the rescue of Europe's Jews.[31]

The Six Day War of June 1967 probably more than any other factor, stimulated interest in the Holocaust in the United States, especially – although by no means exclusively – in the Jewish community. For several days during the conflict, it appeared that Israel might face extinction.

[23] Ernst Nolte, *Der Faschismus in seiner Epoche: Die Action française, der italienische Faschismus, der Nationalsozialismus* (Munich, 1963). On Nolte's role in the *Historikerstreit* of the 1980s, see Charles S. Maier, *The Unmasterable Past: History, Holocaust, and German National Identity* (Cambridge, Mass., 1988).

[24] Andreas Hillgruber, *Hitlers Strategie: Politik und Kriegführung 1940–1941* (Frankfurt am Main, 1965); Hans-Adolf Jacobsen, *Nationalsozialistische Aussenpolitik 1933–1938* (Frankfurt am Main, 1968).

[25] Hans Mommsen, *Beamtentum im Dritten Reich: Mit ausgewählten Quellen zur nationalsozialistischen Beamtenpolitik* (Stuttgart, 1966).

[26] Eberhard Jäckel, *Hitlers Weltanschauung: Entwurf einer Herrschaft* (Tübingen, 1969).

[27] Leon A. Jick, "The Holocaust: Its Use and Abuse Within the American Public," *Yad Vashem Studies* 14 (1981): 303–18.

[28] Raul Hilberg, *The Destruction of the European Jews* (Chicago, 1961).

[29] Judith Doneson, *The Holocaust in American Film* (Philadelphia, 1987), 99–107.

[30] Nora Levin, *The Holocaust: The Destruction of European Jewry, 1933–1945* (New York, 1968).

[31] Arthur Morse, *While Six Million Died: A Chronicle of American Apathy* (New York, 1968).

The predicament of the tiny Jewish state surrounded by hostile forces intent on its destruction inevitably conjured up comparisons with the Holocaust. Subsequently, the Holocaust would occupy a much more central position in the historical consciousness of Jewish Americans.[32]

In West Germany, the consequences of the Six Day War unfolded amid the domestic tumult of the year 1968. Although hostility toward Israel had generally been associated with the right wing in Germany, the "Third World," anticolonial orientation of many young Germans endowed the New Left with a marked hostility toward the Zionist project. What was more, the "antifascist" critique that achieved intellectual and political fashion among New Left adherents often tended to see Nazism more as a form of class oppression and economic exploitation than of anti-Semitism.

Ironically, some German conservative politicians emerged from the late 1960s as ardent supporters of Israel. Although some acted from the most sincere of motives, others were guided by party-political opportunism and the exigencies of Cold War alliances. German conservatives could now win political points at home by posturing against fashionable New Left anti-Zionism and, in the process, align Germany's policy toward the Middle East with that of its American ally. Whatever the motive, the open sympathy for Israel helped break down psychological and political barriers to a more active West German engagement with the legacy of the Holocaust in the 1970s.

Both Americans and Germans grew considerably more aware of the Holocaust through the 1970s, while the 1980s and 1990s would witness an explosion of Holocaust memory. A detailed analysis of these developments is beyond the scope of this article, but several of the more important factors can be mentioned: the further maturation of West Germany's democratic political culture, in which the darker side of the nation's history could be discussed yet more openly; the assertive institutionalization of Holocaust memory by the American Jewish community, motivated in part by a desire to memorialize the experience of Holocaust survivors who were nearing the end of their life expectancy; the "Americanization" of the Holocaust, that is, the embrace of the Holocaust by American popular culture as a morality tale of good versus evil; and, finally, the end of the Cold War and the unification of Germany, which provoked intense discussions on both sides of the Atlantic about the legacy of German national identity and German power.[33]

---

[32] Judith Apter Klinghoffer, "The Transformation of the Holocaust Legacy," *Shofar* 14, no. 2 (1996): 53–75.

[33] See the chapters by Jeffrey Peck, vol. 2, Culture, and Shlomo Shafir, vol. 2, Society.

SOCIETY

America and Social Change in Germany

Volker R. Berghahn

There can be little doubt that West German society underwent significant change in the two decades after the end of World War II caused in part by the influence of the United States in a period of often fierce competition and conflict with the Soviet bloc and its societal model. The degrees of social change and American hegemonic pressure, which varied from issue to issue, are reflected in the contributions to this section. They show that in some instances the transformations were quite dramatic, whereas other areas of society saw a type of reconstruction that restored what had existed before the rise of the Nazi dictatorship but did not recast it.

This introduction grapples with the question of restoration or reform in the western parts of Germany after the Nazi dictatorship and total war, on the one hand, and the American impact on German society during the two decades after 1945, on the other. I am concerned with the country's basic social structure as it emerged from the rubble of the "German catastrophe"[1] after 1945 and try to address complex problems of social change and of influences that the United States, the hegemonic power of the West, may have exerted.[2]

[1] Friedrich Meinecke, *Die deutsche Katastrophe: Betrachtungen und Erinnerungen* (Wiesbaden, 1946).
[2] See Robert G. Moeller, ed., *West Germany Under Construction: Politics, Society, and Culture in the Adenauer Era* (Ann Arbor, 1997).

SOCIAL RESTORATION OR REFORM?

Whoever visited Germany's bombed-out cities and devastated industries in 1945, and whoever saw millions of destitute people walking along the country roads back to what was left of their former homes, was bound to come away with the impression that nothing less than a social revolution was underway. Some eleven million refugees and expellees from the East had lost everything. Further wandering millions were made up of mothers and their children who had been evacuated from the cities to the rural areas to escape aerial warfare. A third group was the demoralized and emaciated soldiers, many of them crippled for life, of Hitler's once imperious Wehrmacht, most of whom were gradually being released from Allied POW camps. Finally, there were the Displaced Persons (DPs) who had survived Nazi concentration and extermination camps or a life as slave laborers on farms and in factories and whose lives had been shattered and families destroyed. Conservative estimates have put the total loss in human lives as a result of Hitler's war at over fifty million. Of these, the Wehrmacht accounted for some seven million fatalities.

Without wishing to play down the extent of the tragedies that the war had inflicted upon millions of non-Germans, the latter figure is important in our context to illustrate the war's impact on the German family as a central element of society: The losses, also of women and children, had turned the traditional two-parent, "happy" family into a myth and a distant dream of post-war family politicians and church leaders. The reality of 1945 was the widespread emergence of the one-parent family, with a working or "for-aging" mother and two or three children often kept alive only with the help of CARE and other food-aid programs.[3] In observing these conditions, most contemporaries were understandably convinced that German society was in the midst of a major social revolution.

In the 1960s and again in the 1980s, historians and social scientists argued that Germany's early postwar social revolution had, in fact, started in 1933. Ralf Dahrendorf was among the first to assert that the impact of the Nazi regime on German society had triggered a fundamental change even before the war's end.[4] Twelve years of Hitler's ruthless policies, he believed, had broken traditional structures and milieus. Social revolution had not been a deliberate aim, Dahrendorf thought, but the effect of Hitler's policies was nevertheless to catapult a backward Germany into the twentieth century. This was the unintended but positive outcome of Hitler's unprecedented radicalism at home and abroad.

At about the same time as Dahrendorf developed his hypotheses, David Schoenbaum postulated that the "traditional class structure" of German society had broken down during the Nazi years and that the Third Reich had produced "a classless reality" even before the impact of total war could be felt.[5] Dahrendorf's and Schoenbaum's studies led to a good deal of argument among historians and social scientists concerning the revolutionary or counterrevolutionary character of Nazism. Although this debate had petered out by the late 1970s,[6] it was revived in the late 1980s by challenges to the *Sonderweg* (special path) view of German history formulated by a number of social historians. Perhaps the most prominent example is Detlev Peukert, who stressed the relative modernity of German society (rather than its relative backwardness) compared to other industrialized urban societies.[7]

Rainer Zitelmann raised the stakes further when he began to expound the view that Hitler was not only a man who tried to revolutionize German society but also a purposeful modernizer.[8] Far from rejecting industrialization, urbanization, secularization, and political participation – as the "relative backwardness" school of thought had maintained – the Nazi leader had actually actively supported and consciously promoted such modernizing developments. In other words, he was not a counterrevolutionary like the agrarian "blood-and-soil" ideologues in his party who dreamt of returning to a premodern society.

Despite the attention given to the postwar transformation of German society and to the impact of the Hitler regime, social change in the Federal Republic was, on the whole, slower than the political and economic transformations that the country experienced in 1945–68 and indeed in this century. Instead, German society resembled a big ocean liner or supertanker, which will continue on its course for a good distance even after it is compelled to make a sharp turn. Sociological research has demonstrated that the notion of a social revolution taking place in 1945 was largely an exaggeration, albeit an understandable one, on the part of contemporaries. Elite circulation and change at the top of the social scale, for example, remained surprisingly low. If in 1900 some 5 percent of the population

---

[3] See the chapter by Godehard Weyerer in this section.

[4] Ralf Dahrendorf, *Society and Democracy in Germany* (London, 1968).

[5] David Schoenbaum, *Hitler's Social Revolution: Class and Status in Nazi Germany, 1933–1939* (New York, 1967).

[6] See, for example, Henry A. Turner, ed., *Reappraisals of Fascism* (New York, 1975).

[7] Detlev J. K. Peukert, *The Weimar Republic: The Crisis of Classical Modernity* (New York, 1992) and *Inside Nazi Germany: Conformity, Opposition, and Racism in Everyday Life* (New Haven, 1987). More generally: Geoff Eley and David Blackbourn, *The Peculiarities of German History* (Oxford, 1984).

[8] Rainer Zitelmann, *Hitler: Selbstverständnis eines Revolutionärs* (Stuttgart, 1990). See also his contributions in Rainer Zitelmann and Michael Prinz, eds., *Der Nationalsozialismus und Modernisierung* (Darmstadt, 1991).

had belonged to the upper stratum of society, this figure was still the same some 60 years later. The six decades since the turn of the century had seen a slow and continuous growth of the middle classes from about 25 percent to 33 percent by 1930, and to just under 50 percent by 1960. The percentage of those belonging to the lower strata had seen a corresponding change from more than 66 percent to about 50 percent.[9]

Some social mobility, therefore, did take place, but, just as in other industrialized countries, this was a long-term phenomenon and there had been no sudden, radical shifts as a result of Nazism and war. Elite circulation remained lower than might have been expected. Thus, over the long term, the rate of self-recruitment among the economic elites remained high, with the rest of the "new men" being drawn from the educated and administrative elites.[10] There were no ruptures or rapid shifts in these patterns that would have confirmed the impression of contemporaries in the early postwar period that a social revolution was underway.[11] As Harmut Kaelble observed:

The rate of self-recruitment declined continuously. Whereas under the Empire and in the Weimar Republic at least every other entrepreneur had an entrepreneur as his father, in the Federal Republic of the 1960s only every third to fifth entrepreneur appears to have come from a family belonging to this social group. At the same time the percentage of entrepreneurs of upper-middle-class background declined somewhat, without it being clear whether this change set in toward the end of the Weimar Republic, during the Nazi regime, or only in the early years of the Federal Republic. . . . Those who moved up from the lower middle class and, by the same token, from working-class families, increased in number.[12]

The notable exceptions were, of course, the once-so-powerful East Elbian Junkers and high-ranking military officers, who lost all they possessed in the East. However, the large-scale landowners in the Western zones of occupation suffered no such losses and hence experienced no downward social mobility. On the contrary, many of them retained their elite status at least regionally. Furthermore, the Prussian nobility saw some recovery of its fortunes once the Bundeswehr and a West German foreign service had been reestablished. Other members of the old noble families found careers in industry and banking.

Nor do data on wealth and income support the notion that a social revolution had occurred by the early postwar period. It is now clear that the currency reform of June 1948 did not mean – as contemporary myth had it – that all West Germans restarted their lives with forty marks of new money in their pockets. It is true that the conversion of savings from Reichsmark to Deutsche Mark at an unfavorable rate caused losses of wealth among holders of large accounts. But once the rebuilding and the economic boom began, the value of physical assets like factories, machines, or real estate – much of which had been nearly worthless in 1945 due to wartime destruction – began to rise at three or four times the rate of inflation. People who had held on to their stocks, which were scraps of paper in 1945, saw their value increase by leaps and bounds. There was some redistribution as a result of the Equalization of Burdens Law designed to compensate those refugees who had lost everything in the East; but even these measures and the welfare support offered to war victims did not change the basic trend in wealth structure. By 1963, some 10 percent of all households again owned almost 40 percent of the national wealth. As for incomes, in 1970, 0.1 percent of all workers and 10.8 percent

[9] Wolfgang Zapf, *Wandlungen der deutschen Elite: Ein Zirkulationsmodell deutscher Führungsgruppen 1919–1961* (Munich, 1965). See also Wilhelm Bürklin et al., *Eliten in Deutschland: Rekrutierung und Integration* (Leverkusen, 1997).

[10] See, for example, Helge Pross and Karl W. Boetticher, *Manager des Kapitalismus: Untersuchung über leitende Angestellte in Grossunternehmen* (Frankfurt am Main, 1971), 33–7.

[11] Hartmut Kaelble, "Long-term Changes in the Recruitment of the Business Elite," *Journal of Social History* 13 (1979–80): 404–23.

[12] Hartmut Kaelble, *Soziale Mobilität und Chancengleichheit im 19. und 20. Jahrhundert: Deutschland im internationalen Vergleich* (Göttingen, 1983), 103–4.

of employees had a monthly net income of more than 1,800 marks, but 33.1 percent of the self-employed were in this category.[13] Apart from undermining Zitelmann's arguments, these sociological data also call into question Martin Broszat's hypotheses that, even if Germany did not undergo a revolution in the 1930s, it experienced one between Stalingrad in 1942 and the 1948 currency reform.[14]

All this seems to argue against the notion that a social revolution happened in Germany somewhere around the 1940s. However frantically Hitler may have turned the wheel of the German ocean liner, its course did not change in any radical way. The transformation of society occurred gradually and over longer periods of time. After 1945, this tendency was reinforced by the actions and policies of strategic elite groups. Hitler may have seen himself as a revolutionary, but his successors after 1945 were social conservatives who responded to the turmoil around them in ways typical of societies in crisis: They did not charge forward with societal experiments but tried to uphold and restore what they thought to be the "good" traditions and values. Their reconstruction effort consisted in restoring rather than recasting. To be sure, there were forces on the far left advocating radical change but, facing the beginning of the Cold War and the deterrent example of developments in the Soviet zone of occupation, most West Germans similarly shied away from social experimentation.

These basic attitudes and the upsurge in Christian religiosity after the defeat of the "atheistic Nazis" explain why the churches, almost by definition conservative institutions, quickly emerged as key organizations in the reconstruction process.[15] They influenced educational policies and curricula, particularly with regard to religious instruction, and advocated the rebuilding of the traditional "Christian" family. Restoring education proved relatively easy. In Bavaria, the minister of culture, Alois Hundhammer, was particularly successful in his archconservative quest; he quickly dashed hopes of introducing a more egalitarian, American-style high school system.[16] But even a city such as Hamburg, ruled by Social Democrats, did not escape the trend. By the late 1950s, two of its most elite and time-honored gymnasia, the Johanneum and the Christianeum, which had introduced curricula in modern languages and sciences, reverted to an exclusively classical canon of ancient Greek and Latin.

Rebuilding the traditional family turned out to be somewhat more complicated, largely because the objective could not be brought into line with social reality. The "intact family" that politicians inside and outside the churches were talking about simply did not exist in postwar Germany, where millions of children either lived in single-parent units with a working mother or in "sinful" common-law marriages between partners who wanted to preserve pension entitlements from deceased spouses.[17] However, these realities did not prevent interested people and groups from arguing, with some justification, that the family had demonstrated its worth as a haven in times of crisis. For them, this was a powerful reason for pleading that the traditional family – with its traditional gender relationships – should be restored.[18]

As several of the articles in this section demonstrate, the rebuilding of institutions and organizations, the extolling of "family values" by legislators, churchmen, educators, and businessmen reflected great efforts in time and

---

[13] Michael Jungblut, *Die Reichen und die Superreichen in Deutschland* (Reinbek, 1973).

[14] Martin Broszat et al., eds., *Von Stalingrad zur Währungsreform: Zur Sozialgeschichte des Umbruchs in Deutschland* (Munich, 1988). For critical analyses, see Heinrich A. Winkler, "Sozialer Umbruch zwischen Stalingrad und Währungsreform?" *Geschichte und Gesellschaft* 3 (1990): 403–9; Mark Roseman, "World War II and Social Change in Germany," in Arthur Marwick, ed., *Total War and Social Change* (London, 1988), 58–78.

[15] See the chapter by Mark Ruff in this section.

[16] See, for example, Roger Tilford and Richard C. J. Preece, *Federal Germany: Political and Social Order* (London, 1969), 47–9.

[17] Robert G. Moeller, *Protecting Motherhood: Women and the Family in the Politics of Postwar West Germany* (Berkeley, 1993).

[18] See the chapter by Hanna Schissler in this section.

money to reconstruct West German society according to principles that Nazism was thought to have assaulted and at least partly undermined. There was a marked willingness to turn the political and economic system in new directions. By contrast, as far as society was concerned, the tendency was to reconstruct it along traditional lines; this caused actual changes in the social structure to be slower and much less dramatic than observers at the end of the war had assumed. Nevertheless, even if it was slower than expected, social change did occur. But how?

THE AMERICAN IMPACT ON WEST GERMANY

One fruitful approach to the question of social change in Germany is to examine generational shifts. After all, it was almost to be expected that the younger generation would rebel against the social conservatism of its elders. The rebellion began, often quite timidly and reluctantly, in the 1950s and can even be detected in the Catholic youth movement.[19] It manifested itself in politics – for example, in the opposition to West German rearmament – but also in gender relations and popular culture, until it reached a crescendo in the late 1960s. Still, even for the early phase of the 1950s, it remains doubtful if the younger generation would have been as effective as it later was in challenging received norms, values, and social conventions, had it not been for the Western Allies and the United States.

The appearance of the United States as a societal model and cultural power, rather than just a military and economic factor, in the evolution of Germany was nothing new after World War II. However, recent scholarly attempts to assess the American impact have generated a good deal of controversy;[20] in particular,

the earlier notion that the Federal Republic underwent a process of "Americanization" has recently been challenged by a number of social and cultural historians. Although the Americanization paradigm had never assumed that the Germans were simply steamrollered by the American "model" and emphasized the blending of indigenous with American elements, some critics continued to espouse the view that what happened in West Germany after 1945 was not unique to the German-American relationship but part of an inexorable process of modernization typical of all urbanized and industrialized societies. Other skeptics preferred to operate with the somewhat vague concept of "Westernization."

However this debate may end, the fact remains that America had come onto the German stage long before 1945. Its impact was particularly strong in the increasingly important areas of economic organization and production techniques. After World War I, concepts of rationalized production spread to most branches of German industry,[21] and German engineers and managers were sent to the centers of American assembly-line production to assess, as Wichard von Moellendorff, I.G. Farben's emissary, put it, the "transferability of experiences to Germany."[22]

However, Germany's bourgeois elites were reluctant to accept the democratic implications of mass production. As Daimler-Benz, the famous car manufacturer, stated rather haughtily: "Over here we are still a long way from the American situation where every Mr. Jones owns a car. With us the automobile is for the most part a vehicle for the better-off classes."[23] When cheaper cars also began to be produced in Germany in the mid-1920s, it was not just this elitist resistance that impeded an expansion of the

[19] See the chapter by Mark Ruff in this section.
[20] See the chapters by Philipp Gassert, Raimund Lammersdorf, and Axel Schildt in this section. See also Anselm Doering-Manteuffel, "Dimensionen von Amerikanisierung in der deutschen Gesellschaft," *Archiv für Sozialgeschichte* 35 (1995): 1–34.

[21] See Mary Nolan, *Visions of Modernity: American Business and the Modernization of Germany* (New York, 1994).
[22] Wichard von Moellendorff, *Volkswirtschaftliche Elementarvergleiche zwischen den Vereinigten Staaten von Amerika, Deutschland, Grossbritannien, Frankreich, Italien* (Berlin, 1930), 1:4.
[23] Quoted in Anita Kugler, "Von der Werkstatt zum Fliessband," *Geschichte und Gesellschaft* 3 (1987): 316–17.

market in consumer durables; by comparison with the United States, prices remained too high and living standards too low to put a small car within reach of the average family.[24] If it had been Henry Ford's argument that rationalized manufacturing should lead to a lowering of prices to make mass-produced goods available to all, Fordism in this sense was not seriously taken up by German industry until after World War II. Only then, when the Americans had obtained the leverage against German industry to force it to abandon its anticompetitive and anticonsumerist habits, did the West German entrepreneurial class (*Wirtschaftsbürgertum*) slowly shed its resistance to Fordism. For the majority of the working population, which in the 1950s was emerging from the deprivations of wartime and the early postwar period, access to goods that had once been available only to the wealthy and privileged few came to be seen as a democratic right.[25] The argument that a society based on the principle of equality before the law and at the ballot box should also provide equal access to consumer goods seemed irrefutable in a parliamentary-democratic republic, which West Germany had become with the adoption of the Basic Law in 1949.

Yet, this Fordist vision of a mass production and mass consumption society, with its "vulgar" Americanizing tendencies, also raised fresh anxieties among the country's economic, political, and intellectual elites. The fears were particularly strong among family politicians and churchmen devoted to social restoration.[26] To them, it looked as if the Americans were not only recasting the country's industrial organization by dissolving cartels, pushing business into a competitive capitalism, instituting new labor relations,[27] and introducing new management methods[28] and marketing techniques;[29] it also seemed as if they were trying to revamp German society.

The larger democratizing implications of Fordism had not been fully appreciated even by the U.S. occupation authorities when they arrived in defeated Germany in 1945. In fact, the early occupation had been characterized by social policies that were themselves quite conservative. When General Lucius D. Clay arrived in Germany as deputy leader of the U.S. military government, he, like most of his contemporaries, was overwhelmed by the destruction that he saw. Originally a hardliner who favored punishing the Germans, he quickly came to believe that the country had already seen enough social change. The only person in the political leadership in Washington whose plans may be said to have had more far-reaching "social revolutionary" implications was Treasury Secretary Henry Morgenthau Jr.[30] But his motives were not inspired by a desire for revolution. The notorious Morgenthau Plan was soon shelved and replaced by the more benign occupation policy and more conservative approach to German social reconstruction promoted by the War and State Departments in Washington.[31] In this context, the interplay between official policymaking and American public opinion was of key importance.[32]

What encouraged the protagonists of social conservatism was the negative example of East Germany, where the Soviets had embarked on a program of socioeconomic reorganization involving large-scale expropriations of estates and businesses.[33] This was, of course, a model that neither the overwhelming majority of Germans

---

[24] See, for example, Werner Abelshauser et al., eds., *Sozialgeschichtliches Arbeitsbuch 1914–1945* (Munich, 1978), 98, 101, 107.

[25] See the chapter by S. Jonathan Wiesen in this section.

[26] See, for example, Uta Poiger, "Rebels with a Cause?" in Reiner Pommerin, ed., *The American Impact on Postwar Germany* (Oxford, 1995), 93–124.

[27] See, for example, Volker R. Berghahn, *The Americanisation of West German Industry, 1945–1973* (New York, 1987).

[28] See, for example, Giuliana Gemelli, *From Imitation to Competitive Cooperation* (San Domenico, 1997).

[29] See the chapter by Ingrid Schenk in this section.

[30] See Volker R. Berghahn, "America and Social Change in Germany, 1933–1955," in Gunther Mai and Günter Bischof, eds., *Allied Enemies* (Baton Rouge, forthcoming).

[31] See the chapters by Klaus-Dietmar Henke in this section and by Wilfried Mausbach, vol. 1, Economics.

[32] See the chapter by Thomas Reuther in this section.

[33] See, for example, Norman M. Naimark, *The Russians in Germany: A History of the Soviet Zone of Occupation, 1945–1949* (Cambridge, Mass., 1995).

nor the Americans wanted to see introduced in the Western zones. The developments in the East also help to explain why the policies of nonfraternization and ostracism that had been decreed early in the occupation were soon abandoned and replaced by the first amnesties and humanitarian-aid programs.[34] An intriguing aspect of early U.S. policy toward German society is how it treated gender relations.[35] In a lively debate over this question, Hermann-Josef Rupieper argued that American policy succeeded in "bringing democracy to the frauleins." He was subsequently criticized by Rebecca Boehling, who demonstrated that official U.S. policy toward women was much more traditional than Rupieper had assumed and, indeed, was in line with the larger quest for social stabilization that marked American policies at the beginning of the Cold War.[36] Further, American women who had been recruited in larger numbers into the war industries during the 1940s were urged by their own family politicians and churchmen to devote themselves exclusively to homemaking again.

AMERICA AND THE DEBATE ON MASS SOCIETY

However uninterested official policy was in effecting tangible social change, the renewed American presence and the adoption of Fordism during the 1950s had real, if indirect, consequences. Many German conservatives began to ask whether the rise of American-style mass production and mass consumption would generate a volatile and purely materialistic *mass society* of the kind that many educated people believed existed in Soviet Russia.

Anxieties about the masses and their power in politically highly mobilized societies had existed in Europe since the nineteenth century; they escalated in the interwar years with the growth of mass movements all over Europe. By the end of World War II, the lines between the regimes of Hitler and Stalin, on the one hand, and the West, on the other, were already clearly drawn: The former were held to have emerged from situations of extreme social crisis in which the elites had lost control over the masses, which ran amok and left behind a trail of physical and sociopsychological devastation. "Totalitarianism" was the concept under which the Nazi and Stalinist dictatorships were subsumed. To Hannah Arendt, totalitarianism represented a modern type of rule and society in which the lonely and isolated individual confronted, rather helplessly, both faceless and inhuman bureaucracies and the crowds of cruel and irrational "mass men" (*Massenmenschen*).[37]

In the view of many conservatives and liberals in Western Europe and the Federal Republic, mass man had shown his ugly face not merely in Nazi Germany and Stalinist Russia: He also lurked behind American society. The idea of the United States as a system in which the masses reigned supreme had first gained wider currency among the bourgeoisie during the 1920s, when dark images of crime-ridden Chicago and of the demagogy of populist politicians circulated in Europe. After 1945, these images receded into the background as the world became ideologically divided into Stalin's totalitarian empire and the Atlantic alliance of open societies for which the United States, the hegemonic power of the West, became the shining example. But soon the rise of McCarthyism helped to revive older European images of the dangers of mass democracy and populism. Some intellectuals even came to believe that America was about to produce a fascist system of the kind Europe had seen in

---

[34] See the chapters by Klaus-Dietmar Henke, Godehard Weyerer, and Petra Gödde in this section.

[35] See the chapters by Petra Goedde and Hanna Schissler in this section.

[36] Hermann-Josepf Rupieper, "Bringing Democracy to the Frauleins," *Geschichte und Gesellschaft* 17 (1991): 61–91; Rebecca Boehling, "'Mütter' in die Politik: Amerikanische Demokratisierungsbemuhungen nach 1945. Eine Antwort auf Hermann-Josef Rupieper," *Geschichte und Gesellschaft* 19 (1993): 504–11; for the American side of the picture, with a differentiation of Betty Friedan's arguments, see Joanne Meyerowitz, "Beyond the Feminine Mystique: A Reassessment of Postwar Mass Culture," *Journal of American History* 79 (1993): 1455–82.

[37] Carl Joachim Friedrich and Zbigniew K. Brzezinski, *Totalitarian Dictatorship and Autocracy* (Cambridge, Mass., 1956); see also Hannah Arendt, *The Origins of Totalitarianism* (New York, 1951).

the interwar period. It was no coincidence that these pessimists rediscovered José Ortega y Gasset, who in 1930 had first summarized the anxieties of bourgeois intellectuals in his somber book, *The Revolt of the Masses*. In the 1950s, the Spanish philosopher toured Germany to lecture before audiences of worried elite groups, such as the "cultural circle" of the Federal Association of German Industrialists.[38]

However, there were also the optimists who, though convinced that Stalinist totalitarianism could never be reformed, believed that Western democracies had already found the key to "taming" the masses without resorting to authoritarianism and repression: to accept and promote mass consumption and popular culture. Thus, enthusiasm for American rock bands, for example, which had unleashed riots by mainly lower-class youth in the concert halls of major cities and been seen by family politicians and church leaders as a political threat, was effectively de-politicized by 1960.[39]

While European intellectuals "spent a lot of time worrying and stewing and griping about the United States, about American domination, about the inferiority of American values,"[40] cultural pessimists across the Atlantic were conducting a similar debate. Perhaps the most prominent among them was the essayist and journalist Dwight Macdonald, who argued vigorously for the indispensability of elites and their creative contributions to society and warned of the onslaught of mass society and "primitive" popular culture against the founding values of the United States.[41] It is possible that these critics took some of their arguments from the scathing but highly structuralist analyses that refugees from Nazism like Theodor W. Adorno had first produced in the 1930s and had reformulated after World War II.[42] However, Macdonald and others also felt confirmed in their views by the empirical hypotheses of American sociologists such as David Riesman, who had discovered the "outer-directed man" of the modern age.[43] As in Europe, the "aristocratic" pessimists were countered by social scientists like Edward Shils and Daniel Bell who began to postulate "the end of ideology."

Bell's influential book of that title contains a number of essays that, with the benefit of hindsight, may be seen as antidotes to the critics of American society on both the Right and the Left.[44] Bell tries to disown the notion of America as a standardized and conformist society by stressing its complexity. Behind critics' notions of a disorganized mass society, he detects "a defense of an aristocratic cultural tradition . . . and a doubt that the large mass of mankind can ever become truly educated or acquire an appreciation of culture." He recognized the critics' concern for the meaning and preservation of liberty in the face of collectivism, demagogy, and leveling tendencies but rejected the "narrow conception of human potentialities" that informed their "aristocratic" stances. For Bell, American society was not on the verge of collapse and, although it was superficial, acquisitive, and status-hungry, it also upheld "the right to privacy, free choice of friends and occupation, status on the basis of achievement rather than ascription, a plurality of norms and standards, rather than the

---

[38] See Jonathan Wiesen, *West German Industry and the Challenge of the Nazi Past, 1945–1955: How West German Industrialists Rehabilitated Their Tarnished Image* (Chapel Hill, 2001), and his chapter in this section.

[39] See the chapter by Uta G. Poiger, vol. 1, Culture.

[40] Thus said Waldemar Nielsen (Ford Foundation) in a report of July 19, 1959, on the Lourmarin conference of European intellectuals, Dartmouth College Library, Shepard Stone Papers, Drawer "Countries," folder: W. A. Nielsen memos.

[41] See Michael Wreszin, *A Rebel in Defense of Tradition: The Life and Politics of Dwight Macdonald* (New York, 1994).

[42] Theodor W. Adorno, *The Dialectic of Enlightenment* (New York, 1972). The essay was originally written during World War II with the ideas probably going back to discussions at the New School for Social Research in New York in the 1930s and the copyright held by the Social Studies Association, New York, 1944. The first German edition appeared with Querido in Amsterdam in 1947.

[43] David Riesman, with Nathan Glazer and Reuel Denney, *The Lonely Crowd: A Study of Changing American Character* (New Haven, 1950).

[44] Daniel Bell, *The End of Ideology: On the Exhaustion of Political Ideas in the Fifties* (Glencoe, 1960). The following quotes are on 27, 28, and 29.

exclusive and monopolistic social controls of a single dominant group." This is why communism or fascism never gained "a real foothold" in the United States.

Overall, Bell's book was designed to refute the "ideological" theories of mass society advanced by Macdonald and others and offer, by contrast, empirically based accounts of contemporary life in America at the "end of ideology." His eloquent defense of American society included a positive view of Keynesianism as presented in John Kenneth Galbraith's *The Affluent Society*[45] and a much less alarmist analysis of McCarthyism, which Bell thought to be an articulation of middle-class status anxiety and part of the price to be paid for an open society.

To be sure, Bell's arguments convinced few of the cultural pessimists, whereas on the Left scholars like C. Wright Mills put forward their highly critical analyses of who really ruled the United States.[46] However, Bell had now established a counterposition to the conservative theories of American mass society that harmonized with contemporary notions of pluralism and modernization. It was based on the assumption that all the fundamental problems of modern industrial and democratic societies had been solved and that, henceforth, it was merely a matter of managing and, where necessary, gradually reforming the system.

These arguments were soon taken up by social analysts in West Germany. The idea that all problems of modern liberal societies were manageable and that cultural conflicts could be depoliticized held great attraction to many of them at a time when American mass culture began to flood the German market, reinforcing elite anxieties and reviving a debate about technology and technocracy in which Americans were castigated as naive adherents of technological panaceas and perfectionism.[47]

By the late 1950s, it was not only mass-produced goods – refrigerators, modern furniture, small cars, and motorcycles – that were coming within reach of the average family; it was also the time when icons of American popular culture – above all Elvis Presley and Bill Haley – became roaring successes with young Germans. Youth rallies and riots continued to be grist for the mills of the cultural pessimists, but the protagonists of the "end of ideology" asserted that the perceived threat had been effectively defused. As far as the struggle against communism and the Soviet bloc was concerned, Bellite societal and technological optimism had even been turned into an asset.[48] While Nikita Khrushchev thundered his "We will bury you" across the Cold War divide, Bell and other scholars opposed to the pessimistic interpretation of American "mass society" presented the United States as the superior system that had solved the problems of modern industrial society.

These ideological and generational divisions are quite neatly reflected in the wide-ranging opinion surveys that polling institutes conducted among the West Germans at regular intervals.[49] The results are of considerable interest, not only for assessing the changing political culture of the Federal Republic in the 1950s and 1960s, but also for what they tell us about changing lifestyles.[50]

MASS CULTURE AND THE CHANGING STRUCTURE OF GERMAN SOCIETY

Impressions of contemporaries notwithstanding, no social revolution occurred in the western

nisierung und Sowjetisierung in Deutschland 1945–1970 (Frankfurt am Main, 1997), 315–34.

[45] John Kenneth Galbraith, *The Affluent Society* (Boston, 1958).

[46] C. Wright Mills, *The Power Elite* (New York, 1956). On Mills, see David Halberstam, *The Fifties* (New York, 1993), 527–36.

[47] See, for example, Michael Ermarth, "'Amerikanisierung' und deutsche Kulturkritik 1945–1965," in Konrad Jarausch and Hannes Siegrist, eds., *Amerika-*

[48] See Uta G. Poiger, *Jazz, Rock, and Rebels: Cold War Politics and American Culture in a Divided Germany* (Berkeley, 2000).

[49] See the chapters by Knud Krakau and Philipp Gassert in this section.

[50] See Elisabeth Noelle-Neumann and Erich Peter Neumann, eds., *The Germans: Public Opinion Polls, 1947–1966* (Allensbach and Bonn, 1967).

parts of Germany in 1945 as a consequence of Nazism and war; the structures of German society proved more durable. What social change did take place was part of a long-term process that began in the late nineteenth century and was related to the country's inexorable industrialization, urbanization, and secularization. This also means that later studies by historians who wrote about "Hitler's social revolution" must be modified. There was some social modernization, but it was far less radical than they assumed. After 1945, as we have seen, conservative family politicians, churchmen, and pessimistic intellectuals tried to restore what they believed the Nazis had destroyed.

By contrast, the Western Allies, led by the Americans, did not aim for straightforward restoration. Although they, too, did not want to unleash a social revolution, they thought in terms of a recasting. The Allies were most persistent in the area of political culture, where they supported the creation of a firmly rooted parliamentary-democratic constitutional order, and in the area of "industrial culture," where they encouraged the German entrepreneurial class to build a liberal-capitalist mass production and mass consumption society. The latter effort generated fresh anxieties among the German bourgeoisie about "the revolt of the masses" they believed the country had experienced under Hitler and might still be looming in the age of democracy.

Against this background, it is not too difficult to see that the interpretations of "mass man's" role in American society that Bell and others had developed were reassuring to many though not to all. Maybe American-style "mass society" and "mass culture" were indeed less dangerous than the "aristocratic" pessimists had assumed in their reworking of Arendt's notion of totalitarianism. Arendt herself noted that Europeans had long dreaded "Americanization" but, she added, "whether or not European federation will be accomplished by the rise of anti-American, pan-European nationalism, as one may sometimes fear today, unification of economic and demographic conditions is almost sure to create a state of affairs which will be very similar to that existing in the United States."[51]

Many of the contributions to this section examine conflicts that the German-American relationship and the perplexities of modern "mass society" engendered. They deal with images of America and with what kind of society West Germany was evolving into.[52] Looking back from the beginning of the twenty-first century, the Federal Republic seems to have become an American-style mass production and mass consumption society and its economic, political, and intellectual elites have accepted, albeit grudgingly, the idea of a liberal-democratic mass society. Germany became a "leveled middle-class society" in a way that it was not yet in the 1950s, when Helmut Schelsky coined the term.[53] As Kaspar Maase described German society in 1997: "The right to enjoy the bliss of common culture is freely claimed in the upper echelons of business and politics, science and technology, and among the academically trained professions. Popular art and entertainment have become a culture for all."[54] The same point can be found in Dietrich Schwanitz's recent novel *Der Campus*:

That same evening Bernie lounged around in his easy chair and watched an episode of the German detective series *Derrick*. Being a professor, Bernie had a guilty conscience when he watched television. It was a pure waste of time and unworthy of an intellectual. Rather than watching this show he could be reading a few scholarly articles or writing an article on "The Ironic Use of Experienced Speech in Flaubert."[55]

---

[51] Hannah Arendt, "The Threat of Conformism," (1954) quoted in Michael Ermarth, "German Reunification as Self-Inflicted Americanization," unpubl. manuscript, 1996, 34.

[52] See the chapters by Axel Schildt, Raimund Lammersdorf, Thomas Reuther, Knud Krakau, Rainer Schnoor, and Philipp Gassert in this section.

[53] Helmut Schelsky, *Die Wandlungen der deutschen Familie in der Gegenwart: Darstellung und Deutung einer empirisch-soziologischen Tatbestandsaufnahme* (Dortmund, 1953).

[54] Kaspar Maase, *Grenzenloses Vergnügen: Der Aufstieg der Massenkultur* (Frankfurt am Main, 1997), 274–5.

[55] Dietrich Schwanitz, *Der Campus* (Munich, 1996), 229.

But Bernie did not switch off his set; instead, he enjoyed the cultural trash on the tube. Naturally, this would not prevent him from pontificating about the problems of mass society and mass culture. Nor does it prevent middle-class parents from taking their little ones to the local McDonald's, even if with an air of disapproval.

But there is the other side of this coin. As West Germany's middle classes gradually lost their antidemocratic cultural elitism and their suspicion of the "masses," the attitudes and mentalities of those "masses" were changing as well. The dissolution of bourgeois perceptions of society was paralleled by a gradual transformation of proletarian consciousness and milieus.[56]

By 1914, German society had produced a social structure in which class had become the crucial category, dividing blue-collar workers from the bourgeoisie and the upper classes. Workers had a lower life expectancy, were less healthy, lived in cramped accommodation, and enjoyed a less-than-adequate diet. And beyond the provision with goods and the "exterior life situation," there was also the "inner existential predicament" (Max Weber) of a growing sense of social isolation and ostracism. With the dawning age of universal suffrage and mass participation in politics, such material conditions and feelings soon translated into political support for the main working-class party, the Social Democrats (*Sozialdemokratische Partei Deutschlands*, or SPD). The socialist trade unions saw even steeper increases in their membership than the SPD. Nothing did more to polarize Wilhelmine society, however, than the sharply negative reaction of the upper classes to working-class demands that the representatives of the proletariat articulated. This conflict continued with varying degrees of intensity for much of the Weimar period until the Nazi dictatorship proscribed and ruthlessly suppressed all manifestations of working-class opposition after 1933.

At the end of World War II, morally in a strong position because of their anti-Hitler stance, Social Democratic leaders and the unions once again pushed for a major shift in the balance of power between employers and workers, between working class and bourgeoisie. Talk of a socialization of major industries was widespread. However, the American occupiers adamantly opposed a fundamental restructuring of economy and society of this kind. Representatives not just of industry and diplomacy but also of the AFL/CIO did their best to nudge the West German working-class movement toward the American model of labor relations and liberal-capitalist economic management.[57] By the mid-1950s and especially after the death of SPD chairman Kurt Schumacher in 1952, moderate Social Democrats slowly began to gain the upper hand over the more radical reformers. They paved the way that finally led the SPD to adopt the Bad Godesberg program of 1959. In it, the party accepted the country's capitalist system, which by then had begun successfully to deliver the material prosperity that "the masses" had so long hoped to share.

From the perspective of industrial workers, the evolution of West Germany's societal structures in the two decades after 1945 afforded them the opportunity to abandon their traditional confrontationist posture. In turn, the evolution of the industrial working class promoted the slow emergence of a more egalitarian society. The long-term structural shifts were consequently accompanied by adaptations in outlook and lifestyles among all of the major social groups.

On the occasion of its fiftieth anniversary, *Der Spiegel* published a special issue in which Christian Graf von Krockow described the 1950s as a "great, leaden time."[58] It was not quite so leaden, even if social change came more slowly than many had hoped. The overwhelming majority of West Germans learned to accept and even enjoy the fruits of a mass production and

---

[56] Josef Mooser, "Abschied vom 'Proletariat': Sozialstruktur und Lage der Arbeiterschaft in der Bundesrepublik in historischer Perspektive," in Werner Conze and M. Rainer Lepsius, eds., *Sozialgeschichte der Bundesrepublik: Beiträge zum Kontinuitätsproblem* (Stuttgart, 1983), 143–86.

[57] See the chapter by Michael Fichter in this section.
[58] *Der Spiegel*, Sonderausgabe 1947–1997 (1997): 36–45.

mass consumption society that came to them between 1945 and 1967.

SUGGESTIONS FOR FURTHER READING

The first comprehensive analyses of the evolution of German society after the collapse of the Nazi dictatorship were produced by sociologists; both Helmut Schelsky's *Die Wandlungen der deutschen Familie in der Gegenwart: Darstellung und Deutung einer empirisch-soziologischen Tatbestandsaufnahme* (Dortmund, 1953) and Ralf Dahrendorf's *Demokratie und Gesellschaft in Deutschland* (Munich, 1965: published in translation as *Society and Democracy in Germany* New York, 1967) still form a good starting point. The most recent English-language retrospective, with contributions on West German society and many helpful bibliographical references in the footnotes, is by Robert G. Moeller, ed., *West Germany Under Construction: Politics, Society and Culture in the Adenauer Era* (Ann Arbor, 1997). Major German-language treatments: Axel Schildt and Arnold Sywottek, eds., *Modernisierung im Wiederaufbau: Die westdeutsche Gesellschaft der fünfziger Jahre* (Bonn, 1993); Axel Schildt, *Moderne Zeiten: Freizeit, Massenmedien und "Zeitgeist" in der Bundesrepublik der 50er Jahre* (Hamburg, 1995); Michael Wildt, *Am Beginn der "Konsumgesellschaft": Mangelerfahrung, Lebenshaltung, Wohlstandshoffnung in Westdeutschland in den fünfziger Jahren* (Hamburg, 1993). Also important are the quantitative studies on elite circulation by Wolfgang Zapf, *Wandlungen der deutschen Elite: Ein Zirkulationsmodell deutscher Führungsgruppen 1919–1961* (Munich, 1965) and most recently by Wilhelm Bürklin et al., *Eliten in Deutschland: Rekrutierung und Integration* (Leverkusen, 1997). The sociologists were subsequently joined by the social historians, in particular Hartmut Kaelble, *Social Mobility in the 19th and 20th Centuries: Europe and America in Comparative Perspective* (Leamington Spa, 1986); also Werner Conze and M. Rainer Lepsius, eds., *Sozialgeschichte der Bundesrepublik: Beiträge zum Kontinuitätsproblem* (Stuttgart, 1983); Werner Abelshauser, *Die langen Fünfziger Jahre: Wirtschaft und Gesellschaft in der Bundesrepublik, 1949–1966* (Düsseldorf, 1987).

All these authors stressed the slow and long-term changes in Germany's social structures, in contrast to David Schoenbaum, *Hitler's Social Revolution: Class and Status in Nazi Germany, 1933–1939* (London, 1967) and more recently Rainer Zitelmann, *Hitler: Selbstverständnis eines Revolutionärs* (Stuttgart, 1987), who postulated that German society underwent a revolutionary change in the 1930s. Dissociating himself from this latter view, Martin Broszat et al., *Von Stalingrad zur Währungsreform: Zur Sozialgeschichte des Umbruchs in Deutschland* (Munich, 1988) nevertheless discerned fundamental shifts as having taken place between 1942 and 1948 that paved the way for the very different society that West Germany represented in the 1950s. Broszat's arguments were also directed against Eberhard Schmidt, *Die verhinderte Neuordnung 1945–1952: Zur Auseinandersetzung um die Demokratisierung der Wirtschaft in den westlichen Besatzungszonen in der Bundesrepublik Deutschland* (Frankfurt am Main, 1966), who asserted that sociopolitical restoration is the key to understanding West Germany's postwar development and that the United States played a major role in engineering it. More recent work, on the other hand, has tended to assume that there was both a "new beginning" and "restoration" (Jürgen Kocka, "1945: Neubeginn oder Restauration?" in Carola Stern and Heinrich August Winkler, eds., *Wendepunkte deutscher Geschichte 1848–1990* [Frankfurt am Main, 1994], 159–92). Robert G. Moeller's *War Stories: The Search for a Usable Past in the Federal Republic of Germany* (Berkeley, 2001) is also pertinent here.

Against the background of these larger debates on social change, there is now a considerable wealth of empirical work on the experiences of the general population and relations within families and between men and women. For example: Richard Bauer, *Ruinen-Jahre: Bilder aus dem zerstörten München 1945–1949* (Munich, 1983); Thomas Berger and Karl-Heinz Müller, eds., *Lebenssituationen 1945–1948: Materialien zum Alltagsleben in den westlichen Besatzungszonen 1945–1948* (Hannover, 1983); Frank Grube and Gerhard Richter, *Die Schwarzmarktzeit: Deutschland zwischen 1945 und 1948* (Hamburg, 1979); Lutz Niethammer, ed., *"Hinterher merkt man, dass es richtig war, dass es schief gegangen ist"* (Bonn, 1983); Friedrich Prinz, *Trümmerzeit in München: Kultur und Gesellschaft einer deutschen Großstadt im Aufbruch 1945–1949* (Munich, 1984); Doris Schubert, ed., *Frauen in der deutschen Nachkriegsgeschichte*, vol. 1, *Frauenarbeit 1945–1949* (Düsseldorf, 1984); Annette Kuhn, ed., *Frauen in der deutschen Nachkriegsgeschichte*, vol. 2, *Frauenpolitik 1945–1949* (Düsseldorf, 1986); Anna-E. Freier and Annette Kuhn, eds., *"Das Schicksal Deutschlands liegt in der Hand seiner Frauen"* (Düsseldorf, 1984); Eva Schulze, *Wie wir das alles geschafft haben: Alleinstehende Frauen berichten über ihr Leben nach 1945* (Munich, 1985); Eva Kolinsky, *Women in Contemporary Germany: Life, Work and Politics* (Oxford, 1993); Robert G. Moeller, *Protecting Motherhood: Women and the Family in the Politics of Postwar West Germany* (Berkeley, 1993); Ute Frevert, *Women in German History: From Bourgeois Emancipation to Sexual Liberation* (Oxford, 1989).

If political scientists and economic historians had long been studying the impact of the United States as an occupying power upon West Germany's political and economic reconstruction, the proliferating interest in grassroots history, as reflected in the studies cited herein, also stimulated work on how America influenced German society in the postwar decades, raising the question of how far that society became "Americanized." In addition to the articles in this section, a few examples of scholarly work concerned with this question are Anselm Doering-Manteuffel, "Dimensionen von Amerikanisierung in der deutschen Gesellschaft," *Archiv für Sozialgeschichte* 35 (1995): 4–34; Konrad Jarausch and Hannes Siegrist, eds., *Amerikanisierung und Sowjetisierung in Deutschland 1945–1970* (Frankfurt am Main, 1997); Ralph Willet, *The Americanization of Germany, 1945–1949* (London, 1989); Heide Fehrenbach, *Cinema in Democratizing Germany: Reconstructing National Identity After Hitler* (Chapel Hill, N.C., 1995); Jeffry M. Diefendorf et al., eds., *American Policy and the Reconstruction of West Germany, 1945–1955* (Cambridge and New York, 1993); Michael Ermarth, ed., *America and the Shaping of German Society, 1945–1955* (Oxford, 1993); Alf Lüdtke, Inge Marßolek, and Adelheid von Saldern, eds., *Amerikanisierung: Traum und Alptraum im Deutschland des 20. Jahrhunderts* (Stuttgart, 1986); Rainer Pommerin, ed., *The American Impact on Postwar Germany* (Oxford, 1995); Heinz Bude and Bernd Greiner, eds., *Westbindungen. Amerika in der Bundesrepublik* (Hamburg, 1999); Heide Fehrenbach and Uta Poiger, eds., *Transactions, Transgressions, Transformations* (New York, 2000); Uta G. Poiger, *Jazz, Rock, and Rebels: Cold War Politics and American Culture in a Divided Germany* (Berkeley, 2000); Maria Höhn, *GIs and Fräuleins: The German-American Encounter in 1950s West Germany* (Chapel Hill, 2002).

CHAPTER ONE

Gentle Conquest in the West

Americans and Germans, 1944–1945

Klaus-Dietmar Henke

Translated by Sally E. Robertson

A FRIENDLY ENEMY

The transformation of Germany into a stable democracy and Western-style civil society began with the American occupation from September 1944 onward. At the time, it seemed impossible to predict or even hope for such a development. The Americans' objective was to force the Third Reich into unconditional surrender, eradicate all vestiges of National Socialism, and ensure that Germany – now reduced in size by the loss of its eastern territories – would never again be capable of waging war. This meant putting strict regulations in place and, if possible, laying the ground for the best guarantee of future security: fusing the postwar government and society to democratic structures and shifting the orientation of German elites from the anti-Western ideas prevailing in 1914 to the ideas of 1789.[1]

Establishment of an enduring open society in Germany and, thereby, the solid normalization and demilitarization of the country would be possible only if the German population gradually accepted and ultimately desired it. The long process of democratization in West Germany

could hardly have gotten off to a better start than with the occupation by the "friendly enemy" that the American army proved itself to be in 1944–5.[2] All in all, this gentle occupation had a practical and fundamentally humane character, which is all the more evident when one casts an eye to the brutal postwar beginnings in East Germany. The population there had to contend with the violence of the Red Army; given German atrocities perpetrated in the Soviet Union, it was psychologically inevitable that the Soviets would see the occupation of Germany as a continuation of the war.[3] This was the worst imaginable start for the establishment of dictatorship east of the Elbe and for the communist cause, which a majority of Germans had traditionally and repeatedly rejected. The eastern and western experience of the end of the war in 1944–5 thus differed as fundamentally as the entire subsequent development of the two parts of Germany. Allied institutions and declarations associated with the coalition of convenience against Hitler maintained the illusion

[1] See Hans-Peter Schwarz, *Vom Reich zur Bundesrepublik: Deutschland im Widerstreit der aussenpolitischen Konzeptionen in den Jahren der Besatzungsherrschaft 1945–1949*, 2d expanded ed. (Stuttgart, 1980); and Herman Graml, *Die Alliierten und die Teilung Deutschlands: Konflikte und Entscheidungen 1941–1948* (Frankfurt am Main, 1985).

[2] Klaus-Dietmar Henke, "Der freundliche Feind: Amerikaner und Deutsche 1944/45," in Heinrich Oberreuter and Jürgen Weber, eds., *Freundliche Feinde? Die Alliierten und die Demokratiebegründung in Deutschland* (Munich, 1996), 41–3. This article is based on Klaus-Dietmar Henke, *Die amerikanische Besetzung Deutschlands* (Munich, 1995).

[3] Norman M. Naimark, *The Russians in Germany: A History of the Soviet Zone of Occupation, 1945–1949* (Cambridge, Mass., 1995), 109.

of commonality for a time. However, this alliance disintegrated rapidly after May 8, 1945,
and the overriding political reality in occupied
Germany immediately became a power struggle
between the rule and tenets of Western democracy and those of communist dictatorship.

At the time of the American occupation,
German political, military, economic, and administrative leaders and the general public
strayed from acceptable – even imaginable –
behavior in the eyes of the civilized world.
Before the United States entered the war, the
émigré-observer Thomas Mann attempted in
his famous radio broadcasts to show his compatriots that all previously accepted standards of
civilization were being violated. While Hitler
was still at the peak of his power, Mann recognized that Germany still had to go the final
and most difficult stretch of its unique path, its
Sonderweg, to one day resume "political life on
a democratic basis . . . and peaceful cooperation
in international life," as the Potsdam protocol of
August 2, 1945, put it. The self-destruction of
state and regime and the conscious discrediting
of chauvinist, racist traditions were the necessary
prerequisites for normalization and civilization.
Only if Germany were completely reduced to
ashes, said Mann, could the occupying powers
push it into making a turnaround and beginning
anew. The totalitarian (Nazi) regime and its ideology obviously never received this chance for
a new beginning from the occupying powers,
but the German population did.[4] The American
occupation of Germany certainly brought punishment of Nazi criminals, reparations, demilitarization, decentralization, and democratization;
it hardly set the stage for permanent degradation
of a key European nation.

It is now commonly accepted that the end of
the war, although certainly an important political turning point, was not a "zero hour" and
that many substantive continuities bridged past
and future. Nonetheless, as early as the 1950s,
Helmut Schelsky looked back on 1945 as an

"unparalleled revolution."[5] The years between
Stalingrad and the currency reform seemed revolutionary not only because of the Reich's
defeat, loss of the eastern territories, and disem-
powerment of the old aristocratic upper class.
The evacuations that began even before the war
ended and the great migration of displaced peoples rocked all of German society. Even before
Germany capitulated, this process began to dismantle the old, rigidified political, social, religious, and cultural institutions that had crippled
the Weimar Republic.

The failure of traditional norms, emergence
of new outlooks, and creation of democratic
institutions in the mid-1940s were not accompanied by a revolutionary public consciousness.
This was not only because of the presence of
occupation forces and the exhaustion of the
soldiers and civilian population. Rather, it can
probably be attributed largely to the fact that
much of the "*obrigkeitlichen Volksferne*,"[6] the
aloofness of the traditional governmental structures, had disappeared from German society as
a result of the mobilizing effects of Nazi rule,
particularly of total war.

GERMAN–AMERICAN ALLIANCES
PROMOTING STABILITY

The relatively painless way in which the war
ended in the West left a lasting impression, as
did the pragmatic manner in which the defeated Germans and their Americans conquerors
treated one another during the critical weeks
and months in which the Americans occupied a zone stretching from Aachen to Leipzig
and from Weimar to Linz.[7] This positive initial

---

[4] See Thomas Mann, *Politische Reden und Schriften*, 3
vols., vol. 2 *Essays*, ed. Hermann Kurzke (Frankfurt am
Main, 1986).

[5] See Martin Broszat, Klaus-Dietmar Henke, and
Hans Woller, eds., *Von Stalingrad zur Währungsreform:
Zur Sozialgeschichte des Umbruchs in Deutschland* (Munich,
1998), xxv–xxvii.

[6] Martin Broszat, "Grundzüge der gesellschaftlichen
Verfassung des Dritten Reiches," in Martin Broszat and
Horst Möller, eds., *Das Dritte Reich: Herrschaftsstruktur
und Geschichte* (Munich, 1983), 52.

[7] The following largely follows Klaus-Dietmar
Henke, "Deutschland," in Ulrich Herbert and Axel

experience laid the foundation and created the prerequisites for a twofold success: Western democracy gradually taking root in Germany and West Germany rapidly converging with the West.

Before the Americans first advanced into German territory, between Aachen and Schnee-Eifel, on September 11, 1944, the German population's main concern was whether – in the face of German crimes against humanity – the American army and its military government would actually demonstrate the degree of fairness and humanity that the people had come to expect despite anti-American propaganda. The Americans were even more uncertain what they would encounter east of the Siegfried Line – perhaps the vaunted solidarity between the German public and leadership, perhaps guerrilla warfare. The American intelligence service, the Office of Strategic Services (OSS), suggested: "Nazi brigands will probably be at large throughout Germany, ready to assassinate anyone, military or civilian, who tries to work with us."[8]

Another reason for the pronounced uncertainty and apprehension was that the Allies did not recognize until August 1944 that the war would not end along the lines of 1918; rather, the Reich would have to be conquered foot by foot. This undermined all of the careful plans that had assumed they would be taking over a largely intact country and would not need to rule with a strong hand. At the same time, when Henry Morgenthau and the president personally intervened in the plans of the civilian and military staffs, occupation policy came under tighter control, although more in appearance than in reality. As a result, the mood in General Dwight D. Eisenhower's headquarters was one of considerable apprehension, even alarm, as the mission in Germany was to begin. Furthermore, it was

clear that the occupation would end in disaster without the cooperation of the defeated Germans. A stable victory was impossible without their help.

For a range of reasons, the population gladly offered the enemy its support. Although no one at the end of 1944 still believed in Germany's ultimate "final victory," some held out hope that the war could somehow be brought to a painless end. In January 1945 at the latest – after the failure of the Ardennes offensive – even the truest believers began to realize that Hitler let the Wehrmacht continue fighting on German soil to win a reprieve for his regime that could only be temporary – an act as inexplicable to the Germans as it was to the Americans. It was this realization as much as anything that released enormous energy reserves among soldiers and civilians in the sixth year of the war. However, they now rushed to the other extreme. Where they had previously embraced extreme faith in Hitler, raison d'état, and readiness for war, they now fled to the opposite extreme of autonomy, self-interest, and the will to survive. The goals of this quiet mass movement by exhausted soldiers and war-weary civilians proved very concrete: first, to "remain"[9] (übrigbleiben), to emerge somehow from the war in one piece; second, to protect property and save one's belongings; third, to come under the authority of the Americans or British if possible, the French if necessary, but definitely not the Soviets.

When the Americans began capturing rural districts in the vicinity of Aachen in September 1944, the inhabitants greeted them warmly, to the dismay of Himmler; these cooperative citizens of "Transylvania" (as the Allied Supreme Command sometimes called it) were not unshakably loyal to the Nazi cause, as official propaganda had suggested. Despite the hardships associated with a military regime, the very first encounters of victors with the defeated population began on mutually friendly footing. By the time summer arrived again, American field officers were amazed at the catastrophes that had

Schildt, eds., *Das Kriegsende in Europa 1945*. Edward N. Peterson, *The Many Faces of Defeat: The German People's Experience in 1945* (New York, 1990) to a large degree offers an opposing view and evaluation of the American occupation of Germany.

[8] OSS Report A-36028, August 14, 1944, National Archives, RG 226, no. 86618.

[9] This is the fitting title of Wolfgang Franz Werner, *Bleib übrig: Deutsche Arbeiter in der nationalsozialistischen Kriegswirtschaft* (Düsseldorf, 1983).

not occurred during the occupation of Germany. Apart from the political leadership surrounding Hitler, most of the SS, a few career soldiers, local Nazi desperados, and other agents of state terror, Germans and Americans were soon united by a clear inclination toward pragmatic cooperation and the determination to stabilize the complicated situation together.

Beneath the political and strategic level, a considerable consensus between the prospective winners and losers thus existed. This harmony of interests, transcending ideological politics and warfare, gave rise to a tight network of hundreds of thousands of small, even minute German-American alliances, ties that ultimately stretched across the entire occupation zone. These small-scale alliances among the occupying army, civil administrators, and the population had strictly local roots. And they were no less important to occupiers than to the occupied populace. Both sides faced the dire situation soberly and worked to institute desperately needed practical measures – repairing bridges and utilities lines, halting epidemics, making food and drugs available from American army supplies, setting up emergency administrative bodies, boosting coal production. The American soldiers and the German population were equally surprised and relieved at this cooperative start.

The widespread surrender of villages and cities without a fight was the prelude to the more far-reaching collaboration between the German population and its friendly enemy. Prudent Wehrmacht officers and low-level party functionaries frequently supported these citizens' initiatives to protect human life and preserve material assets, efforts that prevented much bloodshed on both sides. Only local initiatives of this kind were in a position to assess somewhat reliably the risks and best timing for such potentially dangerous actions after closely observing the balance of power on the ground and foreseeable movements of German and American troops in the immediate vicinity. This de facto aid and the thousands of aforementioned small-scale stabilization pacts helped Eisenhower's troops in capturing German territory. For their part, the Americans showed their gratitude to the civilian population by being very accommodating. They realized in the first weeks of the occupation that an unbridgeable gulf had opened up between the German people and their leaders.[10]

From the end of 1944 on, there was a quiet move toward autonomy behind a facade of loyalty to the regime across all sections of German society: workers and managers, farmers and civil servants. This movement included an uncompromising pursuit of private commercial interests against the interests of state as defined by Hitler. Since summer 1944, the primary goal of most businesses' managers and employees alike was to preserve company assets until the end of the war at all costs. This trend was helped by the increasing seriousness of the situation. The increasing division of authority throughout the country and intensification of terror led to the creation of countless pockets of anarchy and, in the last three months of the war, a zone that was ultimately devoid of law, a space in which civil courage and independent initiative and judgment could more effectively come into their own. No one wanted to be pulled down along with the regime. Everyone put personal interests first and abandoned the worn-out national interest that had been trumpeted for so long. One could even claim that German society had largely distanced itself not only from National Socialist ideology but also from the Nazi regime long before the unconditional surrender on May 8, 1945, sealed its collapse.

In addition to the failure of National Socialism, a failure underlined by Germany's devastating military defeat, this popular self-distancing from the regime in almost every district of the country had another cause: the personal cowardice of Nazi officials. As the first American tank approached, they usually dropped their rhetorical posturing and beat a hasty retreat, usually taking with them the community's last food and gasoline supplies. They had missed the only opportunity in their careers to prove

---

[10] See the overview by Norbert Frei, "Der totale Krieg und die Deutschen," in Norbert Frei and Hermann Kling, eds., with the assistance of Margit Brandt, *Der nationalsozialistische Krieg* (Frankfurt am Main, 1990), 283–5.

personally that they had meant what they preached to their fellow citizens. With this demonstration of hypocrisy, they exposed Nazi ideology to contempt and even ridicule in a way that might have undermined it more effectively than the reeducation efforts the military government implemented soon thereafter.

For American observers, the behavior of lower-level party officials stood in stark contrast with the state-sponsored terrorism. From the time of the war crisis of 1942–3, and particularly after the failed assassination attempt on Hitler on July 20, 1944, on through the last minute before the arrival of the enemy, the regime intensified its assault on the exhausted men and women who had already sacrificed so much for "Führer, Volk und Vaterland" in the five years of the war, even to the point of denouncing them as defeatists. Like the organization of the German *Volkssturm* (militia) in fall 1944, the objective of which was less military than to identify every last man and bring him under the jurisdiction of the military courts, the draconian measures in the final phase of the war rarely served their stated purpose. They were mostly despotic acts thinly cloaked in law, and their purported "punitive goal" – to consolidate resistance against the enemy – became an excuse for the regime to engage in widespread criminality. A few may have still listened to appeals for sacrifice, particularly because the Nazis were adding ever more fuel to what proved a quite reasonable fear of the Russians. But very few were willing to continue submitting themselves to the self-denial and self-sacrifice demanded by the archaic rhetoric of sacrifice.

In the critical days of the invasion, in which each person had to pass from war to peace through "the eye of a needle" (Reinhold Maier),[11] the bulk of the German population in the west had moved closer to the sober, pragmatic military regime of the Americans and the British than to what everyone now saw as a criminal Nazi regime. Although most found it difficult to admit this openly or even to themselves, they well knew that it was the enemy who had freed them from the yoke of their own countrymen and ended the period of "hanging and shooting," as the mayor of Aalen called it.[12] And Eisenhower's soldiers knew it as well. In their reports from April and May 1945, they asserted that the German population appeared to have a genuine feeling of relief and liberation from three fears: "Fear of the Jabos [fighter bombers], fear of the heavy bombers, and fear of the Gestapo."[13]

The German population had a generally positive experience with a friendly enemy in a decisive historic phase. Each individual German had his or her own experience in a key defining moment. These moments became all the more deeply engraved on the collective memory of the nation because of the stark contrast between the liberation from war and terror west of the Elbe and the Mulde Rivers, and the tragedy that began for those in the East as soon as the war ended. "*Weg vom Iwan, hin zum Ami*" ("Away from Ivan to the Yanks") was a popular slogan at the time. Millions of people became part of an exodus to the West long before the Potsdam agreements on expulsions were signed. It began at the end of 1944 and continued after the Soviet offensive began in January 1945 and the Red Army advanced across the Oder River in mid-April. The Soviet advance also forced Germans to make a fundamental choice: Most opted to throw their lot in with the enemy in the West.

The Americans and British did not disappoint German expectations. They made a particularly striking impression, for example, on the demarcation line between the armed forces of the Western Allies and the Red Army on the Elbe, in Mecklenburg, and elsewhere with a series of spectacular acts to help Germans escape from the Russian zone. In a true act of humanitarianism (one that was an extraordinary surprise to the German generals), the victors in the West allowed hundreds of thousands of Germans to

---

[11] Reinhold Maier, *Ende und Wende: Das schwäbische Schicksal 1944–1946. Briefe und Tagebuchaufzeichnungen* (Stuttgart, 1948), 231.

[12] *Bericht: Die letzten Kriegstage von Aalen*, Oct. 9, 1948, Hauptstaatsarchiv Stuttgart, J 170, bundle 1.

[13] SHAEF, G-5, *Weekly Journal of Information*, May 11, 1945, National Archives, RG 331, 131.11, SHAEF, G-5, Information Branch, Entry 54.

slip behind their own lines prior to the capitulation. Documents from the time refer to the American bank of the Elbe as the "friendly side of the river." The Americans dubbed this trick, by which they saved German soldiers from becoming prisoners of war in Russia, as "individual surrender." This gesture became part of the family history of a considerable portion of the population after 1945.[14]

PRAGMATISM WITHOUT NAÏVETÉ

The American occupiers moved into Germany with their eyes wide open. Just as their military superiority did not lead to reckless or malicious outbursts, their pragmatism and fundamentally humane orientation did not allow them to lose sight of the fact that they had been sent by President Roosevelt, ideologically and politically the antithesis of German racism and expansionism, on a "crusade in Europe" (Eisenhower) to eradicate "Hitlerism." The German elites, members of the security apparatus, murderers and oppressors, and many beneficiaries and nominal members of the Nazi party realized this with considerable discomfort in 1945. For a start, the American army placed more than 100,000 officials, suspects, and potential troublemakers under quarantine in internment camps. It was the Americans who most vigorously pushed for judicial reckoning for the elites and personnel of the Nazi's killing operations. No one took the political cleansing more seriously than the Americans, although they sometimes overreached as well. They considered it important to carefully examine the people establishing the new parties and to strictly regulate the newly approved media. Students naturally required decisive reeducation, not to mention their teachers, who were not exactly heralds of democratic thought.

The leaders of German corporations were also not handled with kid gloves by these soldiers from the Eldorado of free enterprise. Later accounts tended to leave out the fact that the

leading entrepreneurs of the Ruhr region felt "hunted down" at the end of 1945.[15] It was not war and capitulation, not upheaval or some overexaggerated claims about a "workers' initiative" that upended the position of the elites of German industry from one day to the next. It was the American and British occupation units. For those affected, it was a lesson as brutal as it was unforgettable. This was the first demonstration for the leaders of industry that even the Western Allies considered them to be a social group that bore considerable responsibility for Nazi rule in Germany and Europe. This did not fully dawn on most industrial leaders until their fall from power and subsequent enforced leave. During the first phase of the occupation, most of them had already returned to a "business as usual" mentality, convinced that they were indispensable during this crisis. "Confidence must substitute distrust," urged a memorandum to the astonished military government from no less a figure than the supremely self-confident chairman of the board of Krupp in late May 1945. During the war, he had been personally involved in the construction of Krupp production facilities at Auschwitz and the use of Jewish concentration camp inmates as forced laborers. In 1948, the Americans sentenced him to twelve years in prison in the Krupp trial.

The captains of industry were not accorded preferential treatment, nor did labor and its representatives suffer any particular disadvantages under Allied rule. The "unpolitical policies" of a military government constantly trying to balance military and political necessities did not really cripple German political initiatives, or did so only in the sense of stigmatizing forces that were nationalistic, nationalist apologists, or antagonistic toward the occupation forces. The "Left" was not really suppressed, but there was indeed a healthy skepticism toward the sporadic activities of old communists, a group that was isolated not only from the population at large but

---

[14] For details, see Henke, *Die amerikanische Besetzung*, 674–6.

[15] Hermann Höpker-Aschoff to Alfred Müller-Armack, December 28, 1945, cited in Werner Plumpe, "Auf dem Weg zur Marktwirtschaft," in Gerhard Brunn, ed., *Neuland Nordrhein-Westfalen und seine Anfänge nach 1945/46* (Essen, 1986), 69.

also from the large, decidedly nonradical labor force. In their stronghold in the Ruhr region, for example, they continued to indulge in a kind of misled radicalism until early summer 1945, unaware of the new general party line of the German Communist Party (*Kommunistische Partei Deutschlands*, or KPD) that Ulbricht was propagating in the Soviet zone. Dogmatic communists were generally classified as troublemakers not only by the occupation forces but also frequently by their own colleagues as well.

A pragmatic occupation policy did not mean naïveté on the part of the victors. Harmony between victors and vanquished did not mean that the occupation forces were taken in by the defeated Germans. Beginning around 1947 or 1948, as the international situation fundamentally changed and the key positive experiences with a friendly enemy became overshadowed by the misery of the years of famine and the insult of living under the rule of an occupying force, an offended national narcissism began to spread in Germany. One occupational group after the other set about producing legends aimed at excusing its past behavior: physicians, judges, civil servants, officers. All seemed to have been caught unawares by Hitler, the usurper; Nazi rule was cast as a kind of foreign domination. For many people two or three years after the war, memory was clouded by concern for their very existence, by helplessness in the face of the total defeat of their fatherland, or by a realization that the sacrifices they had made in the preceding years were futile. Still, the core of positive existential experience with the gentle conquest of 1944–5 in the West remained unscathed.

When the Americans instituted the Berlin airlift in 1948, transforming themselves definitively from an occupying power to a protective power, neither the winners nor losers of the war found it difficult to pick up on their common experience from the end of the war. General Eisenhower's soldiers had laid the groundwork. In the name of pragmatism and the spirit of exerting positive control, they behaved in accordance with their own feelings of responsibility and in the tradition of the army without being caught up in the political tempests of Washington. That tradition had long demanded that an occupation be strict but humane and just. Considering the two burdens of guilt that weighed on Germany – the murder of Europe's Jews and unleashing World War II – the occupation by the Western powers was almost humiliatingly fair and constructive (if one disregards the behavior of the small French contingent supported by the United States). If the war of 1941–5 was a "good war"[16] for the Americans, then the years after 1944–5 were a "good occupation" for the Germans. A gentle occupation conducted by a friendly enemy was a significant prerequisite enabling a Western system of state and society to take root and eventually gain acceptance. The American occupation forces first won the country and the trust of its people and then worked step by step together with the Germans to implement a model of society in which the highest objective was not to create a nation and *Volk* fit for war, as under Hitler, but to protect human dignity.[17]

---

[16] Studs Terkel, *The Good War: Oral History of World War Two* (New York, 1984).

[17] See the chapter by Raimund Lammersdorf in this section.

CHAPTER TWO

Gender, Race, and Power
American Soldiers and the German Population

Petra Goedde

More than two million American soldiers moved into southern and western Germany at the end of World War II. The troops who participated in the invasion in 1944–5 knew that some of them would be called upon to stay as occupation forces. Yet, few of them could have imagined that American forces would remain in Western Germany for decades to come. Nor could they have predicted that with the beginning of the Cold War, the troops' role in Germany would change from occupiers to guarantors of West German and West European security – a role they continued to play long after the end of the Cold War and Germany's division.

American troops, which numbered fewer than 80,000 in 1950 and between 250,000 and 300,000 thereafter, became a permanent fixture of postwar German society.[1] American Army bases were located in Bavaria, Hessen, parts of Baden-Württemberg, West Berlin, Bremen, and, after 1950, in Rhineland-Palatinate. Between the end of World War II and the early 1970s, social relations between American troops and German civilians in these areas reflected the shifting balance of economic and social power. At the end of the war, American troops possessed greater wealth than Germans and the social prerogatives of victors. During the 1950s and 1960s, however, differences in wealth and

power narrowed. By the beginning of the 1970s, Germans were both more prosperous than most GIs and no longer socially deferent to American military personnel. These changes led to considerable strains in the relationship between troops and civilians.

Race and gender were signifiers of the shifting power relations between Americans and Germans. Throughout the 1940s and 1950s, popular attention in both countries focused on sexual liaisons between German women and GIs. In the immediate aftermath of the war, women's relationships with GIs symbolized the power inequalities between Germans and Americans. Many women became dependents of American GIs during the occupation, and many Germans likewise saw themselves as dependents of the United States, a view many Americans shared. Race assumed greater importance in German-American social relations in the 1950s as Germans became increasingly aware of racial discrimination within the armed forces. This awareness led to a resurgence of racism among Germans in the 1950s, noticeable above all in the increase in complaints about the conduct of black GIs issued to a predominantly white military administration. By the early 1970s, however, in the wake of the American civil rights movement and the Vietnam War, Germans increasingly criticized the American military for its internal racial strife, attempting thereby to claim a higher moral ground. Race became a means for Germans to chip away at the facade of American social and moral superiority.

[1] The figures on troop strength are taken from Daniel J. Nelson, *A History of U.S. Military Forces in Germany* (Boulder, Colo., 1987), 45, 81, 103.

German deference to American troops was at its highest during the military occupation between 1945 and 1949, when most Germans not only accepted the presence of foreign troops on their soil but even welcomed the Americans as liberators. In part because of the friendly reception they received, American soldiers soon developed cordial relations with the local population in spite of their official role as occupiers. In their social interactions with German civilians, GIs acted as providers and protectors toward individual Germans long before economic aid and Germany's security became official American Cold War policy. As the troops settled into German communities and developed personal ties to the local population – primarily to young women and children – they increasingly treated German civilians as victims of the war rather than as former enemies.[2]

The soldiers' friendly attitude toward Germans in the early postwar period obstructed the implementation of a punitive occupation policy and undermined the military government's ban on fraternization.[3] Even though the official military definition of fraternization denoted all informal interactions between members of the American armed forces and German nationals, its colloquial meaning soon changed to refer primarily to soldiers' sexual relationships with German women. Because of the sexual connotations of fraternization, most GIs felt little compunction about violating the ban. They saw their relationships with women as personal affairs that did not jeopardize the mission of the occupation. Informal polls taken between VE Day and the end of September 1945 showed

that the vast majority of GIs had some form of contact with the local population.[4] Faced with such massive defiance, military officials in Germany terminated the order on October 1, 1945, except for a ban on billeting with German families and marriages to German nationals.

Just as male GIs craved female companionship in Germany, many German women actively sought the company of American soldiers. The demographic and social upheavals of the early postwar period, combined with the relative wealth of American GIs, predisposed women toward the foreign soldiers. Wartime casualties among German men had been extremely high: In the age group between 20 and 40, there were 160 women for every 100 German men. Because of this gender imbalance, women bore the brunt of Germany's social and economic reconstruction, becoming the main breadwinners for their families and clearing away the rubble from the ruined cities. As single and widowed women faced the possibility of remaining unmarried for the rest of their lives, they increasingly sought out potential husbands among the occupation forces. A more pressing need for women than marriage, however, was access to food and essential goods. Americans had plenty of both and gave freely. Many young women, therefore, offered companionship and sex in return for American army rations. As a result, the borderline between romantic courtship and prostitution became blurred.

The longer American GIs stayed in Germany, the more they treated Germans – both male and female – as victims of the war suffering from food shortages and living under harsh material conditions. The soldiers responded to the deprivations by organizing food drives and holiday parties, recreational activities, and helping out with scarce goods wherever they could. Food,

[2] For more detail on GI relationships with German civilians, see Petra Goedde, *GIs and Germans: Culture, Gender, and Foreign Relations, 1945–1949* (New Haven, 2003) (Ph.D. diss., Northwestern University, 1995), forthcoming Princeton University Press; Petra Gödde, "From Villains to Victims: Fraternization and the Feminization of Germany, 1945–1947," *Diplomatic History* 23 (1999): 1–20.

[3] Directive to the Commander-in-Chief of the United States Forces of Occupation Regarding the Military Government of Germany, May 10, 1945, in U.S. Department of State, *Documents on Germany, 1944–1985* (Washington, D.C., 1985), 15–32.

[4] For more detail about the polls, see Office of the Chief Historian, European Command, *Fraternization with the Germans in World War II* (Frankfurt am Main, 1947), 46. The figures ranged from 15 percent in some regiments to all members in others. The low figures might have been the result of dishonesty toward the pollsters (because fraternization was still illegal at that time), lack of opportunity to meet Germans, or hatred of Germans because of the regiment's wartime experience.

in fact, became a central aspect of German–American relationships.

Two of the consequences of German–American sexual relationships were a dramatic rise in sexually transmitted diseases and illegitimate births. Unofficial estimates placed the total number of German-American offspring at 94,000 over the course of the military occupation.[5] A surprisingly high number of GIs actually took steps to adopt the children they had fathered or marry their German girlfriends. The military government received marriage petitions from servicemen as early as 1944, when even talking to Germans was still a violation of military regulations. Some GIs married Germans in defiance of the fraternization ban, risking court-martial or removal from Germany. Others waited patiently for the lifting of the marriage ban, which finally occurred in December 1946. By June 1950, according to immigration statistics, 14,175 German wives, 6 husbands, and 750 children of "citizen members of United States Armed Forces" had entered the United States under the provisions of the so-called War Brides Act passed by Congress in December 1945.[6] Only Great Britain, where American soldiers had been stationed during the war, sent more spouses and children to the United States.

The few African-American soldiers who applied for permission to marry German women were much less likely to have their requests granted than their white compatriots. The racial discrimination they faced within the still segregated army presented a sharp contrast to their experience with German civilians. In the 1940s, few Germans appeared to distinguish between white and black GIs in public, treating them with equal deference. African-American soldiers – who made up just under 6 percent of the occupation forces – also found Germans to be more tolerant of interracial liaisons than their own white compatriots. Around 3 percent of the postwar children born out of wedlock had nonwhite fathers.[7] However, black soldiers' positive experience in Germany did not mean that racism had vanished from the German consciousness with Hitler's defeat; it simply surfaced in more subtle ways. For example, the number of German official complaints about troop misconduct was far higher for blacks than whites. This discrimination was often encouraged by white military officials who themselves were biased against black soldiers.[8]

The issue of interracial sexual relations was problematic for both Germans and Americans. Even though the vast majority of relationships between German women and black GIs occurred on a voluntary basis, accusations of rape surfaced far more often in conjunction with African-American than with white GIs. Both German and American racism contributed to this disequilibrium. The expectation of African-American misconduct increased both the readiness of Germans to complain about black soldiers and the willingness of white occupation officials to discipline them. German and American racial prejudices thus reinforced each other at the very moment when American reeducation officials were supposed to extinguish the Nazi ideology of racial supremacy from the German mind.[9]

Rape by occupation soldiers was a real threat to women in all parts of Germany, including

---

[5] Barbara Willenbacher, "Zerrüttung und Bewährung der Nachkriegs-Familie," in Martin Broszat, Klaus-Dietmar Henke, and Hans Woller, eds., *Von Stalingrad zur Währungsreform: Zur Sozialgeschichte des Umbruchs in Deutschland* (Munich, 1988), 600–1. The unofficial estimate was made by Hans Habe in *Our Love Affair with Germany* (New York, 1953), 10.

[6] The War Brides Act, as Public Law No. 271 was called, went into effect in December 1945. It was initially designed to allow the spouses and children of American GIs from Allied countries to enter the United States. See *Congressional Record*, 79th Cong., 1st sess., 91, pt. 9: 11738, 12342, 12547. For statistics, see U.S. Immigration and Naturalization Service, *Annual Report, 1950*, table 9A, and *Annual Report, 1949*, table 9A.

[7] Heide Fehrenbach, "Rehabilitating Fatherland: Race and German Remasculinization," *Signs* 24 (1998): 107–27; Signe Seiler, *Die GIs: Amerikanische Soldaten in Deutschland* (Reinbeck, 1983).

[8] See, for example, Headquarters USFET, Report, Subject: Survey of Colored Troops By IG for period 10–31 May, 1946, 19 July 1946, file 291.2, ETO/USFET, RG 332, National Records Center, Suitland, Maryland.

[9] See the chapter by Cornelia Rauh-Kühne, vol. 1, Politics.

the American zone. The evidence remains slim as to the frequency of sexual assaults because women were often reluctant to report them. Yet, even occupation officials in the American zone acknowledged that rapes by GIs, black and white, occurred much more often than the official records showed.[10] Because Germans evaluated the conduct of the soldiers in the context of the early postwar period, American offenses against women appeared mild in comparison to the wave of rapes that swept over the Soviet-occupied part of the country.[11] In the face of such extremes, Germans regarded American troops as benign.

Sexual liaisons between GIs and German women also served as touchstones for German opposition to the American occupation. Many German veterans saw the women's relationships with American GIs as a betrayal of their wartime sacrifices. Yet, most of them turned against the women rather than GIs, publicly deriding them as "Ami whores" or cutting off their hair. Clashes between German men and occupation troops over fraternization occurred less frequently but nonetheless caused enough alarm to lead one occupation official to remark in a report that "the GI and the German Fräulein is Germany's primary social problem."[12]

In spite of such frictions, most Germans saw the presence of American troops as beneficial. During the early phase of the occupation, those benefits were primarily material. With the onset of the Cold War, however, Germans began to see their occupiers also as protectors against the Soviet Union. One single event, the Berlin airlift of 1948–9, epitomized this dual American role. The airlift, more than anything else, reflected Germany's acceptance of its economic and military dependence on the United States, casting Germans in the role of dependents and Americans in the role of providers and protectors. Just as American GIs had provided for German women during the early phase of the occupation, the United States was providing for West Berlin and, by extension, West Germany, during the airlift.

By the end of the airlift in 1949, the American presence in Germany had shrunk to around 80,000 troops. With the onset of the Korean War in 1950, however, military and political officials became convinced that the communist threat required an expansion of troop strength in Western Europe, particularly Germany. The Truman administration, therefore, raised the number of troops in Germany to more than 300,000 over the next three years.[13] In metropolitan areas, the arrival of the new troops changed existing social and economic structures only slightly. Many of the new troops moved, however, into rural areas, whose inhabitants spent the better part of the 1950s adjusting to the demographic upheaval. Most people living in these areas welcomed the economic development but resented the social and cultural changes that came with the American presence.[14] In the town of Baumholder in Rhineland-Palatinate, for instance, the arrival of American troops ended local unemployment, which had been at more than 24 percent. The construction of roads, military facilities, and housing, as well as the relative wealth of the American troops, boosted the local economy.

[10] Report by Ninth Army Courier Leiser, Mar. 14, 1945, File 250.1–1, G-1 Division (Personnel), SHAEF, RG 331, National Archives, Washington, D.C.

[11] For more detail, see Norman M. Naimark, *The Russians in Germany: A History of the Soviet Zone of Occupation, 1945–1949* (Cambridge, Mass., 1995), 69–140, esp. 115. See also Atina Grossman, "A Question of Silence: The Rape of German Women by Occupation Soldiers," *October* 72 (Spring 1995): 43–62.

[12] Information Control Division (ICD) Survey in the American Zone, cited in "U.S. Survey Discloses Returning German Soldiers' Views," *New York Times*, Aug. 23, 1945.

[13] See David J. Nelson, *A History of U.S. Military Forces in Germany* (Boulder, Colo., 1987), 45. See also the chapter by Frank Schumacher, vol. 1, Politics, and by Fred Zilian, vol. 1, Security.

[14] Much of the information on the 1950s relies on Maria Höhn's book, *GIs and Fräuleins: The German-American Encounter in 1950s West Germany* (Chapel Hill, 2002). Höhn studied the changes that occurred in the town of Baumholder and the slightly larger city of Kaiserslautern, both in the state of Rhineland-Palatinate, as a result of the influx of large numbers of American troops.

Within only a few years, the region experienced rapid urbanization and modernization.[15]

The social and cultural modernization that accompanied economic change gave rise to tensions in the region. Cultural change was welcomed mainly by the young and was disturbing to many older people. New bars and nightclubs emerged around army bases, catering to the GI clientele and attracting women, including prostitutes, from all over the region. These developments concerned local authorities, who feared the corruption and moral decay of their youth.[16] Their response was to harass all women who moved to the area to be with an American soldier or who frequented nightspots popular with GIs. Local courts began prosecuting women as prostitutes even if they were actually involved in a long-term relationship with American soldiers.

In an effort to counter the moral reservations of community leaders, military officials sponsored a host of social and cultural activities designed to foster good relations between the military and local communities, including church festivals, Christmas parties, recreational activities, and open houses on the bases. The Americans also subsidized the building of public facilities such as schools, gymnasiums, and athletic fields in financially strapped communities.[17] These efforts muted some of the German complaints about the negative consequences of the troops' presence.

Most social interaction between soldiers and civilians, however, occurred in nightclubs, dance halls, and pubs. As in the 1940s, soldiers sought primarily the company of young single women, including prostitutes who targeted American army bases as their primary market. Yet, many more women were involved in serious relationships with GIs that often led to marriage. In the 1950s, the marriage rate between Germans and American citizens increased at the same rate as troop deployment in Germany.[18] In Baumholder alone, about half of the wedding ceremonies performed between 1954 and 1962 were between Germans and Americans.[19]

In towns like Baumholder, treatment of women who were involved in permanent relationships with American GIs improved gradually during the 1950s. Early in the decade, every woman seen with a GI in Baumholder risked the label "Ami whore." By the late 1950s, however, as economic conditions for Germans improved, most Germans accepted these relationships as long as they appeared permanent and were with white GIs. Women dating black GIs continued to face public and legal persecution. The proportion of prostitution cases in local courts involving black GIs rose dramatically in the second half of the 1950s, to 70 to 80 percent of all prostitution trials, compared to about a third of all cases before.[20] Discrimination against black GIs was apparent in other areas as well, such as in the greater number of police raids of bars patronized by African-Americans. Official American reactions to these forms of discrimination depended on the initiative of individual commanders, many of whom shared the German prejudice against black GIs. This informal German-American alliance against black troops allowed Germans to claim social equality with white Americans and superiority over black Americans.

Racism persisted in German society during the 1950s and 1960s but was expressed far more subtly than it had been during the Third Reich. Under the American military government, Germans had eliminated all forms of legal racism, yet social, economic, and cultural discrimination against nonwhites remained. Especially in the 1950s, an image of blacks as crude, uncivilized, and naive resurfaced in newspaper editorials, cartoons, novels, and films. Ironically, many young Germans were drawn toward

---

[15] Ibid., 31–51.
[16] Ibid., 155–76.
[17] Ibid., 69–70.
[18] For exact figures, see U.S. Immigration and Naturalization Service, *Annual Report, 1950–1968*

(Washington, D.C., 1950–68), esp. tables on "Immigrant Aliens Admitted by Classes under the Immigration Laws and Country or Region of Birth." Special categories in these tables were "Wives, Husbands, and Children of U.S. Citizens."
[19] Höhn, "GIs, Veronikas, and Lucky Strikes," 74.
[20] Ibid., 192.

African-Americans precisely because of those stereotypes. They sought the company of black soldiers and listened to jazz, swing, and rock 'n' roll as a way of rebelling against the established social and cultural norms in their society.[21] Black GIs provided an escape from the constraints of "Western civilization" into the perceived "wilderness" of nonwhite, non-Western culture.[22] It did not matter that black soldiers from the United States were as much a product of Western culture as white Americans or Germans themselves.

For African-American soldiers, German racism was less visible than the discrimination they experienced within their own society. They were able to date German women, and they found nightclubs that catered to their interests. Bars that denied them entrance often were off-limits to white GIs as well, thus making it harder for them to discern whether the discrimination was based on race or their status as foreign soldiers. Black GIs from the American South, in particular, experienced Germany as a country of racial tolerance and personal freedom.

By 1960, communities surrounding American bases had largely adjusted to the changing circumstances. The German "economic miracle" (*Wirtschaftswunder*) narrowed the economic gap between GIs and Germans and led to more equitable social relations. As the Germans became less dependent on the Americans economically, they tended to see the United States more as a NATO ally than an occupation force. German public opinion of Americans also improved steadily, peaking in 1965 when 58 percent of Germans declared that they liked the Americans. Two years later, however, the figure dropped to 47 percent, reflecting a significant deterioration in relations.[23] The reasons for this

decline were related to the American involvement in Vietnam.

The Vietnam War not only called into question the Cold War consensus of the Western alliance but also forced the American military to withdraw many of its most qualified officers and enlisted men from overseas bases, particularly Germany. Those areas were left with a force of diminished quality and steadily decreasing morale. Drug abuse, disciplinary problems, and crime increased on American bases in Germany, while the sharp decline of the dollar against the Deutsche Mark in the early 1970s significantly lowered the living standard of American troops, making it almost impossible to live off base.[24] By the time the United States withdrew from Vietnam in 1973, the once rich and powerful American army in Germany appeared but a shadow of its former self.

The decline of the American military's prestige during the late 1960s and early 1970s strained the relationship between GIs and Germans. The German media began to openly criticize the conduct of American troops, pointing to the dramatic increase in robberies and assaults committed by GIs and the growing intensity of racial strife among them.[25] Germans began to question the assumptions they had held since the end of World War II about the moral superiority of American society. This disillusionment was compounded by the inability of American personnel to live or spend money outside the army compounds, which diminished their interaction with the German population. As contacts decreased, Americans and Germans felt increasingly alienated from each other. By the early 1970s, the balance of economic and social power had shifted decisively toward Germany, creating among Germans a sense of economic and social superiority.

Social relations between American troops and the German population since World War II mirrored the postwar political relationship between Germany and the United States. Germans always regarded the troops' presence as a vital

[21] See the chapters by Edward Larkey and Uta G. Poiger, vol. 1, Culture; see also Uta G. Poiger, *Jazz, Rock, and Rebels: Cold War Politics and American Culture in a Divided Germany* (Berkeley, Calif., 2000).

[22] Rosemarie K. Lester, *Trivialneger: Das Bild der Schwarzen im Westdeutschen Illustriertenroman* (Stuttgart, 1982); Poiger, *Jazz, Rock, and Rebels*.

[23] Figures quoted from Daniel J. Nelson, *Defenders or Intruders: The Dilemma of U.S. Forces in Germany* (Boulder, Colo., 1987), 66.

[24] Nelson, *History of U.S. Military Forces*, 83–105. See also the chapter by T. Michael Ruddy, vol. 2, Security.

[25] Nelson, *History of U.S. Military Forces*, 105–7.

element of their nation's security. In the early postwar period, Germans behaved like dependents of the Americans, glad to abdicate their responsibility for the security of the state. This sense of dependency was reflected in the social relationships between Germans and GIs throughout the first decade of the Cold War. Only with Germany's political and economic emancipation in the 1960s did a social emancipation in the population's relationship with American soldiers also occur, leading to mutual tensions.

Germans held the troops in high regard as long as they represented a strong military, economic, and political power. When America's economic and political prestige declined in the late 1960s, social tensions between GIs and Germans increased. However, even as tensions grew, Germans never seriously challenged the legitimacy of the American military presence on their soil. The reciprocal nature of social and political-military relations created a volatile yet firm partnership that would bind the two states together throughout the Cold War.

CHAPTER THREE

CARE Packages

Gifts from Overseas to a Defeated and Debilitated Nation

Godehard Weyerer

Translated by Eric Weinberger

Germany miscalculated and did so twice. Each time, it challenged first Europe, then the rest of the world; once in 1914 and again in 1939. A devastating defeat in the first war did not deter the Germans from unleashing the second. The question of how to deal with Nazi Germany in the wake of World War II was a source of heated controversy in the United States. Hardliners, conscious of the mass extermination and the disregard of human life shown by the Nazi regime, blamed the German people as a whole for the atrocities. They supported the Morgenthau Plan and came to exert a great deal of influence under President Franklin D. Roosevelt. Opposing them were the so-called soft peace boys from the Departments of State and Commerce, especially the brothers Allen and John Foster Dulles. These moderates warned against the adoption of any postwar policy that would single Germany out for punishment, and a range of ecclesiastical organizations sided with them. They feared that such a course would isolate Germany and perpetuate the kind of instability that had unsettled the old world following World War I. In autumn 1945, church welfare organizations founded CARE, and in February 1946 President Harry S. Truman gave permission for humanitarian relief supplies to be shipped to Germany.

CARE packages were probably the most famous packages in history. They would help countless people to survive the worst of the misery left in the wake of the war. For President Truman and General Dwight D. Eisenhower,

they embodied a humane expression of international goodwill.[1]

The acronym "CARE" stood for "Cooperative for American Remittances to Europe." Twenty-two American welfare agencies joined this effort, including the Quakers, Mennonites, Church of Brothers, and even trade unions and the Salvation Army; their desire was to help the people suffering from the devastation in Europe. When the organization was formed in New York in November 1945, Europe was not thought to include Germany. However, the land that had sworn unconditional allegiance to Adolf Hitler now stood in ruins. Its cities had been levelled, and their inhabitants longed for some sign of sympathy for their predicament. True to the biblical precept of helping even an enemy in distress, the first CARE packages arrived in postwar Germany in August 1946, five months after Truman had given his consent and fourteen months after the unconditional surrender.

The eagerly awaited aid entered Germany through Bremen, the port through which

---

[1] ABC appeal for donations, Deutsches Rundfunkarchiv, Frankfurt, 78 U 3625/3: "A person-to-person expression of international goodwill, in the way many prominent people including President Truman and General Eisenhower have described CARE, the agency that sends needed food-packets overseas. If you would like to order a CARE packet, just send 10 Dollars to CARE, New York. Give your name and address and specify to whom you are sending the packet. This is ABC, the American Broadcasting Company."

supplies for the American troops were channeled. From Bremen, the CARE packages, officially referred to by the Germans as *Liebesgaben* or gifts, were distributed to the American and British occupation zones. Later the French zone also received deliveries, and some packages even made their way into the Soviet zone, albeit not by conventional or official means.

Until March 1947, CARE packages simply consisted of surplus American army rations that had originally been intended for the war in the Pacific. Because the fighting in that part of the world had come to an end a year earlier than expected, 2.8 million ration kits were left over and made available for sale to CARE. Once these had been used up, CARE designed two model packages of its own. One contained canned meat, cooking fat, sugar, dried milk, flour, chocolate, coffee, soap, chewing gum, and cigarettes; the other, woolen blankets, sewing notions, clothing, and shoes. CARE bought in bulk and put the packages together at a warehouse in Philadelphia. The number of different model packages available for purchase by American donors gradually grew to fifteen. By June 1960, when the relief operation came to an end in the western part of Germany, eight million CARE packages had passed through the port of Bremen and been distributed around the country. Some packages contained tools for carpenters and emigrants; others held bottles, milk powder, and diapers for babies. A holiday package even became available beginning in autumn 1949, including a complete seven-pound turkey preserved in lard. Packages also contained baby food, wool for knitting, lard, household linen, and English reading matter, including a dictionary. The variety of supplies offered by CARE was unusually broad for a relief organization. It functioned as a cooperative and, although it was not set up to make a profit, CARE had been designed to be run like a business. Any surpluses were rolled back into its humanitarian operations. Because large numbers of Americans were of German descent, CARE insisted from the outset on being permitted to send packages to Germany as well; packages sent to that devastated country accounted for 60 percent of CARE's business in the years that followed.

The agencies that founded CARE contributed $1 million of initial capital to the umbrella organization, and CARE offices opened their doors in New York and all other major American cities. Packages ordered by U.S. donors were shipped to Europe, and when recipients picked them up, they filled out receipts. These went back to the donors to assure them that their requests had been filled. The initial price for a standard package was $15, which covered the cost of the contents as well as transportation to their final destination. The U.S. government soon assumed the cost of shipping to Europe, which enabled CARE to reduce the price of a standard package to $10. A package of lard cost $4, a holiday package $20. The extremely low administrative expenses for this humanitarian operation, which was run on strict business principles, demonstrated the program's highly effective management and organization.[2]

With a mixture of pride and envy, postwar Germany accorded the status of "aunts" and "uncles" to donors on the other side of the ocean even though very few such relatives had actually achieved wealth or prosperity in America. Little mail was more popular with Germans in the early years after the war than the neatly packed brown boxes with the black metal strips. People waited expectantly for their turn to receive a card from the post office announcing arrival of such a package. For some, a CARE package was nothing less than a gift from heaven, the only ray of hope in their hour of greatest need. "Dear Eva," wrote a German emigrant who had just received a letter from his old home for the first time in twelve years, "I was delighted and amazed to receive your letter. Delighted to know that you are still alive,

---

[2] Karl Ludwig Sommer is currently working on a monograph describing the work of different agencies, which will be published by the Bremen State Archives (Staatsarchiv Bremen). Sommer puts the administrative expenses at 10 percent. According to his research, the first director general had three times the salary of a member of the U.S. government. One-fourth of the initial capital had already been spent on salaries and office rents before the first package was sold. Sommer interprets this as an indication that CARE was professionally managed and a reason for the great success of the operation.

and amazed, because we were never really that close. But the package is already on its way."[3] One young woman, advertising in the newspaper for a husband, wrote: "Two rooms available, two CARE packages per month." She received 2,437 responses.[4] CARE made it all possible.

Why all this concern for a defeated enemy? First, many family ties and bonds of friendship existed between Germans and German-Americans. American soldiers stationed in Germany also reported to friends and family back home on the misery they witnessed in Europe. Reports in the press, on the radio, and in newsreels that revealed what life was like in the shadow of hunger and misery aroused further sympathy. Photographs showing burned facades of houses and basements filled with rubble. Men in tattered German army uniforms scoured the streets for cigarette butts discarded by occupation troops. Women, children, and elderly men would rummage for anything edible in the piles of trash and garbage cans outside Allied officers' mess halls. The pictures and reports showed even more: The people who had set out to rule the world were unable to endure this degradation except in total apathy, in somber, sullen silence.[5]

From the Allied viewpoint, reeducation was the central concern of the hour. Although CARE packages were intended to alleviate suffering, they were also meant to promote the concept of democracy in Germany. The reeducation program represented an unprecedented attempt to revive the democratic traditions of a people that had lost them; it would play a major role in laying the ground for democratic identity in what became the Federal Republic of Germany. The success of the program was not clear at the outset. While advancing militarily into Germany, the Allies had anxiously witnessed how smoothly the Nazi machine continued to function; it did so up to the final day of its existence and despite ever-growing destruc-

tion and the inevitability of a German defeat. Allied forces had, therefore, feared that fanatical hordes of German hold-outs and paramilitaries would fight back as soon as they set foot on German soil. Surprisingly, this did not turn out to be the case.

General Lucius D. Clay, the deputy military governor of the American occupation zone, put his signature to the CARE treaty on June 6, 1946, in Stuttgart. Two weeks later, on June 21, his counterpart in the British zone did the same. Distribution and delivery of CARE packages now became possible in both zones. German welfare agencies oversaw this work, in particular the Catholic organization *Caritas* and the Protestant *Innere Mission*.[6] Before they were allowed to assume this responsibility, however, military authorities required them to reach agreement on a division of labor between their denominations or organizations. It was in this context that the *Zentralausschuss der Spitzenverbände der freien Wohlfahrtspflege*, an umbrella organization for private welfare agencies, was founded to handle the receipt and distribution of charitable donations from abroad. The revived *Arbeiterwohlfahrt* (the Social Democrats' welfare organization, banned in the Nazi period) joined in autumn 1946, as did the German Red Cross and a new, nonaligned agency under the name *Paritätischer Wohlfahrtsverband* a short time later.

The umbrella organization set up its headquarters in Bremen. CARE had established its German headquarters in the city's *Haus des Reiches* (House of the Reich), which at one time housed Germany's financial administration and had been requisitioned by American military authorities at the end of the war. The *Zentralausschuss* acquired an office in the same building, next door on the same floor. Its manager was Pastor Heinrich Johannes Diehl. A former seafarers' chaplain who had looked after

---

[3] "Wunderdosen aus dem braunen Karton: Vor 25 Jahren kamen die ersten CARE-Pakete nach Deutschland," *Süddeutsche Zeitung*, May 8, 1971.

[4] *Bremer Nachrichten*, Feb. 12, 1948.

[5] See the chapter by Thomas Reuther in this section.

[6] Hans-Josef Wollasch, *Humanitäre Auslandshilfe für Deutschland nach dem Zweiten Weltkrieg: Darstellung und Dokumentation kirchlicher und nichtkirchlicher Hilfen* (Freiburg im Breisgau, 1976). This source focuses mainly on the work of Catholic welfare agencies.

the German communities in Southampton and Newcastle until September 1939, he possessed one of the most valued skills of the postwar period: He spoke fluent English. As a liaison to British military authorities, Diehl helped to rebuild the Protestant charity *Evangelisches Hilfswerk* after the war. In January 1946, he had a first meeting with a representative of the CARE organization and, from then until the 1960s, he worked closely with the Americans. Because the packages already bore addresses, the German welfare agencies had no influence over who received them. The agencies nonetheless fell under some suspicion of giving preferential treatment to people who regularly attended church services. On the side, however, some farmers also appear to have hoarded CARE packages from relatives in the United States and refused to share them with the refugees huddled in their barns and struggling to survive.

According to a survey conducted in January 1950 on behalf of the Allied High Commission, 80 percent of those questioned knew that the CARE packages came from America. For every person who had received a package, nine others had not. The most common complaint directed at the scheme thus concerned unfair distribution of the donations.

A CARE package had a long way to travel before it actually reached its intended recipient. Hardly any roads remained intact when the war was over, and the few surviving railroad lines were hopelessly overloaded. Many trucks stood available for use, but most sat parked on their wheel rims because tires remained in short supply. The CARE office in Bremen raised the matter with the British military authorities, who allowed tires to be shipped from Hanover. The canteen of the tire manufacturer Continental received some CARE packages in return. Gasoline also remained a precious commodity. CARE again took care of the problem, shipping five million liters all the way from the United States. Occupation authorities gave vouchers for the gasoline to the German welfare agencies, and the trucks were back on the road.

CARE packages were not the only relief supplies distributed through Bremen. The Amer-

ican agencies that founded CARE set up a second organization in February 1946, the Council of Relief Agencies Licensed for Operation in Germany, otherwise known as "CRALOG." In areas of America with a large number of people from German backgrounds, CRALOG organized "canning days" for collecting donations of nonperishable food items in cans and jars. In autumn 1947, a "friendship train" also crossed the American Northwest to gather up whatever people had to give, be it clothing, shoes, or medicine. So-called friendship ships carried the donations to Bremen, where German welfare agencies received them for free distribution.

CRALOG ultimately transferred 323,000 tons of relief supplies to devastated postwar Germany, four times the amount that entered the area in the form of CARE packages. Yet, the CARE packages continued to be much better known than the CRALOG donations, probably because of the personal connections existing between donor and recipient. As the 1940s drew to a close and private donations fell off, American farm surpluses made up the slack; the federal government bought surpluses and gave them free of charge to the CRALOG agencies. The organization even shipped more than 2,000 head of cattle, which went to ethnic German farmers from Eastern Europe. Although the two American organizations had identical goals and received support from the same agencies, CARE and CRALOG remained separate. Vast quantities of American relief supplies thus made their way to postwar Germany through two different channels, with representatives of both organizations advising and assisting distribution agencies in Germany. Some misunderstandings were inevitable, for example, when General Clay tried to obtain more food for Germany during the second winter after the war. The official ration had fallen below 1,000 calories per day, and Clay asked the German representative what was needed to improve conditions. The answer, in German, was *Korn*, meaning grain, such as rye or wheat. However, the interpreter translated this as "corn." The mistake was not discovered until a whole shipload of maize was on its way to Germany, and it cost the Americans a great deal of goodwill in Germany. Some commented acerbically, "First they let us starve, then they give us chicken feed."[7]

The Soviet Union had suffered particularly from the destruction caused by the German army. Food shortages there led to full-blown famine after the war. The French and British also starved and froze during the two hard winters that followed the end of hostilities. The only one of the Allies in a position to help was the United States. America's willingness to rise to this challenge was anything but a matter of course for a victor and represented an undeserved act of magnanimity toward a former enemy.

In the French occupation zone, savings banks (*Sparkassen*) distributed CARE packages rather than the welfare agencies. This solution, born of necessity, was the brainchild of the Norwegian Arne Torgersen, the CARE mission's representative in the zone. In contrast to the other two western zones, the welfare agencies had not been able to guarantee distribution throughout the area under French jurisdiction because the French military authorities had been slow to permit the establishment (or reestablishment) of organizations and political parties. The French military governor, General Pierre Koenig, did not even sign the CARE treaty until December 1946, half a year after his American and British counterparts had put their signatures to it. CARE had simply failed to notice that the Yalta conference had provided for the creation of an extra occupation zone, to be administered by the French. Arne Torgersen sensed that the proud French would be slow to forgive such an oversight and, as it turned out, the French military government at first did refuse to co-operate with CARE. The first CARE packages for the zone arrived in Freiburg on December 24, and by this time Torgersen had managed to enlist the services of the savings banks. "During

a walk I suddenly saw a sign on a small building that was sandwiched between piles of rubble: ÖFFENTLICHE SPARKASSE FREIBURG ("Freiburg Public Savings Bank"). We had banks like that back home, and there were branches in every village."[8] On Christmas Eve, the names of all those for whom a CARE package was waiting in Freiburg were read out over the radio. All night long a steady stream of hungry, exhausted, and emaciated figures emerged from buildings unfit for human habitation and moved through the snow-covered ruins of the medieval city on their way to the savings bank. The branch manager personally placed the packages into waiting arms. A mother with two children made the deepest impression on Arne Torgersen.

> The young woman trembled with excitement as the package was handed over to her, and she could hardly even sign the receipt. She pressed the package to her body and cried so hard that her thin body shook. Her two children huddled silently against her and stared at us with accusing eyes for being so unkind to their mother and making her cry.[9]

Everyone in the French zone who entered a savings bank to exchange a card for a CARE package was considered a potential customer for the better days that would surely come. Savings bank associations in the other two Western zones attempted to follow the example of their colleagues in the French area, but the welfare agencies, particularly the churches, prevented them from doing so. The reason was obvious: Those who handled the distribution received free packages in return.

The stream of CARE packages reached its greatest volume between 1947 and 1949. In the 1950s, CARE gave increased support to individual charities, such as the *Anstalt Bethel*, or helped refugees and resettlers from the East. By 1960, the western part of Germany had undergone an economic revival, and CARE closed down its operation there in June of that year. Its work in West Berlin came to an end two

---

[7] Conversation with Pastor Heinrich Johannes Diehl, Aug. 22, 1995, Archiv Diehl, archives of the Diakonisches Werk Deutschland, Berlin. (A wealth of archive material is available here for a study of the work by the Protestant agencies: 25 meters of files, some of which have yet to be analyzed.)

[8] Arne M. Torgersen, *Nach Ihnen, Herr General! Humanitäre Abenteuer eines Norwegers im Nachkriegseuropa* (Stuttgart, 1971), 21.

[9] Ibid., 26.

years later. CRALOG continued to provide aid to West Germany until 1962 and to West Berlin for another two years beyond that.

Humanitarian assistance also served propaganda purposes during the Cold War, and CARE was no exception. In fact, it became an integral part of American foreign policy. The organization provided development aid at a sub-government level, for example, in the wake of the uprising in the German Democratic Republic (GDR) on June 17, 1953. CARE shipped $15 million in food aid to West Berlin, paid for by the American government. The plan envisioned East Berliners receiving food if they showed their identity cards. The East German leadership, however, described the offerings as "corruption packages," and if the East German police found that people had more than one identity card on them, they did not allow them to continue on to West Berlin. Nevertheless, 60,000 so-called eastern zone packages found their way into East Germany over the following four years. Church organizations in West Germany took CARE packages and disguised them as private parcels, occasionally enlisting the help of Danish haulage contractors for delivery. However, a humanitarian operation of this magnitude could probably not have been carried out if East German authorities had not looked the other way.

The eight million packages that CARE sent to Germany had a total value of DM 360 million, the aid supplied by CRALOG DM 700 million. The value of the food imported by the military government, the meals program for children, the crop seeds, and the food and material supplied to hospitals and orphanages was even greater. Aid also flowed in from Switzerland, Sweden, Canada, and many other countries against which Germany had declared war just a few years earlier. The hour of total collapse, as Thomas Mann announced in his radio address on May 10, 1945, signified Germany's return to the fold of humanity, even though it had not been able to do so on its own strength. The first CARE packages arrived in Bremen, the port of entry for U.S. military supplies, in August 1946. In the words of General Clay, there was "no place for hunger where the American flag was flying."[10] He knew that "we could not arouse political interest for a democratic government in a hungry, apathetic population."[11] By contrast, not a few Germans regarded the packages from America as reasonable and obvious compensation for the destruction and deprivation caused by Allied bombing raids during the war.

---

[10] "From the first I begged and argued for food because I did not believe that the American people wanted starvation and misery to accompany occupation..." (Lucius D. Clay, *Decision in Germany* [Garden City, N.Y., 1950], 263).

[11] Ibid.

CHAPTER FOUR

Remigrants and Reconstruction

Claus-Dieter Krohn

Translated by Alison Sondhaus Carroll

EXILES, EMIGRANTS, AND REMIGRANTS

Those who returned to Germany after being driven out by the Nazis are an inseparable part of the story of democratic reconstruction in West Germany. Yet, there has been no systematic investigation of this group of people and the history of their influence.[1] It is not even clear who can be counted as remigrants. Are they only those people and groups who had kept a close watch on Germany in their years of exile, waiting for the first opportunity to return? Or should one also consider those who temporarily returned to Germany, who came as members of the occupying forces but contributed to reeducation and the country's reorganization along constitutional lines?

This group could also include so-called cultural multipliers, especially the scholars who came individually as guest professors and played a part in helping the Federal Republic rejoin the international community. Because their expulsion from Germany after 1933 virtually wiped out German cultural life, the remigrants' reversal of the "brain drain" was of particular significance. The emigrants had made a large

contribution to the leading position claimed by American scholarship since the 1930s. The blending of theoretically oriented and philosophically based traditions brought from Europe with American pragmatism qualified the former refugee intellectuals as interlocutors and interpreters between former compatriots and their liberators after 1945.

Only estimates can be made of the numbers of remigrants. No reliable figures exist even for those expelled by the Nazi regime, because the countries that received them did not distinguish statistically between ordinary emigrants and refugees. Research on exile indicates that around 500,000 people were expelled from Germany, Austria, and the German-speaking portion of Czechoslovakia during the years of Nazi rule. Of these, about a fourth went to the United States. Moreover, it is often impossible to make definitive statements about the reasons – whether "racial" or political – for their expulsion or persecution. Yet, these reasons were of prime importance in many people's decision whether to return to Europe. According to the *International Biographical Dictionary of Central European Emigrés*, about 60 percent of the political refugees returned, whereas the share of Jewish remigrants remained at only about 4 percent.[2]

---

[1] For further information, see Claus-Dieter Krohn et al., eds., *Exilforschung: Ein internationales Jahrbuch 9*, "Exile and Remigration" (Munich, 1991); Claus-Dieter Krohn and Patrick von zur Mühlen, eds., *Rückkehr und Aufbau nach 1945: Beiträge deutscher Remigranten zur politischen Kultur der Bundesrepublik* (Marburg, 1997).

[2] Werner Röder and Herbert A. Strauss, eds., *International Biographical Dictionary of Central European Emigrés, 1933–1945*, 3 vols. (Munich, 1980–3).

No organized return process was ever set up. A person's return to Europe depended on old social networks and personal relations. According to an Allied Control Council announcement in September 1945, entrance permits could only be obtained through a prior request of the German authorities, and Americans and Britons at first distributed them very hesitantly. Allied interrogations of German prisoners of war revealed that returning exiles would face considerable hostility from the German population.

Despite the resentment and opposition of the Germans to the return of their former countrymen on the one hand, and tactical considerations and caution on the part of the remigrants on the other, the latter were able to make significant contributions to the reorganization of West Germany even though their influence was often only indirect or only took hold very gradually. This influence extended both to the strengthening of democracy under the supervision of the occupation forces and, more importantly, to the general modernization of German society and culture.

Mainly, Social Democrats remigrated into the Western zones, as few Germans from middle-class circles had gone into exile. In all, approximately 6,000, about 60 percent, of the political refugees returned. Among professional groups, the share never rose above 25 percent; in the case of journalists, for example, fewer than 500 remigrated out of a total number of 2,000 emigrants. Among scholars, scarcely 250, or about 12 percent returned to Germany. In absolute numbers, most remigrants came from the United States. In relative terms, however, fewer returned from the United States than from any other country, an indication of their successful acculturation.

GERMAN OPPOSITION TO THE REMIGRANTS

Immediately after the end of the war, the writer Frank Thiess set the standard by which his exiled compatriots should be judged in Germany. Some suggested that they had "watched the German tragedy in comfort from theater boxes and orchestra seats in foreign countries," while the "stay-at-homes" had "experienced the unspeakable hell of suffering and horror."[3] It is not difficult to see the after effects of the Nazi ideology of national solidarity ("*Volksgemeinschaft*") in such pronouncements, now additionally burdened by guilty conscience. Remaining in Nazi Germany could be justified through "inner emigration," another newly coined word that Thiess popularized. Accordingly, only those taking this kind of journey had the right to speak in the name of Germany. The newspaper *Die Gegenwart*, published by former editors of the liberal *Frankfurter Zeitung*, upheld this line in its first issue in December 1945, writing "Anyone who has gone abroad, according to a singular, inexorable law, can no longer relate to the matters of his homeland. . . . He no longer acts on the stage, the play continues without him."[4] The returnees were disparagingly dubbed as "retired emigrants." Even in 1948, the weekly *Die Zeit* suggested "that one cannot oppose the totalitarian state as a pensioner or an emigrant, only as a participant."[5] Such attitudes dominated views of remigration well into the 1950s. Thus, Hannah Arendt would express astonishment in her famous 1950 report on her first visit back to Germany that the Germans stubbornly refused to take note of what had happened; they narcissistically lamented their own fate without questioning their responsibility and guilt.[6]

Against this background, the Americans in particular doubted that the remigrants could be useful in the task of political reconstruction.

[3] Thomas Mann, Frank Thiess, and Walter von Molo, *Ein Streitgespräch über die äussere und die innere Emigration* (Dortmund, 1946), 3, 6.

[4] "Briefe von draussen: Antworten von drinnen," *Die Gegenwart* 1 (Dec. 24, 1945): 16.

[5] Quoted in Hans Georg Lehmann, *In Acht und Bann: Politische Emigration, NS-Ausbürgerung und Wiedergutmachung am Beispiel Willy Brandts* (Munich, 1976), 165.

[6] Hannah Arendt, "The Aftermath of Nazi Rule: Report from Germany," *Commentary* 10 (Oct. 1950): 342–53. See also Theodor W. Adorno, *Eingriffe* (Frankfurt am Main, 1963), 25–146. See also Norbert Frei, *Vergangenheitspolitik: Die Anfänge der Bundesrepublik und die NS-Vergangenheit* (Munich, 1996).

They eased their entry policy in 1946 only when they saw how the Soviet Union was drawing on communist emigrants for the reconstruction of the Soviet occupation zone. The French followed a similar policy; their zone was particularly heavily settled by returnees who had belonged to the Catholic Center Party. The official policy in the Soviet occupation zone had also strengthened broad resentment toward returnees since the end of the 1940s; as the Socialist Unity Party of Germany (*Sozialistische Einheitspartei Deutschlands*, or SED) was Stalinized, "West emigrants" were politically excluded.

Of greater importance, however, was the fact that the political returnees, especially the Social Democrats, had by and large accepted Western models and norms during their exile. On the one hand, this transfer of ideas from the West had a corrective effect on the national course of the Schumacher's Social Democratic Party (*Sozialdemokratische Partei Deutschlands*, or SPD). On the other, it became strategically important in burgeoning East-West antagonism. The basic conflict of the Cold War between democracy and totalitarianism had already broken out among the German political exiles at a time when the Western Allies and the Soviet Union were still partners in an anti-Hitler coalition. The Moscow Trials of 1936 and the Hitler-Stalin Pact of 1939 had utterly compromised the Soviet brand of communism for noncommunist exiles, so that their antifascist position could broaden out to include a general anticommunism after 1945. In this sense, their opinions coincided to some degree with the "stay-at-homes" who, after the beginning of the Cold War, gave proof of their new democratic convictions by displaying a vehement anticommunism.[7]

The option of turning toward the West, however, could not gloss over the differences among German political emigrants. Not even the Social Democrats had spoken with one voice during their years in exile. Isolated from the situation in Europe, the representatives of the small German Labor Delegation (GLD) in the United States, for example, saw themselves as future activists in a territorially intact Germany within the boundaries of the Versailles Treaty. Full of illusions, they even felt entitled to claim that "the Allied forces should not be allowed to interfere in any way in the domestic problems of Germany,"[8] much to the irritation of their close American associates.

In Great Britain, the Social Democrats surrounding the old exile leadership – under the pragmatic influence of the Labor Party – more realistically sought a new "third way." They wanted to prevent a restoration of the rusty old party apparatus and to find new solutions through social and economic policy. Adoption of the "Keynesian model" of indirect economic regulation, for instance, which was to release the SPD from its traditional Marxism, can be attributed to this impulse. The remigrants from England sought to make an important contribution to redefining the SPD program after 1945, a process that culminated in the Godesberger Program of 1959. A similar movement toward modernization came from returning trade unionists. The revised program of the Federation of German Trade Unions (*Deutscher Gewerkschaftsbund*, or DGB) in 1963 was based on such initiatives by former exiles. Union policy no longer aimed to "smash" capitalism but rather to "tame" it.[9]

---

[7] Not by chance, the debate over totalitarianism after 1945 lost its former character, in which emigrants had given great emphasis to their own experience with Nazi Germany (conducted by Emil Lederer, Franz Neumann, Sigmund Neumann, and others); through a more intense concentration on the Soviet Union, it increasingly took on the form of an ideological battle strategy in the Cold War. See, among others, Carl J. Friedrich, ed., *Totalitarianism: Proceedings of a Conference Held at the American Academy of Arts and Sciences, March 1953*

(Cambridge, 1954); Martin Jänicke, *Totalitäre Herrschaft: Anatomie eines politischen Begriffs* (Berlin, 1971); Karl Graf Ballestrem, "Aporien der Totalitarismus-Theorie," *Politisches Denken: Jahrbuch 1991* (Stuttgart: 1992), 50–67.

[8] See Max Brauer's speech in *Orlando*, 3 February 1942, printed in Christa Fladhammer and Michael Wildt, eds., *Max Brauer im Exil: Briefe und Reden aus den Jahren 1933–1946* (Hamburg, 1994), 299. For American reactions, see, among others, Walter L. Dorns, ibid., 302ff. and 320ff.

[9] See the study written by Paul Sering during World War II (i.e., Richard Löwenthal), *Jenseits des Kapitalismus: Ein Beitrag zur sozialistischen Neuorientierung*

Such long-term influence, however, gives no hint of the immediate difficulties that remigrants faced after 1945. Although Erich Ollenhauer of the old exile leadership was voted deputy head of the SPD at its first convention in May 1946, and although the party leadership in the coming years would be composed mainly of remigrants, their return proved anything but smooth sailing. Reservations about the new arrivals came even from within the party's own ranks. The Social Democrat Erich Brost, who had returned in 1945 and who had become the publisher of the *Westdeutsche Allgemeine Zeitung* after 1948, was unable to find "any aversion against emigrants per se." However, he added, "it can arise naturally if people come who do not understand the situation or are detached from it." And that was increasingly the case. Returnees were expected "to behave with the greatest of humility." They, in turn, could hardly understand the "people thoroughly confirmed in the old ways" whose guiding principles had remained almost unchanged from the period before 1933.[10]

The Germans who stayed never desired or organized a remigration. The first returnees came of their own volition and then brought in more colleagues from their political ranks. For instance, Max Brauer, a former mayor of Altona and the first postwar mayor of Hamburg, came to Germany as a GLD representative with an American trade union delegation from New York. Accompanying him was his party colleague Rudolf Katz, who became Minister of Justice in Schleswig-Holstein in 1947, a member of the parliamentary council in 1948–9, and vice president of the Federal Constitutional Court beginning in 1951. They quickly decided to stay in the country. At the first conference of the heads of German regional states held in Munich in June 1947, Brauer and his Berlin colleague Ernst Reuter – who had remigrated from Turkey – announced a comprehensive initiative to invite those who had been driven out by the Nazis to return to "their homeland." Leaders of the other states also voiced their support for the initiative because they viewed remigrants as potential mediators "between us and the rest of the world." Finally, they made a point of mentioning "that our people are still healthy deep down."[11] This well-intentioned appeal, however, went unheeded, and remigration continued to depend on personal initiative and individual ties.

Brauer reappointed, among others, Herbert Weichmann, the former personal adviser to Minister President Otto Braun of Prussia. The example of Weichmann who, after 1940, had built a new life in New York as a chartered accountant, shows that both party activists and members of the former ruling elite of the Weimar Republic made up the ranks of the political remigrants. While they – like those who had stayed behind – could claim administrative experience, the remigrants also had the advantage over them of having gained new professional experience in exile. With the benefit of their expert knowledge, they gave important creative impetus to the project of democratic reconstruction. Weichmann – comptroller general of Hamburg after 1948, secretary of finance after 1958, and mayor beginning in 1965 – reformed his city-state's government accounting practices so decisively through economic efficiency controls that it became the model for other German states. It meant a departure from the old, authoritarian statist traditions in favor of free enterprise mechanisms based on public finance principles that were anchored in a social policy framework.

Not because but despite the fact that they were emigrants were these experts accepted. Returning specialists who went to work for municipalities found particularly good opportunities in working for pragmatic reconstruction

(Nuremberg, 1946); Julia Angster, "Wertewandel in den Gewerkschaften: Zur Rolle gewerkschaftlicher Remigranten in der Bundesrepublik der 1950er Jahre," in Krohn and von zur Mühlen, eds., *Rückkehr und Aufbau*, 93–120.

[10] For further examples, see Jan Foitzik, "Die Rückkehr aus dem Exil und das politisch kulturelle Umfeld der Reintegration sozialdemokratischer Emigranten in Westdeutschland," in Manfred Briegel and Wolfgang Frühwald, eds., *Die Erfahrung der Fremde* (Weinheim, 1988), 255–70.

[11] The Deutsche Ministerpräsidenten-Konferenz, held in Munich, n.p., n.d., (1947), 114–5.

from below. Politicians did well to refrain from making moralistic claims. Remigrants comprised close to 20 percent of the SPD representatives and 7 percent of all officeholders in the first two West German parliaments (with similar numbers represented in regional state parliaments). They held numerous ministerial posts and sat in the uppermost ranks of the trade unions.[12] Still, the returnees' exile experiences were as little discussed as those of the antifascist resistance in Germany. Only decades later did remigration become part of the story that social democracy offered about its history.

The parliamentary work of the returnees focused instead on practical issues. During the debates over the Basic Law in the parliamentary council, they were able to make their mark through codification of Article 116, which reversed the measures that had stripped people of citizenship during the Nazi period. On their initiative, too, legislation was passed to introduce the "constructive no-confidence vote" (*konstruktives Mißtrauensvotum*, Article 67) and, in the 1950s, on the office of commissioner for the armed forces based on the Swedish model (Article 45b).

Debates about fundamental issues concerning the Nazi past were out of place. The general population, which had gained self-confidence after the founding of the Federal Republic and with the advent of the "economic miracle," could at any time turn against the former emigrants and accuse them of secretly being traitors. The relentless attacks, even in the 1960s, on the Social Democratic candidate for chancellor, Willy Brandt, provide a striking example.

REMIGRATION AND REEDUCATION

Those emigrants who returned with the occupation forces as new American citizens, collo-

quially tagged "avenging angels" or "Morgenthau boys," ran up against more serious rejection.[13] Under the title, "Get the Scoundrel Out of Germany," *Stern* magazine at the beginning of the 1950s took revenge on the "reeducator" Hans Habe, who allegedly viewed anyone who had the slightest bit to do with the Nazi period as a potential "German danger to the world." At the same time, the journal *Quick* heaped scorn and mockery on the former senior government counselor and in-house counsel to the police department in the Prussian Department of the Interior, Robert Kempner; as acting American chief prosecutor during the Nuremberg Trials, Kempner supposedly had urged "breaking the necks of his former colleagues." With his desperate attempts to acquire an "American accent," the journal reported that he had demonstrated how little he still felt tied to Germany.[14]

Together with other emigrants such as the writer Stefan Heym, the historian Golo Mann, and the journalist Ernst Wollenberg, Habe belonged to a group of prominent cultural officers who were responsible for rebuilding the German press and other media as part of the project of denazification. Emigré German intellectuals such as Herbert Marcuse and Franz Neumann had developed basic plans for this effort. The related program of democratization – conforming with the Potsdam Accords – can be traced back to the early social-psychological research conducted by German emigrants such as Kurt Lewin. However, these plans were only partially realized; even those Germans with a clean record resisted attempts to treat an entire people as "a bunch of backward elementary school students," according to a 1948 observation made by Eugen Kogen, a political scientist who had spent time as a concentration camp inmate.[15]

Habe and his colleagues clearly understood these shortcomings. For this reason, the *Neue Zeitung*, which they published in Munich, did

[12] Hartmut Mehringer, Werner Röder, and Dieter Marc Schneider, "Zum Anteil ehemaliger Emigranten am politischen Leben der Bundesrepublik Deutschland, der Deutschen Demokratischen Republik, und der Republik Österreich," in Wolfgang Frühwald and Wolfgang Schieder, eds., *Leben im Exil: Probleme der Integration deutscher Flüchtlinge im Ausland 1933–1945* (Hamburg, 1981), 207–23.

[13] Bernd Greiner, *Die Morgenthau-Legende: Zur Geschichte eines umstrittenen Plans* (Hamburg, 1995).

[14] Michael Schornstheimer, *Bombenstimmung und Katzenjammer. Vergangenheitsbewältigung: Quick und Stern in den 50er Jahren* (Cologne, 1989), 84, 238.

[15] See Jost Hermand, *Kultur im Wiederaufbau: Die Bundesrepublik Deutschland 1945–1965* (Munich, 1985), 90.

not set itself up a mouthpiece of the Americans but rather sought an independent, middle position. The interests of the reader were equally important as the goals of the occupation forces. This principle soon led to serious conflicts. The newspaper drew fire when it did not report on the Nuremberg trials in the expected manner, and the tense situation came to a head in spring 1946 when Habe, the editor-in-chief, declined to place Winston Churchill's Fulton, Missouri, speech on the "iron curtain" on the first page. The strongly anticommunist Habe was less concerned about the contents of the speech than the military authorities' authoritarianism and interference with free speech. He and Heym returned resignedly to the United States. Habe later settled in Switzerland – a destination also chosen by many writers after their remigration – while Heym immigrated to the German Democratic Republic. Despite this break, these cultural officers – who advocated separation of news and commentary on the Anglo-Saxon model – still offered the future German press new standards of reporting, which were carried on by close to fifty trained journalists and editors at the *Neue Zeitung* alone. Among them were Egon Bahr, Hildegard Hamm-Brücher, and Peter Boenisch.[16]

The difficulties that former emigrants experienced working in the service of the Americans were hidden from the German public. The public saw neither their earnest attempts to mediate in conflicts nor what these attempts cost them in personal terms. At the beginning of 1946, Gerhard Colm, once an economist in Kiel, was sent to Germany to prepare for the currency reform. The plan devised by him and the bankers Joseph Dodge and Raymond Goldsmith – the latter a fellow exile from Berlin – would later become famous by its initials as the CDG Plan. It attempted to tie the currency reform to a strict equalization of burdens in order to avoid favoring those who possessed real assets at the expense of those who had savings. Washington officials, however, considered this an unacceptable policy of redistribution. Colm paid for his commitment to German reconstruction with loss of his position as a presidential adviser.[17]

REMIGRATION OF SCHOLARS

University professors returned to Germany later than most political remigrants, more typically arriving from 1948 on. At first, they came only on a temporary basis as guest professors and traveling lecturers because none of them received offers for reinstatement in their old positions. Opportunities for returning to German universities permanently could only come about through the normal selection process when new academic positions became available. Conditions in the countries to which they had fled and the quality of their professional positions inevitably influenced their decisions on returning. After a single lecture tour, for instance, emigrants from Turkey thought the situation in Germany so rosy they accepted offers of academic chairs without hesitation. Their colleagues from America, by contrast, were much more skeptical. The Western Allies' open fondness for the conservative powers in the Christian Democratic Union (CDU) and German nationalism, which had even reached into the ranks of the SPD (a development cited in countless letter exchanges), fed their doubts about whether Germans had truly embraced a democratic new beginning. Torn by contradictory feelings and opinions, they struggled for a long time with the decision to give up newly won positions for an uncertain and sometimes openly hostile climate in postwar Germany. Max Horkheimer was not the only one who finally resolved this inner conflict with the hope that his work for the United States and for peace in Europe would prove much more effective in Germany. Political persecution in the United States during the McCarthy years in turn made the decision easier for others.[18] Many returnees kept their American

---

[16] Marita Biller, *Eine empirische Untersuchung zur Emigration und Remigration deutschsprachiger Journalisten und Publizisten* (Munster, 1994).

[17] Claus-Dieter Krohn, *Intellectuals in Exile: Refugee Scholars and the New School for Social Research* (Amherst, Mass., 1993), 169.

[18] Exchange of letters by Alexander Rüstow with the Rockefeller Foundation, Mar. 6, 1950, Rockefeller Archives, Tarrytown, N.Y., R.G. 1.1/805/1/13;

citizenship as insurance in the event that they wanted to return.

Despite the considerable resistance to their presence and reservations about them, the remigrating professors contributed to the prestige of many scholarly fields and made it possible for the Federal Republic to join the international community of scientists and scholars. This was particularly true for the social sciences, which were reimported by returning scholars as a theoretical foundation in the project of rebuilding Germany democratically.[19] The professionalization of these disciplines had been an achievement of Weimar-era German scholars who were among the first to be driven out by the Nazis. Their work on modern industrial society, totalitarianism, social psychology, and mass culture, which had mostly originated during their time in the United States, also paved the way for a realistic analysis of the recent past. It is no accident that several of these scholars remain among the German authors with the most far-reaching international reputations today.

This recent past was just as rarely the subject of self-conscious, critical debate at the universities as anywhere else in postwar German society. It is true that at some colleges the professors who had been dismissed during the Nazi period and who had not emigrated again received appointments, but they did not necessarily regain their former, more prestigious positions. There were numerous open positions – approximately 20 percent of the teaching body – as a result of the Allies' dismissal of scholars tainted

by Nazi connections. But most universities did not consider taking up contact with former colleagues driven out under the previous regime. Lists of emigrants were occasionally posted under pressure from Allied cultural officers, and discussions about their potential reinstatements also took place at conferences on higher education held in southern and northwestern Germany. However, these proved little more than verbal concessions. In addition, administrative problems complicated matters, first among the military authorities themselves, and then in the German cultural and financial administrations, as educational policy became a German responsibility with the establishment of Bizonia at the beginning of 1947. At this point, higher priority was accorded the professors who had been expelled from the eastern territories and their colleagues who had been stripped of posts after 1945.[20] The Implementing Act for Article 131 of the Basic Law of 1951 thus came as little surprise. It covered reinstatement of those who had been expelled from the East and civil servants dismissed by the occupation administration. The law not only put an official end to denazification, it also guaranteed the continuity of the old Nazi administrative and governing elite in the Federal Republic. Reintegration of the emigrants ceased to be a concern. The law regulating compensation for former civil servants, enacted the same day, did little to change this situation; it only held out some prospect of financial restitution and provisions for those who had lost positions after 1933.[21]

The chance for former emigrants to obtain new university posts depended on individual initiatives launched by committed colleagues and forward-looking cultural officials. As had been the case with political remigrants, the first

---

Adolph Lowe, "Social Research in Europe," Nov. 1948 memorandum, Archives of the New School for Social Research; Max Horkheimer, exchange of letters 1941–1948, from *Gesammelte Schriften*, 19 vols. (Frankfurt am Main, 1996), 17:1002ff.; in addition, see the many letters in the files of the Society for Protection of Science and Learning, Bodleian Library, Oxford.

[19] This has already been indicated by Franz Neumann, *Behemoth: The Structure and Practice of National Socialism* (New York, 1942), 475–6. See also M. Rainer Lepsius, "Die sozialwissenschaftliche Emigration und ihre Folgen," in M. Rainer Lepsius, ed., "Soziologie in Deutschland und Österreich 1918–1945: Materialien zur Entwicklung, Emigration und Wirkungsgeschichte," *Kölner Zeitschrift für Soziologie und Sozialpsychologie*, special issue 23 (1981): 461–500.

[20] Manfred Heinemann, ed., *Nordwestdeutsche Hochschulkonferenzen 1945–1948*, 2 vols. (Hildesheim, 1990); Anikó Szabó, "Verordnete Rückberufungen: Die Hochschulkonferenzen und die Diskussion um die emigrierten Hochschullehrer," in Marlis Buchholz, Claus Füllberg, and Hans-Dieter Schmid, eds., *Nationalsozialimus und Region* (Hannover, 1996), 339–52.

[21] Constantin Goschler, *Wiedergutmachung: Westdeutschland und die Verfolgten des Nationalsozialismus 1945–1954* (Munich, 1992), 234ff.

scholars who returned to Germany smoothed the way for those who followed. This was clearly true for sociologists and political scientists. Their representatives left a distinctive mark on these disciplines, even where they did not completely re-create them; major innovators included the core group of the Frankfurt Institute for Social Research, including Max Horkheimer, Theodor W. Adorno, and Friedrich Pollock, or the founding generation of the revived Hochschule für Politik (College of Political Science) in Berlin, including Ernst Fraenkel, Ossip Flechtheim, and Arkadius Gurland. The sociologist René König, who had returned from Switzerland and became a major figure for scholarship in Cologne, attested that after 1945 his field had become a "sorry remnant," reduced under National Socialism to a meaningless pseudoscience of supposed national characteristics, and that it needed to be completely overhauled.[22]

The return of these scholars was a long, drawn-out process lasting more than a decade. Among political scientists, Arnold Bergstraesser came to Freiburg in 1954, Eric Voegelin to Munich in 1958, and Richard Löwenthal to Berlin from London in 1961. The Otto Suhr Institute of the Free University of Berlin, which had the political science faculty under its roof, held fully ten of the twenty-four chairs for political science in the Federal Republic at this time. Until well into the 1950s, the returnees faced a hostile body of West German university heads, which saw the dictates of the American victor written all over the field of political science; these officials, wedded to a conservative, neohumanist point of view, doubted whether this discipline – seen at best as a "pedagogy for democracy" – could rise to the challenge of becoming an autonomous, rigorous discipline at the university level. It was,

above all, the early returnees in this department field who, through cooperative agreements and a lively exchange of scholars and students with American universities, broke through the resistance of an elite German tradition and helped to put the field of political science in the American sense on solid footing. Almost all the younger social scientists who took over academic chairs in the 1960s had long periods of study and research in the United States behind them; they could finally complete the process begun by the returnees of moving German scholars "out of the backwaters" and into the mainstream of intellectual life. It remains unclear as yet whether this process took place in a similar way in the natural sciences.[23]

Many who returned from exile personified the great innovations made in the social sciences in the 1920s and were shaped politically by the experience of exile. They came to represent a new type of political scholar.[24] They brought to Germany new methods of empirical social research and new theoretical, interdisciplinary, and comparative research approaches from the United States. Their works, conceived in the United States, have long since become classics and were to influence an entire generation in the 1960s. The new epoch marked by the student protest movement would not have been conceivable without the inspiration of that "other Germany."[25]

[22] René König, *Soziologie in Deutschland: Begründer, Verfechter, Verächter* (Munich, 1987), 346.

[23] None of the biologists returned from the United States. See Ute Deichmann, *Biologen Unter Hitler: Vertreibung, Karrieren, Forschung* (Frankfurt am Main, 1992), 51ff.

[24] Alfons Söllner, *Deutsche Politikwissenschaftler in der Emigration: Studien zu ihrer Akkulturation und Wirkungsgeschichte* (Opladen, 1996), 27.

[25] Claus-Dieter Krohn, "Die Entdeckung des 'anderen Deutschland' in der intellektuellen Protestbewegung der 1960er Jahre in der Bundesrepublik und den Vereinigten Staaten," in Claus-Dieter Krohn et al., *Exilforschung: Ein internationales Jahrbuch*, 13: "Kulturtransfer im Exil" (Munich, 1995), 16–51.

CHAPTER FIVE

Immigration and Emigration Before 1968

Dietrich Herrmann

Translated by Richard Sharp

The term "immigration" remains controversial[1] in the Federal Republic of Germany, especially in political discourse. This article uses it in an inclusive sense, encompassing not only foreign "guest workers" (*Gastarbeiter*) but also "displaced persons" (DPs), refugees, ethnic Germans expelled from Eastern Europe during or just after World War II, postwar ethnic German immigrants from the East (*Spätaussiedler*), former residents of the German Democratic Republic (GDR), and workers with temporary contracts in the GDR.

Historical differences between Germany and the United States became readily evident in the two countries' immigration policies in the twenty years following World War II. West Germany's policy reflected the problems arising from the loss of Germany's former eastern territories and the division of the country. The need to integrate refugees from the eastern territories and the GDR meant that the concept of German descent and common culture, laid down in the Imperial Citizenship and Nationality Law (*Reichs- und Staatsangehörigkeitsgesetz*) of 1913 and elsewhere, became fixed as the dominant principle of West German immigration policy. In the United States, universalistic and liberal principles traditionally shaped that policy. In the 1950s and 1960s, the influence of these ideas on migration policy increased, in part because they reflected the political values that the United States had espoused in its ideological confrontation with the fascist and totalitarian states. In part, the socioeconomic and political rise of recent immigrant groups had also created a strong social base advocating these policies.

Common to both countries was a strong commitment to taking in refugees and victims of political persecution. The incorporation of the right to asylum into the Basic Law, West Germany's constitution, was based on a sense of obligation that grew out of the confrontation with the Nazi past. In the United States, a more liberal policy on refugees reflected the earlier failure to help the victims of Hitler's tyranny in Europe; at the same time, it also represented another element of Cold War ideological confrontations. In practice, however, American admission of refugees was often linked to their professional expertise or special skills, and few asylum-seekers entered the Federal Republic before the end of the 1970s. In both countries, refugees from the Soviet-controlled areas received preferential treatment.[2]

---

[1] Klaus J. Bade, "Zuwanderung und Eingliederung in Deutschland seit dem Zweiten Weltkrieg," in Klaus J. Bade, ed., *Fremde im Land: Zuwanderung und Eingliederung im Raum Niedersachsen seit dem Zweiten Weltkrieg* (Osnabrück, 1997), 9–44.

[2] Monika Bethscheider, "Flucht und Migration in der Bundesrepublik Deutschland," in Cornelia Schmalz-Jacobsen and Georg Hansen, eds., *Ethnische Minderheiten in der Bundesrepublik Deutschland: Ein Lexikon* (Munich, 1995), 160; Roger Daniels, *Coming to America: A History*

IMMIGRATION INTO GERMANY

The National Socialist policy of active resettlement, summed up in the slogan "Home to the Reich" (*Heim ins Reich*), resulted in the resettlement of hundreds of thousands of ethnic Germans, mainly from South Tyrol, Galicia, Transylvania, and the Baltic states, during World War II and the expulsion of "ungermanizable" (*nicht eindeutschbarer*) inhabitants of the annexed territories. Between 1939 and 1944, some one million so-called *Volksdeutsche* (ethnic Germans) were resettled, many of them in the annexed areas of Poland; about 1.2 million Poles and Jews were simultaneously driven out of these areas.[3] After the war, the borders that had been set by the Allies led to the flight or expulsion of several million people of German origin from East Prussia, Pomerania, Silesia, and the Sudetenland.

For German authorities, the most pressing task of postwar migration policy was, first of all, simply coping with the practical problems caused by massive numbers of new immigrants. Their efforts can hardly be described as policy in the sense of setting and pursuing longer-term objectives.[4]

By the early 1950s, some eight million refugees and expellees had poured into the Western occupation zones/Federal Republic of Germany (FRG). In the same period, about four million entered the Soviet zone/GDR. Of the more than 10 million former forced laborers and camp prisoners from more than twenty countries held in Germany at the end of the war, some 1.7 million, now reclassified as DPs, remained in the Western occupation zones at the end of 1945. The "repatriation," mostly forced, of DPs from the Soviet Union was halted only in the second half

of 1946 as the East-West conflict became more acute. Various countries in Western Europe and abroad (the United States, Australia, and Canada) took in more than 700,000 DPs beginning in 1947, most of them of Polish, Ukrainian, or Baltic origin. An estimated 150,000 DPs – most of them elderly or ill as a result of having served as forced laborers – remained in West Germany. The German population and the authorities alike viewed them as alien elements and a variety of factors, such as their often long residency in camps after the war and administrative discrimination, prevented their integration into postwar German society.[5]

The Allies made integration of expellees mandatory during the postwar occupation. For instance, expellees were not allowed to form their own political organizations or parties. Most expellees were sent to predominantly agricultural states, and many residents considered the distribution of expellees among the states unfair. Expellees comprised more than 20 percent of the population in Bavaria and Lower Saxony, 33 percent in Schleswig-Holstein, and 42.5 percent in Mecklenburg.[6] When the Federal Republic was founded in 1949, some 8.1 million expellees were living in the western part of Germany, and by 1961 an additional 2.7 million refugees had arrived from the GDR.

Public debate on the problem of integrating expellees took on a different tenor in the Western zones/FRG than in the Soviet zone/GDR. This was the result of a taboo imposed by the Cold War on the subject of "flight and expulsion," the circumstances being reversed in the two cases.

Despite many conflicts, the integration of refugees, former GDR residents, and ethnic German newcomers from Eastern Europe into West German society proceeded swiftly. The occupying powers and the German administration tried to distribute the expellees as efficiently

---

of *Immigration and Ethnicity in American Life* (New York, 1990), 329, 335–7.

[3] Wolfgang Benz, "Fremde in der Heimat: Flucht – Vertreibung – Integration," in Klaus J. Bade, ed., *Deutsche im Ausland, Fremde in Deutschland: Migration in Geschichte und Gegenwart* (Munich, 1992), 375–8.

[4] Bade, ed., *Zuwanderung und Eingliederung*, 14–5.

[5] Wolfgang Jacobmeyer, "Ortlos am Ende des Grauens: 'Displaced Persons' in der Nachkriegszeit," in Bade, ed., *Deutsche im Ausland*, 367–73.

[6] Benz, "Fremde in der Heimat," 382.

as possible, taking into consideration food supplies and the availability of housing and jobs, but
their success was limited on account of the short
period in which the refugees arrived. During
1945–7, housing shortages in particular created
serious conflicts between long-term residents,
refugees, and the authorities, who occasionally
resorted to draconian measures. The occupation
authorities pressed for a rapid resettlement of
refugees in individual housing units, for the alternative – some sort of mass accommodation –
threatened to be politically explosive; moreover,
they did not want to encourage hopes that the
expulsions might not be permanent. Complete
integration was the goal and, for this reason,
the expellees were barred from creating autonomous political organizations during the occupation period.

The *Lastenausgleich* (equalization of burdens)
made an important contribution to the newcomers' economic integration. Refugees were
initially granted financial assistance for integration and later received a graduated compensation package based on the value of property they
had lost. By 1979, DM 113.9 billion had been
distributed in this way, most of it financed by
taxes on private assets.

Election results provide some indication of
the gradual success of the integration process.
The expellee political party BHE (*Block der
Heimatvertriebenen und Entrechteten*) enjoyed significant support during the early 1950s; its best
result was 23.4 percent of the vote in the 1950
Schleswig-Holstein state election. Its support
quickly dwindled, however, and by 1966 the
party was no longer represented in any state
legislature. It only succeeded in sending members to the Bundestag during the 1953–7 legislative period, when it briefly contributed two
ministers to Konrad Adenauer's second cabinet.[7] West German governments of the 1950s

and 1960s always had to keep in mind the
political potential of the deliberately named
Heimatvertriebenen ("the driven-from-home").
At the same time, the expellees were an important weapon in the ideological confrontations
of the Cold War. The West Germans repeatedly criticized the restrictions on foreign travel
by people of German origin imposed in the
countries falling under Soviet influence. Withholding recognition of Poland's western border
and making references to the expellees' right of
domicile became a means of exerting pressure
on Poland and Czechoslovakia but also imposed
constraints on West German Ostpolitik. In
the GDR, where the expellees were described
as resettlers (*Umsiedler*), the Socialist Unity
Party of Germany (*Sozialistische Einheitspartei
Deutschlands*, or SED) rigidly enforced integration and suppressed possible conflicts; in the
early 1950s, integration was officially declared
complete.[8]

Immigration exceeded emigration to other
parts of Western Europe (about 180,000 between 1945 and 1952) and abroad (nearly
800,000 by 1961), but West Germany nonetheless came to experience a labor shortage.
Without taking a hard look at the possible
demographic consequences, the West German
government concluded a labor recruitment
agreement with Italy in 1955 that was later followed by similar agreements with Spain, Greece,
Turkey, Morocco, Portugal, Tunisia, and Yugoslavia. These agreements launched the influx
of foreign *Gastarbeiter* that would continue until a temporary recruitment freeze was imposed
amid the 1973 oil crisis. Employers could recruit workers through a strictly regulated procedure, initially for set periods of time. The
time limit and principle of rotation built into
this kind of employment were gradually abandoned because longer-term arrangements were
in the interests both of employers and employees. Here again, short-term economic considerations took precedence over a more farsighted
immigration policy. Between 1955 and 1973, a
total of some fourteen million foreign workers

---

[7] Ibid., 382–6; Franz J. Bauer, "Aufnahme und
Eingliederung der Flüchtlinge: Das Beispiel Bayern
1945," in Wolfgang Benz, ed., *Die Vertreibung der
Deutschen aus dem Osten: Ursachen, Ereignisse, Fol-
gen* (Frankfurt am Main, 1985), 158–72; Reinhold
Schillinger, "Der Lastenausgleich," in Benz, ed., *Die
Vertreibung der Deutschen*, 183–92.

[8] Bade, "Zuwanderung und Eingliederung," 12–4.

entered the country, of whom eleven million later returned to their countries of origin. By 1973, the number of foreign workers employed in the Federal Republic had reached its absolute peak of nearly 2.6 million, representing almost 10 percent of the total workforce. Altogether 3,966,000 foreigners lived in the Federal Republic and comprised 6.5 percent of the total population. Of this foreign population, 910,500 came from Turkey, 701,600 from Yugoslavia, 630,700 from Italy, 407,600 from Greece, 287,000 from Spain, and 112,000 from Portugal. Most found jobs in manufacturing, which resulted in the creation of a stratum of workers below the native labor force. Foreign workers also served to absorb the impact of economic crises such as the recession of 1966–7, when approximately half of them left the country.[9]

In contrast to expellees, former GDR residents, or postwar ethnic German newcomers from the East, the foreign workers had not been integrated within West German society by the end of the 1960s. The widely used term "guest worker" hardly encouraged either host country or the workers themselves to assume that an unlimited stay with full social integration was on offer. The initially widespread provision of mass dormitory-style accommodations, the high turnover rate and short periods of residence that resulted, and a legal status tied strictly to employment hindered even timid attempts at integration, such as those made by individual trade unions. All political parties rejected the possibility that a large proportion of those who came as "guest workers" might settle permanently in the Federal Republic.[10]

[9] Klaus J. Bade, "Einheimische Ausländer: Gastarbeiter – Dauergäste – Einwanderer," in Bade, ed., *Deutsche im Ausland*, 393–8; see also the tables in Schmalz-Jacobsen and Hansen, eds., *Ethnische Minderheiten*, 558, appendix.
[10] Hedwig Rudolph, "Die Dynamik der Einwanderung im Nichteinwanderungsland Deutschland," in Heinz Fassmann and Rainer Münz, eds., *Migration in Europa: Historische Entwicklung, aktuelle Trends und politische Reaktionen* (Frankfurt am Main, 1996), 161–81; Klaus J. Bade, *Vom Auswanderungsland zum Einwanderungsland? Deutschland 1880–1980* (Berlin, 1983), 67–95.

IMMIGRATION TO THE UNITED STATES

In the period after World War II, American immigration policy underwent radical changes. The ethnicities of the immigrants, their integration into American society, their numbers, as well as the political conditions surrounding immigration policy, underwent rapid changes.

Although immigration numbers had declined during World War II (1941–5: 170,952), they rose again very quickly after the war ended (864,087 in 1946–50, 2,515,479 in 1951–60, and 3,321,677 in 1961–70). This was made possible partly by exemptions from the discriminatory quotas prescribing a maximum number of immigrants from each ethnic group that applied in principle until 1968. A growing number of immigrants did not fall under the existing quotas. The War Brides Act of 1945 permitted entry of some 120,000 members of American soldiers' families. Against the background of the Cold War, nearly 450,000 DPs gained entry between 1948 and 1952, most of them originally from countries and regions occupied by the Soviet Union. In line with the quotas law of 1924, the American authorities allowed immigrants to be selected according to their professional qualifications, even those who were taken in as refugees. This again, however, resulted indirectly in a form of ethnic discrimination.[11]

While the United States had adopted a very restrictive entry policy toward people suffering from Nazi persecution, its Refugee Relief Act of 1953 introduced the first special arrangement made for refugees. Between 1953 and 1956, the United States accepted more than 200,000 refugees and victims of persecution from communist states. Although European refugees received ongoing preferential treatment, this law allowed in 5,000 Asian refugees. The influence of the Cold War resonated in the special arrangements made later for refugees from Hungary and Cuba. Between 1962 and 1979, nearly

[11] Daniels, *Coming to America*, 288; Thomas J. Archdeacon, *Becoming American: An Ethnic History* (New York, 1983), 180–1; Reed Ueda, *Postwar Immigrant America: A Social History* (Boston, 1994), 36–7.

700,000 Cubans immigrated to the United States, representing about 30 percent of all the refugees admitted between 1945 and 1980. And, finally, close relatives of U.S. citizens were not subject to the quota system.[12]

The McCarran-Walter Act of 1952 for the first time codified in a single instrument the rules on immigration and naturalization that had previously been scattered through a mass of individual acts. It confirmed the principle of a quota system based on national origin, as introduced by the National Origins Act of 1924, and also reaffirmed the clear preference given migrants from Western and Northern Europe. The ban on naturalization for Asians was repealed in full. (It had already been lifted for Chinese in 1943 and for Filipinos and Indians in 1946.) The McCarran-Walter Act imposed minimum national immigration quotas for those Asian countries from which no immigration had been permitted since 1924. This shift represented an attempt by Congress, in the ideological context of the Cold War, to take the sting out of the accusation that the ban on immigration was racially motivated. President Harry S. Truman justified his veto of the act, later overridden, by citing his preference for Northern and Western Europeans.[13]

In 1965, after further prodding by Presidents Eisenhower, Kennedy, and Johnson, Congress approved the Immigration Reform Act, which replaced the national quotas with an alternative preference system, but without significantly increasing the total number of visas granted (eastern hemisphere 170,000, western hemisphere 120,000, with a maximum of 20,000 for any one country of origin). While the McCarran-Walter Act had given special preference to highly qualified, educated immigrants, the criterion of close kinship to an American citizen has had priority since 1965. (Other favored criteria include professional qualifications and kinship with foreigners permanently residing in the United States.) Six percent of entry visas were reserved

for refugees. Several factors combined to assist passage of the bill. First was the conviction that the United States, as the leading power in the democratic world, could not continue to maintain an immigration policy based on ethnic discrimination. The altered composition of Congress and its committees also influenced the decision, along with the increased power base of those ethnic groups (Italians, Greeks, and Poles) that, along with Asians, had in the past experienced the greatest disadvantages under the reigning "national origins" principle. Finally, supporters and opponents of the bill alike expected that in practice the origin of future immigrants would hardly change; in other words, they expected that the majority would continue to be from Europe. This expectation proved unfounded in subsequent years, as immigration from Asia and Latin America expanded enormously.[14]

Immigration from Latin America, and especially from Mexico, rose steadily after World War II, in part through the officially sanctioned Bracero Program, which allowed Mexican farm laborers into the country for a limited period, and in part by an increase in the number of illegal immigrants. "Operation Wetback," the attempt by the U.S. federal government to halt illegal immigration from Mexico by deporting 3.8 million Mexicans between 1950 and 1955, entailed frequent human-rights violations. By the end of 1967, 4.7 million Mexicans had entered the country under the terms of the Bracero Program; the end of the program that same year resulted in a further increase in illegal immigration.[15]

Progress in the integration of immigrants is suggested by the drop in the portion of foreign-born Americans in the total population between

---

[12] Daniels, *Coming to America*, 335–7; Ueda, *Postwar Immigrant America*, 49–52.

[13] Daniels, *Coming to America*, 332–3; Ueda, *Postwar Immigrant America*, 43–4.

[14] David M. Reimers, "An Unintended Reform: The 1965 Immigration Act and Third World Immigration to the United States," *Journal of American Ethnic History* 3 (1983): 9–28; David M. Reimers, *Still the Golden Door: The Third World Comes to America* (New York, 1985), 61–76; Edward M. Kennedy, "The Immigration Act of 1965," *Annals of the American Academy of Political and Social Science* 367 (1966): 137–49.

[15] Daniels, *Coming to America*, 312; Ueda, *Postwar Immigrant America*, 34.

1950 (6.9 percent) and 1970 (4.7 percent) that resulted from restrictive entry policies. At the same time, the proportion of mixed marriages, across religious as well as national boundaries, increased markedly. By the end of the 1960s, immigrants of Eastern and Southern European origin, regarded as unassimilable at the start of the century, had become socially, economically, and politically integrated with older immigrant groups.[16]

GERMAN IMMIGRATION INTO THE UNITED STATES

German emigration to other Western European and overseas countries began again immediately after the war, and all host countries made a concerted effort to attract people with skills. By 1948, the United States had succeeded in recruiting more than 500 highly trained specialists and scientists to come live in America through "Operation Paperclip."[17] German authorities, by contrast, attempted to control and restrict emigration out of Germany – and not just that of highly skilled personnel – fearing a drain on human resources after the war. The Allied occupation authorities in Germany similarly worked to strictly control emigration.[18]

The number of German immigrants arriving in the United States rose from an official figure of 2,598 in 1946 to a peak of 128,592 in 1950, but then dropped sharply (to 29,452 in 1960, 10,632 in 1970, for a total of 888,475 from 1945 through 1970). Although the yearly quota for immigrants from Germany was just over 25,000, the other Germans entered the country as relatives of residents or DPs.[19]

As Europe experienced an economic upturn, emigration from Germany to the United States slowed significantly. The new arrivals were generally quick to integrate, linguistically and culturally as well as economically and socially. Unlike earlier immigrants and other recent arrivals from other lands, these German Americans had no strong organizational structures tying them together. Paradoxically, though, as the significance of the German-American organizations dwindled, the German Americans' identification with Germany as the country of their ancestors grew stronger, to the point where it is now greater than that of any other national or ethnic group. The number of people claiming German ancestry in 1980 (49.2 million) was about equal to the number claiming English (49.6 million). By 1990, however, when a survey question about these ties was worded slightly differently, the corresponding figures were nearly 58 million Americans with German ancestry as compared with 39 million Irish and 33 million British.[20]

Kathleen Neils Conzen's 1980 assessment captures the trends at work here well:

> By the last third of the 20th century, the end of immigration, the shock of the two world wars, and high loss of ethnic self-identification, encouraged by diverse occupational paths, movement away from German neighborhoods, and frequent intermarriage, made the United States' largest immigrant group one of its least distinctive.[21]

COMPARATIVE ASPECTS

Migration policies and patterns developed in Germany and the United States in the twenty-five years after World War II that were shaped by the two nation's histories and hardly comparable. The aftereffects of the war, the division

---

[16] Daniels, *Coming to America*, 404; Ueda, *Postwar Immigrant America*, 83–111.

[17] See the chapter by Michael Neufeld, vol. 1, Security.

[18] Daniels, *Coming to America*, 331; Johannes-Dieter Steinert, "Drehscheibe Westdeutschland: Wanderungspolitik im Nachkriegsjahrzehnt," in Bade, ed., *Deutsche im Ausland*, 386–92.

[19] U.S. Department of Commerce, Bureau of the Census, *Historical Statistics from Colonial Times to 1970* (Washington, D.C., 1975), 105–6.

[20] Ueda, *Postwar Immigrant America*, 104–5; U.S. Department of Commerce, Bureau of the Census, *Statistical Abstract of the United States* (Washington, D.C., 1996), 53, table 56.

[21] Kathleen Neils Conzen, "Germans," in Stephen Thernstrom, Ann Orlov, and Oscar Handlin, eds., *Harvard Encyclopedia of American Ethnic Groups* (Cambridge, Mass., 1980), 423.

of Germany, and the huge numbers of expellees and newcomers from the GDR and Eastern Europe exerted a powerful influence on the situation in the Federal Republic. In the United States, by contrast, carefully regulated immigration had begun immediately after the war at a much higher level than before. Some provisions of U.S. immigration policy, above all the admission of DPs, were possible only in the context of the Cold War.

Until the 1970s, no collaboration existed between the Federal Republic and United States on immigration policy aside from technical coordination of the emigration of Germans to North America. The way in which the two countries viewed their respective situations was too different, and the climate of public debate also precluded such an exchange. In the United States, the debate over the need to restrict the numbers of immigrants and how to integrate those who came dated back to the turn of the last century.[22] By contrast, the Federal Republic had never seen itself as a society of immigrants; public debates on the aims and methods of migration policy thus seemed unnecessary. Although the problems created by the "guest workers" in the Federal Republic and the *braceros* in the United States certainly seemed similar, neither in this area nor in policy on political refugees and asylum-seekers did any substantive exchange of experiences between Germany and America occur before the end of the 1970s.[23]

---

[22] Dietrich Hermann, *"Be an American!" Amerikanisierungsbewegung und Theorien zur Einwandererintegration* (Frankfurt am Main, 1996), chap. 1.

[23] Until very recently, American studies in Germany did not systematically address the problem of integration of immigrants into American society but mainly concentrated – both during the period under review and thereafter – on German emigration to the United States. See also the chapter by Willi Paul Adams, vol. 2, Culture.

CHAPTER SIX

The German Churches and the Specter of Americanization

Mark E. Ruff

When National Socialist rule collapsed in May 1945, many Germans thought the "hour of the churches" was upon them. Almost alone among German institutions, the churches emerged from twelve years of Nazi rule with their moral authority strengthened for having spoken out against Nazi injustice at home and abroad. Protestants and Catholics alike sought to recast German society to conform to Christian principles. They spoke of the need to rebuild the Christian West and to roll back the tide of bolshevism and secularism sweeping across Europe. Most importantly, they saw themselves as spokesmen for the defeated German nation at a time when other native political and social institutions had ceased to exist. As one historian described the situation, "In the beginning were the churches – and no state."[1]

For these reasons, the American military government sought to enlist the churches in its efforts to reconfigure German institutions and society along democratic lines. It rapidly initiated contact with both churches and soon extended privileges to church leaders still unavailable to other institutions and individuals in Germany. Yet, within months, relations between the churches and the American and British occupiers had soured.[2] The churches rejected – publicly as well as privately – not just specific occupation policies but also values, traditions, and ideas they associated with the Americans. Despite wide areas of agreement between the Americans and the churches, such criticism remained a mainstay of church teachings and policy for the better part of the 1950s, long after the period of occupation had ended.

At the heart of this sometimes tumultuous relationship lay the churches' peculiar self-understanding, which had emerged in response to challenges posed by National Socialist rule but had roots predating the year 1933. Just as in the Weimar era, the churches saw themselves as warriors in a colossal ideological struggle that pitted the German national cause against the forces of materialism, liberalism, bolshevism, nihilism, and secularism. They argued that the liberal policies espoused by the Americans – democratization, decartelization, and reeducation[3] – could lead only to chaos.[4]

This article traces how the churches' own sense of self shaped their response to the Americans in Germany from 1945 to the late 1960s. I argue that the often hard-line positions taken by the churches in the immediate postwar years

---

[1] Martin Greschat, *Protestanten in der Zeit: Kirche und Gesellschaft in Deutschland vom Kaiserreich bis zur Gegenwart* (Stuttgart, 1994), 180.

[2] Frederic Spotts, *The Churches and Politics in Germany* (Middletown, Mass., 1973).

[3] See the chapters by Barbara Fait, vol. 1, Politics; Regina Gramer, vol. 1, Economics; James F. Tent, vol. 1, Culture.

[4] On the churches and materialism, see Maria Mitchell, "Materialism and Secularism: CDU Politicians and National Socialism, 1945–1949," *Journal of Modern History* 67 (1995): 278–308.

vis-à-vis the Americans led others in the subsequent decades to call the authority of the churches into question. As a result, the self-understanding of both churches began to unravel by the 1960s. To recount the history of both Protestant and Catholic churches over a span of more than twenty years, finally, necessitates simplification. Both churches were far from monolithic entities. The Evangelische Kirche in Deutschland (EKD) first came into existence in 1945 as a confederation of traditional regional churches (*Landeskirchen*) and schismatic movements that had arisen during the 1930s.[5] Even the Catholic Church, though relatively homogeneous, was home to diverse lay movements and organizations – "the church" certainly did not always speak with one voice.[6]

As they have in other areas of German society, historians and contemporaries have wrestled with the question of whether the year 1945 heralded a "new beginning" for both churches or merely restored old values and ideas. Twelve years of National Socialist rule reconfigured but did not fundamentally alter basic preconceptions and tenets held dear by both Christian churches prior to 1933. Indeed, the Nazi years actually strengthened their critique of materialism, secularism, and liberalism, which dated back to the nineteenth century. The Catholic bishops (and many Protestants as well) remained convinced that these forces in modern society had so sapped the vitality of the German people that a collapse of some sort had been largely inevitable. According to this interpretation, Nazism and the destruction brought by the war were the punishment for having fallen away from God.

At the same time, both churches declared themselves victors in the so-called church struggle (*Kirchenkampf*) of the 1930s. As Cardinal Frings of Cologne triumphantly declared in October 1946, "The Catholic Church proved to

be the strongest bulwark against the National Socialist ideology."[7] The Protestant Church, by contrast, acknowledged – albeit begrudingly – in the Stuttgart Declaration of Guilt its own responsibility in the spread and triumph of Nazism.[8] Yet, even the Protestants could use the experiences of the *Kirchenkampf* – evidence in their eyes of their "resistance" to Nazism – to elevate themselves in the moral conscience of the German nation. As Bishop Wurm put it in a letter to the Americans, "the church also has the duty to stand up for truth and justice, wherever these may be violated."[9]

As a result, both churches could present themselves with some legitimacy as defenders of the national cause while avoiding the stigma of National Socialism. Albert Stohr, Bishop of Mainz, declared proudly in June 1945, a mere one month following unconditional surrender:

> For us Catholics, the love of the fatherland is certainly more than a simple natural feeling for the nation. It is, for us, a special way of strengthening the will, whose goal is the community of blood and conscience of all German brothers and sisters that God himself desires.... After religion, the German fatherland is, for me, the highest (goal), and I am also, as a result, prepared to sacrifice all of my personal interests to it.[10]

For Stohr, the German nation had not been liberated by the Allies; it had been overrun by foreign powers.

Men like Stohr harbored bitter memories of German defeat in 1918. These included those conservatives who were to give the Americans and British such trouble – von Galen of Münster, Michael Faulhaber of München, Conrad Gröber of Freiburg – all fervent nationalists but also, for the most part, ardent opponents of National Socialism. By contrast, thousands

---

[5] Karl Herbert, *Kirche zwischen Aufbruch und Tradition: Entscheidungsjahre nach 1945* (Stuttgart, 1989). See also Gerhard Besier, Jörg Thierfelder, and Ralf Tyra, *Kirche nach der Kapitulation*, vol. 1: *Die Allianz zwischen Genf, Stuttgart und Bethel* (Stuttgart, 1989).

[6] See Ulrich von Hehl and Heinz Hürten, *Der Katholizismus in der Bundesrepublik Deutschland 1945–1980: Eine Bibliographie* (Mainz, 1983).

[7] Wolfgang Löhr, ed., *Dokumente Deutscher Bischöfe*, vol. 1: *Hirtenbriefe und Ansprachen zu Gesellschaft und Politik 1945–1949* (Würzburg, 1985), 125.

[8] The Catholic Bishops made a more limited statement of guilt on Aug. 23, 1945. See Ludwig Volk, *Akten deutscher Bischöfe* (Mainz, 1985), 6:689.

[9] Clemens Vollnhals, *Entnazifizierung und Selbstreinigung im Urteil der evangelischen Kirche: Dokumente und Reflexionen 1945–1949* (Munich, 1989), 38.

[10] Löhr, *Dokumente*, 33.

of Protestant clergy had joined the Nazi party or lent support to the German Christian movement during the 1930s. Many pastors had been schooled in the monarchical "National Protestant" tradition. Even Martin Niemöller, jailed in 1937 and later sent to Dachau for denouncing state attacks on the church, petitioned party leaders upon the outbreak of war in 1939 to allow him to return to his position as a U-boat leader.

In 1945, the military government began to extend to the churches travel and publishing rights that went well beyond those granted to other German institutions. The initial goodwill quickly wore off. Some officials within the military government regarded the churches as reactionary and even subversive, attitudes that naturally vexed German church leaders. Other military officials were put off by the strident antibolshevism of church leaders from both denominations. As Marshall Knappen, leader of the Religious Affairs Branch, was to comment, "Our encounters with Bishop Wurm and others of his type left us almost belligerently determined to find a basis of cooperation with the Russians and so make a success of quadripartite occupation."[11]

In light of these preconceptions, it is not at all surprising that relations took a decisive turn for the worse once the Americans began to bring war criminals to justice and push through policies on denazification.[12] Like almost all groups in German society, the clergy reacted strongly to accusations of collective guilt. The Americans had hung posters bearing pictures of heaps of bodies from concentration camps that bore the inscription, "You did it." Denazification and even war-crimes trials, the bishops argued, had to be decided on a case-by-case basis; punishment had to be restricted to those who were truly guilty. Yet, the sincerity of the bishops on this point can easily be called into question. In sundry letters to Allied officials, Wurm and Neuhäusler, the Auxiliary Bishop of Munich-Freising, urged American officials

to grant clemency to convicted war criminals, including leaders of SS troops responsible for the deaths of millions of Jews in Eastern Europe and SS leaders who had carried out a massacre of American POWs near the Belgian town of Malmedy.[13] As some contemporaries remarked, if these men were not guilty, then who was? Faulhaber and Meiser justified their position in a joint letter to the Americans: "Nothing could be further from our minds than to withhold punishment from those who are truly guilty, whereby, however, it is privilege of the church and its godly task to appeal for mercy even for criminals." Wurm, as EKD council chairman, pushed his critique one step further and declared denazification and war-crimes proceedings null and void: "The church cannot recognize that a human authority attempts to punish what can be judged a wrong by God's authority alone."[14]

Why did the churches seek to obstruct denazification in its entirety? In the case of the EKD, one explanation is that denazification threatened to deplete its clergy because many had been compromised by pro-Nazi behavior. Some of the Landeskirchen (as in Hessen-Nassau) did carry through denazification programs in earnest, but these remained the exception. However, this argument cannot explain the attitude of the Catholic Church, which quickly took disciplinary measures against those few clergy and brothers who had voluntarily joined the Nazi party. Both churches seem to have feared the political consequences of a thorough denazification of German society. They recognized that removing former Nazis from their positions in government, industry, and politics would have left former communists and socialists at the helm. The Americans did not fail to notice this anxiety. One official noted that the Catholic organizations had "a pathological fear of anything smacking of Socialism."[15]

---

[11] Spotts, *Churches and Politics in Germany*, 79.
[12] See the chapter by Cornelia Rauh-Kühne, vol. 1, Politics.

[13] Frank M. Buscher, *The U.S. War Crimes Trial Program in Germany* (New York, 1989).
[14] Vollnhals, *Entnazifizierung und Selbstreinigung*, 118.
[15] German Youth Between Yesterday and Tomorrow, Apr. 30, 1948, National Archives (hereafter NA), Record Group (hereafter RG) 287, 12.

Both churches tended to see themselves, and the German nation, as the ultimate victims of the war and of National Socialism. The bishops tended to see the hardships of the occupation – hunger, ruin, scarcity, the expulsion of Germans from the East – as sufficient atonement for the sins of the past. Pastoral statements from the occupation years show a marked lack of interest and sympathy for the sufferings of the other victims of the Nazi years – Jews, gypsies, communists, homosexuals. Instead, many bishops felt called upon to defend the fatherland and all Germans, even former National Socialists and former perpetrators, in its hour of need. Bishop Wurm, in a revealing interview with the American publication *The Christian Century*, commented on the internment in Schwäbisch Hall of the alleged perpetrators of the Malmedy massacre: "Never will the people of Schwäbisch Hall, who in the nights heard the cries of pain of the tortured beyond the prison walls, be made to believe that these investigators were servants of justice and not of revenge."[16]

The issue of rearmament put the relations between the churches and the Americans back on a more even keel by more or less uniting both against the common communist enemy. However, rearmament also exposed rifts both within and between the two churches and, as a result, forced religious leaders to decide how to align Germany within the emerging Cold War.[17] A Protestant member of Chancellor Konrad Adenauer's cabinet, Gustav Heinemann, and his ally, Martin Niemöller, waged an extensive campaign within the EKD to turn popular opinion against rearmament. Although Heinemann and Niemöller were able to muster considerable support within the EKD (and alarm American officials) early in 1950, by the end of the year, opinion within the EKD had turned decisively against them. As one American intelligence report observed, "while some of Niemoeller's ideas may not be as absurd or unsound as

generally believed and might even be capable of being developed into powerful instruments of persuasion if propagated and presented by an accomplished demagogue and clear thinker, they will never amount to much if confined to Niemoeller's rather confused and unimpressive oratory."[18] The Catholic Church, by contrast, was able to drum up solid – though by no means unanimous – support for rearmament.

In supporting rearmament, the Catholic Church was put in the awkward position of having to defend itself against the charge that it was encouraging a revival of militarism. Prominent Catholics defended the church against this charge by putting rearmament in the context of the larger unity of Europe. Josef Gockeln, head of the Catholic Labor Movement (*Katholische Arbeiterbewegung*, or KAB), maintained that the churches had the duty to think not only of their people but also of the larger Christian order in Europe. Josef Rommerskirchen, the head of the German Catholic Youth League (*Bund der deutschen katholischen Jugend*, or BDKJ), drew upon the notion of totalitarianism, which equated Nazism and bolshevism. He argued that rearmament provided the means to instill values of "civil courage and freedom" within German youth so long as the army posed no threat to the democratic state.[19] Catholic youth could thus serve as a "bulwark against Bolshevik totalitarianism." Catholic leaders understood the consequences of these actions, however: Integrating West German troops into a Western European defense scheme meant foregoing the unification of the Eastern and Western zones of Germany.

These positions raised the ire of leading voices within the Protestant Church. Heinemann, in particular, described the emerging East-West conflict as a civil war likely to destroy the German nation forever. Adenauer's policies made German unification all but impossible, the "zonal boundary which tears our

---

[16] Buscher, *U.S. War Crimes Trial in Germany*, 100.

[17] Johanna Vogel, *Kirche und Wiederbewaffnung: Die Haltung der Evangelischen Kirche in Deutschland in den Auseinandersetzungen um die Wiederbewaffnung der Bundesrepublik 1949–1956* (Göttingen, 1978).

[18] Interview with Pastor Martin Niemoeller, June 10, 1952, NA, RG 59, box 3867, Dec. file 1950–4, 762a.00/4–152–5–3052.

[19] Anselm Doering-Manteuffel, *Katholizismus und Wiederbewaffnung: Die Haltung der deutschen Katholiken gegenüber der Wehrfrage 1948–1955* (Mainz, 1981).

nation apart" also tore at the very fabric of the German soul. In rhetoric reminiscent of Weimar nationalism, Protestant leaders issued scarcely veiled threats to the Western powers: "All exhortations to think in a peaceful frame of mind will fall short as a result of the passionate desire of an entire people to regain its destroyed community. Europe will not find peace in this manner."[20] Further, Protestants no longer commanded a decisive majority within parliament, and Niemöller, like many others, complained vociferously about the newly found parity between Catholics and Protestants within the Federal Republic. Rearmament also brought to light the clashing national visions of the two churches: a reunified, largely Protestant German state along the Prussian model, neutral in the East-West conflict, or a unified West German state, fully integrated within the Christian West.

By the late 1950s, these issues had faded into the background. Fears of an "Americanization" of German society, however, lingered, in part because of the continued presence of hundreds of thousands of American troops on German soil.[21] Unlike the French and British occupations, the American soldiers left a permanent mark on German society. To meet the military demands of the Cold War, the Americans built new bases (often in rural regions of the Eifel or in Bavaria), expanded cities, and, in turn, offered employment to thousands of German civilians. At the same time, the Americans fundamentally changed the social landscape of the cities and small villages they entered. Off-duty GIs flocked to newly established bars, which, as is to be expected, soon attracted scores of young "Fräuleins" looking for love, sex, adventure, and, in many cases, hard-earned American dollars.[22] German observers were quick to note the bustling atmosphere and frantic tempo of work (Arbeitswut) that reminded them of scenes of the Wild West.[23]

The reaction of local clergy to the American presence mirrored the ambivalent response toward the "modernization" of German society as a whole. Many clergy sadly noted that "the city had come to the village." Of course, many villages far removed from the actual physical presence of the Americans were undergoing a similar process of transformation. But it was those regions closest to the Americans – "occupation-endangered areas" ("besatzungsgefährdete Gebiete") as they came to be known – that attracted most critical attention. A Protestant pastor from Kaiserslautern saw the American tailfin cars, American street signs, and women with makeup, and concluded that his hometown had become an American city. Local clergy responded differently to the Americans. One military official in Hessen associated with the German Youth Activities Program noted that whenever black soldiers appeared to supervise events, the local Catholic children quickly vanished. Catholic youth leaders were quick to accept donations of money and equipment (e.g., tents, musical instruments) but refused to revamp youth work along the lines recommended by the Religious Affairs Branch of the American military government. The Americans called for more individualistic and democratic forms of youth work – clubs, hobbies, jazz dancing, elections of officers – whereas German youth leaders hoped to retain the contours of the "free youth movement" from the 1920s. Many German clergy, similarly, continued to condemn American mass culture – films, comic books, rock 'n' roll – and passed laws to restrict their spread to youth.

But, by the late 1950s and early 1960s, this picture began to change. Faced with mounting pressure from within their own ranks (many youth wore makeup or listened to jazz regardless of clergy dictates), Catholic leaders began to open their doors to American mass culture. A young priest in Cologne hung up posters asking, "Is the church against rock 'n' roll?" and invited local youth to come dance at a local parish

[20] Vogel, Kirche und Wiederbewaffnung, 112–13.
[21] See the chapter by Axel Schildt in this section.
[22] See the chapter by Petra Goedde in this section.
[23] Maria Höhn, "GIs, Veronika and Lucky Strikes: German Reaction to the American Military in the

Rhineland-Palatinate During the 1950s" (Ph.D. diss., University of Pennsylvania, 1995).

hall. The event brought in throngs of youth and immortalized the chaplain as the *Tanzkaplan*.[24] Even conservative religious leaders began to embrace the notions of individualism and materialism as a weapon with which to attack socialist institutions in the East. On a much larger scale, the Second Vatican Council of 1962–5, in which members of the German episcopate played a central role, set a new tone. It recast the relationship between the church and the modern world in the form of a dialogue instead of condemnation.[25]

The German-American partnership, moreover, began to reap the rewards from exchange programs that the occupational authorities and the churches themselves had put in place in the late 1940s. The German-American relationship after 1945 was shaped not just by individuals in the highest positions of power and authority within the churches and the American government but ultimately by those students and young people who had benefited from trips across the Atlantic. Already in 1946 and 1947, many American churches – particularly those, like the Lutheran Church Missouri Synod, whose members tended to be of German descent – set up relief programs and distributed food and clothing to the German population. Much of this assistance was delivered by American relief workers, who spent anywhere from several weeks to several years in Germany organizing and distributing these shipments. These programs, naturally, fostered much goodwill between the two nations.

More significant, however, were the many exchange programs set up by the National Catholic Welfare Conference (NCWC). Catholics in America invited young German Catholics to meet their leaders and spend time in homes, schools, and universities for stays of up to a year. According to one follow-up report by the NCWC in 1951, many German participants came to the United States skeptical of American culture. Most, however, returned with glowing praise for Catholic institutions in the United States and, more generally, for the American way of life. Although some participants noted that the Catholic Church in America lagged behind its German counterpart in the "philosophical and scholarly treatment of religious problems," others marveled at the vitality of American Catholic institutions. These young men and women saw American priests not as the distant and aloof authority figures they had known back home but as friends and comrades who played basketball and football with the kids. As one German participant on an exchange program between 1949 and 1951 noted, "It is easier to see the Pope himself than a German bishop." On returning to Germany, the participants were encouraged to make presentations to German audiences about their time spent in America. Although the response there to their travelogues was often skeptical, the organizers of the program were more than satisfied with the results. "Yet, I am inclined to think that many listeners were stimulated to think over what they had heard, and gather information about conditions in America, whereas previously they had a totally one-sided (and unfavorable) view."[26] As the number of exchange programs grew during the 1950s and 1960s, young persons returned to Germany with many ideas for the reform and renewal of their native institutions.

Yet, by the late 1960s, the hard-line stances many religious leaders had taken often spelled consequences for their institutions. By using their bully pulpit so strongly in the immediate postwar years on such questions as denazification and rearmament, they set the stage for an equally vitriolic public reexamination of the image they had fashioned for themselves. For the first time, the church's conduct during

---

[24] "Rock 'n Roll ist prima," sagte der Kaplan, n. d., Historisches Archiv des Erzbistums Köln, Gen 23.11, 10.

[25] Franz-Xaver Kaufmann and Arnold Zingerle, eds., *Vatikanum und Modernisierung* (Paderborn, 1996).

[26] German Catholics See America: An Evaluation of the Experiences of 82 Germans Who Visited the United States at the Invitation of the Department of State during the years 1949–51, and Who Were Sponsored during Their Stay in America by the National Catholic Welfare Conference, National Catholic Welfare Conference, box 29, Education: Educational Institutions, Catholic University Archives, Washington, D.C.

the Third Reich was publicly called into question by playwrights, Catholic intellectuals, and students. Some attacked the church's support for the Concordat of 1933; others derided the self-isolation, the *Ghettohaltung*, they believed lay at the heart of Catholic society; and still others denounced both churches as authoritarian and intolerant. Many participants in exchange programs during the 1960s were party to the mounting criticism of authority during the Vietnam era and returned home determined to apply it to their own society.

Religious leaders in the immediate postwar era sought integration in the West – democracy, capitalism, the social market economy – while rejecting its wider societal implications – materialism, individualism, and liberalism. They remained nationalists at heart but, with the exception of Niemöller and other Protestants,

wedded themselves to the West European and American security, economic, and political systems. They supported the "modernization" of the German economy while pushing through an agenda of social conservatism. By the 1960s, as prosperity helped produce the very materialism they condemned and as younger Germans looked askance at the nationalism that, to them, the churches embodied, religious leaders experienced a serious crisis of identity. The relationship with America – as seen in the reaction to policies of the military government, to rearmament, and to American mass culture – underscores the larger transformation that took place within religious institutions: They staked their identity on an opposition to much of what the Americans stood for but, by the 1960s, were forced to open the door to the ideals and visions of the modern world embodied by the Americans.

CHAPTER SEVEN

From Negation to First Dialogues

American Jewry and Germany in the First Postwar Decades

Shlomo Shafir

The American Jewish community, one of the most faithful supporters of the administration of Franklin D. Roosevelt, failed in its efforts for refuge and rescue of fellow Jews before and after the United States entered World War II. Although in the late 1930s it contributed, together with other segments of society, to shifting American public opinion from isolationism to face the Nazi German threat, it had no influence on the making of wartime policies and did not carry much weight in the government's handling of defeated Germany. Because of the Third Reich's persecution of the Jews, which culminated in the wartime murder of millions, American Jewry became consistently anti-German and remained so long after the internal American discussion about the postwar German settlement had been decided in favor of West Germany's economic reconstruction and its inclusion in the Western community. In the confrontation between the supporters of a soft and a hard peace, most American Jews preferred the latter, though the organized community refrained from taking a stand on the harsh anti-German recommendations of Secretary of the Treasury Henry Morgenthau Jr., the only Jew in Roosevelt's close circle who was deeply affected by the Holocaust.[1]

Jewish demands with regard to Germany prior to its expected defeat spelled out severe punishment of German leaders and Nazi officials who had committed crimes against the Jewish people, not only during the war but since Hitler's ascent to power. They called for far-reaching denazification and democratization of German society, eradication of anti-Semitism, restitution of property and compensation for losses suffered by Jewish communities, and indemnification of Jewish victims. These demands were repeated when the war in Europe ended.[2] The five major Jewish cooperating organizations soon became involved in the first steps taken by the Office of the Military Government of the United States (OMGUS) to return confiscated property and indemnify survivors. After restitution of identifiable property had been imposed in 1947 by Military Law 59, the military government pressed the nascent German federal states (*Länder*) to conclude their legislation for individual indemnification, which eventually was enacted under the General Claims Law in 1949. The Jewish Restitution Successor Organization (JRSO), which dealt with restitution issues in

---

[1] Henry L. Feingold, *Bearing Witness: How America and Its Jews Responded to the Holocaust* (Syracuse, N.Y., 1995); Shlomo Shafir, *Ambiguous Relations: The American Jewish Community and Germany Since 1945* (Detroit, 1999), chaps. 1–2.

[2] American Jewish Committee, *To the Counsellors of Peace: Recommendations of the American Jewish Committee* (New York, 1945), 1–9, 101–8; memorandum of the American Jewish Conference to Secretary of State Edward R. Stettinius Jr., Apr. 2, 1945, Central Zionist Archives, Jerusalem, Israel Goldstein papers, A364/1956; statement by the World Jewish Congress (hereafter WJC) on a peace settlement with Germany, *Congress Weekly*, Mar. 21, 1947, 14–15.

the American zone of occupation, was set up in 1948. However, all these issues were overshadowed by American Jewry's concern with the fate and security of the camp survivors and the growing number of refugees from Eastern Europe who filled the displaced persons (DPs) camps in the American zone, mainly in Bavaria. The advisers on Jewish affairs to the American commander-in-chief were of great importance in this context. The small reviving German-Jewish communities received much less attention from Jews abroad, some of whom regarded their reestablishment on German soil as ambiguous. However, their importance was to grow in the eyes of the West German government, which hoped that its official philo-Semitic policy would improve its image in Western public opinion.[3]

MODERATES AND RESOLUTE OPPONENTS

Despite the Jewish consensus on restitution and indemnification, denazification, and punishment of Nazi perpetrators, significant differences of opinion soon cropped up among Jewish groups. The elitist American Jewish Committee (AJC), which generally enjoyed the best contacts with the administration, argued that an active Jewish involvement in liberal democratic reform in Germany served both American national interests and the status of the Jewish community in American society. The AJC insisted that anti-Semitism had not disappeared despite the total defeat of the Nazi state and that the democratic reeducation of the German people was a precondition for successfully fighting it. Moreover, reshaping Germany's political culture was seen as an essential guarantee against a renewal of the German threat after two world wars. Particularly at a time when Western Germany was emerging as an ally of the United States in its confrontation with the Soviet Union, the AJC was also concerned that any

organized opposition by American Jews against the new foreign and security policy could isolate them in the eyes of the non-Jewish majority. This concern was heightened by the hostile rhetoric of right-wing politicians, who often alluded to the prominent part of Jews in the Communist Party and among its fellow travelers before and during the war. Thus, although in principle the AJC preferred a united Germany, its president Joseph M. Proskauer was the first Jewish leader to endorse, in fall 1948, the creation of a separate West German state.[4] In May 1951, two years after the establishment of the Federal Republic of Germany, the AJC called a democratic Germany "the best safeguard against the threat of Communism today and neo-Nazism in the future."[5]

During the early debate in 1950 on German participation in the defense of the West, the Citizens Council for a Democratic Germany, sponsored by the National Jewish Community Relations Advisory Council, publicly opposed as premature all plans for German rearmament. However, an AJC subcommittee recommended acceptance of a West German military contribution on the condition that German units not be placed under German command but form a part of an international Western European or United Nations army.[6] Later, the AJC, although recognizing American Jewish anxiety about German rearmament, alerted Jewish communal agencies against engaging in joint activities with communist groups. But the AJC's tough anticommunist stand became highly controversial and raised strong objections from the liberal parts of the community.

---

[3] See Frank Stern, "Philosemitism – The Whitewashing of the Yellow Badge: Antisemitism and Philosemitism in West Germany, 1945–1952," *Holocaust and Genocide Studies* 4 (1989): 463–77.

[4] U.S. Department of State, Policy Planning Staff, Special Counseling Group in Germany, Sept. 15–16, 1948, Joseph M. Proskauer papers RG1, EXO 16, Steering and Foreign Affairs Committees, 1945–1948, elitist American Jewish Committee (hereafter AJC) Archives, New York.

[5] *Committee Reporter* 8 (May–June 1951): 1,7; transcript of the AJC executive committee meeting, May 5–6, 1951, New York, AJC, Blaustein Library, New York.

[6] AJC Staff Committee on Germany, Dec. 28, 1950, YIVO Archives, New York, AJC Records, FAD-1, box 26; and Draft Statement on the Rearmament of Germany, Jan. 15, 1951, ibid., box 22.

Another faction that took a moderate attitude toward Germany and its people was the Jewish Labor Committee (JLC). It was less influential than the larger organizations. On the eve of and during World War II, the JLC's socialist leadership had supported German and other European social democrats and trade-union activists in exile. It disapproved of collective guilt accusations despite the more critical and emotional sentiments of its constituent agencies. After the war, the JLC continued its relationship with German social democrats and expressed their support for Kurt Schumacher and other politicians in the German Social Democratic Party (*Sozialdemokratische Partei Deutschlands*, or SPD) during their visits to the United States. On what would be his only visit to the United States, Schumacher was also welcomed by leading members of the AJC in fall 1947 but, because of political and ideological differences, these initial links were not institutionalized.[7] The moderate stance of American Council for Judaism (ACJ) resulted from its ideological confrontation with the Zionists, many of whom had endorsed an outspoken anti-German line. Rabbi Elmer Berger, until 1968 ACJ's executive head, rather early expressed the view that Jewish life in Germany after the defeat of Hitler had to be reinstated. The problem as he saw it was "what shall be done with Germany so that there emerges a nation in which Jews as well as other people will be able to live upon a basis of freedom and equality."[8] The post-1933 immigrants from Germany and Central Europe at first expressed doubts about postwar German leaders' good will, but their attitude gradually mellowed. This group, though not at all representative of the American Jewish community, was consistently courted by West Germany's first diplomats in the United States.

But although most of them joined in paying lip service to the need to change German society and political culture, these issues, the majority of organized Jewry represented by such bodies as the American Jewish Conference (until its disbandment in 1948), the World Jewish Congress (WJC) and American Jewish Congress, the Zionist groups, and the various East European fraternal associations did not care much about the future development of German democracy. Their attitude was dominated by the Jewish tragedy in Europe. As U.S. citizens, they could hardly ignore American national interests, but they were slow to adjust to the substantial change in Germany's status so soon after the war. In the meantime, they protested against German visitors and German-sponsored events in the United States, stressing the shortcomings of denazification, the leniency toward Nazi officials and war criminals, and the prevalence of anti-Semitism. In 1947, the American Jewish Conference, which included all Zionist and pro-Zionist groups, rejected the Marshall Plan because of its intended rehabilitation of German industry. At its first postwar plenary assembly in Montreux in summer 1948, the WJC, an umbrella group of different organizations and communities, opposed the "reconstitution of the German state as an economic and political and therefore military power as a threat to Jewish security and place in the world" and reiterated "the determination of the Jewish people never again to settle on the blood-stained soil of Germany." Neither before the proclamation of the West German Basic Law nor after the first Bundestag election did the WJC regard the granting of sovereignty to Germany as justified.[9] An influential exception was Nahum Goldmann, WJC acting president after the death of anti-German Rabbi Stephen Wise in 1949. Goldmann would soon play a major role in the negotiations on German *shilumim* (in German, *Wiedergutmachung*, or reparations in both the

---

[7] Shlomo Shafir, "Eine ausgestreckte Hand: Frühe amerikanisch-jüdische Kontakte zu deutschen Sozialdemokraten in der Nachkriegszeit," *Internationale Wissenschaftliche Korrespondenz zur Geschichte der deutschen Arbeiterbewegung* 25 (June 1989): 174–87.

[8] Elmer Berger, *The Jewish Dilemma* (New York, 1945), 24.

[9] Resolution of the WJC Second Plenary Assembly, Montreux, July 5, 1948, American Jewish Archives (hereafter AJA), Cincinnati, Ohio, World Jewish Congress Collection (hereafter WJCC), box A46/5.

moral and political sense). He understood that the congress movement would not gain support among the American public by opposing West Germany's economic self-sufficiency and, therefore, rejected calls to boycott West German products. He also rejected as unrealistic the demand that no Jew should ever live in Germany.[10] Conversely, the liberal American Jewish Congress, at that time the WJC's American constituency, took a consistently critical view of Germany and usually clashed with the AJC in the deliberations of the National Jewish Community Relations Advisory Council, the common forum.

Because of the rapid change of postwar American policy, the Jewish War Veterans (JWV), a small but vocal organization, found itself in a quandary. On the one hand, it supported the administration's anti-Soviet policy and, therefore, endorsed qualified acceptance of the rapprochement between West Germany and the United States. On the other hand, it remained a critical force that monitored German developments with suspicion and periodically participated in anti-German protests. Among the religious streams, both Zionists and the non-Zionist Orthodox usually took the strongest anti-German stand. For Rabbi Joseph B. Soloveitchik, the most respected intellectual voice in American Orthodox Judaism, anti-Semitism was "not related in any way to the political form or structure of a government . . . [but] to the fascist totalitarian mentality of a people."[11] This differed from the more moderate nuances among the Conservative and Reform congregations and rabbinical groups, although German rearmament, for instance, encountered much criticism at the Reform rabbis' annual meetings. Abba Hillel Silver, the most prominent American Zionist leader in the 1940s, happened to be among the staunchest critics of American support of West Ger-

man rearmament and preferred a neutralized, disarmed, united Germany.[12] It was no wonder that Jewish communists, who opposed West German rearmament according to the Party line, commented favorably on Silver's statements and speeches. Even after the expulsion from the American Jewish Congress of procommunist groups such as the Jewish People's Fraternal Order and the American Jewish Labor Committee, their supporters attracted numerous sympathizers at anti-German rallies conducted in cooperation with East European fraternal associations and a few left-wing trade unions. Nevertheless, the ranks of Jewish communists and fellow travelers gradually diminished.

Whatever their differences over the future of Germany and postwar Jewish-German relations, American Jewish organizations were frustrated by the lack of individual and collective German soul-searching about the murder of millions of Jews. The disappointment applied not only to the indifference of the German masses but also to the evasiveness of most German politicians. Anti-Semitism had, of course, ceased to be part of official German ideology. But although fears of German anti-Semitism were often exaggerated, Jewish expectations that the revelation of Nazi atrocities would cause a German change of heart did not materialize. The restitution of individual and communal Jewish property that began in the late 1940s encountered bureaucratic obstacles and caused hostile reactions among the German owners, adding another point of friction. The churches, too, were slow in taking responsibility for what happened to the Jews during the Nazi period. The Protestants, for example, did not refer to the murder of the Jews in their 1945 "Confession of Guilt." Jewish anxiety about Germany was also reinforced by the massive return of former Nazis and Nazi

---

[10] Minutes of Enlarged Meeting of the European Members of the WJC Executive, Paris, Aug. 25–28, 1949, and Minutes of the WJC Executive (American branch), Oct. 1, 1950, AJA, WJCC, box 3A/3.

[11] *Jewish Advocate*, May 23, 1946, 11.

[12] "Shall We Re-arm Germany?" address delivered by Rabbi Abba Hillel Silver at the Temple, Mar. 4, 1951, Cleveland, Ohio, 9–10; see also his address, "American Stake in Human Freedom," Dec. 12, 1953, in Daniel Jeremy Silver, ed., *In Time of Harvest: Essays in Honor of Abba Hillel Silver on the Occasion of his Seventieth Birthday* (New York, 1963), 89–90.

collaborators to influential posts in government; by clashes between Jewish demonstrators and German police; the prosecution and trial of Philipp Auerbach, the head of the Bavarian office of indemnification; and other affairs. Elliot Cohen, the founding editor of *Commentary* and the first Jewish intellectual to address a German forum after the war, complained particularly about the continuing silence on the part of German religious leaders, scholars, historians, poets, and novelists.[13]

SHILUMIM AS A MITIGATING FACTOR

With the inauguration of the first West German government under Konrad Adenauer, the semisovereign Federal Republic ceased to be an object and became an active protagonist in the American Jewish-German relationship, though at first American Jews were still reluctant to engage in direct contacts with Bonn and preferred to present their views to the American authorities. John J. McCloy, who replaced General Lucius D. Clay when the military government ended, had not been responsive to Jewish requests in the past and also disappointed Jewish spokesmen by commuting the sentences of numerous Nazi criminals and former high-ranking officials. However, because of his interest in forging a close relationship between the United States and the Federal Republic and improving Germany's standing in American public opinion, McCloy supported Jewish demands for restitution of property and *shilumim*.[14] Adenauer himself, in his first address to the Bundestag, condemned anti-Semitic manifestations and called for punishment of those "really guilty of the crimes committed during the Nazi era and in the war." However, he balanced this statement with a critique of denazification, which he said had caused "much misery and much harm." The chancellor did

not at all satisfy Jewish expectations, nor did his subsequent proposal to supply Israel with goods to the value of DM 10 million as a first step of recompense.[15] As Adenauer confided to McCloy, among the German people the National Socialist tradition was still most effective with regard to the "Jewish question."[16] At the same time, a well-informed German diplomatic observer in the United States alerted the chancellery of the importance of conciliating American Jews as an internationalist-minded force and the probable impact of Germany's attitude to the new state of Israel on future American Jewish-German relations. That view was shared by some of the chancellor's closest advisers in Bonn, in particular by Herbert Blankenhorn.[17] Thus, besides a certain moral urge, Adenauer became convinced that his qualified recognition of German responsibility (though not collective guilt) for past crimes against the Jews and West Germany's material amends to Israel and the Jewish people might contribute to the West's acceptance of the Federal Republic as an equal partner. This was the rationale for his September 1951 statement before the Bundestag.[18]

---

[13] "What Do the Germans Propose to Do?" *Commentary* 10 (Sept. 1950): 225–8.

[14] Thomas A. Schwartz, *America's Germany: John J. McCloy and the Federal Republic of Germany* (Cambridge, Mass., 1991), 175–84.

[15] *Verhandlungen des Deutschen Bundestages*, 1. leg. period, 5. sess., Sept. 20, 1949, 22–30, 27. The interview Adenauer granted to Karl Marx and that appeared in the *Allgemeine Wochenzeitung der Juden in Deutschland* on Nov. 25, 1949, is reprinted in Rolf Vogel, ed., *Deutschlands Weg nach Israel: Eine Dokumentation* (Stuttgart, 1967), 17–19.

[16] Wortprotokoll der Sitzung vom 17. November 1949, Hans-Peter Schwarz, ed., in cooperation with Reiner Pommerin, *Akten zur Auswärtigen Politik der Bundesrepublik Deutschland* (Munich, 1989), 1:18–35, 25–6.

[17] Alexander Böker, Report on American Policy Toward Germany, Feb. 2, 1950, Herbert Blankenhorn papers 351/3, Bundesarchiv Koblenz (hereafter BAK); Report on the American Position on Germany, Jan. 15, 1950, Politisches Archiv des Auswärtigen Amtes, Bonn (hereafter PA/AA), II 210–01/80, vol. 262.

[18] *Verhandlungen des Deutschen Bundestages*, 1st leg. period, 165th sess., Sept. 27, 1951, 6697–700; Adenauer to Hermann J. Abs, Apr. 8, 1952, in Konrad Adenauer, *Briefe 1951–1953*, ed. Hans Peter Mensing, Adenauer Rhöndorfer Ausgabe, Rudolf Morsey, and Hans-Peter Schwarz (Berlin, 1987), 198–9; Adenauer at the CDU federal executive committee, Sept. 2, 1952, in Günter Buchstab ed., *Adenauer: "Es musste alles neu gemacht werden:" Die Protokolle des CDU-Bundesvorstandes 1950–1953* (Stuttgart, 1986), 140–1; Adenauer, Tee-Empfang, May

However, Israel continued to need economic and financial assistance, and organized American Jewry continued its struggle for *shilumim*. Both, therefore, concluded that they had to approach Bonn directly. This laid the groundwork for the 1952 negotiations between the West German government and Israel, as well as the Conference on Jewish Material Claims Against Germany (Claims Conference), which twenty-two Jewish groups had established in fall 1951 in preparation for the German-Israeli negotiations. The signing of the Luxembourg Treaty in September 1952 ushered in a new chapter in Jewish-German institutional relations much earlier than expected. The negotiations benefited from AJC president Jacob Blaustein's acquaintanceship with McCloy and his contacts with the Democratic administration; Goldmann's main contribution – besides gaining the chancellor's confidence – lay in convincing the generally anti-German majority of American and Diaspora Jewry that there was no alternative to direct negotiations with the Federal Republic. These efforts were, of course, coordinated with the Israeli government. The *shilumim* agreement and its subsequent implementation partially reduced the anti-German sentiment of the Zionist and pro-Zionist American Jewish leadership, except for the Zionist Revisionists and the Orthodox. In 1953, the anti-German WJC refrained from repeating expressly hostile statements it had made before Luxembourg and, in 1954, Goldmann, though a hidden neutralist and supporter of an East-West thaw, vetoed resolutions against German rearmament lest they imperil his relationship with Adenauer.[19]

Another significant outcome of the Luxembourg Agreement was the reversal of the attitude of B'nai B'rith and its Anti-Defamation League (ADL), which became the first American Jewish organization to accept an invitation to visit Germany. Philip Klutznick, B'nai B'rith's president in the 1950s who intermittently continued to serve both the Jewish community and the U.S. government, based his commitment to an equitable relationship with regard to the Federal Republic on American national interest and Israel's dependence on German deliveries.[20] Similarly, congressmen with strong links to the Jewish community, such as Jacob Javits and Emanuel Celler, also favored a more positive approach toward Germany.[21] However, despite the bitterness and resentment the extermination of a major part of European Jewry had caused, the German "problem" was not as central to the American Jewish agenda (nor was Holocaust consciousness until the 1970s) as domestic issues and the security and well-being of the state of Israel.

The Luxembourg Agreement was made possible only by the solid support of the Social Democratic oppositions in the Bundestag; nevertheless, both the agreement and Adenauer's refusal to succumb to American pressure and suspend reparation shipments after Israel's invasion of Sinai enhanced the chancellor's standing among most American Jewish leaders. When addressing Jewish audiences, German diplomats and official visitors often referred to *shilumim* and the improvements of the individual compensation payments for Nazi victims. Jewish leaders must also have been aware of the growing importance to Israel of the German arms shipments that started in the late 1950s following an understanding reached between West

---

28, 1952, in Konrad Adenauer, *Teegespräche 1950–1954*, ed. Hanns Jürgen Küsters, Adenauer Rhöndorfer Ausgabe, ed. Rudolf Morsey and Hans-Peter Schwarz (Berlin, 1984), 278–94, 284–5.

[19] WJC, minutes of the executive (American branch), Apr. 20, 1954, and Dec. 18, 1954, AJA, WJCC, 3A/4. Goldmann had convened the Claims Conference in 1951 and served as its chairman until his death in 1982.

[20] Klutznick, written interview with the author, June 15, 1988. The three-man ADL delegation went to Germany in March 1954 as part of a visitors' exchange of twenty-eight Americans from different walks of life. Its report, "Germany – Nine Years Later," criticized the still existing potential of anti-Semitism but noted the positive change of mind among young Germans, many of whom were much more liberal than their parents and not at all keen to be drafted into a new army.

[21] Javits to Adenauer, Oct. 27, 1959, National Archives, RG 59, FW 762.00/10–2759; for Celler's views, see his "Random Thoughts on Germany," *Congressional Record*, 85th Cong., 1st sess., July 13, 1957, App., A 5790–1.

German Defense Minister Franz Joseph Strauss and Israeli Director-General of Defense Shimon Peres. In another attempt to mollify American Jewish hostility, the German diplomatic mission hired the Roy Bernard Company, a rather mediocre Manhattan firm owned by Jews, to manage its public relations. Later, it was assisted by General Julius Klein, a leader of the JWV who became a lobbyist for the West German government and German industrial corporations. Klein had frequent access to State Secretary Hans Globke, the head of the chancellor's office, and on several occasions became involved in German-Israeli contacts.[22] In March 1960, a few weeks after an outbreak of anti-Semitic manifestations in West Germany, Adenauer and Israeli Prime Minister David Ben-Gurion met at the Waldorf Astoria hotel in New York. At this meeting, Adenauer promised more military and economic assistance to Israel, partly in order to improve the image of the Federal Republic among organized Jewry. However, the issue of establishing diplomatic relations was again evaded.[23]

CONCERN ABOUT
ANTI-SEMITIC MANIFESTATION

An issue on which no meeting of the minds took place between Jewish Americans and Germans was the prevailing anti-Semitism among a rather substantial portion of the German people. Jewish representatives often exaggerated the threat, whereas their German counterparts tended to belittle it. AJC lay leaders and professionals placed special emphasis on the education of the younger German generation and the development of new educational techniques in dealing with Germany's recent past. Subsequently, the AJC, together with the Ford Foundation and the Institute of International Education, launched a

German Educators Program. Adenauer, for his part, insisted in his talks with Jewish spokesmen that communism and the East German communist dictatorship were the main danger and that the Eastern bloc was trying to discredit West Germany abroad. Because of the constant Soviet pressure on Berlin and his fear that Washington might withdraw its support for the divided city, Adenauer thought he might find support for his views also among American Jews. In the same vein, after the Berlin Wall was built in August 1961, the chancellor advised his emissary Kurt Birrenbach to try to obtain the backing of Jewish leaders by comparing divided Berlin to divided Jerusalem.[24] The continuing involvement of competing American Jewish organizations in German developments aroused the ire of Hendrik van Dam, the secretary general of the Central Council of the Jews in Germany. He advised the German government to beware of spending too much time with Jewish leaders from abroad except "really competent personalities" such as David Ben-Gurion and Nahum Goldmann. Later, he argued that the real issue of "criticism of Germany abroad was not German anti-Semitism but foreign anti-Germanism."[25] However, the American Jewish organizations rebuffed what they called van Dam's "Monroe Doctrine." In their opinion, the postwar Jewish community in Germany was too weak to cope alone with a spate of anti-Semitic events.[26]

The rash of swastika graffiti and anti-Semitic occurrences in the Federal Republic in the winter of 1959–60 temporarily revived Jewish

---

[22] For Klein's involvement, see his secret memorandum of Mar. 3, 1965, which tends, however, to exaggerate his achievements. B'nai B'rith Archives, Washington, D.C.

[23] "David Ben-Gurion and Chancellor Adenauer at the Waldorf Astoria," *Israel Studies* 2 (spring 1997): 56–71.

[24] Adenauer's letter to the AJC, Mar. 6, 1959, AJC news release, and Adenauer to Z. Shuster for I. Engel, Oct. 28, 1959, YIVO, AJC Records, FAD-1, box 34; Shuster to John Slawson, July 27, 1959, ibid., box 21. On Birrenbach's mission to Washington in Oct. 1961, see Kurt Birrenbach, *Meine Sondermissionen: Rückblick auf zwei Jahrzehnte bundesdeutscher Aussenpolitik* (Düsseldorf, 1984), 16, 36, 63.

[25] H. G. van Dam, Pawns in the Quest for Publicity: A World Jewish Affairs Feature, Nov. 5, 1959, YIVO, AJC Records, FAD-1, box 21; Timmermann (German Foreign Office), note about a conversation with van Dam, Feb. 25, 1960, PA/AA, 305 81.12/1 – 91.36, vol. 118.

[26] Shuster to E. Hevesi, Nov. 17, 1959, YIVO, AJC Records, FAD-1, box 21; E. Sterling to Shuster, Nov. 22, 1959, ibid., box 30.

worries. Government spokesmen in Bonn pointed to the imitative behavior of juvenile delinquents and to East German support of at least a part of the instigators. But these accusations, though plausible, were hard to prove at the time, and the American Jewish community put the blame on the West German government. Sensitive to Jewish criticism and fearing the negative impact on American and Western public opinion, Bonn took steps to improve the teaching of contemporary history in schools and toughen the law against preaching racial hatred. A few months later, the most prominent ex-Nazi in the cabinet, Theodor Oberländer, vacated his post. In what would prove to be his only visit to a concentration camp, Adenauer attended a memorial service at Bergen-Belsen with a Jewish delegation. Political scientist Eleonore Sterling, reporting from Germany for the AJC, regarded the impressive Bundestag debate in January 1960 and the disgust expressed by tens of thousands of young Germans who participated in anti-Nazi protest marches in major cities throughout West Germany as a significant positive change in the Federal Republic's political culture.[27] However, the impact of her insights seems to have been marginal. A few months later, the ADL of B'nai B'rith, which had taken the most moderate attitude during the crisis, initiated the first Jewish-West German exchange program aimed at introducing young German community leaders and officials to the American experience of voluntary association. Although a group of Germans from various walks of life came to the United States in 1961 and a team of ADL civil-rights specialists paid a return visit to Germany in 1963, the program soon petered out and was revived only after Germany's reunification.[28]

The Israeli capture of Adolf Eichmann in 1960 and his trial in Jerusalem soon eclipsed American Jewish concern about anti-Semitism in Germany. In the short run, the affair affected the domestic American Jewish scene more than the community's attitude toward Germany. The Jewish establishment and committed intellectuals soon became embroiled in a confrontation with critics of the trial, particularly with Hannah Arendt, the German-born philosopher and essayist who had become a leading voice among American intellectuals. At the same time, Jewish organizations tried to further understanding among the American public for Eichmann's seizure and trial. Because of West Germany's interest in preserving its image and Israel's interest in continuing German military assistance, diplomats from both countries cooperated in emphasizing the difference between the Federal Republic's firmly established democratic system and Germany's Nazi past.[29] In the long run, however, the Eichmann trial spurred Holocaust consciousness, which would reach its peak in the following decades, and thereby impeded any major improvement of the American Jewish perception of Germany.

THE STRUGGLE FOR AMENDING THE STATUTE OF LIMITATIONS

Two years after the Eichmann trial, the Jewish community became deeply involved in the campaign to amend the German statute of limitations, under which suspected Nazi war criminals could not be prosecuted after May 1965. It was feared that those criminals who had successfully evaded detention and indictment would live out the rest of their lives in impunity. The changing atmosphere in East-West relations made the Jewish community more resolute, and although Ben-Gurion's successor, Levy Eshkol, was aware of the importance of Germany's military and

[27] Sterling to Shuster, Jan. 26, 1960, YIVO, AJC Records, FAD-1, box 31.

[28] Benjamin Epstein to Georg Federer, May 26, 1960, and Mission to Germany in summer 1960 by ten B'nai B'rith representatives, ADL FC Germany, Exchange Program 1960–1961, ADL Archives, New York; "The ADL Exchange: Exposure to American Democracy," *ADL Bulletin* 18 (Nov. 1961): 4, 5, 8; Statement of the ADL Study Group, Bonn, Sept. 25, 1963, ADL

FC Germany; Reva Price, "Building Bridges," *Jewish Monthly* 106 (Feb. 1992): 17–18.

[29] German Consulate General, New York, Apr. 13, 1961, PA/AA, 305 82–91.36, vol. 168; M. Arnon to Israel Foreign Ministry, Feb. 10, 1961, Israel State Archives, Foreign Ministry Records, 3059/4.

economic assistance to Israel, he and Foreign Minister Golda Meir took a more critical view of Bonn's policy. Their attitude was reinforced by Egypt's employment of German scientists and technical experts in its armament industry and West Germany's continuing refusal to establish full diplomatic relations with Israel. The crisis peaked with Bonn's suspension of arms shipments to Israel in early 1965. The American Jewish pressure, including boycott threats and picketing of German consulates all over the United States, eventually contributed to Chancellor Ludwig Erhard's solitary decision to offer Israel full diplomatic relations. It also influenced German deliberations regarding the statute of limitations, which was extended until 1969 and then for another ten years until it was finally abolished in 1979.[30]

Some leading American Jewish officials thought the establishment of diplomatic relations between West Germany and Israel and the changes to the statute of limitations had opened the path to a revision of the attitude toward Germany. For the ADL national director, Benjamin Epstein, the time had come to transcend mere criticism, censure, or condemnation of German antidemocratic behavior or anti-Jewish hostility. His advice was to pay more attention to positive factors in Germany, such as the democratic mass media, labor unions, youth and student groups, and the genuinely democratic politicians from the major parties. Will Maslow of the American Jewish Congress paid tribute to German assistance to Israel, but reserved to American Jewry the right of independent judgment on such issues as German reunification or German nuclear development.[31] Two years later, Marvin Kalb, the renowned TV commentator, addressed the AJCs annual meeting in 1967 and sounded a

cautiously optimistic note about the future of German democracy despite recent electoral successes of the right-wing National Democratic Party (*Nationaldemokratische Partei Deutschlands*, or NPD). Yet, his view was not accepted by John Slawson, the AJC's veteran vice president, who detected a fundamental authoritarian streak in German culture and education.[32]

Some individual exchange initiatives were undertaken at this time. Rabbi Joseph Asher's proposal to send German-speaking rabbis to Germany to teach German youth and leaders about Jews and Judaism was implemented in 1966.[33] Brandeis University served as a venue for the first public dialogue between German ambassador Karl Heinrich Knappstein – who enjoyed the confidence of the Jewish community thanks to his role during the 1964–5 crisis – and Rabbi Joachim Prinz, chairman of the Presidents Conference of the Major Jewish Organizations and a former Liberal rabbi in Berlin.[34] Prinz also participated in the high-level German-Jewish dialogue arranged by Nahum Goldmann during the WJC plenary assembly in Brussels in 1966.[35] But all these exchanges produced no concrete results. Except for its scrutiny of West Germany's extreme right and issues connected with Israel, organized American Jewry's interest in Germany declined and would revive only at the end of the next decade. The Germans, despite their persistent interest in conciliating American Jewry, directed their main efforts toward Israel. There they succeeded in lifting a great many barriers in a remarkably short period. This was particularly true after the German show of solidarity during the Six Day War, though political differences were soon to emerge as a result of Israel's decisive military victory.

---

[30] For a detailed description of the crisis leading to Erhard's decision, see Horst Osterheld, *Aussenpolitik unter Bundeskanzler Ludwig Erhard: Ein dokumentarischer Bericht aus dem Kanzleramt* (Düsseldorf, 1993), 149–73. See also Shafir, *Ambiguous Relations*, 234–47; Niels Hansen, "Geheimvorhaben 'Frank/Kol': Zur deutsch-israelischen Rüstungszusammenarbeit 1957 bis 1965," *Historisch-Politische Mitteilungen, Archiv für Christlich-Demokratische Politik*, 6 (1999): 229–64.

[31] NCRAC executive committee, minutes, May 2, 1965, AJA, Lou H. Silverman papers, box 2/1.

[32] AJC Sixty-First Annual Meeting, May 18–21, 1967, New York, transcript, Blaustein Library, New York.

[33] Joseph Asher, "Our Attitude to the Germans – A Time for Reappraisal?" *Pointer* (Summer 1966), Blaustein Library, New York.

[34] Joachim Prinz, "The Germans and the Jews: The Truths That Must Be Faced," and Heinrich Knappstein, "Our Steps Toward Reconciliation," *Congress Bi-Weekly*, Mar. 7, 1966, 6–10.

[35] WJC, Fifth Plenary Assembly, Brussels, Session on Germans and Jews.

CHAPTER EIGHT

German and American Women Between Domesticity and the Workplace

Hanna Schissler

In 1948, a young psychiatrist who worked for the Information Control Division of the American military government in Germany published his research on "the Father Land." According to this study, the German married woman "is completely dependent on her husband." The secondary position of the "German Mother" in the family was assumed to be because of two factors: "her subjugation to the undisputed authority of the father, and her abandonment of those qualities associated with 'femininity' which would make her a colorful, self-reliant personality instead of an insecure passive drudge." The German husband and father, however, behaved like a tyrant and wielded "absolute power" over his wife and children. The children, who only knew their father as an omnipotent presence at home, were shocked to see his subservience toward his superiors.[1] According to the author, these gender-specific behavior patterns within the family continually socialized Germans into specific forms of authoritarianism; it was only a small step from authoritarian family life in Germany to fascism. These and similar ideas were widespread within the American occupation force when it set out to reeducate the Germans and cure them from Nazism.[2]

However, not all researchers accepted the stereotype of the authoritarian Germans falling for Hitler en masse. Howard Becker, for example, stated in 1951: "It seems to me that the attempt to trace authoritarianism in German public life back to 'its family roots' is revealed as foredoomed to failure." Although the observation that German families are more authoritarian than American families seemed to be accurate, according to Becker, this was not a particularly German but rather a European trait. They were more authoritarian than American families only in the sense that parents seemed to have more control over their children. Becker observed "genuine partnership" between husband and wife in Germany, but he also realized that gender determined men's and women's tasks rather rigidly.[3]

Another shrewd observer of conditions in Germany in the immediate postwar period was the movie director Billy Wilder. In his famous movie *A Foreign Affair*, he commented on some salient aspects of the immediate postwar period, especially fraternization and reeducation. Skillfully playing on the cultural stereotypes about German and American women, Wilder juxtaposed Marlene Dietrich as Erika von Schlütow, a postwar German fraternizer/seductress and anything but an "insecure passive drudge," and

---

[1] Bertram Schaffner, *Father Land: A Study of Authoritarianism in the German Family* (New York, 1948), 34; see also 15–17.

[2] See the chapters by Cornelia Rauh-Kühne, vol. 1, Politics, and James F. Tent, vol. 1, Culture.

[3] Howard Becker, "German Families Today," in Hans Morgenthau, ed., *Germany and the Future of Europe* (Chicago, 1951), 18, 23–4.

Jean Arthur as Congresswoman Phoebe Frost from Iowa, a "straight arrow" with rigid moral standards and initially little taste for vices of any sorts. The male protagonist, Captain John Pringle (played by John Lund), starts out as Erika von Schlütow's lover/supporter but in the end chooses Frost, the all-American girl, who is now softened, less rigid, and ready for marriage. The film ends with a rather ambiguous scene: The soldiers sent by Colonel Plummer (played by Millard Mitchel) to observe the former Nazi collaborator von Schlütow follow her and stumble on the stars in helpless anticipation of erotic excitement. The colonel rubs his nose, wondering about the success of the mission on which he has sent his men. This scene can be read as a symbol of American self-doubt about the success of the reeducation effort. *A Foreign Affair* was not shown in Germany at the time of its release in 1948 because the American occupation force felt it was too ironic and too critical of Americans. Perhaps another concern was that the film showed too much sympathy for postwar conditions in Germany, especially for women's struggles to survive amid the rubble of its bombed-out cities.[4]

In the first two or three years, the American occupation force did not devote much attention to women at all. Nevertheless, women constituted the majority of the population after the war, and it quickly became clear that they would have to play an important role in rebuilding the country. The systematic approach toward women and "women's issues" undertaken by the Soviets in their zone of occupation also demonstrated the need for action on the part of the Americans as well, not only to catch up with the Soviets in the field of women's policies but also to contain communist influence on women and women's organizations in the West.[5]

The American response was the founding of the Women's Affairs Section in the Office of the Military Governor of the United States (OMGUS) in 1948.[6] The Office of the Director of Intelligence assigned the Women's Affairs Section the task of observing the "ever-tightening ring of directions from Moscow" on the Democratic Women's League of Germany (*Demokratischer Frauenbund Deutschlands*, or DFD), which, while trying to expand into the Western zones, was monopolizing all activities of women's groups in the East.[7] The founding of the Women's Affairs Section was also a response to the pressure from American women's groups – mainly the League of Women Voters and some prominent American journalists – to pay more attention to women's issues.[8]

The Women's Affairs Section was intended to help women, whom the American occupation authorities considered to have been totally oppressed and muted by the Nazis, to gain a stronger political voice. It also was meant to help reestablish women's groups in order to contribute to a policy of equal rights and citizenship education for women. But the section's budget was small; as part of the Cultural Relations Division, its power and range of responsibilities were limited.[9] Indeed, the activities of the Women's Affairs Section and the circumstances in which it was founded showed that the American

Record Group (hereafter RG) 260, box 149, folder 5/297–1/1.

[6] Hermann-Josef Rupieper, "Bringing Democracy to the German Frauleins: Frauen als Zielgruppe der amerikanischen Demokratisierungspolitik in Deutschland 1945–1952," *Geschichte und Gesellschaft* 17 (1991): 61–91.

[7] Office of the Director of Intelligence, Comment to Memorandum No. 348, Soc. 15 and 16, WNRC, RG 260, box 149, folder 5/297–1/1.

[8] Hermann-Josef Rupieper, *Die Wurzeln der westdeutschen Nachkriegsdemokratie* (Opladen, 1993); Rebecca Boehling, "'Mütter in die Politik': Amerikanische Demokratisierungsbemühungen nach 1945," *Geschichte und Gesellschaft* 19 (1993): 522–9.

[9] Henry P. Pilgert, *Women in West Germany*, Historical Division, Office of the Executive Secretary, Office of the U.S. High Commissioner for Germany, 1952, 7, 9–11.

[4] See Emily Rosenberg, "'Foreign Affairs' after World War II: Connecting Sexual and International Politics," *Diplomatic History* 18 (1994): 59–70.

[5] See Intelligence Officer, Office of the Director of Intelligence, OMG Baden Württemberg, ODI Weekly Report no. 76, Oct. 25 1947, Washington National Records Center, Suitland, Md. (hereafter WNRC),

occupation force did not have a clear concept of gender policies and was mostly reacting to what others – mainly the Soviets – accomplished with greater dispatch and skill.

The Women's Affairs Section had a political concept closely modeled after the American experience: Women were encouraged to do voluntary work in commissions and women's organizations. Following the model of "Republican motherhood" in the United States, forms of politics for women were promoted in which women's private roles, their "motherly qualities," were supposed to serve the public. The German tradition of women's political involvement in unions and political parties was overlooked because it did not correspond to Americans' image of the subdued, politically passive German housewife. Although it helped German women to found new organizations and to revive those the Nazis had banned, this concept did not threaten the traditional division of labor between men and women; "motherly politics" found many followers in the Western zones of occupation. In a country where many of the adult men had either died or were still in POW camps, the role of women was widely discussed. "True partnership between men and women" could be set against the communist threat of "forced and mechanical emancipation," which would – according to the public rhetoric in the West – destroy the foundations of the family by instrumentalizing women for state purposes, something that the Nazis had done in the past and the communists were doing in the present. Gabriele Strecker, a leading member of the Christian Democratic Union (CDU), was happy that women in the difficult postwar situation were again willing to accept their traditional roles and that the "murky stream of rebellious and risky ideas" did not gain ground among women in the West.[10]

In Germany and the United States, married women with children had been pulled into the labor force in great numbers to replace the men who had gone to war.[11] During the war, the proportion of employed women in the United States rose from 28 to 37 percent. Because of its emergency character, women's employment was considered to be only temporary, even by women themselves. The "emancipatory" power of women's immersion into the labor force during the war proved limited; "Rosie the Riveter" was a temporary phenomenon.[12] Women's participation in the labor force was viewed with ambivalence in both the United States and western Germany[13] and did not constitute a claim on the labor market for equal access or equal pay after the war. In both countries, women were sent back into the home once the war was over.

In Germany, the numerical imbalance and deep rupture between men and women was one of the outcomes of World War II. As late as 1950, nearly one-third of Germany's fifteen million households were headed by single women – either war widows, single mothers, or divorcées.[14]

---

[10] Nori Möding, "Die Stunde der Frauen? Frauen und Frauenorganisationen des bürgerlichen Lagers," in Martin Broszat, Klaus-Dietmar Hebke, and Hans Woller, eds., *Von Stalingrad zur Währungsreform: Zur Sozialgeschichte des Umbruchs in Deutschland* (Munich, 1988), 641.

[11] Elaine Tyler May, *Homeward Bound: American Families in the Cold War Era* (New York, 1988), chap. 3; Sara Evans, *Born for Liberty: A History of Women in America* (New York, 1989), chap. 10; William H. Chafe, *The Paradox of Change. American Women in the 20th Century* (New York, 1991), pt. 3; Carl N. Degler, *At Odds: Women and the Family in America from the Revolution to the Present* (Oxford, 1980), 419–22, 426. On Germany, see Dörte Winkler, *Frauenarbeit im Dritten Reich* (Hamburg, 1977); Ludwig Eiber, "Frauen in der Kriegsindustrie: Arbeitsbedingungen, Lebensumstände und Protestverhalten," in Martin Broszat, ed., *Bayern in der NS-Zeit*, 6 vols. (Munich, 1977–83), 3:569–644.

[12] Sherna Berger Gluck, *Rosie the Riveter Revisited: Women, the War and Social Change* (New York, 1987).

[13] Traditional female gender roles in the United States grew stronger in the 1940s. See Susan Hartmann, *The Home Front and Beyond: American Women in the 1940s* (Boston, 1982), 190–2.

[14] Adelheid zu Castell, "Die demographischen Konsequenzen des Ersten und Zweiten Weltkriegs für das Deutsche Reich, die Deutsche Demokratische Republik und die Bundesrepublik Deutschland," in Waclaw Dlugoborski, ed., *Zweiter Weltkrieg und sozialer Wandel* (Göttingen, 1981), 117–37; Annette Kuhn, ed., *Frauen in der deutschen Nachkriegszeit*, 2 vols. (Düsseldorf, 1984–1986); Hanna Schissler, "Women in West Germany,"

Whereas the American soldiers came home as victors, returning German soldiers had to confront the shame of defeat, the atrocities they had committed or witnessed, and the consequences of their inability to protect women and children in the last phase of the war.[15] Many had difficulty fitting into family structures that the war had since changed.[16] In both Germany and the United States, it fell mainly to women to reintegrate their men into civilian life – an aspect of postwar reality that was pervasively portrayed in popular culture, especially in movies. A German example is the film *Die Sünderin*; an American example is *The Best Years of Our Lives*.[17]

Although civilians across Germany, particularly women and children, suffered from the bombing raids toward the end of the war, it was in the East that people were hardest hit. Many lost their homes and fled the approaching Red Army or later became expellees. Some forms of victimization were unique to women. Although sexual assaults and rapes occurred all over occupied Germany, it was mostly in Soviet-occupied territory that women were raped by the victorious soldiers in great numbers.[18] In the Western zones, relationships between the occupiers and civilians were much more benign. The initial ban on fraternization the Americans had issued was quickly lifted. Relationships between German women and American soldiers unfolded in the triangle of sexual adventures, (hunger-) prostitution, but also genuine love. Numerous American-German marriages resulted from those relationships.[19]

The end of the war in Germany empowered women because it was women on whom the survival of the family mostly depended. However, women's position after the war was strengthened mainly in their traditional role as homemakers, not in the labor market or in politics.[20] This continued to be the case after the end of the occupation and the founding of the Federal Republic of Germany.[21] Although the power shift that had taken place in families proved irreversible, efforts to turn women's newly won independence and strength into political leverage encountered formidable resistance. An equality clause for women and men was included in the Basic Law in 1949 only after women's groups had put massive pressure on the Parliamentary Council. In 1957, the

---

in Michael Hülshoff, Andrei S. Markovits, and Simon Reich, eds., *From Bundesrepublik to Deutschland: German Politics After Unification* (Ann Arbor, Mich., 1993), 117–36; Ute Frevert, *Women in German History: From Bourgeois Emancipation to Sexual Liberation* (Oxford, 1989), pt. 5.

[15] Robert Moeller, "War Stories: The Search for a Usable Past in the Federal Republic of Germany," *American Historical Review* 101 (1996): 1008–48; Frank Biess, "Survivors of Totalitarianism: Returning POWs and the Reconstruction of Masculine Citizenship in West Germany, 1945–1955," in Hanna Schissler, ed., *The "Miracle" Years: A Cultural History of West Germany, 1949–1968* (Princeton, 2000).

[16] One result was a sharp increase in divorces, which reached its peak in 1948. On the situation of families and male-female relationships generally, see Sibylle Meyer and Eva Schulze, *Von Liebe sprach damals keiner: Familienalltag in der Nachkriegszeit* (Munich, 1985); on the situation of war veterans, see James M. Diehl, *The Thanks of the Fatherland: German Veterans After the Second World War* (Chapel Hill, N.C., 1993).

[17] On *The Best Years of Our Lives*, see Tyler May, *Homeward Bound*, 65–6; on *Die Sünderin*, see Heide Fehrenbach, *Cinema in Democratizing Germany: Reconstructing National Identity After Hitler* (Chapel Hill, N.C., 1995), chap. 3; see also the chapter by Daniel J. Leab, vol. 1, Culture.

[18] Annemarie Tröger, "Between Rape and Prostitution: Survival Strategies and Possibilities of Liberation of Berlin Women in 1945–48," in Judith Friedlander et al., eds., *Women in Culture and Politics: A Century of Change* (Bloomington, Ind., 1986); Ingrid Schmidt-Harzbach, "Eine Woche im April: Berlin 1945: Vergewaltigung als Massenschicksal," in Helke Sander and Barbara Johr, eds., *BeFreier und Befreite: Krieg, Vergewaltigungen, Kinder* (Munich, 1992); Atina Grossmann, "A Question of Silence: The Rape of German Women by Occupation Soldiers," in Robert Moeller, ed., *West Germany Under Construction: Politics, Society, and Culture in the Adenauer Era* (Ann Arbor, Mich., 1997), 33–52; Norman M. Naimark, *The Russians in Germany: A History of the Soviet Zone of Occupation* (Cambridge, Mass., 1995), chap. 2.

[19] See the chapter by Petra Goedde in this section.

[20] Barbara Willenbacher, "Zerrüttung und Bewährung der Nachkriegsfamilie," in Martin Broszat, Klaus-Dietmar Henke, and Hans Woller, eds., *Von Stalingrad zur Währungsreform: Zur Sozialgeschichte des Umbruchs in Deutschland* (Munich, 1989), 605–6.

[21] Rene König, "Family and Authority: The German Father in 1955," *Sociological Review* 5 (1957): 107–27.

Bundestag finally passed a law on equal rights for men and women, ending a decade of ideological warfare on the role of women (and men) in West German society.[22]

In the East, the Soviets passed laws immediately after the war that stipulated women's equality in all fields of life. With a firm belief that only complete immersion in the labor force would "emancipate" women, Soviet-zone officials set the stage for the German Democratic Republic's (GDR) policies toward women.[23] In the GDR, women's equality was also driven by the regime's desperate need for laborers as it built up the new state's heavy industry and, until the building of the Berlin Wall in 1961, tried to compensate for the flight of qualified laborers to West Germany.

Policies for women in the Federal Republic during the 1950s tended to sacrifice women's equality for the protection of the family. The Basic Law stated that "men and women are equal" but also put the family under the special protection of the constitution. Thus, policies in the 1940s and 1950s that "ostensibly protected the family were in fact policies that defined the social and political status of women."[24] The West German government tried to avoid any form of state intervention in family life that even remotely resembled the practices of the Nazi state in this area or the "forced emancipation"

in East Germany. As a result, it had to walk a fine line between noninterference in gender relations and protective laws for working mothers. Marriage and the two-parent family became the norm. Despite evidence of the large number of single women and the growing number of employed married women, women's equality was largely limited to questions of "partnership" within marriage between a male breadwinner and a homemaker wife.

While the West Germans tried obsessively to "normalize" gender relations, women in the East were quickly and ruthlessly integrated into the labor force according to a rather mechanical understanding of equality. The beginning of the Cold War had a tremendous impact on how women's policies were defined, as each emerging German state tried to model itself in deliberate contrast to the other. In the West, the "forced emancipation" of women in the GDR was used as a pretext for abstaining from policies to promote the equality between men and women stipulated in the Basic Law. In women's and gender politics, the Federal Republic and the GDR generally followed their respective occupation "models." The Cold War reinforced and represented the alignment of each German state with its ally.[25]

In the culture of domesticity that prevailed in both the United States and West Germany in the 1950s, unions and state and local bureaucracies in West Germany tried to push women out of the labor force to create jobs for men, particularly for war veterans and family fathers.[26] In the United States, nearly all the jobs that women had occupied during the war went back to men once the war was over. The sociologist Willard Waller claimed that women in the United States had gotten "out of hand" during the war and that things now needed to return to "normal."[27] West Germany took measures

[22] Robert Moeller, *Protecting Motherhood: Women and the Family in the Policies of Postwar Germany* (Berkeley, Calif., 1993); Eva Kolinsky, *Women in Contemporary Germany: Life, Work, and Politics* (Providence, R.I., 1993).

[23] Hildegard Maria Nickel, "Women in the German Democratic Republic and in the New Federal States: Looking Backwards and Forwards," *German Politics and Society* 24–25 (1991–2): 53–66; Hildegard Maria Nickel, " 'Mitgestalterinnen des Sozialismus' – Frauenarbeit in der DDR," in Gisela Helwig and Hildegard Maria Nickel, eds., *Frauen in Deutschland 1945–1992* (Bonn, 1993), 233–56; Jutta Gysi and Dagmar Meyer, "Leitbild: Berufstätige Mutter – DDR-Frauen in Familie, Partnerschaft und Ehe," in Gisela Helwig and Hildegard Maria Nickel, eds., *Frauen in Deutschland 1945–1992* (Bonn, 1993), 139–65.

[24] Robert Moeller, "Reconstructing the Family in Reconstructing Germany: Women and Social Policy in the Federal Republic, 1949–1955," *Feminist Studies* 15 (1989): 137.

[25] See Tyler May, *Homeward Bound*, 92–113.

[26] See Glenna Matthews, *"Just a Housewife": The Rise and Fall of Domesticity in America* (New York, 1987); Helge Pross, *Die Wirklichkeit der Hausfrau* (Reinbek, 1976); Klaus-Jörg Ruhl, *Frauen in der Nachkriegszeit 1945–1963* (Munich, 1988).

[27] As quoted in Tyler May, *Homeward Bound*, 68–9.

against households with two wage earners, passed special laws regulating women's work, constructed a system of family allowances, and tried to firmly establish the male family wage. These measures, which were strongly supported by the churches, the unions, and other political forces, regulated women's work and tried to keep women at home, especially if they had small children.

Such measures generally met with little opposition in West Germany and the United States. Not even female union members challenged the assumption that women's place was at home with their children.[28] German organized labor had fought for the male family wage since the nineteenth century; now it was within reach.[29] Nevertheless, a significant number of women still wanted to hold on to their jobs, either because they refused to be sent back into the home or because they were without a male provider and needed the income.[30] Stigmatized during the 1950s in both the United States and the Federal Republic, these women had to confront an overwhelming social consensus that women were not entitled to employment or independence. Single women – who were particularly numerous in postwar Germany – felt isolated in an atmosphere where the "normal family" became one of the main pillars of social stability and was equated with Western values. Amid the highly charged anticommunism of the 1950s, single women often were accused of

being *Flintenweiber* – communist subversives who supposedly tried to undermine the sanctity of marriage and family life.[31] In the United States as well, women's employment was considered an assault on the nation and associated with communism and subversion in the 1950s. The prospect of women remaining in the labor force instead of becoming mothers provoked fears in the United States of "race suicide."[32] The West German government, concerned with the decline in family size, tried to stimulate married couples' willingness to produce the next generation. The system of family allowances was designed to allow women to stay at home, raise a family, and avoid the fate of their East German sisters.

These ideological barriers were eventually overcome by a combination of economic need, rising expectations, and West Germany's "economic miracle" in the 1950s and 1960s. Women with or without children were pulled into the workforce. Between 1950 and 1975, the rate of female employment increased from 47.4 to 54.0 percent. The increase seems moderate compared with the GDR, where female employment increased from 52.4 to 81.5 percent between 1950 and 1975.[33] More significant in the West German case, however, was the disproportionate increase in *married* women's employment, which rose from 25 percent in 1950 to 42 percent in 1982.[34] Because women's increasing participation in the labor market took place amid unrealistic social norms, women were pushed into menial jobs, chose part-time over full-time employment, and in general were considered unreliable, secondary, and substitute

[28] Deutscher Gewerkschaftsbund, *"Da haben wir uns alle schrecklich geirrt..."*: *Die Geschichte der gewerkschaftlichen Frauenarbeit im Deutschen Gewerkschaftsbund von 1945 bis 1960* (Pfaffenweiler, 1993); Hanna Schissler, "Social Democratic Gender Policies, the Working Class Milieu, and the Culture of Domesticity in West Germany in the 1950s and 1960s," in David E. Barclay and Eric D. Weitz, eds., *Between Reform and Revolution: Studies in the History of German Socialism and Communism from 1840 to 1990* (Providence, R.I., 1998).

[29] Josef Mooser, *Arbeiterleben in Deutschland 1900–1970: Klassenlagen, Kultur und Politik* (Frankfurt am Main, 1984).

[30] Sibylle Meyer and Eva Schulze, "Von Wirtschaftswunder keine Spur: Die ökonomische und soziale Situation alleinstehender Frauen," in Angela Delille und Andrea Grohn, eds., *Perlonzeit: Wie die Frauen ihr Wirtschaftswunder erlebten* (Berlin, 1985), 92–8.

[31] Angela Vogel, "Familie," in Wolfgang Benz, ed., *Die Geschichte der Bundesrepublik Deutschland: Gesellschaft* (Frankfurt am Main, 1989), 42.

[32] "Public health professionals argued that inside as well as outside the home, women who challenged traditional roles placed the security of the nation at risk." Tyler May, *Homeward Bound*, 99, 100.

[33] Castell, "Die demographischen Konsequenzen," table 10, 137, and table 7, 135.

[34] Statistisches Bundesamt, *Datenreport: Zahlen und Fakten über die Bundesrepublik Deutschland* (Bonn, 1983), 84; Statistisches Bundesamt, *Frauen in Familie, Beruf und Gesellschaft* (Stuttgart, 1987), 62–3.

workers. In the 1950s and 1960s, gender segregation on the labor market was pervasive.[35] This showed most clearly in the wage differential: In the 1950s, female industrial wages in West Germany were 45.7 percent lower and female white-collar wages 43.7 percent lower than the corresponding male wages. Whereas women were made into subsidiary workers on a low level, male workers in West Germany enjoyed a collective upgrade; their advancement to the official category of skilled workers (*Facharbeiter*) was largely attributable to women's cheap labor (and later also to so-called guest workers). The ambivalence about women's employment during the war also reinforced a sex-segregated labor force in the United States, where the war had highlighted women's role as homemakers as much as their roles as consumers and workers.[36] The pervasiveness of the male breadwinner role triggered social criticism of the "organization man" (William F. Whyte) and eventually of the "feminine mystique" (Betty Friedan).[37]

Whereas the West German state was discriminatory in its policies toward women, the GDR fiercely defended women's right and even their duty to work. As much as the GDR provided a framework for women's work, however, it did practically nothing to change gender roles. What in retrospect was sometimes praised as a paradise for working women[38] for its generous maternity leave, child care, and other benefits had only developed in the 1970s after the regime grew alarmed at the declining birth rate. The state considered it of utmost importance that

women produce the next generation of socialist workers; their employment situation had to be harmonized with this goal. The resulting regulations, therefore, pertained mainly to women of child-bearing age.[39] By securing women's reproductive and productive capacities in the interests of the socialist state, the GDR aimed to reconcile "motherhood and profession," not parenthood and work. It consequently left men out of its deliberations and did nothing to make their roles more compatible with fatherhood. In defining women's emancipation as a structural problem of organizing the workplace, providing educational chances for women, steering girls into jobs that were "suitable" for them, and providing special arrangements to allow mothers to combine work and family, the state actually reinforced existing gender roles. Women were supposed to be emancipated as well as feminine.

In the Federal Republic and in the United States, women's paid labor expanded in spite of the culture of domesticity. However, this put women into a difficult situation because it privatized a structural problem of late industrial societies at their expense.[40] The state in the GDR, by contrast, "emancipated" women from above, at first pulling them into employment without any consideration for their roles as mothers but eventually providing the framework in which to reconcile motherhood and work. In the West, the inability to reconcile repressive norms with an increasingly diverse social reality for women resulted in the New Women's Movement of the 1970s; in the GDR, the favorable regulations to combine work and family were taken for granted by both women and men.

---

[35] Josef Mooser, "Arbeiter, Angestellte und Frauen in der 'nivellierten Mittelstandsgesellschaft': Thesen," in Axel Schildt and Arnold Sywottek, eds., *Modernisierung im Wiederaufbau: Die westdeutsche Gesellschaft der 50er Jahre* (Bonn, 1993), 362–76.

[36] Tyler May, *Homeward Bound*, 75.

[37] See the chapter by Hanna Schissler, vol. 2, Society.

[38] Dorothy Rosenberg, "Shock Therapy: The Effect of Unification on Women in Germany," *Signs* 17 (1991): 129–51.

[39] Myra Marx Ferree, "The Rise and Fall of 'Mommy Politics': Feminism and Unification in (East) Germany," *Feminist Studies* 19 (1993): 89–115.

[40] Hanna Schissler, "The Project of 'Normalization': Thoughts on Gender in West Germany," in Schissler, ed., *The "Miracle" Years*.

CHAPTER NINE

Support and Dissent

German and American Labor's Transnational Ties

Michael Fichter

The interaction between German and American trade unions in the period 1945–68 mirrored the special relationship between the United States and Germany. From the outset, it focused on issues of concern to both labor movements in Germany and Europe. In contrast to the period 1968–90, it was driven more by international political considerations than economic or social issues. As international conditions changed, so did the transnational relations of American and West German trade unions.

U.S. and German unions were unequal partners in 1945. The American unions could provide support and exert influence, but the German unions were unable to reciprocate. In part, this was the result of the destruction of the organized labor movement in Germany at the hands of National Socialism. When the war ended, trade unions had to be completely rebuilt, and German unionists were dependent on and grateful for support from their American counterparts – the American Federation of Labor (AFL) and the Congress of Industrial Organizations (CIO). The original imbalance between the American and German federations was also predicated on the dominant role of the United States and the ability of both the AFL and the CIO to influence American policy toward Germany.

By the mid-1950s, however, the unions of the German Trade Union Federation (*Deutscher*

Gewerkschaftsbund, or DGB)[1] had achieved a strong membership basis and were recognized as key social and economic actors in the institutional framework of negotiated settlements that provided a basis for the German economic miracle. This organizational success contributed to changes in the DGB's relations with the AFL and the CIO over the years. The powerful position held by the American unions during the occupation period gave way to a role marked by valuable political support for the DGB on domestic issues combined with a critical stance on foreign policy matters. As German domestic and foreign policy continued to evolve in the late 1960s, the remaining instances of federation-level dialogue deteriorated into a noncommunicative standoff.[2]

AFL AND CIO RIVALRY OVER POLICY IN GERMANY

The bitter rivalry between the AFL and the CIO directly influenced American trade union support for the reconstruction of the German

---

[1] Besides the DGB, the other unions of note are the *Deutsche Angestellten-Gewerkschaft* (DAG), which organizes only salaried employees (*Angestellte*), and the *Deutscher Beamtenbund* (DBB) for civil servants (*Beamte*) and other public service employees.

[2] See the chapter by Michael Fichter, vol. 2, Society.

trade unions during the Allied occupation. In 1944, the AFL set up a Free Trade Union Committee (FTUC) as its own policy arm for the postwar world. Its brand of anticommunism had found little support in international labor circles, and its plans for the reconstruction of German trade unions had been rejected at a meeting of the International Labor Organization (ILO). Under the direction of the top AFL leadership (William Green, George Meany, Matthew Woll, and David Dubinsky), the FTUC and the AFL International Labour Relations Committee were largely independent of any effective internal union control. With their sizable budget, they were able to finance a wide range of activities in the Western occupation zones and elsewhere in Europe.[3]

The CIO, by contrast, was politically more heterogeneous than the AFL; many of its leading activists had Socialist or Communist Party backgrounds. Dedicated to supporting Roosevelt's policy of Allied cooperation, the CIO was ready to assume the international role vacated by the AFL. Sidney Hilman became the CIO spokesman on international affairs and in 1945 helped found the World Federation of Trade Unions (WFTU), which included communist unions and the mass labor organizations of the Soviet bloc. The CIO regarded the WFTU as the proper organization to guide the reconstruction of trade unions in Germany.

Despite their basic differences over policy toward the Soviet Union, both labor federations – first the AFL and then the CIO – supported the goals of "one-world multinationalism": to reconstruct Europe, raise productivity and output, and provide the expanded American economy with necessary export markets.[4] In Germany, American labor unequivocally advocated the earliest possible reconstruction of the trade unions but disagreed strongly over how this goal should be pursued. Whereas the AFL gave its undivided support to the surviving social democratic union leaders, Hilman was highly critical of their failure to thwart the National Socialists' rise to power and advocated a grassroots renewal under new leadership.

As the United States stepped up its preparations for the occupation of Germany in 1944, American labor leaders vied to make their views known and influence the planning. Officers with both AFL and CIO backgrounds joined the Manpower Division of military government and began debating the course of union revival to be followed. However, in the first months of occupation, military government programs were subordinated to occupation prerequisites for security, which rarely included the reconstruction of unions. Not until after the formation of trade unions was recognized in the Potsdam Agreement of August 1945 did the military government apply a unified policy throughout the American zone.[5] Even then, organizational development remained sluggish. Unions had to conform to a highly restrictive and regulated process of rebuilding, beginning at the local level and advancing progressively through regional and state-level approval. This was the conservative military approach to trade union revival and not Hilman's grassroots policy. Both the CIO and the AFL complained about the restraints, but the AFL at least was satisfied to see the pre-1933 unionists back at the helm.[6]

---

[3] Roy Godson, *American Labor and European Politics: The AFL as a Transnational Force* (New York, 1976), 32–7.

[4] Charles S. Maier, "The Politics of Productivity: Foundations of American International Economic Policy After World War II," *International Organization* 31 (1977): 607–34.

[5] The reconstruction of the German unions during the occupation period is extensively documented in Hermann Weber and Siegfried Mielke, eds., *Quellen zur Geschichte der deutschen Gewerkschaftsbewegung im 20. Jahrhundert*, 9 vols. (Cologne, 1985–99), vol. 6: *Organisatorischer Aufbau der Gewerkschaften 1945–1949.*

[6] Michael Fichter, *Besatzungsmacht und Gewerkschaften: Zur Entwicklung und Anwendung der US-Gewerkschaftspolitik in Deutschland 1944–1948* (Opladen, 1982), 140–75.

Despite military government restrictions and the difficulties of communication brought on by destruction and dislocation, local union groups throughout Germany agreed on the need to overcome the political divisions of the union movement that had hampered the fight against National Socialism. This was the birth of the German "unitary union" (*Einheitsgewerkschaft*), a concept with roots in the Weimar period that could address the need for a complete organizational reconstruction. Unionists of Christian, social democratic, and communist persuasion worked together on the basis of "one workplace – one union" (*ein Betrieb – eine Gewerkschaft*) to launch large industrial unions. Initially, many of the local unions also were highly centralized. Their supporters believed this necessary for coping with the challenge of rebuilding and using local resources most efficiently.

Beyond the immediate organizational ramifications, the *Einheitsgewerkschaft* also represented the organizational basis for the goals of economic restructuring (*Neuordung der Wirtschaft*) and economic democracy (*Wirtschaftsdemokratie*), which included the socialization of major industries and the introduction of codetermination at the company and industrial-branch levels. Having returned to their largely destroyed workplaces, labor activists formed works councils (*Betriebsräte*) and began organizing union locals while directing the repair and rebuilding process. Although American union representatives in the U.S. military government would have preferred replacing works councils with union shop stewards, overriding political concerns about the policy of the Soviet Union in its occupation zone forced them to accept the rebirth of works councils.[7]

The foremost interest of both the AFL and the CIO was to ensure democratic membership participation and prevent the new unions from becoming highly centralized bodies resembling the National Socialist labor organization, the *Deutsche Arbeitsfront*. Initially, that meant blocking the regional merger of central-

ized local union bodies. Later in the occupation, the AFL linked this goal to its battle to eliminate communist influence within the unions of the Western zones and prevent their merger with the centralized trade union in the Soviet zone, the *Freier Deutscher Gewerkschaftsbund* (FDGB).

By mid-1946, cooperation between the AFL and the CIO, as well as with the U.S. military government on trade union policy, had improved greatly. Indeed, the strict organizational controls the military government had imposed actually lent support to those German union leaders who sought to create strong and financially independent industrial unions united in a federation but not ruled by its headquarters. The restrictions were a hindrance to the pursuit of an encompassing economic *Neuordnung* (of which the American unions were skeptical), but did not have a noticeably detrimental effect on the rapid growth of membership. Material support for the rebuilding effort came from the AFL and, to a lesser extent, from the CIO in the form of donations of office supplies, equipment, and CARE packages for selected union officials. Both federations helped the DGB regain possession of property confiscated by the Nazis. By 1947, the military government, in cooperation with the AFL and the CIO, had also inaugurated a program that brought in American labor experts to give support and advice and report home on the progress being made.

THE COLD WAR AND THE UNIONS

As relations between the Western Allies and the Soviet Union deteriorated, the AFL stepped up its attacks on both the WFTU, which it accused of unauthorized meddling in the affairs of German unions, and the FDGB in the Soviet zone. Its goal was to thwart interzonal union cooperation and prevent the German unions from joining the WFTU. Although the CIO initially defended the WFTU and its activities in Germany, it inevitably had to reassess its position in 1947 after the WFTU rejected the Marshall Plan. At home, the CIO had eliminated communist supporters from its leadership, and its underwriting of the the Marshall Plan moved

---

[7] Ibid., 176–91.

it into line with AFL international trade union policy.

Similar, if less pronounced, policy controversies existed also among German union leaders. Although they largely accepted the de facto division of Germany and its labor movement and supported the nationalist course of Kurt Schumacher, chairman of the Social Democratic Party (*Sozialdemokratische Partei Deutschlands*, or SPD), noncommunist German union leaders accepted the Marshall Plan as the only realistic path toward economic recovery for Germany and Europe. Union leaders did continue to campaign for the socialization of basic industries, but this goal would soon prove illusory. Parallel to the Marshall Plan's discouragement of such "experiments," the military government pursued a policy of "prejudicing by banning all prejudicing,"[8] suspending parliamentary decisions on socialization at the state (*Land*) level.

The AFL (and eventually the CIO) was fundamentally opposed to the socialization program advocated by the German unions. Nevertheless, both federations tried to promote understanding in the United States for the context and historical background of their German counterparts' demands.[9] The AFL attributed German unionists' sympathy for socialist goals to the devastation and deprivation of postwar Europe, because "empty stomachs are susceptible to all conceivable forms of totalitarianism."[10] It tried to persuade German unionists to renounce socialization and was relieved that the DGB was willing to put the issue in the hands of a western German constitutional assembly. At the same time, the AFL told the military government that, ultimately, demands for socialization could be successfully countered only by rebuilding the economy and integrating the trade unions into a new political democracy. AFL representatives

Irving Brown and Jay Lovestone regarded Germany as the economic heartland of Europe and the German labor movement as the key to establishing "free trade unionism"[11] there, an essential goal for the well-being and prosperity of American labor. Together with the CIO, they argued that with trade union participation, the Marshall Plan would be a powerful means to this end.[12]

As early as 1947, both the AFL and the CIO were calling for an end to the dismantling of industrial facilities, which they felt starkly contradicted the overall policy goals of the Marshall Plan. German and American trade unions cooperated closely in opposing such actions. One example is the unions' successful transnational intervention in 1950 to prevent the dismantling of the Salzgitter industrial complex.[13]

HICOG AND GERMAN LABOR

Military government ended in Germany with the founding of the Federal Republic of Germany in late 1949. However, under the auspices of the United States High Commission for Germany (HICOG), the successor organization to the military government with oversight powers, the American unions continued to battle communism and promote the "American way of life" in their contacts with the German unions. As had been the case with the Manpower Division of the military government, both the AFL and the CIO were consulted in the process of selecting HICOG staff members to deal with labor. High Commissioner John J. McCloy chose Harvey Brown, the president of the International Association of Machinists (AFL), to be his director of the HICOG Office of Labor Affairs.

A major concern of HICOG labor officers was fighting communism, and Brown especially perceived a need to combat the belief in German trade union circles that a communist could also

[8] Hans-Hermann Hartwich, *Sozialstaatspostulat und gesellschaftlicher status quo* (Opladen, 1970), 66–7. See also John Gimbel, *The American Occupation of Germany: Politics and the Military, 1945–1949* (Stanford, Calif., 1968).

[9] Werner Link, *Deutsche und amerikanische Gewerkschaften und Geschäftsleute 1945–1975: Eine Studie über transnationale Beziehungen* (Düsseldorf, 1978), 74.

[10] Quoted in Alfred Hero and Emil Starr, *The Reuther-Meany Foreign Policy Dispute* (New York, 1970), 56.

[11] Fichter, *Besatzungsmacht und Gewerkschaften*, 36–42.

[12] Frederico Romero, *The United States and the European Trade Union Movement, 1944–1951* (Chapel Hill, N.C., 1992), 178–82.

[13] Link, *Gewerkschaften*, 60–2. See also the chapter by Jörg Fisch, vol. 1, Economics.

be a good trade unionist. The role of communists within the unions had been a major issue for the DGB since the Berlin Blockade and the controversies over the Marshall Plan. Although communist unionists had contributed substantially to the reconstruction of the unified union movement, the number of them still holding office had diminished considerably. Nevertheless, with East-West tensions mounting, DGB leaders began to consider administrative action. The DGB executive committee was in close contact with the HICOG labor office on this issue; in October 1950, it served notice that it would fire any union official who openly acknowledged support for the German Communist Party (*Kommunistische Partei Deutschlands*, or KPD). Six months later, after the KPD officially declared its intention to create opposition cells within the unions – a move reminiscent of the disastrous communist tactics of the Weimar period – communist union officials had to choose between allegiance to the party or keeping their union job.[14]

In the following years, the American unions directed their attacks on communism against the German Democratic Republic (GDR). The AFL revived underground contacts with social democrats and noncommunist trade unionists in the GDR that the SPD had arranged in exchange for newsprint. Following the East German workers' uprising of June 17, 1953, the AFL and the CIO joined together with the DGB to step up their underground work in the GDR and to support East German refugees who had fled to the West. Along with the noncommunist International Confederation of Free Trade Unions (ICFTU), they founded a Berlin Committee, whose monthly budget of DM 40,000 was financed in large part by the American (50 percent) and the German (33 percent) union federations.[15]

In the fight against communism, HICOG's Office of Labor Affairs (OLA) regarded its program for sending labor leaders to the United States "as the most important part of the labor re-orientation effort." By September 1950, 138 Germans had participated in such programs. For 1951, OLA planned to send 150 German unionists on ninety-day tours and some 100 younger unionists to study for a year. Competition for inclusion in these trips was stiff. Both the DGB and the white-collar union *Deutsche Angestellten-Gewerkschaft* (DAG) lent their full support to this program as a step toward reestablishing international contacts after the Nazi years of isolation.[16]

A vivid indication of the effectiveness of OLA's study tours is reflected in a report by the president of the Michigan State CIO Council, August Scholle, whom OLA invited to Germany to assess the impact of the program. After a month of interviews, Mr. Scholle reported virtually unanimous agreement among German unionists that the opportunity to visit the United States "had revised many of their pre-conceived notions." "The visits have been the best form of visual education. Visitor after visitor told me that he could not understand what Americans were talking about in telling of democratic institutions and processes until he made his trip to America." Mr. Scholle went on to note that the visitors had also been "keenly observant" of negative aspects "not to the credit of democracy," including racial discrimination and the lack of political organization in the United States labor movement. But overall, he concluded, "the visits have helped answer affirmatively the question of whether democracy can fulfill the needs and aspirations of working people."[17]

Reactions to the reports of participants who wrote and spoke about their experiences upon their return to Germany also confirmed the effectiveness of the visits. Although most audiences reacted positively and were quite

---

[14] Michael Fichter, "HICOG and the Unions in West Germany," in Jeffry M. Diefendorf, Axel Frohn, and Hermann-Josef Rupieper, eds., *American Policy and the Reconstruction of West Germany, 1945–1955* (New York, 1993), 266–7. Michael Fichter, *Einheit und Organisation: Der Deutsche Gewerkschaftsbund im Aufbau 1945 bis 1949* (Cologne, 1990), 73–4.

[15] Link, *Gewerkschaften*, 69.

[16] J. F. J. Gillen, *Labor Problems in West Germany* (Frankfurt am Main, 1952), 66.

[17] August Scholle, Appraisal of Cultural Exchange Program, Aug. 28, 1951, National Archives, Record Group 59, Box 5201, 862a.062/9-1751.

interested in learning about conditions in the United States, communists often launched bitter attacks on both the reports and the program itself.[18]

THE ISSUE OF CODETERMINATION

In the early 1950s, codetermination (*Mitbestimmung*) became a major economic issue for the DGB. The AFL and the CIO supported this goal, not least because, as the CIO put it, without codetermination there would be class conflict. Although the American union federations would have preferred to see the German unions use collective bargaining instead of demanding legislation to attain it, they were ready to back the DGB in its efforts. During the occupation period, AFL and CIO leaders felt that General Clay's military government was too conservative and often biased toward employers; they protested strongly when Clay suspended the economic codetermination provisions of *Land* laws in fall 1948. Under HICOG, the American unions lobbied for reinstating the provisions, and they claimed success when High Commissioner McCloy complied in spring 1950. For its part, the DGB mounted a great effort to stop the new German government under the conservative chancellor Konrad Adenauer from eliminating the existing regulation of codetermination in the iron and steel industry (*Montanindustrie*). As part of its strategy, DGB leaders held talks with American government officials and trade union representatives in hope of preventing HICOG from intervening on behalf of the government and the employers. HICOG's leading labor officer and AFL unionist, Harvey Brown, fully understood the implications of a possible HICOG involvement in the dispute and conveyed the message to McCloy, warning that the United States would be "bitterly condemned" if it were to take sides with the employers or give the impression that they were "picking the German Government's chestnuts out of the fire."[19] HICOG remained neutral,

and Chancellor Adenauer, after weighing the likely political and economic consequences of a strike, agreed to extend the provisions of *Montanmitbestimmung* to German law. The DGB leadership publicly thanked the AFL for its support in securing codetermination in this one key sector and rallied its American allies behind the goal of extending full codetermination to the rest of the economy. This was the beginning of "transnational block building" (*transnationale Frontbildung*). The AFL and the CIO joined in support of the DGB, whereas American business interests backed the attempts of German employers and business interests to prevent the spread of codetermination.[20]

For the DGB, codetermination was more than an instrument of participation in economic decision-making processes; it was also a means of assuring that there would be no uncontrolled economic power that could lead the country into war again. This was indeed an issue of deep concern for the unions, as was the question of military alignment and West Germany's contribution to its own defense. Whereas AFL representative Henry Rutz had begun calling for rearming Germany (against the Soviet Union) soon after the war, German unionists were generally more concerned about eradicating German militarism. But after the two German states were founded in 1949 and West Germany became increasingly connected to the Western Alliance, some union leaders began to reevaluate their rejection of German rearmament. In a meeting with McCloy in August 1950 shortly after the outbreak of the Korea crisis, DGB chairman Hans Böckler stated that, in light of the danger posed by the Soviet bloc, it would be absurd for West Germans to do nothing and expect others to defend their freedom. Although Böckler and his like-minded colleagues also realized that they could not prevent the re-creation of a military establishment, they wished to use their influence to prevent the old guard from assuming a dominant role and posing

[18] Gillen, *Labor Problems*, 68–9.
[19] Fichter, "HICOG and the Unions," 274.

[20] Link, *Gewerkschaften*, 79. American business lobbyists proclaimed that U.S. investors would shun Germany if codetermination were to be adopted throughout the economy. See also Fichter, "HICOG and the Unions," 271.

a threat to the democratization of Germany. Böckler found a majority in the DGB's executive committee for this position, but opposition to rearmament remained widespread within individual member unions.[21]

UNION DIVISION OVER FOREIGN POLICY ISSUES

After Böckler's death in early 1951 and the subsequent failure of the unions to achieve their full codetermination demands, the DGB reasserted its opposition to the Adenauer government's policies of rearmament and Western integration. Despite repeated attempts by American union leaders to swing DGB opinion to support Adenauer, including the pressure of public pronouncements, the DGB refused to be swayed. In March 1955, it called on the Bundestag "to exhaust all possibilities of reunification in peace and freedom before ratifying the treaties" on NATO membership for West Germany and the abolition of the Occupation Statute.[22] Although unsuccessful, the DGB remained undeterred alongside the SPD in its opposition to rearmament. The willingness of the DGB and the SPD to consider peace initiatives from the Soviet bloc provoked criticism from the AFL-CIO[23] and prompted its president, George Meany, to support Adenauer's foreign policy openly. A deepening of differences was temporarily averted after the SPD modified its party platform in 1959 and declared its acceptance of German participation in NATO the following year.[24] After the building of the Berlin Wall in 1961, the DGB also revised its platform to reflect the new political circumstances.

With this foreign policy dispute resolved, relations between the DGB and the AFL-CIO improved again, though in a much different context than in the immediate postwar period. The DGB was now a powerful and integrated organization that had an acknowledged role in setting economic policy in the Federal Republic.[25] The unions also had stepped up their reliance on collective wage-bargaining in the wake of their codetermination defeat of 1952, a policy shift that was introduced as a move toward American-style "business unionism."[26] German unionists, many of whom participated in HICOG's study tours to American unions and industrial sites, were often fascinated not only by the dynamics and technological achievements of the American economy but also by the high standard of living, which they attributed to the successful work of the unions.[27]

But, again, it was foreign policy that finally drove a wedge between the German and American union federations. In 1966, the DGB passed a resolution at its national congress in favor of study trips to the Soviet bloc, excluding East Germany. Several union delegations visited the Soviet Union and a Soviet labor delegation came to West Germany. This was the beginning of a trade union Ostpolitik, an attempt to reduce East-West tensions and open a dialogue. Such an approach ran counter to the foreign policy principles of the AFL-CIO. At the next meeting of the ICFTU, George Meany openly criticized the DGB for its decision, arguing that it violated a 1955 agreement against contacts with communist labor organizations. Although the DGB's initiative scarcely had been launched when Soviet troops invaded Czechoslovakia in August 1968 and all contacts to Soviet bloc organizations were frozen, it had been taken as an unfriendly act by the AFL-CIO leadership and set the stage for a growing estrangement between the two national federations.

---

[21] Fichter, "HICOG and the Unions," 278–9.

[22] The resolution and the controversy with the AFL is documented in Klaus Schönhoven and Hermann Weber, eds., *Quellen zur Geschichte der deutschen Gewerkschaftsbewegung im 20. Jahrhundert*, vol. 11, *Der Deutsche Gewerkschaftsbund 1949 bis 1956* (Cologne, 1996), 667–72.

[23] In 1955, the AFL and the CIO merged to form the AFL-CIO.

[24] See the chapter by Ronald J. Granieri, vol. 1, Politics.

[25] Werner Abelshauser, *Wirtschaftsgeschichte der Bundesrepublik Deutschland 1945–1980* (Frankfurt am Main, 1983), 81. The AFL had advocated a similar role for itself in the economic conversion process at the end of World War II.

[26] Andrei S. Markovits, *The Politics of the West German Trade Unions* (New York, 1986), 84–5.

[27] Fichter, "HICOG and the Unions," 261, 264. Exchanges of delegations and study trips continued at a high frequency up through the mid-1960s.

CHAPTER TEN

Study Tours, Trade Fairs, Publicity Campaigns

German–American Business Encounters and Cold War Anxieties

S. Jonathan Wiesen

For historians of postwar Germany and America, writing about "business relations" poses a formidable challenge. Although such a study might begin with a focus on finance and trade, one quickly discovers that "business" always transcends the realm of the economy proper.[1] After 1945, transatlantic business relations were not only about trade or corporate partnerships, they were also about the transmission of mentalities and ideas. Postwar business relations entailed a collection of "sociopolitical," "socioeconomic," and "sociocultural interlacings."[2] Whether over a glass of wine or at a seminar on management strategies, whether in New York or in Frankfurt, American and West German businessmen met regularly to forge a vibrant transatlantic relationship. Corporate executives, company managers, economic publicists, and entrepreneurs came together to discuss not only business ventures and export statistics but also the political developments in both countries, the spiritual condition of "the West," and the nature of democracy and totalitarianism. If we could eavesdrop on these private dialogues from 1945 to 1968, we would discover that West German and American businessmen were not immune to the broader preoccupations of the postwar period.

This article focuses on two areas that had a particularly strong bearing on the relationship between businessmen in West Germany and the United States: the legacy of National Socialism and the Cold War antagonism between East and West. In their joint attempt to revive the European economy and to establish healthy Atlantic trading ties, American and West German businessmen were forced to confront the legacy of past business behavior under Nazism and their present responsibilities in the fight against Soviet communism.

EARLY POSTWAR CONTACTS

In the immediate aftermath of World War II, the condition of the German economy was foremost on the minds of American politicians and business leaders: Would the country recover from its material devastation? How quickly could German industry be rebuilt? Would West Germany adopt a capitalist or a socialist economy? As the Allies asked these urgent questions in spring 1945, American businessmen were already traveling to Germany to get a firsthand view of the destruction. These initial visitors did not venture into occupied Germany for

---

[1] On postwar German-American trade, see Reinhard Neebe, *Überseemärkte und Exportstrategien in der westdeutschen Wirtschaft* (Stuttgart, 1991); Manfred Knapp, *Sorgen unter Partnern: Zum Verhältnis zwischen den USA und der Bundesrepublik Deutschland* (Hannover, 1984).

[2] Werner Link, *The Contribution of Trade Unions and Businessmen to German-American Relations, 1945–1975* (Bloomington, Ind., 1978), 1. For the most comprehensive studies on the topic of German-American business relations, see Link and Volker R. Berghahn, *The Americanisation of West German Industry, 1945–1973* (Cambridge, 1986).

humanitarian reasons. Rather, they hoped to inspect the damage to their branch installations
and reestablish business connections that had
been severed during the war. This influx of
Americans sparked fears on both sides of the
Atlantic that this was the beginning of a wholesale foreign takeover of West German industry.
To assuage these fears, in 1945 the United States
prohibited direct foreign investment in the West
German economy until 1950, thereby declaring
its commitment to free trade and economic interdependence; West Germany would not become an economic protectorate of the United
States.

Although American businessmen were intent
on discovering new markets in a defeated Germany, they also recognized that their colleagues
across the Atlantic faced tremendous hardships.
Beginning in June 1946, organizations like the
National Association of Manufacturers (NAM)
sponsored a number of goodwill delegations to
West Germany.[3] These trips revived contacts
between American and West German industry as businessmen met with old friends and
spoke of mutual aid and future business relations. However, the majority of American businessmen who traveled to West Germany in the
late 1940s did so under the official sponsorship
of the U.S. occupation authorities, not as private citizens. Their task was to provide technical
assistance to destroyed companies and survey
the overall condition of German industry.[4]
The U.S. government coordinated these visits according to the broader humanitarian and
political aims of the Marshall Plan.[5] By establishing personal contacts between businessmen
and by (re)introducing West Germans to free
enterprise, the United States was pursuing an
explicit policy aim: the containment of communism through the creation of an economically healthy Europe.

This early transatlantic flow of businessmen
was not unidirectional. In fall 1947, West Germans were granted permission to conduct business in the United States, and they quickly
headed overseas in large numbers. Many German businessmen had already come to the
United States during the 1920s and 1930s to
get a firsthand view of the most advanced economy in the world. After a stint in an American
factory, they returned home with an enthusiasm
for the Fordist and Taylorist assembly line and
time-management innovations, along with a respect for the United States as a model of capitalist success.[6] After World War II, West German
industrialists were eager to resume their transatlantic visits. Working and traveling in the United
States brought them into contact with business
practices and attitudes that they hoped to integrate into existing German business structures.[7]

These renewed visits to the United States
were ostensibly geared toward the reestablishment of personal contacts and the discovery
of new export markets for German products,[8] but they were also conceived as "study
tours" in which German entrepreneurs could
learn about "democratic" business attitudes
and management styles. In 1949, the Rockefeller Foundation helped establish the International Work-Study Exchange (*Internationaler
Werkstudenten-Austausch*), which was jointly
directed by prominent Americans and West

---

[6] On Fordism and Taylorism and German business in
the 1920s, see Mary Nolan, *Visions of Modernity: American Business and the Modernization of Germany* (Oxford,
1994); Charles S. Maier, "Between Taylor and Technocracy: European Ideologies and the Vision of Industrial
Productivity in the 1920s," *Journal of Contemporary History* 5, no. 2 (1970): 27–61.

[7] One of the great obstacles to this process was the
persistent enthusiasm for cartels by a number of German industrialists. See Berghahn, *Americanisation*, 21–3.
See also the chapter by Regina Gramer, vol. 1, Economics.

[8] On German trade with the United States, see
Heinz Hartmann, *Amerikanische Firmen in Deutsch-
land* (Cologne, 1963); Rationalisierungs-Kuratorium der
Deutschen Wirtschaft (RKW), *Die Vereinigten Staaten
von Amerika als Markt für deutsche Erzeugnisse: Bericht einer
Studienreise* (Heidelberg, 1961).

---

[3] Link, *Contribution of Trade Unions*, 65.

[4] For one account of these business missions to West
Germany, see Lewis H. Brown, *A Report on Germany*
(New York, 1947).

[5] See the chapter by Gerd Hardach, vol. 1, Economics.

German figures, including Hermann Reusch of the *Gutehoffnungshütte*. The program's goal was to teach postwar European youth the concepts of "self-help" in the country that prided itself on its individualistic spirit.[9] Back in Germany, these future entrepreneurs would apply the practical lessons of market capitalism while inculcating in their colleagues a devotion to freedom and private property.

One participant in these study trips was Ludwig Vaubel, the future director of the *Vereinigte Glanzstoff*.[10] In 1950, Vaubel traveled to America to study management and public speaking at Harvard Business School. He kept a diary that offers a fascinating glimpse into the dynamics of cultural encounter after the war. With an infectious enthusiasm, Vaubel detailed his first contacts with Americans' habits and their attitudes about business, labor, racial relations, money, wealth, leisure, and National Socialism.[11]

Ludwig Vaubel's activities make clear that German-American business relations were as much about cultural and ideological exchange as they were about trade and finance. Mary Nolan and Volker Berghahn, in their respective studies of the Weimar and post–World War II years, have traced the transatlantic flow of manufacturing techniques, business philosophies, company and labor organizational methods, and "industrial cultures."[12] America was feared, revered, reviled, and respected as the model of the successful economy and, despite their many misgivings, Germans were looking westward. "Americanization," to invoke the much contested term, was slow and partial, with much indigenous resistance. But in the minds of many West German industrialists, it was undeniably taking hold.[13]

Even if individual businessmen in both countries remained ambivalent about the habits of their counterparts across the Atlantic, the multiple avenues of exchange created in the 1940s and 1950s fostered a spirit of openness and diminished the mistrust that only recently had existed between former enemies. Another sign of this renewed esprit de corps was the reappearance and popularization of trade fairs in both countries. In April 1949, the New York Museum of Science and Industry, in conjunction with the American military government in Germany, sponsored the *Germany 49* exhibition, which brought 500 West German companies to the United States to highlight their latest goods and machinery.[14] The following year, West Berlin hosted the first annual German Industry Exhibition (*Deutsche Industrie-Ausstellung*), which devoted dozens of pavilions and thousands of feet of floor space to the newest products emerging from West Germany's ascendant companies. In order to keep abreast of the innovations across the Atlantic, American companies sent representatives to Berlin to report on the exhibition. While forging new contacts and rediscovering old ones, Americans could also tour the "George C. Marshall House," which housed an exhibit on industry, trade, and labor in the United States along with a separate presentation on the workings of the American government.[15] Amidst such celebrations of Western economic and cultural unity, American

[9] On these international exchange programs from 1949 and 1950, see Nachlass Hermann Reusch, 400101460/0, Rheinisch-Westfälisches Wirtschaftsarchiv, Cologne.

[10] See Ludwig Vaubel, *Unternehmer gehen zur Schule: Ein Erfahrungsbericht aus USA* (Düsseldorf, 1952); Ludwig Vaubel, *Zusammenbruch und Wiederaufbau: Ein Tagebuch aus der Wirtschaft 1945–1949*, ed. Wolfgang Benz (Munich, 1984).

[11] See Vaubel Sammlung ED 321/1–18, vol. 17, Harvard-Tagebuch, Sept. 8, 1950-Dec. 21, 1950, Institut für Zeitgeschichte, Munich. For a discussion of Hamburg industrialist Otto A. Friedrich's trip to the United States in 1949, see Volker R. Berghahn and Paul J. Friedrich, *Otto A. Friedrich: Ein Politischer Unternehmer* (Frankfurt am Main, 1993).

[12] See Nolan, *Visions of Modernity*; Volker R. Berghahn, "West German Reconstruction and American Industrial Culture, 1945–1960," in Reiner Pommerin, ed., *The American Impact on Postwar Germany* (Providence, R.I., 1995), 65–81.

[13] See the chapter by Axel Schildt in this section.

[14] *Germany 49* [Industry Show, New York Museum of Science and Industry, R.C.A. Building, Apr. 9–24, 1949] (New York, 1949).

[15] Pressestelle der Deutschen Industrieausstellung, no. 13, July 19, 1950, Landesarchiv Berlin. See also *Deutsche Industrieausstellung Berlin 1950: Veranstalter,*

businessmen were getting their first glimpse of an economy on the verge of a miraculous comeback. The explosion of trade fairs throughout West Germany became one of the most potent symbols of the new state's postwar economic miracle (*Wirtschaftswunder*) and its growing confidence in the world market.

Another manifestation of this transatlantic relationship was the establishment of private organizations expressly devoted to business relations between the United States and the Federal Republic of Germany. The U.S.-German Chamber of Commerce was founded in 1947 and had an official employee roster of one person and a support staff of fifteen. It served as a lobbying agency for small and medium-sized companies that came to America to conduct business. In 1959, the organization combined with the German-American Trade Promotion Office (GATPO) to form the German-American Chamber of Commerce, and it soon became the most significant gathering place for German businessmen in America, eventually establishing branches in Washington, D.C., and San Francisco and publishing a newsletter, *German-American Trade News*.[16] The equivalent organization in West Germany was the American Chamber of Commerce (ACC) in Germany, which was reestablished in 1949 after having being dissolved during the war. The ACC, headquartered in Frankfurt am Main, served as the representative body for American business interests in West Germany. Its chief function was to bring its members into contact with fellow businessmen and U.S. consular representatives.[17]

Both these organizations catered to small and middle-sized firms, but big business in both countries also maintained regular contacts. In 1950, Fritz Berg, the president of the newly established Federal Association of German Industry (*Bundesverband der deutschen Industrie*,

or BDI), led the first of what would be an annual delegation of German industrialists to the United States. Often under the aegis of NAM, the BDI representatives met with politicians and prominent New York and Washington businessmen.[18] "The BDI's main committee," stated the delegation report, "went with the recognition that it is in the USA that the great decisions about political and economic issues are made."[19]

All of these organizations, regardless of the constituencies they represented, had a similar raison d'être – one that was as ideological as it was economic. In promoting an expressly "Atlantic" commercial partnership, they were serving the broader aim of building an economic bulwark against communism. In the 1940s, the Marshall Plan had initiated the goal of building and safeguarding a democratic Europe through a healthy economy. Long after the program had concluded, businessmen in both countries continued to draw a link between political democracy and economic prosperity. They demonstrated their commitment to free economic and political exchange (in explicit contrast to the repressive practices in the Soviet bloc) not only through the promotion of active trading relations but also by participation in seminars, roundtable discussions, and social gatherings. On the surface, these contacts were not primarily about the struggle between capitalism and communism. Businessmen often claimed their interests were inherently apolitical and that they simply wanted to create a friendly environment for international business. But in the climate of the Cold War, when a businessman promoted his company's burgeoning success or celebrated his country's financial

---

Berliner Ausstellungen, Eigenbetrieb Gross-Berlin (Berlin, 1950).

[16] My thanks to Dick Jacob in the New York City office of the German-American Chamber of Commerce for talking to me about the early history of the organization.

[17] Link, *Contribution of Trade Unions*, 92.

[18] Fritz Blumrath, "Die internationale Arbeit des Bundesverbandes der Deutschen Industrie von 1945 bis 1954," in BDI, *Fünf Jahre BDI*, (Bergisch-Gladbach, 1954), 169–202.

[19] Bericht über die Reise der Delegation des BDI nach den USA von Juli 1951, Anlage zur Niederschrift über die Hauptausschuss-Sitzung, Sept. 27, 1951, Nachlass Otto Vogel, box 203, Industrie-und Handelskammer Augsburg und Schwaben, Augsburg. NAM representatives continued to come regularly to the Federal Republic as well. In 1950 and 1951, they conferred with German business over the issue of codetermination.

health, he was simultaneously indicting the West's ideological opponent.

PUBLIC RELATIONS AND THE LEGACY OF NATIONAL SOCIALISM

One cannot consider the revival of postwar business relations during the Cold War without addressing the theme of National Socialism. During the period of economic reconstruction, German industrialists were constantly reminded of the actual and reputed help that companies and business leaders had lent to the Nazi economy during the 1930s and 1940s. In the minds of many West German and American businessmen, this legacy had a direct influence on the struggle against communism. Images of slave labor, tanks, armaments contracts, and Zyklon B pursued West Germany into the postwar years, and as long as these examples of "capitalist complicity" remained political issues, industrialists in the United States and West Germany felt that the political interests of the Atlantic nations would be jeopardized. The constant attack on industrialists would, they felt, feed into the rhetoric of the Soviet Union by calling into question the moral credentials of capitalism.

Although most of the references to big-business crimes came from the Left and the Soviet bloc, the Americans were also intent on holding accountable those business leaders who had actively contributed to the Nazi effort. In 1947 and 1948, the Americans conducted three separate trials of Krupp, I.G. Farben, and Flick officials in Nuremberg. Dozens of company directors were prosecuted and convicted of using forced labor, supporting the SS, and plundering businesses in occupied territories during the war. Although the imprisonment of a top executive could have a devastating effect on a company's reputation, industrialists saw Nuremberg as an opportunity to marshal their financial and intellectual resources to counter the familiar images of German business complicity.[20] Even

before Nuremberg, companies called on their contacts in the United States to lobby against the punitive aspects of American foreign policy. Appealing to the themes of unity and transatlantic goodwill, they wrote to old business acquaintances, asking them to ignore the accusations that the American government and the European left were leveling against Germany's "war criminal firms."[21]

This struggle against the "Nuremberg complex" converged with attempts to halt the dismantling of firms the Allies had designated as war-production facilities. In both campaigns, German and American businessmen consulted over how to prevent what they saw as the foolhardy destruction and demoralization of companies so vital to the economic reconstruction of Western Europe. While American businessmen lobbied Washington to halt dismantling and free convicted businessmen, German companies distributed apologetic pamphlets to American businessmen and politicians,[22] and heavy industry hired a lobbyist to shuttle between the Ruhr and Washington, D.C., in the quest to prevent further damage to German industry.[23]

These efforts persisted in the 1950s, when major firms set up public relations branches in the United States and enlisted the help of American businessmen, politicians, and journalists to defend the reputation of German industry. Perhaps the most active American spokesman for German industry was Julius Klein, a retired Jewish army general, former commander of the Jewish War Veterans of America, and director of a public-relations firm in Chicago.[24]

Elisabeth Binder, *Die Entstehung unternehmerischer Public Relations in der Bundesrepublik Deutschland* (Münster, 1983).

[21] See, for example, Hanns-Henning von Pentz to Benjamin O'Sheah, Greuelpropaganda über den Siemens-Konzern, Apr. 8, 1947, Nachlass Fritz Jessen, 11/La 176, Siemens-Archiv, Munich.

[22] See, for example, August Heinrichsbauer, *Schwerindustrie und Politik* (Essen-Kettwig, 1948).

[23] See Hanns D. Ahrens, *Demontage: Nachkriegspolitik der Allierten* (Munich, 1982).

[24] On the career of Klein, see Benjamin Ferencz, *Less than Slaves* (Cambridge, 1979), 134–6; James Boyd, *Above the Law* (New York, 1968), 206. Among his other

[20] S. Jonathan Wiesen, "Overcoming Nazism: Big Business, Public Relations, and the Politics of Memory, 1945–50," *Central European History* 29 (1996): 201–26;

Throughout the 1950s and early 1960s, Klein's task was to deny accusations of industrial complicity in Nazi crimes. He represented a number of German firms, including Bayer, Mannesmann, Rheinmetall, Daimler-Benz, and the Flick concern.

These publicity and lobbying efforts met with some success, no doubt fueled by the Cold War urge to protect Germany's reascendant industries and their directors during this sensitive period. Dismantling ground to a halt in 1949, High Commissioner John McCloy granted amnesty to Germany's imprisoned industrialists in 1951, and many of West Germany's largest companies, regardless of past contributions to the Nazi war effort, were able to find a viable market in the United States.[25]

Whether these developments can be attributed in part to the transatlantic publicity campaigns is hard to say. But the anti-Nuremberg and antidismantling campaigns did lead to a heightened understanding among West German and American businessmen that the economic revival in the Federal Republic would be incomplete without an image makeover. Without a concerted transatlantic effort, the persistent pictures of the authoritarian *Herr im Hause* and "Nazi industrialist" could not be supplanted by that of the democratic and socially conscious business leader. Like many aspects of German-American history after 1945, this cooperative effort resembled the relationship between teacher and student. American industry presented itself as the model to be imitated, and in this realm of image-making, Germans had little doubt that they could learn a few things. One person who benefited greatly from the American example was Carl Hundhausen, one of the earliest and most vocal proponents of aggressive marketing and public-relations techniques. In the 1930s and 1940s, Hundhausen made a number of trips to the United States and shared

his insights in a 1950 publication entitled *Winning the Public Trust*, the first true PR bible in West Germany.[26] In this book and throughout his career, Hundhausen promoted public relations as the "fourth pillar" of every German company, next to production, sales, and finance. As chief articulator of this new science, Hundhausen made what was perhaps a natural and predictable career move: In 1950, he returned to his old company, Krupp (a firm in the greatest need of an image makeover), as head of public relations.[27]

Other West German businessmen returned from their American travels with an increased sensitivity to the power of public relations and, by extension, of human relations. In the late 1940s and early 1950s, West German and American businessmen shared a common fear that European industry would become "socialized." Consequently, they began calling for companies to pay more attention to the workers as people, whose loyalty to the firm and commitment to the market economy depended upon the promise of a high wage packet and a healthy stake in the postwar prosperity. This new strategy came to the fore in the early 1950s, when West German industrialists fought an unsuccessful battle against industrial codetermination by portraying the proposed participation of labor representatives on company managing boards as the first step toward a union dictatorship.[28] In this highly politicized atmosphere, human relations was seen as a tool not only to pacify the workers but also to keep them free from the clutches of socialist thinking and labor organizing. Some of these new insights about human relations and public relations were embodied in the *Deutsches Industrieinstitut* (DI), a nationwide public-relations agency and clearinghouse founded in 1950 to educate small entrepreneurs

---

activities, Klein ran unsuccessfully for the U.S. Senate in 1954 as the Republican candidate from Illinois.

[25] See Thomas Alan Schwartz, *America's Germany: John J. McCloy and the Federal Republic of Germany* (Cambridge, Mass, 1991).

[26] Carl Hundhausen, *Werbung um öffentliches Vertrauen: "Public Relations"* (Essen, 1951).

[27] See Heinz Flieger and Franz Ronneberger, eds., *Public Relations Anfänge in Deutschland: Festschrift zum 100. Geburtstag von Carl Hundhausen* (Wesseling, 1993).

[28] On the theme of codetermination, see Berghahn, *Americanisation*, esp. chap. 3.

and industrialists in all matters relating to the economy, politics, and publicity.[29]

The increasing turn to public relations and advertising indicates that postwar transatlantic business relations were as much about the image of capitalism and the past behavior of German "capitalists" as they were about trade and the material success of companies. Against the backdrop of Nazism and the Cold War and in the age of the mass media, it was not enough for businessmen to boast impressive sales and trade figures; they would also have to demonstrate their own moral worth. They would have to not only prove their credentials as defenders of free-market ideals but also promote those personalities and those products that were the visible manifestations of the Western economic system. In coming to the defense of German industry, in teaching Germans about the importance of image and marketing, in promoting more humane relations between employees and management, American businessmen ultimately felt they were doing their part in the defense of Western values. They saw themselves as part of an international milieu of businessmen who understood each other and the necessities of their age. They drew upon their pre-Hitler contacts, their affinities as "men of business," and their professed disdain for Nazism in order to forgive German capitalism any previous misdeeds, all in service of the united struggle against totalitarianism.

FREE ENTERPRISE AND ATLANTIC UNITY

Between 1945 and 1968, the relations between West German and American business leaders changed profoundly. What began as an unequal relationship between victor and vanquished matured into a balanced partnership defined by open dialogue, mutual exchanges, and liberalized trade relations. The year 1968 saw the balance of trade between West Germany and the United States tip in favor of the former for the first time since World War II. After two decades of cooperation, German businessmen were proving to be a permanent presence in the United States.[30]

The symbolic importance of this maturing commercial partnership cannot be overestimated. Behind the export and import figures lay the mutual recognition that both American and West German business played a vital role in the economic and political security of the West. From the early postwar years, most American policymakers considered the reconstruction of European business and the consolidation of free enterprise as the sine qua non of an effective defense against Soviet military and ideological expansion. West Germany, in short, became not only a trading partner but, in the words of Manfred Knapp, a "system partner," committed to upholding an economic system based on free-market ideals.[31] With the help of individuals on both sides of the Atlantic, the West German economy became the front line in a battle between communism and capitalism.

This is not to suggest that German industrialists blindly conformed to every aspect of American business culture. Many Germans saw their economy as a third way between the oppressive collectivism of the Soviet bloc and the cutthroat competition of the United States. And as they traveled through the United States, they did wonder whether America's loyalty to the mass consumer was anathema to the German tradition of manufacturing high-quality products for the discriminating buyer.[32] Many also feared the arrival in Germany of the faceless

---

[29] The DI published a number of publications in the 1950s and 1960s, including *Rundfunkspiegel, Schnelldienst, Unternehmerbrief,* and *Vortragsreihe des deutschen Industrieinstituts.* In the early 1970s, the organization changed its name to the Institut der Deutschen Wirtschaft.

[30] See Hartmann, *Amerikanische Firmen.*

[31] Knapp, *Sorgen unter Partnern,* 57.

[32] For an introduction to the theme of consumer culture in the 1950s, see Michael Wildt, *Am Beginn der "Konsumgesellschaft": Mangelerfahrung, Lebenshaltung, Wohlstandshoffnung in Westdeutschland in den fünfziger Jahren* (Hamburg, 1994); Erica Carter, *How German Is She? Postwar West German Reconstruction and the Consuming Woman* (Ann Arbor, 1997). See also the chapter by Ingrid Schenk in this section.

"manager" so familiar to American business. This would spell the end of a cherished tradition of the business owner conducting the day-to-day affairs of his company. Despite these misgivings, West German industry did eventually temper its hostility to mass markets as it grew into an oligopolistic, consumer-friendly economy. Throughout the 1950s and 1960s, West Germany underwent a slow but definite acclimation to "American" mass-marketing techniques, managerial structures, and consumerist philosophies, while never abandoning a pride in its own economic traditions. By 1968, the "democratization" of the West German economy had firmly taken hold. American and West German businessmen played a decisive role in this process. When they traveled to each other's countries to pursue a healthy commercial relationship, they were simultaneously preserving "Atlantic unity" in the face of the communist enemy and containing the memory of Germany's own totalitarian past.

CHAPTER ELEVEN

Producing to Consume Becomes Consuming to Produce

Advertising and Consumerism in German-American Relations

Ingrid Schenk

When discussing the origins of the Federal Republic of Germany, it is necessary to shift focus from a famous hour – the *Stunde Null*, or Zero Hour, of May 8, 1945 – to a famous day: *der Tag X*, the day of the Deutsche Mark's arrival in the American, British, and French occupation zones. For many, the defining experience of rupture was not the cessation of hostilities but an end to the hardships of the peace. With regard to the black market and ration policies, the war's end began an escalation in illegal trade and ongoing shortages rather than a fundamental change of direction.[1] However, in the minds of Germans living in the West, the currency reform of June 20, 1948,[2] connected the transformation in shop windows they clearly observed with the de facto division between East and West caused by the Berlin Blockade, which began four days after the Deutsche Mark's arrival. The three Western zones of Germany were united by a currency before they had a constitution; subsequently, national identity, economic policy, and daily life remained intimately intertwined during the years of the economic miracle in the 1950s.

If the period 1945–8 encompassed a combination of ruptures, continuities, and transitions at the level of daily life, this was also the case with German-American relations. In economic policy, the most significant change was the move away from the Morgenthau Plan in favor of the European Recovery Program. Support for wide-scale dismantling as allowed for in JCS 1067 seemed unworkable in the long term, especially to General Lucius D. Clay, given that U.S. military government personnel found themselves assigned the task of preventing disease and unrest while confronted by a population both increasingly hungry and unemployed.[3] On the other hand, the European Recovery Program, and especially the Joint-Export-Import Agency, not only guaranteed a return on American aid designated in the form of investments but also provided West German

---

[1] For continuities and ruptures in ration policies, see Rainer Gries, *Die Rationen-Gesellschaft: Versorgungskampf und Vergleichsmentalität: Leipzig, München und Köln nach dem Kriege* (Münster, 1991). On barter and the black market, see Willi A. Boelcke, *Der Schwarzmarkt 1945–1948: Vom Überleben nach dem Kriege* (Braunschweig, 1986).

[2] Some scholars have examined West Germany in the 1950s as an example of a developing economy, pointing to how a post–Cold War context and cross-cultural comparisons may necessitate modifications of the conception of a German *Sonderweg* (special path) to modernity. See Martin Broszat, Klaus-Dietmar Henke, and Hans Woller, eds., *Währungsreform: Zur Sozialgeschichte des Umbruchs in Deutschland* (Munich, 1988). Michael Wildt, *Am Beginn der "Konsumgesellschaft": Mangelerfahrung, Lebenshaltung, Wohlstandshoffnung in Westdeutschland in den fünfziger Jahren* (Hamburg, 1994), provides a wealth of detail not only in its appendices but also in its treatment of household account books. For a cross-cultural comparison, see Victoria de Grazia, ed., *The Sex of Things: Gender and Consumption in Historical Perspective* (Berkeley, Calif., 1996).

[3] See the chapter by Wilfried Mausbach, vol. 1, Economics.

businesses with opportunities eagerly awaited by both entrepreneurs and workers.[4]

Although the economic miracle of the 1950s fostered a greater degree of rationalization in mass production than efforts to rationalize during the 1920s,[5] the rationalization and/or modernization of industry is not necessarily equivalent to Americanization.[6] A German consumer culture began to emerge during the late 1920s and early 1930s, producing such "American" items as Coca-Cola and cars priced for middle-class buyers.[7] In addition to realizing a potential that had existed since the 1920s, the initial push supplied by the Marshall Plan[8] (and its reinforcement during the Korean War) allowed West Germans to proclaim "We are somebody again" ("*Wir sind wieder wer*") through the strength of export production. The pride in the label "Made in (West) Germany" connected citizens of the Federal Republic to a tradition of superior production for export extending back to the late nineteenth century.[9]

If they took pride in the role exports played in increasing national status on an international level, West Germans also reestablished themselves domestically through patterns of consumption. However, these patterns were articulated against recent memories of the past as well as against the image of a decadent America and a deprived German Democratic Republic. During the 1950s and 1960s, West Germans consumed to produce. The fact that they could consume set them apart from East Germans.

How they did so also set them apart, in their eyes, from most Americans. From the point of view of West German consumers, West German national identity was intimately linked with making both geographical and chronological distinctions. West German advertisers knew this, of course, and they structured advertising strategies with personal and national aspirations in mind.

The following survey of the evolution of West German advertising strategies in 1945–68 illustrates the development of West Germany's consumer society. Key aspects of West German consumer culture, including purchasing patterns, the size of items, and attitudes toward them, are then examined with a comparative focus to stress how they argue against a facile equation of consumerism and Americanization. In conclusion, a brief contrast between East and West in 1990 shows the strength of the correlation between economic progress and German national identity.

Advertising strategies in West Germany paralleled the development of a West German consumer society that, somewhat paradoxically, consumed to produce. As viewed through the tactics used by advertisers, the trajectory of this consumer society's development can be described in four main phases: announcing a product's return to peacetime quality (1948–51), stressing the long-term savings a short-term purchase could guarantee (1951–5), emphasizing how luxury had become necessity (1955–60), and emphasizing the significance of improvements to these new necessities (1960–8). In each of these periods, the West German standard of living experienced a notable improvement. During the first, the purchase of goods long unavailable signaled a return to patterns of purchasing essential to rebuilding a normal life. During the second phase, consumers spent to save in order to consolidate and stabilize this new normality. By the late 1950s, however, former luxuries had become modern necessities, and consumers consumed in order to achieve a more intangible result. They now sought a certain sort of home environment and, with the purchase of consumer durables such as refrigerators, washing machines, and televisions,

---

[4] See Volker R. Berghahn, *The Americanisation of West German Industry, 1945–73* (New York, 1986).

[5] See Mary Nolan, *Visions of Modernity: American Business and the Modernization of Germany* (New York, 1994), 73–4.

[6] Interest in and adoption of American production and management techniques after World War II was a synthetic process tied to a generational shift. See Berghahn, *Americanisation of West German Industry*, 27, 257–8.

[7] Hans Dieter Schäfer, *Das gespaltene Bewusstsein: Über deutsche Kultur und Lebenswirklichkeit 1933–45* (Munich, 1981), 119.

[8] See the chapter by Gerd Hardach, vol. 1, Economics.

[9] Wolfgang J. Mommsen, *Nation und Geschichte: Über die Deutschen und die deutsche Frage* (Munich, 1990), 38–9.

they could create a new level of ease and aesthetic satisfaction. This escalation in consumer standards reached a peak in the mid-1960s, when consumer goals shifted once again. By this final phase, consumers sought goods that signaled both current prosperity and future security – the latest-model television with built-in additional channels, for example.

Advertisements for West German goods celebrated the distance between current circumstances and the widespread scarcity and deprivation experienced in 1945–8. For example, one 1950 advertisement for Persil laundry detergent announced, "The time for makeshift solutions is over! Persil is back again."[10] By 1952, West German consumers wanted to consume quality products, but they wanted to do so as economically as possible. Manufacturers of items from floor wax to refrigerators stressed the care and planning that went into their products in order to convince buyers that spending a bit more in the short run would result in long-term savings. Thrifty housewives were encouraged to use Sigella Wax, which was not an "inexpensive floor wax" but promised to reduce household costs because it was "so spreadable, that it can be applied in an extremely thin film; that means one uses less Sigella, and thus saves cash."[11] During this period, advertisers stressed that one must have a refrigerator because it would preserve expensive food purchases longer; having cool drinks at hand on hot summer days was simply an additional benefit of such an investment.

If spending to save had been the pattern endorsed by West German advertisements during the early 1950s, by the late 1950s luxuries had become necessities, and intangible rewards justified large purchases. For example, advertisements for fully automatic washing machines often mentioned that women who used them had more time for their husbands and children and could better preserve their looks and attitude.[12] Such a purchase – of an item hardly anyone's

parents had owned – was now part of a modern lifestyle and therefore represented a worthy investment. The rising West German standard of living could be seen not only in the high spirits and softness of a well-equipped housewife's hands, but also in the number of roles played by young married women, who increasingly sought part-time employment. Progress brought new economic demands as well as glamorous new possibilities.[13]

By the mid-1960s, West German advertisers shifted their strategy from persuading consumers to make a purchase to showing how a purchase illustrated subtle distinctions. Having more of a certain sort of leisure indicated one's success, as did how comfortably one performed household tasks. By May 1966, 78 percent of households reported that they owned an electric refrigerator, 26 percent owned a fully automatic washing machine, 48 percent owned an automobile, and 68 percent a television set.[14] With regard to automobiles, the level of saturation reached by the mid-1960s is especially striking because only 8 percent of those surveyed in 1954 could claim that they drove a car, and by 1962 this percentage had increased to only 21 percent.[15] During the late 1950s, hybrid vehicles, such as the BMW Isetta, itself an icon of the decade, enjoyed only a brief moment of popularity.[16] West Germans

---

well-cared-for-ness, my good spirits, my free time – all that is made possible for me by the Constructa" (German version: "Was Ihnen bei mir rätselhaft erscheint, mein gutes Aussehen, mein Gepflegt-Sein, meine gute Laune, meine Freizeit – das alles ermöglicht mir die Constructa."), *Der Stern*, June 12, 1955, 32.

[13] If pressing a button to dispatch an onerous household chore indicated a certain level of affluence and success, it was also the case that in working-class or lower-middle-class households these new purchases were financed by a second income. See Elisabeth Pfeil, *Die Berufstätigkeit von Müttern: Eine empirisch-soziologische Erhebung an 900 Müttern aus vollständigen Familien* (Tübingen, 1961), 113.

[14] Elisabeth Noelle Neumann and Erich Peter Neumann, eds., *Jahrbuch der Öffentlichen Meinung 1968–1973* (Allensbach, 1974), 5:399–400.

[15] Elisabeth Noelle Neumann and Erich Peter Neumann, *The Germans: Public Opinion Polls, 1947–1966* (Allensbach, 1967), 325.

[16] Horst Mönnich, *The BMW Story: A Company in Its Time* (London, 1991), 404.

---

[10] *Frankfurter Rundschau*, Oct. 3, 1950, 5.

[11] *Der Stern*, May 18, 1952, 28.

[12] See the AEG washing-machine advertisement in *Der Stern*, November 9, 1957, 81. An advertisement for Constructa washing machines noted, "What to you may seem mysterious about me – my good looks, my

not only wanted to drive to their vacation destinations (or even around town), they also wanted to do so in a vehicle that could seat four comfortably. If comfort was an issue, so was a combination of innovation and durability. Only two years after television sets became widely available for sale in the Federal Republic, one advertisement noted that "every set comes with a remote control for brightness and volume, prepared for the future with reserve-channel and UHF capacity."[17] West German consumers wanted their purchases not just to reflect the moment but also to anticipate the future.

The West German trajectory of prosperity outlined in advertisements began by stressing the actual return of much-longed-for items. Next, it emphasized ownership as a way of increasing efficiency and, paradoxically, practicing thrift. Later, it highlighted the necessity of former luxuries in order to indicate a new level of prosperity. Finally, it stressed subtle distinctions among a multitude of options. This last phase is common to many consumer societies, especially the United States. But increasing affluence in West Germany during the 1950s and 1960s should not be regarded as Americanization. As material circumstances improved, West Germans sought out comforts and conveniences that had formerly been reserved for a local elite or for the upper and middle classes in the United States. However, West Germans did not consume in the same way that Americans did. West German patterns of consumption differed from those in the United States in three significant ways: how consumers paid for new goods, the actual size of the durable goods purchased, and in the attitudes they had toward ownership.

Unlike Americans, West Germans tended to save for an item and pay cash for it, rather than buy on credit and pay off the purchase while using the item. One survey found that one-half of all American heads of households approved of buying on the installment plan, whereas two-thirds or more of all German respondents indicated unqualified opposition to buying on

credit. In 1968, only 14 percent of the most recent durable-goods purchases reported by German consumers were financed by installment debt, compared to 58 percent of cars and 45 percent of household appliances purchased in the United States.[18] Articles in weekly magazines warned that credit purchases could engender financial crises, especially for susceptible young women,[19] and buying on credit remained unpopular even when necessary. As one woman described it:

But we did have one luxury item, even then: a large Bosch refrigerator. That was the only thing that we bought for ourselves, the rest I brought with me as [part of my] dowry.... We paid for this refrigerator in installments. Since then I have never again in my life paid for anything on the installment plan. Completely terrible – I don't know, for five years or something.... You could never get rid of it.[20]

Although more common, credit purchases still retained enough of a stigma that, as one firm's owner reported to the *Süddeutsche Zeitung*, "my clients would rather go hungry than not pay a monthly installment."[21] Americans used an item as they paid for it; West Germans often only purchased an item after they had saved the money.

West German consumption patterns also differed from American in the area of product choice and preference. For example, although by 1962 the majority of West German households owned a refrigerator, the 45-liter (1.59 cubic feet) model found in most of those households was significantly smaller than the 5-cubic-foot (approximately 140 liters) GE Monitor Top

[17] *Der Stern*, Oct. 13, 1956, 35.

[18] George Katona, Burkhard Strumpel, and Ernest Zahn, *Aspirations and Affluence: Comparative Studies in the United States and Western Europe* (New York, 1971), 98–9, 175.
[19] "Die überlistete Hausfrau," *Quick*, May 7, 1950, 626–7.
[20] Michael Wildt, *Am Beginn der "Konsumgesellschaft,"* 148.
[21] "Der 'kleine Mann' zahlt pünktlich," *Süddeutsche Zeitung*, Aug. 3, 1950, 4.

sold in the United States during the late 1920s.[22] Whereas West German companies stressed how superior engineering made the most of 1.59 cubic feet of space, American advertisements illustrated how revolving shelves, in-door juice dispensers, and butter conditioners made for the best buy.[23] The size of refrigerators in West Germany complemented the existing practice of frequent shopping trips, and advertisers described refrigerator ownership as allowing the "working housewife" to take advantage of sales at the grocery store rather than reducing the time and effort she put into household chores.[24]

West German consumers also had a different attitude toward the items they purchased. After the sacrifices of long-term saving or after fulfilling the onerous obligation of monthly credit, West Germans expected goods to last indefinitely. In the 1950s, planned obsolescence typified the United States' automobile industry but was significantly absent from West German advertising and consumer culture. Most German manufacturers needed to persuade consumers to buy rather than trade in or up. Nearly all West German advertisements for automobiles listed gas mileage and operating costs, whereas American advertisements used horsepower as the preferred yardstick for comparison. The 1951 Oldsmobile 88, for example, had 135 horsepower, the Taunus deLuxe only 34.[25] However, the Taunus, which claimed to get approximately 29 miles to the gallon (8.1 liters per 100 kilometers), was probably three times more fuel efficient than the Oldsmobile. Like the refrigerator for a "working housewife," items were purchased not for prestige

or a sense of power but to get something accomplished as inexpensively and efficiently as possible. West Germans consumed in order to produce an outcome – a meal or a vacation trip – with the least possible expenditure. In this regard, everyday life reflected the drive to succeed that lay behind the economic miracle.

It took at least a decade for a consumer society to become established in West Germany. During that time, new desires competed with the experience of having done without, and consumers were often hesitant to spend without a reason that made sense to them. Because rationales for purchase varied between the United States and West Germany – as horsepower differed from fuel efficiency – the emerging West German consumer society of the 1950s was not as much an Americanized version of German society as it was a variant among several European consumer societies emerging simultaneously.[26] By the mid-1960s, when advertisers could assume everyone wanted the goods they offered, affluence was sufficiently widespread to encourage attention to subtle distinctions. In West Germany, these distinctions took the form of improvements in reliable products that would be kept "forever."

In the global marketplace of the end of the twentieth century, national identity cannot be based on economic productivity alone. Although the "apolitical" acquisitiveness of the 1950s was weakened by the student movement of the late 1960s and the experiments in communal living that soon followed, it returned in more intense form during the boom of the mid-1980s. West Germans were recognized (especially abroad during their several weeks of paid vacation) by the prosperity their productivity had generated. If they had consumed during the 1950s in order to produce a household with normal comforts, and during the 1960s in order to illustrate an interest in a progressive lifestyle incorporating the latest technological

[22] Roland Marchand, *Advertising the American Dream: Making Way for Modernity, 1920–1940* (Berkeley and Los Angeles, 1985), 270.

[23] *Saturday Evening Post*, June 4, 1955, 14–5.

[24] In a sample of twenty-six advertisements taken from *Der Stern* and *Quick* between 1951 and 1965, only one dealt specifically with the role of refrigerators in helping the working woman. See *Der Stern*, Apr. 20, 1952, 16.

[25] Karal Ann Marling, *As Seen on TV: The Visual Culture of Everyday Life in the 1950s* (Cambridge, Mass., 1994), 133; *Quick*, Jan. 28, 1954, 124.

[26] For parallel developments in France, see Richard Kuisel, *Seducing the French: The Dilemma of Americanization* (Berkeley, Calif., 1993); Laurence Wylie, *Village in the Vaucluse*, 2d ed. (Cambridge, Mass., 1964).

developments, by the 1980s West Germany had produced a consumer lifestyle par excellence. This became especially obvious in popular West German accounts of differences between West Germans and East Germans during unification. *Wessis* were tanned, Gucci-clad, Jaguar-driving creatures fending off all challenges with the flash of a credit card, while *Ossis* with stringy hair waited forlornly in line for the Aldi to open.[27] Although claims about the decline of the West German work ethic had been made as early as 1963,[28] the contrasts and disparities inherent in unification revealed the role consumption played in West German society. What West Germans created between 1948 and 1989 was not just a consumer society but one so intimately linked with production that consumption became production. West Germans expressed a sense of the significance of their work, their purchases, and themselves accordingly.

[27] "Es ist ein anderes Leben," *Der Spiegel* 44 (Sept. 24, 1990): 34.

[28] "Sind die Deutschen faul geworden?" *Der Stern*, May 5, 1963, 18–29, 118–20.

American Influences on Urban Developments in West Germany

Jeffry M. Diefendorf

In the realm of urban affairs, the nature of German-American relations during the first twenty-five years of the Cold War is best characterized as ambivalent. American attitudes toward and attempts to influence the character of German cities after 1945 shifted radically at the beginning of the period of postwar occupation from a policy of discouraging to one of encouraging urban recovery. Although the Germans themselves mostly abhorred American urban development and did not seek to emulate American cities, at times they also found American models worthy portents of the future.

It is worth recalling that theories of urban planning, housing, and architecture were all part of an international discussion throughout this century, a discussion only suspended by World War II. Through professional publications, international conferences, and individual visits, Germans and Americans remained well informed of developments on both sides of the Atlantic, so the direction of influence was never simply one-sided. For example, the architects Walter Gropius, Ludwig Mies van der Rohe, and other Bauhaus pioneers brought German modernist ideas of planning and architecture with them when they immigrated to the United States in the 1930s. They became Americans, and their ideas gained international currency. Does one consider their influence on Germany after 1945 to be somehow American, a return of German ideas, or both? By the same token, their influence on modern architecture and planning in the United States cannot be denied, but it

had nothing to do with postwar German or German-American relations.

With nearly seventy cities having populations of more than 100,000 and with 75 percent of the population living in or very close to urban centers, West Germany was one of the most urbanized societies on earth. For the most part, West German cities developed autonomously;[1] the degree of direct American influence was, except for the case of West Berlin, relatively modest. Moreover, much of what happened in and to German cities after the war would probably have transpired even without the exigencies of wartime bombing and the Cold War. Suburbanization, the construction of new commercial buildings in city cores and standardized housing tracts on the outskirts, the growth in automobile use and the building of appropriate urban motorways and parking structures, urban renewal projects – these took place in all industrial societies. The fact that Germany was in ruins and impoverished after 1945 meant that it took longer, but what occurred paralleled developments in industrialized nations everywhere.

That is not to say, however, that the Cold War in a broader sense did not affect the course of urbanization in postwar Germany. The division between West and East Germany meant that cities close to that border, like Göttingen, were cut off from their traditional hinterlands

---

[1] See Trevor Wild, ed., *Urban and Rural Change in West Germany* (Beckenham, 1983); and Edgar Wedepohl, *Deutscher Städtebau nach 1945* (Essen, 1961).

and forced to reorient trade and traffic patterns. The combination of that border and the designation of specific corridors for transportation between the two German states meant that the West German Autobahn and rail system developed most highly in a north-south direction and most intensively in the western part of the country along the Rhine.

The West German Autobahn network became justly famous. Neither its system of superhighways nor the increasing motorization of German commerce and society can be necessarily attributed to postwar American influence, even if the postwar revival of automobile factories owned by the Ford Motor Company and General Motors played a significant role in German economic recovery. On the one hand, Germany had itself long been a pioneer in both the development of new types of automobiles and highway construction. On the other, Fordist and Taylorist models for the mass production of automobiles and the American highway system were widely admired in Germany during the Weimar and Nazi periods.[2] Konrad Adenauer, while Cologne's mayor during the Weimar Republic, helped arrange for the establishment of Ford's factory in Cologne-Niehl, and Hitler found inspiration for the Volkswagen in the Model T, but Germany would surely have gone in this direction in any event. If it was not until the early 1950s that personal automobiles and heavy truck transports began to take over some functions of the railroad system, this was mostly because of the pace of the German postwar economic recovery. Between 1960 and 1970, the number of registered private automobiles more than doubled and the size of those cars grew as well. In the same decade, the number of persons using public ground transportation remained about the same, but the number using air transportation quadrupled.[3] By the end

of the 1960s, the West German population was both urban and highly mobile.

The enormous population movement from east to west also helped shape urban areas in West Germany. First, the wave of Germans expelled from Poland, the Soviet Union, and Czechoslovakia and then the flood of people fleeing East Germany swelled urban populations beyond the normal birth and short-distance migration rates. By 1960, the population of most cities was higher than in 1939, and this growth continued throughout the decade. Urban population growth, especially because it occurred during a time when war-damaged housing was still being repaired or replaced, also resulted in burgeoining suburbs and satellite cities, including such suburbs as Munich-Perlach, as well as Gropiusstadt and the Märkisches Viertel in Berlin, which housed 40,000 or more inhabitants. After 1961, an influx of "guest workers" from Italy, Spain, and Greece compensated for some of the flight from city centers to the suburbs. (As suburbs grew, German city centers also experienced a development quite like major American cities – large commercial buildings replaced older residential areas, resulting in markedly reduced population densities in urban cores. This change had a profound impact on the nature of many cities, but it is part of an international trend that had little to do with either American influence or the Cold War.)

The war was catastrophic for Germany's cities. Virtually all cities had been heavily bombed, which resulted in enormous housing shortages, the disruption of public transportation within and between cities, the collapse of urban economies, and urban depopulation. German municipal government had ceased to function. Had the Americans strictly followed the advice of America's wartime secretary of the treasury, Henry Morgenthau Jr., this situation might have been perpetuated. Angry at both Nazi war crimes and the nearly successful attempt to eradicate the Jews, Morgenthau tried to persuade President Franklin Roosevelt that the best guarantee that Germany would never again threaten the peace and people of Europe would be to prevent Germany from reappearing

---

[2] Regina Bittner et al., eds., *Zukunft aus Amerika: Fordismus in der Zwischenkriegszeit: Siedlung, Stadt, Raum* (Dessau, 1995).

[3] Statistisches Bundesamt, *Datenreport 1989. Zahlen und Fakten über die Bundesrepublik Deutschland* (Bonn, 1989).

as an industrial society. He envisioned a pastoralized, nonurban, deindustrialized, nonaggressive Germany.

In fact, Morgenthau's ideas faded rather quickly. The Allies simply were not prepared physically or financially to feed, clothe, and house Germany's largely urban population. With their pragmatic bent, the Americans encouraged the revival of local government and entrusted local officials with clearing rubble and restoring urban services, even at the risk of reemploying former Nazis. More importantly, the Americans quickly realized that if the conditions of 1945 were to continue and if they left the Germans (and other European countries) to their fate, the result would be the collapse of the entire European economy and quite possibly the ascendancy of Soviet dominance on the Continent. The onset of the Cold War accelerated the shift from a policy favoring deindustrialization and deurbanization to a policy favoring German economic revival and with it a revival of urban life.

Central to this shift was the Marshall Plan, announced in June 1947 and authorized by Congress in 1948. It is commonly assumed that the physcial rebuilding of Germany, including the rebuilding of the bombed cities, was in good part made possible by generous American aid, but this was not the case. It is important to realize that the Marshall Plan was not specifically directed at urban reconstruction. The purpose of the plan was to help revive the German economy within a multilateral European context, which meant that most of the aid was directed into areas considered bottlenecks, such as coal production, electrical power generation, and railroads.[4] However, as German industrial and financial concerns sprang back to life, they naturally not only repaired industrial plants but also corporate offices in central urban areas, and

American corporations, such as Ford and IBM, also invested in German industry. American aid and investment thus played an indirect role in the rebuilding of West Germany's devastated cities.

Housing was the one general area where the United States did try to shape urban reconstruction by using European Cooperation Administration (ECA)/European Recovery Program (ERP) funds deriving from the Marshall Plan. The motivation behind these efforts was fear that the massive shortage of housing, especially for workers and refugees, would provoke political discontent, increase support for leftist political groups, and weaken the fragile new democracy of the Federal Republic. Believing that German adherence to traditional masonry construction and high construction standards generally was slowing new housing construction, the Americans in 1951 sponsored a nationwide competition for over 3,300 new housing units to be built in model developments in fifteen cities.[5] The goal was to encourage German architects, planners, and urban authorities to build low-cost, standardized housing on a large scale. The competition attracted 725 entries, including submissions from some of Germany's best-known architects. Of the completed developments, only one, in Bremen, was situated in a bombed-out inner-city area; the rest were built on the outskirts of cities. A second ECA-sponsored housing construction project directly encouraged by the Americans led to the building of nine housing settlements containing some 5,000 dwellings for coal miners, mainly in the Ruhr. Here, the goal was not so much to build model housing as to aid miners' families and thereby raise coal production.

Given the fact that over four million prewar housing units in West Germany had been totally destroyed or very seriously damaged, the housing projects directly sponsored by the Americans

---

[4] Michael J. Hogan, *The Marshall Plan: America, Britain, and the Reconstruction of Western Europe, 1947–1952* (Cambridge, 1987); and the essays in Charles S. Maier and Günter Bischof, eds., *The Marshall Plan and Germany: West German Development within the Framework of the European Recovery Program* (New York, 1991).

[5] Hermann Wandersleb and Hans Schoszberger, eds., *Neue Wohnbau*, vol. 1: *Bauplanung* (Ravensburg, 1952); and Hermann Wandersleb and Georg Günthert, eds., *Neue Wohnbau*, vol. 2: *Durchführung von Versuchssiedlungen: Ergebnisse und Erkentnisse für heute und morgen. Von ECA bis Interbau* (Ravensburg, 1958).

were but a drop in the bucket. It is difficult to assess the impact of these projects. On the one hand, they received considerable publicity and were carefully studied by German housing authorities for strengths and weaknesses. The American-sponsored projects reinforced German inclinations toward standardized, industrialized housing construction, which had roots in the Bauhaus, Nazi-era housing projects, and immediate postwar design competitions.[6] On the other hand, Germans continued to prefer more traditional if more costly modes of construction. Of the DM 31.6 billion invested in housing between 1950 and 1954, only 1.63 percent came from the Marshall Plan, a good indicator of the limits of American influence on urban housing during German reconstruction.[7]

The great exception is West Berlin, the divided city that truly embodied and best symbolized the Cold War. Even as the United States and the Federal Republic of Germany firmly committed themselves to a democratic, West German state with a capital in Bonn and with close political and economic ties to Western Europe and America, the Americans also helped keep alive the idea that Berlin would someday be united and serve as Germany's capital city again. In the meantime, West Berlin had to recover and be maintained as a viable metropolis and a showcase of Western values situated in the middle of communist East Germany. Here, American influence was pronounced, going well beyond the famous airlift that supplied the city during the Berlin Blockade, and this influence was manifested in several ways.

In addition to having been the seat of the national and Prussian state governments, Berlin had also been Germany's largest population center and its largest industrial and financial center. After the war, Berlin lost much of its service sector (Frankfurt becoming the chief financial center for the Federal Republic), industrial

production fell drastically, and, cut off from its natural hinterland, West Berlin lost nearby markets for its products. More than in any other city, Marshall Plan aid came to the rescue, as more than a third of all ERP counterpart funds were channeled to Berlin.[8] This financial aid helped underwrite the construction of housing, schools, hospitals, and churches. Loans helped rejuvenate the machine-building, electrical, and textile industries by supporting factory construction and underwriting contracts for raw materials. By helping to rebuild hotels, restaurants, and infrastructure, aid also enticed tourists and businessmen to again visit the city.

The Americans also sponsored individual projects that were highly visibile in the context of the Cold War. When the division of the city during the Blockade led to the establishment of the Free University in the American sector, the United States provided funds for new buildings. Notable here was the Ford-Bau, sponsored by the Ford Foundation. The Amerika-Haus in West Berlin's new "center" at the head of the Kurfürstendamm symbolized American culture, as did the American Memorial Library a few blocks south of Checkpoint Charlie. ERP funds helped finance the new housing blocks in the Hansaviertel, the key project implemented as part of the 1957 Berlin International Building Exhibition. Located near the Tiergarten, the Hansaviertel was intended to exemplify urban modernism to both the Soviet bloc and to the rest of Europe. The most politically important and typically "American" contribution to the 1957 exhibition was the Congress Hall.[9] Sited near the sector border and the Brandenburg Gate, on the edge of the area foreseen as a potential new government center for a unified German state, this building was to host Berlin meetings of the Bundestag and other meetings and exhibits that would embody Western and American ideas of freedom and liberty. The person most instrumental in gaining American

[6] See Tilman Harlander, *Zwischen Heimstätte und Wohnmaschine: Wohnungsbau und Wohnungspolitik in der Zeit des Nationalsozialismus* (Basel, 1995), 237, 281.

[7] Jeffry M. Diefendorf, *In the Wake of War: The Reconstruction of German Cities After World War II* (New York, 1993), 137–44.

[8] Bundesministerium für wirtschaftlichen Besitz des Bundes, *ERP und die Stadt Berlin* (Vienna, 1961).

[9] Barbara Miller Lane, "The Berlin Congress Hall 1955–57," *Perspectives in American History*, n. ser., 1 (1984).

support for the construction of the Congress Hall was Eleanor Dulles, who persuaded her brother, Secretary of State John Foster Dulles, to create the Benjamin Franklin Foundation that served as the conduit for funding the Congress Hall. Here, Cold War politics and modern architecture, myths of freedom and industriousness, and urban design all came together.

Berlin was exceptional: American aid and influence on urban life was most tangible there. The influence of America on German urban development consisted of more than money and formal policies, however. German planners and intellectuals had long been aware of and had formed conflicting judgments about developments in American cities, and these ideas influenced the evolution of German town planning. Thus, at the beginning of the century and again in the 1920s, critics compared Berlin to Chicago, denouncing both cities for epitomizing the worst excesses of modernity.[10] Decrying sprawling neighborhoods, the mixing of races and ethnic groups, violent gangsters, moral corruption, and shallow, materialistic, presentist culture, they advocated the rebirth of idealized, homogeneous, traditional German towns.

Such thinking persisted after 1945. During postwar reconstruction, those resisting the implementation of modern planning models and architecture worried about the Americanization of their treasured hometowns. Indeed, in their own occupation zone and then in the Federal Republic, the American authorities themselves discouraged plans to rebuild bombed cities using radically changed street layouts because they believed that such sweeping land reform smacked of socialism and threatened the success of West Germany's recovering capitalist economy. In any case, most German citizens wanted to see city silhouettes dominated by the familiar spires of rebuilt churches and town halls, not skyscrapers. They preferred the ancient pattern of narrow, crooked streets to wide avenues suitable for masses of automobiles. Frankfurt am Main, the city which more than any other opted for wide

streets and tall new buildings, was frequently castigated as "Mainhattan," the most Americanized of German cities. Reacting to the growth of automobile traffic, in 1962 the mayor of Munich contrasted the "nightmare" of a faceless city like sprawling Los Angeles to his historic city, which still put people above machines.[11]

In spite of popular hostility toward modern planning, most German planners in the first fifteen years after the war endorsed modernist planning models that had evolved since the appearance of the garden-city movement late in the nineteenth century and continued to enjoy international currency. They believed that modern cities, including Germany's, should feature strict functional zoning, wide streets, and modern buildings constructed to maximize the exposure to sunlight and fresh air.[12] For these planners, American models had great appeal, because prosperous America seemed to presage the future, but they were also attracted to Swedish and English models.

Readily agreeing with this assessment, the Americans supported the return of Bauhaus modernism to Germany. General Lucius Clay invited Walter Gropius to Berlin in 1947 to advise the Americans on reconstruction. Gropius then made a highly publicized tour to several other cities, but he ultimately declined to remain in Germany.[13] In 1948, the Americans helped distribute a German version of a book on contemporary American architecture published by New York's Museum of Modern Art showing elegant housing and skyscrapers. In 1955, the High Commission on Germany supported

---

[10] This theme is present in several of the essays in Charles W. Haxthausen and Heidrun Suhr, eds., *Berlin: Culture and Metropolis* (Minneapolis, 1990).

[11] Quoted by Winfried Nerdinger, "München: Bewährte Kontinuität," in Klaus von Beyme et al., eds., *Neue Städte aus Ruinen: Deutscher Städtebau der Nachkriegszeit* (Munich, 1992), 344.

[12] See Diefendorf, *In the Wake of War*, chaps. 6–7; von Beyme et al., eds., *Neue Städte*; Werner Durth and Niels Gutschow, *Träume in Trümmern: Planungen zum Wiederaufbau zerstörter Städte im Westen Deutschlands 1940–1950*, 2 vols. (Braunschweig, 1988).

[13] Jeffry M. Diefendorf, "America and the Rebuilding of Urban Germany," in Jeffry M. Diefendorf, Axel Frohn, and Hermann-Josef Rupieper, eds., *American Policy and the Reconstruction of West Germany, 1945–1955* (Cambridge, 1993).

the founding of the *Hochschule für Gestaltung* in Ulm, a design academy along the lines of the Bauhaus.[14] Amerika-Haus cultural centers were built in many German cities to inform Germans about American life through exhibits and literature. Partly an outgrowth of the Cold War, these centers became integrated into the urban fabric, only to become after 1968 the focus of demonstrations by young Germans protesting against America's role in Vietnam and supposed domination of Western Europe.

In addition to exposing the German populace to aspects of American urbanization, Americans encouraged German planners and architects to visit the United States. After such a visit in the 1950s, Düsseldorf planner Friedrich Tamms designed a two-level, 800-meter-long motorway through central Düsseldorf that was influenced by Tamms's enthusiasm for Los Angeles. Tamms, who had worked on Autobahn design in the Third Reich, became one of West Germany's leading advocates of urban freeway construction.[15] Also in Düsseldorf, the architect Helmut Hentrich designed the famous and, for Germany, pathbreaking Dreischeibenhaus skyscraper for the Thyssen firm. America also offered educational fellowships to German town planners. For example, Gerd Albers, one of the most influential town planners from the 1960s through the 1980s, traveled to Chicago in 1948 on a fellowship from the American Friends Service Committee to study for two years with Mies van der Rohe and Ludwig Hilberseimer at the Illinois Institute of Technology, where he became familiar with a blend of Bauhaus and modern American planning and architecture.[16]

Some German town planners continued to be attracted to certain aspects of American urban planning throughout the 1960s. Because the growth in motor vehicle use seemed inexorable, Germans paid close attention to American urban highway construction.[17] A 1965 pamphlet published by the Deutscher Städtetag (German Cities Association), for example, featured a photo of Boston's Southeast Expressway as a model of good traffic planning.[18] In the early 1960s, however, both countries began almost simultaneously to develop a new critical perspective on existing trends in urban development. In a 1960 speech to the annual meeting of the Deutscher Städtetag, Edgar Salin called for turning away from rigid models of functional zoning in favor of the kind of greater "urbanity" (*Urbanität*) that arose from densely populated, mixed-usage neighborhoods.[19] The following year, Jane Jacobs published a similar plea in her book criticizing the destruction of urban neighborhoods in America by supposedly progressive planners – a book that was translated into German in 1963.[20] Both of these critics feared that excessive construction of high-rise, monofunctional commercial buildings in city centers and the top priority given traffic problems by urban planners would deprive cities of human interaction and vitality. Widely discussed in professional journals and schools, these ideas led to a sea change in thinking about urban planning.[21]

[14] Paul Betts, "Die Bauhaus-Legende: Amerikanisch-Deutsches 'Joint-Venture' des Kalten Krieges," in Alf Lüdtke, Inge Marssolek, and Adelheid von Saldern, eds., *Amerikanisierung: Traum und Alptraum im Deutschland des 20. Jahrhunderts* (Stuttgart, 1996).

[15] See Werner Durth, "Düsseldorf: Demonstration der Modernität," in von Beyme et al., eds., *Neue Städte*, 239–40, 364, n. 36.

[16] Klaus Borchard, "Laudatio," in Klaus Borchard et al., eds., *Zwischen Transformation und Tradition: Städtebau in der zweiten Hälfte des 20. Jahrhunderts. Gerd Albers zum 60. Geburtstag* (Munich, 1979).

[17] Hans Bernhard Reichow, *Die autogerechte Stadt: Ein Weg aus dem Verkehrs-Chaos* (Ravensburg, 1959); Friedrich Tamms, "Städtebau und Verkehr," in Rudolf Hillebrecht, ed., *Die Auswirkungen des wirtschaftlichen und sozialen Strukturwandels auf den Städtebau* (Cologne, 1964); Josef Walter Hollatz and Friedrich Tamms, eds., *Die kommenden Verkehrsprobleme in der Bundesrepublik Deutschland: Ein Sachverständigenbericht und die Stellungnahme der Bundesregierung* (Essen, 1965).

[18] "Einleitung," in von Beyme et al., eds., *Neue Städte*, 27.

[19] Edgar Salin, "Urbanität," in *Erneuerung unserer Städte*, Neue Schriften des Deutschen Städtetages, Heft 6 (Stuttgart, 1960).

[20] Jane Jacobs, *The Death and Life of Great American Cities* (New York, 1961).

[21] Hans Paul Bahrdt, *Humaner Städtebau: Überlegungen zur Wohnungspolitik und Stadtplanung in einer nahen*

The turn to new planning motifs like urbanity took place against dramatic political changes. The gradual turn toward détente with Eastern Europe exposed West German planners to the massive, prefabricated apartment blocks and badly maintained city centers in Eastern bloc cities – a hostile urban environment that westerners did not want to emulate. In the other

direction, extensive race riots in major American cities in the mid-1960s were well-publicized events that tarnished the image of the United States, as did the prolonged war in Vietnam. The Cold War continued, but to younger Germans and to many younger Americans, the American model lost its glitter. A new generation of urban planners that coincided with the student generation of 1968 began in the 1970s to preserve or reintroduce urbanity to cities in Germany and America – probably with greater success in the former, where traditions of urban life and urban loyalties were deeper and longer standing.

Zukunft (Hamburg, 1968); Hans Paul Bahrdt, *Die moderne Grossstadt* (Reinbeck bei Hamburg, 1961); Heide Berndt, *Das Gesellschaftsbild bei Stadtplanern* (Stuttgart, 1968); Werner Durth, *Die Inszenierung der Alltagswelt: Zur Kritik der Stadtgestaltung* (Braunschweig, 1977).

CHAPTER THIRTEEN

Blurred Sovereignty

The German-American Media Relationship in the Postwar Era

David Braden Posner

The framers of American occupation policy viewed the reshaping of Germany's media land-scape as a central element in the process of democratization. Like their British, French, and Soviet counterparts, the American military government (OMGUS) placed strict controls on German press activity, but it also led the way in establishing procedures and institutions that rapidly returned democratically minded Germans to lightly supervised, effectively self-censoring control of key media outlets. Compared with other "sociopolitical" reorientation efforts undertaken by the Western Allies (e.g., in the field of educational reform), media reform came very close to fulfilling the promise of pre–Cold War expectations; in the field of print journalism, the American contribution was the driving force behind this development.[1]

OMGUS aimed initially at establishing a complete media blackout in occupied Germany. After banning preexisting publications in the areas they controlled, the American army groups issued "overt" newspapers, which served to communicate official notices to the population; ten such overt papers were being published by summer 1945. By that time, OMGUS had also begun to allow Germans who met certain anti-Nazi licensing requirements to reenter the publishing field. The first such licensed paper, the *Frankfurter Rundschau*, was approved at the end of July. By the end of November, there were 19 more licensed papers; at the close of the year, the number had risen to 23, one for every large city in the American zone, with a combined twice-weekly circulation of 3,170,000.

The licensed press represented a dramatic departure from previous German publishing arrangements, especially from those that had held sway outside of large cities. Most of the licensed papers were conceived of as regional organs designed to replace a previously far larger number of financially strapped *Heimatzeitungen*, or local papers. The licensed papers also strictly separated news coverage and editorial commentary, thereby stressing a journalistic propriety seldom adhered to by the *Heimatzeitungen*. To be sure, American licensing procedures furthered a process of consolidation begun under the auspices of the Third Reich, but they also connected this economical rationalization with the adoption of a more inclusive and (self-)critical conception of news-gathering and dissemination. Sixty-two licensed papers were in operation in the American zone by the time licensing requirements ceased in mid-1949. Not all survived the return of competition, and many were indeed forced to make concessions to publishers who had been banned during the occupation.

---

[1] See Norbert Frei, *Amerikanische Lizenzpolitik und deutsche Pressetradition: Die Geschichte der Nachkriegszeitung Südost-Kurier* (Munich, 1986), esp. 8. More critical of American press policy, especially of its political sensibilities vis-à-vis licensees, is Harold Hurwitz's *Die Stunde Null der deutschen Presse: Die amerikanische Pressepolitik in Deutschland 1945–1949* (Cologne, 1972).

Nevertheless, the example set by the licensed papers did much to determine the shape of print journalism in the early Federal Republic.[2]

Although the licensed papers were remarkable evidence of American readiness to permit Germans to resume control of their own media, there was no abandonment of American media control during the occupation. The licensed papers were subject to steady postpublication review. Moreover, OMGUS did not cease to maintain media organs with which it could directly reach German audiences. A more elaborate development of the overt papers, *Die Neue Zeitung*, was launched in Munich in October 1945, and it soon expanded to include Frankfurt and Berlin editions; by the end of 1945, the paper's circulation had reached 1.3 million.[3] OMGUS also offered several magazines, among them *Heute*, a biweekly pictorial; *Neue Auslese*, an Anglo-American readers' digest; and *Die Amerikanische Rundschau*, a highbrow cultural periodical. Radio broadcasting was firmly in the hands of the military government, and an Anglo-American weekly newsreel, *Welt im Film*, was a required part of cinema programs.

After the founding of the Federal Republic, the High Commissioner's Office (HICOG) continued to exert a direct influence over West Germany's media. *Die Neue Zeitung* soldiered on until January 30, 1955, and, additionally, there were Cold War periodicals like *Der Monat* and *Ost-Probleme*. An official news service, *Amerika Dienst*, supplied large amounts of material to West German newspapers and wire services; as of late 1951, it was providing 10 percent of the foreign news and 90 percent of the America coverage distributed by the *Deutsche Presse Agentur* (DPA), the largest West German wire service. West German radio stations were not only monitored, they were also required to carry the *Voice of America* (VOA) for thirty minutes a day, though in April 1951 this requirement was cut back to fifteen minutes, six days a week. Showings of *Welt im Film* ceased to be compulsory after the promulgation of the Occupation Statute, but the Americans kept this newsreel in production until June 1952, at which time it was being shown in more than half of West Germany's theaters and reaching a monthly audience of twenty-five million. HICOG also exercised a (perhaps too) watchful interest in American reporters who were covering the Federal Republic for papers back in the United States. For instance, after he reported on subjects like neo-Nazism and the failure of denazification, Drew Middleton, the *New York Times*'s chief Germany correspondent, found himself under attack both by the government of Chancellor Konrad Adenauer and by American High Commissioner John J. McCloy.[4]

American reporters had been in Germany since the closing days of the war and they, too, played a considerable role in both rebuilding and restructuring the media in the Western zones of occupation. Consider the case of the Associated Press (AP).[5] Although the Gestapo closed the wire service's Berlin office on December 11, 1941, and interned its American staff members, one of the AP's German employees, Rudi Josten, continued to file reports through an Argentine news agency until May 1942. Nearly three years later, Josten, still in possession of his AP press card, met up in Weimar with Edward Ball, a veteran of the prewar Berlin bureau who had penetrated into eastern Germany along with the troops of the American Army. Josten and Ball soon opened an AP office in Frankfurt's Park Hotel.

Berlin served as the seat of the AP's German operations during most of the occupation. Soon

---

[2] For a contemporary American account, see Henry P. Pilgert, *Press, Radio and Film in West Germany, 1945–1953* (n.p., 1953).

[3] On this paper, see Jessica C. E. Gienow-Hecht, *Transmission Impossible: American Journalism as Cultural Diplomacy in Postwar Germany, 1945–1955* (Baton Rouge, La., 1999).

[4] Drew Middleton, *Where Has Last July Gone? Memoirs* (New York, 1973), 172–4.

[5] My thanks to Stephen Miller, the AP's current bureau chief in Germany, for providing me with a detailed history of the AP's German operations (e-mail communication, Stephen Miller to author, Feb. 12, 1997).

after the Reich capital fell to the Soviets, Wes Gallagher, the AP's first postwar bureau chief in Germany, set up a makeshift shop in Berlin with some teletype machines salvaged in Belgium and powered by a generator run on black-market gasoline he purchased from a Red Army officer.[6] By late 1945, the AP was working on establishing a German-language news service, reviving a plan that had been abandoned after the Nazis had come to power in 1933. Rudi Josten became the first editor of this service; there was also a female editor whose presence, Wes Gallagher recalled, caused the male German staff to threaten to walk out. The service overcame this and other hurdles and began to send reports to its first subscriber, the *Wiesbadener Kurier*, in June 1946. By the end of the 1940s, the AP had offices or correspondents in Hamburg, Bonn, Munich, Hannover, and Stuttgart. In 1950, the AP's administrative offices moved to Frankfurt, while the Berlin office retained twenty Americans and Germans staffers who directed operations in Eastern Europe.

Although the AP was well situated to provide German news to the American media, the larger American newspapers and magazines maintained their own correspondents in Germany. During the early postwar years, Delbert Clark ran the *New York Times's* German bureau out of Berlin.[7] When Drew Middleton took over as bureau chief in May 1948, the paper had three other reporters in Germany.[8] As was the case with so many Americans, Middleton was deeply impressed by the resistance put up by the Berlin population during the blockade,

and his admiration did much to lessen the disgust he had felt for the Germans following the war.[9]

Beginning in January 1946, *Time* operated a bureau in Berlin.[10] In April 1951, the magazine moved its German bureau to Frankfurt, though only for three months; in July 1951, the bureau moved to Bonn. Eric Gibbs ran the Frankfurt office during its brief existence and remained in charge in Bonn until February 1952. He was succeeded there by Frank White, James Bell, Edward Hughes, Robert Ball, John H. Mechlin, and Herman Nickel. Not all of the staff were Americans, however; at least one of Time-Life's German reporters, Friedrich Wilhelm Heinz, also served in the intelligence service that Adenauer's security adviser Count Gerhard von Schwerin began setting up in the summer of 1950.[11]

Although *U.S. News & World Report* relied on far fewer personnel than *Time*, it too maintained a bureau in Germany from 1946 onward. Initially based in Berlin, *U.S. News's* German operation did not weather the blockade there; the magazine moved its offices to Frankfurt in late August 1948, where it stayed until moving to Bonn in August 1952.[12] From then until 1965, *U.S. News's* Central European coverage was the responsibility of Kurt Lachmann, an early refugee from Nazism whose father had been murdered in the Theresienstadt concentration camp.[13]

Lachmann was one of the many refugees and émigrés who helped to shape the postwar German-American media relationship.

---

[6] Gallagher served in Germany until the early 1950s. He later became the head of the *AP*'s worldwide operations. See *Dictionary of Literary Biography*, vol. 127: *American Newspaper Publishers, 1950–1990*, ed. Perry J. Ashley (Detroit, 1993), 91–8.

[7] Clark was especially critical of the military government for its willingness to subordinate the goal of denazification to the perceived demands of anticommunism. See Hermann-Josef Rupieper, *Die Wurzeln der westdeutschen Nachkriegsdemokratie: Der amerikanische Beitrag 1945–1952* (Opladen, 1993), 72–5.

[8] Ed Morrow (not the CBS radio reporter) in Berlin, Jack Raymond in Frankfurt, and Kathleen McLaughlin in Munich.

[9] See Middleton, *Where Has Last July Gone?* 166–72.

[10] The office was run by John Scott until March 1948, when Emmet Hughes, previously the magazine's Rome correspondent, took over. Hughes was followed in 1950 by Enno Hobbing, who headed the bureau until April 1951.

[11] David Clay Large, *Germans to the Front: West German Rearmament in the Adenauer Era* (Chapel Hill, N.C., 1996), 59.

[12] During the Frankfurt years, the bureau was run by Robert Kleiman.

[13] See *International Biographical Dictionary of Central European Emigrés 1933–1945*, vol. 2, pt. 2: *The Arts, Sciences, and Literature* (Munich, 1983), 681–2.

Refugees and émigrés had been instrumental in the production of the overt publications put out by the American military government; one refugee, Hans Habe, had been press chief of the American zone and chief editor of *Die Neue Zeitung*.[14] While Lachmann and Habe returned to live in postwar West Germany, many other refugees chose permanent exile; still, even this latter group influenced the West German media, above all by serving as low-rent foreign correspondents at a time when few West German news organs were financially capable of maintaining staff overseas. The left-liberal *Frankfurter Rundschau* relied especially heavily on émigrés for American coverage, most enduringly on Heinz Pol, who reported from New York from 1949 through 1971.[15] For most of West Germany's other large dailies, however, reliance on émigrés lasted generally only until the mid-1950s. Hans Steinitz, who had spent the war in Switzerland and then settled in the United States in 1947, strung articles about America for many German-language papers, including the *Stuttgarter Zeitung* and *Die Welt*,[16] but both these papers engaged permanent Washington correspondents in 1956 (the former with Marlene Manthey, who served through 1963; the latter with Herbert von Borch, who served through 1965). The *Süddeutsche Zeitung* received American news from George-Henri Martin of the *Journal de Genève* until the beginning of 1954, when the paper employed Walter Gong, previously the press attaché at the West German embassy in Washington.[17] In July 1960, Emil Walter, formerly of the DPA, replaced Gong. Walter kept this post until 1965, at which time the *Süddeutsche Zeitung* engaged Borch – who had decided to leave the increasingly conservative *Die Welt*.[18] The *Frankfurter Allgemeine Zeitung* retained its first full-time American correspondent in late 1954, when Jan Reifenberg, who had worked for the DPA in Washington, began an eleven-year stint as the paper's correspondent in the American capital.[19] Beginning in 1961, the *Frankfurter Allgemeine* added a New York correspondent, Sabina Lietzmann.

West German weeklies were slower in dispatching full-time representatives to the United States. Despite the fact that coverage of America – and a supposedly American journalistic style – was a major component of *Der Spiegel*'s fledgling identity,[20] the magazine did not dispatch its first American-based reporter until 1959, when Kurt J. Bachrach-Baker began submitting from New York. In contrast to *Der Spiegel*, *Die Zeit* did not keep personnel in America. This is not to say that *Die Zeit*'s staff in Germany was unfamiliar with the United States; for instance, when future editor Theo Sommer joined the paper in the 1950s, he had already spent two years studying in the United States,[21] just one of many thousands of West Germans who benefited from government-sponsored programs for travel and study in America.[22]

For all its rapid growth, the German-American media relationship did not always ensure accurate reporting; indeed, the closeness of the relationship – itself a product of Cold War political convergence – did not prevent official obstruction of objective reporting. Some idea of the character and etiology of this failure can be glimpsed in the media coverage

---

[14] Ibid., vol. 2, pt. 1, 446.

[15] See *Biographisches Handbuch der deutschsprachigen Emigration nach 1933*, vol. 1: *Politik, Wirtschaft, öffentliches Leben* (Munich, 1980), 568–9.

[16] Ibid., 728.

[17] See Heinz-Dietrich Fischer, "Berichterstattung aus den USA – Skizzen ihrer Entwicklungsgeschichte," in Erika J. Fischer and Heinz-Dietrich Fischer, eds., *Den "American way of life" entlang: Berichte deutscher Journalismus Stipendiaten des John-J.-McCloy Austauschprogramms* (Berlin, 1989), 17–8.

[18] See "Gesicht und Gesichter," *Der Spiegel* 19 (Dec. 29, 1965): 22–3.

[19] See *Frankfurter Allgemeine Zeitung*, Mar. 1, 1958, 42.

[20] Front covers of *Der Spiegel* featuring American subjects: 1947, no. 10; 1948, no. 11; 1949, no. 5; 1950, no. 8; 1951, no. 17; 1952, no. 9; 1953, no. 10; 1954, no. 9; 1955, no. 7; 1956, no. 7; 1957, no. 4; 1958, no. 3; 1959, no. 4.

[21] Fischer, "Berichterstattung aus den USA," 19; Theo Sommer, foreword to Fischer and Fischer, eds., *Den "American way of life" entlang*, 9.

[22] Media representatives made up a significant percentage of exchange program participants; see Rupieper, *Wurzeln*, 400. On exchange programs, see the chapter by Karl-Heinz Füssl, vol. 1, Culture.

of Supreme Court Chief Justice Earl Warren's visit to the Federal Republic in August 1959. Some of West Germany's most major newspapers either ignored Warren's involvement with the Civil Rights issue altogether[23] or went so far as to present him as an advocate of states' rights. In the latter vein, the *Münchner Merkur* described the chief justice as a man who had always been "against an excessive centralization of state powers and for States' rights."[24] For its part, the *Süddeutsche Zeitung* did note Warren's stand against segregation, but it, too, saw him as "always opposed to an excessive centralization of federal powers" and as one who "promoted the rights of the individual American States."[25] At a time when the term "states' rights" was already a sure marker of segregationist opposition to the Warren Court, Munich's papers were certainly offering an unusual description of the chief justice's political reputation, and it is worth considering just how these misrepresentations may have come to pass.

Warren toured the Federal Republic as a private guest of the West German government, but the costs of the chief justice's international travel to and from Germany were covered by the U.S. government.[26] On July 27, during the planning for the Berlin visit, the American mission in that city had suggested to the State Department that a "civil rights lecture theme would be appropriate and have definite interest

and appeal . . . [and] should concentrate on [the] courts' role in racial integration."[27] Two days later, however, the State Department informed Berlin that the "Chief Justice declin[ed] to speak on integration or other objects [of] current juridical or political controversy in [the] U.S."[28] Similar information was conveyed to the West German embassy in Washington, which reported to the Foreign Ministry in Bonn that Warren was willing to talk only before select groups and would avoid controversial subjects.[29] What the ministry told the press is unclear, but we do know what kind of biographical material it prepared for West German President Theodor Heuss well before the chief justice was written up in the Munich papers; in preparation for his meeting with Warren, Heuss was given to understand that his guest was "an opponent of the excessive centralization of federal power and promotes states' rights. This position has served him very well and, despite the reserve he has shown in political matters recently, has earned him the trust of all groups and interests in the United States."[30]

---

[23] In the days following Warren's arrival, *Die Welt* carried two sizable articles on the chief justice, neither of which made the slightest mention of his connection with civil rights. See Hans-Joachim Kausch, "Oberster US-Bundesrichter in Berlin," *Die Welt*, Aug. 18, 1959, 1; Hans-Joachim Kausch, "Earl Warren – ein Kreuzfahrer für das Recht," *Die Welt*, Aug. 20, 1959, 2.

[24] See *Münchner Merkur*, Aug. 27, 1959.

[25] See Martin Rehm, "Amerikas höchster Richter auf Besuch," *Süddeutsche Zeitung*, Aug. 28, 1959.

[26] See telegram from Dillon, Department of State, to USBER Berlin, July 15, 1959, National Archives (hereafter NA), Record Group (hereafter RG) 59, 033.1100/7-1659, box 134; telegram from Dillon, Department of State to USBER Berlin, July 31, 1959, NA, RG 59, 033.1100/7-3059, box 134. See also copy of undated letter from Foy D. Kohler, Acting Assistant Secretary of State for European Affairs, to Earl Warren, NA, RG 59, 033.1100/7-1559, box 134.

[27] See telegram from Gufler (Berlin Mission) to secretary of state, July 27, 1959, NA, RG 59, 033.1100/7-2759, box 134.

[28] Telegram from Dillon, Department of State, to USBER Berlin, July 29, 1959, NA, RG 59, 033.1100/7-2759, box 134.

[29] See telegram from Washington embassy to AA, July 29, 1959, Politisches Archiv des Auswärtigen Amtes, Ref. 305, Bd. 75; Polit. Beziehungen der BRD-USA.

[30] Document prepared in Auswärtiges Amt by Abteilung 5, Ref. 500, August 19, 1959, Bundesarchiv Koblenz, B 122/492. As for the public-relations efforts of the American mission in Berlin, it was instructed by the State Department to encourage press coverage "with emphasis where possible on the two-way flow of American-German exchange activities and on such aspects of the American judicial and political tradition as may emerge from Mr. Warren's remarks." See Department of State Instruction to American Embassies Copenhagen, Helsinki, Bonn, and Moscow; American consuls general Hamburg, Munich, and Stuttgart; and USBER Berlin, July 31, 1959, NA, RG 59, 033.1100/7-3159, box 134. The mission apparently provided the press with "a detailed biography," which I, however, have been unable to locate; see dispatch from Charles F. Blackman, Public Affairs Officer, U.S. Mission Berlin to Department of State, Washington, D.C., Sept. 2, 1959, NA, RG 59, 033.1100/9-259, box 134, 1.

Although Germany and America quickly developed close media ties after the war, their domestic media establishments possessed distinctly national characteristics during the first two postwar decades. Americans enjoyed technological and financial advantages during these years, particularly in broadcasting. The American networks had unmatched resources for gathering news footage around the globe, and American entertainment programming often saw the world as its stage, as on September 7, 1961, when NBC talk-show host Jack Paar decided to tape his program in the shadow of the recently erected Berlin Wall, joined by Peggy Cass and fifty armed GIs.[31] German radio and television developed both more slowly and along the British model of public broadcasting.[32] Undoubtedly, the most influential West German broadcaster working in America during the 1950s was Peter von Zahn. Beginning in 1952, Zahn did weekly radio broadcasts for the German state radio consortium, the ARD. In the middle of the decade, Zahn also began producing monthly half-hour television programs; these "pictures from the new world" were first broadcast in October 1955. Zahn has often been criticized for presenting German audiences with an idealized vision of America, but his reports were not completely uncritical; in his memoirs, he recounts how he felt the need to address the issue of American race relations in order to avoid alienating his audience even though this attention cost him the funding from the United States Information Agency (USIA) that had paid most of the series' costs during its first years.[33]

Zahn remained the mainstay of the West German broadcasting presence in the United States until 1960. In September of that year, Thilo Koch took over as the ARD's radio broadcaster in Washington; he held this job until 1970. Koch was also responsible for television reporting for North German Radio (NDR). In 1964, West German Radio (WDR) began regular television operations in the United States, when Gerd Ruge began his five-year tenure as Washington correspondent.[34] The newly founded Second German Television (ZDF) opened a Washington bureau in April 1963 under the direction of Klaus Harpprecht; however, Harpprecht's tenure lasted only two years, throughout which he continued to contribute regular essays on America to the weekend section of the *Süddeutsche Zeitung*. Although the wordy Harpprecht was perhaps an odd choice for a television correspondent, his unsuitedness showed the degree to which West German television news remained in the shadow of the nation's print media. Nevertheless, West German television news was making rapid strides during the early 1960s, in no small part because of the European Broadcasting Union's Eurovision service. Eurovision provided increasing amounts of satellite news coverage, quite extensively so during the funeral of President John F. Kennedy.[35] By November 1963, West Germans and Americans, it seemed, could simultaneously mourn a shared tragedy.

The Kennedy assassination unleashed a wellspring of German-American (and European-American) identification, but the unifying power of this moment was fleeting. Racial turmoil and the bloody entanglement in Vietnam were soon to darken the vision of America abroad. The rise of anti-Americanism in 1960s West Germany is a topic that reaches beyond the scope of this article, but it can hardly be denied that the Federal Republic's mainstream media gradually began to look more critically at America in this period.[36] To be sure, this increase in critical attention does not necessarily indicate a resurgence in German cultural sovereignty, for the American media continued to set the tone for coverage of civil rights and counterinsurgency even as they responded to German and other foreign criticism. Still, even if only a close analysis can reveal the particular national aspects of the German media's coverage

---

[31] "50 U.S. Soldiers in Action for TV," *New York Times*, Sept. 8, 1963, 63.

[32] Wilson P. Dizard, *Television: A World View* (Syracuse, N.Y., 1966), 162, 6.

[33] Peter von Zahn, *Reporter der Windrose: Erinnerungen 1951–1964* (Stuttgart, 1994), 237–9.

[34] Fischer, "Berichterstattung aus den USA," 23.

[35] Dizard, *Television*, 87–8.

[36] See the chapter by Philipp Gassert in this section.

of these and other issues,[37] it is worth stressing, as Richard Pells has recently done, that West Europeans, Germans included, were never subjected to anything as monolithic as a hypothetical "Americanization."[38] On the contrary, they transformed American ideals and practices for European use and, in turn, influenced American developments. In the German-American case, this relationship may have been far from one of complete parity, but it was complicated enough to defy the ascription of distinct national boundaries.

[37] I have tried to do this for civil rights in my "Afro-America in West German Perspective, 1945–1966" (Ph.D. diss., Yale University, 1997), chap. 5.

[38] See Richard H. Pells, *Not Like Us: How Europeans Have Loved, Hated and Transformed American Culture Since* *World War II* (New York, 1997), esp. 279–83 and 313–24. See also the chapter by Axel Schildt in this section.

CHAPTER FOURTEEN

In Hitler's Shadow

American Images of Germany

Thomas Reuther

The "American image of Germany" can be understood as the "cognitive representation of qualities"[1] that the American public attributes to Germany and Germans. "The" image of Germany is, of course, as much an ideal type and construct as "the" American public. In reality, a whole range of different images of Germany has always existed and continues to coexist; political scientists correctly argue that the existence of diverse, not entirely autonomous, politically defined publics must be assumed. Retaining a sense of the ambiguity of these terms is thus important. Nevertheless, when I use both concepts in singular form here, I do so with the conviction that such simplification can provide useful insights. As recent research into images of nation has found, "the" image that Americans have of Germany is a product of the "cultural system" of the society that receives and absorbs the image; stereotypes of itself and of outsiders, self-images and images of foreigners, all flow into each other.[2]

A modern synthesis of the American image of postwar Germany has not as yet been done using all available source material, be it opinion

polls or current literature or artistic debates on Germany. One must inevitably rely on some older representations that describe the American image of Germany through the lens of history.[3]

STARTING POINT, 1945: AN "OTHER GERMANY" TWICE OVER

With the advance of Allied troops in spring and summer 1945, the full extent of the Nazis' extermination policy became apparent. It added a new dimension to the American image of Germany. It almost seemed as though the United States recognized its foe's true character only after it had conquered it. The American public had known since 1933 that Jews and other minorities in German society had been subject to numerous forms of harassment, persecution,

---

[1] As outlined by Kurt H. Stapf, Wolfgang Stroebe, and Klaus Jonas, *Amerikaner über Deutschland und die Deutchen: Urteile und Vorurteile* (Opladen 1986), 16.

[2] Knud Krakau, "Einführende Überlegungen zur Entstehung und Wirkung von Bildern, die sich Nationen von sich und anderen machen," in Willi Paul Adams and Knud Krakau, eds., *Deutschland und Amerika: Perzeption und historische Realität* (Berlin, 1985), 9–18.

[3] Henry Cord Meyer, *Five Images of Germany* (Washington, 1960). Norbert Muhlen, *Das Deutschlandbild der Amerikaner: Eine Untersuchung der öffentlichen Meinung* (Hamburg, 1960); Christine M. Totten, *Deutschland. Soll und Haben: Amerikas Deutschlandbild* (Munich, 1964). See also Manfred Koch-Hillebrecht, *Das Deutschenbild: Gegenwart, Geschichte, Psychologie* (Munich, 1977); Paul Monaco, "Stereotypes of Germans in American Culture: Observations from an Interdisciplinary Perspective," *American Studies* 31 (1986): 403–11; Eckhard Marten, *Das Deutschlandbild in der amerikanischen Medienberichterstattung: Ein kommunikationswissenschaftlicher Beitrag zur Nationenbildforschung* (Wiesbaden, 1989); David E. Barclay and Elisabeth Glaser-Schmidt, eds., *Transatlantic Images and Perceptions: Germany and America Since 1776* (Cambridge, 1997).

and cruelty. However, this did not attract much attention, especially because American editors treated news of atrocities with extreme caution after their experiences with the exaggerated British propaganda of World War I. They also could not verify the full extent of Nazi terror from the ever smaller trickle of news from Europe, particularly after 1941. Beyond this, some latent anti-Semitism may have also contributed a measure of indifference to their stance.

With the discovery of the first concentration camps, journalists who issued reports on what they saw and then the broader public underwent a learning process. The "war as Holocaust" caught up with Americans in spring 1945. In a letter to his wife, the commander of the American troops, Dwight D. Eisenhower, described what many Americans would soon also feel: "I never dreamed that such cruelty, bestiality, and savagery could really exist in this world! It was horrible."[4]

The reports of the discoveries at Buchenwald and Dachau aroused great interest back in the United States. At the same time, they induced an "elemental revulsion"[5] that has continued to weigh heavily on the American image of Germany up to the present. Opinion polls indicate that the demand for a "harsh peace" soon reached its highest level. In July 1945, 92 percent of those questioned supported the permanent disarmament of Germany, 86 percent supported long-term occupation by Allied troops, 62 percent supported sending German labor to those areas of Europe destroyed by the war, and 60 percent backed the dismantling of key industries. Yet, even at this point, the concept of a "Carthaginian peace," as the plans of Henry Morgenthau at the Treasury Depart-

ment were repeatedly described, found no majority support: 55 percent called for UN support in rebuilding a German peacetime economy; 52 percent for military intervention to prevent widespread famine; and even at this moment of peak hostility toward Germany, only 41 percent supported a division of Germany. At a time when the image of Germany had reached an absolute nadir in the United States, Americans were still more favorably disposed toward Germans than toward the Japanese.[6]

With the occupation of Germany, however, the Americans experienced a positive surprise that decisively helped to improve the image of the conquered foe. Reports in American newspapers had given the impression to both the government and public that the Allied entry into the heart of the German Reich would result in numerous American fatalities and provoke bitter opposition from a fanatical people and constant terrorist attacks by the "werewolf" bands. Reality did not match this picture at all. Most of the population, worn out both inwardly and outwardly by war, bombardment, and defeat, met the American troops (and the correspondents who accompanied them) in part thankfully and enthusiastically, in part apathetically and unresisting, but rarely in a belligerent and aggressive manner. At first, the Americans did not realize that their preconceived picture of the occupation would not overlap much with GIs' actual experiences. Many journalists, especially members of the East Coast press who were particularly critical of the Germans, continued to pick up on any indications that might conform with their set ideas about a peculiar German national character.[7] In spite of this, the comparatively smooth transition from war to occupation contributed to easing strained relations.

---

[4] Letter from Dwight D. Eisenhower to Mamie Eisenhower, Apr. 15, 1945, Dwight D. Eisenhower, *Letters to Mamie*, ed. John S. D. Eisenhower (Garden City, N.Y., 1978), 248.

[5] Konrad H. Jarausch, "Das amerikanische Deutschlandbild in drei Jahrhunderten," in Klaus Weigelt, ed., *Das Deutschland- und Amerikabild: Beiträge zum gegenseitige Verständnis beider Völker* (Melle, 1986), 16. For greater detail, see Robert H. Abzug, *Inside the Vicious Heart: Americans and the Liberation of Nazi Concentration Camps* (New York, 1985).

[6] Office of Public Opinion Studies, 1943–1965, *Public Attitudes on Foreign Policy*, Special Report no. 63, July 2, 1945, in National Archives (hereafter NA), College Park, Md., Record Group (hereafter RG) 59. *Special Reports on Attitudes Toward Foreign Policy, 1943–1965*, box 1: NA, RG 59, OPOS.

[7] Klaus-Dietmar Henke, *Die amerikanische Besetzung Deutschlands* (Munich, 1995), 160ff. Ferdinand A. Hermens, "The Danger of Stereotypes in Viewing Germany," *Public Opinion Quarterly* 9 (1945): 418–27.

During the early occupation period, the American public viewed the Germans with a mixture of mistrust and a readiness to help them. The latter approach soon prevailed over the former, especially because it was tied to the widespread conviction that Europe could not recover without a revitalized German industry. At least since the time of the Stuttgart speech of Secretary of State James F. Byrnes, which was also much discussed in the United States, this belief joined forces with the anticommunist convictions held by an ever-increasing number of Americans. Brewing international tensions had increasingly centered the image of the enemy abroad on the Soviet Union. For Germany, the wartime enemy of yesterday, this anticommunist basis offered the unexpected chance of achieving a political, economic, and – at least partially – moral rehabilitation much more quickly than at first anticipated. Cold War conditions in no way automatically led to a positive image of Germany, though. On the contrary, Germany's image in the United States was still characterized in far greater measure by the deepseated ambivalence that had prevailed since the beginning of the century.

THE AMERICAN DEBATE OVER THE GERMAN
QUESTION, 1946/47–55

By 1946, it was already becoming increasingly clear through the public treatment of the German question that the context in which Germany's future was being discussed had changed radically. As the Cold War began, public discussions shifted more and more away from the problem of how Europe and the world could protect themselves from a new German "grab for world power" and toward the question of how and to what extent this Germany should be drawn into the consolidation of the Western world against the Soviet threat. This development took place in stages and suffered some interruptions. True acceptance of the enemy as an ally was long in the making. For a range of reasons, this was accomplished more quickly and easily in the United States than in most European countries. First, a much broader anticommunist domestic consensus existed in the United States than in most European countries. Through its special geographical position, the United States had also been spared the destruction of the war; it was the only major victor of World War II not to experience the terrors of Hitler's warfare on its own terrain. With the Nuremberg war trials, which the American media described in detail, punishment of the major guilty parties seemed to have been carried through. Already by mid-1946, most Americans felt that the objectives of denazification had also largely been accomplished.[8]

Americans after 1946 were drawn in by European matters primarily through the world economy, just as they had been after World War I. Although many American correspondents had reported from the occupied zones since the end of the war, a broad public discussion did not take off until early 1946. Political experts, business executives, and members of Congress traveled to Western and Central Europe to form a picture of the economic situation. Most significantly, the visit of former American President Herbert Hoover, who toured the Western zones for the first time in April 1946, drew the attention of many Americans to the desperate material deprivation reigning in Central Europe. The two most significant arguments in favor of quick economic reconstruction in the Western zones were, first, the idea that a general European recovery – viewed as the most important requirement for the stabilization of the liberal-democratic system – could not be attained without the "economic locomotive" of Germany; and second, the warning that the "bill" for a misguided (meaning too destructive) occupation policy would have to be paid by the American taxpayer. The same segments of the American population that had been put on the defensive during the war because of their pro-German sentiments now increasingly found an audience. These included liberal-conservative emigrants such as Gustav Stolper,

[8] National Opinion Research Center, "Public Attitudes Toward Germany and Japan," NA, RG 59, OPOS, box 34, Folder "Germany 1947–1948," Feb. 3, 1947, p. 4.

whose influential book – *German Realities* – appeared in 1946; former "isolationists" who in the 1930s had already considered the threat of communism to be more dangerous than fascism; and German-Americans, some of whom were also influential representatives of the American business world, who wanted to build on the cooperation of the 1920s.

Many voices could still be heard pointing out the potential dangers they saw in the imminent reintegration of the Western occupied zones into an American and West European economic and trade system. These included the "Vansittartists," an increasingly marginal group mostly of intellectuals and journalists who believed in an unchanging negative continuity in the German national character and advocated through the "Society for the Prevention of World War III" maintaining a policy of strict supervision over Germany. Other voices of caution included commentators of widely varied political origins, such as Walter Lippmann and James Paul Warburg, who held fast to the demand for an occupation policy in harmony with the security interests of the Soviet Union, which, from their point of view, were understandable. Finally, a number of left-liberals from New Deal circles articulated their unease and persisted in the critical view held by Franklin D. Roosevelt toward Germany; they continued to see Germany, not the Soviet Union, as *the* chief danger for European peace. The fact that the latter groups were particularly heavily represented in the press and other media explains somewhat the curious discrepancy between public opinion, which took a basically positive view of rebuilding Germany, and the often much more critical opinions found in print.

One basic issue further refined through public discourse was the evaluation of the German national character. Resolving this issue would reveal how feasible a liberal democratic social order on German soil was. Were the Germans a people, who "like other peoples, are made up of individuals, who are partly good and partly bad," as James Paul Warburg maintained, a people that had proved itself capable of learning and that could become part of the Atlantic-European community? Or were the fears of Max

Lerner justified when, in 1949, he diagnosed the crucial weakness of German "reconstruction" as the lack of a "moral awakening" and thus looked on the future success of democracy on German soil with skepticism?[9] The American public itself seemed to be undecided about this question. In 1949, according to a Gallup poll, a majority of 55 percent still did not believe that the Germans were in a position to govern themselves in a democratic manner. Public opinion supported a carefully controlled, step-by-step democratization process, one that was very much in keeping with the government's actual policy.

These questions, revolving around the German problem at the end of the 1940s against a backdrop of turbulent political developments, took West German society as their point of reference. By contrast, the Soviet occupation zone remained a *quantité négligeable*. During the Berlin Blockade and the Korean War, numerous reports appeared on conditions in eastern Germany. The publications of the conservative publisher Henry Luce compared socialists' displays with those of the Nazis and the leader cult around Ulbricht and the *Sozialistische Einheitspartei Deutschlands* (SED, or Socialist Unity Party of Germany) with that surrounding Hitler. Yet, thorough analyses of the situation in "the other Germany" were much more rare. After its founding, the new German Democratic Republic remained a Soviet satellite of only passing significance in the American consciousness; in effect, it did not exist for Americans.

By contrast, the political evolution of the Federal Republic under Chancellor Konrad Adenauer attracted great interest. It seemed in many ways to support those who had advocated the experiment of a Western industrial state founded on the territory of the former German empire occupied by the Atlantic-Western European victorious powers; it lent support to those who had spoken out against the alternatives of either a territorial partition and economic suppression or a policy of neutralizing Germany

---

[9] James Paul Warburg, *Deutschland: Brücke oder Schlachtfeld* (Stuttgart, 1949): 130. Max Lerner, "Germany Rebuilds: For What?" *New York Post*, June 28, 1949.

(following, for example, Lippmann and War-burg). The Berlin Blockade and the American view that the people of Berlin had demonstrated courageous support for basic democratic values; the foundation of the Federal Republic, with its constitution modeled on Western examples; the readiness to take part in the defense of Western Europe with its own troops through the EDC or NATO; Adenauer's alliance policy in general; and finally, the "economic miracle" following the currency reform, which to many appeared modeled on American economic principles: All of these factors contributed to the gradual for-mation of a more positive image of Germany. The stereotypes that from the American point of view had always exemplified German "as-sets" – industriousness, thrift, scientific talent, and technical efficiency – were reactivated and gradually eclipsed the image of the Third Reich.

In contrast, "intellectual Germany," which Americans had admired up until World War I and then again in the 1920s, long remained compromised. Although traces of this high re-gard for German intellectual accomplishments can certainly still be found, from the American standpoint, victory in World War II confirmed the cultural superiority of the "American way of life." The New World had emancipated itself from the Old World intellectually.

The other image of the militaristic, aggressive, antidemocratic, and racist Germany lived on in two ways. First, the folly of the wicked Nazis in American popular culture offered a seem-ingly perfect foil for the merits and virtues of Americans. The Nazi German became a cliché figure of countless films, television shows, war novels, and fiction, although ever more strongly beginning in the 1960s.[10] Second, particularly after the appearance of William L. Shirer's best-seller *The Rise and Fall of the Third Reich*, a flood of nonfiction books that dealt with Na-tional Socialism in the most disparate ways began to appear, a publishing phenomenon that

has not ceased to this day.[11] The experience of this "other" Germany of the National Socialist and war period remained an enduring theme in scholarly and popular culture and, at the same time, became a mirror in which the demo-cratic development of the Federal Republic was sharply scrutinized time and again. The first ma-jor moment came in the debate beginning in 1950 over German rearmament, in which the danger of a remilitarization and re-Nazification of German society became a theme for crit-ical journalists. This debate over rearmament happened to coincide with the emergence of apparent neo-Nazi tendencies, recorded in the short-lived electoral successes of the *Sozialis-tische Reichspartei* (SRP), and it seemed to con-firm the fears of these commentators who had mistrusted the U.S. government's vision of democracy in the Western zones from the be-ginning.

With the collapse of the right-wing rad-ical parties, the American news media's re-portage on Germany became more generous. The positive image of the first German chan-cellor contributed significantly to this shift. Initial skepticism about the advanced age, con-servatism, and autocratic governing style of Konrad Adenauer was soon superseded by the image of a statesman concerned with achiev-ing equilibrium with his European neigh-bors and a strong alliance with the United States. Adenauer's first visit to the United States, coming before the Bundestag elections in 1953, was almost unanimously hailed as a public-relations success; as Great Britain and France increasingly distanced themselves from the American vision for Europe, the chancel-lor of the Federal Republic became Washing-ton's most important European interlocutor. In 1953, *Time* even chose Adenauer as "Man of the Year," a visible sign that the American media

[11] Shirer's book sold more than three million copies in the United States between 1960 and 1975. The lead-ing scholarly book, Karl Dietrich Bracher's *Die Deutsche Diktatur*, had sales of only 40,000 in the 14 years after its publication. Fritz Stern, "Deutsche Vergangenheit aus amerikanischer Sicht: Hundert Jahre amerikanische His-toriographie," in his *Verspielte Grosse: Essays zur deutschen Geschichte* (Munich, 1996), 120.

[10] See Beverly Crawford and James Martel, "Rep-resentations of Germans and What Germans Repre-sent: American Film Images and Public Perceptions in the Postwar Era," in Barclay and Glaser-Schmidt, eds., *Transatlantic Images*.

knew enough to value his importance for
German-American relations and the European
idea:

Konrad Adenauer had already guided the hated home
of the Hun and Nazi back to moral respectability
and had earned a seat in the highest councils of
Western powers.... No longer the passive object of
other forces, Germany in 1953 was again one of the
formidable forces of history and Konrad Adenauer
one of history's makers.[12]

The growing respectability of the Federal Republic in the United States, to which the restitution agreement with Israel had contributed, was
noticeably enhanced by the circumstances of the
Cold War, although this process reflected more
than just the East-West conflict. The rather poor
view taken of the Social Democrats can certainly also be understood in this context. Their
neutral foreign policy and (in American eyes)
socialist domestic goals formed a perceptible
barrier until the party's Godesberger Program.
The Americans had tied the success of their European policy since the Korean crisis to Konrad Adenauer, and they offered him assistance
in the elections of 1953, in essence supporting a conservative chancellor who stood for full
German rights among nations and rearmament.
This shows how decisively the foreign-policy
terrain had changed since 1945. It was a transformation that had been carried along by large
segments of the public and published opinion in
the United States.

AMBIVALENT NORMALIZATION: THE
AMERICAN IMAGE OF GERMANY, 1955–68

In 1955, the process of integrating West Germany into the Atlantic-Western European security community was provisionally completed
with the declaration of the Federal Republic's
sovereignty and its entry into NATO and the
West European Union (WEU). The American
public followed the evolution from enemy to
U.S. ally with a critical eye but also with growing
sympathy. The friendly rapport between Ade-

nauer and U.S. Secretary of State John Foster
Dulles most clearly reflected the close relationship between the two states. Questions about the
dependability of German democracy had not
yet disappeared. However, as long as Adenauer
stood at the helm of the West German state,
the danger of a neutralization and a new revanchism seemed averted. To some degree, the
Americans took over Adenauer's self-perception
in these matters. It was less German society as a
whole than the political leadership of the young
republic that had won the trust of the United
States.

The German "economic miracle" had also
gained the respect of the American public.
West German society appeared to rise from
the ruins of the Third Reich like a proverbial phoenix; it almost seemed as though the
"American Dream" had taken on a new form
on German soil. In the second half of the 1950s
and even more in the 1960s, the Mercedes
hood ornament and the Volkswagen Beetle advanced to the rank of German trademarks,
seemingly symbolizing German society even
more effectively than sauerkraut and spiked military helmets (Pickelhaube). The creed of the
occupation period, whereby economic stability was the prerequisite for the establishment
of a healthy, democratic community, seemed
confirmed. The Marshall Plan and Berlin Airlift became in hindsight the twin symbols of
a German-American alliance of interests and
ideas that seemed to become increasingly self-
evident.

Yet, the 1960s also brought difficulties to
the fore. With the second Berlin Crisis and
the building of the Berlin Wall in 1961, the
American people became aware that the policy
direction toward Germany introduced by the
Truman and Eisenhower administrations and
continued by John F. Kennedy had its price:
Berlin would continue to be a source of conflict
and Germany would remain divided. The Berlin
problem clearly carried more weight in the
United States, which is explained by two factors.
First, it was the confrontations over Berlin that
carried the danger of an escalation into a third
world war. Second, since 1948, the divided city
had been a symbol of America's German policy

---

[12] Time, Jan. 4, 1954, 18.

as well as its commitment to Europe; as the front line of the Cold War, Berlin simultaneously embodied the superiority of the American-style democratic system.[13] The mayors of Berlin, most notably Ernst Reuter and Willy Brandt, enjoyed a popularity in the American media otherwise attained only by Konrad Adenauer. The image of the German Democratic Republic remained indistinct in comparison, even at the time of the second Berlin Crisis. The uncompromising rhetorical commitment to reunification made by the Eisenhower and Kennedy administrations in deference to the West German government did not discomfort the American public. Only an occasional invocation of the "Rapallo complex" (i.e., the fear that West Germany could seek a political settlement with the Soviet Union for the sake of reunification) caused some disquiet in the American media. This occurred first in 1948–9 and later in the context of the Stalin memos, at the time of Adenauer's visit to Moscow in 1955, and, more markedly, in the context of Ostpolitik during the 1970s.

A certain mistrust in German society's "fitness for democracy" remained under the surface. An unusual shift from the usual thrust of U.S. domestic policy made this clear: American trust in the German government was far stronger than in Germany's "man on the street." The change in U.S. policy toward Germany, moving from confrontation to cooperation, had also mirrored the shift that had occurred in the Federal Republic. Questions about the causes of the failure of Weimar and the rise of National Socialism, discussed intensively during the war, had been driven into the background with the outbreak of the Cold War. At the beginning of the 1960s, however, the appearance of Shirer's book released a first wave of publications about the Third Reich, and the Eichmann trial brought the horrors of the Nazi regime of violence back into the American consciousness.[14] However, it would be a misunderstanding to speak of a general worsening of Americans' image of Germany in the 1960s. Not least, the Cuban Missile Crisis and the Vietnam War prompted Americans to develop a certain nostalgia for the last "good war" and, in this connection, to return in part to the debates of the last years of the war.[15]

In 1969, three American social psychologists published the results of a survey among Princeton University students.[16] Using questions asked by earlier studies in the years 1933 and 1951, they asked students for their opinions of ten ethnic groups, including Germans. The result brings the American image of Germans during the late 1960s into sharp relief. The most frequently cited traits were "industrious," "scientifically minded," and "methodical." "Extremely nationalistic" and "aggressive" continued to appear but had decreased noticeably in comparison to the 1951 survey, where they were still among the most frequently named traits. One could conclude from this that the American image of Germany in the postwar period had changed for the better, but that the experiences of the Nazi era continued to occupy a place in the American subconscious and could be reactivated at any time (set off by such events as the electoral success of the *National-Demokratische Partei Deutschlands* [NPD] in 1967–8). One can thus speak of an ambivalent normalization in attitudes toward Germany. Beginning in the mid-1950s, West German society became increasingly "Western" for most Americans. But the impressions garnered from the years from 1933 to 1945 remained vivid enough to repeatedly evoke a certain mistrust about the stability of German democracy. Americans did not again feel entirely at ease with Germans after 1945.

---

[13] See the chapter by Diethelm Prowe, vol. 1, Politics.
[14] Irving Crespi, "Public Reaction to the Eichmann Trial," *Public Opinion Quarterly* 28 (1964): 91–103. See also the chapter by Alan E. Steinweis, vol. 1, Culture.

[15] In July 1962, only 17 percent of those questioned in a Gallup poll indicated that the news reports on the Eichmann trial had negatively influenced their attitudes toward the Germans; 55 percent denied this. Gebhard Schweigler, *Politikwissenschaft und Aussenpolitik in den USA. Am Beispiel der europäisch-amerikanischen Beziehungen* (Munich, 1977), 268.
[16] Marvin Karlins, Thomas L. Coffman, and Gary Walters, "On the Fading of Social Stereotypes: Studies in Three Generations of College Students," *Journal of Personality and Social Psychology* 13, no. 1 (1969): 1–16.

CHAPTER FIFTEEN

Old Stereotypes and New Realities

The West German Image of the United States

Knud Krakau

Translated by Sally E. Robertson

The West German image of America between 1945 and 1968 cannot be understood without looking at an earlier history that stretches back to the late eighteenth century. The most important elements of this image included positive attitudes of Germans in liberal, bourgeois, intellectual, and leftist circles toward American values such as freedom, democracy, and constitutional rule; a converse, negative attitude toward the United States among more traditional and reactionary-conservative social groups; the educated classes' denigration of American "civilization" and their elevation of German and European "culture"; admiration for American technological innovation and rationalization techniques that produced new levels of efficiency in industrial production, trade, and organized labor; and finally, a radical Marxist, socialist, and communist critique of capitalism in its American form.

Germans have always embraced a variety of images of America, not just one picture. These images have been ambivalent or multivalent, even contradictory,[1] and "anti-Americanism" has long constituted an integral part of this general history of transatlantic perceptions.[2]

1945: A NEW IMAGE OF AMERICA

Long-standing, older images of America retained a place in the German mental landscape even after 1945.[3] At the same time, as Germans sorted through their experiences of World War II, they formed new images of America or adapted older perceptions to reflect more recent experiences. Up to that point, America had been a distant "Other" that provoked interest among only certain sectors of German

[1] David Large, "America in the Consciousness of the Germans," in Frank Krampikowski, ed., *Amerikanisches Deutschlandbild und deutsches Amerikabild* (Baltmannsweiler, 1990), 199–210; David E. Barclay and Elisabeth Glaser-Schmidt, eds., *Transatlantic Images and Perceptions. Germany and America Since 1776* (New York, 1997).

[2] Ernst Fraenkel, *Amerika im Spiegel des deutschen politischen Denkens* (Cologne, 1959); Frank Trommler, "The Rise and Fall of Americanism in Germany," in Frank Trommler and Joseph McVeigh, eds., *America and the Germans: An Assessment of a Three-Hundred-Year History*, vol. 2: *The Relationship in the Twentieth Century* (Philadelphia, 1985), 332–42; Dan Diner, *Verkehrte Welten: Antiamerikanismus in Deutschland; Ein historischer Essay* (Frankfurt am Main, 1993).

[3] To date, no comprehensive analysis of West German images of America after 1945 has been done. The abundant literature investigates only aspects of the subject or individual, often earlier, periods; see Günter C. Behrmann, "Geschichte und aktuelle Struktur des Antiamerikanismus," *Aus Politik und Zeitgeschichte* B 29/30 (1984): 3–14; Günter Moltmann, "Deutscher Anti-Amerikanismus heute und früher," in Otmar Franz, ed., *Vom Sinn der Geschichte* (Stuttgart, 1976), 85–105.

society – above all, journalists, writers, intellectuals, politicians, representatives of industry, travelers, and emigrants. With the collapse of state institutions and many social institutions in Germany after 1945, however, encounters between Germans and Americans took on a dramatically and historically novel form through the "overwhelming presence of the occupying forces."[4] Germans now experienced Americans in a direct and unmediated way as the victors of the war and an occupying power.

In 1945, Germans experienced America as a kind of revolutionary import, as prosecutor, judge, and reeducation official bent on radically altering German government, society, and economy and imposing a new system of values on the German people. Before long, however, a new American policy had emerged that aimed for political, economic, and even military reconstruction and viewed the restoration of sovereignty to this German half-state as its ultimate goal. Sovereignty, however, was subject to certain reservations *and* contingent on the integration of West Germany into Western European and transatlantic political, economic, and military structures ("double containment").[5] The unique conditions reigning between 1945 and 1955 and the near "normal" quality of subsequent relations between the two countries would leave a strong imprint on West German images of America in later years.

PUBLIC OPINION

It is astonishing at first glance that the "harsh" early phase of the occupation did not induce Germans to embrace a completely negative image of America, criticism and protests on

individual matters notwithstanding. On the contrary, the general attitude toward America remained highly positive. Opinion polls conducted in the American zone of occupation after 1945 by the U.S. military government and the U.S. High Commission confirmed this, as did later surveys undertaken by German research institutes, primarily the *Institut für Demoskopie*, a public opinion research center in Allensbach.

The denazification program was a particularly controversial measure among the German public. Although 65 percent of those surveyed in 1949 criticized its implementation, an equally high percentage approved of its underlying intent.[6] Whereas many of the Germans surveyed in 1946 still considered National Socialism to be a good idea that had been poorly executed, nearly 60 percent did not feel that the occupation was a national humiliation, instead emphasizing the salutary contribution that the Americans had made to reconstruction. The overwhelmingly positive attitude toward the United States surfaced in responses to questions about such issues as general congeniality, the Allied occupation as a national disgrace, whether America would treat Germany fairly, the justifications for and effects of the Nuremberg trials, how America might lend support to German reconstruction efforts (even before the Marshall Plan), close cooperation with America on the basis of common interests and values, guarantees of friendship and security, the presence of American troops in Germany, America's future influence in international politics and confidence in its leadership role in the preservation of peace, and more generally, the extent to which the United States could serve as a model for German development.[7] The polls by the

---

[4] Ralph Willet, *The Americanization of Germany, 1945–1949* (London, 1989), 1.

[5] Ernst-Otto Czempiel, "Die Bundesrepublik und Amerika. Von der Okkupation zur Kooperation," in Richard Löwenthal and Hans-Peter Schwarz, eds., *Die zweite Republik: 25 Jahre Bundesrepublik Deutschland; Eine Bilanz* (Stuttgart, 1974), 554–79.

[6] Anna J. Merritt and Richard L. Merritt, eds., *Public Opinion in Occupied Germany: The OMGUS Surveys, 1945–1949* (Urbana, Ill., 1970), no. 182: 304–5; no. 22: 103–6; no. 60: 160–3.

[7] See the responses and analysis in ibid., nos. 17, 60, 68, 77, 86, 100, 104, 150, 175; see also Anna J. Merritt and Richard L. Merritt, eds., *Public Opinion in Semisovereign Germany: The HICOG Surveys, 1949–1955* (Urbana, Ill., 1980); Richard L. Merritt, *Democracy*

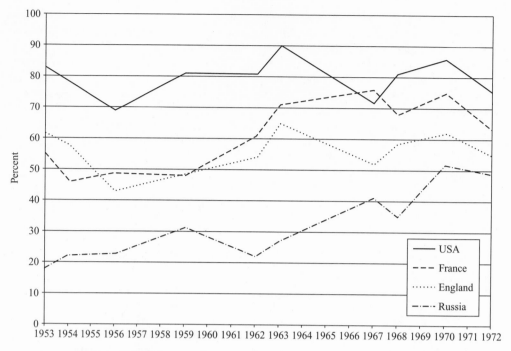

Source: Allensbacher Jahrbücher der öffentlichen Meinung, vols. 1–5.

Graph 1. "With which of these countries should we work together as closely as possible?"

military government as a whole showed an impressively high level of positive feelings toward the United States, despite many fluctuations produced by such events as the Berlin Crisis and the Korean War. This attitude was to remain fairly steady and significantly more positive, in fact, than West Germans' attitudes toward the other occupying powers and later allies. In some areas, German feelings toward the United States even became more favorable. Only once, in 1967, at the height of the public controversy over the Non-Proliferation Treaty and the low point of German-American relations, did more West German citizens support closer

Imposed. U.S. Occupation Policy and the German Public, 1945–1949 (New Haven, Conn., 1995), 239–69; for later years, see Gerhard Herdegen and Elisabeth Noelle-Neumann, "Gute Freunde, schlechte Kritik. Aktuelle Notizen über das Amerikabild der Deutschen," *Die politische Meinung* (Jan.-Feb. 1984): 4–13; Hans J. Kleinsteuber, "Ansichten vom 'grossen Bruder.' Amerikafreundlich oder antiamerikanisch? USA-Stereotypen in der Bundesrepublik im Spiegel von Umfrageergebnissen," *Amerikastudien* 36 (1991): 241–68.

cooperation with France than with the United States (see Graph 1).

Favorable attitudes toward the Americans, already visible soon after the occupation began, grew markedly among Germans as the Cold War advanced. Only the United States offered a bulwark against the Soviet threat. German approval climbed to a new peak during the period of the Berlin Airlift and the Marshall Plan. It included, on the one hand, a high degree of emotional affinity with the Americans and relief as soon as the Soviet blockade proved ineffective. On the other hand, it was mixed with more traditional German admiration for American technical and organizational efficiency. Not even the low point of support – brought on by American passivity during the building of the Berlin Wall in 1961 – could permanently shake a basic German acceptance of America's role as a guarantor of security, as protector and friend. The storm of enthusiasm that greeted President John F. Kennedy's visit barely two years later confirmed the fundamental esteem that Americans enjoyed in Germany. The consistently

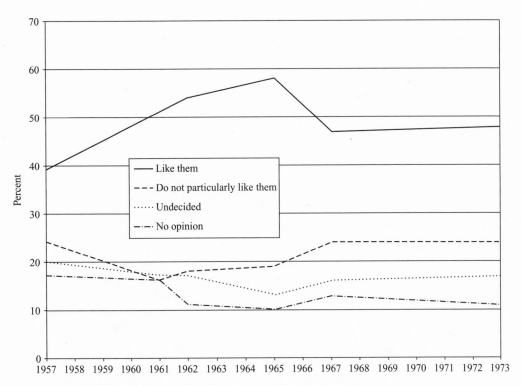

Source: Allensbacher Jahrbücher der öffentlichen Meinung, vols. 1–5.

Graph 2. "Do you actually like the Americans, or do you not particularly like them?"

positive results of polls recorded by the Allensbach Institute also demonstrated this. Beginning in the mid-1950s, the Allensbach polls regularly asked its German respondents, "Do you like the Americans?" (see Graph 2).

The reasons for these sustained positive attitudes toward America by the majority of Germans from an early point are obvious. Even before the end of hostilities, Germans began to ignore Nazi propaganda and to side with the Americans mentally and – where possible – even physically. Their hopes were not miscast. Despite all the inevitable hardships, the Germans viewed the American occupation overall as a "good" occupation.[8] The identity vacuum and disorientation produced by the collapse of all values and institutions apparently created a willingness among Germans to accept both the means and ends of American occupation policy;

they came to view it not only as inevitable, but ultimately as legitimate and reasonable as well. The majority of the population accepted this reorientation and reeducation, with their emphasis on moving toward more democratic values and behavior. And they particularly welcomed the gradual reconstruction of political institutions, the media, and the economy. Most even accepted denazification to some degree. The Germans did not always let the clumsiness and contradictions of these various policies pass without notice (e.g., the fact that a hierarchical military structure was to serve as the guiding hand of democracy).[9] But they gave credence to the underlying premises on which the policies rested.[10]

[8] See the chapter by Klaus-Dietmar Henke in this section.

[9] Norbert Muhlen, "America and the American Occupation in German Eyes," *Annals of the American Academy of Political and Social Sciences* 295 (1954): 55, 57.

[10] Czempiel, "Die Bundesrepublik und Amerika," 561.

Above and beyond the particulars of occupation policy, the moral and political vacuum of 1945 produced a far-reaching consensus that Germany had to open itself up to America and accept the United States as a model. A "positive image" of America thus formed. By contrast, Germany and Europe seemed old and used up; they had been unable to free themselves from the totalitarian yoke of National Socialism on their own. Europe owed its salvation to the vitality and endless resources of America. Few contemporaries would object when Golo Mann offered his accolades: "[U]ndeniably, America has helped more people, helped to create more human happiness, than any other country; the rise of America is undeniably the most amazingly fortunate event of the last hundred and fifty years."[11] Marion Gräfin Dönhoff retrospectively expressed the experience of an entire generation:

After the collapse and long years of moral perversion, intolerance, and intellectual barrenness, the modern, open society of the United States, with its tradition of free debate, its optimism and confidence in the future was for . . . us . . . a revelation. . . . [S]tudents, scholars, and politicians who became acquainted with America in those years returned with the impression that this society was the model for modern society in general.[12]

Disappointments and corrections were, of course, inevitable. One overly psychological interpretation saw the affinity for America as a simple exchange of the externalized superego of Hitler for a new one, a surrogate identity that attempted to overcome the trauma of Hitler by refusing to come to terms with its own past.[13] Such an interpretation fails to acknowledge the real psychic and moral needs of those years and, above all, fails to realize that coming to terms with one's past in fact required some such distance from it. Of course, misunderstandings

arose, for example about the Nuremberg trials. Americans understood these proceedings as offering the Germans a trial based on the rule of law rather than summary justice imposed by the victors; they saw them as a source of information and enlightenment, perhaps even offering a cathartic effect. However, even detailed and engaged reporting in the German media was able to convey neither the horror of the crimes nor who was truly responsible for them. In the press and "on the street," however, people welcomed the judgments and even suggested that the acquitted be brought to trial in German courts because many Germans had succumbed to the "autosuggestion that they had been the first and greatest victims of National Socialism." The judgments appeared as a liberating, exonerative "final stroke, an acquittal of the Germans as a whole. . . . [T]he selective assigning of guilt to members of the accused organizations" seemed to undermine the argument that Germans bore a collective burden of guilt for what had transpired.[14]

ECONOMY AND POLITICS

The economic and political arenas also reveal much. German trade unions for the most part developed a positive image of America and maintained close relationships with American unions. The military government, however, countered "bottom-up" reconstruction efforts by unions in an effort to ward off demands for codetermination and to secure its influence on the labor movement.[15] Leading industrialists soon took advantage of the opportunities arising from the early triumph of groups in America that saw an open, liberal, worldwide system of trade as the best guarantee for the well-being and security of the United States and the world. In this view, the economic and political reconstruction of Europe, and thus of Germany,

---

[11] Golo Mann, *Vom Geist Amerikas*, 2d ed. (Stuttgart, 1955), 28.

[12] Marion Gräfin Dönhoff, *Amerikanische Wechselbäder: Beobachtungen und Kommentare aus vier Jahrzehnten* (Stuttgart, 1983), 7.

[13] Horst-Eberhard Richter, "Amerikanismus, Antiamerikanismus – oder was sonst?" *Psyche* 40 (1986): 583–99.

[14] Anneke de Rudder, "'Warum das ganze Theater?' Der Nürnberger Prozess in den Augen der Zeitgenossen," *Jahrbuch für Antisemitismusforschung* 6 (1997): 236.

[15] See the chapter by Michael Fichter in this section.

was an absolute prerequisite. Unlike the advocates of a "harsh peace," supporters of economic reconstruction saw this route not as an abandonment of the goal of eliminating German aggressive potential but as the most effective means of achieving it.

Many industrialists had been deeply involved in National Socialism. The policy of reconstruction allowed them to return to old, familiar roles, often in their former positions, simply because they were seen as "indispensable." By the 1950s at the latest, the values and business interests of this group were firmly oriented toward the Western democracies. A phase of defiance and resistance toward the United States and a search for a "third way" between American capitalism and Soviet communism preceded this reorientation.[16] The concept of the third way was, however, based on self-delusion about the actual scope of the German defeat and illusions about the opportunities to extend German economic hegemony in Central Europe – where America had once been the main competitor – beyond 1945.[17]

Many entrepreneurs believed the situation after 1945 to be much more open than it actually was. One can, therefore, interpret their choice of the American model as a belated insight into historical change, a choice made freely above and beyond any tactical or opportunistic considerations, a new positive image of America based on a real change in perspective. Traditional admiration for American efficiency in production and organization certainly facilitated this shift. Its manifestations included broad acceptance and adoption of American antitrust and anticartel principles, management training, introduction of efficiency measures into economic concerns, product standardization, and Fordism.[18]

In the realm of politics, both the prominent role of Konrad Adenauer and the significance of the Social Democratic opposition must be scrutinized.[19] Adenauer's image of America assumed a "close correspondence in the thinking and feeling" of the two nations, with their shared Christian and Western ethics, ethics that were threatened by the "destructive forces of godless totalitarianism." Adenauer knew that the United States and, in particular, his friend John Foster Dulles concurred in this assumption. He shared America's concern that no "third way" for Germany could exist and that the country's survival as a Christian nation would be possible only within a framework of close ties to the West and the United States. Nevertheless, he pursued what he perceived to be German (and European) interests pragmatically and without illusions. He knew how to extract incremental concessions from the United States in the interests of German autonomy and to exact security guarantees from the Americans. Yet, he was unable to use these gains effectively to resolve the dilemma facing him in the Gaullist variation on the European "third way." Adenauer denounced, inaccurately, any sign that America might become weary of Europe's isolationism. His main concern was that the superpowers would reach agreement at the expense of Germany and that Germany might be tempted to drift off into neutrality. He thus remained quite pragmatic in stifling criticism of America after the building of the Berlin Wall: "Without the United States, we could not even stay alive. That is clear as day."[20] At the same time, however, he viewed the situation as a crisis of confidence and feared that German interests would be "sold out."[21] Although his view of America was not free of stereotypes, he did know that

[16] See the chapter by Jonathan Wiesen in this section.
[17] Volker R. Berghahn, ed., *Quest for Economic Empire: European Strategies of German Big Business in the Twentieth Century* (Providence, R.I., 1996).
[18] Volker R. Berghahn and Paul J. Friedrich, *Otto A. Friedrich. Ein politischer Unternehmer: Sein Leben und seine Zeit 1902–1975* (Frankfurt am Main, 1993).

[19] On the following subject matter, see the chapter by Ronald J. Granieri, vol. 1, Politics.
[20] Hans-Jürgen Grabbe, "Das Amerikabild Konrad Adenauers," *Amerikastudien* 31 (1986): 315–23, quotations on 316, 317, 318; Hans-Jürgen Schröder, "Chancellor of the Allies? The Significance of the United States in Adenauer's Foreign Policy," in Barclay and Glaser-Schmidt, *Transatlantic Images*, 309–31.
[21] Joachim Arenth, "Die Bewährungsprobe der Special Relationship. Washington und Bonn (1961–1969)," in Klaus Larres and Torsten Oppelland, eds., *Deutschland und die USA im 20. Jahrhundert. Geschichte der politischen Beziehungen* (Darmstadt, 1997), 155–60.

America was indispensable for Germany's reconstruction and security. To this extent, his oft-repeated "profession of faith in Western culture, in the democratic view of life and government, and...a sense of community with America" had a calculated, tactical element in it.[22]

The Social Democrats' charge that Adenauer was "the Allies' chancellor" surely said more about the disappointed opposition and the SPD's lack of foreign policy alternatives than about its own image of America. Traditional negative stereotypes of America were common within the SPD. Even someone as intelligent as Fritz Erler lamented that Americans worshipped material wealth as the highest good at the expense of "human warmth," "depth," "introspection," and "a culture of the heart." Yet, at the same time, more positive alternative assessments could also be found, including Gustav Heinemann's openly declared respect for America's tradition of liberal democracy.[23] SPD opposition to rearmament posed a greater problem, for it signaled sympathy for the idea of Germany becoming a political neutral and threatened to lead the country into fundamental conflict with American policy.[24] In the national tradition articulated by Kurt Schumacher, the SPD feared creation of strong ties to the West at the expense of possible reunification, or even (just as Adenauer feared) a new American isolationism that might abandon Germany to the Soviet Union. The party did not overcome this conflict until the emergence of Willy Brandt as candidate for the chancellorship in 1960–1. The SPD accepted his declaration of "friendship with America" as a "centerpiece of West German foreign policy" and thereafter, whether the party was in power or in the opposition, no longer questioned that position.[25]

NEW AND OLD CRITICISMS OF AMERICA FROM THE RIGHT AND THE LEFT

Inevitably a range of critical and negative voices began to mix with the chorus of voices friendly to America. These voices made up an integral component of the German image of America, although "anti-Americanism,"[26] or its definition, is not the primary subject here. Feelings of resentment festered against individual aspects of the American occupation and American policy toward Germany; against American global policies; and, in general, against the political, economic, and cultural hegemony of the United States. The objections ranged from doubts about the credibility of the American guarantees of security for Germany to the Vietnam War, to "Coca-Colonization," and they succeeded in negatively influencing not only the German but also the European image of America.[27] The traditional criticism of American culture found its spokesmen in certain old-school conservatives such as Hans Zehrer, Hans Freyer, Arnold Gehlen, and Dieter Oberndörfer. However, this criticism from German quarters did not become coherent and was not publicly articulated until a real neoconservatism emerged.[28] This process began in the 1960s after the founding of the European Community and the economic acceleration that followed; German dependence on the United States, which had been comprehensive up to that point, eventually became asymmetrical. Continuing dependence in the security field contrasted with West Germany's gradually increasing economic and political independence. Two well-known essays by Norbert Muhlen diagnosed and bemoaned a firm West German "anti-Americanism" as early as 1953 and 1954. Because the rigid friend-or-foe thinking of the day tolerated no middle ground, the very

---

[22] Konrad Adenauer, *Erinnerungen 1945–1953* (Stuttgart, 1965), 413.

[23] Hans-Jürgen Grabbe, *Unionsparteien, Sozialdemokratie und Vereinigte Staaten von Amerika 1945–1966* (Düsseldorf, 1983), 51–76.

[24] See the chapter by David Clay Large, vol. 1, Security.

[25] See Grabbe, *Unionsparteien, Sozialdemokratie,* 205–30, 245–55.

[26] See the chapters by Philipp Gassert, vols. 1 and 2, Society.

[27] Rob Kroes and Maarten van Rossem, eds., *Anti-Americanism in Europe* (Amsterdam, 1986); Marcus Cunliffe, *In Search of America: Transatlantic Essays, 1951–1990* (New York, 1991), chaps. 17 and 21.

[28] Heimo Schwilk and Ulrich Schacht, eds., *Die selbstbewusste Nation. "Anschwellender Bocksgesang" und weitere Beiträge zu einer deutschen Debatte,* 3d ed. (Berlin, 1995).

discussion of neutrality in those years was misunderstood as "anti-Americanism."[29]

The neoconservative Right began by criticizing specific political projects. Caspar von Schrenck-Notzing denounced American reeducation policy after 1945 as a kind of national castration, as a "long-term alteration of the German character." In doing so, he ignored the fact that the influential contemporary theories about the "authoritarian" personality had originally targeted American anti-Semitism. To the extent that these theories informed policy on Germany and cast National Socialism in psychopathological terms, they ultimately had an exonerative effect. For Schrenck-Notzing, this "character cleansing" was equivalent to the political obliteration of Germans' very substance. Despite the trend toward increased independence, he claimed, developments beginning in 1957 with the Treaties of Rome were once again characterized by "abdication of sovereignty, self-determination, and equal rights," and by "again giving in to the kind of international political system that . . . Roosevelt had envisioned." He also did not fail to mention the enemy state clauses in the United Nations Charter, and he made America unambiguously responsible for all these developments.[30]

German critics of America seized on the Morgenthau Plan as their most favored negative symbol.[31] Even if Morgenthau's basic ideas – which aimed at structurally incapacitating Germany's potential for military aggression – did influence American policy on Germany and the occupation, historians have shown that the political influence of the plan has been greatly overestimated.[32] Uninfluenced by such work,

critics have denounced Morgenthau's concept, with a grotesque verbal twist, as the "final solution to the German problem."[33] The supposed reduction of Germany to the role of a "potato supplier" did not in any way correspond to actual postwar developments.[34] Both formulas, however, were highly convenient pretexts for many Germans to avoid facing historical responsibility for the past and for allowing them to project their anxieties and unease onto America.

The neoconservatives enthusiastically rekindled an old history of criticism of America. The "materialistic" and "uncultured" America, the banality and meaninglessness of its consumer society were set off against loftier German values (sometimes trotted out as European values) of introspection, intellectual pursuit, community, and culture. This criticism tied older traditions of the nineteenth and early twentieth centuries to the 1950s and 1960s. Moreover, it united criticism of America from the Right and the Left.[35] Anxiety about modernization and envy stemming from perceived lagging modernization were and continue to be projected onto America.[36] Marcus Cunliffe, therefore, spoke of Europe falling victim to an "Athenian complex" when America left it behind in terms of industrial and political development; Europe saw itself "as the older and finer culture ousted by the crude new 'Roman' one."[37]

Probably the best collection of malicious America clichés was compiled by Carl Zuckmayer, who in 1948 looked back with an element of self-mockery, recalling the ideas of America that he and Franz Werfel had harbored before emigrating:

A land of fantastic standardization, shallow materialism, and soulless mechanics. A land without

---

[29] Muhlen, "America and the American Occupation"; Muhlen, "German Anti-Americanism: East and West Zones," *Commentary* 15 (1953): 121–30.

[30] Caspar von Schrenck-Notzing, *Charakterwäsche: Die Politik der amerikanischen Umerziehung in Deutschland* (Frankfurt am Main, 1965), 182, 125–6, 213–4.

[31] Klaus Rainer Röhl, "Morgenthau und Antifa: Über den Selbsthass der Deutschen," in Schwilk and Schacht, eds., *Selbstbewusste Nation*, 85–100; Klaus-Dieter Henke, *Die amerikanische Besetzung Deutschlands* (Munich, 1995), 107–17.

[32] Bernd Greiner, *Die Morgenthau-Legende: Zur Geschichte eines umstrittenen Plans* (Hamburg, 1995);

Wilfried Mausbach, *Zwischen Morgenthau und Marshall: Das wirtschaftliche Deutschlandkonzept der USA 1944–1947* (Düsseldorf, 1996).

[33] Schrenck-Notzing, *Charakterwäsche*, 79.

[34] Rolf Winter, *Ami Go Home: Plädoyer für den Abschied von einem gewalttätigen Land* (Hamburg, 1989), 11.

[35] Behrmann, "Geschichte und aktuelle Struktur," 11; Diner, *Verkehrte Welten*.

[36] Arnold Bergstraesser, "Zum Problem der sogennanten Amerikanisierung Deutschlands," *Jahrbuch für Amerikastudien* 8 (1963): 16–18.

[37] Cunliffe, *In Search of America*, 400.

tradition, without culture, without a drive toward beauty or form, without metaphysics and without new wine, a land of chemical fertilizers and can openers, without grace and without dung heaps, without the classics and without shoddiness, without melos, without Apollo, without Dionysus . . . the tyranny of the dollar, of business, of advertising, of violent superficiality.[38]

Even radical Marxist and communist leftists could not think up anything new about America in the 1960s. Criticism of capitalism and America became one. For many, America was a failed love affair. Members of the younger generation in particular believed with conviction and commitment in the American – or universal – ideals of democracy, freedom, and responsibility. President Kennedy appeared to embody these values. America became a surrogate object of identification. Disillusionment over American policies in Cuba, Berlin, Vietnam, and the Third World turned into sharp criticism. German leftists nonetheless continued to project their own dreams onto at least some segments of America, on what they defined as the "other" or "better America,"[39] a perspective that also characterized the official image of America in the GDR.[40] These Germans avoided dealing with America as a whole in all its complexity and, ignoring portions (the "official America"), took the remaining, likeable parts for the whole. The same mechanisms of partial identification and partial rejection operated in the bourgeois milieu, even if they ran in another direction.

Even leftist intellectuals who were not dogmatic Marxists clung to a radical negative image of the United States in the late 1960s. One well-known example was Hans Magnus Enzensberger, who gave up a fellowship at the Wesleyan Center for Advanced Studies in January 1968 and later moved to Cuba. America,

he argued, was no longer the liberator, protector, mediator, and guarantor of democratic values but had itself become the greatest threat to humanity and democracy. Enzensberger considered "the class that rules in the United States of America and the government that carries out the business of this class" to be "a public enemy" because it threatened "every one of us." It was waging a war against more than a billion people, he said, "with all available means, from genocidal bombardment to the most elaborate techniques of mind control. Its goal is to rule the world politically, economically, and militarily. Its lethal enemy is revolution." He asserted that America's "repressive tolerance" destroyed all criticism of America; the purpose of Enzensberger's guest status, he wrote, was "to disarm me so that I would lose my credibility by accepting your fellowship and your stipend, and so that the mere fact that I am here, as your guest, would undermine the point of what I had to say."[41]

Recovering credibility seemed possible only by fleeing out of the reach of comfortably tolerant but ultimately stifling American imperialism. The sharp, undifferentiated, popular Marxist interpretation of American politics elevated a traditional criticism of capitalism to an accusation that U.S. imperialism had permeated the world and would find its climax in a genocide directed against social revolution anywhere. This sentiment found great acceptance in Germany at the time and added to the growing current of anti-Americanism in the late 1960s and 1970s.

Any outside criticism of America essentially has an easy ride, for "[t]here is no anti-Americanism as eloquent as that of the native American."[42] German cultural critics of the 1950s and 1960s had their American counterparts in David Riesman, C. Wright Mills, William H. Whyte,

---

[38] Cited in Wolfgang Wagner, "Das Amerikabild der Europäer," in Karl Kaiser and Hans-Peter Schwarz, eds., *Amerika und Westeuropa. Gegenwarts- und Zukunftsprobleme* (Stuttgart, 1977), 24.

[39] Ekkehart Krippendorff, "Die westdeutsche Linke und ihr Bild von den USA," in Willi Paul Adams and Knud Krakau, eds., *Perzeption und historische Realität* (Berlin, 1985), 39–46.

[40] See the chapter by Rainer Schnoor in this section.

[41] Hans Magnus Enzensberger, "Warum ich Amerika verlasse," *Die Zeit*, Mar. 1, 1968; see Charlotte Melin, "A Look at Enzensberger's America Before and After 'On Leaving America,'" in Heinz D. Osterle, ed., *Amerika! New Images in German Literature* (New York, 1989), 293–313.

[42] Cunliffe, *In Search of America*, 327, 395.

Vance Packard, and John Kenneth Galbraith, just as the Left during the 1960s and 1970s had Paul A. Baran, David Horowitz, V. Leo Huberman, Noam Chomsky, and Paul M. Sweezy. It is ironic that in the face of this criticism, America has often portrayed itself as hopelessly divided or extreme. Yet, simultaneously, it is being seen in the positive light of an open society, "*liked* for its candor and freshness."[43]

[43] Ibid., 397.

CHAPTER SIXTEEN

The Good and the Bad America

Perceptions of the United States in the GDR

Rainer Schnoor

Translated by Margaret Ries

East Germans' images of America were decisively shaped by the historic constraints facing their country immediately after World War II and during the Cold War. These constraints included the collapse of the Nazi regime and the struggle for survival after 1945; consciousness of the catastrophe; the discussion of guilt and a search for alternatives; the disintegration of the anti-Hitler coalition and rise of two enemy camps; and the gradual takeover by German communists under the protection, toleration, and control of the Soviet occupation authority.

Against this backdrop, the variant of Marxism-Leninism that the new regime imported from the Soviet Union – with its corresponding understanding of history and society – established itself piece by piece as the dominant "official ideology." One component of this ideology was an "official" image of America. Those in power would have preferred it to remain the exclusive image of that country, but their desire was only partially realized. The reach of both this new system and its ideology in the end remained limited throughout the life of the Soviet occupation zone in Germany and the German Democratic Republic (GDR).[1]

Three different but closely related basic images of America operated in East Germany. The first of these was the aforementioned "official" image that the dominant voice of the state, the Socialist Unity Party (*Sozialistische Einheitspartei Deutschlands*, or SED), propagated. The government, together with the media, mass organizations, and educational institutions, promoted this vision. Second, "private" opinions that "average" citizens formed about the United States grew alongside the official picture, impressions rooted in daily life and culture, and dependent on individuals' age, sex, profession, interests, education, and political position. Third, mediating between the official and private images, an "intellectual" image developed within the ranks of social scientists and writers.

One needs to consider how this general subdivision evolved from decade to decade as certain ideological assumptions in East Germany endured. The second half of the 1940s – strongly shaped by the aftermath of social breakdown and reconstruction efforts – cannot, for example, be compared to the heyday of Stalinism in the 1950s.

The self-confident, moderate Stalinist orthodoxy of the Ulbricht years after the Wall was built again gave rise to a different social course until it was ultimately superceded by the seeming liberalization that occurred under Erich Honecker at the beginning of the 1970s. That stands in contrast, in turn, to the "stop-and-go" cultural policy that followed the expulsion

---

[1] Rolf Badstübner, *DDR: Gescheiterte Epochalternative, Aufbruch in die Sackgasse oder was sonst? Versuch einer Annäherung*, Hefte zur DDR-Geschichte 19 (Berlin, 1994), 13.

of Wolf Biermann in 1976 and to the intensifying crisis of legitimacy during the Gorbachev years (1985–90).[2]

During the entire period discussed here, the official image of America shaped East Germans' private images of the United States to only a small degree despite the efforts of a formidable ideological apparatus. The two visions rarely coincided as, for example, on specific American foreign and military policies (e.g., the threat of American military power, the Korean War, Cuba, Vietnam, the deployment of new weapons, SDI, Grenada). Partial agreement between the official and the private views also existed over America's glaring social problems, including social polarization, poverty, homelessness, racism, crime, and drug abuse.

Despite comprehensive indoctrination with official anti-Americanism – at first blatant and later more moderate – the East German population was not markedly anti-American. Criticism of the American "arrogance of power" certainly existed but was tempered by a vital curiosity about the country and its inhabitants, its history, culture, science, and technology. The reasons for this curiosity had historical roots: A certain enthusiasm for the United States stretched back into the nineteenth century. In addition, the GDR lacked a real social base for nurturing anti-Americanism among an educated populace. Further, discrediting the National Socialists implicitly included discrediting their anti-American sentiments. East Germans' interest in America was also linked to positive projections of what they felt their country lacked. The mass media played an important role here: Almost from the outset, the GDR had a "dual voiced" media because of the possibility of receiving radio and, from 1960s on, television broadcasts from the West.[3]

THE OFFICIAL IMAGE OF AMERICA

The SED and government's official picture of the United States rested to a large extent on the worldview held by Walter Ulbricht, Wilhelm Pieck, and their fellow German antifascists and communists who held political power after returning from exile in the USSR. Their view had its roots in Lenin's theory of imperialism as the highest and last stage in the development of capitalism and in Dimitrov's theory of fascism as the dictatorship of the most reactionary elements of finance capital.

In this conception of the world, the United States, having caused the break-up of the anti-Hitler coalition, became the "bulwark of reaction" and the "center of capitalist regimes, of war-mongering, and of reactionary and exploitative elements."[4] To avoid the imminent crisis of overproduction after the war – so ran the official argument – the "terrorist international of murderers on Wall Street"[5] had to resort to aggression to expand and prepare for world domination. West Germany, rearmed by the United States, was to serve as the deployment zone and arsenal for this thrust, with West Berlin as the bridgehead. The previous concept of the enemy as fascism evolved into a new depiction of the enemy as U.S. imperialism, a shift also reflected in reigning terminology. Not only through its foreign and military policy but also its ideology and culture, the United States led the forces of reaction and was at the center of imperialist cultural decline. Because of its geographical position and still open border, the Soviet occupation zone and, later, the GDR were at on the frontlines of the defense against "imperialist aggression" and "cultural decadence." East Germany's official image of the United States could never be more liberal or nuanced than the Soviet Union's. This became evident in the application of Stalin's theory of the intensification of class struggle in socialism,

[2] See Rolf Reissig, "Das Scheitern der DDR und des realsozialistischen Systems: Einige Ursachen und Folgen," in Hans Joas and Martin Kohli, eds., Der Zusammenbruch der DDR: Soziologische Analysen (Frankfurt am Main, 1993).

[3] See Heinz Niemann, Hinterm Zaun: Politische Kultur und Meinungsforschung in der DDR: Die geheimen Berichte an das Politbüro der SED (Berlin, 1995), 100.

[4] Eckhard Müller and Günter Benser, eds., Dokumente zur Geschichte der SED, 3 vols. (Berlin, 1981–86), 2:168.

[5] Erich Honecker and Hermann Axen, Die Jugend baut eine neue Welt (Berlin, 1949), 9.

when terrorist "purges" against "deviants" and "weaklings" were organized. The reality of subversion and espionage on both sides fed the fatal paranoia about subversion and espionage that existed in both camps of the Cold War.

Both the rulers and many of the governed in East Germany perceived the threat from the West, the United States in particular, as completely real: Did Truman not propose marching on to Moscow when he visited U.S. troops as a senator during World War II? Was the United States not the first country to have dropped the atomic bomb on civilians? Had Anglo-American bombers not destroyed German cities? Had the United States not employed plague bacteria in Korea?

Both the party press and papers tied to the block parties, forced to conform and adapt to the SED's political line during the 1950s, repeated and spread these pronouncements. The following excerpt from an article appearing in the *Tägliche Rundschau* on June 6, 1951, serves as a good example:

The ideal of American robber imperialism is world domination, the preparation and unleashing of a new world war, and the extermination of other peoples. It has created a "culture" corresponding to these objectives. The highest values of this culture are the dollar and naked power, biological warfare and the dissemination of the Colorado beetle [supposedly dropped from planes flying over the GDR], the execution of peaceful individuals, the bestial bombing of hospitals, children and the aged.[6]

During the 1950s, figures such as Harry S. Truman, Dwight D. Eisenhower, John Foster Dulles, Allen Dulles, Joseph R. McCarthy, General Matthew B. Ridgway, and Francis Cardinal Spellman personified this image of the enemy.

Newspaper cartoons were also instrumental in constructing images of the enemy. Stereotypical caricatures cropped up repeatedly in the press: Uncle Sam standing on the globe with a bomb in his hand; the archetypal U.S. monopoly capitalist, dressed in a black suit and bowler, his hand clutching the throat of the proletariat; a snake with a dollar sign for a tongue.

Any attempt to replace any of the slowly ossifying ideas of Marx, Engels, and Lenin – as well as the Stalinist monopoly on their interpretation – encountered stiff opposition. "Modernism," "cosmopolitanism," "objectivism," "skepticism," "Americanism" (American models in art and architecture, for example), and "decadence" were denounced, and their putative or actual representatives removed from teaching positions and editorial offices. The 1950s and, to a lesser extent, the 1960s were marked by a series of campaigns against "bourgeois ideology" as well.

Official circles also took a stand against the products of the "American way of life," especially those associated with popular culture pouring in from West Germany. In the 1940s and 1950s, jazz musicians and aficionados in East Germany were watched with mistrust, attacked in the media, and subjected to regulations; in the 1960s, it was the fans of rock 'n' roll and beat music.[7] Officials equated the American way of life with hooliganism and took a hostile view of crêpe-soled shoes, "Texas shirts," petticoats, jeans with studs, fancy anklets, and nylon stockings, which were particularly common in the Berlin region before 1961. During the 1950s, crew cuts were taken as a sign of philo-American or Western leanings; in the 1960s, long hair on men could signal these tendencies. Having cola and American cigarettes such as "Lucky Strikes" in one's possession was also suspect.[8]

Schools as well as the youth organizations Young Pioneers (*Jungpioniere*, or JP) and Free German Youth (*Freie Deutsche Jugend*, or FDJ) played an important role in the fight against the products of American "cultural barbarism," for children and adolescents were seen as highly susceptible to their influence. Officials regularly conducted spot checks and searches for "trashy

---

[6] Quoted in Manfred Jäger, *Kultur und Politik in der DDR 1945–1990* (Cologne, 1995), 43.

[7] Michael Rauhut, *Beat in der Grauzone: DDR-Rock 1964–1972* (Berlin, 1993).

[8] Uta G. Poiger, "Rock 'n' Roll, Female Sexuality, and the Cold War Battle over German Identities," *Journal of Modern History* 68 (1996): 577–616.

and smutty literature," during which they confiscated and destroyed the entire spectrum of
unacceptable material from Mickey Spillane to
Mickey Mouse.

Teachers interpreted these orders from above
in markedly different ways. Many teachers followed the hard line zealously, whereas others
remained more pragmatic or even unenthusiastic about enforcing strict standards. A few
completely disregarded the orders, which they
considered pointless, a path that inevitably led
to clashes with higher authorities.[9]

The generally negative official image of the
United States did contain one somewhat more
positive component, however: It drew a distinc-
tion between "U.S. imperialists" and the American people. Taking their cue from the "classic"
thinkers – Marx, Engels, Lenin, and, until the
late 1960s, also Stalin – GDR decision makers
contrasted American politicians, military, and
"monopolists" with the "other America." This
latter group consisted of the masses, who were
oppressed but were fighting back; in the 1950s,
for example, the African American singer and
actor Paul Robeson came to personify this resistance.

The attempt by the SED and the government
to use a cultural Sovietization to counter the cultural Americanization that had overtaken East
Germany before the Wall was built was largely
unsuccessful. The kinds of measures that authorities implemented in the economy and politics
found little approval in the cultural realm. Such
was the fate of the cultural policy official Alfred Kurella's idea in 1957 to foster dance music
from the Soviet Union instead of the uncultured
dances from the West.[10]

[9] See Brigitte Hohlfeld, *Die Neulehrer in der
SBZ/DDR 1945–1953: Ihre Rolle bei der Umgestaltung
von Gesellschaft und Staat* (Weinheim, 1992); Dorothee
Wierling, "Die Jugend als innerer Feind: Konflikte in
der Erziehungsdiktatur der sechziger Jahre," in Hart-
mut Kaelble, Jürgen Kocka, and Hartmut Zwahr, eds.,
Sozialgeschichte der DDR (Stuttgart, 1994), 404–25.
[10] Siegfried Prokop, *Sozialgeschichte der ostdeutschen
Intellektuellen 1945–1961: Zeittafel*, Heft zur DDR-
Geschichte 10 (Berlin, 1993), 47.

PRIVATE IMAGES OF AMERICA

For the middle-aged and older generations of
East Germans, questions of survival and securing
the bare necessities of life, such as food, housing, and clothing, took priority over everything
else during the second half of the 1940s and the
1950s. For many of them, America was far away
"over there." Their conception of the United
States, if they had one, was a colorful, eclectic
collage, pieced together from orally transmitted myths about America, traditional German
literary accounts, and occasionally, before the
Wall, personal encounters with the results of
Americanization in West Germany, especially
in West Berlin. From the 1960s on, images of
the United States disseminated by the mass media, particularly television, increasingly eclipsed
these experiences. The majority of the younger
generation of East Germans found themselves
in a slightly different position. Set against the
bleakness and monotony of the postwar years,
the expanse, beauty, freedom, and abundance in
the United States fired their imaginations and
fed their dreams.

Despite the demands of everyday life in the
GDR, the United States always enjoyed a presence as either a concrete alternative (by emigration through West Germany until 1961) or as
the idea of "the other," of a strange, completely
different society. This sense of the United States
stemmed in part from the traditional German
view of the country – one typified by Indians, cowboys, prairies, the frontier, and gold
rushes – that novelists such as Karl May and
Friedrich Gerstäcker offered up to readers. The
same could also be found in the works of popular American writers such as Mark Twain and
Jack London. The stories and experiences re-
counted by emigrants and prisoners of war returning home from the United States added to
popular conceptions of America, as did memories of the Weimar period, when a clear trend
toward Americanization had become particularly visible in Berlin's urban culture.

The influence of West Berlin as the "show-
place of the free world" became increasingly
important after the war. Apart from those

individuals who were not allowed, on professional grounds, to travel to West Berlin (e.g., members of the military, party members, government officials), there were few citizens of the GDR who had not made the trip at least once. The results of the Marshall Plan also became evident there by 1947. No one who had experienced it could forget the contrast between the dull S-Bahn stations in East Berlin, some still in ruins, and the colorful stations in West Berlin, where American consumer culture was in evidence. The reigning exchange rate was four East German marks to one West German mark. With painstakingly saved money, individuals could fill some of their most fervent desires – a pair of modern shoes, a chic jacket, nylons, chewing gum, citrus and tropical fruit for their children – things that were difficult or impossible to obtain among the limited consumer offerings in the GDR during the 1950s. Anyone acquiring goods in the West risked having East German border guards confiscate them. The gap between official propaganda and individual experience quickly came to light through these visits: glimpses of the real situation in the West showed that the theory about the impoverishment of the masses through the Marshall Plan was absurd. Although East Germany ultimately abandoned its stance against consumerism in the second half of the 1950s, the West remained the promised land of plenty.[11]

The building of the Wall drastically changed both the sources for private images of America as well as their content. Because East Germans could no longer form opinions of the West based on personal experience, the electronic mass media, mainly television, became their most important source of information. After humble beginnings in the 1950s, television (both East German and Western stations) extended its technological reach by the end of the 1960s to most of the GDR. Only a few areas, such as the Elbe valley around Dresden or parts of Mecklenburg, could not receive Western television. The number of television sets in the GDR also increased dramatically, from seventy-five in 1952 to more than 4 million in 1968. We can, therefore, assume that the large majority of East Germans could get Western channels and also regularly watched them. This was officially forbidden, however, and the prohibition was occasionally enforced through warnings and collective discussions in schools, universities, and other institutions. After 1961, a campaign began in which FDJ members who were particularly loyal to the party turned TV antennas – against the will of their owners – in the "correct" direction for receiving East German stations. Actions such as these, however, proved useless in the long run. GDR citizens built up a "spontaneous network of informal communication, free of supervision" for themselves and resisted, actively and passively, attempts to regulate it.[12]

Because of the strains of meeting the needs of everyday life, the middle-aged and older generation could not devote much attention to a growing feeling of being locked in. The younger generation, however, particularly those who had grown up in the 1960s and had no direct experience of the other side, suffered from a far deeper sense of deprivation. East German adolescents in the 1950s, especially those living close to West Berlin, still had access to the "other world" and its goods (clothing, records, or films in cinemas on the border, where tickets cost the same in East and West German currency). Their successors in the next generation only knew about this world through hearsay. The GDR's restrictive, unimaginative youth and cultural programs were not designed to create or permit attractive alternatives. Most young people considered folkdancing groups and choirs boring. Ulbricht's 1958 "Ten Commandments of Socialist Ethics and Morality,"[13] with their overblown didactic message, also failed to offer adolescents an

---

[11] See Stephan Merl, "Sowjetisierung in der Welt des Konsums," in Konrad Jarausch and Hannes Siegrist, eds., *Amerikanisierung und Sowjetisierung in Deutschland 1945–1970* (Frankfurt am Main, 1997), 167–94.

[12] Heide Riedel, ed., *Mit uns zieht die neue Zeit . . . 40 Jahre DDR-Medien* (Berlin, 1993), introd., 18; Gunter Holzweissig, *Massenmedien in der DDR* (Berlin, 1989).

[13] See Antonia Grunenberg, *Aufbruch der inneren Mauer: Politik und Kultur in der DDR 1971–1990* (Bremen, 1990), 51–2.

appealing guide for how to live their lives. In a society based on equality and collectivity, the growing pressure to conform only intensified the urge for nonconformity.

Against this background, the image of the West, particularly of West Germany and the United States, increasingly offered a positive projection that could counter feelings of deprivation. For many East Germans, the United States became "the land of dreams." They compared East Germany's restrictions on travel to America's supposedly boundless opportunities for movement, travel, and personal freedom. They contrasted the modesty and monotony of everyday life in the GDR to the abundance of variety and color in America; the rigid, dogmatically fixed modes of thought and behavior of their own country to Americans' pragmatic willingness to experiment and their relaxed attitudes.

Schools could not and did not want to exist as the institutional space in which adolescents expressed their yearnings. Their task was to impart knowledge and ideology affirmatively and in an accessible way. Despite the efforts of many English teachers, English classes – which up until the end of the GDR focused almost solely on Great Britain – consisted primarily of learning the language and remained relatively unimaginative. The few sections of the schoolbooks that actually addressed such subjects as British and American culture, history, or geography offered only black-and-white depictions of exploitative imperialists, on the one hand, and exploited masses and militant, cheerful young communists on the other.

Pen pals were officially supported in Russian classes but were seen as undesirable when they were pupils from English-speaking countries. Many English teachers risked disciplinary action when, with the best of intentions, they handed out foreign addresses. Unnerved by this restrictive atmosphere, numerous teachers left the GDR before 1961. Many of the remaining English teachers continued to walk the tightrope between communicating the officially supported image of America and their own more nuanced understanding of the country developed through professional engagement.

Good English teachers were considered experts on the United States and Great Britain and thus useful contacts for fulfilling a variety of wishes tied to those two countries: providing information, finding pen pals for their students, translating difficult letters, and transcribing songs of their students' favorite rock and pop groups.

This was not enough for youth in the GDR. Beginning with the craze for Elvis Presley and Bill Haley in the 1950s, they created a second or alternative reality for themselves based primarily on pop culture. Sometimes jazz and sometimes rock and pop took precedence in this world.[14] Since the early 1960s, jazz had slowly freed itself from the negative associations foisted on it by East Germany's official cultural policy. One indication of this was the tolerance and even support for the enormously popular "Jazz and Poetry" events (with, for example, Manfred Krug) staged in the mid-1960s and Louis Armstrong's legendary East German tour in 1965.

Professional and amateur bands, modeling themselves on the Beatles and American rock groups, sprang up all over the country in the 1960s. GDR bureaucrats responsible for enforcing the country's cultural policy found themselves at a loss in the face of these groups' spontaneity and creativity. They took recourse in creating regulations of all kinds. They tried to control what groups performed (as of 1958, at least 60 percent of the songs had to be "made in the East" and the remaining 40 percent could be from the West), prohibited bands from giving themselves English names, and barred some groups from performing.[15]

Screenings of American films in East German cinemas during the 1960s were rare. This restrictive policy ensured that those films that were shown frequently acquired cult followings. Such was the fate of *The Magnificent Seven*, which quickly disappeared from the theaters because

---

[14] See the chapter by Edward Larkey, vol. 1, Culture.
[15] See Peter Wicke, "Zwischen Förderung und Reglementierung. Rockmusik im System der DDR-Kulturbürokratie," in Peter Wicke and Lothar Müller, eds., *Rockmusik und Politik: Analysen, Interviews und Dokumente* (Berlin, 1996), 11–27.

it allegedly promoted violence. The American television shows aired regularly on West German TV also made a great impact on the East German population. Even without empirical evidence, one can assume that shows such as *Bonanza, Lassie, 77 Sunset Strip, Gunsmoke,* and others profoundly shaped the GDR vision of life in America, both past and present. The same holds true for other programs about the United States that were broadcast in the West, such as *New York, New York* and other shows produced by Thilo Koch and Werner Baecker.

The average GDR citizen gained some impressions of protest movements in the United States, but these came with a time lag and offered relatively vague information filtered through the media. The assassinations of John F. Kennedy and Martin Luther King Jr. shocked the population, leaving a deep and lasting impression that terrible things were happening "on the other side." These resulted in a form of hero worship that in Kennedy's case remained officially undesirable, but in King's was tolerated and sometimes even instrumentalized to accuse the United States of racism.

GDR officials also exploited Joan Baez, Pete Seeger, and Bob Dylan's stance against the Vietnam War for their own inflammatory ends. But this also proved beneficial for the musicians' GDR fans and to those generally interested in the United States, for their albums subsequently became available in the country and could, for example, be used in English classes. From the mid-1960s and early 1970s onward, the FDJ's "song movement," promoted by North Americans living in East Germany (Victor Grossman or Perry Friedman from Canada), began to explore themes from American folklore. And Jimi Hendrix, Janis Joplin, Country Joe McDonald, and Woodstock – symbols of the Sixties – became important for the private, pop culture–centered images of America in East Germany. Yet, hardly anyone in the GDR reflected on the psychosocial changes associated with the 1960s in the Western world, particularly in the United States. The geographical distance and distance between the two political systems was simply too great.

INTELLECTUAL IMAGES OF AMERICA

The majority of East German intellectuals were without doubt "supporters of the state," either consciously or unconsciously. They were actively involved in consolidating the system, often with real conviction. Nonetheless, one must differentiate in considering the work of teachers, university professors, writers, and journalists, and their role as intermediaries. There were obviously many hardliners among them who served the political and ideological system loyally in their respective fields and specific capacities. Their view of America frequently only replicated the reigning official image of the country.

More interesting were those writers and academics who walked the fine line between demonstrating ideological engagement and intellectual honesty, who tried to convey a fairly objective picture of the United States.[16] This goal was all but impossible in the 1950s. By the 1960s, it had become slightly more feasible and – despite some self-imposed limits – did become possible in the 1970s and 1980s.[17] These individuals needed to employ a varied repertoire of strategies and compromises in pursuit of their goal. They had to navigate between fundamental ideological principles that they frequently shared, on the one hand, and, on the other, the facts about the United States and the public's desire for information.

---

[16] See Daisy Wessel, *Bild und Gegenbild: Die USA in der Belletristik der SBZ und der DDR (bis 1987)* (Opladen, 1989); Rainer Schnoor, "Ideological Commitment and Intellectual Pursuit: Evolutions in East German American Studies Since the 1960s," in Günter H. Lenz and Klaus J. Milich, eds., *American Studies in Germany: European Contexts and Intercultural Relations* (Frankfurt am Main, 1995), 37–43.

[17] Eberhard Brüning, "Die Amerikanistik an der Universität Leipzig (1950–1990): 40 Jahre Gratwanderungen eines ungeliebten Faches," in Rainer Schnoor, ed., *Amerikanistik in der DDR: Geschichte – Analysen – Zeitzeugenberichte* (Berlin, 1999); interview with Eva Manske in Robert von Mallberg, ed., *Literary Intellectuals and the Dissolution of the State: Professionalism and Conformity in the GDR* (Chicago, 1996), 53–60.

Émigrés returning from the United States took the first steps toward reconciling these two paths. These returnees included such figures as Bertolt Brecht, Stefan Heym, Jürgen Kuczynski, Maximilian Scheer, Wieland Herzfelde, and Herman Budzislawski. The doyens of American studies in the GDR, Karl-Heinz Schönfelder and Eberhard Brüning, both of whom had been prisoners of war in America, also contributed to this effort, along with many other teachers and professors. Although a world-famous playwright and author like Brecht could dare to be plainspoken, others had to make compromises in their work, steering between prescribed dogma and their own experience and knowledge of the United States. This, however, put them on a collision course with hardliners in the SED and government bureaucracy.[18] Many talented specialists in American studies could not tolerate these working conditions and consequently left for the West. The younger generation of intellectuals, educated in the 1950s and 1960s, set to work from a different starting position. Their conception of the world – as well of that of America – had developed without personal contact with the United States and was shaped by the Cold War, McCarthyism, the Cuban Revolution, hopes for the Third World, and the social movements of the 1960s.

For English teachers, translators, and interpreters educated in the GDR, the most decisive factor in forming their image of America was the GDR's version of American studies. The scope of their discipline, initially very limited, gradually expanded during the 1960s for two important reasons. The first was the contradictory policy of peaceful coexistence that the Soviet Union promoted under Khrushchev. Second, after years in which an almost exclusively negative image of the United States prevailed, Lenin's theory that two cultures exist in every national culture – a democratic, socialist one and an archreactionary one – was given a

new spin. The Soviet America expert Georgi Arbatov utilized this theory in his thesis that two class profiles, the democratic and the reactionary, ran through American history and culture. This later became the bedrock of American studies in the GDR.[19]

By invoking this view and quoting from the works of Marx, Engels, and Lenin, academics could now explore "modernist," "decadent" writers such as Norman Mailer and James Baldwin, even though they still had to do so in a critical vein. The fertile field of the "other America" could now be tilled, resulting in scholarly work on the contrast between progressive and reactionary tendencies in American history, politics, society, culture, and literature. The limits of such a dichotomous, profoundly undialectical approach are obvious. Nonetheless, this involvement with leftist, progressive literature and culture in the United States opened up many new possibilities, particularly at a time when they were being ignored in the West.

University English departments left the study of U.S. economics, politics, and history almost exclusively to other disciplines. In the 1950s, hardliners dominated these disciplines and advanced theories about the impoverishment and radicalization of the working class through imperialism, the intensification of class struggle, and the conspiracy of politics and monopoly capitalism against the "forces of peace, the proletariat and socialism." Alongside documents from the Communist Party of the Soviet Union and the SED, William Z. Foster's *Abriss der politischen Geschichte beider Amerika (An Outline of the Political History of the Two Americas)* (published in New York in 1951 and East Berlin in 1957) and the writings and speeches of American Communist Party leader Gus Hall were the basic texts for teaching. The work of Jürgen Kuczynski played a special role in the gray area between Marxist orthodoxy and more unorthodox approaches in the academy. Given the dearth of scholarly literature in the 1950s and 1960s, his

---

[18] For this, see Jürgen Kuczynski, *Dialog mit meinem Urenkel. Neunzehn Briefe und ein Tagebuch* (Berlin, 1983); Jürgen Kuczynski, *Ein Leben in der Wissenschaft der DDR* (Münster, 1993).

[19] See W. I. Lenin, *Werke*, 40 vols. (Berlin, 1968), 20:8.

writings on U.S. economic and social history both set the standard and were indispensable for many East German specialists in American studies.[20]

East German academics long found it almost impossible to obtain new scholarly literature from the West, works that would have served as important sources for their understanding of the United States. Procuring such materials was complicated even before 1961 because of limited financial resources and the ban on private contacts in the West, a regulation that academics often secretly circumvented. Old materials left over from the pre-Nazi period, review copies, and book donations from Amerika-Häuser and colleagues in the West helped to alleviate this scarcity. Library stocks were meager and interlibrary loans hopelessly bureaucratic. After the Wall was built, the situation deteriorated further. In an effort to close the gap and to make an independent contribution to the field, the first East German reference work on American literature was published in 1963.[21] Cheap, mass-produced editions of American classics published in the Soviet Union or by the GDR paperback series Panther Books and Seven Seas Books ensured that at least a small amount of original literature remained available.

Despite these limitations, a modest – in comparison to West Germany – yet still impressive corpus of literature from and about the United States had been built up by the time of the GDR's collapse.[22] The GDR's journal for British and American studies, the *Zeitschrift für Anglistik und Amerikanistik* (founded 1953), offered relatively liberal opportunities for publishing articles and reviewing literature. And from the 1960s on, American studies scholars in the GDR actively supported publication of important works of American literature.[23]

Specialists in American studies also used daily and weekly newspapers to offer information to an audience interested in the United States, an audience that extended far beyond the circle of university students and professors. They also used the popular press to exercise their role as mediators between official and private images of the United States. Conflicts between orthodox editors and the authors inevitably occurred at SED newspapers. Individuals who wanted to write factual and objective articles about the United States had to be willing to pay the price of making compromises and accepting editorial cuts. The conditions proved more favorable at certain weekly newspapers and monthly magazines, such as *Forum, Sonntag, Weltbühne, Neues Leben, Magazin*, or *Weimarer Beiträge*, where the editors were used to taking risks and receiving constant reprimands for their liberal views. Offering lectures with a more popular bent also offered academics a good opportunity to present a realistic picture of the United States; held in such venues as the popular educational organization URANIA, the Kulturbund (Cultural Alliance), and adult education centers, these talks were only rarely subject to censorship, apart from that imposed by speakers on themselves.

In summary, there was not, as often assumed, one homogeneous, compulsory East German image of the United States. Rather, "official," "private," and "intellectual" views of America were intricately intertwined.

---

[20] Jürgen Kuczynski, *Die Geschichte der Lage der Arbeiter in den Vereinigten Staaten von Amerika von 1789 bis in die Gegenwart* (Berlin, 1948).

[21] Eberhard Brüning, *Meyers Taschenlexikon Amerikanische Literatur* (Leipzig, 1963).

[22] "Select Bibliography of Works Relevant to American Studies Published in the GDR," in Rainer Schnoor, ed., *Aspects of the USA: Society – Politics – Ideology* (Potsdam, 1990), 215–25. This piece only lists books, however, and does not take poetry and fiction into account.

[23] Eberhard Brüning, "US-amerikanische Literatur in der DDR seit 1965," *Zeitschrift für Anglistik und Amerikanistik* 28, no. 4 (1980): 293–319.

CHAPTER SEVENTEEN

Neither East Nor West

Anti-Americanism in West Germany, 1945–1968

Philipp Gassert

Translated by Tradukas

Anti-Americanism has accompanied the military, political, economic, and cultural rise of the United States in the twentieth century. It has long constituted a response to the role of the United States in international politics. At the same time, German criticism of America has reflected internal debates over Germany's path into modernity since the early nineteenth century.[1] Critics of the "Western" model, which America seemed to embody more than any other country, juxtaposed "special German consciousness" against the political ideals of the late-eighteenth-century transatlantic revolutions. This difference found its expression in the familiar dichotomies of Western "society" and national "community," of German "culture" and Western "civilization."[2] The discussion of American modernity along these lines peaked in the 1920s[3] and World War II, which the National Socialists interpreted as a conflict of *Weltanschauungen* not only with the East, Bolshevism, and the Soviet Union, but also with "Americanism," liberalism, and Western democracy.[4]

Even after 1945, German criticism of the United States fell back upon the clash between Western, American civilization and traditional German (and European) culture. In contrast to the 1920s and 1930s, however, anti-Americanism in the postwar "post-totalitarian ideological landscape"[5] constituted an important but not formative force in West Germany's political culture. Although large parts of the population may have harbored inner reservations about the West, anti-Americanism essentially remained the domain of fringe groups on the Left and Right. In the anticommunist atmosphere of the 1950s and 1960s, America was seen as the better alternative. This attitude appeared to change only recently, after the end of the Cold War, when young conservatives of the post-1960s generation once again revived anti-Americanism.[6] Latent anti-Western attitudes, largely overlooked in research fixated on the anti-American left, had in fact a distinct influence on West Germany's intellectual climate well into the 1960s.[7] This influence persisted even though the experience of the Nazi period had largely robbed nationalist ideologies of their appeal and the Soviet threat soon

---

[1] Alexander Schmidt, *Reisen in die Moderne: Der Amerika-Diskurs des deutschen Bürgertums vor dem Ersten Weltkrieg im europäischen Vergleich* (Berlin, 1997).

[2] Ferdinand Tönnies, *Gemeinschaft und Gesellschaft: Grundbegriffe der reinen Soziologie* (Berlin, 1912).

[3] Mary Nolan, *Visions of Modernity: American Business and the Modernization of Germany* (Oxford, 1994).

[4] Philipp Gassert, *Amerika im dritten Reich: Ideologie, Volksmeinung und Propaganda 1933–1945* (Stuttgart, 1997).

[5] Hans-Peter Schwarz, *Die Ära Adenauer 1949–1957: Gründerjahre der Republik* (Stuttgart, 1981), 430.

[6] See Richard Herzinger and Hannes Stein, *Endzeitpropheten oder Die Offensive der Antiwestler: Fundamentalismus, Antiamerikanismus und Neue Rechte* (Reinbek, 1995).

[7] See the chapter by Raimund Lammersdorf in this section.

brought about a broad consensus in favor of co-operation with the United States, a shift that left anti-Americanism without a foreign policy adversary.[8]

At its core, anti-Americanism represents a special form of criticism of the "West" (meaning the liberal-capitalist system or modern consumer society) and the attempt to counteract the real or supposed Westernization (or "Americanization") of Germany. In the eyes of many Germans, the United States embodied the "West" to an even greater extent in the Cold War period than it had before 1945. Anti-Americanism has thus not been identical to criticism of U.S. foreign policy or individual decisions made by American politicians, although it was contingent on America's role as a world power and superpower. Nor has anti-Americanism been restricted to a perpetuation of negative stereotypes in Germans' image of America, even if it has regularly drawn on these sources. Rather, anti-Americanism is much more a political ideology possessing the "quality of anticommunism or anti-Semitism."[9] This means that anti-Americanism is embedded in the everyday attitudes and experience of Germans, as demonstrated by the widespread complaints about an "Americanized mass culture" in West Germany, about American "dollar imperialism," and the

discussion about how to stop "American conditions" in the workplace and in the social welfare system. Sometimes anti-Americanism has also included traces of a xenophobic reaction to the presence of Americans such as soldiers and tourists in Germany.[10]

Since 1945, significant numbers of Germans have taken a negative or skeptical view of the United States. Although many Germans saw the arrival of the Americans in 1945 as a deliverance from the horror of war, the terror of the Nazi regime, and the air raids,[11] they only briefly experienced it as a liberation and far more often as a defeat. The German population often approached American troops with a mixture of curiosity and fear, and with the guilty conscience of the defeated. While the younger generation, especially those who had served in the antiaircraft auxiliaries, saw Americanism as the antithesis to Prussian militarism and a strict authoritarianism, older people were generally much more reserved, as for instance the woman in Heidelberg who watched in dismay as long rows of "gum-chewing" Americans trooped by.[12] In Berlin, where the arrival of the Western Allies brought an end to exclusive Soviet rule, a short phase of euphoria soon turned to disappointment.[13] Disillusionment also spread quickly among the captured soldiers in American POW camps; as Hans Werner Richter suggested in his influential novel *Die Geschlagenen* (*Beyond Defeat*), they even compared the treatment of German prisoners of

---

[8] No systematic investigation of right-wing anti-Americanism in the Federal Republic has been done. One pioneering study is Michael Ermath's "'Amerikanisierung' und deutsche Kulturkritik 1945–1965: Metastasen der Moderne und hermeneutische Hybris," in Konrad Jarausch and Hannes Siegrist, eds., *Amerikanisierung und Sowjetisierung in Deutschland 1945–1970* (Frankfurt am Main, 1997), 315–34. See also Dan Diner, *America in the Eyes of the Germans: An Essay on Anti-Americanism* (Princeton, 1996). The concentration on the anti-Americanism of the left since the 1960s is particularly evident in Günter Moltmann, "Deutscher Anti-Amerikanismus heute und früher," in Otmar Franz, ed., *Vom Sinn der Geschichte* (Stuttgart, 1976), 85–105; Emil-Peter Müller, *Antiamerikanismus in Deutschland: Zwischen Care-Paket und Cruise Missile* (Cologne, 1986); Günter C. Behrmann, "Antiamerikanismus in der Bundesrepublik, 1966–1984," *Amerikastudien* 31 (1986): 341–53.

[9] Peter Lösche, "Antiamerikanismus in der Bundesrepublik? Stereotype über Ronald Reagan in der deutschen Presse," *Amerikastudien* 31 (1986): 354.

[10] See the chapters by Petra Gödde, Klaus-Dietmar Henke, and Knud Krakau in this section.

[11] See the oral history interview in Siegrid Westphal and Joachim Arendt, *Uncle Sam und die Deutschen: 50 Jahre deutsch-amerikanische Partnerschaft in Politik, Wirtschaft und Alltagsleben* (Bonn, 1995), 33.

[12] Friederike Reutter, *Heidelberg 1945–1949: Zur politischen Geschichte einer Stadt in der Nachkriegszeit* (Heidelberg, 1994), 3; Rolf Schörken, *Luftwaffenhelfer und Drittes Reich: Die Entstehung eines politischen Bewusstseins* (Stuttgart, 1984), 142–3; see also Johannes Kleinschmidt, *"Do not fraternize": Die schwierige Anfänge deutsch-amerikanischer Freundschaft 1944–1949* (Trier, 1997).

[13] Harold Hurwitz, *Die politische Kultur der Bevölkerung und der Neubeginn konservativer Politik* (Cologne, 1983), 105–6.

war in American camps to National Socialist methods.[14]

In the early postwar years, the economic situation in Germany brought negative connotations to the word "democracy." It became "equated with defeat, hunger, misery, corruption, and bureaucracy."[15] Holding the occupying powers responsible for growing poverty in Germany became all too tempting. Confidence in the occupiers, including the Americans, fell off steadily during the occupation period, a trend not reversed until the Marshall Plan was announced.[16] Traditional anti-American attitudes, which National Socialist propaganda had extensively promoted, also emerged in the immediate postwar period, even if most Germans, with good reason, favored the Americans over the other occupiers. Many Germans nonetheless suspected that American foreign policy harbored imperialist tendencies and were disturbed by social conditions in the United States. In particular, discrimination against African Americans remained an oft-cited problem.[17] Although a majority of Germans supported foreign policy cooperation with the West, even in the 1960s a significant minority – up to one-third of the population – endorsed a neutral course. Until the 1950s, the Americans still had not achieved much popularity in opinion polls, and the real turnaround did not come until the early 1960s. From that point on, about half the respondents reported that they "like the Americans," while about a fourth still did "not particularly" like them.[18] Anti-Western sentiment no longer found support among the majority of intellectuals in the Federal Republic but represented a significant minority opinion in the West German population.

OCCIDENTALISM: THE ANTI-AMERICANISM OF THE RIGHT, 1945–68

Disassociation from National Socialism in Germany had already begun during World War II. After the war, reformed conservatives such as the sociologists Hans Freyer and Arnold Gehlen; the jurist Ernst Forsthoff; and the journalists Hans Zehrer, Giselher Wirsing, and Ferdinand Fried, who had written for the young conservative journal *Die Tat* during the Weimar Republic, renounced the radicalism of the 1920s and 1930s and came to terms, perhaps reluctantly, with liberal democracy. They declared their faith in the Christian Occident and propagated a moderate cultural anti-Americanism as critics of modern "mass society." Their approach was characterized by the idea that the Europeans would assume the intellectual leadership in the transatlantic community, while military and political dominance would fall to the Americans. After 1945, German intellectuals likened the relationship between America and Europe to that between Rome and Greece, because conquerors had often adopted the culture and values of the vanquished in the past.[19] Such reservations can even be found in Konrad Adenauer's concept of Western integration. Although cooperation with the United States was an axiom of state policy for Chancellor Adenauer, he nonetheless opposed any "Americanization" of

[14] Hans Werner Richter, *Beyond Defeat* (New York, 1950); see Gabriela Wettberg, *Das Amerika-Bild und seine negativen Konstanten in der deutschen Nachkriegsliteratur* (Heidelberg, 1987), 26–34.

[15] Hermann Glaser, *Kleine Kulturgeschichte der Bundesrepublik Deutschland 1945–1989* (Munich, 1991), 21–2.

[16] In November 1945, 70 percent of the population in the American zone believed that the American occupation had brought economic progress, but the figure had fallen to 44 percent by April 1947. See Anna J. Merritt and Richard L. Merritt, *Public Opinion in Occupied Germany: The OMGUS Surveys, 1945–1949* (Urbana, Ill., 1970), 161, report no. 60, April 1947, "Trends in German Public Opinion"; ibid., 211, report no. 100, March 1948, "Trends in German Public Opinion."

[17] Ibid., 180–1, report no. 76, October 29, 1947, "German Attitudes Toward the Four Occupying Powers"; ibid., 177–8, report no. 73, October 28, 1947, "A Guide to Some Propaganda Problems."

[18] See Anna J. Merritt and Richard L. Merritt, *Public Opinion in Semisovereign Germany: The HICOG Surveys, 1949–1955* (Urbana, Ill., 1980), 24–30; Elisabeth Noelle-Neumann and Edgar Piel, eds., *Allensbacher Jahrbuch der Demoskopie 8* (1978–83): 606.

[19] Jerzy Z. Muller, *The Other God That Failed: Hans Freyer and the Deradicalization of German Conservatism* (Princeton, 1987), 335–6.

Germany and disputed that the Americans had even "one really viable idea" with which to offer "resistance to the incursion of totalitarian atheism from Russia." Adenauer saw the "Christian humanism" of the Western Europeans as the only bulwark against the threat of Bolshevism.[20]

In the early years of the Federal Republic, only a few critics stuck to consistent anti-Western positions. The foremost in the Christian Democratic Party (*Christlich-Demokratische Union*, or CDU) was Jakob Kaiser, the former head of the East German CDU and Federal Minister for All-German Affairs (1949–57), who rejected Western integration, both social and political. Promoting a concept of Germany as a "bridge between East and West," Kaiser lobbied not only for a foreign policy of neutrality but also for a social and political "third way" between Marxism and liberalism.[21] The ideological fronts of the Cold War meant that such ideas had little influence among the Right. It was only with the growing disillusionment after the building of the Berlin Wall that opponents of integration into the Western alliance became more vocal; this was the case, for example, with Paul Sethe, coeditor of the *Frankfurter Allgemeine Zeitung* from 1949 to 1955, whose concept of neutrality did not have a hard-edged social and political anti-American flavor.[22] Armin Mohler, secretary to Ernst Jünger and confidant of Carl Schmitt, was highly critical of West Germany's media-driven mass democracy

as well. Following the example of groups in the Christian Democratic parties, he demanded a "German Gaullism" between East and West.[23]

Moderate conservative critics of "Americanism" pointed out the costs of the modernization process emanating from the United States but avoided the kind of radical slogans that had been heard in the Weimar Republic. However, nationalist and radical conservative authors such as Gottfried Benn, Hans Grimm, Ernst von Salomon, and Carl Schmitt advocated a consistent anti-American position even after 1945, rejecting cultural and social westernization as well as the integration of West German foreign policy into the Western alliance. The starting point for their criticism was American planning for the postwar period during World War II and the post-1945 occupation. Ernst von Salomon's autobiographical novel *Der Fragebogen* (*The Questionnaire*) was probably the most influential anti-American book of the early years of the Federal Republic, and it marked the literary zenith of criticism of the unpopular denazification programs, which ran aground politically in the same period.[24] Salomon, a former member of the Freikorps who had served six years in prison for participating in the 1922 murder of Walther Rathenau, derided the American attempt to call the Germans to account politically through denazification. He did not confine his sneering reckoning with the victors of World War II to attacks on the arrogant posturing of the educated classes, a target favored by moderate conservative critics. His portrayal of the manifest bureaucratic failings of denazification was peppered with invectives against the Americans, whom he depicted as brutal, degenerate, dumb, and mean. For Salomon, the real victors were the Germans, who faced the justice

[20] Konrad Adenauer in interviews with the London *Times* journalist Leslie Hargrove on January 25, 1961, and with *New York Times* editors on February 20, 1962; quoted from Hans-Jürgen Grabbe, "Das Amerikabild Konrad Adenauers," *Amerikastudien* 31 (1986): 315–23.

[21] See Jakob Kaiser, *Wir haben Brücke zu sein: Reden, Aufsätze und Äusserungen zur Deutschlandpolitik* (Cologne, 1988), Christian Hacke, ed.; Rainer Zitelmann, *Adenauers Gegner: Streiter für Deutschland* (Erlangen, 1991), 29–52.

[22] Paul Sethe, *Öffnung nach Osten: Weltpolitische Realitäten zwischen Bonn, Paris und Moskau* (Frankfurt am Main, 1966); Paul Noack, "Paul Sethe: Publizistische Opposition gegen Adenauer," in Josef Foschepoth, ed., *Adenauer und die deutsche Frage* (Göttingen, 1988), 235–48.

[23] Armin Mohler, *Was die Deutschen fürchten: Angst vor der Politik, Angst vor der Geschichte, Angst vor der Macht* (Stuttgart, 1965).

[24] See Norbert Frei, *Vergangenheitspolitik: Die Anfänge der Bundesrepublik und die NS-Vergangenheit* (Munich, 1996). Intellectuals in particular rejected denazification; see Merritt and Merritt, *Public Opinion*, 304–5, report no. 182, 11 July 1949, "German Views on Denazification."

of the victors unbowed, while the ignorant and incompetent Americans revealed their own inferiority.[25]

A literary genre dealing with reeducation blossomed in West Germany in the 1950s and 1960s, much of it anti-American. Although not representative of the academic discussion in Germany, books such as *Auf dem Bauche sollst Du kriechen* by two *Zeit* editors, Richard Tüngel and Hans Rudolf Berndorff, and *Charakterwäsche* written by Caspar von Schrenck-Notzing (later editor of the neoconservative periodical *Criticon*) did have considerable influence on the educated public, as demonstrated by the large print runs and many reprints.[26] Apart from this, it was principally neo-Nazi splinter groups such as the *Deutsche Gemeinschaft* (DG) and the *Deutsche Reichspartei* (DRP), which quickly abandoned their initial anti-Soviet Western orientation in favor of a national pro-neutral position and fought vehemently against "reeducation of the Germans." Anti-Western and anti-American ideology found a home in the journal *Nation Europa*, which was founded in 1951 and remains to this day one of the most important theoretical organs of the extreme right. Its columns were filled with radical criticism of Western policy toward Germany. Drawing on National Socialist propaganda, *Nation Europa* published endless variations of the old myths of "Wilson's betrayal," "Roosevelt's war guilt," the "influence of the Jews" on American policy, the "spirit of vengeance embedded in the Morgenthau Plan," and the "division of Europe in Yalta." Akin to the National Socialists' plans for Europe, the publishers argued for a European nationalism and called for the defense of the Occident's cultural and racial heritage against Americanism and Bolshevism.[27]

The double front fought against East and West and the pessimistic cultural criticism of technological civilization – the great theme of the conservative revolution of the 1920s and 1930s – was a leitmotif running through anti-American writing of the postwar era. In 1951, Giselher Wirsing, one of the leading journalists in the Nazi period and editor of *Christ und Welt* after the war, advised the Europeans to immunize themselves against Stalinism and Americanism. Hans Grimm, author of the best seller *Volk ohne Raum* and an esteemed authority on poetry during the Third Reich, accused East and West of a tendency toward "massification," whereas Eugen Gürster saw a disquieting affinity between "modern Russia" and "modern America" despite their irreconcilable antagonism in international politics.[28] Eminent cultural critics such as the jurist Carl Schmitt (seen as one of the progenitors of the new right, alongside author Ernst Jünger and philosopher Martin Heidegger) had already before 1945 asserted a convergence of Americanism and Bolshevism. The two blocs were much more similar than one might think, argued Schmitt in 1952, for both originated "from the same source, the historical philosophy of the eighteenth and nineteenth centuries." He saw Americanism and Bolshevism as expressions of a "leveling" industrial and technical civilization and the precursors to an international uniformity he held in low regard.[29]

---

[25] Ernst von Salomon, *Fragebogen: Questionnaire* (Garden City, N.Y., 1955). A reprint of the paperback edition, first published in 1961, indicates that 90,000 copies had been printed by 1991.

[26] Richard Tüngel and Hans Rudolf Berndorff, *Auf dem Bauche sollst Du kriechen . . . Deutschland unter den Besatzungsmächten* (Hamburg, 1958); Caspar von Schrenck-Notzing, *Charakterwäsche: Die amerikanische Besatzung in Deutschland und ihre Folgen* (Stuttgart, 1965), updated reprint (Frankfurt am Main, 1993).

[27] On *Nation Europa*, see Uwe Backes and Eckhard Jesse, *Politischer Extremismus in der Bundesrepublik* (Bonn, 1993), 73–5; see, for example, the special issues on the United States: *Nation Europa* 1, no. 11 (1951): 2, no. 2 (1952); see also Erwin Schönborn, *Los von Amerika: Eine nationaldemokratische Analyse* (Kalbach, 1966).

[28] Giselher Wirsing, *Schritte aus dem Nichts: Perspektiven am Ende der Revolutionen* (Düsseldorf, 1951), 304–6; Hans Grimm, "Reich Europa," *Nation Europa* 1, no. 3 (1951): 3–10; Eugen Gürster, "Geistige Aspekte der amerikanischen Zivilisation II," *Neue Rundschau* 62 (1951): 24–6.

[29] Carl Schmitt, "Die Einheit der Welt," *Merkur* 6, no. 1 (1952): 9.

A common theme of post-1945 German cultural criticism was the idea of *Posthistoire*, that the technological age would bring to an end the "historical" confrontation between capitalism and socialism that begain in the nineteenth century.[30] Ernst Jünger, an extremely influential figure in postwar German nationalistic journalism, noted "the similarity of style" in the "world civil war" between the two superpowers after 1945. The "nihilism" of technology had led to a "horrific hoarding of missiles" in East and West, "calculated for the undifferentiated annihilation of the human race."[31] Referring to Alexis de Tocqueville's famous prediction, Jünger foresaw a "planetary order" rising on the horizon of world history as a result of the "similarity of the two giant partners," the United States and the Soviet Union. This would end in the establishment of a "world state" that would distinguish itself from all previous cultures through a general *Nivellement*, "with the differences between the sexes disappearing," a "leveling of the races, ranks, classes and even the great natural phenomena such as the seasons, or day and night."[32]

UTOPIA AND DISAPPOINTMENT: THE
ANTI-AMERICANISM OF THE LEFT, 1945–68

Until well into the 1960s, few on the left opposed "Americanization" as a model for the internal Western orientation of the Federal Republic. Only in East Germany, where official propaganda railed against "U.S.-American imperialism" and "the revanchist tendencies of U.S. capital," was radical anti-Americanism propagated from an orthodox Marxist standpoint.[33] Unlike most conservative intellectuals,

many leftists had been forced into emigration. They saw the "Westernization" of Germany as a guarantee for a political new beginning after the disaster of National Socialism. Although Kurt Schumacher and the later Social Democratic Party (*Sozialdemokratische Partei Deutschlands*, or SPD) member Gustav Heinemann rejected Adenauer's policy of integration into the Western alliance because of its consequences for German unity, they maintained a fundamental Western orientation in domestic policy.[34]

Until the early 1960s, most serious leftist criticism came from writers. For example, Hans Werner Richter, a cofounder of the "Gruppe 47" and former editor of the periodical *Der Ruf* (which was banned by the occupation authorities), held the Americans responsible, at least indirectly, for supporting a conservative restoration in the Federal Republic.[35] Wolfgang Koeppen also cloaked his analysis of West Germany in anti-Americanism.[36] The increasingly frequent expressions of disappointment with the Americans, a central motif of moderate literary criticism of America, prepared the way for a shift in the left's image of America in the 1960s. Before that shift, the tradition of German anti-American travel writing inspired by the American Progressives was maintained above all by Leo L. Matthias. Matthias, who had lived in the United States and Latin America during World War II and did not return to Germany until 1947, portrayed "American civilization" in classic anti-American style as a class society guided exclusively by pecuniary interests, with no "ranks" based on merit or moral authority, only "profit" and "the desire to buy." Although his first book on America, *Die Entdeckung Amerikas Anno 1953 oder das geordnete*

---

[30] Lutz Niethammer, *Posthistoire: Ist die Geschichte zu Ende?* (Reinbek, 1989), 82–104.

[31] Ernst Jünger, "Über die Linie," in *Werke*, 10 vols., vol. 5: *Essays 1* (Stuttgart, year not indicated [1960]), 5:245–89. See Elliott Neaman, *A Dubious Past: Ernst Jünger and the Politics of Literature After Nazism* (Berkeley, 1998).

[32] Ernst Jünger, "Der Weltstaat: Organismus und Organisation," in Ernst Jünger, *Werke*, 5:495–538, 504–5, 520–1.

[33] See the chapter by Rainer Schnoor in this section.

[34] Hans-Jürgen Grabbe, *Unionsparteien, Sozialdemokratie und Vereinigten Staaten von Amerika 1945–1966* (Düsseldorf, 1983), 51–7, 205–30.

[35] Hans Werner Richter, *Linus Fleck oder der Verlust der Würde* (Munich, 1959); Wettberg, *Amerika-Bild*, 47–55.

[36] Wolfgang Koeppen, *Pigeons on the Grass* (New York, 1988); *Amerikafahrt* (Stuttgart, 1959); see also Ulrich Ott, *Amerika ist Anders: Studien zum Amerika-Bild in deutschen Reiseberichten des 20. Jahrhunderts* (Frankfurt am Main, 1991), 315–59.

Chaos, received little notice on the left-wing scene,[37] the second, *Die Kehrseite der USA* (1964), was widely read. Matthias became an authority for left-wing anti-Americanism and served as a source for Rolf Hochhuth's play *Guerillas*, which Hochhuth dedicated to him "with gratitude."[38]

The decisive factor for the development of left-wing anti-Americanism was the escalation of the Vietnam War after 1964. In Germany, as in almost all Western countries, this radicalized the protest movement.[39] In November 1965, members of the "Gruppe 47" published a "Declaration on the War in Vietnam" in which they declared their solidarity with the American civil rights movement, fiercely criticized the American government for its policies in Southeast Asia, and called on the West German government to account for its moral and financial support for the United States.[40] Whereas the SPD had become the "guarantor of pro-American foreign policy" since the early 1960s (Hans-Jürgen Grabbe), the German New Left turned away from the United States. The shift to anti-Americanism was supported by a neo-Marxist critique of capitalist industrial society (often originating in the United States and reimported by returning German emigrants). These theoretical underpinnings resembled the axioms of liberal modernization theory in that they saw the United States as the prototype of Western development. Criticism of the United States was thus, in final measure, also an expression of cultural Westernization.[41] Moreover, the activists of the West German student movement had in many cases been politically sensitized while studying in the United States. In borrowing the nomenclature of the American New Left – from *Blumenkind* (flower child) to teach-in – they adopted not only its vocabulary but also its style and forms of protest.[42]

In February 1968, the author Hans Magnus Enzensberger, editor of *Kursbuch*, the leading periodical of the German New Left, and one of the intellectual mentors of the student movement, renounced a scholarship at Wesleyan University in Connecticut. This sensational step symbolized a whole generation's break with America.[43] After the end of National Socialism, America had seemed "a utopian place" for Enzensberger and many others, and the younger generation looked to the American constitution and political culture for an alternative. Now America itself was in the wrong.[44] Enthusiasm for Kennedy gave way to disillusionment over the Vietnam War. The Civil Rights movement and the culture of protest at American universities still inspired the activists of the German student movement. But the social order of the United States was no longer a source of emancipation and progress, and it was now seen as the guarantor of the status quo in Germany and the cause of oppression in Africa, Asia, and South America.[45] Accordingly, Third World liberation movement theorists such as Frantz Fanon and

---

[37] See Golo Mann's review and Matthias's reply in *Merkur* 8 (1954): 390–4, 796–800.

[38] Leo L. Matthias, *Die Entdeckung Amerikas anno 1953 oder Das geordnete Chaos* (Hamburg, 1953); *Die Kehrseite der USA* (Reinbek, 1964) (fifth reprint 1967); Rolf Hochhuth, *Guerillas: Tragödie in fünf Akten* (Hamburg, 1970); see Ott, *Amerika ist anders*, 306–7.

[39] See the introduction to Carole Fink, Philipp Gassert, and Detlef Junker, eds., *1968: The World Transformed* (Cambridge, 1998).

[40] "Erklärung über den Krieg in Vietnam," *Der Spiegel* 51 (Dec. 12, 1965): 24, quoted from Ingo Juchler, *Die Studentenbewegungen in den Vereinigten Staaten und der Bundesrepublik Deutschland der sechziger Jahre: Eine Untersuchung hinsichtlich ihrer Beeinflüssung durch Befreiungsbewegungen und -theorien aus der Dritten Welt* (Berlin, 1996), 90–1.

[41] See the chapter by Raimund Lammersdorf in this section.

[42] Doug McAdam and Dieter Rucht, "The Cross National Diffusion of Movement Ideas," *Annals of the American Academy of Political and Social Sciences* 528 (1993): 56–74; Philipp Gassert, "Atlantic Alliances: Cross-Cultural Communication and the 1960s Student Revolution," in Jessica C. E. Gienow-Hecht and Frank Schumacher, eds., *Culture and International Relations* (New York, 2003); and the chapter by Claus Leggewie, vol. 2, Society.

[43] Hans Magnus Enzensberger, "On Leaving America," *New York Review of Books*, Feb. 29, 1968.

[44] See the interview with Enzensberger in Heinz D. Osterle, *Bilder von Amerika: Gespräche mit deutschen Schriftstellern* (Münster, 1987), 41–75.

[45] See Ekkehart Krippendorff, "Die westdeutsche Linke und ihr Bild von den USA," in Willi Paul Adams

Herbert Marcuse; revolutionaries such as Fidel Castro, Ho Chi Minh, and Ernesto Che Guevara; the teachings of Mao; and the Chinese Cultural Revolution became the basis not only for radical criticism of First World "imperialism" but also for a fundamental rejection of the social order in Germany and the United States. Thus, it is right to characterize the protest movement's criticism "of America

and Knud Krakau, eds., *Deutschland und Amerika: Perzeption und historische Realität* (Berlin, 1985), 39–46.

through America" as anti-Americanism, for it encompassed not just American foreign policy or particular American politicians but also a fundamental critique of the liberal capitalist system. Although starting from diametrically opposed ideological positions and in no agreement over political goals, the radical right and the radical left both now opposed the Western development model embodied by the United States. By 1968, not only the German right but also the left advocated a "third way" between East and West.

CHAPTER EIGHTEEN

Americanization

Axel Schildt

Translated by Tradukas

The term "Americanization" has circulated in Germany since the turn of the last century and with increasing frequency since the 1920s. In everyday language and the pages of the popular press, it refers to a process of cultural and social cultural adaptation to the standards set by the society of the United States.[1] According to the simple monolinear model of cultural transmission behind this notion, commodities from the United States and the ideas associated with them have flooded German society and remolded it on the pattern of "the American way of life." Although this cliché remains suggestive and widely used, it should be carefully differentiated from the debate in contemporary history over the degree of American influence on German society and on West German society since World War II in particular, the subject of the second half of this article.

The popular image of American society, which has offered Germans a misleading vision of their own future, encompasses a collection of enduring clichés: Although the United States leads in technology and entices with many of the comforts of civilization, it is a money-driven society lacking culture or a soul.[2] The principal negative, psychosocial consequences attributed to the ongoing rationalization and homogenization associated with Americanization have been "softness" and "feminization" (the loss of male authority) as well as loss of individuality and a unique identity. The completely "other-directed" Americans[3] were helpful and friendly but also naive and conformist. That applied even to the superficial American flirt and the Americans' standardized sexuality, which Sigmund Freud thought had to be distinguished from the Europeans' more profound love relationships.[4]

This stereotypical image that the term "Americanization" commonly invokes has changed little since the turn of the last century. However, even during the interwar period, some journalists pointed out that in the final measure it represented a German or European projection. They observed that Americanization had become a code to describe firsthand experience of modernization and that criticism of Americanization expressed fears about modernization's consequences. The observation that

---

[1] It probably first appeared in the book by the English journalist William Thomas Stead, *The Americanization of the World, or: The Trend of the Twentieth Century* (New York, 1901); for the development of discourses on Americanization, see "Einleitung" in Alf Lüdtke, Inge Marssolek, and Adelheid von Saldern, eds., *Amerikanisierung: Traum und Alptraum im Deutschland des 20. Jahrhunderts* (Stuttgart, 1996), 7–33.

[2] See Axel Schildt, *Moderne Zeiten: Freizeit, Massenmedien und Zeitgeist in der Bundesrepublik der 50er Jahre* (Hamburg, 1995), 398–423.

[3] David Riesman, with Nathan Glazer and Reuel Denney, *The Lonely Crowd: A Study of the Changing American Character* (Garden City, N.Y., 1953), 61.

[4] Sigmund Freud, *Wir und der Tod* (1915), in *Die Zeit* 45, July 20, 1990.

attitudes toward America and Americanization coincided with attitudes toward modern society and modernization helps to show that the fundamental differences between the United States and Germany (or Europe) are hardly clear-cut or absolute. From this point of view, Americanization is a cultural transfer not from a completely different society but from one that is merely more technically and culturally developed yet built on the same foundations.[5] The stereotypes of an "alienated" and soulless "Americanized" future have been largely impervious to this insight. Yet, even if "Americanization" had (and has) largely negative connotations, it has also had (and has) more positive associations. For instance, since the 1920s, Americanization has also been understood in terms of technical and social liberation from traditional hierarchies, as a path to less inhibited, less stiff interpersonal relations. Yet, here the clichés of America were merely reversed without their basic validity being questioned.

DIMENSIONS OF AMERICANIZATION

The concept of Americanization current in contemporary historical research is based on the assumption that "since the turn of the century the United States has unquestionably had a profound influence on the development of German society, not only in military and political terms, but also in economics and culture."[6] But works on the Weimar Republic and the Third Reich have, to date, given scant attention to this hypothesis. The influence of American popular music in urban Germany in the 1920s and 1930s, the image of a Hitler youth downing a bottle of Coke, the popularity of Hollywood films, and other irksome features of American mass cul-

ture in the Third Reich have been noted but not subjected to serious social-historical analysis and classification.[7]

Far-reaching Americanization is assumed to have taken hold even more forcefully in western Germany. According to this view, 1945 irreversibly opened all the floodgates; the end of Germany's *Sonderweg* brought with it the uninhibited acceptance of American goods and ideas, and thereby Americanization.[8] This assumption might be very plausible, for the United States played the leading role among the Western Allies and made enormous efforts to lay the institutional groundwork for parliamentary democracy, to reeducate and reorient the West German population. Yet, the real extent of American influence after the end of occupation has not received much close scrutiny. The sweeping proposition that West German society had "fewer traditional reserves than the French or English"[9] to fend off Americanization and was integrated "with particular intensity in this new, predominantly American-influenced civilization"[10] still awaits comparative study.

Two methodological steps are necessary to investigate the scope and depth of Americanization of West German society. The first is to acknowledge that Americanization will be difficult to separate analytically from general developments in modernization. Each aspect requires discrete consideration to determine

---

[5] On this, see Hannah Arendt, "Europa und Amerika (1954)," in *Zur Zeit: Politische Essays* (Berlin, 1986), 71–93.

[6] Volker Berghahn, "Deutschland im 'American Century' 1942–1992: Einige Argumente zur Amerikanisierungsfrage," in Matthias Frese and Michael Prinz, eds., *Politische Zäsuren und gesellschaftlicher Wandel im 20. Jahrhundert: Regionale und vergleichende Perspektiven* (Paderborn, 1996), 791.

[7] See Detlev J. K. Peukert, *The Weimar Republic: The Crisis of Classical Modernity* (New York, 1992); Hans Dieter Schäfer, *Das gespaltene Bewusstsein: Über deutsche Kultur und Lebenswirklichkeit 1933–1945* (Munich, 1981); the first broader survey is Philipp Gassert, *Amerika im Dritten Reich: Ideologie, Propaganda und Volksmeinung 1933–1945* (Stuttgart, 1997).

[8] See, for example, Ralph Willett, *The Americanization of Germany, 1945–1949* (London, 1989). For an overview of the literature, see Bernd Greiner, "'Test the West': Über die 'Amerikanisierung' der Bundesrepublik Deutschland," *Mittelweg* 36, no. 6 (1997): 4–40.

[9] Richard Löwenthal, "Kulturwandel und Generationswechsel im westlichen Nachkriegsdeutschland," in James A. Cooney et al., eds., *Die Bundesrepublik und die Vereinigten Staaten von Amerika: Politische, soziale und wirtschaftliche Beziehungen im Wandel* (Stuttgart, 1985), 63.

[10] Dietrich Thränhardt, *Geschichte der Bundesrepublik Deutschland* (Frankfurt am Main, 1986), 131.

whether certain ideas, patterns, and forms already existed – with external influences merely providing the impetus that propelled them to center stage – or whether features that had originated elsewhere were introduced or modified to fit existing indigenous cultural patterns. It is often difficult to untangle the relationship between objects or trends that had been imported from the United States and those that merely imitated them, reflected some American influence, or testified to some parallel development in Germany. Furthermore, identifying "genuine" American imports raises the question of whether these were themselves preceded by export of German and European ideas. (The contributions of post-1933 emigrants spring to mind here.)

Second, different domains pose distinct analytical challenges; American influence in such sectors as politics, the economy, society, and culture call for separate consideration. Such an investigation needs to be periodized in terms of major political events (first and foremost, the end of the occupation period and the founding of the Federal Republic in 1949) as well as in terms of social developments. The West German *Zusammenbruchsgesellschaft*[11] ("collapse society") of the immediate postwar period differed fundamentally from the period of prosperity that began in the late 1950s. And this fundamental social transformation was accompanied by the rise of a new generation that was of great importance for the acceptance of American products and ideas. Finally, of crucial analytical importance are the enormous differences between southern Germany – the American zone of occupation and after 1949 the region where American troops were stationed – and northern Germany, where most people had no personal contact with representatives of the "New World."[12]

The two postwar decades, the "pivotal period of Americanization in the whole twentieth-century modernization process," are examined separately in the following sections. This is imperative because the mid-1950s represent a distinct break, the point at which the Federal Republic gained (almost) complete foreign policy sovereignty through the Paris Treaty and NATO membership. This caesura divides two clearly identifiable phases of Americanization.[13] Whereas the first ten years after World War II can be characterized as "Americanization from above," the following decade can best be described as "Americanization from below."

THE FIRST POSTWAR DECADE

"Americanization from above" predominated in the first postwar decade, driven by the Allies' strategic goal of eliminating a German threat for all times. With the beginning of the Cold War, the Allies' initial leanings toward punishing Germany and strictly enacting denazification soon gave way to efforts to integrate the western part of Germany into the transatlantic community of democratic states. Reeducation or reorientation efforts, viewed as core elements in this integration process, focused on the introduction of democratic parliamentary structures. Initially launched at the local level, they concentrated most strongly on education and cultural policy.[14] Among these initiatives was a flood of German-language American periodicals, aimed mainly at German intellectual elites, that offered up pragmatic Anglo-Saxon philosophy and openness in problem-solving as an alternative to rigid ideological doctrines.[15] Radio programming mirrored these literary efforts.[16]

[11] Christoph Klessmann, *Die doppelte Staatsgründung: Deutsche Geschichte, 1945–1955* (Göttingen, 1982), 37.

[12] For a comprehensive study, see Klaus-Dietmar Henke, *Die amerikanische Besetzung Deutschlands* (Munich, 1995).

[13] Anselm Doering-Manteuffel, "Dimensionen von Amerikanisierung in der deutschen Gesellschaft," *Archiv für Sozialgeschichte* 35 (1995): 11.

[14] See the chapters by Barbara Fait and Cornelia Rauh-Kühne, vol. 1, Politics; see also the chapters by Rebecca Boehling, Jessica C. E. Gienow-Hecht, and James F. Tent, vol. 1, Culture.

[15] See the chapter by Frank Trommler, vol. 1, Culture.

[16] See Rüdiger Bolz, *Rundfunk und Literatur unter amerikanischer Kontrolle: Das Programmangebot von Radio München 1945–1949* (Wiesbaden, 1991); Ulrich M. Bausch, *Die Kulturpolitik der US-amerikanischen*

Amerika-Häuser (America Houses) were another important vehicle in this process, and
several were opened after the end of the occupation in cities that had not been in the American zone.[17] Travel programs to the United States
were also important, allowing some 10,000
leading public figures, politicians, local administrators, journalists, judges, trade unionists, academics, clergymen, and officials from youth and
women's organizations to visit the United States
between 1948 and 1953. Applicants to these programs were selected according to their ability
and willingness to act as cultural multipliers in
passing on experiences gained in America.

It is hard to determine whether this "Americanization from above" put down deep roots.
Opinion polls commissioned by American authorities in the early and mid-1950s show at the
very least that the old patterns of prejudice that
saw the United States as a leading civilization –
but culturally backward – had not disappeared.[18]
Efforts to reform schools and universities largely
failed in the face of resistance and continued adherence to traditional German thinking on education. And in the culture of the early 1950s as

a whole, elements of continuity far outweighed
manifestations of Americanization.[19] Increasing
endorsement of a westward-looking politics in
this period went hand in hand with psychological resistance against a culture imposed by the
victors, a phenomenon comparable to the situation in the American South after the Civil
War.[20]

Ideological imports would have little impact
on postwar Germans. In a representative opinion poll in 1950, two-thirds of the respondents
in the former American zone reported that they
had never heard of a special reorientation program, although a large majority knew of American economic aid. The relative popularity of
the American occupying power was connected
to the food, cigarettes, and other commodities
from a faraway world of prosperity proffered
by the Americans, objects that possessed an almost erotic aura. The image of the black American soldier offering Chesterfields to the German
Fräulein, described in Wolfgang Koeppen's 1948
novel Pigeons on the Grass (Tauben im Gras), embedded itself in the collective memory of the
inhabitants of the American zone. These associations held fast even though in a representative
opinion poll conducted at the end of 1949, more
than two-thirds of the respondents said they had
not made closer acquaintance with Americans
since the end of the war. Those who stated they
knew members of the occupying forces well or
very well, about 15 percent, for the most part
held senior positions in business, administration,
and cultural affairs, and had corresponding educational backgrounds. Only about 5 percent
of the population could speak English. In this
respect, the long-lasting, close relationships that
developed in the areas of Bavaria, Hesse, Baden-
Württemberg, and Rhineland-Palatinate where

Information Control Division in Württemberg-Baden
1945–1949: Zwischen militärischem Funktionalismus und
schwäbischem Obrigkeitsdenken (Stuttgart, 1992).

[17] See Axel Schildt, "Die USA als 'Kulturnation': Zur
Bedeutung der Amerikahäuser in den 1950er Jahren,"
in Alf Lüdtke, Inge Marssolek, and Adelheid von
Saldern, eds., Amerikanisierung: Traum und Alptraum im
Deutschland des 20. Jahrhunderts (Stuttgart, 1976), 257–69;
Maritta Hein-Kremer, Die amerikanische Kulturoffensive:
Gründung und Entwicklung der amerikanischen Informa-
tion Centers in Westdeutschland und West Berlin 1945–1955
(Cologne, 1996).

[18] Schildt, Moderne Zeiten, 404–5; for a sociological investigation of the reeducation and reorientation
programs, see Anna J. Merritt and Richard L. Merritt, Public Opinion in Occupied Germany: The OMGUS
Surveys, 1945–1955 (Urbana, Ill., 1970); Anna J. Merritt
and Richard L. Merritt, Public Opinion in Semisovereign
Germany: The HICOG Surveys, 1949–1955 (Urbana, Ill.,
1980); Hans Braun and Stephan Articus, "Sozialwissenschaftliche Forschung im Rahmen der amerikanischen Besatzungspolitik 1945–1949," Kölner Zeitschrift
für Soziologie und Sozialpsychologie 36 (1984): 703–37; see
the chapter by Knud Krakau in this section.

[19] Norbert Finzsch and Jürgen Martschukat, eds., Dif-
ferent Restoration, Reconstruction and 'Wiederaufbau' in the
United States and Germany: 1865–1945–1989 (Providence,
R.I., 1996).

[20] Hans-Peter Schwarz, "Die Westdeutschen, die
westliche Demokratie und die Westbindung im Licht
von Meinungsumfragen," in Cooney et al., eds., Die
Bundesrepublik, 87–144.

American troops had a large presence were interesting exceptions.[21]

"AMERICANIZATION FROM BELOW"

"Americanization from above" came to an end in the mid-1950s. West German parliamentary democracy had proved to be stable and viable, and it no longer seemed to need the organized importation of ideas from the United States. The network of Amerika-Häuser became sparser, and radio stations discontinued their special *Voice of America* programs. "Americanization from below" eclipsed and replaced "Americanization from above," a process that culturally bolstered the Federal Republic's Western political orientation but cannot be seen as a long-term strategic plan for mapping out the future.[22]

Trips by individuals, mostly businesspeople, came to outnumber governmentally and institutionally sponsored travel programs in the West German–American travel statistics in the course of the 1950s.[23] The number of visitors to the United States increased tenfold during the 1950s, eventually reaching 40,000 in 1960. The number of American tourists visiting West Germany doubled, reaching about 140,000 over the same period and, as opinion polls showed, West Germans preferred American guests over all other foreign visitors, regarding them as free-spending, congenial, and friendly.

Growing economic links between the two countries represented another facet of "Americanization from below."[24] The amount of American capital invested in the Federal Republic grew fivefold between 1950 and 1960, reaching approximately DM 1 billion. In 1954–5, about 50 American firms could be found in the Federal Republic, a figure that had grown to 420 by 1960. Two-thirds of these were located in the Rhine-Main region, another indication of significant regional differences in the American presence.[25] However, the growth of American capital – about a third of total foreign capital in the Federal Republic at the time – cannot be taken as a straightforward index of Americanization. The share of U.S. imports to the Federal Republic fell from more than 15 percent (1950) to 14 percent in 1960 and dropped further to about 8 percent in the mid-1970s. Rising U.S. capital investments were plainly caused in part by the failure of trade to keep

---

[21] See Dewey Arthur Browder, "The Impact of the American Presence on Germany and German-American Grass-Roots Relations in Germany, 1950–1960" (Ph.D. diss., Louisiana State University, 1987), which includes examples from the Zweibrücken base; Winfried Herget, Werner Kremp, and Walter G. Rödel, eds., *Nachbar Amerika: 50 Jahre Amerikaner in Rheinland-Pfalz* (Trier, 1995).

[22] This is the tendency in Wolfgang Kreuter and Joachim Oltmann, "Coca-Cola statt Apfelmost: Kalter Krieg und Amerikanisierung," *Englisch-Amerikanische Studien* 6 (1984): 22–35. For the latest overview, see Richard Pells, *Not Like Us: How Europeans Have Loved, Hated, and Transformed American Culture Since World War II* (New York, 1997).

[23] Schildt, *Moderne Zeiten*, 416–7.

[24] See Volker Berghahn, *The Americanization of West German Industry, 1945–1973* (New York, 1986); Volker Berghahn, "West German Reconstruction and American Industrial Culture, 1945–1960," in Reiner Pommerin, ed., *The American Impact on Postwar Germany* (Oxford, 1994), 65–81; for a provocative discussion of this approach, see Paul Erker, "'Amerikanisierung' der westdeutschen Wirtschaft? Stand und Perspektiven der Forschung," in Konrad Jarausch and Hannes Siegrist, eds., *Amerikanisierung und Sowjetisierung in Deutschland 1945–1970* (Frankfurt am Main, 1997), 137–45; Harm G. Schröter, "Zur Übertragbarkeit sozialhistorischer Konzepte in die Wirtschaftsgebiete," in Jarausch and Siegrist, *Amerikanisierung*, 147–65.

[25] Hubert Kiesewetter, "Amerikanische Unternehmen in der Bundesrepublik Deutschland 1950 bis 1974," in Hartmut Kaelble, ed., *Der Boom, 1948–1973: Gesellschaftliche und wirtschaftliche Folgen in der Bundesrepublik Deutschland und in Europa* (Opladen, 1992), 63–81; Alexander von Plato examines American influences in business at the biographical level in "Wirtschaftskapitäne: Biographische Selbstkonstruktionen von Unternehmern der Nachkriegszeit," in Axel Schildt and Arnold Sywottek, eds., *Modernisierung im Wiederaufbau: Die westdeutsche Gesellschaft der 50er Jahre* (Bonn, 1993), 377–91; Volker R. Berghahn and Paul J. Friedrich, *Otto A. Friedrich, ein politischer Unternehmer: Sein Leben und seine Zeit 1902–1975* (Frankfurt am Main, 1993).

pace, as well as by the fact that wage levels remained lower in West Germany than the United States. In the 1950s, whoever wanted to sell products successfully in the Federal Republic had to make them appear German (meaning reliable) and market them in a German manner (relying on a factual rather than humorous sales pitch). American goods did not have a particularly good reputation. What can be regarded as Americanization, however, was the West German advertising sector's use of U.S. agencies as a model and the advance of more aggressive, enterprising marketing concepts.[26] Terms such as *"Managerkrankheit"* ("managerial stress syndrome") also entered the German vocabulary in the 1950s. Still, the extent to which American influences found in German economic culture can be regarded as an innovative transfer from America remains questionable. Contemporary experts – in human relations, for example – found only a few departures from the modern German management methods of the interwar period.[27]

The broad and diffuse field of popular culture and aesthetic patterns in everyday life demands closer examination. Here, too, it will not be possible to fully resolve the problems of analytically distinguishing between Americanization and what were simply general developments connected with the advance of modernity. The German language serves as an example. A huge number of Americanisms entered the German language during and after the 1950s, such as "comics," "fan," "hobby," "job," "okay," and "quiz." Translations that borrowed from English terminology were even more typical in fields such as business, technology, the military, the mass media, and fashion, although the difference between Americanisms and Anglicisms is not always clear. The news magazine

Der Spiegel was surely the main journalistic point of entry for linguistic Americanization.[28]

The most important opening for "Americanization from below" was the new youth culture that began to develop in the last third of the 1950s.[29] Young people's preference for American products – from jeans to James Dean films and, above all, rock 'n' roll and the idols Bill Haley and Elvis Presley – was associated with adoption of cultural models deemed American and thereby in conflict with traditional, authoritarian, and educational values. Informality, casualness, and uninhibited vulgarity in clothing, personal style, and music provoked parents, youth workers, teachers, and the clergy. And for the first time, the entertainment industry became an ally for young people.[30] Initially restricted to urban, male, working-class youths (*"Halbstarke"*), the rebellion grew into a fullfledged intergenerational conflict. It became increasingly clear that a section of the younger generation equated Americanization with liberation. Still, British influences (e.g., beat music from Liverpool, fashion from London) in fact had a much greater influence on youth culture than direct imports from the United States in the first half of the 1960s, which speaks against a linear process of Americanization. Conservative commentators of the day nonetheless took to labeling British influences as American decadence and lack of culture; many even saw the Beatles as *"Amimist"* ("American trash").

---

[28] See the chapter by Heidrun Kämper, vol. 2, Culture.

[29] Christopher W. E. Bigsby, ed., *Superculture: American Popular Culture and Europe* (London, 1975); Mel van Elteren, "Dutch Youths and American Mass Culture in the 1920s and 1950s: Responses to Modernity and the Western Civilization Process," in Kaspar Maase, Gerd Hallenberger, and Mel van Elteren, *Amerikanisierung der Alltagskultur? Zur Rezeption US-amerikanischer Populärkultur in der Bundesrepublik und in den Niederlanden* (Hamburg, 1990), 57–82; Robert Kroes, Robert W. Rydell, and Doelo F. J. Bosscher, eds., *Cultural Transmissions and Receptions: American Mass Culture in Europe* (Amsterdam, 1993).

[30] See Kaspar Maase, *BRAVO Amerika: Erkundungen zur Jugendkultur in der Bundesrepublik in den fünfziger Jahren* (Hamburg, 1992).

[26] See Harm G. Schröter, "Die Amerikanisierung der Werbung in der Bundesrepublik Deutschland," *Jahrbuch für Wirtschaftsgeschichte* (1997), 1: 93–115.

[27] See Heinz Hartmann, *Amerikanische Firmen in Deutschland: Beobachtungen über Kontakte und Kontraste zwischen Industriegesellschaften* (Cologne, 1963), 173–8.

AMERICANIZATION AND MODERNIZATION

Most important but most difficult to interpret are the changes in West German lifestyle and the question of how far those changes can be seen as the results of Americanization. Real net wages doubled as poverty gave rise to prosperity between 1950 and 1963. A significant segment of the population was rehoused in the course of an unprecedented reconstruction program that saw five million new housing units built during the 1950s. This flurry of construction was accompanied by a far-reaching suburbanization process as ever more families moved to large housing subdivisions on the outskirts of urban centers. In the 1950 census, 18 percent of the economically active population reported being "commuters"; by the next census in 1961, the figure had risen to 31 percent. This suburban lifestyle was increasingly associated with the purchase of a car, initially very small, to end dependence on public transportation. The number of automobiles increased eightfold during the 1950s to about four million (1960) and, by 1962–3, every third working household had its own "wheels." The number of automobiles tripled again during the 1960s.

A lifestyle centered on an apartment or owner-occupied house in the suburbs, a car of one's own for traveling to work, and leisure time shaped by television became an ever more pronounced pattern during the 1960s, albeit initially for those in residential developments filled with the bungalows of the prosperous middle classes. Television, however, was a mass medium for the entire population from the outset. In 1960, just one in four households had a television set; by 1968, more than two-thirds did.

Even if some households had a swing hammock (*Hollywoodschaukel*) standing in the garden or could count a hula hoop among their exercise equipment – both leisure products from around 1960 that were seen as distinctly American – "Americanization" can furnish only a very incomplete and superficial understanding of the new West German lifestyle. If anything, elements of Americanization surfaced here within a general process of modernization. As the country attained new prosperity, aspects of a lifestyle that the white American middle classes had known for two decades began to arrive. That said, a sometimes considerable backlog existed in the availability of consumer durables. In 1960, only one West German household in seven had a telephone, for example, and self-service stores were still largely unknown.

It is open to question how far this process of modernization – of catching up to the United States materially – can be described as cultural Americanization.[31] The development of television was just as frenzied as in the United States a decade earlier, but the number of directly imported American television programs remained very low in 1960. They were limited to a few afternoon and early evening series such as *Fury, Corky*, and *Texas Rangers*.[32] If anything, we are dealing with "indirect Americanization" here: for example, the borrowing of particular models for entertainment programs such as quiz shows. A precise historical reconstruction would reveal many German traditions at work – some from as early as the 1930s – as radio and television pilots offered up modern forms of entertainment. Even camping, the most modern form of vacation, can claim German roots dating back to the pre–World War I era, long before its sudden rise in popularity at the end of the 1950s.[33]

Many of the new consumer phenomena of the 1950s and early 1960s exhibited a distinct mixture of German traditions and imported American features. This was true even of the streamlined design of technical consumer durables that were widely seen as purely American. It is thus not possible to speak unequivocally of an Americanized society and culture. Instead,

---

[31] Arnold Sywottek, "The Americanization of Everyday Life? Early Trends in Consumer and Leisure-Time Behavior," in Michael Ermarth, ed., *America and the Shaping of German Society, 1945–1955* (Providence, R.I., 1993), 132–52.

[32] See Irmela Schneider, *Amerikanische Einstellung: Deutsches Fernsehen und US-amerikanische Produktionen* (Heidelberg, 1992); see also the chapter by Michael Geisler, vol. 2, Culture.

[33] Schildt, *Moderne Zeiten*, 197–8.

the emergence of a lifestyle similar to that found among the white East Coast middle classes in American society accompanied the new, still unfamiliar prosperity of West Germans. In this way, the Federal Republic – like other West European countries – opened up to embrace the products of American mass culture in the boom during and after the 1960s. The story of this period of social history in the Federal Republic awaits further, more in-depth investigation.

The role played by generational change demands special attention. The new political and social elites had taken part in the reeducation and reorientation programs as young people. This meant that for the first time, politics, society, and culture were being shaped by an elite for whom a westward-looking politics and cultural orientation came together. For this generation, America and Americanization were not negative signs of things to come but a positive vision of liberal freedom. This was particularly conspicuous in the presentation of Willy Brandt as the "German Kennedy" in the 1961 German parliamentary elections. Model schools popular in the United States – which brought together students with diverse abilities into one comprehensive system – often figured in the debates over modernizing the German educational system. The Vietnam War debate also made visible a new generational constellation. Whereas a majority of the middle-aged generation defended American government policies, parts of the younger "rock 'n' roll generation" protested while also expressing solidarity with their American contemporaries in the struggle against the "establishment."[34] German political protests against the United States in the second half of the 1960s overlapped with their participants' enduring, heightened admiration for American pop music, films, and subculture. By the end of the decade, around 1970, West German society had plainly reached a point more favorable than ever to the reception of American mass culture: a new level of prosperity, a modern lifestyle for the middle classes, and a new generation with less resentment toward the United States and greater knowledge of the English language. The subsequent triumph of American television shows and fast food has not yet been subjected to thoroughgoing historical examination, nor has the American influence – through the mass media above all – on the second German state, the German Democratic Republic. East German propaganda perpetually criticized the Americanization of West Germany, but the GDR was also forced to recognize that the virus of rock 'n' roll had infected its own youth organizations.[35] There is, thus, reason to see the 1950s and early 1960s as an incubation period and the time since the 1970s as the actual phase of "Americanization from below."

---

[34] See the chapter by Claus Leggewie, vol. 2, Society.

[35] See Uta G. Poiger, "Rock 'n' Roll, Kalter Krieg und deutsche Identität," in Jarausch and Siegrist, eds., *Amerikanisierung*, 275–89; see also the chapter by Edward Larkey, vol. 1, Culture.

CHAPTER NINETEEN

Westernization

The Transition in Political Culture

Raimund Lammersdorf

Translated by Margaret Ries

The Federal Republic of Germany's Western orientation in politics, state, and society has been a central element of its self-image from the outset. A self-evident and unambiguous allegiance to the community of Western values remains part of the Federal Republic's raison d'être.[1] Although the developments and decisions that led to this Western orientation on the economic, political, and military level have been extensively discussed, the westernization of Germany's political culture has not been sufficiently explained, despite its importance for understanding the evolution of West German democracy.[2]

The westernization of Germany could simply be equated with the adoption of Western democratic principles for the creation of a new German republic. But more than pure constitutional history is at issue. There is a difference between form and content, between simply founding a democratic state by adopting a constitution based on the principles of liberty and a society embracing democracy as a way of life. The mere existence of a democratic form of

government reveals little about whether democracy will be accepted and ultimately lived by its citizens. This article understands westernization not as a change in constitutional principles but as the transition of West Germany's political culture from authoritarianism to liberal democracy.[3]

The term "political culture" denotes a body of convictions, based upon historical traditions and collective as well as individual experiences, about how society should be organized, how political decisions should be made and carried out, and, above all, how the relationship between the individual and society should be structured.[4] Political culture revolves around definitions of the core values and ideas that determine a society's political assumptions and practices. The term "westernization" thus describes in multiple ways, if not exhaustively, the process of change in all categories of the state's and society's thinking and behavior in West Germany.

West Germans were to develop a particular German variant of westernness. Westernization worked because the new values appeared to be variations on inherited and treasured German values. The partial retention of old governmental structures and their personnel and a revival of

---

[1] See Beate Lindemann, *Amerika in uns: Deutsch-amerikanische Erfahrungen und Visionen* (Mainz, 1995); Walther Leisler Kiep, *Good-bye Amerika, was dann? Der deutsche Standpunkt im Wandel der Weltpolitik* (Stuttgart-Degerloch, 1972).

[2] Anselm Doering-Manteuffel, "Dimensionen von Amerikanisierung in der deutschen Gesellschaft," in *Archiv für Sozialgeschichte* 35 (1995): 1–34; compare to Adolf M. Birke, *Die Bundesrepublik Deutschland: Verfassung, Parlament und Parteien* (Munich, 1997), 55–6.

[3] Cf. Ernst Fraenkel, *Deutschland und die westlichen Demokratien* (Stuttgart, 1964), 8–9.

[4] Cf. Dirk Berg-Schlosser and Jakob Schissler, eds., *Politische Kultur in Deutschland: Bilanz und Perspektiven der Forschung* (Opladen, 1987).

some traditional pre-Nazi values allowed many Germans to experience the process of westernization not as one of alienation but often as the rediscovery of an older, better self. In this way, traditional concepts of order and the state, adapted and redefined until they fit into newly available categories, were carried forward into the new democracy.

These changes were directly connected to the Cold War, which clearly delineated each society's position and simplified ideological difference. Although the Cold War created a strong sense of shared interests and values, it also helped to conceal the differences that existed between the political cultures within each bloc. Besides the Federal Republic's strategic importance, the unifying enmity toward the East facilitated the country's ideological integration into the West while at the same time accelerating westernization within its borders.

An interpretation along these lines explains this transformation as an interplay of ruptures and continuities within West German political culture against the background of international political developments. Evidence for this type of westernization of the Federal Republic can be found, for example, by comparing the concept of "the West" in the United States and Germany, considering the ideological orientation of the Christian Democrats (CDU/CSU) and the Social Democrats (SPD) after 1945, or analyzing the development of public political discussion and the behavior of citizens.

THE WEST AS GEOGRAPHICAL METAPHOR

American planning for a new Germany after World War II aimed at helping the Germans to orient themselves morally and spiritually toward the West. Americans did not, in fact, use the term "westernization" for these plans. From their perspective, it was only with the advent of the Cold War that the West became a geographical metaphor for their own liberal-democratic ideology. The roots of the ideas of liberty embedded in the Atlantic Charter can be traced back to the Enlightenment in Western Europe. Yet, Americans did not acknowledge limits on the geographic reach of their conceptions of democracy. These were understood as "natural" values that simply needed to be given a chance to develop in other cultural settings and countries.

It was only in response to the Stalinist threat after 1947 that the chance geographical divide between East and West in the Cold War became synonymous with the antagonism between totalitarian and free systems. American liberal values became specifically western values only after they were excluded from eastern regions. They were, however, still considered to be valid worldwide. The West was simply the area where they currently held sway and that area would quite naturally expand to encompass the eastern regions once the expected collapse of communism occurred.[5]

This political-ideological American concept of "westernness" differs from the concept of a Western European culture encompassing the entire course of European civilization from antiquity through Christianity, the Middle Ages, the Reformation, and the Enlightenment, on into the modern age.[6] From an American point of view, this conception of civilization was not necessarily determined by nation or race. Pre-1914 Germany, as one of the main bearers of western civilization, was counted among the truly civilized nations. Its complete cultural and moral collapse during the National Socialist dictatorship was, therefore, all the more serious. The United States did not attribute Germans' mistakes to the inferiority of their civilization; rather, more critically, it came down to the failure of a civilized people, otherwise capable of uprightness, and liberty, to develop the necessary republican virtues. For centuries, their development was handicapped by absolutist oppression and stunted by Prussian military

[5] Peter Duignan and Lewis H. Gann, *The Rebirth of the West: The Americanization of the Democratic World, 1945–1958* (Cambridge, Mass., 1992); Tony Smith, *America's Mission: The United States and the Worldwide Struggle for Democracy in the Twentieth Century* (Princeton, N.J., 1994).

[6] See James Davison Hunter, *Culture Wars: The Struggle to Define America* (New York, 1991); Stephen J. Whitfield, *The Culture of the Cold War*, 2d ed. (Baltimore, 1996).

culture. German history, particularly in comparison to the relatively linear course of American history, seemed to have taken a deviant path – a *Sonderweg* – that could and should be corrected.[7]

Although different factions in the Roosevelt and Truman administrations fought bitterly about the right course for Germany's future, they all agreed that the main objective of the war – a final pacification of Germany in Europe – could only be achieved by fundamentally restructuring the country so that it conformed to America's own ideas of democracy.[8] Germany's new polity would be built on the same foundation as America's own political self-understanding: the individual as a free citizen who acts and makes decisions in an independent and responsible manner. A democratic system of government, in conjunction with the elimination of nationalism, militarism, and National Socialism, provided only the formal structure for a citizens' democracy. The principle of self-government would be not merely a form of government but a way of life in a civil society in the making.[9]

An integral component of Germany's democratization consisted, consequently, of democratic reeducation to turn the *Volksgenosse* (member of the *Volk*) into a citizen. Germans were supposed to develop a sense of liberty, individual responsibility, and respect for the rights of others. These civic virtues, the respect for law founded on liberty, and a healthy mistrust of all state authority were the basis for a new republican form of self-government. In general, westernization as a process of democratic reeducation did not occur in terms of "forcing" Germans to fall into line with democratic principles but rather as an Enlightenment project designed to help them, in the Kantian sense, emerge from their self-imposed immaturity.[10]

Although the United States considered its values as universal, Germans clearly saw the proffered democratic principles as decidedly western or West European and, therefore, not necessarily German. The important role that geographical metaphors have played in Germany's political tradition is evident here.[11] And they remain important today because only Germans use the term "westernization" in connection with the democratization of West Germany.

Due to its geopolitical position at the center of Europe, Germany traditionally regarded itself as the meeting point of different cultural and political value systems that were in competition in Germany itself. Anti-liberals and nationalists developed a cultural geography based on cultural-anthropological and racial theories that formed the basis of German politics in the 1930s and 1940s. National Socialist ideologues crudely distinguished between the "Jewified" (*verjudet*) peoples of the modernist, liberal West and the communist, Slavic East. The "Nordic race" of Germans, they complained, was being crushed between them.[12]

Even after 1945 and the break with National Socialism, German discourse on the West was still shaped by traditional geopolitical and ideological ideas.[13] This was evident in the new political conservatism that developed after the

[7] See Michaela Hönicke, "Know Your Enemy: American Interpretations of National Socialism in World War II" (Ph.D. diss., University of North Carolina at Chapel Hill, 1998).

[8] Anton Kaes, "What to Do with Germany? American Debates About the Future of Germany, 1942–1947," in *German Politics and Society* 13 (1995): 130–41; Bernd Greiner, *Die Morgenthau-Legende: Zur Geschichte eines umstrittenen Plans* (Hamburg, 1995).

[9] See Louis Hartz's classic *The Liberal Tradition in America: An Interpretation of American Political Thought Since the Revolution* (New York, 1955); see also Carl J. Friedrich, *The New Belief in the Common Man* (Boston, 1942).

[10] See the chapters by Cornelia Rauh-Kühne, Barbara Fait, and Hermann-Josef Rupieper, vol. 1, Politics; also see the chapter by James F. Trent, vol. 1, Culture, and the chapter by Axel Schildt in this section.

[11] See David Thomas Murphy, *The Heroic Earth: Geopolitical Thought in Weimar Germany, 1918–1933* (Kent, Ohio, 1997); Rainer Sprengel, *Kritik der Geopolitik: Ein deutscher Diskurs 1914–1944* (Berlin, 1996).

[12] For this, see, of course, Adolf Hitler, *Mein Kampf* (Munich, 1925). See also Karl Haushofer, *Das Reich: Grossdeutsches Werden im Abendland* (Berlin, 1943).

[13] On the theme of continuity and rupture, see Martin Broszat, ed., *Zäsuren nach 1945: Essays zur Periodisierung der deutschen Nachkriegsgeschichte* (Munich, 1990); Everhard Holtmann, ed., *Wie neu war der Neubeginn? Zum deutschen Kontinuitätsproblem nach 1945* (Erlangen, 1989).

war. One of the Federal Republic's principal political-ideological problems during its founding years was to integrate the predominantly undemocratic political and bureaucratic class into the new system. Its expertise was seen as indispensable for postwar reconstruction; its resistance to democratization would have created insurmountable obstacles for the survival of the new republic. This conservative and reactionary side of the political spectrum had suffered the greatest ideological losses because the National Socialists had appropriated key conservative principles and ideas and ultimately discredited them. The conservatism of the future had to exclude militarism, authoritarian thinking, racism, and anti-Semitism. A new integrative political conservatism had to be found that clearly distanced itself from National Socialism but embraced former Nazi supporters and lead them closer to the democratic middle to prevent reactionary or even fascist resurgence.[14]

Western European Christianity provided a message broad enough to find an audience among the great majority of these Germans. Christian Democracy bridged the gap between conservative desires for order and democratic ideals of freedom. Both a trust in authority and the democratic safeguarding of individual rights could be derived from the fear of God and brotherly love. Repentance and forgiveness, in turn, aided Germany's internal efforts to overcome National Socialist evil and facilitated eager efforts to achieve reconciliation with former enemies.[15]

Naturally, this shift in values could never be as complete as purported. German conservatives expressed their attitude toward the West and its

values by taking positions that reflected traditional German ideological views. West German democracy was to be built on familiar ground. Resort to the Christian belief system was deliberately linked with a turn to the West. However, the German jeremiad called for a return to the Christian occident and European cultural traditions, rather than turning toward the United States, which the German bourgeoisie, Auschwitz notwithstanding, considered to be uncultured and inferior.[16]

It was only in the context of U.S. engagement in protecting West Germany and West Berlin from the Stalinist threat and in providing economic and humanitarian aid for the Germans that the conservative elite – like the population as a whole – began to develop a bond to the Americans. The United States continued to demonstrate the greatest willingness to accept German gestures toward reconciliation, helped to readmit Germany into the civilized world, and promoted the Federal Republic's integration into Europe. Christian Democrats were grateful and loyal toward Americans, yet they never completely overcame their own nationalistic resentment and feelings of cultural superiority.[17]

By contrast, the Social Democratic Party (SPD), the most "western" of the political parties, did not see the need to move closer to the West. A restored German social democracy could continue in the spirit of its democratic traditions and did not require reorientation in order to establish its political identity after the war. The SPD under the leadership of Kurt Schumacher saw itself as the single legitimate political power in Germany. It had never stopped fighting the National Socialist regime, had always considered itself part of western democratic culture, and maintained a radically anticommunist stance. The democratic tradition of the party did indeed correspond to many facets of American

[14] Maria Mitchell, "Materialism and Secularism: CDU Politicians and National Socialism, 1945–1949," *Journal of Modern History* 67 (1995), 278–308; Ulrich Brochhagen, *Nach Nürnberg: Vergangenheitsbewältigung und Westintegration in der Ära Adenauer* (Hamburg, 1994); Norbert Frei, *Vergangenheitspolitik: Die Anfänge der Bundesrepublik und die NS-Vergangenheit* (Munich, 1996).

[15] Little has been done on this subject. Karin Walter, *Neubeginn, Nationalsozialismus, Widerstand: Die politisch-theoretische Diskussion der Neuordnung in CDU und SPD 1945–1948* (Bonn, 1987), 20–118.

[16] See the chapter by Philipp Gassert in this section.

[17] Hans Jürgen Grabbe, *Unionsparteien, Sozial-demokratie und Vereinigte Staaten von Amerika 1945–1966* (Düsseldorf, 1983); see also the chapters by Philipp Gassert and Knud Krakau in this section.

liberalism. In many areas, its political objectives overlapped with those of the New Deal.

However, the party's fundamental critique of capitalism rendered these commonalities irrelevant, especially because the New Dealers had lost most of their influence during the Truman administration and the Republican-dominated Congress was successfully dismantling economic regulations. The SPD's positions confused American observers. The party was clearly democratic; at the same time, it wanted to severely limit property rights, which Americans saw as an unconditional prerequisite for freedom. The Social Democrats' plans for the future of West Germany were not rejected solely because they ran counter to U.S. economic interests, but because Americans believed they would result in an authoritarian regime that could no longer offer guarantees of individual freedom. This fear was further compounded by the centralist agenda and nationalism of the Social Democratic party leader. With all due respect for Schumacher's and the Social Democrats' uncompromising resistance to National Socialism, the U.S. military government could hardly have been expected to work with the SPD when cooperation with the Christian Democrats was much easier to achieve.[18]

THE INTERNATIONAL CONTEXT

Along with the willingness of many Germans to embrace democratization and the occupying powers' supervision of this process, it was the Cold War that ensured the success of westernization. The confrontation between the superpowers proved to be a stroke of luck for the development of democracy in West Germany. It is true the Cold War brought denazification to a standstill and partly reversed the process. It did also lead to a limited remilitarization of society and facilitated the return of authoritarianism in many areas of public life.

Yet, at the same time, the Cold War strengthened Germany's economic and security ties to the West, ensured greater ideological clarity and unity, and, in the long run, made the growth of a democratic political culture possible.

The inclusion of Germany, the former enemy, into the front against communism brought about a psychologically important national rehabilitation. The West's foreign policy not only gave Germans the sense of being needed again, it also allowed Germany to continue its hostility toward the Soviet Union, albeit now as an expression of a western, prodemocratic stance. Already in the last stages of the war, Germans' fears about the Morgenthau Plan were tempered by the equally widespread hope that the Western Allies would join together with the German Wehrmacht to fight against the "Russian hordes." West German resistance to communist aggression would be recognized as a struggle for Europe's freedom. In this way, democratic and reactionary anticommunism, fused with traditional and new hatred toward the Russians, became a central stabilizing feature of the new political culture in the growing democracy.

The West's recognition of Germany made it easier for Germans to ignore their own guilt and responsibility for the war and the Holocaust and to emphasize instead German suffering. The multiple traumas of national division, loss of the eastern territories, and expulsion were the result of the German war of aggression and extermination. In the context of the Cold War, however, Germans could recast this self-inflicted catastrophe to portray themselves as the first victims of communist aggression. Germany's victim mentality[19] found encouragement through growing support from the Americans, who saw the West Berliners in particular as the "frontiersmen" of Western values in an outpost of freedom. CARE packages and free school meals, the Marshall Plan, and the Berlin Airlift not only engendered German sympathy and gratitude toward the United States, they

---

[18] Daniel E. Rogers, *Politics After Hitler: The Western Allies and the German Party System* (New York, 1995).

[19] Omer Bartov, "Defining Enemies, Making Victims: Germans, Jews and the Holocaust," *American Historical Review* 103 (1998): 771–816.

could also be viewed as compensation for the sacrifices made by Germans. The highpoint of this type of recognition of Germany was John F. Kennedy's 1963 Berlin speech in which he cast the West Berliners as the defenders of Western values.[20]

The Cold War also had a direct effect on the German population's acceptance of the Bonn Republic. It reestablished the primacy of foreign policy in West Germany and resurrected traditional ideas of state sovereignty, thereby counteracting American occupation officers' efforts to introduce the principle of popular sovereignty. Whereas Americans believed in democracy from the bottom up, the German constitutional tradition defined sovereignty from the perspective of a supreme central government (*Staat*). A return to authoritarian governmental structures was blocked, however, by Germany's ties to the West and abandonment of the belief in the necessity of an autonomous German foreign policy. Chancellor Konrad Adenauer's successful efforts to maximize the Federal Republic's sovereignty in foreign policy within the Western framework strengthened domestic respect for the new democratic state. This acceptance complemented Adenauer's patriarchal "chancellor democracy," which served Germans' need for strong political leadership. The chancellor proved that a republican government in Germany could function at home and find acceptance abroad.

Even the division of Germany and the loss of the eastern territories were advantageous for the westernization of West Germany's political culture. The eastern part of Germany had long been regarded as a stronghold of antiliberal conservatism and militarism. Separated from it, West Germany was freed from the influence of the Prussian Junkers. A liberal Catholicism and a more urbane population would now dominate a political culture whose leader, Adenauer, had always harbored strong misgivings about the Germany east of the Elbe.

The only negative aspect of westernization was the apparent abandonment of reunification. The closer the Federal Republic tied itself to the West, the smaller the chances of overcoming the division. This fundamental criticism of Westpolitik became moot because the government could publicly pursue reunification without having to expect success under the conditions laid down by Moscow and the West. The openness of the German national situation left room for a contradictory yet successful policy, which proved to be beneficial for the westernization of the Federal Republic. Moreover, the longer the division lasted and the greater the economic and political success of West German society, the weaker the West Germans' desire for unconditional reunification and the deeper their ideological ties to the West became.

Considerable differences in German and American thinking were obscured or overlooked amid the feeling of solidarity in resisting the Stalinist threat. This was also true for the differences among the other western nations. The western community of values seemed to define itself less by common values than by a common enemy. In far too many instances, the American government, despite its rhetoric of freedom, accepted and supported brutal authoritarian regimes as long as they adhered to the anticommunist line.[21] In a similar fashion, albeit under far less odious circumstances, Americans pushed aside their considerable doubts about the success of the democratization of West Germany and the democratic character of the chancellor democracy.[22] In the shadows of global conflict, the Federal Republic had the opportunity to overcome its democratic shortcomings and to construct its own western-style democracy without external intervention or pressure.

[20] See the chapter by Diethelm Prowe, vol. 1, Politics.

[21] An exemplary apologia for this stance is contained in Jeane J. Kirkpatrick, "Dictatorships and Double Standards," *Commentary* 68, no. 5 (1979): 34–45.

[22] The United States' often harsh criticism of the West German democracy has scarcely been addressed. Hans-Jürgen Schröder provides a first impression in "Die Anfangsjahre der Bundesrepublik Deutschland: Eine amerikanische Bilanz 1954," *Vierteljahreshefte für Zeitgeschichte* 37 (1989): 323–51.

DEMOCRATIZATION AND WESTERNIZATION
AFTER 1968

In light of Germany's prior antidemocratic and authoritarian political culture, the conservative consolidation of the Federal Republic during the 1950s seems like an extremely successful and fundamental change. Although liberal and democratic traditions did initially lose some ground in federal politics and the bureaucracy during the Adenauer era, their place in public discourse was secured by a consistently democratic and frequently critical media, progressive trade unions, and skeptical intellectuals. The Social Democrats departed from their polarizing radicalism and expanded their base beyond the working class, thereby bringing the German party system a little closer to its American counterpart.

This gradual transition, carried by the republican elite, seemed to have helped the largely unreconstructed population to accept the new democratic system of government. At the same time, the continuing influence of authoritarian traditions increased discrepancies between the form and the content of the republic. Above all, young students in the 1960s, the first generation raised democratically, were sensitive to these inherent contradictions. Cultural and political westernization had particularly spoken to this generation, which had not experienced the triumph of National Socialism but only the misery left in its wake. Their schools had provided them with high moral standards, which, as politically aware teenagers and university students, they later sought to apply. Disappointment and indignation with the West German republic developed when they realized that the supposedly democratic political elite was permeated with old Nazis and that Nazi criminals had been pursued only with extreme reluctance. The newly won democracy was apparently being undermined by the misuse of power, the taint of corruption, and the enactment of emergency powers. The natural conflict between generations was increased even further by the cultural divide between young and old, which initially manifested itself in a relatively harmless clash over "Negro music" and blue jeans but quickly took on a more substantial form.[23]

In the 1960s, the success of westernization caught up with the conservative republic and led to confrontations about the character of the country, the vehemence of which had not been seen since the Weimar Republic. The Federal Republic's political culture was not westernized enough to tolerate opposition coming from outside of parliament, parties, or other established institutions. During the era of the Christian Democratic–Social Democratic "Grand Coalition," street protests became the only means by which young people could make their dissenting voices heard. Neither the general public nor the government was willing to accept these demonstrations as legitimate expressions of political will. At times, West Germany and West Berlin took on the character of a police state, unwittingly proving the younger generation's point.

But West Germany's incomplete westernization was evident on both sides of the barricades. The authoritarian hard line of the establishment matched the illiberal attitudes of West Germany's young people. Instead of striving to liberalize the Federal Republic, they propagated Marxist-Leninist or even Maoist views. The lack of strong liberal models and traditions in Germany became apparent. The association of liberal liberalism and German authoritarian conservatism discredited western values in the eyes of the protesting youth. Even the guardian of western ideas, the United States, betrayed its own values daily in Vietnam and in its inner-city ghettos, and it thus could not serve as a guide to the generation of 1968.[24]

Democratization of the young had been enough of a success, however, that neither the belief in democratic principles nor the

---

[23] See Lothar Voigt, *Aktivismus und moralischer Rigorismus: Die politische Romantik der 68er Studentenbewegung* (Wiesbaden, 1991), 211–62. Also see the chapters by Uta Poiger and Edward Larkey, vol. 1, Culture.

[24] Hildegard Weiss, *Die Ideologieentwicklung in der deutschen Studentenbewegung* (Munich, 1985), 39–42.

conviction that they were still worth working for vanished after the much-anticipated world revolution failed to occur. Only a relatively small part of this generation disappeared into the anti-liberal political milieu of communist splinter groups or turned to political violence. The vast majority kept their antiauthoritarianism alive as they themselves assumed positions in the establishment. In the long term, this "long march through the institutions," as the retiring revolutionaries described it in ironic Maoist terms, contributed decisively to affecting real democratic change in the political culture.[25] The apparent resignation of the revolutionaries and the adjustment of many former commune dwellers to middle-class life became an important element of German westernization. The renunciation of revolution, the belief in reform, the recognition of the Federal Republic's legitimacy, the acceptance of the Basic Law, and the development of a "constitutional patriotism" signified that western democracy had also become the norm for the rebels of 1968. Today, this generation of fifty- to sixty- year-olds constitutes a large part of the ruling establishment of teachers, judges, administrators, and politicians. Their realization that there was no alternative to the liberal-bourgeois social system, despite its many shortcomings, grew out of the failure of a revolt for a more humane world – not, as for their parents, out of defeat in a war of extermination. One can safely assume that members of the 1968 generation's thoughts and feelings about democracy are not only different than those of the 1950s generation but also more deeply rooted.

The westernization of West Germany continued in its citizens' increasing willingness to get involved politically, particularly in locally organized citizens' initiatives, and a growing mistrust of government and the political parties went hand in hand with a greater faith in the individual's capacity for self-government. In retrospect, these grassroots movements appear as a belated success of American efforts to build German democracy from the ground up. The extreme uneasiness with which federal and local governments, bureaucracies, and parties initially reacted to this circumvention of their authority showed that the citizens themselves had actually become more westernized than the institutions of the democratic state.[26]

During the early 1990s, the strength of this feeling of civic responsibility manifested itself in impressive mass protests against racist violence. Here, too, citizens revealed that they were more democratically minded than an apparently indifferent government; the masses of demonstrators proved how far Germans had moved away from a traditional, nonwestern political culture. This divide between citizen and state represents a natural tension in western democracies. Germans' distrust of the state, their *Staatsverdrossenheit*, can be compared to the healthy mistrust that American citizens demonstrate toward government. Traditionalist political scientists may see it as a danger to Germany's democratic system, but from the outside it appears to be evidence of the successful westernization of the Federal Republic.

[25] See the chapter by Philipp Gassert in this section; Karl-Heinz Heinemann and Thomas Jaitner, *Ein langer Marsch: 1968 und die Folgen. Gespräche mit Lutz von Werder, Thomas Ziehe, Kurt Holl, Rolf Trommershauser* (Cologne, 1993).

[26] See the chapter by Carl Lankowski, vol. 2, Society.

Index